COMPETITION LAW OF THE
EUROPEAN COMMUNITY

Preface to the Third Edition

Together with trade policy, competition policy is one of the areas where the Community authorities, and especially the Commission, enjoy wide investigative and regulatory powers. Building on art. 85 and 86 of the EC Treaty, the Commission has over the years constructed an increasingly complex body of rules and regulations. In enforcing art. 85 and 86, the Commission has not limited itself to intervention against the 'traditional' antitrust offences such as price-fixing, market-sharing, exploitation of market power and the like. It has set out in an ambitious effort to regulate major aspects of business transactions in increasing detail. As a result, it has become hazardous to draft a distribution, licensing or joint venture agreement, to cite only a few examples, without having regard to EC competition law. Another factor which has increased the cost of non-compliance with EC competition rules is the Commission's policy of imposing increasingly severe fines which, in *several* cases, have exceeded ECU 10 m.

The purpose of this book is to provide a comprehensive and up-to-date analysis of the EC competition rules as developed by the Commission, the Court of First Instance and the Court of Justice. What distinguishes this book from other books written on the same subject is the perspective chosen by its authors: drawing on their experience as practitioners, they have attempted to cut through the theoretical underpinnings of EC competition law to expose its actual impact on business. The book combines a critical commentary on the rules with practical guidance on their application. It should, therefore, prove to be useful to both businessmen and their legal advisers.

The third edition of this book on EC competition law updates all chapters of the second edition to the end of 1993. The chapter on mergers and acquisitions has been revised in its entirety to include a thorough review of decisions taken under the merger control regulation during its first three years of operation. Significant procedural developments are discussed, including those relating to the application of EC competition law at the national level and the initial experiences with the Court of First Instance. The growing importance of EC competition law in the global arena is reflected in new sections dealing with the competition provisions of the EEA Agreement and the co-operation agreement between the US and the EC.

Two new chapters reflect the growing impact of competition law in the public

v

sector. First, a chapter on state aids deals with the rapidly expanding case law in this field. Second, the growing emphasis placed on the decentralised enforcement of EC competition rules by national courts is treated in a chapter on EC competition law and the member states. This same chapter deals with the application of EC competition law to member states, particularly with regard to the deregulation of sectors traditionally controlled by the member states. In this connection, the Third Edition also offers expanded coverage of sectors in which the competition laws have been applied, including banking, insurance, air transport, marine transport and telecommunications.

We wish to acknowledge gratefully the assistance we have received from our associates and staff in the preparation of the third edition of this book. In particular we wish to thank David Hull, Andrzej Kmiecik, Peter L'Ecluse, James Flett, Daniel Lawton, Guy Evans, Jean-Michel Coumes, Ciaràn Keaney, Kris Van Hove, Erik Hellners, Pastora Valero and Laura De Sanctis for their valuable contributions.

Ivo Van Bael
Jean-François Bellis

Foreword to the First Edition

The Community's competition policy is designed to prevent artificial distortions on the market. It stimulates the free enterprise system on which Europe's market economy is based. It also provides for an environment where weak and small operators are protected against the possible excessive use of market power by dominant firms.

From its inception, the maintenance of effective competition has been one of the cornerstones of the Common Market. Initially, the vigorous enforcement of the competition rules was mainly perceived as a necessary tool to foster market integration; today, it is also advocated as a means to help European industry compete on a global scale.

Enforcement of the EC competition rules is essentially in the hands of the Commission. Competition policy is so far the only area of activity where the EC Commission holds considerable direct powers. The advantage of the Commission's autonomy in this respect is that it is capable of swift action and of setting its objectives without needing a consensus from the Council of Ministers, something which in other Community policies inevitably leads to compromise solutions whereby the Commission's initial proposals tend to be watered down to the lowest common denominator.

However, in view of the Commission's sole responsibility for the application of the competition rules, it is all the more important that its policy be sufficiently precise and transparent to remain subject to public scrutiny. Indeed, the Commission's wide powers to shape economy policy through the use of art. 85 and 86 of the EC Treaty call for a system of checks and balances. In this connection, it is to be regretted, for example, that the Commission has not allowed the European Parliament to play a formal role in the elaboration of block exemption regulations. Yet, it is undeniable that the Commission, as the Community's executive branch, would benefit from the input of the European Parliament in the performance of such far-reaching legislative tasks.

Since the Community's competition policy is said to be enforced in favour of the 'man in the street', it would be desirable if, from time to time, a committee of outside experts were to provide a critical analysis of the achievements and shortcomings of the Commission's enforcement of the competition rules from the point of view of consumer welfare. Without such a critical assessment, theories conceived by officials in an ivory tower may produce the wrong results when applied to the realities of the market place.

The book co-authored by Messrs Van Bael and Bellis offers valuable insight into the Commission's approach to the various business practices it seeks to control and regulate. The book's 'no nonsense' style is refreshing because, all too often, academic circles in Europe have tended to endorse and/or paraphrase whatever the authorities have said or done. As experienced practitioners, the authors of this book have succeeded in unravelling the mystery surrounding some of the basic principles on which the Community's competition policy is based. This proves to be a most helpful exercise because the effectiveness of the Community's competition policy has to be judged by the real benefits which it brings or fails to bring to European citizens.

Baroness Elles
Vice-President
European Parliament

About the Authors

Ivo Van Bael and Jean-François Bellis are members of the Brussels Bar. Their experience in EC antitrust and trade law results from many years of practice, both before the EC Commission and the Court of Justice.

Mr Van Bael obtained his PhB and JB from the University of Louvain. Mr Bellis graduated from the University of Brussels Law School. Both also studied at the University of Michigan Law School and, in the initial stages of their careers, have been associated with New York law firms. Mr Van Bael lectures on EC antitrust and anti-dumping procedure at the College of Europe (Bruges), at the University of Amsterdam and at Tokyo University. Mr Bellis lectures on EC trade law at the European Law Institute (Brussels) and at the University of Liège Law School. Mr Van Bael was Chairman of the Antitrust and Trade Law Committee, Section on Business Law, International Bar Association (1987–89).

About the Publisher

CCH Editions Limited is part of a world-wide group of companies that specialises in tax, business and law publishing. The group produces a wide range of books and reporting services for the accounting, business and legal professions. The Oxfordshire premises are the centre for all UK and European operations.

All CCH publications are designed to be practical and authoritative and are written by CCH's own highly qualified and experienced editorial team and specialist outside authors.

In the UK CCH Editions currently produces a comprehensive series of reporting services on UK and international tax, business and law, and many books covering specific areas of interest for accountants, lawyers and business managers. Irrespective of the subject matter being discussed or the depth and scope of its treatment, the material is always dealt with in the same clear and concise manner.

CCH is committed to you and your information needs, and this commitment is reflected in the constant updating and development of our reporting services and the expansion of our range of publications.

If you would like to know more about our books or loose-leaf services telephone (01869) 253300 in the UK.

Contents

Part III – Procedure

Part IV – State Aids

PART I

INTRODUCTION

1 Introduction

¶101 General

Before examining the substance of EC competition law, it is appropriate to describe the role of the various authorities involved in the enforcement of the EC competition policy, i.e. the Council of Ministers, the Commission, the Court of First Instance, the Court of Justice, national courts, the European Parliament and the Economic and Social Committee. As a result of the entry into force of the Treaty on European Union on 1 November 1993, the denominations of the Council of Ministers, the Commission and the Court of Justice have been changed to 'Council of the European Union', 'European Commission' and 'European Court of Justice' (see ¶102–¶109). Thereafter, the broad policy goals of the EC competition policy are discussed (¶110–¶113), together with the characteristic features of its enforcement technique (¶114). The competition law aspects falling within the purview of the ECSC Treaty and the particular aspects of the application of EC competition rules to enterprises governed by the EURATOM Treaty are not discussed here.

ENFORCEMENT AUTHORITIES

¶102 Summary of authorities

Enforcement of the EC competition rules rests primarily with the Commission, the executive branch of the European Communities.

The Commission's enforcement policy is formulated within the legal framework laid down by the Council of Ministers, the legislature of the Community, which acts in close co-operation with the Advisory Committee on Restrictive Practices and Monopolies, which consists of representatives of the member states whose advice must be sought on every case before a decision can be validly adopted.

In recent years the Commission's competition policy has also been under increasing scrutiny from the European Parliament.

Finally, the Court of First Instance, the Court of Justice and the national courts play an important role in the application of the rules of competition.

¶103   The Council of Ministers

The Council of Ministers, the secretariat of which is based in Brussels, consists of one delegate from each member state. The identity of the delegate varies depending upon the subject matter of the Council's deliberations. Each member state is in charge of the presidency of the Council for a six-month period on a rotating basis. In a number of cases the Council may only act by a qualified majority vote on a proposal from the Commission.

The Council is, in practice, the main legislative body of the Community.

The legislative work of the Council is prepared by the Commission which alone has the right to initiate a proposal for any legislative action in the more important policy areas.

The Council is assisted by a Committee of Permanent Representatives (COREPER) with ambassadorial rank.

The practical organisation of Council meetings is governed by rules of procedure adopted by the Council in 1979, as modified in 1987.[1]

In the competition field, the Council has issued Regulation 17/62 setting out the basic rules of procedure to implement art. 85 and 86 of the EC Treaty[2] and Regulation 2988/74 introducing limitation periods in competition proceedings.[3] Moreover, when, after a few years of the implementation of Regulation 17/62, it became apparent that the Commission lacked the manpower to cope effectively with the flood of notifications for individual exemptions, the Council adopted enabling legislation authorising the Commission to issue block exemptions covering certain categories of agreements.[4] The categories of agreements covered are those that had been most commonly notified, i.e. exclusive dealing and purchasing agreements, certain agreements covering industrial property rights and certain co-operation agreements.

¶104   The Commission

The Commission can be regarded as the executive branch of the EC. It is entrusted with the task of implementing and executing Council decisions and submitting proposals to the Council for legislative action.

The Commission is composed of 17 members: two for each of the larger member states (France, Italy, Germany, Spain and the UK) and one for each of

---

[1] Rules of procedure of the Council, OJ 1979 L268/1, amended in OJ 1987 L291/27.

[2] Regulation 17 of the Council implementing art. 85 and 86 of the Treaty, JO 1962 13/204; amended JO 1962 58/1655, JO 1963 162/2696, JO 1971 L285/49. The Council has also issued regulations with respect to the procedure for the application of the competition rules in some sectors which do not fall within the scope of Regulation 17/62, see note 10 below.

[3] Regulation 2988/74 of the Council concerning limitation periods in proceedings and the enforcement of sanctions under the rules of the European Economic Community relating to transport and competition, OJ 1974 L319/1.

[4] See below ¶225 to ¶232.

the smaller member states (Belgium, Denmark, Ireland, Luxembourg, Greece, Netherlands and Portugal).

The Commission plays the preponderant role in the enforcement of EC competition law.

The Commission has the power to prosecute cases and to adopt decisions requiring the termination of infringements of the rules on competition. To that effect, the Commission has important powers of investigation, including the power to compel companies to disclose information requested and to submit to on-the-spot investigations. The Commission may also impose fines and order injunctive relief. In urgent matters the Commission is entitled to grant interim relief, pending the outcome of the proceedings.

The Commission is also the only body authorised to grant a negative clearance or an individual exemption from the ban in art. 85(1) of the treaty on agreements and practices notified to it.

In addition to its power to deal with individual cases, the Commission is also acting in a legislative capacity when it issues regulations implementing the regulations of the Council. Thus, the Commission adopted Regulation 27/62, dealing with the form, content and other details concerning applications and notifications and Regulation 99/63 on the hearings provided for in art. 19(1) and (2) of Council Regulation 17/62.[5]

Furthermore, in an attempt to reduce the number of notifications for individual exemption, the Commission has made use of the authority granted by the Council to issue block exemptions for certain categories of agreements.

In principle, these block exemptions do away with the need to file individual notifications for all those agreements of which the terms are not more restrictive than the permissible restrictions on competition set out in the relevant block exemption.

In addition to implementing Council regulations and adopting its own regulations pursuant to authority delegated by the Council, the Commission has also given shape to the rules of procedure by taking certain measures or developing a given practice on its own initiative.

Thus, for example, in an effort further to promote legal certainty and alleviate the administrative burden on its staff in areas where it had not been specifically empowered by the Council to adopt block exemptions, the Commission has resorted to the publication of notices. In such a notice, the Commission examines the status of certain agreements or practices in the light of art. 85(1) of the treaty and offers useful guidelines and clarifications on the issues involved.

---

[5] Regulation 27 of the Commission of 3 May 1962 implementing Council Regulation 17, JO 1962 35/1118, amended JO 1968 L189/1, OJ 1975 L172/11, OJ 1985 L240/1; Regulation 99/63 of the Commission of 25 July 1963 on the hearings provided for in art. 19(1) and (2) of Council Regulation 17, JO 1962 127/2263.

¶104

The Commission's staff of about 16,500 officials is mainly based in Brussels. It is organised in 23 departments called 'Directorates-General' ('DGs'). The Directorate-General in charge of competition matters (DG IV) is currently composed of five directorates and a Merger Task Force, organised as follows.

Directorate A: general competition policy and co-ordination

(1) General policy and international aspects – relations with the European Parliament and the Economic and Social Committee.

(2) Legal and procedural problems, regulation, infringement procedures and intra-community dumping.

(3) Economic questions and studies.

(4) Co-ordination of competition decisions:

    (a) horizontal agreements and abuse of dominant positions, joint ventures and mergers;

    (b) industrial and intellectual property rights, research and development.

(5) Public enterprises and state monopolies, implementation of art. 101–102.

Directorate B: restrictive practices, abuse of dominant position and other distortions of competition I

(1) Electrical and electronic manufactured products, information industries and telecommunications.

(2) Mechanical manufactured products, textiles, clothing, leather and other manufacturing industries.

(3) Banking, insurance and other service industries.

(4) The media, consumer electronics, music publishing and distributive trades.

Directorate C: restrictive practices, abuse of dominant position and other distortions of competition II

(1) Non-ferrous metals, non-metallic mineral products, construction, timber, paper, glass and rubber industries.

(2) Energy (other than coal), basic products of the chemical industry.

(3) Processed chemical products, agricultural products and foodstuffs.

¶104

Directorate D: restrictive practices, abuse of dominant position and other distortions of competition III

(1) Steel and coal.

(2) Inspections in the steel and coal sector.

(3) Transport and tourist industries.

(4) Motor vehicles and other means of transport, and associated mechanical manufactured products.

Directorate E: state aids

(1) General aid schemes.

(2) Aids to research and development.

(3) Regional aids.

(4) Sectoral aids I.

(5) Sectoral aids II.

(6) Inventory and analysis.

Merger Task Force

(1) Operating Unit I

(2) Operating Unit II

(3) Operating Unit III

This structure was introduced through a re-organisation of DG IV in 1985 and fine-tuned in 1987. Out of the five directorates, three deal with individual cases only (Directorates B, C and D). They are subdivided in sectors according to specific industries and types of services. The case handlers do their fact-finding themselves while previously there existed an inspection directorate. Directorate A, in addition to dealing with general competition policy questions, has the task of ensuring that the case-handlers take into account the current thinking and policy of DG IV on the legal issues involved.

The aim of this structure was to increase fairness and efficiency by having the same team deal with the different phases of the procedure.[6] However, some of the increased efficiency may have been obtained at the expense of certain guarantees of objectivity which existed under the previous set-up due to the separation of the investigating staff from the case-handlers. It may now be more difficult for the case-handlers to distinguish the facts from the issues because of

---

[6] Fourteenth Report on Competition Policy, point 47.

¶104

their direct involvement in both the establishment of the facts and the formulation of the issues.[7]

At the end of 1992, DG IV had a staff of 407 officials. Of this staff, 44 per cent were working on art. 85 and 86 cases, 12 per cent on merger control cases, three per cent on art. 90 cases, 21 per cent on state aids cases, nine per cent on international relations and co-ordination, and 11 per cent on data processing, documentation and similar duties. These comprise grade A officials, i.e. officials with university training, grade B officials, i.e. clerks, and at least 100 grade C officials, i.e. secretaries. In addition, a small number of officials from national administrations is seconded to DG IV. This is a small number of staff in view of the Commission's heavy workload in the competition and merger control field.[8]

In addition to the central role which the staff of DG IV plays in the preparation and implementation of the Commission's policy, mention should also be made of the influence of the Commission's Legal Service. Indeed, a lawyer of the Commission's Legal Service intervenes at every important step in the Commission's administrative procedure and will eventually be entrusted with the defence of the interests of the Commission, should the matter end up before the court.

¶105   The authorities in member states

Pursuant to art. 9(3) of Regulation 17/62, the national antitrust authorities remain competent to apply art. 85(1) and 86 of the treaty in accordance with art. 88 as long as the Commission has not 'initiated any procedure'.[9]

Due to the adoption by the Council of regulations laying down detailed rules for the application of art. 85 and 86 to the transport sector, the national authorities lost a substantial part of their jurisdiction over this matter, which they had before under art. 88 of the treaty.[10]

The national authorities have generally co-operated fully with the Commission's enforcement efforts under art. 85 and 86. This co-operation

---

[7] See, e.g. point 14 of the resolution of the European Parliament on the Nineteenth Report on Competition Policy, annex to the *XXth Report on Competition Policy*, at p. 251; point 44 of the resolution of the European Parliament on the Eighteenth Report on Competition Policy, annex to the *Nineteenth Report on Competition Policy*, at p. 240.

[8] See, e.g. point 10 of the resolution of the European Parliament on the Nineteenth Report on Competition Policy, annex to the *XXth Report on Competition Policy*, at p. 250.

[9] The term 'initiation of any procedure' has been interpreted to mean 'an authoritative act of the Commission evidencing its intention of taking a decision'. An action such as an acknowledgement of receipt is considered to be merely administrative and therefore does not constitute such an 'authoritative act'. See *Brasserie de Haecht v Wilkin* (*Haecht II*) [1973] ECR 77, at pp. 87–88 (para. 14–18).

[10] Regulation 1017/68 applying rules of competition to transport by rail, road and inland waterway, JO 1968 L175/1; Regulation 4056/86 laying down detailed rules for the application of art. 85 and 86 of the treaty to maritime transport, OJ 1986 L378/4; Regulation 3975/87 laying down the procedure for the application of the rules on competition to undertakings in the air transport sector, OJ 1987 L374/1 as amended by Regulation 1284/91, OJ 1991 L122/2; Regulation 2410/92, OJ 1992 L240/18.

takes place through the advisory committees, the most important among them being the Advisory Committee on Restrictive Practices and Monopolies. Unfortunately, the consultation process within this Advisory Committee would not seem to have had much impact on the further course of proceedings and has often degenerated into a mere 'ritual' in cases brought under Regulation 17/62. To avoid a similar result in cases arising under the merger regulation (Regulation 4064/89), the member states secured much tighter language in the regulation on the required consultation procedure.

The national authorities are likely to be increasingly active in exercising their residual jurisdiction at the national level as a number of member states have recently adopted national competition laws.[11]

¶106   The Court of First Instance and the Court of Justice

The Court of First Instance

The establishment of the Court of First Instance, pursuant to art. 168A of the treaty as inserted by the Single European Act ('SEA'),[12] led to a welcome change in the whole judicial review process regarding the Commission's decisions in competition matters. This new court first convened on 1 November 1989. In the first three years of its operation, it rendered 38 judgments, five in 1990, 15 in 1991, and 18 in 1992, while the Court of Justice decided only seven competition cases in 1991.

In competition cases, the Court of First Instance exercises jurisdiction at first instance:

'in actions brought against an institution of the Communities by natural or legal persons [pursuant to the second paragraph of art. 173 and the third paragraph of art. 175 of the EC Treaty] relating to the implementation of the competition rules applicable to undertakings.'[13]

Where such an action is accompanied by an action for compensation for damage caused by a Community institution through the act or failure to act which is being challenged, the court also has jurisdiction to hear the action for compensation.

In addition to competition cases, the Court of First Instance has jurisdiction over other matters that generally involve complex factual situations such as

---

[11] See Chapter 13 below as regards the co-existence of Community competition rules with member states' competition legislation and ¶629ff. with respect to merger control.

[12] Council Decision 88/591 of 24 October 1988, OJ 1988 L319/1, amended OJ 1993 L144/21.

[13] Ibid. art. 3(1)(c) (as amended by Decision 93/350, OJ 1993 L144/21).

state aid and anti-dumping cases.[14] By hearing such cases at first instance, the Court of First Instance frees the Court of Justice to devote more of its time to cases of broader constitutional significance such as those concerning the institutional balance within the Community.

For details about this court and its procedure, see the section on judicial review in Chapter 11.

The Court of Justice

The Court of Justice of the European Communities is, like the Court of First Instance, based in Luxembourg. Under art. 164 of the treaty, its function is to 'ensure that in the interpretation and application of this Treaty the law is observed'. Since the Court of First Instance first convened, the Court of Justice has become a court of appeal in so far as competition decisions of the Commission are concerned. However, the court still enjoys exclusive jurisdiction as regards preliminary rulings originating from member states' courts and neither the SEA nor the treaty revisions under the Maastricht Treaty allow these cases to be referred to the Court of First Instance. See the judicial review section in Chapter 11 for details.

An appeal against a decision of the Court of First Instance must be brought within two months of the notification of the decision. An appeal may be brought against final decisions of the Court of First Instance and also against decisions which only partially dispose of the substantive issues, or which dispose of a procedural issue which concerns a plea of lack of competence or inadmissibility. The appeal may be brought by any party which is unsuccessful, either wholly or partially, in its submissions. Interveners other than member states and Community institutions may only bring such an appeal where they are directly affected by the decision of the Court of First Instance. Member states and Community institutions may also appeal against a decision in which they had not intervened (except in cases involving disputes between the Communities and their servants).

---

[14] In addition to competition cases, the following actions brought by natural or legal persons are included in the jurisdiction of the Court of First Instance:

   (1) staff cases;
   (2) certain categories of actions brought under the Coal and Steel Treaty;
   (3) actions for annulment and failure to act in the field of state aid;
   (4) actions for annulment and failure to act concerning trade protection measures in the field of dumping and subsidies;
   (5) actions for annulment and failure to act in the fields of agriculture, fisheries, the European funds (regional and social) and transport; and
   (6) all actions for damages caused by the Community's institutions or by its servants in the performance of their duties.

See Council Decision 88/591/ECSC, EEC, EURATOM, of 24 October 1988, establishing a Court of First Instance of the European Communities, OJ 1988 L319/1, corrected version OJ 1989 C215/1, and Council Decision 93/350/EURATOM, ECSC, EEC of 8 June 1993 amending Council Decision 88/591/ECSC, EEC, EURATOM establishing a Court of First Instance of the European Communities, OJ 1993 L144/21.

¶106

In addition to handling the appeals from decisions of the Court of First Instance, the Court of Justice has jurisdiction pursuant to art. 177 of the treaty to give 'preliminary rulings' at the request of national courts on questions concerning the interpretation or validity of provisions of Community law. Any national court or tribunal may request a preliminary ruling if it considers that a decision on a question of Community law is necessary to enable it to render a judgment. A court or tribunal from which there is no appeal must make such a request. When such a request is made, the proceedings in the national court are generally suspended until the Court of Justice gives a ruling. In the context of a preliminary reference, the court has the power to interpret Community law, but not to apply it to the facts of the case. After the court has issued a ruling, the case is sent back to the national court which applies the ruling to the facts of the case.

¶107 National courts

The role of national courts in the enforcement of art. 85 and 86 is explored in detail in Chapter 13. Here, only the basic principles will be reviewed.

The Court of Justice has made it clear that:

'as the prohibitions of Article 85(1) and 86 tend by their very nature to produce direct effects in relations between individuals, these Articles create direct rights in respect of the individuals concerned which the national courts must safeguard.'[15]

Hence, the breach of art. 85 or 86 may be the subject of a private action in a national court or arbitration tribunal.

To give effect to the principle of subsidiarity and in an effort to reduce the workload of its limited staff, the Commission actively encourages private actions before national courts and has issued a notice concerning the application of art. 85 and 86 by national courts.[16] In this connection, the Commission intends to give priority to cases of particular Community interest from a political, economic or legal standpoint.[17]

The power of the national courts to apply art. 85(1) necessarily includes the power to apply para. 2 of that article, and thus to declare void any agreements

---

[15] *Belgische Radio en Televisie & Anor (BRT) v SV SABAM & Anor* [1974] ECR 51, at p. 62 (para. 16).

[16] Notice on the co-operation between national courts and the Commission in applying art. 85 and 86 of the EC Treaty, OJ 1993 C39/6. See generally, *XXIst Report on Competition Policy – 1991*, points 69 and 70; *XXth Report on Competition Policy*, point 4.

[17] Notified agreements not presenting a Community interest will be settled by a comfort letter issued by the Commission. Complaints that do not deal with issues of Community interest will be referred back to national courts. See *Automec Srl v EC Commission ('Automec II')*, [1992] ECR II–2223.

prohibited pursuant to art. 85(1).[18] With respect to the application of art. 85(3), this remains within the exclusive jurisdiction of the Commission,[19] though national courts have the power to determine whether an agreement falls within the terms of a block exemption.[20] National law also governs the much-debated issue of whether and to what extent damages may be awarded by a national court for an infringement of the EC competition rules.[21]

¶108   The European Parliament

The European Parliament, the plenary sessions of which are generally held in Strasbourg while its committee meetings are held in Brussels, and the secretariat of which is based in Luxembourg, is composed of members who are chosen in direct elections held every five years. The Parliament exercises what are essentially advisory and supervisory powers. In many instances, the treaties provide that the Parliament must be consulted before a Commission proposal can be adopted by the Council, but the Parliament's opinion is generally not binding upon either the Council or the Commission.

The powers of the European Parliament were enlarged by the Single European Act, which provided for a specific co-operation procedure with the European Parliament with respect to several provisions of the treaty which are relevant to the internal market. The Treaty on European Union further increased the powers of the European Parliament, to which a right of co-decision has been granted with regard to certain matters.

Each year the Parliament adopts a resolution on the Commission's Annual Report on Competition Policy. The Parliament also influences competition policy by means of special resolutions and oral or written questions put to the Commission.[22]

On balance, however, it is fair to say that Parliament has not yet been able to play the role it could and should in the area of competition law. Indeed, more often than not, the Parliament has not been consulted on draft competition legislation, notwithstanding its repeated requests to that effect.[23]

---

[18] In the interest of legal certainty, the Court of Justice has made an exception to the national courts' otherwise unrestricted power to apply art. 85(2). See Chapter 11 where the so-called 'provisional validity' doctrine is explained, at ¶1125(2).

[19] Regulation 17/62, art. 9(1).

[20] See *SA Fonderies de Roubaix-Wattrelos v Société Nouvelle des Fonderies A Roux & Anor* [1976] ECR 111 (para. 11).

[21] See, e.g. Answer to Written Question 519/72, OJ 1973 C67/54. See also *Fifteenth Report on Competition Policy*, point 41, announcing the publication of a new report on the subject.

[22] In 1992, Members of Parliament raised 141 written and 66 oral questions. *XXIInd Report on Competition Policy – 1992*, point 540.

[23] See, e.g. item 3 in resolution on the XXth Report on Competition Policy, annex 1 to *XXIst Report on Competition Policy – 1991*.

¶109   The Economic and Social Committee

The Economic and Social Committee is a consultative body composed of 189 representatives divided into three groups: employers, trade unions and 'other interests' (e.g. consumers, farmers). These representatives are appointed by the governments of the member states for their expert knowledge.

The Secretariat of the Economic and Social Committee is located in Brussels, where all plenary and section meetings are held.

The Economic and Social Committee is consulted on Commission proposals before they are adopted by the Council. The committee also issues every year an opinion on the Commission's Annual Competition Report in which it assesses the Commission's competition policy in some detail.

ENFORCEMENT POLICY

¶110   Introduction

The purpose of this section (¶110 to ¶114) is to analyse the broad outlines of the EC competition enforcement policy with specific reference to:

- vertical agreements and practices (¶111);
- horizontal agreements and practices (¶112);
- abuses of a dominant position (¶113);
- enforcement technique (¶114).

¶111   Vertical agreements and practices

The Commission's attitude towards vertical agreements has been dominated by two main concerns: the promotion of the geographic integration of the common market and the protection of the independence of intermediaries.

Single market integration

From its inception EC competition policy has essentially been geared to the speeding-up of single market integration. This all-out effort of the Commission to promote the geographic unity of the common market has had a profound impact on the priorities it established in its initial enforcement programme. Rather than pursuing horizontal price cartels, viewed as the more damaging antitrust offence by those who adopt consumer welfare as the decisive criterion, the Commission went on the warpath against any agreement which tended to keep the common market partitioned along national boundaries. In particular, it moved against vertical arrangements whereby a manufacturer would entrust the distribution of his product to a separate distributor or licensee in each of the member states and prohibit 're-exports', thereby preventing parallel 'imports'.

¶111

Nobody denounces the enthusiasm with which the Commission and the courts pursue that goal in their respective activities. However, in the field of territorial restrictions there are instances where, in terms of consumer welfare, it would pay to adopt a 'rule of reason' or the doctrine of ancillary restraints instead of the per se approach hitherto followed.

It would seem that too many of the cases brought by the Commission proceed on the assumption that the industry concerned is operating in a truly common market. Yet, this ideal may not correspond to reality. There remain a number of market imperfections for which governments, not industry, are to blame. For example, in the *BMW Belgium* case,[24] the Commission and court dealt with the matter as if there had been a classical export prohibition without any objective justification. Yet, at the root of the problem one found Belgian price control measures causing prices for BMW cars to be lower in Belgium than in Germany, a matter clearly beyond the control of the manufacturer. Similarly, in *Distillers*,[25] the Commission condemned a dual pricing system as a disguised 'export ban' between the UK and the continent. Yet, to an economist, the continued existence of differing prices throughout the EC need not mean anything else than that the various markets or regions in the EC are not yet fully uniform, for a variety of reasons (e.g. tax structure, currency changes, standard of living and distribution pattern).

Another area where the Commission's drive towards single market integration could benefit from further reflection concerns the licensing of industrial property rights. Admittedly, the jurisprudence in this field is largely based on art. 30ff. of the EC Treaty, dealing with the free flow of goods, rather than on art. 85 and 86. However, the net effect of the application of art. 30 likewise serves the aim of opening up national markets to parallel imports.

In its *Deutsche Grammophon* ruling,[26] the Court of Justice developed what is commonly referred to as the 'Community-wide exhaustion' doctrine. Pursuant to that doctrine, the owner of an industrial property right may not avail himself of such right to block imports into a member state of products which have been sold by himself or with his consent in another member state. Such prevention of imports would conflict with the principle of free movement of goods enshrined in art. 30ff. of the EC Treaty in that the exercise of the industrial property right 'exhausts' any such rights he may enjoy within the EC with respect to such goods by putting the product for the first time on the market anywhere within the EC. Hence, the criteria underlying the selection of the first market must include the repercussions that such a decision may have on the other potential markets for the product. As a result, the decision to market a product could well

---

[24] *BMW Belgium*, OJ 1978 L46/33; on appeal: *BMW Belgium SA & Ors v EC Commission* [1979] ECR 2435.
[25] *The Distillers Co Ltd – Conditions of Sale and Price Terms*, OJ 1978 L50/16.
[26] *Deutsche Grammophon GmbH v Metro-SB-Großmärkte GmbH* [1971] ECR 487.

¶111

be delayed and certain member states could be systematically avoided, trade thereby being deflected, due to market imperfections which continue to exist throughout the EC.

Protection of intermediaries
The Commission's approach to the manufacturer-distributor or licensor-licensee relationship would seem to be inspired by notions of fair trade rather than competition law; the distributor or licensee should be protected against the possible greater bargaining power of the supplier.

Examples of the attitude of the Commission abound not only in its case law, but also in the various block exemptions which the Commission has issued in the field of licensing and distribution. Thus, for instance, a licensor may not have any influence over the licensee's output or sales policy. Similarly, a supplier's control over his distributor's performance is made difficult, if not impossible, in several respects. Yet, the manufacturer has a legitimate business interest in supervising the manner in which his products are marketed to the public. The supplier's interest clearly survives the transfer of title at the first sale of his product. It extends throughout the pipeline through which the product reaches the end-consumer. The supplier's reputation for quality, i.e. his goodwill, and, accordingly, his competitive position, depend upon the methods utilised further down the line in the marketing of the product. To the extent that the Commission is reducing a manufacturer's control over the distribution chain, the efficiency of the system, and hence consumer satisfaction, is bound to suffer. The Commission's restrictive policy on distribution and licensing arrangements may well provide an incentive for manufacturers to integrate vertically, eliminating the local middlemen over which they are no longer allowed to exercise sufficient control.

¶112   Horizontal agreements and practices
The Commission's enforcement policy concerning horizontal agreements and practices presents two basic characteristics: a generally hostile attitude with respect to price-fixing, market-sharing, boycotts and the like, the so-called 'bad' agreements (to use the terminology of French competition law); and a basically favourable attitude with respect to industrial co-operation agreements, the so-called 'good' agreements, especially between small and medium-sized undertakings.

'Bad agreements'
The Commission has consistently held that price-fixing, market-sharing, boycotts and other forms of horizontal anti-competitive conduct fall under the prohibition of art. 85(1) and are ineligible for an exemption under art. 85(3).

The Commission's hostility toward price-fixing agreements has also been extended to exchanges of price and other sensitive market information. In accordance with the wording of art. 85(1), the Commission has not limited its enforcement activity to agreements but has also prosecuted concerted practices. On this point, however, the Commission has tended easily to infer the existence of a concerted practice from the existence of a parallel course of conduct even in the absence of any evidence of illegal contacts between the parties concerned.

'Good agreements'

As far as co-operation agreements are concerned, the Commission has tended to take a generally liberal attitude. Some tentative, but positive, comments on a number of co-operation agreements were set out in the 1968 notice on co-operation agreements. Block exemptions have been issued with respect to specialisation and R&D agreements. Here also, however, the bias against large enterprises which often underlies the Commission's antitrust policy has led to these block exemptions being reserved to undertakings with limited market shares and turnover.

As far as joint ventures are concerned, the Commission has selected the approach which enables it to exercise a constant supervision over the operation of the joint venture; instead of applying the provisions of art. 85(1) liberally, it has preferred to deal with joint ventures in the context of art. 85(3) in which notifications are required and conditions for the grant of an exemption may be imposed.

Since Regulation 4064/89 (the 'merger regulation') came into force in September 1990, so-called concentrative joint ventures may fall within the scope of the merger regulation, whereas so-called co-operative joint ventures continue to be dealt with under art. 85 and Regulation 17/62.

During the first few years of operation of the merger regulation, the expeditious and pragmatic attitude of the Merger Task Force has provided a welcome contrast to the traditionally slow and less user-friendly approach of DG IV. Consequently, DG IV has been under pressure to streamline its procedure and criteria of assessment in order to reduce somewhat the difference in treatment between the two types of joint ventures. The publication by the Commission of its notice concerning the assessment of co-operative joint ventures pursuant to art. 85 of the EC Treaty constitutes a long overdue attempt to clarify the situation.

¶113   Abuses of a dominant position

Article 86 prohibits abuses of a dominant position. The Commission, with the support of the courts, has turned this provision into an instrument of control over the conduct of large enterprises. This result has been achieved through an extensive interpretation of the concepts of 'dominant position' and 'abuse'. The concept of dominant position has been watered down to that of pre-eminent position; any large undertaking whose market share is significantly higher than that of its next competitors will easily be found to have a dominant position under the criteria applied by the Commission and the Court of Justice in *United Brands*[27] and subsequent cases. The Commission has also extended considerably the scope of application of art. 86 by resorting to sometimes extremely narrow market definitions in which a relevant market may be limited to the products or services of the undertaking under investigation, thus leading to a finding of dominance regardless of the competitive position of the undertaking concerned in the overall market.[28] A characteristic feature of many art. 86 cases prosecuted by the Commission is its propensity to delineate the relevant market in such a way as to magnify the market share of the undertaking under investigation rather than the other way around.

It is interesting to note that the classic interpretation of what constitutes a dominant position under art. 86 would not always seem to be followed by the Merger Task Force when it has to determine whether a given merger or acquisition gives rise to the creation or strengthening of a dominant position within the meaning of the merger regulation. Indeed, whereas under art. 86 the analysis tends to focus on past conduct, the merger regulation is concerned about the future. It concentrates on the question whether the structure of competition in a market will be so affected by the concentration as to allow the combined firms in the future to act without the constraint of their competitors. It is not surprising, therefore, that the Merger Task Force has placed great emphasis in its analysis on the constraints which possible future market entrants will place on the conduct of the merged entity, and in doing so has been able to find no dominance even in the face of very high combined market shares.

Extensive interpretations also characterise the concept of 'abuse'. Whereas the text of art. 86 clearly suggests that this provision is only concerned with instances of exploitation of market power, the Commission and the Court of Justice have construed the concept of abuse to include monopolisation practices such as mergers and acquisitions.[29] As a result, art. 86 has been

---

[27] *Chiquita*, OJ 1976 L95/1, on appeal: *United Brands Co and United Brands Continentaal BV v EC Commission* [1978] ECR 207.

[28] See, e.g. *General Motors Continental*, OJ 1975 L29/14, on appeal: *General Motors Continental NV v EC Commission* [1975] ECR 1367; *ABG Oil Companies operating in the Netherlands*, OJ 1977 L117/1, on appeal: *Benzine en Petroleum Handelsmaatschappij (BP) & Ors v EC Commission* [1978] ECR 1513; *Hugin/Liptons* OJ 1978 L22/23, on appeal: *Hugin Kassaregister AB & Anor v EC Commission* [1979] ECR 1869.

[29] *Continental Can Co* OJ 1972 L7/25, on appeal: *Europemballage Corp and Continental Can Co Inc v EC Commission* [1973] ECR 215; *British American Tobacco Co Ltd & Anor v EC Commission* [1987] ECR 4487.

¶113

developed as a provision which allows the Commission to regulate a wide range of unilateral practices by large undertakings.

¶114   Enforcement technique

The legal technique followed by the Commission has been to regulate business under art. 85(3) instead of developing a more flexible interpretation of art. 85(1). This approach has slowed down the administrative process. However, notwithstanding the rather limited number of decisions which the Commission is able to adopt every year, its deterrent effect is considerable, as a result of the high fines that are being imposed. The procedure leading to the decision-making is largely inquisitorial in that the powers of fact-finding, prosecution and decision-making are all vested in the Commission.

Legal technique

In terms of legal technique, the Commission has, since the early days of the enforcement of the competition provisions, preferred to regulate business under art. 85(3) instead of adopting a more realistic interpretation of the required restrictive effect on competition under art. 85(1) as first advocated by the Court of Justice in *Société Technique Minière*.[30] Under the Commission's approach, the mere fact that a party's freedom of action is restricted is sufficient to establish a restriction of competition which infringes art. 85(1). This is so even if the overall effect of this restriction is beneficial and pro-competitive. For example, any exclusive distribution agreement is generally viewed by the Commission as restricting competition under art. 85(1) even though it is ready to admit that, in most instances, exclusive distribution agreements increase competition and thus qualify for an exemption under art. 85(3).

As a result of this policy, the Commission has been flooded with notifications. Indeed, if virtually everything is deemed to be restrictive of competition under art. 85(1) and if a 'rule of reason' treatment is generally only applied by the Commission under art. 85(3), business has little choice but to file individual notifications.

The congestion resulting from the rigid legal technique followed by the Commission is aggravated by its constant search for wider powers than those originally entrusted to it under the treaty rules on competition and the implementing legislation. Thus, for example, the Commission sought and obtained from the Court of Justice the power to control mergers under art. 86.[31]

---

[30] *Société Technique Minière v Maschinenbau Ulm GmbH* [1966] ECR 235. The interpretation of the required restrictive effect on competition under art. 85(1) may differ depending on the subject-matter, and is often influenced by the fact that it is the court rather than the Commission which sets the parameters for the EC competition law analysis in relation to a given subject-matter for the first time. See, e.g. *Pronuptia de Paris v Pronuptia de Paris Irmgard Schillgalis* [1986] ECR 353.
[31] *Continental Can Co*, OJ 1972 L7/25, on appeal: *Europemballage Corp and Continental Can Co Inc v EC Commission* [1973] ECR 215; *British American Tobacco & Anor v EC Commission* [1987] ECR 4487.

Similarly, the Commission received the power to adopt interim measures notwithstanding the absence of any provision to that effect in Regulation 17/62.[32]

At times, the Commission has not even hesitated to use its powers under the competition rules to pursue aims which go beyond the parameters of a competition policy, as generally understood. For example, the block exemption dealing with the selective distribution of automobiles contains provisions covering the required notice period to be given when a dealer is dismissed, which is clearly a matter of social policy.[33] The same block exemption also provides for the harmonisation of car prices throughout the Community, a matter which can be said to pertain more to the commercial, fiscal and industrial policy of the Community than to competition policy.[34]

Proposals for reducing the backlog

The Commission's refusal to adopt a rule of reason approach under art. 85(1), its constant quest for wider powers under the competition rules, combined with its pursuit of objectives other than those that can be said to relate directly to the competitive process, have led to a situation where the Commission's workload has outgrown its capacity by far. Over the years, the backlog of pending cases and unprocessed notifications has reached unacceptable proportions. The Commission blames staff shortages, the necessary translation work and the requirements of due process for slowing down the administrative process and proposes to remedy this state of affairs by issuing more block exemptions, by including so-called 'opposition procedures' in such block exemptions, by a more widespread use of comfort letters and by encouraging more settlements and private enforcement in national courts.

While comfort letters and settlements may be helpful devices to speed up procedures, they do not offer the same legal value as an exemption decision under art. 85(3).

Admittedly, the adoption of block exemptions would, in principle, do away with the need for filing individual notifications to the extent that the terms of the agreement or practice fall squarely within the permissible bounds set out in the block exemption. Unfortunately, however, several of the block exemptions contain so many 'ifs and buts' that the Commission felt obliged to issue a set of

---

[32] *Camera Care Ltd v EC Commission* [1980] ECR 119.

[33] Commission Regulation 123/85 on the application of art. 85(3) of the treaty to certain categories of motor vehicle distribution and servicing agreements, art. 5(2)(2)–(3), OJ 1985 L15/16.

[34] Regulation 123/85, art. 10(3), (4) and Commission notice concerning Regulation 123/85 on the application of art. 85(3) of the treaty to certain categories of motor vehicle distribution and servicing agreements, OJ 1985 C17/4, II.

clarifying guidelines.[35] This indicates that legal certainty is not necessarily enhanced by the issuing of block exemptions.

Very often also, the block exemptions contain detailed lists ('white' or 'black') of clauses over which the Commission passes a judgment based more on considerations of equity or reasonableness than on an analysis of their actual impact on the market. The result is that contractual relationships are being codified in abstracto and in considerable detail, irrespective of the market position of the parties involved and the effect on the market at large.

As to the Commission's policy actively to encourage private enforcement before national courts, including the possibility of claiming damages, it seems questionable whether such decentralised enforcement will actually reduce the burden of the Commission. On the contrary, companies may file even more notifications to the Commission in order to seek protection against national enforcement. In addition, the Commission's promotion of national enforcement is likely to have other undesirable side-effects, such as forum shopping in the various member states, for example.

In any event, with the European Economic Area ('EEA') having come into effect on 1 January 1994, the extended geographic scope of application of EC competition law will put further strains on the already limited capacity of DG IV. From this perspective, it is imperative for DG IV to take a close look at its bureaucratic process to see where it could learn from the hitherto successful experience of the first few years of operation of the Merger Task Force. Indeed, the Commission seems ready to modify its decision-making process so as to accelerate the procedure (see Chapter 11, ¶1127).

Deterrent effect

Due to its limited resources, the Commission, on average, is only able to issue some ten to 20 decisions a year. Notwithstanding this very small number, the Commission nevertheless manages to ensure a fair degree of overall compliance because the amount of fines it has imposed on defendants in recent years has increased to the point at which very few companies could still afford to take the risk of being caught.

While such a policy of imposing stiff fines may be warranted as long as the infringements are obvious and serious, it becomes highly questionable when severe fines are being imposed for infringements which could only be established by developing or stretching the law further than in its earlier interpretation. Furthermore, the virtually unlimited discretion enjoyed by the Commission in setting the amount of the fine has, at times, given rise to unequal

---

[35] See, in addition to the Commission notice concerning Regulation 123/85, the Commission notice concerning Regulations 1983/83 and 1984/83 on the application of art. 85(3) of the treaty to categories of exclusive distribution and exclusive purchasing agreements, OJ 1984 L101/2.

¶114

treatment of defendants, despite the similarity of the infringement and the surrounding circumstances.

Inquisitorial procedure

The proceedings before the Commission are of an administrative nature, largely written instead of oral, and inquisitorial in that the Commission combines the roles of prosecutor and judge.

Initially, the critical comments from legal and business circles regarding the Community's procedures in the antitrust field tended to be brushed aside. This attitude has changed. The Community authorities have realised that their procedures must become more transparent in order not to lose credibility. The Commission has implemented a number of improvements that are essentially designed to alleviate shortcomings in the discovery procedure and in the organisation of the hearing.[36] The Commission continues, however, to reject suggestions that it should distinguish between its roles as prosecutor and judge for the purposes of its internal procedure, asserting that the current procedures achieve a fair balance between the need for efficiency and respect for the rights of the defendant.[37]

It is interesting to note that several of the procedural improvements have been adopted by the Commission on its own initiative rather than being compelled by rulings of the Court of Justice. It is paradoxical that the Commission, notwithstanding its role as prosecutor has, over the years, proved to be more liberal than the court on issues of due process.

Notwithstanding this improved climate resulting from the Commission's efforts, the proceedings remain administrative in nature. The Commission as a collegiate body is not seen to participate in the proceedings: the defendant's

---

[36] *Eleventh Report on Competition Policy*, points 14–18; *Twelfth Report on Competition Policy*, points 29–37; *Thirteenth Report on Competition Policy*, points 70–76.

[37] *XXth Report on Competition Policy*, point 89, see also *XXIst Report on Competition Policy – 1991*, p. 232, where the Commission replied as follows to the concern expressed by the European Parliament about the concentration of powers in a single body:

'The Commission fulfils in competition cases at one and the same time the functions of inquiry, decision and sanction. This reflects an essential part of the Continental European law tradition and it has been embodied first into the ECSC Treaty and later into various Council regulations implementing the EEC Treaty. The Court of Justice has on several occasions confirmed that the current system is compatible with the legal order of the European Community as long as the relevant administrative decisions are subject to a strict judicial control which relates to both the factual and the legal findings of the Commission. Such a control is fully guaranteed by the two instances of the European Court.

In addition, the administrative procedure of the Commission is governed by a system of checks and balances. Each decision, before being adopted by the Commission, is examined by the Co-ordination Unit of DG IV, by the Legal Service and by the Advisory Committee on Restrictive Practices and Dominant Positions. Furthermore, the role of the Hearing Officer ensures that the rights of defence on interested and third parties are fully respected.

Under these circumstances the Commission does not see any need for a change of its procedural rules. Splitting up the above-mentioned functions between several bodies would lead to a considerable loss of efficiency and would therefore be contrary to the interest of the Community.'

¶114

fate is sealed in an ex parte meeting. Furthermore, the Commission is not a tribunal but rather a political institution. As a result, its decisions are not made on purely legal grounds but emerge in a political context.

A system of checks and balances is required when so much power is vested in the Commission as enforcer of the competition rules.

In this regard, it is too early to assess whether the Court of First Instance will give a higher priority than the Court of Justice to the rights of the defendant in Commission proceedings. Based upon recent judgments, the Court of First Instance would appear inclined to investigate in greater detail the workings of the Commission's internal procedure leading up to the adoption of the final decision, but is more reluctant to review more substantive issues such as the discretionary power exercised by the Commission when imposing fines.

¶114

2 Basic Provisions

ARTICLES 85 AND 86: THE TWO BASIC PROVISIONS AND THEIR SCOPE OF APPLICATION

¶201 Introduction

The EC rules on competition are set out in art. 85 to 94 of the treaty. The chapter of the treaty containing these provisions is subdivided into three sections. Section 1 deals with 'rules applying to undertakings' and consists of art. 85 to 90. Section 2 consists of only one provision, art. 91, dealing with intra-Community dumping. Section 3 contains art. 92 to 94 dealing with state aid, a factor which in the same way may distort competition.

The two pillars of the EC competition rules applying to private undertakings are art. 85 and 86. Article 85 prohibits agreements or concerted practices which have an anti-competitive objective or effect. Article 86 prohibits the abuse of a dominant position.

Pursuant to art. 90 of the treaty, the competition rules are also applicable to public undertakings, provided however, that 'the application of such rules does not obstruct the performance, in law or in fact, of the particular tasks assigned to them'.

Article 87 of the treaty leaves it to the Council of Ministers to adopt the regulations necessary to enforce the principles laid down in art. 85 and 86.[1]

Articles 88 and 89 of the treaty deal with the respective powers of the Commission and the local authorities in the member states to apply art. 85 and

---

[1] The basic implementing regulation is Regulation 17/62 of the Council implementing art. 85 and 86 of the treaty, JO 1962 13/204, amended by JO 1962 58/1655, by JO 1963 162/2696 and by JO 1971 L285/49.

A major implementing regulation was adopted in 1989 for mergers: Council Regulation 4064/89 on the control of concentrations between undertakings, OJ 1990 L257/13. See Chapter 6.

The following specific implementing regulations were issued for the transport sector:

(1) Council Regulation 1017/68 applying rules of competition to transport by rail, road and inland waterway, JO 1968 L175/1.
(2) Council Regulation 4056/86 laying down detailed rules for the application of art. 85 and 86 of the treaty to maritime transport, OJ 1986 L378/4.
(3) Council Regulation 3975/87 laying down the procedure for the application of the rules on competition to undertakings in the air transport sector, OJ 1987 L374/1, as amended by Council Regulation 1284/91, OJ 1991 L122/2.

86 during the interim period, pending the adoption of the implementing legislation by the Council pursuant to art. 87.

Even though art. 85 is meant to cover concerted action as opposed to abusive conduct covered by art. 86, these provisions need to be interpreted in conjunction with each other.[2] As the court said in *Continental Can*, 'Articles 85 and 86 cannot be interpreted in such a way that they contradict each other, because they serve to achieve the same aim'.[3] Thus, it is important that art. 85 and 86 be applied in a manner consistent with the objectives of the common market as set out in art. 2 and 3 of the treaty.[4]

Both art. 85 and 86 may apply to the same agreement or practice.[5] For example, in *Flat Glass*,[6] the Commission found that the parties had entered into restrictive agreements in violation of art. 85, and had abused a collective dominant position – established on the basis of those agreements – in violation of art. 86. In practice, the parallel application of art. 85 and 86 may give rise to difficulties, which stem largely from the need to achieve logical coherence in the application of these provisions. In *Tetra Pak*,[7] the issue arose of whether the exemption of an agreement under art. 85(3) precludes the application of art. 86. The Court of First Instance held that 'in the scheme for the protection of competition established by the Treaty the grant of exemption, whether individual or block exemption, under Article 85(3) cannot be such as to render inapplicable the prohibition set out in Article 86'.[8]

---

[2] See *Europemballage Corp and Continental Can Co Inc v EC Commission* [1973] ECR 215, at p. 244 (para. 25). For a recent application of this principle, see *Decca Navigator System* [1989] 1 CEC 2 & 137; OJ 1989 L43/27, para. 122. See also *Flat Glass*, OJ 1989 L33/44; on appeal: *Società Italiano Vetro SpA & Ors v EC Commission* [1992] 2 CEC 33, where both art. 85 and art. 86 were applied to the same facts.

[3] *Europemballage Corp and Continental Can Co Inc v EC Commission* [1973] ECR 215, at p. 244 (para. 25).

[4] Article 3(f) of the EEC Treaty (art. 3(g) of the EC Treaty) in particular is frequently referred to in competition cases. This paragraph provides for 'the institution of a system ensuring that competition in the common market is not distorted'.

[5] In *Hoffmann-La Roche v EC Commission* [1979] ECR 461, at p. 550 (para. 116), the court stated:

'... the fact that agreements of this kind might fall within Article 85 and in particular within paragraph 3 thereof does not preclude the application of Article 86, since this latter article is expressly aimed in fact at situations which clearly originate in contractual relations so that in such cases the Commission is entitled, taking into account the nature of the reciprocal undertakings entered into and the competitive position of the various contracting parties on the market or markets in which they operate to proceed on the basis of Article 85 or Article 86.'

See also *Ahmed Saeed Flugreisen & Anor v Zentrale zur Bekämpfung unlauteren Wettbewerbs* [1989] ECR 803, at pp. 849 (para. 37); *Tetra Pak Rausing SA v EC Commission* [1990] ECR II-309, at p. II-356 (para. 21).

[6] *Flat Glass*, OJ 1989 L33/44, on appeal: *Società Italiano Vetro SpA & Ors v EC Commission*, [1992] 2 CEC 33. For examples of other cases in which both art. 85 and 86 have been applied, see *French-West African Shipowners' Committee*, OJ 1992 L134/1; *Cewal, Cowac and Ukwal*, OJ 1993 L34/20; *Decca Navigator System*, OJ 1989 L43/27.

[7] *Tetra Pak Rausing SA v EC Commission* [1990] ECR II-309.

[8] Id., at p. II-358 (para. 25). The court noted, however, that the application of art. 86 could be different, depending on whether the agreement benefited from an individual exemption or a block exemption. Since an individual exemption under art. 85(3) necessarily involves a positive assessment of the individual case, findings made in making such an assessment must be taken into account in applying art. 86 unless circumstances have changed. In contrast, that an agreement may benefit from a block exemption does not involve such an individualised assessment, so the exemption does not influence the application of art. 86. Id., at pp. II-359–II-360 (para. 28–29).

¶201

In order for the EC authorities to have jurisdiction over a practice, the agreement or conduct must have an effect on trade between member states. This requirement constitutes the natural dividing line between the enforcement of the treaty rules on competition and national competition laws. However, in practice the 'effect on trade' concept has been broadly interpreted by both the Commission and the court. Consequently, the co-existence of both the EC and national rules of competition has at times given rise to concurrent enforcement. This issue is treated in Chapter 13.

Similarly, the requirement of an effect on trade defines the jurisdictional scope of the EC competition rules with respect to third countries. To the extent that agreements or conduct outside the EC may have an effect on trade within the EC, such practices may fall within the purview of art. 85 and 86.

Finally, within the scope of application of art. 85 and 86, regard must be given to the fact that a number of special sectors of the economy are exempt, either in whole or in part, from the application of the EC competition rules. The application of art. 85 and 86 to a number of special sectors is discussed in Chapter 10.

ARTICLE 85: CONCERTED ACTION RESTRICTIVE OF COMPETITION

¶202   Text of the article

The text of art. 85 provides that:

'1. The following shall be prohibited as incompatible with the common market: all agreements between undertakings, decisions by associations of undertakings and concerted practices which may affect trade between member states and which have as their object or effect the prevention, restriction or distortion of competition within the common market, and in particular those which:

(a) directly or indirectly fix purchase or selling prices or any other trading conditions;

(b) limit or control production, markets, technical development, or investment;

(c) share markets or sources of supply;

(d) apply dissimilar conditions to equivalent transactions with other trading parties, thereby placing them at a competitive disadvantage;

(e) make the conclusion of contracts subject to acceptance by the other parties of supplementary obligations which, by their nature or according to commercial usage, have no connection with the subject of such contracts.

2. Any agreements or decisions prohibited pursuant to this article shall be automatically void.

3. The provisions of paragraph 1 may, however, be declared inapplicable in the case of:

– any agreement or category of agreements between undertakings;

– any decision or category of decisions by associations of undertakings;

– any concerted practice or category of concerted practices;

which contributes to improving the production or distribution of goods or to promoting technical or economic progress, while allowing consumers a fair share of the resulting benefit, and which does not:

(a) impose on the undertakings concerned restrictions which are not indispensable to the attainment of these objectives;

(b) afford such undertakings the possibility of eliminating competition in respect of a substantial part of the products in question.'

Thus, the first paragraph of the article sets out the prohibition of concerted action, the second paragraph mentions automatic nullity as the sanction for the violation of this prohibition and the third paragraph provides for exemption from the prohibition if certain conditions are met.

ARTICLE 85(1): THE PROHIBITION OF CONCERTED ACTION

¶203   Conditions of prohibition

For the prohibition contained in art. 85(1) to apply there must be:

● some form of concerted action between undertakings (see ¶204–¶213);

● which perceptibly restricts or is intended to restrict competition within the common market (see ¶214–¶219);

● which may affect trade between member states (see ¶220–¶224).

¶204   Concerted action between undertakings

The wording of art. 85(1) makes it clear that there must be at least two undertakings, acting in concert.

The term 'undertaking' is not defined anywhere in the treaty. The Court of Justice has ruled that the concept of 'undertaking' embraces any entity carrying on an economic activity regardless of its legal status or the way it is financed.[9] According to the Commission:

'the term "undertaking" must be viewed in the broadest sense covering any entity engaged in economic or commercial activities such as production, distribution or the supply of services and ranging from small shops run by one individual to large industrial companies.'[10]

Indeed, from the cases it appears that virtually every natural or legal person participating in the economic process will qualify as an undertaking. For example, in addition to companies and associations of various kinds, individuals have likewise been held to constitute an undertaking within the sense of art. 85.[11] The nationality or location of the undertaking has no bearing on the issue.[12] Similarly, it is irrelevant whether the undertaking is privately or publicly owned.[13] Even state-controlled trade organisations of east-European countries have been considered to fall within the scope of the undertaking concept.[14]

Although the member states as such do not qualify as 'undertakings' and are therefore not the addressees of art. 85 and 86, these treaty provisions coupled with art. 3(g) (formerly art. 3 (f)) and 5 of the treaty are increasingly used by the

---

[9] *Höfner and Elsner v Macrotron* [1991] ECR I-1979, at p. I-2016 (para. 21). See also *1990 World Cup*, OJ 1992 L326/31.

[10] EEC Competition Rules – Guide for Small and Medium-Sized Enterprises, (1983) European Documentation, at p. 17.

[11] See, e.g. *AOIP/Beyrard*, OJ 1976 L6/8 (inventor); *Reuter/BASF*, OJ 1976 L254/40 (inventor); *RAI/UNITEL*, OJ 1978 L157/39 (artists); *Vaessen/Morris*, OJ 1979 L19/32 (inventor); *Toltecs/Dorcet*, OJ 1982 L379/19 (businessman); *Nutricia*, OJ 1983 L376/22 (businessman).

[12] From the table of cases (see Annex 4 below), it is readily apparent that many undertakings from third countries have suffered the rigours of EC competition law.

[13] Article 90(1) of the EC Treaty confirms the broad principle that public undertakings are subject to the rules of competition. However, art. 90(2) provides for an important qualification of that principle. In *Bodson v Pompes Funèbres des Régions Libérées* [1988] ECR 2479, at p. 2512 (para. 18), the court ruled that a contract pursuant to which a commune acting in its capacity as a public authority conferred an exclusive licence on a company for the operation of funeral services was not an agreement 'between undertakings' for art. 85 purposes.

[14] *Aluminium Imports from Eastern Europe*, OJ 1985 L92/1, at p. 37, where the Commission stated:

'The foreign trade organizations Raznoimport, Impexmetal, Metalimex, Metalimex/Kerametal and Intrac are also undertakings for the purposes of Article 85. The function of each of the organizations was to engage in the import and export of a range of goods. In the matters concerned by these proceedings each of the foreign trade organizations was engaged in selling aluminium, one of the activities for which each had been specifically established under the law of the country in which it was situated. Entities which engage in the activity of trade are to be regarded as undertakings for the purposes of Article 85, whatever their precise status may be under the domestic law of their country of origin, and even where they are given no separate status from the State.

It follows that the applicability of Article 85, since it relates to trading activities, is not defeated by claims of sovereign immunity. Such claims are properly confined to acts which are those of government and not of trade. Even if the foreign trade organizations were indistinguishable under Socialist law from the State, no sovereign immunity would attach to their participation in the Brandeis agreements since this was an exclusively commercial activity. Furthermore the domestic law of Member States does not accord sovereign immunity to foreign trade organizations of the type concerned by these proceedings.'

¶204

court to scrutinise the effects of national legislation upon competition (see Chapter 13).

¶205   Concerted action: plurality of actors

The concept of concerted action implies the involvement of at least two parties acting in concert. In this connection the question arises whether an employee or agent of a company is capable of independent action (see ¶206 and ¶207 respectively). Similarly, the question to what extent a subsidiary company or one controlled by other means, may nevertheless be regarded as a separate undertaking from the parent or controlling company must be considered (see ¶208).

¶206   Employee relationship

Employees are normally acting on behalf of an undertaking and therefore do not constitute an undertaking themselves.[15] However, from the moment an employee pursues his own economic interests, and where they are different from his employer's interests, he might well become an undertaking within the sense of art. 85.[16]

¶207   Agency relationship

In 1962, the Commission issued a notice on exclusive dealing contracts with commercial agents, i.e. intermediaries negotiating transactions on behalf of and for the benefit of another enterprise.[17] The notice discusses the possible impact on competition of agreements with commercial agents from two perspectives. It examines the competitive conditions on both the market for the provision of goods and on the market for the provision of services consisting of the negotiation and conclusion of transactions.

The notice does not consider an exclusive dealing contract with commercial agents to have a restrictive effect on the market for the provision of goods, provided the agent does not assume any financial risk resulting from the transaction. According to the notice, the commercial agent in that case only performs an auxiliary function, acting on the instructions and in the interest of the enterprise on whose behalf he is operating.

Factors which may indicate that an exclusive dealing contract does have a

---

[15] See *Suiker Unie & Ors v EC Commission* [1975] ECR 1663, at p. 2007 (para. 539); see also Answer to Written Question No. 2391/83, OJ 1984 C222/21, dealing with the status of professional soccer players under the EC competition rules.

[16] See, e.g. *Reuter/BASF*, OJ 1976 L254/40, where the Commission dealt with a non-competition clause between a company and a former employee.

[17] Commission notice on exclusive dealing contracts with commercial agents, OJ 1962 139/2921.

restrictive effect upon the market for the provision of goods and is therefore subject to the application of art. 85(1) are:

(1) the fact that the agent is required to keep, or does in fact keep, a considerable stock of contract products as his own property;

(2) the fact that the agent is required to organise or provide a substantial service to customers free of charge at his own expense;

(3) the ability for the agent to determine prices or conditions of sales.

As regards the typical market for the provision of services by an intermediary, i.e. the negotiation and/or conclusion of transactions, the notice does not perceive any restriction of competition where an agent acts in an auxiliary capacity according to the criterion described above: namely where the agent suffers no financial risks and works exclusively for one principal for a certain period of time. At the time of publication of the notice, the Commission indeed considered the exclusive devotion of an agent to one principal for a certain period of time to be the result of the special obligation between the commercial agent and his principal to protect each other's interests.[18]

Subsequent case law of the Commission and the court has demonstrated the need for caution in the reliance on the principles contained in the notice. The case law typically consists of a rejection of the defence that art. 85 is not applicable because a company was acting in the role of an agent.[19] In *Pittsburgh Corning Europe*,[20] for instance, the Commission declared the notice inapplicable in the absence of economic dependence between agent and principal. In *Aluminium Imports from Eastern Europe*, the Commission intimated that even if a company were to be considered to be an agent, it could still be subject to art. 85(1) where the decision to enter into or remain within an agency agreement placed restrictions upon competition in the market for the provision of an agent's services.[21] The Court of Justice for its part gave the opinion that travel agents operating in the name and on behalf of tour operators organising the travel in question are nevertheless independent intermediaries as they sell travel organised by a large number of different tour operators and the tour operators in turn sell their products through a very large number of travel agents.[22] As a result, the court condemned a system of government-backed resale price maintenance as contrary to art. 85(1).[23]

Agency agreements may equally be scrutinised under art. 86. In the *Sugar*

---

[18] Ibid.
[19] See ¶315.
[20] *Pittsburgh Corning Europe – Formica Belgium – Hertel*, JO 1972 L272/35.
[21] *Aluminium Imports from Eastern Europe*, OJ 1985 L92/1, at p. 37.
[22] *Vereniging van Vlaamse reisbureaus v Sociale Dienst van de plaatselijke en gewestelijke overheidsdiensten* [1987] ECR 3801.
[23] Id., at p. 3828 (para. 20 and 21).

Cartel case[24] the court stated that a contractual clause prohibiting competition between a principal, occupying a dominant position, and his agent may constitute an abuse within the meaning of art. 86 when the agent performs duties which, from an economic point of view, are approximately the same as those carried out by an independent dealer.[25]

There has been a substantial evolution in the Commission's reasoning concerning this subject since the ruling by the court in the *Vlaamse Reisbureaus* case.[26] As a result the Commission has begun to prepare new guidelines on the status of agency agreements under EC competition law which are discussed in Chapter 3.

¶208   Related companies: the 'economic entity'

Are agreements between connected undertakings within the scope of art. 85(1)? The Commission tackled the question of so-called 'intra-enterprise conspiracy' in *Christiani & Nielsen*[27] where it concluded that a market-sharing agreement between a Danish company and its wholly-owned Dutch subsidiary was outside the scope of art. 85 because there was no competitive relationship existing between the two companies capable of being restricted. In the Commission's view, the agreement was 'only a division of labour within the same economic entity'. In contrast, the Commission has determined that the fact that electricity producers co-operate so closely that they can be said to form 'one indivisible system of public supply' in providing electricity to the public does not mean that they form a single economic unit, particularly when they are separate legal entities that pursue independent pricing policies.[28]

The court has endorsed the Commission's 'economic entity' approach, ruling that art. 85 does not apply to a parent-subsidiary relationship because the subsidiary, 'although having separate legal personality, enjoys no economic

---

[24] *Suiker Unie & Ors v EC Commission* [1975] ECR 1663.

[25] Id., at p. 1998 (para. 482–483). The court went on to recognise that even clauses prohibiting competition imposed by an undertaking occupying a dominant position on its trade representatives may constitute an abuse if foreign competitors are unable to find independent operators who can market their products on a sufficiently large scale.

[26] *Vereniging van Vlaamse reisbureaus v Sociale Dienst van de plaatselijke en gewestelijke overheidsdiensten* [1987] ECR 3801.

[27] *Christiani & Nielsen*, JO 1969 L165/12. Similarly, in *Kodak*, JO 1970 L147/24, at p. 25, the Commission stated that '[w]hen it is established, as is so in this case, that the subsidiary companies in question are exclusively and wholly subject to their parent company, and that the latter in fact exercises its power of control by issuing to them precise instructions, it is impossible for them to behave independently inter se in the areas governed by the parent company'. In the context of joint ventures, the Commission has stated that art. 85(1) does not apply to 'JVs formed by parents which all belong to the same group and which are not in a position freely to determine their market behaviour: in such a case its creation is merely a matter of internal organization and allocation of tasks within the group.' (Commission notice concerning the assessment of co-operative joint ventures pursuant to art. 85 of the EEC Treaty, OJ 1993 C43/2).

[28] *IJsselcentrale*, OJ 1991 L28/32, at p. 40.

independence'.[29] In a subsequent case, the court applied the same reasoning where the undertakings form an economic unit within which the subsidiary has no real freedom to determine its course of action in the market. The court added one further qualification by saying that the reasoning applied only if the agreements or practices are concerned merely with the internal allocation of tasks as between the undertakings.[30] This leaves the way open to an application of art. 85 to agreements and practices between members of the same group 'where such instruments and practices have the object or effect of restraining competition from third parties'.[31]

Thus far, the Commission and the court have rarely had to deal with the issue of what gives a company control over another as most cases have involved a parent and a wholly-owned subsidiary. In one case, however, the Commission found that a company was not in a position to control the commercial activity of another because it only held 50 per cent of the shares, only appointed half of the board members and the subsidiary had substantial independence in that it distributed other brands and had its own sales force.[32] Also, it would seem conceivable that under certain circumstances, a minority shareholding by one company could provide effective control over another company. Hence, its dealings with that 'subsidiary' company would fall outside the scope of art. 85(1) as it could no longer be considered a competitor.[33]

---

[29] See *Béguelin Import v GL Import Export* [1971] ECR 949, at p. 959 (para. 8); see also *ICI & Ors v EC Commission* [1972] ECR 619, at p. 662 (para. 132–134); *Commercial Solvents v EC Commission* [1974] ECR 223, at pp. 253–254 (para. 37).

[30] *Centrafarm v Sterling Drug* [1974] ECR 1147, at p. 1167 (para. 41). See also *Bodson v Pompes Funèbres* [1988] ECR 2479, at p. 2513 (para. 19); [1990] 1 CEC 3; *Hydrotherm v Compact* [1984] ECR 2999. The Court of First Instance may soon have the opportunity to address this issue. In a pending case, *VIHO Europe BV v EC Commission*, Case T-102/92, not yet decided, one of the issues raised on appeal is whether an agreement between a parent and its subsidiaries concerning matters relating to the distribution of goods is caught by art. 85(1).

[31] See the opinion of Advocate General Trabucchi in *Centrafarm v Sterling Drug* [1974] ECR 1147, at pp. 1179–1180. In *Bodson v Pompes Funèbres des Régions Libérées* [1988] ECR 2479, at p. 2513 (para. 20), the court suggested that art. 85(1) may apply to holders of concessions belonging to the same group if they pursued different marketing strategies.

[32] *Gosme/Martell-DMP*, OJ 1991 L185/23, at p. 28 (para. 30). See also *1990 World Cup*, OJ 1992 L326/31, in which the Commission discussed the nature of the relationship between various entities for purposes of allocating responsibility for infringements of art. 85(1).

[33] In the Complementary Note to Form A/B, a group relationship is deemed to exist where a firm:

(1) owns more than half the capital or business assets, or
(2) has the power to exercise more than half the voting rights, or
(3) has the power to appoint more than half the members of the supervisory board, board of directors or bodies legally representing the undertaking, or
(4) has the right to manage the affairs of another, (para. IX 3.1).

This definition is in line with the definition of 'connected undertakings' contained in block exemptions issued by the Commission. However, parties filing Form A/B are also requested to provide the following information: 'If you have a substantial interest falling short of control (more than 25 per cent but less than 50 per cent) in some other company competing in a market affected by the arrangements, or if some other such company has a substantial interest in yours, give its name and address and brief details.' (para. IX 3.5.) In a recent decision, the Commission considered that '[a] mere 25.001 per cent interest does not give rise, in view of the larger shares held by other companies . . ., to a parent–subsidiary relationship . . .'. *Welded Steel Mesh* [1989] 2 CEC 2,051; OJ 1989 L260/1, para. 178. Cases decided under the merger regulation may also shed light on the elusive concept of control. See Chapter 6.

It should be noted that the economic entity theory is not only relevant in establishing whether there are at least two undertakings acting in concert, but that it has also been used by the Commission to impose liability on the parent company for the activities of its subsidiary.[34] In this regard, the economic unit theory has been used by the Commission to attack companies situated outside the EC.[35]

¶209   Form of concerted action

The language of art. 85(1) is very broad in that it prohibits 'all agreements between undertakings, decisions by associations of undertakings and concerted practices'. The prohibition is considered in detail at ¶210–¶213.

¶210   Agreements

For art. 85(1) to apply to an agreement, it suffices that a provision expresses the intention of the parties without it being necessary for it to constitute a valid and binding contract under national law.[36] Thus, a so-called 'gentlemen's agreement' has been held to constitute an agreement within the sense of art. 85(1).[37] Furthermore, both horizontal agreements (i.e. between parties

---

[34] See, e.g. *Peroxygen Products*, OJ 1985 L35/1, at p. 14, where the Commission stated:

'For the purpose of the present proceedings the Commission does not consider the Interox grouping as an undertaking possessing an identity sufficiently distinct from that of its two parent companies so as to absolve Solvay and Laporte themselves (as opposed to Interox) from liability under EEC competition rules. The Interox operation is simply the framework in which the activities of Solvay and Laporte in the peroxygen sector are coordinated and profits shared and all major policy decisions are taken by the parent companies. The Interox companies do not determine their market behaviour autonomously but in essentials follow directives issued by the parent companies.'

[35] See ¶255.

[36] *Sandoz v EC Commission* [1990] ECR I-45, at I-45–I-46 (para. 2 of summary judgment). See also *Franco-Japanese ballbearings agreement*, OJ 1974 L343/19, at p. 24. Furthermore, it should be noted that the 'voluntary' limitation of one's freedom does not exclude a situation where certain parties were subject to some pressure. For example, in *Wood Pulp*, OJ 1985 L85/1, at p. 23; on appeal: *Åhlström & Ors v EC Commission*, interim decision, [1988] ECR 5193, the Commission stated:

'The Commission recognizes the difficulty for an undertaking in a weaker position and not being a traditional supplier in resisting the pressure exerted by the stronger ones and in staying out of a concertation. Nevertheless, that behaviour is the expression of the independent will of the undertakings concerned and each must consequently be considered responsible for its own behaviour. The different positions of these undertakings will be taken into account in fixing the fines.'

See also *Fisher-Price/Quaker Oats Ltd – Toyco*, OJ 1988 L49/19, at p. 21.

[37] *ACF Chemiefarma v EC Commission* [1970] ECR 661, at p. 693. In *Polypropylene*, OJ 1986 L230/1, at p. 26, the Commission reiterated the principle as follows:

'It is not necessary, in order for a restriction to constitute an agreement within the meaning of Article 85(1) for the agreement to be intended as legally binding upon the parties. An agreement exists if the parties reach a consensus on a plan which limits or is likely to limit their commercial freedom by determining the lines of their mutual action or abstention from action in the market. No contractual sanctions or enforcement procedures are required. Nor is it necessary for such an agreement to be made in writing.'

See also *Flat Glass* [1989] 1 CEC 2,077; OJ 1989 L33/44; on appeal, *Società Italiano Vetro SpA & Ors v EC Commission* [1992] 2 CEC 33. *PVC*, OJ 1989 L74/1; *LdPE* [1989] 1 CEC 2,193; OJ 1989 L74/21.

operating at the same level of trade) and vertical agreements (i.e. between parties operating at different levels of trade) fall within the scope of art. 85(1).[38]

Standard conditions of sale have frequently been treated as an agreement between the seller and the buyers.[39] Even the acts of unilaterally discontinuing sales, announced in a circular letter, and the refusal to approve the entry of a dealer into a selective distribution system, have been held to come within the scope of art. 85(1).[40]

¶211   Decisions by associations of undertakings

Article 85 is not limited in application to situations where undertakings enter into an agreement with each other, but it also applies when they act in concert through the intermediary of an association.

The term 'decision' has been interpreted to include non-binding recommendations whenever compliance with the recommendation by the members of the association has an appreciable effect on competition.[41]

Agreements between associations of undertakings likewise fall within the scope of art. 85.[42]

The legal form of the association is irrelevant.[43] Furthermore, the fact that the association is entrusted with a public function does not take it outside the scope of art. 85(1).[44]

However, where the association does not play a separate role in the implementation of an anti-competitive arrangement and where the acts of the association cannot be distinguished from the respective acts of the members,

---

[38] *Consten and Grundig v EC Commission* [1966] ECR 299, at p. 339; *Italy v Council and EC Commission* [1966] ECR 389, at p. 407.

[39] See, e.g. *Kodak*, JO 1970 L147/24; *Distillers*, OJ 1978 L50/16; *Sandoz*, OJ 1987 L222/28; *Bayer/Dental*, OJ 1991 L351/46.

[40] See *Ford Werke AG and Ford of Europe Inc v EC Commission* [1985] ECR 2725, at p. 2743 (para. 21), where the court stated:

'Such a decision on the part of the manufacturer does not constitute, on the part of the undertaking, a unilateral act which, as the applicants claim, would be exempt from the prohibition contained in Article 85(1) of the Treaty. On the contrary, it forms part of the contractual relations between the undertaking and its dealers. Indeed, admission to the Ford AG dealer network implies acceptance by the contracting parties of the policy pursued by Ford with regard to the models to be delivered to the German market.'

See also *AEG v EC Commission* [1983] ECR 3151, at p. 3195 (para. 38–39)(concerning a refusal to appoint a dealer); *Tipp-Ex v EC Commission* [1990] ECR I-261; *Eco System/Peugeot*, OJ 1992 L66/1.

[41] See, e.g. *Vereniging van Cementhandelaren v EC Commission* [1972] ECR 977; *Frubo v EC Commission*, [1975] ECR 563; *Van Landewyck v EC Commission* [1980] ECR 3125; *IAZ v EC Commission* [1983] ECR 3369; *Verband der Sachversicherer v EC Commission* [1987] ECR 405.

[42] See, e.g. *CECIMO*, JO 1969 L69/13; *CEMATEX*, JO 1971 L227/26; *NAVEWA-ANSEAU*, OJ 1982 L167/39; *Milchförderungsfonds*, OJ 1985 L35/35; *French inland waterway charter traffic: EATE levy*, OJ 1985 L219/35; *Uniform Eurocheques* [1989] 1 CEC 2,111; OJ 1989 L36/16.

[43] See, e.g. *Milchförderungsfonds*, OJ 1985 L35/35, involving a milk promotion fund, set up by decision of the Presidents of the German Farmers' Union and the German Raiffeisen Association.

[44] *Pabst & Richarz/BNIA*, OJ 1976 L231/24; *NAVEWA-ANSEAU*, OJ 1982 L167/39; *International Energy Agency*, OJ 1983 L376/30.

the association may avoid liability of its own under art. 85 or, at least, the imposition of fines.[45]

¶212   Concerted practices

A concerted practice is a more informal form of collusion than an agreement or a decision of an association of undertakings. The purpose of including concerted practices in the scope of art. 85 is to avoid the possibility of undertakings evading its application by operating via less formal means than a full-fledged agreement.[46] Thus, in *Dyestuffs*, the court defined the term 'concerted practice' as 'a form of co-ordination between undertakings which, without having reached the stage where an agreement properly so-called has been concluded, knowingly substitutes practical cooperation between them for the risks of competition'.[47] One year later, in the *Sugar Cartel* case, the court refined its definition of a concerted practice by explaining the terms 'co-ordination' and 'co-operation' used in the earlier definition as not requiring 'the working out of an actual plan' but as meaning 'that each economic operator must determine independently, the policy which he intends to adopt' and that, therefore, there should not be 'any direct or indirect contact between such operators, the object or effect whereof is either to influence the conduct on the market of an actual or potential competitor or to disclose to such a competitor the course of conduct which they themselves have decided to adopt or contemplate adopting on the market.'[48]

The following elements are essential for a concerted practice to exist:

(1) there must be a form of co-ordination or practical co-operation between undertakings which replaces their independent action;

(2) this co-ordination needs to be achieved through direct or indirect contact; and

---

[45] *Åhlström & Ors v EC Commission ('Wood Pulp')* [1988] ECR 5193, at p. 5245 (para. 27); *Welded Steel Mesh* [1989] 2 CEC 2,051; OJ 1989 L260/1, at p. 42.

[46] In *Soda-ash – Solvay, ICI*, OJ 1991 L152/1, the Commission stated that 'there are many forms and degrees of collusion and it does not require the making of a formal agreement. An infringement of Article 85 may well exist where the parties have not even spelled out an agreement in terms, but each infers commitment from the other on the basis of conduct'. See also *Flat Glass*, OJ 1989 L33/44; *PVC*, OJ 1989 L74/1.

[47] *ICI v EC Commission* [1972] ECR 619, at p. 655 (para. 64). See also *Soda-ash–Solvay, ICI*, OJ 1991 L152/1, at p.12.

[48] *Suiker Unie & Ors v EC Commission* [1975] ECR 1663, at p. 1942 (para. 173–174). See also the opinion of Advocate General Darmon in *Åhlström & Ors v EC Commission ('Wood Pulp')* [1993] 1 CEC 466, at p. 505 (para. 172). In *Petrofina v EC Commission* [1991] ECR II-1087, at p. II-1156 (para. 213), the court found that the plaintiff had taken part in meetings having as their object the fixing of prices and sales volumes in which competitors exchanged, inter alia, information on the prices that they wished to see on the market, and on the prices that they envisaged implementing. Such participation, in the court's view, amounted to a concertation designed to influence the parties' behaviour on the market (para. 214). The plaintiff had the object of eliminating in advance the uncertainty as to the future behaviour of its competitors and had, directly or indirectly, used the information obtained at the meetings to determine the policy that it itself intended to follow on the market.

(3) the aim must be to remove 'in advance any uncertainty as to the future conduct of their competitors'.[49]

The second requirement, i.e. direct or indirect contact, may have more to do with the necessary proof of the concerted practice than with the concept itself. Indeed, the court has consistently held that the mere parallel action of competitors does not constitute sufficient evidence to establish the existence of a concerted practice.[50] As the court stated, the EC treaty does not 'deprive economic operators of the right to adapt themselves intelligently to the existing and anticipated conduct of their competitors'.[51] However, parallel conduct may amount to strong evidence of a concerted practice if it leads to conditions of competition that do not correspond to the normal conditions of the market, having regard to the nature of the products, the size and number of the undertakings and the volume of the said market.[52] Any additional evidence must be 'sufficiently precise and coherent . . . to justify the view that the parallel behaviour . . . was the result of concerted action'.[53]

In *Dyestuffs* the defendant companies had argued that their parallel pricing conduct was the normal response of an oligopolistic industry to price increases made by the price leader in each market. The Commission, however, found it inconceivable that without detailed prior agreement the producers concerned would:

(1) repeatedly increase prices of numerous products by identical percentages, at practically the same time in different markets;

(2) use similar wording in their instructions to their subsidiaries to make the price increases.

---

[49] *Suiker Unie & Ors v EC Commission* [1975] ECR 1663, at p. 1942 (para. 175).

[50] For example, in his opinion, in *Åhlström & Ors v EC Commission ('Wood Pulp')* [1993] 1 CEC 466 (para. 175 and 191), Advocate General Darmon noted that it is necessary that the competitors' knowledge of each other's conduct stems from communications between them, and not simply from monitoring the market. See the judgment of the court in *Züchner* [1981] ECR 2021, where it is stated at para. 21 that a national court 'must consider whether between the banks conducting themselves in like manner there are contacts or, *at least, exchanges of information*' (emphasis added).

[51] *Suiker Unie & Ors v EC Commission* [1975] ECR 1663, at p. 1942 (para. 174); see also *ICI v EC Commission* [1972] ECR 619, at p. 660 (para. 118); and *Züchner v Bayerische Vereinsbank* [1981] ECR 2021, at p. 2031 (para. 14).

Advocate General Darmon in *Åhlström & Ors v EC Commission ('Wood Pulp')* [1993] 1 CEC 466 stated (at para. 177) that

'parallel conduct is not necessarily the result of prior concertation. It can be explained or even dictated by the very structure of certain markets . . . The first situation involves a concentrated oligopoly, in which undertakings are independent: each undertaking must take account in its decisions of the conduct of its rivals. Alignment on each other's conduct constitutes a rational response, independently of any concertation. "Price leadership" constitutes the second situation: undertakings align themselves on a "price leader" on account of the latter's power on the market. Mention may also be made of spontaneous alignment on a price leader which acts as a barometer, with its decisions reflecting changes in market conditions for reasons linked, for instance, to its previous knowledge of that market.'

[52] *ICI v EC Commission* [1972] ECR 619, at p. 655 (para. 66).

[53] *CRAM and Rheinzink v EC Commission* [1984] ECR 1679, at p. 1702 (para. 20). This would seem to suggest that it is necessary to establish a degree of certainty that goes beyond any reasonable doubt.

The Commission's investigations had also established that the producers had met frequently and discussed prices. The court confirmed the Commission's decision essentially because it was 'hardly conceivable that the same action could be taken spontaneously at the same time, on the same national markets and for the same range of products'.[54] The court did not really consider the other circumstantial evidence relied upon by the Commission, i.e. the identical wording of the pricing instructions and the frequent organisation of industry meetings.

In contrast, in the *Sugar Cartel* case, the court carefully reviewed the documentary evidence (e.g. correspondence, telex messages and minutes of meetings) which the Commission had adduced to establish the existence of a concerted practice among sugar producers. The court confirmed the Commission's findings, except for the alleged concerted practice between a German producer and two Dutch producers relating to the Dutch market.[55]

In a case dealing with an alleged concerted action designed to prevent parallel imports of rolled zinc, the court quashed a Commission finding that a refusal to supply had occurred as a result of a concerted practice.[56] On this occasion, the court formulated the following general principle:

'The Commission's reasoning is based on the supposition that the facts established cannot be explained other than by concerted action by the two undertakings. Faced with such an argument, it is sufficient for the applicants to prove circumstances which cast the facts established by the Commission in a different light and thus allow another explanation of the facts to be substituted for the one adopted by the contested decision.'[57]

---

[54] *ICI v EC Commission* [1972] ECR 619 at p. 659 (para. 109).

[55] *Suiker Unie & Ors v EC Commission* [1975] ECR 1663, at pp. 1946–1948 (para. 199–210). The court found that the documentary evidence against the German producer was 'too vague and general' and that as the German price level was not below that of the Netherlands, the court felt that it might 'not have been in the interests of Pfeifer & Langen to investigate the Netherlands market in order to sell sugar there on an occasional and sporadic basis instead of continuing to supply its long established customers who usually provided it with a guaranteed market' (para. 209).

[56] *CRAM and Rheinzink v EC Commission* [1984] ECR 1679.

[57] Id., at p. 1702 (para. 16). In this connection, reference should be made to the judgment in the *Pioneer* case where the court confirmed the Commission's finding that Pioneer's European headquarters had participated in a concerted practice with both its English and German distributors in order to protect its French distributor against parallel imports from England and Germany (*Musique Diffusion française v EC Commission* [1983] ECR 1825). In the absence of any direct evidence of Pioneer's participation in the concerted practice with its English distributor, the court relied on the fact that a meeting had been held on the premises of Pioneer in Antwerp where the distributors concerned discussed complaints by the French distributor against parallel imports. As a consequence of the meeting, the English distributor had sent letters to its customers in order to dissuade them from engaging in exports to France. Under these circumstances, the court concluded that, 'Pioneer, which had called the meeting and presided over it, must accept responsibility for that consequence, regard being had to the position which it occupies in relation to its national distributors, as described above', id. at p. 1899 (para. 79).

As to the concerted practice between Pioneer and its German distributor, the court relied on the fact that Pioneer had forwarded to that distributor the complaints of the French distributor as well as information on import licences granted by the French authorities. According to the court 'such a communication *appears* to have been an *implied* incitement to Melchers to try to discover the source of those imports and to put a stop to them', id. at p. 1898 (para. 76) (emphasis supplied). The lesson to be drawn from the Pioneer judgment is that the

Admittedly, this raises the issue of whether it is fair to base a decision solely on the 'supposition' that the facts cannot be explained in any other way. At times it might be unfair for the Commission to discharge its burden of proof by advancing a logical hypothesis and, by so doing, shifting the burden of proof on to the defendant who must then come up with adequate proof of his innocence.[58]

In *Wood Pulp*,[59] the Court of Justice accepted the alternative explanations for the parallel conduct offered by the defendants. Before rejecting the Commission's claim that the system of quarterly price announcements constituted evidence of concertation at an earlier stage, the court examined the evidence presented by the Commission which consisted of the parallel conduct of the pulp producers from 1975–1981 and different kinds of direct and indirect exchanges of information such as telexes and documents. The court excluded the documentary evidence from consideration as the Commission was unable to state between which producers the concertation established by the documentation took place.[60]

In so far as the parallel conduct was concerned, this consisted essentially of the system of quarterly price announcements, in the simultaneity or near-simultaneity of the announcements and in the fact that the announced prices were identical. As the Commission had no direct evidence to establish concertation between the producers, it was necessary to consider whether the 'parallelism of price announcements as found during the period from 1975 to 1981 constitute a firm, precise and consistent body of evidence of prior concertation'.

The court held that parallel conduct does not furnish proof of concertation unless this is the only plausible explanation of the conduct. Therefore, it was necessary to ascertain whether this parallel conduct, taking into account the nature of the products, the size and the number of undertakings and the volume of the market in question, could be explained otherwise than by concertation. The court concluded that concertation was not the only plausible explanation for the conduct:

'To begin with, the system of price announcements may be regarded as constituting a rational response to the fact that the pulp market constituted a long-term market and to the need felt by both buyers and sellers to limit commercial risks. Further, the similarity in the dates of price announcements may be regarded as a direct result of the high degree of market transparency,

---

organisation of a meeting or the forwarding of information may make one liable for what is said at the meeting or for what is subsequently done with the information.

[58] *Åhlström & Ors v EC Commission* ('*Wood Pulp*') [1993] 1 CEC 466.

[59] *Åhlström & Ors v EC Commission* ('*Wood Pulp*') [1993] 1 CEC 466, at p. 593 (para. 126).

[60] In the court's opinion, the identity of the persons taking part in the concertation is one of the constituents of the infringement.

which does not have to be described as artificial. Finally, the parallelism of prices and price trends may be satisfactorily explained by the oligopolistic tendencies of the market and by the specific circumstances prevailing in certain periods. Accordingly, the parallel conduct established by the Commission does not constitute evidence of concertation. In the absence of a firm, precise and consistent body of evidence, it must be held that concertation regarding announced prices has not been established by the Commission. Article 1(1) of the contested decision must therefore be annulled.'[61]

Thus, the court appeared to give greater weight to economic arguments submitted by the defendants in *Wood Pulp* than it had in *Dyestuffs*. It may also have tried to set a minimum evidentiary standard below which the existence of a concerted practice becomes doubtful.

The third essential element for a concerted practice is that the aim of the co-ordination or co-operation must be to remove in advance any uncertainty as to the future conduct of competitors. In *ICI v EC Commission*,[62] the Commission said, 'it is enough that they [the competitors] *let each other* know beforehand what attitude they intend to adopt, so that each of them could regulate his conduct, *safe in the knowledge* that his competitors would act in a similar fashion'.[63]

In *Wood Pulp*,[64] the Court of Justice rejected the Commission's claim that a system of quarterly price announcements in itself constituted an infringement of the treaty or that such a system provided evidence of concertation on announced prices which took place at an earlier stage. The court held that:

'In this case, the communications arise from the price announcements made to users. They constitute in themselves market behaviour that does not lessen each undertaking's uncertainty as to the future attitude of its competitors. At the time when each undertaking engages in such behaviour, it cannot be sure of the future conduct of the others.'[65]

The definition of a concerted practice has also been held to cover the involvement of undertakings 'which were on the periphery of the cartel but co-operated with it and knowingly associated themselves with its overall objective'.[66] In *LdPE*,[67] the Commission classified the producers into two broad

---

[61] *Åhlström & Ors v EC Commission* [1993] 1 CEC 466, at p. 593 (para. 126–127).
[62] *ICI v EC Commission*, [1972] ECR 619, at p. 639.
[63] Emphasis supplied.
[64] *Åhlström & Ors v EC Commission* ('*Wood Pulp*') [1993] 1 CEC 466.
[65] Id., at p. 586 (para. 64).
[66] *LdPE* [1989] 1 CEC 2,193; OJ 1989 L74/21; *Petrofina SA v EC Commission* [1991] ECR II-1087, at p. 1150 (para. 194).
[67] *LdPE*, OJ 1989 L74/21.

¶212

categories: those who actually took part in the establishment and development of the cartel, and those who played only a peripheral role in the cartel. As regards the latter group, the Commission noted that, while mere knowledge of the existence of a cartel does not constitute involvement in the infringement, an undertaking which is in direct or indirect contact with the cartel and attaches itself to the unlawful enterprise may still be a party to a concerted practice even if it does not play a major role in the overall cartel. Occasional telephone calls and local meetings with a member of the cartel where proposed price increases were exchanged, were held to be sufficient to amount to unlawful contact and to constitute a concerted practice.[68]

Similarly, the Commission has held that the involvement of an undertaking 'which co-operated with a cartel without being a full member, and was able to adapt its own market behaviour in the light of its contacts with the cartel',[69] could amount to a concerted practice.

In the *LdPE* and *PVC* cases,[70] involving horizontal cartels of almost all the Community producers of the bulk thermoplastics LdPE (low density polyethylene) and PVC (polyvinylchloride), the Commission further elaborated on the concept of concerted pricing practices. In both cases, the producers were said to have held regular secret meetings in order to co-ordinate their commercial behaviour, including pricing behaviour. In its decisions, the Commission relied on 'a substantial body of direct documentary evidence relating to the facts in issue' in order to prove that those meetings actually took place. This evidence primarily included minutes and documents from the meetings found with some of the participating producers. Nevertheless, the Commission found it necessary to state that 'it is inherent in the nature of the infringement . . . that any decision will to a large extent have to be based upon circumstantial evidence: the existence of the facts constituting the infringement of Article 85 may have to be proved by logical deduction from

---

[68] One of the parties only indirectly involved in the LdPE cartel, Shell, claimed not to have given any precise information on its sales in the European market to one of the cartel's participants, ICI. The Commission rejected this defence stating that Shell had not made any effort to rebuff ICI's approaches. In addition, according to the Commission,

'[Shell's] admitted telephone contacts with ICI and the participation of the Shell UK operating company in local meetings at the very least constituted a channel for a two-way flow of information to the mutual benefit of Shell and members of the cartel.'

Another company accused of a mere 'peripheral involvement' was tackled by the Commission along the same lines (*LdPE* [1989] 1 CEC 2,193; OJ 1989 L74/21 at pp. 30–31 (para. 33)):

'No documentary evidence was available of Monsanto's commercial policy or pricing policy but its participation in local meetings in which, at the very least, ICI informed the others of its proposed prices . . . is sufficient to implicate it in the infringement.'

[69] *PVC* [1989] 1 CEC 2,167; OJ 1989 L74/1. See also *Polypropylene*, OJ 1986 L230/1, at p. 28 (para. 87), where the Commission held that a concerted practice may be found where 'in a complex cartel, some producers at one time or another might not express their definite assent to a particular course of action agreed by the others but nevertheless indicate their general support for the scheme in question and conduct themselves accordingly'.

[70] *LdPE* [1989] 1 CEC 2,193; OJ 1989 L74/21; *PVC* [1989] 1 CEC 2,167; OJ 1989 L74/1.

other proven facts.'[71] Providing a list of the direct documentary and circumstantial evidence, the Commission rejected what it held to be the producers' approach of considering each single item of the evidence in isolation. Instead, it took the view that the items had to be regarded together and concluded that 'each element of proof reinforces the others with respect to the facts in issue and leads to the conclusion that a market-sharing and price-fixing cartel was being operated in LdPE.'[72]

It is also worth noting that a series of events can be qualified as one single violation if they are all inspired by the same anti-competitive intention.[73] In addition, such a single complex violation may be qualified as an agreement *and* concerted practice meaning a complex of facts of which some may be qualified as agreements and others as concerted practices.[74] However, it is still not totally clear whether it is necessary for the Commission to identify each objectionable event as an agreement or as a concerted practice.[75]

Finally, the fact remains that the Commission has to prove that each undertaking participated in the different events which constituted an infringement. Indeed, Advocate General Vesterdorf as well as the court refuses to accept the principle of collective responsibility.[76] This means that

---

[71] *PVC* [1989] 1 CEC 2,167; OJ 1989 L74/1, at p. 3; *LdPE* [1989] 1 CEC 2,193; OJ 1989 L74/21 at p. 28.

[72] *LdPE* [1989] 1 CEC 2,193; OJ 1989 L74/21, at p. 29. See also *PVC* [1989] 1 CEC 2,167 OJ 1989 L74/1, at p. 9.

[73] *Rhône-Poulenc v EC Commission* [1991] ECR II-867 (at para. 125–126); *Petrofina v EC Commission* [1991] ECR II-1087 (at para. 217–218); *BASF v EC Commission* [1991] ECR II-1523 (at para. 244–245); *Enichem Amic v EC Commission* [1991] ECR II-1623 (at para. 203–204); *Hercules v EC Commission* [1991] ECR II-1711 (at para. 262–263); *DSM v EC Commission* [1991] ECR II-1833 (at para. 233–234); *Hülls v EC Commission* Case T-9/89 (at para. 297–298); *Hoechst v EC Commission* Case T-10/89 (at para. 293–294); *Shell v EC Commission* Case T-11/89 (para. 304–305); *Solvay v EC Commission* Case T-12/89 (at para. 258–259); *ICI v EC Commission* Case T-13/89 (at para. 259–260); *Montedipe v EC Commission* Case T-14/89 (at para. 237–238); *Chemie Linz v EC Commission* (at para. 307–308) [1992] ECR II-1275. In these cases, the Court of First Instance stated that the object of trying to alter the normal evolution of prices on the polypropylene market bound all the different events together into one single violation.

[74] *Polypropylene*, OJ 1986 L230/1, (at para. 86); on appeal: *Rhône-Poulenc v EC Commission* [1991] ECR II-867 (at para. 127); *Petrofina v EC Commission* [1991] ECR II-1087 (at para. 219); *BASF v EC Commission* [1991] ECR II-1523 (at para. 246); *Enichem Amic v EC Commission* [1991] ECR II-1623 (at para. 205); *Hercules v EC Commission* [1991] ECR II-1711 (at para. 264); *DSM v EC Commission* [1991] ECR II-1833 (at para. 235); *Hülls v EC Commission* Case T-9/89 (at para. 299); *Hoechst v EC Commission* Case T-10/89 (at para. 295); *Solvay v EC Commission* Case T-12/89 (at para. 260); *ICI v EC Commission* Case T-13/89 (at para. 261); *Montedipe v EC Commission* Case T-14/89 (at para. 236); *Chemie Linz v EC Commission* (at para. 309) [1992] ECR II-1275. See also: *PVC*, OJ 1989 L74/1 at p. 11; *LdPE*, OJ 1989 L74/21 at p. 32.

[75] In the *Polypropylene* case, the Commission had qualified each event as an agreement or concerted practice and the court declined to say whether or not this had been necessary. See *Rhône-Poulenc v EC Commission* [1991] ECR II-867 (at para. 118). However, in view of what the court said with regard to the qualification of a complex single violation (see above), it is unlikely that such a qualification of each individual event is still necessary. In addition, reference should be made to the opinion of Avocate General Vesterdorf of 10 July 1991. According to the Avocate General, no distinction should be made between the two types of infringement because in each category the undertakings no longer determine independently the policies they will pursue and there is thus a risk that conditions not corresponding to the normal conditions on the market will be created (see opinion of Avocate General Vesterdorf in the *Polypropylene* cases, [1991] ECR II-867, at p. II-944).

[76] Opinion of Avocate General Vesterdorf of 10 July 1991 ([1991] ECR II-867, at p. II-950ff.); *Petrofina v EC Commission* [1991] ECR II-1087 (at para. 234–236); *BASF v EC Commission* [1991] ECR II-1523 (at para. 254–256); *Hercules v EC Commission* [1991] ECR II-1711 (at para. 289–291); *Hülls v EC Commission* (para. 327) Case T-10/89 (judgment of 10 March 1992) (not yet reported).

¶212

each undertaking cannot be held liable to a greater extent than that of its own participation.

In the *Polypropylene* cases, the court has also dealt with the question whether proof of an anti-competitive effect on the market is necessary if the Commission has already found the existence of concertation. The court followed the opinion of Advocate General Vesterdorf.[77] According to the Advocate General, 'in principle concertation will automatically trigger subsequent [anti-competitive] action on the market ... [because] these undertakings will necessarily act on the market in the light of the knowledge and on the basis of the discussions which have taken place in connection with the concertation'.[78] However, parties can still try to prove that their action subsequent to the concertation was not inspired by the knowledge they got from the concertation.[79]

¶213   Government compulsion

The concepts of agreements, decisions of associations and concerted practices all imply a degree of freedom, without which there could be no violation of art. 85(1). In this connection the question arises as to the impact of government interference on the existence of an agreement, decision or concerted practice within the sense of art. 85(1).

The influence of government action was discussed for the first time in relation to so-called voluntary restraint agreements entered into by non-EC producers. The Commission, in its *Third Report on Competition Policy*, distinguished the situation where such agreements are being 'imposed' by the governments of third countries, from the situation where the agreements are merely 'authorised' by the government.[80] Only in the former situation would art. 85 not apply.

A few months later the Commission had occasion to deal with the matter more extensively in its decision on the *Franco-Japanese ballbearings agreements*.[81] This time the Commission distinguished between four types of situations:

'(a) measures taken in pursuance of trade agreements between the Community and Japan.

These are acts of external commercial policy, which as such are outside the scope of Article 85 of the EEC Treaty.

---

[77] Opinion of Advocate General Vesterdorf in e.g. *Solvay v EC Commission* Case T-12/89 (judgment of 10 March 1992) (at para. 255–256).

[78] Id., at p. II-941.

[79] Id., at p. II-943.

[80] *Third Report on Competition Policy*, point 20.

[81] *Franco-Japanese ballbearings agreements*, OJ 1974 L343/19.

(b) measures imposed on Japanese undertakings by the Japanese authorities.

These measures are also outside the scope of Article 85.

However, in both cases, Article 85 could be applicable to any agreements or concerted practices additional to such measures.

(c) measures resulting from agreements or concerted practices between undertakings which are merely authorized by the Japanese authorities under Japanese law.

Such an authorization, while required for the measures to be lawful in Japan, would not necessarily mean that Article 85 could not apply since it would in no way alter the fact that the undertakings concerned were free to refrain from entering into an agreement or engaging in concerted practices.

(d) measures resulting solely from agreements, concerted practices, or decisions by associations of undertakings, entered into or engaged in either unilaterally by Japanese undertakings or in concert with the appropriate European undertakings.

These measures of a private nature may also come within the provisions of Article 85. The Commission has expressly drawn the attention of undertakings to this point by an opinion[82] published in the Official Journal in October 1972.'

In later decisions the Commission substantially confirmed its initial position. For example, in the *Aluminium* case,[83] the German and English defendants argued that the joint purchasing arrangements to which the Commission took exception were the acts of their governments and as such were outside the scope of art. 85. This argument was rejected outright by the Commission because 'the agreements were neither acts to which the governments were signatory, nor did governments oblige the undertakings to enter into the arrangements'.[84]

The defendants then argued that as the governments concerned encouraged and supported the arrangements, they were consequently part of the external commercial policy of the states concerned and therefore outside the scope of art. 85(1). The Commission dismissed the argument with respect to the German defendants on the facts because it found that at best the German government

---

[82] Notice concerning imports into the Community of Japanese goods falling within the scope of the Rome Treaty, OJ 1972 C111/13.
[83] *Aluminium Imports from Eastern Europe*, OJ 1985 L92/1.
[84] Id., at pp. 37–39. See also *Åhlström & Ors v EC Commission* ('*Wood Pulp*') [1988] ECR 5193, at p. 5244 (para. 20).

¶213

had tolerated rather than encouraged the arrangements. As for the UK defendants, the Commission rejected the argument on its merits as follows:

'The Commission accepts as fact that, from 1965 onwards, the UK Government gave support to the UK-based undertakings to enter into the Brandeis arrangements. This does not mean that the encouragement and support of the UK Government reflected a sovereign decision that Community trade should be affected. The fact that the UK Government, in pursuit of its own legitimate national interests, permitted a private restriction upon competition within the Community does not mean that it either sought or desired a breach of the law within the Community and still less that it favoured that breach. Even if the UK Government had intended such a breach (which the Commission does not believe was ever the case), that would not alter the position of the undertakings.'[85]

Since overt support and encouragement by a government is not enough to take an agreement or practice outside the ambit of art. 85, it is obvious that the mere knowledge or awareness of an agreement by government authorities – or by the Commission for that matter – will similarly not cause the agreement to fall outside the scope of art. 85. Thus, for example, in *Zinc producer group*[86] the Commission stated on this point:

'The firms also submit that government agencies in the Member States and the relevant Commission departments were aware of the price-fixing agreements and support measures and that some Member States' authorities had expressly approved them. However, the fact that Member State authorities had knowledge of, participated in or approved price-fixing agreements does not protect them from the application of the EEC competition rules.

The Commission was aware of the existence of a "zinc producer price" and of cuts in production. At no time was it known to the Commission officials concerned that the producer price was collusive, nor that production cuts were collusive. If a "producer price" is published in the technical press it cannot be assumed in principle that this necessarily implies an infringement of Article 85. The members of a trade association may in that association recognize that there is overcapacity without colluding over reductions of capacity. The attempts in the present case to infer that, because an authority knew some of what was going on, it must have known all of the facts, must be rejected.

---

[85] Id, at p. 39.
[86] *Zinc producer group*, OJ 1984 L220/27, at p. 39; see also *BNIC v Aubert* [1987] ECR 4789, at p. 4813 (para. 13); *Jahrhundertvertrag*, OJ 1993 L50/14; *French-West African Shipowners' Committees*, OJ 1992 L134/1, at pp. 12–14; *French inland waterway charter traffic: EATE levy*, OJ 1985 L219/35, at p. 44.

The same can probably be said for the involvement of authorities of the Member States. At any rate, undertakings cannot obtain protection from the application of the rules on competition merely by allegations that some government department knew or even approved of the utilization of a producer price.'

Thus, it is clear that only compulsion by a government authority will take an agreement or practice outside the scrutiny of art. 85. Lesser forms of government involvement like authorisation, encouragement, approval or tolerance could at best justify a plea in mitigation.

¶214   Restriction of competition

For a concerted action to be caught by art. 85(1), it must have as its 'object or effect the prevention, restriction or distortion of competition within the common market'. ¶215–¶219 contain a detailed analysis of this wording.

¶215   'Object or effect'

As a result of the wording in the alternative, the court has ruled that 'for the purpose of applying art. 85(1), there is no need to take account of the concrete effects of an agreement once it appears that it has as its object the prevention, restriction or distortion of competition'.[87] Likewise, the court has ruled that even if an agreement does not have the object of restricting competition within the meaning of art. 85(1), it is nevertheless necessary to ascertain whether it has the effect of restricting competition.[88] Even if this were not the case, as a practical matter, it is at least to some extent necessary to verify the effect of an agreement or practice, even if its purpose would be clearly anti-competitive. Indeed, pursuant to art. 85(1) it is in any event mandatory to examine whether the agreement 'may affect trade between member states'. Furthermore, in view of the court's subsequent case law it is also essential to assess the agreement in

---

[87] *Consten and Grundig v EC Commission* [1966] ECR 299, at p. 342; see also *Sandoz v EC Commission* [1990] ECR 47, and *Société Technique Minière v Maschinenbau Ulm* [1966] ECR 235, at p. 249, where the court stated:

'This interference with competition referred to in Article 85(1) must result from all or some of the clauses of the agreement itself. Where, however, an analysis of the said clauses does not reveal the effect on competition to be sufficiently deleterious, the consequences of the agreement should then be considered and for it to be caught by the prohibition it is then necessary to find that those factors are present which show that competition has in fact been prevented or restricted or distorted to an appreciable extent.'

For applications of this principle by the Commission see, e.g. *Zinc producer group*, OJ 1984 L220/27, at p. 38 (para. 71), ('In any case, for Article 85(1) to be applicable, it is sufficient for there to have been the intention to restrict competition; it is not necessary for the intention to have been carried out, in full or only in part, that is to say, for the restriction of competition to have been put into effect.'); *Fire insurance (D)*, OJ 1985 L35/20, at p. 24; *PVC* [1989] 1 CEC 2,167; OJ 1989 L74/1, at p. 13 (para. 37); *LdPE* [1989] 1 CEC 2,193; OJ 1989 L74/21, at p. 34 (para. 44).

[88] *Delimitis v Henninger Bräu* [1991] ECR I-935, at p. I-984 (para. 13).

its economic context and to see whether the effect on competition is 'appreciable', rather than de minimis.[89]

The court's requirement that an agreement needs to be considered in the economic context in which it is to be applied implies that 'the competition in question must be understood within the actual context in which it would occur in the absence of the agreement in dispute . . .'[90] This means that the effects an agreement has must be considered 'in their surrounding economic and legal circumstances within which they may, together with other factors, have a cumulative effect on competition'.[91]

The effect of an agreement should not be examined in isolation, but in the context of other similar agreements to determine their cumulative effect on competition.[92] In *Delimitis*,[93] a case involving a tied-house contract between a brewery and a publican, the Court of Justice elaborated upon the factors to be taken into account when applying this so-called 'network effect theory'. First, it is necessary to determine the effects of the network of agreements on the opportunities of competitors to gain access to the national market or to increase their market share. The court stated that the effect of a network of agreements on access to the market 'depends specifically on the number of outlets thus tied to the national producers in relation to the number of [untied outlets], the duration of the commitments entered into, the quantities of [the product] to which those commitments relate, and on the proportion between those quantities and the quantities sold by free distributors.'[94] Aside from the

---

[89] *Völk v Vervaecke* [1969] ECR 295, at p. 302 (para. 5–7), where the court stated:

'Those conditions [i.e. effect on inter-state trade and the restrictive object or effect] must be understood by reference to the actual circumstances of the agreement. Consequently an agreement falls outside the prohibition in Article 85 when it has only an insignificant effect on the markets, taking into account the weak position which the persons concerned have on the market of the product in question. Thus an exclusive dealing agreement, even with absolute territorial protection, may, having regard to the weak position of the persons concerned on the market in the products in question in the area covered by the absolute protection, escape the prohibition laid down in Article 85(1).'

[90] *Société Technique Minière v Maschinenbau Ulm* [1966] ECR 235, at p. 250. For an application of this principle see, e.g. *BPCL/ICI*, OJ 1984 L212/1, at p. 7, where the Commission stated:

'The parties maintain as a reason for excluding the agreement from the scope of Article 85(1) that the decisions to withdraw from the UK market by ICI and BPCL in LdPE and PVC respectively were inevitable since these decisions were in line with their respective long-term strategies. It is true that competition on the respective markets seemed to be forcing ICI and BPCL to run down their activities but this run-down would not have amounted in the short and medium term to a total withdrawal. In the absence of the agreements, each party would have continued operation even if only on a reduced scale in the areas which it was obliged to abandon. The sale both of the most modern plant and of the goodwill were the instruments that determined the actual closures and their timing. Therefore it may be concluded that the agreements entailed as an immediate and inevitable consequence a specialization of production and a closure of capacity, and as such fall within the scope of Article 85(1).'

[91] *Suiker Unie & Ors v EC Commission* [1975] ECR 1663, at pp. 2008–2009 (para. 548).

[92] See *Delimitis v Henninger Bräu* [1991] ECR I-935; *Brasserie de Haecht v Wilkin ('Haecht I')* [1967] ECR 407; *Optical Fibres*, OJ 1986 L236/30; *Deutsche Castrol Vertriebsgesellschaft*, OJ 1983 L114/26; *Breeders' rights — roses*, OJ 1985 L369/9.

[93] *Delimitis v Henninger Bräu* [1991] ECR I-935.

[94] Id., at p. I-985 (para. 19).

effect of the network of contracts itself on possibilities of access to the market, it is necessary to examine whether there are 'real concrete possibilities' for a new competitor to penetrate the bundle of contracts by acquiring a supplier already established on the market together with its network of sales outlets, or to circumvent the bundle of contracts by opening new outlets.[95] Also, the presence of wholesalers on the market is a factor capable of facilitating a new producer's access to the market because it can use the wholesaler's distribution networks.[96]

Secondly, the court ruled that the competitive forces on the market must be examined to assess the number and size of the producers present on the market as well as the degree of saturation of that market and customer loyalty to existing brands, for it is generally more difficult to penetrate a saturated market in which customers are loyal to a small number of large producers than a market in full expansion in which a large number of small producers are operating without any strong brand names.[97]

¶216   Nature of competition

The term 'competition' has been interpreted as referring not only to actual but also to potential competition.[98] When examining the possibility of potential competition, the Commission pays attention to the parties' technical, financial and marketing capabilities.[99]

The prohibition contained in art. 85 applies not only to restrictions of inter-brand competition but also to restrictions of intra-brand competition.[100]

---

[95] Id., at pp. I-985–I-986 (para. 21).

[96] Id.

[97] Id., at p. I-986 (para. 22).

[98] For example, in *ACF Chemiefarma v EC Commission* [1970] ECR 661, at pp. 701–702, the court ruled that a commitment not to manufacture a product, undertaken by a firm not presently capable of manufacturing such product, constituted a restriction of competition. See also *Eirpage*, OJ 1991 L306/22, and the Commission notice concerning Commission Regulations 1983/83 and 1984/83 on the application of art. 85(3) of the treaty to categories of exclusive distribution agreements and exclusive purchasing agreements, OJ 1984 C101/2. In *UK Agricultural Tractor Registration Exchange*, OJ 1992 L68/19, at p. 29, the Commission stated:

'Article 85(1) must be interpreted as including potential anticompetitive effects because the objective of that provision is the maintenance of an effective competitive structure within the meaning of Article 3(f)[now art. 3(g)]. This objective is particularly material in a highly concentrated market where an information exchange creates a structure of transparency which prevents hidden competition and increases barriers to entry for non-members.'

[99] See, e.g. *Eirpage*, OJ 1991 L306/22. For a more detailed discussion of the concept of potential competition as applied to joint ventures, see Chapter 5.

[100] *Consten and Grundig v EC Commission* [1966] ECR 299, at p. 342, where the court held that:

'[t]he principle of freedom of competition concerns the various stages and manifestations of competition. Although competition between producers is generally more noticeable than that between distributors of products of the same make, it does not thereby follow that an agreement tending to restrict the latter kind of competition should escape the prohibition of Article 85(1) merely because it might increase the former.'

For other examples of this approach, see, e.g., *UK Agricultural Tractor Registration Exchange*, OJ 1992 L68/19; *Distribution system of Ford Werke AG*, OJ 1983 L327/31, at p. 36. In *Vichy*, OJ 1991 L75/57, the Commission noted that inter-brand competition was not sufficiently strong to counterbalance the agreement's restrictive effect on intra-brand competition. This approach is in contrast with the current attitude of the US authorities who put more emphasis on aspects of inter-brand competition and who are more inclined to tolerate certain

An unlawful restriction of competition may not only occur between the parties to an agreement or practice but may also be found to exist between parties to the agreement and third parties.[101]

Restrictions on allegedly 'unfair' competition have also been held to run foul of art. 85(1). In a case involving a purchasing cartel of aluminium originating in eastern Europe the defendants argued that the competition presented by the 'dumped' eastern metal 'was not competition in the context of a lawful free enterprise economy, so that Article 85(1) could not apply'.[102] The Commission rejected their argument because private parties may not arrogate to themselves public functions:

'Even if it were proved that the governments of all the European States concerned might have taken measures having the same effects in all respects as the Brandeis and Eisen und Metall agreements, for all the aluminium products concerned, undertakings are nevertheless not entitled to pre-empt such measures by deciding for themselves how much competition there should be in Western Europe, or how much aluminium should circulate in those territories.'[103]

In one case, however, the Commission and the court were of the opinion that it would be 'unfair' to require a manufacturer to offer the same conditions to a wholesaler as to a retailer.[104] The judgment of the court in this case is also noteworthy for the court's acceptance of the principle that price competition is not the only effective form of competition:

'It is true that in such systems of distribution [i.e. selective distribution

---

restrictions on intra-brand competition. The Commission explains this difference by pointing to the already high degree of integration and competition prevailing on the US market. See *Thirteenth Report on Competition Policy*, point 25.

[101] *Consten and Grundig v EC Commission* [1966] ECR 299; more recently see, e.g. *Astra*, OJ 1993 L20/23, *UK Agricultural Tractor Registration Exchange*, OJ 1992 L68/19.

[102] *Aluminium Imports from Eastern Europe*, OJ 1985 L92/1, at p. 43.

[103] id., at p. 44. For an earlier case in which the Commission had ruled against self-protection against unfair trade, see *IFTRA rules for producers of virgin aluminium*, OJ 1975 L228/3.

[104] *Metro v EC Commission* [1977] ECR 1875, at pp. 1908–1909 (para. 28–29), where the reasoning was as follows:

'The Commission considers that, apart from the fact that this limitation on the activity of wholesalers is in accordance with the requirements of German legislation, it does not constitute a restriction on competition within the meaning of Article 85(1) of the Treaty because it corresponds to the separation of the functions of wholesaler and retailer and because if such a separation did not obtain the former would enjoy an unjustified competitive advantage over the latter which, since it would not correspond to benefits supplied, would not be protected under Article 85.

It is established that various Member States have enacted legislation entailing obligations and charges, in particular in the field of social security and taxation, which differ as between the retail and wholesale trades, so that competition would be distorted if wholesalers, whose costs are in general proportionally lighter precisely because of the marketing stage at which they operate, competed with retailers at the retail stage, in particular on supplies to private customers.

The Commission did not infringe Article 85(1) in considering that this separation of functions is in principle in accordance with the requirement that competition shall not be distorted.'

¶216

systems] price competition is not generally emphasized either as an exclusive or indeed as a principal factor.

This is particularly so when, as in the present case, access to the distribution network is subject to conditions exceeding the requirements of an appropriate distribution of the products.

However, although price competition is so important that it can never be eliminated, it does not constitute the only effective form of competition or that to which absolute priority must in all circumstances be accorded.

The powers conferred upon the Commission under Article 85(3) show that the requirements for the maintenance of workable competition may be reconciled with the safeguarding of objectives of a different nature and that to this end certain restrictions on competition are permissible, provided that they are essential to the attainment of those objectives and that they do not result in the elimination of competition for a substantial part of the Common Market.

For specialist wholesalers and retailers the desire to maintain a certain price level, which corresponds to the desire to preserve, in the interests of consumers, the possibility of the continued existence of this channel of distribution in conjunction with new methods of distribution based on a different type of competition policy, forms one of the objectives which may be pursued without necessarily falling under the prohibition contained in Article 85(1), and, if it does fall thereunder, either wholly or in part, coming within the framework of Article 85(3).

This argument is strengthened if, in addition, such conditions promote improved competition inasmuch as it relates to factors other than prices.'[105]

Equally interesting is the court's development of the notion 'workable competition':

'The requirement contained in Articles 3 and 85 of the EEC Treaty that competition shall not be distorted implies the existence on the market of workable competition, that is to say the degree of competition necessary to ensure the observance of the basic requirements and the attainment of the objectives of the Treaty, in particular the creation of a single market achieving conditions similar to those of a domestic market.

In accordance with this requirement the nature and intensiveness of competition may vary to an extent dictated by the products or services in question and the economic structure of the relevant market sectors.

---

[105] Id., at pp. 1904–1905 (para. 21).

¶216

In the sector covering the production of high quality and technically advanced consumer durables, where a relatively small number of large- and medium-scale producers offer a varied range of items which, or so consumers may consider, are readily interchangeable, the structure of the market does not preclude the existence of a variety of channels of distribution adapted to the peculiar characteristics of the various producers and to the requirements of the various categories of consumers.

On this view the Commission was justified in recognizing that selective distribution systems constituted, together with others, an aspect of competition which accords with Article 85(1), provided that resellers are chosen on the basis of objective criteria of a qualitative nature relating to the technical qualifications of the reseller and his staff and the suitability of his trading premises and that such conditions are laid down uniformly for all potential resellers and are not applied in a discriminatory fashion.'[106]

¶217   Relevant market

In order to determine whether actual or potential competition is being restricted it may be necessary to define the relevant product market to see whether the parties to a given agreement or practice are in competition with each other or with certain third parties. This raises the question of the interchangeability of the products concerned.[107]

Admittedly, the difficult question of properly defining the relevant product market is usually more important for the correct application of art. 86 than art. 85. However, there are instances where the application of art. 85 likewise depends on the definition of the relevant product market.[108]

¶218   Influence of external circumstances

In a number of cases the defendants pleaded that the challenged agreement or concerted practice could not be said to restrict competition because competition was already fundamentally restricted by factors beyond their

---

[106] Id., at p. 1904 (para. 20).

[107] This matter is discussed in greater detail at ¶237 to ¶242, in connection with the application of art. 86. However, for purposes of the application of art. 85, some guidance can be found in art. 3 of Commission Regulation 1983/83 on the application of art. 85(3) of the treaty to categories of exclusive distribution agreements, OJ 1983 L173/1, and in art. 3 of Commission Regulation 1984/83 on the application of art. 85(3) of the treaty to categories of exclusive purchasing agreements, OJ 1983 L173/5, where the Commission refers to manufacturers of identical goods or of goods which are considered by users as equivalent in view of their characteristics, price and intended use. In the first case where the Commission applied this provision, it concluded that gin and whisky do not belong to the same product market (*Sole distribution agreements for whisky and gin*, OJ 1985 L369/19, at p. 23).

[108] See the cases cited below at note 136 in connection with the application of the de minimis rule. In its notice of 3 September 1986 on agreements of minor importance (OJ 1986 C231/2), the Commission defined the relevant market (paras. 10–14). See ¶224 below.

control. The argument was successful in the *Sugar Cartel* case where the court annulled that part of the Commission's decision which dealt with the control of sugar supplies on the Italian market because competition was already substantially restricted by the special organisation of that market.[109] Subsequently, however, the argument failed in a case involving price-fixing practised by cigarette manufacturers on the Dutch market.[110] Their defence that the Dutch excise tax legislation combined with the interference of the Ministry of Economic Affairs in the setting of the price level left no scope for competition, met with little sympathy from the court:

'[A]lthough the Netherlands legislation gives the tobacco manufacturer less scope for price competition, it does leave him the means of creating a price difference between his products and those of his competitors, by reducing his prices or by holding them at the same level while other manufacturers increase theirs. . . .

The fact that it was in the interest of the manufacturers to avoid, by means of a collective effort, the constraints which the operation of the market imposed on each of them individually does not make their agreements compatible with competition law.'[111]

¶219   Anti-competitive effect within common market

Article 85(1) condemns restrictions of competition 'within the common market' to the extent they may affect 'trade between member states'. With regard to EC competition law, the territory of the common market consists of: Belgium, Denmark, France (including the overseas departments Guadeloupe, French Guiana, Martinique, Réunion and Saint-Pierre-et-Miquelon),[112] Germany,[113] Greece, Ireland, Italy, Luxembourg, the Netherlands,[114] Portugal

---

[109] *Suiker Unie & Ors v EC Commission* [1975] ECR 1663, at pp. 1917–1924 (para. 30–73).

[110] *Stichting Sigarettenindustrie & Ors v EC Commission* [1985] ECR 3831, at pp. 3866–3871 (para. 18–37).

[111] Id., at p. 3869 (paras. 29 and 32). See also *Agreements and concerted practices in the flat glass sector in the Benelux countries*, OJ 1984 L212/13, at p. 18, where the Commission rejected the argument that price control in Belgium was responsible for the identical prices:

'[W]hilst it is true that this price control may have prevented, delayed or limited price rises announced by the producers, the decision to propose a price rise, the amount proposed and finally how the rise was actually implemented in the price lists and when it took effect were in fact the subject of agreement or consultation between the producers.'

[112] EC competition law does not apply, however, in dependent overseas territories (art. 227(3) of the treaty).

[113] Since 3 October 1990, the Community's competition rules have been fully applicable in the territory of the former German Democratic Republic. Agreements already in force on that date which are incompatible with art. 85(1) should have been amended within three months of unification. Firms wishing to claim exemption for existing agreements under art. 85(3) should have submitted an appropriate notification to the Commission within six months of unification. Council Regulation 4064/89 of 21 December 1989 on the control of concentrations, OJ 1990 L257/13, has applied since unification. *XXth Report on Competition Policy*, points 39–40. For a summary of major cases involving the former GDR, see id., points 33–38.

[114] EC competition law does not apply, however, in dependent overseas territories (ibid.).

(including the autonomous regions of the Azores and Madeira),[115] Spain (including the Canary Islands, Ceuta and Melilla) and the UK (Gibraltar included).

It should be noted that EC competition law does not apply to the Principalities of Andorra[116] and Monaco,[117] the Republic of San Marino,[118] the Vatican City, the Faroe Islands and Greenland,[119] the Channel Islands (Jersey and Guernsey) and the Isle of Man.[120]

¶220   Effect on inter-state trade

Agreements, decisions or concerted practices which restrict competition within the common market are only caught by the prohibition contained in art. 85(1) if they 'may affect trade between member states' (see ¶221–¶224).

¶221   Required effect

As the words 'may affect' suggest, for the requirement to be satisfied it suffices that the agreement, decision or practice 'may have an influence, direct or indirect, actual or potential, on the pattern of trade between member states'.[121]

The required effect on trade has been held to exist also in a situation where the agreement concerned caused the volume of trade between member states to increase rather than decrease.[122]

The requisite effect on 'trade' has been defined both in terms of a change to

---

[115] EC competition law does not apply in Macao (see answer of the Commission to Written Question No. 401/85, OJ 1985 C251/26).

[116] See Answers of the Commission to Written Question No. 191/78, OJ 1978 C238/14, and to Question No. 113/81, OJ 1981 C153/19.

[117] See Answer of the Commission to Written Question No. 213/81, OJ 1981 C210/14.

[118] See Smit and Herzog, *The Law of the European Community*, 6–210.

[119] See the Treaty amending, with regard to Greenland, the Treaties establishing the European Communities, OJ 1985 L29/1.

[120] The EC Treaty shall not apply to the Sovereign Base Areas of the United Kingdom of Great Britain and Northern Ireland in Cyprus (art. 227(5)(b) of the treaty). The same applies with regard to dependent overseas territories (art. 227(3) of the treaty).

[121] *Société Technique Minière v Maschinenbau Ulm* [1966] ECR 235, at p. 249.

[122] *Consten and Grundig v EC Commission* [1966] ECR 299, at p. 341. In *Eirpage*, OJ 1992 L306/22, at p. 29, the Commission found that a joint venture to provide a nationwide paging service would have both a detrimental and a beneficial impact on trade between member states. Since the joint venture would initially be the only provider of such services in Ireland, it could dissuade competitors from other member states from entering the Irish market (presumably because it would be difficult to compete against a network that was already established). On the other hand, the joint venture could make the paging concept more popular, which would attract providers of complementary paging services from other member states.

the normal pattern of trade[123] and in terms of a change to the competitive structure of the market.[124]

¶222   Evidence required

The court has held that 'it must be possible to foresee with a sufficient degree of probability on the basis of a set of objective factors of law or of fact' that the agreement or practice may affect trade between member states.[125]

In practice, very little evidence needs to be adduced by the Commission to satisfy the effect on inter-state trade requirement.[126] Only exceptionally has the court failed to endorse the Commission's findings in this respect. In *Papiers peints de Belgique*, the court found the Commission's reasoning in support of its determination that inter-state trade was affected to be insufficiently precise.[127]

However, in two judgments on references for a preliminary ruling the court went as far as stating that inter-state trade was affected even though the product concerned was only traded in the Cognac region in France.[128]

¶223   Trade between member states

In its *Grundig* judgment, the court enunciated the basic principle that the purpose of the 'effect on inter-state trade' criterion is to set the limit between the areas covered by EC and national law respectively. According to the court:

'[i]t is only to the extent to which the agreement may affect trade between

---

[123] *Société Technique Minière v Maschinenbau Ulm* [1966] ECR 235, at p. 249; *Coöperatieve Stremsel-en Kleurselfabriek v EC Commission* [1981] ECR 851, at p. 867 (para. 14).

[124] This approach is favoured in cases dealing with art. 86. See *Commercial Solvents v EC Commission* [1974] ECR 223, at p. 252 (para. 32). For other examples of the application of this principle by the Commission, see *ECS/AKZO*, OJ 1985 L374/1; *British Sugar/Napier Brown*, OJ 1988 L284/41; *London European–Sabena* [1989] 1 CEC 2,278; OJ 1988 L317/47; *Flat Glass* [1989] 1 CEC 2,077; OJ 1989 L33/44 and *Decca Navigator System* [1989] 1 CEC 2,137; OJ 1989 L43/27.

[125] *Société Technique Minière v Maschinenbau Ulm* [1966] ECR 235, at p. 249; see also *Coöperatieve Stremsel-en Kleurselfabriek v EC Commission* [1981] ECR 851, at p. 867 (para. 14).

[126] For example, in *Bayo-n-ox*, OJ 1990 L21/71, at p. 77, the Commission stated:

'The actual effects of an agreement which by its nature may affect trade have to be determined precisely in only a very small number of cases. Article 85(1) does not require that an agreement in restraint of competition must be successful in achieving its desired effect.'

[127] *Papiers peints de Belgique v EC Commission* [1975] ECR 1491, at p. 1514 (para. 32) where the court stated:

'With regard to the finding in the decision of the territorial protection arising from the restrictive practice and the closing off of the national market, the decision does not clearly set forth the grounds on which the Commission found them to exist, the mere reference to an earlier case constituting insufficient explanation.'

[128] *Bureau National Interprofessionnel du Cognac v Clair* [1985] ECR 391, at p. 425 (para. 29) and *Bureau National Interprofessionnel du Cognac v Aubert* [1987] ECR 4789, at p. 4814 (para. 18); [1989] 1 CEC 363. In *Clair* the court stated that:

'any agreement whose object or effect is to restrict competition by fixing minimum prices for an intermediate product is capable of affecting intra-Community trade, even if there is no trade in that intermediate product between the Member States, where the product constitutes the raw material for another product marketed elsewhere in the Community. The fact that the finished product is protected by a registered designation of origin is irrelevant.'

Member States that the deterioration in competition caused by the agreement falls under the prohibition of Community law contained in Article 85; otherwise, it escapes the prohibition. In this connection, what is particularly important is whether the agreement is capable of constituting a threat, either direct or indirect, actual or potential, to freedom of trade between Member States in a manner which might harm the attainment of the objectives of a single market between States.'[129]

This straightforward pronouncement of the court notwithstanding, the Commission has been quick to seize jurisdiction over agreements or practices between companies all located in the same member state, even when the agreement or practice was not import or export oriented. The court, more often than not, has confirmed the Commission's theories in that respect.[130] In *Delimitis*,[131] however, the court suggested that a liberal interpretation of this requirement is not always appropriate. In that case, the court stated that a beer supply arrangement limited to a single member state is not in principle capable of affecting trade between member states if it contains an access clause that mitigates the restrictive effect of the agreement by giving a national or foreign supplier a realistic possibility of supplying the distributor.[132]

The Commission's decision condemning a premium recommendation issued by a German association of property insurers provides a good illustration of how far the Commission's long arm stretches.[133] Even though the recommendation covered only the German market and had been duly filed with the German supervisory authorities, the Commission nevertheless concluded that inter-state trade was affected because some of the members of the German association were branch offices of Community fire insurers having their head offices outside Germany. The Commission came to this conclusion notwithstanding the fact that the branch offices concerned represented only a small share of the insurance business involved. This interpretation would appear far-reaching since it implies that a local scheme may become

---

[129] *Consten and Grundig v EC Commission* [1966] ECR 299, at p. 341.

[130] See, e.g., *Brasserie de Haecht v Wilkin ('Haecht I')* [1967] ECR 407, at pp. 415–416, dealing with the tied house contracts of a small Belgian brewer; *Vereniging van Cementhandelaren v EC Commission* [1972] ECR 977, at p. 991 (para. 29), where the court stated that:

'[a]n agreement extending over the whole of the territory of a Member State by its very nature has the effect of reinforcing the compartmentalization of markets on a national basis, thereby holding up the economic interpenetration which the Treaty is designed to bring about and protecting domestic production.'

[131] *Delimitis v Henninger Bräu* [1991] ECR I-935.

[132] Id., at p. I-989 (para. 32). The court suggested that such a possibility is more likely to exist where the reseller may sell beers imported from other member states by other undertakings in addition to any beer that he himself may import. Id., at p. I-988 (para. 29).

[133] *Fire insurance (D)*, OJ 1985 L35/20, affirmed by the court in *Verband der Sachversicherer v EC Commission* [1987] ECR 405.

transnational in nature from the moment one of the participants is related to a company having its offices outside the area concerned.[134]

In addition to the problem of delineating the Commission's jurisdiction with respect to purely national arrangements, the inter-state trade requirement also raises the question of the scope of application of art. 85 to trade with third countries. In this connection, the Commission has found that an agreement affects trade between member states if it affects competition among Community companies in markets outside the Community.[135] For a discussion of the issue of to what extent restrictive conduct taking place outside the Community may be said to affect trade within the Community, see ¶255 and ¶256.

¶224   Effect on competition and trade must be appreciable

Even though the wording of art. 85 suggests that any effect on competition and trade between member states is sufficient to bring an agreement or practice within the scope of the prohibition, the court in 1969 established a de minimis rule requiring that the effect be appreciable. This development occurred in *Völk v Vervaecke*, where the court ruled that:

'an agreement falls outside the prohibition in Article 85(1) when it has only an insignificant effect on the markets, taking into account the weak position which the persons concerned have on the market of the product in question.'[136]

Shortly thereafter, in 1970, the Commission issued a notice concerning agreements of minor importance[137] offering some guidance as to its understanding of what is meant by a significant or appreciable impact on the market in question. The notice quantifies the de minimis concept by a reference to both market share and turnover. The 1970 Notice was updated in 1977 and 1986.[138] The latest version provides that normally agreements or practices will not be caught by art. 85(1) if the following two conditions are satisfied:

(1) market share: the goods or services which are the subject of the

---

[134] See also *Assurpol*, OJ 1992 L37/16, at p. 22; *Eirpage*, OJ 1991 L306/22, at p. 29. In *Assurpol*, the Commission went so far as to suggest that interstate trade is affected because property covered by local insurance contracts was owned by foreign companies.

[135] See *French-West African Shipowner's Committees*, OJ 1992 L134/1, where the Commission found that an agreement affected trade between member states because, inter alia, it gave French shipping lines an advantage over shipping lines of other member states in trade with certain African countries.

[136] *Völk v Vervaecke* [1969] ECR 295, at p. 302 (para. 5–7); see also *Louis Erauw-Jacquery v La Hesbignonne* [1988] ECR 1919; [1989] 2 CEC 637; *APB* [1990] 1 CEC 2,060; OJ 1990 L18/35, at p. 39 (para. 41–42).

[137] Commission notice on agreements of minor economic importance which do not fall under art. 85(1) of the treaty establishing the European Economic Community, JO 1970 C84/1.

[138] OJ 1977 C313/3; OJ 1986 C231/2.

agreement together with the participating undertakings' other goods or services which are considered by users to be equivalent in view of their characteristics, price and intended use must not represent more than five per cent of the total market for such goods or services in the area of the common market affected by the agreement;

(2) turnover: the aggregate annual turnover of the participating undertakings must not exceed ECU 200m.

Notwithstanding the fact that, at the time of the 1986 amendment, the turnover threshold was increased from ECU 50m to 200m, a great number of agreements continue to miss the benefit of the de minimis rule. This is because the limit is calculated on the turnover of the full product range, not just of the product or service in question, and on a consolidated basis in relation to the turnover of the entire corporate group. The term 'participating undertakings' is, indeed, defined in the notice as comprising not only the parties to the agreement but related companies as well.[139]

Another difficulty with the application of the notice concerns the vagaries inherent in the definition of the relevant product or service market in order to determine the share of the market which is affected by the agreement or practice in question.[140]

Thus, apart from the fact that the notice is offered for purposes of 'guidance' only, already the sheer practical difficulties that may arise when applying the terms of the notice to the facts of a particular situation would dictate great

---

[139] Under the terms of the notice 'participating undertakings' are defined as follows:

'(a) undertakings party to the agreement;
(b) undertakings in which a party to the agreement, directly or indirectly,
  – owns more than half the capital or business assets, or
  – has the power to exercise more than half the voting rights, or
  – has the power to appoint more than half the members of the supervisory board, board of management or bodies legally representing the undertakings, or
  – has the right to manage the affairs;
(c) undertakings which directly or indirectly have in or over a party to the agreement the rights or powers listed in (b);
(d) undertakings in or over which an undertaking referred to in (c) directly or indirectly has the rights or powers listed in (b);

Undertakings in which several undertakings as referred to in (a) to (d) jointly have, directly or indirectly, the rights or powers set out in (b) shall also be considered to be participating undertakings.'

[140] For example, in *Wea-Fillipacchi*, JO 1972 L303/52 the Commission refused to consider the record market as a whole but distinguished between the markets for classical, light and pop music. Similarly, in *Hasselblad v EC Commission* [1984] ECR 883, the court endorsed the Commission's narrow market definition, i.e. the market in medium-format reflex cameras (where Hasselblad's market share ranged between 25 per cent to 50 per cent) instead of the wider market of reflex cameras in general (where Hasselblad's share was less than one per cent).

¶224

caution before placing too much reliance on it.[141] This is all the more so in view of the fact that at times the Commission continues to make reference to the principle that it need not prove any effect on competition or trade from the moment the anti-competitive intent is clear.[142]

Finally, an agreement may be deemed to have an appreciable effect on competition if other companies in the sector use agreements comprising similar restrictions of competition. In such cases, the appreciable nature of the restriction is derived from the cumulative effect of these agreements.[143]

ARTICLE 85(3): EXEMPTION FROM THE PROHIBITION

¶225   The scope of the exemption

The prohibition contained in art. 85(1) is not absolute. Article 85(3) enables the Commission to declare the prohibition inapplicable if the benefits of the agreement, decision or concerted practice concerned outweigh the harm to competition caused by it.

When balancing the benefits and harms of a particular agreement or practice, the Commission needs to verify whether the four substantive conditions set out in art. 85(3) are satisfied (see ¶226–¶231).

As to the mechanics of the application of art. 85(3), an exemption can be granted by the Commission either individually or by way of a block exemption (¶232).

¶226   The four substantive conditions

Article 85(3) lays down four conditions that must all be met before an exemption can be granted:

  (1) the agreement or practice must contribute to improving the production or distribution of goods or to promoting technical or economic progress (¶227);

---

[141] Misinterpretation of the terms of the notice by counsel for the defendants did not prevent the Commission from imposing a fine in *Kawasaki*, OJ 1979 L16/9. The 1986 amendment to the notice sets out the Commission's current attitude on the application of the notice and the question of fines. In para. 5 of the notice it is stated that:

'Where, due to exceptional circumstances, an agreement which is covered by the present Notice nevertheless falls under Article 85(1), the Commission will not impose fines. Where undertakings have failed to notify an agreement falling under Article 85(1) because they wrongly assumed, owing to a mistake in calculating their market share or aggregate turnover, that the agreement was covered by the present Notice, the Commission will not consider imposing fines unless the mistake was due to negligence.'

[142] See, e.g. *Polistil/Arbois*, OJ 1984 L136/9.

[143] See, e.g. *Parfums Givenchy*, OJ 1992 L236/11, at p. 18, where the Commission noted that 'the agreements notified form part of an economic context in which selective distribution systems comprising restrictions of competition similar to those described above are the rule and that, consequently, the appreciable nature of the restrictions noted may be said to derive from the cumulative effect inherent in such a distribution structure'.

(2) consumers must obtain a fair share of the resulting benefits (¶228);

(3) the restrictions imposed need to be indispensable to the attainment of the beneficial results (¶229);

(4) the parties to the agreement or practice may not be afforded the possibility of eliminating competition in respect of a substantial part of the products in question (¶230).

A few general observations may be appropriate regarding these four criteria, although one should bear in mind that a functional analysis of each category of agreement or practice offers a more reliable basis for anticipating the Commission's reaction to a particular agreement or practice.

¶227 Contribution to production or distribution or to technical or economic progress

Article 85(3) describes the necessary benefits in general terms, i.e. the improvement of production or distribution of goods and the promotion of technical or economic progress.

For those agreements or practices belonging to a category for which a block exemption has already been issued, the preamble to the regulation in question provides a useful indication of the kinds of benefits that are typically deemed to result from the category of agreement concerned:

(1) for exclusive distribution agreements:[144]

  (a) manufacturer (especially small and medium-sized), by dealing with only one dealer, can more easily overcome difficulties in international trade resulting from linguistic, legal and other differences;

  (b) rationalisation of distribution, more intensive marketing, continuity of supplies;

  (c) increased inter-brand competition.

(2) for exclusive purchasing agreements:[145]

  (a) improved sales planning and assurance that reseller's requirements will be met;

  (b) more intensive marketing;

---

[144] Commission Regulation 1983/83 on the application of art. 85(3) of the treaty to certain categories of exclusive distribution agreements, OJ 1983 L173/1.

[145] Commission Regulation 1984/83 on the application of art. 85(3) of the treaty to certain categories of exclusive purchasing agreements, OJ 1983 L173/5.

(c) increased inter-brand competition;

(d) sometimes the only way for small or medium-sized manufacturers to penetrate a new market.

(3) for patent licence agreements:[146]

(a) patentees more willing to grant licences;

(b) licensees more inclined to undertake the investment required to manufacture, use and put a new product on the market or to use a new process;

(c) access to new technology;   .

(d) increase in the number of production facilities and the quantity and quality of goods purchased in the common market.

(4) selective distribution agreements for motor vehicles:[147]

(a) manufacturers and selected dealers need to co-operate to provide specialised service;

(b) rapid availability of spare parts, including those with a low turnover;

(c) incentive for dealer to develop sales and servicing.

(5) for specialisation agreements:[148]

(a) the companies concerned can concentrate on the manufacture of certain products, which allow them to operate more efficiently and supply the product more cheaply.

(6) research and development agreements:[149]

(a) improved dissemination of technical knowledge;

(b) avoidance of duplication of efforts;

(c) stimulation of new advances through the exchange of complementary technical knowledge;

(d) rationalisation of the manufacture of the products or application of the processes resulting from the research.

---

[146] Commission Regulation 2349/84 on the application of art. 85(3) of the treaty to certain categories of patent licensing agreements, OJ 1984 L219/15.

[147] Commission Regulation 123/85 on the application of art. 85(3) of the treaty to certain categories of motor vehicle distribution and servicing agreements, OJ 1985 L15/16.

[148] Commission Regulation 417/85 on the application of art. 85(3) of the treaty to categories of specialisation agreements, OJ 1985 L53/1.

[149] Commission Regulation 418/85 on the application of art. 85(3) of the treaty to categories of research and development agreements, OJ 1985 L53/5.

¶227

(7) for franchise agreements:[150]

    (a) limited investments for franchisor facilitating new entries on the market;

    (b) easier establishment of outlets by independent traders thanks to franchisor's experience and assistance.

(8) for know-how licensing agreements:[151]

    (a) improved transfer of technology;

    (b) increased number of production facilities and quality of goods produced;

    (c) expanded possibilities of further development of licensed technologies.

Similarly, notices which the Commission issues from time to time in order to clarify its general position regarding certain types of agreements offer a valuable insight into the kind of considerations by which the Commission will be guided when applying art. 85(1) to the category of agreements involved. Thus, the notices on co-operation agreements and on subcontracting agreements[152] reflect the Commission's overall favourable attitude toward such agreements. Parties entering into similar agreements can expect to benefit from such favourable bias.

As to agreements that are not comparable to any of the broad categories of agreements for which a block exemption or notice already sheds light on the advantages typically derived from them, the parties can be expected to have to discharge the burden of proving on an ad hoc basis why the agreement or practice is beneficial.[153] In this connection, the court has pointed out that the

---

[150] Commission Regulation 4087/88 on the application of art. 85(3) of the treaty to categories of franchise agreements, OJ 1988 L359/46.

[151] Commission Regulation 556/89 on the application of art. 85(3) of the treaty to certain categories of know-how licensing agreements, OJ 1989 L61/1.

[152] Notice concerning agreements, decisions and concerted practices in the field of co-operation between enterprises, JO 1968 C75/3, and Commission notice concerning its assessment of certain subcontracting agreements in relation to art. 85(1) of the EEC Treaty, OJ 1979 C1/2.

[153] For recent examples, see e.g.:

Fiat/Hitachi, OJ 1993 L20/10: a joint venture for the manufacture, distribution and sale of hydraulic excavators. Benefits:

– better excavators due to incorporation of technically better components;

– improved distribution due to merger of separate and largely complementary distribution systems of the parties.

¶227

benefits need to be assessed objectively rather than from the subjective viewpoint of the parties to the agreement.[154]

¶228   Fair share to consumers

Once it is established that an agreement or practice produces certain benefits, it is also necessary to determine that such benefits do not accrue exclusively in favour of the parties but that interested outsiders, i.e. the users and ultimate consumers, likewise obtain their fair share.

Generally speaking, this second requirement tends to be satisfied more easily than the first because the Commission will readily assume that, as long as the market in question is subject to effective competition, the parties will not be able to keep the benefits but will be forced to pass them on further down the line.[155]

It is interesting to note that the Commission tends to interpret the 'fair share' concept in terms of lower prices rather than in terms of improved service or other more intangible values. A good illustration of the Commission's thinking in this respect can be found in the Flemish book case where the defendants claimed that the consumers received a fair share from the benefits resulting from resale price maintenance in that a broader range of titles is available than would otherwise be the case and in that, without resale price maintenance, booksellers would be unable or unwilling to provide ancillary services such as providing full information to customers and passing on individual orders. The Commission rejected these arguments as follows:

'As far as the production or publishing of books is concerned, [the parties]

Ford/Volkswagen, OJ 1993 L20/14: a joint venture for the development and production of a multi-purpose vehicle.
Benefits:

– rationalisation of product development and manufacturing;
– pooling of existing technical knowledge for establishment of a plant using latest production technology;
– development of a more advanced vehicle.

Moosehead/Whitbread, OJ 1990 L100/32: trade mark licence agreement and related agreements for the production and sale of beer.
Benefits:

– lower production costs;
– improved distribution because one party is given access to the other's distribution system.

[154] *Consten and Grundig v EC Commission* [1966] ECR 299, at p. 348.
[155] See, e.g. *Rockwell/Iveco*, OJ 1983 L224/19, at pp. 25–26; *Carbon Gas Technologie*, OJ 1983 L376/17, at p. 20; *Iveco/Ford*, OJ 1988 L230/39, at p. 45 (para. 41).

have maintained that a broader range of titles is available than would be the case without resale price maintenance. In view, among other things, of the fact that many publishers do not publish both general-interest and less-popular books, but restrict themselves to the one or other type, this condition is not considered to be satisfied. Nor can the argument go unchallenged that booksellers would be unable or unwilling to provide ancillary services such as providing full information to customers and passing on individual orders unless there is a system of resale price maintenance. As long as they are able to earn a fair return for the services they provide there is no reason why booksellers should not be able to carry on a normal business without resale price maintenance. Moreover, this system denies the consumer the opportunity of deciding for himself whether to buy books at a price that includes a service charge or to take his custom to a bookseller who does not provide any services and from whom he can buy books more cheaply. The consumer pays the same price for a Dutch-language book published in the other country regardless of his preferences as to additional services; and he is obliged to pay the service charge even if he does not wish to use the service, as is apparently often the case.

Secondly, it must be pointed out that even if a wide range of titles and the availability of services are to be regarded as benefiting the consumer, the consumer generally cannot benefit from the advantages of any rationalisation that takes place in the book trade. Booksellers are not allowed to grant discounts to good customers. Since the price of the product is, for many consumers, an important element in their decision to purchase – and this applies to books as much as to other products – the Commission considers that the consumer is not receiving a fair share of any benefits resulting from the agreement to which this Decision relates.

A further result of the system of collective resale price maintenance for Dutch-language books is that the main group of consumers, which tends to favour the more popular books, is forced to contribute to the cost of publishing short-run titles, which are generally intended for a smaller part of the population. In assessing the relative advantages and disadvantages of any agreement such as that concerned in this case, it cannot be accepted that the advantages it involves for a small minority of the population outweigh the disadvantages for the majority of consumers.'[156]

While the Commission tends to focus on the pricing in assessing the benefit to consumers, other factors are also taken into consideration. For instance, better

---

[156] *VBBB/VBVB*, OJ 1982 L54/36, at pp. 47–48. See also Answer to Written Question No. 307/84, OJ 1984 C243/2.

¶228

service or a broader range of products may be taken into account[157] as well as more esoteric considerations.[158]

¶229   Indispensability of the restriction

This third requirement raises the question of whether less restrictive means exist to achieve the desired benefits. This gives the Commission a chance to intervene and suggest less harmful alternatives than those adopted by the parties. Thus, for example, in *Bayer/Gist-Brocades*, the Commission caused the joint subsidiaries set up for the production of certain pharmaceuticals to be replaced by reciprocal supply arrangements.[159] In *Optical Fibres*, a series of joint-venture arrangements were substantially modified both as to the structure of the joint ventures and the rights and obligations of the parties.[160] In *Jahrhundertvertrag*, the Commission required the parties to change the coverage of an exclusive purchasing commitment.[161]

¶230   No elimination of competition

Pursuant to the fourth requirement, the agreement may not afford the parties an opportunity to exclude competition in respect of a substantial proportion of the goods in question. Thus, the Commission needs to delineate the relevant market[162] and to establish how the share of the market affected by the agreement relates to the unaffected portion.[163]

At times the Commission has stretched the non-exclusion of competition concept in order to accommodate a cartel which, for reasons of industrial and social policy, was deemed to be desirable. For example, in *Synthetic Fibres*, the Commission granted an exemption to a crisis cartel set up in order to reduce the structural overcapacity in the sector.[164] Even though the cartel grouped the ten largest European manufacturers of synthetic fibre and concerned the closure of 18 per cent of their production capacity for six types of synthetic textile, the Commission nevertheless came to the conclusion that competition was not eliminated. In addition to invoking the limited duration of the arrangement, the

---

[157] See, e.g. *Ford/Volkswagen*, OJ 1993 L20/17; *Parfums Givenchy*, OJ 1992 236/11; *Eirpage*, OJ 1991 L306/22. The Commission is generally favourably disposed towards arrangements that benefit small and medium-sized enterprises ('SMEs'). For example, in *Assurpol*, OJ 1992 L37/16, at p. 23, the Commission noted that co-operation among insurance companies would make it possible 'to cover both the risks of SMEs and those of larger enterprises'.

[158] For instance, in *Parfums Givenchy*, OJ 1992 236/11, consumers were deemed to benefit from the fact that the selective distribution system insured that the luxury product would not become an everyday product.

[159] *Bayer/Gist-Brocades*, OJ 1976 L30/13, at p. 16.

[160] *Optical Fibres*, OJ 1986 L236/30.

[161] *Jahrhundertvertrag*, OJ 1993 L50/14.

[162] See, e.g., *Kali und Salz v EC Commission* [1975] ECR 499, where the court annulled the Commission's decision for failure to demonstrate that two types of fertiliser constituted separate markets.

[163] See, e.g., *Carlsberg*, OJ 1984 L207/26, at p. 30.

[164] *Synthetic Fibres*, OJ 1984 L207/17. See also *BPCL/ICI*, OJ 1984 L212/1, likewise involving plant closures.

Commission pointed to the presence on the Community market of products from third countries and of substitute products such as cotton and wool. The Commission also emphasised the fact that the crisis cartel did not provide for any co-ordination of the parties' commercial behaviour in general, in that the co-ordinated reductions involved only one of the participants' commercial strategies.[165]

¶231   The Commission's approach

A review of the Commission's decisions under art. 85(3) reveals that the nature of the agreement and the position of the parties on the market tend to be the two most important factors in determining whether an agreement qualifies for an exemption or not.

Thus, it is clear that certain kinds of agreements will hardly ever receive the benefit of an exemption – e.g. price-fixing and market-sharing agreements, export bans – while other types of agreements have been held more often than not to be eligible for an exemption – e.g. licensing, distribution, specialisation and joint venture agreements.

By the same token, it is fair to say that it is relatively easier for small or medium-sized firms to qualify for an exemption than for large undertakings.[166]

Although the Commission's decisions whereby exemptions are granted or refused are subject to judicial review, the court has made it clear from the outset that it would avoid interfering with the Commission's discretion. In *Consten and Grundig*, the court stated that the exercise of the Commission's powers under art. 85(3):

'[n]ecessarily implies complex evaluations on economic matters. A judicial review of these evaluations must take account of their nature by confining itself to an examination of the relevance of the facts and of the legal consequences which the Commission deduced therefrom. This review must in the first place be carried out in respect of the reasons given for the decisions which must set out the facts and considerations on which the said evaluations are based.'[167]

The wide discretion enjoyed by the Commission under art. 85(3) has allowed

---

[165] In this connection it is interesting that the Commission's decision 'is subject to the condition that the signatories shall refrain from communicating data on their individual output and deliveries of synthetic fibres to one another either directly or through a trustee body or a third party', *Synthetic Fibres*, OJ 1984 L207/17, at p. 24 (art. 2). In other words, the Commission only allowed parties to exchange information on their respective capacity cutbacks but not on their actual output.

[166] See, e.g., *Transocean Marine Paint Association*, JO 1967 163/10, where the Commission accepted that a commission was payable whenever a member of the association sold for the first time paints into the area of primary responsibility of another member. However, when the exemption was for the first time extended, this restriction on competition had to be struck from the agreement. See *Transocean Marine Paint Association*, OJ 1974 L19/18.

[167] *Consten and Grundig v EC Commission* [1966] ECR 299, at p. 347.

it to put pressure on parties to amend their agreement in line with the Commission's policy on the subject[168] or to agree to certain conditions such as the submission to the Commission of periodic reports.[169] In addition, the Commission has used its discretionary powers to reconcile the requirements of its competition policy with the broader needs of the Community for an industrial and/or social policy.[170] Reasons of opportunism have likewise been involved.[171]

At times, exemptions have been granted in which the Commission's reasoning as to whether the four criteria of art. 85(3) were satisfied, did not cover more than one paragraph or a few lines.[172] This creates the danger that it becomes difficult, if not impossible, for outsiders as well as for the court, to verify whether the Commission has adequately applied the four criteria to the agreement or practice in question.

¶232   Individual or block exemptions

Exemptions pursuant to art. 85(3) are granted by the Commission either by way of an individual decision or by the application of a block exemption.

In order to be eligible for an individual exemption, the agreement or practice needs to be notified to the Commission or to be dispensed from the notification requirement under Regulation 17/62.[173] In order to determine whether the four criteria are fulfilled, the parties must co-operate with the Commission to establish the relevant facts.[174]

With respect to air and sea transport, specific procedures for the grant of

---

[168] See, e.g., *Parfums Givenchy*, OJ 1992 L236/11.

[169] See, e.g., *Ford/Volkswagen*, OJ 1993 L20/14; *Parfums Givenchy*, OJ 1992 L236/11; *Eirpage*, OJ 1991 L306/22.

[170] See, e.g. *Ford/Volkswagen*, OJ 1993 L20/14, where, in granting an exemption to a joint venture between two of the world's largest motor vehicle manufacturers, the Commission took into account the large number of jobs that would be created by the joint venture in one of the Community's poorest regions.

[171] See, e.g. *P & I clubs*, OJ 1985 L376/2 where the Commission exempted mutual non-profit-making associations providing certain types of marine insurance. One of the considerations mentioned by the Commission, at p. 13, was 'that a prohibition of the IGA could have the effect that a large proportion of members in the clubs, at least those who are not established in the Community, would decide to leave the club and set up new P & I clubs outside the Community'.

[172] See, e.g. *BP/Kellogg*, OJ 1985 L369/6; *Sole distribution agreements for whisky and gin*, OJ 1985 L369/19.

[173] For the procedural aspects, including the duration of and special conditions which may be attached to an exemption decision, see Chapter 11.

[174] See *Consten and Grundig v EC Commission* [1966] ECR 299, where the court, at p. 349, stated:

'The applicants, supported on several points by the German Government, allege inter alia that all the conditions for application of the exemption, the existence of which is denied in the contested decision, are met in the present case. The defendant starts from the premise that it is for the undertakings concerned to prove that the conditions required for exemption are satisfied.

The undertakings are entitled to an appropriate examination by the Commission of their requests for Article 85(3) to be applied. For this purpose the Commission may not confine itself to requiring from undertakings proof of the fulfilment of the requirements for the grant of the exemption but must, as a matter of good administration, play its part, using the means available to it, in ascertaining the relevant facts and circumstances.'

individual exemptions exist under Regulation 3975/87[175] and Regulation 4056/86.[176]

Article 85(3) of the treaty expressly provides for the possibility that a 'category' of agreements receive an exemption from the prohibition of art. 85(1). Pursuant to enabling regulations of the Council of Ministers, the Commission has thus far enacted several block exemptions, i.e. regulations whereby certain categories of agreements are exempted as a group:

- exclusive distribution agreements;[177]
- exclusive purchasing agreements;[178]
- patent licence agreements;[179]
- selective distribution agreements for motor vehicles;[180]
- specialisation agreements;[181]
- research and development agreements;[182]
- franchise agreements;[183]
- know-how licensing agreements;[184]
- agreements between carriers concerning the operation of scheduled maritime transport services;[185]
- agreements between transport users and conferences concerning the use of scheduled maritime transport services;[186]
- agreements concerning joint planning and co-ordination of capacity,

[175] Council Regulation 3975/87 of 14 December 1987 laying down the procedure for the application of the rules on competition to undertakings in the air transport sector, OJ 1987 L374/1.

[176] Council Regulation 4056/86 of 22 December 1986 laying down detailed rules for the application of art. 85 and 86 of the treaty to maritime transport, OJ 1986 L378/4.

[177] Commission Regulation 1983/83 of 22 June 1983 on the application of art. 85(3) of the treaty to categories of exclusive distribution agreements, OJ 1983 L173/1.

[178] Commission Regulation 1984/83 of 22 June 1983 on the application of art. 85(3) of the treaty to categories of exclusive purchasing agreements, OJ 1983 L173/5.

[179] Commission Regulation 2349/84 of 23 July 1984 on the application of art. 85(3) of the treaty to categories of patent licence agreements, OJ 1984 L219/15.

[180] Commission Regulation 123/85 of 12 December 1984 on the application of art. 85(3) of the treaty to categories of motor vehicle distribution and servicing agreements, OJ 1985 L15/16.

[181] Commission Regulation 417/85 of 19 December 1984 on the application of art. 85(3) of the treaty to categories of specialisation agreements, OJ 1985 L53/1.

[182] Commission Regulation 418/85 of 19 December 1984 on the application of art. 85(3) of the treaty to categories of research and development agreements, OJ 1985 L53/5.

[183] Commission Regulation 4087/88 of 30 November 1988 on the application of art. 85(3) of the treaty to categories of franchise agreements, OJ 1988 L359/46.

[184] Commission Regulation 556/89 of 30 November 1988 on the application of art. 85(3) of the treaty to certain categories of know-how licensing agreements, OJ 1989 L61/1.

[185] See art. 3, 4 and 5 of Council Regulation 4056/86 of 22 December 1986 laying down detailed rules for the application of art. 85 and 86 of the treaty to maritime transport, OJ 1986 L378/4.

[186] See art. 4 and 6 of Council Regulation 4056/86 of 22 December 1986 laying down detailed rules for the application of art. 85 and 86 of the treaty to maritime transport, OJ 1986 L378/4.

¶232

consultations on tariffs on scheduled air services and slot allocation at airports;[187]

- agreements relating to computer reservation systems for air transport services;[188]
- agreements concerning ground handling services;[189]
- agreements in the insurance sector.[190]

In principle, these block exemptions do away with the need for filing individual notifications for agreements the terms of which are not more restrictive than the clauses specifically allowed in the block exemption. They are generally aimed at promoting legal certainty and alleviating the burden on the Commission staff.[191] Unfortunately, however, the block exemptions on exclusive distribution and exclusive purchasing, for example, contain so many 'ifs and buts' that within months of their publication the Commission felt obliged to issue a set of clarifying guidelines.[192] This goes to show that legal certainty is not necessarily enhanced by the block exemptions. As a result, the number of individual notifications may rise rather than fall, thereby increasing the workload of the Commission staff and further burdening the Commission's process.

Several block exemptions[193] provide for opposition procedures whereby the exemption may be extended to agreements containing restrictions of competition which are not expressly admitted without having been explicitly excluded, if the Commission does not oppose such exemption within six months from the day of notification of the agreement.

---

[187] Commission Regulation 84/91 of 5 December 1990 on the application of art. 85(3) of the treaty to certain categories of agreements between undertakings, decisions of associations of undertakings and concerted practices concerning joint planning and co-ordination of capacity, consultations on tariffs on scheduled air services and slot allocation at airports, OJ 1991 L10/14.

[188] Commission Regulation 83/91 of 5 December 1990 on the application of art. 85(3) of the treaty to certain categories of agreements between undertakings relating to computer reservation systems for air transport services, OJ 1991 L10/9.

[189] Commission Regulation 82/91 of 5 December 1990 on the application of agreements between undertakings, decisions of associations of undertakings and concerted practices concerning ground handling services, OJ 1991 L10/7.

[190] Commission Regulation 3932/92 of 21 December 1992 on the application of art. 85(3) of the treaty to certain categories of agreements, decisions and concerted practices in the insurance sector, OJ 1992 L398/7.

[191] Due to a shortage of staff, the delays involved in obtaining an individual decision can be formidable. For example, the Velcro/Aplix agreement of 14 October 1958 had been notified to the Commission on 30 January 1963 while a decision was only issued on 12 July 1985. See *Velcro/Aplix*, OJ 1985 L233/22.

[192] Commission Notice concerning Commission Regulations 1983/83 and 1984/83 of 22 June 1983 on the application of art. 85(3) of the treaty to categories of exclusive distribution and exclusive purchasing agreements, OJ 1984 C101/2.

[193] Regulation 2349/84 (patent licence agreements), Regulation 417/85 (specialisation agreements), Regulation 418/85 (research and development agreements), Regulation 4087/88 (franchise agreements) and Regulation 556/89 (know-how licensing agreements).

¶232

ARTICLE 85(2): THE NULLITY SANCTION

¶233 Scope and application of the sanction

Pursuant to art. 85(2) any agreement or practice which violates art. 85(1) 'shall be automatically void'. No prior decision to that effect is required.[194]

Since arts. 85 and 86 are 'directly applicable' in the member states,[195] the automatic nullity cannot only be established by the Commission but also by a national court.[196]

The rigour of the automatic nullity concept is tempered in three ways.

First, art. 85(3) provides for the possibility of obtaining an exemption from the ban contained in art. 85(1).

Secondly, the court, for the sake of legal certainty, has established the 'provisional validity' doctrine pursuant to which a national court may only declare so-called 'old' and 'accession' agreements, which have been notified in time or which are exempt from the notification requirement, to be automatically void after the Commission has taken a decision under art. 85(3) whereby the exemption is refused.[197]

Thirdly, the court has made it clear that nullity as a civil law consequence of breaches of arts. 85 and 86 only applies to those provisions or features in the agreement or practice which violate art. 85(1) or art. 86.[198] In other words, the remaining provisions are unaffected by the nullity sanction, provided they are severable. The question of severability is a matter to be decided by reference to the law applicable to the agreement or practice in question.[199]

---

[194] Regulation 17/62, art. 2.

[195] The fact that art. 85 and 86 are directly applicable means that these provisions create rights and obligations for private persons which are immediately enforceable by national courts. See *BRT v SABAM (BRT I)* [1974] ECR 51, at p. 62 (para. 16):

'As the prohibitions of Articles 85(1) and 86 tend by their very nature to produce direct effects in relations between individuals, these Articles create direct rights in respect of the individuals concerned which the national courts must safeguard.'

The Commission has established as a priority the reinforcement of the role which national courts play in the enforcement of the EC Treaty's competition rules. See Chapter 13.

[196] As to the problems arising from this concurrent jurisdiction, see Chapter 13.

[197] *Brasserie de Haecht v Wilkin (Haecht II)* [1973] ECR 77, at pp. 87–88 (para. 9). So-called 'old' agreements are agreements which were in existence on the date of entry in force of Regulation 17/62, i.e. 13 March 1962. So-called 'accession' agreements are agreements which were in existence on the date of accession of new member states, i.e. 1 January 1973 for the UK, Ireland and Denmark, 1 January 1981 for Greece, and 1 January 1986 for Portugal and Spain. The 'provisional validity' doctrine is discussed further in Chapter 11.

[198] *Société Technique Minière v Maschinenbau Ulm* [1966] ECR 235.

[199] *Soc. de vente de ciments et bétons v Kerpen & Kerpen* [1983] ECR 4173, at p. 4185, where the court held:

'The automatic nullity decreed by Article 85(2) of the Treaty applies only to those contractual provisions which are incompatible with Article 85(1). The consequences of such nullity for other parts of the agreement, and for any orders and deliveries made on the basis of the agreement, and the resulting financial obligations are not a matter for Community law. Such consequences are to be determined by the national court according to its own law.'

¶233

ARTICLE 86: ABUSE OF A DOMINANT POSITION

¶234   The scope of the Article

The text of art. 86 provides that:

'Any abuse by one or more undertakings of a dominant position within the common market or in a substantial part of it shall be prohibited as incompatible with the common market in so far as it may affect trade between Member States.

Such abuse may, in particular, consist in:

(a) directly or indirectly imposing unfair purchase or selling prices or other unfair trading conditions;

(b) limiting production, markets or technical development to the prejudice of consumers;

(c) applying dissimilar conditions to equivalent transactions with other trading parties, thereby placing them at a competitive disadvantage;

(d) making the conclusion of contracts subject to acceptance by the other parties of supplementary obligations which, by their nature or according to commercial usage, have no connection with the subject of such contracts.'

Thus the first paragraph of the article sets out the prohibition of any abuse of a dominant position within the common market if it may affect trade between member states. The second paragraph contains a list of examples of abusive practices.

The examples of abusive conduct listed in art. 86 correspond largely to the examples of illegal agreements mentioned in art. 85. Both articles also contain the same jurisdictional requirement that trade between member states must be affected. The main distinguishing features between the two provisions, therefore, are (1) that under art. 86 an individual firm's practice may come under scrutiny, while under art. 85 a plurality of actors is required, (2) that for art. 86 to apply the firm(s) concerned must hold a 'dominant' position on the market, whereas under art. 85 it suffices that the effect on competition be 'appreciable', and (3) that the abuse of a dominant position cannot receive the benefit of an exemption, unlike agreements or practices caught by the ban in art. 85(1) which may be exempted pursuant to art. 85(3).

The wording of art. 86 makes it clear that it is not market dominance as such which is prohibited, but its abuse. Furthermore, the dominant position may be that of a single firm or a collective dominant position, held by several firms.

What is to be understood by the concept of dominant position is not defined in art. 86 but has been clarified by the case law of the Commission and court as meaning a degree of market control which enables a firm to behave to an appreciable extent independently of its competitors and customers. As a prerequisite for the application of this definition, it is essential to first establish the relevant product and geographic market within the boundaries of which the market power of the firm concerned is to be measured. Depending on how narrowly or broadly the parameters of the relevant market are drawn, a finding of dominance will be easier or more difficult to establish. The Commission's discretion in this area has proven to be formidable.

As to the concept of abuse, the list of examples contained in art. 86 is not exhaustive. The most important abusive practices in the light of the Commission's practice and the jurisprudence of the court are discussed in Part II of this book under Chapter 9.

The required effect on trade between member states referred to in art. 86 gives rise to the same considerations as under art. 85. It should be noted, however, that under art. 86 the required effect on trade has been inferred from the impact of the abuse on the 'competitive structure' within the common market.

ARTICLE 86: THE RELEVANT MARKET

¶235 Definition

Any inquiry into the applicability of art. 86 to a particular set of facts typically starts with a definition of the relevant market. As stated by the court in *Continental Can*, the definition of the relevant market is of essential significance for the appraisal of a dominant position because 'the possibilities of competition can only be judged in relation to those characteristics of the products in question by virtue of which those products are particularly apt to satisfy an inelastic need, and are only to a limited extent interchangeable with other products'.[200] The Commission adopts a similar approach. It considers that 'the object of market delineation is to define the area of commerce in which conditions of competition and the market power of the dominant firm is to be assessed'.[201]

Since market power is the ability to behave to a significant extent independently in the market, or to prevent the maintenance of effective competition,[202] the measurement of market power must take into account those undertakings which through their restraining influence prevent other

---

[200] *Europemballage Corp and Continental Can Co Inc v EC Commission* [1973] ECR 215, at p. 247 (para. 32).
[201] *ECS/AKZO*, OJ 1985 L374/1, at p. 17.
[202] See Chapter 9.

undertakings from behaving independently. The process of identifying those undertakings is the inquiry into what constitutes the relevant market. For example, those firms which prevent an undertaking from raising its prices to supra-competitive levels because they would then offer equivalent goods or services at a better price are part of the relevant market. Undertakings are only capable of exerting a restraining influence on other undertakings when they provide goods or services which the customers regard as reasonably interchangeable, and which are available to them within a certain geographical area. Thus, the relevant market should be identified both from the point of view of the product involved (¶236–¶242), and from the point of view of geography (¶243–¶245).[203]

¶236   Relevant product market

The decisive test for defining whether products belong to the same market or not is the criterion of 'interchangeability'. The difficulty in using this criterion is that it leaves open the threshold question of 'how much' goods need to be interchangeable to pertain to the same market (see ¶237–¶241). Examples from the Commission's case law highlight the fact that the Commission tends to select those markets where the defendant's market share is the highest. This provides a good illustration of the Commission's desire to extend the boundaries of its jurisdiction under art. 86.

¶237   Interchangeability of products

According to *Continental Can*, products which are only to a limited extent interchangeable with other products are not part of the relevant market.[204] Those that are reasonably interchangeable will be considered part of the relevant market.

Interchangeability, sometimes also referred to as 'substitutability', must be considered from the viewpoint of the customer. To judge whether goods are interchangeable, the nature of the goods, their price and use can be considered.[205] However, an inquiry into the relevant product market limited to

---

[203] Sometimes, discussions of the relevant market inquiry mention a third aspect, the temporal aspect. As this aspect has not yet given rise to problems, it will not be discussed separately. It goes without saying that the relevant market, as well as the position of a particular undertaking within that market, may change over time. If the alleged abuse is said to have been committed over a relatively long period of time it may be worthwhile to investigate whether at all times during the investigated period the defendant undertaking was in a dominant position. For example, in *Soda-Ash – Solvay*, OJ 1991 L152/21, at p. 31, the Commission noted that Solvay's 'historic market share of some 70% in continental western Europe over the whole of the period under consideration is in itself indicative of a significant degree of market power'. On this matter see generally Baden Fuller, 'Article 86 EEC: Economic Analysis of the Existence of a Dominant Position', (1979) 4 E.L. Rev. 423.

[204] *Europemballage Corp and Continental Can Co Inc v EC Commission* [1973] ECR 215, at p. 247 (para. 32).

[205] See, e.g., *Chiquita*, OJ 1976 L95/1, at pp. 11–12; Commission Notice on agreements of minor economic importance, OJ 1986 L231/2, at para. 11. For a market definition in a case where products can be used for different purposes, see *Hoffmann-La Roche v EC Commission ('Vitamins')* [1979] ECR 461, at pp. 515–517 (paras. 24–30).

a study of the objective characteristics of the products involved would be insufficient. In *Michelin* the court held that in addition to the objective characteristics of the products involved, 'the competitive conditions and the structure of supply and demand on the market must also be taken into consideration'.[206] In other words, even goods which based on their objective characteristics (nature, price, use) could be considered as being reasonably interchangeable, may be used by different categories of customers, who are part of a different competitive environment. Under these circumstances it may be appropriate to treat the different categories of customers as belonging to separate markets. In *Michelin*, where the alleged abuse related to discounts to tyre dealers, the parties agreed that new, original-equipment tyres should be excluded from the relevant market because these tyres were directly ordered by car manufacturers. Owing to that particular 'structure of demand', competition in that sphere was considered to be governed by completely different factors and rules than in the replacement-tyre market.[207] For similar reasons, the court endorsed the Commission in its exclusion of car and van tyres from the relevant market.[208]

¶238   'Reasonable' interchangeability of products

Some products are more interchangeable than others. In *Continental Can* the court ruled that products which are only to a limited extent interchangeable with other products should not be considered part of the same relevant market.[209] This obviously raises the question of what is meant by the requirement that, to be part of the same relevant market, products should be interchangeable to more than just a limited extent.[210]

While no rule of thumb exists in Community law which would help to

---

[206] *Michelin v EC Commission* [1983] ECR 3461, at pp. 3504–3505 (para. 37).

[207] *Michelin v EC Commission* [1983] ECR 3461, at p. 3505 (para. 38).

[208] *Michelin v EC Commission* [1983] ECR 3461, at pp. 3505–3506 (para. 39–41). See also *International Express Courier Services*, OJ 1990 L233/19, where the Commission treated basic postal service and international express delivery as separate markets because these services are used by different categories of customers. The basic service meets the needs of the general public where the price of the service is at least as important as the speed while express courier service meets the needs of business customers who must have a guarantee that their packages will be delivered within a given time period. Similarly, in *Soda-Ash – Solvay*, OJ 1991 L152/21, and *Soda-Ash – ICI*, OJ 1991 L152/40, the Commission held that, while caustic soda could replace soda ash for certain manufacturing applications, this possibility did not constitute a substantial limitation on the dominant producer's market power in the soda-ash market. In this connection, the Commission stressed that the principal buyers of soda ash were glass manufacturers, for whom caustic soda was not a good substitute for soda ash.

[209] *Europemballage Corp and Continental Can Co Inc v EC Commission*[1973] ECR 215, at p. 247 (para. 32).

[210] In *Michelin v EC Commission* [1983] ECR 3461, at p. 3508 (para. 48), the court held that:

'[a]lthough the existence of a competitive relationship between two products does not presuppose complete interchangeability for a specific purpose, it is not a pre-condition for a finding that a dominant position exists in the case of a given product that there should be a complete absence of competition from other partially interchangeable products as long as such competition does not affect the undertaking's ability to influence appreciably the conditions in which that competition may be exerted or at any rate to conduct itself to a large extent without having to take account of that competition and without suffering any adverse effects as a result of its attitude.'

¶238

determine whether, in a given case, the degree of interchangeability between certain products is sufficient, the case law of the court and of the Commission shows that generally a very high degree of interchangeability is required for products to be part of the same market. For example, in *United Brands* the existence of seasonal interchangeability between bananas and other fresh fruits was held to be insufficient because bananas were available in sufficient quantities throughout the year.[211] Similarly, in *Michelin*, the fact that a number of customers expressed certain reservations regarding the use of retread tyres, particularly on the front axle, was deemed to be sufficiently important to exclude them from the market for new replacement tyres.[212]

One reason that a high degree of interchangeability is generally required is that the time period over which interchangeability is measured, whether from the demand or supply side, tends to be short. For example, in *Tetra Pak II*,[213] the Commission stressed that the analysis used to define a market should cover only a short period because it 'corresponds more to the economic operative time during which a given company exercises its power on the market'. Over longer periods, technological progress may occur, and consumer habits and market structures may change, so that the boundaries between markets may shift.[214]

¶239   Cross-elasticity of demand

Data concerning the cross-elasticity of demand can be useful for the inquiry into whether goods are interchangeable. Where there is a high cross-elasticity of demand between certain products, a slight increase in the price of one product causes a considerable number of customers to switch to other products, thereby indicating that the products compete in the same relevant market. Cross-elasticity of demand therefore directly measures the degree of interchangeability of certain products.[215]

---

[211] *United Brands v EC Commission* [1978] ECR 207, at pp. 272 (para. 27–29) and 273 (para. 32–33).
[212] *Michelin v EC Commission* [1983] ECR 3461, at p. 3508 (para. 49).
[213] *Tetra Pak II*, OJ 1992 L72/1, at p. 18.
[214] Id.
[215] In *United Brands v EC Commission* [1978] ECR 207, the court briefly discussed the cross-elasticity of demand between bananas and other fruits. It held that, although during the summer months and at the end of the year bananas were exposed to competition from other fruits, there was no significant long-term cross-elasticity of demand between these products. That was one of the reasons why bananas where held to constitute a market separate from the market for other fresh fruits. For a critical comment on this aspect of the case, see Baden Fuller, 'Article 86: Economic Analysis of the Existence of a Dominant Position', (1979) 4 E.L. Rev. 423, at p. 426.
In *Tetra Pak I* (BTG licence), OJ 1988 L272/27, at pp. 35–37, the Commission thoroughly discussed at length the cross-elasticity of demand between different types of milk packages and their associated machines. The Commission stated that the lack of price sensitivity, i.e. the fact that a rise in the price of aseptic packages or the machines for packaging would not cause a significant reduction in demand for those products, allows producers to act independently and that the test of price elasticity accordingly is closely and logically linked to determining the existence of dominance. The Commission mentioned two causes which contributed to making cross-elasticity of demand low. The first cause was that packages and their associated machines only represent a small proportion of the price of milk. Any changes in the relative price of milk packages or of machines would not cause any

¶240 Supply substitutability

Interchangeability or substitutability should not only be considered from the demand side. It may be that certain companies, which do not offer interchangeable products, could easily alter their existing production methods and start supplying products which are considered interchangeable by the purchasers. For example, in *Continental Can* the court held that a dominant position in the market for light metal containers for meat and fish cannot be decisive as long as it has not been proved that producers in other sectors of the market for light metal containers are not in a position to enter this market, by a simple adaptation, with sufficient strength to create a serious counterweight.[216]

The assessment of whether there is elasticity of supply between certain products takes into account elements such as differences in production techniques and in the plant and tools needed to manufacture the goods in question. If a manufacturer needs considerable time and investment to adapt his production lines to make competing goods, he should not be considered part of the relevant market. In *Michelin*, car tyres were excluded from the market for heavy vehicles on these grounds.[217] Similarly, in *Tetra Pak* the Commission considered the market for carton packaging machines for fresh milk to be different from that for carton packaging machines for UHT milk.[218] The Commission noted that access to technology and know-how to build machines for packaging fresh milk did not permit entry into the UHT milk packaging machine market since technology in the latter market was particularly difficult to master and partially covered by patents. The existence of high entry barriers had been demonstrated by other companies' lengthy and costly attempts to develop acceptable products.

High entry barriers to a market may also exist in the form of regulatory restrictions. For example, in *British Midland v Aer Lingus*,[219] the Commission found that supply substitutability was limited because only three airlines were authorised to operate scheduled services on the route in question.

---

appreciable difference in the retail price for the customer. The Commission provided an example in that a significant price change of milk packages (±10 per cent) would only affect the retail price of milk to a small extent (±1 per cent). The second cause was that different types of milk and their associated packages were not regarded by consumers as perfect substitutes. Each type of milk had a different taste and preservation quality, and each type of milk was associated with certain types of packaging. On appeal, Tetra Pak only challenged the parallel application of art. 85 and 86, *Tetra Pak Rausing SA v EC Commission* [1990] ECR II-309. See also *Eurofix-Bauco v Hilti*, OJ 1988 L65/19, at pp. 32–33 (para. 60–65).

[216] *Europemballage Corp and Continental Can Co Inc v EC Commission* [1973] ECR 215, at pp. 247–248 (para. 33).

[217] *Michelin v EC Commission* [1983] ECR 3461, at p. 3506 (para. 41).

[218] *Tetra Pak I* (BTG licence), OJ 1988 L272/27, at pp. 37–38.

[219] *British Midland v Aer Lingus*, OJ 1992 L96/34. The Commission also noted that, even if other airlines were authorised to operate on the route, it is doubtful that they would choose to do so because of high opportunity costs.

¶241   Captive users

Sometimes a product is used by several categories of buyers who may not regard the availability of substitutes in the same way. Some categories of buyers may be more willing to switch to different products than others. This element should be taken into account when assessing the availability of interchangeable products. Where a particular category of customers, for certain reasons, cannot switch to other products – so-called 'captive users' – the market definition tends to be restrictive. For example, in *United Brands*, one of the reasons for restricting the market to bananas, and not to the fresh fruit market in general, was the existence of a particular group of users, namely the very young, the old and the sick, for which only bananas displayed the proper characteristics to satisfy their needs.[220]

¶242   Examples of market definitions

The following examples of market definitions used by the court and/or the Commission illustrate the tendency to use narrow market definitions:

(1) the market for raw materials for the production of ethambutol, as opposed to the market in which ethambutol competed with other anti-tuberculosis drugs;[221]

(2) the banana market, as opposed to the market for fresh fruit;[222]

(3) the market for cash register spare parts supplied to independent servicing undertakings, as opposed to the market for cash registers as a whole;[223]

(4) the markets of bulk vitamins (A, B1, B2, B3, B6, C, E, H, B12, D, PP, K and M), each group forming a market of its own;[224]

(5) the services rendered in response to applications for vehicle approval and the issue of certificates of conformity;[225]

(6) the market for new replacement tyres for heavy vehicles, not including retread tyres;[226]

(7) the market for the management of royalties due to performing artists as a result of secondary exploitation of their performances, as opposed to the market for the exchange of services in the field of performance of artistic works;[227]

---

[220] *United Brands v EC Commission* [1978] ECR 207, at p. 273 (para. 31).
[221] *Commercial Solvents v EC Commission* [1974] ECR 223, at pp. 248–249 (para. 19–22).
[222] *United Brands v EC Commission* [1978] ECR 207, at p. 273 (para. 31).
[223] *Hugin v EC Commission* [1979] ECR 1869, at pp. 1895–1897 (para. 3–10).
[224] *Hoffmann-La Roche v EC Commission ('Vitamins')* [1979] ECR 461, at pp. 514–515 (para. 21–24).
[225] *General Motors Continental v EC Commission* [1975] ECR 1367, at pp. 1377–1378 (para. 4–10).
[226] *Michelin v EC Commission* [1983] ECR 3461, at pp. 3503–3510 (para. 32–52).
[227] *GVL v EC Commission* [1983] ECR 483, at pp. 506–507 (para. 42–45).

(8) the market for premium and standard grade motor spirit for carburation in four-stroke engines;[228]

(9) the organic peroxides market;[229]

(10) the market for the supply of information relating to national type-approval certification needed by an importer seeking to license a BL vehicle for use on the roads in Great Britain;[230]

(11) the market for the management of rights of authors of musical works;[231]

(12) the market for weekly television programme listings and the television guides of each individual television station in which they are published rather than broadcasting services or the market for information on television programmes in general;[232]

(13) the market for aseptic milk-packaging machines as opposed to the market for machines for packaging fresh milk;[233]

(14) the market for flat glass as distinguished from the market for hollow glass;[234]

(15) the market for granulated sugar sold to retail and industrial customers as distinct from specialty sugars, liquid sugars and syrup;[235]

(16) the service market of DNS radio signals as opposed to the market of radio signals in general and the product market of DNS compatible receivers for commercial use as opposed to the market of receivers in general;[236]

(17) the market for Hilti-compatible cartridge strips as opposed to the market for cartridge strips in general and the market for Hilti-compatible nails for nail guns as opposed to the market of such nails in general;[237]

(18) the market for funeral services;[238]

---

[228] *ABG oil companies operating in the Netherlands*, OJ 1977 L117/1, at p. 3.

[229] *ECS/AKZO*, OJ 1985 L374/1, at p. 3.

[230] *BL*, OJ 1984 L207/11, at p. 14.

[231] *GEMA v EC Commission* [1979] ECR 3193.

[232] *Magill TV Guide/ITP, BBC and RTE* [1989] 1 CEC 2,223; OJ 1989 L78/43, at p. 48; on appeal: *Radio Telefis Eireann & Ors v EC Commission* [1991] ECR II-485; *British Broadcasting Corporation and BBC Enterprises v EC Commission* [1991] ECR II-535; *ITP v EC Commission* [1991] ECR II-575. ITP and Radio Telefis Eireann appealed the decision to the Court of Justice; Cases C-241/91 and C-242/91P.

[233] *Tetra Pak I* (BTG licence), OJ 1988 L272/27, at pp. 33–38; on appeal: *Tetra Pak Rausing v EC Commission*, [1990] ECR II-309.

[234] *Flat Glass* [1989] 1 CEC 2,077; OJ 1989 L33/44, at p. 65; on appeal: *Società Italiano Vetro SpA & Ors v EC Commission* [1992] 2 CEC 33.

[235] *Napier Brown-British Sugar*, OJ 1988 L284/41, at p. 50 (para. 42).

[236] *Decca Navigator Systems* [1989] 1 CEC 2,137; OJ 1989 L43/27, at pp. 39–40 (para. 83–87).

[237] *Eurofix-Bauco v Hilti*, OJ 1988 L65/19, at pp. 31–33 (para. 55–65); on appeal: *Hilti AG v EC Commission* [1991] ECR II-1439; on appeal to the Court of Justice, [1994] 1 CEC 590.

[238] *Bodson v Pompes Funèbres* [1988] ECR 2479; [1990] 1 CEC 3.

(19) the market for plasterboard;[239]

(20) the market for musical instruments for brass bands, as opposed to the total market for musical instruments and to the rest of the market for wind or brass instruments;[240]

(21) the market for express courier services as distinguished from the market for basic postal services;[241]

(22) the market for the provision and sale of air transport between Dublin and London (Heathrow) as opposed to the market for surface transport or air travel between Dublin and other London airports.[242]

¶243   Relevant geographic market

Article 86 applies only in case of an abuse of a dominant position in a substantial part of the common market. That condition implies first that an area within the common market has to be defined which can be considered relevant for purposes of the proceeding (see ¶244). Secondly, the area which has thus been defined should be important enough to be considered 'substantial' within the meaning of art. 86 (see ¶245).

¶244   Geographic delineation of the market

The geographic relevant market is that area where the allegedly dominant firm faces competition in respect of the practices which are considered abusive.[243] The definition of the relevant geographic market therefore depends on the location of the company which is the object of the investigation and on the nature of the practices which are being investigated.[244] The relevant geographic market should moreover be characterised by homogeneous competitive conditions.[245] Thus, for example, in the *United Brands* case, France, the UK and

---

[239] *BPB Industries plc* [1989] 1 CEC 2,008; OJ 1989 L10/50, at pp. 63–64 (para. 106–109).

[240] *BBI Boosey & Hawkes: interim measures*, OJ 1987 L286/36, at p. 40 (para. 17).

[241] *International Express Courier Services*, OJ 1990 L233/19.

[242] *British Midland v Aer Lingus*, OJ 1992 L96/34.

[243] *Michelin v EC Commission* [1983] ECR 3461, at p. 3502 (para. 26).

[244] In his opinion in *Michelin v EC Commission* [1983] ECR 3461, at pp. 3534–3535, Advocate General VerLoren van Themaat stressed that the relevant geographic market cannot be defined in the abstract. See also *Società Italiano Vetro SpA & Ors v EC Commission* ('*Flat Glass*') [1992] 2 CEC 33, where the Court of First Instance suggested that it is not enough to simply allege that high transport costs mean that the geographic market should be limited to the member state or portion of the member state in which production facilities are located. Rather, the analysis of the relevant geographic market should examine whether, in reality, transport costs are significant.

[245] In *United Brands v EC Commission* [1978] ECR 207, at p. 274 (para. 44), the court held that the geographic market 'is an area where the objective conditions of competition applying to the product in question must be the same for all traders'. However, in *Soda-Ash – Solvay*, OJ 1991 L152/21, the Commission held that the relevant geographic market consisted of those member states that fell within Solvay's 'sphere of influence', even though it acknowledged that the Community market was divided along national lines and that there were price differences between the various national markets. The Commission noted that, even if each national market were considered separately, Solvay would still be dominant in each one. In *Hilti AG v EC Commission* [1991] ECR II-1439, the Court of First Instance upheld the Commission's determination that the relevant geographic market was the

Italy were excluded from the relevant geographic market because in these countries national market organisations discriminated against United Brands' bananas in favour of bananas of a different source.[246] In the other six member states, market conditions – such as tariff provisions and transport costs – were different, but not discriminatory.[247] Since the conditions of competition were the same for all suppliers of bananas in these member states, they were considered part of the same relevant geographic market.

In *Michelin*, the Netherlands were considered the relevant geographic market.[248] The decision dealt with discounts granted by Michelin NV – the Dutch subsidiary of the Michelin group – to its dealers. The reasons invoked for confining the relevant geographic market to the Netherlands were that Michelin NV's activities were concentrated on the Netherlands market, and that, in practice, the Dutch tyre dealers obtained their supplies only from suppliers operating in the Netherlands.[249] Moreover, Michelin's competitors were organised in the same way: they carried on their activities in the Netherlands through Dutch subsidiaries of their respective groups.

The Commission has on various occasions considered one member state to be the relevant geographical market.[250] In *Alsatel v Novasam*[251] it even tried to have the court declare the Alsace region to be the relevant market.[252] The court refused to follow the Commission's suggestion, since the company whose conduct was examined, a company authorised by the French Telecommunications' Administration to supply and maintain telephone sets, was authorised to operate on the entire French territory.[253]

---

entire Community on the grounds that parallel trade in Hilti products between member states was likely due to low transport costs and large price differences. Presumably, the court had decided that these price differences were due to attempts by Hilti to erect artificial barriers to trade between member states. Otherwise, price differences would seem to suggest that the Community market could not be considered as homogeneous. For appeal to the European Court of Justice see [1994] 1 CEC 590.

[246] Id., at pp. 274–275 (para. 44–51).

[247] Id., at p. 276 (para. 52).

[248] *Michelin*, OJ 1981 L353/33, at p. 35.

[249] In his opinion in *Michelin v EC Commission* [1983] ECR 3461, at p. 3535, Advocate General VerLoren van Themaat stated that even if dealers could obtain their supplies from abroad, the Netherlands could still be regarded as the relevant market for purposes of the proceeding.

[250] See, e.g. *Flat Glass* [1989] 1 CEC 2,077; OJ 1989 L33/44, at p. 65 where the Commission considered Italy to constitute the relevant geographic market. The producers sold most of their products on the home market since transport costs were high and the products' competitiveness decreased in proportion with the distance between the production centre and the point of supply. The Court of First Instance rejected the Commission's analysis of the geographic market noting that Italian producers were obliged to take into account the competitive effect of imports from other countries. *Società Italiano Vetro SpA & Ors v EC Commission* [1992] 2 CEC 33. The costs of transport were also taken into account in *Napier Brown-British Sugar*, OJ 1988 L284/41, at pp. 50–52, where the Commission was of the opinion that Great Britain, excluding Northern Ireland, constituted the relevant market. In *British Midlands v Aer Lingus*, OJ 1992 L96/34, the UK and Ireland were considered to be two separate geographic markets because the sale of airline tickets is organised on a national level and there are significant price differences between fares charged in these countries.

[251] *Alsatel v Novasam* [1988] ECR 5987; [1990] 1 CEC 248.

[252] Id., at para. 13.

[253] Id., at para. 14–16.

¶245 'Substantial part' of the common market

Pursuant to the wording of art. 86, the relevant geographic market must amount to a substantial part of the common market. In *Suiker Unie*, the court stated that:

'for the purpose of determining whether a specific territory is large enough to amount to "a substantial part of the common market" within the meaning of Article 86 of the Treaty the pattern and volume of the production and consumption of the said product as well as the habits and economic opportunities of vendors and purchasers must be considered.'[254]

On these grounds the Belgo–Luxembourg market and the southern part of Germany were considered a substantial part of the common market.[255]

In most art. 86 cases, the relevant market comprised the territory of at least one member state, thus, quasi-automatically satisfying the substantiality requirement.[256] *Suiker Unie* and *Hugin* moreover indicate that even a part of a member state may qualify as a substantial part of the common market within the meaning of art. 86.[257]

ARTICLE 86: DOMINANT POSITION

¶246 Definition

In *United Brands* the court defined the concept of a dominant position as:

'a position of economic strength enjoyed by an undertaking which enables it to prevent effective competition being maintained on the relevant market by giving it the power to behave to an appreciable extent independently of its competitors, customers and ultimately of its consumers.'[258]

---

[254] *Suiker Unie & Ors v EC Commission* [1975] ECR 1663, at p. 1977 (para. 371).

[255] Id., at pp. 1977 (para. 375) and 1993 (para. 448). See also *Magill TV Guide/ITP, BBC and RTE* [1989] 1 CEC 2,223; OJ 1989 L78/43 at p. 48 (para. 21) where the Commission held Ireland and Northern Ireland to constitute a substantial part of the common market; on appeal: *Radio Telefis Eireann & Ors v EC Commission* [1991] ECR II-485; *British Broadcasting Corporation and BBC Enterprises v EC Commission* [1991] ECR II-535; *ITP v EC Commission* [1991] ECR II-575. ITP and Radio Telefis Eireann appealed the decision to the Court of Justice (Cases C-241/91 and C-242/91P).

[256] In his opinion in *BP v EC Commission* [1978] ECR 1513, at p. 1537, Advocate General Warner indicated, in an aside, that Luxembourg would have to be regarded as a substantial part of the common market despite its population being at that time a mere 0.23 per cent of the total population in the Community.

[257] In *Suiker Unie & Ors v EC Commission* [1975] ECR 1663: the southern part of Germany; in *Hugin v EC Commission* [1979] ECR 1869: the city of London. See also *Bodson v Pompes Funèbres* [1988] ECR 2479; [1990] 1 CEC 3, where the court held, in reply to a request for a preliminary ruling, that art. 86 might be applicable to activities carried out in only a part of the territory of a member state, while leaving it to the national court to decide if there was in fact a dominant position in a substantial part of the common market.

[258] *United Brands v EC Commission* [1978] ECR 207, at p. 277 (para. 65).

This definition has become the standard in subsequent applications of art. 86.[259]

Admittedly, this definition is concerned with the dominant position of a seller. It is clear, however, that art. 86 would also be applicable to abusive conduct of a dominant buyer.[260]

The court's definition of dominance specifies that a dominant undertaking must be capable of acting independently 'to an appreciable extent', and of hindering the maintenance 'of effective competition'. On the one hand, this qualification indicates that art. 86 is not concerned with the minimal amount of market power that most undertakings enjoy. On the other hand, it is clear that not all competition has to be eliminated for an undertaking to be in a dominant position.[261]

---

[259] *Hoffmann-La Roche v EC Commission ('Vitamins')* [1979] ECR 461, at p. 520 (para. 38); *Michelin v EC Commission* [1983] ECR 3461, at p. 3503 (para. 30); *CBEM – Télémarketing SA v Compagnie Luxembourgeoise de Télédiffusion (CLT) and Information Publicité Benelux SA (IFB)* [1985] ECR 3261, at p. 3275 (para. 16).

[260] According to the Commission, one of the 'basic principles governing the implementation of the Community competition rules' is that 'any public or private undertaking in a dominant position as a purchaser of goods or services is subject to obligations equivalent to those incumbent on an undertaking which is in a dominant position as a supplier of goods or services'. *XXth Report on Competition Policy*, point 115. See also *XXth Report on Competition Policy*, point 107; *Eurofima, Third Report on Competition Policy*, points 68–69. In *Filtrona Española*, OJ 1989 C211/9, the Commission rejected a complaint by Filtrona Española, a cigarette filters manufacturer, against Tabacelera, an undertaking having the state monopoly for cigarette manufacturing in Spain. Tabacelera had decided to increase its own production of ordinary cigarette filters from 44 per cent to 100 per cent of its requirements, thus severing its commercial relationship with Filtrona. The Commission closed the file after deciding that Tabacelera did not have a dominant position as a buyer since the relevant geographical market to consider was not the Spanish but the world market. Filtrona lodged an appeal against this Commission decision which was dismissed as inadmissible. See *Filtrona Española v EC Commission* [1990] ECR II-393.

[261] *United Brands v EC Commission* [1978] ECR 207, at p. 283 (para. 113–117) where the court stated as follows:

'However an undertaking does not have to have eliminated all opportunity for competition in order to be in a dominant position.

In this case there was in fact a very lively competitive struggle on several occasions in 1973 as Castle and Cooke had mounted a large-scale advertising and promotion campaign with price rebates on the Danish and German markets.

At the same time Alba cut prices and offered promotional material.

Recently the competition of the Villeman & Tas firm on the Netherlands market has been so lively that prices have dropped below those on the German market which are traditionally the lowest.

It must however be recorded that in spite of their exertions these firms have not succeeded in increasing their market share on the national markets where they launched their attacks.'

Temple Lang commented as follows on this aspect of the case:

'The Court's view that the failure of competitors' sales campaigns is evidence of dominance is important and perceptive. It is the ability to contain competition, not the ability to ignore it, which is characteristic of dominance. Dominant firms can overcome competition, but very few of them can disregard it. The power to plan and choose a controlled response to competitors' efforts, sufficient to ensure no significant long term loss of market share, is typical of dominant firms. As market leader a dominant firm is often able to adopt a strategy advantageous to itself and disadvantageous for the rest of the industry, without using overtly exclusionary practices, which will maintain its market in spite of some competition. Such a strategy may be adopted on the dominant firm's own initiative or in response to competitors' actions. Since dominance does not mean absence

¶246

Dominance needs to be established on all segments of the relevant market. In *London European-Sabena* the relevant market was found to have two facets. The market for the provision of computerised reservation services by an operator of computerised reservation systems to one or more air carriers and the market for the supply of such systems by that operator to travel agencies.[262] The Commission concluded that, to determine whether Sabena infringed art. 86, it should examine whether the company in question held a dominant position on both markets.[263]

¶247   Collective dominance

Article 86 prohibits not only an abuse of a dominant position by a single firm, but also abuse by 'one or more' firms acting together. Despite the explicit language of art. 86, the case law on the notion of collective dominance is sparse and the Court of Justice has yet to address the subject. In recent years, however, the Commission has resorted to the concept of collective dominance with increasing frequency in an attempt to strengthen its arsenal in art. 86 cases.

In *Alsatel*,[264] the Commission tried to convince the Court of Justice to apply the concept of collective dominance to a situation where several companies had been given the exclusive right to install telecommunications equipment and, in carrying out this activity, pursued a parallel course of conduct with respect to prices and trading conditions. While the court declined to rule on this issue because it was unconnected with the facts before the national court, the case is interesting because the Commission suggested that the mere parallel conduct

---

of competition, or even absence of effective competition, clearly it does not mean freedom to disregard competition. It follows that dominance can exist even if the dominant firm is compelled to react to its competitors' activities.' Temple Lang, 'Some Aspects of Abuse of Dominant Positions in European Community Antitrust Law', (1979) 3 Fordham Int. L. Forum 1, at pp. 11–12

See also *British Midland v Aer Lingus*, OJ 1992 L96/34, where the Commission held that Aer Lingus had a dominant position even though British Midland had been able to obtain a significant market share. In that case, the key factor for the Commission was not any absence of competition, but rather that Aer Lingus had been able to contain competition at a relatively low cost to itself.

[262] *London European-Sabena* [1989] 1 CEC 2,278; OJ 1988 L317/47, at p. 50 (para. 13–15).

[263] Id., at p. 50 (para. 15) and 52 (para. 23).

[264] *Alsatel v SA Novasam* [1988] ECR 5987. Prior to this case, the notion of collective dominance was relied upon sporadically in the 1970s. In *European Sugar Industry*, OJ 1973 L140/17, the Commission considered two Dutch sugar producers – Suiker Unie and Centrale Suiker Maatschappij – jointly to hold a dominant position on the Dutch sugar market. This finding was based on the close commercial relationship between the two firms: joint purchase of raw materials, rationing of production, collaboration in the use of intermediary products, pooling of research, co-operation on market research, advertising and sales promotions and the harmonisation of ex-factory prices and conditions of sales. Another reference to joint dominance in the Commission's practice can be found in the *Fourth Report on Competition Policy*, where it was reported that seven large oil suppliers received statements of objections alleging that they had abused their collective dominant position on the Dutch market by refusing supplies to an independent network. However, the Report does not elaborate on the notion of joint dominance and the final decision was not based on a joint dominance theory. Instead, each individual oil company was held to be in a dominant position vis-à-vis its own customers. See *ABG oil companies operating in the Netherlands*, OJ 1977 L117/1.

of independent companies might constitute the basis for a finding of collective dominance.[265]

In *Flat Glass*,[266] the Commission found three companies to occupy a collective dominant position on the Italian market for flat glass. The companies concerned allegedly presented themselves on the market 'as a single entity and not as individuals' because they jointly maintained special links with a group of wholesalers, took business decisions displaying a marked degree of interdependence and established structural links relating to production through the systematic exchange of products. On appeal, the Court of First Instance confirmed the notion that companies may hold a collective dominant position on a market.[267] On the facts of the case at hand, however, the court found that the Commission had failed to establish the existence of a collective dominant position because it had failed to produce evidence substantiating the assertion that the companies acted 'as a single entity rather than as individuals'. While the court failed to give much guidance as to the kind of evidence necessary to establish the existence of a collective dominant position, it did note that it was insufficient to simply 'recycle' facts constituting an infringement of art. 85.[268]

In two cases involving international maritime transport, the Commission relied on the notion of collective dominance to find that members of ship owners' committees or shipping conferences held a dominant position over shipping between certain member states and certain African countries. In *French-West African Shipowners' Committees*,[269] the Commission based this finding on the following facts: some of the members were linked by shareholdings; there was no competition between the members; and the committee members presented a united front to shippers, particularly with regard to the fixing of rates. In *Cewal*,[270] the Commission noted that the conference agreement created very close economic links between its members as evidenced by the existence of a common scale of freight rates.

---

[265] *Alsatel v SA Novasam* [1988] ECR 5987, at p. 6011 (para. 21); Report for the Hearing, pp. 5993–5994.

[266] *Flat Glass*, OJ 1989 L33/44.

[267] *Società Italian Vetro & Ors v EC Commission* [1992] 2 CEC 33. The Court of First Instance stated (at para. 38):

'There is nothing, in principle, to prevent two or more independent economic entities from being, on a specific market, united by such economic links that, by virture of that fact, together they hold a dominant position vis-à-vis the other operators on the same market. This could be the case, for example, where two or more independent undertakings jointly have, through agreements or licences, a technological lead affording them the power to behave to an appreciable extent independently of their competitors, their customers and ultimately of their consumers.'

[268] Id., at para. 360.

[269] *French-West African Shipowners' Committees*, OJ 1992 L134/1, at p. 17.

[270] *Cewal*, OJ 1993 L34/20, at p. 31.

¶247

¶248   Relevant criteria for measuring economic strength

The foremost test for determining whether or not a company enjoys a dominant position has been to establish its market share. However, the lower a company's market share, the more additional factors have been relied upon by the Commission and court to support a finding of dominance. Such additional factors have included a number of structural elements, amounting to barriers of entry, as well as certain performance factors. At times the factors retained by the Commission, and more often than not endorsed by the court, appear to be taken from a description of the dominant firm instead of from an analysis of the market. The relevant factors are discussed below (¶249–¶252).

¶249   Market share

The market share held by the undertaking concerned is important because it has been held that an undertaking can only be deemed to be in a dominant position on a market if it has succeeded in winning a large part of this market.[271]

It is accepted that very large market shares are in themselves evidence of a dominant position. In *Hoffmann-La Roche*, the court considered market shares of approximately 93 per cent, 84 per cent, 75 per cent and 65 per cent as evidence of the existence of a dominant position.[272] Likewise, in *Michelin*, a market share of 57 per cent to 65 per cent was considered to be sufficient evidence of the existence of a dominant position.[273] Similarly, in *AKZO*, a market share of 50 per cent was considered to be adequate evidence of the existence of a dominant position.[274] In *United Brands*, however, a market share ranging from 40 to 45 per cent was held not to warrant, in itself, the conclusion that United Brands dominated the market.[275]

Often, the preponderant market share of the dominant undertaking is contrasted with the market shares held by its competitors. When there is a significant gap between the market share of the dominant undertaking and the market shares of its competitors, that element is considered as a confirmation of the existence of a dominant position.[276] By the same token, when competitors

---

[271] *United Brands v EC Commission* [1978] ECR 207, at p. 282 (para. 107).

[272] *Hoffmann-La Roche v EC Commission ('Vitamins')* [1979] ECR 461, at pp. 527–531 (para. 56, 60, 63 and 67).

[273] *Michelin v EC Commission* [1983] ECR 3461, at pp. 3509–3510 (para. 52); *Michelin*, OJ 1981 L353/33, at pp. 40–41.

[274] *AKZO Chemie BV v EC Commission* [1991] ECR I-3359, para. 60.

[275] *United Brands v EC Commission* [1978] ECR 207, at p. 282 (para. 108–109).

[276] *Michelin v EC Commission* [1983] ECR 3461, at pp. 3509–3510 (para. 52); *Hoffmann-La Roche v Commission ('Vitamins')* [1979] ECR 461, at pp. 529–531 (para. 60, 63 and 66). See also *Tetra Pak II*, OJ 1992 L72/1, where Tetra Pak was found to have a dominant position on the market for non-aseptic packaging because, inter alia, it had a 55 per cent market share while its two main competitors only had market shares of 27 per cent and 11 per cent. Similarly, in *London European-Sabena* [1989] 1 CEC 2,278; OJ 1988 L317/47, at p. 52 (para. 23–27), Sabena's dominance in the market for the supply of computerised reservation systems to travel agencies was illustrated by the fact that 118 agencies used Sabena's Saphir system while the five other systems used on the Belgian territory only serviced 20 agencies. As regards the market for the provision of computerised reservation

also have significant market shares, a relatively large market share is not necessarily indicative of dominance.[277]

On the other side of the spectrum, some market shares conclusively show that an undertaking is not in a dominant position. For example, in *Demo Studio*, it was held that an undertaking with a market share of one per cent cannot be considered to be dominant.[278] In *Mecaniver-PPG*, the Commission stated that a transaction by which the market share held by an undertaking increased from four to 11 per cent cannot be regarded as the strengthening of a dominant position, thus implicitly suggesting that a market share of four per cent does not amount to a dominant position.[279] In *Agence et Messageries de la Presse* an undertaking owning 190 retail stores out of a total of 5,500 was held not to be dominant on the retail market.[280] In the *Metro* case, the court rejected the contention that SABA had a dominant position in Germany where it had only five to ten per cent of the leisure electronic equipment market and six to seven per cent of the market for colour television sets.[281]

It follows that, save in exceptional circumstances, a company with a market share of less than ten per cent is unlikely to be considered dominant. However, according to the Commission, a dominant position cannot be ruled out in respect of market shares between 20 and 40 per cent.

As noted earlier in this chapter when discussing the relevant product market, the Commission has at times defined the market very narrowly (see ¶242). For example, in *General Motors* the market retained was not the market for motor cars but the market for issuing certificates of conformity in connection with the type-approval of cars.[282] Similarly, in *Hugin*, instead of taking the market for cash registers as a whole, the market was limited to the manufacturer's own spare parts.[283] In both instances, the selection of a narrow market resulted in a finding of an outright monopoly, whereas on the broader market the firms in question held a relatively insignificant share.

¶250   Dependence

The market share test may not only become meaningless when the product market is defined as the manufacturer's own goods, but also in a situation where, due to special circumstances, the normal competitive process comes to a

---

services to air carriers, the dominance of Sabena resulted from the fact that all but two airlines operating in Brussels were listed in the Saphir system.

[277] See *Metaleurop SA*, OJ 1990 L179/41, where the Commission determined that a firm with shares of 20 per cent and 30 per cent on the relevant markets did not have a dominant position because of the presence of other major producers and the continued flow of a large number of imports onto the market.

[278] *Demo Studio Schmidt v EC Commission* [1983] ECR 3045, at p. 3065 (para. 21).

[279] *Mecaniver-PPG*, OJ 1985 L35/54, at p. 57.

[280] *Binon & Cie v Agence et messageries de la presse* [1985] ECR 2015, at p. 2041 (para. 23).

[281] *Metro v EC Commission* [1977] ECR 1875, at p. 1902 (para. 17).

[282] *General Motors Continental v EC Commission* [1975] ECR 1367.

[283] *Hugin v EC Commission* [1979] ECR 1869.

stop. The Commission was confronted with such a context during the oil crisis and laid down the principle that, when, due to a shortage, customers find themselves in a situation of dependence vis-à-vis their traditional suppliers, each supplier finds himself in a dominant position:

> 'Economic restrictions such as existed in the Netherlands during the oil crisis can substantially alter existing commercial relations between suppliers who have a substantial share of the market and quantities available and their customers. For reasons completely outside the control of the normal suppliers, their customers can become completely dependent on them for the supply of scarce products. Thus, while the situation continues, the suppliers are placed in a dominant position in respect of their normal customers.

> With the general shortage of supplies all the oil companies were faced with the same problem, that of maintaining supplies to their regular customers. Thus they were not able to make up the deficiencies of the other companies with substantial market shares and they were in no way in competition with each other to supply each others' customers.

> In the prevailing circumstances each of these companies found itself in a dominant position relative to its customers.'[284]

¶251   Additional structural factors

When the market share of the allegedly dominant firm is insufficient in itself to establish the existence of a dominant position, other factual elements have been cited by the Commission and court in support of the finding of dominance. Such additional indicators of market dominance include:

- strong vertical integration;[285]
- strict quality control;[286]
- a technological lead over competitors;[287]
- a strong brand name due to large-scale advertising campaigns;[288]
- a highly developed sales network;[289]

---

[284] *ABG oil companies operating in the Netherlands*, OJ 1977 L117/1, at p. 9.

[285] *United Brands v EC Commission* [1978] ECR 207, at pp. 278–279 (para. 70–81). See also *Soda-Ash – Solvay*, OJ 1991 L152/21, at p. 32; *Eurofix-Bauco v Hilti*, OJ 1988 L65/19, at p. 34 confirmed on appeal *Hilti v EC Commission* [1991] ECR II-1439; on appeal to the Court of Justice, [1994] 1 CEC 590.

[286] *United Brands v EC Commission* [1978] ECR 207, at p. 280 (para. 85–87).

[287] Id., at p. 279 (para. 82–84); *Hoffmann-La Roche v EC Commission* (*'Vitamins'*) [1979] ECR 461, at p. 524 (para. 48); *Michelin v EC Commission* [1983] ECR 3461, at p. 3511 (para. 58). See also *Eurofix-Bauco v Hilti*, OJ 1988 L65/19, at p. 34 confirmed on appeal: *Hilti v EC Commission* [1991] ECR II-1439; on appeal to the Court of Justice, [1994] 1 CEC 590.

[288] *United Brands v EC Commission* [1978] ECR 207, at p. 280 (para. 91); see also *BBI/Boosey & Hawkes: interim measures*, OJ 1987 L286/36, at p. 40 (para. 18) where the Commission noted as additional factors supporting a preliminary finding of dominance the strong buyer preference for Boosey & Hawkes instruments and its close identification with the brass band movement.

[289] *Hoffmann-La Roche v EC Commission* (*'Vitamins'*) [1979] ECR 461, at p. 524 (para. 48); *Michelin v EC*

- absence of potential competition;[290]
- an extensive range of products;[291]
- mature market;[292]
- technological and financial resources;[293]
- ability to influence prices;[294]
- competitors' perception that a company is dominant, thus making them reluctant to compete for its traditional customers;[295]
- bias of consumers in favour of a company from their member state.[296]

The use of these additional criteria to establish or to confirm the existence of a dominant position is not very satisfactory. They are generally described as 'competitive' advantages enjoyed by the dominant firm which make it different from its competitors. However, there is little economic analysis, if any, that would help to explain the relevance of some of these factors in terms of barriers to entry or otherwise in connection with the finding of dominance.[297] Furthermore, it is not always clear why a certain combination of competitive

---

Commission [1983] ECR 3461 at p. 3511 (para. 58); *AKZO Chemie BV v EC Commission* [1991] ECR I-3359. See also *Soda-Ash – Solvay*, OJ 1991 L152/21, at p. 32, where the Commission referred to Solvay's excellent 'market coverage' as the exclusive or near exclusive supplier to almost all the major customers in the Community.

[290] *United Brands v EC Commission* [1978] ECR 207, at p. 284 (para. 122); *Hoffmann-La Roche v EC Commission* ('*Vitamins*') [1979] ECR 461, at p. 524 (para. 48); *Ahmed Saeed Flugreisen & Anor v Zentrale zur Bekämpfung unlauteren Wettbewerbs eV* [1989] ECR 803; [1989] 2 CEC 654; *Napier Brown-British Sugar* OJ 1988 L284/41, at pp. 52–53; *Decca-Navigator System* [1989] 1 CEC 2,137; OJ 1989 L43/27, at pp. 28 and 41 (para. 8 and 92); *Flat Glass* [1989] 1 CEC 2,077; OJ 1989 L33/44, at p. 66 (para. 79); on appeal: *Società Italiano Vetro SpA & Ors* [1992] 2 CEC 33, at para. 357–369; *BPB Industries plc* [1989] 1 CEC 2,008; OJ 1989 L10/50, at p. 65 (para. 119–120). In *Soda-Ash – Solvay*, OJ 1991 L252/21, at p. 32, the Commission noted that Solvay was protected against competition from non-Community producers by anti-dumping measures. In *British Midland v Aer Lingus*, OJ 1992 L96/34, at p. 39, the Commission stressed the high barriers to entry to the route in question.

[291] *Michelin v EC Commission* [1983] ECR 3461, at p. 3510 (para. 55); *AKZO Chemie BV v EC Commission* [1991] ECR II-3359, para. 58. See also *Tetra Pak II*, OJ 1992 L72/1, at p. 20, where the Commission stated that one indication of Tetra Pak's market power was 'the diversity of its products and geographical locations, which makes it less dependent on various fluctuations and allows it, if necessary, to make financial sacrifices on one or other of its products without affecting the overall profitability of its operations.'

[292] In *Eurofix-Bauco v Hilti*, OJ 1988 L65/19, at p. 34 (para. 69) confirmed on appeal *Hilti v EC Commission* [1991] ECR II-1439; on appeal to the Court of Justice, [1994] 1 CEC 590, the Commission held that one additional advantage which helped Hilti to reinforce and maintain its position was that the market in question was relatively mature. The Commission considered that this could discourage new entrants since sales or market shares could only be obtained at the expense of existing competitors. See also *Tetra Pak I* (BTG licence), OJ 1988 L272/27, at p. 39 (para. 44).

[293] *BPB Industries plc* [1989] 1 CEC 2,008; OJ 1989 L10/50, at p. 64 (para. 115–116)

[294] See *Soda-Ash – Solvay*, OJ 1991 L152/21, where the Commission referred to Solvay's traditional role as price leader. See also *Metaleurop SA*, OJ 1990 L179/41, where one of the factors that led the Commission to conclude that the company did not have a dominant position was that prices on the relevant markets were formed on public commodity exchanges, so that it was highly unlikely that individual firms could have a decisive influence on prices.

[295] *Soda-Ash – Solvay*, OJ 1991 L152/21.

[296] See *British Midland v Aer Lingus*, OJ 1992 L96/34, where the Commission noted that, as the national airline, Aer Lingus would be the preferred choice of Irish nationals.

[297] Barriers to entry were discussed to some extent in three Commission decisions. In *Tetra Pak I* (BTG licence), OJ 1988 L272/27, at pp. 32, 33 and 39, the Commission emphasised that barriers to entry, in the case at hand the difficulties to master the relevant technology, were particularly high, although the 91.8 per cent market share of Tetra Pak constituted conclusive evidence of a dominant position, on appeal *Tetra Pak Rausing v EC*

advantages gives the undertaking a sufficient competitive edge over its competitors to be called dominant. The statement that the dominant position results from the cumulative effect of certain factors, which taken separately may not be decisive, is not very helpful in this respect. If one takes a realistic look at the case law under art. 86, it is clear that the elusive concept of 'dominance' often boils down to that of 'pre-eminence': any large company whose share of any particular market significantly exceeds that of its next competitors can easily be found dominant regardless of its market performance and the overall degree of competition in that market.

¶252 Performance

In addition to structural factors pointing to the existence of a dominant position, the Commission and the court have also had the occasion to discuss certain features of the market conduct of the allegedly dominant firm.

Thus, for example, in *United Brands* the court rejected United Brands' contention that its losses were incompatible with the Commission's finding of dominance:

'However, UBC takes into account the losses which its banana division made from 1971 to 1976 – whereas during this period its competitors made profits – for the purpose of inferring that, since dominance is in essence the power to fix prices, making losses is inconsistent with the existence of a dominant position.

An undertaking's economic strength is not measured by its profitability; a reduced profit margin or even losses for a time are not incompatible with a dominant position, just as large profits may be compatible with a situation where there is effective competition.

The fact that UBC's profitability is for a time moderate or non-existent must be considered in the light of the whole of its operations.

The finding that, whatever losses UBC may make, the customers continue to buy more goods from UBC which is the dearest vendor, is more significant and this fact is a particular feature of the dominant position and its verification is determinative in this case.'[298]

Commission [1990] ECR II 309. In *Napier Brown-British Sugar*, OJ 1988 L284/41, at p. 53, the Commission pointed to the existence of barriers to entry in certain sugar markets. In the beet-origin sugar market they were the well-developed integrated production system of British Sugar and the fact that British Sugar received all of the UK basic quantity of sugar under applicable EEC rules. According to the Commission, it was unlikely that the UK Government would reallocate part of the UK quantity to another producer. In *Eurofix-Bauco v Hilti*, OJ 1988 L65/19, at p. 34, the Commission accepted, among other factors, as evidence of Hilti's dominant position the fact that the market was mature. Such maturity was considered to discourage new entrants since sales or market shares could only be obtained at the expense of existing competitors; confirmed on appeal: *Hilti v EC Commission* [1991] ECR II-1439; on appeal to the Court of Justice, [1994] 1 CEC 590.
[298] *United Brands v EC Commission* [1978] ECR 207, at pp. 284–285 (para. 125–128); see also *Michelin v EC*

In *Hoffmann-La Roche*, the court did not accept the Commission's argument that the ability of the allegedly dominant undertaking to maintain its market share, notwithstanding lively competition, was a factor which could be relied upon to establish a dominant position. According to the court, the retention of market share could as well have resulted from effective competitive behaviour as from a position which ensures that the undertaking can behave independently from its competitors. Where the market share held by a dominant undertaking is stable despite the presence of competition, other elements which account for the stability of the market share must be relied on to establish the existence of a dominant position.[299]

In *Michelin*, the Commission used the finding of abusive conduct as a strong indication of the existence of a dominant position.[300] This theory is based on the premise that only undertakings which wield substantial market power are capable of adopting a course of conduct which amounts to an abuse. On appeal, the court did not address the issue, but the Advocate-General was of the opinion that the 'argument is in fact admissible and sometimes of practical value'.[301] The problem with this approach, however, is that it amounts to circular reasoning: an undertaking is dominant because it has adopted a course of conduct which amounts to an abuse, yet certain courses of conduct only amount to abuses because the undertaking which has adopted them is dominant.

¶253   Effect on trade between member states

Application of art. 86

Article 86 applies only if the abuse of a dominant position is capable of affecting trade between member states. As in the case of art. 85, this requirement is intended to define the sphere of application of Community law in relation to

---

Commission [1983] ECR 3461, at pp. 3511–3512 (para. 53).

[299] *Hoffmann-La Roche v EC Commission ('Vitamins')* [1979] ECR 461, at p. 522 (para. 44).

[300] *Michelin*, OJ 1981 L353/33, at pp. 40–41.

[301] In his opinion in *Michelin v EC Commission* [1983] ECR 3461, at p. 3530, Advocate General VerLoren van Themaat stated:

'Before I consider in turn each of the submissions advanced it would be as well, I think, to point out that this separate examination of them must not obscure the link between the various elements of the prohibition contained in Article 86 of the EEC Treaty. Nor should the nature of that link be forgotten.

First of all, in this case that link is of some relevance to the relationship between the nature of the alleged abuse and the evidence of the existence of a dominant position. As is clear from the last sentence of paragraph 35 and the second subparagraph of paragraph 48 of the contested decision, the Commission considers the existence of a dominant position partly proven by the fact that Michelin NV adopted a course of conduct which an undertaking not having a dominant position could not allow itself to do. In principle I consider that such an argument is in fact admissible and sometimes of practical value. For instance, an undertaking's elimination of its competitors through aggressive price competition consisting in the selling of goods at a loss might in certain circumstances constitute evidence of that undertakings's dominant (financial) position.'

the national laws of the member states.[302] Where the effects of the allegedly abusive behaviour are confined to the territory of a single member state, art. 86 will not apply.[303] In that case, the behaviour will be governed by national law. Conversely, where the agreement or practice may affect trade between member states, Community law applies.[304]

Construction of 'may affect trade between member states'

The notion 'may affect trade between member states' has been defined by the court in the light of the principles governing the EC Treaty. Since the EC Treaty seeks to establish a common market, inter alia, by instituting a system which ensures that competition in that common market is not distorted,[305] the notion 'may affect trade between member states' must be construed to apply to agreements and practices which harm, or threaten to harm, the attainment of the objective of a single market between the member states.[306]

The requirement that trade between member states must be affected is common to art. 85 and 86, and can often be applied in the same way under both articles. For example, where an agreement or practice has the effect of partitioning markets, it will be deemed to affect trade between member states. In *Hoffmann-La Roche*, the court held that some of the contracts used by Roche, containing a so-called 'English clause', had the effect of partitioning markets since the scope of the clause was limited to Roche's guarantee of the best price on the local market.[307] This was one of the reasons why Roche's course of conduct was held to be capable of affecting trade between member states.

Impairment of the competitive structure with the common market

However, in an analysis under art. 86, the demonstration that trade between member states may be affected can take a particular form. In a line of cases the court has inferred the required effect on trade between member states from the repercussions of the abuse on the competitive structure within the common market. In *Commercial Solvents*, the applicants argued that their refusal to

---

[302] *Commercial Solvents v EC Commission* [1979] ECR 223, at p. 252 (para. 31).

[303] *Hugin v EC Commission* [1979] ECR 1869, at p. 1899 (para. 17).

[304] The applicability of Community law does not, of course, necessarily exclude the applicability of national law. Where a conflict between Community law and national law exists, Community law takes precedence. See, e.g. *Wilhelm v Bundeskartellamt* [1969] ECR 1, at p. 14 (para. 6).

[305] Article 3(g) of the EC Treaty.

[306] For art. 85, see *Société Technique Minière v Maschinenbau Ulm* [1966] ECR 235, at p. 249 and *Consten and Grundig v EC Commission* [1966] ECR 299, at p. 341; for art. 86, see *Hugin v EC Commission* [1979] ECR 1869, at p. 1899 (para. 17).

[307] *Hoffmann-La Roche v EC Commission* ('*Vitamins*') [1979] ECR 461, at pp. 544–545 (para. 105). See also *Flat Glass* [1989] 1 CEC 2,077; OJ 1989 L33/44, at pp. 64 and 66. The Commission referred to what it had stated under art. 85 when dealing with the effect on trade between member states under art. 86. The effect concerned was held to be the consolidation of national compartmentalisations which obstruct the economic interpenetration intended by the treaty; on appeal, see *Società Italiano Vetro SpA & Ors* [1992] 2 CEC 33 at para. 357–369.

¶253

supply Zoja with certain raw materials necessary for the production of ethambutol could not affect trade between member states since Zoja exported 90 per cent of its production based on ethambutol outside the common market. Moreover, its sales outlets within the common market were limited due to the existence in several member states of patents held by other competitors, which prevented Zoja from selling drugs based on ethambutol.[308] The court refused to follow this argument and stated that:

> '[W]hen an undertaking in a dominant position within the Common Market abuses its position in such a way that a competitor in the Common Market is likely to be eliminated, it does not matter whether the conduct relates to the latter's exports or its trade within the Common Market, once it has been established that this elimination will have repercussions on the competitive structure within the Common Market.'[309]

The court justified its approach by pointing out that art. 86 not only covers abuses which directly prejudice consumers, but also abuses which indirectly prejudice them by impairing the effective competitive structure within the common market.[310] Since *Commercial Solvents*, this argument has recurred in virtually every case dealing with art. 86.[311]

Examples

The apparent simplicity of the phrase 'may affect trade between member states' is therefore deceptive. It may very well be that the behaviour in dispute does not at all relate to trade between member states.[312] The following activities have been held to be capable of affecting trade between member states:

(1) production intended for export outside the common market;[313]

(2) the provision of services, such as the management of copyrights, in relation to non-member countries where the undertaking involved also provides similar services within the Community;[314]

(3) the application of a discount scheme within a single member state;[315]

---

[308] *Commercial Solvents v EC Commission* [1974] ECR 223, at p. 252 (para. 30).

[309] Id., at pp. 252–253 (para. 33).

[310] Id., at p. 252 (para. 32).

[311] See, e.g. *United Brands v EC Commission* [1978] ECR 207; *Hugin v EC Commission* [1979] ECR 1869; *Greenwich Film Production v SACEM* [1979] ECR 3275; *Michelin v EC Commission* [1983] ECR 3461; *GVL v EC Commission* [1983] ECR 483; *Bodson v Pompes Funèbres* [1988] ECR 2479; [1990] 1 CEC 3. See also the following Commission decisions: *French-West African Shipowners' Committees*, OJ 1992 L134/1; *Soda-Ash – Solvay*, OJ 1991 L152/21.

[312] *United Brands v EC Commission* [1978] ECR 207, at p. 294 (para. 207).

[313] *Commercial Solvents v EC Commission* [1974] ECR 223, at pp. 252–253 (para. 33); *Greenwich Film Production v SACEM* [1979] ECR 3275, at p. 3288 (para. 11).

[314] *Greenwich Film Production v SACEM* [1979] ECR 3275, at p. 3288 (para. 11).

[315] *Michelin v EC Commission* [1983] ECR 3461, at p. 3522 (para. 103).

(4) the import of products from third countries into member states;[316]

(5) exclusionary pricing in export markets;[317]

(6) the provision of funeral services by a group of undertakings holding concessions and enjoying a monopoly over a large part of a member state;[318]

(7) the provision of express delivery services within one member state;[319]

(8) the provision of maritime shipping services between the Community and certain African countries.[320]

In as far as these activities affect the competitive structure within the Community, the requirement that trade between member states must be affected will be deemed fulfilled.

The *Hugin* Case

Although in some cases, the analysis used by the court to establish that trade between member states may be affected appears to be a direct consequence of the finding of an abuse, it would be wrong to hold that this requirement has been read out of the treaty. In *Hugin*, the court annulled the Commission's decision precisely on this ground. It found that Hugin's refusal to supply Lipton with spare parts did not have any effects outside the London region in which Lipton was active. This was due to the nature of Lipton's activities. The maintenance, repair and renting out of cash registers, as well as the sale of used machines, were found not to be profitable beyond a certain area around the commercial base of an undertaking. It appeared from the file that these services were performed by a large number of small, local undertakings. For that reason, Hugin's refusal to supply spare parts to independent companies which specialise in the provision of maintenance services could not be deemed to affect trade between member states.[321] Also, the fact that Lipton had addressed itself to Hugin subsidiaries and distributors located in other member states did not establish either that Hugin's refusal to supply affected trade between member states. In the absence of any allegation of differential pricing by Hugin, and given the fact that the value of the spare parts was held to be relatively insignificant, the court decided that Hugin's refusal to supply spare parts could not be regarded as diverting the movement of goods from its normal

---

[316] *United Brands v EC Commission* [1978] ECR 207, at p. 294 (para. 197–203); *Soda-Ash – Solvay*, OJ 1991 L152/21.

[317] *ECS/Akzo*, OJ 1985 L379/1, at p. 23, on appeal: *AKZO Chemie BV v EC Commission* [1991] ECR I-3359.

[318] *Bodson v Pompes Funèbres* [1988] ECR 2479; [1990] 1 CEC 3.

[319] *Express delivery services*, OJ 1990 L10/47, at p. 50 (para. 15); the court annulled the Commission decision for procedural reasons in *Netherlands v EC Commission, Koninklijke PTT Nederland NV and PTT Post BV v EC Commission* [1992] ECR I-165.

[320] *French-West African Shipowners' Committees*, OJ 1992 L134/1.

[321] *Hugin v EC Commission* [1979] ECR 1869, at p. 1899 (para. 19).

channels.[322] Lipton applied to Hugin subsidiaries and distributors in other member states only because Hugin refused to supply it with spare parts in the UK.

Reconciling the different approaches

However, in other cases such as in *United Brands*,[323] the court stated that it is immaterial whether certain behaviour relates to trade between member states, once it is established that this behaviour may lead to the elimination of a competitor. How can this statement be reconciled with the *Hugin* holding that trade between member states is not affected because Hugin's refusal to supply did not have the effect of diverting the movement of goods from its normal channels? The answer to that question is not entirely clear, but surely Hugin suggests that there are limits to the 'competitive structure' argument. As Advocate General Reischl put it, 'it is not sufficient to find that the structure of competition has been affected in each individual Member State, since those effects may be of a purely local nature ...'.[324] Effect on competition is not the equivalent of effect on trade between member states. The latter element must have an independent meaning. Where larger undertakings are involved, the effect on competition will almost automatically lead to the required effect on trade between member states, or at least to its possibility.[325] In contrast, where purely local undertakings are involved, as in *Hugin*, more must be shown than merely an effect on competition.

THE INTERNATIONAL DIMENSION OF EC COMPETITION LAW

¶254   An outline

The international dimension of the Community's competition policy is of increasing importance.[326] This international dimension has two aspects. First, practices or conduct engaged in outside the EC may fall within the purview of

---

[322] Id., at p. 1900 (para. 23).

[323] *United Brands v EC Commission* [1978] ECR 207, at p. 294 (para. 201). See also *Napier Brown-British Sugar*, OJ 1988 L284/41, at p. 57 (para. 79–80), where the Commission applied the principle contained in *United Brands* to the attempts of British Sugar, an undertaking occupying a dominant position, to remove a competitor whose activities included the import, transformation and resale of a product. It added that while British Sugar's refusal to supply effectively increased the level of trade between member states since the victim of this refusal had to procure its requirements abroad, such increase did not prevent British Sugar's action from affecting trade between member states within the meaning of art. 86.

[324] *Hugin v EC Commission* [1979] ECR 1869, Opinion of Advocate General Reischl, at p. 1920.

[325] *Michelin v EC Commission* [1983] ECR 3461, at pp. 3522–3523 (para. 104) stresses that such possibility is sufficient to meet the requirement.

[326] See generally *XXIInd Report on Competition Policy for 1992*, point 114; *XXIst Report on Competition Policy for 1991*, points 58–65; *XXth Report on Competition Policy*, pp. 12–14.

art. 85 and 86 in so far as they may have an effect on trade within the EC and restrict competition within the EC. The extra-territorial application of EC competition law is dealt with in ¶255 and ¶256. Relatedly, this extra-territorial application creates a need to co-operate with competition authorities from other countries. The EC/US agreement in this area is discussed below at ¶257–¶265.

The second aspect of the international dimension of EC competition policy concerns its role in the process of the gradual widening of the Community, notably in the context of the EEA Agreement and the Europe Agreements. These agreements are reviewed below at ¶266–¶274.

¶255   Extra-territorial reach of EC competition law

Articles 85 and 86 both contain a geographical limitation in that 'trade between member states' must be affected and that the anti-competitive effect of the agreement or practice must occur 'within the common market' or the dominant position must exist 'within the common market or within a substantial part thereof'.[327]

The Commission has interpreted this jurisdictional requirement in terms of the 'effects' which the agreement or practice has within the EC, irrespective of the location, inside or outside the common market, of the parties involved (¶256). The court has not opposed this interpretation, although it has never expressly made reference to the effects doctrine in its judgments.

¶256   The effects doctrine

In 1969, in *Dyestuffs*, the Commission addressed its decision, condemning a concerted practice of price fixing, to both EC and non-EC undertakings:

'The decision is applicable to all the undertakings which took part in the concerted practices, whether they are established within or outside the Common Market ... The competition rules of the Treaty are, consequently, applicable to all restrictions of competition which produce within the Common Market effects set out in Article 85(1). There is therefore no need to examine whether the undertakings which are the cause of those restrictions of competition have their seat within or outside the Community.'[328]

On appeal, the Advocate General endorsed the Commission's approach in so far as the effects within the EC were direct and immediate, reasonably foreseeable and substantial,[329] but the court avoided the issue by relying on the

---

[327] For a listing of the states and territories where the EC rules of competition apply, see ¶219 above.
[328] *Dyestuffs*, JO 1969 L195/11, at p. 16.
[329] See the opinion of Advocate General Mayras in *ICI & Ors v EC Commission* [1972] ECR 619, at

economic unity theory and imputing the conduct of the subsidiaries inside the EC to their parents outside the EC.[330]

In subsequent cases dealing with the application of art. 86, the court continued to base jurisdiction on the economic unity theory by attributing the conduct of the EC subsidiary to its parent outside the EC.[331]

In the mid-1980s, the Commission considered two large price-fixing cases where certain participants were without any physical presence in the form of a subsidiary or a branch in the EC. Consequently, as to those participants, the Commission had no choice but to base its jurisdiction on the pure effects doctrine, without any reference to the economic unity theory.

In one of these cases, *Aluminium*, the Commission cited the court's dictum in *Béguelin*[332] and continued:

'The reasoning must be equally applicable to horizontal agreements between competitors where some are in the Community and some outside. Moreover there is no reason to distinguish in such horizontal agreements between the restrictions accepted towards each other by those within the Common Market and those outside, and those restrictions accepted towards each other by those wholly outside, subject always to the overall requirement that there be a substantial effect on trade between Member States.'[333]

In the other case, *Wood Pulp*, all the parties to a pricing agreement were companies situated outside the Community. Some of them had branches, subsidiaries, agencies or other establishments within the Community. The Commission, however, emphasised the overall impact of shipments of pulp from third countries on the EC market.[334] On appeal the court found that the

---

pp. 695–696. In support of his opinion, the Advocate General made a reference to an obiter dictum of the court in *Béguelin Import v GL Import Export* [1971] ECR 949, where the court, at p. 959 (para. 11), stated that '[t]he fact that one of the undertakings party to the agreement is situated in a third country does not prevent application of [art. 85] since the agreement is operative on the territory of the Common Market'.

[330] *ICI & Ors v EC Commission* [1972] ECR 619, at pp. 662–663 (para. 131–142).

[331] *Europemballage Corp and Continental Can Co Inc v EC Commission* [1973] ECR 215; *Commercial Solvents v EC Commission* [1974] ECR 223; *Centrafarm v Sterling Drug* [1974] ECR 1147; *United Brands v EC Commission* [1978] ECR 207; *Hoffmann-La Roche v EC Commission ('Vitamins')* [1979] ECR 461.

[332] *Béguelin Import v GL Import Export* [1971] ECR 949, at p. 959 (para. 11).

[333] *Aluminium Imports from Eastern Europe*, OJ 1985 L92/1.

[334] *Wood Pulp*, OJ 1985 L85/1, at pp. 14–15. The Commission's reasoning was as follows:

'In this case all the addressees of this Decision were during the period of the infringement exporting directly to or doing business within the Community. Some of them had branches, subsidiaries, agencies or other establishments within the Community. The concertation on prices, the exchange of sensitive information relative to prices, and the clauses prohibiting export or resale all concerned shipments made directly to buyers in the EEC or sales made in the EEC to buyers there. The shipments affected by these agreements and practices amounted to about two-thirds of total shipments of bleached sulphate wood pulp to the EEC and some 60 per cent of EEC consumption. The agreements and practices appear to have applied to at least the vast majority of the sales of the relevant product by the parties to and in the EEC during the relevant periods. The effect of the agreements and practices on prices announced and/or charged to customers and on resale of pulp within the EEC was therefore not only substantial but intended, and was the primary and direct result of the agreements and practices.'

¶256

Commission had not made an incorrect assessment of the territorial scope of art. 85.

The court stated:

'It should be noted that the main sources of supply of wood pulp are outside the Community, in Canada, the United States, Sweden and Finland and that the market therefore has global dimensions. Where wood pulp producers established in those countries sell directly to purchasers established in the Community and engage in price competition in order to win orders from those customers, that constitutes competition within the Common Market.

It follows that where those producers concert on the prices to be charged to their customers in the Community and put that concertation into effect by selling at prices which are actually coordinated, they are taking part in concertation within the Common Market within the meaning of Article 85 of the Treaty.'[335]

The applicants submitted that the decision was incompatible with public international law. The court did not agree:

'It should be observed that an infringement of Article 85, such as the conclusion of an agreement which has had the effect of restricting competition within the Common Market, consists of conduct made up of two elements, the formation of the agreement, decision or concerted practice and the implementation thereof. If the applicability of prohibitions laid down under competition law were made to depend on the place where the agreement, decision or concerted practice was formed, the result would obviously be to give undertakings an easy means of evading those prohibitions. The decisive factor is therefore the place where it is implemented.

The producers in this case implemented their pricing agreement within the Common Market. It is immaterial in that respect whether or not they had recourse to subsidiaries, agents, sub-agents, or branches within the Community in order to make their contacts with purchasers within the Community.

Accordingly the Community's jurisdiction to apply its competition rules to such conduct is covered by the territoriality principle as universally recognized in public international law.'[336]

---

[335] *Åhlström & Ors v EC Commission* ('*Wood Pulp*') [1988] ECR 5193, at p. 5242 (para. 12–13).

[336] Id., at para. 16–18. In *Aluminium Imports from Eastern Europe*, OJ 1985 L92/1, at p. 48, the Commission held that '[t]here is no prohibitive rule of international law which prevents the application of Community law to all the participants in the Brandeis arrangements'.

In *Wood Pulp*, certain applicants argued that the effects doctrine is contrary to international law because it violates the principle of non-interference by arguably opposing the US interest in promoting exports under the

While the court upheld the Commission decision, *Wood Pulp* does not represent an express endorsement of the effects doctrine. The court has arguably adopted a narrower principle than 'effects' by saying that the concertation should be 'put into effect' by the producers. Accordingly, the justification for applying EC competition law to undertakings situated outside the Community appears to rest on the fact that the agreement or concertation has been implemented within the Community. Even though the court does not clearly define what 'put into effect' means, the term seems to require some constituent act or conduct within the Community which gives effect to the agreement.

The Commission's reliance on the effects doctrine does not mean that it turns a blind eye to considerations of comity. In its Eleventh Report, the Commission emphasised that 'active co-operation between the authorities concerned should iron out certain difficulties and at the same time help maintain fair competition in the interests of the continuing growth of international trade'.[337] In *Wood Pulp*, however, the court rejected the argument by the applicants that imposing fines on them was a breach of the principle of international comity. The court held this argument tantamount to calling into question the Community's jurisdiction to apply its competition rules to conduct such as that found to exist in this case.[338] Possibly, the court regards the argument on comity as a political one, which raises no legal restraints on the Commission's power.

In the light of a possible application of the effects doctrine, it is clear that agreements or practices which restrict imports into the EC are likely to have an adverse effect on competition within the EC and thus may violate art. 85(1).[339]

Webb-Pomerene Act. The principle of non-interference prohibits a state from adopting measures under its national law if such measures have an adverse effect on the interests of another state and if those interests outweigh its own. The court, at para. 20, rejected this argument. It found that there was not 'any contradiction between the conduct required by the US and that required by the Community since the Webb-Pomerene Act merely exempts the conclusion of export cartels from the application of US anti-trust laws but does not require such cartels to be concluded.'

[337] *Eleventh Report on Competition Policy*, point 37. See also *Fourteenth Report on Competition Policy*, point 21, where the Commission made reference to three cases where it had consultations with third countries 'to ensure that proposed decisions did not affect important interests of the countries and, possibly, to look for mutually acceptable compromises'. Idem in *Twelfth Report on Competition Policy*, point 157, where the Commission mentioned that 'non-Community antitrust authorities were for the first time admitted as observers at the oral stage of proceedings concerning firms from their countries'. In *Aluminium Imports from Eastern Europe*, OJ 1985 L92/1, at p. 48, the Commission said:

'Moreover there are no reasons of comity which militate in favour of self restraint in the exercise of jurisdiction by the Commission. The exercise of jurisdiction by the Commission does not require any of the undertakings concerned to act in any way contrary to the requirements of their domestic laws, nor would the application of Community law adversely affect important interests of a non-member State. Such an interest would have to be so important as to prevail over the fundamental interest of the Community that competition within the common market is not distorted (Article 3(f) of the EEC Treaty), for that is an essential means under the Treaty for achieving the objectives of the Community.'

[338] *Åhlström & Ors v EC Commission ('Wood Pulp')* [1988] ECR 5193, at p. 5244 (para. 22).

[339] See *EMI Records v CBS* [1976] ECR 811, at p. 848 (para. 28), where the court said:

'A restrictive agreement between traders within the common market and competitors in third countries that would bring about an isolation of the common market as a whole which, in the territory of the Community,

With respect to agreements restricting exports outside the EC, the required effect within the EC may be missing.[340] Furthermore, the more lenient attitude of the EC Commission concerning export cartels, compared to import restrictions, is, of course, quite normal because every authority in the world is in the first place concerned by what happens within its own territory. Needless to say, however, export cartels favoured by one jurisdiction may have damaging effects on another jurisdiction. Thus, for example, in its *Wood Pulp* decision, the Commission condemned the activities of a Webb-Pomerene association.[341] The court, however, declared the decision void in so far as it concerned this association since the association was found not to play a separate role in the implementation of the agreements.[342]

An agreement may affect trade between member states even if it only concerns trade between member states and third countries. For example, in two cases involving international maritime transport,[343] the Commission found that agreements controlling trade between certain Community ports and the ports of third countries had the necessary effect on trade within the Community because it would distort competition between ports within the Community. The Commission also went so far as to suggest that the agreements affected trade because they distorted competition between Community shipping lines on third country markets.[344] While such practices may very well distort competition, it is questionable whether they can be said to distort competition within the Community.

---

would reduce the supply of products originating in third countries and similar to those protected by a mark within the Community, might be of such a nature as to affect adversely the conditions of competition within the Common Market.'

See also *Quantel International-Continuum/Quantel SA*, OJ 1992 L235/9, at pp.14–15; *Siemens/Fanuc*, OJ 1985 L376/29, at pp. 35–36. See also Bellis, 'International Trade and the Competition Law of the European Economic Community', (1979) 16 C.M.L. Rev. 647.

[340] See, e.g. *Iqbal, XXIst Report on Competition Policy for 1991*, p. 334, in which the Commission found that a ban on exports to certain countries outside the EC did not restrict competition. The Commission took the view that, in that case, 'the use of export destination clauses was not connected to actions having the specific intention of preventing trade between Member States'.

[341] *Wood Pulp* OJ 1985 L85/1, at p. 22, where the Commission stated:

'Associations under the Webb-Pomerene Act exporting to the EEC are not as such unlawful under EEC law. They may, however, infringe Article 85 if they restrict competition within the Common Market, and are likely to affect trade between Member States to an appreciable extent. Under the given circumstances of the present case, the agreements and practices of KEA and its members described in paragraphs 28 et seq. above had as their result an appreciable restriction of competition in the EEC. (As to the effect on trade between Member States see paragraphs 136 et seq.) The concertation on prices and the system of recommended prices within the framework of KEA did not only lead to uniform prices charged by the members of KEA but was an important factor in establishing an artificial transparency of the whole market and facilitated a concertation on prices with other producers outside the KEA. The KEA recommended price even served as reference price for other producers.'

[342] *Åhlström & Ors v EC Commission* ('Wood Pulp') [1988] ECR 5193, at p. 5245 (para. 24–28).

[343] *French-West African Shipowners' Committees*, OJ 1992 L134/1; *Cewal, Cowac and Ukwal*, OJ 1993 L34/20.

[344] *French-West African Shipowners' Committees*, OJ 1992 L134/1, at pp. 14–15.

¶257 EC/US Agreement: introduction

On 23 September 1991, the Commission and the US Government entered into an agreement[345] regarding the application of their competition laws.[346] The EC/US Agreement is intended to promote co-operation and co-ordination between the EC and the US and to lessen the possibility of differences in the application of their competition laws or the impact of such differences. Towards this end, the EC/US Agreement contains provisions regarding the notification of one party by the other, provisions regarding meetings between the competition authorities of the two parties and other exchanges of information and provisions regarding co-operation, co-ordination and the avoidance of conflict in enforcement activities.

¶258 EC/US Agreement: notification

Pursuant to the EC/US Agreement, the EC and the US must notify each other in the event that the enforcement activity of either competition authority affects important interests of the other party. Article II of the EC/US Agreement lists certain enforcement activities in connection with which notification to the other party would normally be appropriate. This is the case where one party's enforcement activities are relevant to enforcement activities of the other party, relate to anti-competitive activity conducted in the other party's territory, relate to a merger or acquisition involving a company organised under the laws of one of the other parties' states or member states, relate to conduct understood to be required, encouraged or approved by the other party or involve remedies that would have significant consequences in the other party's territory. In addition, the parties may also be required to notify each other when their competition authorities formally participate in public regulatory or judicial proceedings not arising from enforcement activities, provided the issues which are addressed affect important interests of the other party.

---

[345] This arrangement is an agreement rather than a treaty, which means that its provisions apply within the framework of, and subject to, requirements of EC and US law. See art. IX of the EC/US Agreement.

[346] Agreement between the Commission of the European Communities and the Government of the United States of America regarding the application of their competition laws, 23 September 1991 (the 'EC/US Agreement') 4 Trade Reg. Rpt. (CCH) ¶13,504. With regard to coverage, it should be noted that, for the purposes of the agreement, competition law is not understood to include provisions of the EC Treaty regarding state aid. In a case before the Court of Justice, France attacked the EC/US Agreement's validity, alleging that in concluding the agreement the Commission overstepped its authority under Community law. The Court of Justice has upheld France's complaint, that the agreement should have been concluded by the Council (*France v EC Commission* (Case C–327/91)), judgment of 9 August 1994 (not yet reported). The Commission proposes to take the necessary steps to ensure that the formal requirements for a correct conclusion to the agreement are put into place as soon as possible.

Article II of the agreement also contains provisions regarding the time at which such notification should be made. In general, notification is stipulated upon certain specified events. For example, with respect to the EC Commission, the US authorities should be notified when notice of a concentration under the merger regulation (Regulation 4064/89) is published in the *Official Journal*, when the Commission decides to initiate proceedings under the merger regulation and far enough in advance of a decision to allow the views of the US to be taken into account.[347] Outside the context of the merger regulation, notification should generally be provided to US authorities far enough before the issuance of a statement of objections and the adoption of a decision or settlement to give the US authorities an opportunity to have their views taken into account.

Notifications made in this context must include enough information so as to allow the recipient to make an initial evaluation of the effects on its interests.

¶259　EC/US Agreement: exchange of information

The EC/US Agreement also provides for a significant exchange of information between the EC and the US.[348] This exchange of information occurs in biannual meetings between EC and US competition officials.[349] The purpose of these meetings is to exchange information regarding current enforcement activities, priorities and economic sectors of common interest and to discuss potential policy changes and other relevant matters. In addition, significant information received by one competition authority is provided to the other insofar as it relates to anti-competitive activities that the providing authority believes to be relevant to the receiving authority. Finally, either party may request information that is relevant to ongoing or contemplated enforcement activity.

¶260　EC/US Agreement: co-operation regarding competition enforcement activities

The co-operation envisaged by the EC/US Agreement may arise out of three situations. First, the competition authorities of the EC and the US may both pursue enforcement activities regarding related situations. Secondly, there are situations where one party's enforcement activities might have adverse effects regarding important interests of the other party. Thirdly, there are situations

---

[347] However, the short-time limits under the merger regulation may, in many cases, make it difficult for the views of the US to be taken into account.

[348] EC/US Agreement, art. III. The exchange of information should, however, only be made subject to the requirements of confidentiality to which each party is bound. Therefore, the EC/US Agreement does not, in principle, provide any basis for the exchange of confidential information, see ¶264 below.

[349] In addition, the EC/US Agreement provides that either party will engage in consultations with the other party upon such other party's request.

where anti-competitive activities within the territory of one party may have adverse consequences for the other party.

¶261 EC/US Agreement: co-ordination of enforcement activities

In situations where the competition authorities of both the EC and the US pursue enforcement activities, the EC/US Agreement contains provisions pursuant to which the parties may co-ordinate such activities.[350] Decisions as to whether co-ordination is appropriate should take account of considerations of efficiency, the relative abilities of the competition authorities to obtain information, the overall effects of the co-ordination and the possibility of reducing the investigated party or parties' costs through the co-ordination of enforcement activities, as well as other factors. Even if enforcement activities are co-ordinated, however, the EC/US Agreement makes it clear that participation in co-ordinated activity may be limited or terminated subject to appropriate notice.

¶262 EC/US Agreement: comity

The EC/US Agreement acknowledges that the enforcement activities of one party may adversely affect the other party. Under such circumstances, the parties agree to seek accommodation of their competing interests.[351] Towards this end, the parties will consider a number of factors, including the relevant importance of the conduct in question within the two territories and its effect on both parties, the specific competitive effect of the conduct in the enforcing party's territory, the consistency of the enforcement activities in question with the other party's legal and economic policy and possible effects on such other party's own enforcement activities.

¶263 EC/US Agreement: positive comity

In certain cases, activity carried out within the territory of one of the parties will have an adverse effect on the other party.[352] In such cases, the EC/US Agreement provides that the latter may notify the former and request the

---

[350] EC/US Agreement, art. IV.

[351] EC/US Agreement, art. VI. This process is referred to as comity when an authority in one jurisdiction refrains from exercising jurisdiction over certain conduct out of a recognition that the benefits of exercising jurisdiction are outweighed by the disadvantages which such an exercise would create for the authorities of another jurisdiction. See *XXIst Report on Competition Policy for 1991*, point 64.

[352] For example, anti-competitive activity carried out in one territory may make it difficult for competitors from the other territory to enter and compete in the first territory. See *XXIst Report on Competition Policy for 1991*, point 64.

initiation of enforcement activities,[353] provided that the conduct at issue violates the notified party's competition laws.[354] The notified party will decide in its sole discretion whether or not to initiate enforcement activities or enhance already ongoing activities and communicate its decision to the requesting party. If the notified party decides to act on the request, the requesting party shall be informed of the outcome and, if possible, significant developments. The requesting party will, in any case, not be precluded from itself initiating enforcement activities. These provisions of the EC/US Agreement represent a further development of traditional principles of comity and are therefore often referred to as 'positive comity'.

¶264   EC/US Agreement: confidentiality

Irrespective of any other provisions of the EC/US Agreement, art. VIII of the agreement provides that neither party is required to disclose information to the other party if such disclosure would violate the laws of the disclosing party or be incompatible with important interests of the disclosing party. Interpreted literally, this provision would preclude the Commission from providing the US authorities with any information that the Commission has obtained by way of a request for information, a sector enquiry or an on-the-spot investigation.[355] The Commission would also be precluded from disclosing any other information acquired as a result of the application of Regulation 17/62, provided such information was 'of the kind covered by the obligation of professional secrecy.'[356]

This conclusion would also apply in the context of the merger regulation. Information acquired through requests for information, investigations and hearings in the context of the regulation, may only be used for the purpose of the request, investigation or hearing in question.[357] The Commission is also prohibited from disclosing any other information acquired through the application of the merger regulation which is covered by the obligation of professional secrecy.[358]

In addition, both the EC and the US agree that they will maintain the confidentiality of information received from the other party pursuant to the

---

[353] EC/US Agreement, art. V.

[354] As a result of this requirement, the positive comity provisions of the agreement have no application to conduct that adversely affects one party but which does not violate the competition laws of the party in whose territory the conduct is carried out. For example, an export cartel in the territory of one of the parties which has no effects in such territory is not covered by these provisions.

[355] See Regulation 17/62 of the Council of 6 February 1962 implementing art. 85 and 86 of the treaty, JO 1962 13/204; amended JO 1962 58/1655, JO 1963 162/2696, JO 1971 L 285/48, art. 20(1). The same provision is contained in the transport sector implementing regulations.

[356] Id., at art. 20(2). The same provision is contained in the transport sector implementing regulations.

[357] Council Regulation 4064/89 of 21 December 1989 on the control of concentrations between undertakings, OJ 1990 L257/13, art. 17(1).

[358] Id., art. 17(2).

agreement and resist, as far as possible, applications for disclosure made by unauthorised third parties.[359]

¶265   Consequences of the EC/US Agreement

Although the Commission has referred to the EC/US Agreement as a 'leap forward'[360] it should be considered whether the EC/US Agreement marks any real change in the level and nature of co-operation between the two parties. In examining this question, consideration should be given to two elements of the EC/US Agreement upon which much attention has been focused: the exchange of information and the positive comity provisions.

With regard to the former, there has been some concern that the EC/US Agreement would lead to the disclosure of confidential information held by the competition authorities of one of the parties to the other. Although the EC/US Agreement purports not to alter the parties' obligations to maintain the confidentiality of information, it has been suggested that it will be extremely difficult for the Commission to abide by this requirement.[361] If the Commission does abide by this requirement, the material exchanged will consist of general information to be used in the definition of markets, general analytical determinations, public information regarding the status of ongoing cases or investigations and other non-confidential information. The importance of such 'public information' should not, however, be underestimated, especially in cases where the conduct in question has significant consequences in both jurisdictions.

With regard to positive comity, the inclusion of these provisions within the EC/US Agreement may be deemed to represent an important step in the development of this newly emerging concept. Nonetheless, the practical significance of positive comity in the context of EC/US relations regarding competition policy may still be minimal because both sides are likely to be reluctant to accept the task of carrying out an investigation for the other or, by the same token, to entrust the other with an investigation.

Even though the EC/US Agreement does not provide for any dramatic changes in the relationship between the competition authorities of the EC and the US, the practical significance of the agreement should not be underestimated. The importance of the agreement is as a declaration of the two parties' intent to co-operate in the enforcement of competition law. Although

---

[359] EC/US Agreement, art. VIII(2). This provision does not, however, fit squarely with the announced intention of the EC/US Agreement. If the agreement is not intended to provide a vehicle for the exchange of confidential information, it is difficult to understand the necessity of a provision binding each party to maintain the confidentiality of information provided to it by the other party.

[360] *XXIst Report on Competition Policy for 1991*, point 64.

[361] The Commission has in the past, in the context of a parliamentary question, even declined to reveal the names of entities under investigation on the basis of its confidentiality obligations, Written Question 1740/79, OJ 1980 C140/15.

the mechanisms described in the agreement could have been used before it came into force, the agreement signals the parties' full intention to use them and, as a practical consequence, makes meaningful co-operation more likely.

As a result of such co-operation, the enforcement activities of the parties are brought one step closer together. Such an incremental change makes it more difficult to approach the EC and the US aspects of a competition law problem as two completely independent considerations. Although questions concerning one jurisdiction will of course remain separate from questions concerning the other, the EC/US Agreement may be taken to suggest their potential interdependence and the necessity, in certain cases, of adopting a more global framework of analysis.

¶266   European Economic Area ('EEA'): introduction

The European Economic Area ('EEA') Agreement is designed to strengthen the relationship between the Community and the EFTA states by replacing the series of bilateral free trade agreements in existence since 1973 with a more wide-ranging agreement.[362] The EEA Agreement may be described as a halfway house between the former free trade zone and full-fledged membership in the Community. In large part, the EEA Agreement contains substantive provisions of the EEC Treaty adapted to fit into the context of the EEA. The EEA Agreement extends to the EFTA countries the EC's four freedoms – the free movement of goods, services, persons and capital – and horizontal policies related to the four freedoms such as social policy, consumer protection, company law and competition policy.

The extension of the EC's competition rules to the EFTA states is likely to have a significant impact on how companies operate in the EFTA states because most EFTA states have had weak or non-existent competition laws. The following sections review the main elements of the competition rules established by the EEA Agreement and the institutional structures set up for their enforcement.

---

[362] The EEA Agreement was signed on 2 May 1992 by all Contracting Parties, i.e. the 12 EC member states and the seven EFTA countries namely Norway, Sweden, Finland, Austria, Switzerland, Liechtenstein and Iceland. As a consequence of the non-ratification of the EEA Agreement by Switzerland on 6 December 1992, the originally intended entry into force on 1 January 1993 was postponed. New negotiations were necessary to adopt a protocol excluding Switzerland from the application of the agreement and to make certain adjustments to the provisions concerning a cohesion fund to be financed by the EFTA countries. The EEA Agreement entered into force on 1 January 1994 following completion of the Parliamentary ratification process. It should be noted that, as a result of Switzerland's failure to ratify the EEA Agreement, any reference to the EFTA countries hereafter will not include Switzerland (nor in the short term, Liechtenstein).

¶267   EEA: substantive rules

The competition rules contained in the EEA Agreement mirror those contained in the EC Treaty. They deal with restrictive practices,[363] abuses of dominant positions,[364] mergers,[365] state aids,[366] and public undertakings and undertakings enjoying special or exclusive rights.[367] The basic competition provisions are contained in the EEA Agreement itself. Secondary legislation implementing those rules which corresponds to the equivalent EC legislation, including block exemption regulations, are set out in a number of annexes and protocols and are adapted to the EEA context. Also, in the application of the competition rules, the EEA Agreement provides that the principles and rules contained in the existing EC Commission notices must be taken into account.

It appears that the EEA competition rules are intended to have direct effect like their counterparts in the EC Treaty, and can therefore be directly invoked by private parties before national courts in the EFTA countries.[368]

¶268   EEA: the two-pillar system

Implementation of the EEA competition rules is entrusted to two regulatory agencies – or 'surveillance authorities' – the EC Commission and its equivalent on the EFTA side, the EFTA Surveillance Authority. The EFTA Surveillance Authority is an independent body established by the EFTA states,[369] and is vested with investigative and decision-making powers that parallel those of the EC Commission.[370] This 'two-pillar' approach represents a compromise between having a genuine, independent EEA enforcement authority – which would have been unacceptable for the Community – and having the rules enforced by existing Community institutions – which would have been unacceptable for the EFTA states.

¶269   EEA: 'one-stop-shop' principle

The enforcement of the competition rules set out in the EEA Agreement will be carried out by either the EC Commission or the EFTA Surveillance Authority, but not both. The rules for determining which of these authorities has jurisdiction over a given case are discussed in greater detail below. This

---

[363] EEA Agreement, art. 53.

[364] Id., art. 54.

[365] Id., art. 57.

[366] Id., art. 61–64.

[367] Id., art. 59.

[368] Article 6 of the EEA Agreement provides that provisions that mirror provisions of Community law must be interpreted in accordance with the EC Court of Justice's case law prior to the date of the signature of the agreement, which presumably includes the essential elements of the Community's legal order such as the doctrine of direct effect.

[369] Id., art. 108(1).

[370] Id., Protocol 21, art. 1(1) and 2.

'one-stop-shop' ensures that companies involved in competition proceedings involving the EEA Agreement will only have to deal with one competition authority and that divergent decisions taken by the EC Commission or the EFTA Surveillance Authority with respect to the same individual proceeding cannot occur.

¶270   EEA: jurisdiction allocation criteria

Restrictive agreements, decisions or practices

Pure cases
In cases involving restrictive agreements, decisions or practices that affect trade only within the EC or only within the EFTA territory – so-called 'pure' cases – the allocation of jurisdiction is straightforward. The EFTA Surveillance Authority deals with proceedings involving only the EFTA territory while the EC Commission is in charge of cases where only the EC is affected.[371] The only exception to this rule is in cases where an agreement only has restrictive effects within the EC, but such effects are considered to be de minimis[372] and the turnover of the undertakings involved in the EFTA states equals 33 per cent or more of their turnover in the entire EC.[373]

Mixed cases
In cases involving restrictive agreements that affect trade between the EC member states and the EFTA states – so-called 'mixed' cases – the criteria for the allocation of jurisdiction are more complex. Broadly, these criteria are designed to give the EC Commission jurisdiction over the majority of such cases. The EFTA Surveillance Authority is only given jurisdiction over cases where the turnover of the undertakings concerned in the EFTA states amounts to 33 per cent or more of the total aggregate turnover in the EEA as a whole. There is an important exception to this rule: in cases where trade between EC member states is also affected by the agreement at issue, the EC Commission rather than the EFTA Surveillance Authority has jurisdiction. Finally, there is an exception to this exception: in cases where the agreement's effect on trade in the EC is de minimis (and the turnover criterion of the basic rule is satisfied), the EFTA Surveillance Authority has jurisdiction.

---

[371] Id., art. 56(1)(a) and (c).
[372] To be considered as de minimis, an agreement must meet the criteria set out in the Commission's notice on agreements of minor importance discussed at ¶224 above.
[373] For definitions of 'undertaking' and 'turnover' for the purposes of applying the jurisdiction allocation criteria discussed in this section, see Protocol 22 to the EEA Agreement.

Abuses of dominant positions

In cases involving an abuse of a dominant position, the authority located in the territory in which the dominant position is found to exist has jurisdiction. If dominance is found to exist in both territories – so-called 'double dominance' – the criteria for the allocation of jurisdiction are basically the same as those for restrictive agreements. Thus, the EEA Agreement gives the EC Commission jurisdiction over most cases. The EFTA Surveillance Authority only has jurisdiction in cases where the turnover of the undertakings concerned in the territory of the EFTA states equals 33 per cent or more of their total turnover in the EEA as a whole. There is an exception to this rule: in cases where trade between EC member states is affected, the EC Commission rather than the EFTA Surveillance Authority has jurisdiction. Again, there is an exception to this exception: in cases where the effect on trade in the EC is not appreciable (and the turnover criterion of the basic rule is satisfied), the EFTA Surveillance Authority has jurisdiction.

Merger control

The EEA Agreement introduces a system of control for concentrations based fundamentally on Regulation 4064/89, which governs merger control within the EC.[374] Under the EEA Agreement, the EC Commission retains its existing powers with respect to merger control. Thus, it will continue to have the power to review mergers that fulfil the thresholds set out in Regulation 4064/89.[375] The novelty introduced by the EEA Agreement is that the Commission must take into account the market situation in the EFTA states as well as within the Community when assessing a merger. Thus, the EC Commission may prohibit a merger even if it only gives rise to market dominance in the EFTA states and not within the EC.

The EFTA Surveillance Authority has jurisdiction to deal with cases which do not fulfil the turnover thresholds set out in the EC merger regulation, but which fulfil identical criteria for the EFTA territory.[376] It should be noted that the fact that the EFTA Surveillance Authority has jurisdiction over a particular transaction does not affect the right of EC member states to examine the transaction under their national competition laws, even if the EFTA Surveillance Authority treats the transaction as one having an EFTA dimension. This represents the sole exception to the one-stop-shop principle on which the control of mergers is based.

As a practical matter, these rules may mean that the EFTA Surveillance

---

[374] The basic provision governing merger control in the EEA Agreement is art. 57, which is supplemented by detailed rules set out in Protocols 21 and 24 and Annex XIV. For a detailed review of Regulation 4064/89, see Chapter 6.

[375] EEA Agreement, art. 57(2)(a).

[376] Id., art. 57(2)(b).

¶270

Authority will have jurisdiction over relatively few cases. If the parties to a concentration have an aggregate worldwide turnover of ECU 5,000m and if two of them have within the EFTA a turnover exceeding ECU 250m (conditions for the EFTA Surveillance Authority having jurisdiction), it would seem likely that two of the parties to the concentration will also have a turnover of ECU 250m in the EC, thus giving the EC Commission exclusive jurisdiction over the concentration.

Finally, in the event that each of the undertakings concerned realises more than two-thirds of its turnover in one and the same EEA State, the concentration will in principle escape EC as well as EFTA control.

¶271   EEA: co-operation and exchange of information

The smooth functioning of the system established under the EEA Agreement necessarily relies on substantial co-operation between the EC Commission and the EFTA Surveillance Authority. The EEA Agreement establishes a framework for co-operation and consultation that covers general policy issues as well as individual cases.[377] The information exchanged under the EEA Agreement must be treated confidentially.[378] With respect to general policy issues, the EFTA Surveillance Authority and the EC Commission are required to exchange information and consult with each other.[379]

Co-operation in the context of individual cases involving restrictive practices and abuses of dominant positions is required in the mixed cases described above. Broadly, the co-operation will cover all stages of the proceedings. Copies of notifications and complaints received by one authority must be sent to the other.[380] Each authority as well as the states within their territories may present their views at hearings and at meetings of the Advisory Committees.[381] As for investigations, each authority may request the other to undertake 'on-the-spot' investigations in its territory and may take an active part in the investigation.[382]

In the merger control field, co-operation will take place falling within the EC Commission's jurisdiction[383] and where one of the following criteria is satisfied:

(1) where the combined turnover of the undertakings concerned in the territory of the EFTA states equals 25 per cent or more of their total turnover within the EEA;

---

[377] Article 58 of the EEA Agreement sets out the basic principle of co-operation. Protocol 23 contains detailed rules on co-operation with respect to restrictive practices and abuses of dominant positions. Protocol 24 contains detailed rules on co-operation in the area of merger control.
[378] Protocols 23 and 24, art. 9.
[379] Protocols 23 and 24, art. 1.
[380] Protocol 23, art. 2.
[381] Id., art. 5 and 6.
[382] Id., art. 8.
[383] Protocol 24, art. 1(2).

(2) each of at least two of the undertakings concerned has a turnover exceeding ECU 250m in the territory of the EFTA states; or

(3) the concentration is liable to create or strengthen a dominant position as a result of which effective competition would be significantly impeded in the territories of the EFTA states or a substantial part thereof.[384] The co-operation between the EC Commission and the EFTA Surveillance Authority covers all phases of the proceedings and must take place within the strict time limits followed in the context of the merger regulation.

¶272   EEA: judicial review

Decisions of the EC Commission applying the competition rules of the EEA are subject to the control of the EC Court of First Instance and the EC Court of Justice. Decisions of the EFTA Surveillance Authority are subject to the control of the EFTA Court established under the EEA Agreement.[385]

A major challenge in the implementation of the competition rules of the EEA Agreement will be to ensure the uniform development and application of rules in the future. While various institutional mechanisms have been established in an effort to minimise divergences in the jurisprudence of the EC courts and the EFTA Court, these courts nevertheless remain independent and their jurisprudence may not always be consistent. Likewise, there is a danger that the administrative practice and rules applied by the EC Commission and the EFTA Surveillance Authority may differ, despite various mechanisms designed to achieve uniformity in this area.

¶273   EEA: transitional period

A restrictive agreement that is concluded after the EEA Agreement enters into force must be notified to obtain an individual exemption unless it qualifies for exemption under one of the block exemption regulations.

A restrictive agreement that was already in existence when the EEA Agreement entered into force had to be notified within six months unless it qualified for exemption under one of the block exemption regulations.[386] If the agreement has been notified to the EC Commission, but has not yet received an individual exemption, the notification requirements of the EEA Agreement are deemed to have been complied with and no further action is necessary.[387] If

---

[384] Id., art. 2(1). The protocol also requires co-operation in cases where an EFTA state claims legitimate interests or where it invokes the existence of a separate national market. See art. 2(2).

[385] EEA Agreement, art. 108(2).

[386] Id., Protocol 21, art. 5(1).

[387] Id., art. 8.

the agreement has already received an individual exemption under the EC Treaty, the exemption remains in force until its expiry date and no further action is necessary.[388] No fines may be imposed with respect to any act prior to notification of existing agreements which were notified within six months of the date of entry into force of the EEA Agreement.[389]

¶274   Agreements with eastern European countries

As a result of changes in the political landscape in eastern Europe, the Community has signed a series of bilateral agreements – the so-called Europe Agreements – with Poland, the Czech and Slovak Republics, Hungary, Romania and Bulgaria.[390] These Agreements are broad in scope – covering topics ranging from political dialogue and cultural cooperation to trade and economic co-operation – and are generally considered to constitute a first step towards eventual membership in the Community.

Each of the Europe Agreements contains provisions on competition that are virtually identical.[391] The key provision on competition matters provides that the following are incompatible with the agreement in so far as they may affect trade between the Community and other signatory:

(1) all agreements between undertakings, decisions by associations of undertakings and concerted practices between undertakings which have as their object or effect the prevention, restriction or distortion of competition;

(2) abuse by one or more undertakings of a dominant position in the territories of the Community or of [the other signatory] as a whole or in a substantial part thereof;

(3) any public aid which distorts or threatens to distort competition by favouring certain undertakings or the production of certain goods.

This provision borrows language from the EC Treaty and, indeed, it is expressly provided that 'any practices contrary to this Article shall be assessed on the basis of criteria arising from the application of the rules of Articles 85, 86

---

[388] Id., art. 13.

[389] Id., art. 9.

[390] Since the Community only has the power to conclude international agreements in the commercial field, it has had to submit the Europe Agreements to the member states for ratification because these agreements are not limited to commercial matters, but cover other areas as well such as political co-operation. Pending the ratification of the full texts of the Europe Agreements, the Community proceeded to implement so-called Interim Agreements which contain only the provisions of the Europe Agreements concerning trade and trade-related matters, including competition policy: Poland (OJ 1992 L114/1); Czech and Slovak Republics (OJ 1992 L115/1, additional protocols OJ 1993 L195/47 and 49); Hungary (OJ 1992 L116/1); Romania (OJ 1993 L81/1); and Bulgaria (OJ 1993 L323/1). The full agreements with Poland and Hungary came into force on 1 February 1994 (OJ L348/2 and OJ 1993 L347/2 respectively).

[391] The provisions of the Europe Agreements dealing with competition matters are contained in the so-called Interim Agreements where the full agreements are not yet in force. See note 390.

and 92 of the [EC Treaty].' It should be noted that, in contrast to the corresponding provisions of the EC Treaty, the practices listed above are not 'prohibited' but merely deemed to be 'incompatible with the proper functioning of the Agreement.' This more ambiguous tone suggests that it is unlikely that the competition rules contained in the Europe Agreements would be deemed to be of the precise, unconditional nature necessary for them to have direct effect.[392] Thus, it is questionable whether a private party could invoke these rules before a national court in arguing that a given contract should be nullified as restrictive of competition.

Rules implementing the basic competition provisions are to be adopted within three years from the entry in force of each agreement. In the meantime, if either party considers that a particular practice violates the terms of the provision set out above, and if such practice causes or threatens to cause serious prejudice to the interest of the other party or material injury to its domestic industry, it may take appropriate measures after consultation within the Joint Committee with the other party or within 30 days following referral for such consultation.[393]

The agreements contain special rules on state aid, underscoring that this is a particularly sensitive area for former communist countries and that they will require time to switch over to free-market economies. Until implementing legislation is adopted, the provisions of the agreements on the interpretation and application of art. VI, XVI and XXIII of the GATT must be applied. In addition, it is expressly recognised that, during the first five years of the agreement, each East European signatory will be accorded the status of an economically-depressed region within the meaning of art. 92(3)(a) of the EC Treaty, thus giving it the benefit of a more lenient regime for the assessment of state aid.[394] Also, the agreements provide for the exchange of annual reports concerning state aids as well as information on individual cases upon request.

The Europe Agreements contain a set of rules dealing with the free movement of goods between the Community and the associated countries. Tariff and non-tariff barriers for imports from the associated countries will gradually be dismantled. Consequently the entry into the EC market is facilitated considerably and goods imported from associated countries may move freely within the territory of the EC member states.

---

[392] This position is supported by a Joint Declaration annexed to the Interim Agreement with Poland, which provides as follows:

'Parties may request the Joint Committee at a later stage, and after the adoption of the implementing rules referred to in Article 33(3), to examine to what extent and under which conditions certain competition rules may be directly applicable, taking into account the progress made in the integration process between the Community and Poland.'

[393] In cases involving state aid, any measures taken by a party must be in conformity with the procedures and under the conditions laid down by the GATT and any other relevant instrument negotiated under its auspices.

[394] The agreements leave open the possibility of extending this period for further five-year periods.

¶274

As tariff and non-tariff barriers to the importation of goods into the EC from the East European countries are gradually lowered, it would not be altogether surprising if the EC attempted to apply its competition rules to practices of companies located in East European countries on the basis of the 'effects doctrine'. Such a scenario could become even more likely if there are delays in adopting the legislation necessary to implement the competition rules set out in the Europe Agreements. As time passes and the East European companies become more competitive, the EC may feel compelled to take action to level the playing field.

¶274

PART II
PRACTICES

3 Distribution

THE REGULATION OF DISTRIBUTION

¶301 Introduction

Considerable emphasis is placed on vertical relationships in the enforcement of EC competition rules. A large proportion of the Commission's case law and legislation relates to distribution activities.

An examination of the cases shows that, to a large extent, the Commission is not principally motivated by economic considerations. Economic justifications that certain types of vertical restraints may promote inter-brand competition are virtually ignored by the Commission in so far as they conflict with the political goal of market integration.

There is a high degree of regulation of the distribution function by the EC Commission. Block exemption regulations governing exclusive distribution, exclusive purchase and franchise agreements are already on the books. There have also been regulations issued relating specifically to the distribution of beer, motor vehicle fuels and automobiles. These regulations contain provisions which go beyond what would strictly be necessary for competition law purposes and in fact regulate other aspects of the relationship between the supplier and the distributor.

The first part of this chapter (¶302–¶313) considers the application of general principles of EC competition rules to all forms of distribution. The second part (¶314–¶375) describes the specific rules that have been applied to various types of distribution, and the third part (¶376) deals with certain clauses found in distribution agreements.

GENERAL PRINCIPLES APPLICABLE TO VERTICAL AGREEMENTS

¶302   Common principles of EC competition rules

Although there are various channels or means of distribution that a supplier may use to get his product to the ultimate purchaser, there are certain common principles of the EC competition rules applicable to all forms of distribution. Thus, the cases consistently show that absolute territorial limitations or resale price maintenance provisions are not acceptable (see ¶303–¶310 and ¶311 respectively). Although the case law is not as consistent, there are also general rules relating to customer restrictions (¶312) and restrictions on the use of goods (¶313). Although the Commission's practice in the distribution area has been mainly concerned with the supply of products, it is important to note that the principles of EC competition law established in this field apply without distinction to products and services.[1]

¶303   Territorial restrictions

Since the earliest days of enforcement of EC competition rules, the Commission and the Court of Justice have consistently prohibited absolute territorial protection granted by suppliers to distributors. This prohibition is applied to outright export bans, as well as to other practices that may have the effect of insulating markets, such as price discrimination, denial of guarantees or after-sales service, and the exercise of intellectual property rights or other rights arising under national law.

In one of its first competition decisions, the Commission decided that an agreement whereby the German consumer electronics manufacturer Grundig granted absolute territorial protection to its French exclusive distributor, Consten, violated art. 85(1).[2] The court upheld the Commission's decision with respect to the territorial restrictions.[3]

Three basic justifications for the condemnation of territorial protection can be derived from the Commission decision:

(1) the economic goal of encouraging intra-brand competition;

(2) the political goal of achieving an integrated common market; and

(3) the social goal of protecting the small parallel trader against the power of the large supplier.

---

[1] *ServiceMaster* [1989] 1 CEC 2,287; OJ 1988 L332/38, at p. 39.
[2] *Grundig-Consten*, JO 1964, p. 2545.
[3] *Consten and Grundig v EC Commission* [1966] ECR 299.

¶304   Encouragement of intra-brand competition

On the issue of intra-brand competition, the Commission and the court embarked in *Cousten and Grundig* on a course that has been consistently followed since that time. The Commission examined only price competition between Grundig products and refused to analyse effects on inter-brand competition. The court upheld the Commission's approach stating:

'The principle of freedom of competition concerns the various stages and manifestations of competition. Although competition between producers is generally more noticeable than that between distributors of products of the same make, it does not thereby follow that an agreement tending to restrict the latter kind of competition should escape the prohibition of Article 85(1) merely because it might increase the former.'[4]

The court went on to state that:

'the absence in the contested decision of any analysis of the effects of the agreement on competition between similar products of different makes does not, of itself, constitute a defect in the decision.'[5]

Absolute territorial restrictions have been considered per se violations of art. 85(1) with no requirement of an analysis of the broader economic effects on competition with other brands.

¶305   Market integration

The use of the competition rules to promote the political goal of achieving the integration of the various member state markets into a single market has been the most important basis for the prohibition of export bans.[6] In *Consten and*

---

[4] Id., at p. 342.

[5] Ibid. The failure of the Commission to examine the effect of the export bans on inter-brand competition was criticised by both the government of Germany in its intervention and Advocate General Roemer in his opinion. Id., at pp. 325 and 359–360. The position expressed in *Consten and Grundig* is also reflected in *Sandoz prodotti farmaceutici SpA v EC Commission* [1990] ECR I-45 (summary publication only).

[6] In discussing its basic policy on exclusive dealing agreements the Commission stated:

'The attention given to the exclusive dealing agreements was fundamentally due to the fact that such agreements are particularly likely to create obstacles with regard to the integration of national markets into a single market, to the extent that they guarantee to the holder of the concession not only the exclusive right to obtain supplies direct from the manufacturer but also to be the only distributor allowed to introduce the relevant products into the territory allocated to him.' (*First Report on Competition Policy*, point 45).

A more recent statement of the Commission reflects exactly the same policy:

'Territorial restrictions in distribution agreements cannot be allowed if they give distributors a monopoly of sales in a territory and shield them against parallel imports. Those arrangements deprive consumers in the distributor's territory of the opportunity to make use of the single market by buying a product outside that territory if it is offered there on more attractive terms. Territorial protection must not prevent intermediaries who have obtained a product from reselling it throughout the single market, including in territories in which the manufacturer may have set up different distribution channels' (*XXIst Report on Competition Policy*, point 44).

Grundig, the court stated that as the agreement had the object of isolating national markets:

'It was ... proper for the contested decision to hold that the agreement constitutes an infringement of Article 85(1). No further considerations, whether of economic data (price differences between France and Germany, representative character of the type of appliance considered, level of overheads borne by Consten) or of the corrections of the criteria upon which the Commission relied in its comparisons between the situations of the French and German markets, and no possible favourable effects of the agreement in other respects, can in any way lead, in the face of [the] above-mentioned restrictions, to a different solution under Article 85(1).'[7]

The Commission has tended to reject arguments relating to differences in conditions in national markets. Rather than considering the continuing imperfections in the market, the Commission and the court, for purposes of condemning territorial restrictions, have treated the market as if it were already integrated and have acted as if the actions of companies operating within the Community were the only barriers to trade.

In *Consten and Grundig*, the Commission and the court failed to consider justifications for price differentials such as differences in transportation costs, customs duties or overheads.

¶306   Protection of the parallel trader

The Commission has chosen to protect the parallel trader without any showing that the parallel trader was contributing to price reductions or otherwise benefiting the consumer. In his criticism of the Commission's approach in *Consten and Grundig*, Advocate General Roemer stated:

'Thus, for example, it does not seem to be disputed that retail prices are equally high in France for Grundig equipment, whether they are supplied by Consten or by parallel importers. Consequently, the parallel imports, which the Commission considers necessary, do not lead to favourable prices to the consumer; they even have the result, that the consumers are less well served, if, as Consten asserts, it is true (which would have to be proved) that it supplies better benefits through a good guarantee and after-sales service, a comprehensive stock and the provision of supplies to the whole of the French market. It is even possible that if parallel imports were to increase, that is to say, if the market were exploited in a less well organized and less intensive manner than it is by Consten, the development of sales would deteriorate,

---

[7] *Consten and Grundig v EC Commission* [1966] ECR 299, at p. 343.

with corresponding repercussions on the conditions of production and the structuring of the manufacturer's prices.'[8]

The protection of the parallel trader by the Commission has reached extremes in some cases. For example, the Commission has denounced price reductions granted to exclusive distributors in order to allow the exclusive distributors to compete with parallel traders.[9]

In an early draft of the block exemption for motor vehicle selective distribution agreements, the Commission set out in the preamble the following justification for removing the protection from parallel traders when price differentials between member states reach 12 per cent:

'It may generally be concluded from observations of imports of motor vehicles through distribution channels other than those established by the manufacturer (parallel imports) that the incentive to engage in parallel imports within the common market increases rapidly where recommendations in different Member States produce price variations of more than 12 per cent of the lowest price.'[10]

Thus, the Commission was willing to grant protection to official dealers from parallel traders only for as long as it would be uneconomical to engage in parallel trade.

It is interesting to compare the attempt to harmonise prices through the use of the automobile exemption to a position taken by the Commission in the *Wood Pulp* case. In that case, involving allegations of price-fixing, price uniformity among the various national markets was condemned, inter alia, because it did not allow the development of conditions which would permit the parallel trader to operate.[11]

¶307　Forms of territorial restrictions

Territorial limitations can take a variety of forms ranging from outright bans on exports to differential pricing or restrictions on the provision of after sales service. These forms will be discussed below. In individual cases, the Commission has been confronted with other strategies to impose territorial limitations.[12]

---

[8] Opinion of Advocate General Roemer in *Consten and Grundig v EC Commission* [1966] ECR 299, at pp. 372–373.
[9] See ¶309.
[10] Draft Commission regulation on the application of art. 85(3) of the treaty to certain categories of motor vehicle distribution and servicing agreements, OJ 1983 C165/2, recital 29. See also, Van Bael, 'The Draft EEC Regulation on Selective Distribution of Motor Vehicles: A Daydream for Free Riders – A Nightmare for Industry', (1983) 19 Swiss Rev. Int. Comp. L. 3.
[11] *Wood Pulp*, OJ 1985 L85/1, at p. 24 (para. 136ff.).
[12] See, e.g., *Konica*, OJ 1988 L78/34, at p. 40 (para. 38–40), where the Commission decided that a buying-up operation in relation to parallel traded Konica films had to be regarded as a term of its supply contracts with

In addition (as will be further discussed in Chapter 4 dealing with industrial and commercial property rights) the case law of the court under art. 85–86 and art. 30–36 has severely curtailed opportunities to use industrial and commercial property rights to interfere with parallel imports.

¶308   Export bans

(1)   Export bans within the EC

The Commission has consistently required that export bans be removed from distributor agreements and sales conditions.[13] The only contractual territorial restrictions which have been allowed within the EC are those contained in agreements that are considered to be de minimis given the importance of the parties in the market.[14] Companies, however, must be very careful in determining whether agreements can be considered to be de minimis.[15]

Territorial restrictions are prohibited even if they are not incorporated in a formal written agreement.[16] A company cannot successfully defend itself by showing that an export ban in an agreement has not been enforced.[17] Qualifications stating, for example, that an export restriction applies to the extent that it is permitted by law will not save an otherwise unlawful export restriction.[18]

German dealers whereby Konica Europe undertook to protect its German dealers against competition from parallel imports. A buying-up operation was likewise condemned in *Newitt/Dunlop Slazenger International & Ors*, OJ 1992 L131/32, at p. 42 (para. 58).
[13] See *Kodak*, JO 1970 L147/24; *Omega*, JO 1970 L242/22; *WEA Filipacchi Music SA*, JO 1972 L303/52; *Du Pont de Nemours Deutschland*, OJ 1973 L194/27; *Bayerische Motoren Werke AG*, OJ 1975 L29/1; *Goodyear Italiana-Euram*, OJ 1975 L38/10; *Miller International*, OJ 1976 L357/40; *Junghans*, OJ 1977 L30/10; *GERO-Fabriek*, OJ 1977 L16/8; *Theal Watts*, OJ 1977 L39/19; *BMW Belgium*, OJ 1978 L46/33; *Kawasaki*, OJ 1979 L16/9; *Pioneer Hi-Fi Equipment*, OJ 1980 L60/21; *Johnson and Johnson*, OJ 1980 L377/16; *Hasselblad*, OJ 1982 L161/18; *Moët et Chandon (London) Ltd*, OJ 1982 L94/7; *Polistil-Arbois*, OJ 1984 L136/9; *John Deere*, OJ 1985 L35/58; *Sperry New Holland*, OJ 1985 L376/21; *Sandoz*, OJ 1987 L222/28; *Bayer Dental*, OJ 1990 L351/46; *Gosme/Martell*, OJ 1991 L185/23; *Viho/Toshiba*, OJ 1991 L287/39; *Viho/Parker Pen*, OJ 1992 L233/27.
[14] See *Völk v Vervaecke* [1969] ECR 295, at p. 302 (para. 5–7), where the court said:

'an exclusive dealing agreement, even with absolute territorial protection, may, having regard to the weak position of the persons concerned on the market in the products in question in the area covered by the absolute protection, escape the prohibition laid down in Article 85(1).'

See also the Commission Notice concerning agreements of minor importance which do not fall under art. 85(1) of the EC Treaty establishing the European Economic Community, OJ 1986 C231/2.
[15] See *Kawasaki*, OJ 1979 L16/9, where the turnover limits set out in the notice were misunderstood by Kawasaki's legal advisers.
[16] See, e.g., *National Panasonic*, OJ 1982 L354/28, at p. 32; *Fisher-Price/Quaker Oats Ltd-Toyco*, OJ 1988 L49/19; *Ford Agricultural*, OJ 1993 L20/1.
[17] See *Miller v EC Commission* [1978] ECR 131, at p. 148 (para. 7), where the court stated:

'the fact that the supplier is not strict in enforcing such prohibitions cannot establish that they had no effect since their very existence may create a "visual and psychological" background which satisfies customers and contributes to a more or less rigorous division of the markets.'

See also *Sandoz Prodotti farmaceutici SpA v EC Commission* [1990] ECR I-45 (summary publication only).
[18] In *John Deere*, OJ 1985 L35/58, at p. 62 (para. 27), the Commission stated:

'The export ban contained in these sales conditions is qualified by the words "... as far as no contrary legal

In exemptions under art. 85(3), the Commission has allowed limited restrictions on the activities which a distributor may perform outside of its territory. Thus, in agreements falling within the terms of the exclusive distribution block exemption, a distributor can be prevented from soliciting sales or from maintaining stocks outside of its territory.[19]

(2) Bans on exports outside the EC

The legality of clauses restricting the ability of a distributor to export a product outside the EC must be determined in light of whether the jurisdictional test in art. 85(1) is met. In several early cases, the Commission held that bans on exports outside of the EC would not affect trade between member states because, as a result of the accumulation of profit margins and transport costs as well as the obstacle of the Common Customs Tariff, it was deemed to be unlikely that products exported outside the EC would be reimported into the Community. Even if a product were reimported, it was considered to be unlikely that the product would be re-exported to another member state since the demand in a member state could be met much more readily and at a more favourable price directly from another member state than from a third country to which the products in demand would be first exported from the EC.[20]

In 1976, the Commission modified its views and ruled that a clause prohibiting exports outside the EC in a distribution agreement for the EC would violate art. 85(1) once the relevant products would no longer be subject to customs duties in trade between the EC and the relevant territory.[21] If the product is still subject to customs duties, however, the export restriction will fall outside the scope of the prohibition contained in art. 85(1).[22]

In summary, it appears that the Commission considers that bans on exports to countries outside the EC are prohibited by art. 85(1) with respect to products which can be traded on a duty-free basis. Restrictions on exports to countries outside the EC are outside the scope of art. 85(1) with respect to products which remain subject to a duty.

While the court has not yet had an opportunity to address this issue in detail,

---

regulation prevents ...". However, the Commission holds that such an article constitutes an export ban in spite of this saving clause; the article is worded to read as if exporting is forbidden and imposed without explanation or negotiation by a company that ought to know the law on a multitude of small dealers; such dealers are less likely to know the law and unlikely, in the circumstances, to consult a lawyer; it is most unlikely, therefore, that the dealer would know that an export ban is contrary to Community law and could not in consequence of that fact be enforced against intra-Community exports. In other words, and in view of the fact that export bans are illegal within the common market, the drafting of this export ban constitutes a reversal of a general rule of Community law in respect of what should be only a derogation.'

[19] Commission Regulation 1983/83 on the application of art. 85(3) to categories of exclusive distribution agreements, OJ 1983 L173/1, corrigendum OJ 1983 L281/84, art. 2(2)(c).

[20] See *Kodak*, OJ 1970 L147/24; *Goodyear Italiana-Euram*, OJ 1975 L38/10; *Kabelmetal-Luchaire*, OJ 1975 L222/34.

[21] *SABA*, OJ 1976 L28/19, at p. 22.

[22] *Campari*, OJ 1978 L70/60, at p. 74.

the rare case law on this matter seems to be in line with the above conclusion. In *Bulk Oil (Zug) AG v Sun International Ltd and Sun Oil Trading Company*,[23] the court analysed a destination clause prohibiting buyers from exporting British North Sea crude oil to a destination other than that approved by the exporting countries' government policy. On that basis, British Petroleum, the original supplier, refused to load oil for delivery to Israel on the ground that such delivery was contrary to the policy of the UK. The court ruled, with regard to the compatibility of the destination clause with art. 85(1), that 'a measure such as that in question which is specifically directed at exports of oil to a non-member country is not in itself likely to restrict or distort competition within the common market. It cannot affect trade within the Community and infringe Articles 3(f), 5 and 85 of the Treaty'.[24]

Application of art. 86

Exports outside the EC may not only be restricted by an agreement but also by a refusal to sell to a firm which wants the products for export purposes or by making such a sale conditional upon the acceptance of an obligation not to export the product outside the EC. If the supplier has a dominant position on the market, its refusal to deal may constitute a violation of art. 86, unless the refusal is objectively justified.

The Commission has not yet issued a decision that deals directly with the issue of the compatibility of a ban on exports outside the EC with art. 86. However, in *Polaroid/SSI Europe*, the Polaroid group ended its refusal to supply instant film to SSI Europe, a small Dutch firm, following an action by the Commission under art. 86. SSI Europe had approached Polaroid Nederland with a large order for instant film. Polaroid Nederland, which had previously quoted to SSI Europe for a smaller order, refused to fill the order because the quantities involved exceeded demand on the entire European market. Polaroid UK also refused to fill the order since SSI Europe would not disclose the geographical destination of the goods. Subsequently, SSI Europe lodged a complaint against Polaroid and the Commission began an investigation

---

[23] *Bulk Oil (Zug) AG v Sun International Ltd and Sun Oil Trading Company* [1986] ECR 559.

[24] Id., at p. 589. The case law has also dealt with a different type of destination clause, whereby companies located within the Community are obliged to supply the contract goods to specific countries of destination outside the Community. In *Cram & Rheinzink v EC Commission*, ([1984] ECR 1679, pp. 1703–1705) such a clause was held to violate art. 85(1) of the treaty since it was considered to be designed to prevent the re-export of the goods to the country of production within the Community and to therefore maintain a system of dual prices and restrict competition within the Community. However, in *Iqbal* (*XXIst Report on Competition Policy for 1991*, p. 334), a similar clause was held not to violate EC competition law since the Commission took the view that the use of the export destination clauses was not connected to actions having the specific intention of preventing trade between member states. The Commission stated that 'it is not the purpose of Article 85(1) to prohibit vertical agreements which restrict the intra-brand competition between the Community as a whole and third countries in order to enable the manufacturer to have an independent price policy adapted to the conditions prevailing on those third-countries' markets.' Unless the intentions of the companies involved are given decisive weight, it is not self-evident how to reconcile the positions taken in *Cram & Rheinzink* and *Iqbal*.

¶308

concerning a possible abuse of a dominant position by Polaroid. The Commission carried out an inspection of the premises of Polaroid UK and since, during the inspection, Polaroid agreed to quote to SSI Europe, the Commission decided not to open formal proceedings. In commenting on this case, the Commission emphasised that:

> 'as a general principle ... an objectively unjustifiable refusal to supply by an undertaking holding a dominant position on a market constitutes an infringement of Article 86 and will also be regarded as such when the dominant undertaking makes supply of the product conditional on his having control of its further processing or marketing.'[25]

The Commission's conclusion in this matter would seem anomalous in light of its approach to bans on exports outside the EC under art. 85. It may well be that the significance of this case should be discounted because the investigation was terminated at an early stage, before the facts and issues were allowed to fully develop.

A company which places a restriction or penalty on sales for export outside the EC must be careful that the restriction is not applied within the EC as well.[26]

¶309   Dual pricing systems and discount practices

Even without formal export restrictions, a company could obtain similar results by charging different prices or by granting different discounts depending upon the destination of the product.[27] In order to prevent pricing practices from being used to isolate markets, the Commission has objected to practices that could have such an effect.

The Commission has held that a provision whereby customers have to pay the prices applicable in the country of destination, rather than in the territory where the seller is located, was an illegal restriction of competition.[28] It is also illegal for a company to provide a discount to purchasers based on a showing that the product has not been exported to another member state.[29] More generally, bonus, discount or price schemes which depend on the destination of the sales have been likened to export bans and, for that reason, have been heavily criticised in the Commission's case law. The following are examples of practices that have been condemned by the Commission on that basis:

---

[25] *Polaroid/SSI Europe, Thirteenth Report on Competition Policy*, points 155–157.
[26] In *John Deere*, OJ 1985 L35/58, at p. 62, the Commission discovered evidence that staff had imposed the penalty on sales outside the EC on sales within the Community.
[27] For examples of systems of dual pricing lists see *Newitt/Dunlop Slazenger International & Ors*, OJ 1992 L131/32 and *XXIst Report on Competition Policy for 1991*, point 123.
[28] *Kodak*, OJ 1970 L147/24, at pp. 25–26.
[29] *Pittsburgh Corning Europe–Formica Belgium–Hertel*, JO 1972 L272/35, at p. 38; *Sperry New Holland*, OJ 1985 L376/21, at p. 26; *Ford Agricultural*, OJ 1993 L20/1.

- the complete abolition of all normal discounts in the case of export sales;[30]
- the imposition of less favourable payment terms for goods known to be exported;[31]
- the imposition of a five per cent surcharge on goods known to be exported;[32]
- the reduction of discounts on exports in order to protect the local exclusive distributor;[33]
- a promotional campaign in Belgium and Luxembourg whereby special terms were offered for a short time on selected car models, but only to residents of Belgium and Luxembourg;[34]
- the requirement of evidence of non-re-export in order to allow a particular sale to be taken into account for the application of a bonus scheme;[35]
- the making of discounts conditional on registration within the territory or on the original purchaser retaining and using the purchased vehicle.[36]

Rejection of economic arguments for supporting exclusive distributors

The Commission, in its case law, has not accepted economic justifications for dual pricing systems. In *Distillers*,[37] the Commission objected to an arrangement under which a surcharge was to be paid by wholesalers in the UK whenever the product was exported outside the UK. The difference in price, £5.20 per case of 12 bottles, was said to reflect the considerably higher promotional costs incurred by DCL's sole distributors on the Continent. This in turn was argued to be the result of a major difference between market conditions in the UK and in continental EC countries. In the UK, Scotch whisky is a traditional drink representing more than 50 per cent of the total spirit sales whereas on the Continent, consumer acceptance of Scotch whisky is much lower and, except for Belgium, it must compete against a variety of locally produced spirits, which are often favoured by the relevant tax regime. The UK market could therefore be described as a market which has reached the 'maturity stage' where competition is predominantly based on price and where prices are extremely low as a result of the buying power of the large brewery companies and their retail outlets. In contrast, the continental market was still in the 'expansive phase', facing the competition of cheaper and more

---

[30] *Gosme/Martell–DMP*, OJ 1991 L185/23, at pp. 28–29.
[31] *John Deere*, OJ 1985 L35/38, at p. 61.
[32] Id., see also *Ford Agricultural*, OJ 1993 L20/1.
[33] *Newitt/Dunlop Slazenger International & Ors*, OJ 1992 L131/32, at p. 42.
[34] *Citroën, Eighteenth Report on Competition Policy*, point 56.
[35] *Sperry New Holland*, OJ 1985 L376/21, at p. 26.
[36] *Ford Agricultural*, OJ 1993 L20/1.
[37] *The Distillers Co Ltd – Conditions of Sale and Price Terms*, OJ 1978 L50/16.

¶309

popular local products. In such a market emphasis was on promotional activity rather than on price. According to DCL, it was only 'by energetically reminding the public that Scotch whisky is a high-quality, distinctive product for which it is worthwhile to pay the extra tax' that one could hope to lure away customers from tax-favoured local spirits.[38] In essence, DCL claimed that without the protection of the dual price structure UK wholesalers would take a free ride on the promotional efforts and expenses sustained by its sole distributors on the Continent.

Although the Commission recognised that exclusive distributors outside the UK had higher costs than parallel traders arising from their obligation to promote the product, the Commission nonetheless came down firmly on the side of the free riders.[39]

Although the Commission obviously expected the result of its actions to be the lowering of Scotch whisky prices in markets on the Continent, in fact the result was that DCL chose to protect its distributors on the Continent by withdrawing two of their bestselling brands, Johnnie Walker, Red Label and Dimple, from the UK market.[40] The confusion resulting from this case has been heightened by the announcement by the Commission that they intended to allow Distillers to re-introduce the dual pricing system in order to recommence selling Red Label on the UK market.[41]

Whereas, in *Distillers*, the Commission challenged a surcharge placed on sales to parallel traders, in *Polistil-Arbois*, the Commission was confronted with the other side of the coin, i.e., price reductions granted by a supplier to an exclusive distributor to help him compete with parallel imports. The Commission held that the pricing arrangements were a violation of art. 85(1).[42] As the Commission and the court[43] suggested in earlier cases that one legal alternative to impeding parallel imports would be to lower prices to an

---

[38] *Distillers Company v EC Commission* [1980] ECR 2229, at pp. 2239–2240.

[39] In *The Distillers Co Ltd – Conditions of Sale and Price Terms*, OJ 1978 L50/16, at p. 26, the Commission stated:

'Indeed, sole distributors have higher costs due to their obligations of promoting the spirits. It has been argued that these costs approximate to the difference between the buying price of the parallel importer and that of the sole distributor. However, such differences in the buying price make it distinctly difficult for the DCL United Kingdom trade customers, and even more so, for their subsequent customers to compete with the sole distributors in the other EEC Member States or at the very least, render parallel export unattractive.'

[40] The Commission Decision on Distillers has been the subject of criticism from Advocate General Warner in his opinion on the appeal and by commentators. See the opinion of Advocate General Warner in *Distillers Co v EC Commission* [1980] ECR 2229; see also Korah, 'Goodbye, Red Label: Condemnation of Dual Pricing by Distillers', (1979) 4 E.L.Rev. 1; Baden Fuller, 'Price Variations – The Distillers Case and Article 85 EEC', (1979) ICLQ 128; and Van Bael, 'Heretical Reflections on the Basic Dogma of EEC Antitrust: Single Market Integration', (1980) 10 Swiss Rev. Int. Antitrust L. 39.

[41] Notice pursuant to art. 19(3) of Council Regulation 17/62, *The Distillers Co plc*, OJ 1983 C245/3.

[42] *Polistil-Arbois*, OJ 1984 L136/9, at pp. 12–13. See also *Hennessy-Henkell*, OJ 1980 L383/11, at p. 15; *Newitt/Dunlop Slazenger International & Ors*, OJ 1992 L131/32, at pp. 41–42.

[43] See *The Distillers Co Ltd – Conditions of Sale and Price Terms*, OJ 1978 L50/16, at p. 29, and *Grundig-Consten*, JO 1964, p. 2545, at pp. 2551–2552.

exclusive distributor to take account of its higher costs, it is unfortunate that the Commission has taken a negative view of precisely this type of discount.

The position adopted in *Distillers* and *Polistil-Arbois* seems to be confirmed and probably even strengthened in the Commission's most recent case law. In *Newitt/Dunlop Slazenger International & Ors*,[44] DSI attempted to defend the reduction of discounts granted to parallel traders and the granting of financial support to its exclusive distributor in order to combat parallel imports by referring to the specific costs borne by the exclusive distributor. The Commission dismissed this argument as follows:

'[...] such expenditure is certainly not without benefit to the exclusive distributor in so far as his name – and his title of "exclusive" or "official" distributor – are broadly associated with the brand in the advertising and promotional measures. If there are specific costs, they are thus counterbalanced by specific benefits.

At any rate, the view must be taken that any specific costs borne by exclusive distributors are largely offset by the granting of exclusivity, which constitutes a key commercial advantage. They do not justify the additional application to exclusive distributors of special prices intended to protect them from parallel imports.'[45]

This statement would seem to be taking the protection of the parallel trader to the extreme, while further undermining the protection from which exclusive distributors can benefit.[46]

¶310   Warranty and after-sales service

Even if there is no export restriction, customers could be discouraged from buying products from parallel traders if the manufacturer were to discriminate between products purchased from official distributors and products purchased from other sources with respect to the provision of warranty or after-sales service. The Commission has established the principle that 'a manufacturer's guarantee for the products he distributes must be applicable throughout the Community irrespective of the member state where the product was purchased'.[47] The same principle extends to the provision of after-sales and essential services, including the provision of technical information, in circumstances where the withholding of such services would hinder parallel trade in the products concerned.[48]

---

[44] *Newitt/Dunlop Slazenger International & Ors*, OJ 1992 L131/32.
[45] Id., at p. 42.
[46] See ¶318.
[47] *Matsushita Electrical Trading Company, Twelfth Report on Competition Policy*, points 77 79; *Sixteenth Report on Competition Policy*, point 56; *Sony, Seventeenth Report on Competition Policy*, point 67; *Grundig's EC Distribution system*, OJ 1994 L20/15
[48] *Akzo Coatings, Nineteenth Report on Competition Policy*, point 45.

The Commission has applied this principle in a series of decisions[49] ensuring that a guarantee given by a manufacturer on branded goods would be provided by any approved dealer and not merely by the dealer from which it was purchased. The court has confirmed the Commission's position in *Hasselblad*[50] and *Swatch*.[51]

It is not necessary for a company to provide the same guarantee service in all parts of the Community. If guarantees vary, then it is permissible for a supplier to provide that guarantee service be provided on the terms applied where the product is used rather than where it is bought.[52] The Commission has permitted clauses providing that the user must bear the costs of adaptation of a product to local safety standards if it wishes to take advantage of a local guarantee.[53] It is also permissible to require a user to bear the expense of returning a product to the country of origin 'in [a] case where the model concerned is not of the same type as those marketed in the country of use and the spare parts needed for the repair are unavailable'.[54] It would appear that a system according to which the customer pays for the warranty repair in a country other than the country of purchase and obtains a receipt on the basis of which he can reclaim his expenses in the country of purchase is also admissible.[55]

A distributor may provide its own additional guarantee and reserve that guarantee to its own customers. Thus, in *Hasselblad*, the Commission stated that the non-discrimination requirement 'does not mean that a sole distributor is not allowed to provide any additional guarantee services in respect of goods imported and resold by him. However, parallel import products must not be placed at a disadvantage in so far as the manufacturer's guarantee and the sole distributor's guarantee are identical'.[56]

Restrictions on warranty may have the effect of limiting the distribution of a

---

[49] *Omega*, JO 1970 L242/22; *Bayerische Motoren Werke AG*, OJ 1975 L29/1; *SABA*, OJ 1976 L28/19; *Zanussi*, OJ 1978 L322/26; *IBM Personal Computer*, OJ 1984 L118/24.

[50] *Hasselblad v EC Commission* [1984] ECR 883.

[51] *ETA Fabriques d'Ebauches v DK Investment* [1985] ECR 3933.

[52] See *Zanussi*, OJ 1978 L322/26; see also *ETA Fabriques d'Ebauches v DK Investment* [1985] ECR 3933.

[53] *Moulinex, Tenth Report on Competition Policy*, point 121; *Matsushita Electrical Trading Company, Twelfth Report on Competition Policy*, points 77–78.

[54] Ibid.

[55] *Fourteenth Report on Competition Policy*, point 70. The Fiat guarantee system was approved by the Commission subject to the following changes being made:

(1) the previous requirement of presenting the replaced parts to the dealer who sold the car was changed so as to only require a check of the documents which show that the work had been done;

(2) it was made possible for the customer to obtain reimbursement not only from the original seller but also from the Fiat distribution company issuing the guarantee certificate;

(3) the deadline for applying for a refund was extended from one month to two months after payment had been made for the guarantee work; and

(4) the customer was given the freedom to make his refund application in his own language.

[56] *Hasselblad*, OJ 1982 L161/18, at p. 28. Although the Commission has stated that it was not permissible for the UK Hasselblad distributor to offer faster guarantee service to its own customers, the court stated that it was possible for a distributor to reserve a special 24-hour service to its own customers. *Hasselblad v EC Commission* [1984] ECR 883, at p. 905 (para. 34).

¶310

product to certain sales channels. Thus, the Commission objected to a clause in a contract which limited a warranty on plumbing fittings to those which had been installed by plumbers because this would keep consumers from buying the product from retailers.[57] On the other hand, restrictions on warranty may be valid within the context of a selective distribution system. In *Metro v Curtier*,[58] the court held that a manufacturer operating a selective distribution network may refuse to honour guarantees in respect of goods *bought* outside of that system.

Special rules relating to warranty service have been incorporated in the block exemption for automobile selective distribution agreements[59] and in the block exemption on franchise agreements.[60]

¶311   Resale price maintenance

The Commission and the Court of Justice have recognised that the goal of maintaining a certain minimum price level for a product may be pro-competitive and may serve to improve competition on factors other than price.[61] Nonetheless, the Community authorities have not accepted that resale price maintenance is a legitimate means of guaranteeing such price levels.[62]

---

[57] *Ideal Standard's distribution system*, OJ 1985 L20/38, at p. 42.

[58] *Metro SB Großmärkte Gmbh v Cartier*, Case C-376/92, judgment of 13 January 1994 (not yet reported).

[59] Commission Regulation 123/85 on the application of art. 85(3) of the treaty to certain categories of motor vehicle distribution and servicing agreements, OJ 1985 L15/16, art. 4(1)(6) and 5(1)(1).

[60] Commission Regulation 4087/88 on the application of art. 85(3) of the treaty to categories of franchise agreements, OJ 1988 L359/46, art. 4(b).

[61] In *Metro v EC Commission* [1977] ECR 1875, at p. 1905 (para. 21), the court stated:

'For specialist wholesalers and retailers the desire to maintain a certain price level, which corresponds to the desire to preserve, in the interests of consumers, the possibility of the continued existence of this channel of distribution in conjunction with the new methods of distribution based on a different type of competition policy, forms one of the objectives which may be pursued without necessarily falling under the prohibition contained in Article 85(1), and, if it does fall thereunder, either wholly or in part, coming within the framework of Article 85(3).

This argument is strengthened if, in addition, such conditions promote improvement of competition inasmuch as it relates to factors other than prices.'

[62] Clarifying its position in the *Metro* case, the court stated in *AEG v EC Commission* [1983] ECR 3151, at pp. 3196–3197 (para. 42–43):

'A restriction of price competition must however be regarded as being inherent in any selective distribution system in view of the fact that prices charged by specialist traders remain within a much narrower span than that which might be envisaged in the case of competition between specialists and non-specialist traders. That restriction is counterbalanced by competition as regards the quality of the services supplied to customers which would not normally be possible in the absence of an appropriate profit margin making it possible to support the higher expenses connected with those services. The maintenance of a certain level of prices is therefore lawful, but only to the extent to which it is strictly justified by the requirements of a system within which competition must continue to perform the functions assigned to it by the Treaty. In fact, the object of such a system is solely the improvement of competition in so far as it relates to factors other than prices and not the guarantee of a high profit margin for approved re-sellers.

AEG was therefore not justified in taking the view that the acceptance of an undertaking to charge prices making possible a sufficiently high profit margin constituted a lawful condition for admission to a selective distribution system. By the very fact that it was authorized not to admit to and not to keep in its distribution network traders who were not, or were no longer, in a position to provide services typical of the specialist trade, it had at its disposal all the means necessary to enable it to ensure the effective application of the system. In such

Resale price maintenance has been considered as being a violation of art. 85(1) both in cases where groups of suppliers agree to impose resale prices on their purchasers (collective resale price maintenance)[63] and in cases where a single supplier agrees with its resellers that they will not supply a product below a certain price.[64] In distribution agreements notified for exemption, the Commission has consistently required that the supplier remove restrictions on resale prices.[65]

The Commission is concerned with protecting the distributor's ability to set its prices freely. Thus, in *Hennessy-Henkell*, the Commission objected to a clause whereby a supplier required that its distributor set its prices between a minimum and maximum price level unless the distributor obtained the supplier's consent.[66]

The prohibition on resale price maintenance does not extend to recommended retail price lists as long as they are non-binding.[67]

In order for resale price maintenance to be found to violate art. 85(1), there must be an effect on trade between member states. The Commission suggested in an early policy statement that purely national systems of resale price maintenance do not fall within the prohibition of art. 85(1) if there is no effect on trade between member states. The Commission stated at that time that 'purely national systems' of resale price maintenance would be a matter of national competition policy.[68]

In subsequent cases, however, the Commission and the Court of Justice have

circumstances the existence of a price undertaking constitutes a condition which is manifestly foreign to the requirements of a selective distribution system and thus also affects freedom of competition.'

[63] See, e.g. *VBBB/VBVB*, OJ 1982 L54/36; on appeal: *VBVB/VBBB v EC Commission* [1984] ECR 19; *Publishers Association – Net Book Agreements*, OJ 1989 L22/12.

[64] See, e.g. *Deutsche Philips GmbH*, OJ 1973 L293/40.

[65] See, e.g. *Omega*, JO 1970 L242/22; *SABA*, OJ 1976 L28/19; *Junghans*, OJ 1977 L30/10; *Hasselblad*, OJ 1982 L161/18; *Yves Rocher*, OJ 1987 L8/49. In *Pronuptia*, OJ 1987 L13/39, at p. 41, the Commission insisted that a clause which required the franchisee not to harm the brand image of the franchisor by his pricing level be removed. See also *XXth Report on Competition Policy*, point 48 and *XXIst Report on Competition Policy of 1991*, point 127.

[66] *Hennessy-Henkell*, OJ 1980 L383/11, at p. 16.

[67] See *Pronuptia de Paris v Irmgard Schillgallis* [1986] ECR 353, at p. 384 (para. 27); see also the references to recommended prices in Italian spectacles sector, *Fifteenth Report on Competition Policy*, point 66; the Commission notice concerning Regulation 123/85 on the application of art. 85(3) of the treaty to certain categories of motor vehicle distribution and servicing agreements, OJ 1985 C17/4, at II(1); Commission Regulation 4087/88 on the application of art. 85(3) of the treaty to categories of franchise agreements, OJ 1988 L359/46, art. 5(e).

[68] In the *First Report on Competition Policy*, point 55, the Commission stated:

'Purely national systems of resale price maintenance do not generally come under the Community law prohibiting cartels. To the extent that they are limited to compelling retailers in a Member State to respect certain prices for the resale within that State of products supplied by a manufacturer established on that market or by a concession holder appointed for that territory, trade between Member States will not, generally, be affected within the meaning of Article 85 of the EEC Treaty. That is why the Commission considers that the question of vertical resale price maintenance is essentially a matter of national competition policy. The Commission ensures, however, that intermediaries and consumers are enabled to obtain supplies of the product concerned at the most favourable prices and wherever they choose within the Community.'

See also Answer to Written Question No. 247/71, JO 1971 C115/5.

interpreted the requirement of an effect on trade between member states in ways which would make it ill-advised for a company to impose resale price maintenance even in its own country. In *GERO-Fabriek*, the Commission stated that 'the system of retail prices imposed on dealers would be likely to influence trade between member states by deflecting trade flows away from the channels which they would naturally have if prices were fixed freely'.[69]

In *BNIC v Clair*, the Court of Justice found an effect on trade despite the fact that the product in question, potable spirits for use in the manufacture of cognac, was not generally traded outside the Cognac region of France. The court stated:

'It must be observed in that respect that any agreement whose object or effect is to restrict competition by fixing minimum prices for an intermediate product is capable of affecting intra-Community trade, even if there is no trade in that intermediate product between the Member States, where the product constitutes the raw material for another product marketed elsewhere in the Community. The fact that the finished product is protected by a registered designation of origin is irrelevant.'[70]

Thus, it would appear that since the 1970 statement, the Community institutions have gradually tended to regard national resale price maintenance as falling within their competence.

One exception to the general trend of the Community institutions to bring national resale price maintenance schemes under their jurisdiction should be noted. Although in the *VBBB/VBVB* case, the Commission and the court found a system of collective resale price maintenance for book prices operating across national borders to be a violation of art. 85(1) which could not be exempted, they made it clear that the proceeding did not relate to the purely national aspects of the resale price maintenance systems.[71]

In two cases involving the French law requiring resale price-fixing for books, decided in 1985, the Court of Justice held that:

'As Community law stands, the second paragraph of Article 5 of the EEC Treaty, in conjunction with Articles 3(f) and 85, does not prohibit member states from enacting legislation whereby the retail price of books must be fixed by the publisher or by the importer and is binding on all retailers, provided that such legislation is consonant with the other specific provisions of the Treaty, in particular those relating to the free movement of goods'.[72]

---

[69] See *GERO-Fabriek*, OJ 1977 L16/8, at p. 11.
[70] *Bureau National Interprofessionnel du Cognac (BNIC) v Clair* [1985] ECR 391, at p. 425 (para. 29).
[71] *VBBB/VBVB*, OJ 1982 L54/36; on appeal: *VBVB/VBBB v EC Commission* [1984] ECR 19.
[72] *Leclerc & Ors v Au Blé Vert* [1985] ECR 1 (para. 20); *Saint Herblain Distribution, Centre distributeur Leclerc & Ors v Syndicat des Libraires de Loire-Océan* [1985] ECR 2515.

These judgments should not be interpreted too broadly, however. In a Community with several different languages and cultures, national rules governing prices of books take on a particular significance relating to the protection of cultural identity. Thus, the court was faced with the politically sensitive problem of reconciling EC competition rules with national rules designed to protect cultural identity that were strongly supported by the French Government.

In *Net Book Agreements*,[73] the Commission prohibited agreements on book prices between British publishers in so far as they applied to intra-Community trade. The Net Book Agreements provided for minimum prices and uniform rules on discounts. According to the Commission, these rules were not indispensable to the improvement of the publication and distribution of books since the parties could have used less restrictive means to achieve the same end. Consequently, the agreements could not be exempted under art. 85(3).

¶312   Customer restrictions

It is extremely difficult to discover a coherent pattern underlying the Commission's decisions on the compatibility of customer restrictions with the competition rules. Indeed, in cases decided in 1985, the Commission:

(1) granted a negative clearance stating that art. 85(1) does not apply to agreements under which certain suppliers were allowed to sell certain tableware only to hotels and restaurants;[74]

(2) issued a comfort letter stating that the Commission did not intend to take any action regarding an agreement restricting the sale of tyres to authorised dealers and end-users;[75]

(3) decided that restrictions on the sale of artificial teeth to dentists, dental technicians, laboratories, universities, hospitals and authorised depots fell within the prohibition of art. 85(1), but were capable of exemption;[76] and

(4) required companies to remove from their agreements requirements that eyeglasses be sold only to end-users.[77]

Generally, a restriction that a product be sold only to end-users will be considered a violation of art. 85(1) and not capable of exemption. The Commission considers it to be important for dealers to be able to obtain the

---

[73] *Publishers Association – Net Book Agreements*, OJ 1989 L22/12.
[74] *Villeroy & Boch*, OJ 1985 L376/15.
[75] *Mitsui/Bridgestone, Fifteenth Report on Competition Policy*, point 60.
[76] *Ivoclar*, OJ 1985 L369/1.
[77] *Menrad-Silhouette, Fifteenth Report on Competition Policy*, point 64; *Rodenstock/Metzler*, id., point 65.

product from sources other than the supplier.[78] It is possible to limit a dealer to sell only to other dealers which meet certain requirements within the context of a selective distribution system. Indeed, such restrictions are the essence of a selective distribution system.[79] The Commission, however, has rejected some selective distribution systems because they prevent the product from being sold through other distribution channels.[80]

It is also possible to restrict wholesalers from selling to end-users. In upholding the Commission's decision in SABA,[81] that a restriction on sales by German wholesalers to end-users in Germany did not violate art. 85(1), the court stated that:

> 'The Commission considers that, apart from the fact that this limitation on the activity of wholesalers is in accordance with the requirements of German legislation, it does not constitute a restriction on competition within the meaning of Article 85(1) of the Treaty because it corresponds to the separation of the functions of wholesalers and retailers and because if such a separation did not obtain the former would enjoy an unjustified competitive advantage over the latter which, since it would not correspond to benefits supplied, would not be protected under Article 85.'[82]

The Commission has permitted customer restrictions when they were found to be justified because of the nature of the product. In *Distillers-Victuallers*, products were supplied on a duty-free basis and the following restrictions were allowed:

> '(a) not to resell the products supplied except for the purpose of tax and duty-free consumption (in embassies or in aircraft or as ships' stores), and to resell them only to persons or firms which there is no reasonable cause to believe will resell or use such products otherwise than for duty-free consumption;
>
> (b) to impose an obligation similar in terms to (a) above on the resale of the products supplied and to use their best endeavour to ensure that the same obligation is accepted by all subsequent purchasers of the products supplied.'[83]

The Commission found that, in practice, victuallers were unlikely to supply the ordinary (non-duty free) trade and that if they wished to supply such

---

[78] See ¶304.
[79] See ¶332.
[80] See, e.g. *Ideal Standard's distribution system*, OJ 1985 L20/38, and *Grohe's distribution system*, OJ 1985 L19/17, which excluded any retailer which was not a plumbing contractor.
[81] *SABA*, OJ 1976 L28/19, at p. 22.
[82] *Metro v EC Commission* [1977] ECR 1875, at p. 1908 (para. 28). See also *Grundig's EC distribution system*, OJ 1994 L20/15, at p. 20.
[83] *The Distillers Co Ltd – Victuallers*, OJ 1980 L233/43, at p. 44 (para. 6).

¶312

customers, they would be able to obtain products from the suppliers on which duty and taxes had been paid. The Commission stated:

> 'Consequently it may be concluded that, although in theory the standard agreement notified appears to restrict the victualler's freedom to choose his customers and the terms of the sales agreements to be made with them, it does not in practice result in any real restriction on the victualler's freedom of action. It follows that the obligation imposed on victuallers does not have the effect of appreciably restricting competition in the Common Market. Moreover, the agreement notified restricts them in no other way, for it leaves the victuallers free to sell in all countries of the Common Market – and indeed in the world – without restrictions; it does not prevent them from selling other brands of Scotch whisky which are not covered by the agreement, nor does it affect their freedom to determine their resale prices.'[84]

The Commission adopted similar reasoning in holding that customer restrictions in Villeroy & Boch's specialised sales networks for tableware for hotels and restaurants and for advertising gifts did not violate art. 85(1). According to the Commission, the nature of the resellers' business operations and the nature of the products justified the customer restrictions.[85]

In practice, the Commission is willing to accept customer restrictions which are part of a selective distribution system, or which protect retailers from unfair competition by wholesalers. In addition, the particular nature of a product, such as alcohol labelled 'duty-free', may justify restrictions on the classes of customers which may be served. The Commission will not, however, allow any customer restrictions which completely exclude trade in the product between resellers, such as restrictions that the product be sold only to end-users.

¶313   Restrictions on use

The Commission and the Court of Justice generally take the position that it is a violation of the competition rules for a supplier to impose restrictions on the use which its customer may make of a product.

In *Société de vente de ciments et bétons v Kerpen & Kerpen*, the court stated:

> 'clauses in contracts of sale restricting the buyer's freedom to use the goods supplied in accordance with his own economic interests are restrictions on competition within the meaning of Article 85 of the Treaty. A contract which

---

[84] Id., at p. 45.
[85] In discussing the restriction on sales to hotels and restaurants in *Villeroy & Boch*, OJ 1985 L376/15, at p. 19, the Commission stated:

> 'strictly speaking this entails no restriction of competition since the make-up and appearance of the dinner services are different from those of household dinner services'.

imposes upon the buyer an obligation to use the goods supplied for his own needs, not to resell the goods in a specified area and to consult the seller before soliciting business in another specified area has as its object the prevention of competition within the Common Market.'[86]

Along the same lines, the Commission condemned in *Bayo-n-ox*[87] an 'own-use' requirement under which Bayer's customers could only purchase a particular growth promoter (Bayo-n-ox Premix 10 per cent) to cover their own requirements in their own works. The introduction of the own-use requirement must be seen in the context of the expiry of German patent protection for the active substance included in the growth promoter, which triggered a price decrease for the product. Since patent protection remained available in all other Community countries, Bayer feared competition in those countries from cheaper supplies of Bayo-n-ox coming from the German market. Therefore, German customers were offered attractive prices on the condition that they only used the growth promoter in their own works. The Commission characterised the introduction of the own-use requirement as a serious infringement designed to partition the German market from other Community markets and therefore levied a fine of ECU 500,000.

In *Beecham Pharma–Hoechst*, the Commission objected to clauses in a supply agreement for bulk ampicillin requiring the product to be resold only packaged as medicine for consumers rather than in bulk form, and only for human consumption rather than for veterinary use. The Commission found these restrictions to be unjustifiable, stating:

'restrictions on the form in which a raw material may be resold or on the uses to which it may be put are quite as prejudicial to the maintenance of free competition in the Community as geographical market sharing.'[88]

The Commission is concerned that restrictions on resale of a product in its raw form would mean that purchasers would only be able to obtain the raw product from the original supplier. In several cases, the Commission has objected to clauses imposed by South American coffee suppliers that required purchasers to resell only roasted coffee beans, thus preventing the resale of green coffee beans.[89]

The Commission tends to view such use restrictions as a form of territorial

---

[86] *Société de vente de ciments et bétons v Kerpen & Kerpen* [1983] ECR 4173, at p. 4182 (para. 0).
[87] *Bayo-n-ox*, OJ 1990 L21/71.
[88] *Beecham Pharma-Hoechst*, Sixth Report on Competition Policy, points 129–132. See also, *Billiton and Metal & Thermit Chemicals*, Seventh Report on Competition Policy, point 131.
[89] *Marketing Policy of the Instituto Brasileiro do Café*, Fifth Report on Competition Policy, point 33; *Cafeteros de Colombia*, OJ 1982 L360/31, *Instituto Brasileiro do Café (IBC)*, Sixteenth Report on Competition Policy, point 54.

restriction. In *Cafeteros de Colombia*, the Commission said that by including such a clause in its contracts, the supplier:

'makes any interpenetration of the Colombian green coffee market very difficult or even impossible. It is able to partition the market into as many isolated units as there are buyers of Colombian coffee, especially as it controls the supply of all Colombian green coffee sold to EEC roasting plants.'[90]

Attacking, under art. 86 of the treaty, a similar clause requiring that bananas sold by United Brands be ripened before being resold, the Commission said:

'this requirement also makes it difficult, if not impossible, for trade to be carried on in UBC bananas when green, whether Chiquita or unbranded, either within one member state or between member states. UBC's prohibition on the resale of green UBC bananas therefore amounts to a prohibition on exports and thus maintains an effective market segregation.'[91]

The extent to which safety and public health considerations may justify certain use restrictions must be assessed on a case-by-case basis.

The Commission has allowed, by way of a comfort letter, restrictions to be imposed by a supplier of a chemical product on certain uses of the product, and on the resale of the product, when government health regulations required specific approval for such uses of the product.[92] In the *European Gas Producers' settlement*,[93] the Commission insisted that a prohibition on resale clause be deleted from the standard agreements. If, exceptionally, a supplier wished to include such a clause based on properly justified safety grounds, the contract would have to be notified to the Commission. In *1990 World Cup Package Tours*,[94] the Commission had to analyse the allegation that the organisers of the FIFA World Cup in Italy imposed on the authorised travel agencies (and also other officially appointed distribution channels) an obligation not to resell entrance tickets to non-authorised travel agents. The Commission held that for safety reasons it was acceptable for the authorised agencies to be required to resell the entrance tickets only as part of their package tours. Thus, it would appear that for products which could be dangerous to health or which entail safety risks, the Commission could accept that use restrictions are objectively

---

[90] *Cafeteros de Colombia*, OJ 1982 L360/31, at p. 34.
[91] *Chiquita*, OJ 1976 L95/1, at p. 14.
[92] Notice pursuant to art. 19(3) of Council Regulation 17/62 concerning an application for a negative clearance, *Kathon Biocide*, OJ 1984 C59/6.
[93] *European Gas Producers' settlement* of 7 June 1989, press release IP(89) 426. *Nineteenth Report on Competition Policy*, point 62.
[94] *Re 1990 World Cup Package Tours*, OJ 1992 L326/31.

¶313

justified and not restrictive of competition, or at least eligible for an exemption pursuant to art. 85(3).

RULES APPLIED TO PARTICULAR FORMS OF DISTRIBUTION

¶314   Types of distribution

The EC has adopted specific rules applicable to various forms of distribution. The rules relating to agency agreements are old and have been changed in practice (¶315). Exclusive distribution (¶317–¶333), exclusive purchase (¶363–¶375) and franchising (¶352–¶362) agreements benefit from block exemptions. Finally, the rules governing selective distribution systems vary depending upon the type of product (¶334–¶351).

AGENCY

¶315   Commercial agents: the 1962 Notice

An undertaking may choose to distribute its goods and/or services through a commercial agent rather than through employees or independent distributors. A commercial agent may act in his own name or in the name of his principal, but in either case he acts on behalf of the principal and for the principal's benefit.

In 1962, the Commission issued a Notice on exclusive dealing contracts with commercial agents.[95] The notice discusses the possible impact on competition of agreements with commercial agents from two perspectives: it examines the competitive conditions on both the market for the provision of goods and on the market for the provision of services consisting of the negotiation and conclusion of transactions.

The notice does not consider an exclusive dealing contract with commercial agents to have a restrictive effect on the market for the provision of goods, provided the agent does not assume any significant financial risk resulting from the transaction. According to the notice, the commercial agent in that case only performs an auxiliary function, acting on the instructions and in the interest of the enterprise on whose behalf he is operating.[96]

Factors that point to a contrary conclusion and which therefore tend to expose the exclusive dealing contract to the application of art. 85(1) are:

---

[95] Commission Notice on exclusive dealing contracts with commercial agents, JO 1962 139/2921.

[96] This view is, in principle, supported by the court. See *Suiker Unie & Ors v EC Commission* [1975] ECR 1663, at pp. 2005–2010. See also *Consten and Grundig v EC Commission* [1966] ECR 299, at p. 340 and *Italy v Council and Commission* [1966] ECR 389, at pp. 407–408, *ARG/Unipart*, OJ 1988 L45/38.

(1) the fact that the agent is required to keep or does in fact keep a considerable stock of contract products as his own property;

(2) the fact that the agent is required to organise or ensure at his own expense a substantial service to customers free of charge; and

(3) the possibility for the agent to determine prices or conditions of sales.[97]

As regards the market for the provision of an intermediary's services, i.e. the negotiation and/or conclusion of transactions, the notice holds that there is no restriction of competition where the agent acts in an auxiliary capacity according to the criterion described above (i.e. absence of financial risks on behalf of the agent) and works exclusively for one principal for a certain period of time. At the time of the publication of the notice, the Commission considered such exclusive devotion of an agent to one principal for a certain period of time to be the result of the special mutual obligation of the commercial agent and his principal to protect each other's interests.[98]

Application of the notice's principles

Subsequent case law of the Commission and the court has demonstrated the need for caution in reliance on the principles contained in the notice. This case law typically rejects the defence that art. 85 is not applicable because a company was acting in the role of agent.

The Commission, in *Pittsburgh Corning Europe*,[99] stressed the 'economic reality' of a commercial agency relationship rather than its legal form. In rejecting a defence that the Belgian company Formica was acting as an agent, the Commission stated that it had never indicated in its 1962 Notice that it would consider solely the 'outside appearance' of an agency relationship without considering 'the true character of legal acts, relations between undertakings, and economic conditions'.[100]

Although the formal consequences of the contract provision were respected by the parties,[101] this was irrelevant for determining whether Formica was in a position of economic dependence with regard to PCE. The Commission declared that 'whatever part [the formal aspect of the contract] may have played in the situation when viewed under national law, [it has] no bearing or effect on Community law and particularly on whether Formica during that period was really in a position of economic dependence with regard to PCE'.[102]

In the absence of economic dependence, the notice is inapplicable.

---

[97] For an application of these criteria, see *Re 1990 World Cup Package Tours*, OJ 1992 L326/31, at p. 38.
[98] Commission Notice on exclusive dealing contracts with commercial agents, JO 1962 139/2921.
[99] *Pittsburgh Corning Europe – Formica Belgium – Hertel*, JO 1972 L272/35.
[100] Id., at p. 37.
[101] Ibid. Invoices were prepared by PCE or in its name and Formica was paid a commission during the period in question.
[102] Ibid.

Moreover, the Commission observed that Formica was 'strong enough and independent enough of PCE to be capable of resisting the latter's demand to apply discriminatory price rates which are so obviously contrary to the rules of the Treaty'.[103] The Commission concluded that Formica neither exercised an auxiliary function nor was integrated into PCE's distribution network and that the application of the prices in question therefore resulted from a concerted practice between PCE and Formica in violation of art. 85(1).

Similarly, the Court of Justice applied the prohibition of art. 85(1) to restrictive agreements between sugar manufacturers and large business houses that acted as agents with regard to sugar sales in specified territories, but that also acted as independent dealers on their own account with regard to sugar exports to non-member countries and sugar supplies for denaturing.[104] The court held that:

> 'the creation of such an ambivalent relationship, which in respect of the same commodity only gives the trader the opportunity of continuing to operate independently to the extent to which it is in the interest of his supplier for him to do so, cannot escape the prohibition of Article 85 no matter how such a relationship is regarded under national law.'[105]

In *Vlaamse Reisbureaus*,[106] the court ruled that travel agents operating in the name and on behalf of tour operators are nevertheless independent intermediaries when those agents work for many tour operators and when the tour operators in turn sell their products through many travel agents.[107] The court consequently condemned a system of government-backed resale price maintenance whereby travel agents were prohibited from sharing part of the commission or discounts which they received with their customers. The Commission adopted similar reasoning in more recent case law.[108]

The Commission suggested on another occasion that even if a company were to be considered as an agent, it could still be subject to art. 85(1) if the decision to enter into an agency agreement or to remain bound by one were restrictive of competition in the market for the provision of the agent's services. In *Aluminium Imports from Eastern Europe*,[109] the Commission stated that:

---

[103] Ibid. The Commission found that Formica was directly or indirectly affiliated with a number of other companies and that it derived most of its revenue from the sale of its own manufactured goods and its distribution of the products of other companies.

[104] *Suiker Unie & Ors v EC Commission* [1975] ECR 1663, at p. 2008 (para. 544).

[105] Id., at p. 2008 (para. 547). For another application of art. 85(1) in the case of an agreement concluded by an undertaking acting both as an independent trader and an agent, see *Fisher-Price/Quaker Oats Ltd – Toyco*, OJ 1988 L49/19. But see for a contrary conclusion *ARG/Unipart*, OJ 1988 L45/34.

[106] *Vereniging van Vlaamse Reisbureaus v Sociale Dienst van de plaatselijke en gewestelijke overheidsdiensten* [1987] ECR 3801.

[107] Id., at p. 3829 (para. 20–21).

[108] *Distribution of railway tickets by travel agents*, OJ 1992 L366/47, at p. 57 and *Center Parcs*, XXIInd Report on Competition Policy for 1992, point 581.

[109] *Aluminium Imports from Eastern Europe*, OJ 1985 L92/1.

'neither Brandeis Goldschmidt nor Eisen und Metall were acting under the instructions of any person when they decided to take part in the agreements which are the subject of these proceedings. Brandeis Goldschmidt was under no obligation to enter into the agreements or to assume such a material role in their implementation and enforcement. Brandeis Goldschmidt decided of its own will as independent economic operator to take part in an arrangement which could exclude its competitors from the trade in aluminium in eastern Europe. Both Brandeis Goldschmidt and Eisen und Metall could have withdrawn at any time from the agreements without going out of their line of business. Neither company escapes liability for its participation in a restrictive agreement by alleging that it had no independent status, but merely acted on instructions. The relationship within which those instructions were given arose only from their choice to enter into the restrictive agreement.'[110]

Agency agreements may come with in the ambit of art. 86 as well. In the *Sugar Cartel* case,[111] the court stated that a contractual clause prohibiting competition between a principal occupying a dominant position and his agent may constitute an abuse within the meaning of art. 86 when the agent is given responsibilities which, from an economic point of view, are approximately the same as those carried out by an independent dealer.[112]

The case law concerning agency has severely restricted the scope of the defence that an entity was acting as the agent of the supplier and that its action and the relationship with the supplier may therefore not be considered restrictive of competition. In particular, the court's judgment in *Vlaamse Reisbureaus* has left some commentators wondering whether there remains any possibility of effectively organising a distribution system through agents.[113]

¶316   New guidelines on agency agreements

The Commission is preparing new guidelines on the status of agency agreements under EC competition law.[114] While it is not entirely clear at present what the contents of the new guidelines will be, it may be useful to note that the Commission has introduced in one of its drafts a distinction between so-called integrated and unintegrated agents. Integration has been defined as 'a

---

[110] Id., at p. 37.
[111] *Suiker Unie & Ors v EC Commission* [1975] ECR 1663.
[112] Id., at p. 1998 (para. 482–483). The court added that clauses prohibiting competition imposed by an undertaking occupying a dominant position on its trade representatives may constitute an abuse if foreign competitors are unable to find independent operators who can market their products on a sufficiently large scale.
[113] Koch and Marenco, 'L'article 85 du Traité CEE et les contrats d'agence', Cahiers de droit européen, 1987, 603, at pp. 614–615. But see Van Houtte, 'Les contrats d'agence au regard de l'Article 85 CEE: Agir pour le compte d'autrui et intégration dans son entreprise', Cahiers de droit européen, 1989, 345, at pp. 359–360.
[114] *XXIInd Report on Competition Policy for 1992*, point 300.

situation where the agent has a particularly intensive link with the principal which leads him to subordinate his interests and to dedicate his operations in the field of the product covered by the agency agreement to those of the principal, and which leads customers or suppliers with whom the agent deals not to expect autonomous commercial behaviour from the agent but to identify him with the principal'. Unintegrated agents have in most respects, other than the fixing of prices and conditions, been treated in these drafts as if they were independent traders and the more lenient approach towards agency contracts is reserved only for integrated agents.

Finally, it should be noted that increasing importance is attached to the role of agents (intermediaries) in the context of motor vehicle distribution systems based on Commission Regulation 123/85. The Commission has adopted a notice clarifying the activities of motor vehicle intermediaries.[115]

EXCLUSIVE DISTRIBUTION

¶317   Block exemption

Exclusive distribution and exclusive purchase agreements were the first types of agreements to benefit from a block exemption. For 15 years, Regulation 67/67 applied to both types of agreements.[116] On 1 July 1983, separate regulations applying to exclusive distribution agreements[117] and exclusive purchase agreements[118] replaced Regulation 67/67.

The Commission considers that exclusive distribution agreements fall under the prohibition of art. 85(1) because the supplier limits his freedom in appointing distributors in a territory. Such agreements may benefit from an exemption under art. 85(3), however, because of the improvement in distribution and sales promotion which they allow.[119]

The purpose of adopting a block exemption is to help create legal certainty with respect to a class of agreements and to decrease the necessity for individual notifications. In a series of resolutions, the European Parliament expressed concern that the level of detail set out in the block exemptions for exclusive distribution and exclusive purchase agreements would, in fact, decrease certainty and increase the number of notifications.[120]

---

[115]   OJ 1991 C329/20; see ¶342.
[116]   Regulation 67/67 of the Commission on the application of art. 85(3) of the treaty to certain categories of exclusive dealing agreements, JO 1967 57/849, as last amended by the Act of Accession for Greece.
[117]   Commission Regulation 1983/83 on the application of art. 85(3) to categories of exclusive distribution agreements, OJ 1983 L173/1.
[118]   Commission Regulation 1984/83 on the application of art. 85(3) to categories of exclusive purchasing agreements, OJ 1983 L173/5.
[119]   See Regulation 1983/83 recitals 5–7.
[120]   Resolution on the Eleventh Report of the Commission of the European Communities on competition

Practical experience in applying Regulation 1983/83 suggests, however, that the level of detail contained in the block exemption does not constitute a major problem. In fact, compared to other block exemptions, Regulation 1983/83 does not impose a long list of requirements and is fairly easy to work with. The main difficulty is the absence of detailed information on the interpretation of both the block exemption and the related Commission notice.[121] Practitioners face a number of recurring interpretative difficulties when drafting exclusive distribution agreements based on Regulation 1983/83. Legal certainty and the practical usefulness of Regulation 1983/83 could therefore benefit from increased Commission guidance in the context, for example, of competition policy reports.

Regulation 1983/83 only applies if the exclusive distribution agreement contains only the restrictions of competition which are expressly exempted. The inclusion of additional restrictions of competition will render the block exemption inapplicable to the agreement as a whole.[122] Regulation 1983/83 does not provide for an opposition procedure, nor does it rely on the model used in Regulation 123/85 whereby restrictive clauses specifically mentioned are automatically exempted even if the additional restrictions which are not mentioned in the block exemption are included.

¶318   Nature of agreements exempted

The basic exemption granted by Regulation 1983/83 applies to agreements:

'to which only two undertakings are party and whereby one party agrees with the other to supply certain goods for resale within the whole or a defined area of the common market only to that other.'[123]

The prerequisites for the application of the exemption are considered in detail at ¶319–¶332.

¶319   Territorial exclusivity

The block exemption applies only if the supplier grants territorial exclusivity to the distributor. The exclusivity requirement contained in Regulation 1983/83 implies that there is a single distributor appointed within a given contract territory. Shared exclusivity is not covered by the block exemption.[124] The

---

policy, OJ 1983 C13/225, point 14; Resolution on the proposed Commission amendments to Regulation 67/67, OJ 1983 C184/67, point 5.

[121] Commission Notice concerning Commission Regulation 1983/83 and 1984/83 on the application of art. 85(3) of the treaty to categories of exclusive distribution and exclusive purchasing agreements (hereinafter referred to as the 'guidelines'), OJ 1984 C101/2.

[122] Guidelines, para. 17; *Newitt/Dunlop Slazenger International & Ors*, OJ 1992 L131/32, at p. 43 (para. 60).

[123] Regulation 1983/83, art. 1.

[124] In *Junghans* (OJ 1977 L30/10, at p. 15), the Commission stated that Regulation 67/67 was not applicable 'since Junghans does not supply only one dealer in the contractual territory, as required by Article 1(1)(a) of the

Commission has made it clear, however, that even though the appointment of more than one distributor within a given contract territory puts agreements outside the scope of the block exemption, they may often fulfil the requirements for an individual exemption.[125]

The Commission has had to deal with two interesting interpretative issues relating to the territorial exclusivity requirement:

(1) an agreement concluded by a manufacturer of pharmaceutical products with several traders, relating to the distribution within one member state of identical products which had been registered under separate new brand names, was judged not to be covered by the block exemption;[126]

(2) two distribution agreements entered into by a manufacturer of non-dutiable products with two exclusive distributors operating in the same territory, one in the duty free market and the other in the ordinary market, were said to be exempted under Regulation 1983/83.[127]

While it is clearly preferable that territorial exclusivity is expressly provided for in the distribution agreement in order for Regulation 1983/83 to apply, the regulation does not impose such a formal requirement. In order to meet the territorial exclusivity requirement of the block exemption, it suffices that the parties agree on this point, albeit tacitly. In this regard, even a concerted practice on territorial exclusivity may be enough to bring the block exemption into play.[128]

¶320 Extent of the territory

Under the block exemption, the territory granted to the exclusive distributor must be defined.

Regulation 1983/83 applies to exclusive distribution agreements which grant a territory covering 'the whole or a defined territory of the Common Market'.[129]

Regulation, but three'. The Commission affirmed that the line taken in the *Junghans* decision must also be followed under Regulation 1983/83, *Seventeenth Report on Competition Policy*, point 28.

[125] *Seventeenth Report on Competition Policy*, point 28.

[126] *Nineteenth Report on Competition Policy*, point 17.

[127] *XXIst Report on Competition Policy*, point 112; The Commission considered the two markets to be distinct from the final consumer's point of view, given the built-in price difference and the limited and restricted access to the duty free market.

[128] In its *Seventeenth Report on Competition Policy*, point 28, the Commission stated that a distribution agreement between a propylene manufacturer and its distributor in a member state qualified for the exemption granted by Regulation 1983/83 even though the agreement did not formally confer territorial exclusivity on the distributor. In accordance with art. 9 of Regulation 1983/83 which provides that the regulation applies mutatis mutandis to concerted practices, the Commission found that the manufacturer had treated the distributor as a de facto exclusive distributor for several years and, accordingly, a concerted practice on territorial exclusivity existed.

[129] Regulation 1983/83, art. 1. Regulation 19/65, which gives the Commission the authority to grant a block exemption for exclusive distribution agreements, refers to exclusive supply 'within a defined area of the Common Market'. One author has noted that the Commission's interpretation of the identical phrase in the *Durodyne* decision casts doubts on the authority of the Commission to grant a block exemption to agreements covering the

This language means that it is no longer necessary for parties to follow the absurd practice of carving out a small region of the EC from the scope of the territory granted to an exclusive distributor for the sole purpose of bringing the agreement into the scope of the block exemption. Agreements that grant territories including areas outside the common market may also benefit from the exemption.[130]

While it is now generally accepted that an exclusive distributor's contract territory may encompass the whole of the Community, there is less certainty as to exactly how much freedom parties enjoy in determining the size of their contract territories. One author suggests that parties have considerable discretion and that Regulation 1983/83 'covers a large scale of possible stipulations, ranging from exclusive distributorships for the whole of the Common Market to simple location clauses protecting local sales areas'.[131]

¶321 Territorial protection enjoyed by the exclusive distributor

The regulation limits the extent of the exclusivity which a distributor can expect to obtain. In addition, the guidelines issued by the Commission with the intent of clarifying the regulation instead bring considerable confusion by introducing interpretations that are inconsistent with a straightforward reading of the terms of the regulation. In order to appreciate the level of territorial protection from which an exclusive distributor can benefit, a distinction must be made between

(1) sales by the supplier to other resellers;

(2) sales by other resellers; and

(3) direct sales by the supplier to end-users.

(1) Sales by the supplier to other resellers

Territorial exclusivity does not mean that the exclusive distributor will benefit from complete protection against sales by other distributors in his contract territory. The minimum territorial protection which the distributor in any event enjoys is that the supplier may not appoint other distributors or resellers in the contract territory. Indeed, in order to meet the requirements of art. 1 of Regulation 1983/83, the supplier can only supply one reseller within the contract territory concerned. However, the exclusive supply obligation does not prevent the supplier from providing the contract products to other resellers which afterwards sell them in the exclusive distributor's territory. The

---

entire territory of the common market. See Korah, *Exclusive Distribution and the EEC Competition Rules*, London, 1992, at pp. 84–85.

[130] *Hydrotherm v Compact* [1984] ECR 2999, at p. 3016 (para. 11).

[131] Schröter, 'The Application of Article 85 of the EEC Treaty to Distribution Agreements – Principles and Recent Developments' (1984) Fordham Corporate Law Institute, 375, at p. 402.

guidelines suggest that in such a case the supplier does not act in breach of its contractual obligations to the exclusive distributor provided that:

(1) it supplies these resellers only at their request,

(2) they take delivery of the products outside the territory and

(3) the supplier does not assume the costs of the delivery into the territory.

Thus, under the Commission's interpretation, a supplier does not breach the exclusivity obligation even if it supplies to another reseller established in the territory, provided the aforesaid conditions are met.

In its recent practice, the Commission has taken the approach from the guidelines one step further. In the *Eighteenth Report on Competition Policy*, the Commission's position is summarised as follows:

'[A] manufacturer who has assumed exclusive supply obligations for a territory within the EC may not be prevented from dealing with non-solicited resellers from such a territory as long as the goods are handed over outside the territory, and the buyer assumes both the risk and the cost of transport.

On the other hand, there is no general obligation on a manufacturer under Community competition law to contract with another party, irrespective of the latter's place of residence. There may be valid business considerations for not supplying a particular dealer. Furthermore, the manufacturer may decide not to offer certain discounts because the party in question is not expected to provide the corresponding services, such as for example, stocking or sales promotion. Where, however, a manufacturer refuses custom because the ultimate destination of the goods is in another Member State, the Commission would regard such a policy as pointing to the existence of agreements or concerted practices, whose purpose was the protection of exclusive distributors against bona fide parallel imports.'[132]

In view of the foregoing, it appears not to be possible for a supplier to assume a contractual commitment not to supply independent resellers that are not part of the supplier's distribution network and that the supplier suspects will sell in the exclusive distributor's contract territory.[133] In addition, even in the absence of such a contractual commitment, the supplier would seem not to be allowed to refrain from supplying such resellers if the sole motivation for such refusal relates to the ultimate destination of the products.

The Commission's interpretation of an exclusivity obligation is different from the interpretation which parties to an agreement would normally adopt. In addition, the Commission's interpretation would appear to be contrary to

---

[132] *Eighteenth Report on Competition Policy*, point 21.
[133] *Tipp-Ex*, OJ 1987 L222/1, at pp. 3 and 8.

the language of art. 1 of the regulation. The requirement that the independent reseller rather than the supplier pay for transportation into the territory will provide the exclusive distributor with little protection in cases where transportation costs are low, the territory is small, or the exclusive distributor itself bears transportation costs into the territory.

The Commission's interpretation expressed in the guidelines and the *Eighteenth Report on Competition Policy* leads to a disparity in the protection afforded to exclusive distributors depending upon whether or not the supplier's agreements with one or several exclusive distributors covers the entire territory of the EC. If all of the EC is covered, the supplier will be prevented from supplying independent resellers in the Community by the terms of the exclusive agreements covering each territory. Any hole in the network of exclusive distribution agreements, however, would open the supplier to complaints concerning refusal to supply and would allow independent resellers located in the territory of an exclusive distributor to obtain access to the goods directly from the supplier, which goods could be delivered in the territory not covered by an exclusive agreement.

It may in any event be hoped that a restrictive interpretation will be given to the extract from the *Eighteenth Report on Competition Policy* quoted above.[134] There is indeed no reason to abandon the established principle that non-dominant suppliers that do not operate a selective distribution network should be free to contract with the parties of their choice. Such suppliers should have no duty to justify their decision not to supply a particular reseller. Also, a general policy of the supplier not to supply resellers other than its authorised distributors should be acceptable, provided the requirements of art. 3(c) and (d) of Regulation 1983/83 are respected.

(2)   Sales by other resellers
Territorial exclusivity under Regulation 1983/83 does not imply that other resellers cannot sell into the exclusive distributor's contract territory. The protection which the supplier can offer in this respect is fairly limited. In accordance with art. 2(2)(c) of Regulation 1983/83, the supplier can impose a contractual obligation on his exclusive distributors to refrain from active solicitation outside their respective contract territories. On this basis, exclusive distributors are protected against active marketing efforts in their respective contract territories from other exclusive distributors. However, passive or

---

[134] In *Newitt/Dunlop Slazenger International & Ors*, OJ 1992 L131/32, at p. 42, the Commission stated that 'any specific costs borne by exclusive distributors are largely offset by the granting of exclusivity which constitutes a key commercial advantage'. It would be difficult to reconcile such a statement with attempts to undermine the exclusive distributor's territorial protection to an undue extent. .

unsolicited sales by such exclusive distributors to customers located in another exclusive distributor's contract territory must remain possible.[135]

There is no obligation for the supplier to impose a contractual obligation on his distributors to refrain from active solicitation outside their respective contract territories. In the case of exclusive distributors, such an obligation can benefit from an exemption pursuant to Regulation 1983/83, but is clearly not required by the regulation. In the case of non-exclusive distributors, such an obligation cannot benefit from an automatic exemption and may need to be notified in order to receive an individual exemption.

With regard to independent resellers that are not part of the supplier's distribution system, the supplier can offer its exclusive distributors virtually no territorial protection. Attempts on the part of the supplier to impede sales by independent resellers in an exclusive distributor's contract territory are not exempted by Regulation 1983/83.

(3)   Direct sales by the supplier to end-users

It is possible, but not necessary, for the distribution agreement to restrict the right of the supplier to supply goods to end-users in the contract territory. Article 2(1) of Regulation 1983/83 provides that, apart from the obligation to supply to only one distributor within the territory, 'no restrictions on competition shall be imposed on the supplier other than the obligation not to supply the contract goods to users in the contract territory'.

It is not necessary for the restriction on sales to final users in the contract territory to be absolute. Clauses permitting the supplier to supply only certain specific categories of end-users (e.g. government bodies, the supplier's own personnel, charitable organisations) are also permissible. The distribution agreement may also require the supplier to pay compensation to the exclusive distributor in the case of direct sales to final users. The payment of such compensation is, however, not required under the regulation.[136]

The allowable scope of the restriction pursuant to art. 2(1) of Regulation 1983/83 is very limited. Thus, in its report on the settlement involving the agreements of La Maison des Bibliothèques, the Commission stated:

'Although Article 2(1) of the new block exemption regulation on exclusive distribution agreements permits imposition of an obligation on the supplier not to compete actively with an exclusive distributor in his contract territory, the Commission pointed out that the block exemption is available only if the supplier remains free to deliver goods covered by the contract on his own

---

[135] Guidelines, para. 28.
[136] Guidelines para. 30.

¶321

terms – but outside the contract territory – to customers resident in that territory.'[137]

A similar approach is taken in the guidelines where it is suggested that the position regarding art. 2(1) of the regulation is the same as for supplies by the supplier to independent resellers.[138]

¶322 Goods for resale

Regulation 1983/83 applies only to the distribution of goods and not to services.[139] Customer services incidental to the sale of goods are covered by the regulation.[140] Distribution agreements in which the distributor hires or leases goods, rather than reselling them, will fall within the scope of the block exemption.[141]

The term 'resale' is meant to ensure that the exemption applies only to true distributors and to prevent the exemption from applying to arrangements where the purchaser transforms or processes the product into another good before it is sold.[142] However, the repackaging of goods does not imply that the goods are not resold. Slight transformations, such as 'operations to improve the quality, durability, appearance or taste of the goods (such as rust-proofing of metals, sterilisation of food or the addition of colouring matter or flavourings to drugs)' or the dilution of 'a concentrated extract for a drink', will only take an agreement outside of the scope of the block exemption if there is more than 'a slight addition in value'.[143]

In a notice concerning a notification of certain collaboration agreements between ICL and Fujitsu, the Commission suggested that OEM agreements under which the purchaser sells products under its own trade name as part of its own range of products would not be considered distribution agreements because the purchaser does not hold itself out as a distributor.[144] This limitation would appear to restrict further the notion of resale, as there is no suggestion in the regulation that a reseller may not sell goods under its own trade marks.[145]

---

[137] *Furniture trade, Fourteenth Report on Competition Policy*, point 68.
[138] Guidelines, para. 30. See ¶321 above.
[139] Guidelines, para. 11; *Re 1990 World Cup Package Tours*, OJ 1992 L326/1, at pp. 39–40.
[140] Regulation 1983/83, art. 2(3)(c); guidelines, para. 11.
[141] Guidelines, para. 12.
[142] Id., para. 9.
[143] Id., para. 10.
[144] Notice pursuant to art. 19(3) of Council Regulation 17/62 concerning a request for negative clearance or the application of art. 85(3) of the EEC Treaty, *ICL Fujitsu*, OJ 1986 C210/3, at p. 4; see also *Sixteenth Report on Competition Policy*, point 72.
[145] Article 2(3)(b) merely states that it is permissible for the distributor to undertake 'to sell the contract goods under trade marks, or packed and presented as specified by the other party'.

¶323   Only two undertakings

The exemption is applicable only if there are two undertakings involved, a supplier and a reseller.[146] Undertakings forming one 'economic unit' may be treated as a single undertaking.[147] In the *Hydrotherm* case, the Court of Justice interpreted the same requirement in Regulation 67/67 to be fulfilled if:

> 'one of the parties to the agreement is made up of undertakings having identical interests and controlled by the same natural person, who also participates in the agreement. For in those circumstances competition between the persons participating together, as a single party, in the agreement in question is impossible.'[148] It is also possible for a supplier to delegate performance of certain contractual obligations to a third party.[149] However, such involvement of third parties should be limited to the 'execution of deliveries'.[150]

¶324   Permitted restrictions on competition

The regulation defines the extent of the restrictions on competition that may be imposed on the supplier and the distributor.[151] The use of the term 'restrictions on competition' may be overbroad as there is the possibility that an agreement may restrict competition but not violate art. 85(1).

For example, restrictions on exports outside the EC may be a restriction on competition but are generally considered not to violate art. 85(1) owing to the absence of an effect on trade between member states.[152] However, the Commission takes the view in the guidelines that it is an impermissible restriction on competition for the supplier to agree with his exclusive distributor that he will prevent his other customers from selling into the distributor's territory. This would apply, as well, to an undertaking to prevent customers outside the common market from supplying into the territory of the distributor. Unilateral action by the supplier to prevent such sales would not

---

[146] Guidelines, para. 14. See also *Welded steel mesh* [1989] 2 CEC 2,051; OJ 1989 L260/1, at p. 38, where the Commission found that exclusive distribution agreements were part of a comprehensive market-sharing arrangement involving more than two undertakings and thus did not qualify for an exemption under Regulation 67/67.

[147] Guidelines, para. 13. The scope of this guideline is unclear because the Commission has used the undefined term 'an economic unit' rather than the term 'connected undertaking' which is defined in the regulation (art. 4(2)).

[148] *Hydrotherm v Compact* [1984] ECR 2999, at p. 3016 (para. 11).

[149] Guidelines, para. 15.

[150] Id., para. 16.

[151] Regulation 67/67 had not specifically set out the extent of the restrictions which could be imposed on the supplier. In a court case interpreting Regulation 67/67, Advocate General Reischl had questioned whether, in the absence of such provision, art. 2 of Regulation 67/67 could be interpreted as limiting the restrictions which could be imposed on the supplier. See the opinion of Advocate General Reischl in *Van Vliet Kwastenfabriek v Dalle Crode* [1975] ECR 1103, at p. 1117. Specific language relating to restrictions on the supplier was inserted in Regulation 1983/83 to ensure that the list would be interpreted as exhaustive.

[152] See ¶308.

remove the agreement from the exemption provided by Regulation 1983/83 unless there was no alternative supply available within the common market.[153]

¶325 Permitted restrictions on the supplier

Article 2(1) of the regulation provides that apart from the obligation to supply to only one distributor within the territory, 'no restrictions on competition shall be imposed on the supplier other than the obligation not to supply the contract goods to users in the contract territory'. As discussed above, the scope of the allowable restrictions on competition is very limited.[154]

¶326 Restrictions on competition that may be imposed on the distributor

Certain restrictions on competition may be imposed on the exclusive distributor without taking the agreement outside the scope of the block exemption.

(1) Non-competition clause

It is permissible to impose on the distributor 'the obligation not to manufacture or distribute goods which compete with the contract goods'.[155] Although Regulation 67/67 exempted non-competition clauses which continued for one year after the termination of the agreement,[156] Regulation 1983/83 allows such a clause to be imposed only for the duration of the agreement.[157]

It may be assumed that art. 2(2)(a) of Regulation 1983/83 also exempts partial non-compete obligations. In many sectors, it is indeed customary to include in the distribution agreement an exhaustive list of other brands which the exclusive distributor is entitled to market. Likewise, it would seem to be reasonable to consider clauses aimed at preventing circumvention of the non-compete obligation to be covered by the exemption. Such clauses could make it clear, for instance, that the non-compete obligation is not met in cases where the distributor establishes a separate legal entity in order to manufacture or distribute competing products.

(2) Exclusive purchase obligation

It is permissible to impose an 'obligation to obtain contract goods for resale only from the other party'.[158] An obligation on the part of the exclusive

---

[153] Guidelines, para. 33. See also Regulation 1983/83, art. 3(d).
[154] See ¶321.
[155] Regulation 1983/83, art. 2(2)(a).
[156] Regulation 67/67, art. 2(1)(a).
[157] Guidelines, para. 18.
[158] Regulation 1983/83, art. 2(2)(b).

distributor to purchase the contract goods only from the supplier and other authorised distributors is also possible under Regulation 1983/83.[159]

(3)   Restrictions on activities outside the territory

It is possible to prevent the exclusive distributor from undertaking an active sales policy with respect to customers outside its territory, but not to prevent the distributor from supplying unsolicited requests. The regulation exempts 'the obligation to refrain, outside the contract territory and in relation to the contract goods, from seeking customers, from establishing any branch, and from maintaining any distribution depot'.[160] By analogy to the corresponding provision in Regulation 123/85, advertising in a medium directed to customers in the contract territory but also covering a wider area may not be prevented on the basis of this obligation.[161]

¶327   Impermissible restrictions on the distributor

Restrictions on the distributor's competitive freedom which go beyond those set out in art. 2(2) will take the agreement outside the scope of the block exemption granted by the regulation.[162]

No restrictions may be placed on the ability of the distributor to determine prices or to fill unsolicited orders outside its territory. Although the guidelines suggest that such obligations may be notified for an individual exemption, it is extremely unlikely that an exemption would be granted for absolute export restrictions or resale price maintenance.[163]

Agreements that restrict the exclusive distributor's free choice of customers will not benefit from the block exemption.[164] In the settlement relating to the Mitsui-Bridgestone agreements, the Commission demonstrated its willingness to allow provisions only permitting sales to end-users or other authorised dealers on a case-by-case basis.[165]

¶328   Additional obligations

The regulation sets out the following additional obligations that will not take the agreement outside the scope of the block exemption. The following obligations are permissible:

'(a) to purchase complete ranges of goods or minimum quantities;

---

[159] *Honda motorcycles*, press release of 3 July 1992, IP(92) 544.
[160] Regulation 1983/83, art. 2(2)(c); see also ¶321.
[161] Regulation 123/85, recital 9 and art. 3(8).
[162] Guidelines, para. 17.
[163] See ¶308 and ¶311.
[164] Guidelines, paras. 1) and 29.
[165] *Mitsui-Bridgestone, Fifteenth Report on Competition Policy*, point 60.

(b) to sell the contract goods under trade marks or packed and presented as specified by the other party;

(c) to take measures for promotion of sales, in particular:

- to advertise,
- to maintain a sales network or stock of goods,
- to provide customer and guarantee services,
- to employ staff having specialised or technical training.'[166]

These obligations are listed separately because they are not generally considered restrictive of competition.[167] It would appear that the purpose of specifically mentioning such clauses is to exempt them in the event that they were considered to be a violation of art. 85(1) in specific situations.[168]

The Commission, in the guidelines, interprets the provision permitting obligations for the promotion of sales to allow the reseller to 'be forbidden to supply the contract goods to unsuitable dealers' provided that selection of suitable dealers is based on objective qualitative criteria.[169] Selection of dealers based on quantitative criteria would require an individual exemption.[170] The preamble of Regulation 1983/83, however, states that 'further restrictive obligations and in particular those which limit the exclusive distributor's choice of customers ... cannot be exempted under this Regulation'.[171] Thus, although non-discriminatory selection of dealers on the basis of objective criteria is allowed, limitations on classes of customers would require an individual exemption.[172]

¶329 Situations where the block exemption will not apply

The block exemption will ·not apply to agreements otherwise meeting the conditions for exemption in the following situations:

(1) if manufacturers of identical or equivalent goods enter into reciprocal exclusive distribution agreements (see ¶330);[173]

(2) if a non-reciprocal exclusive distribution agreement is entered into

---

[166] Regulation 1983/83, art. 2(3).
[167] Guidelines, para. 19.
[168] This purpose is specifically mentioned in the preambles to the patent licensing and research and development block exemptions with respect to a similar provision in those regulations.
[169] Guidelines, para. 20. During the notice period before the termination of an exclusive distribution agreement, the exclusive distributor may even be prevented from appointing any new sub-dealers (*XXIst Report on Competition Policy for 1991*, point 113).
[170] *Ivoclar*, OJ 1985 L369/1, at pp. 3–4. For a discussion of objective qualitative criteria and quantitative criteria, see ¶334ff.
[171] Regulation 1983/83, recital 8.
[172] *Ivoclar*, OJ 1985 L369/1, at p. 3. See also ¶325.
[173] Regulation 1983/83, art. 3(a).

between manufacturers of identical or equivalent goods unless one is small (see ¶330);[174]

(3) if users have no alternative sources of supply (see ¶331);[175]

(4) if the parties interfere with parallel trade (see ¶332).[176]

¶330   Agreements between manufacturers of identical or equivalent products

The block exemption will not apply to reciprocal exclusive distribution agreements between 'manufacturers of identical goods or of goods which are considered by users as equivalent in view of their characteristics, price and intended use'.[177] With respect to non-reciprocal agreements between such manufacturers, the exemption only applies if one of the parties has an annual turnover of less than ECU 100m. This turnover threshold refers to all products sold world-wide and includes the turnover of connected undertakings.[178] Thus, the turnover figure is used as a measure of the economic strength of the undertaking rather than a measure of its size in the relevant product or geographic market.[179]

The Commission has made it clear that the concept 'manufacturer' which is used in art. 3 must be given a broad interpretation. A company which has the contract products manufactured for it by a subcontractor or another undertaking associated with it and then markets the products under its own name or trade mark will be considered a 'manufacturer'.[180]

The Commission is concerned that agreements between competitors could lead to or be used to maintain market-sharing arrangements.[181] The Commission is also concerned that agreements between competitors might not lead to an improvement in distribution and therefore not meet the general requirements of exemption set out in art. 85(3) of the treaty.[182] As a result, the

---

[174] Regulation 1983/83, art. 3(b).

[175] Regulation 1983/83, art. 3(c).

[176] Regulation 1983/83, art. 3(d).

[177] Regulation 1983/83, art. 3(a) and (b). See *Fluke-Phillips*, OJ 1989 C188/2; *Nineteenth Report on Competition Policy*, point 47. The Commission indicated that although the product ranges of the parties were largely complementary, the block exemption was nonetheless unavailable because the parties were direct competitors with respect to some products.

[178] Connected undertakings are defined in art. 4 of Regulation 1983/83; see also art. 5.

[179] See guidelines, para. 22.

[180] *XXIst Report on Competition Policy*, point 114.

[181] See *Siemens/Fanuc*, OJ 1985 L376/29, at p. 36; *Sole distribution agreements for whisky and gin*, OJ 1985 L369/19, at p. 23.

[182] Ibid. The Commission has stated at para. 20:

'It is the purpose of Article 3(b) to refuse the benefit of the group exemption to agreements under which a manufacturer entrusts the distribution of his goods to another manufacturer of competing goods, because the requirements of Article 85(3) of the Treaty might not then be fulfilled. It may be doubted whether a sole distributor would be sufficiently prepared to promote the sale of a certain product if he produces a competing product the market position of which might be weakened by such an effort. This conflict of interests could

Commission has suggested that it would prefer to examine such agreements individually.

In *Sole Distribution Agreements for Whisky and Gin*, the Commission adopted reasoning which weakens the confidence which manufacturers of similar products may place in the block exemption as an alternative to an individual exemption. The Commission stated that whisky and gin were not within the same market because 'a consumer looking for whisk(e)y or gin will not readily buy a spirit from another category, if no product belonging to the desired category is available'.[183] An analysis based on a consumer's choice if there are no supplies at all of the product which he seeks would appear to have little relevance for the determination of whether two products are identical or equivalent.

The Commission's suggestion that gin and genever, on one hand, and Scotch whisky, Irish whiskey, bourbon and Canadian whisky, on the other, should be grouped into only two markets for the purposes of art. 3(b) would appear to be a broadening of the notion of identical or equivalent products. Consumers of the products involved would probably find it quite surprising that Scotch whisky and bourbon, for example, are considered identical or equivalent. Indeed, the studies which the Commission relied on for its categorisation of products recognised significant differences in characteristics between products which the Commission grouped together.[184]

The uncertainty introduced by the Commission's reasoning in this decision is particularly unfortunate as it would appear from the legislative history of the regulation that one of the reasons for adopting the more specific language in Regulation 1983/83 was to ensure that in sectors such as alcohol distribution, art. 3(b) would not preclude companies with sales forces selling similar but not identical products the use of from using the most effective channels of distribution.[185]

---

impede the stimulation of competition between products of different manufacturers which Regulation (EEC) No. 1983/83 assumes normally to result from exclusive distributorship (see Recital 6 of the preamble). It may also be imagined that such an agreement could involve an arrangement between the two manufacturers to maintain their respective market shares and not to intensify competition between them.'

[183] *Sole distribution agreements for whisky and gin*, OJ 1985 L369/19, at p. 23.

[184] The Commission referred to its proposal laying down general rules on the definitive description and preparation of spirituous beverages and of vermouths and other wines of fresh grapes flavoured with plants or other aromatic substances, OJ 1982 C189/7. On the basis of this proposal, the Council adopted a regulation laying down general rules on the definition, description and presentation of spirit drinks (Regulation 1576/89, OJ 1989 L160/1). Article 5(3) of this regulation provides that spirit drinks may be given geographical indications, provided that they do not mislead consumers. These geographical designations shall be reserved for spirit drinks in the case of which the production stage during which they acquired their character and definitive qualities took place in the geographical area indicated. Annex II to the regulation lists gin and genever and Scotch and Irish whiskies among the products which can be given geographical designations.

[185] One of the last modifications in art. 3(b) was to change the word 'similar' to 'equivalent'. In its Resolution on the proposed Commission amendments to Regulation 67/67 (OJ 1983 C184/167), adopted on 10 June 1983, the European Parliament said, at point 9, that it:

¶330

¶331   No alternative sources of supply

The block exemption does not apply 'where users can obtain the contract goods in the contract territory only from the exclusive distributor and have no alternative sources of supply outside the contract territory'.[186] This provision should be seen in the light of the Commission's policy of ensuring intra-brand competition. Its purpose is to compel the supplier to supply directly to users within the territory when there is no other alternative source and to prevent the supplier from relying on the exclusive distribution agreement to refuse supplies.[187]

¶332   Interference with parallel imports

The regulation does not apply if either the supplier or the distributor takes steps to interfere with the ability of intermediaries or consumers to obtain goods from other dealers in the EC. In addition, if no alternative sources of supply exist within the common market, no actions should be taken to limit imports from outside of the common market. The relevant language states that the block exemption does not apply where:

> 'one or both of the parties makes it difficult for intermediaries or users to obtain the contract goods from other dealers inside the common market or, in so far as no alternative source of supply is available there, from outside the common market, in particular where one or both of them:
>
> (1) exercises industrial property rights so as to prevent dealers or users from obtaining outside, or from selling in, the contract territory properly marked or otherwise properly marketed contract goods;
>
> (2) exercises other rights or takes other measures so as to prevent dealers or

---

'Believes, in particular, that Article 3(b) concerning non-reciprocal agreements between competing manufacturers still poses considerable problems, and that for instance, it will cause considerable uncertainty on the borderline as to what are and what are not "similar" goods; considers that Article 3(b) will deprive many pro-competitive agreements of the benefit of the block exemption and impair inter-State trade.'

The explanatory statement of the Report of the Parliament's Committee on Economic and Monetary Affairs stated:

'Your rapporteur points out that Article 3(b) could have considerable practical importance in such fields as pharmaceuticals or alcohol spirits distribution, where it may often be the sales force of what the Commission would define as a competing manufacturer which is in the best position to distribute such products, and to permit the penetration of a product into a new market, thus enhancing rather than reducing competition. He would point out additionally that interpretation of the concept of "similar" goods could pose considerable difficulties. Are cognac and whisky similar? Where can the dividing line be drawn?'

European Parliament Working Documents (1983–1984), Document 1–357/83, 30 May 1903, p. 19.

[186] Regulation 1983/83, art. 3(c). See, e.g. *Tipp-Ex*, OJ 1987 L222/1, at p. 9, where the Commission held that certain authorised dealer contracts were outside the scope of Regulation 67/67 since they contained provisions which had the aim of protecting the exclusive distribution from parallel imports.

[187] In *Siemens/Fanuc*, OJ 1985 L376/29, at p. 34, the Commission found that the technical nature of the product was such that parallel imports were 'a less than satisfactory alternative to direct supplies'. See also, Daout 'Distribution under EEC law – An Official View', (1983) Fordham Corporate Law Institute 441, at pp. 445–446.

users from obtaining outside, or from selling in, the contract territory contract goods.'[188]

In *Van Vliet*, the court held that a clause in an agreement requiring the manufacturer to take action to prohibit intermediaries and consumers in the manufacturer's member state from exporting takes an agreement outside the block exemption even where the intermediaries have real possibilities of obtaining the product in other member states.[189]

It is not necessary to provide expressly in an agreement that the parties will not take action to prevent parallel trade. In *Hydrotherm v Compact*, the court interpreted the comparable provision of Regulation 67/67 relating to the exercise of industrial property rights. According to the court, this provision:

'must be interpreted as excluding an agreement from block exemption only if it is clear from the actual terms of the agreement or from the conduct of the parties that they intend to use, or are in fact using, an industrial property right in such a way as to prevent or impede, with the aid of that right parallel imports into the territory covered by the exclusive dealership. The fact that an agreement does not contain any provision to prevent abuse of an industrial property right is not in itself a sufficient reason for excluding that agreement from the application of Regulation No. 67/67.'[190]

The imposition of export bans or the creation of absolute territorial protection has often been held to fall within art. 3(d).[191]

¶333   Withdrawal of the block exemption

Like any exemption, the exclusive distribution block exemption may be withdrawn by the Commission if the agreement has effects that are incompatible with the conditions for exemption set out in art. 85(3) of the treaty.[192] The following examples of situations which could lead to the withdrawal of the exemption are specifically mentioned:

'(a) the contract goods are not subject, in the contract territory, to effective competition from identical goods or goods considered by users as equivalent in view of their characteristics, price and intended use;

(b) access by other suppliers to the different stages of distribution within the contract territory is made difficult to a significant extent;

---

[188] Regulation 1983/83, art. 3(d).
[189] *Van Vliet Kwastenfabriek v Dalle Crode* [1975] ECR 1103, at p. 1113.
[190] *Hydrotherm v Compact* [1984] ECR 2999, at p. 3020.
[191] *Gosme/Martell*, OJ 1991 L185/23; *Newitt/Dunlop Slazenger International & Ors*, OJ 1992 L131/32.
[192] See Regulation 19/65 on application of art. 85(3) of the treaty to certain categories of agreements and concerted practices, JO 1965 36/533, art. 7.

(c) for reasons other than those referred to in Article 3(c) and (d) it is not possible for intermediaries or users to obtain supplies of the contract goods from dealers outside the contract territory on the terms there customary;

(d) the exclusive distributor:

 1. without any objectively justified reason refuses to supply in the contract territory categories of purchasers who cannot obtain contract goods elsewhere on suitable terms or applies to them differing prices or conditions of sale;

 2. sells the contract goods at excessively high prices.'[193]

A withdrawal of the exemption may not be made retroactively and requires a decision of the Commission following the procedure set out in Regulation 17/62.[194]

Regulation 1983/83 constitutes a good starting point for the drafting of exclusive distribution agreements. Its value in creating legal certainty, however, has been reduced, rather than enhanced, by interpretations of the Commission. The suggestions that OEM agreements may not fall within the scope of the exemption may lead to an increase in notifications as such agreements are becoming more widespread. The Commission's broad interpretation of the notion of identical or equivalent products and its narrow interpretation of exclusivity as meaning simply that the supplier will only pay delivery costs on sales to one distributor per territory also cast doubt on the relevance of the block exemption to a large number of other agreements.

SELECTIVE DISTRIBUTION

¶334 Definition

'Selective distribution' is a form of distribution in which a supplier limits the sale of its product to a limited class of wholesalers and/or retailers. The Commission accepts that for certain types of products it is permissible to use distribution systems in which wholesalers and retailers must meet certain requirements. The Commission has said:

'Numerous manufactured products are sold by means of so-called 'selective distribution' systems. Manufacturers that operate such systems determine general rules governing sales with the aim of ensuring that specialized or complex products are properly marketed by the trade. With this in mind,

---

[193] Regulation 1983/83 art. 6.
[194] Guidelines para. 24.

they restrict the number of independent dealers and the location of sales points to degrees that vary according to the stringency of the requirements to be met by dealers seeking appointment and the freedom, retained by manufacturers in certain cases, to choose from various potentially qualified dealers. In many industries – particularly motor vehicles, photographic products, household electrical appliances, consumer electronics and perfumes – selective distribution is especially common.'[195]

Selective distribution systems have been found to be acceptable for consumer electronics products,[196] automobiles,[197] personal computers,[198] jewellery,[199] clocks and watches,[200] perfume,[201] dental products,[202] porcelain tableware,[203] photographic products[204] and newspapers.[205] The necessity of selective distribution systems has been questioned in cases dealing with plumbing fixtures[206] and watches.[207]

In addition to the nature of the product, the extent to which other suppliers of the same product rely on selective distribution systems may be an important factor in assessing a selective distribution system. Thus, in the first *Metro* case, the court mentioned the somewhat rigid price structure within the SABA distribution centre, but accepted that competition in the market had not been restricted. The court stated, however, that 'the Commission must ensure that this structural rigidity is not reinforced, as might happen if there were an

---

[195] *Ninth Report on Competition Policy*, point 5; see also *Thirteenth Report on Competition Policy*, point 33.
[196] *SABA*, OJ 1976 L28/19, on appeal: *Metro v EC Commission* [1977] ECR 1875; *Demo-Studio Schmidt*, *Eleventh Report on Competition Policy*, point 118, on appeal: *Demo-Studio Schmidt v EC Commission* [1983] ECR 3045; *SABA's EC distribution system*, OJ 1983 L376/41, on appeal: *Metro-SB-Grossmärkte GmbH & Co v EC Commission*, Case 354/85, removed by order of 25 February 1987, OJ 1987 C96/10; *Grundig's EC distribution system*, OJ 1985 L233/1. The Commission has renewed the individual exemption originally granted to *Grundig AG* pursuant to art. 8(2) of Regulation 17/62; *Grundig's EC distribution system*, Decision 94/29, OJ 1994 L20/15.
[197] *Bayerische Motoren Werke AG*, OJ 1975 L29/1; *Ford Werke AG*, OJ 1983 L327/31, on appeal: *Ford v EC Commission* [1985] ECR 2736. Regulation 123/85 provides for conditions under which a block exemption may be granted for selective distribution agreements in the automobile industry. For an analysis, see ¶339–¶351.
[198] *IBM personal computer*, OJ 1984 L118/24.
[199] *Murat*, OJ 1983 L348/20.
[200] *Omega*, JO 1970 L242/22; *Junghans*, OJ 1977 L30/10.
[201] *Procureur de la République v Giry and Guerlain* [1980] ECR 2329; *Anne Marty v Estée Lauder* [1980] ECR 2481; *Lancôme v Etos* [1980] ECR 2511; *Yves Saint Laurent Parfums*, OJ 1992 L12/24; *Parfums Givenchy*, OJ 1992 L236/11.
[202] *Ivoclar*, OJ 1985 L369/1.
[203] *Villeroy & Boch*, OJ 1985 L376/15.
[204] *Kodak*, JO 1970 L147/24, *Hasselblad*, OJ 1982 L161/18, on appeal: *Hasselblad v EC Commission* [1984] ECR 883.
[205] *Binon v Agence et Messageries de la Presse* [1985] ECR 2034.
[206] *Grohe's distribution system*, OJ 1985 L19/17, on appeal: *Friedrich Grohe Armaturenfabrik v EC Commission*, removed by order of 30 September 1987, OJ 1987 C307/10; *Ideal Standard's distribution system*, OJ 1985 L20/38, on appeal: *Ideal Standard v EC Commission*, removed by order of 30 September 1987, OJ 1987 C307/10.
[207] *ETA Fabriques d'Ebauches v DK Investment* [1985] ECR 3933. As a product becomes more technically simple, the Commission is apparently unwilling to recognise the need for a selective distribution system. Thus, in the 1970s Omega and Junghans watches were allowed to be distributed by a selective distribution system, but in 1985, the court questioned the need for a selective distribution system for Swatch watches.

¶334

increase in the number of selective distribution networks for marketing the same product'.[208] The structure of the German market for plumbing fixtures played a role in the Commission's rejection of the selective distribution systems notified by Grohe and Ideal Standard.[209] In the perfume cases the Commission noted that all the producers distributed their top-of-the-range articles only through comparable selective distribution networks, but emphasised that a sufficient degree of inter-brand competition was guaranteed as a result of the large number of producers active in the sector.[210]

An essential aspect of a selective distribution system is that the distributors in the system may only supply to end-users and to other distributors meeting the criteria for selection in the system.[210A] Appointment systems that provide a mark of approval to dealers meeting certain conditions but that do not withhold supplies from non-approved channels are unlikely to raise competition law problems in the absence of other restrictions.[211]

Restrictions on sales to unauthorised dealers outside of the selective distribution network are assessed on the same basis as the selection criteria. If the selection criteria do not violate art. 85(1), then the restriction on sales outside of the system will not violate art. 85(1).[212] Systems using selection criteria which would require an exemption will also require an exemption for any accompanying sales restrictions.[213]

For a selective distribution system to be compatible with the competition

---

[208] *Metro v EC Commission* [1977] ECR 1875, at p. 1905 (para. 22). In the second *Metro* case, although Advocate General VerLoren Van Themaat had accepted Metro's argument that the Commission did not adequately investigate the structure of the entire market, the court stated:

'the fact that Metro cannot obtain supplies of SABA products directly does not constitute an elimination of competition within the meaning of Article 85(3) when it is possible for Metro or other self-service wholesalers to market consumer electronics equipment, and colour television sets in particular, obtained from other producers.' (*Metro v EC Commission II* [1986] ECR 3074, at 3021, at p. 3089 (para. 64).)

Likewise, when renewing the individual exemption originally granted to Grundig, the Commission was of the opinion that competition between dealers was not eliminated, since a substantial number of competing manufacturers marketed their products without a selective distribution system. 'Consequently, there is in particular no danger of certain forms of distribution such as discount stores, cash-and-carry wholesalers and retail supermarkets being generally excluded from selling such products.' *Grundig's EC distribution system*, OJ 1994 L20/15, at p. 22 (para. 41).

[209] See *Grohe's distribution system*, OJ 1985 L19/17; *Ideal Standard's distribution system*, OJ 1985 L20/38. John Ferry, then Director of DG IV, stated at a conference that: 'Before you get to feel that we were harsh about the plumbers in Grohe and Ideal-Standard you should remember two things; both those selective distribution systems were installed simultaneously by two companies who between them had almost sixty per cent of the market – don't hold me to that figure, but it was large – and it was done under pressure from the plumbers themselves because they were finding that they were losing considerable money to the do-it-yourself boys. And so, there was a very strong element there of abuse, if you like, although we didn't technically find it.'

[210] *Yves Saint Laurent Parfums*, OJ 1992 L12/24, at pp. 25 and 30; *Parfums Givenchy*, OJ 1992 L236/11, at pp. 12 and 21–22.

[210A] A distribution system does not lose its effective character by virtue of the fact that the goods are distributed in independent channels outside of the Community. See *Metro SB Großmärkte GmbH v Cartier SA*, Case C-376/92, judgment of 13 January 1994 (not yet reported).

[211] *Krups*, OJ 1980 L120/26.

[212] See, e.g. *Murat*, OJ 1983 L348/20.

[213] See, e.g. *SABA's EC distribution system*, OJ 1983 L376/41, at p. 45.

rules, it is important that dealers have the opportunity to obtain their supplies from any source within the system.[214] The Commission has put particular emphasis on this requirement in its most recent case law.[215] In *Yves Saint Laurent Parfums*, for instance, the Commission insisted on the deletion of a provision restricting the ability of authorised retailers to resell the products concerned to network members established in the same member state. As a result of the Commission's intervention, the agreement was amended so as to allow each authorised retailer to resell to or obtain supplies from any other authorised retailer established in any member state, including the member state in which he himself is established.

Finally, systems for policing the compliance with the system's rules on sales outside the system will be treated in the same way as the rules themselves.[216] Nevertheless, the Commission's more recent case law imposes certain limitations on the procedures which may be used in order to monitor such compliance. In *Yves Saint Laurent Parfums*,[217] for instance, the Commission insisted on the deletion of provisions according to which authorised retailers had to communicate systematically copies of invoices or vouchers for each transaction with other authorised retailers. In *Parfums Givenchy*, the right to consult copies of the invoices for resales to other authorised retailers was limited to cases where Givenchy possessed evidence directly suggesting the contractual liability of the authorised retailer.[218]

¶335 Criteria for admission

The Commission has established three broad categories of requirements upon which a selective distribution system may be based:[219]

(1) *Objective qualitative requirements* – These are requirements which relate to the nature of the product which may call for specific technical

---

[214] Id., at p. 50.
[215] *Yves Saint Laurent Parfums*, OJ 1992 L12/24, at p. 27; *Parfums Givenchy*, OJ 1992 L236/11, at p. 14; Notice pursuant to art. 19(3) of Council Regulation 17/62 concerning a notification in cases IV/34.114 – *Kenwood Electronics Deutschland GmbH* (Car audio), IV/34.116 – *Kenwood Electronics Deutschland GmbH* (Amateur-radio equipment) and, IV/23.117 – *Kenwood Electronics Deutschland GmbH* (Hi-fi), OJ 1993 C67/9; *Grundig's EC distribution system*, OJ 1994 L20/15, at p. 22 (para. 39).
[216] *SABA's EC distribution system*, OJ 1983 L376/41, at p. 46. But see *Grundig's EC distribution system*, OJ 1985 L233/1, at p. 5, where policing obligations were said to have no independent anti-competitive character.
[217] OJ 1992 L12/24, at p. 27.
[218] OJ 1992 L236/11, at p. 14. In *Grundig's EC distribution system*, OJ 1994 L20/15, at p. 20 (para. 29–30), authorised dealers, when reselling authorised products, were required to take note of the purchaser, date of purchase and serial numbers of the products resold and pass on this information to Grundig upon request. The Commission considered this provision to be non-restrictive of competition as Grundig's right to request such information was limited 'to cases where checking of distribution appears necessary for technical reasons or because there is a valid suspicion that the EC distribution system has been breached...'. Furthermore, Grundig was under obligation to report to the Commission annually on cases where it made use of its rights to request information.
[219] See, e.g. *Fifth Report on Competition Policy*, point 12.

qualifications regarding the distributor, his staff or business premises (see ¶336).

(2) *Qualitative requirements combined with additional obligations* – This category covers situations in which selection is not based exclusively on the technical expertise required from the distributor but additionally on his willingness to assume certain other obligations (e.g. his co-operation in sales promotion) (see ¶337).

(3) *Quantitative requirements* – This category includes whatever criteria a manufacturer uses to impose quantitative limits on the number of authorised distributors (see ¶338).

¶336   Objective qualitative criteria

In general, objective qualitative criteria are criteria directly related to the nature of the product. Provided that there is no discrimination in the application of such criteria and that the system is open to all potential dealers who meet the criteria, it is well established that such criteria do not violate art. 85(1).

In assessing the compatibility with art. 85(1) of 'simple' selective distribution systems based solely on objective qualitative criteria, it is important to consider two factors:

(1) the presence of similar systems for competing products; and

(2) the nature of the product.

Systems which otherwise would not be found to violate art. 85(1) may be found to restrict competition if the presence of other selective distribution systems prevents particular types of distributors from obtaining products sold under competing brands. In the second *Metro* case, the court stated:

'It must be borne in mind that, although the Court has held in previous decisions that "simple" selective distribution systems are capable of constituting an aspect of competition compatible with Article 85(1) of the Treaty, there may nevertheless be a restriction or elimination of competition where the existence of a certain number of such systems does not leave any room for other forms of distribution based on a different type of competition policy or results in a rigidity in price structure which is not counterbalanced by other aspects of competition between products of the same brand and by the existence of effective competition between different brands.'[220]

---

[220] *Metro v EC Commission (Metro II)* [1986] ECR 3021, at p. 3085 (para. 40). See also *Grundig's EC distribution system*, OJ 1994 L20/15, at p. 22 (para. 41).

¶336

The classification of various criteria as 'objective qualitative criteria' will vary depending upon the nature of the product.[221] In a case involving perfume, the court stated:

'In order to determine the exact nature of such qualitative criteria for the selection of re-sellers, it is also necessary to consider whether the characteristics of the product in question necessitate a selective distribution system in order to preserve its quality and ensure its proper use, and whether those objectives are not already satisfied by national rules governing admission to the re-sale trade or the conditions of sale of the product in question.'[222]

Criteria that may be found not to violate art. 85(1) in distribution systems for one product may be found to violate art. 85(1) when applied to another product.[223]

---

[221] In reply to Written Question No. 2906/87, OJ 1989 C77/9, the Commission stated that it considers taking action against some systems of selective distribution of health care products and it pointed out that it is doubtful that a system of distribution for milk powder and milk-based babyfoods exclusively through chemists satisfies the Commission's policy towards selective distribution. In *APB*, OJ 1990 L18/35, the Commission secured amendments to an agreement concerning the distribution in Belgium of pharmaceutical products in pharmacies. The initial agreement required manufacturers to sell pharmaceutical products bearing the APB guarantee mark only in pharmacies and prohibited the sale of the products concerned (whether stamped with the guarantee mark or not) through distribution channels other than pharmacies. Following a statement of objections, APB amended its agreement so that the exclusivity only applies to products bearing the stamp and the manufacturers are free to sell the same products without a stamp through distribution channels other than pharmacies. In *Vichy*, OJ 1991 L75/57, the Commission decided on the basis of a preliminary examination pursuant to art. 15(6) of Regulation 17/62 that an exemption under art. 85(3) of Vichy's distribution system for cosmetics was not justified. The requirement imposed by Vichy to sell its cosmetics only through pharmacies was considered to be a factor that restricted the number of potential sellers in a quantitative manner. In this context, the Commission noted that a 'producer's freedom of choice in determining the way in which his products are distributed must remain subject to the principle of proportionality between the properties of the product and the selection criteria imposed by the producer' (ibid., at p. 60). The 'sale through pharmacists' criterion was deemed to go beyond what is necessary for maintaining quality and ensuring the proper use of the product. The fact that L'Oréal, one of Vichy's competitors, sells its top-range brands in luxury perfumeries by sales' staff not holding scientific diplomas, but by staff professionally qualified as beauticians, seems to have played a role in the Commission arriving at this determination. The Court of First Instance upheld this decision (*Société d'hygiène dermatologique de Vichy v EC Commission* [1992] ECR II–415).

[222] *L'Oréal v De Nieuwe AMCK* [1980] ECR 3775. at p. 3791 (para. 16).

[223] In *Grohe's distribution system*, OJ 1985 L19/17, at pp. 20–21 (para. 15), the Commission said:

'Since it is doubtful whether plumbing fittings can be considered as technically advanced products and since wholesalers generally do not sell directly to final consumers but to retailers, it is questionable, at least at wholesaler level, whether the characteristics of the products necessitate a selective distribution system in order to preserve their quality and ensure their proper use. It is thus doubtful whether the purely qualitative criteria which Grohe imposes in its dealership agreement with wholesalers are compatible with Article 85(1) of the EEC Treaty.'

See also *Ideal Standard's distribution system*, OJ 1985 L20/38, at p. 41.

On the other hand, when reviewing the exemption originally granted to Grundig, the Commission considered that a selective distribution system at the wholesaler level for consumer electronics products was justified. The

¶337   Additional obligations

Apart from objective qualitative criteria, some selective distribution agreements impose additional conditions which are not directly related to the nature of the goods covered by the system. The effect of such additional requirements is to limit the number of dealers eligible for entry to the system to a class which is smaller than those meeting the objective qualitative requirements. The Commission generally treats such provisions as violations of art. 85(1),[224] but may exempt agreements containing such provisions pursuant to art. 85(3).

¶338   Quantitative criteria

Quantitative limitations are those by which the number of dealers in a selective distribution system is limited. The Commission views quantitative limitations as very restrictive of competition and will only provide an exemption under art. 85(3) in exceptional circumstances.

In its 1970 *Omega* decision,[225] the Commission allowed quantitative limits on the number of dealers allowed to join the system. The Commission's exemption was based on the fact that the products – Omega watches – were luxury products which were produced in limited quantities. This justification for a limited number of dealers has not been repeated in cases since 1970. In fact, in submissions to the court in a later case, the Commission stated that a '[q]uantitative limitation of the number of traders at the distribution level goes beyond the objective requirements for the maintenance of a product as a luxury product'.[226]

Apart from the *Omega* case – which no longer reflects the Commission's thinking – selective distribution systems based on quantitative criteria have also been allowed in the automobile sector based on the understanding that the technical complexity and inherent risks of the product require exceptionally close co-operation between manufacturer and dealer, thus justifying quantitative limitations on the number of authorised dealers.[227]

Commission stressed the retailers' needs, when providing advice and service to the consumer, to receive appropriate information and backing from the wholesalers. Consequently, it is appropriate, under a selective distribution system, for product-related advice and servicing to be provided at all distribution levels, and this justifies requirements along these lines being imposed on wholesalers'. It is interesting to note that Grundig reserved the right to waive individual criteria imposed on wholesalers in member states where 'the wholesale trade ... is generally confined to purely distributive function' and does not imply advice and back-up to specialised retailers; see *Grundig's EC distribution system*, OJ 1994 L20/15, at p. 19 (para. 26(c) and 27).

[224] There are cases where selection criteria that go further than objective qualitative criteria were considered not to violate art. 85(1). See, e.g. *Villeroy & Boch*, OJ 1985 L376/15, at pp. 18–19, where certain sales promotion requirements were held not to violate art. 85(1).

[225] *Omega*, JO 1970 L242/22.

[226] *Procureur de la République v Giry and Guerlain* [1980] ECR 2329, at p. 2352.

[227] In *Bayerische Motoren Werke AG*, OJ 1975 L29/1, at p. 7, the Commission stated:

The Commission has been hostile to quantitative limitations in a number of cases. In a case imposing a fine on a Swedish manufacturer of photographic equipment and its distributors, the Commission stated:

'Hasselblad (GB) refuses to admit dealers to its distribution network for reasons additional to those laid down in the Dealer Agreement and rejects some dealers who satisfy all the terms and conditions of the distribution arrangement. This hinders potential competition within the territories allotted to authorised dealers. Resellers are thus selected not only on the basis of objective criteria of a qualitative nature but on the basis of the quantitative assessment made by Hasselblad (GB).'[228]

In *Vichy*, the Commission considered that the requirement to sell certain products only through pharmacies added to the professional qualification element an additional factor that restricted the number of potential sellers in a quantitative manner. The Commission noted that in eight of the member states a quantitative ceiling to the establishment of pharmacies applied and made reference to the *BINON/AMP* case where the court held that criteria for the selection of sellers based on a minimum number of inhabitants per sales point were quantitative in nature. According to the Commission, the result would be the same if sales were restricted to a certain type of outlet (i.e. pharmacies) the establishment of which is restricted.[229] The Court of First Instance confirmed that through national legislation (the quantitative ceiling for pharmacies) the Vichy selection criteria acquired a quantitative character.[230]

Even though quantitative restrictions that relate to the total number of outlets are unlikely to be exempted, it is possible to limit the number of first-level distributors to one per territory by using the exclusive distribution block exemption.[231] By analogy to the exclusive distribution block exemption, the Commission has granted individual exemptions to selective distribution

---

'Motor vehicles, being products of limited life, high cost and complex technology, require regular maintenance by specially equipped garages or service depots, because their use can be dangerous to life, health and property and can have a harmful effect on the environment.'

This principle is repeated in recital 4 of Regulation 123/85:

'The exclusive and selective distribution clauses can be regarded as indispensable measures of rationalization in the motor vehicle industry because motor vehicles are consumer durables which at both regular and irregular intervals require expert maintenance and repair, not always in the same place. Motor vehicle manufacturers cooperate with the selected dealers and repairers in order to provide specialized servicing for the product. On grounds of capacity and efficiency alone, such a form of cooperation cannot be extended to an unlimited number of dealers and repairers.'

[228] *Hasselblad*, OJ 1982 L161/18, at p. 29. This decision was upheld by the Court of Justice: *Hasselblad v EC Commission* [1984] ECR 883.
[229] *Vichy*, OJ 1991 L75/57, at p. 60.
[230] *Société d'hygiène dermatologique de Vichy v EC Commission* [1992] ECR II–415 at pp. 442–443 (para. 68).
[231] See ¶317 ff.

¶338

systems which include more than one first-level distributor within a territory, but where the total number of first-level distributors was limited.[232]

¶339   The treatment of particular clauses in selective distribution agreements[233]

The analytical division which is often used by the Commission is not applied clearly in practice. The use of certain selection criteria may be considered a violation of art. 85(1) for one type of product, but not for another product. Identical criteria may fall under different classifications in different cases. Finally, criteria grouped within the same classification may receive different treatment under art. 85(1).

For products for which a selective distribution system is justified, the Commission has generally accepted, as not falling under art. 85(1), selection criteria relating to:

(1) the requirement that the goods be sold in a specialist shop or in a self-contained specialist department;[234]

(2) the technical qualifications and specialised knowledge of the staff;[235]

(3) the fittings and appearance of the shop;[236]

(4) the hours during which the shop is open;[237]

(5) the provision of guarantee and after-sales service;[238]

(6) a favourable banker's reference and credit rating;[239]

---

[232] See, e.g. *Junghans*, OJ 1977 L30/10, at p. 15.

[233] Examples of additional clauses are set out in ¶376 of this chapter and in ¶339–¶351 dealing with automobile selective distribution agreements.

[234] See, e.g. *Murat*, OJ 1983 L348/20, at p. 22; *Villeroy & Boch*, OJ 1985 L376/15, at p. 18; *Yves Saint Laurent Parfums*, OJ 1992 L12/24, at pp. 29–30; *Parfums Givenchy*, OJ 1992 L236/11, at p. 16; Notice pursuant to art. 19(3) of Council Regulation 17/62 concerning a notification in Cases IV/34.114 – *Kenwood Electronics Deutschland GmbH* (Car audio), IV/34.116 – *Kenwood Electronics Deutschland GmbH* (Amateur-radio equipment) and, IV/23.117 – *Kenwood Electronics Deutschland GmbH* (Hi-fi), OJ 1993 C67/9; *Grundig's EC distribution system*, OJ 1994 L20/15.

[235] See, e.g. *Grundig's EEC distribution system*, OJ 1985 L233/1, at p. 4; *IBM personal computer*, OJ 1984 L118/24, at p. 27; *Parfums Givenchy*, OJ 1992 L236/11, at p. 12; *Yves Saint Laurent Parfums*, OJ 1992 L12/24, at p. 25; Notice pursuant to art. 19(3) of Council Regulation 17/62 concerning a notification in Cases IV/34.114 – *Kenwood Electronics Deutschland GmbH* (Car audio), IV/34.116 – *Kenwood Electronics Deutschland GmbH* (Amateur-radio equipment) and, IV/23.117 – *Kenwood Electronics Deutschland GmbH* (Hi-fi), OJ 1993 C67/9; *Grundig's EC Distribution system*, OJ 1994 L20/15.

[236] See, e.g. *Grundig's EC distribution system*, OJ 1985 L233/1, at p. 4; *Murat*, OJ 1983 L348/20, at p. 22; *Yves Saint Laurent Parfums*, OJ 1992 L12/24, at p. 29 and *Parfums Givenchy*, OJ 1992 L236/11, at p. 16.

[237] See, e.g. *Demo-Studio Schmidt*, *Eleventh Report on Competition Policy*, point 118; *Grundig's EC Distribution system*, OJ 1994 L20/15.

[238] See, e.g. *Junghans*, OJ 1977 L30/10, at p. 14; *IBM personal computer*, OJ 1984 L118/24, at p. 27; *SABA's EC distribution system*, OJ 1983 L376/41, at p. 45; Notice pursuant to art. 19(3) of Council Regulation 17/62 concerning a notification in Cases IV/34.114 – *Kenwood Electronics Deutschland GmbH* (Car audio), IV/34.116 – *Kenwood Electronics Deutschland GmbH* (Amateur-radio equipment) and, IV/23.117 – *Kenwood Electronics Deutschland GmbH* (Hi-fi), OJ 1993 C67/9; *Grundig's EC distribution system*, OJ 1994 L20/15).

[239] See, e.g. *IBM personal computer*, OJ 1984 L118/24, at p. 25.

(7) the requirement that the retailer undertakes to have his staff attend training sessions.[240]

In the first *SABA* decision, the Commission stated that the obligation for a wholesaler to participate in the setting up of a distribution system would not violate art. 85(1).[241] However, the Court of Justice overruled the Commission on this point. As justification, the court put forward a particularly one-sided conception of the role of a wholesaler, stating:

'However, the Commission maintains (paragraph 28 of the decision) that the obligation upon wholesalers to participate "in the creation of a distribution network" does not constitute a restriction on competition coming within the ambit of Article 85(1).

That appraisal does not take proper cognizance of the scope of that provision since the function of a wholesaler is not to promote the products of a particular manufacturer but rather to provide for the retail trade supplies obtained on the basis of competition between manufacturers, so that obligations entered into by a wholesaler which limit his freedom in this respect constitute restrictions on competition.'[242]

The view that an undertaking to take action on behalf of a particular supplier may reduce the attention a distributor can devote to other products underlies the Commission's thinking with respect to several clauses.[243]

Thus, in its second *SABA* decision, the Commission found that requirements obliging distributors to carry a full range of products, to maintain sufficient stocks, and to agree to annual sales targets required a particular sales effort in relation to SABA products and were therefore contrary to art. 85(1), but granted an exemption under art. 85(3). The Commission stated that:

'These obligations in terms of sales effort also restrict dealers who join the network in their competitive behaviour. By forcing them to make a special effort to promote SABA products, they restrict the dealers' freedom to pursue their own sales policy vis-à-vis their retailer or consumer customers, taking advantage of competition between different manufacturers.'[244]

Although in *SABA* and *Grundig* the Commission concluded that these types of requirements might reduce the freedom of distributors to sell competing products, similar requirements have been found not to violate art. 85(1) in

---

[240] *Yves Saint Laurent Parfums*, OJ 1992 L12/24, at p. 29 and *Parfums Givenchy*, OJ 1992 L236/11, at p. 16.
[241] See *SABA*, OJ 1976 L28/19, at p. 25.
[242] *Metro v EC Commission ('Metro I')* [1977] ECR 1875, at p. 1914 (para. 40).
[243] See, e.g. *Ideal Standard's distribution system*, OJ 1985 L20/38, at p. 42.
[244] *SABA's EC distribution system*, OJ 1983 L376/41, at p. 46; see also *Yves Saint Laurent Parfums*, OJ 1992 L12/24, at p. 30 and *Parfums Givenchy*, OJ 1992 L236/11, at p. 30; *Grundig's EC distribution system*, OJ 1994 L20/15, at p. 21.

other cases. In *Murat*, an obligation to take at least three months supplies at one time was considered to be not restrictive of competition because such a quantity was 'less than that customary in the trade.'[245] In *Villeroy & Boch*, the Commission found that obligations to maintain adequate stocks and to display a wide range of Villeroy & Boch products was not restrictive of competition because the market was very competitive and because Villeroy & Boch itself encouraged retailers to carry the products of other porcelain manufacturers.[246]

In several cases, especially those concerning consumer electronics, the Commission has tried to ensure that selective distribution systems allow dealers the freedom to sell competing products. Nevertheless, for other products, the Commission has permitted restrictions placed on a dealer's activities with respect to competing products. In *BMW*, the Commission allowed a prohibition on the sale by BMW dealers of motor vehicles of other makes and of parts not complying with BMW's quality standards of quality. The agreement, however, allowed dealers to request that the prohibition on dealing in competing products should be lifted if they could show reasonable cause. In addition, the dealers were free to sell competing accessories which were not 'particularly important' for the safety of the vehicle.[247]

The Commission has also permitted an obligation on dealers not to mix products of a similar appearance but different quality with the product supplied under the selective distribution agreement.[248]

The Commission has permitted suppliers to place certain restrictions on the advertising of products by distributors in a selective distribution system. If the selective distribution agreement contains an obligation to provide advisory or after-sales services, the distributor may be prohibited from advertising products at 'cash-and-carry, self-service or take-away prices' because this would be an encouragement to the customer to waive services that the distributor should supply.[249] The Commission has also permitted as compatible with art. 85(1) the requirement that a dealer submit advertising to the supplier prior to use, provided that the advertising does not show prices.[250]

In the perfume cases, the Commission not only permitted requirements on the achievement of minimum annual purchases, the maintenance of certain stocks and co-operation in advertising and promotion activities, it also

---

[245] *Murat*, OJ 1983 L348/20, at p. 22.

[246] *Villeroy & Boch*, OJ 1985 L376/15, at p. 18.

[247] *Bayerische Motoren Werke AG*, OJ 1975 L29/1, at p. 8.

[248] See, e.g. *Murat*, OJ 1983 L348/20, at p. 22; In *Yves Saint Laurent Parfums*, OJ 1991 L12/24, at p. 29 and *Parfums Givenchy*, OJ 1992 L236/11, at p. 16, the Commission considered a ban on selling other goods which, through their proximity, are liable to detract from the product's brand image to be non-restrictive. The Commission accepted that this obligation was merely intended to safeguard, in the public's mind, the aura of prestige and exclusivity inherent in the products in question, thus preventing any association with lower quality goods.

[249] *Grundig's EC distribution system*, OJ 1994 L20/15, at p. 20.

[250] *IBM personal computer*, OJ 1984 L118/24, at p. 26.

¶339

exempted an obligation on authorised retailers in whose territory a new product had not yet been launched to refrain from engaging in active sales of such product for one year after the date on which it was first launched in the Community.[251]

¶340 The process of approving dealers

The Commission is concerned that selective distribution systems should not be applied in a discriminatory manner and that all potential dealers meeting the selection criteria be admitted as dealers. In its *Eleventh Report on Competition Policy*, the Commission stated:

'Where refusal to appoint a dealer results from discriminatory application of a distribution system, its compatibility with Article 85 is brought into question. An obligation may then be imposed on the manufacturer to refrain from impeding the dealer's access to his products.'[252]

Although the refusal to approve a dealer may appear to be a unilateral act by the manufacturer, the Commission and the Court of Justice have readily inferred the existence of an agreement so as to justify the application of art. 85.

In *AEG-Telefunken*, a case in which the Commission decided that AEG was misusing its selective distribution system by refusing to supply dealers who did not comply with its pricing policy, the Court of Justice stated:

'The view must therefore be taken that even refusals of approval are acts performed in the context of the contractual relations with authorised distributors inasmuch as their purpose is to guarantee observance of the agreements in restraint of competition which form the basis of contracts between manufacturers and approved distributors. Refusals to approve distributors who satisfy the qualitative criteria mentioned above therefore supply proof of an unlawful application of the system if their number is sufficient to preclude the possibility that they are isolated cases not forming part of systematic conduct.'[253]

The Court of Justice has held that the refusal to supply a dealer not meeting

---

[251] *Yves Saint Laurent Parfums*, OJ 1992 L12/24, at p. 30 para. 6(b),(c), (d) and p. 34; *Parfums Givenchy*, OJ 1992 L236/11, at p. 17, para. 6(b), (d), (e) and p. 20.

[252] *Eleventh Report on Competition Policy*, point 11.

[253] *AEG v EC Commission* [1983] ECR 3151, at pp. 3195–3196 (para. 39). It should be noted that the 'systematic conduct' was based on approximately 20 cases out of a system of 12,000 dealers.

objective qualitative criteria is not a discriminatory application of a selective distribution system.[254]

The Commission has introduced safeguards to prevent abuse in the selection process.[255] Thus, in *Murat*,[256] the Commission required the supplier to amend its standard form agreement so that retailers would be free to sell the products to any retailers meeting the prescribed technical and professional requirements regardless of whether they had been authorised by the supplier. Any retailer can check himself whether these requirements are met.

In its renewal of the *SABA* exemption[257] the Commission required SABA to adopt the following procedure as regards admission and expulsion:

(1) each application for admission must be decided upon by SABA within four weeks and in the absence of a decision within the prescribed time limit the applicant must be deemed admitted;

(2) all SABA wholesalers must also be entitled to admit dealers that satisfy the selection criteria, subject to SABA's right to expel dealers who have been wrongly admitted;

(3) dealers can be expelled only for cause and if they object final expulsion is only possible after a decision by a court.

The selective distribution system considered in the *IBM personal computer*[258] decision provides for the following admission and expulsion terms:

(1) dealers are appointed for a three-year term, which is renewable. The dealer may terminate the agreement at any time but IBM may terminate the agreement only if IBM completely ceases distribution by dealers or as a result of a breach of contract by the dealer;

(2) a dealer may nominate other prospective dealers and IBM undertakes to process such nominations within two months.

In *Villeroy & Boch*, however, the Commission stated:

'The principle that the producer should himself verify the qualifications of specialised retailers admitted to the network is necessary to ensure that the

---

[254] *Demo-Studio Schmidt, Eleventh Report on Competition Policy*, point 118.

[255] In the *Thirteenth Report on Competition Policy*, point 33, the Commission stated:

'An enquiry which the Commission conducted in 1979 among a number of firms in the consumer electronics sector following a succession of complaints, revealed that where only the manufacturer or the exclusive distributor had the right to recognize dealers' qualifications, they could use it to refuse admission to and thereby neutralize qualified retailers who were suspected of price undercutting or exporters/importers thought to be exploiting differences in the prices of the manufacturer's products in different parts of the common market. The enquiry also revealed that dealers already in the network who acted in this way had been excluded from it or threatened with exclusion or subjected to other pressures.'

[256] *Murat*, OJ 1983 L348/20.

[257] *SABA's EC distribution system*, OJ 1983 L376/41, at pp. 47–49.

[258] *IBM personal computer*, OJ 1984 L118/24, at p. 26.

selective distribution system is uniform and remains closed. In as much as it is accessory to the main obligation of specialization incumbent on the retailer, and contributes to ensuring compliance with that obligation, the principle that the producer should himself control the access of specialised retailers to the network does not go beyond what is necessary to maintain the network.'[259]

Although this statement appears to go back to the Commission's pre-*AEG-Telefunken*[260] approach concerning selection, the liberal approach taken in *Villeroy & Boch* may be a result of the fact that Villeroy & Boch's system was relatively open.

In *Yves Saint Laurent Parfums*[261] and *Parfums Givenchy*[262] cases, the Commission held that the admission procedure was contrary to art. 85(1) of the treaty, but was entitled to an exemption pursuant to art. 85(3). Both admission procedures essentially consist of an inspection of the retail outlet to determine whether the necessary qualitative requirements are met. This inspection must be carried out within a maximum period of three months, in the case of Givenchy, and five months, in the case of Yves Saint Laurent. The inspection results in one of the following outcomes :

- If the inspection reveals that the application does not even approach the qualitative criteria, the applicant must be informed thereof in writing and reasons must be provided.

- If the application is capable of meeting the qualitative requirements, but certain additional work is necessary, the applicant is informed in writing and is given three months (which period may be extended to six months at his request) to carry out the necessary work. If the work is completed within that period, the account will be opened within nine months from the date of initial inspection.

- If the application satisfies the qualitative criteria, the applicant is informed accordingly in writing and its account will be opened within a period of nine months following the inspection date.

The duration of the application procedure was found to be likely to affect competition since it could discourage certain potentially qualified candidates. Nevertheless, the Commission exempted the procedure since it was considered necessary to ensure the flexible integration of new resellers into the distribution network and to facilitate the transition from a closed distribution system based on quantitative criteria to a system based only on qualitative criteria.

---

[259] *Villeroy & Boch*, OJ 1985 L376/15, at p. 18.
[260] *AEG-Telefunken AG v EC Commission* [1983] ECR 3151.
[261] *Yves Saint Laurent Parfums*, OJ 1992 L12/24 , at pp. 26, 30, 32 and 33.
[262] *Parfums Givenchy*, OJ 1992 L236/11, at pp. 13, 17, 18 and 20.

¶340

In its renewal of the Grundig exemption[263] (*Grundig's EC distribution system*, OJ 1994 L20/15, at p. 20), the Commission considered that the procedure for admission and exclusion of wholesalers and retailers was 'unobjectionable'.

¶341   The use of the selective distribution rules to regulate an industry: the case of motor vehicles

Selective distribution of motor vehicles is governed by Regulation 123/85, which grants a block exemption to certain categories of motor vehicle distribution and servicing agreements.[264]

Viewed from the standpoint of competition policy, the significance of this regulation is two-fold. First, it is a striking example of the Commission's desire to regulate contractual relations in a specific economic sector in minute detail.[265] Secondly, by exerting pressure on motor vehicle manufacturers to realign their prices throughout the EC, the regulation represents an attempt to use competition rules to regulate pricing. It is questionable whether either of these goals belong to competition law as properly understood.

The provisions of Regulation 123/85 are considered at ¶342–¶351.

---

[263] The provisions for admission and exclusion are as follows:

(1) applications for admissions are decided upon within an appropriate period of four weeks;
(2) ordinary notice to terminate may only be given by Grundig in the event of the entire distribution network being abandoned;
(3) notice on important grounds and/or the withholding of supplies may be decided by Grundig in the event of unfair competition, if the allegations are not denied or have been proved in court.

[264] Commission Regulation 123/85 on the application of art. 85(3) of the treaty to certain categories of motor vehicle distribution and servicing agreements, OJ 1985 L15/16.

See *Seventeenth Report on Competition Policy*, point 34: After adoption of this regulation, the Commission informed motor vehicle manufacturers and traders that had notified agreements '... that although the general block exemption regulations for exclusive distribution and exclusive purchasing agreements (No. 1983/83 and 1984/83) were inapplicable to motor dealerships because the contracts prohibited resale to dealers not in the official distribution network, any agreement satisfying the conditions of Article 1 to 6 of Regulation No. 123/85 was already exempt and so did not require individual exemption to give the parties legal security'. In this regard, any notification of a motor vehicle manufacturer's agreement (unless it applied for individual exemption of restrictive clauses going beyond those exempted by the regulation) was considered as having lapsed on 1 July 1985 and the file was considered closed.

[265] Commenting on the draft regulation on the applicability of art. 85(3) of the treaty to certain categories of motor vehicle distribution and servicing agreements, OJ 1983 C341/18, the Economic and Social Committee stated that:

'A regulation laying down a standard contract governing relations between manufacturers and dealers is not regarded as desirable. Nor would this seem to be the Commission's intention. Under these circumstances the Committee considers that the draft Regulation must not go beyond the definition of some fundamental principles governing relations between manufacturers and dealers, and that sufficient scope should be left for the exercise of contractual freedom within a framework of genuine consultation.

The Committee has already voiced its views on this subject on a separate occasion ... and believes that the Commission should not adopt too many specific regulations applicable to individual economic sectors.'

¶342   Motor vehicle distribution: territorial exclusivity

Regulation 123/85 exempts motor vehicle distribution agreements to which only two undertakings are party and in which one party agrees to supply motor vehicles[266] and spare parts[267] within a defined territory of the EC:

(1) only to the other party, or

(2) only to the other party and to a specified number of other undertakings within the distribution system.[268]

The exemption also applies where the supplier is required not to sell contract goods to final consumers or to provide them with servicing for contract goods in the contract territory.[269] The territorial protection extended to the dealer may be diluted during the course of the agreement in so far as the supplier may appoint additional dealers within the contract territory if the supplier is able to show that objectively valid reasons exist for doing so.[270] For example, if there is sudden increase in demand caused by a change in traffic patterns or the opening of new offices to which the original dealer is unable to respond as a result of limited space or capital, the supplier could presumably appoint an additional dealer within the territory.[271]

The loose notion of exclusivity adopted in Regulation 123/85 results from the Commission's attempt to bring this regulation within the terms of Regulation 19/65, the enabling regulation that empowers the Commission to issue block exemptions to categories of bilateral agreements, including exclusive supply agreements 'whereby one party agrees with the other to supply only to that other certain goods for resale within a defined area of the Common Market.'[272] The difficulty encountered by the Commission in seeking to inject the necessary element of exclusivity into Regulation 123/85 was the industry practice according to which dealers were granted areas of primary responsibility which could be altered when necessary, rather than exclusive

---

[266] The scope of the regulation is limited to 'motor vehicles intended for use on public roads and having three or more road wheels'. Agricultural machinery (*XXth Report on Competition Policy*, point 42) and motorcycles (*XXIst Report on Competition Policy for 1991*, point 123) do not fall within the scope of the regulation. Moreover, the Commission has made it clear that distribution agreements for agricultural machinery and motorcycles that are modelled after Regulation 123/85 are in principle not eligible for an individual exemption (ibid.).

[267] In *ARG/Unipart*, OJ 1988 L45/34, the Commission stated that since Regulation 123/85 only governs agreements for the combined distribution of new motor vehicles and parts thereof, an agreement concerning the co-ordination of the purchase of parts from third parties as well as restrictions on distribution and on product range was not covered by the regulation.

[268] Regulation 123/85, art. 1.

[269] Regulation 123/85, art. 2. This provision would not seem to deprive the supplier of the possibility of reserving the right to supply certain categories of customers, such as public authorities, fleet owners and diplomats. See Stöver, speech delivered at the Law Society, Solicitors' European Group, 28 November 1985.

[270] Regulation 123/85, art. 5(2)(1)(b).

[271] See Stöver, speech delivered at the Law Society, Solicitors' European Group, 28 November 1985.

[272] Regulation 19/65.

sales territories.[273] The Commission's solution to this problem was to adopt a loose notion of exclusivity.

This loose notion of exclusivity is materially different from the exclusivity concept used in Regulation 1983/83. The following differences between the two regulations are noteworthy in this respect:

- the application of Regulation 1983/83 is strictly dependent on the appointment of one dealer per contract territory, while Regulation 123/85 allows the appointment of any fixed and limited number of dealers (one or more) in any given contract territory; and

- under Regulation 123/85 the supplier is entitled to reserve the right to appoint additional dealers or to alter the contract territory on the condition that there are objectively valid reasons for doing so. The same reservation would not seem to be possible in the context of Regulation 1983/83.

¶343 Motor vehicle distribution: non-competition obligation

The territorial protection accorded to the dealer finds its counterpart in the dealer's non-compete obligation.[274] This obligation is justified on the grounds that it ensures that dealers will concentrate their efforts on the distribution and servicing of the manufacturer's products, thus stimulating both intra-brand and inter-brand competition.[275] The regulation fails to define the term 'competing motor vehicles'. The most workable definition would seem to be one based on generally accepted categories of vehicles, i.e. passenger cars, trucks and vans.

The specific non-compete obligations relating to motor vehicles that may be imposed under Regulation 123/85 are the following. The dealer may be prevented from :

(1) concluding a distribution agreement for competing motor vehicles (art. 3(5));

(2) concluding a servicing agreement for competing motor vehicles (art. 3(5));

---

[273] This practice is not surprising since a selective distribution system is not inherently based on an exclusive supply obligation involving the appointment of a single dealer within a given territory. Rather, the distinguishing feature of a selective distribution system is the obligation placed on dealers to sell only to other authorised dealers and final customers.

[274] Regulation 123/85, art. 3(2)–(5). For a discussion of the dealer's non-competition obligation with respect to spare parts, see ¶343.

[275] Id., recital 7. In the case of selective distribution of motor vehicles, it is generally recognised that the promotion of inter-brand competition between rival distribution networks takes precedence over intra-brand competition between dealers belonging to the same network. See *Fourteenth Report on Competition Policy*, point 37.

(3) selling new competing motor vehicles, even outside the framework of an established distribution relationship with a third party (art. 3(3));[276] and

(4) selling new non-competing vehicles of other manufacturers at the premises used for the distribution of the motor vehicles covered by the dealer agreement (art. 3(3)).

However, the dealer agreement must provide that the supplier will release the dealer from these non-compete obligations if the dealer shows that there are objectively valid reasons for doing so.[277] Such objectively valid reasons could consist in a permanent (i.e. other than a purely temporary) decline in turnover in the manufacturer's vehicles which necessitates a supplementary turnover in the sale and servicing of vehicles of other manufacturers.[278]

¶344   Motor vehicle distribution: sales outside distribution network

Regulation 123/85 exempts a prohibition imposed on dealers with regard to sales outside of the manufacturer's distribution network, which lies at the heart of any selective distribution system for motor vehicles.[279] The Commission recognises that consumers benefit from such closed dealer networks, particularly in so far as they promote the quality of after-sales service.[280]

Although dealers may be prevented from selling vehicles to parallel traders to preserve the integrity of the manufacturer's selective distribution system, the regulation explicitly sanctions sales to 'intermediaries', i.e. agents acting on behalf of the final customer. Dealers may require the intermediary to produce written authorisation from the customer[281] as well as a copy of the customer's passport or identity card.[282] To protect the manufacturer's distribution system further, the regulation provides that a dealer may be prevented from supplying motor vehicles to a third party who represents himself as an authorised reseller

---

[276] In reply to certain questions of the UK Monopolies and Mergers Commission, the services of the EC Commission suggested that this specific non-competition obligation must be geographically limited to the dealer's contract territory. This narrow interpretation of art. 3(3) seems unjustified and the textual arguments invoked in its support are not convincing.

[277] Regulation 123/85, art. 5(2)(1)(a).

[278] See Stöver, speech delivered at the Law Society, Solicitors' European Group, 28 November 1985.

[279] Regulation 123/85, art. 3(10)(a). With respect to spare parts, the dealer must remain free to sell to independent dealers and repair shops which need the parts for the repair of a vehicle, Regulation 123/85, art. 3(10)(b).

[280] Regulation 123/85, recital 4.

[281] Regulation 123/85, art. 3(11).

[282] See *Alfa Romeo, Fourteenth Report on Competition Policy*, point 72.

of the vehicles or carries on an activity equivalent to that of a reseller.[283] The important distinction between lawful intermediaries and unauthorised resellers has received considerable attention over the past few years. The debate was triggered by the dispute between Peugeot and Ecosystem[284] and has led to the adoption of a Commission notice clarifying the activities of motor vehicle intermediaries.[285] The Commission notice provides practical criteria (relating to the validity of the authorisation given to the intermediary, the nature of the services which he provides, the intermediary's advertising activities and the supplies made to the intermediary) on the basis of which it can be assessed whether the entity in question is an intermediary for the purposes of Regulation 123/85.

¶345 Motor vehicle distribution: spare parts

The dealer's obligation not to deal in products which compete with those covered by the distribution agreement only has limited application to spare parts. In the Commission's view, competition in the spare parts market would be stifled if dealers were prevented from obtaining supplies from independent spare parts manufacturers.[286] Thus, except in cases of guarantee work, free servicing or vehicle recall work, a dealer must be allowed to sell and use spare parts of another brand which 'match the quality of the contract goods.'[287] The regulation gives little guidance as to the meaning of this critical phrase. The preamble deals with the easiest case, where the parts are produced by a subcontractor who supplies the motor vehicle manufacturer as well as

---

[283] Commission Notice concerning Regulation 123/85 on the application of art. 85(3) of the treaty to certain categories of motor vehicle distribution and servicing agreements, OJ 1985 C17/4, para. 1(3).

This statement, however, has to be interpreted carefully. The Commission has always declined to accept, as a valid ground for refusing to sell to an intermediary who has a written order to purchase a new vehicle, the fact that he is collecting orders professionally or is charging for his services. *Sixteenth Report on Competition Policy*, point 30. The intermediary is responsible for providing the dealer with documentary evidence that he is acting on behalf and for the account of the consumer. Notice, para. 1(3).

[284] *Eco System/Peugeot*, OJ 1992 L66/1. The position defended by the Commission in this case was upheld by the Court of First Instance in *Automobiles Peugeot SA and Peugeot SA v EC Commission* Case T-9/92, judgment of 22 April 1993 (not yet reported). In this regard, the court pointed out that the usual activities of a professional intermediary may include:

(1) the possibility to carry out promotion and advertising campaigns;
(2) the possibility to concentrate activities on certain makes of car;
(3) the acceptance of the commercial risks which are usually linked to service providers' activities such as storage liability.

[285] OJ 1991 C329/20.

[286] For example, the Commission considered that the discount system offered by Fiat to its distributors was intended to dissuade them from buying spare parts from competing spare parts manufacturers. As a result of the Commission's intervention, Fiat decided to abandon its discount system and, more particularly, the special bonus rewarding the distributors' fidelity to Fiat. Fiat also undertook to remove the purchase threshold the distributors had to reach in order to benefit from the discount system. IP/94/159 (24 April 1994).

[287] Regulation 123/85, art. 3(4) and art. 4(1)(7).

independent dealers in spare parts.[288] Other cases may prove more difficult. It would seem that the concept of quality should embrace the functional as well as technical characteristics of spare parts as it is conceivable that spare parts may be of equal quality, but may not be used interchangeably.[289]

The dealer may be obliged to inform customers in a general manner of the extent to which spare parts from other sources may be used for the repair or maintenance of the manufacturer's motor vehicles.[290] The dealer may also be required to inform customers whenever spare parts from other sources have been used for the repair or maintenance of motor vehicles in cases where spare parts within the contract programme were also available.[291] In addition, the dealer may be required to maintain a minimum stock of the manufacturer's spare parts.[292]

Since the non-competition obligation discussed here applies only to spare parts and not to accessories, the question may arise as to whether a particular item is a spare part or an accessory. The regulation provides that spare parts are to be distinguished from other parts and from accessories according to 'customary usage in the trade'.[293] In the *BMW* decision, the Commission suggested that spare parts are parts that are 'particularly important' for the safety of the vehicle.[294]

Regulation 123/85 does not exempt a non-competition obligation relating to accessories, lubricants, brake-fluid and similar products. The regulation does not, however, prevent the supplier from imposing limitations on the dealer's choice of such products. In *D'Ieteren motor oils*,[295] the Commission decided that the imposition of certain objective quality standards of a technical nature was not contrary to art. 85(1) of the treaty. Moreover, nothing would seem to prevent suppliers from structuring the distribution of their accessories in accordance with Regulation 1983/83. On that basis, a full non-competition obligation for accessories could be imposed.

Concerning selectivity, Regulation 123/85 contains specific rules that can be imposed in relation to spare parts. Dealers may be prevented from selling spare parts within the contract programme to unauthorised resellers for the purposes

---

[288] Even in this easy case, the presumption that spare parts produced by a subcontractor 'match the quality of' the manufacturer's spare parts might be rebutted in cases where the manufacturer carries out additional quality controls on the parts.

[289] Such a concept would appear desirable in so far as it would reduce the risk that the use of independent spare parts would be detrimental to the safety of a vehicle. In this connection, it should be noted that the Economic and Social Committee objected to the inclusion of spare parts in the regulation on the grounds that 'it is of vital importance to safeguard the interests of consumers, particularly in respect of spare-part availability, price, quality and guarantees'. Opinion of the Economic and Social Committee on the draft regulation, OJ 1983 C341/18.

[290] Regulation 123/85, art. 4(1)(8).

[291] Regulation 123/85, art. 4(1)(9).

[292] Regulation 123/85, art. 4(1)(4).

[293] Regulation 123/85, art. 13(6).

[294] *Bayerische Motoren Werke AG*, OJ 1975 L29/1, at p. 8.

[295] *D'Ieteren motor oils*, OJ 1991 L20/42; See also *XXIst Report on Competition Policy for 1991*, point 123.

¶345

of resale by the latter. However, they must be free to supply such unauthorised resellers with spare parts if they will be used by such resellers for the repair or maintenance of a motor vehicle.[296]

¶346   Motor vehicle distribution: guarantees

The supplier may require the dealer to perform guarantee work, free servicing and vehicle recall work on the motor vehicles.[297] The dealer must perform such work even if the vehicle was sold by another dealer within the manufacturer's EC distribution network.[298] The straightforward application of this Community-wide guarantee principle may raise problems because the extent of the manufacturer's guarantee may differ from one member state to another. For instance, a manufacturer's guarantee may include rust-proofing treatment in Germany while such treatment would not be included in the guarantee offered in Italy. The regulation offers a solution to this problem. It provides that the dealer must perform guarantee work to an extent that corresponds to the dealer's obligations for vehicles that he supplied himself, but that need not exceed the guarantee obligation imposed upon the selling dealer or accepted by the manufacturer when supplying the vehicles. Taking the example mentioned above, German dealers would not be obliged to provide rust-proofing in the case of vehicles bought in Italy. Logically, Italian dealers should only be obliged to apply the Italian guarantee. This approach avoids a situation where Italian dealers must be equipped to perform rust-proofing or other services which would not normally be offered in Italy.[299] However, it is arguably inconsistent with the Community-wide guarantee principle. One means of avoiding this problem would be for the servicing dealer to honour always the customer's guarantee and then seek reimbursement from the selling dealer or the manufacturer. In the alternative, the customer could pay for the repairs himself and obtain a refund from the selling dealer or the manufacturer.[300]

---

[296] Regulation 123/85, art. 3(10)(b).

[297] Regulation 123/85, art. 4(1)(6). The dealer must be required to impose an obligation upon sub-dealers to honour guarantees and to perform free servicing and vehicle recall work at least to the extent to which the dealer is so obliged. Regulation 123/85, art. 5(1)(1)(b).

[298] Regulation 123/85, art. 5(1)(1)(a). This principle of a Community-wide guarantee was explicitly established with respect to motor vehicles in *Ford Garantie Deutschland, Thirteenth Report on Competition Policy*, points 104–106. See also *ETA Fabriques d'Ebauches v DK Investment* [1985] ECR 3933 and the *XXIst Report on Competition Policy for 1991*, point 123.

[299] This interpretation is similar to the position adopted by the Commission with respect to electrical appliances where the Commission has been satisfied with an obligation on the dealer to provide guarantee work in accordance with the terms of the local guarantee, even in cases where the product was bought elsewhere. See ¶310.

[300] This approach was approved by the Commission in *Fiat, Fourteenth Report on Competition Policy*, point 70. Under the original system, the guarantee would only be honoured outside the country of purchase if the work was examined by the dealer who originally sold the car, and both the supporting documents and the parts replaced were produced. These requirements created difficulties for customers who bought their cars in member states other than the member states in which guarantee servicing was sought. Therefore, Fiat was required to change its guarantee system as follows:

¶347   Motor vehicle distribution: control over dealers

Regulation 123/85 allows the supplier to impose minimum standards upon the dealer with regard to the equipment of the business premises, training of staff, advertising, the collection, storage and delivery of vehicles and spare parts, and the servicing of vehicles.[301] The dealer may also be required to observe certain time limits in ordering vehicles, to endeavour to sell a minimum quantity of vehicles, to maintain minimum stocks and to perform guarantee work.[302] These types of boiler-plate clauses do not generally pose problems, but it is nevertheless surprising that the Commission deems it necessary to enter into such details as defining acceptable periods for placing orders. In practice, a problem may arise concerning the minimum quantities provision. In light of the 'best efforts' principle embodied in this provision, it is uncertain whether the dealer may be obliged to sell a minimum quantity of the manufacturer's vehicles.[303] Arguably, a persistent failure to sell agreed minimum quantities would give the supplier the right to appoint additional dealers within the contract territory.[304]

¶348   Motor vehicle distribution: sub-dealers

The supplier may reserve the right to approve appointments of sub-dealers by the dealer;[305] however, the supplier may not withhold such approval without objectively valid reasons.[306] Sub-dealers may be held to the same obligations as the main dealers.[307]

¶349   Motor vehicle distribution: price differentials

The Commission may withdraw the benefit of the block exemption accorded by Regulation 123/85 'where, over a considerable period, prices or conditions of supply for contract goods or for corresponding goods are applied which differ

---

'(1) it is no longer necessary to present the parts replaced to the Fiat dealer who originally sold the car, but merely to have a check done of the documents showing that the work was done;

(2) the refund can be obtained not only from the seller but also directly from the Fiat distribution company which issued the guarantee certificate;

(3) the application for a refund may be submitted up to two months after payment is made for the work, instead of one month, and could be made out in the language of the customer.'

[301] Regulation 123/85, art. 4(1)(1).

[302] Regulation 123/85, art. 4(1)(2)–(6).

[303] It is, however, certain that dealers do not have to respect prices determined in the manufacturer's list. In the *Spanish cars* settlement, the Commission required that Spanish car importers agreed to send circulars to their dealers and agents indicating that the list prices for the resale of vehicles and spare parts were to be considered as recommendations and were not binding on the dealers. See IP(89) 639 (9 August 1989).

[304] Art. 5(2)(1)(b) allows the supplier to appoint additional dealers where he can show 'objectively valid reasons' for such an action. According to recital 19, 'this is ... the case where there would otherwise be reason to apprehend a serious deterioration in the distribution or servicing of contract goods.'

[305] Regulation 123/85, art. 3(6).

[306] Regulation 123/85, art. 5(1)(2)(a).

[307] Regulation 123/85, art. 3(7) and art. 5(1)(1)(b).

substantially as between Member States, and such substantial differences are chiefly due to obligations exempted by this Regulation'.[308]

The Commission notice[309] published in conjunction with Regulation 123/85 offers guidance in the interpretation of the broad and often vague terms of this critical provision. This notice is not legally-binding and failure to follow the guidelines does not therefore give rise to any automatic legal effects. By the same token, compliance with the guidelines does not guarantee protection against an investigation by the Commission. However, the guidelines contained in the notice are nonetheless important because they indicate how the Commission intends to interpret and apply certain provisions of Regulation 123/85.

According to the guidelines, the Commission may withdraw the benefit of the exemption where list prices (i.e. recommended net prices for resale to final consumers) differ by more than 12 per cent, or by more than 18 per cent for a period of less than one year.[310] The version of this so-called '12 per cent clause' contained in the draft regulation was severely criticised.[311] As a result of such criticism, it was left out of the text of the regulation itself and was softened in the guidelines through an extension of the relevant time period.[312] More significantly, the Commission made it clear that even if price differences exceed these limits for a significant proportion of the motor vehicles, this is not enough to trigger the withdrawal of the block exemption. It must also be determined that the obligations exempted by the regulation are in fact the principal cause of the price differences.[313] In other words, the Commission considers that

---

[308] Regulation 123/85, art. 10(3).

[309] Commission notice concerning Regulation 123/85 on the application of art. 85(3) of the treaty to certain categories of motor vehicle distribution and servicing agreements, OJ 1985 C17/4.

[310] See notice, para. II.1(a). These differences may be greater when an insignificant portion of the motor vehicles within the contract programme is involved.

[311] In its opinion on the draft regulation, OJ 1983 C341/18, the Economic and Social Committee noted that 'the maximum permitted price difference, as referred to in the draft Regulation, must be regarded in the first instance as an objective without any automatic legal force. The more complete the process of European integration, the easier it will be to achieve this objective.'

The Section for Industry, Commerce, Crafts and Services unanimously agreed that 'the responsibility for price differences did not lie primarily with manufacturers; they could be attributed to a variety of factors, including exchange rates, interest rates, different rates of inflation, taxes in some countries ... price controls ... and, in some respects, production costs'. IND/196, 20 September 1983. In its resolution on the draft regulation, OJ 1984 C172/81, the European Parliament recognised 'the right of manufacturers to determine their own prices for different markets' and recommended that the Commission delete the provision on price differentials.

[312] Under art. 7(1)(a) of the draft Commission regulation on the application of art. 85(3) of the treaty to certain categories of motor vehicle distribution and servicing agreements, OJ 1983 C165/2, the exemption was rendered automatically inapplicable if recommended retail prices differed by more than 12 per cent for a period of six months.

[313] The benefit of Regulation 123/85 may only be withdrawn where price differences are 'chiefly due' to the obligations exempted by Regulation 123/85, see art. 10(3). The notice states that whether the Commission will open a procedure to withdraw the benefit of the Regulation will depend on whether the exempted agreement is the 'principal cause' of actual price differences, see para. II(3). This requirement that price differences should, principally, be a result of the agreement was not contained in the draft regulation. Its inclusion reflected the concerns expressed within the Economic and Social Committee (see the opinion of the Economic and Social Committee on the draft Regulation, OJ 1983 C341/18, and the report of the Section for Industry, Commerce,

legitimate price comparisons may only be made for the purposes of Regulation 123/85 if factors other than the agreements themselves are not taken into consideration.[314]

Price differentials may exceed the stated limits where they are attributable to taxes, charges or fees amounting to more than 100 per cent of the net price in one of the member states.[315] Price differentials may also exceed the stated limits where they are attributable to national measures lasting longer than one year in one of the member states restricting directly or indirectly the freedom to set the price or margin for the resale of the vehicle.[316]

The Commission notice also lists other factors that are to be taken into account when making price comparisons. Alterations in the parities within the European Monetary System and fluctuations in exchange rates will be considered by the Commission in making price comparisons.[317] Price comparisons will be based on prices net of discount in so far as the discounts are public knowledge.[318] Finally, price comparisons will take into account differences in equipment and specifications as well as the extent of the guarantee, delivery services and registration formalities in the member states.[319]

In its notice, the Commission also recognises that '[p]rice differentials for motor vehicles as between member states are to a certain extent a reflection of the particular play of supply and demand in the areas concerned.'[320] Thus, to the

---

Crafts and Services, 20 September 1983, IND/196) as well as by the motor vehicle industry (see reply by the CCMC and CLCA, 24 October 1983). See also Written Question No. 2001/86 to the Commission, OJ 1987 C157/28.

[314] In the *Fourteenth Report on Competition Policy*, point 40, this principle was articulated as follows:

'The Commission has always stressed that it has neither the desire nor the power to take interventionist measures to harmonize car prices across the common market. It cannot satisfy demands to abolish price differentials between Member States which are in fact partly a reflection of the particular play of supply and demand in the regions concerned. However, where price differentials are substantial, there may be reason to suspect that national measures or private restrictive measures are behind them and very large, long lasting price differentials between Member States can thus result in the withdrawal of the benefit of exemption in individual cases.'

See Written Question No. 200/88 to the Commission, OJ 1989 C57/17.

[315] See notice, para. II(1)(b). See Written Question No. 200/88 to the Commission, OJ 1989 C57/17 where Commissioner Sutherland recalled that certain countries had to be excluded from the comparison of prices in so far as their prices are distorted by legal price restraints or by extremely high taxation.

[316] Notice, para. II(1)(b).

[317] Ibid.

[318] Ibid.

[319] Notice, para. II(2).

[320] Notice, para. II. See also Written Question No. 200/88 to the Commission, OJ 1989 C57/17.

¶349

extent that price differences are due to differences in competitive environments, consumer preferences, and similar factors extraneous to the agreement itself, the distribution agreement should remain eligible for exemption.[321] In connection therewith, differences in inflation rates and the purchasing power of consumers should also be taken into account when making price comparisons.[322]

In order to address complaints received from the European Consumer Organisation and a member of the European Parliament, the Commission launched a price inquiry in April 1990 in order to investigate the price differentials of new cars in the Community. Fifteen European and five Japanese manufacturers were involved in the inquiry. The Commission's findings were published in 1992 in the '*Intra-EC Car Price Differential Report*'. The outcome of the inquiry was that there exist high car price differentials, but that the linkage between these differentials and the obligations exempted by the regulation had not been established beyond doubt. On that basis, the Commissioner in charge of competition policy informed the car manufacturers that the Commission did not intend to withdraw or amend Regulation 123/85 prior to its expiry date, i.e. 30 June 1995.

---

[321] Differences in competitive environments among member states seem to explain, to a large extent, price differentials. For instance, a car manufacturer may temporarily charge relatively low prices for a new model in order to attract potential purchasers away from more established competitors.

If the difference in relative prices between the equivalent versions of the same car in two member states is due, for example, exclusively to its popularity in one of those member states where it commands a relatively high price and to consumer indifference in the other member state, where, in order to sell the cars, the manufacturer has substantially reduced his price, the distribution agreement should continue to benefit from the block exemption.

The second-hand market may have an influence on prices. In certain member states, such as the UK, there is a highly developed, well-served second-hand car market which offers consumers service comparable with that for buyers of new cars, e.g. pre-delivery inspection and after-sales service. This is not the case in all countries. In other member states, there is no commercial second-hand car market, which depresses the residual value of cars and reduces the price of a new car.

In some member states – particularly the UK – large fleet car markets have developed, the existence of which tends to bolster new car sales. Also, since fleet buyers generally demand a substantial discount, this may be transmitted into higher retail prices for private cars.

In this regard, it may be noted that cultural differences may help explain price differentials among member states. For example, the popularity of the bicycle in the Netherlands depresses car usage and this may have an effect on car prices.

Public transportation systems may also have an effect on car prices, particularly in member states that discourage car ownership by giving financial incentives to users of public transport.

[322] The Commission has recognised that differences in the business cycle, differing rates of inflation and disparities in purchasing power contribute to price differences among member states. *Eleventh Report on Competition Policy*, point 266.

¶349

¶350   Motor vehicle distribution: full-line availability

One of the Commission's overriding concerns in the motor vehicle sector is to ensure that European consumers are free to purchase cars wherever they wish within the Community.[323] Thus, in *Distribution system of Ford Werke AG*,[324] the Commission condemned the decision by Ford Germany to cut off supplies of right-hand drive cars to its dealers. Prior to this decision, German dealers had sold substantial quantities of Ford vehicles to British consumers who had come to Germany to take advantage of lower German prices. The Commission held that the refusal by Ford to supply right-hand drive cars could not be exempted because it impeded parallel imports and, consequently, led to the partitioning of national markets.

The Commission was careful to note, however, that its decision did not oblige Ford Germany to practise 'full-line availability', that is, to make available to its German dealers all of the series production cars marketed by Ford in the Community. In particular, the Commission stated that Ford Germany was not obliged to supply cars having minor features which were not important to a significant number of consumers and which could be installed easily and cheaply by the consumers themselves. Moreover, if Ford Germany no longer manufactured right-hand drive cars, it would not be under an obligation to supply right-hand drive cars to its dealers.

In Regulation 123/85, the Commission reaffirmed the importance of ensuring that consumers may purchase motor vehicles wherever prices are most favourable in the Community.[325] The regulation provides that, for the purpose of the performance of a contract of sale concluded between the dealer and a final customer in the EC, the dealer must be supplied with any passenger car:

---

[323] In the *Citroën* settlement, the Commission compelled the Belgian subsidiary of Citroën to terminate a limitation on a series of special offers which were to discriminate against nationals of other countries. *Eighteenth Report on Competition Policy*, point 56. Likewise, the Danish importer of Nissan was compelled to withdraw a price list which provided for considerably higher prices in cases where cars were to be exported to other member states. *XXIst Report on Competition Policy for 1991*, point 123.

[324] *Distribution system of Ford Werke AG*, OJ 1983 L327/31 and *Ford Werke AG and Ford of Europe Inc v EC Commission* [1985] ECR 2725, where the court confirmed the lawfulness of the Commission's decision. See *Fifteenth Report on Competition Policy*, point 125.

[325] See *Fiat, Fourteenth Report on Competition Policy*, point 70, and *Alfa Romeo, Fourteenth Report on Competition Policy*, point 72, where, following intervention by the Commission, the two manufacturers agreed to remove obstacles to the purchase of right-hand drive (RHD) cars in Belgium and Luxembourg by British nationals. In *Peugeot*, OJ 1986 L295/19, the French manufacturer adopted dissuasive measures for the sale of RHD-vehicles in Belgium and Luxembourg, namely, the list prices for such vehicles were increased to approximately the price level in the United Kingdom with the result that a sharp price difference between RHD and left-hand drive (LHD) cars was created, which amounted to 31 per cent for Peugeot and 47 per cent for Talbot cars. The decision of the Commission, refusing an exemption under art. 85(3) for the distribution system in question, is in line with the Commission's policy previously set out in the *Ford* case. *Sixteenth Report on Competition Policy*, point 52.

(1) which corresponds to a model within the contract programme, i.e. which is:

    (a) manufactured or assembled in volume by the manufacturer;

    (b) identical as to body style, drive-line, chassis and type of motor with a vehicle within the dealer's contract programme;

(2) which is marketed by the manufacturer or with his consent in the member state where the passenger car is to be registered.[326]

This provision is generally referred to as the 'full-line availability clause'. This is a misnomer since the provision does not oblige the supplier to make available to dealers in a member state all of the models marketed by the manufacturer in the Community, but only those models that are already marketed by the dealer or that 'correspond' to such models.[327] In this connection, it is interesting to note that the Commission has abandoned two conditions contained in the *Ford* decision. Under the regulation, the fact that Ford Germany no longer manufactured right-hand drive cars would not justify a refusal to supply such cars to its dealers. In addition, the regulation would oblige Ford Germany to supply cars with all of the minor features available in the consumer's home country, although the consumer may be charged a supplement for those features not available on German models.

When supplying cars in accordance with the full-line availability clause, the supplier must not apply prices or conditions which are not objectively justifiable and which have the object or effect of partitioning the common market.[328]

In its notice, the Commission warns that the consumer must not be subject to abusive hindrance, either in the exporting country where he wishes to buy the vehicle, or in the country where he seeks to register it.[329] Thus, manufacturers and their importers must co-operate in the registration of vehicles that have been imported from other member states and should avoid abnormally long delivery periods.[330]

In supplying passenger cars under the full-line availability clause, the supplier may charge a supplement in those countries where official measures

---

[326] Regulation 123/85, art. 5(1)(2)(d).

[327] See the *Volkswagen AG* settlement; *Nineteenth Report on Competition Policy*, point 48.

[328] Regulation 123/85, art. 10(4). See *Seventeenth Report on Competition Policy*, point 34.

[329] Notice, para. I(2).

[330] Ibid. In this connection, it should be noted that the amount charged by manufacturers for the issuance of certificates of conformity required under national legislation must be based on cost factors, *British Leyland*, OJ 1984 L207/11; *General Motors v EC Commission* [1975] ECR 1367.

    See also *Sixteenth Report on Competition Policy*, point 30 and *Seventeenth Report on Competition Policy*, point 34.

    Regarding delivery periods, the Commission stated that they should normally not exceed the longer of the delivery times for the vehicles in the exporting or importing country. *Sixteenth Report on Competition Policy*, point 30 and the *Volkswagen AG* settlement, *Nineteenth Report on Competition Policy*, point 48.

such as very high taxes (e.g., Denmark) or price controls (e.g., Belgium) distort the manufacturer's list prices.[331] This supplement may not lead to a price which exceeds the price that would be charged in similar cases in a member state not subject to such measures in which the lowest price net of tax is recommended for sale to a final consumer.[332] For example, a manufacturer or its importer in Denmark could charge a supplement representing the difference between the price of the vehicle in Denmark and the price in the member state which has the lowest price (net of tax) and which does not have very high taxes or price controls. In addition to the supplement designed to compensate for national measures, the supplier may also charge an objectively justifiable supplement for special distribution costs and any differences in equipment and specification.[333]

¶351   Motor vehicle distribution: duration and termination

In cases where the dealer assumes obligations for the improvement of the distribution and servicing of motor vehicles, certain rules governing the duration and termination of the agreement must be adhered to if the exemption is to apply to the dealer's obligation not to sell competing vehicles and not to conclude distribution agreements with third parties.[334] Such distribution agreements may be for a definite period of at least four years, with a six-month notice period of the intention not to renew, or for an indefinite period with notice for termination of the agreement of at least one year.[335] The stated purpose of these requirements is to prevent the dealer from becoming overly dependent on the supplier as a result of a short-term agreement or one which may be terminated on short notice.[336]

In *VAG v Magne*,[337] a dealer in motor vehicles supplied by VAG France argued that VAG France was required to enter into a new four-year dealer agreement which was in accordance with the provisions of Regulation 123/85.[338] The court held that Regulation 123/85 does not lay down any mandatory provisions directly affecting the validity or content of contractual provisions in motor vehicle distribution agreements, nor does it require the contracting parties to adapt the contents of such agreements. According to the court, the

---

[331] Notice, para. II(2).
[332] Ibid.
[333] Ibid.
[334] Regulation 123/85, art. 5(2). See also *Seventeenth Report on Competition Policy*, point 34.
[335] Regulation 123/85, art. 5(2)(2) and (3).
[336] Regulation 123/85, recital 20.
[337] *VAG France SA v Établissements Magne* [1986] ECR 4071; see also *Sixteenth Report on Competition Policy*, point 117.
[338] *Sixteenth Report on Competition Policy*, point 117.

regulation merely sets out the conditions which, if satisfied, exclude certain contractual provisions from the art. 85 prohibition.[339]

It would seem that the longer the agreement, the more likely dealers are to become dependent on the supplier. More importantly, the minimum duration and notice requirements prevent the manufacturer from readily replacing weak dealers, thus injecting an element of rigidity into distribution systems which could increase costs and lower the quality of services rendered to the customer.

There are two exceptions to these rules. First, if the supplier is obliged by national law or by special agreement to pay appropriate compensation on termination of the agreement, the period of notice for regular termination may be less than one year.[340] Secondly, if the dealer is a new entrant to the distribution system and the term of the agreement, or notice-period for regular termination, is the first such term or notice-period agreed upon by that dealer, then the term or notice-period may be less than the periods specified above.[341] Since new dealers would seem to be more dependent upon suppliers than established dealers, it is questionable whether this second exception is compatible with the stated goal of lessening dealers' dependence on suppliers.

FRANCHISING

¶352   Introduction

Franchising is a form of commercial marketing whereby goods and/or services are distributed at the retail level under the same trade mark or trade name through a network of similar, yet economically independent, retail outlets.[342]

---

[339] *VAG France SA v Établissements Magne* [1986] ECR 4071.

[340] Regulation 123/85, art. 5(2)(2). For a discussion of the relationship between Regulation 123/85 and the Belgian law concerning the termination of distribution agreements, see Willemart, 'Distribution Automobile' (1983) 11 RDCB 677.

[341] Regulation 123/85, art. 5(2)(2).

[342] The 'European Code of Ethics for Franchising', drafted by the EC Commission and the European Franchising Federation, defines 'franchising' as 'a method of contractual collaboration between parties which are legally independent and equal: on the one hand a franchising firm, the franchisor, and on the other hand one or several firms, the franchisee(s)'. It lists the following elements as characteristic of franchise agreements:

    (1) ownership by the franchisor of a company name, a trade name, initials or symbols; or a trade mark of a business or a service, and know-how, which is made available to the franchisee(s);

    (2) control of a range of products and/or services presented in a distinctive and original format, and which must be adopted and used by the franchisee(s), the format being based on a set of specific business techniques which have been previously tested, and which are continually developed and checked as regards their value and efficiency;

    (3) a payment made in one form or another by the franchisee to the franchisor in recognition of the service supplied by the franchisor in providing his name, format, technology and know-how;

    (4) acceptance by both parties of important obligations to one another, over and above those established in such conventional trading relationships as sales agreements or licence concession contracts;

    (5) a guarantee by the franchisor of the validity of its rights over the brand, sign, initials, slogan, etc. and the grant to franchised firms of the unimpaired enjoyment of any of these which it makes available to them;

Development of Community policy

Franchising has developed into a very important mode of commercial activity since its introduction in the early 1970s. In its *Fifteenth Report on Competition Policy*,[343] the Commission recognised franchising as 'a rapidly developing form of distribution and commercialisation in Europe', and concluded that the effects of such agreements are 'generally positive' in that they increase competition and contribute to the creation of a unified European market. Nevertheless, the Commission warned, such agreements can have a negative effect on competition if they include restrictions that are normally prohibited, such as market division and resale price maintenance. Furthermore, the block exemptions available at that time[344] were not normally applicable to franchise agreements because such agreements 'may contain elements of exclusive and/or selective distribution, and trade mark, patent and know-how licensing'.[345] It was recognised that a greater degree of certainty was desirable as to the application of the competition rules to franchising.

In January 1986, the court delivered a judgment in the *Pronuptia*[346] case, which involved a distribution franchise for the sale of a line of bridal wear and other wedding articles.

The court held that franchise agreements were distinguishable from other distribution systems. A franchise system must fulfil two fundamental conditions in order to operate:

(1) communication of the franchisor's know-how;

(2) protection of the franchisor's identity and reputation.

---

(6) selection and acceptance by the franchisor of those franchise candidates who possess the qualification required by the franchise, all discrimination based on politics, race, language, religion or sex being excluded from the qualifications;

(7) specification in particular of the following points, it being understood that the provisions adopted will be consistent with national or community law:

    (a) the method and conditions of payment of fees and royalties;

    (b) the duration of the contract, the basis for its renewal, and the time and duration of notice;

    (c) the rights of the franchisor prior to assignment by the franchisee;

    (d) the definition of 'open territorial rights' granted to the franchisee, including options (if granted) on adjoining territories;

    (e) the basis for distribution of the assets affected by the contract, if the contract is terminated;

    (f) distribution arrangements relative to supply of goods, including responsibility for transport and transport charges;

    (g) terms of payment;

    (h) services provided by the franchisor (e.g. marketing assistance, promotion and advertising; technology and know-how; managerial, administrative and business advice; financial and taxation advice, and the conditions under which these services are to be provided and the relevant charges; and training); and

    (i) obligations of the franchisee (e.g. to provide accounts and operating data; to receive training; and to accept inspection procedures).

[343] *Fifteenth Report on Competition Policy*, point 25.

[344] i.e., Commission Regulations 1983/83 and 1984/83 on exclusive dealing agreements, and Commission Regulation 2349/84 on patent licensing agreements.

[345] *Fifteenth Report on Competition Policy*, point 25.

[346] *Pronuptia de Paris v Irmgard Schillgalis* [1986] ECR 353.

¶352

The franchisor must be able to communicate its know-how to franchisees and to provide them with the necessary assistance to enable them to apply its methods, without running the risk that such know-how or assistance could benefit, however indirectly, its competitors. Article 85(1) does not prohibit clauses essential to achieve that objective.

The franchisor must be able to take whatever measures are necessary to safeguard the identity and reputation of the distribution network symbolised by the franchised trade mark or trade name. Any clauses which provide the necessary control to achieve these objectives do not restrict competition within the meaning of art. 85(1).

However, the court held that certain clauses often found in distribution franchise agreements are not justified by the need to protect the franchisor's know-how or preserve the identity and reputation of the franchise system. Such clauses fall within the prohibition of art. 85(1). This is the case, in particular, as regards clauses which:

(1) result in market divisions between the franchisor and the franchisees or among the franchisees; and

(2) restrict and distort price competition among franchisees.

The Commission took account of the principles outlined in the judgment when examining several of the franchise agreements which had been notified, in order to gain enough experience to draft a block exemption regulation for franchise agreements. A regulation in draft form, based on this approach, was circulated in 1987[347] and the Commission received various comments from interested parties as a result. As required under Regulation 19/65,[348] the Advisory Committee on Restrictive Practices and Monopolies was consulted, and eventually Regulation 4087/88[349] was adopted by the Commission on 30 November 1988.

¶353   Block exemption: object and scope

The purpose of the regulation is to define certain types of franchise agreements which can be assumed to meet the conditions required in art. 85(3) in order to be exempted from art. 85(1).

The regulation applies to distribution franchises (involving the sale of goods) and service franchises (involving the supply of services), but not to industrial franchises which differ in that they usually govern relationships between producers.[350]

---

[347] Draft·Commission regulation on the application of art. 85(1) of the treaty to categories of franchise agreements, OJ 1987 C229/3.
[348] Regulation 19/65, art. 6.
[349] OJ 1988 L359/46.
[350] Regulation 4087/88, recital 4.

It covers franchise agreements between two undertakings, the franchisor and the franchisee,[351] although it also applies to agreements involving a master franchisee. Wholesale franchise agreements are not within the scope of the regulation as the Commission has had very little experience in this area.

A franchise agreement is defined in art. 1(3)(b) as:

'an agreement whereby one undertaking, the franchisor, grants the other, the franchisee, in exchange for direct or indirect financial consideration, the right to exploit a franchise for the purpose of marketing specified types of goods and for services; it includes at least obligations relating to:

– the use of a common name or shop sign and a uniform presentation of contract premises and/or means of transport;

– the communication by the franchisor to the franchisee of know-how;

– the continuing provision by the franchisor to the franchisee of commercial or technical assistance during the life of the agreement.'

The franchise itself is defined in art. 1(3)(a) as a package of industrial or intellectual property rights relating to trade marks, trade names, shop signs, utility models, designs, copyrights, know-how or patents, to be exploited for the resale of goods or the provision of services to end-users.

The franchise agreement must satisfy certain conditions in order to benefit from the block exemption.

Direct or indirect financial consideration

In the cases that have been decided to date, the Commission has emphasised the obligation of the franchisee to pay remuneration for the right to use the franchise. This is one of the factors which differentiates a franchise from other types of distribution arrangements. In *Pronuptia*, there was an initial once-off payment calculated in proportion to the population of the area, combined with monthly royalties of four per cent to five per cent of the total turnover from the direct sale of franchise goods from the shop.[352] In *Yves Rocher*,[353] the franchisee had the choice of paying a substantial initial licence fee or of paying a lesser initial fee combined with an annual royalty of one per cent of the turnover.[354] It

---

[351] On the issue of whether the extension of certain obligations imposed on a franchisee to its individual shareholders by a separate agreement with the franchisor takes the franchise agreement outside the scope of Regulation 4087/88 because it may cover more than two undertakings, see *XXIst Report on Competition Policy*, point 128.

[352] *Pronuptia*, OJ 1987 L13/39, at pp. 40, 44 (para. 11, 26). A minimum amount of royalties was to be paid each year.

[353] *Yves Rocher*, OJ 1986 L8/49, at p. 52 (para. 24).

[354] See also *Computerland*, OJ 1987 L222/12, at pp. 14, 19 (para. 11, 24(i)); *ServiceMaster* [1989] 1 CEC 2,287; OJ 1988 L332/38, at pp. 39, 40 (para. 5, 19); *Charles Jourdan* [1989] 1 CEC 2,119; OJ 1989 L35/31, at p. 34 (para. 14).

¶353

can be seen that the financial consideration involved has so far been substantial. If the consideration is too low, there is a risk that the Commission would regard it as merely symbolic, rather than as sufficient consideration constituting one of the essential conditions of the franchise.

Use of a common name or shop sign and uniform presentation of the contract premises

This obligation also constitutes one of the essential characteristics of a franchising system. In *Pronuptia*, the franchisee had undertaken not to use the Pronuptia trade mark and logo other than in conjunction with his own business name, which was followed by the phrase: 'Franchisee of Pronuptia de Paris'. In addition, it was agreed that the franchise business would be carried out in the particular manner developed by the franchisor, exclusively from the premises approved by the franchisor and fitted and decorated according to its instructions.[355] However, it should be noted that art. 4(c) of the regulation stipulates that notwithstanding these obligations, the franchisee must also clearly indicate its status as an independent undertaking.[356]

Communication of know-how

The know-how which must be communicated should consist of a package of non-patented practical information, resulting from experience and testing by the franchisor, which is secret, substantial and identified.[357]

The type of information communicated obviously will vary to some extent from sector to sector. In general, the regulation provides that the know-how can include information pertaining to the presentation of goods for sale, the processing of goods in connection with the provision of services, methods of dealing with customers, administration and financial management advice.[358]

In *Yves Rocher*[359] the know-how covered technical, commercial, promotional, administrative and financial matters, staff training and general administration. In the *Charles Jourdan*[360] decision, the information provided

---

[355] *Pronuptia*, OJ 1986 L13/39, pp. 40, 44 (para. 11, 25). See also *Yves Rocher*, OJ 1986 L8/49, at pp. 51, 52 (para. 20, 25). The procedures to be followed in running the business were set out in the operating manual. 'This covers the following aspects …: decor, lighting, fitting-out in accordance with plans and specifications which Yves Rocher causes to be drawn up at its own expense, layout and furnishing of Centres, presentation of products …' Id., at p. 52 (para. 25). See also, *Computerland*, OJ 1987 L222/12, at pp. 13, 17, 18 (para. 5, 23(ii), (v)); *Charles Jourdan*, OJ 1989 L35/31, at pp. 33, 35 (at. para. 9, 10, 11, 23).

[356] *Computerland*, OJ 1987 L222/12, at p. 13 (para. 4). There the franchisee had to put up a 'sign indicating that the franchisee independently owns and operates the business under a franchise from Computerland, conspicuously posted in the store'. The franchisee in that case also had to form a corporation for the purpose of running his business. See also *Yves Rocher*, OJ 1986 L8/49, at p. 51 (para. 17).

[357] Regulation 4087/88, art. 1(3)(f). For a fuller discussion of this concept, see ¶434.

[358] Regulation 4087/88, art. 1(3)(h).

[359] *Yves Rocher*, OJ 1987 L8/49, at p. 52 (para. 22).

[360] *Charles Jourdan*, OJ 1989 L35/31, at p. 34 (para. 11).

¶353

was mainly commercial, relating to purchasing (season's collection, fashion trends), and the decoration concept which was to be followed, but also covered management aspects.

Continuing provision of commercial and technical assistance

This is the fourth essential condition of a franchise agreement within the meaning of the regulation. The type of assistance intended is illustrated by the decisions to date. In *Pronuptia*,[361] the franchisor assisted the franchisee in the selection of the site and the premises, shop fitting and stocking, regular training, promotion, advertising and continuing information and advice on innovations, promotions, market analysis, purchasing and so on. In *Computerland*,[362] the continuing support services provided included training, information, advice, guidance and know-how concerning shop management, operation, financing, advertising, sales and inventory and other matters.[363]

¶354   Territorial protection: limitation of the number of resellers

Obligations relating to territorial protection constitute one of the main subjects of the regulation. As noted above, in the *Pronuptia* case,[364] the court held that provisions organising a sharing of markets between the franchisor and franchisees or among the franchisees fall under the prohibition of art. 85(1). This may occur when a provision obliges the franchisee to sell only from the contract premises, while at the same time he is granted exclusivity in a given territory for the use of the licensed sign. This makes quantitative selection of the franchisees possible. However, the court was prepared to exempt such provisions to ensure a minimum profit for the franchised outlets.

In the regulation, such provisions are similarly held to be restrictive of competition but to merit an exemption. The regulation is slightly stricter than the court judgment, in that the territorial exclusivity and the 'contract premises' clause are treated as two separate restrictions, whereas the court had held that it was their combination which was restrictive.

In *Computerland* in particular, the prohibition on opening further outlets was considered restrictive. This was because the outlets were medium-sized enterprises, for whom expansion could be both 'logical and desirable'.[365]

Article 2 of the regulation specifies that the franchisor may be obliged, in the contract territory, not to:

---

[361] *Pronuptia*, OJ 1987 L13/39, at p. 40 (para. 11)
[362] *Computerland*, OJ 1987 L222/12, at p. 12 (para. 2).
[363] See also *Yves Rocher*, OJ 1987 L8/49, at p. 52 (para. 23); *Charles Jourdan*, OJ 1989 L35/31, at p. 34 (para. 11).
[364] *Pronuptia de Paris v Irmgard Schillgalis* [1986] ECR 353, at p. 385.
[365] *Computerland*, OJ 1987 L222/12, at p. 19 (para. 25).

– grant the right to exploit all or part of the franchise to third parties,

– itself exploit the franchise, . . .

– itself supply the franchisor's goods to third parties.'

¶355   Territorial restrictions on the franchisee

Location

Article 2(c) of Regulation 4087/88 exempts an obligation on the franchisee to exploit the franchise only from the contract premises. However, art. 3(2)(i) provides that the fact that the franchisee can exploit the franchise only from premises approved by the franchisor is not a restriction of competition.

Various forms of location restrictions have been allowed by the Commission. In *Yves Rocher*,[366] the Commission approved of the procedure the franchisor used in establishing the location of the contract premises. This consisted of a preliminary market and location survey which the franchisor carried out, on the basis of which the franchisor proposed to the franchisee the most promising location. The exact location was determined by the franchisees with the franchisor's consent. In *Computerland*,[367] the franchisor's prior approval was required for the location of the store, and the objective criteria used by Computerland in its site approval were set out in the operator's manual.[368]

Restrictions on the activities of franchisees outside their contract territory

Under the regulation, a restriction on active sales by franchisees outside their respective territories is exempted. Article 2(d) provides that the franchisee may be obliged to refrain from seeking customers from outside the contract territory for the goods or the services which are the subject-matter of the franchise.

Passive sales must, however, always be allowed, in conformity with the Commission's position regarding other distribution systems. Article 5(g) prevents an obligation on the franchisee 'not to supply within the common market the goods or services which are the subject-matter of the franchise to end-users because of their place of residence'.

It is also provided that the benefit of the regulation could be withdrawn if one of the parties prevented end-users, because of their place of residence, from obtaining the goods or services which constitute the subject-matter of the franchise.[369]

On the other hand, art. 3(1)(c) states that art. 85(1) will not be infringed if the

---

[366] *Yves Rocher*, OJ 1987 L8/49, at p. 54 (para. 42).
[367] *Computerland*, OJ 1987 L222/12, at p. 17 (para. 23).
[368] See also *Pronuptia*, OJ 1987 L13/39, at p. 43 (para. 25).
[369] Regulation 4087/88, art. 8(c).

franchisee must undertake not to engage, directly or indirectly, in any similar business in a territory where it would compete with a member of the franchise network or the franchisor.[370]

¶356   Non-competition clauses

There are two different types of non-competition obligations that are relevant to franchise agreements. The first concerns the obligation which may be imposed on the franchisee not to deal in competing goods, the second concerns an obligation on the franchisee not to be involved in a competing business.

No competing goods

The regulation differentiates between the franchisor's goods that are the subject-matter of the franchise, and spare parts or accessories for the franchisor's goods. Article 2(e) allows an obligation on the franchisee not to manufacture, sell or use in the course of the provision of services, goods competing with the franchisor's goods which are the subject-matter of the franchise. It is a restriction of competition because franchisees are prevented from selling goods of the same quality. However, it is exempted because it guarantees that the franchisor's know-how is used only to sell the franchisor's products.

This obligation may not be imposed in respect of spare parts or accessories for these goods since the same standard of protection is not appropriate. In *Yves Rocher*,[371] for example, the franchisee was allowed to sell competing accessories (brushes, tweezers, nail scissors and other products) with Yves Rocher's prior consent, although for the rest of the stock he could sell only products bearing the Yves Rocher trade mark.

The regulation also distinguishes between the franchisor's goods which are the subject-matter of the franchise and other types of goods. The choice of other types of goods may be subject only to certain obligations which the regulation treats as non-restrictive, in so far as they are necessary to protect the franchisor's know-how or maintain the common identity of the network. The franchisee may not be prevented from selling other types of goods altogether, but may be obliged to sell, or use in the course of the provision of services, only goods which match minimum objective quality specifications laid down by the franchisor.[372] The franchisee can be obliged to sell, or use in the course of the provision of services, only goods which are manufactured by the franchisor or by third parties designated by it, 'where it is impracticable, owing to the nature

---

[370] See ¶354.
[371] *Yves Rocher*, OJ 1987 L8/49, at p. 52 (para. 26).
[372] Regulation 4087/88, art. 3(1)(a).

of the goods which are the subject-matter of the franchise, to apply objective quality specifications'.[373]

This is based on the *Pronuptia*[374] judgment of the court, where the court accepted that objective quality specifications were sometimes impracticable, either because of the nature of the products or because of the large number of franchisees. This latter factor, however, was considered too subjective a criterion to include in the regulation itself.

In *Yves Rocher*,[375] the Commission considered that an exclusive dealing agreement, allowing the franchisees to sell only products bearing the Yves Rocher trade mark, fell outside art. 85(1). However, this approach could not be taken in the regulation because it was based on the specific facts of the case, and in particular on the structure of the market in question.[376]

It is provided that the exemption will not apply if the franchisor refuses to designate third parties as authorised manufacturers, where spare parts, accessories and types of goods other than those that are the subject-matter of the franchise are concerned, for reasons other than the 'protection of the franchisor's industrial property rights, or maintaining the common identity and reputation of the network'.[377]

In *Computerland*,[378] the franchisee was allowed to sell only products and perform services 'specifically authorised in the operator's manual or in other instructions from CLE, or products and services of equivalent quality, subject to prior approval by CLE, which will not be unreasonably withheld'. This was exempted by the Commission, which held that since there was such a wide product range, and technological evolution on the product market was so rapid, objective quality specifications were indeed impracticable. It would be detrimental to the franchisees' freedom to sell the most up-to-date products to lay down specifications. The Commission also drew attention to the fact that franchisees participate in regular 'European Network Product Councils' where they can propose products for approval. Such approval also covers all relevant accessories and future improvements. Therefore, it was accepted that such a method of choosing goods was reasonable.

Non-competition obligation
Where necessary, the franchisee can be obliged:

'not to engage, directly or indirectly, in any similar business in a territory

---

[373] Regulation 4087/88, art. 3(1)(b).
[374] *Pronuptia de Paris v Irmgard Schillgalis* [1986] ECR 353, at p. 383 (para. 21).
[375] *Yves Rocher*, OJ 1987 L8/49, at p. 55 (para. 45).
[376] See de Cockborne, 'The New Block Exemption on Franchising', Fordham International Law Journal, Winter 1989, 242, at p. 275.
[377] Regulation 4087/88, art. 5(c). See also *XXth Report on Competition Policy*, point 48.
[378] *Computerland*, OJ 1987 L222/12, at p. 14 (para. 8).

¶356

where it would compete with a member of the franchised network, including the franchisor.'[379]

This is also a clause based on the court's judgment in *Pronuptia*.[380] The clause further specifies that:

'the franchisee may be held to this obligation after termination of the agreement, for a reasonable period which may not exceed one year, in the territory in which it has exploited the franchise.'[381]

In *Charles Jourdan*,[382] the franchisee was prohibited from operating within the allocated territory any other shop franchised by another company 'unless such other shop sells articles which because of their price and style cannot be regarded as competing with Charles Jourdan products'.

In *Computerland*,[383] the agreement as notified had a non-competition obligation which continued for three years after the termination of the agreement within a certain distance of the ex-franchisee's former outlet, for two years after termination within a given distance of any Computerland store and for one year after termination at any location. After discussions with the Commission, CLE decided that a non-competition obligation of one year after termination within a radius of ten kilometres of the ex-franchisee's former outlet would be sufficient to safeguard the confidentiality of the know-how transmitted during the agreement.

In order to prevent a conflict of interest it is also possible, where necessary, in addition to the non-competition obligation, to oblige the franchisee not to acquire financial interests in the capital of a competing undertaking which would give the franchisee the power to influence the economic conduct of the undertaking.[384]

In *Yves Rocher*,[385] the franchisee was free to acquire financial interests in the capital of a competitor of Yves Rocher, 'provided this investment does not involve him personally in carrying on competing activities'. *Computerland*[386] was more lenient, stipulating only that the franchisee could acquire a financial

---

[379] Regulation 4087/88, art. 3(1)(c).

[380] *Pronuptia de Paris v Irmgard Schillgalis* [1986] ECR 353, at p. 382 (para. 16).

[381] de Cockborne, in 'The New Block Exemption Regulation on franchising', Fordham International Law Journal, Winter 1989, 242, states, at p. 282, that one year is the maximum that should be allowed and that a 'shorter period should often be considered as reasonable'.

[382] *Charles Jourdan* [1989] 1 CEC 2,119; OJ 1989 L35/31, at p. 34, (para. 15). See also *ServiceMaster* [1989] 1 CEC 2,287; OJ 1988 L332/38, at pp. 39–40 (para. 10).

[383] *Computerland*, OJ 1987 L222/12, at p. 15 (para. 12). See also *Pronuptia*, OJ 1986 L13/39, at p. 41 (para. 11), where the restriction was equivalent to that contained in the regulation. In *Yves Rocher*, OJ 1987 L8/49, at p. 52 (para. 26), the franchisee was expressly forbidden to carry on either directly or indirectly, whether in return for payment or not, any business which competes with an Yves Rocher Beauty Centre.

[384] Regulation 4087/88, art. 3(1)(d).

[385] *Yves Rocher*, OJ 1986 L8/49, at p. 52 (para. 26).

[386] *Computerland*, OJ 1987 L222/12, at p. 15 (para. 12).

interest in a competing enterprise, provided it did not allow him effectively to control such business.

The *ServiceMaster*[387] agreement contained a similar clause, except that it was specified that the financial interest could not exceed five per cent of the capital of a publicly-quoted company. The Commission explained that such a clause might sometimes be restrictive, but that it was not so here since the franchisees were generally small undertakings and such a restriction did 'not normally constitute a real hindrance in the development of their own activities'. The obligation on the franchisee, after termination, not to be involved in a competing business for one year within any territory in which he had provided services during the franchise agreement was not considered restrictive. Nor was a 'non-solicitation obligation', which meant that the franchisee could not solicit people who had been customers during the two years prior to termination for one year after the end of the agreement.[388]

¶357   Protection of know-how

It is recognised that a ban on the disclosure of know-how is not restrictive, since it is clearly necessary to prevent others benefiting from the know-how supplied by the franchisor. Article 3(2)(a) provides that the franchisee may be held to this obligation not to supply know-how to others even after the termination of the agreement. However, it is forbidden to prevent the franchisee from continuing to use the licensed know-how after termination of the agreement where the know-how has become generally known or easily accessible.[389]

It can also be stipulated that the franchisee must communicate to the franchisor any experience gained in exploiting the franchise and that the franchisor and the other franchisees must be granted a non-exclusive licence for the know-how which results from this experience.[390] The franchisee may not be prohibited, however, from challenging the validity of the industrial or intellectual property rights.[391]

¶358   Selling prices

Article 5(e) forbids the practice of resale price maintenance; wherever this is present the exemption will not apply.[392] The franchisor may, however,

---

[387] *ServiceMaster* [1989] 1 CEC 2,287; OJ 1988 L332/38, at p. 39 (para. 10).

[388] Ibid., at p. 40 (para. 11).

[389] Regulation 4087/88, art. 5(d). See also *Computerland*, OJ 1987 L222/12, at p. 13 (para. 5), where it was provided that upon termination, the franchisee had to stop using the franchisor's names, marks and system, but that he could continue to use any of his own improvements which were 'demonstrably separable from the operation of the Computerland store and system'.

[390] Regulation 4087/88, art. 3(2)(b).

[391] Regulation 4087/88, art. 5(f).

[392] See also *XXth Report on Competition Policy*, point 48; *XXIst Report on Competition Policy for 1991*, point 127.

recommend sales prices to the franchisee. In the *Pronuptia* judgment,[393] the court stated that the suggestion of prices for the guidance of franchisees was not restrictive of competition, as long as there was no concerted practice between the franchisor and the franchisees, or between the franchisees themselves for the application of such prices.

In the *Pronuptia* proceeding, the franchisor deleted the clause that had provided that the franchisee should not harm the brand image of the franchisor by his pricing level. Instead, it was merely recommended to the franchisee not to exceed the maximum prices quoted by the franchisor in advertising and promotions.[394]

Yves Rocher[395] deleted its resale price maintenance provisions (which were not applied in practice) at the request of the Commission, and issued a circular to franchisees stressing that the recommended prices were purely guidelines. It also undertook to avoid any reference in its circular to a 'maximum price', and to mention in its future catalogues that the prices quoted are recommended prices only. In *Computerland*,[396] franchisees were free to determine their own resale prices, while in *ServiceMaster*[397] sales prices were recommended.

¶359   Customer restrictions

It is considered in the regulation to be non-restrictive to oblige the franchisees to sell the products that are the subject-matter of the franchise only to end-users or to other members of the network.[398] Where the products are also sold to other resellers outside the network with the manufacturer's consent, the franchisee may also supply these resellers.[399]

In *Computerland*, it was specified that an obligation not to supply resellers outside the network would be considered restrictive when the franchisees are selling the products of other manufacturers. In this situation franchisees should not be prevented from supplying other qualified resellers.[400]

In *ServiceMaster*, the franchisee was obliged to resell home care products

---

[393] *Pronuptia de Paris v Irmgard Schillgalis* [1986] ECR 353, at p. 388 (answer 1(e)).
[394] *Pronuptia*, OJ 1987 L13/39, at p. 41 (para. 12).
[395] *Yves Rocher*, OJ 1987 L8/49, at p. 53 (para. 30).
[396] *Computerland*, OJ 1987 L222/12, at p. 14 (para. 8).
[397] *ServiceMaster* [1989] 1 CEC 2,287; OJ 1988 L332/38, at p. 41 (para. 21). See also *Charles Jourdan* [1989] 1 CEC 2,119; OJ 1989 L35/31, at p. 35 (para. 18).
[398] Regulation 4087/88, art. 3(1)(e).
[399] From the answer provided by the Commission to a question dealing with the sales restrictions that can be imposed on a master-franchisee outside his contract territory, it follows that a master-franchisee must be free to sell to other master-franchisees, franchisees and other channels of distribution supplied by the manufacturer or with its consent. However, if these customers are located outside the master-franchisee's contract territory, their orders must be unsolicited and may not be the result of active marketing outside the contract territory. The master-franchisee may be prevented from selling to final consumers and resellers that are not within the channels of distribution supplied by the manufacturer or with its consent. This prohibition applies both within and outside the master-franchisee's contract territory (*XXIst Report on Competition Policy for 1991*, para. 126).
[400] *Computerland*, OJ 1987 L222/12, at p. 19 (para. 26).

¶359

only with the franchisor's consent and only to customers of the franchisee. This restriction on the resale of home care products was allowed by the Commission because it was 'based on the legitimate concern that the franchisee must concentrate on his primary business which is the provision of services, rather than the resale of goods'.[401]

¶360   Cross sales

The franchisee must be allowed to supply other franchisees: the exemption will not apply if this is not possible. Article 4(a) stipulates that cross sales must always be allowed.

The *Yves Rocher* contracts were modified to provide for the possibility of cross sales.[402] The *Computerland* contracts allowed franchisees to choose any source of supply they wished.[403] The Commission also insisted that cross supplies be allowed in the *Charles Jourdan* case where the agreement as exempted provided that 'as a general rule, cross supplies between distributors of products bearing the Group's trade marks are allowed, provided that the principal activity of the franchisee or franchise-corner-retailer is not that of wholesaler'.[404]

Article 4(a) further provides that where the goods are also distributed through another network of authorised distributors, the franchisee must be free to obtain the goods from such network. The concept 'another network of authorised distributors' must be interpreted to mean only a selective distribution network supplied by the franchisor (and its associated companies and subsidiaries) anywhere within the Community in which the dealers fulfil certain objective qualitative criteria or are otherwise selected and are prevented from selling the relevant products to other non-qualified or non-selected resellers.[405]

¶361   Other obligations relating to control of the network

Article 3(1)(f) provides for other obligations which may be imposed, where necessary, on the franchisee without being considered restrictive. The franchisee may have to use his 'best endeavours' to sell the goods or provide the services as intended under the franchise. He may also have to 'offer for sale a minimum range of goods, achieve a minimum turnover, plan its orders in advance, keep minimum stocks and provide customer and guarantee services'. These obligations would be considered restrictive in a selective distribution

---

[401] *ServiceMaster* [1989] 1 CEC 2,287; OJ 1988 L332/38, at p. 41 (para. 21).
[402] *Yves Rocher*, OJ 1987 L8/49, at p. 53 (para. 31).
[403] *Computerland*, OJ 1987 L222/12, at p. 18 (para. 23(vi)).
[404] *Charles Jourdan* [1989] 1 CEC 2,119; OJ 1989 L35/31, at p. 35 (para. 16).
[405] *XXIst Report on Competition Policy*, para. 125.

system but are treated differently in this context owing to the particular characteristics of a franchise agreement.[406]

In *Pronuptia*, the franchisee undertook to cover, in advance, at least 50 per cent of his estimated sales, based on sales in previous years and also to have in stock the articles shown in the catalogue.[407]

In *Yves Rocher*, the franchisee undertook 'to devote all his energy and as much time as necessary to promoting the sale of Yves Rocher products and beauty treatments and agree[d] not to carry on any activities incompatible with those of a Beauty Centre'.[408] The franchisor may also reserve the right to inspect franchisees' stock levels, accounts and balance sheets.[409] This is considered not to be restrictive of competition because the inspection merely verifies franchisees' compliance with obligations which themselves fall outside art. 85(1). In the case of *Yves Rocher*,[410] the inspection especially ensured that products were not stocked for so long that their quality was affected. The Commission did, however, reserve the right to intervene if such controls were used by the franchisor to affect the freedom of the franchisees to fix their selling prices.

The *Computerland* contracts obliged franchisees to submit regular financial statements, including balance sheets and profit-and-loss statements.[411] They also stipulated that CLE's representatives 'must be allowed into the premises during working hours in order to inspect the operation of the store, including the quality of the goods being sold, the supplies on hand and the services rendered'.[412]

In *ServiceMaster*, the franchisee was obliged to devote the necessary time and attention to the ServiceMaster business and to use his best endeavours to promote and increase the turnover of that business. The Commission considered this obligation acceptable 'in light of the concern to preserve the reputation and uniform identity of the network by creating an efficient franchise system devoting all its efforts to the provision of the *ServiceMaster* services'.[413]

Other obligations which relate to the protection of know-how and the maintenance of the franchisor's reputation are not considered restrictive:

---

[406] See de Cockborne, 'The New Block Exemption Regulation on Franchising', Fordham International Law Journal, Winter 1989, 242, at p. 286, where it is pointed out that such obligations may be applied only to preserve the identity and reputation of the network. In particular, they should be applied to franchisees in a non-discriminatory way.

[407] *Pronuptia*, OJ 1987 L13/39, at p. 40 (para. 11).

[408] *Yves Rocher*, OJ 1987 L8/49, at p. 53 (para. 29).

[409] Regulation 4087/88, art. 3(2)(h).

[410] *Yves Rocher*, OJ 1986 L8/49, at p. 56 (para. 50).

[411] *Computerland*, OJ 1987 L222/12, at p. 14 (para. 11).

[412] Ibid.

[413] *ServiceMaster* [1989] 1 CEC 2,287; OJ 1988 L332/38, at p. 40 (para. 16). See also *Computerland*, OJ 1987 L222/12, at p. 14 (para. 6), where the franchisee was obliged to devote his 'best personal efforts' to the enterprise.

attendance at training courses, application of the commercial methods devised by the franchisor, and assignment of the rights under the agreement only with the franchisor's consent.[414] For the same reason, the franchisors are allowed considerable discretion as to their choice of franchisees.[415]

Certain obligations relating to advertising are also considered non-restrictive. Article 3(1)(g) allows an obligation on the franchisee (where necessary) to pay the franchisor a certain proportion of its revenue for advertising. It may also be obliged to conduct advertising itself, obtaining the franchisor's prior approval for such advertising.[416]

The contract in *Yves Rocher*[417] specified that the control which the franchisor exercised extended 'only to the nature of the publicity and not to the retail prices quoted therein'. This was to ensure that there was no deviation 'from the theme of natural beauty from plants, on which the network's image is based'.[418]

¶362   Opposition procedure and withdrawal of exemption

As well as an opposition procedure, set out in art. 6, which closely resembles the procedure in the know-how licensing block exemption regulation,[419] the regulation also sets out the conditions under which the block exemption may be withdrawn. Article 8 provides that wherever there are agreements which, although exempted, have effects incompatible with art. 85(3), the benefit of the regulation may be withdrawn.

This may occur if access to the relevant market is restricted as a result of the 'cumulative effect of parallel networks of similar agreements', or if the goods and services concerned do not face effective competition in a substantial part of the common market. It may also be withdrawn if end-users are prevented from obtaining the goods due to their place of residence, as mentioned above,[420] or if differences in specifications concerning the goods are used to isolate markets.

If concerted practices relating to the sales prices of the goods or services are engaged in, the regulation will be withdrawn, as will be the case if the franchisor

---

[414] Regulation 4087/88, art. 3(2)(e), (f), (j). See *Charles Jourdan* [1989] 1 CEC 2,119; OJ 1989 L35/31, at p. 36 (para. 27), where it was held that the provision 'prohibiting the franchisee from transferring its franchise contract, subletting its shop, setting up a subfranchise, placing its business under management by a third party or appointing a salaried shop manager without the express approval of the group' was not restrictive.

[415] See *Computerland*, OJ 1987 L222/12, at p. 13 (para. 4): 'Franchisees are chosen on the basis of their personal and financial standing and their prior experience in the retail trade, and subject to successful completion of a training programme organised by CLE, employees are also expected to be fully trained in the Computerland system.' See also *Charles Jourdan*, OJ 1989 L35/31, at p. 33 (para. 8), and *Yves Rocher*, OJ 1987 L8/49, at p. 51 (para. 16).

[416] See *Pronuptia*, OJ 1987 L13/39, at p. 40 (para. 11), where the franchisor's approval had to be obtained for local advertising.

[417] *Yves Rocher*, OJ 1987 L8/49, at p. 52 (para. 25).

[418] Id., at p. 55 (para. 44). See also *Computerland*, OJ 1987 L222/12, at pp. 14 and 18 (para. 8 and 23(vii)), and *Charles Jourdan*, OJ 1989 L35/31, at p. 36 (para. 28).

[419] See ¶436.

[420] See ¶353.

misuses its right to check the contract premises and means of transport of the franchisee. This procedure has not yet been put into practice.

REQUIREMENTS CONTRACTS AND EXCLUSIVE PURCHASE

¶363   General rules

Exclusive purchase agreements have been defined by the Commission as:

> 'agreements under which the purchaser accepts an obligation to purchase particular goods from a single supplier only over a relatively long period. They have an important business function in that they give a guarantee of ensured sales to one party and a guarantee of continuous supplies to the other.'[421]

Such agreements may be entered into by purchasers that will use the product in producing other products or by purchasers intending to resell the product.

Article 86 considerations

When the supplier is in a dominant position, exclusive purchase agreements may give rise to problems under art. 86 as they could be a tool for limiting access to the market for the dominant supplier's competitors.[422]

Article 85: network effect

An exclusive purchase agreement may also fall under the prohibition of art. 85(1). In *Brasserie de Haecht ('Haecht I')*, the court stated:

> 'Agreements whereby an undertaking agrees to obtain its supplies from one undertaking to the exclusion of all others do not by their very nature necessarily include all the elements constituting incompatibility with the Common Market as referred to in Article 85(1) of the Treaty. Such agreements may, however, exhibit such elements where, taken either in isolation or together with others, and in the economic and legal context in which they are made on the basis of a set of objective factors of law or of fact, they may affect trade between Member States and where they have either as

---

[421] *Seventh Report on Competition Policy*, point 9.
[422] See *Suiker Unie & Ors v EC Commission* [1975] ECR 1663; *Hoffmann-La Roche v EC Commission* (*'Vitamins'*) [1979] ECR 461. See also the memorandum sent by the Commission to the various national railway companies, *XXth Report on Competition Policy*, point 115.

their object or effect the prevention, restriction or distortion of competition.'[423]

Agreements between two parties established in the same member state may fall within the prohibition of art. 85(1), even though the amount of trade covered by the particular agreement is very small, 'because of the cumulative effect produced by the existence of one or more networks of similar agreements'.[424]

Exclusive purchase obligation combined with other obligations

A restriction on competition may also arise from the combination of an exclusive purchase obligation and other obligations. Thus, in *Billiton and Metal & Thermit Chemicals*, the Commission objected to three provisions in the agreement: the exclusive purchase obligation, the restriction on the purchaser's freedom to manufacture the product delivered by the supplier, and the prohibition on resale of the product.[425]

In *BP Kemi-DDSF*, one of the reasons given by the Commission for not exempting the exclusive purchase agreement was that:

'[i]n the present case the exclusive purchasing obligation is inseparably linked with a number of supplementary restrictions; these are the arrangements between BP Kemi and DDSF on sales quotas and compensation, prices and conditions of payment, customer-market sharing and exchange of information as well as the English clause.'[426]

Possibility of exemption

The Commission recognises that exclusive purchase agreements may be beneficial even if they are found to technically violate art. 85(1). Thus, the Commission has been willing to grant individual exemptions under art. 85(3).[427] A block exemption regulation has also been issued for exclusive purchase agreements where the purchaser resells the products.[428]

In a policy statement setting out its views on the grant of individual exemptions, the Commission stated:

'The Commission considers that exclusive purchasing agreements can

---

[423] *Brasserie de Haecht v Wilkin ('Haecht I')* [1967] ECR 407, at pp. 416–417.

[424] *De Norre v Brouwerij Concordia* [1977] ECR 65, at p. 95 (para. 31). See also *Seventeenth Report on Competition Policy*, point 29, about an enquiry addressed to the Commission by German civil courts to help them decide whether the tied-house networks existing in Germany tended, by their cumulative effect, to seal off the German beer market from those of other member states, so affecting intra-Community trade. In the *XXIInd Report on Competition Policy*, point 195, the Commission sets out an extremely broad 'three-tier test' for determining the cumulative effect of exclusivity agreements.

[425] *Billiton and Metal & Thermit Chemicals*, *Seventh Report on Competition Policy*, point 131.

[426] *BP Kemi-DDSF*, OJ 1979 L286/32, at p. 48.

[427] See, e.g. *Schlegel/CPIO*, OJ 1983 L351/20.

[428] See ¶363.

¶363

contribute to improving the production and distribution of goods, because they make it possible for the parties to the agreement to plan their production and sales more precisely and over a longer period, to limit the risk of market fluctuation and to lower the cost of production, storage and marketing. And in many cases agreements of this kind give small and medium-sized firms their only opportunity of entering the market and thus increasing competition.

However, exemption can only be given where the firms involved do not retain the whole of the benefit. Customers must be allowed their fair share as well. The benefits must also be great enough to balance out the restrictions of competition they bring with them. These tests are not satisfied if the exclusive arrangements make it more difficult for other firms to sell on the market, and especially if they raise barriers to market entry. In such cases an application for exemption will usually fail, because the agreements will afford the parties the possibility of eliminating competition in respect of a substantial part of the products in question, and this is in direct conflict with Article 85(3)(b).'[429]

Importance of market share in assessing agreements

It is clear that market access concerns underlie the Commission's policy in relation to exclusive purchasing. Therefore, it should not come as a surprise that assessment of exclusive purchasing cases focuses on the market share of the suppliers or purchasers.[430]

Outlet exclusivity

The dispute between Mars and Langnese-Iglo and Schöller is an interesting example of a case where market entry considerations were relevant to an assessment of the restrictive impact of 'outlet exclusivity', according to which

---

[429] *Seventh Report on Competition Policy*, point 15.

[430] The size of the suppliers was an important factor in *BP Kemi-DDSF*, OJ 1979 L286/32, and *Billiton and Metal & Thermit Chemicals, Seventh Report on Competition Policy*, point 131. See also *Soda Ash, Eleventh Report on Competition Policy*, points 73–76, where the Commission required the two largest suppliers of soda ash to change their contracts from long term exclusive purchase agreements to contracts for fixed tonnage that would normally not exceed two years. In *Spices*, OJ 1978 L53/20, at p. 24, the Commission was concerned not only with the size of the supplier, but also with the fact that the three purchasers accounted for approximately 30 per cent of the distribution of spices in the Belgian market.

The Commission has also adopted two decisions in the energy sector. In *IJsselcentrale & Ors*, OJ 1991 L28/32, the agreements concerned involved four Dutch electricity generators and their jointly-owned subsidiary. Under these agreements, the four companies had the exclusive right to import and export electricity and imposed an import and export ban on their distributors as well as an exclusive purchasing obligation. The imposition of an import and export ban coupled with an exclusive purchasing obligation was found to infringe art. 85(1) and not to qualify for an exemption. An application for partial annulment of the Commission decision was dismissed, *Rendo NV & Ors v Commission* [1992] II-2417.

In *Scottish Nuclear*, OJ 1991 L178/31, the agreement at issue contained an obligation to purchase on a take or pay basis, an exclusive supply obligation and fixed prices. The agreement was part of the UK Government's proposal for the privatisation of the electric industry in Scotland and was granted an individual exemption by the Commission.

retailers were obliged to sell in a particular outlet only the products of Langnese-Iglo and Schöller.[431] The Commission concluded that the agreements requiring such outlet exclusivity infringed art. 85(1) and were incapable of benefiting from an individual exemption. In so far as it may have applied to the agreements, the benefit of the block exemption was withdrawn. Moreover, Langnese and Schöller were prohibited from concluding 'outlet exclusivity' agreements until after 31 December 1997.[432]

This decision was reached in view of the fact that Langnese and Schöller operated a duopoly on the relevant market and access to the market was made even more difficult by freezer exclusivity arrangements.[433] In this situation, any further strengthening of Langnese and Schöller's position by exclusivity agreements could not be accepted.[434]

¶364   Agreements to purchase only part of requirements

Agreements by which the buyer purchases less than 100 per cent of its requirements from the supplier may also be prohibited under art. 85 or art. 86. With respect to art. 86, the Commission has stated:

'For a finding of abuse there is no need, in the Commission's view, to show that customers take their supplies of the products covered by the agreement exclusively from the dominant manufacturer. It is enough if supplies from him account for the major part of their requirements. Nor is there any need of a legal obligation on the customer to obtain his supplies exclusively or mainly from the dominant firm. Where there is no express provision to this effect in the agreement, it is sufficient if the expected result is actually achieved. There may be abuse if the dominant manufacturer's terms of sale make it economically attractive for customers to take their supplies exclusively or mainly from him. By what means this is done is immaterial. The dominant firm may offer financial advantages (special or fidelity and other rebates) or threaten financial disadvantages (demands for the return of rebates given, refusal to allow any price concessions in future).'[435]

---

[431] This dispute involved a complaint by Mars against these practices and the granting of interim measures which were partially suspended by the Court of First Instance, see order of 16 June 1992, *Langnese-Iglo GmbH and Schöller Lebensmittel GmbH & Co KG v Commission* [1992] ECR II-1839. The court also partially suspended the final decision of the Commission, see Order of 19 February 1993, 1993 II-131.

[432] Schöller Lebensmittel GmbH & Co KC, OJ 1993 L 183/1; Langnese-Iglo GmbH, OJ 1993 L 183/19

[433] In its complaint, Mars also sought action against 'freezer exclusivity', according to which manufacturers provide retailers with freezers which may only be used to sell such manufacturers' products. The interim measures granted by the Commission and the final decision only concerned outlet exclusivity. Ibid.

[434] Actions to annul this final decision were brought by Langnese-Iglo GmbH on 19 January 1993 (OJ 1993 C54/6) and by Schöller Lebensmittel GmbH & Co on 20 January 1993 (OJ 1993 C62/7).

[435] *Seventh Report on Competition Policy*, point 12; see also *Hoffmann-La Roche v EC Commission* ('*Vitamins*') [1979] ECR 461, at p. 541. In the *Italian Coca-Cola* settlement (*Nineteenth Report on Competition Policy*, point 50) the Commission intervened against a fidelity rebate system which encouraged distributors to sell only Coca-Cola, thereby hindering competing producers from entering the Italian market. In *BPB Industries plc*

Article 85 may also apply to contracts for less than 100 per cent of a company's requirements. In *Spices*, the Commission found that the contracts entered into by Liebig with the three largest food retail chains in Belgium violated art. 85(1) even though the companies were able to sell spices under their own brand names in addition to those purchased from Liebig.[436]

In *Carlsberg* the Commission found that a long-term contract for purchases of minimum quantities of lager by a British brewing group, Grand Metropolitan (GM), came within the prohibition of art. 85(1). Despite the fact that the volume amounted to only approximately half of the purchaser's annual purchases of lager, the Commission stated that the obligation 'is restrictive of competition because it prevents GM from producing this volume itself or purchasing it from other producers possibly on more favourable terms'.[437] The Commission also found that the agreement constituted a restriction on the supplier (Carlsberg Ltd) 'because it deprives Carlsberg Ltd of control over more than half of its present output which it would otherwise be able to sell to other breweries or on the free market through its agencies'.[438] The supply agreements nonetheless benefited from an exemption under art. 85(3).

¶365   Purchase of goods for processing

Agreements for the purchase of goods which the purchasing party transforms or processes into other goods are not covered by Regulation 1984/83[439] and, hence, do not benefit from a block exemption. The Commission's settlement practice demonstrates that the dividing line for the EC competition law analysis of such requirements contracts is not between art. 85 and art. 86 of the treaty. The fact that an undertaking in a dominant position is involved does not necessarily mean that a radically different analysis of the agreements will be made. The outcome of the Commission's review depends rather on the nature of the market concerned, the nature of the purchase obligation and the duration of the agreement. In *BP-Kemi-DDSF*, the Commission stated in this respect:

'When a purchaser undertakes to buy all his requirements for a given product

---

[1989] 1 CEC 2,008; OJ 1989 L10/50, the Commission held that British Gypsum Ltd infringed art. 86 because it aimed at exclusivity or 'loyalty' thereby preventing the merchants concerned from purchasing and selling imported plasterboard.

[436] The agreement limited the number of spices that could be sold under the distributor's own name and placed conditions on how such spices could be displayed: *Spices*, OJ 1978 L53/20.

[437] *Carlsberg*, OJ 1984 L207/26, at p. 33.

[438] Ibid. This finding of a restriction on Carlsberg's freedom demonstrates the excessively broad reading which the Commission gives to art. 85(1). The output to which the Commission refers is not the total output of the Carlsberg group but merely the output of a single brewery that had originally been set up as a joint venture between Carlsberg and Grand Metropolitan as a means of giving Carlsberg greater access to the British market. In its assessment under art. 85(1), the Commission did not consider the availability of the identical product from other Carlsberg breweries or from Carlsberg licensees.

[439] Commission Regulation 1984/83 on the application of art. 85(3) of the treaty to categories of exclusive purchasing agreements, OJ 1983 L173/5.

from one manufacturer during a certain period, other manufacturers of the product in question are prevented from supplying the purchaser with the product during the period concerned. Thus, all competition between the manufacturer who gets such a contract and other manufacturers of the product is excluded during this period in so far as supplies to the purchaser in question are concerned. Depending inter alia, on the length of the period and on the economic context, including the market shares and positions of the purchaser and seller such a purchasing obligation may constitute a restriction of competition within the meaning of Article 85(1).'[440]

A purchasing obligation which in practice meant that all foreign suppliers were prevented for a period of six years from selling to DDSF, which represented not only the largest, but also in a number of respects the only practical sales possibility in Denmark, was held to run counter to art. 85(1).[441] Since the agreement had not been notified and was not covered by Regulation 67/67, it was not necessary for the Commission to consider the question of an exemption pursuant to art. 85(3).[442]

In the *Solvay-ICI* settlement,[443] the Commission investigated a number of long-term supply contracts which the EC producers of soda ash had entered into with their major customers on their domestic markets, mainly in the glass manufacturing industry. The contracts were for five years or more and tied the glass manufacturers to one supplier, to the exclusion of all other sources, even for occasional or additional supplies. The Commission requested that Solvay and ICI change their agreements so as to make them non-exclusive for fixed tonnages and to provide for contract periods not exceeding two years.

The *Istituto/IMC and Angus* settlement[444] concerned an investigation by the Commission of the practices of two American firms which held a dominant position in the market for aminobutanol. Following the intervention of the Commission, IMC and Angus terminated their exclusive purchasing agreements and replaced them with new contracts for the delivery of fixed amounts of aminobutanol over a period of two years with automatic renewal of one year unless terminated with six months' prior notice. In the Commission's opinion, this arrangement gave the contracting parties a sufficiently long period for planning production and delivery without excluding the dominant firms' competitors.

In *Nutrasweet*,[445] the Commission secured amendments to contracts between the Nutrasweet Company, the world's largest producer of aspartame, and

---

[440] *BP-Kemi-DDSF*, OJ 1979 L286/32, at pp. 40–41.
[441] Ibid.
[442] Ibid., at pp. 47–48.
[443] Bull. EC 1-1982, point 2.1.17. See also *Eleventh Report on Competition Policy* points 74–76.
[444] *Sixteenth Report on Competition Policy*, point 76.
[445] *Eighteenth Report on Competition Policy*, point 53.

Coca-Cola Company and Pepsico Inc., respectively the largest and second largest purchasers of aspartame within the EC. The amended agreements no longer contained an exclusive purchasing requirement and provided that Coca-Cola and Pepsico would purchase minimum fixed quantities of aspartame from Nutrasweet for two years.

Following an investigation into the industrial gases sector,[446] the Commission required the world's major producers of industrial gases to amend clauses in their sales contracts for oxygen, nitrogen and argon. Any clause which committed customers to obtain all, or a fixed percentage, of their requirements of any gas from one supplier had to be deleted. Instead, the supply and purchasing commitments had to be related to quantities falling within a fixed minimum/maximum range (on-site or pipeline contracts) or quantities up to a fixed maximum (liquid in bulk gas contracts). As to the duration of the agreements, the Commission took into account the high level of investment necessary to make supplies possible under on-site or pipeline contracts and permitted a duration of 15 years. The duration of liquid in bulk agreements, however, had to be reduced from five to three years.

The Commission issued a comfort letter regarding supply contracts entered into by British Shotton Paper Company with two waste paper collectors. Under the agreements, the waste paper suppliers were required to deliver waste paper in response to requests from Shotton up to an amount substantially equal to Shotton's requirements.[447] Shotton was bound to purchase at least 85 per cent of such amount. If increased quantities were required by Shotton, it could request supplies from either or both wastepaper collectors but could also obtain such additional supplies from any other source. The agreements were entered into for a five-year period. The Commission approved the agreements, but only after amendments were introduced regarding a prior obligation on Shotton to purchase all of its requirements, the price calculation and the right of Shotton to obtain third-party supplies.

¶366 'English clauses'

Exclusive purchase agreements may contain 'English clauses' which allow the purchaser to obtain the product from a source other than the other party to the contract when the alternative source offers better conditions. In principle, such clauses should reduce the element of foreclosure of outlets. In guidelines interpreting the block exemption for exclusive purchasing agreements, the

---

[446] *European Gas Producers* settlement, press release of 7 June 1989, IP(89) 426 and *Nineteenth Report on Competition Policy*, point 62.
[447] Notice under art. 19(3) of Regulation 17/62, OJ 1990 C106/3 and *XXth Report on Competition Policy*, point 93.

Commission stated that such clauses would be allowed.[448] In fact, for certain types of long-term tenancy agreements between a brewer and a pub operator leasing his premises from the brewer, the block exemption requires such a clause to be in the agreement.[449]

In *Hoffmann-La Roche*,[450] it was stressed that the English clause does not in fact remedy to a great extent the distortion of competition caused by a requirements clause and fidelity rebates on a market where an undertaking in a dominant position is operating and where for this reason the structure of competition has already been weakened.

Under certain conditions, an English clause could even be found to compound the perceived restriction on competition. In *BP Kemi-DDSF*, the Commission objected to an English clause because it could only be invoked if the alternative supplier made an offer corresponding to the annual requirements of the purchaser. As the agreement did not allow the purchaser to obtain smaller quantities from alternative sources and as BP could meet any competing offer, the Commission found that the exclusive purchasing obligation was relaxed only to an insignificant extent. The Commission also decided that the clause would give BP Kemi valuable access to information on offers made by competitors which it could not obtain otherwise.[451] Although the Commission went into great detail discussing the evils of the English clause in this case, it is important to remember the context in which this discussion took place. In denouncing the English clause, the Commission was responding to a defence to an exclusive purchasing obligation which it objected to in any event. Therefore, the rather harsh criticism of the English clause in this case has little relevance to the legality of such a clause in an agreement which the Commission finds otherwise acceptable.

In the *European Gas Producers* settlement,[452] the Commission made the clause conditional upon a request by the customer for its inclusion and upon a guarantee that the anonymity of the supplier making the better offer would be preserved.

---

[448] Commission notice concerning Regulation 1983/83 and 1984/83 on the application of art. 85(3) of the treaty to categories of exclusive distribution and exclusive purchasing agreements (hereinafter referred to as 'guidelines'), OJ 1984 C10/82, para. 35.

[449] Regulation 1984/83, art. 8(2)(b).

[450] *Hoffmann-La Roche v EC Commission* [1979] ECR 461, at p. 545.

[451] *BP Kemi-DDSF*, OJ 1979 L286/32, at pp. 41–42. See also *Hoffmann-La Roche v EC Commission* [1979] ECR 461, at p. 545.

[452] Press release of 7 June 1989, IP(89) 426 and *Nineteenth Report on Competition Policy*, point 62.

¶366

¶367   Block exemption

Background to Regulation 1984/83

Regulation 67/67, on its face, applied to exclusive purchase agreements whereby the purchaser agreed to purchase certain goods for resale only from the other party, even in the absence of any form of territorial exclusivity granted to the reseller.[453] Nonetheless, as an intervener before the Court of Justice, the Commission suggested that Regulation 67/67 was not meant to apply to exclusive purchase agreements that did not provide for territorial exclusivity or to agreements in which both the supplier and the reseller were established in the same member state. The court rejected the interpretation suggested by the Commission relying on the language of the regulation rather than on the unexpressed intent claimed by the Commission.[454] The court also rejected the Commission's suggestion that Regulation 67/67 did not apply to agreements between parties in the same member state. In doing so it rejected the express language of the regulation which states that the exemption 'shall not apply to agreements to which undertakings from one Member State only are party and which concern the resale of goods within that Member State'.[455] The court chose to rely on the intention expressed in the preamble.[456] As a result of these judgments, the Commission found it necessary to issue a

---

[453] Article 1(b) of Regulation 67/67 states that the exemption applies to agreements whereby 'one party agrees with the other to purchase only from that other certain goods for resale'.

[454] In *De Norre v Brouwerij Concordia* [1977] ECR 65, at p. 92 (para. 10), the court stated:

'It is impossible to accept the contention of the Commission that, despite its wording, this provision does not apply to agreements such as that involved in this case since they do not define the area of the common market within which resale of the products concerned is to take place.

The fact that the inclusion of such a territorial stipulation in the agreements is an express condition of the application of Article 1(1)(a) of Regulation No. 67/67, which relates to agreements embodying an undertaking for exclusive supply, is explained by the fact that, in the case of such agreements, the definition of the area to which they are to apply is inherent in this type of contract.

On the other hand, in the case of exclusive purchase agreements, an express definition of the area to which they apply is generally unnecessary, in particular in case of brewery contracts such as that in question, since, necessarily, it is only on his own premises that the café owner sells beverages covered by the contract.

Consequently, agreements such as that in question fulfil the conditions laid down in Article 1(1)(b) of Regulation No. 67/67.'

[455] Regulation 67/67, art. 1(2).

[456] In *Fonderies Roubaix v Fonderies Roux* [1976] ECR 111, at pp. 120–121, the court stated:

'The effect of [art. 1(2) of Regulation 67/67], is thus to exclude from the scope of Article 85(1) and, therefore, from Regulation No. 67/67, exclusive dealing agreements which are purely domestic in nature and are not capable of significantly affecting [trade] between Member States. On the other hand its purpose is not to

separate regulation for exclusive purchasing agreements taking into account the specific problems relating to such agreements.[457]

Scope of Regulation 1984/83

Regulation 1984/83 sets out general rules relating to exclusive purchase agreements (see ¶368–¶372) and specific rules relating to certain types of beer supply agreements and service station agreements (see ¶373–¶375). According to the Commission, 'the underlying principle of the Regulation is that the problem of market foreclosure is directly linked to the duration and the scope of the exclusive purchasing agreement. Also relevant is the limit on the commercial freedom of the resellers.'[458]

¶368   Nature of agreements exempted

The block exemption applies to agreements:

'to which only two undertakings are party and whereby one party, the reseller, agrees with the other, the supplier, to purchase certain goods specified in the agreement for resale only from the supplier or from a connected undertaking or from another undertaking which the supplier has entrusted with the sale of his goods.'[459]

As with exclusive distribution, the block exemption only applies to agreements relating to goods resold by the purchaser.[460] In the guidelines, the Commission states that it is necessary to specify the goods 'by brand or denomination in the agreement'.[461]

---

exclude from the benefit of the exemption by categories those agreements which, although concluded between two undertakings from one Member State, may nevertheless by way of exception significantly affect trade between Member States, but which, in addition, satisfy all the conditions laid down in Article 1 of Regulation 67/67.'

See also *De Norre v Brouwerij Concordia* [1977] ECR 65, at p. 93 (para. 18–21).

[457] In response to a parliamentary question concerning brewery agreements, Commissioner Andriessen stated:

'It was only in 1977 in the Concordia case that the Court held that Regulation No. 67/67/EEC was applicable to national exclusive purchasing agreements, and in particular to networks of brewers agreements; the Commission's administrative practice had previously been based on the view that it was not. There is no provision whatsoever in the regulation dealing with the problems specific to exclusive purchasing agreements and it is difficult to see it as having stood the test of time as a tool for dealing with them.'

Answer to Written Question No. 1764/82, OJ 1983 C93/22, at p. 23.

[458] *Thirteenth Report on Competition Policy*, point 29.

[459] Regulation 1984/83, art. 1. In *VBA/Bloemenveilingen Aalsmeer*, OJ 1988 L262/27 at p. 42, the Commission held that, although certain competitive restrictions had the same effect as exclusive purchasing agreements, the block exemption was inapplicable because the formal definition set out in art. 1 was not met.

[460] See ¶318 for an explanation of these provisions.

[461] Guidelines, para. 36.

There must only be two undertakings party to the agreement, but the regulation specifically allows for the intervention of connected undertakings or suppliers entrusted with the sale of goods.[462]

It is essential for the application of the block exemption that the reseller undertakes to purchase exclusively from the supplier. The regulation will not exempt agreements involving anything less than the total requirements of the reseller.[463] The Commission takes the position, however, that it is permissible to insert clauses allowing the reseller to obtain goods from sellers supplying at lower prices or on more favourable conditions than those applied by the other party to the agreement.[464] It is also possible to insert a clause releasing the reseller from its exclusive purchasing obligation if the supplier is unable to fill his orders.[465]

The main distinction between the exclusive distribution regulation and the exclusive purchase regulation is that the former requires territorial exclusivity while the inclusion of territorial exclusivity will render the latter inapplicable.[466]

¶369   Permissible obligations: restrictions on competition

The regulation specifically lists permissible restrictions on competition which may be placed on the supplier and the resellers and excludes other restrictions. Unfortunately, loose language in some Commission decisions in this field may weaken the legal certainty which the block exemption would be expected to give.

In *BP Kemi-DDSF*, for example, the Commission referred to an English clause as a restriction on competition.[467] In the guidelines to the block exemption, however, such clauses are considered permissible by the Commission.[468] It would appear that the conclusion that an English clause may be a restriction of competition is limited to the facts of the *BP Kemi-DDSF* case.[469]

---

[462] Although Regulation 1983/83 does not contain the specific language set out in art. 1 of Regulation 1984/83, the guidelines extend this possibility to agreements falling under Regulation 1983/83. See ¶320.

[463] The Commission, following the position stated in para. 35 of the guidelines, confirmed that a contract under which a retailer is obliged to take only 90 per cent of his requirements of the contract goods from the supplier is not an 'exclusive purchasing agreement' for the purposes of Regulation 1984/83, *Seventeenth Report on Competition Policy*, point 29.

[464] Guidelines, para. 35. In past cases, however, the Commission has viewed such clauses as restrictive of competition. See, e.g. *BP Kemi-DDSF*, OJ 1979 L286/32, at p. 41.

[465] Guidelines, para. 35.

[466] Regulation 1984/83, art. 16.

[467] See *BP Kemi–DDSF*, OJ 1979 L286/32, at p. 41.

[468] Guidelines, para. 35. See the *European Gas Producers*, *Nineteenth Report on Competition Policy*, point 62.

[469] See ¶361, above. But see *Hoffmann-La Roche v EC Commission* ('*Vitamins*') [1979] ECR 461, at pp. 545–546 (para. 107–108).

In *Carlsberg*, the Commission stated that:

'The obligations upon each party to furnish the other four times a year with a rolling forecast of its sales and supply requirements and to consult with one another about such sales forecasts are restrictions of competition which are linked to the purchase and supply commitments.'[470]

Forecasting of supply capability and purchasing requirements would appear to be an essential aspect of an exclusive purchase agreement. Indeed, one of the benefits of exclusive purchasing agreements which justifies their exemption is that:

'They enable the supplier to plan the sales of his goods with greater precision and for a longer period and ensure that the reseller's requirements will be met on a regular basis for the duration of the agreement.'[471]

It is unfortunate, therefore, that the Commission did not clarify the scope of the above-quoted statement in the *Carlsberg* case.

Restrictions on the supplier
The regulation provides that:

'No other restriction of competition shall be imposed on the supplier than the obligation not to distribute the contract goods or goods which compete with the contract goods in the reseller's principal sales area and at the reseller's level of distribution.'[472]

Thus, it is permissible for the supplier to undertake not to compete with the reseller in the principal sales area of the reseller with respect to sales at the level of trade at which the reseller sells.

If the agreement allows the supplier to compete with the reseller, it must be allowed to compete freely. In *BP Kemi-DDSF*, the Commission stated:

'Of course a producer is not obliged to enter the territory of his sole distributor, but if circumstances prompt him to do so, either directly or through a subsidiary or affiliated company, he becomes an operator on the market in the territory like the distributor. Economically he then exercises

---

[470] *Carlsberg*, OJ 1984 L207/26, at p. 33.
[471] Regulation 1984/83, recital 5.
[472] Regulation 1984/83, art. 2(1).

¶369

functions on the market similar to those of the distributor, and any restriction of his free behaviour on the market becomes a restriction of competition just as a restriction in an agreement between two distributors on the market.

To exclude the relationship between a manufacturer and his distributor in a given territory from the application of the rules of competition would mean that they could freely agree to sell at identical prices or to divide customers between them. The producer and the dealer may have completely different views on sales policy, which will find their expression in different prices, terms and customer services, to the advantage of the customer.'[473]

It is not permissible for restrictions to be placed on the freedom of the supplier to appoint other resellers in the same area or to supply to parallel traders who will resell the product in the area.[474]

Restrictions on the reseller

Apart from the exclusive purchase obligation,

'no other restriction of competition shall be imposed on the reseller than the obligation not to manufacture or distribute goods which compete with the contract goods.'[475]

Such non-competition clauses cannot be extended beyond the period of the agreement.[476] Contrary to the exclusive distribution block exemption,[477] no form of territorial restriction on the activities of the reseller is allowed.

¶370   Permissible obligations: additional

The regulation lists the following additional obligations which are not ordinarily considered to be restrictions on competition which may be imposed on the reseller:

'(a) to purchase complete ranges of goods;

(b) to purchase minimum quantities of goods which are subject to the exclusive purchasing obligation;

(c) to sell the contract goods under trademarks, or packed and presented as specified by the supplier;

(d) to take measures for the promotion of sales, in particular:

---

[473] *BP Kemi–DDSF*, OJ 1979 L286/32, at p. 44.
[474] Guidelines, para. 37.
[475] Regulation 1984/83, art. 2(2).
[476] Guidelines, para. 18.
[477] Regulation 1983/83, art. 2(2)(c).

- to advertise;
- to maintain a sales network or stock of goods;
- to provide customer and guarantee services;
- to employ staff having specialised or technical training.'[478]

The list is identical to that in the exclusive distribution block exemption except for the explicit statement that the obligation to purchase minimum quantities can only relate to the goods subject to the exclusive purchasing obligation. This is related to the withdrawal of the block exemption in case of tying of exclusive purchase obligations for unrelated products.[479]

¶371   Situations where the block exemption will not apply

The block exemption will not apply to agreements otherwise meeting the conditions for exemption in the following situations.

(1) If manufacturers of identical or equivalent goods enter into reciprocal exclusive purchase agreements.[480]

(2) If a non-reciprocal exclusive purchase agreement is entered into between manufacturers of identical or equivalent goods unless one manufacturer is small.[481]

(3) If the exclusive purchase obligation relates to more than one type of goods not connected by their nature or commercial usage.[482]

(4) If the agreement is for an indefinite period or for a period of more than five years.[483]

The first two situations are comparable to those under Regulation 1983/83 and the same considerations apply to them.[484]

Tying

The block exemption is not applicable where:

'the exclusive purchasing obligation is agreed for more than one type of goods where these are neither by their nature nor according to commercial usage, connected to each other.'[485]

---

[478] Regulation 1984/83, art. 2(3).
[479] Regulation 1984/83, art. 3(c).
[480] Regulation 1984/83, art. 3(a).
[481] Regulation 1984/83, art. 3(b).
[482] Regulation 1984/83, art. 3(c).
[483] Regulation 1984/83, art. 3(d).
[484] See ¶329.
[485] Regulation 1984/83, art. 3(c).

According to an internal memorandum which accompanied the draft regulation at the time it was adopted, this provision 'is chiefly intended to counteract the practice of large industrial groups selling an enormously wide range of products to tie important customers such as department stores to buy all their products.'[486]

In order to be eligible for the exemption, the exclusive purchasing agreement should be 'concluded for a specified product or range of products'.[487] The guidelines suggest three possible types of relationships which can be considered to determine if goods fall within the same range of products:

(1) technical ('a machine, accessories and spare parts for it');

(2) commercial ('several products used for the same purpose'); or

(3) trade usage ('different goods that are customarily offered for sale together').[488]

If an agreement relates to goods that do not normally fall within the same range then it would be necessary to seek an individual exemption.

Agreements must be for a definite period not exceeding five years

The exemption does not apply if 'the agreement is concluded for an indefinite duration or for a period of more than five years'.[489]

The Commission is concerned that long-term agreements will restrict access to distributors by other suppliers.[490] The Commission considers fixed-term agreements with automatic renewal provisions to be indefinite.[491] Thus, a new agreement would have to be negotiated at least once every five years. In a settlement involving exclusive purchase agreements in Germany for ice cream, however, the Commission issued a comfort letter for standard contracts for an indefinite period which allowed termination with six months' notice after two years. In practice, the average duration of the contracts was three years.[492]

---

[486] Explanatory Memorandum, para. 25.

[487] Regulation 1984/83, recital 11.

[488] Guidelines, para. 38.

[489] Regulation 1984/83, art. 3(d). See *VBA/Bloemenveilingen Aalsmeer*, OJ 1988 L262/27, at p. 43; the Commission held that certain agreements involving the rental of processing rooms did not qualify for the block exemption because the obligations therein were of indefinite duration. The agreements, entered into between a co-operative society and the dealers established on the premises, included a requirement that the dealers purchase products only from the co-operative society. In reaching its decision, the Commission rejected the possible application of art. 8(2)(a) and 12(2) of the regulation which exempt obligations throughout the duration of leases or from the whole period of actual occupation. According to the Commission, these provisions only apply to the retail level of the specific markets identified therein (i.e., beer supply agreements and service-station agreements) and therefore were not applicable in the case in question.

[490] Regulation 1984/83, recital 11.

[491] Guidelines, para. 39.

[492] *Fifteenth Report on Competition Policy*, point 19.

¶371

¶372   Withdrawal of the block exemption

The block exemption may be withdrawn if the conditions for exemption in art. 85(3) are not met in particular situations. The following examples of reasons for withdrawal are set out in the regulation:

'(a) the contract goods are not subject, in a substantial part of the common market, to effective competition from identical goods or goods considered by users as equivalent in view of their characteristics, price and intended use;

(b) access by of [sic] other suppliers to the different stages of distribution in a substantial part of the common market is made difficult to a significant extent;

(c) the supplier without any objectively justified reason:

(1)refuses to supply categories of resellers who cannot obtain the contract goods elsewhere on suitable terms or applies to them differing prices or conditions of sale;

(2)applies less favourable prices or conditions of sale to resellers bound by an exclusive purchasing obligation as compared with other resellers at the same level of distribution.'[493]

¶373   Beer supply and service station agreements

Regulation 1984/83 was the first block exemption under which the Commission used its powers of exemption to regulate the activities of sectors of the economy. The regulation contains specific provisions governing the contractual relations between breweries and pub operators (¶374) and between fuel suppliers and service stations (¶375).

According to the Commission,

'the rationale of Regulation No. 1984/83 on exclusive purchasing agreements is that agreements of this kind covering the purchase of goods for resale display similar features in almost all sectors of the economy, so that they can be brought under a common set of rules. Brewery and filling station agreements, however, show clear differences from other exclusive purchasing agreements so that special rules were necessary for those sectors.'[494]

The Commission goes on to say that 'normally, beer supply and service-station agreements entail a considerable financial involvement on the part of

---

[493] Regulation 1984/83, art. 14.
[494] *Thirteenth Report on Competition Policy*, point 29.

the supplier, which may thus justify binding the reseller for a longer period of time than in other sectors'.[495]

Although the regulation provides for longer periods for such agreements, it would appear that this was not an initial motivation behind the establishment of separate rules. Indeed, early drafts would have made the exemption inapplicable to agreements which did not contain clauses allowing the dealer to terminate the agreement after five years.[496] Thus, it would appear that the primary motivation behind the specific rules was the regulation of contractual arrangements in these sectors.

¶374　Beer supply agreements

The special provisions of the regulation are contained in its Title II and will be discussed hereunder.

Scope of application

Title II of Regulation 1984/83 applies to agreements meeting all of the following conditions:[497]

- only two undertakings are party;

- one party (the reseller) undertakes to purchase certain beers, or certain beers and certain other drinks, specified in the agreement only from the other party (the supplier). Agreements which relate only to certain drinks (not including beer) are not covered by Title II of the regulation. The beer, or beer and drinks, must be specifically designated in the agreement. Any extension of the product range covered by the exclusive purchasing obligation requires an additional agreement which must meet the conditions of Title II;

- the products are resold in premises which are used for the sale and consumption of drinks, and which are specified in the agreement. Such premises include all bars, pubs, cafes, restaurants and other establishments, but not off-licence shops such as liquor stores and supermarkets.[498] Similarly, an agreement between a brewery and an

---

[495] Id., point 30.

[496] A July 1982 draft contained provisions that the exemptions for beer and service station agreements shall not apply where:

'the agreement contains no clause entitling the dealer to terminate the agreement at any time on or after five years from the date on which the agreement entered into force by giving prior notice of not more than one year and making good any benefits conferred by the supplier for which the supplier has not yet been compensated.'

Draft Commission regulation on the application of art. 85(3) of the treaty to certain categories of exclusive purchasing agreements, OJ 1982 C172/7, art. 8(1)(c) and 11(1)(c).

[497] Regulation 1984/83, art. 6(1).

[498] Guidelines, para. 42.

importer/distributor will not be considered a beer supply agreement within the meaning of Title II of the regulation;

- the exclusive purchasing obligation is the counterpart of special commercial or financial advantages granted by the supplier to the reseller. Examples of special commercial or financial advantages are loans on favourable terms, contributions by the supplier to the installation of the premises used by the reseller and the provision of certain equipment free of charge.

Permitted restrictions on the reseller

The following restrictions may be imposed on the reseller without taking the agreement outside the scope of the block exemption:

- not to sell in the contract premises beers and other drinks supplied by companies other than the supplier, and which are of the same type as the beers and drinks specified in the agreement.[499] By way of illustration, this obligation would allow a supplier of one brand of lager to impose an obligation on his reseller not to sell in the contract premises a competing brand of lager. According to the regulation, types of beers are determined by their composition, appearance and taste.[500] Beers are of different types if they are clearly distinguishable on the basis of these criteria;

- to sell in the contract premises beers of a different type than those specified in the agreement only in bottles, cans or other small packages, unless it is customary or necessary to satisfy demand to sell such beers in draught form;[501]

- to advertise products supplied by companies other than the supplier only in proportion to the share of these products in the turnover realised in the sales premises;[502]

- to purchase complete ranges of beers, or beers and other drinks;

- to purchase minimum quantities;

- to sell the beers, or beers and other drinks, under trade marks, or packed and presented as specified by the supplier; and

- to take measures for the promotion of sales.

The regulation does not allow parties to impose other obligations on the reseller that are restrictive of competition[503] such as, for example, resale price maintenance. On the other hand, the regulation has no bearing on clauses in the

---

[499] Regulation 1984/83, art. 7(1)(a).
[500] Regulation 1984/83, art. 7(2).
[501] Regulation 1984/83, art. 7(1)(b).
[502] Regulation 1984/83, art. 7(1)(c).
[503] Guidelines, para. 46.

¶374

agreement which do not affect competition. In this respect, parties are free to structure the agreement as they see fit.

In *Delimitis v Henninger Bräu AG*, the court made it clear that beer supply agreements that do not satisfy all of the above requirements cannot benefit from the block exemption.[504] In such a case, every contractual clause must be assessed on its own merits as to its compatibility with art. 85(1). Clauses found to be contrary to art. 85(1) are void pursuant to art. 85(2). In accordance with established case law, the court added that a void clause could result in the nullity of the entire agreement if the void clause is found not to be severable from the rest of the agreement.[505]

Duration of the agreement
Beer supply agreements that cover certain beers and certain other drinks may not have a duration which exceeds five years.[506] If the beer supply agreement covers only certain beers, the maximum duration allowed by the regulation is ten years.[507] Beer supply agreements which have an indefinite duration, or which exceed the maximum duration allowed by the regulation, lose the benefit of the block exemption.

The provision regarding the maximum duration of beer supply agreements may not be circumvented by the use of automatic renewal clauses, i.e. clauses pursuant to which the agreement is automatically renewed upon its expiry unless the reseller expressly serves notice of his intention not to continue the agreement.[508]

The only exception to the maximum durations described above is when the contract premises used by the reseller are let to him by the supplier, or when the supplier allows the reseller to occupy these premises on some basis other than a lease agreement. In such case, the obligations on the reseller which are exempted by the regulation may be imposed for the entire period during which the reseller operates from such premises.[509]

Effect on trade between member states
While exclusive supply arrangements and non-competition clauses are often found to be contrary to art. 85(1), such a finding is not made unless these clauses also affect to an appreciable extent trade between member states. The required impact on trade between member states was at issue in *Delimitis v Henninger*

---

[504] *Delimitis v Henninger Bräu AG* [1991] ECR I-935, at p. I-990 (para. 39).
[505] Ibid., at p. I-990 (para. 40).
[506] Regulation 1984/83, art. 8(1)(c). See Commission notice under art. 19(3) of Regulation 17/62 *Bass Standard Tenancy Agreements*, OJ 1988 C285/5.
[507] Regulation 1984/83, art. 8(1)(d).
[508] Guidelines, para. 39.
[509] Regulation 1984/83, art. 8(2)(a).

¶374

Bräu AG, since both the supplier and the reseller were established in Germany.[510]

In *Brasserie de Haecht v Wilkin ('Haecht I'),*[511] the court had ruled that a 'tied house' agreement under which a Belgian cafe proprietor agreed to purchase his supply of beer and other drinks exclusively from one Belgian brewery might infringe art. 85(1) if the agreement is part of a network of agreements that, taken together, appreciably restrict competition on the Belgian market. The court held that inter-state trade may be affected by the foreclosure of competition, which makes it difficult for other breweries to find outlets for their products. In addition to the possible existence of a network of agreements, the court ruled that consideration should be given to the whole economic and legal context in which the contract operates. In *Delimitis v Henninger Bräu AG,* the court added a further requirement that must be satisfied for an exclusive supply agreement between parties located in one member state to infringe art. 85(1). The court stated that the agreement should to a considerable extent itself contribute to the foreclosure of competition resulting from the overall network of similar agreements and other relevant economic and legal factors. According to the court, the importance of such contribution by the individual agreement in question should be assessed in view of the market position of the contracting parties and the duration of the agreement.[512]

It would seem that, by adding a second condition for the fulfilment of the effect on trade requirement under art. 85(1), the court intended to remove a larger number of contracts from the scope of art. 85.

Commission notice on agreements of minor importance

Following the industry-wide inquiry regarding the brewery sector in the Community conducted by the Commission in 1990[513] and the court's judgment in *Delimitis v Henninger Bräu AG,* the Commission published a notice setting out the criteria according to which certain types of exclusive supply agreements for beer may be of minor importance and thus fall outside the scope of art. 85(1) of the treaty.[514]

According to the notice, agreements for the exclusive supply of beer involving small breweries fall outside EC competition law if the following three conditions are satisfied:

---

[510] *Delimitis v Henninger Bräu AG* [1991] ECR I-935.
[511] *Brasserie de Haecht v Wilkin ('Haecht I')* [1967] ECR 407.
[512] *Delimitis v Henninger Bräu AG* [1991] ECR I-935, at p. I-987 (para. 25–26).
[513] *XXth Report on Competition Policy,* point 84.
[514] Commission notice modifying the notice concerning Commission Regulations 1983/83 and 1984/83 of 22 June 1983 on the application of art. 85(3) of the EC Treaty to categories of exclusive distribution and exclusive purchasing agreements, OJ 1992 C121/2.

¶374

(1) the brewery's share of the market for the resale of beer in premises, such as bars, hotels and restaurants, does not exceed one per cent;

(2) the production of the brewery is not more than 200,000 hectolitres of beer per year; and

(3) the duration of the exclusive beer supply agreement does not exceed 7½ years where the agreement covers the exclusive supply of both beer and other drinks, or 15 years if the agreement only relates to the supply of beer.

The threshold of 200,000 hectolitres was set by the Commission in order to limit the exception to a small segment of the beer market. The Commission indicated that, in individual cases, beer supply agreements that do not satisfy these de minimis requirements may still be considered to be of minor importance and to fall outside of EC competition law if the number of tied outlets of a particular brewery is limited compared to the total number of outlets on the market.

¶375   Service station agreements

Title III applies to exclusive purchase agreements for petroleum-based motor vehicles fuels for resale in service stations.[515] The motor vehicle fuels can be for land, water or air vehicles[516] and for stations along public roads or on private property and not open to the public.[517]

In addition to motor vehicle fuels, exempted agreements may cover:

(1) other petroleum-based fuels;[518]

(2) lubricants or related petroleum-based products, if the supplier or a connected undertaking has supplied or financed the reseller's lubrication bay or motor vehicle lubrication equipment;[519] and

(3) servicing of equipment owned or financed by the supplier or a connected undertaking.[520]

---

[515] Regulation 1984/83, art. 10. In connection with its review of the relationship between Italian oil companies and their trade association Unione Petrolifera, the Commission stated, in a particular case, that the fact that a contract is formally between three parties does not prevent the block exemption from applying. For further details, see *Seventeenth Report on Competition Policy*, point 29.

[516] Guidelines, para. 59.

[517] Id., para. 60.

[518] Regulation 1984/83, art. 10. See also guidelines, para. 58.

[519] Regulation 1984/83, art. 11(b).

[520] Regulation 1984/83, art. 11(d).

No further exclusive purchasing or other obligations not mentioned in Title III may be imposed.[521]

The agreement may be for a maximum period of ten years[522] except in the case of service stations let to the reseller, in which case the agreement may extend for the entire period of the operation of the premises.[523] The reseller may not be obliged to impose any longer term on his successor.[524]

CLAUSES IN DISTRIBUTION AGREEMENTS

¶376   Summary

The table below provides an overview of the substantive treatment under EC competition law of the following clauses in distribution agreements:

- territorial protection clauses,
- non-competition clauses,
- prohibition against selling to non-authorised resellers,
- obligation to buy the contract goods exclusively from the supplier/ franchisor,
- purchase and sales obligations,
- advertising obligations,
- resale price maintenance clauses,
- duration and termination clauses.

The table is intended as a general checklist which must be used together with the sections of this chapter discussing the different distribution systems. The following distribution systems are referred to in the table: exclusive distribution; exclusive purchasing (i.e. non-exclusive distribution coupled with an exclusive purchasing obligation); motor vehicle distribution; franchising and selective distribution.

---

[521] Regulation 1984/83, art. 12(1)(a). For a discussion of the obligation imposed on service station operators to return storage tanks to the petroleum company at the expiry of the contract, see *Eighteenth Report on Competition Policy*, point 22. In *VEB/Shell*, *Sixteenth Report on Competition Policy*, points 26 and 55, the Commission formally rejected the complaint that Shell's contract with its petrol station tenants in the Netherlands violated the competition rules on the grounds that the discount system operated by Shell amounted to indirect resale price maintenance and price discrimination. The Commission found that the discount system was operated to support the margin of retailers who were forced to reduce their pump prices to counter local competitors and did not involve indirect resale price maintenance.

[522] Regulation 1984/83, art. 12(1)(c).

[523] Regulation 1984/83, art. 12(2).

[524] Regulation 1984/83, art. 12(1)(d).

Exclusive distribution agreements and Regulation 1983/83[525] are dealt with in ¶317–¶333. Exclusive purchasing agreements and the conditions that they must meet in order to benefit from an automatic exemption under Regulation 1984/83[526] are discussed in ¶363–¶375. The Commission notice[527] to which reference is made in the second and the third column of the table is referred to as the 'guidelines' in the preceding parts of the chapter. The rules relating to selective distribution systems and to the distribution of motor vehicles under Regulation 123/85[528] are set out in ¶334–¶351. As far as Regulation 4087/88[529] on franchise agreements is concerned, reference is made to ¶352–¶362.

---

[525] Regulation 1983/83 of 22 June 1983 on the application of art. 85(3) of the treaty to categories of exclusive distribution agreements, OJ 1983 L173/1.

[526] Regulation 1984/83 of 22 June 1983 on the application of art. 85(3) of the treaty to categories of exclusive purchasing agreements, OJ 1983 L173/5.

[527] Commission notice concerning Commission Regulations 1983/83 and 1984/83 on the application of art. 85(3) of the treaty to categories of exclusive distribution and exclusive purchasing agreements, OJ 1984 C101/2.

[528] Regulation 123/85 of 12 December 1984 on the application of art. 85(3) of the treaty to certain categories of motor vehicle distribution and servicing agreements, OJ 1985 L15/6.

[529] Regulation 4087/88 of 30 November 1988 on the application of art. 85(3) of the treaty to certain categories of franchise agreements, OJ 1988 L359/46.

Clauses in distribution agreements	Exclusive distribution Reg. 1983/83 and Commission notice	Exclusive purchasing Reg. 1984/83 and Commission notice	Motor vehicle distribution Reg. 123/85	Franchising Reg. 4087/88	Selective distribution case law of the court and the Commission
I. Territorial protection					
grant of exclusive territory to reseller/franchisee	essential (art. 1)	impossible (art. 16)	essential, but shared exclusivity is possible (art. 1)	possible (art. 2(a))	territorial protection in distribution agreements is rarely exempted by the Commission
appointment of additional resellers/franchisees	impossible but eligible for an individual exemption	essential (para. 4 and 37 of the Commission notice)	possible (art. 5(2)(1)(b))	possible	essential, but the reseller must fulfil the objective qualitative requirements for admission
restriction on active sales policy outside territory	possible (art. 2(2)(c))	impossible (para. 4 of the Commission notice)	possible (art. 3(8))	possible (art. 2(c) and (d))	impossible in principle (exceptions in case law)
location clause	impossible	impossible	impossible, but the business premises may have to meet minimum standards	possible (art. 2(c) and 3(2)(i))	impossible in principle (exceptions in case law)
obligation on supplier not to sell directly to users within the territory	possible (art. 2(1), para. 30 of the Commission notice)	possible with regard to the reseller's principal sales area and at the reseller's level of distribution (art. 2(1), para. 37 of the Commission notice)	possible (art. 2)	possible (art. 2(a))	impossible
restriction on wholesaler/master franchisee to appoint resellers/franchisees only within his territory	possible (art. 2(2)(c))	impossible	possible (art. 3(9))	possible (art. 2(b))	impossible

Clauses in distribution agreements	Exclusive distribution Reg. 1983/83 and Commission notice	Exclusive purchasing Reg. 1984/83 and Commission notice	Motor vehicle distribution Reg. 123/85	Franchising Reg. 4087/88	Selective distribution case law of the court and the Commission
II. Non-competition clauses					
prohibition against selling competing products	possible (art. 2(2)(a))	possible (art. 2(2))	possible (art. 3(3))	possible with regard to goods competing with the subject-matter of the franchise and with regard to other goods only under specific circumstances (art. 2(e), 3(1)(a) and 3(1)(b))	impossible
prohibition against selling competing spare parts	possible (art. 2(2)(a))	possible (art. 2(2))	possible (art. 3(4))	impossible, unless, owing to the nature of the goods which are the subject-matter of the franchise, it is impracticable to apply objective quality specifications (art. 2(e), 3(1)(a) and 3(1)(b))	impossible
prohibition against selling competing accessories	possible (art. 2(2)(a))	possible (art. 2(2))	possible under strict conditions	impossible, unless, owing to the nature of the goods which are the subject-matter of the franchise, it is impracticable to apply objective quality specifications (art. 2(e), 3(1)(a) and 3(1)(b))	impossible

Clauses in distribution agreements	Exclusive distribution Reg. 1983/83 and Commission notice	Exclusive purchasing Reg. 1984/83 and Commission notice	Motor vehicle distribution Reg. 123/85	Franchising Reg. 4087/88	Selective distribution case law of the court and the Commission
III. **Prohibition against selling to non-authorised resellers**	impossible in principle (para. 17 and 29 of the Commission notice) possible to limit to a small extent sales to unsuitable dealers (para. 20 of the Commission notice)	impossible in principle (para. 17 of the Commission notice) possible to limit to a small extent sales to unsuitable dealers (para. 20 of the Commission notice)	possible within certain limits (art. 3(10) and (11))	franchisees may be required to sell the goods which are the subject-matter of the franchise only to end-users, to other franchisees and to resellers within other channels of distribution supplied by the manufacturer of these goods (art. 3(1)(e))	essential
IV. **Obligation to source the contract goods only from the supplier/ franchisor**	possible (art. 2(2)(b))	essential (art. 1) clause permitting the reseller to obtain goods from other sellers supplying them at lower prices or on more favourable terms than those applied by the supplier is allowed (para. 35 of the Commission notice)	no specific provision	the franchisee cannot be prevented from sourcing the goods from the other franchisees in the network and, where the goods are also distributed through another network of authorised distributors, from the authorised distributor within such other network (art. 4(a))	the resellers may not be prohibited from obtaining supplies from sellers belonging to the distribution network

Clauses in distribution agreements	Exclusive distribution Reg. 1983/83 and Commission notice	Exclusive purchasing Reg. 1984/83 and Commission notice	Motor vehicle distribution Reg. 123/85	Franchising Reg. 4087/88	Selective distribution case law of the court and the Commission
V. **Purchase and sales obligations which can be imposed on the resellers/franchisees**	reseller may be required to ● purchase complete ranges of goods ● purchase minimum quantities ● sell the contract goods under trade marks, or packed and presented as specified by the supplier ● take measures for the promotion of sales (art. 2(3))	reseller may be required to ● purchase complete ranges of goods ● purchase minimum quantities of the contract goods ● sell the contract goods under trade marks, or packed and presented as specified by the supplier ● take measures for the promotion of sales (art. 2(3))	reseller may be required to ● observe minimum standards for distribution and servicing ● endeavour to sell minimum quantities of contract goods ● keep minimum stocks ● perform guarantee work (art. 4)	franchisee may be required to ● offer for sale a minimum range of goods ● achieve a minimum turnover ● keep minimum stocks ● provide customer and warranty services (art. 3(1)(f))	depending on the circumstances, a reseller may normally be required to ● maintain adequate stocks ● have a sufficiently wide range of contract goods an obligation to achieve a sales target may need an individual exemption
VI. **Advertising obligations which can be imposed on the resellers/ franchisees**	reseller may be required to advertise the contract products (art. 2(3)(c))	reseller may be required to advertise the contract products (art. 2(3)(d))	reseller may be required to observe minimum standards relating to advertising the contract products (art. 4(1)(c))	franchisee may be required to pay to the franchisor a specified proportion of its revenue for advertising franchisee may be required to obtain franchisor's approval as to the nature of its advertising (art. 3(1)(g))	reseller may be required to advertise the contract products reseller may be required to obtain supplier's approval as to the nature of the advertising

¶376

Clauses in distribution agreements	Exclusive distribution Reg. 1983/83 and Commission notice	Exclusive purchasing Reg. 1984/83 and Commission notice	Motor vehicle distribution Reg. 123/85	Franchising Reg. 4087/88	Selective distribution case law of the court and the Commission
VII. **Resale price maintenance**	impossible (para. 17 of the Commission notice)	impossible (para. 17 of the Commission notice)	impossible (art. 6(2))	impossible (art. 5(e))	impossible
VIII. **Duration and termination** fixed term	possible	maximum 5 years (art. 3(d))	at least 4 years (art. 5(2)(2))	possible	possible
automatic renewal	possible	impossible (para. 39 of the Commission notice)	essential, unless 6 months prior notice (art. 5(2)(3))	possible	possible
indefinite term + notice	possible	impossible (art. 3(d))	at least 1 year notice for termination (art. 5(2)(2))	possible	possible

4 Industrial and Commercial Property Rights

INTRODUCTION

¶401 Overview

Industrial and commercial property rights broadly remain governed by member state legislation.[1] As the abundant case law of the court and a number of decisions of the Commission have shown, however, the exercise of industrial and commercial property rights may come within the scope of the treaty

---

[1] In recent years, the Commission has pursued a wide-ranging legislative programme to harmonise or regulate in part member state legislation with respect to intellectual property rights. This has already resulted in the adoption by the Council of the following legal instruments:

- Council Directive 87/57 of 16 December 1986 on the legal protection of topographies of semiconductor products, OJ 1987 L24/36;
- Council Directive 89/104, first Council directive of 21 December 1988 to approximate the laws of the member states relating to trade marks, OJ 1989 L40/1, as amended, OJ 1992 L6/35;
- Council Directive 91/250 of 14 May 1991 on the legal protection of computer programs, OJ 1991 L122/42, repealed in part at OJ 1993 L290/9;
- Council Regulation 1768/92 of 18 June 1992 concerning the creation of a supplementary protection certificate for medicinal products, OJ 1992 L182/1;
- Council Regulation 2081/92 of 14 July 1992 on the protection of geographical indications and designations of origin for agricultural products and foodstuffs, OJ 1992 L208/1;
- Council Directive 92/100 of 19 November 1992 on rental right and lending right and on certain rights related to copyright in the field of intellectual property, OJ 1992 L346/61, repealed in part at OJ 1993 L290/9;
- Council Directive 93/83 of 27 September 1993 on the co-ordination of certain rules concerning copyright and rights related to copyright applicable to satellite broadcasting and cable retransmission, OJ 1993 L248/15;
- Council Directive 93/98 of 29 October 1993 harmonising the term of protection of copyright and certain related rights, OJ 1993 L290/9;
- Council Regulation 40/94 of 20 December 1993 on the Community trade mark, OJ 1994 L11/1.

Further proposed measures harmonising rules in fields as diverse as databases, biotechnological inventions, plant variety rights and design rights are at various stages of the legislative pipeline. In contrast, efforts to create specific uniform, truly EC-wide intellectual property rights have proved difficult thus far. For example, member states are still divided over the question how to proceed with the ratification of the 1989 Agreement relating to Community patents (OJ 1989 L401/1). Similarly, only in late 1993 were the member states able to break the stalemate over a Commission proposal almost 20 years old regarding a single Community trade mark (see Regulation 40/94 above).

provisions. This chapter analyses the restrictions on the exercise of industrial and commercial property rights imposed by Community law, i.e.:

(1) restrictions on the enforcement of industrial and commercial property rights: it is clear from a series of judgments of the court that treaty provisions, essentially art. 85–86 and 30–36, may be relied upon as a defence against the enforcement of industrial and commercial property rights in certain circumstances;

(2) licences: licences of industrial and commercial property rights may fall under the prohibition of art. 85 where they contain provisions that the Commission and the court consider to be impermissible restrictions of competition. Patent and know-how licences are now comprehensively regulated under the provisions of Regulation 2349/84 and Regulation 556/89. Other types of licences – e.g., trade mark, copyright or breeders' rights – similarly may be scrutinised for possible violations of art. 85;

(3) trade mark delimitation agreements: another type of agreement involving industrial property is the so-called 'trade mark delimitation agreement' under which owners of confusable trade marks make arrangements concerning the use of such trade marks. Here also, art. 85 may be applicable.

Apart from the matters discussed in this chapter, the exercise of industrial or commercial property rights may fall under the prohibition on abuses of a dominant position laid down in art. 86. Reference should therefore be made to Chapter 9 on this point.

RESTRICTIONS ON ENFORCEMENT OF INDUSTRIAL AND COMMERCIAL PROPERTY RIGHTS

¶402   Introduction

As already stated, one of the characteristic features of EC competition policy is its concern for parallel trading. It rapidly became apparent in the early years of EC competition enforcement that the territorial protection granted by industrial and commercial property legislation in the member states might constitute a serious obstacle to parallel imports. In the first case in which the Commission issued a decision of infringement – *Grundig-Consten*[2] – Grundig's exclusive distributor in France had tried to rely on its trade mark registration in France to oppose parallel imports of Grundig products from other member

---

[*] *Grundig-Consten*, JO 1964 p. 2545; on appeal: *Consten and Grundig v EC Commission* [1966] ECR 299.

states. This was one of the factors relied upon by the Commission in concluding that Grundig's exclusive distribution agreement violated art. 85.

¶403 Articles 85 and 86 as a defence against enforcement of industrial and intellectual property rights

A few years later, the court was asked whether art. 85 and 86 could be raised as a defence in an action brought by the holder of an industrial or intellectual property right against infringing imports. The case – *Parke, Davis*[3] – involved imports into the Netherlands of pharmaceuticals originating in Italy where such products did not enjoy patent protection. The court ruled that the existence of patent rights granted by a member state is not affected by the prohibitions contained in art. 85(1) and 86. The court added that the exercise of such rights cannot of itself fall either under art. 85, failing the existence of an agreement or concerted practice, or under art. 86 in the absence of any abuse of a dominant position.[4]

The question referred to the court in *Parke, Davis* was put to the court again in the 1970 *Sirena*[5] case. The case involved an action by the Italian owner of a trade mark against imports into Italy of products bearing the trade mark in question which had been manufactured by the (unrelated) German owner of this trade mark. The Italian company had acquired its trade mark rights as a result of an assignment made in 1937 with the original American owner of the trade mark. The court ruled that:

'Article 85 ... is applicable to the extent to which trade mark rights are invoked so as to prevent imports of products which originate in different member states, and bear the same trade mark by virtue of the fact that the proprietors have acquired it, or the right to use it, whether by agreements between themselves or by agreements with third parties.'[6]

The court said that, if the agreements in question were concluded before the treaty entered into force, it is both necessary and sufficient that they continue to produce their effects after that date.

Until *Sirena* the focus of the Court's approach to the question of industrial and commercial property rights had been on art. 85 and 86. It was becoming increasingly clear, however, that art. 85 and 86 offered only limited possibilities for imposing restrictions on the use of industrial and commercial property rights against parallel imports. Article 86 requires the abuse of a dominant

---

[3] *Parke, Davis v Centrafarm* [1968] ECR 55.
[4] The distinction between the existence and the exercise of intellectual property rights drawn by the court was confirmed by the Commission in the policy guidelines that it issued in adopting its initial proposal for a Council directive on the legal protection of computer programs (OJ 1989 C91/16).
[5] *Sirena v Eda* [1971] ECR 69.
[6] Ibid., at p. 83 (para. 11).

position.[7] As the court rightly observed in *Parke, Davis*, the owner of an industrial or commercial property right does not enjoy a dominant position within the meaning of art. 86 merely because he is in a position to prevent third parties from putting into circulation products that infringe upon his right. Article 85, for its part, requires the existence of an agreement or a concerted practice.[8] It may be difficult in practice to establish that the enforcement of an industrial or intellectual property right against parallel imports is the result of an agreement or a concerted practice. The court stretched the concept of restrictive agreement beyond its reasonable limit when it suggested in *Sirena* that art. 85 may be applicable to a mere assignment of trade marks even in the absence of any evidence of continuing concerted practices[9] between the assignees of the trade marks. As a matter of fact, it would seem that the court reversed its *Sirena* ruling in *EMI v CBS*.[10]

¶404   The exhaustion rule

The 1971 *Deutsche Grammophon* judgment marked a radical departure from the approach followed by the court in previous cases.[11] The case involved an attempt by Deutsche Grammophon to use its exclusive rights under German sound recording legislation to stop parallel imports into Germany of records put on the market by its subsidiary in France. Questions on the possible

---

[7] See for recent applications: *Basset v SACEM* [1987] ECR 1747; *Consorzio Italiano della Componentistica di Ricambio per Autoveicoli and SpA Maxicar v Régie Nationale des Usines Renault* [1988] ECR 6039; *AB Volvo v Erik Veng (UK) Ltd* [1988] ECR 6211; *Ministère Public v Tournier* [1989] ECR 2521; *Lucazeau v SACEM, SACEM v Debelle* and *SACEM v Soumagnac* [1989] ECR 2811; *Tetra Pak I*, OJ 1988 L272/27, on appeal : *Tetra Pak Rausing SA v EC Commission* [1990] ECR II-309; *Magill TV guide ITP, BBC and RTE*, OJ 1989 L78/43, on appeal : *Radio Telefis Eireann v Commission* [1991] ECR II-485, *British Broadcasting Corporation and BBC Enterprises Limited v Commission* [1991] ECR II-535 and *Independent Television Publications Ltd v Commission* [1991] ECR II-575, on further appeal : OJ 1991 C307/5 and C307/6, not yet decided. The abuse of a dominant position by owners of intellectual property rights is discussed in Chapter 9.

[8] See for recent applications concerning concerted practices: *Ministère Public v Tournier* [1989] ECR 2521; *Lucazeau v SACEM, SACEM v Debelle* and *SACEM v Soumagnac* [1989] ECR 2811.

[9] In *Warner-Lambert/Gillette & Ors and BIC/Gillette & Ors*, OJ 1993 L116/21 the Commission took issue with a number of agreements in relation to the sale of the Wilkinson Sword wet-shaving business by the Swedish company Stora Kopparbergs Bergslags AB. The Dutch company Eemland Holdings NV ('Eemland') acquired the EC and US part of this wet-shaving business while The Gillette Company ('Gillette') obtained the relevant business interests in the rest of the world. Gillette became at the same time a shareholder in and a creditor of Eemland. In addition, Gillette and Eemland entered into a number of agreements, including a non-Community sale agreement and an intellectual property agreement resulting, inter alia, in the division of the Wilkinson Sword trade mark along the frontiers that separate the Community from third countries. The Commission was of the opinion that these agreements created an artificial separation of markets that did not correspond with economic reality. According to the Commission, the parties would be obliged to co-operate at least in relation to neighbouring markets on both sides of the Community borders. The Commission concluded that the non-Community sale and intellectual property agreements violated art. 85(1) and did not qualify for an exemption under art. 85(3).

[10] *EMI Records v CBS UK* [1976] ECR 811, at p. 848 (para. 28–32). An application made by one of the parties to the *Sirena* case requesting the court to clarify its judgment in the light of subsequent developments of the jurisprudence was rejected, *Sirena v Eda* [1979] ECR 3169. The Commission, however, applied the *Sirena* approach in *Advocaat Zwarte Kip* OJ 1974 L237/12, where it held a 1938 trade mark assignment agreement to violate art. 85(1).

[11] *Deutsche Grammophon v Metro* [1971] ECR 487.

applicability of art. 85 and 86 were referred to the Court of Justice. Instead of examining the issue from the angle of art. 85 and 86, as it had done in previous cases, the court relied on art. 30 and 36, the treaty provisions dealing with the free movement of goods. It held that:

> '... it would be in conflict with the provisions prescribing the free movement of products within the Common Market for a manufacturer of sound recordings to exercise the exclusive right to distribute the protected articles, conferred upon him by the legislation of a member state, in such a way as to prohibit the sale in that state of products placed on the market by him or with his consent in another member state solely because such distribution did not occur within the territory of the first member state.'[12]

In other words, the mere enforcement of an industrial or commercial property right constitutes an illicit 'exercise' of the right where it is directed against parallel imports. Under this new approach, it is no longer necessary to show that the enforcement of the right is the result of a restrictive agreement or concerted practice or that the party enforcing the right holds a dominant position. Another significant difference between the new approach adopted in *Deutsche Grammophon* and that followed in previous cases such as *Parke, Davis* or *Sirena* is that the illicit exercise of the right is now defined as the enforcement of the right against imports of products placed on the market by the holder of the right or with his consent in another member state. With *Deutsche Grammophon* the court thus introduced into EC law the concept of 'exhaustion', which is part of a number of national trade mark laws. As subsequent cases show, however, the concept of 'Community-wide exhaustion' defined by the court is both broader and narrower in scope. It is broader in that it applies indiscriminately to all industrial property rights whereas national doctrines of exhaustion tend to be confined to certain specific rights, for instance trade marks. But it is also narrower in scope in that, unlike equivalent national doctrines which operate on a world-wide basis, the Community doctrine is confined to intra-EC trade.[13]

¶405 'Community-wide exhaustion': a summary of the rules

This section will address the rules concerning 'Community-wide exhaustion' based on *Deutsche Grammophon* and the line of cases that have followed it.

---

[12] Id., at p. 500 (para. 13).
[13] Bellis, 'After Polydor – The Territoriality of the Community Doctrine of Exhaustion of Industrial Property Rights' (1982) 16 Swiss Rev. Int. Comp. L. 17.

General principles

In general, under the exhaustion doctrine, the owner of an industrial or commercial property right is legally barred from invoking his right to prevent the importation of products which have been sold by himself, an affiliated company or a licensee in another member state.

The rule applies to all types of industrial or commercial property rights as may be recognised by member state law, including patents,[14] trade marks,[15] copyrights (see below), designs and models[16] and other laws such as the law on unfair competition.[17]

The exhaustion rule applies whether or not the owner of the right enjoys equivalent protection in the member state from which the product is imported.[18]

The exhaustion rule extends to imports of products which have been repackaged by the importer if:

(a) it is established that the use of the trade mark right by the proprietor, having regard to the marketing system which he has adopted, will contribute to the artificial partitioning of the markets between member states, and

(b) it is shown that the repackaging cannot adversely affect the original condition of the product, and

(c) the proprietor of the mark receives prior notice of the marketing of the repackaged product, and

(d) it is stated on the new packaging by whom the product has been repackaged.[19]

The exhaustion rule does not extend to products sold under a different trade mark in another member state unless it is established that the proprietor of different marks has followed the practice of using such marks for the purpose of artificially partitioning the markets.[20]

The exhaustion rule does not apply to products which have been

---

[14] *Centrafarm v Sterling Drug* [1974] ECR 1147.
[15] *Centrafarm v Winthrop* [1974] ECR 1183.
[16] *Keurkoop v Nancy Kean Gifts* [1982] ECR 2853.
[17] *Dansk Supermarked v Imerco* [1981] ECR 181.
[18] *Merck v Stephar and Exler* [1981] ECR 2063.
[19] *Hoffmann-La Roche v Centrafarm* [1978] ECR 1139. In *Bayer Dental*, OJ 1990 L351/46, the Commission found a specific provision of Bayer Dental's General Conditions of Sales and Delivery to be contrary to art. 85(1) because it prohibited original packages of the seller which carry registered trade marks from being supplied to a third party in opened form. The Commission was of the opinion that this prohibition did not take account of forms of packaging which do not affect the original state of the goods. Resellers would as a result be discouraged from reselling repacked products. See also *Pfizer v Eurim-Pharm* [1981] ECR 2913 (imports of pharmaceuticals by a parallel importer held to be admissible where only the external wrapping was removed, the trade mark affixed by the manufacturer to the internal wrapping was visible and it was stated on the wrapping that the product had been manufactured by a subsidiary of the owner of the mark and repackaged by the parallel importer).
[20] *Centrafarm v American Home Products Corporation* [1978] ECR 1823.

¶405

manufactured in another member state by the holder of a compulsory licence granted in respect of a parallel patent held by the same proprietor.[21]

Copyright – mechanical rights

In the area of copyright and related rights, the exhaustion doctrine applies to the exercise of rights with respect to the importation and putting on the market of the physical carrier of a work, such as audio and video cassettes ('mechanical rights').[22] In *Musik-Vertrieb Membran v GEMA* the court held that it was inconsistent with art. 30 and 36 for GEMA, a German collecting society, to claim from a parallel importer the difference between the royalties ordinarily paid in Germany and the lower royalties paid in the UK where the records had been put into circulation with the consent of the copyright owner.[23] In *EMI Electrola GmbH v Patricia Im-und Export & Ors* the court distinguished between records placed on the market with the consent of the copyright owner and records lawfully put into circulation due to the expiration of the period in which the rights of the copyright owner are protected.[24] In the latter case the exhaustion doctrine does not apply. The case involved differences in the member states' rules regarding the term of copyright protection. The court held that, in respect of products initially put on the market in a member state where copyright protection had expired, the right owner could prevent the sale in another member state where copyright protection still applied.[25]

In the *Cinéthèque* case,[26] the question arose whether French legislation prohibiting the simultaneous exploitation of films in cinemas and in video-cassette form was compatible with art. 30 and 36 of the EC Treaty. Phrased differently, the issue could have been whether the public performance of a film exhausted the right to put the film on the market in the form of a physical carrier. The court did not tackle the case from that perspective but simply ruled that national legislation may

> 'prohibit ... th[e] simultaneous exploitation [of films] in cinemas and in video-cassette form for a limited period, provided that the prohibition applies to domestically produced and imported cassettes alike and any barriers to intra-Community trade to which its implementation may give rise do not exceed what is necessary for ensuring that the exploitation in cinemas

---

[21] *Pharmon v Hoechst* [1985] ECR 2281.
[22] *Deutsche Grammophon v Metro* [1971] ECR 487.
[23] [1981] ECR 147. For a general discussion of the status of collecting societies under EC law, see Bellis, 'Collecting Societies and EEC Law' in Peeperkorn, Van Rij (eds.), *Collecting Societies in the Music Business* (Apeldoorn, Antwerpen, 1989), MAKLU Publishers.
[24] [1989] ECR 79.
[25] The terms of copyright protection in the member states are to be harmonised with effect from 1 July 1995 by virtue of Directive 93/98, OJ 1993 L290/9.
[26] *Cinéthèque & Ors v Fédération nationale des cinémas français* [1985] ECR 2605.

of cinematographic works of all origins retains priority over other means of distribution.'[27]

Copyright – performing rights

The exhaustion rule does not apply to performing rights: this issue was addressed by the court in cases involving performing rights in a film and rights related to the public performance of sound recordings. In *Coditel v Ciné-Vog Films (Coditel I)*, it was held that the owner of a performing right in a film may rely on his right in a member state to prohibit public performance of the film in the member state in question.[28] The case involved the showing of a film on German television with the rightholder's consent. The television signal was subsequently picked up by a Belgian cable operator who retransmitted the film to its subscribers in Belgium. This retransmission was successfully opposed by the Belgian rightholder.[29] In *Ministère Public v Tournier* the court ruled that art. 30 and 59 do not preclude the application of national legislation which treats as an infringement of copyright the public performance of protected musical works by means of sound recordings without payment of a royalty in a case where a royalty in respect of the manufacture and sale of the sound recordings has already been paid in another member state.[30]

Copyright – other rights

The court has also addressed cases involving other types of rights associated with copyright, such as a rental right in relation to video cassettes and a supplementary royalty on the public performance of sound recordings. In *Warner Brothers Inc. & Metronome Video Aps v Erik Viuff Christiansen*, the court held that art. 30 and 36 do not prohibit the application of national legislation which gives an author the right to make the hiring-out of video-cassettes subject to his permission when the video-cassettes in question were put into circulation with his consent in another member state whose legislation enables the author to control the initial sale without, however, giving him the right to prohibit hiring-out.[31] In two similar cases, *Basset v SACEM*[32] and *Cholay and Société 'Bizon's Club' v SACEM*,[33] the court held that art. 30 and 36 of the EC Treaty are fully compatible with national legislation allowing a national copyright management society to charge a royalty called a

---

[27] Ibid., at pp. 2626–2627 (para. 24).
[28] [1980] ECR 881 (performing rights fall under art. 59 of the treaty dealing with services and not under art. 30).
[29] Copyright-related issues of, inter alia, cable retransmission have been harmonised in Council Directive 93/83 on the co-ordination of certain rules concerning copyright and rights related to copyright applicable to satellite broadcasting and cable retransmission, OJ 1993 L248/15.
[30] [1989] ECR 2521.
[31] [1988] ECR 2605.
[32] [1987] ECR 1747
[33] [1990] ECR I-4607.

¶405

'supplementary mechanical reproduction fee', in addition to a performance royalty, on the public performance of sound recordings, even where such a supplementary fee is not provided for in the member state where the sound recordings were lawfully placed on the market.

Geographical scope

The exhaustion doctrine is based on art. 30, which prohibits quantitative restrictions and measures of equivalent effect between member states, and applies only to imports from EC member states.[34] In general, parallel imports from non-EC countries, including countries with which the Community has entered into free trade agreements, do not benefit from the exhaustion rule.[35] The position is different with respect to imports into the EC from EFTA member states that are party to the Agreement on the European Economic Area ('EEA Agreement') (Austria, Finland, Iceland, Norway and Sweden (i.e. all EFTA countries except Switzerland and, for the present, Liechtenstein)) which entered into force on 1 January 1994. Pursuant to the EEA Agreement, the exhaustion doctrine fully applies to goods originating in an EEA member state. As a result, a record producer who has consented to the marketing of a record with EEA origin in Sweden, will be unable to object under copyright law to the subsequent sale of that record in Belgium. As regards goods that do not have EEA origin, the application of the exhaustion doctrine upon their importation into the EC is disputed.[36] It is argued that, in this situation, the exhaustion doctrine will not apply.[37]

---

[34] Compare: *EMI Records v CBS UK* [1976] ECR 811, at p. 848 (para. 28–29).

[35] *Polydor Ltd & RSO Records Inc v Harlequin Record Shops & Simans Record Ltd* [1982] ECR 329.

[36] See on this issue, Abbey, 'Exhaustion of IP Rights under the EEA Agreement does not apply to Third Country Goods' (1992) ECLR 231 and Prändl, 'Exhaustion of IP Rights in the EEA applies to Third-country Goods placed on the EEA Market' (1993) ECLR 43.

[37] Article 30 of the EC Treaty, which enshrines the principle of free movement of goods between the member states, is reproduced in art. 11 of the EEA Agreement. Article 36 of the EC Treaty, which contains a limited number of strictly construed exceptions to the free movement principle, has a corresponding rule in art. 13 of the EEA Agreement. Article 6 of the EEA Agreement states that the provisions of the agreement shall be interpreted in accordance with the existing case law of the EC Court of Justice when these provisions are identical in substance to corresponding rules of the EC Treaty. It follows that the system of free movement of goods operative in the EEA is similar to that presently existing in the EC. However, as the EEA is not a customs union but merely a free trade zone, it would seem that the principle of free movement will only apply to specific categories of goods that have EEA origin (see EEA Agreement, art. 8(2)). The goods at issue are defined in general terms in art. 8(3) of the EEA Agreement.

Pursuant to art. 36 of the EC Treaty, a rightholder is entitled to rely on his intellectual property right to prevent the importation of goods that would violate his exclusive right. However, pursuant to the exhaustion doctrine a rightholder will not be allowed to invoke his right to prevent the importation of products that were previously put on the market in another member state by himself or with his consent, for instance by an affiliate or an unrelated licensee. This rule will also apply to the trade of goods with EEA origin by virtue of art. 2 of Protocol 28. It should be noted that, as regards patent rights, EEA member states are permitted to delay by a maximum of one year after the entry into force of the EEA Agreement the application of the exhaustion doctrine (i.e. until 1 January 1995)(see art. 2(2), Protocol 28).

National legislation

In a number of cases the court has further examined to what extent the derogations from art. 30 which are provided for in art. 36 or in the jurisprudence of the court, may cover national legislation on industrial and commercial property rights.[38]

According to art. 36, the provisions of the treaty on the free movement of goods do not preclude prohibitions or restrictions on imports justified on grounds of the protection of industrial and commercial property.[39] However, this article provides also, as confirmed in *Basset*[40] and *Thetford*,[41] that such prohibitions or restrictions must not constitute a means of arbitrary discrimination or a disguised restriction on trade between member states. In *Allen and Hanburys v Generics (UK)*[42] the court applied those principles to a law in the UK under which any person was entitled as of right to a licence under certain patents so as to manufacture the invention in the UK against payment of a royalty. This law also provided that licences of right may impose a prohibition on importing the product covered by the patent. The court held that the provisions of art. 36 on the protection of industrial and commercial property could not justify the enforcement of such a prohibition on importation since that protection is not 'necessary in order to ensure that the proprietor of such a patent has, vis-à-vis importers, the same rights as he enjoys against producers who manufacture the product in the national territory'.[43] The court also considered that art. 30 and 36 prohibit the competent administrative authorities from imposing on a licensee terms impeding the importation from other member states of a product covered by a patent endorsed 'licences of right' where those authorities may not refuse to grant a licence to an undertaking which would manufacture the product in the national territory and market it there.

UK patent legislation has been found to be contrary to art. 30 and 36 on two further occasions. First, the court rules in *Commission v United Kingdom*[44] that under the provisions regarding the free movement of goods, it is wrong for

---

[38] Or rules laid down in a bilateral agreement between member states: in *Exportur v LOR and Confiserie du Tech* [1992] ECR I-5529, the court held that art. 30 and 36 do not preclude the application of specific rules protecting appellations of origin as laid down in a bilateral agreement between France and Spain, provided the appellations have not become generic in their country of origin.

[39] See, for example, Case C-317/91, *Deutsche Renault AG v Audi AG*, judgment of 30 November 1993, not yet reported (owner of the German trade mark 'quattro' for a type of four-wheel drive vehicles allowed under art. 30 and 36 to prevent the use of the trade mark 'quadro' by a competitor, even though that competitor has lawfully used its mark in other member states).

[40] *Basset v SACEM* [1987] ECR 1747.

[41] *Thetford Corporation & Anor v Fiamma SpA & Ors* [1988] ECR 3585.

[42] *Allen and Hanburys Ltd v Generics (UK) Ltd* [1988] ECR 1245.

[43] Ibid., at para. 14.

[44] *EC Commission v United Kingdom* [1992] ECR I-829. See, for a similar case, *EC Commission v Italy* [1992] ECR I 777.

national patent law provisions to allow the grant of a compulsory licence for an alleged lack of sufficient exploitation of the patented invention, when the demand for the patented product is satisfied on the UK market by imports from other member states. Second, in *Generics (UK) v Smith Kline and French Laboratories*,[45] the court maintained that art. 30 and 36 do not permit national patent authorities to prevent the holder of a so-called 'licence of right' from importing patented goods when the original patent owner produces the goods in the UK, while allowing such importations when the original patent owner imports the patented goods himself from another member state.[46]

¶406   Trade marks with a 'common origin'

An issue similar to that raised in *Sirena* arose in the 1974 *Hag* case.[47] The case involved an attempt by the holder of the Hag trade mark in Belgium and Luxembourg to stop imports of products bearing the Hag trade mark exported by the holder of the mark in Germany. The Hag trade mark in Belgium and Luxembourg, which prior to World War II had been assigned by the initial German holder of the mark to its subsidiary in Belgium, had been confiscated as enemy property after the War and there were, as a result, no legal or economic links between the holder of the mark in Belgium and Luxembourg and the initial holder in Germany. The question was whether the current owner of the trade mark in Belgium and Luxembourg was legally entitled to enforce its rights against the imports of products bearing the initial holder's trade mark from Germany. Frequent references to the *Sirena* judgment were made throughout the pleadings in this case. In a barely reasoned judgment the court held that:

> '. . . to prohibit the marketing in a member state of a product legally bearing a trade mark in another member state, for the sole reason that an identical trade mark having the same origin exists in the first State, is incompatible with the provisions providing for free movement of goods within the Common Market.'[48]

---

[45] *Generics (UK) Ltd and Harris Pharmaceuticals v Smith Kline and French Laboratories* [1992] ECR I-5335.
[46] Principles ensuring the free movement of goods worked to the advantage of the holder of an intellectual property right in *Pall Corp v P J Dahlhausen & Co* [1990] ECR I-4827, where the court held that art. 30 precludes the application of a national law on unfair competition in order to prevent the import of goods from another member state bearing the encircled letter (R) with a trade mark, which indicates that the mark has been registered in the other member state, on the grounds that an indication of this nature might lead to the allegedly confusing suggestion that it has been registered in the member state of import.
Similarly in *Verband Sozialer Wettbewerb v Clinique Laboratories SNC and Estée Lauder Cosmetics GmbH* (Case C-315/92) [1994] 1 CEC 577 the court held that art. 30 and 36 of the treaty preclude a product bearing the name 'Clinique' from being banned in a specific member state under the pretext that the name is misleading, when the product is being sold lawfully in other member states under that same name.
[47] *Van Zuylen v Hag* [1974] ECR 731.
[48] Ibid., at p. 744 (para. 15).

In *Terrapin v Terranova* the court repeated that the holder of a trade mark right may not rely on his right to prevent the importation of a product which has lawfully been marketed in another member state by the proprietor himself or with his consent:

'... when the right relied on is the result of the subdivision, either by voluntary act or as a result of public constraint, of a trade mark right which originally belonged to one and the same proprietor. In these cases the basic function of the trade mark to guarantee to consumers that the product has the same origin is already undermined by the subdivision of the original right.'[49]

The *Hag* judgment gave rise to severe criticism. One respected commentator was so outraged by the judgment that he advised national courts to stop referring questions on intellectual property rights to the Court of Justice.[50]

The fundamental problem with the *Hag* case was that the ownership of the trade marks had been broken by government expropriation. There were, as a result, two totally independent sources generating goods with the same trade mark. It was therefore unrealistic to regard the Benelux and German goods as being of the same origin and thus not requiring trade mark protection to maintain their respective identities.

The court was presented with an occasion to review the same issue when CNL-Sucal, the new owner of the *Hag* trade mark in the Benelux, attempted to import and market Café Hag coffee in Germany. The German company Hag AG sought to rely on its German trade mark rights to prevent this. In *Hag II*,[51] the court was thus asked to assess facts that were the exact reverse of those in the earlier *Hag* case. The court emphasised the consent of the right holder as being the factor which exhausts the right to use the trade mark to block imports.[52] It accordingly overturned the position it had adopted 16 years earlier accepting that as a consequence of the expropriation of the Belgian marks in the Second World War, the common ownership was broken, and the marks

---

[49] *Terrapin v Terranova* [1976] ECR 1039, at p. 1061 (para. 6). This judgment put to rest fears that the court would extend its case law to cover cases where the marks are confusingly similar but had no common origin. The court held that a trade mark owner was entitled to enforce his rights against imports of products bearing identical or confusingly similar trade marks in the absence of common origin. The court suggested, however, that art. 30 might still apply if the rights are not exercised with the same strictness whatever the nationality of the party responsible for the infringement.

[50] Mann, 'Industrial Property and the EEC Treaty', (1975) 24 I.C.L.Q. 31.

[51] *SA CNL-SUCAL NV v HAG GF AG* [1990] ECR I-3711 ('*Hag II*').

[52] In contrast, in *Chiquita/Fyffes*, the Commission reviewed an agreement between Fyffes plc and Chiquita whereby Chiquita was granted the exclusive right to use the Fyffes trade mark outside the UK and Ireland for a period of three years. The trade mark agreement further contained a non-use clause prohibiting Fyffes from using the trade mark outside the United Kingdom and Ireland at the latest until the year 2006. The Commission maintained that Chiquita would not be allowed under art. 30 and 36 to rely on the trade mark legislation of certain member states to block the importation of goods with the Fyffes brand if these goods had been lawfully marketed in another member state. According to the Commission, this resulted from the fact that Chiquita had consented to the division of the ownership of the Fyffes trade mark in different member states through a partial assignment of the mark. *Chiquita/Fyffes*, *XXIInd Report on Competition Policy for 1992*, point 169–176.

thenceforth served to guarantee independently the authenticity of products from two separate sources.[53]

In spite of the ostensible emphasis placed by the court on the absence of consent on the part of the rightholder as a reason for accepting a partitioning of the market, specific commentators maintain that a division of markets brought about by a trade mark assignment should receive the same favourable treatment. Accordingly, if the owner of a trade mark in several member states assigns this mark for one of those states to another unrelated party, it is argued that the assignor should be permitted to prevent in the countries where he has retained ownership of the mark to block the importation of goods produced under the same trade mark by the assignee.[54] This reasoning is based on the idea that an assignment, like an expropriation, deprives the assignor from any means to determine the quality of the goods produced by the assignee. As a result, the trade marks should be able to ensure the genuine character of the products of two different sources, i.e. assignor and assignee. The court has been requested to give a ruling on this issue.[55]

PATENT LICENCES

¶407   Regulation of patent licences

Patent licences are currently regulated by Commission Regulation 2349/84 of 23 July 1984 on the application of art. 85(3) of the treaty to certain categories of patent licensing agreements.[56] This regulation grants an exemption to patent licensing agreements from 1 January 1985 to 31 December 1994.[57] The adoption of Regulation 2349/84 was the last major step in a series of developments that started in 1962 with the publication of the Commission's notice on patent licensing agreements (the so-called 'Christmas message')[58] and included:

(1) the adoption in the 1970s of a series of individual decisions in which the

---

[53] For detailed comments, see Joliet, 'Trade Mark Law and the Free Movement of Goods: The Overruling of the Judgment in Hag I', 22 IIC 303 (1991).

[54] Joliet, *supra* note 53, at p. 317. See also Kunze, 'Waiting for Sirena II – Trademark Assignment in the Case Law of the European Court of Justice', 22 IIC 319 (1991).

[55] Case C-9/93, *IHT Internationale Heiztechnik & Ors v Ideal-Standard GmbH & Ors*, OJ 1993 C-35/8, not yet decided.

[56] Commission Regulation 2349/84 on the application of art. 85(3) to certain categories of patent licensing agreements, OJ 1984 L219/15, corrigendum OJ 1985 L113/34, as amended by Commission Regulation 151/93, OJ 1993 L21/8. On this matter see, e.g. Korah, *Patent Licensing and EEC Competition Rules, Regulation 2349/84* (1985) E. S. C.; Venit, 'EEC Patent Licensing Revisited: The Commission's Patent Licensing Regulation', (1985) Antitrust Bulletin 457.

[57] At the beginning of 1994, the Commission was in the process of preparing a new regulation that would merge the block exemptions on patent licensing and know-how licensing into one regulation.

[58] Notice on patent licence agreements ('Christmas message'), JO 1962 C139/2922.

Commission reversed some of the liberal positions taken with respect to patent licence restrictions in the 1962 Christmas Message;[59]

(2) the publication in 1979 of a draft regulation intended to codify the Commission's practice with respect to patent licensing agreements[60] (hereafter 'the 1979 draft') – Regulation 2349/84 is based on this draft;

(3) the court's judgment in the *Maize seed* case.[61]

Regulation 2349/84 is itself the product of a lengthy consultation process with member state competition authorities and other interested parties,[62] initiated after the publication of the 1979 draft. As is shown below, the regulation is significantly more liberal than the draft in its treatment of a number of restrictions commonly found in patent licensing agreements, notably exclusivity and territorial restrictions. Another innovation introduced by the regulation is the setting up of a fast-track 'opposition procedure' under which patent licensing agreements containing restrictive clauses which are neither expressly permitted nor expressly prohibited by the regulation may be notified to the Commission and are deemed to be exempt if the Commission raises no objection within six months.[63]

With its comprehensive lists of permissible and prohibited clauses the regulation is designed to serve as a guide for the drafting of patent licensing agreements effective in the common market. Patent licensing agreements which meet the conditions set out in the regulation are automatically exempted from the prohibition of art. 85(1) as long as the exemption is not withdrawn without it being necessary to notify them to the Commission.[64]

This section is divided into two parts. The first part (¶408–¶414) analyses the scope and procedural provisions of Regulation 2349/84, while the second part (¶415–¶430) discusses the substantive treatment (in the light of Regulation 2349/84 and other relevant authority) of a number of clauses commonly found in patent licensing agreements.

---

[59] The Christmas message was formally withdrawn by a notice published after the adoption of Regulation 2349/84, OJ 1984 C220/14. The notice said that no fines would be imposed on undertakings whose agreements complied with the Christmas message until the entry into effect of the regulation.

[60] Proposal for a Commission regulation on the application of art. 85(3) of the treaty to certain categories of patent licensing agreements, OJ (1979) C58/12. The basis for the group exemption is Regulation 19/65, JO 1965 p. 36/533.

[61] *Nungesser v EC Commission* ('*Maize seed*') [1982] ECR 2015.

[62] Hearings with representatives of industry and the legal profession on the draft were held on 9–11 October 1979.

[63] This procedure is provided for in all group exemptions issued afterwards. See, e.g., research and development agreements (Regulation 418/85) and specialisation agreements (Regulation 417/85).

[64] But see *Tetra Pak Rausing SA v EC Commission* [1990] ECR II-309, where the court held that compliance with the regulation does not preclude the application of art. 86.

¶407

¶408   Substantive scope of Regulation 2349/84 – types of agreements covered

Article 1 of Regulation 2349/84 provides that it applies to 'patent licensing agreements,[65] and agreements combining the licensing of patents and the communication of know-how,[66] to which only two undertakings are party' and which include one or more of the seven obligations spelt out in art. 1. In other words, the regulation applies to patent licensing agreements (whether exclusive or not) as well as to certain combined patent and know-how licensing agreements (whether exclusive or not), but not to pure know-how licensing agreements.[67] The regulation makes it clear that it also applies to:

(1) agreements relating to the exploitation of an invention if a patent application is made in respect of the invention for the licensed territory within one year from the date when the agreement was entered into (art. 10(2));

(2) patent licensing agreements where the licensor is not the patentee but is authorised by the patentee to grant a licence or sub-licence (art. 11(1));

(3) assignments of a patent or of a right to a patent where the sum payable in consideration of the assignment is dependent upon the turnover attained by the assignee in respect of the patented products, the quantity of such products manufactured or the number of operations carried out employing the patented invention (art. 11(2));

(4) patent licensing agreements in which rights or obligations of the licensor or the licensee are assumed by undertakings connected with them (art. 11(3)).[68]

Finally, art. 10(1) of the regulation provides that it applies to:

(1) patent applications;

(2) utility models;

(3) applications for registration of utility models;

(4) 'certificats d'utilité and 'certificats d'addition' under French law;

(5) applications for 'certificats d'utilité' and 'certificats d'addition' under French law.

---

[65] Patent licensing agreements are defined in recital 2 as 'agreements whereby one undertaking, the holder of a patent (the licensor), permits another undertaking (the licensee) to exploit the patented invention by one or more of the means of exploitation afforded by patent law, in particular manufacture, use or putting on the market'.

[66] Know-how is defined in recital 9 as secret technical knowledge which permits a better exploitation of the licensed patents.

[67] On this matter see ¶432.

[68] On the concept of 'connected undertakings', see art. 12 of the regulation.

¶408

¶409　Agreements specifically excluded from the scope of the regulation

A number of types of agreements are specifically excluded from the scope of the regulation. Article 5(1) provides that the regulation does not apply to the following.

(1) Agreements between members of a patent pool that relate to the pooled patents.[69]

(2) Patent licensing agreements between competitors who hold interests in a joint venture or between one of them and the joint venture, if the licensing agreements relate to the activities of the joint venture.[70] However, the regulation applies to agreements by which a parent company of a joint venture grants the joint venture a patent licence on the condition that the products which are the subject of the agreement, in addition to any equivalent products of the parties, do not represent more than (i) 20 per cent of the market where the licence is limited to production and (ii) ten per cent for licences covering production and distribution (art. 5(2)(a)). If these market shares are exceeded during any period of two consecutive financial years by not more than one-tenth, the regulation will continue to apply. If this limit is also exceeded, the regulation will only apply for a period of six months following the end of the financial year in which this limit was exceeded (art. 5(3)).

(3) Agreements under which one party grants to the other party a patent licence and that other party, albeit in separate agreements or through connected undertakings, grants to the first party a licence under patents or trade marks or reciprocal sales rights for unprotected products or communicates to him know-how, where the parties are competitors in relation to the products covered by those agreements. The regulation will nonetheless apply provided the parties are not subject to any territorial restriction within the common market with regard to the manufacture, use or putting on the market of the contract products or the use of the licensed processes (art. 5(2)(b)).

---

[69] Even though there has been no formal decision dealing with patent pools yet, the Commission indicated that patent pools may come under the ban of art. 85(1) when:

(1) they tend to stifle competition as regards technical innovation and provide participants with a substantial competitive advantage; and

(2) the exercise of the patent rights concerned has exclusionary effects. See *Concast/Mannesmann, Eleventh Report on Competition Policy*, point 93; *IGR Stereo-Television*, id., point 94,

See also two notices published pursuant to art. 19(3) of Regulation 17/62, *Philips/Matsushita – D2B*, OJ 1991 C220/2 and *Philips/Matsushita DCC*, OJ 1992 C333/8 where the Commission, without elaborating, mentions the potential anti-competitive effects of the pooling of patents and know-how.

[70] On this matter see Chapter 5.

(4) Licensing agreements in respect of plant breeders' rights.

In addition, as is made clear in recital 7, the regulation does not apply to mere sales licences unrelated to a licence to manufacture or use. If exclusive, sales licences are covered by Regulation 1983/83 on exclusive distribution agreements.

¶410   Territorial scope

The regulation applies to patent licensing agreements containing obligations which relate to territories within the common market. Recital 4 makes it clear that the regulation applies to agreements that contain obligations relating not only to territories within the common market but also to non-member countries. The presence of the latter does not prevent the regulation from applying to the obligations relating to territories within the common market. In addition, recital 5 indicates that agreements for non-member countries or for territories that extend beyond the frontiers of the Community, having effects within the common market that may fall within the scope of art. 85(1), may also be covered by the regulation.[71]

¶411   Clauses specifically reviewed in the regulation

The substantive core of the regulation consists of three descriptive lists of provisions commonly included in patent licensing agreements.

(1) The first list to be found in art. 1 includes seven provisions that the Commission considers to fall within art. 85(1) but to qualify for an exemption under art. 85(3). Article 1(3) of the regulation makes it clear that the exemption also applies 'where in a particular agreement the parties undertake obligations of one or more of the types referred to in that paragraph but with a more limited scope than is permitted by the paragraph'.

(2) The second list to be found in art. 2 includes 11 provisions that the Commission considers not to be restrictive of competition and which may accordingly be inserted in a patent licensing agreement without giving rise to any exposure under art. 85. For this reason this list is generally referred to as the 'white list'. In order to avoid any doubt as to the legality of any of these provisions, art. 2(2) states that, if, because of particular circumstances, the obligations referred to in art. 2(1) fall within the scope of art. 85(1), they shall also be exempted even if they are

---

[71] See, e.g., *Raymond-Nagoya*, JO 1972 L143/39 (grant-back imposed by a French licensor on a Japanese licensee). On this matter generally, see Bellis, 'International Trade and the Competition Law of the European Community', (1979) 16 C.M.L.Rev. 647.

¶411

not accompanied by any of the obligations exempted by art. 1. Here also, the exemption applies to obligations of the types referred to in art. 2(1) but with a more limited scope than that permitted by that paragraph.

(3) The third list to be found in art. 3 includes eleven provisions that the Commission considers not to be permissible under the regulation: the inclusion of one of these provisions in a patent licensing agreement will render the group exemption inapplicable. This list is generally referred to as the 'black list'.

¶412   Opposition procedure

Article 4 provides that agreements containing provisions restrictive of competition that are neither expressly permitted nor expressly prohibited by the regulation may be covered by the exemption provided that:

(1) the agreement is notified to the Commission with complete information (art. 4(3)(b)) and express reference is made to art. 4 in the notification or in a communication accompanying it (art. 4(3)(a)); and

(2) the Commission does not oppose such exemption within a period of six months.

It is important to note that the benefit of the opposition procedure may be claimed for agreements notified before the entry into force of Regulation 2349/84 by submitting a communication referring expressly to art. 4 and to the notification (art. 4(4)).

Rules governing the opposition procedure are set out in art. 4(5)–(9). The Commission is required to oppose the exemption if it is requested to do so by a member state within three months of the transmission to the member state of the notification or communication. The Commission may withdraw its opposition at any time if certain conditions are met.

¶413   Withdrawal of the exemption

Article 9 provides that the Commission may withdraw the benefit of the exemption where it finds in a particular case that an agreement exempted by this regulation nevertheless has certain effects that are incompatible with the conditions laid down in art. 85(3) of the treaty[72] and in particular where:

(1) such effects arise from an arbitration award;

(2) the licensed products or the services provided using a licensed process

---

[72] In *Tetra Pak I*, OJ 1988 L272/27, on appeal: *Tetra Pak Rausing SA v Commission* [1990] ECR II-309, the Commission explained the reasons for which it would have applied this provision if the exclusivity of the licence had not been abandoned.

are not exposed to effective competition in the licensed territory from identical products or services, or products or services considered by users as equivalent in view of their characteristics, price and intended use;

(3) the licensor does not have the right to terminate the exclusivity granted to the licensee at the latest five years from the date the agreement was entered into and at least annually thereafter if, without legitimate reason, the licensee fails to exploit the patent or to do so adequately;

(4) without prejudice to art. 1(1)(6), the licensee refuses, without objectively valid reasons, to meet unsolicited demand from users or resellers in the territory of other licensees;

(5) one or both of the parties:

   (a) without any objectively justified reason, refuse to meet demand from users or resellers in their respective territories who would market the products in other territories within the common market, or

   (b) make it difficult for users or resellers to obtain the products from other resellers within the common market, and in particular where they exercise industrial or commercial property rights or take measures so as to prevent resellers or users from obtaining outside, or from putting on the market in, the licensed territory products which have been lawfully put on the market within the common market by the patentee or with his consent.

¶414 Application to existing agreements

Articles 6 to 8 set out the rules applicable to agreements in existence or notified to the Commission prior to the entry into force of the Regulation (e.g. so-called 'old' agreements in existence on the date of entry into force of Regulation 17/62 or the dates of the accession of the new member states).

As regards 'old' notified agreements or agreements exempted from notification under art. 4(2)(2)(b) of Regulation 17/62, art. 7 provides that the exemption applies with retroactive effect to those agreements amended before 1 April 1985 and where the amendment was communicated to the Commission prior to 1 July 1985.

¶415 Clauses in patent licensing agreements

The following paragraphs (¶416–¶430) analyse the substantive treatment under EC competition law of the following clauses in patent licensing agreements:

* exclusivity,
* restrictions on the licensee's activities outside the licensed territory,

- use of trade mark and get-up,
- tying,
- field of use,
- no challenge,
- grant back,
- non-competition,
- price restrictions,
- customer restrictions,
- output restrictions,
- royalties,
- post-term bans on use,
- duration, and
- other clauses.

¶416 Exclusivity

Patent licensing agreements commonly include exclusivity provisions whereby the licensor undertakes not to grant licences to any other person for the licensed territory (a 'sole licence') or not to exploit the patent himself within the licensed territory (an 'exclusive licence'). The question of whether or not exclusivity provisions in patent licences fall under the prohibition of art. 85(1) has long been a subject of controversy. The initial position taken by the Commission was that exclusivity provisions do not come within the scope of art. 85(1). In its 'Christmas message' of 24 December 1962, the Commission said:

> 'By the undertaking ... not to authorise the use of the invention by any other person ... the licensor forfeits the right to make agreements with other applicants for a licence. Leaving out of account the controversial question whether such exclusive undertakings have the object or effect of restricting competition, they are not likely to affect trade between member states as things stand in the Community at present. The undertaking not to exploit the patented invention oneself is closely akin to an assignment of right and accordingly does not seem/to be open to objection.'[73]

By 1971, however, it was clear that this liberal attitude had been abandoned by the Commission. In *Burroughs* the Commission stated that 'in some cases an

---

[73] Notice on patent licence agreements ('Christmas message'), JO 1962 C139/2922, at para. IV. On this matter generally see Jeanrenaud, 'Exclusive Licences of Patent Rights and Territorial Restraints in the EEC: Certainty vs Flexibility', (1986) 26 Swiss Rev. Int. Comp. L. 21.

exclusive manufacturing licence may ... restrict competition and come within the prohibition of Article 85, paragraph 1'.[74] In a subsequent case, *Davidson Rubber*,[75] the Commission actually ruled that the exclusive rights granted in a patent licence were not contrary to art. 85(3) because of the contribution to technical progress made by the licences and the existence of a sufficient degree of competition on the market. The same principles have been applied by the Commission in subsequent cases.[76]

The question of whether or not exclusivity provisions fall under the prohibition of art. 85(1) was submitted to the court for the first time in the famous *Maize seed* case.[77] Even though the case did not involve a patent licence, but rather a plant breeder's right licence, much was expected from the judgment of the court; so much so that final adoption of what was to become Regulation 2349/84 was delayed to await the judgment. The least that can be said is that those who expected the court to decide clearly which of the two inconsistent positions taken by the Commission – that of the 1962 Christmas message or that applied in the line of decisions since the 1971 *Burroughs* decision – was the correct one were disappointed in reading the *Maize seed* judgment. The court, taking over a distinction between 'open exclusivity' and 'absolute territorial protection' made in its 1960s case law on exclusive distribution agreements, stated that 'the grant of an open exclusive licence, that is to say a licence which does not affect the position of third parties such as parallel importers and licensees for other territories, is not in itself incompatible with Article 85(1) of the Treaty'.[78] The context in which this statement was made, however, suggested that this positive conclusion was warranted only in cases involving 'new technology' and that there might then be situations where exclusivity, instead of being perceived as pro-competitive, might be considered to have anti-competitive effects caught by art. 85(1).

From a practical viewpoint, the treatment of exclusivity provisions has been considerably clarified by Regulation 2349/84. Articles 1(1)(1) and (2) of the regulation exempt agreements which include:

(1) 'an obligation on the licensor not to license other undertakings to exploit[79] the licensed invention in the licensed territory, covering all or part of the common market, in so far and as long as one of the licensed patents remains in force'; and

(2) 'an obligation on the licensor not to exploit the licensed invention in the licensed territory himself in so far as and as long as one of the licensed

---

[74] *Burroughs-Delplanque*, JO 1972 L13/50.
[75] *Davidson Rubber*, JO 1972 L143/31.
[76] See, e.g., *Kabelmetal-Luchaire*, OJ 1975 L222/34; *AOIP-Beyrard*, OJ 1976 L6/8.
[77] *Nungesser v EC Commission* ('*Maize seed*') [1982] ECR 2015.
[78] Ibid., at p. 2069 (para. 58).
[79] The term to 'exploit' is defined in recital 2 as including manufacture, use or putting on the market.

¶416

patents remains in force'. By virtue of art. 1(2), this obligation is exempted only if the licensee manufactures the licensed product himself or has it manufactured by a connected undertaking or by a subcontractor.

In other words, a patent licensing agreement may validly contain provisions protecting the licensee, for the life of the licensed patent, from the grant of licences to other licensees in the licensed territory or from any form of competition by the licensor, including selling activities.[80] On the latter point, Regulation 2349/84 is considerably more liberal than the 1979 proposal under which the exemption for prohibitions on sales by the licensor in the licensed territory would have been restricted to cases where the licensee would be an undertaking with a total annual turnover of not more than ECU 100m.

Even if an exclusive licence does not contain any restriction going beyond those described in art. 1 and 2 of Regulation 2349/84, the automatic exemption provided for in that regulation remains subject to the provisions of art. 9 thereof. This article empowers the Commission to withdraw this exemption if the conditions of art. 85(3) are no longer fulfilled.[81] Article 9(3) provides, for instance, that the exemption may be withdrawn where the licensor does not have the right to terminate the exclusivity granted to the licensee at the latest five years from the date the agreement was entered into and at least annually thereafter if, without legitimate reason, the licensee fails to exploit the patent or to do so adequately.

¶417   Restrictions on licensees' activities outside the licensed territory

A closely related question is what type of restrictions may be validly imposed on licensees' activities outside the licensed territory. Protection from competition by the licensor may bring little comfort to a licensee if other licensees may freely operate in the licensed territory. The same would apply to a licensor who decides to exploit the licensed invention himself in part of the common market. He might also need to be protected from competitive activities by his licensees outside their licensed territory. On this point, again, the solutions upheld by Regulation 2349/84 go much further than those suggested in the 1979 proposal. Without any limitation as to the turnover of the

---

[80] Article 1(3) makes it clear that the exemption also applies where obligations with a more limited scope are imposed limiting the number of licences which the licensor may grant. In the light of *Bronbemaling-Heidemaatschappij*, OJ 1975 L249/27, a clause subjecting the grant of further licences to organised concertation between the licensor and the licensees would not be covered by the exemption (the undertaking by a licensor to grant additional licences only with the prior consent of a majority of the parties was held to infringe art. 85).

[81] See *Tetra Pak I*, OJ 1988 L272/27, at p. 43 (para. 58 and 59), on appeal: *Tetra Pak Rausing SA v EC Commission* [1990] ECR II-309.

party whose market is to be protected by the restrictions, art. 1(1)(3)–(1)(6) of Regulation 2349/84 exempt the following obligations.

(1) 'An obligation on the licensee not to exploit the licensed invention in territories within the Common Market which are reserved by the licensor, in so far and as long as the patented product is protected in those territories by parallel patents' (art. 1(1)(3)).

The licensee may thus be prohibited from engaging in any form of exploitation of the licensed invention – manufacture, sale, lease, etc. – in the territories which are reserved for the licensor,[82] and this for the life of the patent. The only prerequisites are that these territories be covered by a parallel patent, i.e., a patent covering the same invention;[83] that no licence be granted for such territories and that the licensee manufactures the licensed product himself or through a connected undertaking or a subcontractor.[84] The licensor is not required to exploit the invention in these territories. He may reserve these territories for future exploitation by himself or by a licensee. As soon as a licensee is appointed, the applicable rules are those set out in art. 1(1)(4)–(6).

(2) 'An obligation on the licensee not to manufacture or use the licensed product, or use the patented process or communicated know-how, in territories within the common market which are licensed to other licensees, in so far and as long as the licensed product is protected in those territories by parallel patents' (art. 1(1)(4)).

In other words, it is legally permissible for a licensor to grant exclusive manufacturing rights to his licensees. Licensees in other territories may be prohibited from manufacturing or using the licensed product, or using the patented process or know-how in other licensees' 'territories protected by parallel patents for the life of such patents'.[85]

(3) 'An obligation on the licensee not to pursue an active policy of putting the licensed product on the market in the territories within the Common Market which are licensed to other licensees, and in particular not to engage in advertising specifically aimed at those territories or to establish any branch or maintain any distribution depot there, in so far

---

[82] In *Pilkington/Covina, Nineteenth Report on Competition Policy*, point 60, the Commission stated that a patent holder who had granted sales licences within certain territories to licensees producing within other territories cannot be deemed to have reserved these territories for himself within the meaning of art. 1(1)(3).

[83] See Regulation 2349/84, recital 12.

[84] Ibid., art. 1(2).

[85] The imposition on a licensee of an obligation not to manufacture in a country where the licensor has no patent protection violates art. 85. The Commission in *Windsurfing International*, OJ 1983 L229/1, at p. 14, and the court in *Windsurfing International v EC Commission* [1986] ECR 611, at p. 662 (para. 85), condemned a clause in a patent licensing agreement allowing the licensor to terminate the agreement immediately should the licensees start production in a territory not covered by a patent.

¶417

and as long as the licensed product is protected in those territories by parallel patents' (art. 1(1)(5)).

The licensor may impose on the licensee (whether exclusive or not) essentially the same restrictions as regards active sales outside the licensed territory as may be imposed on an exclusive distributor under Regulation 1983/83. Here again, the licensed product must be protected in territories concerned by parallel patents and the licensee in such territories must manufacture the licensed product himself or have it manufactured by a connected undertaking or a subcontractor.[86]

Subject to the possibility provided for in art. 1(1)(6), the prohibition on active sales allowed by art. 1(1)(5) represents the maximum restriction on competitive selling activities in other licensees' territories which may be lawfully imposed on a licensee.[87] As provided for in art. 3(11), the exemption does not apply if one or both of the parties are required to refuse without any objectively justified reason to meet demand from parallel exporters in their territories or to make it difficult, in particular through the exercise of industrial or commercial property rights, for users or resellers to obtain the products from other resellers within the common market. In addition, art. 9(4) of Regulation 2349/84 empowers the Commission to withdraw the benefit of the exemption if 'the licensee refuses, without objectively valid reason, to meet unsolicited demand from users or resellers in the territory of other licensees'. By virtue of art. 9(5), the exemption may also be withdrawn where 'one or both of the parties, without any objectively justified reason, refuse to meet demand from users or resellers in their respective territories who would market the products in other territories within the Common Market' or 'make it difficult for users or resellers to obtain the products from other resellers within the Common Market', in particular through the exercise of industrial and commercial property rights. In other words, trade must remain totally unrestricted at the level of users and resellers.

(4) 'An obligation on the licensee not to put the licensed product on the market in the territories licensed to other licensees within the Common Market for a period not exceeding five years from the date when the product is first put on the market within the Common Market by the

---

[86] Regulation 2349/84, art. 1(1) and (2).

[87] In *Pilkington/Covina, Nineteenth Report on Competition Policy*, point 60, the Commission required the contracting parties to amend their patent and know-how licensing agreement to bring it in line with Regulation 2349/84. In the version initially notified, the agreement prohibited the licensee from exporting to specific Community countries for the duration of the licence (ten years) and for ten additional years after the expiry of the agreement. This had been done without regard to the protection afforded by parallel patents in these countries. The parties modified the licence agreement at the request of the Commission. As a result, the territorial restrictions thenceforth only precluded the licensee from pursuing an active sales policy. In addition, their application was limited to the territories where patents were enforced during their time of validity.

¶417

licensor or one of his licensees, in so far and as long as the product is protected in these territories by parallel patents' (art. 1(1)(6)).

Under certain circumstances, the licensee may even be prohibited from engaging in passive sales in other licensees' territories, i.e., simply responding to requests which he has not solicited from users or resellers established in the territories of other licensees.[88] This possibility was included in one of the last drafts of the regulation.[89] The essential prerequisite is that the product must have been put on the market[90] for less than five years in the common market by the licensor or one of his licensees. As is the case with the other restrictions on a licensee's activities outside the licensed territory, the protected territories must be covered by a parallel patent still in force. By virtue of art. 1(2), the restriction is covered by the exemption only if the licensee manufactures the licensed product himself or has it manufactured by a connected undertaking or a subcontractor. Even in cases where passive sales may be restricted for five years, no licensee will benefit from 'absolute territorial protection' since no restriction may be imposed on competitive activities of users or resellers (other than the licensees) in the licensed territory. Any concerted attempt by the licensor and the licensee(s) to interfere with the activities of parallel traders will lead to the inapplicability of the exemption,[91] if non-concerted, the same activities may warrant the withdrawal of the exemption.[92]

¶418   Use of trade mark and get-up

A licensor may make the grant of the licence conditional upon the licensee's undertaking to use only the licensor's trade mark or get-up. This particular form of tying was specifically black listed in the 1979 proposal as an illicit restriction of competition.[93]

The Commission has contradicted itself on this point in Regulation 2349/84. Article 1(1)(7) of the regulation now specifically exempts the imposition of 'an obligation on the licensee to use only the licensor's trade mark or the get-up

---

[88] Ibid., recital 12.

[89] Without this possibility, Regulation 2349/84 would not have allowed any restriction on licensees' export sales going beyond those which can be lawfully imposed on an exclusive distributor under Regulation 1983/83, a paradoxical result in view of the Commission's apparent determination to provide more protection for licensees in a patent licensing context.

[90] According to Korah, 'Patent Licensing and EEC Competition Rules, Regulation 2349/84' (1985) E. S. C., at 4.4.3.1., sales to customers for experimentation or clinical trials should not amount to 'putting on the market': only sales in commercial quantities should be taken into account for purposes of determining the start of the five-year period.

[91] Regulation 2349/84, art. 3(11).

[92] Ibid., art. 9(4) and (5).

[93] Subject to the licensor's right to require the licensee to make such use of the licensor's trade mark as is necessary to preserve its validity, id., art. 3(9).

¶418

determined by the licensor to distinguish the licensed product, provided that the licensee is not prevented from identifying himself as the manufacturer of the licensed product'. In recital 10 of the regulation, the Commission stated that the provisions will allow the licensee to avoid having to enter into a new trade mark agreement with the licensor when the licensed patents expire in order not to lose the goodwill attaching to the licensed product. As illustrated by *Velcro-Aplix*, however, attempts by the licensee to retain his goodwill under a new trade mark may give rise to serious practical difficulties.[94]

Instead of requiring the licensee to use his trade mark, the licensor may restrict himself to imposing on the licensee an obligation to mark the licensed products with an indication of the patentee's name, the licensed patent or the patent licensing arrangement. This obligation is included in the white list in art. 2 of Regulation 2349/84 (art. 2(1)(6)) as not involving any restriction of competition.[95]

¶419   Tying

A patent licensing agreement may contain a clause requiring the licensee to buy specified products or services from the licensor or an undertaking designated by the licensor. Such a clause will not fall under the prohibition of art. 85(1) 'in so far as such products or services are necessary for a technically satisfactory exploitation of the licensed invention'.[96] If the products or services are not necessary for that purpose, the imposition of a tie will make the exemption inapplicable.[97]

Article 3(9) of Regulation 2349/84 also makes it clear that the exemption is inapplicable where 'the licensee is induced at the time the agreement is entered into to accept further licences which he does not want or to agree to use patents ... which he does not want, unless such patents ... are necessary for a technically satisfactory exploitation of the licensed invention'. This provision may offer unlimited possibilities of evasion and give rise to serious difficulties of application: licensees wishing to escape from the contract may well claim that

---

[94] *Velcro-Aplix*, OJ 1985 L233/22.

[95] The notice should only be placed on components protected by the patent. In *Windsurfing International v EC Commission* [1986] ECR 611, at p. 660 (para. 73), the court condemned a clause in a patent licence for windsurfer rigs requiring the licensees to affix a notice referring to the licensor's name to the windsurfer board on the implausible ground (Advocate General Lenz dissented) that 'by requiring such a notice [the licensor] encouraged uncertainty as to whether or not the board too was covered by the patent and thereby diminished the consumer's confidence in the licensees so as to gain a competitive advance for itself'.

[96] Regulation 2349/84, art. 2(1)(1).

[97] Ibid., art. 3(9). In *Vaessen/Moris*, OJ 1979 L19/32, the Commission condemned a provision in a patent licensing agreement imposing an exclusive purchasing requirement on the licensee; this requirement was held to violate art. 85 even though it was a substitute for the charging of royalties (the Commission took into account the fact that no royalties were charged and that the licensee was only required to obtain all its supplies of the relevant product from the licensor as a ground for refraining from imposing a fine). See also *Velcro-Aplix*, OJ 1985 L233/22.

they were 'induced' to accept licences which they did not want. Such claims may involve difficult inquiries into the record of the negotiation.

Another form of tying includes the obligation imposed on the licensee to use only the licensor's trade mark (see ¶418). This specific form of tying is expressly exempted by Regulation 2349/84.[98]

¶420   Field of use

When a patented invention is capable of being used in different ways, a licensor may wish to restrict his licensee to a distinct field of use. In its *Fourth Report on Competition Policy*, the Commission stated that field-of-use restrictions might fall under art. 85(1) where a segregation of different fields of use is shown to be the result of an agreement to eliminate competition between the licensees or between the parties.[99] Field-of-use restrictions are nevertheless included in the white list of Regulation 2349/84. Article 2(1)(3) provides that no restriction of competition is involved in 'an obligation on the licensee to restrict his exploitation of the licensed invention to one or more technical fields of application covered by the licensed patent'.

The concept of 'field of application' is not defined in Regulation 2349/84. Article 2(1)(1) of the 1979 proposal provided that 'there are different fields of application where the relevant products in each of the fields from which the licensee is excluded differ in a material respect from the products for which the licence is granted'. In *Windsurfing*, the Commission argued that '(r)estrictions on the field of use of the products may be acceptable but only if they relate to different products belonging to different markets'.[100] In this case the Commission and the court condemned a provision in a licence for a windsurfer rig under which the licensee could use the rig with only certain types of boards. This restriction, which was perceived by the court as being motivated by the licensor's interest in ensuring that 'there was sufficient product differentiation between its licensees' sailboards to cover the widest possible spectrum of market demand', was condemned because the restrictions on use were 'within the same technical field of application, namely the construction of sailboards for use on water'.[101] In *Suralmo*,[102] an informal settlement, a clause requiring a licensee to obtain prior approval from the licensor before granting sub-licences for military as opposed to civilian use was held to constitute a field-of-use restriction and could therefore fall within the prohibition of competition under art. 85(1).

---

[98] Regulation 2349/84, art. 1(1)(7).
[99] *Fourth Report on Competition Policy*, point 28.
[100] *Windsurfing International v EC Commission* [1986] ECR 611, at p. 654 (para. 42).
[101] Ibid., at p. 656 (para. 49).
[102] *Suralmo, Ninth Report on Competition Policy*, point 114.

¶421   No challenge

The licensing agreement may not contain a clause requiring the licensee to acknowledge the validity of the patent or to refrain from challenging it. No-challenge clauses have been consistently held by the Commission to violate art. 85(1) and to be ineligible for an exemption.[103] This position was upheld by the court in *Windsurfing*.[104] Article 3(1) of Regulation 2349/84 codifies this rule against no-challenge clauses by providing that the exemption does not apply where 'the licensee is prohibited from challenging the validity of licensed patents or other industrial or commercial property rights[105] within the Common Market belonging to the licensor or undertakings connected with him, without prejudice to the right of the licensor to terminate the licensing agreement in the event of such a challenge'.

In *Bayer v Süllhöfer*,[106] the court seems to have softened the position adopted in its previous line of cases. In this case the court stated that a no-challenge clause in a patent licensing agreement might, depending on the legal and economic context, restrict competition within the meaning of art. 85(1). In the opinion of the court, it is immaterial whether the no-challenge clause forms part of an agreement whose purpose it is to put an end to litigation or of an agreement concluded with other aims in mind. The court held that a no-challenge clause does not restrict competition where the licence agreement in which it is contained is granted free of charge and the licensee does not, therefore, suffer the competitive disadvantage involved in the payment of royalties. No-challenge clauses in respect of licences granted subject to payment of royalties do not infringe art. 85(1) if the licence relates to a technically out-dated process not used by the firm accepting the clause. The Commission commented on the case by stating that the court seemed to focus more on the competitive position of the parties and less on the public interest in eliminating the barriers to economic activity which might arise from a wrongly issued patent.[107]

¶422   Grant back

Codifying the consistent practice of the Commission in a series of individual decisions,[108] Regulation 2349/84 includes grant-back provisions in the white list

---

[103] See, e.g., *Davidson Rubber*, JO 1972 L143/31; *Kabelmetal-Luchaire*, OJ 1975 L222/34; *AOIP-Beyrard*, OJ 1976 L6/8; *Vaessen-Moris*, OJ 1979 L19/32; *Windsurfing International*, OJ 1983 L229/1; *Breeders' rights – roses*, OJ 1985 L369/9.

[104] *Windsurfing International v EC Commission* [1986] ECR 611, at p. 663 (para. 92).

[105] In *Windsurfing International v EC Commission* [1986] ECR 611, the Commission and the court condemned a clause in a patent licensing agreement whereby the licensee acknowledged the validity of the licensor's trade marks and logo. The inclusion of such a provision in an agreement would make the exemption unavailable.

[106] *Bayer AG & Maschinenfabrik Hennecke GmbH v Süllhöfer* [1988] ECR 5249.

[107] *Eighteenth Report on Competition Policy*, point 104. With respect to no-challenge clauses in trade mark licences, see *Moosehead-Whitbread*, OJ 1990 L100/32.

[108] *Raymond-Nagoya*, JO 1972 L143/39; *Davidson Rubber*, JO 1972 L143/31; *Kabelmetal-Luchaire*, OJ 1975

if they are reciprocal and non-exclusive. Article 2(1)(10) provides that no restriction of competition is involved in:

'an obligation on the parties to communicate to one another any experience gained in exploiting the licensed invention and to grant one another a licence in respect of inventions relating to improvements and new applications, provided that such communication or licence is non-exclusive.'[109]

As illustrated by the individual decisions, the terms on which the reciprocal grant of non-exclusive licences is made need not be identical: for instance, the licensee's licence may be restricted to his territory while the licensor's licence may encompass a wider territory.[110] An arrangement under which only the licensee would be required to grant a non-exclusive licence for improvements or new applications would fall outside art. 2(1)(10) and might have to be notified under the opposition procedure.

¶423   Non-competition

As early as 1974, the Commission indicated in the *Fourth Report on Competition Policy* that it regarded non-competition clauses in patent licences as being covered by art. 85(1). Possibilities of exemption under art. 85(3) could only arise in special situations, particularly cases relating to specialisation agreements.[111] Accordingly, art. 3(3) of Regulation 2349/84 blacklists clauses whereby:

'one party is restricted from competing with the other party, with undertakings connected with the other party or with other undertakings within the Common Market in respect of research and development, manufacture, use or sales, save as provided in Article 1 and without prejudice to an obligation on the licensee to use his best endeavours to exploit the licensed invention.'

A patent licensing agreement may therefore not impose on the licensee an obligation not to manufacture or sell a product which might compete with the licensed products. The maximum restriction that may be imposed on the licensee is an obligation to use 'his best endeavours' to exploit the licensed invention coupled with a minimum quantity or royalty obligation (see ¶426

L222/34; *Velcro-Aplix*, OJ 1985 L233/22; *Breeders' rights – roses*, OJ 1985 L369/9.

[109] This provision is to be read jointly with art. 3(8) which blacklists provisions whereby 'the licensee is obliged to assign wholly or in part to the licensor rights in or to patents for improvements or for new applications of the licensed patents'.

[110] See *Raymond-Nagoya*, JO 1972 L143/39.

[111] *Fourth Report on Competition Policy*, point 30. See also *Spitzer/Vanttool, Twelfth Report on Competition Policy*, para. 86; *Velcro-Aplix*, OJ 1985 L233/22.

below).[112] The Commission justifies its hostility toward non-competition provisions in a patent licensing context on the ground that patent licences often have a horizontal character, an assumption which is not necessarily correct.

¶424   Price restrictions

Restrictions on prices are included in the black list of Regulation 2349/84. Article 3(6) declares the exemption to be inapplicable where 'one party is restricted in the determination of prices, components of prices or discounts for the licensed products'.

In addition to restrictions on prices, the 1979 draft also blacklisted 'recommendations from one party to the other concerning any of such matters'. This provision has not been taken over in Regulation 2349/84. Price recommendations would therefore appear to be permissible.

¶425   Customer restrictions

Customer restrictions are blacklisted by Regulation 2349/84. By virtue of art. 3(7), the exemption is inapplicable where:

> 'one party is restricted as to the customers he may serve, in particular by being prohibited from supplying certain classes of users, employing certain forms of distribution or, with the aim of sharing customers, using certain types of packaging for the products, save as provided in Article 1(1)(7) and Article 2(1)(3).'

It is clear from this provision that, except for valid field-of-use restrictions covered by art. 2(1)(3) or the requirement to use the licensor's trade mark or get-up exempted pursuant to art. 1(1)(7), any form of restriction on the licensee's marketing policy (including, presumably, the charging of higher royalties for sale to certain classes of customers) is outlawed by Regulation 2349/84.

¶426   Output restrictions

For the purposes of Regulation 2349/84, restrictions on the quantity of products manufactured by the licensee fall into two classes.

(1) Minimum quantity obligations: art. 2(1)(2) states that no restriction of competition is involved in 'an obligation on the licensee to pay a minimum royalty or to produce a minimum quantity of the licensed product or to carry out a minimum number of operations exploiting the licensed invention'.

---

[112] Regulation 2349/84, art. 2(1)(2).

The rationale is that such a provision only aims at ensuring adequate exploitation by the licensee of the licensed rights.[113] Minimum quantity obligations may take a variety of forms: a specified weight or number of products, a specified sales target or even less precise formulas such as the obligation to produce 'in sufficient quantities', cleared by the Commission as being outside art. 85(1) in *Burroughs-Delplanque*. A minimum quantity obligation may be imposed whether or not the licence is exclusive. The provision in art. 9(3) of the 1979 draft allowing the Commission to withdraw the exemption if the licensee does not have the right to terminate his obligation to pay a minimum royalty within five years from the date when the agreement was entered into and at least yearly thereafter subject to his giving up any exclusivity is not incorporated in Regulation 2349/84.

(2) Maximum quantity restrictions: In contrast, any attempt by a licensor to impose a maximum quantity restriction on the licensee will result in the unavailability of the exemption. Article 3(5) of Regulation 2349/84 provides that the group exemption does not apply when 'the quantity of licensed products one party may manufacture or sell or the number of operations exploiting the licensed invention he may carry out are subject to limitations.'

In the *Fourth Report on Competition Policy*,[114] the Commission had already stated that it views such clauses as contrary to art. 85(1) since they tend to make the licensee less effective as a competitor and, if imposed on a number of licensees, may have similar effects as export bans, a rationale repeated in recital 23 of Regulation 2349/84. In *Maize seed*, the Commission condemned a provision under which the licensee was required not to produce more than one third of its requirements and to purchase the remainder from the licensor as an impermissible interference with the licensee's production policy.[115]

¶427 Royalties

The following rules regarding royalties result from Regulation 2349/84 and other relevant authority.

(1) Minimum royalties: As stated above, it is permissible for a licensor to provide for the payment of minimum royalties in the patent licensing agreement.[116]

---

[113] *Burroughs-Delplanque*, JO 1972 L13/50.
[114] *Fourth Report on Competition Policy*, point 31.
[115] *Breeders' rights – Maize seed*, OJ 1978 L288/23, at p. 32.
[116] See ¶426.

(2) Royalties on unpatented products: art. 3(4) of Regulation 2349/84 provides that the exemption does not apply where 'the licensee is charged royalties on products which are not entirely or partially patented or manufactured by means of a patented process, or for the use of know-how which has entered into the public domain otherwise than by the fault of the licensee or an undertaking connected with him'. This provision applies where the patents have expired or are invalidated or where the products on which the royalties are charged are not made on the basis of the licensed patent or know-how.

In *Windsurfing*, the Commission acknowledged that it may for practical reasons be necessary not to take the individual items covered by the licensed patent as the basis for calculating royalties, but to refer instead to a product at a more advanced stage of the manufacturing process, into which the patented item is incorporated and in conjunction with which it is marketed. The Commission stated that:

'[t]he reason for this may be, for example, that the number of items manufactured or consumed or their value are difficult to establish separately in a complex production process, or that there is for the patented item on its own no separate demand which the licensee would be prevented from satisfying through such a method of calculation'.[117]

In this case the Commission objected to a method of calculation by which royalties for the licence of a rig for sailboards were calculated on the basis of the net selling price of a complete sailboard supplied by the licensee, thus creating a disincentive for the licensee to supply rigs and boards separately.[118]

(3) Royalties after expiry of the patent: As stated in (2) above, the charging of royalties after the expiry of the patent will normally lead to the loss of the exemption. Article 3(4) of Regulation 2349/84, however, authorises 'arrangements whereby, in order to facilitate payment, the royalty payments for the use of a licensed invention are spread over a period extending beyond the life of the licensed patents or the entry of the know-how into the public domain'. In addition, the court held in *Ottung*[119] that an agreement providing for the payment of royalties or after expiry of the patent did not violate art. 85 if the agreement provided the licensee with the right to terminate the agreement upon giving

---

[117] *Windsurfing International*, OJ 1983 L229/1, at p. 13.

[118] The Commission decision was partly annulled by the court on this point on the ground that this arrangement did not restrict separate sales of rigs – only those of boards – because in the new agreements the licensees agreed to pay a higher rate of royalty once the licensor's remuneration had been calculated on the basis of the price of the rig alone: *Windsurfing International v EC Commission* [1986] ECR 611, at p. 659 (para. 66).

[119] *Ottung v Klee & Weilbach A/S & Thomas Schmidt A/S* [1989] ECR 1177.

¶427

reasonable notice. In the light of a clear ban on payment of royalties on unpatented items laid down in art. 3(4), the arrangements concerning payment of royalties should not involve any payment of royalties based on sales made after the expiry of the patents.

Another ground on which payments of royalties might continue after the expiry of the patents is that set out in art. 3(2) of Regulation 2349/84 acknowledging the licensor's right 'to charge royalties for the full period during which the licensee continues to use know-how communicated by the licensor which has not entered into the public domain, even if that period exceeds the life of the patents'. Regulation 2349/84 does not incorporate the provision in the 1979 draft that the royalties charged in respect of patents or parts of patents that remain in force or of know-how that has not entered the public domain should be 'appropriately reduced'.[120] Whether there should be a reduction in the royalties charged on account of the remaining patents or know-how depends in each case upon the relative significance of the expired patent in the total licensed package. If the expired patent played a significant part in the total licensed package, the charging of an unchanged rate of royalty may be inconsistent with art. 3(4).[121] The same considerations may apply where the patent licence is combined with a trade mark licence: art. 3(5) of the 1979 draft blacklisted any obligation on the part of the licensee to continue, after expiry of the patent, to pay the full royalties stipulated by the licence for the use of a patent and a trade mark. Even though this provision has not been taken over in Regulation 2349/84, it may still provide guidance as to how art. 3(4) of Regulation 2349/84 could be construed by the Commission: if royalties for the use of the patent and those for the use of the trade mark are not separately itemised, the trade mark licence may be analysed as a means of unlawfully extending the effects of the patent if full royalties continue to be charged after the expiry of the patent.

¶428   Post-term bans on use

Article 2(4) of Regulation 2349/84 provides that no restriction of competition is involved in 'an obligation on the licensee not to exploit the patent after the termination of the agreement in so far as the patent is still in force'.[122]

---

[120] Regulation 2349/84, art. 3(4).

[121] It should be noted, however, that recital 22 suggests that art. 3(4) applies only where the licensee is required 'to continue to pay royalties after all the licensed patents have ceased to be in force and the communicated know-how has entered into the public domain'.

[122] A post-term ban on the production and marketing of products after the expiry of the patents may, however, fall within the prohibition of art. 85(1) (see *Ottung v Klee & Weilbach A/S & Thomas Schmidt A/S* [1989] ECR 1177).

This provision is restricted to exploitation of the patent. No provision of Regulation 2349/84 deals with post-term bans on use of know-how. The regulation does not incorporate the provision in the 1979 draft blacklisting post-term bans on know-how subject to payments for the use of such know-how 'for an appropriate period' after the expiry of the agreement. In view of the silence of Regulation 2349/84 on this point, post-term bans on use of know-how are not covered by the group exemption and might have to be notified, for instance, in the context of the opposition procedure.

¶429   Duration

Article 3(2) of Regulation 2349/84 provides that the exemption does not apply where:

> 'the duration of the licensing agreement is automatically prolonged beyond the expiry of the licensed patents existing at the time the agreement was entered into by the inclusion in it of any new patent obtained by the licensor, unless the agreement provides each party with the right to terminate the agreement at least annually after the expiry of the licensed patents at the time the agreement was entered into ...'

As is made clear in art. 3(2), this provision is without prejudice to the right of the licensor to charge royalties for the use of know-how after the expiry of the patents.[123]

Provisions automatically extending the term of the agreement by the inclusion, for instance, of improvement patents have been condemned in several individual cases.[124] As the Commission stated in recital 20 of Regulation 2349/84, the parties are free to agree subsequently to extend the term of the original agreement by entering into new agreements.[125] What is prohibited is an automatic extension of the agreement, i.e. in the absence of a specific new agreement to that effect.

¶430   Other clauses

Patent licensing agreements also commonly contain one or more of the following provisions which generally should not raise difficulties from the standpoint of art. 85 as construed by the Commission and the court:

> (1) Restrictions on sub-licensing: art. 2(1)(5) (the 'white list') of Regulation 2349/84 expressly provides that no restriction of competition is involved

---

[123] On this matter, see ¶427.
[124] *AOIP-Beyrard*, OJ 1976 L6/8; *Peugeot-Zimmern, Sixth Report on Competition Policy*, point 159; *Velcro-Aplix*, OJ 1985 L233/22.
[125] See also *AOIP-Beyrard*, OJ 1976 L6/8, at p. 13.

in 'an obligation on the licensee not to grant sub-licences or assign the licence';[126]

(2) Confidentiality: another type of obligation included in the 'white list' (art. 2(1)(7)) is 'an obligation on the licensee not to divulge know-how communicated by the licensor; the licensee may be held to this obligation even after the agreement has expired';

(3) Assistance over patent infringement: also included in the 'white list' (art. 2(1)(8)) are –

'obligations:

(a) to inform the licensor of infringements of the patents;

(b) to take legal action against an infringement;

(c) to assist the licensor in any legal action against an infringer, provided that these obligations are without prejudice to the licensee's right to challenge the validity of the licensed patent';

(4) Quality specifications: the licensor may also lawfully impose quality specifications on the licensee. Article 2(1)(9) of Regulation 2349/84 condones the imposition of 'an obligation on the licensee to observe specifications concerning the minimum quality of the licensed product, provided that such specifications are necessary for a technically satisfactory exploitation of the licensed invention, and to allow the licensor to carry out related checks';

(5) Most favoured licensee: the patent licence may contain 'an obligation on the licensor to grant the licensee any more favourable terms that the licensor may grant to another undertaking after the agreement is entered into'. This type of provision is included in the 'white list' (art. 2(1)(11));

(6) Arbitration clause: the Commission has traditionally been suspicious of arbitration awards. Article 4 of the 1979 draft required the parties to communicate the terms of any arbitration award dealing with provisions covered in the exemption or the black list.[127] Article 9(5) empowered the Commission to withdraw the exemption where art. 4 was infringed or an arbitration award communicated under that article did not state the reasons on which it was based. These provisions are not included in Regulation 2349/84. Article 9(1) only states that the exemption may be withdrawn where an agreement has effects which are incompatible with art. 85(3), in particular where 'such effects arise from an arbitration award'. Regulation 2349/84 does not lay down any obligation to

---

[126] In *Suralmo, Ninth Report on Competition Policy*, point 114, the Commission objected to a provision requiring the licensor's prior consent before granting sub-licences for military as opposed to civilian use.
[127] See also *Kabelmetal-Luchaire*, OJ 1975 L222/34.

¶430

systematically communicate arbitration awards to the Commission. The licensing agreement may validly contain an arbitration clause.

KNOW-HOW LICENCES

¶431   Regulation of know-how licences

The Commission has adopted Regulation 556/89 of 30 November 1988 on the application of art. 85(3) of the treaty to certain categories of know-how licensing agreements.[128] Know-how licensing agreements which meet the conditions set out in the regulation are automatically exempted from the prohibition of art. 85(1) without prior notification to the Commission. The regulation entered into force on 1 April 1989 and will apply until 31 December 1999.[129]

The Commission had already issued guidelines in respect of pure know-how agreements in a draft working paper submitted for the comments of the member states in June 1986.[130] Between 1986 and 1988, the Commission also granted individual exemptions to some know-how licensing agreements,[131] and in the light of the experience acquired decided to adopt the block exemption on know-how licences.

The reasons for the adoption of Regulation 556/89 are set out in recitals (2) and (7): recital (2) states that 'the increasing economic importance of non-patented technical information commonly termed know-how ... and the fact that the transfer of know-how is, in practice, frequently irreversible, make it necessary to provide greater legal certainty' to agreements licensing the exploitation of such information. Recital (7) states that the obligations contained in the regulation 'encourage the transfer of technology and thus generally contribute to improving the production of goods and to promoting technical progress by increasing the number of production facilities and the quality of goods produced in the common market ...'.

Recital (6) of Regulation 556/89 refers to the solution adopted by the court in the *Maize seed* case,[132] i.e., that exclusive know-how licences that do not place restrictions on third parties might not be caught by the prohibition of art. 85(1) where they are concerned with the introduction of a new technology.

Regulation 556/89 is drafted according to a structure similar to Regulation

---

[128] Commission Regulation 556/89 on the application of art. 85(3) of the treaty to certain categories of know-how licensing agreements, OJ 1989 L61/1, as amended by Commission Regulation 151/93, OJ 1993 L21/8.
[129] At the beginning of 1994, the Commission was in the process of preparing a new regulation that would merge the block exemptions on know-how licensing and patent licensing into one regulation.
[130] The treatment of know-how licensing under the competition rules, 86/EN-1.
[131] *Boussois-Interpane*, OJ 1987 L50/30; *Rich Products-Jus Rol*, OJ 1988 L69/21; *Delta Chemie-DDD* [1989] 1 CEC 2,234; OJ 1988 L309/34.
[132] *Nungesser v EC Commission ('Maize seed')* [1982] ECR 2015.

2349/84 on patent licensing agreements.[133] Some provisions are common to both, while others result from the specific nature of know-how.

¶432   Substantive scope of Regulation 556/89 – types of agreements covered

Article 1 of Regulation 556/89 provides that it applies to 'pure know-how licensing agreements and to mixed know-how and patent licensing agreements not exempted by [Regulation 2349/84], including those agreements containing ancillary provisions relating to trade marks or other intellectual property rights, to which only two undertakings are party', and which include one or more of the eight obligations spelt out in art. 1. Article 1(7)(6) of the regulation defines the mixed know-how and patent licensing agreements concerned as 'agreements not exempted by [Regulation 2349/84], under which a technology containing both non-patented elements and elements that are patented in one or more Member States is licensed'. Accordingly, in order to define the scope of application of Regulation 556/89, it is important to specify whether or not a mixed agreement is covered by Regulation 2349/84. Mixed know-how and patent licensing agreements are covered by Regulation 2349/84 where, pursuant to the provisions of recital 9 of this regulation, 'the know-how is secret and permits a better exploitation of the licensed patents', although 'only in so far as the licensed patents are necessary for achieving the objects of the licensed technology and as long as one of the licensed patents remains in force'.

On the basis of recital 9, the Commission decided in *Boussois-Interpane*,[134] that the licensing of a complete package including patented and non-patented technology was outside the scope of Regulation 2349/84. The Commission justified the non-availability of Regulation 2349/84 by the fact that the 'detailed body of know-how was the dominant element', particularly because the use of the patents was required for only one type of the processes concerned, because the licensee was not obliged to exploit the patents throughout the term of the contract and was not obliged to pay royalties if he did not do so. Moreover, the type of process for which the patents were required was not 'even partially protected by patents in five Member States'.

Article 1(1)(3) and (1)(4) of Regulation 2349/84 provides that restrictions on the exploitation of the licensed technology may only be imposed in member states where the technology is protected by parallel patents. In other words, territorial restrictions cannot be exempted by Regulation 2349/84 if they concern territories without patent protection. Many mixed agreements are therefore outside the scope of Regulation 2349/84. The Commission opted to

---

[133] Commission Regulation 2349/84 on the application of art. 85(3) to certain categories of patent licensing agreements, OJ 1984 L219/15, as amended by Commission Regulation 151/93, OJ 1993 L21/8.
[134] *Boussois-Interpane*, OJ 1987 L50/30, at p. 35 (para. 19).

¶432

fill the gap by way of Regulation 556/89; recital 2 of Regulation 556/89 provides that the block exemption will apply in particular to:

'– mixed agreements in which the licensed patents are not necessary for the achievement of the objects of the licensed technology containing both patented and non-patented elements; this may be the case where such patents do not afford effective protection against the exploitation of the technology by third parties;

– mixed agreements which, regardless of whether or not the licensed patents are necessary for the achievement of the objects of the licensed technology, contain obligations which restrict the exploitation of the relevant technology by the licensor or the licensee in Member States without patent protection, in so far and as long as such obligations are based in whole or in part on the exploitation of the licensed know-how and fulfil the other conditions set out in this Regulation.'

The regulation makes it clear that it also applies to:

(1) agreements where the licensor is not the developer of the know-how but is authorised by the developer to grant a licence or a sub-licence (art. 6(1));

(2) assignments of know-how when the risk associated with exploitation remains with the assignor (art. 6(2));

(3) pure know-how or mixed agreements in which rights or obligations of the licensor or the licensee are assumed by undertakings connected with them (art. 6(3));

(4) agreements, including the licensing of intellectual property rights other than patents (trade marks, copyright and designs) or the licensing of software, where these rights or the software are of assistance in achieving the object of the licensed technology, and there are no obligations restrictive of competition other than those also attached to the licensed know-how and exempted under the regulation (art. 5(1)(4)).

¶433   Agreements specifically excluded from the scope of the regulation

A number of types of agreements are specifically excluded from the scope of the regulation. Article 5(1) provides for the same categories of exclusion as in Regulation 2349/84, i.e.:

(1) 'agreements between members of a patent or know-how pool which relate to the pooled technologies' (art. 5(1)(1));

(2) 'know-how licensing agreements between competing undertakings

which hold interests in a joint venture, or between one of them and the joint venture, if the licensing agreements relate to the activities of the joint venture' (art. 5(1)(2). However, the regulation applies to agreements by which a parent company of a joint venture grants the joint venture a know-how licence, on the condition that the products which are the subject of the agreement, in addition to any equivalent products of the parties, do not represent more than (i) 20 per cent of the market where the licence is limited to production and (ii) ten per cent for licences covering production and distribution (art. 5(2)(a)). If these market shares are exceeded during any period of two consecutive financial years by not more than one-tenth, the regulation will continue to apply. If this limit is also exceeded, the regulation will only apply for a period of six months following the end of the financial year in which this limit was exceeded (art. 5(3));

(3) 'agreements under which one party grants the other a know-how licence and the other party, albeit in separate agreements or through connected undertakings, grants the first party a patent, trade mark or know-how licence or exclusive sales rights, where the parties are competitors in relation to the products covered by those agreements' (art. 5(1)(3)). The regulation will nevertheless apply to reciprocal licences within the meaning of point 3 of paragraph 1, provided the parties are not subject to any territorial restriction within the common market with regard to the manufacture, use or putting on the market of the contract products or the use of the licensed processes' (art. 5(2)(b)).

The regulation also makes it clear that it does not apply to agreements concluded 'solely for the purpose of sale, except where the licensor undertakes for a preliminary period before the licensee himself commences production using the licensed technology, to supply the contract products for sale by the licensee'.[135] Also excluded from the scope of the regulation are 'agreements relating to marketing know-how communicated in the context of franchising arrangements' (recital 5), and agreements including the licensing of intellectual property rights other than patents, in so far as they are not ancillary to the know-how (art. 5(1)(4)).[136]

---

[135] Recital 5. See *Delta Chemie-DDD* [1989] 1 CEC 2,254; OJ 1988 L309/34, where a distribution agreement was concluded before the grant of the know-how licence.

[136] In *Moosehead-Whitbread*, OJ 1990 L100/32, at p. 36 (para. 16), the Commission looked to the principal interest of the parties in assessing whether the trade mark licence was ancillary to the know-how licence:

'In the present case the principal interest of the parties lies in the exploitation of the trade mark rather than of the know-how. The parties view the Canadian origin of the mark as crucial to the success of the marketing campaign, which promotes the product as a Canadian beer. Under these circumstances, the provision of the agreement relating to the trade marks is not ancillary and Regulation 556/89 therefore does not apply.'

¶433

¶434　Definition of know-how

According to art. 1(7)(1) 'know-how means a body of technical information that is secret, substantial and identified in any appropriate form'.

Secrecy

Secrecy is the fundamental characteristic of know-how. Although patents are publicly revealed, they are also protected by the grant of a monopoly in favour of the patent holder. Know-how, however, is only protected as long as it is secret. Once the product is on the market, every competitor can buy it and try to find out the method of production through reverse engineering without infringing the inventor's rights, as would be the case for patents. For the Commission, as stated in art. 1(7)(2), secrecy should not be taken to mean that each individual component of the know-how should be totally unknown or unobtainable outside the licensor's business. Article 1(7)(2) makes it clear that 'the term "secret" means that the know-how package as a body or in the precise configuration and assembly of its components is not generally known or easily accessible, so that part of its value consists in the lead-time the licensee gains when it is communicated to him'.[137]

Substantiality

Substantiality is the basic condition in order to ensure that know-how licensing agreements and the restrictions included therein are not a disguised way of sharing the market by licensing worthless and trivial know-how, since unlike a patent, the value of the know-how is not controlled by a public authority. Pursuant to art. 1(7)(3), substantiality means 'that the know-how includes information which is of importance for the whole or a significant part of (i) a manufacturing process, or (ii) a product or service, or (iii) for the development thereof, and excludes information which is trivial. Such know-how must thus be useful, i.e. can reasonably be expected at the date of conclusion of the agreement to be capable of improving the competitive position of the licensee, for example by helping him to enter a new market or giving him an advantage in competition with other manufacturers or providers of services who do not have access to the licensed secret know-how or other comparable secret know-how'.[138] The Economic and Social Committee argued in its additional opinion

---

[137] In *Boussois-Interpane*, OJ 1987 L50/30, at p. 30 (para. 2), the Commission considered that the know-how licensed to Boussois was secret 'in the sense that, although its individual components might not be totally unknown or unobtainable, particularly for qualified engineers in the industry, the know-how package as a whole was not readily available, and could therefore be said to be not in the public domain'.

[138] In *Rich Products-Jus Rol*, OJ 1988 L69/21, at p. 22 (para. 4), the licence concerned a yeast freezing process which enabled the licensee to extend its range of products. The Commission stated that the know-how was of significant importance for the production of this new range of products and 'had to be considered as substantial and capable of improving the performance of the licensee who was thus willing to pay royalties for it'.

In *Delta Chemie-DDD* [1989] 1 CEC 2,254; OJ 1988 L309/34, at p. 35 (para. 4 and 5), the know-how permitted

on the draft regulation[139] that practitioners might have difficulty in estimating the usefulness of the know-how as no precise reference level was clearly defined by the Commission.

Identification

In order to control whether the criteria of secrecy and substantiality are fulfilled, the know-how must be identified, i.e., according to art. 1(7)(4), 'described or recorded' in such a manner as to make it possible to verify that the first two conditions are fulfilled, and 'to ensure that the licensee is not unduly restricted in his exploitation of his own technology. In order to be identified the know-how can either be set out in the licence agreement or in a separate document or recorded in any other appropriate form'.[140]

Article 1(3) also makes it clear that the obligation of identification concerns 'any subsequent improvements' to the basic know-how 'which become available to the parties and are communicated to the other party pursuant to the terms of the agreement'.

Whatever the form of the identification, art. 1(7)(4) provides an important time condition: the know-how must be identified at the latest when it is transferred or shortly thereafter.

¶435   Territorial scope

Recital 4 provides that where a know-how licensing agreement contains not only obligations relating to territories within the EC, but also obligations relating to non-member countries, the presence of the latter does not prevent Regulation 556/89 from applying to the obligations relating to territories within the EC. However, where know-how licensing agreements for non-member countries or for territories which extend beyond the frontiers of the Community have effects within the EC that may fall within the scope of art. 85(1), such agreements should be covered by Regulation 556/89 to the same extent as would agreements for territories within the Community.

---

principally the manufacture of specific stain removers. The Commission estimated that the know-how was substantial in so far as it concerned the manufacture, packaging and sale of a range of original products which satisfied specific needs, and differed from universal stain removers which might be used for all types of stains.

[139] Additional opinion on the draft Commission regulation on the application of art. 85(3) of the treaty to certain categories of know-how licensing agreements, OJ 1988 C134/10, point 2.2.

[140] Some examples of different means of identification of know-how may usefully be provided by certain Commission decisions. In *Boussois-Interpane*, OJ 1987 L50/30, at p. 30 (para. 2), identification consisted, e.g., of providing plans, drawings, descriptions of materials and operations which were attached to the contract, together with specifications of the performance characteristics of the plant and each type of product, lists of the materials and consumables the licensee had to keep in stock etc.; in *Rich Products-Jus Rol*, OJ 1988 L69/21, at p. 22 (para. 4), the know-how included both written information on the process used for manufacturing the licensed product, and notes of oral discussions between the employees of the two parties with a view to the delivery of technical information; in *Delta Chemie-DDD*, OJ 1988 L309/34, at p. 35 (para. 5), the know-how was described in formulae and technical documents disclosed to the licensee. In addition, the licensor gave the licensee all appropriate advice, and put specialised technicians at his disposal.

¶436   Opposition procedure

Regulation 556/89, like Regulation 2349/84, contains an opposition procedure whereby, pursuant to art. 4(1), agreements containing provisions restrictive of competition which are neither expressly permitted nor expressly prohibited by the regulation may be covered by the exemption if they are notified to the Commission in accordance with the provisions of Regulation 17/62 and if the Commission does not oppose such exemption within a period of six months.

Regulation 556/89 is original in that it provides an example of a provision that might be subject to the opposition procedure. Article 4(2) provides that this procedure:

> 'shall apply to an obligation on the licensee to supply only a limited quantity of the licensed product to a particular customer, where the know-how licence is granted at the request of such a customer in order to provide him with a second source of supply within the licensed territory. The provision shall also apply where the customer is the licensee and the licence, in order to provide a second source of supply, provides for the customer to make licensed products or have them made by a sub-contractor'.

In recital 18 of Regulation 556/89, the Commission has explained the reasons why this particular clause is subject to the opposition procedure: in one respect it is restrictive of competition in so far as there is a risk of the second supplier being deprived of the possibility of developing his own business in the fields covered by the agreement, but on the other hand it may contribute to the improvement of the production of goods and to the promotion of technical progress by further disseminating the technology.

¶437   Withdrawal of the exemption

The five first cases of withdrawal are similar to Regulation 2349/84, i.e.:

(1)   when anti-competitive effects that are incompatible with the conditions laid down in art. 85(3) of the treaty arise from an arbitration award (art. 7(1));

(2)   when 'the effect of the agreement is to prevent the licensed products from being exposed to effective competition in the licensed territory from identical products or products considered by users as equivalent in view of their characteristics, price and intended use' (art. 7(2));

(3)   when 'the licensor does not have the right to terminate the exclusivity granted to the licensee at the latest five years from the date the agreement was entered into and at least annually thereafter, if without legitimate reason, the licensee fails to exploit the licensed technology or to do so adequately' (art. 7(3));

(4) when the licensee, after the expiry of the period provided for in art. 1(1)(6), refuses without objectively valid reasons, to meet unsolicited demand from users or resellers in the territory of other licensees (art. 7(4));

(5) when one or both parties:

   '(a) without objectively justified reason, refuse to meet demand from users or resellers in their respective territories who would market the products in other territories within the common market; or

   (b) make it difficult for users or resellers to obtain the products from other resellers within the common market and, in particular, where they exercise intellectual property rights or take measures so as to prevent resellers or users from obtaining outside, or from putting on the market in the licensed territory products which have been lawfully put on the market within the common market by the licensor or with his consent' (art. 7(5)).

Articles 7(6), 7(7) and 7(8) provide three other cases of withdrawal that are specific to Regulation 556/89 and which will be discussed below.

¶438   Application to existing agreements

Articles 8 to 10 set out the rules applicable to agreements in existence or notified to the Commission prior to the entry into force of the regulation. Article 8 provides that for 'old' agreements and agreements dispensed from notification under art. 4(2)(2)(b) of Regulation 17/62, the exemption shall have retroactive effect from the time at which the conditions for application of Regulation 556/89 were fulfilled. For the same category of agreements, art. 9 provides that the exemption will be applicable with retroactive effect if those agreements are amended before 1 July 1989 and if the amendment is communicated to the Commission prior to 1 October 1989.

¶439   Exclusivity and territorial restrictions

Before the publication of Regulation 556/89, the Commission granted individual exemptions to some know-how licensing agreements whereby the licensor granted exclusive licenses to the licensee and imposed territorial restrictions on him.[141] The Commission has justified this attitude, stating that

---

[141] *Boussois-Interpane*, OJ 1987 L50/30, where the licensee was granted an exclusive licence for the manufacture and sale of the product in France for the first five years after signature of the agreement; *Rich Products-Jus Rol*, OJ 1988 L69/21, where the licensor granted to the licensee an exclusive right to manufacture the licensed product that was restricted to the UK and a non-exclusive right to sell the licensed product in all the member states; *Delta Chemie-DDD* [1989] 1 CEC 2,254; OJ 1988 L309/34, where the licensor granted to the licensee an exclusive licence for the manufacture of the products limited to the licensed territory, and had undertaken not to appoint any distributor other than the licensee in the territory in relation to the distribution and sale of the products.

exclusivity and territorial restrictions may be necessary to induce both the licensor and the licensee to enter into a licensing agreement. It is clear that a proliferation of non-exclusive licences creates a considerable risk of the licensor's know-how being divulged. On the other hand, the licensee may have time to recoup his investment without having to face competition from other members of the network. Accordingly, Regulation 556/89 exempts from the prohibition of art. 85(1) a certain number of provisions concerning exclusivity and territorial restrictions. These provisions are similar to those exempted in Regulation 2349/84. However, the basic difference between the two regulations concerns the duration of these exemptions. In the context of patent licences, they last as long as the patent itself is in force, i.e. for a maximum of 20 years. In contrast, the length of time for which the know-how is entitled to protection depends in each case on how long the know-how remains secret. The Commission, however, has refused to exempt indefinite territorial restrictions inserted in a know-how licence and has therefore fixed the duration of the exemption itself.

Obligations permitted under the regulations
Accordingly, Regulation 556/89 exempts from the prohibition of art. 85(1) for a limited period the following obligations:

(1) 'An obligation on the licensor not to license other undertakings to exploit the licensed technology in the licensed territory' (art. 1(1)(1));

(2) 'An obligation on the licensor not to exploit the licensed technology in the licensed territory himself' (art. 1(1)(2));

(3) 'An obligation on the licensee not to exploit the licensed technology in territories within the Common Market which are reserved for the licensor' (art. 1(1)(3)).

For the sake of clarity, Regulation 556/89 provides a list of definitions in art. 1: the term 'licensed products' refers to 'goods or services the production of which requires the use of the licensed technology' (art. 1(7)(9)); 'licensed territory' means 'the territory covering all or at least part of the Common Market where the licensee is entitled to exploit the licensed technology' (art. 1(7)(11)); and 'exploitation' broadly refers to 'any use of the licensed technology, in particular in the production, active or passive sales ... even if not coupled with manufacture ... or leasing of the licensed products' (art. 1(7)(10)).

It is also important to specify that 'territory reserved for the licensor' refers to 'territories in which the licensor has not granted any licences and which he has expressly reserved for himself' (art. 1(7)(12)). Accordingly, the licensor

¶439

must indicate precisely the territories he wants to reserve for himself, and there should be no doubt between the parties on this issue after the conclusion of the agreement.

As far as the duration of the restrictions listed in art. 1(1)(1), (2) and (3) is concerned, art. 1(2) provides for their exemption 'for a period not exceeding for each licensed territory within the EEC ten years from the date of signature of the first licence agreement entered into by the licensor for that territory in respect of the same technology'.

Restrictions on relations between licensees
Articles 1(1)(4), 1(1)(5) and 1(1)(6) concern the restrictions which can be imposed on the relations between licensees. In this respect, the following obligations are exempted from the prohibition of art. 85(1):

(1) 'An obligation on the licensee not to manufacture or use the licensed product, or use the licensed process, in territories within the common market which are licensed to other licensees' (art. 1(1)(4));

(2) 'An obligation on the licensee not to pursue an active policy of putting the licensed product on the market in the territories within the common market which are licensed to other licensees, and in particular not to engage in advertising, specifically aimed at those territories or to establish any branch or maintain any distribution depot there' (art. 1(1)(5));

(3) 'An obligation on the licensee not to put the licensed product on the market in the territories licensed to other licensees within the common market' (art. 1(1)(6)).[142]

Article 1(2) sets out the maximum duration of these restrictions. The ban on the manufacture and use of the product and the ban on active sales are exempted 'for a period not exceeding ten years from the date of signature of the first licence agreement entered into by the licensor within the EEC in respect of the same technology'.

The ban on passive sales is exempted 'for a period not exceeding five years from the date of the signature of the first licence agreement entered into by the licensor within the EEC in respect of the same technology'.

---

[142] In *Boussois-Interpane*, OJ 1987 L50/30, at p. 35 (para. 20), the Commission considered that protection of the licensee and other potential future licensees against passive competition from one another was particularly important 'in view of the fact that the products' were 'sold to people in the trade who were well-informed and that there were only eight suppliers of the products in the Community. In these circumstances, a protection of licensees inter se which only covered active competition would be ineffectual as their customers would then be able to "shop around" all the potential sources of supply in the Community, leaving the licensee completely unprotected during the initial period of launch of the product'.

General provisions

As far as all the restrictions of art. 1 of Regulation 556/89 are concerned, art. 1(3) makes it clear that the exemption applies 'where the parties have identified in any appropriate form the initial know-how and any subsequent improvements to it ... and only for as long as the know-how remains secret and substantial'. In addition, the restrictions on putting the licensed product on the market resulting from the obligations referred to in paragraphs 1(2), (3), (5) and (6) are exempted only 'if the licensee manufactures or proposes to manufacture the licensed product himself or has it manufactured by a connected undertaking or by a subcontractor' (art. 1(5)).

Also, Regulation 556/89 does not apply if a licensing agreement allows the parties to benefit from absolute territorial protection. In other words, any attempt by the parties to prevent parallel imports falls within the black list (art. 3(12)). The Commission may also withdraw the benefit of the exemption in such a case (art. 7(5)).

The ten-year time limit

It must be pointed out that the Commission does not give any justification for the choice of a ten-year period as the time limit of the exemption in Regulation 556/89. In *Boussois-Interpane*, *Rich Products-Jus Rol* and *Delta Chemie-DDD*, different time limits were provided by the parties and the Commission decided to limit the exemption of the territorial restrictions to the duration necessary to preserve the average life cycle of the technology and to allow the licensee to recoup his investment.[143] The time allowed was fixed at ten years in Regulation 556/89 for the same reason.[144] Under art. 1(4) it may be possible to extend this duration 'for territories including Member States in which the same technology is protected by necessary patents'. This refers to a situation which could arise where mixed agreements benefit in some member states from patent protection, while in other member states patent protection was not applied for or was not granted, for whatever reason. Under those circumstances, the parties may rely on Regulation 556/89 and the exemption provided for will

---

[143] In *Boussois-Interpane*, OJ 1987 L50/30, at p. 36 (para. 21), the exclusive manufacturing and sales licence was granted to the licensee for the first five years following the signature of the agreement, and afterwards on a non-exclusive basis for an indefinite period. The Commission considered it appropriate to grant an exemption until the end of the five-year period of territorial protection provided for in the contract; in *Rich Products-Jus Rol*, OJ 1988 L69/21, at p. 28 (para. 45), the Commission did not consider that the period of ten years set by the parties for an exclusive manufacturing licence granted to the licensee was excessive, due to the existence both of many other competing products on the market and the possibility of the licensee selling the product freely throughout the Community; in *Delta Chemie-DDD* [1989] 1 CEC 2,254; OJ 1988 L309/34, at p. 43 (para. 47), the Commission, for the same reasons, and taking into account the considerable investment of the licensee, granted an exemption for the length of the agreement, i.e. 20 years.

[144] After the criticisms of the member states and interested parties, the Commission increased the duration originally provided in the draft regulation which was limited to seven years from the date of signature of the first licence agreement entered into by the licensor within the EC. See draft Commission regulation on the application of art. 85(3) of the treaty to certain categories of know-how licensing agreements, OJ 1987 C214/2, art. 1(2).

'extend for those Member States as long as the licensed product or process is protected in those Member States for such patents'. Therefore, the exemption could last for up to 20 years in such a case.

It is important to note that an automatic extension of the exemption beyond the ten-year limit is not possible, since any restrictions exceeding the period permitted under Regulation 556/89 are blacklisted (art. 3(11)). In other words, longer periods of territorial protection can only be granted by an individual exemption,[145] 'in particular to protect expensive and risky investment, or where the parties were not already competitors before the granting of the licence' (recital 7). Recital 7 likewise provides that:

> 'the parties are free to extend the term of their agreement to exploit any subsequent improvements ... However, in such cases, further periods of territorial protection starting from the date of licensing of the improvements in the EEC may be allowed only by individual decision, in particular where the improvements to or new applications of the licensed technology are substantial and secret and not of significantly less importance than the technology initially granted, or [where they] require new, expensive and risky investment.'

As far as the date of commencement of protection is concerned, the choice of the 'first signature of the agreement' either within the licensed territory or within the EEC, represents a date which is easier to ascertain than the 'first time the product is put on the market'. This is especially true where the licence is negotiated after the goods or services incorporating the technology have proved successful on the market, according to the wording of recital 7.[146]

Moreover, when successful reverse engineering is thought to be possible within a short time-period, it is not worthwhile for the parties to have their agreement covered by the block exemption only from the date of the first marketing of the product.

Problems may, nevertheless, arise when the starting point of the exemption is the 'first signature within the EEC', since the first appointed licensees will be prevented from manufacturing or selling the licensed product outside their territory for a maximum period of ten years, whereas licensees appointed later will be subject to the same prohibition for a shorter period of time.

---

[145] See *BBC Brown Boveri* [1989] 1 CEC 2,234; OJ 1988 L301/68, where the parties concluded co-operation agreements aimed at the constitution of a joint venture between them, whose business was to carry out research and development in the field of sodium–sulphur batteries. The parties granted to the joint venture exclusive licences to use their technology which included considerable know-how. The Commission considered that application of Regulation 418/85 was not possible, since one party was prohibited under the agreement from selling the products concerned or pursuing an active sales policy in the territories within the EC which were reserved for the other party, after the end of the period of five years provided for in art. 4(1)(f) of Regulation 418/85. Accordingly, the agreement could only be exempted by an individual decision.

[146] For an illustration of this situation, see *Delta Chemie-DDD* [1989] 1 CEC 2,254; OJ 1988 L309/34, where an exclusive distribution agreement was concluded before the grant of the know-how licence.

Nevertheless, it can be assumed that everyone benefits fairly from this, since the first licensees will benefit in return from a longer period of protection and from the head start acquired in being the first to exploit the technology.[147] Finally, it has to be stressed that art. 1(2) concerns the signature of the first licence agreement 'in respect of the same technology'. Article 1(7)(8) makes it clear that the term 'the same technology' includes 'the technology as licensed to the first licensee and enhanced by any improvements made thereto subsequently . . .' This concept otherwise could have raised important problems for the parties in the case of know-how.

¶440   Use of trade mark and get-up

Article 1(1)(7) exempts the obligation on the licensee to use only the licensor's trade mark or get-up, provided that the licensee is not prevented from identifying himself as the manufacturer of the licensed products. In contrast, the obligation on the licensee to mark the product with the licensor's name is not restrictive of competition (art. 2(1)(11)).

Such an obligation may be justified by the need to keep the goodwill attached to the trade mark. It might also encourage the licensee to maintain more stringent standards concerning the quality of the products or to redouble his 'best endeavours' when the reputation of a trade mark is at stake.

¶441   Minimum quality and tying

Minimum quality specifications and tying are grouped together in art. 2(1)(5) of Regulation 556/89 which provides that an obligation on the licensee to observe minimum quality specifications or to procure goods or services from the licensor or an undertaking designated by him, are not caught by art. 85(1) in so far as they are:

(1) necessary for a technically satisfactory exploitation of the licensed technology; or

(2) to ensure that the production of the licensee conforms to the quality standards that are respected by the licensor and other licensees.

If one of these conditions is not fulfilled, Regulation 556/89 will be inapplicable.

The reference to 'quality standards' is absent from Regulation 2349/84. This concept presupposes that a minimum quality obligation may be used to ensure

---

[147] The Economic and Social Committee had proposed in its additional opinion on the draft Commission regulation on the application of art. 85(3) of the treaty to certain categories of know-how licensing agreements, (OJ 1988 C134/10, at point 2.4.6) to oblige the licensor to disclose for each agreement entered into by a new licensee the number of licensees already appointed in the network in order to make the new licensee fully aware of the situation.

compliance of the licensee's production with high quality standards, if these are the standards respected by the licensor and the other licensees.

Article 3(3) also makes it clear that Regulation 556/89 does not apply when the licensee is obliged to accept quality specifications or further licences which he does not want at the time the agreement is entered into. This may offer the same possibilities of evasion for the licensee as under the patent regulation.

¶442   Field-of-use restrictions

Article 2(1)(8) of Regulation 556/89 provides that an obligation on the licensee to restrict exploitation to one or more technical fields of application of the technology or to one or more product markets is not caught by art. 85(1). The Commission has thus reversed its initial position since it considered in its working paper that this type of clause was a restriction of competition, although it could be exempted under art. 85(3).

A field-of-use restriction may be an incentive for the licensor to license his technology since he is allowed to reserve for himself the sectors he is interested in exploiting. This is especially interesting for small and medium-sized undertakings which can thus be protected against powerful licensees.

Since art. 2(1)(8) refers to 'one or more product markets', one may assume that Regulation 556/89 is less restrictive on this point than Regulation 2349/84 which does not provide for this possibility. However, the distinction between a field-of-use restriction and a disguised customer restriction may be difficult to define.[148]

¶443   No-challenge clause

Article 3(4) of Regulation 556/89 maintains the traditional prohibition on no-challenge clauses, already contained in Regulation 2349/84, which would weaken the licensee's position on the market vis-à-vis other competitors who remain free to challenge the secrecy of the know-how.[149] The licensee may, nevertheless, be prevented from challenging the secrecy of the know-how 'if he has in some way contributed to its disclosure' (art. 2(1)(6)).

However, the licensee may be less inclined to make such a challenge if post-disclosure royalties are provided for in the licence, since he will be held, in any event, to the payment of these royalties. Moreover, art. 3(4) states that the inclusion of no-challenge clauses in the black list is without prejudice to the

---

[148] Guttuso, S., proposed in his comments on the working paper (Know-how agreements, Fordham Corporate Law Institute, 1986, 477 et seq.) that in order to determine whether a field-of-use or a customer restriction was involved it should be determined whether or not the restriction applies to the same product market: 'if it does, the provision will normally constitute a customer restriction'. However, this proposal does not stand any more. See art. 2(1)(8) of Regulation 556/89.

[149] But see *Moosehead-Whitbread*, OJ 1990 L100/32, with respect to no-challenge clauses in trade mark licences.

¶443

right of the licensor to terminate the agreement in case of such a challenge by the licensee. Accordingly, the licensee may be deterred from challenging the know-how in order not to lose the benefit of the whole agreement and this threat may be used by the licensor to impose a stand-still obligation on him.

¶444   Post-term use ban

Article 2(1)(3) of Regulation 556/89 provides that an obligation on the licensee not to exploit the licensed know-how after termination of the agreement is not caught by art. 85(1) 'in so far and as long as the know-how is still secret'. In contrast, a post-term use ban imposed on the licensee where the know-how has meanwhile fallen into the public domain 'other than by the action of the licensee in breach of the agreement' is blacklisted (art. 3(1)).

The Working Paper, taking into account the licensee's interests, had first provided that a post-term use ban was not restrictive of competition in certain specific cases only, i.e. where the know-how had been licensed with the purpose of using the technology for carrying out a specific project or where the ban on use was limited to three years after the end of the agreement. However, the Commission has renounced these conditions in Regulation 556/89. Before the entry into force of the regulation, the Commission stated in the *Thomasson* complaint that post-term use bans in know-how licences were outside the scope of art. 85(1) on the grounds that 'otherwise any transfer of technology would necessarily be a permanent one, a condition under which few companies would be prepared to disseminate their know-how'.[150]

Article 7(6) provides, nevertheless, that in a particular case, the Commission may withdraw the benefit of the exemption when 'a post-term use ban prevents the licensee from working an expired patent which can be worked by all other manufacturers'.

Difficulties may also arise in another kind of situation each time a post-term use ban prevents the licensee from making use of his own improvements.

¶445   Post-term use ban, grant-back clause and improvements

The treatment of the improvements made to the basic know-how by the licensee may be complicated by the existence of factors such as the insertion of

---

[150] Complaint of *Thomasson International v Elliot Machinery Corporation*, IP(88) 612 of 12 October 1988. See also *Rich Products-Jus Rol*, OJ 1988 L69/21, at p. 26 (para. 34), where the Commission stated that a post-term use ban 'would become anti-competitive if the know-how became freely accessible through no fault of the licensee or if the licensee had freely acquired identical knowledge from a third party'. Except in such hypothetical situations, the ban on using the know-how following termination of the agreement did not fall within art. 85(1) of the treaty; *Delta Chemie-DDD* [1989] 1 CEC 2,254; OJ 1988 L 309/34, at p. 40 (para. 32), where the Commission stated that 'the commercial value of know-how rests very largely in its confidential character. ... [A]n obligation [not to divulge the know-how even after the expiry of the licence] must be considered necessary in the context of the present type of agreement.'

a post-term use ban in the agreement or the necessity for the licensor to preserve the secrecy of the know-how.

Article 3(2) of the regulation makes it clear that the obligation on the licensee to assign in whole or in part to the licensor rights to improvements is a restriction of competition which may not be exempted. The communication of the improvements must be carried out on a non-exclusive and reciprocal basis between the parties. Nevertheless, the situation differs according to whether or not the improvements made by the licensee are severable from the basic technology.

(1) The improvements are severable: the licensee must be free to use them during and after the term of the agreement, which implies that sub-licensing of these improvements must be possible. However, such sub-licensing must not disclose the basic know-how, communicated by the licensor, which is still secret. An obligation on the licensee to seek the licensor's prior approval before granting sub-licences to third parties, is not considered restrictive of competition, provided that the approval may not be withheld unless there are objectively justifiable reasons to believe that licensing improvements to third parties will disclose the licensor's know-how.[151]

(2) The improvements are not severable from the basic know-how: sub-licensing the improvement to third parties will be equivalent to disclosing the basic know-how and the licensor is entitled to take all measures necessary to preserve the secrecy. A ban on sub-licensing is deemed not to be restrictive of competition.[152]

However, the situation is more complex when the licence contains both a grant-back clause and a post-term use ban. In this case the parties are not on an equal footing if the licensor can benefit from the exploitation of the technology enhanced by the licensee's improvements, whereas the licensee will be obliged to renounce the exploitation of the whole package including his own improvements, after the end of the agreement, as a consequence of the post-term use ban. Accordingly, art. 3(2)(c) provides that when the agreement contains a post-term use ban, a grant-back clause even on a non-exclusive and reciprocal basis, will fall within the black list if the licensor's right to use the improvements that are not severable from the basic know-how is of a longer duration than the licensee's right to use the licensor's know-how, except for

---

[151] Article 2(1)(4). See on this point *Rich Products-Jus Rol*, OJ 1988 L69/21, at p. 26 (para. 33); *Delta Chemie-DDD* [1989] 1 CEC 2,254; OJ 1988 L309/34, at p. 41 (para. 36).
[152] Article 2(1)(2).

¶445

termination of the agreement because of breach by the licensee.[153] This provision is generally considered as an incentive for the parties to re-negotiate the agreement and for the licensee to make substantive and valuable improvements to the basic technology in order to be in a strong bargaining position at the time of the re-negotiation.

¶446   Non-competition clause

Article 3(9) blacklists a prohibition imposed on one party not to compete with the other party or with other undertakings in respect of research and development, production or use of competing products and their distribution.[154] However, the licensor has a legitimate interest in having his technology exploited to the full extent and in having it effectively used for the manufacture or the exploitation of the goods or services subject to the licence. Accordingly, the obligation on the licensee to use his best endeavours in exploiting the technology or to prove that the know-how is not used for the production of goods and services other than those licensed, is not caught by art. 85(1). For the same purpose, art. 2(1)(12) provides that an obligation on the licensee not to use the know-how to construct facilities for third parties is not restrictive of competition.

However, the Commission, although stating that the licensee theoretically is free to deal in competing products, in practice discourages him from doing so: art. 3(9) makes it clear that the prohibition of non-competition clauses is 'without prejudice to the right of the licensor to terminate the exclusivity granted to the licensee and cease communicating improvements in the event of the licensee's engaging in any such competing activities'.

¶447   Obligation not to grant sub-licences

Article 2(1)(2) provides that an obligation on the licensee not to grant sub-licences falls outside the prohibition of art. 85(1). This may be explained by the needs to preserve the secrecy of the know-how, and the character *intuitu personae* of know-how licences, where it is important for the licensor to be able to choose his licensees.

However, this prohibition cannot prevent the licensee from sub-licensing his own improvements in so far as they are severable from the basic know-how and

---

[153] In *Delta Chemie-DDD*, OJ 1988 L309/34, the parties had to modify the provisions of their agreement at the request of the Commission, in order to provide the same length for both the right of the licensee to use the licensed technology and the right of the licensor to use the improvements communicated to him.

[154] The Court of Justice has reserved a more favourable treatment to non-competition clauses concerning commercial know-how which is excluded from the scope of Regulation 556/89, In the *Pronuptia* case ([1986] ECR 373), the court considered that a non-competition clause inserted in a franchising arrangement was not caught by art. 85(1) because it intended to prevent competitors from indirectly benefiting from the know-how and assistance provided by the franchisor.

when there is no risk that such sub-licensing may disclose the licensor's know-how (see ¶445).

¶448 Output restrictions

The provisions relating to the quantity of products manufactured by the licensee can be divided into two parts.

Minimum quantity

Article 2(1)(9) states that an obligation on the licensor to produce a minimum quantity of the licensed product or to carry out a minimum number of operations exploiting the licensed technology falls outside the scope of art. 85(1). This obligation represents the licensor's interest in having his technology effectively exploited by the licensee. This quantity should not be fixed at a level so high that it has the same effect as a non-competition clause.[155] However, the Commission reserves the right to withdraw the exemption in cases where 'the parties were already competitors before the grant of the licence and obligations on the licensee to produce a minimum quantity or to use his best endeavours . . . have the effect of preventing the licensee from using competing technologies' (art. 7(8)).

Quantity restrictions

Article 3(7) prohibits clauses which impose quantity restrictions on the licensee concerning manufacture, sale or the number of operations he may carry out. Recital 19 provides that quantity restrictions, by limiting the extent to which the licensee can exploit the know-how, may weaken his competitive position and have the same effect as export bans. However, art. 1(1)(8) exempts an obligation on the licensee 'to limit his production of the licensed products to the quantities he requires in manufacturing his own products and to sell the licensed product only as an integral part of or a replacement part for his own products'. Article 1(1)(8) of Regulation 556/89 exempts such a provision provided that the quantities referred to above are freely determined by the licensee. Another exception is set out in art. 4(2) which subjects to the opposition procedure an obligation on the licensee to supply only a limited quantity of the licensed product to a particular customer in order to provide him with a second source of supply.

¶449 Royalties

The provisions of Regulation 556/89 related to the payment of royalties may be divided into three parts:

---

[155] Gutusso, 'Know-How agreements', Fordham Corporate Law Institute, 1986, 477, at p. 500.

Payment of minimum royalties

Article 2(1)(9) provides that the obligation on the licensee to pay a minimum royalty is not caught by art. 85(1). This also is intended to ensure the licensor's right to have his technology exploited to the full.

Payment of post-disclosure royalties

The draft regulation provided that post-disclosure royalties were not prohibited by art. 85(1) if they were limited to three years after the disclosure of the know-how in order not to impose an unjustifiable financial burden on the licensee at a moment when the know-how can be freely used by all his competitors on the market.[156] The Commission has, however, modified its position in Regulation 556/89 and art. 2(1)(7) clearly states that 'an obligation on the licensee, in the event of the know-how becoming publicly known other than by action of the licensor, to continue paying until the end of the agreement the royalties in the amounts, for the periods, and according to the methods freely determined by the parties' is not prohibited by art. 85(1) 'without prejudice to the payment of any additional damages in the event of the know-how becoming publicly known by the action of the licensee in breach of the agreement'.

Recital 15 of Regulation 556/89 justifies this approach, pointing out that the parties should not be restricted in their choice of the appropriate means of financing the transfer of know-how. Post-disclosure royalties, according to the same recital, allow the parties to spread the payments over a period of time and 'prevent the licensor demanding a high initial payment up front with a view to diminishing his financial exposure in the event of premature disclosure'. In this way, the risks connected to such a premature disclosure are shared between the parties. Post-disclosure royalties are also a means of permitting the licensor to receive compensation for the lead-time he granted to the licensee, vis-à-vis other competitors who did not have access to the technology before its disclosure. Recital 15 also makes it clear that post-disclosure royalties are allowed 'in cases where both parties are fully aware that the first sale of the product will necessarily disclose the know-how'.

Nevertheless, post-disclosure royalties may lead to the withdrawal of the exemption in some circumstances: art. 7(7) provides that the Commission may withdraw the exemption if the period of post-disclosure payments 'substantially exceeds the lead-time acquired by the licensee because of the head start in production and marketing, and this obligation is detrimental to competition in the market'.

---

[156] Draft Commission regulation on the application of art. 85(3) of the treaty to certain categories of know-how licensing agreements, OJ 1987 C214/2, art. 2(1)(9).

¶449

Disguised royalties
Article 3(5) blacklists the charge of royalties 'on goods or services which are not entirely or partially produced by means of the licensed technology or for the use of know-how which has become publicly known by the action of the licensor or an undertaking connected with him'. This provision prevents the situation which may exist in the case of mixed agreements where, in fact, post-disclosure royalties on know-how represent a disguised royalty on an expired patent. It should be remembered that recital 15 specifies that the mere sale of the product by the licensor or an undertaking connected with him which would result in disclosure of the know-how does not constitute an 'action of the licensor' of the kind referred to above in art. 3(5).

¶450   Obligation on the licensee to preserve the secrecy of the know-how

This type of obligation is not prohibited by art. 85(1). The licensee may be held to an obligation 'not to divulge the know-how communicated by the licensor' and 'may be held to this obligation after the agreement has expired' (art. 2(1)(1)). This provision may be considered essential in a know-how licensing agreement, since secrecy, as seen above, is one of the fundamental elements of definition of the know-how.

¶451   Other clauses

Misappropriation or infringement of know-how
Article 2(1)(6) allows an obligation on the licensee to inform the licensor of misappropriation of the know-how, or of infringements of the licensed patents, or to take or to assist the licensor in taking legal action against such misappropriation or infringements.

Favourable terms
Article 2(1)(10) considers to be outside the scope of art. 85(1) the obligation on the licensor to grant the licensee any more favourable terms that the licensor may grant to another undertaking after the agreement is entered into.[157]

Inclusion of improvements
Article 3(10) provides that any automatic prolongation of the agreement by the

---

[157] A most-favoured-licensee clause might be restrictive of competition, e.g., where the market situation is such that the only way to find other licensees is to grant them more favourable terms than those granted to the first licensee: *Kabelmetal-Luchaire*, OJ 1975 L222/34, at p. 37 (para. 8(i)).

inclusion in it of any new improvements communicated by the licensor falls within the black list, unless the licensee has the right to refuse such improvements or each party has the right to terminate the agreement at the expiry of the initial term of the agreement and at least every three years thereafter. However, the parties are free to extend their contractual relationship by entering into new agreements.

Price or customer restrictions

Articles 3(6) and (8) prohibit, as in the patent regulation, price or customer restrictions.

LICENCES OF OTHER INDUSTRIAL OR COMMERCIAL PROPERTY RIGHTS

¶452   Introduction

The principles laid down in Regulation 2349/84 and Regulation 556/89 may be applicable to licences of rights other than patents and know-how. The number of cases dealing with such licences, however, has been rather limited thus far.

¶453   Trade mark licences

There have thus far been two Commission decisions dealing with trade mark licences.[158]

Campari

The first decision, *Campari*,[159] exempted licence agreements between Campari-Milano and a number of licensees in various EC countries, authorising the licensees to manufacture and sell Campari subject to a number of restrictions.

---

[158] See also *Tepea BV v EC Commission* [1978] ECR 1391, where the Court of Justice, in confirming a Commission decision (*Theal Watts*, OJ 1977 L39/19), found an oral exclusive trademark licensing agreement, concluded in conjunction with an oral exclusive distribution agreement, to be contrary to art. 85(1) and not worthy of an exemption under art. 85(3) as the two agreements sought to secure absolute territorial protection for the licensee/distributor.

[159] *Campari*, OJ 1978 L70/69; see also *Campari, Eighteenth Report on Competition Policy*, point 69, which indicates that the Commission granted a comfort letter to Campari, which had replaced and amended the agreements exempted in 1977. On this matter see Joliet, 'Territorial and exclusive trade mark licensing under EEC law of competition', (1984) I.I.C. 21.

Restrictions not within art. 85(1)

The following restrictions were found not to come within the prohibition of art. 85(1):

(1) a ban on exports outside the EC: this restriction was held not to infringe art. 85(1), even with respect to EFTA countries, on the ground that the relevant product remains subject to excise duties and taxes in trade between the EC and third countries;

(2) a restriction of the licence to those plants which are capable of guaranteeing the quality of the product;

(3) an obligation to follow the licensor's instructions relating to the manufacture of the product and the quality of the ingredients;

(4) an obligation to buy certain secret raw materials from the licensor: this restriction was considered to be necessary in order to ensure that the product manufactured by the licensee has the same quality as that of the original product manufactured by the licensor;

(5) an obligation not to divulge the manufacturing processes to third parties;

(6) an obligation to maintain continuous contact with the customer and to spend minimum amounts on advertising;

(7) a ban on assignments of the contract.

Restrictions subject to exemption under art. 85(3)

The following restrictions were found to come under art. 85(1) but to meet the conditions for an exemption under art. 85(3):

(1) the exclusivity provisions: under the terms of the licence, Campari-Milano undertook not to appoint other licensees in the allocated territory nor to manufacture itself the products bearing the trade mark there;

(2) a non-competition clause: the licensees were prevented from dealing in competing products. That restriction was exempted under art. 85(3) on the ground that it was necessary to concentrate the sales efforts of the licensees on Campari products;

(3) a prohibition against active sales outside the territory imposed upon the licensees;

(4) an obligation imposed upon the licensees to supply to diplomatic corps, ship victuallers, foreign armed forces and all organisations with duty-free facilities the original product manufactured by Campari-Milano rather than that which they themselves manufactured. This restriction was exempted on the ground that it was necessary in order to assure uniformity of the product sold in that segment of the market.

¶453

Moosehead-Whitbread

The second Commission decision dealing with trade mark licences is *Moosehead-Whitbread*.[160] The agreements at issue in this case involved the granting by Moosehead, a Canadian company, to Whitbread, a UK company, the sole and exclusive right to produce, promote, market and sell a type of beer under the trade mark 'Moosehead' in the UK, the Channel Islands and the Isle of Man. The Commission found the following restrictions not to be contrary to art. 85(1):

(1) the obligation not to challenge the ownership or validity of the trade mark. For the restriction on challenging ownership, the Commission found that whether or not the licensor or licensee has ownership of the trade mark, the use of it by any other party is in any case prevented and competition would thus not be affected. As for the restrictions on challenging its validity, the Commission found that this could be an appreciable restriction on competition, but was not so in the present case because the trade mark in question was comparatively new. In addition, its ownership and use was not considered to be a significant advantage to a company entering or competing in any given market.[161]

(2) the obligation to use know-how granted only for the manufacture of the product in question and to keep this know-how confidential. The Commission found that the know-how was not exclusive and the obligations imposed on Whitbread were simply ancillary to the grant of the trade mark licence and enabled the licence to take effect;

(3) the obligation to purchase yeast only from Moosehead. The Commission found that this was necessary to ensure a technically satisfactory exploitation of the licensed technology and also a similar identity between the lager produced by Moosehead and the similar lager produced by Whitbread.

The following restrictions were found by the Commission to be contrary to art. 85(1) :

(1) the exclusive trade mark licence for the production and marketing of the product;

(2) the prohibition of active sales by Whitbread outside the territory;

(3) the obligation on Whitbread not to produce or promote within the territory any other beer identified as a Canadian beer.

---

[160] *Moosehead-Whitbread*, OJ 1990 L100/32.

[161] In contrast, in *Toltecs-Dorcet*, OJ 1982 L 379/19, a fine of ECU 50,000 was imposed on account of the no-challenge clause contained in the trade mark delimitation agreement objected to by the Commission in that case.

¶453

In respect of the restrictions contrary to art. 85(1), the Commission found that the provisions of the Commission block exemption Regulation 556/89 on know-how licences could not be relied on. The Commission was of the opinion that the requirement in art. 1(1) of this regulation that the trade mark element of the agreement be 'ancillary' to the know-how element of the agreement was not satisfied. The parties to the agreement indeed viewed the Canadian origin of the mark as crucial to the success of the marketing campaign. Nevertheless, the Commission concluded that these restrictions met the conditions for an exemption under art. 85(3).

Block exemption
Further guidance on the issue of trade mark licensing can be found in the Commission's block exemption regulations.

Article 2(3)(b) of Regulation 1983/83 regarding exclusive distribution agreements and art. 2(3)(c) of Regulation 1984/83 regarding exclusive purchasing agreements provide that the block exemption applies notwithstanding an obligation on the reseller to sell the contract goods under trade marks as specified by the supplier.

The scope of Regulation 2349/84 on patent licensing agreements[162] and Regulation 556/89 on know-how licensing agreements[163] likewise covers agreements containing ancillary provisions relating to trade marks. Article 1(1)(7) of Regulation 2349/84 provides that the block exemption applies to 'an obligation on the licensee to use only the licensor's trade mark ..., provided that the licensee is not prevented from identifying himself as the manufacturer of the licensed product'. Article 1(1)(7) of Regulation 556/89 exempts a similar obligation. However, art. 5(1)(4) of Regulation 556/89 excludes the application of the block exemption to know-how licensing agreements including the licensing of trade marks, where the trade marks are not of assistance in achieving the object of the licensed technology or where the agreements contain restrictions of competition other than those also attached to the licensed know-how and exempted under the regulation.

Since trade marks are often included in the package of industrial or intellectual property rights which the franchisor places at the disposal of his franchisees, Regulation 4087/88 regarding franchise agreements inevitably touches on the issue of trade mark licensing.

---

[162] Recital 10 of Regulation 2349/84 adds the condition that the trade mark licences may not be used to extend the effects of the licence beyond the life of the patents.
[163] Recital 2 of Regulation 556/89.

First Council directive to approximate the laws of the member states relating to trade marks

Finally, it is useful to refer to the first Council directive to approximate the laws of the member states relating to trade marks.[164] Article 8 of the directive provides in relation to trade mark licensing:

> 'A trade mark may be licensed for some or all of the goods or services for which it is registered and for the whole or part of the Member State concerned. A licence may be exclusive or non-exclusive.
>
> The proprietor of a trade mark may invoke the rights conferred by that trade mark against a licensee who contravenes any provision in his licensing contract with regard to its duration, the form covered by the registration in which the trade mark may be used, the scope of the goods or services for which the licence is granted, the territory in which the trade mark may be affixed, or the quality of the goods manufactured or of the services provided by the licensee.'

¶454   Copyright licences

In *Decca Navigator System*,[165] the Commission stated that 'the Community system of competition does not allow an improper use of rights under national copyright laws which frustrate competition law'. Recently, the Commission affirmed that the relation between the Community's competition rules and copyright is governed by the court's distinction between the existence and the exercise of the intellectual property rights in question.[166] Any arrangement or measure which goes beyond the existence of copyright can be subject to control under the competition rules.

The court's position

In *Coditel v Ciné-Vog Films*,[167] the court applied this distinction by holding that the grant of an exclusive right to exhibit a film restricted to a specified member state is not, as such, subject to the prohibition of art. 85. The court added, however, that the exercise of such a right may, depending on the accompanying legal or economic circumstances, result in a restriction of competition, regard naturally being had not only to the contractually agreed scope for the exercise of the right, but also to its actual exercise. The court stated that:

---

[164] Directive 89/104, first Council directive of 21 December 1988 to approximate the laws of the member states relating to trade marks, OJ 1989 L40/1; amended OJ 1992 L6/35.
[165] *Decca Navigator System* [1989] 1 CEC 2,137; OJ 1989 L43/27, at p. 42 (para. 104).
[166] Commission conclusions decided on the occasion of the adoption of the Commission's proposal for a Council directive on the legal protection of computer programs, OJ 1989 C91/16. For the relation between copyright and art. 30 to 36 see ¶404 and ¶405. The applicability of art. 30 to the exercise of copyright is discussed in Chapter 9.
[167] *Coditel v Ciné-Vog Films* ('*Coditel II*') [1982] ECR 3381.

'it is for national courts, where appropriate, . . . to establish whether or not the exercise of the exclusive right to exhibit a cinematographic film creates barriers which are artificial and unjustifiable in terms of the needs of the cinematographic industry, or the possibility of charging fees which exceed a fair return on investment, or an exclusivity the duration of which is disproportionate to those requirements, and whether or not, from a general point of view, such exercise within a given geographic area is such as to prevent, restrict or distort competition within the common market.'[168]

Needless to say, this statement opens the door to unlimited discussions as to whether an exclusive exhibition licence creates 'artificial and unjustifiable' barriers in a particular case. The shadow cast over the legality under art. 85(1) of exclusive exhibition licences by the court's language in *Coditel* may make it prudent to consider notification of such agreements.

Commission settlements

The Commission has also indicated in informal settlements, that principles laid down with respect to licences of other intellectual property rights may equally apply to copyright licences.[169]

In *Neilson-Hordell/Richmark*,[170] for instance, the Commission confirmed this approach stating that a no-challenge clause, a non-competition clause, a clause requiring the payment of royalties on products not protected by any copyright of the licensor and a clause requiring the licensee to transfer to the licensor the title to any copyright of the licensee in improvements made to the licensed products, would normally be regarded as infringing art. 85(1) of the EC Treaty and as being incapable of exemption under art. 85(3).

The relevant factors

The above judgment and settlements suggest that a number of factors will come into play in determining the compatibility of a copyright licence with art. 85. These factors include, inter alia, the scope of the licence, the geographic area covered by the licence, the number of forms of exploitation licensed, the duration of the licence and the special characteristics of the industry. In *Film purchases by German Television Stations*,[171] the first decision of the

---

[168] Id., at p. 3402 (para. 19).

[169] See *English Football League/London Weekend Television*, *Ninth Report on Competition Policy*, point 116, and Commission press release IP(93) 614 of 20 July 1993 (exclusive right to record and transmit Football League matches challenged by the Commission); *Stemra*, *Eleventh Report on Competition Policy*, point 98 (export ban); *Neilson-Hordell/Richmark*, *Twelfth Report on Competition Policy*, point 88 (exclusive grant-back for improvement); *RAI/UNITEL*, *Twelfth Report on Competition Policy*, point 90 (exclusive performance rights); *Knoll/Hille-Form*, *Thirteenth Report on Competition Policy*, points 142–146 (exclusive licence of copyrights relating to design furniture).

[170] *Neilson-Hordell/Richmark*, *Twelfth Report on Competition Policy*, points 88–89.

[171] *Film Purchases by German TV Stations* [1989] 2 CEC 2,109; OJ 1989 L284/36.

¶454

Commission dealing specifically with copyright licences, the Commission focused on two of these factors, i.e., the scope and the duration of the licence. In this case, the Commission reviewed agreements under which exclusive rights to the television broadcasting of films were granted to a German broadcasting organisation. The Commission stated that:

'taking into account the principles set out in the Coditel II judgment of the Court, the restriction of competition derives ... from the duration and scope of the exclusivity.'[172]

To assess the extent of the contractual scope and the length of the contract term, the Commission partly relied on industry practice and on previous contracts concluded by the licensee. After the parties had substantially altered the contract terms, the Commission granted an individual exemption pursuant to art. 85(3).[173]

Council directive on the legal protection of computer programs

A further illustration of the Commission position on the applicability of the competition rules to copyright is provided in the context of the Council directive on the legal protection of computer programs,[174] which provides for the legal protection of computer programs by means of copyright law. In its policy guidelines[175] which were published with its initial proposal for this directive, the Commission confirmed that any arrangement going beyond the existence of copyright can be subject to control under the competition rules.

'This means that for example any attempt to extend by contractual agreements or other arrangements the scope of protection to aspects of the programs for which protection under copyright is not available for the right owner may constitute an infringement of the competition rules.'

¶455   Software licensing

Software licensing agreements may come under the scope of the patent licensing[176] or the know-how licensing block exemption regulations.[177] The patent licensing block exemption is mainly concerned with patent licences but

---

[172] Ibid., at p. 41 (para. 41).

[173] See also the parliamentary question of MEP Banotti and the answer of Commissioner Van Miert, OJ 1993 C195/14.

[174] Council Directive 91/250 on the legal protection of computer programs, OJ 1991 L122/42.

[175] Commission conclusions decided on the occasion of the adoption of the Commission's proposal for a Council directive on the legal protection of computer programs, OJ 1989 C91/16.

[176] Commission Regulation 2349/84 on the application of art. 85(3) of the treaty to certain categories of patent licensing agreements, OJ 1984 L219/15, corrigendum OJ 1985 L113/34, as amended by Commission Regulation 151/93, OJ 1993 L21/8.

[177] Commission Regulation 556/89 on the application of art. 85(3) of the treaty to certain categories of know-how licensing agreements, OJ 1989 L61/1, as amended by Commission Regulation 151/93, OJ 1993 L21/8.

also covers mixed know-how and patent licences if the patented invention is the dominant element in the licensed technology.[178] This block exemption may therefore serve as a legal framework for a software licensing agreement on the rare occasions where the licensed software qualifies for patent protection.

The know-how licensing block exemption primarily concerns licences in which know-how constitutes the dominant element. However, the know-how block exemption will not apply to agreements which include a licence of software unless that software is 'of assistance in achieving the object of the licensed technology and there are no obligations restrictive of competition other than those also attached to the licensed know-how and exempted under the [know-how block exemption] Regulation'.[179]

If copyrighted computer software forms part of the package of intellectual property rights licensed in connection with a franchise agreement, Regulation 4087/88 may apply.[180]

More often than not, the clauses of a software licensing agreement will have to be assessed individually in the light of the Court of Justice's case law and the Commission's practice with respect to copyright,[181] patent and know-how licensing agreements. To date no cases have dealt specifically with software licensing agreements. The Commission has made it clear, however, that any arrangement that goes beyond what is essential to the preservation of the copyright may run counter to art. 85.[182]

The status of specific clauses in a software licensing agreement is as follows.

(1) *Exclusivity*: an obligation on the licensor not to license the software to third parties, nor to exploit itself the licensed software in the contract territory may constitute an infringement of art. 85(1).[183] If the licence agreement will introduce a new technology into the licensed territory, exclusivity is likely not to be contrary to art. 85, provided the exclusivity is indispensable for the protection of the licensee's investment costs associated with the production and sale of a novel product unknown to potential buyers.[184]

---

[178] *Boussois-Interpane*, OJ 1987 L50/30.

[179] Regulation 556/89, art. 5(1)(4).

[180] Commission Regulation 4087/88 on the application of art. 85(3) of the treaty to categories of franchise agreements, OJ 1988 L359/46, art. 1(3)(a).

[181] Pursuant to Council Directive 91/250 on the legal protection of computer programs, OJ 1991 L122/42, member states are required to afford copyright protection to computer programs as if these were literary works within the meaning of the Berne Convention for the Protection of Literary and Artistic Works (art. 1(1)).

[182] Commission conclusions decided on the occasion of the adoption of the Commission's proposal for a Council directive on the legal protection of computer programs, OJ 1989 C91/16. See Sucker 'Lizenzierung von Computersoftware', Computer und Recht, 1989, 353 and 468; Downing, 'EEC Competition Law and software licences' (1992) 3 EBLR Rev. 63; Forrester, 'Software licensing in the light of current EC Competition Law considerations', ECLR, 1992, 5; Vinje, 'Compliance with Article 85 in software licensing', ECLR, 1992, 165.

[183] But see *Coditel SA & Ors v Ciné-Vog Films & Ors* [1982] ECR 3381.

[184] *Nungesser v EC Commission* [1982] ECR 2015.

¶455

(2) *Territorial restrictions*: software licensing agreements in which the licensee is not the end-user of the software but in which he intends to develop the software further before selling the enhanced computer programs, may contain provisions aiming at giving the licensee some form of territorial protection against other licensees. It would appear that such provisions may be held to be contrary to art. 85(1). The provisions may, however, qualify for an individual exemption if they are limited in time and do not prevent parallel trade in the products generated with the help of the licensed software.[185]

(3) *Location clause*: limiting the use of the software to particular premises may run counter to art. 85(1),[186] but may qualify for an exemption.

(4) *Ban on sub-licensing*: an obligation on the licensee to grant sub-licences does not infringe art. 85(1).[187]

(5) *Ban on copies*: a prohibition on the licensee to make copies in addition to a back-up copy does not infringe art. 85(1).[188]

(6) *Tying*: making the licensing of software dependent on (i) the licensee concluding further agreements for the licensing of additional software, (ii) the licensee buying certain hardware from the licensor[189] or (iii) the licensee concluding a separate maintenance and support contract with the licensor may be caught by art. 85(1). However, the tying provision may fall outside the scope of art. 85(1) if it can be demonstrated that the additional software, the hardware or the maintenance contract is necessary for a technically satisfactory exploitation of the licensed software.[190]

(7) *Developments*: preventing the licensee from making further developments of the licensed software in a manner that restricts the licensee's ability to observe, study or test the program[191] or to decompile the program in order to achieve the interoperability of an independently created program will be contrary to art. 85(1).[192]

---

[185] Compare the principles regarding exempted territorial restrictions contained in art. 1(1) of Regulation 2349/84 and art. 1(1) of Regulation 556/89.

[186] Compare art. 2(c) of Regulation 4087/88.

[187] Compare art. 2(1)(5) of Regulation 2349/84 and art. 2(1)(2) of Regulation 556/89.

[188] See art. 4(a) and 5(2) of Council Directive 91/250 on the legal protection of computer programs, OJ 1991 L122/42.

[189] Compare *IBM settlement, Fourteenth Report on Competition Policy*, points 94–95, where it is reported that IBM allegedly had the opposite practice of refusing to supply its System/370 central processing units unless the basic software was included in the price. According to the Commission, this constituted an abuse of IBM's supposed dominant position in the market for the supply of the key products for System/370.

[190] Compare art. 3(9) of Regulation 2349/84 and art. 3(3) of Regulation 556/89.

[191] Articles 4(b) and 5(3) of Council Directive 91/250 on the legal protection of computer programs.

[192] Articles 4(b) and 6 of Council Directive 91/250 on the legal protection of computer programs.

¶456   Licences of plant breeders' rights

In the *Maize seed* case,[193] the court defined plant breeders' rights as follows:

> 'breeders' rights are those rights conferred on the breeder of a new plant variety or his successor in title pursuant to which the production, for purposes of commercial marketing, of the reproductive or vegetative propagating material, as such, of the new variety and the offering for sale or marketing of such material are subject to the prior authorization of the breeder.'

The court stated in the same case that it is:

> 'not correct to consider that breeders' rights are a species of commercial or industrial property right with characteristics of so special a nature as to require, in relation to the competition rules, a different treatment from other commercial and industrial property rights.'[194]

Decisions of the Commission and judgments of the court illustrate the application of the EC competition rules to licences of plant breeders' rights.

(1) *Exclusivity*: in the *Maize seed* judgment,[195] the court concluded that, having regard to the specific nature of the products in question, the grant of an open exclusive licence, that is to say a licence which does not affect the position of third parties such as parallel importers and licensees for other territories, is not in itself incompatible with art. 85(1) of the treaty.[196]

(2) *Territorial protection*: in *Maize seed*,[197] the court also upheld the decision of the Commission in so far as it considered that the absolute territorial protection granted to the licensee infringed art. 85(1). This protection resulted from an obligation upon the licensor to prevent third parties from exporting into the licensed territory and the licensee's undertaking to use his exclusive rights to prevent parallel imports.

(3) *Sale and export restrictions*: in *Erauw-Jacquery v La Hesbignonne*,[198] a provision of an agreement concerning plant breeders' rights, which prohibited the licensee from selling and exporting the basic seed, was found to be compatible with art. 85(1) in so far as it was necessary in order to enable the breeder to select the growers who were to be the

---

[193] *Nungesser v EC Commission* [1982] ECR 2015, at p. 2054 (para. 2); see also Van Bael, 'Réflexions sur l'arret *«semences de maïs»*: des semences d'espoir?', (1983) Cahiers de droit européen 176–185.
[194] Ibid., at p. 2065 (para. 43).
[195] Ibid., at p. 2069 (para. 58).
[196] See ¶416 above.
[197] *Nungesser v EC Commission* [1982] ECR 2015, at p. 2070 (para. 60–66).
[198] *Erauw-Jacquery v La Hesbignonne* [1988] ECR 1919.

licensees. The Commission emphasised that this ruling has a limited scope and may not be construed as a general assessment of prohibitions on exports.[199]

(4) *Price-fixing*: the court has indicated that a provision fixing minimum prices may be found to infringe art. 85(1).[200]

(5) *Other clauses*: the Commission has also condemned other provisions, for instance, customer restrictions,[201] output restrictions,[202] a non-competition clause,[203] a grant-back clause imposed on a sub-licensee[204] and a no-challenge clause.[205]

TRADE MARK DELIMITATION AGREEMENTS

¶457   Application

It may prove useful under certain circumstances for owners of identical or confusingly similar trade marks or trade names to enter into arrangements (sometimes referred to as 'delimitation agreements') relating to the use of such trade marks or trade names. In *BAT v EC Commission*, the court acknowledged that 'agreements known as "delimitation agreements" are lawful and useful if they serve to delimit, in the mutual interest of the parties, the spheres within which their respective trade marks may be used, and are intended to avoid confusion or conflict between them'.[206] The court added,

---

[199] *Eighteenth Report on Competition Policy*, point 103. See however, *Standard Seed Production and Sales Agreements in France*, OJ 1990 C6/3, in which the Commission indicated, inter alia, that it would take a favourable view of restrictions on a licensee in the standard agreement in question from exporting certified seed (i.e. a direct descendant of basic seed and which is not intended for the production of seed but for direct or indirect sale to farmers for sowing).

[200] *Erauw-Jacquery v La Hesbignonne* [1988] ECR 1919, at pp. 1939–1941 (para. 12–20).

[201] *Breeders' rights – Maize seed*, OJ 1978 L286/23, at p. 36.

[202] Ibid.

[203] Ibid.

[204] *Breeders' rights – roses*, OJ 1985 L369/9, at p. 15.

[205] Ibid., at p. 16.

[206] *BAT Cigaretten Fabriken v EC Commission* [1985] ECR 363, at p. 380 (para. 14–15). See, however, *Bayer AG & Maschinenfabrik Hennecke GmbH v Süllhöfer* [1988] ECR 5249, at pp. 5285–5286 (para. 14–15), where the court observed in relation to no-challenge clauses in patent licensing agreements:

'In the Commission's view, an undertaking not to challenge an industrial property right included in a licensing agreement should, in principle, be considered to be a restriction of competition. Such a clause is, however, compatible with Article 85(1) of the EC Treaty when it is included in an agreement whose purpose is to put an end to proceedings pending before a court, provided that the existence of the industrial property right which is the subject-matter of the dispute is genuinely in doubt, that the agreement includes no other clauses restricting competition, and that the no-challenge clause relates to the right in issue.

The point of view put forward by the Commission cannot be accepted. In its prohibition of certain "agreements" between undertakings, Article 85(1) makes no distinction between agreements whose purpose is to put an end to litigation and those concluded with other aims in mind. It should also be noted that this assessment of such a settlement is without prejudice to the question whether, and to what extent, a judicial settlement reached before a national court which constitutes a judicial act may be invalid for breach of Community competition rules.'

however, that '[t]hat is not to say . . . that such agreements are excluded from the application of Article 85 of the Treaty if they also have the aim of dividing up the market or restricting competition in other ways'.[207]

The Commission has already had occasion to apply art. 85 to a number of trade mark delimitation agreements. The rules which emerge from these cases are as follows:

Agreements not to use trade marks in certain member states

The Commission will view with suspicion any agreement under which the parties undertake not to use certain trade marks in specified member states. The Commission will easily tend to regard these agreements as a form of market-sharing. Extreme caution should therefore be exercised in entering into trade mark delimitation agreements even where these agreements are entered into with a view to settling a trade mark infringement action. In *Sirdar-Phildar*,[208] the Commission held that an agreement, under which two companies had undertaken not to use their respective trade marks (Sirdar and Phildar) in each other's home markets (France and the UK), was illegal because the parties had accepted the co-existence of the two trade marks in question in other territories. In the *BAT* case the Commission[209] and the court condemned a settlement between a major cigarette producer (BAT) and a smaller Dutch producer under which the latter undertook not to export certain tobacco products into Germany under its 'Toltecs' trade mark. The settlement marked the conclusion of a suit brought by BAT for alleged infringement of its 'Dorcet' trade mark. The court said that BAT's purpose in bringing the action was to prevent export sales by the Dutch company on the German market and that BAT's use of its 'Dorcet' trade mark – an unused, dormant trade mark – constituted an abuse of the right conferred by the trade mark ownership.[210]

In *Synthex-Synthelabo*[211] the Commission reviewed a trade mark agreement whereby two pharmaceutical companies, in order to avoid confusion, undertook not to use the trade mark Synthelabo or Synthelab in the UK. The Commission found that this agreement, which made it more difficult for Synthelabo to sell its products in the UK, infringed art. 85(1). The Commission also refused to grant an exemption since the agreement would not improve the production or distribution of goods and less restrictive solutions could have

---

[207] *BAT Cigaretten Fabriken v EC Commission* [1985] ECR 363, at p. 385 (para. 33).
[208] *Sirdar-Phildar*, OJ 1975 L125/27.
[209] *Toltecs-Dorcet*, OJ 1982 L379/19.
[210] *BAT Cigaretten-Fabriken v EC Commission* [1985] ECR 363.
[211] *Synthex-Synthelabo*, press release of the Commission of 28 February 1989 (IP(89) 108). Commenting on this case, the Commission made it clear that it is more likely to intervene 'in cases where available evidence points to the inability of a party to legally enforce its claim of invalidity of the other party's trade mark. If it is evident that through such actions one party may legally exclude the other from selling in certain Member States, an agreement between the two companies having the same effect would not restrict competition.' *Nineteenth Report on Competition Policy*, point 59.

¶457

been adopted. Furthermore, consumers were unlikely to receive a fair share of the benefits resulting from this agreement. The Commission closed the file after both parties had agreed to amend the agreement, which now provides that the trade marks of both companies co-exist in all member states.

In *Chiquita/Fyffes*,[212] Chiquita sold Fyffes group Ltd., an English company trading bananas in the UK under the Fyffes trade mark, to the Irish company Fyffes plc. In an accompanying trade mark agreement, Chiquita was granted the exclusive right to use the Fyffes trade mark outside the UK and Ireland for a period of three years from 1986. In addition, Fyffes plc was prevented under a non-use clause from using the Fyffes mark for the sale of fresh fruit, including bananas, outside the same territories until the year 2006, or such earlier date to be decided by Chiquita. According to the Commission, to the extent the non-use clause applied beyond the initial three-year period following the transfer of the Fyffes business, it could not be regarded as securing the protection of any Chiquita goodwill attached to the Fyffes trade mark. The clause was considered to be contrary to art. 85(1).[213] Following the issue of two statements of objections, Chiquita agreed with Fyffes to cease blocking access for Fyffes' bananas under the Fyffes trade mark to the continental banana market.

Unhampered movements of goods bearing the mark
In contrast, the Commission will tend to view with favour trade mark delimitation agreements under which the free movement of the products bearing the disputed trade mark within the Community remains unhampered and parties do not have to recreate their goodwill under other trade marks. An example of the type of trade mark delimitation agreements favoured by the Commission is provided by the *Persil Washing Powder*[214] case in which the parties, under pressure from the Commission, agreed to abandon their objections to the use of the Persil trade mark – which they both owned in different member states – by the other party in each other's territories. Instead, it was agreed that one party would use the Persil trade mark in red letters with the name of the company in smaller letters in a red oval while the other party would use a green Persil trade mark. Arrangements concerning the presentation of trade marks will be considered to fall outside art. 85 where none of the parties is prevented from using its own trade marks.

---

[212] *Chiquita/Fyffes, XXIInd Report on Competition Policy for 1992*, points 168–176.

[213] The Commission also found that Chiquita had abused its dominant position by relying on the non-use clause since 1989.

[214] *Persil Washing Powder, Seventh Report on Competition Policy*, point 138. See also *Penneys*, OJ 1978 L60/19 (agreements under which all rights to the Penneys trade mark in dispute between the parties were transferred to one party for the whole Community but the other party retained the right to use the name Penneys as a business name for its retail shops in one Member State); *Bayer-Tanabe, Eighth Report on Competition Policy*, point 125; *Osram-Airam, Eleventh Report on Competition Policy*, point 97.

¶457

It may be questioned whether, on this point, the Commission does not underestimate the difficulties faced by companies as a result of the coexistence of identical or confusingly similar trade marks in the same territory. Different presentations of the same trade mark may not eliminate confusion; requiring owners of trade marks to resolve their conflicts preferably through the use of arrangements on presentation may cause the trade marks in question to lose much of their value.

Another example of the type of trade mark delimitation agreement supported by the Commission is provided by the *Hershey/Hershi*[215] case. In this case, the Commission cleared, on an informal basis, a trade mark delimitation agreement between two companies, one of which used the 'Hershey' trade mark and the other used the 'Hershi' trade mark. According to the agreement, the company owning the 'Hershi' mark would assign its mark to the other company for valuable consideration and would receive a licence from the other company to use the mark on an exclusive basis for five years (renewable on request) in respect of a defined group of products. The original owner of the 'Hershi' mark also undertook not to introduce new products with the 'Hershi' mark and not to continue using Hershi as a corporate name after a specified time. The Commission indicated that the arrangement did not impede competition, particularly as no partition of the EC market was envisaged and suggested that the terms of this settlement might form the basis of future trade mark dispute settlements.

---

[215] *Hershey/Hershi*, Commission press release of 2 February 1990, *XXth Report on Competition Policy*, point 111.

5 Co-operation Agreements

INTRODUCTION

¶501 Overview

This chapter examines the application of EC competition law to various forms of co-operation between enterprises including joint ventures (¶502–¶511), joint research and development programmes (¶512–¶516) and specialisation arrangements (¶517–¶521). The analysis also covers sub-contracting (¶523), joint purchasing (¶524) and joint selling (¶525) agreements, as well as miscellaneous types of co-operation arrangements (¶526–535). On the whole, the Commission has been favourably disposed towards such agreements in so far as they promote the goal of an integrated European market.

In its 1968 notice on co-operation agreements, the Commission first set out its views with regard to various forms of co-operation arrangements. Since that time, the Commission has issued block exemption regulations covering specialisation agreements and joint research and development agreements as well as a notice on sub-contracting agreements. In addition, numerous individual decisions dealing with various forms of co-operation agreements have been published. The Commission has recently issued a notice which gives guidance on the assessment of joint ventures under EC competition rules.[1]

JOINT VENTURES

¶502 General

Joint ventures are generally defined as 'undertakings jointly controlled by two or more economically independent firms'.[2] Depending upon the nature of the operation, the legality of joint ventures is assessed under art. 85 or under the Council Regulation on the control of concentrations between undertakings (the 'merger regulation').[3]

---

[1] Commission notice concerning the assessment of co-operative joint ventures pursuant to art. 85 of the EEC Treaty, OJ 1993 C43/2 (hereinafter cited as the 'joint venture guidelines').

[2] *Fourth Report on Competition Policy*, point 37; *Thirteenth Report on Competition Policy*, point 53;

[3] Council Regulation 4064/89 of 21 December 1989 on the control of concentrations between undertakings, OJ 1990 L 257/13. The merger regulation entered into force on 21 September 1990.

¶501

In the sphere of joint ventures, the Commission's traditional approach has been to afford a wide definition to the scope of art. 85(1). A mere finding that the parties to the agreement were actual or potential competitors[4] or that the de minimis rule had been breached or indeed the inclusion of express restrictions[5] on the parties sufficed, without any in-depth economic analysis, for a finding that the agreement contravened art. 85(1) and required exemption under art. 85(3).

The consequences of such a policy are obvious: parties notifying agreements to the Commission exposed themselves to inordinate delays and legal uncertainty due to the time necessary to obtain an exemption (sometimes frustrating the very objectives of the co-operation); parties to complex transactions, which required speedy approval and who, as a result, chose not to notify, ran the risk of nullity and fines; national authorities were unable to clear transactions as only the Commission has power to grant exemptions and exemptions granted under art. 85(3) were made subject to conditions and were only granted for a limited amount of time.

The *Thirteenth Report on Competition Policy* opened the way for a more realistic approach to joint ventures. This, coupled with certain recent decisions[6] and policy initiatives undertaken by the Competition Directorate,[7] suggest a gradual and positive evolution in this difficult area.[8] The Commission, on 23 December 1992, adopted the following measures to reinforce its policy that co-operative joint ventures generally deserve favourable treatment under the EC competition rules:

(1) it widened the scope of its block exemption regulations, enabling joint ventures to be exempted from the competition rules more often and more quickly, provided that they meet the relevant conditions;

(2) it adopted a notice on the assessment of co-operative joint ventures under art. 85(1) and art. 85(3) in order to improve the legal certainty for undertakings by explaining the legal and economic criteria which will guide it in its future policy towards joint ventures; and

(3) it has decided to speed up its proceedings in all cases involving so-called 'co-operative' joint ventures; see ¶1127.

---

[4] *GEC-Weir Sodium Circulators*, OJ 1977 L327/26.

[5] *Rockwell/Iveco*, OJ 1983 L224/19.

[6] *Elopak/Metal Box-Odin*, OJ 1990 L209/15, *GEC-Siemens/Plessey*, OJ 1990 C239/2, *Mitchell Cotts/Sofiltra*, OJ 1987 L41/31.

[7] See IP(92)1009 of 8 December 1992. Sir Leon Brittan, 'Strategic Alliances – An Old Problem and a New Challenge to the Commission's Competition Policy' speech delivered in Berlin, 25 May 1992; Sir Leon Brittan, 'The Future of EC Competition Policy' speech delivered at the Centre of European Policy Studies, Brussels, 7 December 1992.

[8] Note however the decisions of *KSB/Goulds/Lowara/ITT*, OJ 1991 L19/25, and *Cekacan*, OJ 1990 L299/64, which suggest that a consistent and coherent Commission policy in this area is not yet in existence.

¶503   The standard of legality: art. 85 or the merger regulation

A threshold question which arises with regard to the assessment of a joint venture under the EC competition rules is whether it is to be judged under art. 85 or under the principles laid down in the merger regulation.

The legality of a joint venture will be assessed under the merger regulation if it can be characterised as a 'merger' or 'concentration', whether total or partial.[9] In all other cases, the standard of legality will be art. 85.[10]

The particularly difficult issue of delineating partial concentrations and joint ventures is dealt with in Chapter 6.

¶504   The assessment of joint ventures under art. 85

Joint ventures which do not involve a concentration, either total or partial, are to be judged according to the standards of art. 85. This involves a two-step enquiry:

(1) Does the joint venture come under the prohibition of art. 85(1) (¶505–¶507)?

(2) If it falls under art. 85(1), does it qualify for an exemption under art. 85(3) (¶508–¶511)?

¶505   Application of art. 85(1) to joint ventures

A joint venture will fall under art. 85(1) if (a) the creation or the activities of the joint venture have as their object or effect an appreciable restriction or

---

[9] The merger regulation confers exclusive power on the Commission to assess the legality of concentrations with a Community dimension. For an analysis of the system established by the merger regulation, see Chapter 6. In 1990, the Commission issued a notice clarifying the concepts of concentration and co-operation under the merger regulation (OJ 1990 C203/10). The Commission notice is be discussed in Chapter 6.

[10] It should, however, be noted that art. 86 is applicable to joint ventures involving a dominant undertaking. In the *Eighth Report on Competition Policy*, point 136 the Commission stated:

'The joint venture agreements could in this case have additionally amounted to an abuse of ICI's dominant position in the UK blackpowder market.'

See also *Fiat/Hitachi*, OJ 1993 L20/10, at p. 12, where the Commission held that under the circumstances of the case, the joint venture was co-operative in nature. Its creation would have led to co-ordination of competitive behaviour between the parent companies on the one hand, and between the parent companies and the joint venture on the other hand, even if the parties had not included restrictive clauses in their contractual arrangements.

In the joint venture guidelines, para. 10, the Commission states that:

'according to Article 3(2) of Regulation (EEC) No. 4064/89, any JV which does not fulfil the criteria of a concentration, is co-operative in nature. Under the second sub-paragraph, this applies to:
   – all JVs, the activities of which are not to be performed on a lasting basis, especially those limited in advance by the parents to a short time period,
   – JVs which do not perform all the functions of an autonomous economic entity, especially those charged by their parents simply with the operation of particular functions of an undertaking (partial function JVs),
   – JVs which perform all the functions of an autonomous economic entity (full function JVs) where they give rise to co-ordination of competitive behaviour by the parents in relation to each other or to the JV.'

distortion of competition (¶506) within the common market, and (b) these activities are likely to affect trade between member states (¶507). Co-operative joint ventures not fulfilling these criteria do not fall within art. 85(1). The Commission has set out in the joint venture guidelines,[11] a list of joint ventures that do not have as their object or effect the prevention, restriction or distortion of competition. These consist of:

- joint ventures formed by parents which all belong to the same group and which are not in a position freely to determine their market behaviour;
- joint ventures of minor economic importance within the meaning of the 1986 notice; and
- joint ventures with activities neutral to competition in the sense of the 1968 notice on co-operation between enterprises.

Any joint ventures that do not fall into any of these categories must be individually examined to see whether they restrict competition.[12]

¶506   Appreciable restriction of competition

A joint venture will be found to restrict competition where:

(1) the partners in the joint venture are actual or potential competitors. In the case of a full-function joint venture, the relationship between the parents and the joint venture will also be relevant; or

(2) the partners in the joint venture are neither actual or potential competitors, but the joint venture either forms part of a network of interrelated joint ventures that has an anti-competitive effect or affects the market position of third parties in downstream or upstream markets.

Actual competitors

A joint venture between actual competitors will easily be found to restrict competition either directly or indirectly.[13] 'Actual competitors' refers to those who operate on the joint venture's geographic and product market or in an adjacent market.[14] According to the joint venture guidelines, in the case of a

---

[11] Joint venture guidelines, para. 15.

[12] For a discussion of the criteria to be used when assessing such joint ventures, see the joint venture guidelines, para. 17 et seq.

[13] See *Astra*, OJ 1993 L20/23 at p. 28. This is, of course, assuming that the restrictive effects on competition in the relevant market and the effect on inter-state trade are perceptible. *Thirteenth Report on Competition Policy*, point 55.

[14] See *KSB/Goulds/Lowara/ITT*, OJ 1991 L19/25, p. 30. In *Elopak/Metal Box-Odin*, OJ 1990 L209/15, the parties could not be actual competitors where one had technology relating to the making and filling of cartons in aseptic conditions and the other had technology relating to metal containers, but neither party had technology in the same product market. In effect, they were in different areas of the packaging industry. See also *Cekacan*, OJ 1990 L299/64, at p. 68, *IVECO/Ford*, OJ 1988 L230/39, *Olivetti/Canon*, OJ 1988 L52/51.

full-function joint venture, a separate assessment of the relationship between the parents and the joint venture is also required[15] when the joint venture is in competition with, or is a supplier or a customer of, at least one of the parents. This is because anti-competitive behaviour between the joint venture and one of the parents will always affect relationships between the parents.[16] When assessing a full-function joint venture it is essential to assess whether the activities of the joint venture are closely linked to those of the parents in addition to examining the activities of the parents in relation to each other.[17] Where a full-function joint venture operates in the same product market as its parents, it is likely, not to say inevitable in some cases, that competition between the participating undertakings will be restricted.[18] Such anti-competitive behaviour can, according to the joint venture guidelines, occur between the parents or between one of the parents and the joint venture.[19] If however, the full-function joint venture operates on a market adjacent to that of its parents, competition can only be restricted where there is a high degree of interdependence between the two markets.[20]

If the joint venture combines research and development activities, the Commission will consider that the establishment of the joint venture between actual competitors restricts competition by preventing either from gaining an advantage over the other, a restriction which may be particularly serious where innovation is critical to a firm's competitive ability.[21] In the area of production,

---

[15] Joint venture guidelines, para. 17.

[16] Ibid., para. 21, 22.

[17] Ibid., para. 35. The joint venture guidelines go on to state that:

'if the JV trades in a product market which is upstream or downstream of the market of a parent, restrictions on competition can occur in relation to third parties, if the participants are undertakings with market power. If the market of the JV is upstream of the market of one of the parents and at the same time downstream of the market of another parent, the JV functions as a connection between the two parents and also possibly as a vertical multi-level integration instrument. In such a situation the exclusive effects with regard to third parties are reinforced. Whether it fulfils the requisite minimum degree for the application of Article 85(1) can be decided only on an individual basis.'

[18] Joint venture guidelines, para. 35, 41. *Screensport/EBU-Eurosport*, OJ 1991 L63/32; *Konsortium ECR 900*, OJ 1990 L228/31; *Olivetti/Canon*, OJ 1988 L52/51; *Mitchell Cotts/Sofiltra*, OJ 1987 L41/31.

[19] Ibid., para. 17, 21. The restriction of competition between parents and the joint venture typically manifests itself in the division of geographical markets, product markets (especially through specialisation) or customers. In such cases, the participating undertakings reduce their activity to the role of potential competitors. If they remain active competitors, they will usually be tempted to reduce the intensity of competition by co-ordinating their business policy, especially as to prices and volume of production or sales or by voluntarily restraining their efforts. Id., para. 22. See also *Olivetti/Canon*, OJ 1988 L52/51, at p. 57 ; *Fiat/Hitachi*, OJ 1993 L20/10.

[20] The joint venture guidelines, para. 41. Note that the joint venture guidelines go on to say that where co-operation in the form of a joint venture is the only objective possibility for competing parents to enter a new market or to remain present in a market, the joint venture will neither reduce existing competition nor prevent potential competition and thus not come within art. 85(1), provided that the presence of the parents on that market will strengthen competition or prevent it from being weakened; see *Metaleurope*, *XXth Report on Competition Policy*, point 117; *Elopak/Metalbox-Odin*, OJ 1990 L209/15; *Konsortium ECR 900*, OJ 1990 L228/31.

[21] See, e.g. *Beecham-Parke Davis*, OJ 1979 L70/11; *Henkel-Colgate*, OJ 1972 L14/14; *Elopak/Metal Box-Odin*, OJ 1990 L209/15. This is also the case where the results of the research and development are restricted, see the joint venture guidelines, para. 37; 1968 notice on co-operation, II, pt. 3; Regulation 418/85 (fn 7). In *Alcatel Espace/AWT Nachrichtentechnik*, OJ 1990 L32/19, the Commission determined that the joint venture was caught by art. 85(1) because the parties were actual competitors. To support this approach, the Commission noted that,

¶506

the formation of a joint venture will generally be deemed to restrict competition because, on the supply side, the parties forgo the opportunity of manufacturing the products independently and selling them on the market as competitors,[22] and, on the demand side, the consumer's range of choice is reduced.[23]

Sales joint ventures, selling the products of competing manufacturers, restrict competition between the parents on the supply side and limit the choice of purchasers.[24] Purchasing joint ventures set up by competitors can give the participants an advantage on the demand side and reduce the choice of suppliers.[25] Such co-operation can lead to a weakening of price competition between the participating undertakings. If however, the joint venture competes on a market that is different from that of the parents, the fact that the parents are actual competitors would not necessarily imply the application of art. 85(1).[26]

Potential competitors

Where the parent companies are not actual competitors, the formation of the joint venture may nevertheless fall within the scope of art. 85 if it sufficiently impairs potential competition. In the *Thirteenth Report on Competition Policy*, the Commission stated that a realistic approach must be taken in addressing the

---

as a result of their co-operation, only one of the parties would have undertaken research and development on specific projects whereas both might otherwise have done so.

[22] In *Olivetti/Canon*, OJ 1988 L52/51, the parents were actual competitors for copying machines of the low-end speed range as both manufactured and sold these machines. They were also actual competitors for facsimile products as Canon is an important manufacturer and Olivetti is a supplier on an OEM basis with an important volume in Italy (24 per cent of all sales there). The Commission found that the setting-up of the joint venture restricted competition between the parent companies as they would no longer compete at the production stage (a) as to copying machines for over half of the low-range market, and (b) in future possibly also for the mid-range and facsimile. See also *Rockwell-Iveco*, OJ 1983 L224/19.

[23] See *De Laval-Stork*, OJ 1977 L215/11, at p. 16; *VW-MAN*, OJ 1983 L376/11.

[24] See *Olivetti/Canon*, OJ 1988 L52/51, at p. 57. See also *VW-MAN*, OJ 1983 L376/11; *Sopelem-Vickers*, OJ 1978 L70/47, OJ 1981 L391/1; *UIP*, OJ 1989 L226/25; joint venture guidelines, para. 38. In *Alcatel Espace/ANT Nachrichtentechnik*, OJ 1990 L32/19, the Commission found that the choice of one of the parties to market the products eliminated one supplier from the market and consequently restricted competition. In addition, the joint venture restricted competition vis-à-vis third party suppliers. The Commission applied art. 85(1) even though it had noted the following market characteristics:

(1) the unique character of each project, which required highly adapted research and development and a very high degree of co-operation between all the parties involved, made R & D very expensive;

(2) the large number of competitors in the EC and worldwide and certain non-European manufacturers who, benefiting from their strong worldwide positions, had R & D budgets far superior to those of their European competitors so that non-European competitors had won contracts for a number of recent EC projects;

(3) the main customers for the products (national telecommunications administrations, space agencies and organisations or direct broadcast satellite consortia) were not numerous and as a result had considerable buying power; and

(4) certain regulatory barriers prevented the provision of services on an international basis.

[25] *Ijsselcentrale* OJ 1991 L28/32. See joint venture guidelines, para. 39.

[26] *Elopak/Metal Box*, OJ 1990 L209/15; See joint venture guidelines, para. 36.

¶506

question of whether the formation of a joint venture sufficiently restricts potential competition.[27] More specifically, the Commission stated that the following individual questions may be relevant to the issue of potential competition:

'Input of the joint venture
Does the investment expenditure involved substantially exceed the financing capacity of each partner? Does each partner have the necessary technical know-how and sources of supply of input products?

Production of the joint venture
Is each partner familiar with the process technology? Does each partner itself produce inputs for or products derived from the joint venture's product and does it have access to the necessary production facilities?

Sales by the joint venture
Is the actual or potential demand such that it would be feasible for each of the partners to manufacture the product on its own? Does each have access to the necessary distribution channels for the joint venture's product?

Risk factor
Could each partner bear the technical and financial risks associated with the production operations of the joint venture alone?'[28]

According to the joint venture guidelines, an economically realistic approach is necessary in the assessment of any particular case to ensure that each parent alone was not in a position to fulfil the tasks performed by the joint venture and that it did not forfeit its ability to do so by setting up the joint venture.[29] Here also, the Commission has advocated a sophisticated concept of potential competition which would proceed from a weighing of all relevant economic factors in order to determine whether the partners could reasonably be expected to act individually on the market.[30]

The earlier decisions of the Commission witnessed an eagerness to conclude that parties were potential competitors. Little evidence of the extent or importance of this potential competition was offered. The prerequisites to such a finding were the existence of technological expertise in fields other than those in which the joint venture was operating and the financial resources of the parties,[31] whether the parties had simply engaged in research and development

---

[27] *Thirteenth Report on Competition Policy*, point 55.
[28] Ibid. These factors are repeated in the joint venture guidelines. See *Astra*, OJ 1993 L 20/23, where these factors were considered more in the art. 85(3) analysis than in that of art. 85(1).
[29] Joint venture guidelines, para, 18
[30] Ibid., para 19
[31] *Carbon Gas Technologie*, OJ 1983 L376/17.

of the product,[32] or the fact that the parties were competitors in upstream or downstream markets of the product.[33]

As already noted, in the *Thirteenth Report on Competition Policy*, the Commission signalled the adoption of a realistic approach by insisting on a more substantive finding in determining whether the formation of a given joint venture restricted potential competition. This resulted in a change in the criteria used to make this assessment. A review of the cases reveals that this more realistic approach has not always been applied consistently.

Mitchell Cotts-Sofiltra

In *Mitchell Cotts-Sofiltra*, the Commission found that one of the founding companies of a joint venture, set up for the manufacture of high-efficiency air filters, was not a potential competitor because it lacked the requisite know-how and research and development facilities for the production of the filters.[34] The Commission stated that the mere availability of purchases or licences from other sources did not alter this analysis because of the company's evident economic and commercial interest in developing its own technology in the field.

Olivetti-Canon

In *Olivetti-Canon*, the Commission found that Olivetti, in spite of its financial means, was not a potential competitor of Canon in the market of laser printers.[35] The Commission based this decision on the following economic considerations:

(1) Olivetti would need a certain amount of time to achieve the necessary skills and technology to convert plants;

(2) the conversion would need substantial investments in machines and plant extensions;

(3) at the speed of the technological progress in this sector, Olivetti could not risk entering the market with an out-of-date product while many competitors were already well established in that market and in a position to keep pace with the technology.

---

[32] *GEC/Weir Sodium Circulators*, OJ 1977 L327/26.

[33] *Vacuum Interrupters II*, OJ 1980 L383/1. In this case, the Commission found the parties to be potential competitors even though it had been shown to be economically unfeasible for the companies to develop the product independently. In *Sopelem-Vickers*, OJ 1978 L70/47, the Commission found that two companies which set up a joint venture for the development, manufacture and distribution of advanced microscopes were potential competitors because the said companies had 'a certain amount of expertise and skill' in producing other types of microscopes and because one of the parents was active in the joint venture's sphere of activity.

[34] *Mitchell Cotts-Sofiltra*, OJ 1987 L41/31. A similar finding was made in *Optical Fibres*, OJ 1986 L236/30, which concerned several joint ventures set up by the same parent. None of the parties to the respective joint ventures had experience in the other parties' field, a fact which led the Commission to conclude that they were not potential competitors.

[35] *Olivetti-Canon*, OJ 1988 L52/51.

The Commission decided on the basis of these criteria that it did not appear that Olivetti, in spite of its financial means, could reasonably bear alone the high financial risks associated with the production of laser printers. This decision constitutes a clear departure from earlier cases such as *Vacuum Interrupters* and *Carbon Gas Technologie* that interpreted the notion of potential competition in a much looser fashion.

In the same decision, however, the Commission held that Olivetti was a potential competitor in mid-range copying machines. The Commission decided that Olivetti could bear alone the technical and financial risks associated with the production of mid-range machines because:

(1) Olivetti had an insignificant level of activity on the market of mid-range machines a long time ago. This market is adjacent to the market of low-range machines and Olivetti could re-enter the market of mid-range copiers and stay there alone;

(2) Olivetti's skills and technology for copying machines could be extended to higher-range (i.e. mid-range) models;

(3) the input products for low-range and mid-range copiers are largely the same;

(4) demand is sufficient to support such business;

(5) mid-range machines permit higher resources and higher profits;

(6) Olivetti is a profitable and healthy group.

This product-by-product analysis is in line with the Commission's earlier statement 'that the degree of potential competition depends largely on the nature of the product manufactured'.[36]

Elopak/Metal Box-Odin

In *Elopak/Metal Box-Odin*,[37] Elopak and Metal Box created for an indefinite period of time a 50/50 joint venture named Odin to research, develop and exploit a new type of container for UHT processed foods. The Commission found that the founding companies were not potential competitors in the relevant product market as 'neither party could in a short term enter the market alone as such entry would require a knowledge of the other party's technology which could not be developed without significant and time-consuming investment'.

The Commission continued:

'Both Metal Box's and Elopak's experience and resources are necessary to

---

[36] *Thirteenth Report on Competition Policy*, point 55.
[37] *Elopak/Metal Box-Odin*, OJ 1990 L209/15.

¶506

develop the new product which will be a combination of their respective technical and commercial know-how. The technical risks involved in carrying out research for a brand new product yet to be proven and which involves a whole new area of technology for each partner and the risks involved in developing the new filling, sealing and handling machinery necessary, would realistically preclude each party from attempting to carry out research and development on its own.'

This decision suggests a much greater flexibility in the way the Commission treats the issue of potential competition and confirms the trend towards the more realistic approach heralded in its *Thirteenth Report on Competition Policy*.[38]

Konsortium ECR 900
In *Konsortium ECR 900*,[39] the Commission concluded that the formation of a consortium for the development, manufacture and joint distribution of a pan-European digital cellular mobile telephone system did not fall under art. 85(1) because no single member of the consortium would have undertaken the project individually. The Commission noted that the development and manufacture by individual companies would not take place because of the extremely high costs involved and the very limited time schedule given for the development of the project.

The Commission also stressed that the parties to the agreement could not be expected to bear alone the financial risk involved in the project, in particular, considering the very limited demand (the only potential customers being 15 national network operators) and the fact that it was only if they achieved a big award that the companies would be able to amortise the very high development costs. Thus, following closely the approach articulated in both the *Thirteenth Report on Competition Policy* and *Elopak/Metal Box-Odin*, the Commission stated that 'realistically' there is no scope for companies to act individually.

---

[38] The novelty about *Odin* compared with other cases, in particular, *BBC Brown Boveri*, OJ 1988 L301/68, is that the Commission did not limit its analysis to the issue of potential competition after the joint venture was formed and the product being produced and marketed. On the contrary, it first ruled that, at the moment the joint venture was formed, Elopak and Metal Box were not potential competitors in the field covered by Odin since neither would have developed the new product alone. It also decided that the joint venture and Metal Box could not have been potential competitors at the time the joint venture was formed because the new product had not yet been developed and Metal Box would not have been able to produce it alone. On the other hand, it conceded that, once the product was being developed, the joint venture might become a competitor of Metal Box. However it concluded that sufficient safeguards had been built in to the agreements, particularly in the obligations of the founder companies relating to the dissolution of the joint venture, to avoid falling within art. 85(1).
[39] *Konsortium ECR 900*, OJ 1990 L228/31.

Cekacan

The Commission has not been entirely consistent in applying this more realistic analysis. For example, the approach in *Cekacan* appears reminiscent of that used in cases decided prior to the *Thirteenth Report on Competition Policy*. In *Cekacan*,[40] a Swedish group, A&R, whose activities included packaging (essentially for foodstuffs), and ECA, a German manufacturer of paperboard and paperboard packaging, formed a joint venture to develop and market a new packaging technology. ECA had not been independently producing paperboard laminated with plastics and aluminium foil, as would have been used in the new packaging. A&R however, had been carrying out research into packaging systems employing the same materials as those to be used in the new packaging. The Commission decided that the parties 'must be considered as potential competitors in the use of methods similar to Cekacan methods and producing and selling laminates'.

In the words of the Commission:

> 'ECA is a major producer of corrugated and flexible paperboard. In order to be able to produce paperboard laminated with plastics and aluminium foil, it would merely need to acquire the requisite know-how and make the necessary investments or, alternatively, link up with a firm in possession of such know-how. The same applies to the use of packaging systems which could replace the Cekacan packaging.'[41]

Although the reasoning behind this decision is not altogether clear, it may be that the Commission did not require a meaningful analysis to conclude that the parties could develop the package separately without having to engage in investment of a disproportionate amount.

KSB/Goulds/Lowara/ITT

Similarly, in *KSB/Goulds/Lowara/ITT*,[42] an agreement was reached by four pump manufacturers to form a joint venture to research and develop components for a chrome nickel stainless steel pump. While only one of the parties had the technology to develop these components, all of the parties were held to be potential competitors in the market for components as they all had the financial capability to develop the components alone. The Commission concluded that in view of their size, it must be assumed that each of the parties could develop the components alone. In addition, the other three parties could have acquired the technical knowledge necessary by way of a licence from third

---

[40] *Cekacan*, OJ 1990 L299/64.
[41] Ibid, See also *Fiat/Hitachi*, OJ 1993 L20/10, at p. 12.
[42] *KSB/Goulds/Lowara/ITT*, OJ 1991 L19/25. See also *Ford/Volkswagen*, OJ 1993 L20/14, at p. 16.

¶506

parties. Finally, the parties could have used the volume of units necessary for cost-effective production by licensing or producing for third parties.

Conclusion

Recent cases seem to confirm the Commission's intention to apply greater flexibility in the way it treats the issue of potential competition, thereby following the trend towards a more realistic approach enunciated in the *Thirteenth Report on Competition Policy*.[43] However, several cases suggest that the Commission is prone to occasionally lapsing into its former approach where a mechanical conclusion was reached to the exclusion of a genuine economic analysis.[44] As each case is decided on its own facts, caution should be exercised in attaching too much precedential value to cases decided in this fast-evolving area.

A review of the decisions suggests that different weight is attached to the various factors to be taken into account in assessing whether a joint venture restricts potential competition. One way of reconciling the case law may be to attach in a realistic manner primary importance to the financial cost and risk to be incurred in entering the market of the joint venture.[45] In any event, the actual content and relative weight of the criteria used remain uncertain and do not seem to limit the Commission's discretion.[46]

---

[43] Confirmed in the joint venture guidelines. See also *Konsortium ECR 900*, OJ 1990 L228/31; *Elopak/Metal Box*, OJ 1990 L209/15; *Olivetti-Canon*, OJ 1988 L52/51; *Mitchel Cotts-Sofiltra*, OJ 1987 L41/31; *Optical Fibres*, OJ 1986 L236/30.

[44] *KSB/Goulds/Lowara/ITT*, OJ 1991 L19/25; *Cekacan*, OJ 1990 L299/64. See, e.g. *De Laval-Stork*, OJ 1988 L59/32, in which the Commission did not make a product-by-product analysis comparable to that which was made in *Olivetti-Canon*, OJ 1988 L52/51. The Commission even seemed to suggest that the legal right for one of the partners to re-enter the joint venture's market in case the other partners were to withdraw from it was one of the factors conferring the status of potential competitor on the former partner. It is submitted that such an analysis is hardly realistic. The Commission's concise analysis with regard to the aspect of potential competition in *BBC Brown Boveri*, OJ 1988 L301/68, is also open to criticism. In this case, the Commission decided that one of the parent companies was a potential competitor because it would get access to the technology newly-developed by the joint venture in the field of high-performance batteries. The Commission did not enquire whether it was economically and financially feasible for the parent company to acquire the technology independently. The analysis is even more suspect because the same parent company was a ceramics manufacturer without any technical knowledge whatsoever in the field of batteries.

[45] In *KSB/Goulds/Lowara/ITT*, OJ 1991 L19/25, all of the parties were already manufacturers of conventional water pumps. The Commission said that 'in view of their size it must be assumed that each group of undertakings would have been in a financial position to develop the components alone'. See also the joint venture guidelines, para. 20, where it is stated that the parents of a joint venture are potential competitors if they could reasonably be expected to act autonomously. In that connection, analysis must focus on the various stages of the activity of an undertaking. In *Cekacan*, OJ 1990 L299/64, the parties were already in similar markets and the financial costs and risks involved may not have been prohibitive in order for the parties to develop the new product separately. In *Konsortium ECR 900*, OJ 1990 L228/31, the cost factor involved in developing the digital cellular mobile phone system was deemed to be 'so great that realistically there is no scope for companies to act individually'. In *Elopak/Metal Box*, OJ 1990 L209/15, it was felt that 'neither party could in a short term enter the market alone as such entry would require a knowledge of the other party's technology which could not be developed without significant and time consuming investment'. In *Olivetti-Canon*, OJ 1988 L52/51, it did not appear that Olivetti could reasonably bear alone the high financial risks associated with the production of laser printers.

[46] See *Fiat/Hitachi*, OJ 1993 L20/10; *KSB/Goulds/Lowara/ITT*, OJ 1991 L19/25. In *IVECO/FORD*, OJ 1988 L230/39, the Commission inferred from activities of the parent companies in the joint venture's sphere of activity in geographic markets other than the EC (the US in particular) that the parent companies remained potential

The parties to the joint venture must be actual or potential competitors in the same product *and* geographical market.[47] The geographical market is usually the EC. In *Olivetti/Canon*, the Commission stated that

'for all the products involved the EEC represents an area in which the conditions of competition are similar for all suppliers. National laws do not make trade between Member States difficult, nor do costs of transport or consumer preference.'[48]

However, when defining the geographical market, it is necessary to ensure that the competitive conditions are broadly similar for the product in question. In *Mitchell/Cotts-Sofiltra*, as this condition was fulfilled throughout the common market, the Commission held the whole of the EC to be the relevant geographic market in order to assess the parties' positions.

In addition to considering whether the parents are actual or potential competitors in deciding on the applicability of art. 85(1) to the agreement in question, the degree of 'appreciability' of the restriction of competition that might take place as a result of the formation of the joint venture must also be taken into account. This 'appreciability' test was first developed in *GEC-Siemens/Plessey*,[49] where certain aspects of the joint venture not having an appreciable effect on competition were held not to come within art. 85(1) at all, even though the parties to the joint venture were actual competitors. The Commission had previously relied on such reasoning to exempt an agreement under art. 85(3) or to not oppose a concentration.

This case involved the joint acquisition by Siemens and GEC of a wide range of Plessey's activities. In some of these areas, such as public switching systems, large private switching systems and transmission systems, the Commission found an appreciable restriction on competition with the resulting applicability of art. 85(1). However, as regards small private switching systems and Plessey's traffic control system, the Commission was of the opinion that the

---

competitors. A genuine economic analysis would not have warranted such a mechanical conclusion because a number of cost factors (e.g. economic feasibility of exports or overall financial resources) would have to be taken into account in order to reach such a conclusion.

[47] In *Mitchell/Cotts-Sofiltra*, OJ 1987 L41/31, the Commission stated, 'the question arises whether the participating undertakings are competitors within the relevant geographical and product markets'.

[48] *Olivetti/Canon*, OJ 1988 L52/52, at p. 52. In *Fiat/Hitachi*, OJ 1993 L20/10, the Commission found that the parents to the joint venture were at least potential competitors in Europe and worldwide after the joint venture was formed. Fiat and Hitachi were actual competitors in Europe and worldwide before they entered into the agreement to create their joint venture. They have remained at least potential competitors thereafter. Hitachi operates on the same product markets as Fiat-Hitachi in Japan and in the Far East and indirectly, through its joint venture with Deere, also in the US. Fiat continues to develop, manufacture and sell its product range based on its own technology through Fitallis Latino-Americana and to operate in the other subsectors of the earthmoving machinery market. Both parent companies have retained their technologies for the production of hydraulic excavators and components and merely granted a licence to their joint venture and the relevant agreements are to terminate in the event of liquidation of the joint venture. As exclusive supplier of motors and hydraulics, they are furthermore actively interested in the production and marketing activities of Fiat-Hitachi.

[49] *GEC-Siemens/Plessey*, OJ 1990 C239/2.

appreciability threshold had not been reached, with the result that art. 85(1) did not apply.

In reaching this conclusion, the Commission applied a so-called 'structural analysis' to the joint venture. This entailed increasing the threshold of the appreciable effect on competition and involved the examination of many diverse factors such as the number of competitors at European level, actual and potential competition from outside the EC, the size and importance of the parties, the market shares of the parties, barriers to entry, and specialisation by the parties as well as the need for international alliances.

Although this reasoning represents a departure in the analysis of joint ventures under art. 85, its scope and conditions of application are uncertain. Although the same analysis was also used in *Elopak-Metal Box/Odin*[50] where the Commission decided that the entire agreement did not appreciably restrict competition, more recent cases place in question the Commission's willingness to engage in an in-depth structural analysis.[51] Secondly, the concept of structural as opposed to behavioural analysis has yet to be defined. Further, it is unsure whether the application of this new test will be restricted to 'merger fall-out' cases that would, but for the level of co-operation between the parties, otherwise fall within the merger regulation or indeed whether it will be applied to co-operative joint venture cases in general.[52] Finally, it is not clear at what stage the restrictive effects on competition become appreciable enough to warrant the application of art. 85.

Network effect

Even in cases where the joint venture partners are neither actual nor potential competitors, the Commission may find that the joint venture agreement falls within the scope of art. 85(1). In *Optical Fibres*,[53] the Commission objected to the joint venture agreements concluded by Corning with local partners in

---

[50] *Elopak-Metal Box/Odin*, OJ 1990 L209/15. This case also addresses the issue left unresolved by the *Thirteenth Report on Competition Policy* that, where only one of the parents is a potential competitor of the joint venture, art. 85(1) may not apply if there are sufficient provisions in the agreement to ensure that the relationship between the joint venture and the parents does not give rise to restrictions of competition.

[51] In *Alcatel Espace/ANT Nachrichtentechnik*, OJ 1990 L32/19, the Commission chose not to attach importance to structural factors. See also *Cekacan*, OJ 1990 L299/64, and *KSB/Goulds/Lowara/ITT*, OJ 1991 L19/25. However, in *Fiat/Hitachi*, OJ 1993 L20/10, the Commission seemed to return to the 'appreciable restriction on competition' test by considering factors such as non-compete clauses, a ban on active imports into the Community and a market share in the EC of 16 per cent after the creation of the joint venture, in order to find that the agreements would appreciably restrict competition. This analysis was made in spite of the fact that the parties were clearly potential competitors after they entered into the agreement to create the joint venture.

[52] These questions are unlikely to be satisfactorily resolved as the Commission has announced its intention to clear joint venture agreements in the future by comfort letter. See ¶1126.

[53] *Optical Fibres*, OJ 1986 L236/30. It should be noted that the Commission confirmed its 'network theory' in *Elopak/Metal Box-Odin*, OJ 1990 L209/15 at p. 19 and in *Mitchell Cotts-Solfiltra*, OJ 1987 L41/31 at p. 35. In these decisions, the Commission excluded the application of art. 85(1) to an agreement for joint manufacturing because, inter alia, the agreement did not involve 'the creation of a network of competing joint ventures'.

different member states on the sole ground that Corning was in a position to prevent the joint ventures from competing with each other:

'Corning's active participation in the joint ventures cannot be compared with a straightforward financial investment in or licensing of several independent third parties. Firstly, the joint ventures depend fully on Corning's technology and its implementation by a Technical Manager appointed by Corning. Secondly, the fact that Corning is a partner in each joint venture creates a network of closely inter-related companies which are otherwise competitors. Given this network of inter-related joint ventures and the technological dependence of the joint ventures on a common partner, they cannot be expected to compete with each other to the same extent as if they were unrelated competitors relying on different partners and different technologies.'[54]

This 'network theory' enabled the Commission to exercise jurisdiction over Corning's joint venture arrangements under art. 85(1) and to condition the grant of an exemption under art. 85(3) on the willingness of the parties to make a number of modifications.[55]

The joint venture guidelines state that joint venture networks can particularly restrict competition through increasing the influence of the individual joint venture on the business policy of the parents and on the market position of third parties. In some cases, restrictions on competition will only be brought about by the creation of additional joint ventures. Thus, the assessment under competition law must take into account the different ways of arranging joint venture networks just as much as the cumulative effects of parallel existing networks.[56]

---

[54] *Optical Fibres*, OJ 1986 L236/30, at p. 52.
[55] The modifications included the following:

(1) a reduction of Corning's voting and management rights;
(2) the possibility for the partners to veto certain decisions;
(3) the termination of exclusive sales licences; and
(4) each partner was given the rights unilaterally to require expansion of the joint venture's production capacity.

[56] The joint venture guidelines at para. 27 ff. go on to say that

'often competing parent companies set up several joint ventures which are active in the same product market but in different geographical markets. On top of the restrictions of competition which can already be attributed to each joint venture, there will then be those which arise in the relationships between the individual joint ventures. The ties between the parents are strengthened by the creation of every further joint venture so that competition existing between them will be further reduced.

The same is true in the case where competing parents set up several joint ventures for complementary products which they themselves intend to process or for different products which they themselves distribute. The extent and intensity of the restrictive effects on competition are also increased in such cases. Competition is most severely restricted where undertakings competing within the same oligopolistic sector set up a multitude of joint ventures for related products or for a great variety of intermediate products. These considerations are also valid for the service sector.

¶506

Effect upon third parties

Even where a joint venture is established between companies that are neither actual nor potential competitors, the formation of the joint venture may affect competition between the partners or the joint venture and third parties in an upstream or downstream market.[57] This type of restriction of competition may also bring art. 85(1) into play. Indeed, in *Alcatel Espace*,[58] the Commission held that the procedure under the agreement for the procurement by one party of the equipment manufactured by the other party, although leaving the former the possibility of using another supplier, tended to eliminate the competition of third party suppliers.[59] Competition was consequently restricted. Where the joint venture handles the parent companies' purchases or sales, the choice available to suppliers or customers may be appreciably restricted.[60]

The same is true when the joint venture manufactures primary or intermediate products for its parents or processes products which they themselves have produced.[61] In *Mitchell Cotts/Sofiltra*,[62] competition was not restricted as only one of the parties had the technology to make filters, and the aggregate market share of the parties was too small to foreclose others. In *Elopak/Metal Box*,[63] it was determined that the creation of the joint venture was not likely to foreclose similar possibilities of collaboration for other potential competitors. Such risks of foreclosure may not be present when there are a number of other undertakings competing in the relevant product and geographic markets.[64]

Foreclosure may also occur by the granting of exclusive licences. The

---

Even where a joint venture is created by non-competing firms and does not on its own cause any restriction of competition, it can be anti-competitive if it belongs to a network of joint ventures set up by one of the parents for the same product market with different partners, because competition between the joint ventures may then be prevented, restricted or distorted. If the different partners are actual or potential competitors, there will additionally be restrictive effects in the relationships between them.

Parallel networks of joint ventures, involving different parent companies, simply reveal the degree of personal and financial connection between the undertakings of an economic sector or between several economic sectors. They form, in so far as they are comparable to the degree of concentration on the relevant market, an important aspect of the economic environment which has to be taken into account in the assessment from a competition point of view of both the individual networks and the participating joint ventures.'

[57] In the joint venture guidelines, para. 23, the Commission states that the restrictive effect on third parties depends on the joint venture's activities in relation to those of its parents and on the combined market power of the undertakings concerned.

[58] *Alcatel Espace/ANT Nachrichtentechnik*, OJ 1990 L32/19.

[59] See also *Astra*, OJ 1993 L20/23, at p. 31.

[60] In *Olivetti-Canon*, OJ 1988 L52/51, the parties were required to amend a provision allowing either party to authorise sales by a third party of products developed by the joint venture only when the other party consented. Such consent could only be required where the product was based on the technology of that other party. See also the joint venture guidelines, para. 24.

[61] *Vacuum Interrupters I*, OJ 1977 L48/32; *GEC/Weir*, OJ 1977 L327/26; *Continental Michelin*, OJ 1988 L305/33; joint venture guidelines, para. 24.

[62] *Mitchell Cotts/Sofiltra*, OJ 1987 L41/31.

[63] *Elopak/Metal Box-Odin*, OJ 1990 L209/15.

[64] Ibid. In that case, the Commission noted that 'there are several other very large metal-can makers in the EEC who have at least equivalent technical know-how to Metal Box's.' See also *GEC-Siemens/Plessey*, OJ 1990 C239/2 ; *Mitchell Cotts/Sofiltra*, OJ 1987 L41/31.

¶506

granting of such licences to the joint venture by the parent companies precludes the granting of licences to third parties. For instance, in *Optical Fibres*,[65] the Commission was prepared to grant an exemption only if the licences were amended to be non-exclusive. Similarly, in *Continental/Michelin*,[66] the Commission requested that the parties be offered licences of the new technology in the joint venture on reasonable terms.

In *Screensport/EBU Members*,[67] the Commission refused to grant an exemption to a series of agreements because of their exclusionary effect on third parties. Certain members of the European Broadcasting Union ('EBU'), an association consisting primarily of public service broadcasters, had created a joint venture operating the transnational satellite television sports channel Eurosport. Following a complaint lodged by another sports channel service, Screensport, the Commission objected to the Eurosport venture because, inter alia, as a result of the exclusive rights acquired by the EBU and its members to which Eurosport had unrestricted and privileged access, third parties seeking to broadcast sports events were severely restricted in their ability to obtain broadcasting rights, in particular because they could only rely on sub-licences available from EBU members.

Appreciable restriction of competition
A finding that the parents are actual or potential competitors is not sufficient to bring a joint venture within art. 85(1). There must also be an appreciable restriction of competition resulting from the formation of the joint venture. It was originally believed that the 1986 Commission notice[68] would be used to assess whether competition had been restricted appreciably. This notice states that agreements between undertakings engaged in the production or distribution of goods or in the provision of services generally do not fall under the prohibition of art. 85(1) if:

(1) the goods or services which are the subject of the agreement together with the participating undertakings' other goods or services which are considered by users to be equivalent in view of their characteristics, price and intended use, do not represent more than five per cent of the total market for such goods or services in the area of the common market affected by the agreement;

---

[65] *Optical fibres*, OJ 1986 L236/30.
[66] *Continental/Michelin*, OJ 1988 L305/33.
[67] *Screensport/EBU members*, OJ 1991 L63/32. A modified scheme submitted to the Commission was subsequently exempted; see IP/93/158.
[68] Commission notice of 3 September 1986 on agreements of minor importance which do not fall under art. 85(1) of the treaty establishing the European Economic Community, OJ 1986 L231/2.

(2) the aggregate annual turnover of the participating undertakings does not exceed ECU 200m;[69] and

(3) the above-mentioned market share or turnover is not exceeded by more than one tenth during two successive financial years.

The Commission's notice on de minimis agreements should, however, be applied with caution. In *Floral*,[70] for instance, three leading French manufacturers of fertilisers entered into a co-operation agreement whereby a joint organisation for exports of compound fertilisers to Germany ('Floral') was set up. This co-operation agreement was held to cause an appreciable restriction of competition in spite of the fact that exports through the Floral venture only represented two per cent of total German consumption of compound fertilisers. The Commission considered that the oligopolistic structure of the German fertiliser market was a factor of greater importance than the actual market share of the parties to the joint venture.[71]

The Commission has even gone so far as to take the range of products of the joint venture into consideration in establishing that an appreciable restriction of competition was caused by an agreement between the parent companies.[72]

In *Olivetti-Canon*,[73] however, it was found that the restrictions brought about by the joint venture were appreciable in the market for mid-range copiers even though Olivetti was not in this market and Canon's EC market share was only 6.7 per cent. The Commission said that: 'In mid-range machines Canon has a market share of 6.7%, which is not negligible. Olivetti is currently only a potential competitor in that market, but it could be expected that if it re-entered it would rapidly acquire a market share of a few points, on the strength of the name it already has in this sector.'[74]

---

[69] In a prior notice on agreements of minor importance (OJ 1977 C313/3) the annual turnover threshold was fixed at ECU 50m.

[70] *Floral*, OJ 1980 L39/51.

[71] The Commission stated (Ibid., at p. 57):

'Moreover, account must be taken of the structure of competition on the market concerned, that is the German market. The number of competitors on the German market is very small. By far the largest are Ruhrstickstoff, BASF and Hoechst, which together have an exceptional position on the market, although, in terms of size, they are comparable as manufacturers of compound fertilizers with the three French manufacturers concerned.

On a market with such an oligopolistic structure, if three of the few suppliers (who despite their size have only a small share of that market) standardize their supply through a joint sales organization, the oligopoly merely becomes tighter. Even relatively small quantities can, if put on the market by the suppliers individually, have an appreciable impact on market conditions. The share of the market captured by the three French manufacturers seemed to them significant enough to warrant planning and effecting a scheme of co-operation to standardize their supplies, and there is no evidence that their influence on this market could not be increased through changes in competitive conditions, market structure and their own sales policy.'

[72] *GEC-Weir Sodium Circulators*, OJ 1977 L327/26 See also *GEC-Siemens/Plessey*, OJ 1990 C239/2. This decision does not state the level of market shares of the parties although it may be that they exceeded the thresholds contained in the 1986 notice. Sir Leon Brittan, 'Strategic Alliances – An Old Problem and a New Challenge to Commission's Competition Policy', speech delivered in Berlin, 25 May 1992.

[73] *Olivetti-Canon*, OJ 1988 L52/51.

[74] Ibid., at p. 59.

The joint venture guidelines state that joint ventures of minor economic importance within the meaning of the 1986 notice do not appreciably restrict competition and accordingly fall outside art. 85(1).[75] However, the guidelines go on to set out a number of factors which are to be taken into account when assessing the appreciable effect of restrictions on competition, only one of which is market share.[76] This apparent contradiction is unfortunate in an area where it was hoped that the uncertainty would be cleared up by the joint venture guidelines. Until that time arrives, however, it would seem imprudent to place too much emphasis on market share figures alone in assessing appreciability.

According to the guidelines, acceptable market shares for production joint ventures cannot be fixed. However, a 20 per cent market share limit can serve as a starting point in such cases. For full-function joint ventures (which include distribution) to be generally compatible with the competition rules, the aggregate market share of the participating undertakings must not exceed ten per cent. Below this threshold, it can be assumed that the effect of exclusion from the market of third parties and the danger of creating or reinforcing barriers to market entry will be kept within justifiable limits, so that the market structure will further guarantee effective competition. If this threshold is exceeded, the guidelines state that an exemption will only be considered after a careful examination of the individual case.

Ancillary restrictions

This section examines the treatment afforded by the Commission to ancillary restrictions, i.e. those restrictions that are necessary for the setting-up and proper operation of the joint venture.

In *BP/Kellogg*,[77] the Commission accepted that the parties were not potential competitors, but nevertheless found that restrictions that were ancillary to the collaboration of the parties, while being reasonable and necessary, restricted

---

[75] The joint venture guidelines, at para. 15, state that there is no appreciable restriction of competition where the combined turnover of the participating undertakings does not exceed ECU 200m and their market share is not more than five per cent.

[76] See ¶502 et seq. The joint venture guidelines state at para. 26 that the scale of a joint venture's effects on competition depends on a number of factors, the most important of which are:

- the market shares of the parent companies and the joint venture, the structure of the relevant market and the degree of concentration in the sector concerned;
- the economic and financial strength of the parent companies, and any commercial or technical edge which they may have in comparison with their competitors;
- the market proximity of the activities carried out by the joint venture;
- whether the fields of activity of the parent companies and the joint venture are identical or interdependent;
- the scale and significance of the joint venture's activities in relation to those of its parents;
- the extent to which the arrangements between the firms concerned are restrictive;
- the extent to which market access by third parties is restricted.

[77] *BP/Kellogg*, OJ 1985 L369/6.

¶506

competition and required exemption. An exemption under art. 85(3) was accordingly granted as the restrictions were indeed reasonable and necessary. The question may reasonably be asked why the restrictions fell within art. 85(1) in the first place if they were reasonable and necessary for the collaboration to take place.

Since this case, the Commission has sought to enunciate a more coherent position with regard to ancillary restraints. In *Mitchell Cotts-Sofiltra*,[78] the Commission was of the view that agreements or restrictions that are ancillary to the joint venture agreement i.e. strictly necessary for the creation and proper operation of the joint venture, would be treated in the same way as the joint venture agreement itself and would not require a separate analysis. On the other hand, agreements or restrictions that are not ancillary to the joint venture would require a separate analysis under art. 85(1) irrespective of whether the joint venture itself did not restrict competition.

The Commission stated:

'Since the parties are not competitors and there is no loss of competition involved and no foreclosure risk, and the agreement does not involve the creation of a network of competing joint ventures, the agreement to undertake joint manufacturing does not *in itself* fall within the terms of art. 85(1).'[79]

The restrictions that were considered ancillary to the joint venture included an obligation on the joint venture to maintain confidentiality, not to grant sub-licences, to disclose to Sofiltra any improvements developed or acquired by the joint venture, and not, due to the specific circumstance of the case, to manufacture or deal in products competing with the licensed products.[80] However, restrictive clauses granting to the joint venture an exclusive licence to manufacture air filters in Ireland and the UK were not deemed ancillary.

Elopak/Metal Box-Odin[81] would seem to represent another step towards the development of a genuine theory of ancillary restraints under art. 85(1). Here, the Commission held that the restrictions which 'cannot be dissociated from the creation of [the joint venture] without undermining its existence and purpose will fall outside the scope of art. 85(1)'.[82] After granting a negative clearance to the joint venture itself, the Commission analysed the ancillary provisions to ensure that they were no more than was necessary to ensure the establishment

---

[78] *Mitchell Cotts/Sofiltra*, OJ 1987 L41/31.
[79] Ibid., at p. 35.
[80] Ibid., at p. 35.
[81] *Elopak/Metal Box-Odin*, OJ 1990 L209/15.
[82] Ibid., at p. 21.

and proper functioning of the joint venture. On the basis of this doctrine, the Commission decided that the following restraints did not infringe art. 85(1):

- an exclusive licence granted to the joint venture to exploit, even beyond the starting-up period for new technology, the proprietary know-how of the parent companies;

- the obligation on each parent not to allow a competitor of the other parent to use that other parent's know-how or improvements made by the joint venture for five years following the break-up of Odin;

- a provision giving the seller of shares of the joint venture a right of first refusal in case of a further sale.[83]

In *Konsortium ECR 900*,[84] a party excluded from the consortium for breach of contract forfeited its right to use the technical documentation of the other parties. The Commission found that such a clause did not restrict competition as the use of the other's documentation in such a case would allow that party to receive unjustified benefits which would lead to an undeserved competitive advantage vis-à-vis the other parties. Such competition not based on performance was held not to be protected by art. 85. The Commission also found that an obligation on the parties not to compete with each other during the term of the agreement did not amount to a restriction on competition.

Following *Elopak/Metal Box*, the Commission issued a press statement[85] to the effect that

'where the setting up of a joint venture does not in itself infringe the rules of competition, any reasonable restrictions which are necessary for the setting up and the efficient operation of the joint venture are also compatible with the rules of competition ... [O]ther restrictions such as ODIN's exclusive right to exploit the parents' know-how in the field of the agreement do not in this case restrict competition, as such restrictions cannot be disassociated from the creation of the joint venture without undermining its existence.'

These cases suggest that restrictions that would on their own, restrict competition, but which are ancillary to a joint venture agreement which is itself cleared, would also escape the provisions of art. 85(1). Caution should however be exercised as each case would seem to turn on its own facts.[86]

---

[83] The treatment afforded by the Commission to the exclusive licence to manufacture which was granted to the joint venture may be distinguished from that in *Mitchell/Cotts* as, in *Elopak/Metal Box-Odin*, neither of the parents were capable of developing the product individually.

[84] *Konsortium ECR 900*, OJ 1990 L228/31.

[85] Press Release IP(90)582 of 23 July 1990.

[86] The approach taken in *Odin* is consistent with the approach adopted in art. 8(2) of the merger regulation which provides that 'the decision declaring the concentration compatible shall also cover restrictions directly related and necessary to the implementing Commission Notice regarding restrictions ancillary to concentrations.'

The joint venture guidelines also signal an emerging ancillary restraints doctrine. Here, the Commission distinguishes between restrictions of competition that are caused by the creation and operation of the joint venture, and additional agreements that would, on their own, constitute restrictions of competition by limiting the freedom of action in the market of the firms concerned. Such additional agreements are either directly related and necessary to the establishment and operation of the joint venture in so far as they cannot be dissociated from it without jeopardising its existence, or are simply concluded at the same time as the joint venture is created without having those features.

Additional agreements that are directly related to the joint venture and necessary for its existence must be assessed together with the joint venture. They are treated as ancillary restrictions if they remain subordinate in importance to the main object of the joint venture. Additional agreements that are not ancillary to the joint venture normally fall within the scope of art. 85(1) even though the joint venture may not. For them to be granted an exemption under art. 85(3), a specific assessment of their benefits and disadvantages must be made. This assessment must be carried out separately from that of the joint venture.[87]

¶507 Effect on trade between member states

In the joint venture guidelines, the Commission makes it clear that the question of whether agreements, decisions or concerted practices are likely to affect trade between member states, can only be decided on a case-by-case basis. Where the joint venture's actual or foreseeable effects on competition are limited to the territory of one member state or to territories outside the Community, art. 85(1) will not apply.[88]

However, trade between member states will be affected where the joint venture's production will be marketed in more than one member state.[89] Trade between member states may also be affected whether the parties are from the same member state or from different member states.[90] In *Ford/Volkswagen*,[91] an agreement was held appreciably to affect trade between member states as it was concluded between two internationally active car manufacturers concerning the joint development and production of a product which was to be sold throughout the Community. In *Ansac*,[92] an agreement between six US

---

[87] See joint venture guidelines, para. 65 et seq.
[88] Ibid., para. 14.
[89] *Auditel*, OJ 1993 L306/50; *KSB/Goulds/Lowara/ITT*, OJ 1991 L19/25; *Olivetti/Canon*, OJ 1988 L52/51; *Mitchell Cotts/Sofiltra*, OJ 1987 L41/31.
[90] *Alcatel Espace/ANT Nachrichtentechnik*, OJ 1990 L32/19; *Mitchell Cotts/Sofiltra*, OJ 1987 L41/31.
[91] *Ford/Volkswagen*, OJ 1993 L20/14.
[92] *Ansac*, OJ 1991 L152/54.

producers of natural soda-ash to the effect that nearly all export sales by them or by any subsidiary would be made through Ansac, a US association, was held to affect trade between member states.

The Commission said:

> 'If Ansac enters the EEC soda-ash market on the terms set out in the notification there will be only one new operator on the market. Trade within the Community will necessarily be conducted on different terms from those which would prevail if all or any of Ansac's members were to enter the market individually. The notified arrangements are thus liable to affect trade between member states.'[93]

In *UIP*,[94] the Commission found that trade between member states was affected because the pooling of distribution activities for films by three of the largest film producers in the Community 'necessarily means that trade will develop under conditions different from those which could have existed in the absence of such pooling of functions'.[95]

In *ENI-Montedison*, the Commission held that trade between member states was affected because, as a result of the agreements, 'the whole structure of competition is substantially changed from the point of view of consumers and of other producers in Italy and the rest of the EEC'.[96]

¶508   Exemption: application of art. 85(3) to joint ventures

Joint venture agreements falling under the prohibition of art. 85(1) must be analysed under the four criteria of art. 85(3) before an exemption may be granted. The agreement must contribute to improving the production or distribution of goods or to promoting technical or economic progress, while allowing consumers a fair share of the resulting benefit. Further, the agreement must not impose restrictions which are not indispensable to the attainment of these objectives nor afford the possibility of eliminating competition in respect of a substantial part of the products in question.

While the four criteria for exemption are cumulative, particular importance appears to be attached to an objective improvement such as technological development, output expansion or efficiency gain, as well as ensuring that the competitive structure of the market is maintained.[97] These two criteria are regarded by the Commission as the keys in deciding whether a joint venture can

---

[93] Ibid., at p. 58.
[94] *UIP*, OJ 1989 L226/25.
[95] Ibid., at p. 30.
[96] *ENI-Montedison*, OJ 1987 L5/13, at p. 18.
[97] Sir Leon Brittan, 'Strategic Alliances An Old Problem and a New Challenge to Commission's Competition Policy', speech delivered in Berlin, 25 May 1992; *Fifteenth Report on Competition Policy*, point 26.

be exempted under art. 85(3).[98] In practice, the issue of indispensability is also examined in detail. Should these criteria be satisfied, then it is generally assumed that there will be a fair outcome for consumers.[99]

The Commission is particularly accommodating in respect of joint ventures that contribute to the integration of the internal market, promote the innovation and transfer of technology, develop new markets, promote risk sharing, improve the competitiveness of the Community industry, strengthen the competitive position of small and medium-sized firms and eliminate structural overcapacity.[100] Favourable treatment may also be afforded to joint ventures that increase the development of high technology within the Community.[101]

The Commission views full-function joint ventures, in so far as they are not price fixing, quota-fixing or market-sharing cartels or vehicles for the co-ordination of the investment policies conducted by the parents which go beyond the individual case, as forming elements of dynamic competition and deserving a favourable assessment.[102] However, as is the case with the Commission's interpretation of joint ventures under art. 85(1), many cases turn on their own particular facts, making the setting out of rules difficult and the exercise of caution a necessity.[103]

A review of the cases shows that, save for rare exceptions,[104] the joint ventures that were found by the Commission to fall under art. 85(1), have received exemptions under art. 85(3).

The policy followed thus far by the Commission under art. 85(3) is summarised at ¶509 to ¶511.

---

[98] Ibid. The joint venture guidelines state that:

'In order to fulfil the first two conditions of Article 85(3) the JV must bring appreciable objective advantages for third parties, especially consumers, which at least equal the consequent detriment to competition.

Advantages in the above-mentioned sense, which can be pursued and attained with the aid of a JV, include, in the Commission's opinion, in particular, the development of new or improved products and processes which are marketed by the originator or by third parties under licence. In addition, measures opening up new markets, leading to the sales expansion of the undertaking in new territories or the enlargement of its supply range by new products, will in principle be assessed favourably. In all these cases the undertakings in question contribute to dynamic competition, consolidating the internal market and strengthening the competitiveness of the relevant economic sector. Production and sales increases can also be a pro-competitive stimulant. On the other hand, the rationalization of production activities and distribution networks are rather a means of adapting supply to a shrinking or stagnant demand. It leads, however, to cost savings which, under effective competition, are usually passed on to customers as lower prices. Plans for the reduction of production capacity however lead mostly to price rises. Agreements of this latter type will be judged favourably only if they serve to overcome a structural crisis, to accelerate the removal of unprofitable production capacity from the market and thereby to re-establish competition in the medium term.'

[99] Ibid., at para. 54, 55.
[100] *Fifteenth Report on Competition Policy*, point 26.
[101] *Ford/Volkswagen*, OJ 1993 L20/14
[102] The joint venture guidelines, para. 64.
[103] See, e.g. *Ford/Volkswagen*, OJ 1993 L20/14, where the Commission was willing to grant an exemption to the joint venture due to certain unusual features of the case such as the fact that the joint venture would create jobs in one of the less-developed regions of the Community.
[104] *Screensport/EBU Member*, OJ 1991 L63/32; *Ansac*, OJ 1991 L152/54; *WANO-Schwarzpulver*, OJ 1978 L322/26.

¶508

¶509   Permissibility of the joint venture

The assessment by the Commission of whether or not the formation of a particular joint venture can be exempted under art. 85(3) will be guided by the following four criteria:

(1) Does the joint venture contribute to improving the production and distribution of goods or to promoting technical or economic progress?

(2) Do consumers receive a fair share of the resulting benefit?

(3) Is the joint venture 'indispensable' or are there less restrictive means to realise the benefits expected of the joint venture?

(4) Will competition be eliminated or reduced to an unacceptable level as a result of the formation of the joint venture?

(1)   Improvement in production or distribution or promotion of technical or economic progress[105]

As joint ventures that are innovative in nature invariably lead to an objective improvement in technical or economic progress, this condition is generally fulfilled without too much difficulty. Benefits found by the Commission to meet this condition to date include: facilitating the entry by one or both of the parents into a new geographic or product market,[106] sharing financial and other risks in connection with the development of advanced-technology products,[107] placing the manufacture of intermediate products used by the parents on a profitable footing,[108] simplification and acceleration of the transition of technology from the planning and research stage to that of large scale industrial application,[109] reduction of overcapacity,[110] utilisation of a greater amount of existing capacity through the emergence of a new and efficient competitor,[111] production of a wider range of sophisticated equipment at competitive prices,[112] regaining competitiveness and progressively reducing losses through closure of plants, reduction in surplus capacity, optimisation of transportation costs[113] and energy saving.[114]

Several cases give an indication of the Commission's approach in this area. In *Alcatel Espace/ANT Nachrichtentechnik*,[115] the Commission granted a ten-year

---

[105] See generally joint venture guidelines, para. 53 et seq.; Sir Leon Brittan, 'Strategic Alliances – An Old Problem and a New Challenge to Commission's Competition Policy', speech delivered in Berlin, 25 May 1992; *Fifteenth Report on Competition Policy*, point 26.

[106] *Apollinaris/Schweppes, XXIst Report on Competition Policy*, point 87; *De Laval-Stork*, OJ 1977 L215/11.

[107] *Vacuum Interrupters*, OJ 1980 L383/1.

[108] *Seventh Report on Competition Policy*, point 117–119.

[109] *Carbon Gas Technologie*, OJ 1983 L376/5.

[110] *Bayer/BP Chemicals*, OJ 1988 L150/35.

[111] *Rockwell/Iveco*, OJ 1983 L224/19.

[112] *Alcatel Espace/ANT Nachrichtentechnik*, OJ 1990 L32/19

[113] *Enichem/ICI*, OJ 1988 L50/18.

[114] *BP/Kellogg*, OJ 1985 L369/6.

[115] *Alcatel Espace/ANT Nachrichtentechnik*, OJ 1990 L32/19.

exemption to the co-operation agreement on the research, development, production and marketing of electronic components for satellites. The Commission noted that the joint research and development program was likely to promote technical and economic progress as the effects and risks involved, even if they could be supported independently by the parties, would most certainly not lead to results as rapid, efficient and economic as those envisaged. Similarly, in *Olivetti/Canon*[116] the same conclusion was reached concerning the design, development and manufacture of certain photocopying machines. The Commission explained:

'On all the markets involved, and in which the parties are competing, the technology is fast-moving and the degree of competition high. In order to compete efficiently, the undertakings on those markets have to offer products which are the result of the most up-to-date technology, at competitive prices. Up-to-date technologies, however, require large investments in research and development. The expansion of production in the EEC which is the effect of the joint venture enables the parties to spread the costs of these investments over a larger number of products: otherwise the costs of those products would be too high for producers to be able to sell them at a competitive price.'[117]

In *KSB/Goulds/Lowara/ITT*,[118] an agreement by four conventional pump manufacturers for the joint research, development and production of a chrome nickel steel pump was said to contribute to the improvement in the production of goods and to promote technical progress. This was so in view of the fact that the new pump had significant advantages over conventional pumps resulting from the material used (anti-corrosive) for the wet end components and from its construction. In addition, the new pump would be made with a higher capacity, by mass production and with savings or materials (light-weight construction). The Commission also noted in this case that 'under art. 85(3) a *mere* contribution to the promotion of technical or economic progress is required, whereas under art. 2(d) of Regulation ... 418/85, this contribution must be *substantial*'.[119]

In *Ansac*,[120] an agreement between six American producers of natural soda-ash to channel most of their export sales to the Community through

---

[116] *Olivetti/Canon*, OJ 1988 L52/51.
[117] Ibid., at p. 60.
[118] *KSB/Goulds/Lowara/ITT*, OJ 1991 L19/25.
[119] *KSB/Goulds/Lowara/ITT*, OJ 1991 L19/25, p. 33 (emphasis supplied). For further examples, see *Ford/Volkswagen*, OJ 1993 L20/14; *Fiat/Hitachi*, OJ 1993 L20/10; *De Laval-Stork*, OJ 1988 L59/32; *Carbon Gas Technologie*, OJ 1983 L376/17; *Rockwell/Iveco*, OJ 1983 L224/19; *Vacuum Interruptors Ltd*, OJ 1981 L383/1; *Enichem/ICI*, OJ 1991 C74/7; *Optical Fibres*, OJ 1986 L236/30; *Bayer/BP Chemicals*, OJ 1988 L150/35.
[120] *Ansac*, OJ 1991 L152/54.

¶509

Ansac was viewed by the Commission as not contributing to improving production or promoting technical progress in spite of the arguments in favour of the use of natural, rather than synthetic soda-ash. These environmental arguments had no bearing on the marketing of the product, which was the only factor of interest to Ansac. In addition, the Commission stated:

> 'Ansac has also failed to demonstrate that its proposals will lead to an improvement in the distribution of soda-ash or promote economic progress in the common market. *To be exempted under Article 85(3) restrictions should bring about an objective improvement over the situation which would have existed in their absence.*'[121]

Finally, in *Astra*,[122] the Commission, in refusing an exemption under art. 85(3), stated that:

> 'An agreement concluded for the purpose of facilitating or complying with a procedure in which the entry of new competitors is subject to the approval of existing competing marketing participants cannot benefit from an exemption under Article 85(3), the requirements of which relate to objective advantages such as improvements in production, distribution or technical and economic advances.'

(2)   Consumers receiving a fair share of the resultant benefit

This condition is usually fulfilled once it is shown that the joint venture leads to an improvement in production or distribution or to the promotion of technical or economic progress[123] as this would normally lead to new products becoming available,[124] an improvement in the service being provided[125] or to a reduction in costs.[126] In *Ford/Volkswagen*,[127] the Commission held that the European consumer could expect to benefit directly from the joint venture. As a result of the co-operation, mainly due to the sophisticated production technology and the economies of scale, the consumer would be offered two versions of a high-quality and reasonably priced multi-purpose vehicle which would be

---

[121]   Ibid., at p. 59 (emphasis supplied).

[122]   *Astra*, OJ 1993 L20/23, at p. 33.

[123]   This is, of course, assuming that sufficient competition exists. In a speech delivered in Berlin on 25 May 1992, 'Strategic Alliances – An Old Problem and a New Challenge to Commission's Competition Policy', Sir Leon Brittan stated that 'If a competitive structure is maintained, we can be reasonably confident that the forces of competition will ensure a fair outcome for consumers.'

[124]   See *KSB/Goulds/Lowara/ITT*, OJ 1991 L19/25; *Cekacan*, OJ 1990 L299/64; *Vaccum Interruptors Ltd*, OJ 1977 L48/32.

[125]   See *Bayer & Hoechst*, Commission press release IP(90)857; *UIP*, OJ 1989 L226/25; *Rockwell/Iveco*, OJ 1983 L224/19.

[126]   See *Alcatel Espace/ANT Nachrichtentechnik*, OJ 1990 L32/19; *BBC Brown Boveri*, OJ 1988 L301/68; *Olivetti/Canon*, OJ 1988 L52/51; *Optical Fibres*, OJ 1986 L236/30. The joint venture guidelines at para. 54, state that 'in order to fulfil the first two conditions of Article 85(3), the joint venture must bring appreciably objective advantages for third parties, especially consumers, which at least equal the consequent detriment to competition.'

[127]   *Ford/Volkswagen*, OJ 1993 L20/14.

¶509

distributed in the whole Community through the extensive sales networks of the partners. Ford and Volkswagen would be forced to pass on the benefits to the consumer, because, as a result of their entry, along with that of other manufacturers into the expanding MPV segment, there would be an increased competitive pressure on all suppliers leading to a more balanced segment. Moreover, with Ford and Volkswagen, further competitive European car manufacturers would be present in this market segment.

However, in *Ansac*,[128] the only advantages that Ansac's entry into the Community market could offer consumers flowed from the economies of scale achievable by shipping and storing soda-ash in much larger quantities than would have been possible for any of Ansac's members acting individually. The Commission noted, however, that Ansac itself did not intend for these economies of scale to be passed on to the customer in the form of lower prices. Its own forecasts showed that it intended to charge slightly higher prices in the EC than it believed would be achieved by the individual US producers.

(3) Indispensability

(a) *Formation of the joint venture*

The Commission is only likely to grant an exemption if it is satisfied that the benefits expected of the joint venture cannot be realised through less restrictive means such as a licensing arrangement, a specialisation arrangement or a sub-contracting agreement.[129] For example, in *Screensport/EBU Members*,[130] the Commission stated that it was not

> 'convinced that a transnational sports channel such as Eurosport could only come into existence on the basis of such a joint venture between a group of members of the EBU with the backing of the organization itself and the most likely main competitor capable of creating an alternative venture ... [T]he creation of a joint venture on the basis of the present agreement is excessive and the implied restrictions of competition cannot be regarded as indispensable to the establishment of a dedicated sports channel with a transnational dimension capable of rivalling other sports channels to the benefit of consumers'.[131]

---

[128] *Ansac*, OJ 1991 L152/54.
[129] See *Mitchell Cotts/Sofiltra*, OJ 1987 L41/31.
[130] *Screensport/EBU Members*, OJ 1991 L63/32.
[131] Ibid., at p. 44; see also *Astra*, OJ 1991 L20/23 at p. 33; *Cekacan*, OJ 1990 L299/64. In *Bayer/Gist-Brocades*, OJ 1976 L30/13, the Commission did not authorise the parties to enter into a joint venture agreement since the benefits sought could be attained more simply through a reciprocal long-term supply contract, covering the products in which each party was specialising. See also *Olivetti-Canon*, OJ 1988 L52/51, at p. 60: 'The grant of a licence would not have allowed the transfer of technology to the same extent as i[s] allowed by a joint venture. The major involvement of the partners inherent in a manufacturing joint venture permits a permanent and intense flow of technology'.

¶509

The formation of the joint venture is likely to be considered as indispensable where the product is complex and its development necessitates a close, continuous co-operation between the parties which could not be achieved through a looser form of co-operation. In *Ford/Volkswagen*,[132] the Commission held that:

> 'The co-operation enables the partners to competitively offer a high-quality product, designed for the specific needs of European consumers in a relatively new and low-volume MPV market segment in a comparatively short time. The examination of the case leads the Commission to accept the partners' arguments that the beneficial results of the co-operation could not to that extent, be achieved otherwise. The partners, each acting on its own, could not develop and produce the MPV in the same conditions so rapidly and efficiently in Portugal as their co-operation will enable them to do.'

The Commission is also prepared to grant exemptions to joint ventures where the product necessitates very high development costs which could be justified economically only if there are economies of scale. For example, in *KSB/Goulds/Lowara/ITT*,[133] the Commission observed that 'it is understandable that KSB and Lowara preferred co-operation with Goulds and ITT to other arrangements, despite the above-mentioned effects on competition. The arrangement they opted for has the advantage of combining the benefits of technical co-operation in research and development and an assured volume of the wet end components.'[134]

In cases where one of the partners is established outside the EC, the Commission appears particularly inclined to accept the joint venture form as it

---

[132] *Ford/Volkswagen*, OJ 1993 L20/114. In *GEC-Weir Sodium Circulators* (OJ 1977 L327/26), the Commission accepted that the joint venture form was indispensable:

'A more independent and looser form of co-operation than a joint venture could not in this case be expected to lead to so coherent or comprehensive a development. A cross-licensing and disclosure of information agreement, for example, would not result in a sufficiently close sharing between the parties of all their complementary skills and facilities. A specialization agreement would not give to each party sufficient experience of or insight into the work of the other.'

See also *UIP* [1989] 2 CEC 2,019; OJ 1989 L226/25:

'The formation of the joint venture itself is indispensable to continuation of the international distribution of the parent companies' films. Alternatives less restrictive of competition, such as relying on independent distributors throughout the Community for their international distribution, would not provide the benefits expected of UIP.'

[133] *KSB/Goulds/Lowara/ITT*, OJ 1991 L19/25.

[134] Ibid., at point 29. In *GEC-Siemens/Plessey*, OJ 1990 C239/2, the Commission said (at point 31) that

'in the particular circumstances of this case, an arrangement along the lines envisaged is indispensable to the attainment of the benefits outlined above, and a co operation agreement between Plessey and Siemens, even if one could be clearly envisaged, does not seem likely to provide comparable benefits. In particular, companies are unlikely to share their most sensitive technological advances, which would result in real savings of research and development costs, with competing companies with whom no irreversible tie exists.'

¶509

is more conducive to a transfer of technology and ensures that the European partner is kept up-to-date with the latest technological developments.[135]

(b) *Activities of the joint venture*

Apart from the question of whether the formation of the joint venture may be justified as indispensable, there is also the question of whether the restrictions placed on the parties in connection with the activities of the joint venture are indispensable. Generally, it must be shown that such restrictions are ancillary to the formation of the joint venture itself.[136]

Non-competition clause

An obligation imposed upon the parties not to compete in the joint venture's field of activity during its initial phase is generally regarded as indispensable to

---

[135] In *Rockwell/Iveco*, OJ 1983 L224/19, the Commission noted that:

'Rockwell's participation in the joint venture ensures that the latter will be provided for several years with up-to-date information, which is of particular importance in view of rapid technical development. This advantage will result from Rockwell's own interest in the prosperity of the joint venture. It would be less certain if Rockwell were merely to grant Iveco the right to exploit its knowhow.'

For similar reasons, the Commission accepted the joint venture form as indispensable in *Optical Fibres*, OJ 1986 L236/30:

'Other options available to Corning were the marketing in Europe of optical fibres imported from the USA, the establishment by Corning of fully owned plants in the EEC or the grant of simple licences. None of these options would have had the same benefits as the joint ventures. Under the first two options, there would be no transfer of technology to the European companies and therefore no dissemination of Corning's technology. The grant of simple licensing, while increasing competition and encouraging further developments by the licensees, would not facilitate the efficient flow of a technology which is undergoing rapid changes to the same extent as is possible within the framework of a joint venture relationship.'

In *Olivetti-Canon*, OJ 1988 L52/51, the Commission noted that the joint venture agreement enabled a transfer of advanced technology by Canon, a leader of innovation with an R & D-oriented policy, to Olivetti in markets where technology is of crucial importance.

The view of the Commission in *Ford/Volkswagen*, OJ 1993 L20/14, at p. 19, is also worth noting. In the assessment of this case, the Commission also takes note of the fact that the project constitutes the largest ever single foreign investment in Portugal. It is estimated to lead, inter alia, to the creation of about 5,000 jobs and indirectly create up to another 10,000 jobs, as well as attracting other investment in the supply industry. It therefore contributes to the promotion of the harmonious development of the Community and the reduction of regional disparities which is one of the basic aims of the treaty. It also furthers European market integration by linking Portugal more closely to the Community through one of its important industries. This would not be enough to make an exemption possible unless the conditions of art. 85(3) were fulfilled, but it is an element which the Commission has taken into account.

[136] See the joint venture guidelines at para. 65 et seq. In *Cekacan*, OJ 1990 L299/64, the Commission held that clauses governing the provision of supplies to the joint venture by the parent companies (A&R and ECA), which in practice restricted ECA's sales of its cutting and printing services to Germany and at the same time guaranteed ECA a minimum volume of such sales for Cekacan applications, were necessary. Without such restrictions, A&R would not have entered into a co-operation project with ECA but would have embarked alone on the process of introducing its technology in other countries, with all the extra costs and difficulties which that would have entailed. Without those guarantees, ECA would not have agreed to give up the position which it held under its original licence agreement with A&R, which guaranteed its sales in German territory. Furthermore, the option granted to ECA to meet orders from customers outside Germany who refused to go through the joint venture, and exports of packaged finished products would also indirectly guarantee ECA's sales for Cekacan applications outside Germany. In addition, it was considered that the possibility of terminating the co-operation agreement, as a result of which the original licensing agreement would be reactivated and customers shared out between A&R and ECA, was a necessary safeguard allowing the two contracting parties to enter into the envisaged co-operation without too many risks.

¶509

the success of the joint venture as it ensures that the parties will concentrate their development and production efforts on the joint venture.[137]

In *Halifax Building Society and Bank of Scotland*,[138] the Commission considered that the ban on one of the parties (Halifax) promoting within its branches any other credit cards which the other party considered were capable of competing with the credit card the subject of the agreement, restricted competition between the parties because it applied beyond the start-up period 'when such a restriction might be considered reasonably necessary for the establishment of the new card'. The Commission accordingly requested Halifax to reduce the period during which this restraint would apply. Halifax agreed to reduce this period to five years from the date of the agreement. Subsequently, the Commission informed the parties that the agreement was not caught by art. 85(1).

In *Mitchell Cotts-Sofiltra*[139] the Commission decided that the obligation on the joint venture not to manufacture or deal in competing products did not fall under art. 85(1) because it was deemed necessary in view of the need for the joint venture to concentrate on the success of the new production unit. It is not clear why this type of non-competition clause is considered not to fall under art. 85(1) while other kinds of non-competition clauses, e.g. territorial restrictions for parent companies competing with the joint venture,[140] have consistently been held to be contrary to art. 85(1) and thus to necessitate an analysis under art. 85(3).[141] The Commission has even decided that if no express prohibition is imposed on the parent companies to compete with the joint venture, such a prohibition shall nevertheless be assumed because the parties cannot reasonably be expected to compete with a joint venture in which they hold substantial stakes even if they are contractually free to do so.[142] Such an implied non-competition clause is held to be restrictive of competition and can therefore only be exempted under art. 85(3).[143] However, the joint venture

---

[137] *IVECO-FORD*, OJ 1988 L230/39; *Carbon Gas Technologie*, OJ 1983 L376/17; *VW-MAN*, OJ 1983 L376/11. The joint venture guidelines, at para. 70 et seq., state that when the setting-up of the joint venture involves the creation of new production capacity or the transfer of technology from the parent, the obligation imposed on the joint venture not to manufacture or market products competing with the licensed products may usually be regarded as ancillary. The joint venture must seek to ensure the success of the new production unit, without depriving the parent companies of the necessary control over exploitation and dissemination of their technology.

[138] *XXIst Report on Competition Policy for 1991*, at p. 335.

[139] *Mitchell Cotts-Sofiltra*, OJ 1987 L41/31, at p. 35.

[140] Ibid.; see also *IVECO-FORD*, OJ 1988 L230/39, at pp. 43 and 44.

[141] In *Eirpage*, *XXIst Report on Competition Policy*, point 80, a clause prohibiting either party from engaging in a competing wide-area interconnected paging service independently or in association with others, brought the agreement within the prohibition of art. 85(1). See also *Amadeus/Sabre*, *XXIst Report on Competition Policy for 1991*, point 93; *Vacuum Interrupters*, OJ 1980 L383/1, at p. 8.

[142] *GEC-Weir Sodium Circulators*, OJ 1977 L327/26, at p. 31.

[143] Ibid. In the joint venture guidelines, the Commission states that:

'Restrictions which prohibit the parent companies from competing with the joint venture or from actively competing with it in its area of activity may be regarded as ancillary at least during the JV's starting-up period.

¶509

partners must usually remain free to supply customers which the joint venture is unable to supply.[144] Once the initial phase is over, licences granted to the joint venture should no longer be exclusive.[145] Finally, upon the expiry of the joint venture agreement, the parties should be free to compete with one another.[146]

In *Elopak/Metal Box-Odin*,[147] the Commission appears to have taken a more flexible approach to the treatment of non-competition clauses under art. 85(1). It considered that the following clauses did not restrict competition:

(1) an exclusive licence granted to the joint venture, even beyond the starting-up period for new technology, to exploit the proprietary know-how of the parent companies;

(2) the obligation by each parent not to allow a competitor of the other

---

Additional restrictions relating to quantities, prices or customers, and export bans obviously go beyond what is required for the setting-up and operation of the JV.

The Commission has in one case regarded as ancillary, a territorial restriction imposed on a parent company where the JV was granted an exclusive manufacturing licence in respect of fields of technical application and product markets in which both the joint venture and the parent were to be active (*Mitchell Cotts/Sofiltra ...*). This decision was, however, limited to the starting-up period of the JV and appeared necessary for the parents to become established in a new geographical market with the help of the JV. In another case, the grant to the JV of an exclusive exploitation licence without time limit was regarded as indispensable for its creation and operation. In this case the parent company granting the licence was not active in the same field of application or on the same product market as that for which the licence was granted (*Elopak/Metal Box – Odin ...*). This will generally be the case with JVs undertaking new activities in respect of which the parent companies are neither actual nor potential competitors.'

[144] *GEC-Weir Sodium Circulators*, OJ 1977 L327/26; *De Laval-Stork*, OJ 1977 L215/11.

[145] *Rockwell-IVECO*, OJ 1983 L224/19; *De Laval-Stork*, OJ 1977 L215/11.

[146] In *IVECO-FORD*, OJ 1988 L230/39, the Commission exempted a five-year non-competition clause with regard to the distribution of heavy vehicles which would apply until five years after one of the parent companies had withdrawn from the joint venture. In *Roquette-National Starch, Fourteenth Report on Competition Policy*, points 87–89, the Commission accepted the following restrictions imposed upon the parties in connection with the dissolution of their joint ventures:

'(i) Roquette undertook not to make or sell starch for human consumption in the UK for 6 months (9 months in Scandinavia) and National undertook not to make or sell these products for the same period on the former joint venture's exclusive territory.

(ii) Roquette granted National (and the subsidiaries it was to establish in France and Italy) exclusive distribution rights for starch for human consumption in the former exclusive territories for a period of 2 years, thus allowing National to establish contacts with customers and commercial know-how on the continent.

(iii) Roquette undertook to supply National with starch for non-human consumption for a period of 18 months at an advantageous price.

(iv) Roquette undertook not to use for 10 years the name National (except for a 6-month period in order to dispose of stocks) and National granted Roquette a non-exclusive licence for between 4 and 10 years for the trade marks previously used by the joint ventures.

(v) National and Roquette granted each other non-exclusive licences for the patents and know-how used by the joint ventures.'

According to the Commission, these restrictions did not, either in geographical extent or duration, go beyond what was necessary both for the orderly dissolution of the joint ventures and to allow the parties a reasonable possibility to establish themselves as independent producers and sellers of starch on all markets, and to become active competitors with each other in all markets. See *Optical Fibres*, OJ 1986 L236/30; *VW-MAN*, OJ 1983 L376/11. In *Carbon Gas Technologie*, OJ 1983 L376/17, the Commission accepted a five-year non-competition clause regarding the exploitation of know-how operable in the event of one of the parties withdrawing from the joint venture.

[147] *Elopak/Metal Box-Odin*, OJ 1990 L209/15.

¶509

parent to use that other parent's know-how or improvements made by the joint venture for five years following the break-up of the joint venture;

(3) a provision giving the seller of shares of the joint venture a right of first refusal in case of a further sale.

The Commission justified the liberal approach taken in this decision by giving the following reasons:

(1) the proprietary know-how of the parent companies was necessary not only in the development of the new product and the machinery and technology linked to it, but also in the marketing of the product;

(2) the agreement contained no explicit price, quantity, customers or territorial restrictions placed on the joint venture's activities even though the Commission admitted that the joint venture could compete with one of the parent companies;

(3) the exclusivity was limited to the field of the agreement which was very narrowly defined.[148]

Exclusive supply or purchasing
In several cases, the Commission has held that exclusive supply or purchasing obligations were indispensable to the proper functioning of a given joint venture. These obligations ensure that the joint venture has an outlet for its products from the outset, which may be particularly important in cases where the product is new or the market is underdeveloped.[149] In *Rockwell/IVECO*,[150] the Iveco subsidiaries were obliged, for instance, to satisfy their total axle requirement from the joint venture during the first seven years of the latter's production. The Commission found that the above-mentioned obligation, having regard to the difficulties that are likely to be encountered in finding customers, had a direct bearing on the economic success of the joint venture during the initial phase. At the end of the period, however, the Iveco subsidiaries had to be contractually free to satisfy their axle requirements from

---

[148] See also *Konsortium ECR 900*, OJ 1990 L228/31, where the Commission said:

'As a result of the joint distribution requirement in the CEPT countries, the parties to the agreement are prevented during the term of the agreement from competing with one another in the sale of the products in such countries, which include all the Member States. However, this requirement does not amount to a restriction of competition. For the reasons specified above, the parties to the agreement acting on their own would not be in a position to provide a viable source of supply for individual distribution of the GSM system.'

[149] See, e.g. *Vacuum Interrupters II*, OJ 1980 L383/1, where the Commission found that an obligation imposed upon the partners to purchase all of their vacuum interrupters' requirements from the joint venture was reasonable since they remained free to purchase from other sources where one of their customers specified that a vacuum interrupter made by another manufacturer must be used. The joint venture guidelines, at para. 74, state that obligations imposed on the joint venture to purchase from or supply its parents may be regarded as ancillary, at least during the joint venture's starting-up period.

[150] *Rockwell-IVECO*, OJ 1983 L224/19.

¶509

whatever sources they considered to be the most advantageous. In *Olivetti-Canon*,[151] the Commission held that an obligation on the parent companies to purchase a minimum volume of products from the joint venture was indispensable to the correct functioning of the joint venture because:

'The investments in development and production capacities in the framework of a joint venture and the transfer of technology to it would not be conceivable if the partners themselves could, by purchasing substantially elsewhere, hamper the necessary return on capital.'[152]

For similar reasons, the Commission exempted in *Cekacan*[153] the obligation for the joint venture to be supplied exclusively by the parent companies and for it to purchase a minimum volume of the product concerned from one of the parent companies. Similarly in *Fiat/Hitachi*,[154] the Commission was of the view that although the exclusive purchasing provisions, obliging the joint venture to buy all its parts from the Fiat group and all hydraulics which it did not manufacture itself from Hitachi, foreclosed sales opportunities for third party manufacturers of motors and hydraulics, this restriction resulted from the setting up of the joint venture and appeared to be reasonably necessary to its operation.

Joint distribution

Arrangements which provide for joint marketing and distribution through the joint venture or which impose restrictions on the distribution activities of the parties are likely to receive particularly close scrutiny. The Commission has accepted joint distribution arrangements as indispensable where it was anticipated that the market would be difficult to penetrate or where the product was technically sophisticated so that close technical co-operation with customers was necessary.[155]

The joint venture guidelines state that the Commission will in principle assess sales joint ventures negatively as they usually have the object and effect of co-ordinating the sales policy of competing manufacturers. The

---

[151] *Olivetti/Canon*, OJ 1988 L52/51.
[152] *Olivetti-Canon*, OJ 1988 L52/51, at p. 60.
[153] *Cekacan*, OJ 1990 L299/64.
[154] *Fiat/Hitachi*, OJ 1993 L20/10.
[155] In *Rockwell-Iveco*, OJ 1983 L224/19 at p. 26, a joint distribution arrangement was regarded as indispensable on the following grounds:

'These particular difficulties in obtaining customers and the necessary expenditure in time and effort and technical considerations militate in favour of the need for joint marketing through the JVC. Rear-drive axles for commercial vehicles are not finished products in the sense that they can be installed without any difficulty. A customer will place an order only after extensive testing and will, if necessary, expect plans to be drawn up for the incorporation of special design features by the supplier. This calls for close technical co-operation with the customer which can be better achieved by the producer itself, which is the JVC.'

See also *Bayer-BP Chemicals*, OJ 1988 L150/35, at p. 39:

'Agreements between competitor producers for joint selling by their very nature restrict competition; *Rank-Sopelem*, OJ 1975 L29/20.'

¶509

Commmission however takes a positive view of those cases where joint distribution of the contract products is part of a global co-operation project which merits favourable treatment under art. 85(3) and for the success of which it is indispensable.[156] In all other cases, an exemption can be envisaged only in certain specific circumstances.[157]

In *VW-Man*, a joint distributor arrangement whereby the jointly-produced product would be distributed through the established distribution network of one of the parties was regarded as indispensable on the grounds that it would be uneconomical or technically impossible to set up a separate distribution and servicing network.[158] In *Olivetti-Canon*, the parent companies were obliged to sell the joint venture's production only through their own distribution network and under their own brand name, unless the other partner agreed to the contrary.[159] The Commission held that this obligation constituted a tangible restriction of competition because it could, in effect, preclude all OEM sales or sales under other brand names of the joint venture's production, thereby impeding inter-brand competition. The Commission nevertheless exempted this restrictive covenant because it was deemed to be 'economically connected with the joint venture and therefore indispensable for its correct functioning'. This conclusion was based on the consideration that it was the purpose of the joint venture to manufacture captive products for the partners and that it would be contrary to this purpose to allow a third party to use the same products in manufacturing goods competing with the partners' products.

In the case of a network of joint ventures established by one firm with different partners in several member states, the distribution arrangements are viewed as likely to lead to a partitioning of national markets. Thus, in *Optical Fibres*, the Commission required that each joint venture would remain free to sell in the territories of the other joint ventures.[160]

In *UIP*[161] the parent companies granted to UIP an exclusive licence under copyright or otherwise to distribute all feature-length pictures, short subjects and trailer films produced and/or distributed by each parent company or any of its parents, subsidiaries, affiliates and related companies. The exclusivity consisted in effect of a right of first refusal for UIP, i.e. the parent companies could only distribute films outside the UIP vehicle if the product was first offered for distribution to UIP. The Commission found that, in the case at hand,

---

[156] Examples include sales joint ventures between manufacturers who have concluded a reciprocal specialisation agreement, but wish to continue to offer the whole range of products concerned, or sales joint ventures set up for the joint exploitation of the results of joint R&D, even at the distribution stage; see the joint venture guidelines, para. 60.

[157] Ibid.; Papeteries de Golbey, OJ 1993 C254/3.

[158] *VW-MAN*, OJ 1983 L376/11.

[159] *Olivetti-Canon*, OJ 1988 L52/51.

[160] *Optical Fibres*, OJ 1986 L236/30.

[161] *UIP* [1989] 2 CEC 2,019; OJ 1989 L226/25, at p. 32.

¶509

the negative effects which are ordinarily associated with exclusive distribution arrangements of this kind were substantially limited for two reasons:

'In the first place, each parent company retains the right to impose on UIP the distribution of a particular film should the joint venture freely elect not to distribute the film in the entire Community, or may distribute the film on its own or through a third party. Secondly, the parent companies and UIP itself will make themselves available, based upon their commercial judgment, to distribute third parties' films in the Community.'

In *BBC Brown Boveri*[162] the partners to a joint venture for the research and development in the field of high-performance batteries were allowed to agree on exclusive territorial licences for the production and distribution of the ensuing products: one partner could use the technology for the production and sale of the products in Japan and other countries in the Far East, while the other partner was granted an exclusive licence for the manufacture and sale of the products in the Community, North America and a number of other countries. The Commission decided that these exclusive territorial licences were indispensable because of the resistance which was likely to be encountered among customers and industrial users to a fundamentally new product and because the partners could not run the unusually high risk of failure at the marketing stage by being exposed to competition from each other as well as from third parties, especially after having spent exceptionally large amounts on research and development.

In *Alcatel Espace/ANT Nachrichtentechnik*,[163] the Commission exempted a joint venture involving a certain degree of joint marketing. The agreements provided that the exploitation of the results achieved by the joint venture could be carried out through jointly, individually or independently marketed projects. The Commission gave the following reasoning:

'The nature of demand in this case implies that the option of joint R&D, joint manufacturing, but separate marketing is not practical. This results from the close co-operation that is necessary between the customer, prime satellite contractor and subcontractors (such as the parties). Customers and their prime contractors insist on knowing, in great detail, who has manufactured which item, and all the relevant technical detail as there is normally no way of repairing a satellite once in orbit. Competition normally takes place by customers' calling for tenders which are then submitted by consortia formed on a case-by-case basis. If separate marketing were attempted, then in any project for which both parties wished to bid, each party would have, at the

---

[162] *BBC Brown Boveri*, OJ 1988 L301/68, at p. 72.
[163] *Alcatel Espace/ANT Nachrichtentechnik*, OJ 1990 L32/19.

¶509

same time, to promote its own package, and to assist the other in promoting that party's rival package to the final customer, either within one consortium or as part of rival consortia. Thus, the same technical experts would have, twice over, to describe and promote an identical technical package to the same customer. In this context the customer may have doubts as to whether two parties, having failed to co-operate commercially on a joint bid, could in fact successfully co-operate technically. This might lead them to buy elsewhere. This implies that, in this particular case, the benefits of joint R&D and joint manufacture can only be achieved if they are combined with a degree of joint marketing.'

In *Konsortium ECR 900*,[164] the Commission ruled that the joint distribution by the joint venture of a pan-European digital cellular mobile telephone system, did not infringe art. 85(1) because the parties to the agreement would not have been in a position to distribute individually.

(4)   No elimination of competition

If the combined market share of the parties is small and other large competitors co-operate on the market, it is generally assumed that the joint venture will not eliminate competition in a substantial part of the market. The joint venture guidelines state that;

'to assess whether a full function joint venture raises problems of compatibility with the competition rules or not, an important point of reference is the aggregate market share of 10% contained in the group exemption Regulations. Below this threshold it can be assumed that the effect of exclusion from the market of third parties and the danger of creating or reinforcing barriers to market entry will be kept within justifiable limits. A prerequisite is, however, that the market structure will continue to guarantee effective competition. If the said threshold is exceeded, an exemption will be considered only after a careful examination of each individual case.'

The joint venture guidelines go on to state that market share limits cannot be fixed for production joint ventures. The market share of 20 per cent in the group exemption regulations can, however, serve as a starting point for the assessment of production joint ventures in individual cases.[165] In cases where a

---

[164] *Konsortium ECR 900*, OJ 1990 L228/31.

[165] The joint venture guidelines, para. 64; see also *Elopak/Metal Box-Odin*, OJ 1990 L209/15; *VW-MAN*, OJ 1983 L376/11; *Amersham-Buchler*, OJ 1982 L314/34.

However, in *Fiat/Hitachi* OJ 1993 L20/10, the Commission exempted a joint venture that was expected to have 16 per cent of the Community market for excavators. As the parties had undertaken that, in so far as the Community was concerned, the agreements setting up the joint venture would allow passive sales into the other party's exclusive territory, the Commission felt that the creation of the joint venture would bring about a more balanced market structure and the joint venture would operate throughout the Community. As a consequence, the purchasers of tractors should also benefit from the distribution of the products.

¶509

joint venture is formed in an oligopolistic market, problems are likely to arise.[166] However, if the parent companies are not among the largest firms in the industry, an exemption may nevertheless be granted.[167] The Commission has been prepared to exempt an agreement whereby a joint venture was set up by a market leader and another important supplier on the basis that competition in respect of a substantial part of the products was not eliminated.[168]

In *Auditel*,[169] an agreement to use only Auditel's figures for measuring audience ratings was found to provide an opportunity for eliminating competition. Even though there were other valid systems for measuring audience ratings, such potential competition was effectively prohibited, thereby placing Auditel in a *de facto* monopoly position.

In *Amadeus/Sabre*,[170] the Commission was concerned that a joint venture agreement to co-ordinate two independent computer reservation systems as a joint product could afford the parties to the agreement the possibility to eliminate competition in a substantial part of the common market. To avoid this, the parties were required to give detailed undertakings. In *Alcatel Espace/ANT Nachrichtentechnik*,[171] the Commission considered that although one of the parent companies was the world's second largest manufacturer and the other a leading company in Germany, the joint venture did not eliminate competition because there still remained a large number of competitors on the EC market and the combined EC market share of the parties was under 20 per cent. Similarly, in *Du Pont de Nemours/Merck*,[172] the Commission held that the agreement between the parties merited an exemption under art. 85(3) mainly because the creation of the joint venture would add a new and substantial competitor to the world market.

In *Ford/Volkswagen*,[173] the Commission felt that the co-operation between Ford and Volkswagen would not lead to an elimination of competition in the MPV segment. Having regard to the leading position of the Renault 'Espace', it would, on the contrary, stimulate competition through the creation of an

---

[166] See *WANO-Schwarzpulver*, OJ 1978 L322/29, where the Commission held that the joint venture would lead to an unacceptable restriction of competition because it would control 58 per cent of the sales of black powder in the EC and would reinforce ICI's monopoly position in the UK. See also *Sixth Report on Competition Policy*, point 179.

[167] See *De Laval-Stork*, OJ 1977 L215/11, where the joint venture agreement was not considered as giving the parties the possibility of eliminating competition because '[t]hey have a Community market share of between 10 and 15 per cent, and have to compete with some very large groups which sell their goods throughout the world and have capacities and sales often far greater than that of De Laval-Stork'.

[168] *Apollinaris/Schweppes*, *XXIst Report on Competition Policy*, point 87; *Olivetti-Canon*, OJ 1988 L52/51. Another sample of the Commission's liberal attitude with respect to the application of this criterion can be found in *IVECO-FORD*, OJ 1988 L230/39, in which a joint venture was set up between the second largest and the fifth largest manufacturer of heavy vehicles in the Community.

[169] *Auditel*, OJ 1993, L306/50.

[170] *XXIst Report on Competition Policy for 1991*, point 93.

[171] *Alcatel Espace/ANT Nachrichtentechnik*, OJ 1990 L32/19.

[172] *XXIst Report on Competition Policy for 1991*, point 85.

[173] *Ford/Volkswagen*, OJ 1993 L20/14.

¶509

additional choice in this area and lead to a more balanced structure in the MPV market segment. There would also be increased competition concerning price and quality over the coming years with the penetration of the segment by Japanese producers as well as other new entrants. In addition, the Commission looked at competition at the distribution level and decided that the product differentiation and profit margins in the MPV segment would leave sufficient scope for a certain degree of competition between the parties.

The Commission decided in *UIP*[174] that a 22 per cent Community-wide market share held by the joint venture did not eliminate competition in respect of a substantial part of the products because of the local character of the competitive structure of the film industry in the various member states which was due to language barriers, government regulations and different patterns of distribution and exhibition, thereby rendering an economic analysis of the impact of this joint venture based on Community-wide market shares less meaningful.

In many cases, the joint venture will be involved in the development of a new product and, at the outset, there will be no competition on the market. However, an exemption may be granted if any of the following factors can be shown: that other firms are developing new products;[175] strong buyers operate on the market;[176] substitute products are available;[177] or that there is a threat of competition from non-EC firms.[178] Even in the absence of such factors, the Commission has shown willingness to exempt the agreement in exceptional

---

[174] *UIP* [1989] 2 CEC 2,019; OJ 1989 L226/25, at p. 32.

[175] See *BBC Brown Boveri* [1989] 1 CEC 2,066; OJ 1988 L301/68; *Carbon Gas Technologie*, OJ 1983 L376/17; *Vacuum Interrupters II*, OJ 1980 L382/1; *GEC-Weir Sodium Circulators*, OJ 1977 L327/26.

[176] See *GEC-Siemens/Plessey*, OJ 1990 C239/2, at p. 6, where the Commission noted that '[t]he national markets for these products are largely monopsonistic, with purchasing limited to a few entities, typically government agencies. Instead of choosing among a range of existing products, these purchasers tend to specify to potential suppliers the characteristics of the products they wish to purchase. Thus, there is little concern that any reduction in the number of potential competitors may reduce the variety of products available. Moreover, these purchasers are sufficiently powerful to insist on favourable economic terms, eliminating the concern that their arrangements will result in increased prices.' See also *Konsortium ECR 900*, OJ 1990 L228/31, where the only potential customers of a pan-European digital cellular mobile telephone system were fifteen national network operators with the result that the suppliers' prospects of achieving a bid award were limited, and *Optical Fibres*, OJ 1986 L236/30, where the Commission noted that '[t]he main end-users, the PTTs, have exceptionally strong purchasing power; they are able to insist on supplies of both optical fibres and optical cables at world competitive prices and to obtain supplies from non-national producers, including joint ventures which are not established on their own territory, if they so wish.'

[177] See *GEC-Siemens/Plessey*, OJ 1990 C239/2; *BBC Brown Boveri* [1989] 1 CEC 2,234; OJ 1988 L301/68; *Optical Fibres*, OJ 1986 L236/30; *Vacuum Interrupters II*, OJ 1980 L383/1.

[178] See *Philips/Thomson/Sagem* Commission press release IP (93) 322 of 30 April 1993; *Optical Fibres*, OJ 1986 L236/30, at p. 40, where it was noted that:

'The optical fibre market in the EEC is not immune from the pressure of competition of the world market These pressures derive principally from the strong position of US and Japanese producers, in particular AT & T and SUMITOMO. AT & T has a worldwide licence under Corning's basic patents. It could at any time export optical fibres to the EEC or manufacture optical fibres in the EEC.'

See also *GEC-Weir Sodium Circulators*, OJ 1977 L327/26; *Vacuum Interrupters II*, OJ 1980 L383/1; *GEC-Siemens/Plessey*, OJ 1990 C239/2.

¶509

cases if it will lead to the eventual creation of effective competition between the partners once the agreement expires.[179]

¶510   Duration of the art. 85(3) exemption

If an exemption is granted to a joint venture agreement, its duration will be limited in time and certain conditions will be attached. Thus far, the duration of the exemption has ranged from five[180] to 15 years.[181] The exemption is, however, renewable. In renewing the first exemption accorded to the De Laval-Stork[182] joint-venture agreement, the Commission granted a particularly long exemption term of 20 years which, according to the Commission, was warranted by the experience obtained during the ten years in which the original exemption was applicable.

In *Continental-Michelin*[183] the periods of validity of the exemption were differentiated on the basis of the activities involved: ten years for the co-operation in research and development, a subsequent two years for commercial development of the products and an overall period of 20 years for the activity of the joint venture as such.

In cases where the joint venture agreement has been exempted for periods exceeding ten years, the Commission has placed emphasis on the high level of investment involved, the length of the time necessary to achieve an adequate return on capital and the difficulties of introducing a new product on the market.[184] In *BBC Brown Boveri*,[185] for example, an exemption term of ten (vis-à-vis the Japanese partners) and 15 (vis-à-vis other licensees) years has been granted by the Commission to the German partner with respect to its exclusive territorial protection (covering the whole of the EC) to manufacture and sell products ensuing from joint research and development activities. This long term was considered indispensable because of the radically innovative nature of the products involved. By contrast, in *KSB/Goulds/Lowara/ITT*,[186] the Commission considered that since the first series of the new product had already been put on the market, it would only grant a five-year extension as of the first date of marketing by analogy to the block exemption regulation on research and development co-operation agreements.

---

[179] See *United Reprocessors*, OJ 1975 L51/7.

[180] *KSB/Goulds/Lowara/ITT*, OJ 1991 L19/25; *Enichem/ICI*; *XXIst Report on Competition Policy*, at p. 336; *Langenscheidt-Hachette*, OJ 1982 L39/25.

[181] *VW-MAN*, OJ 1983 L376/11; *Optical Fibres*, OJ 1986 L236/30; *Amersham Buchler*, OJ 1982 L314/34; *United Reprocessors*, OJ 1975 L51/7.

[182] *De Laval-Stork II*, OJ 1988 L59/32.

[183] *Continental-Michelin* [1989] 1 CEC 2,241; OJ 1988 L305/33.

[184] See, e.g. *VW-MAN*, OJ 1983 L376/11 at p. 15, where the Commission noted that 'new truck models take an extremely long time to develop and also tend to remain in production and on sale for a long time (long intervals between model changes)'.

[185] *BBC Brown Boveri* [1989] 1 CEC 2,234; OJ 1988 L301/68.

[186] *KSB/Goulds/Lowara/ITT*, OJ 1991 L19/25.

¶511   Conditions attached to the exemption

Exempted joint ventures may be made subject to specific reporting requirements covering such matters as:

- changes in ownership and capital structure;
- interlocking directorates between the joint venture partners;
- new joint ventures;
- new licence agreements;
- amendments to the joint venture agreement or activities;
- financial statements;
- staff allocation in the event of dissolution.

In *IVECO-FORD*[187] the Commission stated that no reporting requirements were imposed on the parties because the exemption period of five years was considered too short.

On the whole, Commission practice has been fairly liberal, especially with respect to actual requirements, as opposed to mere obligations to inform.[188] However, in *Ford/Volkswagen,*[189] the Commission imposed extensive conditions on the parties such as the obligations to take appropriate safeguards to ensure that competitively sensitive information did not reach employees of the other party, to obtain Commission approval for proposals by either party not to market its MPV in any member state and not to expand the range of products to be produced by the joint venture without Commission approval. In addition, Ford was obliged not to use Volkswagen engines in more than 25 per cent of Ford's MPV's over any three-year period.

JOINT RESEARCH AND DEVELOPMENT[190]

¶512   Introduction

In modern economies, industrial competitiveness is increasingly determined by the ability to create new or improved products or services. Co-operation in the

---

[187] *IVECO-FORD*, OJ 1988 L230/39. In *Sopelem-Vickers*, OJ 1978 L70/47, however, a reporting requirement was imposed in spite of a short exemption period of five years.

[188] See, e.g. *BBC Brown Boveri* [1989] 1 CEC 2,234; OJ 1988 L301/68 (no conditions imposed) and *Mitchell Cotts-Sofiltra*, OJ 1987 L41/31 (no conditions imposed).

[189] *Ford/Volkswagen*, OJ 1993 L20/14. Similarly, in *Astra*, OJ 1993 L20/23, the Commission refused an exemption and in addition obliged the parties to inform program providers that they could, within four months of being informed, renegotiate the terms of their contracts or terminate their contracts, taking into account a reasonable period of notice, ibid., at p. 38.

[190] See generally Whish, 'The Commission's Block Exemption on Research and Development Agreements', (1985) ECLR 84; White, 'Research and Development Joint Ventures under EEC Competition Law', (1985) 16 I.I.C. 663; Venit, 'The Research and Development Block Exemption Regulation', (1985) 11 E.L.Rev. 151.

field of research and development is often essential to innovation, particularly in high technology sectors where the technical and financial risks are high. Not only does such co-operation enable firms to share these risks, but it also allows firms with complementary technologies to avoid costly duplication of efforts and promotes economies of scale.

In its 1968 notice on co-operation agreements, the Commission stated that art. 85(1) does not generally apply to agreements on the joint execution of research work or the joint development of the results of research up to the stage of industrial application nor to the exchange of opinion or experience.[191] The Commission, however, stated that art. 85(1) may be applicable where the parties enter into commitments which restrict their own research and development activity or the utilisation of the results of joint work, where certain participants are excluded from the exploitation of the results or where the granting of licences to third parties is expressly or tacitly excluded.[192]

Despite the positive language on 'pure' joint research and development agreements in the notice, subsequent decisions have shown that an agreement relating to the joint carrying out of research and development projects may in itself fall under art. 85(1) where the parties are large undertakings and where competition in the field of research is particularly important.[193] In fact, the Commission made it clear in its *First Report on Competition Policy* that the 1968 notice should be read with 'certain reservations' when large firms are involved in a joint research and development agreement.[194] Since the Commission, however, takes a favourable view of co-operation on research and development, joint research and development agreements falling under art. 85(1) would normally qualify for an exemption under art. 85(3) provided that certain conditions are met.

On 19 December 1984, the Commission adopted Regulation 418/85 granting a block exemption to research and development agreements effective from 1 March 1985 until 31 December 1997.[195] This regulation is aimed at stimulating

---

[191] Notice on agreements, decisions and concerted practices in the field of co-operation, JO 1968 C75/3, corrigendum JO 1968 C84/4 (hereinafter cited as '1968 notice'). In *Eurogypsum* (JO 1968 L57/9) a decision issued a short time before the notice on co-operation agreements, the Commission granted a negative clearance to a joint research and development arrangement by an association under which the parties remained free to engage in research independently, had equal access to the results and there were no discriminating conditions concerning admission to the association. Agreements which have as their sole object joint research and development are exempted from the notification requirement under art. 4(2), (3)(b) of Regulation 17/62.

[192] Notice on agreements, decisions and concerted practices in the field of co-operation, JO 1968 C75/3, corrigendum JO 1968 C84/14, at para. 28–31.

[193] *Henkel-Colgate*, JO 1972 L14/14; *Beecham-Parke Davis*, OJ 1979 L70/11.

[194] *First Report on Competition Policy*, point 32.

[195] Commission Regulation 418/85 on the application of art. 85(3) of the treaty to categories of research and development agreements, OJ 1985 L53/5. The regulation contains provisions dealing with 'old' agreements or agreements dispensed from notification; see art. 11.

¶512

technological innovation in Europe, particularly by creating an environment favourable to transnational co-operation among firms which will enable them to compete more effectively on world markets.[196] Although the Commission has generally shown a favourable attitude towards co-operation in research and development, a block exemption regulation was deemed necessary to create a climate of greater legal certainty for European industry.[197] In this respect, the most noteworthy feature of the regulation is that it covers agreements which extend beyond research and development to include joint exploitation of results, i.e. joint manufacturing and licensing. Initially, the regulation did not cover research and development joint ventures extending to joint distribution or selling which meant that an individual exemption was required if the parents were competitors.[198] This severely restricted the usefulness of the regulation. This situation was remedied however, when the Commission, on 23 December 1992, extended the scope of the regulation to co-operation at the marketing stage.[199]

In line with the other block exemptions, the regulation contains a list of clauses that may validly be inserted in an agreement coming within the scope of the exemption (the 'white list' of art. 5) and of prohibited clauses which cause the exemption not to apply (the 'black list' of art. 6). Like many of the block exemptions, the regulation provides for an opposition procedure[200] whereby agreements containing restrictions not expressly exempted or prohibited by the regulation can be notified to the Commission and are deemed to be exempt unless the Commission opposes exemption within six months.

¶513   Regulation 418/85

Sections ¶514–¶516 analyse successively:

(1) the prerequisites for the grant of the exemption (¶514);

(2) the specific restrictions authorised or prohibited by the regulation (¶515);

(3) procedural mechanisms instituted by the regulation (i.e. the opposition procedure and the withdrawal of the exemption) (¶516).

---

[196] Commission press release of 20 December 1984, IP(84) 471, hereinafter cited as 'press release'). See also *Fourteenth Report on Competition Policy*, point 28.

[197] Press release IP(84) 471.

[198] See, e.g. *Elopak/Metal Box-Odin*, OJ 1990 L209/15; See *Seventeenth Report on Competition Policy*, point 31.

[199] OJ 1993 L21/8. *XXIst Report on Competition Policy for 1991*, point 132.

[200] In 1990, the Commission received four notifications asking for the opposition procedure to be applied, see *XXth Report on Competition Policy*, point 44.

¶514 Prerequisites for the grant of the exemption

Regulation 418/85 basically exempts two types of agreements:[201]

(1) agreements for joint[202] research and development,[203] whether coupled or not with agreements for joint exploitation of the results;[204]

(2) agreements for joint[205] exploitation[206] of the results of the research and development jointly carried out pursuant to a prior agreement between the same undertakings.

In order to benefit from the exemption, agreements must, in addition, fulfil the following conditions:

(1) they must meet the six threshold conditions set out in art. 2 of the regulation;

(2) the parties to the agreement must meet the market share limitations set out in art. 3 of the regulation.

Threshold conditions for exemption

Article 2 of the regulation sets out five threshold conditions which must be met in order for the exemption to apply.

The first three conditions apply to all agreements coming within the scope of the regulation.

(1) The research and development programme must define the objective of

---

[201] Regulation 418/85, art. 1(1).

[202] It is important to note that research and development as well as exploitation of results are deemed to be 'joint' not only when the parties actually carry out the work together, but also when they entrust the work to a third party, perform the work under a specialisation arrangement or collaborate in licensing industrial property rights or know-how to entitle other parties to carry out the work: Regulation 418/85, art. 1(3).

[203] Research and development is defined in art. 1(2)(a) as 'the acquisition of technical knowledge and the carrying out of theoretical analysis, systematic study or experimentation, including experimental production, technical testing of products or processes, the establishment of the necessary facilities and the obtaining of intellectual property rights for the results'. In *KSB/Goulds/Lowara/ITT*, OJ 1991 L19/25, the Commission had to decide whether there had been any real research and development in respect of chrome nickel steel components and whether, in any event, the parties acceding to the co-operation that had already been initiated by the original parties, KSB and Lowara, had taken part in it. The Commission decided that the notion of research and development of products or processes 'is defined so widely in Article 1(2)(a) that the activities of the parties fall within it.'

[204] Provisions of the regulation that only apply to agreements extending to joint exploitation include those dealing with exclusive purchasing and supply, quantities, prices, and field of use and customer restrictions.

[205] Regulation 418/85, art. 1(3). See also the joint venture guidelines, para. 47. In *KSB/Goulds/Lowara/ITT*, OJ 1991 L19/25, the Commission decided that joint exploitation of the results was carried out in accordance with art. 1(3)(a) of Regulation 418/85 where one of the four parties manufactured the products exclusively for the parties to the agreement even though the machine tools were the property of the participants for which the individual units were manufactured.

[206] Exploitation of the results is defined in art. 1(2)(d) as '... the manufacture of the contract processes or the assignment or licensing of intellectual property rights or the communication of know-how required for such manufacture or application'. In *Elopak/Metal Box-Odin*, OJ 1990 L209/15, the clauses in the notified agreement setting up a joint venture (Odin) whereby it would undertake distribution of the new products were, in the view of the Commission, not covered by the term 'exploitation of the results' as defined in art. 1(2)(d) of Regulation 418/85. But see the joint venture guidelines, para. 47.

the work and the field in which it is to be carried out.[207] It should be noted that the defined scope of the programme is important in so far as any restrictions imposed on the activities of the parties are exempted only within the field covered by the agreement. In addition, the purpose of the agreement would also seem to be as relevant a factor as that of defining the scope of the programme. In *Quantel*,[208] the Commission stated that the purpose of Regulation 418/85, which is to encourage joint research and development activities by allowing – under certain conditions – costs and benefits to be shared, is not achieved in a case where the agreement confined itself 'to determining the sharing of the benefits from work which henceforth would be carried out independently by each party, according to the terms of the agreement itself'.

(2) All the parties must have access to the results of the work.[209]

(3) In the case of agreements limited to joint research and development, each party must remain free to exploit the results of the work as well as any pre-existing technical knowledge necessary for such exploitation independently.[210]

The other two conditions only apply to agreements which extend beyond joint research and development to include joint exploitation.

(1) The joint exploitation must relate only to results which are protected by industrial property rights or constitute know-how which 'substantially contributes' to technical or economic progress, and the results must be 'decisive' for the manufacture of the products or application of processes.[211] The purpose of this requirement is to prevent the parties from entering into a joint production arrangement for products which were not developed pursuant to a joint research and development agreement.[212] In such cases, the parties may only co-operate in production by means of other arrangements such as licensing or specialisation, which may benefit from other block exemption regulations. Apart from the ambiguity inherent in terms such as 'substantially contributes' and 'decisive', it may prove difficult to determine at the outset whether the joint research and development programme will produce patentable results or valuable know-how which

---

[207] Regulation 418/85, art. 2(a).
[208] *Quantel International-Continuum/Quantel SA*, OJ 1992 L235/9, at p. 16.
[209] Regulation 418/85, art. 2(b).
[210] Ibid., art. 2(c).
[211] Ibid., art. 2(d). In *KSB/Goulds/Lowara/ITT*, OJ 1991 L19/25, the development of technical knowledge, the granting of a patent without objection being made together with the grant of an innovation prize, in the Commission's view, pointed to the conclusion that the results in question 'contributed substantially to technical or economic progress within the meaning of Article 2(d).' See also the joint venture guidelines, para. 47.
[212] Regulation 418/85, recital 7.

¶514

substantially contributes to technical or economic progress and which is decisive at the manufacturing stage.[213] It is to be hoped that the term 'decisive' will receive a liberal interpretation so that the parties will not have to contend with the risk of losing the benefit of the block exemption if the results are not revolutionary.

(2) Undertakings charged with the manufacture of the products by way of specialisation must be required to fulfil orders from all the parties.[214]

Market-share limitations

The duration and availability of the regulation is dealt with in art. 3 and may be summarised as follows:

(1) where the parties are not competing manufacturers of products capable of being improved or replaced by the contract products, the exemption applies for the duration of the research and development programme and if there is joint exploitation, for five years after the products were first placed on the market in the EC;[215]

(2) where the parties are competitors of products capable of being improved or replaced by the contract products, the exemption applies for the same period as in (1), but only if, at the time of entering into the agreement, their combined production of products capable of being improved or replaced by the contract products does not exceed 20 per cent of the market for such products in the EC or a substantial part thereof;[216]

(3) in both cases, after five years of exploitation, the exemption will continue to apply as long as the parties' combined production of the contract products as well as products considered by users to be equivalent, does not exceed 20 per cent of the total market for such products in the EC or a substantial part thereof;[217]

---

[213] In *KSB/Goulds/Lowara/ITT*, OJ 1991 L19/25, the Commission noted that under art. 85(3) of the treaty a *mere* contribution to the promotion of technical or economic progress is required, whereas under art. 2(d) of Regulation 418/85, this contribution must be *substantial*.

[214] Regulation 418/85, art. 2(e); See also Commission Regulation 151/93 of 23 December 1992, OJ 1993 L21/8. Under Regulation 418/85, an additional condition existed whereby any joint undertaking or third party charged with the manufacture of the products could supply them only to the parties, ibid., art. 2(e). However, this requirement has now been excluded, see Regulation 151/93 of 23 December 1992, OJ 1993 L21/8, art. 2(1). As a result, a third party charged with manufacturing the contract products now also has the freedom to distribute them.

[215] Regulation 418/85, art. 3(1).

[216] Ibid., art. 3(2). In practice, it would seem that this 20 per cent rule is strictly adhered to. In *KSB/Goulds/Lowara/ITT*, OJ 1991 L19/25, the fact that it could not be ruled out that the combined share of the parties for water pumps in the Community was over 20 per cent, coupled with the possibility that one of the parties' market share would rise, at least in the long term, led the Commission to assess the co-operation between the parties under art. 85 of the EC Treaty and not under Regulation 418/85. However, recourse was had to art. 3(2) of Regulation 418/85 when deciding the duration of the exemption to be granted under art. 85(3).

[217] Ibid., art. 3(3). Where contract products are components used by the parties for the manufacture of other products, reference must be made to the markets of such of the latter products for which the components

¶514

(4) where the agreement extends to exclusive distribution of the goods, then, in certain situations,[218] the exemption will apply if the parties' production of the products referred to in (2) and (3) above does not exceed ten per cent for all such products[219] in the EC or a substantial part thereof. It would seem however, that this ten per cent market share limit does not apply to a situation where the parties to the agreement separately distribute the goods in their own defined territories.[220] In such a case, the 20 per cent market share rule would still apply.

Article 3(2) states that the parties' combined production must not exceed 20 per cent of the market for such products, *at the time the agreement is entered into* in order for the block exemption to apply. However, in *KSB/Goulds/Lowara/ ITT*, the Commission included, as part of its reasoning for denying the application of the block exemption, the fact that it could not be ruled out that the combined share of the parties on the market for water pumps in the Community was over 20 per cent. KSB alone exceeded this share in Germany and France and together with Lowara, in Italy. However, the Commission went on to say that '[i]t is also possible that KSB's market share would rise, at least in

---

represent a significant part. The exemption will continue to apply once the market shares in question are exceeded by not more than one tenth during any period of two consecutive financial years; art. 3(4). (This would seem to be the intention of art. 3(4) which, in its present form, appears to contain some typographical errors.) If this threshold is exceeded, the exemption will continue to apply for a period of six months following the end of the financial year during which it was exceeded; art. 3(5). However, in *Continental-Michelin*, OJ 1988 L305/33, the Commission granted an individual exemption for 20 years even though the market shares of the parties exceeded the 20 per cent limit.

[218] See art. 4(1)(fa),(fb) and (fc) of Commission Regulation 418/85. These situations occur where

    (a) one of the parties has the exclusive right to distribute the contract products;
    (b) a joint or third undertaking is granted the exclusive right to distribute the contract products; or
    (c) joint or third undertakings are granted the exclusive right to distribute the contract products in the whole or a defined area of the EC provided that users and intermediaries can also obtain the contract products from other suppliers and are not inhibited by the parties or the joint or third undertakings in so doing

provided that those to whom the exclusive distribution rights have been granted do not distribute products that compete with the contract products.

[219] See art. 3(3a) of Regulation 418/85 (as amended by Commission Regulation 151/93 of 23 December 1992, OJ 1993 L21/8). It seems that 'all such products' in art. 3(3a) should be interpreted as being broader than the term 'Contract Products' in art. 1 of the block exemption. Accordingly, when calculating the ten per cent market share under art. 3(3a), reference should be made to

    (1) the parties' combined production of products capable of being improved or replaced by the contract products,
    (2) the parties' combined production of the contract products, and
    (3) the parties' combined production or other products which are considered by users to be equivalent in view of their characteristics, price and intended use.

Only if the parties' combined production of products in all three categories was no greater than ten per cent of the total market for all three categories in all or a substantial part of the EC would they benefit from the block exemption.

[220] See art. 4(1)(f) of Commission Regulation 418/85. The resulting disadvantage is that this type of agreement would still only be subject to the benefit of the exemption for five years after the goods were placed on the market in the EC (see art. 3(1)) whereas the other exclusive distribution rules in art. 4(1)(fa), (fb) and (fc) are not subject to such temporal limitations. See the joint venture guidelines, para. 48.

the long term, as a result of the increase in turnover which it hopes to achieve through the multi-media pump.'[221] This interpretation of art. 3(2) would seem overly broad.

These rules reflect the Commission's long-standing suspicion of research and development agreements entered into by large firms competing on the same market[222] as well as its desire to ensure that several independent poles of research remain in the Community.[223] Nevertheless, the decision to extend the scope of the block exemption to co-operation at the marketing stage shows a willingness to consider that co-operative joint ventures that perform on a lasting basis all the functions of an autonomous legal entity generally increase competition.[224]

At the time when the agreement is concluded, only actual competitors appear to be subject to the market-share limitation.[225]

In applying these rules relating to the market-share limitation, the critical inquiry concerns the delimitation of the relevant product market. The regulation defines this market as that for 'products capable of being improved or replaced' by those arising out of the joint research and development. This definition poses numerous problems. It assumes that the parties are able accurately to predict at the outset the nature of the products which will result from the project as well as their field of application. Such predictions may prove to be difficult in cases where the project involves a substantial amount of basic research at the outset, which is arguably the type of project most likely to generate significant long-term technological benefits.

Even if it is possible to clearly identify the products which will result from the co-operation in research and development, the parties are still exposed to a high degree of uncertainty. In many cases, the determination of the boundaries of the relevant product market will give rise to complex issues relating to the substitutability of products. Indeed, only in the case of a truly novel product such as a miracle drug will the parties be able to determine with certainty that the exemption is applicable to their agreement since, by definition, the product

---

[221] *KSB/Goulds/Lowara/ITT*, OJ 1990 L19/25 at p. 33; see also *BP Chemicals/Enichem*, OJ 1993 C272/7.

[222] See *Henkel-Colgate*, JO 1972 L14/14; notice on agreements, decisions and concerted practices in the field of co-operation, JO 1968 C75/3, corrigendum JO 1968 L84/14. If a joint R & D agreement is entered into by competing manufacturers with a combined market share in excess of 20 per cent, the parties must apply for an individual exemption; the opposition procedure is not available for this purpose. See, e.g. *Continental-Michelin* [1989] 1 CEC 2,241; OJ 1988 L305/33. As stated in recital 10, the decision will take account of world competition and the particular circumstances prevailing in the manufacture of high technology products.

[223] Regulation 418/85, Recital 8.

[224] *XXIst Report on Competition Policy for 1991*, point 131. See also the joint venture guidelines, para. 48.

[225] This represents a significant departure from the approach generally adopted by the Commission in the past where the focus has been on potential competition as well as actual competition, see e.g. *Vacuum Interpreters I*, OJ 1977 L48/32. In fact, the draft regulation referred to potential competition, but this reference was deleted because it would have proved difficult to apply in practice. Under the draft text, the exemption was only available if not more than one of the three 'actually or potentially' leading undertakings in the sector concerned was a party to the agreement (draft regulation on the application of art. 85(3) of the treaty to categories of research and development co-operation agreements, OJ 1984 C16/3).

¶514

would not improve or replace existing products. In such a case, however, it is likely that the agreement will no longer qualify for the exemption after the initial five-year period since the parties will probably control the entire market or at least a substantial portion of the market for the product. Moreover, there is a risk that the exemption may be withdrawn even earlier as the regulation provides that the Commission may withdraw the exemption where 'the contract products are not subject in the whole or a substantial part of the Common Market to effective competition from identical products or products considered by users to be equivalent in view of their characteristics, price and intended uses.'[226]

In summary, the most critical feature of the entire regulation – the market-share limitation – is also the most nebulous, thus heightening the already significant risk generally attached to research and development projects. Apart from undermining the goal of legal certainty, this limitation also appears inconsistent with the goal of stimulating technological innovation in Europe.

¶515   Specific restrictions covered by the regulation

Articles 4 and 5 of the regulation contain lists of clauses which are specifically allowed. Article 4 lists restrictions that would normally fall under art. 85(1) but benefit from the exemption. Article 5 lists restrictions that would not usually infringe art. 85(1). Articles 4(2) and 5(2) confirm the applicability of the block exemption to obligations with a more limited scope than those set out in art. 4(1) and 5(1) respectively.

The obligations referred to in these two lists fall into the following main categories:

(1)   independent research and development;

(2)   territorial restrictions;

(3)   exclusive purchasing;

(4)   intellectual property rights.

These four broad categories as well as other clauses are briefly reviewed below.

Independent research and development

Restrictions imposed on the parties concerning independent research and development in the same field or a closely connected field generally fall under art. 85(1) since they restrict competition between the parties in the field of research and prevent each from gaining a competitive edge over the other.

---

[226]   Regulation 418/85, art. 10(d).

However, such restrictions, including those concerning co-operation with third parties, are exempted by the regulation as they ensure that the parties will devote their efforts to the project.[227] Accordingly, art. 4(1)(a) and (b) exempt obligations not to carry out independently, or to enter into agreements with third parties on, research and development in the field to which the programme relates or in a 'closely connected' field during the execution of the programme.

Restrictions on independent research and development must not be unduly broad as the exemption does not apply to programmes extending to 'unconnected' fields.[228] For this reason, the parties may be able to protect themselves by giving a wide definition to the programme. The Commission is prepared to approve a clause which obliges parties who want to start joint action in new fields, unconnected to the field of the original agreement, to first invite the other parties to the original agreement.[229] In practice, it may prove difficult to distinguish between 'closely connected' fields and 'unconnected' fields. It would seem that if work carried out independently could be used in the joint programme, such work relates to a 'closely connected' field.

After the joint research and development programme has been completed, no restrictions may be imposed on the parties regarding independent activity.[230] However, an obligation may be imposed on the parties to grant each other non-exclusive licences for inventions relating to improvements or new applications which are developed independently after the completion of the programme.[231]

Territorial restrictions

The regulation exempts certain territorial restrictions concerning both the manufacture and distribution of the products arising out of the joint research and development. As in other areas, such as patent licensing and exclusive distribution, such restrictions may be justified on the ground that they enable firms to concentrate their efforts in a given area, thus facilitating the introduction and promotion of the product on the market. This reasoning would seem particularly cogent in the context of joint research and development programmes, which often give rise to entirely new products unfamiliar to consumers.

The regulation exempts the following two types of territorial restrictions:

(1) As regards manufacturing, the parties may be required not to manufacture the contract products or apply the contract processes in

---

[227] Ibid., art. 4(1)(a)–(b).
[228] Restrictions on independent research activity in unconnected fields are prohibited in art. 6(a).
[229] Commission notice pursuant to art. 19(3) of Council Regulation 17/62, Communication *GEC-ANT-Teletra-SAT*, OJ 1988 C180/3.
[230] Regulation 418/85, art. 6(a).
[231] Ibid., art. 4(1)(h).

territories reserved for other parties.[232] Manufacturing exclusivity is generally considered to have a minimal effect on competition, giving rise to problems only when transportation costs are high enough to generate what may amount to de facto sales exclusivity.

(2) As regards distribution arrangements, the regulation, at first sight, seems to follow the classic approach adopted by the Commission with respect to territorial restrictions imposed in connection with distribution arrangements by exempting restrictions on active sales while preserving the possibility of passive sales.[233] The regulation exempts a ban on active sales[234] only for a five-year period from the time the contract products are first put on the market within the EC, a limitation not found in other areas such as patent licensing and exclusive distribution. However, in *BBC Brown Boveri*, the Commission granted an individual exemption pursuant to art. 85(3) for a ban on exports to the Community during the first ten years after the launching on the market of the product, because the agreement did not eliminate competition in respect of a substantial part of the product in question.[235] Presumably, the temporal limitation of five years the Commission generally applies is deemed necessary due to the strong horizontal element often present in joint research and development programmes even though the market share limitation would seem to constitute an effective deterrent to unacceptable restrictions on competition flowing from co-operation between competing manufacturers.

Passive sales, are not expressly mentioned in art. 4(1)(f). The Commission has stated that such sales are not covered by the block exemption and must be justified on an individual basis.[236] In *Quantel*,[237] the Commission decided that an agreement containing a ban on passive competition was prohibited under art. 4(1)(f) of the regulation. This interpretation appears questionable in view of both the Commission's earlier statement and the fact that art. 4 does not list prohibited clauses, but rather clauses that would ordinarily fall within art. 85(1) yet are nonetheless exempted under the regulation.

---

[232] Ibid., art. 4(1)(d).

[233] Ibid., art. 4(1)(f). Any territorial restrictions on sales activities not expressly exempted in art. 4(1)(f) are blacklisted in art. 6(f) and art. 6(h).

[234] In *Quantel International-Continuum/Quantel SA*, OJ 1992 L235/9, the territorial division clause was held to be of unlimited duration even though it was later modified to limit its duration. The Commission accordingly held it to fall outside Regulation 418/85.

[235] *BBC Brown Boveri*, OJ 1988 L301/68.

[236] *Seventeenth Report on Competition Policy*, point 31.

[237] *Quantel International-Continuum/Quantel SA*, OJ 1992 L235/9.

¶515

Exclusive purchasing

Article 4(1)(c) of the regulation exempts exclusive purchasing obligations to obtain the products only from the parties, joint organisations or third parties charged with their manufacture, thus giving the manufacturer a guaranteed outlet which enables him to achieve rationalisation of production. In contrast to the exclusive purchasing block exemption, the regulation does not allow clauses, including so-called 'English clauses', which prevent the purchaser from buying competing products.

As a corollary to the exclusive purchasing obligation, the parties may be required to supply other parties with minimum quantities of the products.[238]

Intellectual property rights

Regulation 418/85 exempts a number of obligations common to agreements involving intellectual property rights and know-how and which are discussed in detail in the part on patent licensing.[239] However, there are several clauses specific to joint research and development programmes which deserve brief mention.

Although the regulation reflects the Commission's hostility towards no-challenge clauses, there is no absolute ban on these clauses (in contrast to the patent licensing block exemption). Instead, the ban on no-challenge clauses applies only in certain circumstances. If the intellectual property rights existed prior to the joint research and development programme, only no-challenge clauses extending beyond the stage of research and development are prohibited. In the case of intellectual property rights which protect the results of the joint research and development, no-challenge clauses are prohibited if they extend beyond the expiry of the agreement.[240] Thus, the regulation seeks to strike a balance between the anti-competitive effects of no-challenge clauses and the need to allow firms to carry out joint research and development projects in an atmosphere of co-operation. It is important to note that the regulation does not explicitly exempt no-challenge clauses for pre-existing intellectual property rights during the research and development programme nor those for intellectual property rights protecting the results of the joint work

---

[238] Regulation 418/85, art. 5(1)(h).
[239] See the following provisions of Regulation 418/85:

(1) art. 4(1)(e) exempting field of use restrictions except where two or more of the parties are competitors within the meaning of art. 3 at the time the agreement was entered into;
(2) art. 5(1)(c) relating to obligations to maintain in force intellectual property rights for the contract processes or products;
(3) art. 5(1)(d) relating to obligations to preserve the confidentiality of know-how;
(4) art. 5(1)(e) relating to obligations to assist in the protection of intellectual property rights.

See also art. 5(1)(g) providing that no restriction of competition is involved in an obligation to share with other parties royalties received from third parties.

[240] Ibid., art. 6(b).

¶515

before the expiry of the agreement, so it would appear necessary to notify such clauses to the Commission under the opposition procedure in order to obtain an exemption.

The regulation also exempts an obligation to pay royalties or render services to other parties to compensate for unequal contributions to the research and development programme or unequal exploitation of its results.[241]

Miscellaneous clauses

In line with other block exemptions, especially the patent licensing block exemption, art. 6 of the regulation sets out in a list of clauses that are expressly prohibited (i.e. blacklisted). These include, inter alia:

(1) maximum quantity restrictions;[242]

(2) price restrictions;[243]

(3) customer restrictions;[244]

(4) prohibitions on the parties from granting licences to third parties to manufacture the contract products or to apply the contract processes even though exploitation of the results by the parties is not provided for or does not take place;[245]

(5) obligations to refuse without any objectively justified reason to meet demand from users or dealers established in their respective territories who would market the contract products in other territories of the EC or to make it difficult for users or dealers to obtain the contract products from other dealers in the EC.[246]

Other clauses not previously discussed in the text or the notes of this section that are specifically discussed in the regulation are the obligation to communicate necessary technical knowledge[247] or not to use any know-how received from another party for purposes other than carrying out the arrangement.[248] Not unexpectedly, these two clauses are included in the list of provisions normally not coming within art. 85(1).

---

[241] Ibid., art. 5(1)(f).

[242] Ibid., art. 6(c).

[243] Ibid., art. 6(d). See *Alcatel/Espace/ANT Nachrichtentechnik*, OJ 1990 L32/99, where the Commission viewed an agreement to bid jointly for the contract for a satellite as restricting the parties in their determination of prices (as they had to agree on the bid price) as bringing the agreement within the scope of art. 6(d). The regulation could therefore not be applied.

[244] Regulation 418/85, art. 6(e).

[245] Ibid., art. 6(g). See *KSB/Goulds/Lowara/ITT*, OJ 1991 L19/25, at p. 33.

[246] Regulation 418/85, art. 6(h). This clause must be read together with those clauses of the regulation that allow joint manufacture. See also art. 6(f).

[247] Ibid., art. 5(1)(a).

[248] Ibid., art. 5(1)(b).

¶515

¶516   Procedural mechanisms

This section deals with the following two procedural mechanisms:

(1) the opposition procedure; and

(2) the withdrawal of the exemption.

Opposition procedure

Like many of the block exemptions, the regulation provides for a fast-track 'opposition' procedure for agreements containing restrictive clauses which are neither expressly permitted nor expressly prohibited by the regulation.[249] Article 7 stipulates that such an agreement may benefit from the exemption provided that:

(1) the agreement is notified to the Commission with complete and accurate information and express reference is made to art. 7 in the notification or in a communication accompanying it; and

(2) the Commission does not oppose such exemption within a period of six months.[250] These restrictions become exemptible through non-opposition.[251]

The Commission must oppose the exemption if it receives a request to do so from a member state within three months of the forwarding to the member state of the notification or communication.[252] Unless the member state withdraws its request, the Commission may only withdraw its opposition after consultation of the Advisory Committee on Restrictive Practices and Dominant Positions.[253] In all other cases, the Commission may withdraw its opposition at any time.

The exemption normally applies from the date of notification unless the agreement has to be amended to meet the conditions of art. 85(3), in which case the exemption applies from the date of the amendment.[254]

---

[249] The industry has made little use of the opposition procedure contained in art. 7 of Regulation 418/85. Three notifications were made in 1987 (*Seventeenth Report on Competition Policy*, point 31), none in 1988 (*Eighteenth Report on Competition Policy*, point 23), one in 1989 (*Nineteenth Report on Competition Policy*, point 18); four in 1990 (*XXth Report on Competition Policy*, point 44) and one in 1992 (*XXIInd Report on Competition Policy for 1992*, point 27).

[250] Regulation 418/85, art. 7(1). The six-month period starts running from the date of receipt of the notification by the Commission or in cases of notifications made by registered post, the date shown on the postmark of the place of posting art. 7(2).

[251] The Commission services consider that an exemption through non-opposition can generally apply in all the cases where restrictions linked to an exempted field of use restriction occur in agreements between non-competitors, in particular between undertakings from different sectors having complementary expertise or undertakings in a supplier-customer relationship, *Seventeenth Report on Competition Policy*, point 31.

[252] Regulation 418/85, art. 7(5).

[253] Ibid., art. 7(6).

[254] Ibid., art. 7(7) and (8).

Withdrawal of the exemption

Article 10 provides that the Commission may withdraw the benefit of the exemption where it finds in a particular case that an agreement exempted by the regulation nevertheless has certain effects that are incompatible with the conditions laid down in art. 85(3), particularly where:

(1) the existence of the agreement substantially restricts the scope for third parties to carry out research and development in the relevant field because of the limited research capacity available elsewhere;

(2) because of the particular structure of supply, the existence of the agreement substantially restricts the access of third parties to the market for the contract products;

(3) without any objectively valid reason, the parties do not exploit the results of the joint research and development; or

(4) the contract products are not subject in the whole or a substantial part of the common market to effective competition from identical products or products considered by users as equivalent in view of their characteristics, price and intended use.

SPECIALISATION AGREEMENTS

¶517   Introduction

A specialisation agreement is an arrangement whereby either each party gives up the manufacture of certain products in favour of the other or the parties undertake to manufacture or have manufactured certain products only jointly. Such agreements are usually combined with an obligation on the parties to supply the products each has agreed to manufacture to the other on an exclusive basis.

As the undertakings concerned may concentrate on the manufacture of certain products and thus operate more efficiently while at the same time being assured of a supply of the full range of goods, such agreements are likely to be of benefit both to the parties involved and to the consumer.[255] Specialisation agreements normally fall within the prohibition, under art. 85(1), of the limitation or control of 'production, markets, technical development, or investment'. Individual exemption is possible under art. 85(3), and there is also a block exemption for specialisation agreements between small and medium-sized enterprises.

---

[255] On the benefits of specialisation agreements, see the *First Report on Competition Policy*, point 27.

¶518   Regulation 417/85

Specialisation agreements have benefited from a block exemption since 1973. This exemption was initially granted for a period of five years by Regulation 2779/72 of 21 December 1972.[256] The exemption has been extended and amended several times.[257] The current exemption is granted by Regulation 417/85.[258]

The various amendments to the initial Regulation 2779/72 culminating in Regulation 417/85, have extended the scope of the exemption. The initial market share and turnover ceilings of ten per cent and ECU 150m have been raised to 20 per cent and ECU 1,000m respectively except in the case of exclusive distribution by one of the parties or by joint or third undertaking(s) where the market share may not exceed ten per cent.

In 1982, the exemption, which was previously restricted to reciprocal obligations not to manufacture certain products, was extended to agreements in which the parties undertake to manufacture, or have manufactured, certain products only jointly. Another important change made in 1985 was the introduction of the opposition procedure into the exemption mechanism. Under this procedure, which is also available under other block exemptions, specialisation agreements that fall outside the exemption because the parties' turnover is more than ECU 1,000m are nevertheless exempted if they are notified to the Commission and the latter does not react within six months.

¶519   Regulation 417/85: scope of application

Regulation 417/85 applies to any agreement which meets the following three conditions:

(1) the agreement must correspond to the definition set out in art. 1;

(2) the agreement must not contain any restriction of competition other than those set out in art. 2; and

(3) the market share and turnover ceilings set out in art. 3 must not be exceeded.

Specialisation agreements defined

The regulation applies only to agreements whereby, for the duration of the agreement, undertakings accept:

---

[256] JO 1972 L292/23.
[257] OJ 1977 L338/14; OJ 1980 L376/33.
[258] Commission Regulation 417/85 on the application of art. 85(3) of the treaty to categories of specialisation agreements: OJ 1985 L53/1, as amended by Commission Regulation 151/93, OJ 1993 L21/8.

(1) Reciprocal obligations: the exemption does not apply to arrangements imposing unilateral obligations to refrain from manufacturing.[259]

(2) Not to manufacture certain products or to have them manufactured, but to leave it to other parties to manufacture the products or have them manufactured or to manufacture certain products or have them manufactured only jointly: the exemption applies only to agreements relating to the manufacture of products. Agreements relating solely to distribution or research and development fall outside the scope of the exemption.[260]

Permissible restrictions

Article 2(1) of the regulation sets out six restrictions of competition which may validly be imposed on the parties in a specialisation agreement:

(1) an obligation not to conclude with third parties specialisation agreements relating to identical or interchangeable products;[261]

(2) an obligation to procure the products subject to the agreement only from another party, a joint undertaking or an undertaking jointly charged with their manufacture subject to a right to buy elsewhere on more favourable terms which the other party, the joint undertaking or the undertaking charged with manufacture will not match (the 'English clause');[262]

(3) an obligation to grant to the other party (or parties) to the agreement exclusive distribution rights within the whole or a defined area of the EC provided that intermediaries and users can also obtain the products from other suppliers and the parties do not render it difficult for intermediaries and users to thus obtain the products;[263]

(4) an obligation to grant one of the parties to the agreement the exclusive right to distribute products which are the subject of the specialisation provided that that party does not distribute competing products of a third undertaking;[264]

---

[259] Regulation 417/85, art. 1(a). See *PRYM-BEKA*, OJ 1973 L296/24. See also *Seventeenth Report on Competition Policy*, point 30; *Nineteenth Report on Competition Policy*, point 18 and 39; the joint venture guidelines, para. 44.

[260] Regulation 417/85, art. 1(b). As stated in the *Second Report on Competition Policy*, point 9, '… [t]he commitment can refer only to the nature and not to the quantity of the products, and any quantitative limitation of production lies outside the scope of the exemption.' See *Italian cast glass*, OJ 1980 L383/19 and *Seventeenth Report on Competition Policy*, point 30. Note that the scope of the regulation has been extended to cover co-operative joint ventures which perform all the functions of normal undertakings, including sales, see OJ 1993 L151/93. See also *XXIst Report on Competition Policy for 1991*, point 132.

[261] Regulation 417/85, art. 2(1)(a). As stated in art. 2(2), the exemption also applies where the parties undertake obligations of the types referred to in art. 2(1), but of a more limited scope.

[262] Ibid., art. 2(1)(b). See, e.g. notice pursuant to art. 19(3) of Council Regulation 17/62, *Alcatel Espace-ANT Nachrichtentechnik*, OJ 1989 C179/9.

[263] Regulation 417/85, art. 2(1)(c),

[264] Ibid., art. 2(1)(d).

¶519

(5) an obligation to grant the exclusive right to distribute products which are the subject of the specialisation to a joint or third undertaking provided that the joint or third undertaking does not manufacture or distribute competing products;[265]

(6) an obligation to grant the exclusive right to distribute within the whole or a defined area of the EC the products which are the subject of the specialisation to joint or third undertakings which do not manufacture or distribute competing products, provided that users and intermediaries can also obtain the contract products from other suppliers and that neither the parties nor the joint or third undertakings entrusted with the exclusive distribution render it difficult for users and intermediaries to thus obtain the products.[266]

If a specialisation agreement within the meaning of the regulation imposes any restriction on competition other than the six specifically authorised, it will not qualify for the block exemption, although in such circumstances an individual exemption from the Commission under art. 85(3) might be granted.[267]

The regulation also expressly permits three other obligations on the parties that are not considered to be restrictions on competition: to supply the other parties with products meeting minimum quality standards, to maintain minimum stocks of products which are the subject of the specialisation and of replacement parts for them and to provide after-sales, customer and guarantee services for products which are the subject of the specialisation. [268]

Market share and turnover ceiling

Since the regulation is specifically designed to assist small and medium-sized undertakings,[269] the grant of the exemption is conditional upon the parties to the agreements not exceeding the market share and turnover ceilings set out in art. 3. The exemption only applies if:

(1) the products that are the subject of the specialisation (including products considered by users to be equivalent in view of their characteristics, price and intended use) do not represent more than 20 per cent of the market in the EC or a substantial part thereof; and the aggregate annual turnover of all the participants does not exceed ECU 1,000m.[270]

---

[265] Ibid., art. 2(1)(e).
[266] Ibid., art. 2(1)(f). The purpose of art. 2(2) is to confirm the applicability of the block exemption to obligations with a more limited scope than those set out in art. 2(1).
[267] Regulation 417/85, art. 2(2a).
[268] Regulation 417/85, art. 2(3).
[269] See e.g. *Eleventh Report on Competition Policy*, point 31.
[270] Regulation 417/85, art. 3(1), as amended by Commission Regulation 151/93, OJ 1993 L21/8. In order to calculate whether the ceilings are reached, account must be taken of the participating undertakings and related

¶519

(2) where one of the parties or one or more joint or third undertaking(s) is (are) entrusted with the exclusive distribution of the products which are the subject of the specialisation, the exemption will only apply if these products (together with the participating undertakings' other products which are considered by users to be equivalent) do not represent more than ten per cent of the market for all such products in the EC or a substantial part thereof; and the aggregate annual turnover of all the participating undertakings does not exceed ECU 1,000m.[271]

Small variations are allowed under art. 3(3), whereby the exemption continues to apply where the turnover and market share limits are exceeded by not more than one-tenth in any two consecutive financial years.[272]

The restriction is quite severe, particularly as the relevant turnover is the aggregate turnover for all products of the parties to the agreement and their corporate groups.[273]

While the market share ceiling is absolute, the turnover limitation may be exceeded if the agreement is notified to the Commission under the opposition procedure of art. 4, and the Commission does not oppose the exemption within six months.[274]

¶520   Regulation 417/85: withdrawal of the exemption

Under art. 8, the Commission may withdraw the benefit of the exemption where it finds that in a particular case, even though it had been found to meet the formal requirements for exemption under art. 85(3), an agreement has effects incompatible with it; in particular, where:

'(a) the agreement is not yielding significant results in terms of rationalisation or consumers are not receiving a fair share of the resulting benefit; or

(b) the products which are the subject of the specialisation are not subject in the Common Market or a substantial part thereof to effective competition from identical products or products considered by users to be equivalent in view of their characteristics, price and intended use.'

---

undertakings as defined in art. 7. See the *XXth Report on Competition Policy*, point 43, where the Commission stated that it did not oppose an agreement notified under the block exemption regulation concerning a specialisation agreement between firms whose combined turnover exceeded ECU 500m.

[271] Ibid., art. 3(2). The joint venture guidelines, para. 44.

[272] If the limits in art. 3(3) are exceeded, the exemption continues to apply for a period of six months following the end of the financial year during which it was exceeded; art. 3(4).

[273] Regulation 417/85, art. 7. For the determination of the turnover, see art. 6.

[274] See the joint venture guidelines, para. 44, 46. It is conceivable however, that the Commission would attach conditions in such a case, such as, for example, deleting from the agreement in question any reference to a ban on passive sales.

¶521   Individual exemptions

Any agreements that do not qualify under the block exemption have to be notified in order to benefit from an individual exemption. A review of the individual exemption decisions[275] adopted by the Commission shows that:

(1) exemptions have been granted to agreements broader in scope than those covered by the regulation: several of the agreements individually exempted by the Commission have covered not only specialisation in the manufacture of products but also in research and development.[276] In one agreement, *PRYM-BEKA*,[277] the obligation not to manufacture was unilateral and not reciprocal; under another, *VFA/Sauer*,[278] the parties did not cease to manufacture any product but rather in a context of mutual exclusive supply, agreed not to develop certain products. In *ENI/Montedison*,[279] the agreement brought about a de facto specialisation by each party in a complex exchange of assets and supply contracts.

(2) exemptions have been granted to agreements containing restrictions other than those authorised by the regulation: for example, in *Jaz-Peter*,[280] in relation to a reciprocal grant of exclusive distribution rights for the products concerned, the Commission allowed a mechanism by which products made by one party and distributed by the other would be sold under the distributor's trade mark; in *Sopelem/Vickers*,[281] the Commission exempted an agreement under which exclusive distribution rights were granted to a joint venture.

(3) exemptions have been granted to undertakings which exceeded the market share and turnover ceilings: individual exemptions have been extended to far larger companies with higher aggregate turnovers and market shares than the group exemption under the regulation. An extreme example is *Fine Paper*,[282] where the companies held 80 per cent

---

[275] *Clima-Chappée/Buderus*, JO 1969 L195/1; *FN-CF*, JO 1971 L134/6; *Sopelem/Langen*, JO 1972 L13/47; *MAN/SAVIEM*, JO 1972 L31/29; *Fine Paper*, JO 1972 L182/24; *Rank/Sopelem*, OJ 1975 L29/20; *Sopelem/Vickers*, OJ 1978 L70/47, OJ 1981 L391/1; *PRYM-BEKA*, OJ 1973 L296/24; *Jaz-Peter*, JO 1969 L195/5, OJ 1978 L61/17; *Bayer/Gist-Brocades*, OJ 1976 L30/13; *VFA/Sauer, Fifteenth Report on Competition Policy*, point 79; *ENI/Montedison*, OJ 1987 L5/13. See also *BPCL-ICI*, OJ 1984 L212/1.

[276] See e.g. *Sopelem/Vickers*, OJ 1981 L391/1, OJ 1978 L70/47; *Rank/Sopelem*, OJ 1975 L29/20; *MAN/SAVIEM*, OJ 1972 L31/29; *FN-CF*, JO 1971 L134/6.

[277] *PRYM-BEKA*, OJ 1973 L296/24. In *Perlite, Nineteenth Report of Competition Policy*, point 39, another unilateral specialisation agreement was cleared without a formal decision, following the removal of a clause which prevented the party who had agreed not to manufacture the product in question from asking the other party (who he had agreed would be his sole supplier) for supplies above a certain ceiling. The amended clause allowed the purchaser to obtain supplies from other suppliers in quantities exceeding the agreed ceiling.

[278] *VFA/Saver, Fifteenth Report on Competition Policy*, point 79.

[279] *ENI/Montedison*, OJ 1987 L5/13.

[280] *Jaz-Peter*, OJ 1969 L195/5.

[281] *Sopelem/Vickers*, OJ 1981 L391/1, OJ 1978 L70/47.

[282] *Fine Paper*, OJ 1972 L182/24.

of the relevant French, and 70 per cent of the relevant Benelux markets. In *Bayer/Gist*,[283] an eight-year exemption was granted even though the partners accounted for 30 per cent of world production of one of the products in question. Generally, the most common reason for the need for an individual exemption is the size of the undertakings concerned or the groups to which they belong.[284]

(4) certain restrictions have been considered to be unacceptable by the Commission: in a number of cases the Commission compelled the parties to eliminate certain provisions in their arrangements, such as:

   (a) a customer allocation clause in *Prym-Beka*,[285]

   (b) the production allocation quotas in *Fine Paper*,[286]

   (c) the setting up of joint subsidiaries in *Bayer/Gist-Brocades*,[287]

   (d) restrictions on the use of trade marks after the expiry of the agreement in *Rank/Sopelem*,[288] and

   (e) quantitative restrictions, obliging a party to buy solely from one supplier *and* preventing that purchaser from asking that supplier for supplies above a certain ceiling in *Perlite*.[289]

OTHER FORMS OF CO-OPERATION

¶522   Categories of co-operation agreements

The remainder of this chapter examines the following types of co-operation agreements:

   (1) subcontracting agreements (¶523);

   (2) joint purchasing agreements (¶524);

---

[283] *Bayer/Gist-Brocades*, OJ 1976 L30/13.
[284] See *Second Report on Competition Policy*, point 35:

'The adoption of a block exemption regulation for certain production specialization agreements in order to facilitate co-operation between small and medium-sized firms does not mean, in specific cases, that specialization between large firms may not also qualify for exemption. However, owing to the size of the undertakings concerned, such agreements continue to be subject to the individual exemption procedure and also perhaps to the imposition of appropriate charges and conditions under Regulation 17.'

In most individual decisions of exemption, the Commission has required the parties to file reports on a regular basis, so that the Commission is kept informed of such matters as market developments, the interpretation of the agreement and the status of the parties.
[285] *PRYM-BEKA*, OJ 1973 L296/24.
[286] *Fine Paper*, JO 1972 L182/24.
[287] *Bayer/Gist-Brocades*, OJ 1976 L30/13.
[288] *Rank/Sopelem*, OJ 1975 L29/20.
[289] *Nineteenth Report on Competition Policy*, point 39.

(3) joint selling agreements (¶525);

(4) miscellaneous types of co-operation arrangements (¶526 – ¶535).

¶523   Subcontracting

The Commission sought to clarify the status of subcontracting agreements in its notice of 18 December 1978.[290] This notice supplements the 1968 notice on co-operation. Subcontracting agreements are defined as 'agreements under which one firm, called "the contractor", whether or not in consequence of a prior order from a third party, entrusts to another, called "the subcontractor", the manufacture of goods, the supply of services or the performance of work under the contractor's instruction, to be provided to the contractor or performed on his behalf'.[291] In the notice, the Commission said that sub-contracting agreements are not in themselves caught by art. 85(1).

The notice also deals with the permissibility of restrictions on the use by the subcontractor of any such technology or equipment which the contractor provides to the subcontractor. In the Commission's view, art. 85(1) does not apply to clauses:

(1) restricting the use of technology or equipment provided by the contractor for the purposes of the agreement;

(2) forbidding the subcontractor to make such technology or equipment available to third parties; and

(3) imposing on the subcontractor the obligation to supply only to the contractor the goods, services or work resulting from the use of the technology or equipment.

These restrictions are permissible if this technology or equipment is necessary to enable the subcontractor, under reasonable conditions, to perform the agreements if:

(1) the performance of the agreement makes necessary the use by the subcontractor of industrial property rights, know-how, studies or plans prepared by the contractor, dies, patterns or tools and accessory equipment that are distinctively the contractor's;

(2) the subcontractor does not have at its disposal or have reasonable access to the technology and equipment concerned.[292]

---

[290] Commission notice of 18 December 1978 concerning its assessment of certain subcontracting agreements in relation to art. 85(1) of the EEC Treaty, OJ 1979 C1/2.

[291] Ibid., at para. 1.

[292] Ibid., at para. 2.

Other restrictions are referred to as being outside art. 85(1) in the notice, namely,

(1) secrecy obligations;

(2) post-term bans on use;

(3) non-exclusive grant-backs for improvements and new applications when they are incapable of being used independently of the contractor's secret know-how or patents;

(4) bans on the use of the contractor's trade marks or trade-names.[293]

¶524   Joint purchasing

Joint purchasing agreements may restrict competition where the participants represent a significant share of the market, thus affecting the competitive position of suppliers. In the *First Report on Competition Policy*, the Commission said:

'[P]urchasing groups established by commercial enterprises may be an appropriate means of allowing the retail trade access to foreign supply markets and thus overcoming difficulties inherent in their size, in the face of integrated forms of distribution with regard to obtaining advantageous prices and other purchasing conditions which can be passed on to the consumers. But the creation of powerful purchasing groups should be avoided, or at least be kept under control, in view of the repercussions they could have on the position of suppliers. The determination of the overall position on the market of the participating enterprises and the economic power of their aggregate requirements in relation to supply in the various markets concerned is therefore the main problem to be faced if effective competition within the Common Market is to be preserved.'[294]

The Commission has thus far been liberal in its individual decisions concerning joint purchasing agreements. In *SOCEMAS*[295] and *INTERGROUP*,[296] joint purchasing agreements were found not to fall under art. 85(1) on the ground that they did not have any perceptible effect on the position of suppliers because of the small share of the markets for products concerned accounted for by the participants.

In *National Sulphuric Acid Association*[297] the Commission found that a joint buying pool for the purchase of elemental sulphur, set up by an association

---

[293] Ibid., at para. 3.
[294] *First Report on Competition Policy*, point 40.
[295] *SOCEMAS*, JO 1968 L201/4.
[296] *INTERGROUP*, OJ 1975 L212/23.
[297] *National Sulphuric Acid Association*, OJ 1980 L260/24; see also Commission notice in *National Sulphuric Acid Association*, OJ 1988 C164/3 (proposing extension of exemption).

grouping all manufacturers of sulphuric acid in the UK, was restrictive of competition. The joint purchasing agreement was exempted, inter alia, because it allowed its members to achieve a considerable degree of flexibility in the distribution of different sorts of elemental sulphur (solid and liquid) and because it ensured a steady supply of these commodities in times of shortages. It should, however, be added that the Commission decided that it would not exempt any agreement whereby the members of the pool would be obliged to purchase their full requirement of elemental sulphur through the pool. The Commission was nevertheless prepared to accept an obligation on the members to purchase a minimum of 25 per cent of their total requirements exclusively from the pool.

In *Scottish Nuclear, Nuclear Energy Agreement*,[298] an agreement whereby two privatised competing electricity utilities companies were obliged to purchase by way of fixed quota and at the same price, *all* the electricity generated by the publicly owned Scottish Nuclear Ltd., was held to restrict the utility companies' source of supply. Since they could not deviate from the quotas, they could not gain any competitive advantage over one another. However, an exemption was granted as the agreements would gradually allow the utilities to compete in their relations with the customers. In addition, the quotas for the purchase of the nuclear electricity did not reflect the market share of the companies as each one was free to determine individually their output and meet their demand.[299]

¶525   Joint selling

Joint selling arrangements may take many forms. In their most common form, joint selling arrangements involve the grant to a common agent of the right (whether on an exclusive basis or not) to sell the products of the participants in specified areas. In order to ensure that all participants receive the same price per unit regardless of the actual selling prices obtained by the joint agent, joint selling arrangements often provide for equalisation systems.

Since joint selling arrangements have the effect of eliminating competition among the participants, they will fall under art. 85(1) unless the participants' market position is such that no appreciable restriction of competition occurs.[300]

---

[298] *Scottish Nuclear, Nuclear Energy Agreement*, OJ 1991 L178/31.

[299] In *Jahrhundertvertrag*, OJ 1990 C159/7, the Commission issued a notice stating that an agreement obliging electricity supply companies in Germany to purchase a minimum amount of German coal to generate electricity could, in principle, be exempted under art. 85(3) because of the accruing benefits to electricity consumers and the public insofar as the safeguard of supply was concerned. However, the Commission was not convinced that 'the amount of coal specified in the agreement was indispensable to the attainment of this objective and justify the elimination of competition to this extent'. It therefore proposed to impose a cap on the amount of coal that the electricity supply companies could be obliged to purchase.

[300] *First Report on Competition Policy*, point 11. As illustrated by *Wild-Leitz*, JO 1972 L61/27, a joint selling arrangement between firms which are not in competition with each other for the equipment covered by the agreement (various types of microscopes) does not fall under art. 85(1).

As illustrated by the individual decisions adopted thus far by the Commission, joint selling arrangements among firms accounting for a large share of the market concerned will normally be unlawful under art. 85(1) and will be unlikely to benefit from an exemption under art. 85(3).[301]

The same seems to be true for arrangements between potential entrants to the Community market when such parties could be expected to enter the market individually. In *Ansac*,[302] an agreement between six US producers of soda-ash to co-ordinate all their exports sales to the EC through Ansac and preventing them from selling individually (with the exception of sales to associated companies) was held to infringe art. 85(1). An exemption under art. 85(3) was refused as the Commission did not believe that the entry of Ansac into the Community market would enhance competition and improve the oligopolistic market structure. The granting of an exemption would allow Ansac to control and restrict the amount of US soda-ash produced for, imported into and sold within the Community as well as determining the price at which it would be sold. On the other hand, US producers acting independently could compete among themselves and improve competition in the EC soda-ash market.

Reversing a position that it had taken in a series of decisions in the late 1960s,[303] the Commission ruled in 1978 that joint selling arrangements between producers in a particular member state for the sale of the product concerned in that member state and outside the EC (but not to other EC member states) fall under the prohibition of art. 85(1).[304] Article 85(1) is also infringed if undertakings sell jointly to other member states.[305]

---

[301] See e.g. *Kali und Salz/Kali Chemie*, OJ 1974 L19/22 (reversed by the court); *Nederlandse Cement Handelsmaatschappij*, JO 1972 L22/16. However, the recent *UIP* decision, OJ 1989 L226/25 indicates that the Commission does not consider the size of the participants to be the determining factor. This decision concerned the creation of a joint venture (UIP) aiming at the distribution of the products of five large feature film production companies. The Commission considered that the agreements did not afford the parties the possibility of eliminating competition in respect of a substantial part of the products in question, having due regard to the structure of the industry, the nature of the product and the countervailing economic power of competitors. As the Commission found that the other requirements of art. 85(3) were met, it granted an exemption. See also *Arbed SA and Usinor Sacilor SA (Europrofil)*, OJ 1991 L281/17 where the Commission approved a joint selling agreement under art. 65 of the ECSC Treaty. Although the parties to the agreement accounted for 29.1 per cent of Community production, the Commission decided that the existence of other Community producers, including five with market shares ranging from 4.8 to 23.1 per cent of production, together with imports which accounted for 13.1 per cent of apparent consumption, would ensure the maintenance of effective competition.

[302] *Ansac*, OJ 1991 L152/54.

[303] *Supexil*, JO 1971 L10/12; *SEIFA*, JO 1969 L173/8; *CFA*, JO 1968 L274/29; *Cobelaz-Synthetic*, JO 1968 L276/13; *Cobelaz-Cokeries*, JO 1968 L276/19.

[304] *Centraal Stikstof Verkoopkantoor*, OJ 1978 L242/15. In *Laval-Stork*, OJ 1977 L215/11 and *VW/MAN*, OJ 1983 L376/11 and *De Laval-Stork*, OJ 1977 L215/11, the Commission had taken the view that arrangements which did not relate to sales to other EC member states did not affect trade between member states. Note, however, that joint selling arrangements restricted to sales outside the EC do not fall under art. 85 (*DFC* 4, OJ 1904 1 /3/2761).

[305] In *Floral*, OJ 1980 L39/51, the export of fertilisers to Germany from France by a company jointly owned by the three largest French producers was held to have infringed art. 85(1) in spite of the fact that the parties jointly controlled only two per cent of the German market. The Commission decided that the parties could still have offered substantial competition in a market that was tightly controlled by a small number of suppliers. In addition,

The Commission has displayed a more liberal attitude in cases involving joint selling arrangements between small firms. In the notice on co-operation, the Commission said that

'[v]ery often joint selling by small or medium-sized enterprises – even if they are competing with each other – does not entail an appreciable restraint of competition; it is, however, impossible to establish in this Notice any general criteria or to specify what enterprises may be deemed "small or medium-sized".'[306]

Joint selling arrangements between small companies may qualify for a negative clearance under art. 85(1).[307]

¶526 Miscellaneous types of co-operation agreements

Apart from subcontracting, joint purchasing and joint selling, the Commission has also given indications on the permissibility of miscellaneous co-operation agreements of a more limited scope, namely:

(1) joint after-sales service;

(2) joint trade marks;

(3) joint advertising;

(4) joint use of a quality label;

(5) joint use of production facilities;

(6) joint market research;

(7) co-operation in accounting matters;

(8) standard sales conditions;

(9) joint contracts for the common execution of orders.[308]

These agreements are considered at ¶527–¶535.

¶527 Joint after-sales service

The Commission stated in its notice on co-operation agreements that joint after-sales and repair service do not fall under art. 85(1) where the participating undertakings are not competitors with regard to the products or services covered by the agreement. The Commission also said that there is no restraint of competition if several manufacturers, without acting in concert, arrange for

each of the parties were capable of setting up an independent sales organisation. See also *Bayer/BP Chemicals*, OJ 1988 L150/33.
[306] Notice on agreements, decisions and concerted practices in the field of co-operation, JO 1968 C75/3, corrigendum JO 1968 C84/14, at para. II(6).
[307] See e.g. notice pursuant to art. 19(3) of Council Regulation 17/62, *Finnpap*, OJ 1989 C45/4.
[308] See e.g. *SAFCO*, JO 1972 L13/44; *Alliance de constructeurs français de machines-outils*, JO 1968 L201/11.

an after-sales and repair service for their products to be provided by an independent undertaking and this even when they are competitors.[309]

¶528   Joint trade marks

Agreements under which competing firms undertake to sell their products under a joint trade mark are considered by the Commission to involve a restriction of competition falling under art. 85(1). They may, however, qualify for an exemption under art. 85(3) especially in cases where they are entered into by small or medium-sized firms.[310]

¶529   Joint advertising

The Commission said in the notice on co-operation agreements that joint advertising does not fall under art. 85(1) where it is merely designed to draw the buyer's attention to the products of an industry or to a common brand, provided that the participants are not prevented from advertising individually.[311] In the *First Report on Competition Policy*, however, the Commission suggested that, even in that case, joint advertising may be under the ban of art. 85(1) in oligopolistic markets where advertising as a means of competition plays a decisive role.[312]

In *Milchförderungsfonds*, the Commission considered the activities of the Milk Promotion Fund, organised by German dairy producers to finance advertising campaigns, to infringe art. 85(1). The Commission stressed, inter alia, that the support for advertising applied to particular brands of semi-hard cheese in Italy strengthened the competitive position of the supported German exporters, without passing the resulting costs indirectly on to the selling price. However, the Commission stated that in the case of advertising that is not brand oriented, or in the case of advertising that stresses only the special features of the dairy products in question, the measures would not be deemed to restrict competition.[313]

¶530   Joint quality labels

Joint quality labels attesting that particular products meet minimum industry standards do not involve any restraint of competition falling under art. 85(1)

---

[309] Notice on agreements, decisions and concerted practices in the field of co-operation, JO 1968 C75/3, corrigendum JO 1968 C84/14, at para. II(6).

[310] See *Transocean Marine Paint Association*, OJ 1988 L351/40; OJ 1980 L39/73; OJ 1975 L286/24; JO 1967 L163/10 (joint trade mark arrangements between medium-sized producers established in different member states; for an initial period the Commission allowed them to operate a system of reciprocal compensatory commission paid on sales made on other producers' territories).

[311] Notice on agreements, decisions and concerted practices in the field of co-operation, JO 1968 C75/3, corrigendum JO 1968 C84/14, at para. II(8).

[312] *First Report on Competition Policy*, point 36

[313] *Milchförderungsfonds*, OJ 1985 L35/35.

when the label is available to all producers meeting objectively established quality standards and no restriction is imposed on the producers as regards their production, sale, price, and advertising activities.[314] The Commission also made it clear that the obligations to accept quality control of the products covered by the label, to issue uniform instructions for use, or to use the label for the products meeting the quality standards are similarly outside the scope of art. 85.

As illustrated by *NAVEWA-ANSEAU*,[315] however, any attempt to use certification procedures in order to interfere with parallel imports will give rise to a serious violation of art. 85(1).

¶531 Joint use of production facilities, storing and transport equipment

In the notice on co-operation agreements the Commission stated that agreements that have as their sole object the joint use of production facilities and storing and transport equipment do not restrict competition because they are confined to organisational and technical arrangements for the use of facilities. The Commission, however, added in a somewhat cryptic sentence that '[t]here may be a restraint of competition if the enterprises involved do not bear the cost of utilisation of equipment themselves'.[316]

¶532 Joint market research

The notice on co-operation agreements also makes it clear that art. 85(1) is not applicable to agreements having as their sole object:

(1) an exchange of opinion on experience provided that the scope of action of the undertakings is not limited or the market behaviour is not co-ordinated either expressly or through concerted practice;

(2) joint market research;

(3) the joint carrying out of comparative studies of undertakings or industries;

(4) the joint preparation of statistics and calculation models; the Commission, however, stated that calculation models containing specified rates of calculation are to be regarded as recommendations that may lead to restraints of competition.[317]

---

[314] Notice on agreements, decisions and concerted practices in the field of co-operation, JO 1968 C75/3, corrigendum JO 1968 C84/14, at para. II(8).
[315] *NAVEWA-ANSEAU*, OJ 1982 L167/39, amended OJ 1982 325/20, on appeal: *NV IAZ International Belgium & Ors v EC Commission* [1983] ECR 3369.
[316] Notice on agreements, decisions and concerted practices in the field of co-operation, JO 1968 C75/3, corrigendum OJ 1968 C84/14, at para. II(8).
[317] Ibid., at para. II(1)(d).

¶533   Co-operation in accounting, credit guarantee, debt collection and related matters

In the notice on co-operation agreements, the Commission also said that art. 85(1) is not applicable to agreements having as their sole object:

- co-operation in accounting matters;
- joint provision of credit guarantees;
- joint debt collecting associations;
- joint business in tax consultant organisations.[318]

¶534   Standardised forms

As stated in the notice on co-operation agreements, the use of standardised forms does not involve any violation of art. 85(1) as long as their use is not combined with any understanding or tacit agreement on uniform prices, rebates or conditions of sale.[319]

¶535   Setting up of joint ventures for the common execution of orders

In the notice on co-operation agreements, the Commission also said that art. 85(1) does not apply to the setting up of joint ventures for the common execution of orders where:

(1) the participating enterprises are not in competition with each other, or

(2) they cannot execute the specific order by themselves due to lack of experience or specialised knowledge, or for financial reasons. The Commission, however, added that there may be a restraint of competition if the participants undertake to work solely in the framework of the joint venture.[320]

---

[318] Ibid., at para. II(2).

[319] Ibid.

[320] Ibid., at para. II(5). These principles were recently confirmed in *Eurotunnel* [1989] 1 CEC 2,266; OJ 1988 L311/36.

6 Mergers and Acquisitions

INTRODUCTION

¶601 Overview

The EC Treaty, unlike the ECSC Treaty, does not contain any explicit provision on merger control. In the early years of EC antitrust enforcement, however, the Commission took the view that mergers and acquisitions, referred to as 'concentrations', fall under the prohibition of abuses of a dominant position laid down in art. 86.[1] This view, which gave rise to a major doctrinal controversy,[2] was finally upheld by the Court of Justice in the 1973 *Continental Can* judgment.[3] Subsequently, the Commission scrutinised a number of concentrations for their compatibility with art. 86 for the most part in a series of informal decisions reported in summary form in the annual reports on competition policy.

The 1966 Memorandum expressed the opinion that art. 85 does not apply to concentrations between undertakings.[4] The principle of the non-applicability of art. 85 to concentrations was subsequently most clearly reflected in the Commission's case law on partial concentrations. The court's judgment in *British American Tobacco Co Ltd and R J Reynolds Industries Inc v EC Commission*,[5] however, re-opened the debate and led the Commission to claim the power to investigate concentrations on the basis of art. 85.

Nevertheless, an approach based on art. 85 and 86 was bound to remain impractical in most instances. Indeed, art. 86 fails to cover the situation where market dominance is achieved as a result of the merger, whereas art. 85 is in principle only applicable in the context where the companies involved remain independent, i.e. a joint venture set-up as opposed to a merger. Furthermore,

---

[1] *Le Problème de la Concentration dans le Marché Commun*, hereinafter referred to as '1966 Memorandum', (1966) *Etudes CEE, Série concurrence*, No. 3.

[2] Numerous authors argued that art. 86 is solely concerned with exploitative abuses, not with practices which only restrict competition without actually exploiting customers. See, Joliet, *Monopolization and Abuse of Dominant Position: A Comparative Study of American and European Approaches to the Control of Economic Power* (1970).

[3] *Europemballage Corp and Continental Can Co Inc v EC Commission* [1973] ECR 215.

[4] 1966 Memorandum, Pt. III.

[5] *British American Tobacco Co Ltd and R J Reynolds Industries Inc v EC Commission* [1987] ECR 4487 (hereinafter referred to as *BAT and Reynolds v EC Commission*).

art. 85 and 86 do not provide for the prior control of mergers and the nullity sanction embodied in art. 85(2) might be difficult to apply after the merger has been consummated. The possibility of obtaining an exemption under art. 85(3) is also ill-suited, because mergers and acquisitions are usually carried out under great time constraints and require legal certainty, whereas the Commission's decision-making process under Regulation 17/62 has been notoriously slow and exemptions are only granted for a limited period of time, subject to renewal.

Hence, soon after the court's judgment in *Continental Can* in 1973, the Commission introduced its first proposal for a regulation on merger control. However, it would take 16 years before the Council finally concluded that the time was ripe for adopting such a regulation.[6] This happened on 21 December 1989, in the wake of uncertainties resulting from the court's ruling in *BAT and Reynolds v EC Commission* and the Community's 1992 programme calling for substantial restructuring of European industry. Under these circumstances, the Council saw fit to strike the right political compromises necessary to reach the consensus required. The regulation became effective on 21 September 1990.

ARTICLE 86 AND THE CONTROL OVER CONCENTRATIONS

¶602   View of the Court of Justice

The view that concentrations may fall under art. 86, which was expressed by the Commission in the 1966 Memorandum, was upheld by the Court of Justice in *Continental Can*. Even though the court annulled the decision of the Commission for not having sufficiently set out the facts and evaluations on which the market definition was based, it held:

'[Article 86] states a certain number of abusive practices which it prohibits. The list merely gives examples, not an exhaustive enumeration of the sort of abuses of a dominant position prohibited by the Treaty. As may further be seen from letters (c) and (d) of Article 86(2), the provision is not only aimed at practices which may cause damage to consumers directly, but also at those which are detrimental to them through their impact on an effective competition structure, such as is mentioned in Article 3(f) of the Treaty. Abuse may therefore occur if an undertaking in a dominant position strengthens such position in such a way that the degree of dominance reached substantially fetters competition, i.e. that only undertakings remain in the market whose behaviour depends on the dominant one.'[7]

---

[6] Council Regulation 4064/89 of 21 December 1989 on the control of concentrations between undertakings, OJ 1990 L257/13 (hereinafter referred to as the 'merger regulation' or the 'regulation').
[7] *Europemballage Corp and Continental Can Co Inc v EC Commission* [1973] ECR 215, at p. 245 (para. 26).

Thus the court confirmed that concentrations which strengthen an existing dominant position are caught by art. 86. The question whether a concentration which created a dominant position could be caught by art. 86 was not considered, and it was subsequently assumed by the Commission in its case law that it could not.

¶603   Decisions and settlements since Continental Can

The only formal decisions in which the Commission has considered the *Continental Can* doctrine are *Tetra Pak I*[8] and *Metaleurop*.[9] In the former case the Commission considered that Tetra Pak had abused its dominant position when it took over a small competitor, the Liquipak Group, and thereby acquired rights under an exclusive license for a new sterilising process for milk cartons. According to the Commission, the acquisition of the exclusive rights not only reinforced Tetra Pak's dominant position, but also prevented or delayed the entry of new competitors onto the market by denying them access to the crucial technology covered by the licence. Because the abuse consisted of the acquisition of the exclusive licence, the violation only lasted until Tetra Pak renounced all claims to the exclusivity. Tetra Pak was not required to sell the Liquipak Group. In *Metaleurop*[10] the Commission reviewed the merger of the metal activities of Preussag and Penarroya under art. 86. It concluded that neither company had a dominant position prior to the merger, thus excluding the application of the *Continental Can* doctrine. Surprisingly, the Commission still considered the effect of the merger on the structure of competition in the relevant markets, before concluding that there were no grounds for believing that the merger would have the effect of impeding effective competition contrary to the provisions of art. 86. The fact that the decision was taken two months before the entry into force of the merger regulation may account for this apparent willingness to consider whether the merger *created* a dominant position.

Despite the paucity of formal decisions applying the *Continental Can* doctrine, the Commission intervened informally in a number of cases either at the request of the parties contemplating a concentration or at the request of complainants. In some cases, particularly those involving large-scale concentrations, the Commission issued requests for information on its own initiative. The cases of concentrations dealt with informally by the Commission are briefly discussed in the annual reports on competition policy. The reports show that more than 30 cases of concentrations were examined by the

---

[8] *Tetra Pak I (BTG Licence)*, OJ 1988 L272/27.
[9] *Metaleurop*, OJ 1990 L179/41.
[10] Ibid.

Commission.[11] However, given what is already an abundance of case law under the merger regulation, these cases are largely of historical interest.

ARTICLE 85 AND THE CONTROL OVER CONCENTRATIONS

¶604 Cartels distinguished from concentrations

Following the 1966 Memorandum, it became a clearly established principle that art. 85 of the treaty does not apply to concentrations between undertakings. In the memorandum the Commission concluded that art. 85 does not apply to agreements 'whose purpose is the acquisition of total or partial ownership of enterprises or the reorganisation of the ownership of enterprises'. The Commission aimed at distinguishing cartels, which would be primarily controlled under art. 85, from concentrations, which could only be controlled under art. 86.

The distinction between concentration and cartel was blurred when two or more companies placed part of their business under joint control. Although such joint ventures were structural, the Commission was concerned that they could result in collusion among the parent companies in the businesses which they retained and between the parent companies and the joint venture. Thus the Commission adopted a strict approach and 'partial concentrations' were only considered to fall outside the scope of art. 85 where:

(1) the parent companies completely and irreversibly abandoned business in the area covered by the joint venture; and

(2) the transfer of assets did not, even indirectly, restrict competition in areas where the parent companies were still competitors (the so-called 'group-effect').[12]

Guidance on the application of these principles was provided in *SHV/ Chevron*.[13] In that case, the parent companies transferred their distribution networks and all related assets to a network of joint subsidiaries established for the distribution of specified petroleum products. The Commission held that this arrangement was a partial concentration, focusing on the fact that the parents

---

[11] See e.g. *Irish Distillers Group, Eighteenth Report on Competition Policy*, point 80; *British Airways/British Caledonian*, id., point 81; *Klöckner Stahl, Krupp Stahl and Thyssen Stahl*, id., point 88; *TWIL/Bridon, Nineteenth Report on Competition Policy*, point 64; *Ibercombe/Outokumpu*, id., point 65; *Plessey/GEC-Siemens*, id., point 66; *Rhône-Poulenc/Monsanto*, id., point 67; *Consolidated Gold Fields/Minorco*, id., point 68; *Carnaud-Metal Box, Pechiney-American Can*, id., point 69; *Stena-Houlder Offshore*, id., point 70, *Air France/Air Inter/UTA, XXth Report on Competition Policy*, point 116; *European/InterRent*, id., point 118 and *Enasa*, id., point 119.
[12] *Sixth Report on Competition Policy*, point 55.
[13] *SHV/Chevron*, OJ 1979 L38/14.

would no longer retail the relevant products separately and that the subsidiaries were formed for a period of 50 years which evidenced a permanent transfer of assets. Moreover, the agreements did not restrict competition in areas other than those covered by the joint subsidiaries. In *Montedison/ Hercules*[14] the Commission confirmed that a joint venture would only be characterised as a partial concentration if it were an enterprise entirely independent of the parent companies, with regard to both its management and ownership and its market position.[15]

¶605   Agreements producing structural changes

It was not until the court's judgment in *BAT and Reynolds v EC Commission*[16] that the principle that art. 85 does not apply to structural changes in the market was put into question. In the course of the court proceedings, both the intervening parties and the Commission relied on the 1966 Memorandum. The Commission argued that 'as a general rule Article 85(1) does not apply to agreements for the sale or purchase of shares'.[17] The applicants, on the other hand, submitted that, under the circumstances of the case, a per se rule excluding the application of art. 85 could not be relied upon.[18]

The case concerned the acquisition by the cigarette manufacturer Philip Morris of 24.9 per cent of the voting rights in its competitor Rothmans International from Rembrandt. The court held that art. 85 may apply to the acquisition of an equity interest in a competitor if the acquisition serves as an instrument for influencing the commercial conduct of the companies in question so as to restrict or distort competition on the market on which they carry on business.[19] The court explained this principle by stating:

'That will be true in particular where, by the acquisition of a shareholding or through subsidiary clauses in the agreement, the investing company obtains legal or *de facto* control of the commercial conduct of the other company or where the agreement provides for commercial co-operation between the companies or creates a structure likely to be used for such co-operation.

That may also be the case where the agreement gives the investing company the possibility of reinforcing its position at a later stage and taking effective control of the other company. Account must be taken not only of the immediate effects of the agreement but also of its potential effects and of the possibility that the agreement may be part of a long-term plan.

---

[14] *Seventeenth Report on Competition Policy*, point 69.
[15] For further guidance, see also *Kaiser/Estel, Ninth Report on Competition Policy*, point 131; *De Laval-Stork*, OJ 1977 L215/11 and *Mecaniver-PPG*, OJ 1985 L35/54.
[16] *BAT and Reynolds v EC Commission* [1987] ECR 4487.
[17] *Fourteenth Report on Competition Policy*, point 99.
[18] *BAT and Reynolds v EC Commission* [1987] ECR 4487, at p. 4509.
[19] Id., at p. 4577 (para. 37).

Finally, every agreement must be assessed in its economic context and in particular in the light of the situation on the relevant market. Moreover, where the companies concerned are multinational corporations which carry on business on a world-wide scale, their relationships outside the Community cannot be ignored. It is necessary in particular to consider the possibility that the agreement in question may be part of a policy of global co-operation between the companies which are party to it.'[20]

The reference by the court to the possible application of art. 85(1) to an investment whereby the 'investing company obtains legal or *de facto* control', and other similar references,[21] gave rise to particular controversy, as they could be interpreted as permitting the use of art. 85 to control concentrations.[22] However, two points should be made in this regard.

First, on the facts, the court found that Rembrandt would retain sole control of Rothmans International and, furthermore, that there was no reason to believe that there would be collusion between Philip Morris and Rothmans International. Consequently, the court did not have to consider what aspects of a concentration (necessarily involving the acquisition of control) would be subject to review under art. 85. Specifically, the question was not addressed as to whether art. 85 could only be applied to the risk of collusion between two companies which remain independent entities following a change of control (i.e., the buyer and the seller of the shares), or whether it could also be used to control the effect on the structure of competition in the market of a concentration between the buyer of shares and the company in which the shares were bought (i.e., the buyer and the target). Given this, it is submitted that the judgment does not recognise art. 85 as an instrument of merger control.

Secondly, following the entry into force of the merger regulation, the significance of the controversy over the application of this judgment to concentrations is much reduced. An operation giving rise to a change in control will now constitute a concentration subject to review in accordance with the jurisdictional rules of the merger regulation. As was accepted under the partial concentration case law, the exception will be the acquisition of joint control giving rise to co-ordination among the parties, which will not constitute a concentration and will be subject to review under art. 85.[23]

The judgment is of greatest value for what it says on the application of art. 85

---

[20] Id., at p. 4577 (para. 38–40).
[21] See the references to 'taking effective control' (e.g., at p. 4577 at para. 39) and 'intended to result in a take over' (at p. 4578 at para. 45).
[22] Indeed, it would appear that in *GEC-Siemens/Plessey*, OJ 1990 C239/2, the Commission applied art. 85(1) to parts of the transaction which were concentrative, for example Siemens' acquisition of 100 per cent of Plessey's traffic control system. These should be distinguished from other parts of the transaction which concerned the acquisition by GEC and Siemens of parts of Plessey which would be run jointly by the acquirors. As these gave rise to a risk of co-ordination between GEC and Siemens, they would appear not to have been concentrative.
[23] See ¶604.

¶605

to acquisitions which do not give rise to a change in control but which provide for commercial co-operation or create a structure likely to be used for such co-operation. This is discussed further below.

MINORITY SHAREHOLDINGS UNDER ARTICLES 85 AND 86

¶606 Acquisitions of minority shareholdings

The discussion thus far has concentrated on the application of art. 85 and 86 to operations involving an acquisition of control. However, as confirmed by the Court of Justice in *BAT and Reynolds v EC Commission*,[24] art. 85 and 86 may apply to share acquisitions which do not give the acquiror of the shares either sole or joint control of the company in which the shares are purchased (the target).[25] In brief, this may be the case if the target is a competitor of the acquiror, if there are sufficient grounds to believe that the acquisition will lead to the co-ordination of the market behaviour of the acquiror and the target and, for the purposes of art. 86, if there is a pre-existing dominant position.[26]

¶607 Acquisition of a minority stake by a dominant purchaser

The most recent case on the acquisition of a minority shareholding is the Commission's decision in *Gillette*.[27] In the decision the Commission considered the acquisition by Gillette, which held a dominant position in the wet-shaving products market, of a 22 per cent non-voting equity holding in Eemland, the owner in the EC and the US of Wilkinson Sword, arguably Gillette's strongest competitor. Gillette had bought outright the Wilkinson Sword business in the rest of the world from Eemland.[28] In its legal assessment, the Commission stressed the special responsibility incumbent on Gillette as a dominant company not to allow its conduct to impair genuine undistorted competition. Although the shareholding gave Gillette no board representation, no votes and no right of representation at the shareholders' meetings and no access to

---

[24] *BAT and Reynolds v EC Commission* [1987] ECR 4487, at p. 4577 (para. 38), regarding art. 85, and p. 4584 (para. 65), regarding art. 86.

[25] Even in the context of a change of control, art. 85 and 86 could apply to the retention of a minority stake by a vendor company if this stake gives rise to a risk of co-ordination of market conduct between the vendor company and the purchaser/target following the change of control. The Commission considered whether such a risk existed in *Mecaniver-PPG*, OJ 1985 L35/54, but concluded that it did not.

[26] In *BAT and Reynolds v EC Commission* it was the sale of a minority stake by an allegedly *dominant vendor* (Rothmans/Rembrandt) to a competitor (Philip Morris) which was argued by the complainants to constitute an abuse. In *Warner-Lambert/Gillette*, OJ 1993 L116/21, it was the purchase of a minority stake by a *dominant purchaser* (Gillette) which was held by the Commission to constitute an abuse.

[27] *Warner-Lambert/Gillette*, OJ 1993 L116/21.

[28] Following the intervention of the US antitrust authorities, Gillette had been obliged to abandon the planned acquisition of the US business of Wilkinson Sword.

internal information, the Commission none the less found that Gillette would be able by other means to exercise some influence over Eemland's commercial conduct and to weaken the competitive position of Eemland. This was sufficient to result in the finding of an infringement of art. 86. In particular this was achieved by the important pre-emption and conversion rights enjoyed by Gillette, by Gillette's status as the largest creditor of Eemland and by the fact that Gillette had significantly weakened Eemland by acquiring the Wilkinson Sword businesses outside of the EC and the USA.

As for art. 85, the Commission admitted that the acquisition of the equity interest as such did not infringe art. 85. However, the trade mark separation agreement between Eemland and Gillette – whereby Eemland agreed not knowingly to supply products under the Wilkinson Sword trade mark for sale outside of the EC and Gillette agreed not knowingly to supply products under the same trade mark for sale within the EC – was held liable to result in co-ordination between Eemland and Gillette in violation of art. 85. In addition, the purchase by Gillette of products from Eemland for sale outside the EC was also held liable to result in co-ordination between Eemland and Gillette in violation of art. 85.

There are many similarities between the facts of the *Gillette* decision and the judgment in *BAT and Reynolds v EC Commission*: in both cases the shareholding was less than 25 per cent, the investor had no board representation and Chinese walls had been erected to prevent the flow of confidential information. Indeed, in one important respect Gillette's powers were more restricted than those of Philip Morris because no voting rights attached to Gillette's shareholding and it had no right of representation at the shareholders' meeting. Although the markets were highly concentrated in both cases, Gillette – unlike Philip Morris – was dominant.[29] The emphasis placed by the Commission on the special responsibility which this placed on Gillette suggests that the effects of the acquisition of a minority stake by a dominant company may be viewed more strictly under art. 86 than under art. 85. It is noteworthy that in the *Gillette* decision the Commission only found the ancillary trade mark and supply agreements to violate art. 85. The ability of Gillette, arising from the rights it acquired in Eemland, to exercise some influence over the conduct of Eemland was only found to be an infringement of art. 86.[30]

---

[29] In *Gillette* the Commission attempts to distinguish the facts of the case from those of *BAT and Reynolds v EC Commission* by stressing that in the latter case it was the target (Rothmans) and not the acquiror (Philip Morris) which was said to be dominant.

[30] The Court of Justice in *BAT and Reynolds v EC Commission* did not expressly consider whether the acquisition of minority stakes should be viewed more strictly under art. 86 than under art. 85. Instead, the court concluded that, because the facts did not reveal a violation of art. 85, the submission based on art. 86 should also be rejected ([1987] ECR 4487 at p. 4584, para. 65).

¶608   How to determine if a minority stake infringes art. 85 or 86

A comparison of the *Gillette* decision[31] and the judgment in *BAT and Reynolds v EC Commission*[32] reveals to what extent the applicability of art. 85 and 86 to minority shareholdings depends on the precise context of the case. However, from the case law the following factors can be identified as important in this determination:

(1) The structure of the market will be a highly relevant factor. In *BAT and Reynolds v EC Commission* the court stressed that in a concentrated market with high barriers to entry the risk of collusion between competitors through the acquisition of a minority stake must be treated very seriously.[33] As discussed above, if the acquiror is a dominant company, there is a special responsibility on the acquiror not to weaken competition on the market in which it is dominant. On the other hand, in markets in which there is a low level of concentration and the acquiror has a low market share, the risk of an infringement must presumably be judged to be considerably lower.

(2) Depending on the jurisdiction, a certain level of shareholding may give rise to a right to block certain important corporate decisions, which will give a minority shareholder an important say in the affairs of the company in which it holds the shares. In *Hudson's Bay II*,[34] the Commission considered that the purchase of a 35 per cent shareholding by Danish Fur Sales (DPA) in its largest competitor, Hudson's Bay and Annings, would give DPA substantial power in deciding the future conduct of Hudson's Bay, thereby considerably reducing competition between them. On the other hand, according to the judgment in *BAT and Reynolds v EC Commission* a mere hypothetical ability to block certain special resolutions will not give rise to a risk of co-ordination.[35] At the opposite extreme, the *Gillette* decision reveals that even an acquisition which gives no voting rights will not ensure compatibility with art. 86.[36]

(3) Representation on the board of the target will lead to the disclosure of market information concerning the target and the co-ordination of

---

[31] *Warner-Lambert/Gillette*, OJ 1993 L116/21.
[32] *BAT and Reynolds v EC Commission* [1987] ECR 4487.
[33] Id., at p. 4578 (para. 43–45).
[34] Commission Press Release IP(88)810 of 15 December 1988.
[35] *BAT and Reynolds v EC Commission* [1987] ECR 4487, at p. 4579 (para. 49).
[36] *Warner-Lambert/Gillette*, OJ 1993 L116/21, at p. 28 (para. 25).

competitive behaviour. It is notable that in *BAT and Reynolds v EC Commission* the parties had erected Chinese walls between Philip Morris (the acquiror) and Rothmans International (the target). There was no Philip Morris representation on the board of Rothmans International and an undertaking was given that no information concerning Rothmans would be disclosed to Philip Morris which might influence the latter's commercial conduct on the market.[37] In contrast, the erection of Chinese walls did not prevent the finding of an abuse in *Gillette*.[38]

(4) The ability through the operation of pre-emption, option and conversion rights to prevent a third party competitor from acquiring control over the target was seen as one of the means by which Gillette weakened competition in the market for wet-shaving products in violation of art. 86.[39] However, under the art. 85 analysis contained in *BAT and Reynolds v EC Commission* it was stated that such a right 'cannot in itself amount to a restriction of competition'.[40]

(5) The influence of the minority shareholder may be increased significantly if it is also a major creditor of the target.[41]

(6) A mere limited participation in the profits of the target will not give rise to a reduction in competition with the target. It was stressed in *BAT and Reynolds v EC Commission* that this participation would not prevent Philip Morris from competing fully with Rothmans International. Indeed, since Philip Morris' primary interest was in the success of Philip Morris, it retained a considerable incentive to resist any growth in market share by Rothmans at Philip Morris' expense.[42]

(7) Even if the rights attaching to the shareholding itself do not infringe art. 85, ancillary agreements (such as supply agreements, intellectual property agreements, and technical support agreements) may be deemed to provide an instrument for co-ordination.[43]

---

[37] Id., at p. 4570 (para. 9) and at pp. 4578–4579 (para. 46 and 47).
[38] *Warner-Lambert/Gillette*, OJ 1993 L116/21, at p. 28 (para. 25).
[39] *Warner-Lambert/Gillette*, OJ 1993 L116/21, at p. 28 (para. 26–27).
[40] Id., at p. 4581 (para. 56). However, Philip Morris was obliged to notify the Commission within 48 hours of any increase in its shareholding or voting rights so that the Commission could consider the compatibility of such operation with the EC competition rules.
[41] *Warner-Lambert/Gillette*, OJ 1993 L116/21, at p. 28 (para. 25).
[42] *BAT and Reynolds v EC Commission* [1987] ECR 448/ at p. 4580 (para. 50).
[43] *Warner-Lambert/Gillette*, OJ 1993 L116/21, at pp. 29–30 (para. 33–40).

¶609   Consequences of the finding of an infringement

If the acquisition of a minority stake is held to violate art. 86, the acquiror may be required to dispose of the stake. In *Warner-Lambert/Gillette*,[44] the Commission ordered Gillette to dispose of its equity interest in Eemland and its interest as a creditor of Eemland. Furthermore, taking into account both the risk of co-ordination which the Commission found in the markets bordering the EC and the need to strengthen Eemland as a competitive force, Gillette had to re-assign to Eemland the Wilkinson Sword businesses in all the countries neighbouring the EC.

If art. 85(1) is infringed by the acquisition of a minority stake, it may be very difficult to justify an exemption under art. 85(3) on the grounds of compensating benefits. A minority stake which falls short of control is unlikely to bring efficiency benefits through the integration of two companies, and may well be viewed as a naked cartel. In cases in which the acquiror and the target would not together be judged to hold a dominant position, it may be easier to defend the operation under the EC competition rules if the acquiror increases its level of shareholding and rights so as to give rise to a joint venture or an acquisition.

EC REGULATION ON THE CONTROL OF CONCENTRATIONS

¶610   Introduction

Regulation 4064/89 on the control of concentrations between undertakings (the 'merger regulation')[45] was adopted by the Council on 21 December 1989 and became effective on 21 September 1990. The Commission has also adopted a regulation containing provisions concerning notifications, time-limits, hearings and other procedural matters.[46]

The merger regulation applies to concentrations with a Community dimension. These must be notified to the Commission before they are put into effect. There is a special form, Form CO,[47] on which notifications must be made. Notifications are dealt with by part of the Commission specially constituted particularly for that purpose, the Merger Task Force.

The Commission has also adopted two notices dealing with the distinction

---

[44] Ibid., at p. 31.
[45] OJ 1990 L257/13.
[46] Commission Regulation 2367/90 of 25 July 1990 on the notifications, time-limits and hearings provided for in Council Regulation 4064/89 on the control of concentrations between undertakings, OJ 1990 L219/5 (hereinafter referred to as the 'implementing regulation').
[47] Form CO appears in Annex 1 to Regulation 2367/90, as amended by Regulation 3666/93, OJ 1993 L336/1.

between co-operative and concentrative operations[48] and ancillary restrictions.[49]

The analysis of the merger regulation in this chapter addresses the following key points:

- whether or not an operation has a Community dimension (¶611–¶616);

- whether or not an operation is a concentration (¶617–¶628);

- the interface between national and Community control of concentrations (¶629–¶634);

- the criteria by which concentrations will be assessed (¶635–¶641);

- the treatment of ancillary restrictions (¶642, ¶643);

- the notification and other procedural aspects (¶644–¶655);

- conditions and undertakings to which a clearance may be subject (¶656, ¶657).

¶611   Community dimension: introduction

Thresholds

In order to secure the necessary backing from European industry, the Commission initially aimed at establishing the so-called 'one-stop shop principle'. In the end, however, the member states with an active merger control enforcement policy managed to keep their antitrust authorities in the picture.

Germany and the UK, each having a well developed system of merger control, advocated a high turnover threshold as a basis for the Community's exclusive jurisdiction over mergers with a so-called 'Community dimension'. In contrast, smaller member states like Italy and the Netherlands, which at the time did not have a merger control system of their own, preferred the turnover threshold to be low, so that the EC Commission would in effect take care of their merger control.

By way of compromise, relatively high turnover thresholds have been provided for in the regulation. They were reviewed at the end of 1993[50] at which

---

[48] Commission notice regarding the concentrative and co-operative operations under Council Regulation 4064/89 of 21 December 1989 on the control of concentrations between undertakings, OJ 1990 C203/10 (hereinafter referred to as the 'concentrative/co-operative notice').

[49] Commission notice regarding restrictions ancillary to concentrations, OJ 1990 C203/5 (hereinafter referred to as the 'notice on ancillary restrictions').

[50] Regulation 4064/89, art. 1(3). In the meantime, an independent study was commissioned to determine how many concentrations occurred that might affect trade between member states and created or strengthened a dominant position, and how many of those may not have been subject to regulatory control. The Commission had indicated that it considered that the thresholds should be reduced; see notes on Regulation 4064/89, *Bulletin of the European Communities* annex to supplement 2/90, and *Nineteenth Report on Competition Policy*, point 16, where the figure of ECU 2,000m for the overall threshold was suggested. However, consultations with EC industry

time the Council decided to retain the existing thresholds at least until the end of 1996. When the Council reviews the thresholds again at that time, it will act by qualified majority.

Community dimension

Currently, an operation has a Community dimension under the merger regulation, where the total worldwide turnover of the companies concerned exceeds ECU 5,000m, each of at least two of them has an EC turnover of ECU 250m, and provided that each of them does not achieve more than two thirds of its turnover in one and the same member state. Thus, there are three thresholds that a transaction must satisfy in order to come within the regulation. These are basically designed to catch large transactions, involving at least two companies with a reasonably large presence in the EC, the effects of which are not predominantly felt in one member state. At the level at which the thresholds are currently set, it was forecast that there would be about 50 transactions falling within the regulation each year.[51] Right on target, on 1 January 1994, there had been 190 notifications. Out of these, only six operations were found not to have a Community dimension.[52] This is largely because the issue tends to be dealt with during informal contact with the Task Force at the pre-notification stage, even when presented as a hypothetical case by lawyers who do not reveal the identity of their client.[53]

Protection of national interests

At the insistence of the German authorities, art. 9, known as the 'German clause' was introduced in the merger regulation, authorising the Commission to refer a case back to the relevant national authorities even though it has a Community dimension, provided there is a distinct regional impact. This compromise was necessary to allay the fears of the Bundeskartellamt that the Community's merger policy would not be as strict as Germany's enforcement of its own merger control laws.

In addition to the 'German' clause, the regulation in art. 21(3) provides for a

---

revealed broad satisfaction with the status quo, and the Commission's plan faced strong opposition from France, Germany and the UK. The Commission will review the thresholds again before the end of 1996.

[51] *Nineteenth Report on Competition Policy*, point 16. Increased to 60 in *XXth Report on Competition Policy*, point 28.

[52] *Arjomari-Prioux SA/Wiggins Teape Appleton plc*, M025, 1990; *Cereol/Continentale*, M156, 1991 (eventually excluding CAP export subsidies from the turnover calculation); *Solvay-Laporte/Interox*, M197, 1992; *Eurocard/Eurocheque–Europay*, M241, 1992 (in respect of which the notice of decision originally published stated that the regulation was inapplicable because there was no concentration. A later corrigendum stated that in fact the regulation was inapplicable because there was no Community dimension); *Alcatel/STC*, M366, 1993; and *British Telecom/MCI*, M353, 1993 (in relation to one part of the operation).

[53] See Overbury, 'Politics or Policy? The Demystification of EC Merger Control', *Annual proceedings of the Fordham Corporate Law Institute, International Anti-trust Law & Policy*, 1993, at p. 557. See also *XXth Report on Competition Policy*, points 28 and 29; and Regulation 2367/90, recital 8 of the preamble. 399 case numbers had been issued as at 1 January 1993, whilst only 190 formal notifications had been made.

second exception allowing the application of member state law to concentrations with a Community dimension. This exception applies whenever legitimate interests are at stake, i.e. public security, plurality of the media, and prudential rules.

It is also interesting to note that, in accordance with art. 22(3)–(5) of the regulation, the Commission may apply the provisions of the regulation to concentrations not having a Community dimension at the request of a member state. This article, known as the 'Dutch clause', was introduced into the regulation as a result of the concerns of certain member states, namely Belgium, Denmark, Greece, Italy, Luxembourg and the Netherlands, that their less developed merger enforcement systems would not be able to cope with certain concentrations albeit not of a Community dimension. For an example of its application, see *British Airways/Dan Air*, M278, 1992.

Analysis of notified operations

Determining whether or not an operation has a Community dimension is a two-stage analysis, involving first the identification of the undertakings concerned[54] and second, the calculation of their turnovers. In addition, there are special rules covering staged acquisitions, geographical allocation of turnover and banks and insurance undertakings. These, and other issues, are discussed in the following paragraphs, whereas the exceptions to the 'one-stop shop principle', i.e. the so-called 'German' and 'Dutch' clauses and the legitimate interests provision, are dealt with at ¶629–¶633. Suffice it to say here that even in cases that fall squarely within the scope of the regulation, the companies concerned cannot afford to ignore the national competition authorities. Indeed, in view of the existence of the German clause, national authorities are entitled to request the kind of information they need to have in order to determine whether they find themselves in a situation where they could ask the Commission to refer the case back to them.

EEA

Following the entry into force of the EEA, almost identical rules apply in that jurisdiction. Article 57 of the EEA agreement provides that concentrations having a Community or EFTA dimension and which create or strengthen a dominant position as a result of which effective competition would be significantly impeded within the EC/EFTA or a substantial part of it, are prohibited. Subject to a limited number of modifications, the merger control

---

[54] Many Commission decisions do not make explicit the basis on which the turnovers of certain companies are taken into consideration, i.e. whether it is because they are undertakings concerned, or as a result of the operation of Regulation 4064/89, art. 5(4), which provides for the consolidation of group turnover. In many cases this may be unnecessary if it is clear that there will be a Community dimension, but in other cases it may be critical to determining whether or not the operation has a Community dimension.

¶611

regulation will be applied in the EFTA countries in accordance with art. 7 and 60 and Annex XIV of the EEA agreement.

¶612   Thresholds indicating Community dimension

The merger regulation applies to concentrations that have a Community dimension.[55] A concentration has a Community dimension where :

- the combined aggregate worldwide turnover of all the undertakings concerned is more than ECU 5,000m; and

- the aggregate Community-wide turnover of at least two of the undertakings concerned is more than ECU 250m; unless

- each of the undertakings concerned achieves more than two-thirds of its aggregate Community-wide turnover in one and the same member state.[56]

¶613   Application of the thresholds in practice

In applying the thresholds, general questions may arise concerning the undertakings to be included and the calculation and allocation of turnover, and these are discussed more fully below. However, two particular issues may arise, which are worthy of note at this stage.

First, in the case of the second threshold, there must be at least two undertakings concerned with EC turnover in excess of ECU 250m. This makes it of particular importance that it is possible to identify which are the two undertakings concerned, an exercise which may sometimes lead to curious results (see, for example, the discussion at ¶614(5) below concerning the Commission's practice of 'lifting the veil'). Evidently, the Commission's approach has been conditioned by a desire to prevent circumvention of the regulation by the formal restructuring of an operation.

Second, in the case of the third threshold, it appears to be the Commission's view that all undertakings concerned (not simply those with EC turnovers over ECU 250m) are subject to the two-thirds rule. Thus a merger, in which all the undertakings concerned had a combined worldwide turnover in excess of ECU 5,000m, between two companies each with an EC turnover over ECU 250m achieved entirely in, for example, Germany, could theoretically fall within the regulation should there happen to be another undertaking concerned which did not achieve more than two-thirds of its EC turnover in Germany, no matter how small that third undertaking's EC turnover might be.[57] It should be noted

---

[55] Pursuant to art. 22, the regulation may apply, at the request of a member state, to concentrations which do not have a Community dimension. It may be disapplied to concentrations with a Community dimension pursuant to Regulation 4064/89, art. 9 or 21. See ¶629–¶634 below.

[56] Regulation 4064/89, art. 1(2).

[57] See Overbury, 'Politics or Policy? The Demystification of EC Merger Control', *Annual proceedings of the Fordham Corporate Law Institute, International Anti-trust Law & Policy*, 1993, at p. 557.

that the third undertaking might be, for example, a Japanese or American company, with a small turnover in, for example, the UK. In such a case, the Commission has rejected the application of a de minimis rule.[58] Although such a transaction could eventually be referred to the German competition authority,[59] it would apparently first have to be notified to the Commission.

¶614   Undertakings concerned

The merger regulation contains no definition of an undertaking concerned, and there would appear to be no theoretical limit to the number of undertakings that might be concerned by a transaction.[60] In practice, however, the undertakings concerned are likely to be parties to the operation, and not simply concerned in the wider sense, as a result, for example, of having provided finance for an acquisition.[61]

Furthermore, art. 1 of the regulation is based on the assumption that the combination of resources in terms of turnover reflects the economic importance of an operation. As a general principle, therefore, the undertakings concerned would appear to be those that are concentrating or combining their resources, i.e. (in the case of an acquisition) the acquiring undertaking and the undertaking that is acquired. The vendor would not generally appear to be an undertaking concerned.[62] It follows that, for the purposes of satisfying the second threshold, the two undertakings concerned with Community turnovers in excess of ECU 250m should generally each be part of a different group prior to the operation.[63]

---

[58] Regulation 4064/89, recital 11 of the preamble, refers to '*substantial* operations in at least one other Member State'. Furthermore, the Commission has developed a de minimis rule (not provided for in Regulation 4064/89) for determining the scope of the regulation in the context of whether an operation is concentrative or co-operative (discussed below).

[59] Regulation 4064/89, art. 9.

[60] See e.g. *Kelt/American Express*, M116, 1991, where it appears that at least eight undertakings were concerned, referred to by Kleeman, (1991) *Fordham Corporate Law Institute*.

[61] See *CCIE/GTE*, M258, 1992, in which Siemens provided finance for the main purchase of IL by CCIE's subsidiary, EDIL, from GTE. In addition, Siemens' subsidiary, Osram, acquired NAL, which was spun-off by GTE in a 'mutually dependent' transaction. EDIL and Osram also concluded a series of temporary intellectual property and supply agreements. However, neither Siemens nor Osram were cited as undertakings concerned.

[62] See Kleeman, (1991) *Fordham Corporate Law Institute*; and *XXIst Report on Competition Policy for 1991*, Annex III, p. 351.

[63] In the Commission's decisions to date, reference has generally been made, when referring to two companies that have an EC turnover in excess of ECU 250m, to two companies which, prior to the operation, were part of different groups (for the exception, see *ASKO/Jacobs/ADIA*, M082, 1991, discussed below). Although the Commission's practice is inconsistent, it seems that the undertaking concerned is generally the acquiror rather than its parent or another company in the same group, with the parent's turnover being included as a result of the application of Regulation 4064/89, art. 5(4). See e.g., *Torras/Sarrio*, M166, 1992; and *Ifinit/EXOR*, M187, 1992 (but compare the position of CCIEL in *CCIE/GTE*, M258, 1992). The parent or other companies may, however, be undertakings concerned if they are parties to the agreement (where, e.g., they give warranties). In most cases the point should be academic, since the parent's turnover will in any event be included as a result of art. 5(4).

(1) Mergers and de-mergers

In a merger, both merging companies will be undertakings concerned. Thus if A merges with B, both A and B will be undertakings concerned.[64]

In the case of de-mergers, it is probably correct to view the acquisition of each part of the de-mergered entity by a third party as a separate operation, with the acquiring company and the acquired assets being the undertakings concerned.[65] However, the Commission has stated that where there are 'exogenous constraints' imposed on the parties or products, conferring a 'unity of character' on the division, then it may be correct to view the de-merger as one operation. In such a case, each acquiror and each bundle of assets acquired, as well as the undertaking being divided, may be considered as undertakings concerned.[66]

(2) Acquisitions, joint bids and asset swaps

In an acquisition, the acquiror of a sole controlling interest and the acquired company or assets will be undertakings concerned. Thus if company A sells its sole controlling interest in its subsidiary or assets B to company C, B and C will be undertakings concerned.

In the case of a joint bid, where two companies bid together for a target whose assets they intend to divide between themselves immediately in the event of a successful bid, then the transaction may be viewed as two separate operations. In each operation, the bidder and the bundle of assets to be acquired may be treated as undertakings concerned.

In the case of asset swaps, for example where group AB swaps its B assets for group XY's Y assets, then the transaction may be viewed as two separate acquisitions, provided that after the operation each group is entirely dissociated from the assets with which it parted. In such a case, in each operation, the acquiring group and the assets acquired will be the undertakings concerned.

(3) Joint ventures

The Commission's view is apparently that where a joint venture arises, each of the joint controlling parents of the joint venture, as well as the venture itself,

---

[64] For cases involving mergers see e.g., *Renault/Volvo*, M004, 1990 (for the creation of a 'single economic entity'); *Groupe AG/Amev*, M018, 1990 (merger from an economic point of view); *Kyowa/Saitama Banks*, M069, 1991; *Bankamerica/Security Pacific*, M137, 1991; *Eurocom/RSCG*, M147, 1991; *KNP/Bührmann–Tetterode/VRG*, M291, 1992; and *JCSAT/SAJAC*, M346, 1993.

[65] See e.g., *Solvay-Laporte/Interox*, M197, 1991, where one part of the de-merger met the thresholds, but the other did not. See also *CCIE/GTE*, M258, 1992, where Osram's acquisition of NAL appears not to have been notified (even though the two transactions were mutually dependent as to completion), presumably because it did not meet the thresholds. See also the reference to a 'single economic unit' in *SITA-RPC/SCORI*, M295, 1993.

[66] See e.g. *Campsa*, M138, 1991, where the Commission's view was apparently that prohibition of one part of the transaction would effectively have led to prohibition of the whole de-merger, and that it was more efficient for there to be a joint notification.

¶614

will be undertakings concerned. Companies that have an interest in the venture, but do not control or jointly control it, will not normally be undertakings concerned (nor should they generally have their turnover included in the calculation – see ¶615 below concerning the calculation of turnover). Thus if A and B together acquire a sole controlling interest in C, then A, B and C will be undertakings concerned.[67] As a result, if any two of A, B and C have Community turnovers in excess of ECU 250m, then the second threshold will be satisfied.[68]

This appears to be the Commission's view, regardless of how many joint controlling parents there are[69] or of how the joint venture arises, i.e. including situations where the parents contribute assets to a newly created company,[70] where one parent carves a joint controlling interest out of the other parent's pre-existing sole controlling interest,[71] where a new parent steps into the shoes of a departing joint venture partner,[72] or where a non-controlling interest crystallises[73] into a controlling interest.[74]

---

[67] See e.g. *Thomas Cook/LTU/West LB*, M229, 1992; *Del Monte/Royal Foods/Anglo-American*, M277, 1992; and *SITA-RPC/SCORI*, M295, 1993.

[68] This may result in relatively unimportant joint ventures having a Community dimension. If C has a Community-wide turnover of less than ECU 250m, the operation will nevertheless satisfy the second threshold where both A and B have a Community-wide turnover in excess of ECU 250m. See the views expressed by Kleeman, (1991) *Fordham Corporate Law Institute*; and *XXIst Report on Competition Policy for 1991*, Annex III, at p. 351. This was precisely the situation in *Aérospatiale-Alenia/de Havilland*, OJ 1991 L334/42, at p. 43. In such a case, the Commission may reduce the burden of the notification by granting 'waivers' from the information required on the basis of Regulation 2367/90 of 25 July 1990 on the notifications, time-limits and hearings provided for in Council Regulation 4064/89 on the control of concentrations between undertakings, OJ 1990 L219/5, art. 4(3).

[69] See *Drager/IBM/HMP*, M101, 1991 (three); *Philips/Thomson/Sagem*, M293, 1992 (three); *TNT/Canada Post, DBP Postdienst, La Poste, PTT Post and Sweden Post*, M102, 1991 (six); *Kelt/American Express*, M116, 1991 (eight); *Sunrise*, M176, 1991 (five); *Eureko*, M207, 1992 (four); *CEA Industrie/France Telecom/Finmeccanica/SGS-Thomson*, M216, 1993 (three); and *JCSAT/SAJAC*, M346, 1993 (four). It appears that an undertaking which could exercise joint control, though may never do so, may be an undertaking concerned. See *Avesta/British Steel/NCC*, M239, 1992; and *Philips/Thomson/Sagem*, M293, 1992.

[70] *Varta/Bosch*, OJ 1991 L320/26, cited by the Commission in *XXIst Report on Competition Policy for 1991*, Annex III, at p. 351; *Sanofi/Sterling Drug*, M072, 1991; *Ericsson/Kolbe*, M133, 1991; *Ericsson/Ascom*, M236, 1992. In *Avesta/British Steel/NCC*, M239, 1992, it is implied that assets or undertakings transferred to a newly created joint venture may also be undertakings concerned in their own right.

[71] *Mitsubishi/UCAR*, M024, 1990; *Baxter/Néstlé/Salvia*, M058, 1991; *Thomson/Pilkington*, M086, 1991; *Alcan/Inespal/Palco*, M322, 1993; *Toyota Motor Corp/Walter Frey/Toyota France*, M326, 1993; *Fortis/CGER*, M342, 1993; and *Costa Crociere/Chargeurs/Accor*, M334, 1993. See also *Conagra/Idea*, M010, 1991 (purchase of 20 per cent of shares giving rise to a joint controlling interest); and *Elf/Enterprise*, M088, 1991 (purchase of 30 per cent of shares).

[72] See *ASKO/Jacobs/ADIA*, M082, 1991; *RVI/VBC/Heuliez*, M092, 1991; *James River/Rayne*, M162, 1992; *CEA Industrie/France Telecom/Finmeccanica/SGS-Thomson*, M216, 1993; and *Synthomer/Yule Catto*, M376, 1993.

[73] See *Elf/Ertoil*, M063, 1991; *Elf/BC/Cepsa*, M098, 1991; and *UAP/Transatlantic/Sunlife*, M141, 1991.

[74] The Commission's approach may produce some curious results. See e.g., *ASKO/Jacobs/ADIA*, M082, 1991 (and the earlier case of *ASKO/Omni*, M065, 1991). ASKO and Omni jointly controlled Adia, which was transferred to a new joint venture which ASKO and KJJ would jointly control. It appears from the decision to have been sufficient for the purposes of the second threshold that ASKO and Adia had Community-wide turnovers in excess of ECU 250m, despite the fact that they were both, in a sense, part of the same group. If ASKO had sold its interest outright to KJJ, there would apparently have been no Community dimension.

¶614

(4)   Changes from joint to sole control

In cases involving changes from joint to sole control, it appears that the pre-existing joint venture and the new sole controller will be undertakings concerned.[75] Thus if A and B jointly control C, and A acquires sole control, it appears that the undertakings concerned would be A and C. As a result, where A has a shareholding in C of 90 per cent and B a shareholding in C of 10 per cent, but C is jointly controlled by A and B,[76] and A acquires B's interest in C, both A and C may be undertakings concerned for the purposes of the second threshold, even though they may appear at first sight to be members of the same group according to the criteria set out in art. 5(4) of the regulation.

(5)   Lifting the veil

Where two or more companies do not acquire a target company directly, but do so through the medium of a jointly controlled intermediary company, and each of the parents but not the target has a Community-wide turnover in excess of ECU 250m, the Commission's view is that the application of the regulation depends on whether or not it is possible to 'look through' the jointly-controlled intermediary company and treat each of its parents as an undertaking concerned. Otherwise it would not be possible to identify at least two undertakings concerned for the purposes of satisfying the second threshold. The Commission will 'lift the veil' behind the acquiring jointly-controlled intermediary company and regard its parents as undertakings concerned at least in cases where the intermediary company has been specifically (and recently) set up for the purpose of carrying out the joint acquisition, or for the purpose of owning and managing shareholdings in the target. If the intermediary company has few operating assets of its own, does not operate in the target's market, and is basically the 'puppet' of the parents, then the Commission is apparently more likely to lift the veil. The Commission's view appears to be that unless this approach is taken, the parties to a joint acquisition could easily circumvent the regulation by modifying the formal structure of the transaction.[77]

---

[75] *ICI/Tioxide*, M023, 1990.

[76] Such a situation existed in *Thomas Cook/LTU/West LB*, M229, 1992.

[77] Regulation 4064/89, recital 24 of the preamble, may support the view that the regulation was intended to apply in such cases. See also Kleeman, (1991) *Fordham Corporate Law Institute* and *XXIst Report on Competition Policy for 1991*, Annex III, at p. 351. See *ASKO/Jacobs/ADIA*, M082, 1991; *TNT/Canada Post, DBP Postdienst, La Poste, PTT Post and Sweden Post*, M102, 1991; *Kelt/American Express*, M116, 1991; *UAP/Transatlantic/Sun Life*, M141, 1991; *Del Monte/Royal Foods/Anglo-American*, M277, 1992; and *CEA Industrie/France Telecom/ Finmeccanica/SGS Thomson*, M216, 1993 (in relation to France Telecom). In *Eucom/Digital*, M218, 1992, the Commission was prepared to 'lift the veil' behind the intermediary company even though it would not appear to have been set up specifically for the notified transaction, but only for the purposes of projects of that type. In *ABC/Général des Eaux/Canal+/W H Smith TV*, M110, 1991, the Commission looked through two levels of joint ventures in order to identify the undertakings concerned, and apparently considered it sufficient for the purposes of satisfying the second threshold that they together controlled only 50 per cent of the acquiring vehicle. In *Sextant/BTG-VDO*, M290, 1992, Sextant, one of the parents of the joint venture, was itself apparently jointly

¶615   Calculation of turnover

(1)   Definition of turnover

Aggregate turnover within the meaning of art. 1(2) of the merger regulation is defined as:

'the amounts derived by the undertakings concerned in the preceding financial year[78] from the sale of products and the provision of services falling within the undertakings' concerned ordinary activities[79] after deduction of sales rebates and of value added tax and other taxes[80] directly related to turnover.'[81]

For the calculation of turnover in the Community or in a member state, account is taken only of the products sold and the services provided to undertakings or consumers in the Community or in that member state.[82] It is immaterial if the

---

controlled by Aérospatiale and Thomson. Aérospatiale seems to have been treated as an undertaking concerned (particularly for the purposes of satisfying the second threshold), even though Sextant was a well established and substantial operating company. A similar question arises over the inclusion of the turnover of Rhône-Poulenc in *SITA-RPC/SCORI*, M295, 1993, since it had only a 50 per cent holding in TERIS (see *RPC/SITA*, M266, 1992), although the explanation in this case may lie in an interpretation of art. 5(4)(b) of the regulation which would extend it to joint controlling parents (see below). See also *Ahold/Jéronimo Martins/Inovação*, M320, 1993.

[78] Form CO relating to the notification of a concentration pursuant to Regulation 4064/89 ('Form CO'), which appears at Annex 1 to Regulation 2367/90, states at note D that financial data must be provided in ECU at the average conversion rates prevailing for the years or other periods in question. In practice the Commission has looked at the situation prevailing at the time of the concentration, by considering data from the preceding financial year for which audited accounts are available (see *Accor/Wagons-Lits*, OJ 1992 L204/1, at p. 2) and making an adjustment to allow for any material disposals or acquisitions during the intervening period, or for any changes in the borders of a territory (see *Paribas/MBH*, M122, 1991, in relation to the former DDR). Conversion into ECU should be made from the currency of audit using the average annual exchange rates published by DG II.

[79] In *Cereol/Continentale*, M156, 1991, the Commission excluded from the turnover calculation Community aid received by an undertaking concerned (which it was obliged to pass on to third parties) in the framework of the common agricultural policy. The Commission left the more general question open as to whether aid can be taken into account at all in calculating the turnover of an undertaking concerned. In *Accor/Wagons-Lits*, OJ 1991 L204/1, at p. 2, the Commission considered that an item 'other operating profits' should be included in the turnover calculation. The question of which 'other' items, in addition to net sales, would be included in the caculation will be decided by the Commission on a case by case basis. The Commission's approach would appear to broadly follow the accounting distinction between operating and non-operating income. Thus, the following would be strong candidates for inclusion: intellectual property royalties; cash discounts on purchases; interest for late payment on sales; fees for sub-letting plant and production equipment; and income from the lease of property rights. On the other hand the following would be weak candidates for inclusion: interest on investment of sales revenue; regional grants; dividends on minority interests; legal settlements; and capital gains on the sale of operating assets, investments and securities. Evidently, it is unnecessary to enter into the detail of such 'other' income unless it is critical for determining whether or not the relevant threshold is reached.

[80] The most likely candidate would appear to be excise duties, which may be particularly important in cases involving alcohol or tobacco. The point remains to be settled, but the Commission's preliminary view appears to be that excise duties would be excluded from the turnover calculations for manufacturers, but included for others.

[81] Regulation 4064/89, art. 5(1).

[82] Regulation 4064/89, art. 5(1), second sub-paragraph. The Commission apparently uses the turnover of subsidiaries or agents in a particular territory as a starting point, attributing direct exports to the territory of destination, indirect exports to the intermediary territory into which they are delivered, and services to the territory where the customer receives the benefit. In the financial services sector, the Commission considered that in inter-bank lending allocation should be made on the basis of the location of the borrowing bank's branch. See *Hong Kong and Shanghai Bank/Midland*, M213, 1992. In the air transport sector, the Commission has considered three possible ways of making the allocation for operating revenues deriving from international air transportation services: to the country of destination, on a 50:50 ratio between the countries of origin and final destination, or to

concentration is effected by undertakings that do not have their principal fields of activities in the Community or that are not located within the Community.[83] The provisions apply equally to public and private sector companies.[84]

(2)   General principle: consolidated group turnover

The aggregate turnover of an undertaking concerned must be calculated on a consolidated group basis. For the purposes of determining whether two undertakings form part of the same group, it is necessary to consider whether one exercises over the other the rights and powers set out in art. 5(4)(b) of the regulation. These rights and powers refer to the degree of control exercised by one undertaking over another. The concept of control set out in art. 5(4)(b) is not, however, necessarily the same as that which is defined in art. 3, and applied for the purposes of determining whether or not there is a concentration within the meaning of the regulation.[85]

The relevant rights or powers set out in art. 5(4)(b) consist of, directly or indirectly:[86]

● the ownership of more than half the capital or business assets; or

● the power to exercise more than half the voting rights; or

● the power to appoint more than half the members of the supervisory board, the administrative board or bodies legally representing the undertaking; or

● the right to manage the undertaking's affairs.[87]

---

the member state where the ticket sale occurred. See *Delta/Pan Am*, M130, 1991; *Air France/Sabena*, M157, 1992; *British Airways/TAT*, M259, 1992 (on appeal); and *British Airways/Dan Air*, M278, 1992. For the Commission's approach to international submarine telecommunication systems, see *Alcatel/STC*, M366, 1993.

[83]   Regulation 4064/89, recital 11 of the preamble.

[84]   Regulation 4064/89, recital 12 of the preamble states that:

'in the public sector, calculation of the turnover of an undertaking concerned in a concentration needs ... to take account of undertakings making up an economic unit with an independent power of decision, irrespective of the way in which their capital is held or of the rules of administrative supervision applicable to them'.

For examples of cases involving public sector companies, see *Aérospatiale-Alenia/de Havilland*, OJ 1991 L334/42; *Aérospatiale/MBB*, M017, 1991; *BSN-Néstle/Cokoladovny*, M090, 1992; *Koipe-Tabacalara/Elosua*, M117, 1992; *Air France/Sabena*, M157, 1992; *Rhône-Poulenc/SNIA*, M206, 1992; *Eucom/Digital*, M218, 1992; *Elf Aquitaine/Thyssen/Minol*, M235, 1992; and *Rhône-Poulenc/SNIA (II)*, M355, 1993.

[85]   The intention of the regulation would appear to have been that art. 3 is a qualitative test, whereas art. 5 is a more quantitative test, giving more legal certainty. However, the Commission's interpretation of art. 5 has tended to introduce qualitative elements not dissimilar to those used in the application of art. 3.

[86]   This includes control through the medium of one or more other undertakings. The drafting of art. 5(4) means that the word 'indirectly' only applies to art. 4(5)(b), i.e. subsidiaries, and is not referred to again in art. 5(4)(c)–(e), although in practice the Commission has inferred it. There would appear to be no limit to the number of levels of a corporate structure to which art. 5(4) may be applied. See *Eridania/ISI*, M062, 1991 (great grandparent); *La Redoute/Empire*, M080, 1991 (great grandparent); *Rhône-Poulenc/SNIA*, M206, 1992 (great grandparent); *Mondi/Frantschach*, M210, 1992 (4 subsidiaries of great grandparent); *Volvo/Lex*, M224, 1992 (grandparent); and *Del Monte/Royal Foods/Anglo-American*, M277, 1992 (great great grandparent).

[87]   In *Accor/Wagons-Lits*, OJ 1992 L204/1, the Commission took into account the turnover of various companies in which Accor had a minority shareholding, on the grounds that the terms of various contracts

¶615

Article 5(4) of the regulation lists those companies to be included within the group for the purposes of the turnover calculation. It provides that the turnover of an undertaking for the purposes of applying art. 1(2) will consist of:

(a) the turnover of the undertaking concerned; *plus*

(b) the turnover of any undertaking in which the undertaking concerned has the rights or powers listed in art. 5(4)(b) (control of subsidiaries); *plus*

(c) the turnover of any undertaking which has in the undertaking concerned the rights and powers listed in art. 5(4)(b) (control by parents); *plus*

(d) the turnover of any undertaking in which the controlling undertaking referred to in (c) has the rights and powers referred to in art. 5(4)(b) (other undertakings controlled by a parent); *plus*

(e) the turnover of any undertaking in which two or more undertakings referred to in (a) to (d) jointly have the rights or powers referred in art. 5(4)(b) (other group controlled undertakings); *less*

(f) the turnover attributable to the provision of goods and services between any of the undertakings within the group (i.e. excluding intra-group transactions).[88]

(3) Exception: sale of part

By way of derogation from the general principle that turnover should be calculated on a consolidated group basis, art. 5(2) provides that where a concentration consists in the acquisition of parts, whether or not constituted as legal entities, of one or more undertakings, only the turnover relating to the parts which are the subject of the transaction shall be taken into account with regard to the seller or sellers.

Thus if subsidiary A of group ABC purchases subsidiary X of group XYZ, the combined aggregate turnover for the purposes of art. 1(2)(a) will be that of ABC (consolidated) plus X. In addition, for the operation to fall within the regulation, both ABC and X must each have a turnover of ECU 250m. Finally, unless ABC and X both achieve two-thirds of their turnover in one and the same member state, the operation will not be taken outside the scope of the regulation by the final paragraph of art. 1(2).

If the operation involves the creation of a joint venture, both parents will probably be undertakings concerned, and their turnover will therefore have to be taken into consideration (see the discussion above).[89]

---

conferred on Accor the right to manage them (see recital 6 of the decision). See also the position of CCIEL in *CCIE/GTE*, M258, 1992.

[88] Regulation 4064/89, art. 5(1), final sentence.

[89] See e.g. *Promodes/Dirsa*, M027, 1990; and *Digital/Philips*, M129, 1991.

¶615

(4) Relative control

The rights and powers enumerated in art. 5(4)(b) may exist where an undertaking, whilst not having an absolute majority of the voting rights in another undertaking, holds the largest percentage of voting rights and the remaining voting rights are dispersed. Where it can be proved that an undertaking holding such voting rights has actually been able to make the appointments set out in art. 5(4)(b) by controlling more than 50 per cent of the voting rights in the general meeting due to the absence of other voting rights, or more than 50 per cent of the board, it is reasonable to assume that the power referred to in art. 5(4)(b), third indent, exists.

In *Arjomari-Prioux SA/Wiggins Teape Appleton plc*,[90] the turnover of a parent exercising 45.19 per cent of the voting rights present or represented at the last general meeting of Arjomari was not included in the calculation, as a result of which the operation fell below the threshold in art. 1(2)(a) and outside the scope of the regulation. The Commission did not apparently take into consideration changes in voting rights that had occurred since the last annual general meeting. On the other hand, in *Eridania/ISI*,[91] the Commission included the turnover of Eridania's grandparent, Ferruzzi, on the grounds that it controlled 43.69 per cent of the shares in Eridania's parent, Montedison (which controlled Eridania), and had the power to directly or indirectly appoint all of Montedison's board. The remaining shares were dispersed (11.4 per cent amongst the next nine largest shareholders). Furthermore, Eridania's turnover was consolidated in Ferruzzi's accounts, and Montedison had apparently been incorporated by a company forming part of the Ferruzzi group.[92]

(5) Jointly controlling parents and jointly controlled subsidiaries

One reading of art. 5(4) might lead to the conclusion, based on the words 'more than half' in art. 5(4)(b), that a company which owned 50 per cent or less of the voting rights in an undertaking concerned would not (subject to the discussion of 'relative control' above) have its turnover included in the turnover calculations (provided that it did not satisfy any of the other criteria listed in art. 5(4)(b)). The view has been expressed, however, that the turnover of companies which jointly control an undertaking concerned will be included in

---

[90] *Arjomari-Prioux SA/Wiggins Teape Appleton plc*, M025, 1990, discussed in *XXth Report on Competition Policy*, point 150.

[91] *Eridania/ISI*, M062, 1991.

[92] See also *Courtaulds/SNIA*, M113, 1991 (referred to in *XXIst Report on Competition Policy for 1991*, Annex III, at p. 351); *Eurocom/RSCG*, M147, 1991 (45.25 per cent of the shares representing 69.5 per cent, 68 per cent and 77.5 per cent of the votes in the three preceding annual general meetings); *Ifint/EXOR*, M187, 1992 (in relation to IFI, less than 50 per cent shares but more than half the board, in relation to Perrier, 49.31 per cent shares and 52.1 per cent votes in previous general meeting, common President and Director General); *Rhône-Poulenc/SNIA*, M206, 1992 (45.24 per cent capital, more than half the board); and *Société Générale de Belgique/Générale de Banque*, M343, 1993 (change from 20.94 per cent to 25.96 per cent, projected to represent more than 50 per cent of votes present or represented at the next annual general meeting).

¶615

the turnover calculation.[93] This interpretation is based on the fact that art. 5(4)(c) uses the plural 'undertakings'. Together with the Commission's view on relative control, this would effectively sweep away, at least in the case of parents, the relatively precise language of art. 5(4)(b), and replace it with a concept of control or joint control that does not differ materially from that used in the context of art. 3.

With regard to subsidiaries, the view has been expressed that the turnover of a joint venture between an undertaking concerned and a third party should not be included at all in the turnover calculation.[94] It seems to be difficult to justify the inclusion of jointly controlling parents, and the exclusion of jointly controlled subsidiaries. An alternative view (discussed below) is that art. 5(5) may apply in such cases.

(6)   Existing joint ventures between undertakings concerned (art. 5(5))
Article 5(5) provides that where undertakings concerned jointly have control within the meaning of art. 5(4)(b) of a joint venture, in calculating the aggregate turnover of the undertakings concerned, sales of products or the provision of services between the joint venture and the undertakings concerned, or any other undertaking connected with them within the meaning of art. 5(4)(b)–(e), must be discounted. Other turnover of the joint venture will be taken into account, and apportioned equally between the undertakings concerned.

Article 5(5) seems, therefore, to require the turnover of existing joint ventures between undertakings concerned to be consolidated and split equally between them. It does not appear to deal with the case of a 50 per cent joint venture with a third party, and this view is supported by the guidance notes given in the annex to the implementing regulation.[95]

(7)   Multiple staged acquisitions
Two or more transactions involving the sale of part of an undertaking between the same undertakings within two years will be treated together as a concentration occurring on the date of the last transaction. In such a case the turnover of the acquired undertaking will be the aggregate of all the parts acquired during the preceding two years.[96]

---

[93] See Jones and González-Díaz, *The EEC Merger Regulation*, Sweet & Maxwell, 1992, at 2.4.2.1. This may explain the inclusion of Rhône-Poulenc's turnover in *SITA-RPC/SCORI*, M295, 1993. See also *Ahold/Jéronimo Martins/Inovação*, M320, 1993 (in relation to the turnover of Ahold).
[94] See Jones and González-Díaz, *The EEC Merger Regulation*, Sweet & Maxwell, 1992, at 2.4.2.4.
[95] Regard should be had, however, to the *XXIst Report on Competition Policy for 1991*, Annex III, at p. 351, where it is stated that: 'Turnover from companies in which an undertaking concerned exercises joint control with a third undertaking is taken into account as to 50 per cent,' The authority cited is art. 6(1)(c) of *Accor/Wagons-Lits*, OJ 1992 L204/1, although that article does not exist, and the reference probably relates to the legal basis of the decision (art. 6(1)(c) of the merger regulation). The position therefore remains unclear. However, in practice the Commission has been willing to follow the statement in the *XXIst Report on Competition Policy for 1991*, even though this may appear difficult to reconcile with the Form CO guidance notes.
[96] See Regulation 4064/89, art. 5(2), para. 2; *Volvo/Lex*, M224, 1992; *Volvo/Lex (2)*, M261, 1992; *PepsiCo/KAS*, M289, 1992; and *Alcatel/STC*, M366, 1993.

¶616 Special rules for turnover of banks and insurance companies

For credit institutions and other financial institutions and for insurance undertakings, there are special rules for the calculation of turnover. These are set out in art. 5(3) of the merger regulation. They involve the replacement of turnover by a proportion of assets in the case of banks, and by the value of certain premiums in the case of insurance undertakings.

(1) Credit and other financial institutions[97]

In the case of credit and other financial institutions, in calculating whether or not the first turnover threshold is satisfied, one-tenth of total assets should be used instead of turnover.

In calculating whether or not the second and third thresholds are satisfied, Community-wide (or member state) turnover should be replaced by one-tenth of total assets multiplied by the ratio between loans and advances to credit institutions and customers in transactions with Community (or member state) residents and the total sum of these loans and advances.

The view of the Merger Task Force would appear to be that the holding of fixed interest securities is essentially another way of giving credit. Therefore, turnover in a region should be calculated on the basis that fixed interest securities held from issuers resident in that region constitute loans and advances in the sense of art. 5(3) of the regulation.[98]

The geographical allocation of turnover related to inter-bank lending should be made according to the location of the borrowing bank branch, there being a presumption that the location of the branch is the place where the loan will be used.[99] In *Hong Kong and Shanghai Bank/Midland* the parties were required to gather specific data from all subsidiaries and branches in every country in which banking operations were carried out, and to demonstrate that the data reconciled to the audited published accounts.

For the relationship between these provisions and the other provisions of art. 5, see *Groupe AG/Amev*,[100] discussed below.

---

[97] See generally, *BNP/Dresdner Bank*, M021, 1990; *Kyowa/Saitama Banks*, M069, 1991; *Kelt/American Express*, M116, 1991; *BNP/Dresdner Bank–Czechoslovakia*, M124, 1991; *Bankamerica/Security Pacific*, M137, 1991; *Mediobanca/Generali*, M159, 1991 (on appeal); *Torras/Sarrio*, M166, 1992; *Hong Kong and Shanghai Bank/Midland*, M213, 1992; *BHF/CCF/Charterhouse*, M319, 1993; *Schweizerische Kreditanstalt/Schweizerische Volksbank*, M335, 1993; *Deutsche Bank/Banco de Madrid*, M341, 1993; *West LB/Thomas Cook*, M350, 1993; *Société Générale de Belgique/Générale de Banque*, M343, 1993; *Commerzbank/CCR (Paribas)*, M357, 1993; *Fortis/CGER*, M342, 1993; and *BAI/Banca Popolare di Lecco*, M391, 1993.

[98] *Torras/Sarrio*, M166, 1992.

[99] *Hong Kong and Shanghai Bank/Midland*, M213, 1992.

[100] *Groupe AG/Amev*, M018, 1990.

(2) Insurance undertakings[101]

In the case of insurance undertakings, in the place of turnover, the value of gross premiums written should be used. These are defined as follows:

> '... all amounts received and receivable in respect of insurance contracts issued by or on behalf of the insurance undertakings, including also outgoing reinsurance premiums and after deduction of taxes and parafiscal contributions or levies charged by reference to the amounts of individual premiums or the total volume of premiums;'.

Thus for the purposes of calculating Community (or member state) turnover, gross premiums received from Community (or member state) residents should be taken into account. In *Allianz/DKV*[102] the Commission excluded certain excess premiums from the turnover calculation. Had they been included, then apparently the third threshold may not have been met.

In *Groupe AG/Amev*,[103] the Commission decided that the turnover of certain subsidiaries of the insurance undertakings involved active in the building sector should be included with that of the gross premiums of the parents in making the turnover calculations, since investments in the building sector were frequently linked with insurance activities. Without the inclusion of this turnover, the operation would not have satisfied the ECU 5,000m threshold. The Commission went on to state that this would also apply to other kinds of business. This conclusion was reached on the basis that the provisions of art. 5(3)(b) were simply special rules for calculating the turnover resulting from insurance activities, and did not exempt insurance companies from the general provisions of art. 5.

¶617 'Concentration' under the regulation: introduction

The merger regulation applies to 'concentrations'.[104] The concept of concentration is only intended to cover operations bringing about a lasting change in the structure of the undertakings concerned.[105] This basically covers mergers and sole or joint acquisitions of control (including the creation of so-called structural or concentrative joint ventures). Operations which have as their object or effect the co-ordination of the competitive behaviour of undertakings which remain independent will not be concentrations, and will fall outside the scope of the regulation.[106] This basically covers so-called

---

[101] For examples of cases involving the insurance sector, see *Groupe AG/Amev*, M018, 1990; *UAP/Transatlantic/Sun Life*, M141, 1991; *Mediobanca/Generali*, M159, 1991 (on appeal); *Generali/BCHA*, M189, 1992; *Eureko*, M207, 1992; *Allianz/DKV*, M251, 1992; *Zürich/MMI*, M286, 1993; *Codan/Hafnia*, M344, 1993; *AEGON/Scottish Equitable*, M349, 1993; and *VAP/VINCI*, M384, 1993.
[102] *Allianz/DKV*, M251, 1992.
[103] *Groupe AG/Amev*, M018, 1990, discussed in *XXth Report on Competition Policy*, point 149.
[104] Regulation 4064/89, art. 1(1).
[105] Regulation 4064/89, recital 23 of the preamble.
[106] Regulation 4064/89, art. 3(2), para. 1.

behavioural or co-operative joint ventures and other co-operative operations. Co-operative operations may still be examined under art. 85 and 86 of the EC Treaty.[107] A Commission notice[108] gives further guidance on the problematic distinction[109] between concentrative and co-operative operations, particularly joint ventures.[110]

A joint venture may be concentrative only if it performs all the functions of an autonomous economic entity. Furthermore, there must be no risk of co-ordination giving rise to a restriction of competition, either between the parents, or between them and the joint venture.[111] In assessing whether or not a joint venture is concentrative, the Commission will consider particularly whether the parents have withdrawn from the market of the joint venture, and whether they remain active on neighbouring, upstream or downstream markets.

There are certain types of operations (temporary share acquisitions, acquisitions by insolvency practioners, and acquisitions by financial holding companies) which are explicitly excluded from the scope of the regulation.

When considering whether or not a particular case falls within the regulation, it may be useful to bear in mind the following general points. First, the Merger Task Force has tended to prefer interpretations of the regulation which result

---

[107] Regulation 4064/89, recital 23 of the preamble. See e.g. *Renault/Volvo*, M004, 1990, (in relation to cars).

[108] Commission notice regarding the concentrative and co-operative operations under Council Regulation 4064/89 of 21 December on the control of concentrations between undertakings (the 'concentrative/co-operative notice'), OJ 1990 C203/10.

[109] The distinction has been expressed by the Commission as follows:

'Whereas a cartel can be defined as an agreement between enterprises that remain independent relative to certain market practices, the term "concentration of enterprises" is used where several enterprises are brought together under a single economic management at the expense of their economic independence in a manner that indicates permanence. A cartel creates an obligation with regard to *practices*, whereas a concentration of enterprises brings about a modification of the internal *structure* of the enterprises. The distinctions, however, are elusive so that it is hard to say in the abstract exactly where the dividing line between a cartel and a concentration of enterprises falls.' (Emphasis added.) See Competition Series No. 3 (1966), *The Problem of Industrial Concentration in the Common Market*, at p. 32.

[110] The concentrative/co-operative notice states that an operation which includes both lasting structural change and the co-ordination of competitive behaviour will fall to be assessed under the appropriate regulations implementing art. 85 and 86, where the two aspects of the operation are inseparable. If they are separable, the former will be assessed under the regulation and the latter, to the extent that it does not amount to an ancillary restraint within the meaning of art. 8(2), second subparagraph of the merger regulation, will be assessed under regulations implementing art. 85 and 86. For an example of separation, see *Ahold/Jerónimo Martins*, M263, 1992. For examples of a separate analysis of parts of an operation see *Renault/Volvo*, M004, 1990; *Steeley/Tarmac*, M180, 1993; *Solvay-Laporte/Interox*, M197, 1992; and *British Telecom/MCI*, M353, 1993.

[111] Regulation 4064/89 art. 3(2), para. 2. This requirement that there should be no co-ordination in the case of the creation of a joint venture to some extent duplicates the provisions of Regulation 4064/89 art. 3(2), para. 1, which applies to all operations, including the creation of a joint venture. In practice, the Commission has only considered the issue of co-ordination in cases involving joint ventures. In cases involving mergers or acquisitions where the undertakings lose their independence, the issue of co-ordination is irrelevant, unless the operation is linked to a co-ordinative agreement – a particular risk in the case of asset swaps. See the concentrative/co-operative notice, para. 46 and 47.

¶617

in it having a broad jurisdiction.[112] Secondly, it has tended to adopt a pragmatic approach based on economic reality, rather than a dogmatic one based on legal form.[113] Thirdly, it has not always followed the concentrative/co-operative notice.[114] Fourthly, the Commission tends to take a case-by-case approach.[115] Fifthly, difficult jurisdictional questions may be discussed on a 'no-names' basis with the Merger Task Force prior to notification.[116]

¶618   Definition of 'concentration'

The merger regulation applies to concentrations, whether in the public or the private sector.[117] Article 3 of the regulation provides[118] that:

'1. A concentration shall be deemed to arise where:

(a) two or more previously independent undertakings[119] merge, or

(b) – one or more persons already controlling at least one undertaking, or

   – one or more undertakings

---

[112] See e.g. the view that changes from joint to sole control may be concentrations and generally the view that the application of the regulation may be triggered by 'changes in the nature or quality of control' (discussed at ¶621 and ¶622 below).

[113] Sir Leon Brittan, whilst Commissioner responsible for competition, stated that:

'The one point I wish to stress is that our approach is an economic, rather than a legal one. Competition law is rightly concerned with substance rather than form ... The key issue is whether a transaction brings about a lasting change in market structure or merely a temporary change in companies' behaviour. The former is a concentration, the latter is not.' ((1990) 15 E.L.Rev., p. 351.)

See also Regulation 4064/89, recitals 7, 9 and 23 of the preamble; *Renault/Volvo*, M004, 1990 (establishment of a 'single economic entity'); and *Groupe AG/Amev*, M018, 1990 ('merger from an economic point of view').

[114] For example, the concentrative/co-operative notice, para. 20, 25 and 33, suggest that *both* parents must withdraw from a joint venture's market for the joint venture to be concentrative. However, the Merger Task Force has developed a theory of 'industrial leadership' (discussed more fully at ¶626 below) which allows one of the parents to remain in the market in certain circumstances.

[115] This reflects the comparatively short time-limits within which the Commission must make a decision, the Commission's working methods and the fact that the full text of most decisions (usually under Regulation 4064/89, art. 6) are not published in the *Official Journal*. Compare, e.g., the treatment of the ownership of intellectual property rights in *Baxter/Nestlé*, M058, 1991; and *Lucas/Eaton*, M149, 1991, in the context of autonomy (discussed at ¶625 below).

[116] Of 399 case numbers issued to 1 January 1994, only 190 were formally notified. The remainder were either found to be outside the regulation before they were notified or were not continued. Cases may be informally discussed with the Merger Task Force 'even if presented as a hypothetical problem by lawyers who do not reveal the identity of their client'. See Overbury 'Politics or Policy? The Demystification of EC Merger Control', *Annual Proceedings of the Fordham Corporate Law Institute, International Antitrust Law & Policy*, 1993, at p. 557; and Regulation 2367/90, recital 11 of the preamble.

[117] Regulation 4064/89, recital 12 of the preamble states that: 'the control of concentrations should, without prejudice to the provisions of art. 90(2) of the Treaty, respect the principle of non-discrimination between the public and the private sectors'. For examples of cases involving public sector companies, see *Aérospatiale-Alenia/de Havilland*, OJ 1991 L334/42; *Aérospatiale/MBB*, M017, 1991; *BSN-Nestlé/Cokoladovny*, M090, 1992; *Koipe-Tabacalara/Elosua*, M117, 1992; *Air France/Sabena*, M157, 1992; *Rhône-Poulenc/SNIA*, M206, 1992; *Eucom/Digital*, M218, 1992; *Elf Aquitaine/Thyssen/Minol*, M235, 1992; and *Alcan/Inespal/Palco*, M322, 1993.

[118] The concentrative/co-operative notice, para. 1, states that art. 3(1) contains an exhaustive list of the circumstances which fall to be considered as concentrations. Regulation 4064/89, art. 3(2) brings the creation of a lasting, full-function, autonomous, non-co-ordinative joint venture within the meaning of art. 3(1)(b).

[119] The concentrative/co-operative notice, para. 8, defines an undertaking as 'an organised assembly of human and material resources, intended to pursue a defined economic purpose on a long term basis.'

acquire, whether by purchase of securities or assets, by contract or by any other means, direct or indirect[120] control of the whole or parts, of one or more other undertakings.

2. An operation, including the creation of a joint venture, which has as its object or effect the co-ordination of the competitive behaviour of undertakings which remain independent shall not constitute a concentration within the meaning of paragraph 1(b).

The creation of a joint venture performing on a lasting basis all the functions of an autonomous economic entity, which does not give rise to co-ordination of the competitive behaviour of the parties amongst themselves or between them and the joint venture, shall constitute a concentration within the meaning of paragraph 1(b).'

From this provision it appears that the regulation may apply to mergers and to sole or joint acquisitions of control (including the creation of lasting, full-function, autonomous, non-co-ordinative joint ventures).

¶619 Merger[121]

There will be a concentration where two or more previously independent undertakings merge.[122] The regulation does not contain any definition of a merger.[123] Legal mergers, where companies are completely absorbed and lose their legal identity, are unusual, and relatively few[124] cases have been explicitly referred to by the Commission as mergers as opposed to acquisitions.[125]

In *Kyowa/Saitama*[126] the Commission considered a merger in accordance with the statutory provisions of the Commercial Code of Japan to be a

---

[120] Control may certainly be exercised through several intermediary companies. See e.g. *RVI/VBC/Heuliez*, M092, 1991.
[121] The regulation may also apply to de-mergers, either with each acquiror together with its acquired bundle of assets being treated as a separate operation (see *Solvay-Laporte/Interox*, M197, 1992), or with the overall de-merger being treated as one operation (see *Campsa*, M138, 1991).
[122] Regulation 4064/89, art. 3(1).
[123] The concentrative/co-operative notice states that:

'Where the parent companies transfer their entire business activities to the joint venture, and thereafter act only as holding companies, this amounts to complete merger from the economic viewpoint'.

See *Groupe AG/Amev*, M018, 1990.
[124] There were seven operations explicitly referred to as mergers out of 190 notifications to 1 January 1994. The distinction may give rise to some consequences with regard to the obligation to notify. Regulation 4064/89, art. 4(2), provides that mergers must be jointly notified, whereas acquisitions must be notified by the person acquiring control.
[125] Although a strict reading of the regulation does not rule out the possibility that a merger could be considered co-ordinative, it is difficult to imagine such a transaction, and in practice the Commission only considers whether or not there is a risk of co-ordination in joint control cases. See *XXIst Report on Competition Policy for 1991*, Annex III, at p. 352: 'the decisions examine in each case whether the operation creates a situation of sole or joint control and in the case of joint control whether it is a concentrative or cooperative operation'. The operation must not, however, be linked to a co-ordinative agreement – a particular risk in the case of asset swaps. See the concentrative/co-operative notice, para. 46 and 47.
[126] *Kyowa/Saitama*, M069, 1991.

concentration. Under the terms of the agreement between the parties, Kyowa was to absorb Saitama, assuming all the assets, rights, obligations and liabilities of Saitama, which would be dissolved. The shareholders of Saitama were to be issued with shares in Kyowa on a one-for-one basis.

Groupe AG/Amev[127] concerned an operation between two groups, each of which hived down its entire business to a subsidiary. The shares of each of these two subsidiaries were then divided equally between the two ultimate holding companies. The two subsidiaries were subsequently to operate as one single group under a single management, and the members of their decision making bodies were to be appointed equally by the two holding companies. The Commission found that since the two groups had brought together all their activities, on a lasting basis, into a new jointly controlled group, the operation constituted a merger from an economic point of view, and therefore a concentration within the meaning of the regulation.[128]

Cross shareholdings and or directorships may be an indication of co-ordination (discussed more fully below) taking the operation outside the scope of the regulation. However, if sufficiently strong, they may give rise to a 'single economic entity', and a concentration within the regulation.[129]

¶620   Acquisition of control[130]

The application of the merger regulation is triggered by an acquisition of control,[131] whether by purchase of securities or assets,[132] by contract or by any other means. Control for the purposes of the regulation means the possibility[133] of exercising decisive influence[134] on an undertaking. Decisive influence may be

---

[127] *Groupe AG/Amev*, M018, 1990.

[128] See particularly the concentrative/co-operative notice, para. 41, which refers to 'economic concentrations'.

[129] See the concentrative/co-operative notice, para. 40, and *Renault/Volvo*, M004, 1990. For other cases involving mergers, see *Bank America/Security Pacific*, M137, 1991; *Eurocom/RSCG*, M147, 1991; *KNP/Bührmann-Tetterode/VRG*, M291, 1992; and *JCSAT/SAJAC*, M346, 1993.

[130] Regulation 4064/89, art. 3, refers to one or more persons acquiring control – i.e. a sole or joint acquisition of control. This section considers what is required in order to cross that control threshold. Issues relating to joint control are considered in the section on joint ventures.

[131] A strict reading of Regulation 4064/89 suggests that the issue of co-ordination could arise in the context of a sole acquisition of control. However, in practice, the issue of co-ordination will only be considered in joint control situations (unless the operation is linked to a co-ordinative agreement – a particular risk in the case of asset swaps. See the concentrative/co-operative notice, para. 46 and 47).

[132] For asset purchases see *Digital/Philips*, M129, 1991; *Delta/Pan Am*, M130, 1991; *Torras/Sarrio*, M166, 1992; *GECC/Avis Lease*, M234, 1992; *Elf Aquitaine/Thyssen/Minol*, M235, 1992; *Ericsson/Ascom*, M236, 1992; *Volvo/Lex*, M244, 1992; *BTR/Pirelli*, M253, 1992; *Volvo/Lex (2)*, M261, 1992; *Zürich/MMI*, M286, 1993; and *Cyanamid/Shell*, M354, 1993.

[133] Regulation 4064/89, art. 3(3). It is unnecessary to demonstrate that decisive influence has actually been exercised, only that it could be. See particularly *Société Générale de Belgique/Générale de Banque*, M343, 1993, and *Fortis/CGER*, M342, 1993. For an example of a case involving apparently unexercised share options, see *ELF/BC/Cepsa*, M098, 1991 (but compare the suggestion in *Conagra/Idea* M010, 1991 and *British Airways/TAT*, M259, 1992 (on appeal), that these are irrelevant).

[134] Some Commission decisions suggest that a joint controlling interest may in itself give decisive influence, even though the concept suggests a positive control (see *British Telecom/MCI*, M353, 1993), i.e. an ability to proceed against all other interests, rather than a negative control, such as a veto over strategic decisions.

established by any means, including ownership, or contractual or other rights over the use of all or part of the assets of an undertaking, or over the composition, voting or decisions of its organs.[135] Whether or not it is present can only be determined by reference to all the legal and factual circumstances of the case,[136] no one of which will be decisive. In practice the Commission has looked at the size of shareholdings and the right to appoint members of the management bodies, in conjunction with any other relevant factors.

(1) Shareholdings

A 100 per cent shareholding will give rise to control, unless there are exceptional circumstances.[137] Furthermore, in the absence of agreements between shareholders to the contrary, shareholdings or voting rights[138] in excess of 50 per cent are a firm indication of control.[139]

It is not, however, essential to have an absolute majority shareholding in order to have the possibility of exercising control.[140] In assessing whether or not a particular shareholding gives control, the Commission will take into consideration the dispersal of the remaining shares and the involvement of the other shareholders in the management of the undertaking.

In *Arjomari-Prioux/Wiggins Teape Appleton plc*,[141] the Commission found that a 39 per cent shareholding gave rise to decisive influence where the remaining shares were dispersed amongst 107,000 other shareholders, none of whom held more than four per cent and only three of whom held more than three per cent of the issued share capital. This is apparently based on the idea that dispersal results in low attendance at general meetings, and that in the absence of any formal mechanism between the smaller shareholders, they are unlikely, because of their large number, to reach agreement on a combined exercise of their powers. Thus, in considering whether or not a shareholding of a certain size gives rise to the possibility of exercising a decisive influence, the

---

[135] Regulation 4064/89, art. 3(3).

[136] Concentrative/co-operative notice, para. 9.

[137] For examples of 100 per cent acquisitions of share capital, see *Cargill/Unilever*, M026, 1990; *Matsushita/MCA*, M037, 1990; *Elf/Ertoil*, M063, 1991; *Elf/Occidental*, M085, 1991; *ICL/Nokia Data*, M105, 1991; and *Inchape/IEP*, M182, 1991. In *VWAG/VAG (UK)*, M304, 1993, Lonrho's 100 per cent shareholding gave only joint control.

[138] Where the two differ, the latter is the determining factor.

[139] See e.g. *VIAG/Continental Can*, M081, 1991 ('a majority'); *Mannesmann/Boge*, M134, 1991 (50.01 per cent); *Magneti Marelli/CEAc*, OJ 1991 L222/38 (50.1 per cent); *Gehe AG/OCP SA*, M328, 1993 (50.1 per cent); *BSN-Nestlé/Cokoladovny*, M090, 1992, (50.41 per cent); *Mannesmann/VDO*, M164, 1991, (51 per cent); *DASA/Fokker*, M237, 1993 (51 per cent); *Alcatel/Telettra*, M042, OJ 1991 L122/48 (69.2 per cent); *Fiat Geotech/Ford New Holland*, M009, 1991, (80 per cent); concentrative/co-operative notice, para. 12; and *XXIst Report on Competition Policy for 1991*, Annex III, at p. 352. However, the rights of minority shareholders or other parties should always be examined carefully to determine whether or not they in fact exercise control jointly with the majority shareholder. In *Thomas Cook/LTU/West LB*, M229, 1992, a 90:10 division of shares was found by the Commission to give rise to joint control (see the discussion of joint ventures below).

[140] The concentrative/co-operative notice, para. 12, refers to a 'relative majority of the capital'.

[141] *Arjomari-Prioux/Wiggins Teape Appleton plc*, M025, 1990.

Commission may consider what percentage of the votes historically cast at general meetings it represents. In *Mediobanca/Generali*,[142] for example, a 12.84 per cent shareholding which would have represented between 33.24 per cent and 41.24 per cent of the votes cast at ordinary general meetings over the preceding five years, was insufficient to give the possibility of exercising control. On the other hand, in *Société Générale de Belgique/Générale de Banque*,[143] an increase of a shareholding from 20.94 per cent to 25.96 per cent was *projected* to result in control over more than 50 per cent of the votes present or represented at the next annual general meeting, and therefore considered to be a concentration.[144]

Shareholdings of less than 50 per cent may give rise to control not only where the remaining shares are dispersed, but also if they are controlled by passive shareholders.[145] In *RVI/VBC/Heuliez*,[146] RVI's nine per cent stake in an intermediary company which had joint control of the joint venture, where the remaining 91 per cent was held by banks with 'no industrial interest', together with the existence of an exclusive purchasing agreement between the joint venture and RVI which had been operating for ten years, was sufficient to give RVI control with another company over the joint venture.[147]

Minority shareholdings insufficient to achieve the control threshold may nevertheless represent a joint controlling interest if there is another identifiable joint controller. This issue is discussed more fully in the section below concerning joint ventures (¶624). If they do not give rise to either a controlling or a joint controlling interest, they may give rise to a risk of co-ordination.[148] The question of co-ordination is discussed more fully below.

---

[142] *Mediobanca/Generali*, M159, 1991 (on appeal).

[143] *Société Générale de Belgique/Générale de Banque*, M343, 1993.

[144] See also *Solvay-Laporte/Interox*, M197, 1992, where two (non-executive) directors out of ten and a 24.96 per cent shareholding (the next largest being six per cent) did not give control, since this had not represented more than 50 per cent of the votes historically cast at general meetings; and *Del Monte/Royal Foods/Anglo-American*, M277, 1992, where a shareholding of between 50 per cent and 55 per cent gave control, the remaining shares being dispersed amongst 800 other shareholders. This reasoning has also been used by the Commission in the turnover calculation. See e.g. *Arjomari-Prioux/Wiggins Teape Appleton plc*, M025, 1990 (45.19 per cent, excluded); *Eurocom/RSCG*, M147, 1991 (between 68 per cent and 77.5 per cent, included); and *Ifint/EXOR*, M187, 1992 (52.1 per cent, included).

[145] The concentrative/co-operative notice, para. 12, refers to 'passive minority holdings'.

[146] *RVI/VBC/Heuliez*, M092, 1991.

[147] In *Eridania/ISI*, M062, 1991, in an operation preceding the notified operation, the splitting by the Italian state of its 30 per cent shareholding equally between the other two shareholders, each of which already had a 35 per cent shareholding, had not given rise to a concentration, given that the vendor played 'no significant role in ... strategic or material decisions'.

[148] See the concentrative/co-operative notice, para. 37–39.

¶620

(2) Management bodies[149]

Control over an undertaking may be established where one or more undertakings has the right to appoint half[150] or more than half[151] of the board members of that undertaking.

The arguments set out above relating to the dispersal or passiveness of a majority of shares, which result in the possibility of the exercise of control by a minority shareholder, carry less weight in the case of board members, who are more likely to attend meetings and more likely to be sufficiently few to make a common exercise of their voting rights possible. However, para. 12 of the concentrative/co-operative notice suggests that a 'relative majority' of the seats may suffice to control the undertaking in certain circumstances. The ability to appoint particular officers, such as the chairman, managing director or finance director, may increase the degree of influence which may be exercised.[152]

(3) Other factors

A number of other factors have been referred to in cases establishing control. These include, for example, the possession of unexercised options over shares,[153] and the existence of a long-term supply contract.[154] Furthermore, control may also arise from rights over a company's assets, or contractual rights to participate in the running of a company.[155]

Interestingly, in *CCIE/GTE*[156] the provision of substantial finance to support a management buy-out, together with the conclusion of a series of intellectual property and supply agreements, whilst giving a limited temporary influence, were insufficient to give rise to control.

---

[149] See generally, the concentrative/co-operative notice, para. 42–45.

[150] See *UAP/Transatlantic/Sun Life*, M141, 1991, where it appears that either six or seven directors (it is unclear which) out of 14, including the chairman, was sufficient.

[151] See e.g. *Gambogi/Cogei*, M167, 1991 (four of seven).

[152] For example, in *UAP/Transatlantic/Sun Life*, M141, 1991, the undertakings which together exercised decisive influence were able to appoint at most seven of the 14 board members, which included the chairman. See also *BNP/Dresdner Bank*, M021, 1990 (right to appoint managing director). For a case in which voting rights attached to shares were effectively subordinated to board structure, see *Fletcher Challenge/Metharex*, M331, 1993.

[153] See *ELF/BC/Cepsa*, M098, 1991. See, however, *Conagra/Idea*, M010, 1991 and *British Airways/TAT*, M259, 1992 (on appeal), which suggest that share options may not in themselves generally give rise to control.

[154] See *RVI/VBC/Heuliez*, M092, 1991; and *SITA-RPC/SCORI*, M295, 1993 (in relation to VICAT before the operation).

[155] See the concentrative/co-operative notice, para. 10. In the context of joint control the Commission has distinguished between 'strategic decisions' concerning the management of a company and other decisions. A veto over strategic decisions may give rise to joint control, whilst a veto over other decisions will be insufficient. Such contractual rights, if sufficiently strong, may lead to sole control (see the discussion of joint ventures at ¶624 below). See *Arvin/Sogefi*, M360, 1993.

[156] *CCIE/GTE*, M258, 1992.

¶621   Change from joint to sole control

In *ICI/Tioxide*[157] the Commission found that an increase by ICI of its shareholding in Tioxide from 50 per cent (joint control) to 100 per cent (sole control) constituted a concentration within the meaning of the regulation. This was apparently because ICI had one kind of 'decisive influence' before the operation, and another after the operation, and 'decisive influence exercised jointly is different from decisive influence exercised solely'.[158]

¶622   Acquisition of a joint controlling interest

It is clear that an acquisition of control by more than one undertaking, i.e. a joint acquisition of control, (for example, A and B together acquire C) would come within art. 3 of the merger regulation. It appears to be the Commission's view that an acquisition of a joint controlling interest (and more generally a change in the 'nature or quality of control') may in itself trigger the regulation. This in turn raises the question of what amounts to a joint controlling interest, which is discussed more fully below in the section on joint ventures.

¶623   Joint bids

Where two or more undertakings together acquire control of another, the question of whether or not the transaction is concentrative will depend on the application of the principles relating to joint ventures, particularly whether or not the target is a full function autonomous economic entity and whether or not there is a risk of co-ordination. However, where the intention of the parties in bidding is to divide the assets of the target between themselves, and the period of joint control does not go beyond the very short term, the transaction may be treated as two or more separate operations. In each operation the undertakings concerned will be the acquiring bidder and the bundle of assets to be acquired by that bidder.[159]

---

[157] *ICI/Tioxide*, M023, 1990.

[158] The Commission used the same language in *ABB/BREL*, M221, 1992; and *Solvay-Laporte/Interox*, M197, 1992; and similar language in *Accor/Wagons-Lits*, OJ 1992 L204/1; *Eridania/ISI*, M062, 1991; *VWAG/VAG (UK)*, M304, 1993; *West LB/Thomas Cook*, M350, 1993; and *Volvo/Procordia*, M196, 1993. It was less explicit in *Grand Metropolitan/Cinzano*, M184, 1992; and *Philips/Grundig*, M382, 1993. The choice of wording in these cases is generally difficult to defend. The regulation makes no reference to different types of decisive influence. *ICI/Tioxide* could have been decided on the basis that before the operation ICI had no decisive influence, only joint control, whereas afterwards it had decisive influence. The acquisition of decisive influence triggering the regulation is clear. The Commission may have been concerned to establish that a joint controller has decisive influence in its own right in order to ensure its jurisdiction in cases involving acquisitions of a joint controlling interest. This was unnecessary, however, since such cases by definition involve another joint controller, and may therefore be treated as creations of joint ventures within art. 3(2) of Regulation 4064/89, on the grounds that where one party replaces another, a 'new' joint venture is thereby created (see *James River/Rayne*, M162, 1992; and *Sythomer/Yule Catto*, M376, 1993). This approach would have done less violence to the wording of the regulation.

[159] See the concentrative/co-operative notice, para. 48.

¶624   Joint venture

Joint ventures are the most common form of operation notified to the Commission. They may also be the most difficult to classify as either concentrative or co-operative.

In line with the Commission's broadly economic rather than legal approach, the precise legal mechanism by which a joint venture arises is not important. Thus, the merger regulation clearly applies where two or more undertakings together acquire control of a third,[160] or where a new joint venture is created which two or more undertakings agree jointly to control.[161] It also applies where one parent carves out a joint controlling interest from a previously wholly-owned subsidiary of the other parent,[162] to the sale by one joint venture partner of its interest to a third party,[163] and to the crystallisation of joint control out of a dispersed share capital.[164] It may also apply to the division of a joint venture's assets between its parents.[165]

For a joint venture to be concentrative, it must :

- be jointly controlled;[166]

- perform on a lasting basis all the functions of an autonomous economic entity;[167] and

- not give rise to the risk of co-ordination.[168]

(1)   Joint control: two shareholders

(a)   *Reciprocal 50:50 blocking votes*

Joint control exists where the parent companies must agree on decisions concerning the joint venture's activities.[169] This will generally be the case where two undertakings each control half of the shares or board, whether or not there is a shareholders' agreement, since they will be obliged to co-operate in order to avoid a standstill.[170]

---

[160] Regulation 4064/89, art. 3(1). See e.g. *Aérospatiale-Alenia/de Havilland*, OJ 1991 L334/42; *BSN/Nestlé/Cokoladovny*, M090, 1992; and *Del Monte/Royal Foods/Anglo-American*, M277, 1992.

[161] Regulation 4064/89, art. 3(2). See e.g. *Steetley/Tarmac*, M180, 1991.

[162] See e.g. *Mitsubishi/UCAR*, M024, 1990; *Asko/Omni*, M065, 1991; *Péchiney/Usinor Sacilor*, M097, 1991; *Air France/Sabena*, M157, 1992; *Péchiney/VIAG*, M198, 1992; *Northern Telecom/Matra Télécommunication*, M249, 1992; *British Airways/TAT*, M259, 1992 (on appeal); *Ahold/Jerónimo Martins*, M263, 1992; *Alcan/Inespal/Palco*, M322, 1993; *Toyota Motor Corp/Walter Frey/Toyota France*, M326, 1993; *Fortis/CGER*, M342, 1993; and *Costa Crociere/Chargeurs/Accor*, M334, 1993.

[163] See *Asko/Jacobs/ADIA*, M082, 1991; *RVI/VBC/Heuliez*, M092, 1991; *James River/Rayne*, M162, 1992; *CEA Industrie/France Télécom/Finmeccanica/SGS Thomson*, M216, 1993; and *Synthomer/Yule Catto*, M376, 1993.

[164] See e.g. *UAP/Transatlantic/Sun Life*, M141, 1991.

[165] See e.g. *Campsa*, M138, 1991; and *Solvay-Laporte/Interox*, M197, 1992.

[166] Concentrative/co-operative notice, para. 11.

[167] Regulation 4064/89, art. 3(2).

[168] Regulation 4064/89, art. 3(2).

[169] Concentrative/co-operative notice, para. 11.

[170] Concentrative/co-operative notice, para. 13. See e.g. *BNP/Dresdner Bank*, M021, 1991; *Mitsubishi/UCAR*,

On the other hand, if one of the two parents can decide alone on the commercial activities of the venture company, there will be no joint control. In the absence of rights for the minority shareholder to participate in strategic decisions of the venture, this is generally the case where one company owns more than half the capital or assets of the venture, has the right to appoint more than half of the managing or supervisory bodies, controls more than half of the votes in one of those bodies, or has the sole right to manage the venture's business.[171] Thus in *Gambogi/Cogei*, 51 per cent of the share capital of the venture was sufficient to give sole control, where the remaining 49 per cent was held by the other parent.[172]

The fact that one parent may have greater influence in the day-to-day management of the venture in relation to one market, whilst the other parent has greater influence in relation to another, will not necessarily mean that the venture is not jointly controlled, particularly where these influences mirror each other.[173]

(b) *Right to participate in strategic decisions*

Joint control may also arise where a minority shareholder[174] enjoys unusually extensive protection, particularly where a majority shareholder extends to one or more minority shareholders a contractual right to take part in the control of the joint venture.[175] Of particular importance is the existence of a veto over so-called strategic decisions, such as: the approval of annual or pluriannual budgets or strategic business plans; the approval of major investments; the launching of new products; the conclusion of important financial contracts; and the appointment and dismissal of members of the board, management, or senior executives.[176]

M024, 1990; *Flachglass/Vegla*, M168, 1992; *Steetley/Tarmac*, M180, 1991; *Grand Metropolitan/Cinzano*, M184, 1992; *Herba/IRR*, M188, 1992; *Generali/BCHA*, M189, 1992; *Péchiney/Viag*, M198, 1992; *Mondi/Franschach*, M210, 1992; *Eucom/Digital*, M218, 1992; *Fortis/La Caixa*, M254, 1992; *Rhône-Poulenc Chimie/SITA*, M266, 1992; *Waste Management International plc/SAE*, M283, 1992; *Sextant/BTG-VDO*, M290, 1992; *Matra/Cap Gemini Sogeti*, M272, 1993; *Alcan/Inespal/Palco*, M322, 1993; *Harrisons & Crosfield/AKZO*, M310, 1993; and *Hoechst/Wacker*, M284, 1993. For an example of joint control through equal board members in the face of unequal shareholdings, see *Thomson/Shorts*, M318, 1993.
[171] Concentrative/co-operative notice, para. 12.
[172] *Gambogi/Cogei*, M167, 1991. See also *Digital/Kienzle*, M057, 1991 (65:35); and *Fortis/CGER*, M342, 1993.
[173] *Elf Atochem/Rohm & Haas*, M160, 1992; and *Thomson/Shorts*, M318, 1993.
[174] Joint control has been found with a shareholding as low as ten per cent (*Thomas Cook/LTU/West LB*, M229, 1992). In *VWAG/VW (UK)*, M304, 1993, a joint controller had no shares in the jointly controlled venture.
[175] Concentrative/co-operative notice, para. 13.
[176] See e.g. *Varta/Bosch*, OJ 1991 L320/26; *Conagra/Idea*, M010, 1991; *Aérospatiale/MBB*, M017, 1991; *Sanofi/Sterling Drug*, M072, 1991; *Lyonnaise des eaux Dumez SA/Hans Brochier GmbH & CoKG*, M076, 1991, *Elf/Enterprise*, M088, 1991; *BSN-Nestlé/Cokoladovny*, M090, 1992; *Apollinaris/Schweppes*, M093, 1991; *Elf/BC/CEPSA*, M098, 1991; *Ingersoll-Rand/Dresser*, M121, 1991; *Paribas/MTH/MBH*, M122, 1991; *Viag/EB-Brühl*, M139, 1991; *Lucas/Eaton*, M149, 1991; *Air France/Sabena*, M157, 1992; *Elf/Atochem*, M160, 1992; *Péchiney/Usinor-Sacilor*, M198, 1992; *Eucom/Digital*, M218, 1992; *Thomas Cook/LTU/West LB*, M229, 1992; *Ericsson/Ascom*, M236, 1992; *Linde/Fiat*, M256, 1992; *British Airways/TAT*, M259, 1992 (on appeal); *Ahold/Jerónimo Martins*, M263, 1992; *Philips/Thomson/Sagem*, M293, 1992; *Ericsson/Hewlett-Packard*, M292, 1993; *AEGON/Scottish Equitable*, M349, 1993; and *Toyota Motor Corp/Walter Frey/Toyota France*, M326, 1993. For cases

¶624

On the other hand, in *Eridania/ISI*[177] one of the parent undertakings of a 50:50 joint venture acquired 15 per cent of the joint venture's shares from the other parent resulting in a 65:35 shareholding. The Commission found that this constituted a change from joint to sole control.[178] Unanimity was required for decisions concerning changes in the legal form of the venture, its voluntary liquidation, any modification of the existing shareholdings and the relocation of its legal headquarters. However, these were insufficiently 'strategic' to give rise to joint control on the part of the 35 per cent minority shareholder.

In *PepsiCo/General Mills*,[179] PepsiCo had overall responsibility for the day-to-day management of the venture and controlled 59.5 per cent of the shares and four of seven board members. General Mills controlled the remaining 40.5 per cent of the shares and three board members. Board decisions were to be taken by simple majority, except for acquisitions or divestitures involving an affiliate of the parties where the sale price exceeded five per cent of the venture's net asset value. There were also provisions allowing General Mills to monitor the value of and expected earnings from its investment. The Commission none the less considered that PepsiCo had sole control of the venture.[180]

(2)   Joint control: three or more shareholders

Where there are three or more shareholders, control may be exercised jointly by two or more of them, which combine their shareholdings to acquire a majority (or a relative majority) of shares, votes or seats on the board,[181] and develop a deliberate common policy, either through the granting of a veto right to each joint controlling parent[182] (especially over strategic decisions) or through the creation of a joint intermediary company specifically established

---

referring to strategic decisions where there are in any event apparently equal voting rights, see *Elf Atochem/Rohm & Haas*, M160, 1992; *Rhône-Poulenc/SNIA*, M206, 1992; and *Northern Telecom/Matra Télécommunication*, M249, 1992. The Commission's tendency is to stress the importance of control over the business plan and budget (see *SITA-RPC/SCORI*, M295, 1993).

[177]   *Eridania/ISI*, M062, 1991.

[178]   See *ICI/Tioxide*, M023, 1990 and subsequent cases discussed above.

[179]   *PepsiCo/General Mills*, M232, 1992.

[180]   See also *Usinor/ASD*, M073, 1991; *SITA-RPC/SCORI*, M295, 1993; and *DASA/Fokker*, M237, 1993. Compare the finding of joint control in *Fletcher Challenge/Methanex*, M331, 1993, despite the absence of a unanimity requirement for strategic decisions.

[181]   See e.g. *Del Monte/Royal Foods/Anglo-American*, M277, 1992; and *SITA-RPC/SCORI*, M295, 1993.

[182]   See e.g. *Dräger/IBM/HMP*, M101, 1991 (3 joint controllers with a unanimity requirement); *Kelt/American Express*, M116, 1991 (8 joint controllers, with a unanimity requirement); *Sunrise*, M176, 1991 (5 joint controllers, with shareholdings of between 15 per cent and 25 per cent, and a unanimity requirement); and *Del Monte/Royal Foods/Anglo-American*, M277, 1992 (use of voting pool). *Paribas/MBM*, M122, 1991; and *ABB/BREL*, M221, 1992 (both 40 per cent/40 per cent) do not state the basis of joint control by the two main shareholders, although this would appear to be either the dispersal of the remaining shares, or the existence of an agreement between the two main shareholders. *Elf/Ertoil*, M063, 1991, provides an example of a 20.5 per cent shareholding and a 32.1 per cent shareholding not being treated as together giving rise to decisive influence. When, however, these shareholdings were increased to 34 per cent each (*Elf/BC/CEPSA*, M098, 1991), they were treated as together giving rise to decisive influence, especially because each party now had a veto over strategic decisions.

¶624

for the purpose of exercising control over the joint venture.[183] There may also be other circumstances in which parents may be presumed together to exercise control, if the factual and legal circumstances – especially a convergence of economic interests – support the notion of a deliberate common policy.[184]

It appears that where there may be shifting alliances between minority shareholders, so that it is not possible to say which of them will consistently act together and control the venture, there may be no joint control. *Eureko*[185] illustrates the circumstances in which such a common policy may not exist. Four insurance companies established a joint venture to which they transferred their non-life and life insurance business outside their respective home countries. In principle, each party would hold 25 per cent of the venture, although this could fluctuate between about 20 per cent and 30 per cent. New partners would be sought, who would enjoy equal shareholdings with existing participants. The management board was appointed by simple majority of the shareholders' meeting, and each parent nominated two members of the supervisory board, which would approve decisions of the management board by simple or qualified (more than two-thirds) majority. The parents would have no veto in respect of these decisions. The Commission found that in all areas of commercial importance decisions could be taken by simple qualified majority, the only issue requiring unanimity at a shareholders' meeting being amendment to the list of the venture's core business. In the Commission's view these elements indicated that 'there may not be enough grounds to consider that Eureko is jointly controlled. Control would become even more diluted in the event that new shareholders joined Eureko.' In the event, the Commission found it unnecessary to decide on this point, since it found that the venture was co-ordinative and therefore outside the scope of the regulation.[186]

An interesting variation arose in *Avesta/British Steel/NCC*,[187] which concerned a four party joint venture, with the consent of the two major shareholders – together accounting for 65 per cent – and one of the other two

---

[183] See *BSN-Nestlé/Cokoladovny*, M090, 1992 (54.1 per cent); *TNT/Canada Post, DBP Postdienst, La Poste, PTT Post and Sweden Post*, M102, 1991; *ABC/Générale des Eaux/Canal+/W H Smith TV*, M110, 1991; *Kelt/American Express*, M116, 1991; *Paribas/MTH/MBH*, M122, 1991; *Del Monte/Royal Foods/Anglo-American*, M277, 1992; and *CEA Industrie/France Télécom/Finmeccanica/SGS Thomson*, M216, 1993; and *DASA/Fokker*, M237, 1993. In *UAP/Transatlantic/Sun Life*, M141, 1991, prior to the operation two shareholdings of 27.7 per cent in Sun Life did not together give decisive influence, since the parties had no intention of exercising joint control, and organised no mechanism to achieve that end. However, the placing of both shareholdings into an intermediary joint venture, which acquired a further 4.5 per cent of Sun Life, led to a joint acquisition of control.

[184] Concentrative/co-operative notice, para. 13. See e.g. *BNP/Dresdner Bank*, M021, 1990 (right to together effectively manage the venture); *Fletcher Challenge/Methanex*, M331, 1993; and *Philips/Grundig*, M382, 1993.

[185] *Eureko*, M207, 1992.

[186] See also *Koipe-Tabacalera/Elosua*, M117, 1992 (40 per cent: 40 per cent: 20 per cent), where the Commission considered that joint control could not be established with any certainty; and *Fletcher Challenge/Methanex*, M331, 1993, where joint control was established despite the fact that neither party could be sure of not being out voted by the other's alliance with the independent directors. The case may be explained by the fact that the independent directors were initially jointly nominated by the parties.

[187] *Avesta/British Steel/NCC*, M239, 1992.

required for major decisions. The venture was considered to be jointly controlled. The Commission went one stage further in *Philips/Thomson/ Sagem*,[188] finding joint control in an 80 per cent: 10 per cent: 10 per cent venture where strategic decisions required the consent of the majority shareholder and one of the two minority shareholders.

¶625   Enduring autonomous economic entity

If joint control is established, it must further be considered whether or not the joint venture will perform on a lasting basis all the functions of an autonomous economic entity.[189] Of 190 notifications to 1 January 1994, three led to a finding that this condition was not satisfied, and that therefore there was no concentration.[190]

The first requirement is therefore that the venture must be full-function, i.e. it must have all the resources necessary to function as an economically independent concern. Its human and material resources must be such as to ensure its long term existence and independence. This will generally be the case where the parent companies invest substantial financial resources in the joint venture, transfer an existing undertaking or business to it, or give it substantial technical or commercial knowhow.[191] Furthermore, the joint venture will need to be an independent supplier and buyer on the market, i.e., not supplying exclusively its parents, or taking over from its parents partial responsibilities that are merely auxiliary to their commercial activities. The fact that it achieves the majority of its supplies or sales with third parties may be insufficient if it remains substantially dependent on its parents for the maintenance and development of its business.[192]

The second requirement is that the joint venture must have decisional autonomy. Whilst the parents may reserve to themselves the right to take decisions concerning the alteration of the objects or capital, or the application of the profits, the joint venture must be able to exercise its own commercial policy and determine its competitive behaviour autonomously. This will usually not be the case where the joint venture operates in the same market as the parent undertakings, and may not be the case where it operates in adjacent,

---

[188] *Philips/Thomson/Sagem*, M293, 1992.
[189] Regulation 4064/89, art. 3 (2), para. 2.
[190] *Baxter/Nestlé/Salvia*, M058, 1991; *Flachglas/Vegla*, M168, 1992; and *Pasteur Mérieux Merck*, M285, 1993. The autonomy of the joint venture was also in question in *Philips/Thomson/Sagem*, M293, 1992; and in *British Telecom/MCI*, M353, 1993. Few cases have led to a finding that the venture is not a full function autonomous economic entity either because the issue tends to be dealt with at the pre-notification stage, or because the requirement has not been strictly applied by the Commission.
[191] Concentrative/co-operative notice, para. 17. In *CEA Industrie/France Télécom/Finemeccanica/SGS Thomson*, M216, 1993, the Commission considered that before the concentration the joint venture already performed all the functions of an autonomous economic entity.
[192] Concentrative/co-operative notice, para. 16.

upstream or downstream markets (see the discussion of co-ordination in ¶626 below).[193]

The third requirement is that these structural changes to the market must be lasting.

Factors relevant to finding of fully functional autonomy

In the cases to date, the following have been referred to by the Commission in establishing that a joint venture performs on a lasting basis all the functions of an autonomous economic entity:

- the presence or transfer of basic resources necessary to function independently, especially in connection with production,[194] marketing,[195] distribution,[196] finance,[197] management,[198] research and development,[199] stocks,[200] employees,[201] capital,[202] and (of particular importance) intellectual property rights;[203]

- the fact that the joint venture is an independent supplier and buyer on the market;[204]

- the fact that the joint venture is identifiable and distinct from its parents,[205] determines its own commercial policy,[206] intends to build and maintain its own customer base,[207] or has a very specific activity;[208]

---

[193] Concentrative/co-operative notice, para. 17 and 18.

[194] *Sanofi/Sterling Drug*, M072, 1991; *Elf Atochem/Rohm & Haas*, M160, 1992; *Steetly/Tarmac*, M180, 1991; *Péchiney/Viag*, M198, 1992; *Thomson/Shorts*, M318, 1993; and *Hoechst/Wacker*, M284, 1993. Some production facilities may be retained by the parent for R&D purposes (*Péchiney/Viag*, M198, 1992).

[195] *Steetley/Tarmac*, M180, 1991; and *Harrisons & Crosfield/AKZO*, M310, 1993.

[196] *Sanofi/Sterling Drug*, M072, 1991; *Péchiney/VIAG*, M198, 1992; and *Fortis/La Caixa*, M254, 1992.

[197] *TNT/Canada Post, DBP Postdienst, La Poste, PTT Post and Sweden Post*, M102, 1991; *Rhône-Poulenc/SNIA*, M206, 1992; *Fortis/La Caixa*, M254, 1992; and *Waste Management International plc/SAE*, M283, 1992.

[198] *Steetley/Tarmac*, M180, 1991.

[199] *Sanofi/Sterling Drug*, M072, 1991; *BSN-Nestlé/Cokoladovny*, M090, 1992; *Elf/Atochem*, M160, 1992 (own applied laboratories, with possible installation of basic research unit); *Péchiney/VIAG*, M198, 1992 (access to parents' R&D may be sufficient); and *Hoechst/Wacker*, M284, 1993.

[200] *Péchiney/VIAG*, M198, 1992.

[201] *Sanofi/Sterling Drug*, M072, 1991; *Dräger/IBM/HMP*, M101, 1991; *Volvo/Atlas*, M152, 1991; *British Airways/TAT*, M259, 1992 (on appeal); *Ericsson/Hewlett-Packard*, M292, 1993; and *SITA-RPC/SCORI*, M295, 1993 (203 employees).

[202] *BSN-Nestlé/Cokoladovny*, M090, 1992 (prospect of substantial capital injection to modernise machinery and improve productivity and quality control); *Herba/IRR*, M188, 1992; and *Ericsson/Hewlett-Packard*, M292, 1993.

[203] *Sanofi/Sterling Drug*, M072, 1991; *Thomson/Pilkington*, M086, 1991; *Dräger/IBM/HMP*, M101, 1991; *Lucas/Eaton*, M149, 1991; *Volvo/Atlas*, M152, 1991 (use of own trade name); *Elf/Atochem*, M160, 1992; *Péchiney/VIAG*, M198, 1992; *Rhône-Poulenc/SNIA*, M206, 1992; *Eucom/Digital*, M218, 1992; *Ericsson/Hewlett-Packard*, M292, 1993; *SITA-RPC/SCORI*, M295, 1993 (substantial know-how); *Thomson/Shorts*, M318, 1993; and *Hoechst/Wacker*, M284, 1993. See, especially, *Baxter/Nestlé/Salvia*, M058, 1991; and *Lucas/Eaton*, M149, 1991 (discussed below).

[204] *Steetley/Tarmac*, M180, 1991; and *Rhône-Poulenc/SNIA*, M206, 1992.

[205] *Ericsson/Kolbe*, M133, 1991; *Volvo/Atlas*, M152, 1991 (own trade name), *Steetley/Tarmac*, M180, 1991; *Avesta/British Steel/NCC*, M239, 1992 (listed on London and Stockholm stock exchanges); and *Linde/Fiat*, M256, 1992 (own trade name).

[206] *Varta/Bosch OJ* 1991 L320/26; *Mitsubishi/UCAR*, M024, 1990; *Steetley/Tarmac*, M180, 1991.

[207] *Eucom/Digital*, M218, 1992.

[208] *BNP/Dresdner Bank*, M124, 1991 (financial services in Czechoslovakia).

- the fact that the joint venture represents a permanent and durable change in the structure of the market,[209] particularly where the integration and rationalisation of the parents' assets in the joint venture makes reversal unrealistic,[210] or where there are limited and restrictive possibilities for dissolution.[211] The Commission will have regard to the pace and importance of legal and economic changes in the relevant sector in assessing whether or not structural changes should be considered relatively durable. Joint ventures of shorter duration should be possible in sectors experiencing rapid change.[212]

The Commission has found autonomy notwithstanding the following:

- the fact that the parents may appoint the board[213] or the managing director[214] of the joint venture;

- the existence of a contract for the supply of basic raw materials from a parent to the joint venture (particularly where there are very few suppliers on the EC market and it is the industry norm that most production of the raw material is used internally by producing companies);[215]

- provisions for the purchase or partial distribution of the joint venture products by one of the parents,[216] or for contracting out to the parents, particularly where it is not unusual in the industry and the commercial risk remains with the joint venture;[217]

- the existence of contracts between the parents and the joint venture regulating the common use of joint facilities on-site (electricity, gas, steam, effluent treatment, technical service agreements, cleaning, environmental, security, fire, information technology, legal, fiscal, accountancy, etc.),[218] or the leasing of land from one of the parents to the joint venture;[219]

---

[209] *Mitsubishi/UCAR*, M024, 1990 (indefinite); *Elf/Atochem*, M160, 1992 (99 years); *Herba/IRR*, M188, 1992 (58 years); *ABC/Général des Eaux/Canal+/W H Smith TV*, M110, 1991 (50 years); *Air France/Sabena*, M157, 1992 (30 years); *BSN-Nestlé/Cokoladovny*, M090, 1992 (seven years); *British Airways/TAT*, M259, 1992 (6.5 years) (on appeal); and *Volvo/Atlas*, M152, 1991 (five years).

[210] *Steetley/Tarmac*, M180, 1991; and *Péchiney/VIAG*, M198, 1992.

[211] *Elf/Atochem*, M160, 1992; and *Volvo/Atlas*, M152, 1992.

[212] See *British Airways/TAT*, M259, 1992 (on appeal).

[213] *James River/Rayne*, M162, 1992; and *Steetley/Tarmac*, M180, 1991.

[214] *Varta/Bosch* OJ 1991 L320/26; *Aérospatiale/MBB*, M017, 1991; *Dräger/IBM/HMP*, M101, 1991; and *Grand Metropolitan/Cinzano*, M184, 1992.

[215] *Courtaulds/SNIA*, M113, 1991; *Elf/Atochem*, M160, 1992; *Rhône-Poulenc/SNIA*, M206, 1992; *Rhône-Poulenc Chimie/SITA*, M266, 1992; *SITA-RPC/SCORI*, M295, 1993 (20 year contract indicator of autonomy); *Alcan/Inespal/Palco*, M322, 1993 (raw materials apparently supplied to the joint venture by both parents); *Hoechst/Wacker*, M284, 1993; *Rhône-Poulenc/SNIA* (II), M355, 1993; and *Mannesmann/Hoesch*, OJ 1993 L114/34, at p. 35. See also *Lucas/Eaton*, M149, 1991.

[216] *Ericsson/Kolbe*, M133, 1991; *Lucas/Eaton*, M149, 1991; *Generali/BCHA*, M189, 1992; *Ericsson/Ascom*, M236, 1992; *Fortis/La Caixa*, M254, 1992; and *Hoechst/Wacker*, M284, 1993.

[217] *TNT/Canada Post, DBP Postdienst, La Poste, PTT Post and Sweden Post*, M102, 1991.

[218] *Courtaulds/SNIA*, M113, 1991; *Elf/Atochem*, M160, 1992; *Rhône-Poulenc/SNIA*, M206, 1992; *Rhône-Poulenc Chimie/SITA*, M266, 1992; and *Harrisons & Crosfield/AKZO*, M310, 1993.

[219] *Courtaulds/SNIA*, M113, 1991; and *Rhône-Poulenc Chimie/SITA*, M266, 1992.

- the fact that one of the parents retains a 90 per cent (or majority) stake in the subsidiary companies to be managed by the joint venture;[220]
- the existence of a sub-contracting relationship between one of the parents and the joint venture;[221]
- the existence of operating or manufacturing agreements between the parents and the joint venture.[222]

Case illustrations

In *Baxter/Nestlé/Salvia*,[223] Baxter and Nestlé formed a new 50:50 joint venture in Germany, to which the clinical nutritional business of another company, Salvia, described by the Commission as a 'full function' undertaking, was to be transferred. The intellectual property rights, trade marks, manufacturing plant, warehousing facilities, personnel and other logistics of Salvia were transferred to Clintec. However, the parties informed the Commission of their intention to transfer ownership of the intellectual property rights jointly to Baxter and Nestlé, which would then grant an exclusive license to Clintec. In the Commission's view, since a company could only operate in the pharmaceutical market if it had access to technology and patents, this transfer would make Clintec largely dependent on its parents, and would take away the autonomous status which the joint venture would otherwise have enjoyed.[224]

By comparison, in *Lucas/Eaton*,[225] the joint venture was established to design, develop, manufacture, assemble, market and sell heavy duty braking systems. It was found to be autonomous notwithstanding the fact that the parents retained ownership of the relevant intellectual property rights, granting the joint venture exclusive, royalty-free, perpetual licences. Neither parent retained the right unilaterally to terminate the licences, and both concluded a non-competition clause in respect of the joint venture's field of operations. The Commission considered this to amount to a 'de facto transfer of intellectual property'.[226]

Flachglas/Vegla,[227] concerned a German joint venture for recycling glass used in the car and construction industries. The Commission considered that the venture would perform merely an auxilary function for its parents (who were together manufacturers and suppliers of 70 per cent of car glass in the

---

[220] *Waste Management International plc/SAE*, M283, 1992.

[221] *Sextant/BTG-VDO*, M290, 1992.

[222] *Harrisons & Crosfield/AKZO*, M310, 1993. Compare, however, *Pasteur-Mérieux/Merck*, M285, 1993 (discussed below).

[223] *Baxter/Nestlé/Salvia*, M058, 1991.

[224] See, however, *Lucas/Eaton*, M149, 1991, discussed below.

[225] *Lucas/Eaton*, M149, 1991.

[226] The joint venture also sold about 15 per cent of its products through one of the parents, from which it also purchased about one to two per cent of its parts requirements.

[227] *Flachglas/Vegla*, M168, 1992.

Community), and that the availability of a coherent disposal policy would directly affect glass purchasing decisions made by car manufacturers. The Commission also considered that the venture would operate on up-stream and down-stream markets from those of its parents, purchasing significant quantities of scrap glass from them and selling to them significant quantities of products resulting from the recycling. Other factors referred to by the Commission in reaching its finding that the venture was not full-function were: between 75 per cent and 83 per cent of the venture's first five years' budget would be for sub-contracting; the venture would not have any significant know-how or R&D programme; the venture had very few assets and would have to rely on its parents for financial resources; and economic research suggested that the market for recycled glass in Germany could not sustain an independent operation of the kind to be carried out by the venture.[228]

Pasteur-Mérieux/Merck[229] concerned a joint venture in human vaccines in the EEC and EFTA, which the Commission found not to be autonomous. This finding was largely based on the fact that the parents did not transfer their vaccine related R&D activities to the joint venture (they considered it impossible to isolate their human vaccine R&D work from their other R&D activities). The joint venture would have access to the parents R&D activities through a Development Committee created within the joint venture. This Committee could issue recommendations with regard to R&D for products currently marketed; and would have access to, select, fund and direct R&D in relation to products at a late or early stage of development (although all product rights would be retained by the originating parent for use outside the territory). However, the Commission considered that decisions relating to prior research and early development stages would remain with the parents. Since the ability to determine basic research policy independently, at least in relation to new antigens, was considered by the Commission to be a mandatory condition for an independent current and future competitive and commercial vaccine producer, and given the continuing activities of the parents in the vaccines markets outside the territory, the Commission concluded that the joint venture would not be autonomous. Furthermore, the parents did not transfer their vaccine production facilities to the joint venture (similarly, because these could not be isolated from production facilities that would not be transferred). The Commission did not consider that the terms of the manufacturing and supply agreements concluded with the joint venture would allow it to operate autonomously. In addition, the parents retained control over intellectual property rights that would allow them easily to re-enter the market as

---

[228] The autonomy of the venture was also in question in *Philips/Thomson/Sagem*, M293, 1992; and *British Telecom/MCI*, M353, 1993, given that all or a high percentage of the venture's output was likely to be supplied to its parents.

[229] *Pasteur-Mérieux/Merck*, M285, 1993.

independent operators. In the light of these factors, the Commission found the regulation inapplicable.

¶626   Concentration distinguished from co-ordination

(1)   Joint ventures: concentration or co-ordination

Generally, co-ordinative operations will fall outside the merger regulation, but may be considered under art. 85 and 86.[230] In practice the issue of co-ordination is only likely to arise in cases involving joint ventures.[231] Whether or not a joint venture gives rise to a risk of co-ordination depends very much on the particular circumstances of the case, and it is therefore one of the most difficult areas in which to give general guidance. The Commission has recognised this fact, and established a special screening group within the Task Force in order to consider this issue on a case-by-case basis at an early stage. Where the question arises, it is therefore generally desirable that the screening group is consulted as soon as possible.

A joint venture may only be concentrative if it does not have as its object or effect the co-ordination of competitive behaviour between undertakings which remain independent. In particular, there must be no such co-ordination between the parent companies, or between them and the joint venture.[232] If it is reasonably foreseeable that the competitive behaviour of one of the parents or of the joint venture on the relevant market will be influenced, then the joint venture should not be regarded as concentrative.[233] The precise dividing line between the concordance of interests of the parent companies which is necessarily present in the creation of a joint venture, and a co-ordination of competitive behaviour that is incompatible with the notion of a concentration, is problematic. The decisive factor is not the legal form of the relationship between the parent companies and between them and the joint venture. Rather, the direct or indirect, actual or potential effects of the establishment and operation of the joint venture on market relationships have determinant importance.[234] The Commission will examine particularly whether or not the joint venture and the parents remain actual or potential competitors in the

---

[230] Joint acquisitions where the sole object of the agreement is to divide up the assets of the undertaking, and this agreement is put into effect immediately after the acquisition, will fall within the scope of the regulation, and will not be considered as co-ordinative joint ventures. See Regulation 4064/89, recital 24 of the preamble, and the concentrative/co-operative notice, para. 48.

[231] Unless the operation is linked to a co-operative agreement – a particular risk in the case of asset swaps. See the concentrative/co-operative notice, para. 46 and 47.

[232] It appears that a substantial minority shareholder (but not a joint controller) may remain in a neighbouring market without giving rise to co-ordination. See *LEA Industrie/France Télécom/Finemeccanica/SGS Thomson*, M216, 1993, where Thomson CSF (in the semi-conductor market) retained a 49,9 per cent interest in an intermediary company which had joint control of the venture (in the neighbouring market for semi-conductors with military and space applications).

[233] See Regulation 4064/89, art. 3(2), para. 1; and the concentrative/co-operative notice, para. 20.

[234] Concentrative/co-operative notice, para. 23.

relevant market or in upstream, downstream or neighbouring markets,[235] and if so, whether the parents limit their influence over the joint venture, or express only their financial rather than their market oriented interest.[236] Clearly, the definition of the product and geographical markets will be of particular importance.

In practice, the cases decided by the Commission appear to fall into three broad categories: those where neither parent effectively withdraws, those where both parents effectively withdraw, and those where only one parent effectively withdraws. Since cases often appear to be distinguished on their facts, these categories are discussed below with some illustrative examples. Of 190 notifications to 1 January 1994, the Commission ruled the regulation inapplicable to 11 notified operations on the grounds that they gave rise to a risk of co-ordination.[237] In all cases both parents remained actual or potential competitors of the joint venture (or at least two parents remained in the joint venture's market). In practice the Commission has at its disposal a number of

---

[235] For examples of cases discussing neighbouring, upstream or downstream markets, or other possible spillover effects, in the context of a determination that an operation is concentrative, see *Varta/Bosch*, OJ 1991 L320/26 (starter batteries – no co-ordination with other batteries or automotive parts); *Thomson/Pilkington*, M086, 1991 (optronics – no co-ordination with glass and communication systems); *Elf/BP/CEPSA*, M098, 1991 (Spanish petrochemicals – no co-ordination with French petrochemicals); *Dräger/IBM/HMP*, M101, 1991 (computerised health management – no co-ordination with hospital equipment or computerised hospital management); *TNT/Canada Post DPP Postdienst, La Poste, PTT Post and Sweden Post*, M102, 1991 (international express delivery – no co-ordination with other postal services); *Courtaulds/SNIA*, M113, 1991 (acetate filament – no co-ordination with viscose and polyamide yarns); *Ingersoll-Rand/Dresser*, M121, 1991 (industrial pumps – no co-ordination with other types of pumps); *Lucas/Eaton*, M149, 1991 (brakes – no co-ordination with other automotive parts); *Elf Atochem/Rohm & Haas*, M160, 1992 (acrylic glass – no co-ordination with upstream product, MAM); *Péchiney/VIAG*, M198, 1992 (insulated wire – no co-ordination with ferro-alloy powders); *Ericsson/Ascomb*, M236, 1992 (public line transmission – no co-ordination with other telecommunications sectors); *Avesta/British Steel/NCC*, M239, 1992 (stainless steel – no co-ordination with other steel or scrap); *Northern Telecom/Matra Télécommunication*, M249, 1992 (telecommunications equipment – no co-ordination with public digital switching or digital cellular radio systems); *Ahold/Jerónimo Martins*, M263, 1992 (food retail – no co-ordination with luxury confectionary, cash & carry, fats and edible oils, and ice-cream); *Ericsson/Hewlett-Packard*, M292, 1993 (multi-vendor telecommunications network management systems – TNM – no co-ordination with computer networking systems or proprietry TNM systems); *Thomson/Shorts*, M318, 1993 (CAD missiles – no co-ordination with other missiles); *Alcan/Inespal/Palco*, M322, 1993 (aluminium foil containers – no co-ordination with aluminium foil); *Harrisons & Crosfield/AKZO*, M310, 1993 (PVC additives – no co-ordination with other chemicals); *Hoechst/Wacker*, M284, 1993 (PVC – no co-ordination with upstream or downstream markets or other chemicals); *Toyota Motor Corp/Walter Frey/Toyota France* (vehicle distribution in France – no co-ordination with vehicle manufacture or vehicle distribution in other member states); *Arvin/Sogefi*, M360, 1993 (exhaust after market – no co-ordination with original equipment exhaust market); *Allied Signal/Knorr-Bremse*, M337, 1993 (air brakes – no co-ordination with hydraulic brakes); *Fortis/CGER*, M342, 1993 (banking – no co-ordination with credit institutions and mortgages); *SNECMA/TI* (aircraft landing gear – no co-ordination with components, repair and óverhaul); and *Mannesmann/Hoesch*, OJ 1993 L114/34, at p. 36 (steel tubes – no co-ordination with other steel activities). In *CEA Industrie/France Télécom/Finemeccanica/SGS Thomson*, M216, 1993, the Commission considered the market for semi-conductors to be neighbouring but distinct from that for semi-conductors with military and space applications, and that there was no co-ordination between the two.

[236] Concentrative/co-operative notice, para. 20–36. See, especially, the position of ACC in *Del Monte/Royal Foods/Anglo-American*, M277, 1992.

[237] *Baxter/Nestlé/Salvia*, M058, 1991; *Elf/Enterprise*, M088, 1991; *BSN-Nestlé/Cokoladovny*, M090, 1992; *Apollinaris/Schweppes*, M093, 1991; *Koipe-Tabacalera/Elosua*, M117, 1992; *Sunrise*, M176, 1991; *Herba/IRR*, M188, 1992; *Eureko*, M207, 1992; *VTG/BPTL*, M265, 1992; *Philips/Thomson/Sagem*, M293, 1992; and *British Telecom/MCI*, M353, 1993.

¶626

devices which may be used to reach a finding of an absence of co-ordination, including narrowly defined geographical[238] and product markets, high barriers to re-entry, the development of a 'de minimis' rule and, the theory of 'industrial leadership' (discussed below).[239]

(2)   Two or more parents remain competitors of the joint venture

Where both parents remain active on the joint venture's market, or are potential competitors after the creation of the joint venture, then co-ordination of competitive behaviour between them and the joint venture is highly likely, and normally leads to the inapplicability of the merger regulation.[240] A risk of co-ordination may also arise where the parents are in competition with the joint venture on neighbouring, upstream or downstream markets.[241]

In *Baxter/Nestlé/Salvia*[242] the joint venture was to be active on the markets for enteral and parenteral clinical nutrition. Both parents would remain active in these markets, and in the closely related markets of infant and pregnant or nursing mother nutrition, nutritional products delivered to private homes (as opposed to hospitals) and nutritional products sold at retail or food service outlets. In effect, both parents remained actual competitors of the joint venture. The Commission considered that there was a high probability of allocation of product and geographical markets and a corresponding risk of co-ordination. The operation was accordingly found not to be concentrative.[243]

In *Apollinaris/Schweppes*,[244] the joint venture was to manufacture, prepare, bottle, distribute and sell Apollinaris mineral water and soft drinks and Schweppes soft drinks in Germany and Austria. Apollinaris remained in the market for regional mineral water and soft drinks in Germany, whilst Schweppes remained in the soft drinks market in other member states of the Community. The Commission concluded that the joint venture would have the effect of co-ordinating the behaviour of undertakings which remain independent. It stressed the fact that Apollinaris only partially withdrew from the joint venture's market, whilst Schweppes remained a potential competitor of the joint venture since it had the production facilities, know-how and

---

[238]   See e.g. *Thomas Cook/LTU/West LB*, M229, 1992.

[239]   For a particularly striking case, where all of these devices were present together, see *Sextant/BGT-VDO*, M290, 1992.

[240]   See *XXIst Report on Competition Policy for 1991*, Annex III(7)(I), at p. 354.

[241]   But see *Alcan/Inespal/Palco*, M322, 1993; and *Hoechst/Wacker*, M284, 1993.

[242]   *Baxter/Nestlé/Salvia*, M058, 1991.

[243]   For other cases in which at least two parents have remained actual competitors of the joint venture see *Elf/Enterprise*, M088, 1991 (both parents remained active on the joint venture's market – North Sea (UK sector) oil and gas, and the fact that the parents agreed not to compete with the joint venture for licences was considered by the Commission to contribute to the co-ordinative nature of the operation); *Koipe-Tabacalera/Elosua*, M117, 1992 (the parents and the joint venture remained in the market for edible oils in Spain); *Sunrise*, M176, 1991 (where three out of five joint controllers and the joint venture remained competitors for television advertising); and *Philips/Thomson/Sagem*, M293, 1992.

[244]   *Apollinaris/Schweppes*, M093, 1991.

financial means to re-enter the joint venture's market, and was already marketing the product in a different member state. In the Commission's view, re-entry remained a realistic option for Schweppes. The notification was subsequently treated by the Commission as a notification under Regulation 17/62 (a 'comfort letter' clearing the operation was eventually issued).[245]

If both parents are merely potential competitors of the joint venture, even in different markets, a risk of co-ordination may still arise. In *BSN-Nestlé/ Cokoladovny*[246] the parents combined their biscuit (BSN) and chocolate (Nestlé) know-how in a company intended to operate primarily in the former Czechoslovakia, but not restricted from eventually exporting to the Community. The Commission considered that the biscuit and chocolate markets were distinct and that there was no risk of horizontal co-ordination between the parents. However, it also considered that the joint venture might eventually seek to penetrate the Community market, giving rise to a risk of co-ordination. It did not therefore consider the operation to be concentrative.[247]

An interesting contrast to these cases is *Rhône-Poulenc/SNIA*,[248] where the two parents of a joint venture retained respectively one and two installations producing the joint venture product. This did not apparently lead to a risk of co-ordination, given that the entire production was sold to the joint venture.

(3)   No parent remains a competitor of the joint venture

If both parents withdraw entirely[249] and permanently from the market and adjacent upstream and downstream markets (or the joint venture enters a new market), or limit their influence over the joint venture to decisions which express their financial rather than their market-oriented interests, then the risk of co-ordination will not normally arise.[250]

In *Sanofi/Sterling Drug*,[251] concerning the combination of the parties' prescription and non-prescription pharmaceutical activities, the Commission found that, in relation to one part of the notified operation, there was a lasting

---

[245] See *XXIst Report on Competition Policy for 1991*, Annex III, at p. 355. For other cases where one parent has remained an actual competitor of the joint venture, and the other a potential competitor, see *Herba/IRR*, M188, 1992 (a joint venture producing and trading rice, with one parent active in that market, and the other active in the cereals market and therefore a potential competitor).

[246] *BSN-Nestlé/Cokoladovny*, M090, 1992.

[247] For other cases where the parents were potential competitors see *Eureko*, M207, 1992 (co-ordination of international business by national insurance companies); *VTG/BPTL*, M265, 1992 (where the activities of the two parents and the joint venture in respectively road, rail and waterway oil transport were considered to make them potential competitors and to give rise to the risk of co-ordination); *Philips/Thompson/Sagem*, M293, 1992 (a joint venture in flat screens between Philips and Thompson); and *British Telecom/MCI*, M353, 1993 (a joint venture in telecommunications services).

[248] *Rhône-Poulenc/SNIA*, M206, 1992. See also *Rhône-Poulenc/SNIA (II)*, M355, 1993.

[249] Some marginal presence may be tolerable. See the discussion at ¶627 below concerning appreciable effects on competition.

[250] Concentrative/co-operative notice; para. 21–23.

[251] *Sanofi/Sterling Drug*, M072, 1991.

¶626

change in the structure of the undertakings concerned, that the operation implied the parents' effective withdrawal from the relevant markets, and that there was no room for the co-ordination of conduct as between the parents, or between them and the joint ventures. Sterling effectively deprived itself of any realistic opportunity of re-entering the European market and acting as an independent operator on that market.

In reaching this conclusion the Commission emphasised the following points: the merging, transfer, leasing or licensing on a permanent basis of the parents' existing production, distribution and marketing assets, including all material contracts, government permits, licences, manufacturing authorisations and product registrations; the transfer of employees; the marketing of the relevant product ranges under common trade names; the fact that although research would continue to be carried out independently by the parents, further development would only be possible by agreement between the parents, failing which such know-how could only be licensed to third parties; the requirement that new acquisitions be effected jointly; the establishment of a fully integrated management structure; and the equal sharing of profits.

In *Dräger/IBM/HMP*,[252] a 33 per cent: 33 per cent: 33 per cent joint venture in which each parent controlled two out of the six seats on the supervisory board and each appointed directly a managing director, the joint venture was found to be concentrative. The Commission emphasised the transfer of intellectual property rights and personnel to the joint venture, the withdrawal or intended withdrawal of the parents from the relevant market and the existence of an 18-month non-competition agreement between the joint venture and the parents.[253] It also took account of the fact that it would be highly unlikely for any of the three parents to re-enter the market, since such a decision would be commercially unreasonable given the costs and risks involved in relation to the nature and size of the estimated market.

In *BNP/Dresdner Bank*,[254] a French bank and German bank established a joint venture to operate in the Hungarian banking market. The Commission considered that, although they were in competition in many parts of the Community, there was no interaction between the Hungarian banking system and that of the Community, and that there was therefore no risk of co-ordination arising between the two parents in the Community markets.[255]

---

[252] *Dräger/IBM/HMP*, M101, 1991.
[253] See also *Mitsubishi/UCAR*, M024, 1990; *Sanofi/Sterling Drug*, M072, 1991; *ASKO/Jacobs/ADIA*, M082, 1991; and *Péchiney/Usinor-Sacilor*, M097, 1991.
[254] *BNP/Dresdner Bank*, M021, 1991.
[255] See also *Mitsubishi/UCAR*, M024, 1990.

¶626

(4)   One parent withdraws: 'industrial leadership'

If only one parent withdraws from the market, then it may well be that a risk of co-ordination does not arise, where it can be shown that the remaining parent performs the role of 'industrial leader'. The Commission's primary concern would appear to be the risk of the co-ordination of competitive behaviour between parents. It is apparently less concerned with the risk of co-ordination between one parent and its joint venture. It has taken the view in a number of cases that where the relationship between the remaining parent and the joint venture is sufficiently close, there is in fact no competitive relationship, and therefore no risk of co-ordination. In other words, there is no risk of a reduction of competition through co-ordination because there is already no competition, since the parent's industrial leadership deprives the joint venture of independence. This would appear to be a reference to art. 3(2) of the merger regulation, which refers to the risk of co-ordination between undertakings 'which remain independent'. Such an approach sits awkwardly with a finding that the joint venture is a full function autonomous economic entity. It is also difficult to reconcile with a finding that the venture is jointly controlled by both parents, rather than solely controlled by the industrial leader. The Commission's somewhat strained approach is apparently intended to overcome the difficulty that the concentrative/co-operative notice clearly indicates that where one parent remains in the market a risk of co-ordination may arise. Furthermore, a finding of sole control by the industrial leader would result in the exclusion of the other parent as an undertaking concerned and of its turnover in any calculation intended to establish whether or not the thresholds were met and the operation had a Community dimension. In other cases it may make it difficult to identify an acquisition of a controlling interest. Quite a large number of operations might, as a result, be taken outside the scope of the regulation. Characteristically, the Commission's approach effectively widens the scope of the regulation. In the interests of clarity and legal certainty, a preferable solution would have been to amend the notice and accept a more limited application of the regulation.

In *Thomson/Pilkington*[256] the Commission found that there was no risk of co-ordination between the joint venture and Thomson, even though Thomson remained in the joint venture's market. The operation concerned the establishment of a joint venture between Thomson (a French company specialising in military high technology) and Pilkington (a UK company specialising in glass production), in the area of optronics, through the purchase by Thomson of a 49.99 per cent stake in Pilkington's existing optronics subsidiary. The Commission found that a full function joint venture would thereby be established on a permanent basis. The Commission further found

---

[256] *Thomson/Pilkington*, M086, 1991.

that Thomson was already active in optronics and would not withdraw from this field, whilst Pilkington would withdraw (its other worldwide optronics interests being run down, dormant, or not de facto under its management). With regard to the relationship between Thomson and the joint venture, the Commission found that, whilst it was possible that the markets concerned might become more open to intra-Community competition in the foreseeable future, Thomson would continue to focus its activities on the French market, and that Thomson's products were complementary to those of the joint venture. Furthermore, Thomson would have the main responsibility for the market behaviour of the joint venture (the CEO of which would be nominated by the Thomson Board). It was therefore considered that there was no significant room for competition between Thomson and the joint venture, and that the operation was concentrative.

In *Air France/Sabena*,[257] Air France acquired 37.5 per cent of the voting rights in Sabena, the remainder being held by the Belgian state. The President and Vice-President of Sabena were to be elected by simple majority of the shareholders, with Air France's consent required for their nomination. The Belgian state nominated seven representatives of the 14 strong administrative council, whilst Air France nominated five plus the president and vice-president. The Council's decisions were to be by simple majority (three-quarters majority for changes in the business plan, strategy, investment or industrial co-operation). Half of the executive committee were to be nominated by the president of the Administrative Council, and half by Air France. The Commission first found that Sabena was a jointly controlled full function autonomous economic entity. It then found that there was no co-ordination between Air France and Sabena given that Air France had the means to direct the market behaviour of Sabena (i.e. was the 'industrial leader').[258]

(5)   Meaning of 'potential' competitors

If the parents are potential competitors of the joint venture, the Commission will consider the duration and effectiveness of the parents' exclusion from the relevant markets. To that end non-competition agreements may well be treated as ancillary restraints within the meaning of the merger regulation.[259] It may be

---

[257] *Air France/Sabena*, M157, 1992.

[258] For other cases developing the theory of industrial leadership, see *Ericsson/Kolbe*, M133, 1991; *UAP/Transatlantic/Sun Life*, M141, 1991; *Generali/BCHA*, M189, 1992; *Mondi/Frantschach*, M210, 1992; *Fortis/La Caixa*, M254, 1992; *British Airways/TAT*, M259, 1992 (on appeal); *Del Monte/Royal Foods/Anglo-American*, M277, 1992; and *Sextant/BTG-VDO*, M290, 1992. For a case in which a joint controlling parent's continuing presence on the joint venture's market did not give rise to co-ordination, given that the venture was the exclusive agent of the parent, see *SITA-RPC/SCORI*, M295, 1993. In *Degussa/Ciba-Geigy*, M317, 1993, the fact that the joint venture in ceramics continued to manufacture metal oxides for one of the parents did not prejudice the concentrative nature of the operation.

[259] See e.g. *Ingersoll-Rand/Dresser*, M121, 1991; *Generali/BCHA*, M189, 1992; *Avesta/British Steel/NCC*, M239, 1992; and *Ahold/Jerónimo Martins*, M263, 1992.

¶626

sufficient if re-entry is highly unlikely, because it would not, in objective terms, represent a commercially reasonable course,[260] because the parents have transferred all relevant assets and expertise to the joint venture[261] or given the substantial costs and risks involved (i.e. the capital intensive nature of the industry) in relation to the nature and estimated size of the market.[262] The possibility of re-entry by the parent may be acceptable if it is linked to the break up of the joint venture.[263]

Thus in *Thomson/Pilkington*,[264] Pilkington's re-entry to the market was considered improbable given the high technological barriers to entry, the time-scale for showing a profit on new products (typically five to seven years before production commences), the need to recruit a skilled and expert team of scientists and engineers and the substantial capital investment in plant and machinery that would be required.

On the other hand, *Herba/IRR*[265] concerned the establishment of a joint venture between Feruzzi and Herba in the Italian rice merchanting market. Both parents were to withdraw from the market, but Feruzzi remained in the markets for merchanting maize and soya. It was therefore considered as a potential entrant into the joint venture's market, and the operation was found by the Commission to be co-operative.

(6) Types of joint venture

Further guidance may be taken from the role to be performed by the joint venture.

Where a joint venture takes over all (or some, provided that no close economic links remain) of the existing activities of the parents, and the parents withdraw permanently, there is normally no risk of co-ordination. There may be a transitional period, which should not normally exceed one year, for the parents to withdraw. The parents may remain on the same product market on a sufficiently removed geographical market.[266]

Where a joint venture undertakes new activities on behalf of the parents, there is normally no risk of co-ordination where the parents cannot enter the market, or where it would not be commercially reasonable for them to do so,

---

[260] Concentrative/co-operative notice, para. 25; *Ericsson/Hewlett-Packard*, M292, 1993; and *Matra/Cap Gemini Sogeti*, M272, 1993.

[261] *Elf Atochem/Rohm & Haas*, M160, 1992; *Steetley/Tarmac*, M180, 1991; and *AEGON/Scottish Equitable*, M349, 1993.

[262] See *Dräger/IBM/HMP*, M101, 1991; *Rhône-Poulenc/SNIA*, M206, 1992; *Waste Management International plc/SAE*, M283, 1992; *Thomson/Shorts*, M318, 1993; and *Hoechst/Wacker*, M284, 1993.

[263] See *Digital/Kienzle*, M057, 1991.

[264] *Thomson/Pilkington*, M086, 1991.

[265] *Herba/IRR*, M188, 1992.

[266] Concentrative/co-operative notice, para. 25–30.

provided that they are not active in neighbouring, upstream or downstream markets.[267]

Where the joint venture enters the parents' market and the parents remain active on the joint venture's market, there will be a presumption of co-ordination, and the regulation will not apply unless that presumption is rebutted.[268]

Where a joint venture enters an upstream or downstream market to that of the parents, the Commission will examine if their is a risk of co-ordination of selling or purchasing policy between the parents, or if the joint venture makes a substantial measure of its sales or purchases with the parents. The risk of co-ordination on neighbouring markets may depend on whether the joint venture's and the parents' products are technically or economically linked, whether they are both components of another product or are otherwise mutually complementary.[269]

¶627   Appreciable effect on competition: de minimis rule

There is no explicit requirement that the effect on competition arising from the risk of co-ordination need be appreciable in order for the operation to be taken outside the scope of the merger regulation. In practice, the relatively high thresholds will mean that joint ventures under consideration by the Commission are likely to have an appreciable effect on competition. However, in *UAP/Transatlantic/Sun Life*[270] the Commission found that both the parents and their joint venture remained active in the re-insurance market with market shares of 2.4 per cent, 0.016 per cent and 0.007 per cent. Nevertheless, the operation creating the joint venture was considered to be concentrative. The explanation for this finding would appear to be that the small market shares meant that there would be no appreciable effect on competition in the re-insurance market. In *Avesta/British Steel/NCC*,[271] British Steel retained some activities in the market of the joint venture (stainless steel), but these were considered to be negligible. The Commission stated that 'de minimis' activities of this kind would not generally give rise to any likelihood of co-ordination. In *Northern Telecom/Matra Télécommunications*[272] the Commission considered annual European sales of ECU 4m by one of the parents of the joint venture to be insignificant in competition terms. In *Waste Management International plc/SAE*,[273] the agreement establishing the joint

---

[267] Concentrative/co-operative notice, para. 31 and 32. But see *Rhône-Poulenc Chimie/SITA*, M266, 1992.
[268] Concentrative/co-operative notice, para. 33.
[269] Concentrative/co-operative notice, para. 34–36.
[270] *UAP/Transatlantic/Sun Life*, M141, 1991.
[271] *Avesta/British Steel/NCC*, M239, 1992.
[272] *Northern Telecom/Matra Télécommunications*, M249, 1992.
[273] *Waste Management International plc/SAE*, M283, 1992.

venture (concerning waste management in France) contained a de minimis clause permitting the parents to acquire other companies which earned less than 20 per cent of their French turnover in waste management, where that turnover was below FF 10m. This de minimis clause did not prejudice the concentrative nature of the operation.[274]

¶628   Operations outside the scope of the regulation

(1)   Temporary share acquisition

Article 3(5)(a) of the merger regulation provides that a concentration does not arise as a result of an acquisition and temporary holding of securities in an undertaking with a view to resale by a credit or other financial institution or insurance company, the normal activities of which include transactions and dealings in securities for their own account or for the account of others, provided that:

- the financial institution does not exercise voting rights in respect of those securities with a view to determining the competitive behaviour of that undertaking; or

- the financial institution exercises such voting rights only with a view to preparing for the disposal of all or part of the undertaking or its assets, or of the securities, and that any such disposal takes place within one year of acquisition. That period may be extended by the Commission if the financial institution can show that disposal was not reasonably possible within one year of acquisition.

In *Kelt/American Express*[275] the Commission was notified of the proposed acquisition of the whole of the share capital of Kelt Exploration Limited (Keltex), a subsidiary of Kelt Energy PLC (Kelt), as well as certain other Kelt assets, by a company formed by a syndicate of eight banks, led by American Express. The acquisition was a financial restructuring operation, designed to prevent Kelt from going into receivership.

In the decision of non-opposition the Commission concluded that art. 3(5)(a) of the regulation was not applicable, and that the notified operation would therefore result in the establishment of a concentration within the scope of the regulation.

In the part of the decision stating that art. 3(5)(a) did not apply, the

---

[274] For other cases suggesting the existence of a de minimis rule, see *Aérospatiale/MBB*, M017, 1991; *Mitsubishi/UCAR*, M024, 1990; *Elf/BP/CEPSA*, M098, 1991; *Del Monte/Royal Foods/Anglo-American*, M277, 1992; *Matra/Cap Gemini Sogeti*, M272, 1993; *SITA-RPC/SCORI*, M295, 1993; *Hoechst/Wacker*, M284, 1993; *AEGON/Scottish Equitable*, M349, 1993; *Toyota Motor Corp/Walter Frey/Toyota France*, M326, 1993; *Allied Signal/Knorr-Bremse*, M337, 1993; *Fortis/CGER*, M342, 1993; and *Mannesmann/Hoesch*, OJ 1993 L114/34, at p. 36.
[275] *Kelt/American Express*, M116, 1991.

¶628

Commission does not refer explicitly to the question of whether voting rights would be exercised with a view to determining the competitive behaviour of Keltex. It does refer to the 'special circumstances' of the case, particularly the absence of any indication that the banks would dispose of the Keltex securities within one year.

(2)   Insolvency
The merger regulation will not apply where control is acquired by an office-holder of a member state relating to liquidation, winding-up, insolvency, cessation of payments, compositions or analogous proceedings.[276]

(3)   Financial holding companies
The merger regulation will not apply to operations carried out by financial holding companies, provided that the voting rights in respect of the holding are exercised, in particular in relation to the appointment of members of the management and supervisory bodies of the undertakings in which they have holdings, only to maintain the full value of those investments and not to determine directly or indirectly the competitive conduct of those undertakings.[277] Financial holding companies are defined as:

> 'companies the sole object of which is to acquire holdings in other undertakings, and to manage such holdings and turn them to profit, without involving themselves directly or indirectly in the management of those undertakings, the foregoing without prejudice to their rights as shareholders. The limitations imposed on the activities of these companies must be such that compliance with them can be supervised by an administrative or judicial authority.'[278]

¶629   Interplay between EC and national merger control: introduction

In art. 1, 9, 19, 21 and 22, the merger regulation defines the scope of the respective powers of the Commission and the competent authorities of the member states as regards concentrations between undertakings.

The basic principles underlying the regulation in this respect are, first, that the Commission (subject to review by the Court of First Instance and the Court of Justice) has sole competence to take the decisions provided in the regulation[279] and, second, that no member state may apply its national

---

[276]   Regulation 4064/89, art. 3(5)(b).
[277]   Regulation 4064/89, art. 3(5)(c).
[278]   Art. 5(3) of the fourth company law directive (Directive 78/660) on the annual accounts of certain types of companies, OJ 1978 L222/11, as amended by Directive 84/569 revising the amounts expressed in ECU in Directive 78/660, OJ 1984 L314/28.
[279]   Regulation 4064/89, art. 21(1).

legislation on competition to any concentration that has a Community dimension.[280] In this manner, the regulation seeks to avoid the dangers of so-called 'double jeopardy', which refers to the legal uncertainty resulting from the simultaneous review of a transaction by a number of authorities. The essence of the one-stop principle has been amply explained by the Commission, which has stated that:

> 'The basic concept underlying the Regulation is to establish a clear allocation between Community-scale mergers, for which the Commission is responsible, and those whose main impact is in the territory of a member state, for which the national authorities are responsible'.[281]

Despite the practical advantages of this approach for commercial operators, the one-stop principle contained in the regulation has been qualified by certain political considerations expressed by the member states. Consequently, art. 1, 9, 19, 21 and 22 of the regulation, which define the scope of the respective powers of the Commission and the competent national authorities of the member states, have clouded the aforementioned 'clear allocation' of regulatory jurisdiction. The result, while not giving rise to double jeopardy, does nevertheless provide for dual control in certain circumstances. In addition, the residual application of art. 85 and 86 of the EC Treaty by the Commission and in the member states should also be taken into consideration. In short, the one-stop principle has been qualified in the following manner:

(1) even in respect of concentrations having a Community dimension, the Commission is obliged to consult closely with the authorities of the member states by virtue of art. 19 of the regulation (see ¶630);

(2) in certain circumstances the Commission may refer a concentration having a Community dimension to the competent national authorities in conformity with art. 9 of the regulation (see ¶631);

(3) member states may, upon those occasions specified in art. 21(3), apply national law to transactions with a Community dimension in order to protect certain 'legitimate interests' (see ¶632);

(4) the Commission may apply the provisions of the regulation to concentrations not having a Community dimension at the request of a member state by virtue of art. 22(3)–(5) of the regulation (see ¶633);

(5) art. 85 and 86 of the treaty may in certain circumstances be applied to concentrations with (and without) a Community dimension within the member states (see ¶634); and

(6) the Commission may apply the principles contained in art. 85 and 86 of

---

[280] Regulation 4064/89, art. 21(2).
[281] *Nineteenth Report on Competition Policy*, point 16(a).

¶629

the treaty to concentrations without a Community dimension by virtue of its residual authority provided for in art. 89 of the treaty (see ¶634).

¶630   Liaison with the authorities of the member states

Article 19 of the merger regulation provides that the Commission, when acting under the terms of the regulation, must consult with the authorities of the member states, and must transmit copies of notifications to the latter within three working days. Such liaison is particularly important when the Commission is considering a request by a member state for a referral by virtue of art. 9 of the regulation, discussed below (¶631).[282] Article 19 also provides for the creation of a joint committee, composed of one or two representatives of each member state and chaired by the Commission, in which consultation shall take place. In particular, this committee, called the 'Advisory Committee on Concentrations', must be consulted prior to the Commission taking various second phase decisions specified in the regulation.[283]

In general, art. 19 of the regulation mirrors the consultation provisions contained in art. 10 of Regulation 17/62, which has been disapplied from concentrations falling within the meaning of the regulation.[284] However, in several respects the regulation does place greater emphasis on the role of the member state authorities than the provisions of Regulation 17/62. For example, once the committee has delivered its opinion on the Commission's draft decision, the regulation expressly provides that the Commission 'shall take the utmost account of the opinion delivered by the Committee', and 'shall inform the Committee of the manner in which its opinion has been taken into account'.[285] In addition, contrary to the procedure under Regulation 17/62, the Commission may publish the opinions of the committee, having given consideration to the legitimate interest of undertakings in the protection of their business secrets.[286] However, the opinion of the advisory committee is not binding on the Commission.[287]

---

[282] Regulation 4064/89, art. 19(2).
[283] Regulation 4064/89, art. 19(3).
[284] Regulation 4064/89, art. 22(2), discussed below at ¶634).
[285] Regulation 4064/89, art. 19(6).
[286] Regulation 4064/89, art. 19(7).
[287] Although certain minority groups within the advisory committee have on a number of occasions disagreed with certain elements of draft Commission decisions, a more fundamental disagreement arose in *Varta/Bosch*, OJ 1991 L320/26. In this case the advisory committee was of the opinion that the Commission should block the concentration, indicating that the parties' amendments to the deal following the communication of the Commission's statement of objections were insufficient to alter the negative appraisal contained therein. Nevertheless, following such amendments the Commission proceeded to clear the concentration.

¶630

¶631 Referral to the competent authorities of a member state (the 'German clause')

The mechanism contained in art. 9 of the merger regulation, which authorises the Commission to refer a case involving a concentration with a Community dimension back to the relevant national authorities, constitutes a potentially important exception to the one-stop principle discussed above. Article 9, known as the 'German clause', was included in the regulation in order to address the concern expressed by member states in relation to the Commission's likely treatment of concentrations with a Community dimension whose effects are generally limited to the territory of a single member state.

When acting under art. 85 and 86 of the EC Treaty, the Commission had been required to concentrate on those aspects of transactions which may have an effect on trade between member states, without addressing more local policy considerations. As for the regulation, the review criteria contained therein are based on the assumption that concentrations with a Community dimension will generally involve cross-border operations. Member states had expressed the concern that the Commission would, therefore, clear predominantly national concentrations with a Community dimension without giving due consideration to more localised interests. Prior to the entry into force of the regulation, member states had been able to pursue national policies such as consumer welfare by undertaking their own reviews of transactions already addressed by the Commission.[288] However, on a strict application of the one-stop principle contained in the regulation, such parallel national reviews would no longer be possible in respect of concentrations with a Community dimension. Certain member states therefore demanded that they should have the opportunity to obtain jurisdiction over concentrations with largely national effects. Art. 9 of the regulation provides for such an opportunity, subject to certain strict conditions.

(1) Conditions for referral

The pre-conditions for the referral of a concentration with a Community dimension to the national authorities of a member state are:

(1) the existence of a 'distinct market'[289] affected by the concentration located within the territory of the requesting member state; and

---

[288] See e.g. *Coats Patons Ltd/Gütermann & Co., Ninth Report on Competition Policy*, point 132. Despite the Commission having found the proposed take-over to be compatible with art. 86 of the treaty, 'the project was nevertheless abandoned when the German Federal Cartel Office objected on account of its effects on the German market ...'

[289] Art. 9(7) of the Regulation provides:

'[T]he geographical reference market shall consist of the area in which the undertakings concerned are involved in the supply and demand of products or services, in which the conditions of competition are

(2) the existence of a threat to effective competition within that market resulting from the concentration.

In addition, the member state must lodge its request for referral within three weeks of its receipt of the copy of the relevant notification.[290]

Even in the event that these conditions are fulfilled, the Commission may still decide to deal with the case itself.[291] However, should the Commission adopt this course, it is obliged to act 'in order to maintain or restore effective competition on the market concerned'.[292] When a referral is made, the national authorities of the member state are obliged to apply national competition law to the concentration.[293] In the interests of transparency, the member state must publish or announce the findings of its examination of the concentration within four months of the referral by the Commission.[294]

(2) Procedure

Despite the Commission's discretion as to whether or not it should make the requested referral, art. 9 of the regulation contains strict deadlines within which the Commission's decision must be made. If no proceeding is opened by the Commission, a decision on referral must be taken within six weeks of notification.[295] If proceedings are opened by the Commission, but no preparatory steps are taken in order to adopt a decision (for example, no statement of objections is issued), a decision on referral must be taken within three months of notification.[296] If no decision is taken within this three-month period, the referral request is deemed accepted.[297] If proceedings are opened and preparatory steps taken, it would appear that the referral request is deemed rejected without an obligation on the Commission to take a decision to this effect.

(3) Referral requests

To date, there have been six requests by member states for referrals. Only two of these requests have met with a positive response. Such limited recourse to

---

sufficiently homogeneous and which can be distinguished from neighbouring areas because, in particular, conditions of competition are appreciably different in those areas. This assessment should take account in particular of the nature and characteristics of the products or services concerned, of the existence of entry barriers or of consumer preferences, of appreciable differences of the undertakings' market shares between the area concerned and neighbouring areas or of substantial price differences.'

The definition of the relevant geographic market for the purposes of the regulation is discussed at ¶636(2).
[290] Regulation 4064/89, art. 9(2).
[291] Regulation 4064/89, art. 9(3).
[292] Regulation 4064/89, art. 9(3)(a).
[293] Regulation 4064/89, art. 9(3)(b).
[294] Regulation 4064/89, art. 9(6).
[295] Regulation 4064/89, art. 9(4)(a).
[296] Regulation 4064/89, art. 9(4)(b).
[297] Curiously, deemed acceptance only applies if the member state concerned has reminded the Commission of the need to take a decision (art. 9(5)).

the referral procedure is in conformity with a joint policy statement issued by the Council and the Commission,[298] which provides that 'the referral procedure provided for in art. 9 should only be applied in exceptional cases', and should be confined 'to cases in which the interests in respect of competition of the member state concerned could not be adequately protected in any other way'.

Varta/Bosch

The first request for a referral arose in the context of the *Varta/Bosch* case,[299] and was lodged by the German Bundeskartellamt. The Commission announced in a press release concerning the initiation of proceedings in this case that it would not refer the case to the Bundeskartellamt.[300]

Alcatel/AEG Kabel

In the second case, *Alcatel/AEG Kabel*,[301] the Bundeskartellamt again sought a referral, claiming that the German markets for telecommunication cables and power cables constituted distinct geographic markets in which effective competition would be significantly impeded as a result of the transaction. Specifically, the Bundeskartellamt claimed that the transaction threatened to create or strengthen a dominant position through the creation of a three-supplier oligopoly which would hold more than 50 per cent of total sales in the German market. Rejecting the referral request in a decision taken under art. 6(1)(b) of the regulation, the Commission addressed the telecommunication cable and power cable markets separately.

Concerning the telecommunication cable market, the Commission concluded that the relevant geographic market for telecommunication cables was Community-wide. Thus, the first condition for a referral was not met. Secondly, in respect of the geographic market for power cables, the Commission accepted the existence of a national market, largely as a result of the limited effect of Community harmonisation measures in this sector. However, regarding power cables, the second condition for referral was not fulfilled because the Commission did not consider that the concentration threatened effective competition in this German market. In particular, the

---

[298] Accompanying statements entered in the minutes of the EC Council concerning Regulation 4064/89, *Nineteenth Report on Competition Policy*, p. 265.

[299] *Varta/Bosch*, OJ 1991 L320/26.

[300] IP(91)304. Interestingly, despite the apparent decision not to refer contained in this press release, the Commission stated in its *XXIst Report on Competition Policy of 1991* (Annex III, at p. 371) that 'the Commission did not have to decide on the referral request because it took in time the preparatory steps (communication of a statement of objections) . . .'. It is possible that the Commission did not, therefore, consider that the statement in the press release reflected an express decision on referral.

[301] *Alcatel/AEG Kabel*, M165, 1991.

¶631

Commission rejected the Bundeskartellamt's claim that the concentration would create a position of collective dominance.[302]

Steetley/Tarmac
The third request for a referral, submitted by the UK Department of Trade and Industry in the context of the *Steetley/Tarmac*[303] transaction, was granted by the Commission. The notified transaction involved the creation of a joint venture whereby Steetley and Tarmac merged their building materials interests. Although in relation to concrete blocks, structural concrete products and masonry products the Commission examined and cleared the transaction itself, it referred those aspects of the agreement concerning bricks and clay tiles to the UK authorities. In so deciding, the Commission identified two distinct local markets and one national market for these two products respectively. The Commission further found that the merged company would acquire a very high percentage of available capacity in these markets, thereby threatening to create a dominant position as a result of which competition would be significantly impeded. This decision to refer gives rise to two observations.

(a)   Scope of referral
First, the *Steetley/Tarmac* referral resolves the uncertainty which had surrounded the scope of a member state's review following referral under art. 9 of the regulation. Art. 9(3)(a) and (b) provides that the Commission has an option whether to deal with the 'case' itself or refer the 'case' to the national authorities. Doubt had been expressed[304] as to the exact definition of 'case' in this context. One broad interpretation would lead to the entire concentration being referred to the national authorities, while another interpretation would restrict this national intervention only to those aspects of the concentration for which national or regional markets have been identified. The aforementioned distinction drawn by the Commission between the markets for concrete blocks, structural concrete products and masonry products to be reviewed by the Commission, and bricks and clay tiles referred to the UK authorities, would suggest a Commission preference for the latter, more restrictive interpretation.

(b)   Parallel bids
Secondly, the *Steetley/Tarmac* decision also provides an interesting insight into the Commission's referral policy, independent of the requirements of the regulation. In a Commission press release[305] addressing the *Steetley/Tarmac* decision, Sir Leon Brittan stated that,

---

[302] For a further discussion of the substance of this decision, see ¶640.
[303] *Steetley/Tarmac*, M180, 1991.
[304] See Bright, 'The European Merger Control Regulation: Do Member States still have an Independent Role in Merger Control?' [1991] 4 ECLR 139.
[305] IP(92)104.

¶631

'... in any event, had there been any uncertainty in my mind, the (parallel) bid for Steetley plc by Redland might well have tipped the scales in favour of a reference back. That bid is not notifiable to the Commission, because it falls below the threshold, and it is much better for related cases to be dealt with by one regulatory authority if at all possible'.

In the event that two or more bids are made in respect of one target company, and at least one of these parallel bids falls within the jurisdiction of the national authorities of a member state, it would appear that the Commission would view more favourably a request by that member state for a referral of the other bid(s) falling within the Commission's jurisdiction.

However, the limits of this policy were revealed in the Commission's treatment of the bid by the Hong Kong and Shanghai Bank for Midland Bank plc.[306] In an attempt to put an end to the extensive press speculation concerning this issue, the Commission indicated that it would refuse any request for referral which might be submitted by the UK Department of Trade and Industry, despite the fact that Midland Bank plc was at that time also facing a parallel take-over attempt by Lloyds Bank which did not meet the regulation's thresholds.

Mannesman/Hoesch

The fourth referral request was submitted by the German Bundeskartellamt, in connection with the *Mannesman/Hoesch* notification.[307] According to the Commission's press release,[308] the Commission was not required to decide on the referral request since it had been automatically rejected by virtue of the Commission's decision to initiate proceedings on the basis of art. 6(1)(c) of the regulation. However, it would appear from art. 9(4)(b) of the regulation discussed above that such deemed refusal of referral will only arise in the event that both a proceeding has been initiated and preparatory steps have been taken in order to adopt a decision. The mere initiation of proceedings absent such preparatory steps would not appear to allow the Commission to escape from its obligation to adopt a decision on referral within the three month post-notification period in order to avoid a deemed referral. The Commission's decision[309] does not make any reference to the adoption of the requisite preparatory steps within the prescribed time limit.

Siemens/Philips

The fifth referral request was made by the German Bundeskartellamt, and concerned the *Siemens/Philips* concentration in the optical fibre and

---

[306] *Hong Kong and Shanghai Bank/Midland*, M213, 1992.
[307] *Mannesman/Hoesch*, M222, 1992.
[308] IP(92)575.
[309] OJ 1993 L114/34.

telecommunication cable business.[310] Upon opening a second phase proceeding, the Commission indicated in a press release that it did not envisage referring the case back to the German authorities.[311]

The most recent referral request was made by the German Bundeskartellamt in the context of the *McCormick/CPC/Rabobank/Ostmann* notification.[312] As explained in the Commission's press release,[313] referral was made in this case as a result of the 'miscalculation of deadlines'. In particular, the Commission had failed to initiate proceedings within the six-week period prescribed by art. 10(1) of the regulation. According to art. 10(6) of the regulation, the concentration should 'as a general rule' be declared compatible with the common market in such circumstances. Nevertheless, the Commission chose to refer the concentration to the Bundeskartellamt. Furthermore, the referral was made despite doubts concerning the interpretation of art. 9(4)(a) of the regulation, which would appear to preclude a referral after the expiry of the applicable six-week period.[314]

¶632   Protection by a member state of its 'legitimate interests'

In addition to the art. 9 referral procedure (see ¶631), a further exception to the principle of exclusive Commission jurisdiction over concentrations with a Community dimension is contained in art. 21(3) of the merger regulation, whereby national legislation may be applied by a member state[315] in order to protect its 'legitimate interests'.[316] The regulation is therefore consistent with other areas of Community law, in which a member state's ability to invoke considerations of public interest in order to derogate from its Community law obligations has traditionally been recognised.[317]

Certain interests are expressly recognised by the regulation to be 'legitimate', namely public security, the plurality of the media and prudential rules.[318] In the event that a member state seeks to rely upon other, unspecified legitimate interests, it must obtain prior approval from the Commission.

However, Community law does not recognise a member state's unqualified right to derogate from its obligations. Thus, for example, a restrictive interpretation has been adopted of the scope of a member state's right to adopt

---

[310] *Siemens/Philips Kabel*, M238, 1992.

[311] IP(92)1126.

[312] *McCormick/CPC/Rabobank/Ostmann*, M330, 1993.

[313] IP(93)943.

[314] The Commission's decision to refer in these circumstances may be founded on a certain degree of flexibility provided for in the wording of art. 9(4)(a) of the regulation.

[315] One should note that art. 21(3) of the regulation does not provide for exclusive member state jurisdiction and that a simultaneous review of the relevant concentration by the Commission under the regulation is therefore not precluded.

[316] Regulation 4064/89, art. 21(3).

[317] See e g art 26, 40(3) and 56 of the EC Treaty.

[318] Regulation 4064/89, art. 21(3).

public policy measures which are inconsistent with the principles of Community law.[319] Consistent with this approach, the regulation provides for certain limitations on a member state's right to derogate from the one-stop principle in order to protect its legitimate interests. Thus, art. 21(3) provides that a member state may only take measures to protect legitimate interests 'other than those taken into consideration' by the regulation which are 'compatible with the general principles and other provisions of Community law'.

(1) Public security

The exact scope of public security legitimate interests within the meaning of the regulation is not immediately evident. Although a public security interest may, in normal circumstances, be considered to involve considerations of national defence, recital 28 of the preamble to the regulation expressly states that the regulation is without prejudice to the rights held by the member states by virtue of art. 223 of the treaty. This treaty provision would allow a member state to intervene in respect of a concentration connected with the production of or trade in arms, munitions and war material. Thus, since a member state's national security may be protected by virtue of art. 223 of the treaty in any event, the nature of the public security issues remaining relevant under art. 21(3) of the regulation is unclear.

Some guidance regarding this issue may be derived from the joint statement made by the Council and the Commission at the time of the adoption of the regulation.[320] In this statement, it is indicated that there may be wider considerations of public security, in the sense of both art. 224[321] and 36[322] of the treaty, in addition to defence interests in the strict sense.

Thus, it would appear that legitimate public security interests may authorise a member state to adopt measures for the preservation of domestic law and

---

[319] See e.g. *Van Duyn v Home Office* [1974] ECR 1337 at p. 1350.

[320] Accompanying statements entered in the minutes of the EC Council concerning Regulation 4064/89, *Nineteenth Report on Competition Policy*, at p. 267.

[321] Article 224 of the treaty, invoked only rarely by member states, provides for wide-ranging:

'... measures which a Member State may be called upon to take in the event of serious internal disturbances affecting the maintenance of law and order, in the event of war, serious international tension constituting a threat of war, or in order to carry out obligations it has accepted for the purpose of maintaining peace and international security'.

[322] Article 36 of the treaty provides for an exception to art. 30–34 of the treaty, which preclude the imposition by member states of prohibitions or restrictions on the movement of goods imported into, exported out of or in transit through their territory. In particular, art. 36 provides that such prohibitions or restrictions may be permitted 'on grounds of public morality, public policy or public security', provided that they do not 'constitute a means of arbitrary discrimination or a disguised restriction on trade between member states. The reference to art. 36 of the treaty introduces further interests outside the scope of art. 223 or 224. For example, although a member state will not be entitled under art. 223 or 224 to take measures during peacetime with a view to ensuring the security and maintenance of supplies of certain strategic products or services considered of vital or essential interest for the protection of the population's health, such national measures have been authorised by the Court of Justice under art. 36 of the treaty (see e.g. *Campus Oil v Minister for Industry and Energy* [1984] ECR 2727).

¶632

order, for the production of strategic raw materials and for the maintenance of supply of certain strategic products. Such measures may be adopted in both times of stability and in times of domestic upheaval or international crisis. The public security legitimate interest exception to the one-stop principle could, therefore, allow potentially significant member state intervention in respect of concentrations having a Community dimension.

(2) Plurality of the media

According to the joint statement,[323] the right of the member states to plead the 'plurality of the media' recognises the legitimate concern of member states to maintain diversified sources of information for the sake of plurality of opinion and multiplicity of views. Thus, member states are able to apply their national media legislation in order to regulate concentrations which may otherwise undermine the diversified nature of a member state's media.

(3) Prudential rules

Concerning the application of prudential rules by the member states, the joint statement identifies specifically those national prudential, supervisory or cautionary rules 'which relate in particular to financial services'. According to the statement:

> 'the application of these rules is normally confined to national bodies for the surveillance of banks, stockbroking firms and insurance companies. They concern, for example, the good repute of individuals, the honesty of transactions and the rules of solvency. These specific prudential criteria are also the subject of efforts aimed at a minimum degree of harmonisation being made in order to ensure uniform 'rules of play' in the Community as a whole.'

(4) Other legitimate interests

Member states may also seek to take action in respect of concentrations on the basis of the protection of certain additional, yet unspecified, legitimate interests. In this event, the additional legitimate interest must be notified to the Commission, which shall analyse the compatibility of the relevant interest with the general principles and other provisions of Community law as discussed below. The Commission must inform the member state of its decision within one month.[324]

(5) Conditions attached to member state intervention

Despite this potential scope for intervention which the member states appear to enjoy in relation to the protection of their legitimate interests, one should

---

[323] Accompanying statements entered in the minutes of the EC Council concerning Regulation 4064/89, *Nineteenth Report on Competition Policy*, at p. 267.

[324] Regulation 4064/89, art. 21(3).

recall that this is qualified by two restrictions expressly provided for in the regulation.[325] First, the national legislation invoked by the member states in order to protect their legitimate interests should not address interests already protected under the regulation. Secondly, any such measures must respect the general principles and other provisions of Community law.

(a) *Interests already protected under the regulation*
Although the Commission must clearly take into account considerations pertaining to the maintenance of effective competition in the relevant market when reviewing concentrations under the regulation, more specific indications of what exactly is to be considered by the Commission exist in art. 2(1) of the regulation. Furthermore, it is possible that the criteria contained in art. 2(1) are not exhaustive, despite the apparently restrictive wording of this provision. This conclusion could be drawn from recital 13 of the preamble to the regulation, which states that the Commission must place its appraisal within the general framework of the achievement of the fundamental objectives referred to in art. 2 of the treaty, including that of strengthening the Community's economic and social cohesion, referred to in art. 130A.

The scope for member state intervention could be significantly diminished by this obligation on the Commission. However, as yet the Commission has not applied non-competition factors in its evaluation of the compatibility of concentrations with the common market.[326] This leaves open the possibility for member states to claim that they should have the right to invoke industrial or social policy considerations as legitimate interests because these interests are not properly safeguarded by the Commission.

(b) *General principles of Community law*
As regards the general principles of Community law to be respected, the jurisprudence of the Court of Justice requires member states (and Community institutions) to protect the principles of proportionality, legal certainty, legitimate expectation and equality, the protection of fundamental human rights and the principle of good administration. The joint statement[327] goes beyond the jurisprudence of the Court of Justice, indicating that in order that the Commission may recognise the compatibility of the public interest claimed by a member state with the general principles and other provisions of Community law it is essential that prohibitions or restrictions placed on the forming of concentrations should constitute neither a form of arbitrary discrimination nor a disguised restriction on trade between member states.

---

[325] Regulation 4064/89, art. 21(3).
[326] For a further discussion of this point, see ¶639(6).
[327] Accompanying statements entered in the minutes of the EC Council concerning Regulation 4064/89, *Nineteenth Report on Competition Policy*, at p. 267.

(c)   *Other provisions of Community law*

Concerning the 'other provisions' of Community law which must be respected by member states adopting measures in this context, the regulation presumably refers to the provisions of the treaty and secondary legislation such as directives and regulations.

¶633   Application of the regulation to concentrations without a Community dimension (the 'Dutch clause')

In accordance with art. 22(3)–(5) of the merger regulation, the Commission may apply the provisions of the regulation to concentrations not having a Community dimension at the request of a member state. This provision, known as the 'Dutch clause', was introduced into the regulation as a result of the concerns of certain member states, namely Belgium, Denmark, Greece, Italy, Luxembourg and the Netherlands, that their less developed merger enforcement systems would not be able to provide sufficient regulatory control over concentrations outside the jurisdiction of the Commission. This clause constituted an alternative to setting the thresholds provided for in art. 1(2) of the regulation at a lower level, thereby extending the exclusive jurisdiction of the Commission. Such an extension of the Commission's jurisdiction was politically unacceptable to certain other member states. Article 22(6) of the regulation provides that the Dutch clause would only apply until the thresholds had been reviewed.[328] This review having been completed (see ¶611), the Dutch clause should no longer apply.

(1)   Conditions

Three conditions were to be met before the Commission could intervene under art. 22(3). Firstly, the relevant member state had to request the Commission's intervention.[329] Secondly, the concentration had to create or strengthen a dominant position which significantly impeded effective competition within the territory of the requesting member state[330] and, finally, the concentration had to affect trade between member states.

---

[328] See Regulation 4064/89, art. 1(3), which provided that the thresholds laid down in the regulation will be reviewed before the end of the fourth year following that of the adoption of the regulation, i.e. before the end of 1993.

[329] By 1 January 1994, only one such request had been made by a member state. On 30 November 1992, following the Commission's decision in *British Airways/Dan Air*, M278, 1992, that the concentration did not have a Community dimension, and its subsequent clearance by the UK competition authorities, Belgium requested that the Commission should review the effects of the concentration on the London/Brussels route. Following such review, the Commission failed to find that the concentration would create or strengthen a dominant position as a result of which effective competition would be significantly impeded on the London/Brussels route (IP(93)106).

[330] One should note that it was not necessary that the concentration should take place in the territory of the requesting member state, but only that the effects thereof should be felt in that territory. The art. 22(3) mechanism could, therefore, provide a means for one member state to challenge a decision made by the competition authorities of the member state in which the concentration took place.

As for the third condition, in the joint statement[331] the Commission indicated that it did not intend to take action in respect of concentrations with a worldwide turnover of less than ECU 2,000m or below a minimum Community turnover level of ECU 100m, on the grounds that below such levels a concentration would not normally significantly affect trade between member states.

(2) Partial application of the regulation

Once the three conditions were met, and assuming the Commission decided to intervene, art. 2(1)(a) and (b), 5, 6, 8 and 10–20 of the regulation became applicable. Thus, concentrations without a Community dimension would be treated by the Commission in a similar manner to those with a Community dimension, subject to four exceptions. First, there was no need for the undertakings concerned to comply with the prior notification provisions contained in art. 4 of the regulation. Secondly, the mandatory suspension provisions in art. 7 of the regulation were not applicable, thereby reducing the incentive for undertakings which were targets in hostile take-over bids to petition their national authorities to make an art. 22(3) request. Thirdly, the referral procedure contained in art. 9 of the regulation (¶631) was not applicable. Finally, without the application of art. 21(2) and (3), the member states remained free to apply their national competition legislation to the relevant concentration, thereby providing for an additional source of limited double control.

(3) Procedure

The request by a member state for Commission intervention had to be made within one month of the date on which the concentration was effected or the day on which it was made known to the member state.[332] The decision by the Commission whether or not to initiate a proceeding had to be taken within one month of the request being made by the member state to the Commission.[333] Any measures adopted by the Commission on the basis of this procedure had to respect the principle of proportionality, i.e. they had to be limited to those which were strictly necessary to maintain or restore effective competition within the territory of the member state at the request of which it had intervened.[334]

---

[331] Accompanying statements entered in the minutes of the EC Council concerning Regulation 4064/89, *Nineteenth Report on Competition Policy*, at p. 267.

[332] Regulation 4064/89, art. 22(4).

[333] Regulation 4064/89, art. 22(4).

[334] Regulation 4064/89, art. 22(5).

¶633

¶634   Residual application of art. 85 and 86 to concentrations

Subject to the various exceptions cited above, the one-stop principle contained in the merger regulation clearly delimits the regulatory domains of, on the one hand, the Commission applying the regulation and, on the other hand, national authorities applying national competition law. However, such strict delimitation may in certain circumstances be undermined by the residual application of art. 85 and 86 of the treaty to concentrations (with or without a Community dimension) both within the member states and by the Commission.

(1)   Review of concentrations under art. 85 and 86 within member states

In assessing the implications of the regulation for the application within the member states of art. 85 and 86, it is important to distinguish between proceedings brought before the national courts and the regulatory role of the national competition authorities.

(a)   *Proceedings before the national courts*

By virtue of the direct effect of art. 85 and 86 of the treaty, legal or natural persons should, in theory, be able to rely upon these articles in order to initiate proceedings opposing concentrations (with or without a Community dimension) before the national courts. It should theoretically be possible for a national court to apply art. 85 or 86 to a concentration, even when that concentration is or has been under review by the Commission. However, concerning the application of art. 85, it is widely held that a concentration may not constitute an agreement which has the object or effect of restricting competition within the meaning of art. 85(1) of the treaty; the Court of Justice[335] has cast some doubt[336] on any such conclusion.

Consequently, it is not considered likely that art. 85 of the treaty will constitute a fruitful legal basis for proceedings brought before national courts by parties seeking to delay hostile take-overs or other concentrations.

Article 86 of the treaty, on the other hand, could play a most important role concerning the review of concentrations (with or without a Community dimension) by the national courts. As established by the Court of Justice in *Continental Can*,[337] a concentration may constitute an abuse of a dominant

---

[335] *BAT and Reynolds v EC Commission* [1987] ECR 4487.

[336] This doubt is reflected in recital 6 of the preamble to the merger regulation, which provides that although art. 85 and 86 are applicable 'according to the case-law of the Court of Justice, to certain concentrations, [they] are not, however, sufficient to control all operations which may prove to be incompatible with the system of undistorted competition envisaged in the Treaty'.

[337] *Europemballage Corp and Continental Can Co Inc v EC Commission* [1973] ECR 215.

¶634

position in violation of art. 86 of the treaty.[338] However, it should be noted that the jurisprudence of the Court of Justice only allows for the application of art. 86 of the treaty to transactions which *strengthen* a dominant position through concentration. The *creation* of a dominant position via a concentrative arrangement does not fall within the scope of art. 86. Parties seeking to block a concentration which creates a dominant position may, therefore, be better advised to make representations to the Commission or national authorities, depending on which body is conducting the review of the concentration.

In addition to the substantive limitations on the application of art. 85 and 86 by national courts set out above, one should also consider the practice of national courts in proceedings involving transactions under parallel review by the Commission. In such circumstances, national courts have tended to stay the proceedings pending completion of the Commission's review. Thus, the practical utility of national action by parties against concentrations falling within the jurisdiction of the Commission under the regulation may be further reduced.

(b) *National competition authorities (art. 88)*

Article 88 of the treaty requires the authorities of the member states to rule on the admissibility of transactions by virtue of both national law and the provisions of art. 85 (in particular paragraph 3 thereof) and art. 86 of the treaty. However, art. 88 may only be relied on by the national authorities in the absence of implementing legislation adopted pursuant to art. 87 of the treaty. Since the regulation may be deemed to constitute such implementing legislation for the purposes of applying art. 85 and 86 of the treaty to concentrations, it is possible that the national authorities do not, therefore, retain any residual authority to apply art. 85 and 86 of the treaty to concentrations.[339] This would be true of concentrations both with and without a Community dimension.[340]

(2) Residual authority of the Commission to apply principles of art. 85 and 86 (art. 89)

Article 89 provides that the Commission may conduct investigations, either on its own initiative or at the request of a member state, and propose appropriate measures in the event that it finds the existence of an infringement of these principles. In the event that the infringement is not terminated (as a result of undertakings ignoring the measures proposed by the Commission, for

---

[338] See ¶602 above.

[339] Although not beyond all doubt, this view has been endorsed by the English Court of Appeal in *R v Secretary for Trade and Industry, ex parte Airlines of Britain Holdings, The Times*, 10 December 1992. For a discussion of this case, see Levitt, 'Article 88, the Merger Control Regulation and the English Courts: BA/Dan-Air' [1993] 2 ECLR 73.

[340] Regulation 4064/89, art. 22(1).

example), the Commission may publish a reasoned opinion on the basis of which the member states (possibly invoking art. 88) may adopt specific measures in order to remedy the situation.[341]

(a) *Commission intervention in respect of concentrations without a Community dimension*

The use of art. 89 by the Commission in respect of concentrations with a Community dimension is inconceivable given the powers the Commission has under the regulation. However, the same might not be true of concentrations falling below the relevant thresholds. As a result of art. 22(2) of the regulation, the Commission would have no authority to challenge concentrations without a Community dimension except under the limited powers contained in art. 89 of the treaty. Thus it is not inconceivable that the Commission could resort to art. 89 if the relevant national authorities fail to take what the Commission judges to be appropriate action against a concentration without a Community dimension. Indeed, the Commission has adopted this course in the past in respect of restrictive practices in the air transport sector, which were expressly excluded from the scope of Regulation 17/62 and were for a long time not covered by any implementing legislation.[342]

(b) *Commission's statement of policy*

Indeed, the danger of a legal vacuum in the event of member state inactivity against concentrations without a Community dimension has led the Commission expressly to reserve its right to have recourse to this provision. In the joint policy statement issued by the Council and the Commission,[343] the Commission stated that it reserved the right to take action in accordance with the procedures laid down in art. 89 of the treaty for concentrations as defined in art. 3, but which do not have a Community dimension within the meaning of art. 1, in hypotheses not provided for by art. 22 (¶633). However, the extent of this reservation is somewhat circumscribed by the Commission's subsequent comment that it does not intend to take action in respect of concentrations with a worldwide turnover of less than ECU 2,000m or below a minimum Community turnover level of ECU 100m, on the ground that below such levels

---

[341] Unlike art. 88 of the treaty, it does not appear that art. 89 of the treaty may only be relied on in the absence of implementing legislation.

[342] Following the court's removal of the doubt surrounding the general application of the treaty's competition principles to the air transport sector in the absence of implementing legislation (*Ministère Public v Asjes & Ors* [1986] ECR 1425), the Commission commenced several art. 89 proceedings against various Community carriers (see e.g. the *Sixteenth Report on Competition Policy*, point 36 and the *Seventeenth Report on Competition Policy*, point 46). indeed, it was these developments which contributed greatly to the adoption by the Council of Regulation 3975/87 laying down the procedure for the application of the rules on competition to undertakings in the air transport sector (OJ 1987 L374/1).

[343] Accompanying statements entered in the minutes of the EC Council concerning Regulation 4064/89, *Nineteenth Report on Competition Policy*, p. 268.

¶634

a concentration would not normally significantly affect trade between member states.[344]

¶635   Appraisal of concentrations: compatibility with the common market

If a notified operation is deemed to constitute a concentration with a Community dimension, the Commission must establish whether or not it is compatible with the common market. According to art. 2(2) of the merger regulation a concentration will be declared compatible with the common market (and thereby granted clearance) provided that the operation:

'... does not create or strengthen a dominant position as a result of which effective competition would be significantly impeded in the common market or in a substantial part of it'.

Article 2(3) provides that if a concentration does create or strengthen a dominant position which significantly impedes effective competition in at least a substantial part of the common market, the operation will be declared incompatible with the common market and thereby prohibited.

(1)   Dominance

The review of a concentration under the regulation is based primarily on the concept of dominance.

A concentration may be prohibited if it either creates a dominant position or if it strengthens an existing dominant position. The reference to the creation of a dominant position remedies what was one of the main limitations of the application of art. 86 to mergers, namely that it only applied if a merger strengthened a pre-existing dominant position and not if it created a dominant position.[345]

From the decisions taken under the regulation, it is apparent that the Commission regards a merged entity as being dominant if it is able to exercise appreciable influence over price without losing market share, or if it is otherwise able to act to an appreciable extent independently of its competitors.[346] Although this is in keeping with definitions of dominance under

---

[344] In addition, the Commission has subsequently demonstrated restraint in its policy of recourse to art. 89 of the treaty. Thus, upon rejecting a request by British Midland to review the compatibility of the take-over by British Airways of Dan Air (*British Airways/Dan Air* M278, 1992) with art. 86 of the treaty (having previously declined jurisdiction over this transaction under the regulation), Sir Leon Brittan stated that whilst the Commission has a residual power to apply art. 86 by using the procedure set out in art. 89 of the treaty, it will only do so where a very clear case of dominance is established that is not able to be dealt with by national competition authorities. This policy enables the one-stop shop principle to function effectively, and ensures that all concentrations are subject to effective regulatory control in the Community (IP(92)1048).

[345] *Europemballage Corp and Continental Can Co Inc v EC Commission* [1973] ECR 215, at p. 245 (para. 26).

[346] For example, in *Renault/Volvo*, M004, 1990, the Commission decided that the merged entity would not be dominant in the truck market, stating '[i]t appears therefore unlikely that Renault and Volvo will have the power

art. 86, it appears that the Commission has on occasion been more reluctant to find the existence of a dominant position in cases under the regulation than in cases under art. 86.[347] This should not be seen as surprising since the assessment of dominance under art. 86 and under the regulation serve different respective purposes.

Under art. 86, dominance itself is not illegal. What is illegal is an abuse, that is a specific anti-competitive act which a firm is able to commit because its dominant position has weakened the ability of its competitors to react. Consequently, findings of dominance sometimes seem to have been easily made, based upon market shares of above 40 per cent in product and geographic markets narrowly defined.[348] Furthermore, as it is often the legality of past conduct which is at issue in art. 86 cases, in the evaluation of dominance relatively little attention has been given to the constraints placed on a firm by possible future market entrants.

Under the merger regulation, however, it is the creation or strengthening of dominance itself which is at least the principal element of illegality. Consequently, the analysis under the regulation is *ex ante*: it is designed to assess whether the structure of competition in a market will be so undermined by the concentration as to allow the combined firms in the future to act without the constraint of their competitors. It is not surprising, therefore, that the Commission has placed great emphasis in its analysis on the constraints which possible future market entrants will place on the conduct of the merged entity, and in so doing has been able to find no dominance even in the face of combined market shares of 81 and 83 per cent.[349]

(2)   Effective competition

Article 2(2) of the merger regulation provides that a concentration will be incompatible with the common market if it creates or strengthens a dominant position 'as a result of which effective competition would be significantly impeded in the common market or in a substantial part of it'. According to the art. 86 case law, a dominant firm has by definition the ability 'to hinder the maintenance of effective competition on the relevant market'[350] and it is, therefore, strongly arguable that the similar wording in art. 2(2) does no more than explain the concept of dominance. However, it should be noted that in

---

to behave to an appreciable extent independently of these competitors or to gain an appreciable influence on the determination of prices without losing market share'.

[347] For example in *Alcatel/Telettra*, OJ 1991 L122/48, at p. 53 (para. 37), a concentration was cleared even though the merged entity would have market shares of 81 per cent and 83 per cent in certain telecommunications equipment markets in Spain. This should be contrasted with the statement of the Court of Justice in *AKZO Chemie BV v EC Commission* [1991] ECR I-3359, at para. 60, that a market share of 50 per cent, except in exceptional circumstances, in itself establishes dominance.

[348] See ¶234–¶252 on dominance under art. 86.

[349] *Alcatel/Telettra*, OJ 1991 L122/48, at p. 53 (para. 37).

[350] *Michelin v EC Commission* [1983] ECR 3461, at p. 3504 (para. 30).

Aérospatiale-Alenia/de Havilland the Commission did draw a distinction between dominance and effective competition in claiming that a concentration which leads to the creation of a dominant position may be compatible with the common market if the dominance is only temporary and will not significantly impede effective competition.[351] Applying this principle, the Commission was able to declare the concentration between *Mannesmann* and *Hoesch* to be compatible with the common market. Although there was strong evidence that the merged entity would be dominant at the outset in the market for steel gas pipelines, it was concluded that such dominance would only subsist for a limited period of time owing to the high probability of new competition.[352] Finally, the requirement that effective competition be significantly impeded may be of some significance in cases in which one of the parties to a concentration has a dominant position prior to the concentration. In such circumstances the issue is whether the dominance is strengthened by the concentration. The requirement that the concentration should significantly impede effective competition may be said at least to suggest that such strengthening must be appreciable and will not be deemed automatic.[353]

(3) Horizontal, vertical and conglomerate aspects

Section 5 of Form CO[354] reveals that in determining whether a dominant position is created or strengthened so as to impede effective competition, the Commission will examine the effects of a concentration in three ways :

- First, it may consider the effect of the concentration on those markets on which at least two of the parties already compete. These are horizontal relationships and are the primary concern of the Commission.

- Secondly, if one party is operating on a market upstream or downstream of a market on which another party operates, the Commission will consider the effect which the combination of the parties may have on competitors at each level. These are vertical relationships. Most commonly, one party will be a supplier of another party, and the Commission's analysis will focus on whether the access of other suppliers to customers and of other customers to suppliers will be significantly limited as a result of the merger.[355]

- Thirdly, even if the parties do not operate on horizontally or vertically related markets, the Commission may examine the effect of the

---

[351] *Aérospatiale-Alenia/de Havilland*, OJ 1991 L334/42, at p. 56 (para. 53) and p. 60 (para. 72).

[352] *Mannesmann/Hoesch*, OJ 1993 L114/34, at pp. 47, 48 (para. 112–114).

[353] In *Tetra Pak/Alfa-Laval*, OJ 1991 L290/35, the Commission concluded that the pre-existing dominance of Tetra Pak would not be strengthened by the acquisition of Alfa-Laval. For a fuller discussion of concentrations with a de minimis effect see ¶639(5).

[354] Annex 1 to Commission Regulation 2367/90, OJ 1990 L219/5, as amended by Regulation 3666/93, OJ 1993 L336/1.

[355] See ¶639(3) below.

combination of the parties on the position which they hold on unrelated markets – these are the conglomerate features of the concentration. In this respect, the Commission has considered the effect of the combination of the financial resources and of the technical and commercial know-how of the parties to a concentration to evaluate whether this could create or strengthen a dominant position for the merged entity on markets on which only one party to the concentration previously operated.[356] Furthermore, if the parties produce related products which have the same customers, the Commission will be concerned whether the ability of the merged entity to offer a package of such goods will give them a significant competitive advantage.[357]

(4)   Overview of relevant factors in assessing compatibility

Article 2(1) of the regulation sets out the factors which the Commission should take into account in assessing whether a concentration creates or strengthens a dominant position as a result of which effective competition is significantly impeded.

Article 2(1)(a) makes it clear that the assessment is concerned specifically with the promotion of competition – 'the need to maintain and develop effective competition within the common market' – and not with the general public interest.[358] The effect on competition is to be judged in the light of the following factors:

- the structure of all the markets affected by the concentration; and
- the actual or potential competition from firms located within or outside of the EC.

Article 2(1)(b) gives more specific factors which should be taken into account in applying these basic principles of assessment. These are the following :

- the market position and the economic and financial power of the parties to the concentration;
- alternatives available to suppliers and users;
- the access of suppliers to markets and users to supplies;
- any legal or other barriers to entry;

---

[356] See ¶639(4)(b) below.
[357] See ¶639(4)(a) below.
[358] Compare, for example, with UK merger control legislation, which provides that a merger will be assessed in order to determine whether it 'operates, or may be expected to operate, against the public interest' (s. 84 of the *Fair Trading Act* 1973). In addition to the maintenance and promotion of effective competition, other factors which can be taken into account in assessing the public interest include the maintenance and promotion of a balanced distribution of industry and employment in the UK.

¶635

- supply and demand trends for the relevant goods and services;
- the interests of intermediate and ultimate consumers; and
- the development of technical and economic progress provided that it is to the advantage of consumers and does not obstruct competition.

Having first considered how markets are defined for the purpose of the application of these criteria (¶636), consideration will be given to how the principal criteria are applied in practice (¶637–¶641).

¶636   Market definition

In order to be able to analyse the effects of the concentration on competition, the first task of the Commission must be to determine the markets affected by the concentration. This requires the Commission to define both the product or service market(s) and the geographic market(s).

(1)   Product market

The merger regulation offers no guidance on how product and service markets should be distinguished from one another, but Form CO offers the following definition:

'A relevant product market comprises all those products and/or services which are regarded as interchangeable or substitutable by the consumer, by reason of the products' characteristics, their prices and their intended use.'[359]

This definition suggests that a market consists of those products or services which are substitutable for the buyer. Although such demand-side substitutability has been the determining factor in market definition under the regulation, the Commission has also on occasions examined, and made use of, the degree of supply-side substitutability between products (the extent to which products or services are substitutable for the supplier) in defining the market. In *Mannesmann/Hoesch* the Commission explained the circumstances in which supply-side substitutability would be relevant in product market evaluation:

'In the determination of the relevant product market, supply-side substitutability can only be taken into account if manufacturers of products other than the product in question can readily and quickly switch to the production of the latter.'[360]

---

[359] Section 5 of Form CO.
[360] *Mannesmann/Hoesch*, OJ 1993 L114/34, at p. 41 (para. 66). Both the extensive production changes and the considerable time required for manufacturers of other steel tubes to switch production to steel gas-line pipes suggested that steel gas-line pipes and other steel tubes were not sufficiently substitutable for manufacturers to be in the same product market. Likewise in *Nestlé/Perrier*, OJ 1992 L356/1, at pp. 6, 7 (para. 18), on appeal, the

The Commission's approach to market definition appears ad hoc and therefore its definitions are difficult to predict. Market definition is always a somewhat arbitrary exercise, and the extreme time pressure which the Commission faces in carrying out its review (it must send out a decision within one month of notification unless it is prepared to open a full proceeding)[361] makes market definition under the merger regulation no exception. The Commission is often able to avoid taking a final decision on market definition by concluding that, whichever of the alternative definitions in a case is correct, there is no risk of the concentration being declared incompatible with the common market. In cases in which it takes a position on market definition, the Commission has a tendency to define markets narrowly. The high market shares which emerge in narrowly defined markets justify a careful review by the Commisson of the effect of concentrations on competition.

(a)   *Measure of substitutability*
The Commission generally forms a view on substitutability on the basis of a comparison of the characteristics, use and price of the products. The market definition will be based on an overall comparison between products based on these three factors, although in particular cases more weight may be given to one or more of the factors. A decision in which differences in the characteristics and use of the products under comparison was crucial to a finding of distinct markets was *Aérospatiale-Alenia/de Havilland* in which the Commission decided that commuter turboprop aircraft with more than 20 seats occupied three distinct markets: aircraft with 20–39 seats; with 40–59 seats; and with 60 or more seats.[362] The differences in the seat capacities of the aircraft were seen as fundamental because this determined the type of routes on which they could be used. Different product characteristics, therefore, resulted in different use. A decision in which the price differences between the products under

---

Commission stressed the lack of supply-side substitutability between bottled source waters and soft drinks in defining the product market as bottled source waters. On the other hand, in *Elf/Ertoil*, M063, 1991, a number of different refined oil products were held to constitute a product market despite the lack of demand substitutability between them. One reason given for this was the similar conditions under which the different products were produced. For other examples of cases in which the issue of supply substitutability was considered, see, *Metallgesellschaft/Safic Alcan*, M146, 1991 (supply substitutability between natural rubber and latex); *Lucas/Eaton*, M149, 1991 (supply substitutability between different types of braking systems); *Torras/Sarrio*, M166, 1992 (supply substitutability between different types of coated and uncoated papers); *Péchiney/VIAG*, M198, 1992 (supply substitutability between different types of cored wires); *ABB/BREL*, M221, 1992 (supply substitutability between different types of railway vehicles); *Avesta/British Steel/NCC*, M239, 1992 (supply substitutability between different types of stainless steel products); *Linde/Fiat*, M256, 1992 (supply substitutability between different types of warehouse equipment); *PepsiCo/KAS*, M289, 1992 (supply substitutability between different types of carbonated soft drinks); and *Sextant/BGT-VDO*, M290, 1992 (supply substitutability between different types of aircraft components).

[361] Regulation 4064/89, art. 10(1).

[362] *Aérospatiale-Alenia/de Havilland*, OJ 1991 L334/42, at pp. 43ff. (para. 8ff.) confirmed in *DASA/Fokker*, M237, 1993.

¶636

comparision was particularly important in distinguishing product markets was *Nestlé/Perrier*.[363] In this case the Commission decided that bottled source waters constituted a distinct product market from soft drinks, stressing, among other factors, the large price differences between these two types of products (200 to 300 per cent as a general rule).

For an economist this broad approach to assessing substitutability may appear unsystematic. Ideally, the competitive relationship between products should be measured on the basis of the reaction of purchasers to price changes, that is in terms of demand cross-elasticity. If a small price increase for product X causes a large shift in demand in favour of product Y, there is a high level of cross-elasticity suggesting that products X and Y are in the same market. The Commission made a clear statement to this effect in *Du Pont/ICI*:[364]

'For two products to be regarded as substitutable, the direct customer must consider it a realistic and rational possibility to react to, for example, a significant increase in price of one product by switching to the other product in a relatively short period of time.'

In fact, in three major cases, *Tetra Pak/Alfa-Laval*,[365] *Nestlé/Perrier*[366] and *Du Pont/ICI*,[367] the Commission relied partly on the results of demand cross-elasticity studies in deciding that products occupied different markets.[368] In *Tetra Pak/Alfa-Laval*, the Commission distinguished markets for aseptic and non-aseptic carton packaging machines. In so doing, it stated that 75 per cent of customers questioned had responded that it would take a price increase of more than 20 per cent to lead them to change from aseptic to non-aseptic packaging systems.[369] In *Nestlé/Perrier*, the Commission showed that producers of bottled source waters had been able both to increase prices significantly over a period of five years and to increase sales volume at a time when the prices of soft drinks had fallen, thus suggesting a low level of substitutability between bottled source water and soft drinks.[370] In *Du Pont/ICI* the Commission found a low level of cross-price elasticity between polypropylene carpet fibres and nylon carpet fibres: a fall in the price of polypropylene carpet fibres over a

---

[363] *Nestlé/Perrier*, OJ 1992 L356/1, at pp. 3–4, on appeal.
[364] *Du Pont/ICI*, OJ 1993 L7/13, at p. 17 (para. 23).
[365] *Tetra Pak/Alfa-Laval*, OJ 1991 L290/35.
[366] *Nestlé/Perrier*, OJ 1992 L356/1, on appeal.
[367] *Du Pont/ICI*, OJ 1993 L7/13.
[368] See also, *Costa Crociere/Chargeurs/Accor*, M334, 1993.
[369] *Tetra Pak/Alfa-Laval*, OJ 1991 L290/35, at pp. 37–38. The Commission suggested that a reason for the low level of cross-price elasticity was the fact that the packaging process only accounts for 10 per cent of the cost of the final packaged product, and therefore cost increases would have to be substantial to result in substitution. In evaluating the competitive relationship between aseptic packaging machines using carton and aseptic packaging machines using glass or plastic, the Commission again used the low level of cross-price elasticity between the two categories of products as a reason for distinguishing two separate markets.
[370] *Nestlé/Perrier*, OJ 1992 L356/1, at pp. 4–6, on appeal.

period of five years had not reduced the use of nylon carpet fibres even though the price of nylon carpet fibres had risen during the same period.[371]

It seems fair to conclude from the decisions as a whole that a high degree of substitutability will be required for products to be regarded in the same market. Determining what constitutes a high level of substitutabilty is inevitably arbitrary. However, even if the degree of substitutability is not regarded as sufficient to place products in the same market, the Commission may nevertheless take it into account in assessing whether the merged firms will be dominant within that market.[372]

(b) *Market practice*

Given the time constraints under which the Commission must operate in carrying out its review, it relies considerably on the views of the customers and competitors of the parties (who are often required to complete questionnaires) in defining the market.[373] In a number of decisions the Commission has referred specifically to 'market practice' as a relevant factor in market definition.[374] If product categories have been adopted by international organisations, these may be particularly persuasive. For example, in *Sanofi/Sterling Drug* the Commission relied on ATC classifications for pharmaceutical products – which, it noted, are used by the World Health Organisation – in order to establish markets for certain pharmaceutical products.[375]

(c) *Original equipment/service and replacement markets*

In certain decisions the Commission has found different product markets in respect of what might appear to be the same product as a result of the existence of two very different demand structures for that product. With respect to car components, the Commission has distinguished the OEM/OES market from the replacement market, an approach endorsed by the Court of Justice under art. 86 in *Michelin v EC Commission*.[376] The OEM/OES market comprises the supply of components to car manufacturers either for incorporation in new vehicles (OEM) or for supply as spare parts through the car manufacturers' distribution systems (OES). The replacement market comprises the supply of the same components to a wide variety of resellers for use in the independent

---

[371] *Du Pont/ICI*, OJ 1993 L7/13, at pp. 18–19 (para. 28).
[372] See ¶639(1).
[373] For example, in *Aérospatiale-Alenia/de Havilland*, OJ 1991 L334/42, at p. 44 (para. 13) the overwhelming majority of customers and competitors of the merged entity were said to share the Commission's view on market segmentation.
[374] See e.g. *Courtaulds/SNIA*, M113, 1991; and *Metallgesellschaft/Safic Alcan*, M146, 1991.
[375] *Sanofi/Sterling Drug*, M072, 1991.
[376] *NV Nederlandsche Banden Industrie Michelin v EC Commission* [1983] ECR 3461, at p. 3505 (para. 37–38). The decisions relating to car components are *Varta/Bosch*, OJ 1991 L320/26, at pp. 27–28 (para. 12–16) and *Magnetti Marelli/CEAc*, OJ 1991 L222/38, at p. 39 (para. 8–10) (car batteries); and *Mannesmann/Boge* M134, 1991 (shock absorbers).

repair market. At the root of the distinction is the difference in the identity and requirements of the buyers. Car manufacturers are few in number and commercially powerful. Taking shock absorbers as an example, they require a limited range of products, technically tailored to their cars, which satisfy a manufacturer's requirements as to quality and just-in-time delivery. Independent resellers, on the other hand, are far more numerous and less powerful. They stock a very wide variety of shock absorbers to fit all brands of car, and a shock absorber manufacturer may require a distribution network of its own to supply them. All this results in very different conditions of competition in the supply of the product, which also give rise to significant differences in price.[377]

(d) *Service markets*
In defining markets for services, the determining factor for the Commission is, as for product market definition, the level of substitutability between services. Thus train services between Brussels and Paris are not to be regarded as part of the same service market as air services between the same cities because they are only substitutable for limited categories of travellers.[378] A considerable number of cases have involved forms of distribution and retailing services. The Commission has established substitutability by reference to the type of products supplied and/or the way in which they are supplied. In *Promodes/ DIRSA* retailing markets were identified by reference to the size of the shop.[379] This was decisive because the range of products sold and the quantities bought by the customer increased in proportion to the size of the shop. In *KNP/BT/ VRG* the Commission found the distribution of paper through merchants to be a market distinct from direct sales by manufacturers, owing to the different requirements of the customers of merchants and manufacturers respectively.[380]

---

[377] To take a different industry, in *Eridania/ISI*, M062, 1991, the Commission examined direct sales of sugar by manufacturers to industrial customers separately from sales of sugar by manufacturers to retailers.

[378] *Air France/Sabena*, M157, 1992. The Commission has also considered market definition in the air transport sector in *Delta/Pan Am*, M130, 1991 and *British Airways/TAT*, M259, 1992, on appeal. A relevant market will generally be a single route or a bundle of routes to the extent that there is sufficient substitutability between them. In *Air France/Sabena* the Commission found that flights from any airport located in the EC and EFTA countries to a destination in francophone sub-Saharan Africa would be substitutable and constitute a market. In *British Airways/TAT*, on the other hand, the lack of slots at London Heathrow and Gatwick meant that the substitutability between the flights from each of these airports to Paris was not decisive in defining the market.

[379] *Promodes/DIRSA*, M027, 1990.

[380] *KNP/BT/VRG*, OJ 1993 L217/35, at pp. 42–43 (para. 57). Whereas merchants were seen to attract customers requiring quick deliveries of small quantities from a wide range of products, manufacturers were seen to sell to customers requiring bulk deliveries at lower prices. In respect of distribution, see also *Cargill/Unilever*, M026, 1990, in which the markets for agricultural merchants were largely identified by the type of product sold; *OTTO/Grattan*, M070, 1991, and *La Redoute/Empire*, M080, 1991, in which the Commission held the relevant market to be retailing through mail order as opposed to general retailing because, even though the products supplied through both channels are the same, there are significant differences in respect of (1) the manner in which customers purchase goods, (2) the way in which the companies are organised, (3) pricing and credit policy and (4) the type of customer; *Usinor Sacilor/ASD*, M073, 1991 and *Avesta/British Steel/NCC*, M239, 1992, in which the stockholding of steel products was deemed to constitute a market, even though stockholders supplied

In defining service markets the Commission has perhaps shown itself more influenced by supply-side factors than in defining product markets. An illustration of this is *TNT/Canada Post & Ors*, in which the Commission distinguished two markets, one for domestic express deliveries of parcels and documents and the other for international express deliveries.[381] Although an express delivery service to Tokyo is not a substitute for a customer wishing to send a document to New York, the Commission nonetheless regarded these services as part of a single international market as a result of the manner in which the suppliers organised their businesses.

(2)   Geographic market

In addition to defining the product market, the Commission must define the geographic market in order to be able to assess the effects of the concentration. Form CO suggests a geographic market to be the area in which the parties supply goods or services, in which the conditions of competition are sufficiently homogeneous and which can be distinguished from neighbouring areas where the conditions of competition are appreciably different.[382] These rather unrevealing criteria are expanded by reference to the following factors to be taken into account in determining the geographic market:

- the nature of the products or services in question;
- whether there are differing consumer preferences between areas;
- whether there are other entry barriers;
- whether there are substantial price differences between geographic areas; and
- whether the market shares of the parties vary significantly in different areas.[383]

The basic purpose of defining the geographic market is to determine the geographic area or areas in which the merged entity will face actual and potential competition from suppliers of substitutable products or services. The area in which the merged entity will operate may constitute a number of geographic markets if there are entry barriers within the area preventing suppliers extending the scope of their operations beyond a certain part of the

---

a wide range of different products; *Campsa*, M138, 1991, in which the markets for the retail distribution of oil products were distinguished by the type of service offered by the different categories of resellers; and *Inchcape/IEP*, M182, 1991, in which it was not deemed necessary to divide the market for the wholesale distribution of passenger cars and commercial vehicles by sector as cars and vehicles from each sector were generally sold through the same distribution channel.

[381] *TNT/Canada Post, DBP Postdienst, La Poste, PTT Post and Sweden Post*, M102, 1991.

[382] Section 5 of Form CO. See also art. 9(7) of Regulation 4064/89 which repeats these criteria for determining whether a distinct market exists within a member state and, therefore, whether there are circumstances in which the Commission could refer a notified concentration to the competent authorities of a member state (see ¶631).

[383] Ibid.

area. On the other hand, the geographic market may be far larger than the area in which the merged entity will operate if suppliers established far away already ship, or could ship, into that area.

Owing to the difficulty in defining geographic markets, in the decisions the Commission has often declined to decide definitively on the question of the geographic market affected by the concentration, on the ground that, whichever of the possible definitions were correct, there would be no risk of the concentration being judged incompatible with the common market.

(a)   *Different conditions of competition*
The existence of markedly different conditions of competition in different areas suggests the existence of separate geographic markets. The factors which are often considered in the decisions include:

- whether or not there are significant price differences between areas;[384]

- whether or not there is a low level of imports and absence of foreign firms in an area;[385]

- whether or not there are different market leaders and differences in the market shares of the main operators in different areas;[386]

- whether or not the market is at a different stage of development in different areas.[387]

If significant differences are identified between areas, this is consistent with

---

[384] *Magnetti Marelli/CEAc*, OJ 1991 L222/38, at p. 40 (para. 16); *Varta/Bosch*, OJ 1991 L320/26, at p. 28 (para. 18); *Mannesmann/Hoesch*, OJ 1993 L114/34, at p. 37 (para. 28); *KNP/BT/VRG*, OJ 1993 L217/35, at p. 37 (para. 17); *ICI/Tioxide*, M023, 1990; *Mitsubishi/UCAR*, M024, 1990; *AT&T/NCR*, M050, 1990; *Eridania/ISI*, M062, 1991; *Sanofi/Sterling Drug*, M072, 1991; *TNT/Canada Post, DBP Postdienst, La Poste, PTT Post and Sweden Post*, M102, 1991; *Volvo/Atlas* M152, 1991; *Generali/BCHA*, M189, 1992; *Solvay-Laporte/Interox*, M197, 1992; *Thorn EMI/Virgin Music*, M202, 1992; *Thomas Cook/LTU/West LB*, M229, 1992; *Fortis/La Caixa*, M254, 1992; *Del Monte/Royal Foods/Anglo-American*, M277, 1992; *Waste Management International plc/SAE*, M283, 1992; *Alcan/Inespal/Palco*, M322, 1993; *Procordia/Erbamont*, M323, 1993; *Harrisons & Crosfield/AKZO*, M310, 1993; *Costa Crociere/Chargeurs/Accor*, M334, 1993; *Nestlé/Italgel*, M362, 1993; and *GEHE AG/OCP SA*, M328, 1993.
[385] *Alcatel/Telettra*, OJ 1991 L122/48 at p. 52 (para. 34); *Tetra Pak/Alfa-Laval*, OJ 1991 L290/35 at p. 38; *Varta/Bosch*, OJ 1991 L320/26 at pp. 29–30 (para. 31); *Accor/Wagons-Lits*, OJ 1992 L204/1 at p. 8 (para. 25(3)); *Nestlé/Perrier*, OJ 1992 L356/1 at pp. 7–10, on appeal; *Mannesmann/Hoesch*, OJ 1993 L114/34, at p. 37 (para. 28) and p. 38 (para. 35); *KNP/BT/VRG*, OJ 1993 L217/35, at p. 41 (para. 43); *Aérospatiale/MBB*, M017, 1991; *ICI/Tioxide*, M023,1990; *AT&T/NCR*, M050, 1990; *Eridania/ISI*, M062, 1991: *Ingersoll-Rand/Dresser* M121, 1991; *Metallgesellschaft/Safic Alcan*, M146, 1991; *Lucas/Eaton*, M149, 1991; *Volvo/Atlas*, M152, 1991; *Elf Atochem/Rohm and Haas*, M160, 1992; *Torras/Sarrio*, M166, 1992; *Péchiney/VIAG*, M198, 1992; *Thorn EMI/Virgin Music*, M202, 1992; *Avesta/British Steel/NCC*, M239, 1992; *Waste Management International plc/SAE* M283, 1992; *Harrisons & Crosfield/AKZO*, M310, 1993; and *Nestlé/Italgel*, M362, 1993.
[386] *Magnetti Marelli/CEAc*, OJ 1991 L222/38 at p. 40 (para. 16); *Varta/Bosch*, OJ 1991 L320/26 at p. 28 (para. 18); *Mannesmann/Hoesch*, OJ 1993 L114/34, at p. 42 (para. 72, 73); *TNT/Canada Post, DBP Postdienst, La Poste, PTT Post and Sweden Post*, M102, 1991; *Mannesmann/Boge*, M134, 1991; *Metallgesellschaft/Safic Alcan*, M146, 1991; *Mannesmann/VDO*, M164, 1991; *Solvay-Laporte/Interox*, M197, 1992; *Fortis/La Caixa*, M254, 1992; *Linde/Fiat*, M256, 1992; *Harrisons & Crosfield/AKZO*, M310, 1993; and *Costa Crociere/Chargeurs/Accor*, M334, 1993.
[387] *Otto/Grattan*, M070, 1991; *La Redoute/Empire*, M080, 1991; *TNT/Canada Post, DBP Postdienst, La Poste, PTT Post and Sweden Post*, M102, 1991; *UAP/Transatlantic/Sun Life*, M141, 1991; and *AHOLD/Jerónimo Martins/Inovação*, M320, 1993.

different geographic markets, and if they are not, the opposite is true. For example, if prices are significantly higher in one area (area A) than in another area (area B), suppliers in area B would be expected to enter area A to undercut existing suppliers. If they do not do so over a significant period, this would suggest the existence of barriers preventing or discouraging them.

However, these factors (in particular the second and fourth of those listed above) do not show that suppliers in one area would not be able to enter another area should the opportunity arise. Indeed imports may be low and foreign firms may be few because prices are not high enough to encourage entry. However, if the merged entity increased price, this might attract imports and foreign suppliers. It is only by examining the barriers to entry to an area that the Commission can reach a more accurate assessment of the geographic market.

(b)   *Barriers to entry*
The following are types of entry barriers which the Commission has assessed in determining geographic markets:

* national standards and regulatory requirements;[388]
* preference for domestic products;[389]
* national state distribution monopoly;[390]
* differing consumer preferences for product brands;[391]
* the level of transport costs;[392]
* differences in the product ranges and types of service provided in different areas;[393]

---

[388] *Alcatel/Telettra*, OJ 1991 L122/48, at pp. 50–52; *Accor/Wagons-Lits*, OJ 1992 L204/1, at p. 3 (para. 16); *Mannesmann/Hoesch*, OJ 1993 L114/34, at pp. 42–44; *Renault/Volvo*, M004, 1990; *Aérospatiale/MBB*, M017, 1991; *Group AG/Amev*, M018, 1990; *ICI/Tioxide*, M023, 1990; *Otto/Grattan*, M070, 1991; *Sanofi/Sterling Drug*, M072, 1991; *Usinor Sacilor/ASD*, M073, 1991; *La Redoute/Empire*, M080, 1991; *UAP/Transatlantic/Sun Life*, M141, 1991; *Volvo/Atlas*, M152, 1991; *Alcatel/AEG Kabel*, M165, 1991; *EUREKO*, M207, 1992; *Waste Management International plc/SAE*, M283, 1992; *Zürich/MMI*, M286, 1993; *Procordia/Erbamont*, M323, 1993; *Codan/Hafnia*, M344, 1993; *Nestlé/Italgel*, M362, 1993; and *GEHE AG/OCP SA*, M328, 1993.
[389] *Alcatel/Telettra*, OJ 1991 L122/48 at p. 52; *Aérospatiale/MBB*, M017, 1991; *Alcatel/AEG Kabel*, M165, 1991; *Mannesmann/Hoesch*, OJ 1993 L114/34, at p. 43 (para. 78); *Thomson/Shorts*, M318, 1993.
[390] *Elf/Ertoil*, M063, 1991; *Elf/BP/CEPSA*, M098, 1991; and *BP/Petromed*, M111, 1991.
[391] *Magnetti Marelli/CEAc*, OJ 1991 L222/38, at p. 40 (para. 16); *Varta/Bosch*, OJ 1991 L320/26, at p. 29 (para. 25–27); *Nestlé/Perrier*, OJ 1992 L356/1, at p. 10 (para. 33), on appeal; *Eridania/ISI*, M062, 1991; *Sanofi/Sterling Drug*, M072, 1991; and *Grand Metropolitan/Cinzano*, M184, 1992.
[392] *Nestlé/Perrier*, OJ 1992 L356/1, at pp. 8–10, on appeal; *KNP/BT/VRG*, OJ 1993 L217/35, at p. 41 (para. 44); *Eridania/ISI*, M062, 1991; *Usinor Sacilor/ASD*, M073, 1991; *VIAG/Continental Can*, M081, 1991; *BP/Petromed*, M111, 1991; *Courtaulds/SNIA*, M113, 1991; *Campsa*, M138, 1991; *Lucas/Eaton*, M149, 1991; *Volvo/Atlas*, M152, 1991; *Torras/Sarrio*, M166, 1992; *Péchiney/VIAG*, M198, 1992; *Thorn EMI/Virgin Music*, M202, 1992; *ABB/BREL*, M221, 1992; *BTR/Pirelli*, M253, 1992; *Rhône-Poulenc/SITA*, M266, 1992; *Del Monte/Royal Foods/Anglo-American*, M277, 1992; *Waste Management International plc/SAE*, M283, 1992; *Fletcher Challenge/Methanex*, M331, 1993; and *Harrisons & Crosfield/AKZO*, M310, 1993.
[393] *Magnetti Marelli/CEAc*, OJ 1991 L222/38, at p. 40 (para. 16); *Varta/Bosch*, OJ 1991 L320/26, at pp. 28–29 (para. 20–24); *Group AG/Amev*, M018, 1990; *Eridania/ISI*, M062, 1991; *Otto/Grattan*, M070, 1991; *La*

¶636

- differences in distribution channels used by suppliers in different areas;[394]
- the degree to which customers are bound by exclusive purchasing agreements foreclosing potential competing suppliers;[395]
- quantitative import restrictions and import duties;[396]
- linguistic and cultural differences;[397]
- the importance of short delivery times favouring local production;[398]

An analysis of these types of barriers determines how difficult it is for a supplier to enter a geographical area. However, in the decisions the Commission has also placed emphasis on the fact that customers may be strong enough to take supplies direct from suppliers established in a different area should suppliers within their area increase price. In particular, strong industrial buyers of components and raw materials and buyers of sophisticated expensive equipment may be prepared to buy from the best source even if it is situated far away.[399]

(c) *The effect of the single market*
Despite the single market programme, the Commission has confirmed that formidable barriers to trade between member states still exist. Consequently, for many products there are still national markets rather than a single EC market. In certain decisions, however, it has been emphasised that measures taken to complete the single market should in the longer term help to break down these barriers, and it has often been concluded that a market was in a transitional phase at the time of the decision.[400] The process of technical

---

Redoute/Empire, M080, 1991; *Generali/BCHA*, M189, 1992; *Thorn EMI/Virgin Music*, M202, 1992; *Fortis/La Caixa*, M254, 1992; *Del Monte/Royal Foods/Anglo-American*, M277, 1992; *Zürich/MMI*, M286, 1993; *Codan/Hafnia*, M344, 1993; and *GEHE AG/OCP SA*, M328, 1993.

[394] *Magnetti Marelli/CEAc*, OJ 1991 L222/38, at p. 40 (para. 16); *Tetra Pak/Alfa-Laval*, OJ 1991 L290/35, at p. 41; *Varta/Bosch*, OJ 1991 L320/26, at pp. 29–30 (para. 28–30); *Group AG/Amev*, M018, 1990; *Eridania/ISI*, M062, 1991; *Otto/Grattan*, M070, 1991; *Sanofi/Sterling Drug*, M072, 1991; *La Redoute/Empire*, M080, 1991; *Elf/Occidental*, M085, 1991; *UAP/Transatlantic/Sun Life*, M141, 1991; *Torras/Sarrio*, M166, 1992; *Grand Metropolitan/Cinzano*, M184, 1992; *Generali/BCHA*, M189, 1992; *Thorn EMI/Virgin Music*, M202, 1992; *Fortis/La Caixa*, M254, 1992; *Linde/Fiat*, M256, 1992; *Zürich/MMI*, M286, 1993; *Codan/Hafnia*, M344, 1993; *West LB/Thomas Cook*, M350, 1993; and *Costa Crociere/Chargeurs/Accor*, M334, 1993.

[395] *Fiat Geotech/Ford New Holland*, M009, 1991; and *Eridania/ISI*, M062, 1991.

[396] *KNP/BT/VRG*, OJ 1993 L217/35, at p. 41 (para. 46); *Elf/Ertoil*, M063, 1991; *Elf/BP/CEPSA*, M098, 1991; *Courtaulds/SNIA*, M113, 1991; *BP/Petromed*, M111, 1991; *BTR/Pirelli*, M253, 1992; *Fletcher Challenge/Methanex*, M331, 1993; and *Harrisons & Crosfield/AKZO*, M310, 1993.

[397] *ABC/Générale des Eaux/Canal+/W H Smith TV*, M110, 1991; *Eurocom/RSCG*, M147, 1991; *Thorn EMI/Virgin Music*, M202, 1992; *West LB/Thomas Cook*, M350, 1993; and *Costa Crociere/Chargeurs/Accor*, M334, 1993.

[398] *KNP/BT/VRG*, OJ 1993 L217/35, at p. 37 (para. 14, 15) and p. 43 (para. 58); *VIAG/Continental Can*, 1991, M081; *Mannesmann/Boge* M134, 1991; *Torras/Sarrio*, M166, 1992; and *BTR/Pirelli*, M253, 1992.

[399] See for example, *Renault/Volvo*, M004, 1990; *Aérospatiale/MBB*, M017, 1991; *Mitsubishi/UCAR*, M024, 1990; *AT&T/NCR*, M050, 1990; *Mannesmann/Boge*, M134, 1991; *Solvay-Laporte/Interox*, M197, 1992; *Péchiney/VIAG*, M198, 1992; *Rhône-Poulenc/SNIA*, M206, 1992; *BTR/Pirelli*, M253, 1992; *Alcan/Inespal/Palco*, M322, 1993; and *Codan/Hafnia*, M344, 1993.

[400] See *Alcatel/Teletra*, OJ 1991 L122/48, at pp. 49–50 (para. 7–15) (Spanish line transmission and microwave

¶636

standardisation and the liberalisation of public procurement are key elements in this transition, although the pace of change varies considerably between countries and products. In *Accor/Wagons-Lits* the Commission concluded that the directive co-ordinating the procedures for the award of public service contracts would not affect the national nature of the markets for motorway catering services 'until after a very long period'.[401] It has similarly been concluded that the national nature of the markets for defence equipment is unlikely to be affected significantly by EC legislation.[402] Even if the Commission decides that liberalisation measures have not yet dismantled the boundaries of national markets, it may, however, take account of the longer-term effect of these measures (in the form of new entrants or increased imports) in evaluating whether the merged entity will have market power.[403]

(d) *World markets*

A market will only be regarded as a world market if there is a high level of trade between the different parts of the world which results in customers throughout the world relying on the same suppliers. This can only be the case if transport costs and duties are low relative to the value of the product and provided there are no significant import restrictions. On these criteria world markets have been found (or at least considered likely) in respect of civil helicopters,[404] civil aircraft,[405] aircraft components,[406] natural rubber,[407] reinsurance services[408] and semi-conductors.[409] In contrast, in *Courtaulds/SNIA* the Commission rejected the argument of the parties that the market for acetate yarn was a world market, citing an import level into the EC of 16 per cent, a duty of ten per cent

---

transmission equipment markets); *Renault/Volvo*, M004, 1990 (national bus markets); *Ericsson/Kolbe*, M133, 1991 (telecommunications); *Alcatel/AEG Kabel*, M165, 1991 (cables market); *Generali/BCHA*, M189, 1992 (insurance); *ABB/BREL*, M221, 1992 (railway vehicles); and *Fortis/La Caixa*, M254, 1992 (insurance).

[401] *Accor/Wagons-Lits*, OJ 1992 L204/1, at p. 10 (para. 25(4)). See, also, *Mannesmann/Hoesch*, OJ 1993 L114/34, at pp. 43–44. In a number of decisions concerning oil products in Spain (*Elf/Ertoil*, M063, 1991; *Elf/BP/CEPSA*, M098, 1991; *BP/Petromed*, M111, 1991) it was stated that the expiry of the transitional period for the state distribution monopoly for primary oil products (provided in the Spanish Act of Accession to the EC) would not change the national nature of the market in the short to medium term.

[402] See *Aérospatiale/MBB*, M017, 1991, in respect of military helicopters. In *Thomson/Pilkington*, M086, 1991, the Commission pointed out that there is a certain opening up of public procurement in the defence markets. However, the Commission also stressed that the existence of international projects in the defence industry is often not indicative of a broader geographic market, as they are based on agreements between governments under which orders placed with participant companies must correspond to the investment made by the country concerned (principle of 'juste retour').

[403] See ¶638(2)(d) below.

[404] *Aérospatiale/MBB*, M017, 1991.

[405] *Aérospatiale-Alenia/de Havilland*, OJ 1991 L334/42, at p. 47 (para. 20), but note that China and eastern Europe were not deemed part of the world-wide market because there were no sales into those areas by western manufacturers and aircraft produced in those areas were not exported to the west because they did not meet western standards. See, also, *DASA/Fokker*, M237, 1993.

[406] *Sextant/BGT-VDO*, M290, 1992.

[407] *Metallgesellschaft/Safic Alcan*, M146, 1991.

[408] *UAP/Transatlantic/Sun Life*, M141, 1991; *Schweizer Rück/Elvia*, M183, 1991; and *EUREKO*, M207, 1992.

[409] *CEA Industrie/France Télécom/Finmeccanica/SGS-Thomson*, M216, 1993.

¶636

and the differences in the market shares of the market leaders in the different parts of the world.[410]

(e) *Distribution and retailing markets*

At the opposite extreme to world-wide markets, distribution and retail markets are often at most national and, in the case of retail in particular, may be local. For example, in *Promodes/DIRSA* the markets for food retailing in Spain were held to be local and not regional as contended by the parties.[411] For the shopper, the retail market is very limited in its geographic scope, being determined by how far the shopper is prepared to travel to purchase the product in question, which, in the case of food, will be a very short distance, especially in large towns. The retail outlets, however, may be part of national and international chains, and the ability of such chains to compete over broad areas has also to be taken into account in reaching a conclusion on market definition.[412]

Distribution and wholesale markets will normally be wider than retail markets because customers will usually buy from a broader area.[413] As with retail markets, account must also be taken of the way in which the distributors/ wholesalers operate. Thus in *Cargill/Unilever* the Commission suggested that, even though farmers bought from agricultural merchants within a limited range of 100 miles of their farm, the market for agricultural merchants in the UK might be national rather than regional because merchants could and did operate in many regions under similar conditions.[414] In *KNP/BT/VRG* the markets for the distribution of printing presses were held to be national, taking into account that manufacturers organise distribution on a national basis.[415]

---

[410] *Courtaulds/SNIA*, M113, 1991. Despite the finding of a western European market, the Commission stressed the potential competition from imports from the rest of the world in clearing a market share of 65 per cent. The existence of a world-wide market was also rejected in *Elf Atochem/Rohm and Haas*, M160, 1992; *Rhône-Poulenc/ SNIA*, M206, 1992 and *Del Monte/Royal Foods/Anglo-American*, M277, 1992.

[411] *Promodes/DIRSA*, M027, 1990. In *Promodes/BRMC*, M242, 1992 the Commission viewed the effect on competition (in respect of retailing) in France at the level of the *département*. In *Steetley/Tarmac*, M180, 1991, the markets for bricks in the UK were held to be local. See, also, *AHOLD/Jerónimo Martins/Inovação*, M320, 1993.

[412] In *Promodes/BRMC*, M242, 1992, the Commission took this into account in deciding (in respect of retailing) to view the effect of the concentration on competition at the level of the *département*. See also *AHOLD/Jerónimo Martins/Inovação*, M320, 1993.

[413] In *Promodes/BRMC*, M242, 1992, the wholesale market for food and non-food products was held to be at least regional. In *Torras/Sarrio*, M166, 1992, the market for paper merchants in Spain was held to be national, the importance of speed of delivery preventing it being broader. In *Metallgesellschaft/Safic Alcan*, M146, 1991, however, the market for traders of latex was held to be Community-wide.

[414] Similar reasoning was employed in respect of the distribution of steel products in *Usinor Sacilor/ASD*, M073, 1991, despite the fact that customers made purchases locally or regionally. Conversely, in *Avesta/British Steel/NCC*, M239, 1992, which concerned the distribution of stainless steel products, the Commission's preference (although no definitive geographic market definition was adopted) seems to have been for a regional market.

[415] *KNP/BT/VRG*, OJ 1993 L217/35, at p. 37 (para. 14–18).

¶636

¶637   Significance of market shares

Once the market has been defined, the market share of a firm is the starting point for an assessment of dominance, although it should not by itself be sufficient to justify a finding of dominance.

Recital 15 of the preamble to the merger regulation states that a concentration may be presumed to be compatible with the common market if the parties have a limited market share, for in such circumstances the concentration will not be liable to impede effective competition. It is expressly provided that a concentration will be presumed compatible with the common market if the combined market share of the parties is 25 per cent or less.

Although a combined market share of 25 per cent or less may give rise to a presumption of compatibility, there is no suggestion that a combined market share of more than 25 per cent will provide a presumption of incompatibility. Under the art. 86 case law, no firm has been found dominant with a market share of less than 41 per cent,[416] although the Commission has stated that a dominant position could not be excluded in the case of a market share in the range of only 20–40 per cent.[417] As yet there have been few findings of dominance under the regulation, but the 40 per cent threshold has been respected. The lowest market share figures upon which the Commission has been prepared to make findings of dominance were 43 per cent in *Du Pont/ICI*[418] and 44.3 per cent in *Varta/Bosch*.[419]

However, the decisions taken under the regulation reveal that the Commission will only use market shares, even if they are very high, as the starting point for an analysis of actual and potential competition within the market. In *Mannesmann/Hoesch*, the Commission stated:

'Market shares characterize the current market position of an undertaking. High market shares represent an important factor as evidence of a dominant position provided they not only reflect current conditions but are also a reliable indicator of future conditions. If no other structural factors are identifiable which are liable in due course to change the existing conditions of competition, market shares have to be viewed as a reliable indicator of future conditions.'[420]

The result has been that the Commission has been prepared to approve concentrations which result in very high combined market shares (as high as 83 per cent), and which, if viewed under art. 86, might have been expected to have

---

[416] *United Brands Co & Anor v EC Commission* [1978] ECR 207 at p. 282 (para. 108–109).
[417] *Ninth Report on Competition Policy*, point 22.
[418] *Du Pont/ICI*, OJ 1993 L7/13, at p. 20 (para. 32).
[419] *Varta/Bosch*, OJ 1991 L320/26, at p. 30 (para. 32).
[420] *Mannesmann/Hoesch*, OJ 1993, L114/34 at p. 45 (para. 91).

led to a finding of dominance.[421] In *Tetra Pak/Alfa-Laval* the Commission went so far as to say:

'A market share as high as 90 per cent is, in itself, a very strong indicator of a dominant position. However, in certain rare circumstances even such a high market share may not necessarily result in dominance. In particular, if sufficiently active competitors are present on the market, the company with the large market share may be prevented from acting to an appreciable extent independently of the pressures typical of a competitive market.'[422]

It is tempting to see the Commission's approach to market shares under the regulation as being more permissive than the approach of the Commission and the court under art. 86. For example, in *AKZO*[423] the court accepted that a market share of 50 per cent except in exceptional circumstances established dominance under art. 86. Despite this, it is important to emphasise that each case under the regulation is considered very much on its particular merits, and the stance taken by the Commission in *Varta/Bosch*[424] and *Du Pont/ICI*[425] would not support a general conclusion of permissiveness.

Before proceeding to a detailed analysis of the assessment of actual and potential competition in the market, there are a number of factors which should be taken into account in assessing how accurate a reflection a high market share gives of the strength of a company.

(1) In a new market, it is likely that market shares and market leadership may change frequently. Thus a high market share at any one time may

---

[421] See *Alcatel/Telettra*, OJ 1991 L122/48, at p. 53 (para. 37) (market shares in Spain of 81 per cent in the line transmission equipment market and 83 per cent in the microwave equipment market); *Accor/Wagons-Lits*, OJ 1992 L204/1, at pp. 4–5 (para. 17) (market shares of 51 per cent on the German, and 43 per cent on the Spanish group catering markets); *Renault/Volvo*, M004, 1990: (market shares of 54.3 per cent and 51 per cent in France for the intermediate and upper range of trucks respectively and market shares for buses of 69.7 per cent in France (Renault) and 64 per cent in the UK (Volvo)); *Fiat Geotech/Ford New Holland*, M009, 1991 (market share of 58 per cent for combine harvesters in Italy); *Aérospatiale/MBB*, M017, 1991 (market share of 52 per cent in the EC civil helicopter market); *Eridania/ISI*, M062, 1991 (market share in excess of 50 per cent for industrial sugar in Italy); *Sanofi/Sterling Drug*, M072, 1991 (market share of 74 per cent in the Netherlands for cold preparations without anti-infectives); *Courtaulds/SNIA*, M113, 1991 (market share of 65 per cent for acetate yarn in western Europe); *Lucas/Eaton*, M149, 1991 (market share in excess of 50 per cent in certain markets for braking systems); *ABB/BREL*, M221, 1992 (market share of over 50 per cent in the EC and 60 per cent in the UK in certain new-build railway vehicle markets); *Elf Aquitaine/Thyssen/Minol*, M235, 1992 (market share of 76 per cent (1991)/59 per cent (first half of 1992) for distribution of petroleum products in the eastern part of Germany); *Ericsson/Ascom*, M236, 1992 (market share of 61 per cent in Denmark in public line transmission equipment); *British Airways/TAT*, M259, 1992, on appeal (market share of 58.6 per cent on the London–Lyon route (100 per cent from Gatwick) and 52.2 per cent on the London–Paris route (98.6 per cent from Gatwick); *PepsiCo/KAS*, M289, 1992 (69 per cent in lemon-lime carbonated soft drinks in Portugal); *Costa Crociere/Chargeurs/Accor*, M334, 1993 (market share in France of 45 per cent in cruises); *Société Générale de Belgique/Générale de Banque*, M343, 1993 (market share in Belgium of 59 per cent in export finance); and *Rhône-Poulenc/SNIA (II)*, M355, 1993 (market share in the EEA of 43 per cent in nylon textile filament).
[422] *Tetra Pak/Alfa-Laval*, OJ 1991 L290/35, at pp. 38–39.
[423] *AKZO Chemie BV v EC Commission* [1991] ECR I-3359, at para. 60.
[424] *Varta/Bosch*, OJ 1991 L320/26.
[425] *Du Pont/ICI*, OJ 1993 L7/13.

¶637

not give an accurate reflection of the strength of the company concerned.[426]

(2) If orders for particular products are intermittent because, for example, the products are custom-built, produced in small numbers and of particularly high value, market shares viewed over a limited period of time may not accurately reflect the competitive situation. A producer may make no sales for two years, only to take a large part of the market in the third year with one order.[427]

(3) The significance of the market share will be reduced if it has been falling in previous years. In *Fiat Geotech/Ford New Holland,* in which the merged firms had a market share of 58 per cent for combine harvesters in Italy, the Commission cited the decrease in Fiat's market shares in recent years as a factor indicating an absence of a dominant position which could significantly impede effective competition in Italy.[428] Likewise in *Elf Aquitaine/Thyssen/Minol* it was emphasised that the market share of Minol in the market for the distribution of petroleum products in the eastern part of Germany had fallen from 76 per cent in 1991 to 59 per cent in the first half of 1992 in the wake of the restructuring of the economy.[429] By contrast, in *Tetra Pak/Alfa-Laval* the Commission noted that Tetra Pak had held a market share of over 90 per cent for a considerable period of time, thus indicating a position of great market power.[430]

(4) In the service sector in particular, a concentration may result in a loss of future market share because the merged entity may not be able to keep all the clients of the previously independent companies. Clients who are competitors on their own markets may not wish to be represented by the same firm. In *Eurocom/RSCG* the Commission decided that a concentration between two advertising agencies could decrease their combined market share because competing clients would not necessarily

---

[426] This was the case in the workstations market in *Digital/Kienzle*, M057, 1991. According to the Commission:

'High market shares on a new developing market are not extraordinary, and they do not necessarily indicate market power. In fact the development of the market shares of the three leading companies over a period of time shows the dynamic nature of this market. There has been a constant change including a change in market leadership' (id., at para. 20).

This is repeated, virtually verbatim, in *Digital/Philips*, M129, 1991. See also *TNT/Canada Post, DBP Postdienst, La Poste, PTT Post and Sweden Post*, M102, 1991 (international express delivery market subject to rapid growth and fluctuating market shares of service providers).

[427] *ABB/BREL*, M221, 1992 (railway vehicles).

[428] *Fiat Geotech/Ford New Holland*, M009, 1991.

[429] *Elf Aquitaine/Thyssen/Minol*, M235, 1992. See also *Procordia/Erbamont*, M323, 1993. However, in *Du Pont/ICI*, OJ 1993 L7/13, at p. 20 (para. 32), the fact that the market share of Du Pont and ICI had been declining prior to the concentration did not prevent the Commission from concluding that Du Pont would have been dominant following the concentration.

[430] *Tetra Pak/Alfa-Laval*, OJ 1991 L290/35, at p. 38.

¶637

wish to have their advertising campaigns handled by the same agency.[431] In the manufacturing sector, the Commission suggested that the *Mannesmann/Boge* merger in the shock absorber business could result in the loss of some market share as some customers common to the merging firms would transfer demand to other manufacturers to maintain at least dual sourcing.[432]

¶638   The role of actual and potential competitors

The significance of a high market share must be seen in the context of the degree of competition, both actual and potential, which the merged entity faces in the market. From the decisions, it appears that the Commission has placed great stress on the constraining influence of actual and potential competitors on the competitive behaviour of the merged entity, and this has been the single most important factor in enabling it to clear concentrations despite high market shares.

(1)   Actual competition

The strength of actual competitors, and their ability to restrain the market conduct of the merged entity, is judged in terms of such factors as their market share, their production capacity, their financial resources, their access to technology and the effectiveness of their distribution network.

The most obvious indication of the strength of actual competition is the market shares of the competitors of the merged entity. The larger the gap between the market share of the merged entity and those of its nearest competitors, the greater the indication of the ability of the merged entity to act independently of those competitors. In *Accor/Wagons-Lits*, in which the Commission decided that the merged entity would have been dominant in the motorway catering services market in France, it was noted that the merged entity would have had a market share of 89 per cent which would have been 18 times larger than the market share of its next competitor.[433]

The relative size and financial power of competitors is crucial evidence of the strength of actual competition. The decision in *Varta/Bosch* is an interesting

---

[431] *Eurocom/RSCG*, M147, 1991.

[432] *Mannesmann/Boge*, M134, 1991.

[433] *Accor/Wagons-Lits*, OJ 1992 L204/1, at p. 8 (para. 25(4)). In *Magnetti Marelli/CEAc*, OJ 1991 L222/38 at p. 40 (para. 16), the Commission decided that the new entity would have a dominant position in the starter battery market in France with a market share of 60 per cent, some three times larger than its nearest competitor. In *Varta/Bosch*, OJ 1991 L320/26, at p. 30 (para. 32) a finding of dominance was made on the basis of a market share of 44.3 per cent in the starter battery market in Germany, with a lead of some 25 per cent over the next competitor. In *Aérospatiale-Alenia/de Havilland*, OJ 1991 L334/42, at p. 50 (para. 29), the Commission noted that even in the overall turbo-prop market (which the Commission in fact considered to comprise three relevant markets), the merged firms would have had a world market share of around 50 per cent which would have been two and a half times greater than the 19 per cent share of Saab, their nearest competitor. See also *Du Pont/ICI*, OJ 1993 L7/13, at p. 20; *Mannesmann/Hoesch*, OJ 1993 L114/37, at p. 45; and *KNP/BT/VRG*, OJ 1993 L217/35, at p. 38.

example of how crucial this can be to the outcome of the review.[434] The Commission claimed that the new entity would have had a dominant position with a market share of 44.3 per cent, emphasising that its actual competitors were only small and medium-sized companies lacking financial strength. However, the entry onto the market in the course of the review of a strong new competitor, Fiat (which acquired a local company), together with the severance of the structural links between the merged entity and its strongest actual competitor, Deta/Mareg, allowed the Commission to conclude that the new entity would no longer be able to act independently of its competitors. The manner in which actual competition was strengthened by these events was crucial to the Commission's decision. The importance placed by the Commission on the size of actual competitiors is also shown in *Alcatel/Telettra*. The concentration was cleared despite market shares of 81 per cent and 83 per cent, emphasis being placed on the size and resources of the two principal competitors of the merged entity, AT&T and Ericsson.[435] On the other hand, in *Tetra Pak/Alfa-Laval* the Commission was only able to identify one actual competitor (PKL) of Tetra Pak on the aseptic carton packaging machines market, and PKL was judged too weak to act as real restraint on the conduct of Tetra Pak which had a market share exceeding 90 per cent.[436]

In order to prevent customers becoming dependent on the market leader, its competitors will need to have the extra capacity required to supply those customers. In *Varta/Bosch* the Commission emphasised the lack of spare capacity in the market to support a preliminary finding of dominance.[437]

The effectivness of an actual competitor will also depend on the quality of its products. If its products are out-dated or have a poor reputation, the ability of the competitor to restrain the market conduct of the merged entity will be limited.[438] In addition the strength of actual competitors will be limited if they are only able to offer a more limited range of products than the merged entity.[439]

---

[434] *Varta/Bosch*, OJ 1991 L320/26, at p. 30 (para. 32) and p. 33 (para. 58).

[435] *Alcatel/Telettra*, OJ 1991 L122/48, at p. 53. (para. 40).

[436] *Tetra Pak/Alfa-Laval*, OJ 1991 L290/35, at p. 39. Likewise, in *Aérospatiale-Alenia/de Havilland*, OJ 1991 L334/42, at pp. 52–54 (para. 34–41), the Commission concluded that the actual competitors of ATP-de Havilland would be too weak to constrain its competitive conduct given the competitive advantages which the concentration would entail. In *Nestlé/Perrier*, OJ 1992 L356/1, at pp. 15–18 (para. 64–76), on appeal, the competitors of Nestlé and BSN in the bottled source water market in France were small companies which produced local bottled spring waters and whose individual financial strength compared to Nestlé and BSN was judged extremely weak. They were, therefore, unable to constrain the collective market power of Nestlé and BSN which derived from their ownership of all the very strong national brands. See also *KNP/BT/VRG*, OJ 1993 L217/35 at p. 38 (para. 20).

[437] *Varta/Bosch*, OJ 1991 L320/26, at p. 30 (para. 32); *KNP/BT/VRG*, OJ 1993 L217/35, at pp. 41–42; and *Rhône-Poulenc/SNIA (II)*, M355, 1993.

[438] In *Aérospatiale-Alenia/de Havilland*, OJ 1991 L334/42, at p. 57ff. (at para. 57–62), aircraft manufactured in eastern Europe and China were held not to serve as real alternatives for customers in the west as they did not meet western certification standards.

[439] In *Du Pont/ICI*, OJ 1993 L7/13, at p. 21 (para. 38–40), the market leader Du Pont would face competition from very large companies in the nylon carpet fibres market, but these companies were judged unable to restrain the market conduct of Du Pont largely because they could not produce the same range of nylon fibres as Du Pont. See also *Aérospatiale-Alenia/de Havilland*, OJ 1991 L334/42, at p. 51 (para. 32); *KNP/BT/VRG*, OJ 1993 L217/35, at p. 38 (para. 20), but see *Mannesmann/Hoesch*, OJ 1993 L114/37, at p. 45 (para. 95) and *Rhône-Poulenc/SNIA (II)*, M355, 1993.

¶638

(2) Potential competition

The strength of potential competition both from expansion on the part of companies already present on the market and from new entrants depends primarily on the nature of the barriers to expansion or entry to the relevant market. Barriers to entry are of three types: legal, technical and economic. The number and success of new market entrants in the years prior to the concentration may give an indication of the significance of these barriers,[440] but this cannot remove the necessity for an analysis of the nature of the barriers in the context of the market following the concentration.

(a) *Legal barriers to entry*

Legal barriers to entry take the form of legal restrictions on the right to carry on a particular business. Foreign firms may face restrictions on the freedom of establishment and on trade across borders, although within the EC these barriers should have been largely dismantled at least for EC nationals.[441] However, a legally supported monopoly is an insurmountable barrier for all firms, whether domestic or foreign.[442]

An obligation to obtain a licence to operate on a market may be an important barrier to entry for all firms if the pre-conditions which must be met by applicants are particularly onerous. In *Accor/Wagons-Lits* the strict legal framework within which the motorway catering markets in France operate was cited as evidence of the high barriers to entry supporting Accor's very high market shares.[443] In particular, the possibility of obtaining government concessions was strictly limited by the long duration of those already granted and by the fact that the total number of concessions was conditioned on the size of the motorway network. Foreign firms also faced additional barriers.

In *British Airways/TAT* it was noted that the entry into force on 1 January

---

[440] In *Nestlé/Perrier*, OJ 1992 L356/10, at p. 23 (para. 103), on appeal, the failure of foreign companies to establish a significant presence on the French market for bottled source waters was regarded as evidence of the high barriers to entry. In *Thorn EMI/Virgin Music*, M202, 1992, the Commission noted that nine companies had entered the recorded music business in the UK in the five years prior to the concentration, but that they had only achieved an aggregate market share of four per cent. On the other hand, in *Péchiney/VIAG*, M198, 1992, the Commission noted that there had been several entrants since 1985 on the market for cored wires, who had eroded or checked the market shares of Péchiney and VIAG on the affected markets.

[441] For restrictions on the freedom of establishment and on the provision of cross-border services in the insurance sector within the EC, see *Group AG/Amev*, M018, 1990; *UAP/Transatlantic/Sun Life*, M141, 1991; and *Fortis/La Caixa*, M254, 1992. Quantitative restrictions on imports of petroleum products into Spain still existed at the time of a number of concentrations in the oil sector in Spain (see e.g. *BP/Petromed* M111, 1991).

[442] For example, the distribution in Spain of major refined oil products was until 1992 subject to a state distribution monopoly (see e.g. *BP/Petromed* M111, 1991). In *Eridania/ISI*, M062, 1991, it was noted that market entry to the Italian sugar market at the production level was prevented by the national production quotas set under the EEC sugar regime.

[443] *Accor/Wagons-Lits*, OJ 1992 L204/1, at p. 8 (para. 25(4)). In *Group AG/Amev*, M018, 1990, the Commission found high legal barriers to entry to the Belgian insurance market emphasising, among other things, the need for substantial financial and capital reserves to comply with legal and prudential rules. However, in *Promodes/BRMC*, M242, 1992, it was noted that, although the setting up of new retail outlets in France was regulated, this did not constitute a significant barrier to entry as entrants could buy existing outlets or use the franchise system.

¶638

1993 of the third package of EC air transport liberalisation measures would remove important legal barriers to entry, but the lack of slots at London Heathrow and Gatwick still constituted formidable barriers to entry.[444]

(b)   *Technical barriers to entry*

The existence of technical barriers to entry, particularly in the form of intellectual property rights, is an important aspect of the evaluation of the strength of potential competition. In the most extreme case, broad patents may effectively block all market entry, reserving a monopoly for their owner. This was virtually the case in *Tetra Pak/Alfa-Laval*, in which Tetra Pak's market share of over 90 per cent was supported by the many patents which Tetra Pak owned.[445] In addition, in respect of complex products, the degree of specialised know-how and engineering skills required to operate on the market may operate as a considerable barrier to entry,[446] although the significance of this may depend on the experience of potential competitors in other fields.[447] The existence of extensive cross licensing arrangements within an industry may make market entry difficult for new entrants: not only will the parties to such arrangements gain the competitive advantage of having access to their competitors' technology, but new entrants may find it difficult to participate in such exchanges as they will have little to offer.[448]

In contrast, an absence of technical barriers may reduce the significance of a high market share. In *Sanofi/Sterling Drug*, the Commission stressed the low technological content of certain drugs which had been on the market for long periods. Consequently, research and patents played a very limited role in the affected markets, making barriers to entry insignificant.[449]

(c)   *Economic barriers to entry*

The evaluation of potential competition must also consider the economic barriers to expansion on, or entry to, the market. The assessment of the significance of economic barriers will be based on whether it would be economically rational for a firm to enter or expand on the market and how

---

[444] *British Airways/TAT*, M259, 1992, on appeal.

[445] *Tetra Pak/Alfa-Laval*, OJ 1991 L290/35, at p. 39.

[446] In *CCIE/GTE*, M258, 1992, entry into the very concentrated general purpose lamp market was said to be very difficult owing, among other things, to the level of technical and engineering capability required. See also *Tetra Pak/Alfa-Laval*, OJ 1991 L290/35, at p. 39.

[447] In *Courtaulds/SNIA*, M113, 1991, the Commission stressed that strong producers active in the acetate markets could enter the upstream acetate yarn market because they had the fundamental technical know-how as a result of their activities in the acetate markets. See also *Rhône-Poulenc/SNIA*, M206, 1992.

[448] See *CCIE/GTE*, M258, 1992 (difficulty of entry into the very concentrated general purpose lamp market).

[449] *Sanofi/Sterling Drug*, M072, 1991. Likewise in *Alcatel/Telettra*, OJ 1991 L122/48, at p. 53 (para. 42), the Commission noted that the costs of technical adaptation to enter the Spanish markets for line transmission equipment and microwave equipment did not constitute an appreciable barrier to entry for European-based companies and that there was no evidence that intellectual property rights could be used to block entry. See also *Procordia/Erbamont*, M323, 1993.

¶638

quickly it could do so. Economic barriers to entry may often be surmountable by a firm with very large financial resources, but the Commission must be persuaded that, in the case of a price rise by the merged entity, market entry or expansion would be (1) very likely to occur and (2) able to occur in a short enough time period in order to restrain the merged entity.

In this assessment an analysis of demand in the market is fundamental. The existence of excess capacity is clearly a disincentive to market entry.[450] In mature markets market entry may be discouraged by the limited potential for an increase in demand,[451] and the limited possibility of gaining a competitive advantage through technological innovation.[452] On the other hand, in new markets the possibility to develop demand should act as an incentive to market entry.[453] Aside from these considerations, the degree of customer loyalty to existing suppliers[454] and the extent to which customers are tied to existing suppliers[455] may reveal the likelihood of a new entrant being able to tap potential demand in the market.

The cost of market entry is clearly a crucial factor in assessing the significance of economic barriers to entry. The level of start-up costs and the likely rate of return on investment will each be relevant.[456] These factors are, of course, relative to the financial resources of the possible entrants and to the general level of risk involved in market entry.

The decision in *Aérospatiale-Alenia/de Havilland*[457] contains a good example of an evaluation of economic barriers to entry. The Commission determined that market entry was not economically rational for the following reasons: the

---

[450] See e.g. *Mitsubishi/UCAR*, M024, 1990. However, in *Mannesmann/Hoesch*, OJ 1993 L114/34, at p. 46, it was judged that the degree of overcapacity throughout Europe would encourage non-German manufacturers to enter the German market when entry barriers were removed.

[451] See e.g. *Magnetti Marelli/CEAc*, OJ 1991 L222/38, at p. 40 (para. 16(b)); *Aérospatiale-Alenia/de Havilland*, OJ 1991 L334/42, at pp. 56–58 (para. 54, 56 and 63); and *Nestlé/Perrier*, OJ 1992 L356/1, at p. 21 (para. 93–94), on appeal.

[452] See e.g. *Mitsubishi/UCAR*, M024, 1990.

[453] In *Mannesmann/Hoesch*, OJ 1993 L114/34, at p. 46 (para. 106), the high level of demand in Germany following unification was seen as an incentive to market entry.

[454] In *Thorn EMI/Virgin Music*, M202, 1992, the Commission stressed that the recorded music market is dynamic and that demand is fluid. There is little brand loyalty, operators in the market relying heavily on the success of particular artists and hits. However, although this might seem favourable to new entrants, it was pointed out that the five market leaders had retained, and even increased, their strong market positions over the years. Only they had the financial resources to compete for the major artists, who demanded very high advances.

[455] In *Nestlé/Perrier*, OJ 1992 L356/1, on appeal, the rebate system operated by the leading suppliers of bottled source waters in France was judged to tie customers to existing suppliers and foreclose potential entrants. In *Fiat Geotech/Ford New Holland*, M009, 1991, a national exclusive purchase agreement for combine harvesters was held to be an important barrier to entry to the Italian market and, consequently, the agreement was terminated before clearance was granted. See also *TNT/Canada Post, DBP Postdienst, La Poste, PTT Post and Sweden Post*, M102, 1991 (access of the joint venture to postal outlets for the provision of international express delivery services to the public), and *Codan/Hafnia*, M344, 1993 (the influence of the short term duration of insurance contracts).

[456] In *Tetra Pak/Alfa-Laval*, OJ 1991 L290/35, at p. 39, the Commission decided that there was a considerable risk that the investment needed to enter the market would exceed returns given the maturity of the market and the importance for customers of a proven track record in the product.

[457] *Aérospatiale-Alenia/de Havilland*, OJ 1991 L334/42.

¶638

market was approaching maturity and demand was likely to decline and stabilise from the mid 1990s; the costs of entry were very high; and it would take six or seven years to develop, produce and market a new aircraft. Consequently, new entrants would come too late into the market to catch sufficient demand to recoup their very high fixed and sunk costs.[458] In *Accor/Wagons-Lits*, on the other hand, the market for group catering services was expanding at the rate of 15–20 per cent in Germany and ten per cent in Spain, thus making entry to or expansion on markets with no specific legal, technical or economic barriers to entry rational.[459]

(d)   Comparison with geographic market definition

The assessment of potential competition (through an analysis of barriers to entry) is important both in defining the market and in considering the effect of the concentration on competition in the market. However, it is submitted that whereas the definition of a geographic market under the regulation has been largely a recognition of the current conditions of competition in an area, the effect of potential competition has been given greatest weight in the analysis of the extent to which the merged entity will in the future be able to act independently on the market. Thus the durability of the factors supporting the finding of a given geographic market are assessed in the evaluation of the market power of the merged entity. For example, in *Courtaulds/SNIA* the Commission cleared a concentration resulting in a 65 per cent market share in the acetate yarn market partly because of the restraining effect which the threat of increased imports from outside the EC placed on the competitive conduct of the merged entities. This was despite the fact that the level of third-country imports (16 per cent of demand) was not sufficient to support the finding of a world-wide market.[460]

An example of a barrier to entry which has supported findings of national markets, but which viewed in the longer term has been judged as unenduring, is the existence of national buying policies in the context of public procurement. Although the effect of the EC measures to liberalise public procurement has on a number of occasions been insufficient to prevent a finding of national markets, in the longer term these measures have been judged likely to erode

---

[458] Id., at p. 56ff. (para. 53–64).

[459] *Accor/Wagons-Lits*, OJ 1992 L204/1 at p. 4 (para. 17(1)(1)) and p. 5 (para. 17(2)(1)).

[460] *Courtaulds/SNIA*, M113, 1991. In *Eridania/ISI*, M062, 1991, the Commission declined to decide definitively whether imports into Italy extended the geographic markets for industrial and retail sugar beyond Italy, but decided none the less that the potential competition from such imports prevented Eridania obtaining power over price. The Commission noted that a one per cent increase in price had resulted in a 100 per cent increase in imports. In *Accor/Wagons-Lits*, OJ 1992 L204/1, at pp. 4–5, the Commission decided that the markets for group catering services were national, but in assessing the strength of potential competition in those national markets, it emphasised that foreign firms could enter the markets by acquisition, joint venture or establishment of local subsidiaries. See also *Procordia/Erbamont*, M323, 1993.

this important barrier to entry.[461] This apparent willingness on the part of the Commission to take a longer term view with respect to potential competition when assessing the ability of the merged entity to act independently on the market compensates for what is inevitably a certain arbitrariness in the conclusions reached in defining the parameters of the affected markets.

¶639   Other appraisal criteria

(1)   Alternatives for suppliers and customers

Just as the Commission has been willing to consider that the threat of imports into a narrow geographic market may act as a significant check on the market conduct of a merged entity, it has likewise accepted that a degree of demand or supply substitutability between products which it has defined to be in different product markets may be a competitive constraint. For example, in *Courtaulds/ SNIA* the Commission decided that acetate yarn constituted a discrete product market.[462] However, in assessing the significance of the high market share of the merged entity, it was concluded that the threat of customers turning to other partly substitutable yarns acted as a check on the competitive conduct of the merged entity on the acetate yarn market.[463] On the other hand, in *Nestlé/ Perrier* the Commission rejected the argument that a degree of demand

---

[461] The most dramatic example of this can be found in *Mannesmann/Hoesch*, OJ 1993 L114/34 in which the Commission concluded that at the outset the merged entity would have a dominant position in Germany, but that the effect of public procurement liberalisation would contribute to the rapid erosion of its market position. In *Alcatel/Telettra*, OJ 1991 L122/48, at pp. 49–50 and 52–53, public procurement liberalisation was also a factor relied upon to decide that Alcatel and Telettra would not be dominant in the markets for line transmission equipment and microwave equipment in Spain. Likewise in *Volvo/Renault*, M004, 1990, public procurement liberalisation was seen as a significant factor in the conclusion that Renault was not dominant in the bus market in France.

[462] *Courtaulds/SNIA*, M113, 1991.

[463] See also *Accor/Wagons-Lits*, OJ 1992 L204/1, at p. 5 (para. 17(1)(4) and 17(2)(4)), in which the Commission did not decide definitively whether contract group catering services provided by small companies and by independent contractors operating at a local or regional level in Germany and Spain should be regarded to be in the same market as the same services provided by the larger catering firms. However, in deciding that Accor would not be dominant even if the market only included the larger catering firms, the Commission stated that Accor would have to take into account the competitive reaction of the independent contractors or small companies, thus limiting its scope of action in the market. In *Du Pont/ICI*, OJ 1993 L7/13, at p. 22 (para. 45–46), the Commission rejected the argument of the parties that polypropylene carpet fibres are in the same market as nylon carpet fibres, but accepted that there is direct competition between carpets made from each type of fibre at the retail level which acts as a considerable restraint on the competitive conduct of nylon carpet fibre suppliers. In *Sanofi/Sterling Drug*, M072, 1991, the Commission claimed that there was a degree of substitutability between the pharmaceutical products identified as the relevant product markets and a number of alternative products (e.g. homeopathic treatments, dietary products, drugs classified in different therapeutic groups and generic products) which had to be taken into account in assessing the importance of market shares of up to 74 per cent. In *Metallgesellschaft/Safic Alcan*, M146, 1991, the availability of synthetic rubber as a partial substitute for latex was noted by the Commission in deciding that the merged firms would not be able to prevent effective competition in the EC latex market. In *PepsiCo/KAS*, M289, 1992, the degree of substitutability between different flavours of carbonated soft drinks was taken into account in clearing a 69 per cent market share in lemon-lime carbonated soft drinks in Portugal. See also *Alcan/Inespal/Palco*, M323, 1993; and *Costa Crociere/Chargeurs/Accor*, M334, 1993.

¶639

substitutability between waters and soft drinks should be taken into account in assessing the strength of Nestlé and BSN on the bottled source water market.[464]

The same approach has been adopted with regard to supply-side substitutability. For example, in *Lucas/Eaton* the Commission concluded that the threat of entry into the market for certain categories of braking systems by producers of different categories of braking system (which had been held to comprise different product markets) would, to a certain extent, constrain the competitive behaviour of the merged entity. On the other hand, in *Nestlé/ Perrier*, the Commission denied that the supply substitutability between soft drinks and purified tap water limited the market power of Nestlé and BSN on the bottled source water market in France.[465]

This acceptance by the Commission that its market definition practice is to some extent inherently arbitrary is important. Notifying parties will always tend to present a broad market definition to the Commission in an attempt to make their market shares as low as possible. However, it seems that the Commission's practice is to favour narrow market definitions, and subsequently to take into account a broad range of factors in assessing the ability of the merged entity to act independently of its competitors. Consequently, notifying parties should appreciate that the case is unlikely to be won or lost on the question of market definition alone.

(2) The strength of buyers in the market

The Commission has not only cited the power of competing producers as a reason for concluding that a merged entity will not achieve dominance. It has also relied to a significant extent on the strength of its customers. In *Alcatel/Telettra* the Commission stated that:

> '[a] very high share of any market could indicate that a dominant position exists. Such an indication in the case of a supplier may nonetheless be countered, for example by the buying power of a monopsonistic purchaser.'[466]

The Commission emphasised that Alcatel and Telettra had very high market shares because the monopsonistic purchaser of telecommunications equipment, Telefonica, had chosen them as its main suppliers. Telefonica was, however, capable of increasing supplies from other sellers.[467] In *Renault/Volvo*

---

[464] *Nestlé/Perrier*, OJ 1992 L356/1, at p. 23 (para. 106), on appeal.

[465] *Lucas/Eaton*, M149, 1991. See also *Tetra Pak/Alfa-Laval*, OJ 1991 L290/35, at p. 42, concerning the restraining effect of a high level of supply substitutability on the position of the merged entity on the markets for different types of milk and juice processing equipment. *Nestlé/Perrier*, OJ 1992 L356/1, at p. 23 (para. 105), on appeal.

[466] *Alcatel/Telettra*, OJ 1991 L122/48, at p. 53 (para. 38).

[467] Id., at p. 53 (para. 38–40) and p. 54 (para. 47). However, termination of the structural links between Telefonica and the merging companies was a condition of clearance.

the fact that buyers of trucks and buses are fleet buyers able to exert pressure on price by transferring their demand in the EC to wherever prices are lowest was a factor cited by the Commission in denying the dominance of the merged entity.[468] The ability of powerful purchasers to prevent suppliers achieving dominance has been cited in a considerable number of cases.[469]

If a supplier's customer has its own production capacity, this may act as a considerable check on the supplier's power over price in his relations with that customer. At a certain price level, it may be more economical for the customer to increase his own production than to continue to buy from the outside supplier. This was the case in *Lucas/Eaton*;[470] not only was demand for braking equipment concentrated in the hands of a limited number of very large truck and agricultural vehicle producers, but these customers also made their own braking equipment.[471]

In the public sector, the Commission has also emphasised the enhanced bargaining power which public procurement liberalisation should give to customers. In *Alcatel/AEG Kabel* the purchasing power of the public utilities as customers of cable manufacturers was said to be considerable, but it was noted that it would be increased still further by EC liberalisation measures.[472]

The type of buyers that have been regarded as having buying power capable of restraining the conduct of their suppliers have generally been industrial companies, public sector companies or utilities. In contrast, in the case of consumer products with strong consumer brands, the ability even of strong retail chains to constrain the competitive conduct of manufacturers may be limited. In *Nestlé/Perrier* the Commission concluded that, although ten leading retailers would account for around 70 per cent of the turnover of Nestlé and BSN in bottled source waters, the strength of the brands owned by Nestlé and

---

[468] *Renault/Volvo*, M004, 1990.

[469] See, for example, *Tetra Pak/Alfa-Laval*, OJ 1991 L290/35, at pp. 40–42 (buying power of dairies and juice processors with respect to food-processing machines); *Accor/Wagons-Lits*, OJ 1992 L204/1, at p. 5 (para. 17(1)(5)) and p. 7 (para. 21) (bargaining power of industrial buyers of group catering services and bargaining power of tour operators and travel agencies in relation to hotel services); *VIAG/Continental Can*, M081, 1991 (the power of soft drinks manufacturers with respect to beverage packaging); *Thomson/Pilkington*, M086, 1991 (the buying power of the national defence procurement authority with respect to defence equipment); *Péchiney/Usinor-Sacilor*, M097, 1991 (the buying power of car manufacturers with respect to metal alloy components); *Ingersoll-Rand/Dresser*, M121, 1991 (the buying power of large and technically sophisticated industrial customers with respect to pumps); *Mannesmann/Boge*, M134, 1991 (the buying power of car manufacturers with respect to shock absorbers); *VIAG/EB-Brühl*, M139, 1991 (the buying power of car manufacturers with respect to certain car components); *Metallgesellschaft/Safic Alcan*, M146, 1991 (the buying power of tyre manufacturers with respect to solid natural rubber); *ABB/BREL*, M221, 1992 (the buying power of British Rail and the London Underground with respect to railway equipment); *BTR/Pirelli*, M253, 1992 (the buying power of car manufacturers with respect to components); and *Matra/Cap Gemini Sogeti*, M272, 1993 (the buying power of the national defence procurement authority with respect to defence equipment).

[470] *Lucas/Eaton*, M149, 1991.

[471] See also *Mannesmann/Boge*, M134, 1991 (manufacture of shock absorbers by car manufacturers). It should be noted that captive production will not have been included in the total size of the market for the purpose of calculating market shares.

[472] *Alcatel/AEG Kabel*, M165, 1991. See also *Alcatel/Telettra*, OJ 1991 L122/48.

BSN was so great with the consumer that retailers simply could not afford not to sell them.[473] The Commission pointed out that in other decisions under the merger regulation in which the strength of buyers had been held to be a factor in preventing market power:

> '... the products involved were generally intermediary products or products where long-term contracts or cooperation agreements for development of the products were involved which can create a more balanced seller-buyer relationship.'[474]

(3) Access of suppliers to markets and users to supplies: vertical integration

In section 5 of Form CO the parties to a concentration are required to provide information on any market on which one of the parties operates which is upstream or downstream of any market on which another of the parties operates, if any of their market shares is ten per cent or more. It is by means of this information that the Commission will assess the effect on competition of a concentration between a supplier and an actual or potential customer in both the supplier's and the customer's markets.

In its analysis of such vertical links, the Commission has concentrated on the extent to which the market position of the merging companies on each of the vertically linked markets will be strengthened through the foreclosure of their competitors. The Commission has been concerned to assess:

- whether customers will have restricted access to supplies thus strengthening the position of the merged entity on the downstream market, and likewise

- whether the access of suppliers to customers will be significantly limited thus strengthening the position of the merged entity on the upstream market.[475]

---

[473] *Nestlé/Perrier*, OJ 1992 L356/1, at pp. 18–20, on appeal.

[474] Id., at para. 80. Likewise in *Aérospatiale-Alenia/de Havilland*, OJ 1991 L334/42, at p. 54ff. (para. 43–50), it was considered that even airlines and aircaft leasing companies would have limited bargaining power in their relations with ATR/de Havilland. In *Magnetti Marelli/CEAc*, OJ 1991 L222/38, at p. 40 (para. 16(b)) the Commission stressed that the dominance of the merged entity on the replacement starter battery market could not be offset by the purchasing strength of its customers because even the largest of its numerous customers achieved only a fraction of the new entity's turnover. See also *KNP/BT/VRG*, OJ 1993 L217/35, at p. 38 (para. 22).

[475] For a consideration of vertical links, see *ICI/Tioxide*, M023, 1990; *Mitsubishi/UCAR*, M024, 1990; *Cargill/Unilever*, M026, 1990; *AT&T/NCR*, M050, 1990; *Usinor/ASD*, M073, 1991; *VIAG/Continental Can*, M081, 1991; *Paribas/MBH*, M122, 1991; *Delta/Pan Am*, M130, 1991; *ABC/Générale des Eaux/Canal+/W H Smith TV*, M110, 1991; *Metallgesellschaft/Feldmühle*, M119, 1991; *VIAG/EB-Brühl*, M139, 1991; *Eurocom/RSCG*, M147, 1991; *Volvo/Atlas*, M152, 1991; *Air France/Sabena*, M157, 1992; *Solvay-Laporte/Interox*, M197, 1992; *Péchiney/VIAG*, M198, 1992; *Thorn EMI/Virgin Music*, M202, 1992; *Rhône-Poulenc/SNIA*, M206, 1992; *Mondi/Frantschach*, M210, 1992; *ABB/BREL*, M221, 1992; *Elf Aquitaine/Thyssen/Minol*, M235, 1992; *Avesta/British Steel/NCC*, M239, 1992; *BTR/Pirelli*, M253, 1992; *Del Monte/Royal Foods/Anglo-American*, M277, 1991; *Sextant/BGT-VDO*, M290, 1992; *Volkswagen (VWAG)/VAG (UK)*, M001, 1993; *LEA Industrie/France Télécom/Finmeccanica/SGS-Thomson*, M210, 1993; *Fletcher Challenge/Methanex*, M331, 1993; and *GEHE AG/OCF SA*, M328, 1993.

¶639

As a consequence of identifying the possible weakening of third parties through foreclosure as the primary means by which dominance could be achieved through vertical integration, the Commission has placed relatively little emphasis on the competitive advantage which the merged entity may obtain from vertical integration through such factors as the availability of a constant source of supply or demand, protection from market pricing and other cost savings.

The Commission has often found there to have been no significant foreclosure despite apparent high market shares enjoyed by one or more of the parties to the concentration. It has emphasised the availability of alternative suppliers or, as the case may be, alternative customers for competitors of the merging companies;[476] the willingness of the merged firm to supply its competitors on the downstream market and to take supplies from its competitors on the upstream market;[477] and the fact that merged firms will not necessarily rely exclusively on one another for supplies or services even if they operate on vertically related markets.[478] In the few cases in which the foreclosure effect on competitors was seen to be a serious concern, concessions by the parties have been sufficient to allow the Commission to conclude that a dominant position has been neither created nor strengthened.[479]

As far as factors other than foreclosure are concerned, in concluding that dominance does not result from vertical integration the Commission has

---

[476] In *Solvay-Laporte/Interox*, M197, 1992, Interox was the market leader for persalts and Solvay had important market shares for two upstream products, soda ash and caustic soda. The Commission claimed that, as there were a number of strong alternative suppliers on the upstream markets (each with a free market share of over five per cent), there would be no significant foreclosure on the persalts market. In *VIAG/Continental Can*, M081, 1991, VIAG was very strong in aluminium, and Continental Can in packaging. The Commission stressed that the availability of one major alternative non-integrated aluminium supplier to VIAG in each market sector would provide a source for Continental Can's competitors in the packaging markets, thus preventing foreclosure on the packaging markets. It is noteworthy that one of the suppliers which the Commission identified as an alternative was in fact in a joint venture with VIAG.

[477] In *AT&T/NCR*, M050, 1990, the Commission concluded that even if NCR were dominant in the computer workstations business, this dominance would not be strengthened by AT&T's activities on the upstream computer operating systems software market because the competitors of NCR would not be foreclosed access to AT&T's product, UNIX. It was noted that AT&T had granted a large number of generally irrevocable licences of the UNIX source code, enabling licensees to develop their own UNIX-versions, of which about 100 versions were on the market. No change in the licensing policy was expected by the Commission. In *Thorn EMI/Virgin Music*, M202, 1992, it was stated that industry regulation for the most part requires music publishers to grant licences for the exploitation of musical works which they own to all users at regulated royalty rates. Therefore, Thorn EMI would not foreclose competing record companies in acquiring the Virgin Music catalogue. In *Avesta/British Steel/NCC*, M239, 1992, in which there was vertical integration between steel producers and stockholders, it was noted that there would be little incentive for the merged entity to refuse to stock other steel producers' products given the alternative means of distribution available to them. See also *Sextant/BGT-VDO*, M290, 1992.

[478] See *Elf/Occidental*, M085, 1991 (oil companies, in supplying their refineries, use the world-wide crude oil market rather than merely their own oil production); *VIAG/EB-Brühl*, M139, 1991 (EB-B needed supplies of secondary aluminium, but it would purchase from VIAG's competitors as VIAG's own plants would be too distant to make supplies economical); *Péchiney/VIAG*, M198, 1992 (no obligation on the merged entity to take supplies of upstream products from its parent companies and variety of uses of the upstream products); and *Thorn EMI/Virgin Music*, M202, 1992 (in particular, the lack of allegiance of record companies to their integrated music publishers).

[479] See *Air France/Sabena*, M157, 1992 and *Elf Aquitaine/Thyssen/Minol*, M235, 1992, discussed in ¶639(1)(a).

stressed the small relative cost advantage which the vertical link could give on the downstream market,[480] and the constraining power of the ultimate customers of the merged firm despite the vertical integration.[481]

(a)   *Effect of vertical integration on downstream market*

Looking at the effect of the vertical integration on the downstream market, the Commission is concerned to ensure that competitors of the merged entity on the downstream market are not placed at such a competitive disadvantage in obtaining their supplies that the merged entity will be able to act independently of those competitors in selling on the downstream market. This would be the case if competitors on the downstream market became dependent on the merged entity as supplier for supplies from the upstream market. In such circumstances the merged entity as supplier might discriminate in its terms of supply against those customers which compete with it on the downstream market, thus strengthening its market position on the downstream market. Factually this could occur if there is, and there is likely to remain, insufficient capacity from competing suppliers on the upstream market to meet the needs of customers who are not vertically integrated on the downstream market. If other suppliers are also vertically integrated, the effect on customers which are not vertically integrated might be particularly acute.

In *Elf Aquitaine/Thyssen/Minol*, Elf acquired certain oil refining and distribution businesses in the eastern part of Germany including two-thirds of all distribution depot capacity in that area.[482] As a consequence of the acquisition of this depot capacity, the Commission judged there to be a serious risk that companies which competed with Elf in the distribution of petroleum products in the eastern part of Germany would become dependent on Elf for depot capacity. Given that Elf would in any event be the market leader in the distribution of petroleum products, the additional competitive advantage it would gain from the control over depot capacity could have given it market power in the distribution of petroleum products. In response to the arguments of competitors that there would not be sufficient independent depot capacity to meet their requirements, the Commission required Elf to send its competitors legally binding offers to enter into agreements for a period of two years relating to the use of its depot facilities on a cost plus basis. In addition to the issue of

---

[480] In *ICI/Tioxide*, M023, 1990, the relatively low proportion of the total cost of paint represented by the upstream product titanium dioxide (average 18 per cent) limited the possible cost advantages for ICI over its competitors on the paint market resulting from vertical integration. See also *VIAG/EB-Brühl*, M139, 1991.

[481] In *ABB/BREL*, M221, 1992, BREL had a very strong position on the market for certain first-build railway vehicles and ABB was an upstream component manufacturer. In considering the effect of the vertical link on the market position of BREL, the Commission stressed the following factors which weakened BREL's market position: (1) that demand for BREL's products and services was concentrated in just two customers, British Rail and the London Underground; and (2) that there was considerable (50 per cent) overcapacity in the industry.

[482] *Elf Aquitaine/Thyssen/Minol*, M235, 1992.

¶639

depot capacity, the Commission was also concerned by the competitive advantage which Elf could obtain from an arrangement under which it was to take over the operation of certain oil refineries with the benefit of the guarantee that any losses of the refineries would be borne by the German privatisation agency, the Treuhandanstalt. Elf's very strong position on the distribution market could have been strengthened further by the supply of subsidised petroleum products from these refineries. However, the Commission was satisfied with an assurance from the Treuhandanstalt that it would enforce the contractual obligation on Elf to obtain the best terms for the refineries' output by using the inspection rights which were reserved to the Treuhandanstalt.

In *Air France/Sabena* the Commission was concerned whether airlines trying to compete with Air France and Sabena (which would have a dominant position on several markets) would have adequate access to airport facilities and take-off and landing slots at certain airports over which Air France and Sabena had significant control.[483] As part of the conditions of clearance, Air France and Sabena, together with their respective governments, were required to give assurances that airport facilities and slots would be made available to competing carriers and that the merging carriers would restrict the number of slots they held at Brussels. These concessions were regarded as sufficient to ensure access to essential facilities for competing carriers.

(b) *Effect of vertical integration on upstream market*
Looking at the effect of the vertical integration on the market position of the merged entity as supplier on an upstream market, the Commission seems concerned to ensure that competing suppliers are not placed at such a competitive disadvantage in their access to customers that the merged entity as supplier will be able to act independently of them. This could occur if competing suppliers are dependent on the merging customer for demand because insufficient independent demand remains in the market to take up their capacity. In such a case, the merging customer could impose onerous terms on the suppliers which would disadvantage them in their ability to compete with the merging supplier. In *VIAG/Continental Can*[484] the Commission rejected the notion that suppliers of aluminium would become dependent on the merged entity as a customer on the downstream packaging market. The Commission stressed that 40 per cent of demand in the downstream packaging market would continue to come from packaging manufacturers without links to aluminium producers, and that this should be sufficient to prevent VIAG obtaining a dominant position.

---

[483] *Air France/Sabena*, M157, 1992.
[484] *VIAG/Continental Can*, M081, 1991.

¶639

(4)   Competitive advantages
Because so few cases have given rise to even a preliminary finding of incompatibility,[485] a review of the case law under the regulation inevitably results in great emphasis being placed on factors which suggest that a merged entity will not be dominant and that effective competition will not be impeded as a consequence of a concentration. As is clear from the discussion in this chapter thus far, factors such as the strength of actual and potential competitors, the strength of buyers, the competitive pressures exerted both by substitute products and from neighbouring markets, and the absence of foreclosure have all been considered frequently in the case law. On the other hand, discussion of particular competitive advantages which might contribute to the dominance of a merged entity has been rather limited. In the *Tetra Pak/Alfa-Laval* decision,[486] Tetra Pak had two of the most common advantages of dominant firms: financial strength and a technical lead. Tetra Pak had a market share of more than 90 per cent which was protected by patents and by its very considerable financial resources relative to those of its sole competitor.[487]

However, the two main categories of advantages which have been reviewed by the Commission have been those arising from the ability to offer a range of complementary products and those arising from the conglomerate aspects of a concentration. These are each discussed further below.

(a)   *Ability to offer a range of products*
In a number of cases, the Commission has been concerned to evaluate what advantage a merged firm will obtain from the ability to produce complementary products and the effect this will have on its market position in the market for each of these products. The Commission has suggested that this effect will only be significant if two conditions are met: (1) the products are sold together (system selling); and (2) the merged entity is sufficiently strong in sales of one product to be able to exert pressure on customers to buy the other product(s).[488]

In *Tetra Pak/Alfa-Laval*, Tetra Pak was undeniably dominant in the markets for aseptic carton packaging machines.[489] The acquisition by Tetra Pak of Alfa-Laval's food processing machine business (machines which treated foods which would be packaged in aseptic carton packaging machines) was deemed not to strengthen this dominance. The ability to offer processing machines as well as packaging machines did not constitute a competitive advantage

---

[485] In only one case so far, *Aérospatiale-Alenia/de Havilland*, OJ 1991 L334/42, has it been impossible for the parties to avoid a finding of incompatibility by making changes to the concentration.
[486] *Tetra Pak/Alfa-Laval*, OJ 1991 L290/35.
[487] Id., at p. 39. For the discussion of a number of possible competitive advantages, see *Mannesmann/Hoesch*, OJ 1993 L114/34, at pp. 45–46.
[488] *XXIst Report on Competition Policy for 1991*, Annex III(7)(II)(f), at p. 369.
[489] *Tetra Pak/Alfa-Laval*, OJ 1991 L290/35.

¶639

because, among other reasons, the two types of machine were only bought together very rarely and they were not technically interdependent.[490] On the other hand, in *Aérospatiale-Alenia/de Havilland* the fact that ATR would be the only producer able to offer the full range of commuter aircraft was seen as a significant advantage because airlines derive cost benefits from buying different aircraft from the same producer.[491]

In *VIAG/Continental Can* the Commission suggests that the ability to offer complementary products may only be relevant if there is a pre-existing dominant position on one of the product markets.[492] None the less, in other cases the Commission has considered whether a firm could obtain a dominant position by being able to offer complementary products. In *Matsushita/MCA* the Commission had considered whether Matsushita could obtain a dominant position by being able to offer, as a consequence of the acquisition of MCA, film and music software compatible with Matsushita audiovisual products, in particular HDTV products.[493] It concluded that there were many other producers of film and music software able to make products compatible with any audiovisual hardware, which would prevent the merged entity from becoming dominant.[494]

(b)   Conglomerate effects

The Commission has considered the conglomerate effects of concentrations in a number of cases. The purpose of such a review is to assess whether, irrespective of any horizontal or vertical links between the markets on which the parties operate, there are other advantages from which any one of the

---

[490] Id., at p. 40. Both purchasers of aseptic carton packaging machines and the actual/potential competitors of Tetra Pak indicated that the ability of a single undertaking to offer both types of machine was not commercially important. Furthermore, strong actual and potential competition on the processing machine market was found to exist and customers were found to have significant buying power on that market. Similarly in *Mannesmann/VDO*, M164, 1991, there appeared to have been pre-existing dominance in respect of certain car components. One factor supporting the conclusion that any dominance would not be strengthened was the fact that no appreciable advantage would derive from the ability to sell the different products of the parties together. See also *Metallgesellschaft/Feldmühle*, M119, 1991.

[491] *Aérospatiale-Alenia/de Havilland*, OJ 1991 L334/42, at pp. 51–52 (para. 32 and 33). See also *Du Pont/ICI*, OJ 1993 L7/13, at p. 21 (para. 41), in which Du Pont would have a significant competitive advantage after the concentration as a consequence of being the only manufacturer able to offer the full range of nylon carpet fibres; and *Aérospatiale/MBB*, M017, 1991, in which the market position of the merged firms would be strengthened by the ability to offer a broader range of civil helicopters than they could do individually.

[492] In *VIAG/Continental Can*, M081, 1991, the Commission stated:

'... the two parties will have the opportunity to offer customers Gerresheimer glass containers with CCE's metal closures and to jointly develop new product applications specially adjusted to each other. Even if this advantage were to be considered as relevant under Art. 2(1) of the Regulation, it could in general only harm competition if CCE or Gerresheimer were already in a dominant position in their respective market.'

[493] *Matsushita/MCA*, M037, 1990.

[494] See also *Delta/Pan Am*, M130, 1991, in which the Commission considered the competitive advantage Delta would obtain from offering its US domestic services as a feeder to, or extension of, Pan Am's North Atlantic routes. The Commission noted the ability of all US carriers to combine flights in this way, and concluded that the competitive advantage for Delta did not create a dominant position.

¶639

parties could benefit as a consequence of the concentration which might appreciably strengthen its position on its respective markets. As yet, no such advantages have been identified which could create or strengthen a dominant position.

By far the most frequently considered advantage has been the access of one party to the far greater financial resources of another party. The Commission has invariably concluded, however, that the competitors of the merged entity have comparable financial strength, and consequently finance will not give the merged entity the ability to act independently on the market. In *Matsushita/ MCA* the Commission considered the effect of the availability of Matsushita's very substantial financial resources on MCA as a producer of entertainment 'software' products, but decided that the competitors of MCA had adequate access to finance through their shareholders.[495]

Another advantage which has been considered has been the access of one party to the technical resources of another party. In *ATT/NCR*, the Commission considered whether a combination of NCR's strong market position in the computer workstations business together with AT&T's technical and commercial know-how in the telecommunications and network processing business could create or strengthen a dominant position for NCR.[496] The conclusion was that the possible advantages to be derived from the link were theoretical, especially as previous attempts at combining computer and telecommunications businesses had failed or, as yet, had not lived up to expectations.[497] These cases show, it is submitted, that conglomerate effects, given their rather imprecise nature, may rarely be a crucial factor in a substantive review of compatibility under the regulation. More often their function might be to support a finding of dominance based primarily on horizontal or vertical effects.

(5)   De minimis rule and elimination of potential competition between the parties

Many concentrations result in either no increase, or only a very small increase, in the market shares of the parties on the relevant affected markets. In such

---

[495] *Matsushita/MCA*, M037, 1990. In *BP-Petromed*, M111, 1991, the availability of the significant financial resources of BP to Petromed was not considered decisive, especially given that the market leader, Repsol, was state owned and that the number two in the market, CEPSA, also had very significant financial resources. See also, *ICI/Tioxide*, M023, 1990; *TNT/Canada Post, DBP Postdienst, La Poste, PTT Post and Sweden Post*, M102, 1991; *UAP/Transatlantic/Sun Life*, M141, 1991; *James River/Rayne*, M162, 1991; *Mannesmann/VDO*, M164, 1991; *Solvay-Laporte/Interox*, M197, 1992; *Del Monte/Royal Foods/Anglo-American*, M277, 1992; *Sextant/BGT-VDO*, M290, 1992; *Sara Lee/BP Food Division*, M299, 1993; *CEA Industrie/France Télécom/Finmeccanica/SGS-Thomson*, M216, 1993; *Zürich/MMI*, M286, 1993; *West LB/Thomas Cook*, M350, 1993; and *GEHE AG/OCP SA*, M328, 1993.

[496] *AT&T/NCR*, M050, 1990.

[497] For technical advantages see also *Elf/Occidental*, M085, 1991; *Solvay Laporte/Interox*, M197, 1992; and *Sextant/BGT-VDO*, M290, 1992.

circumstances, even when faced with high individual market shares, the Commission has been willing to clear concentrations on the grounds that they do not significantly alter the status quo ante in the affected markets. The best example is perhaps *Tetra Pak/Alfa-Laval* in which the Commission decided that the acquisition by a dominant firm, Tetra Pak, of a company, Alfa-Laval, which was active in neighbouring markets, did not strengthen the dominance of Tetra Pak.[498]

However, even if the parties are not actual competitors, there may none the less be a significant loss of potential competition, especially if the parties are present on different geographic markets, or if they operate on related product markets. The concentration will most likely eliminate whatever realistic potential competition there was between them. The Commission has considered the loss of potential competition in a limited number of cases. In *Mannesmann/VDO*[499] the Commission cleared the concentration despite some very high individual market shares which suggested dominance. In concluding that this dominance would not be strengthened by the concentration, the Commission emphasised that the other party was not an effective source of potential competition in the market. In *Lucas/Eaton*[500] Lucas had certain market shares of around 50 per cent, and in clearing the concentration the Commission stressed forcefully that a very important fact underlying its

---

[498] *Tetra Pak/Alfa-Laval*, OJ 1991 L290/35. In *Aérospatiale/MBB*, M017, 1991, the aggregate market share for civil helicopters in the EC was 52 per cent (44 per cent attributable to Aérospatiale and eight per cent to MBB). In clearing the concentration, the Commission stressed, among other things, that this increase only represented the sale of five extra helicopters a year. In *Mitsubishi/UCAR*, M024, 1990, several factors suggested that UCAR may have had a dominant position prior to the concentration. However, as Mitsubishi did not compete as a manufacturer with UCAR (although it was a trader in the products in question outside of the EC), the Commission concluded that the concentration would have no appreciable effect on competition. In *Digital/Kienzle*, M057, 1991, an increase of four per cent in the market share for workstations was considered insignificant given an expanding market and low barriers to entry. In *Sanofi/Sterling Drug*, M072, 1991, market shares as high as 74 per cent were cleared, the Commission emphasising that the pharmaceutical products marketed by the parties were complementary. In *Mannesmann/VDO*, M164, 1991, individual market shares of up to 90 per cent were noted for certain car components in Germany, but as the other party did not operate on these markets, it was concluded that any existing dominance was not strengthened. In *ABB/BREL*, M221, 1992, market shares as high as 50–60 per cent were mentioned, but the Commission was able to conclude that the concentration would not have a significant effect on competition as there was no increase in market shares on the affected markets. In *Ericsson/Ascom*, M236, 1992, Ericsson had a market share of over 78 per cent in Denmark in public line transmission equipment, but Ascom did not operate in the EC at all and in any event had a low turnover. In *Linde/Fiat*, M256, 1992, the merged entity would acquire a market share of 44 per cent in Germany in fork lift trucks, but, as the merger only increased Linde's previous share by one per cent, this would not appreciably strengthen its position. In *PepsiCo/KAS*, M289, 1992, PepsiCo would have a market share of 69 per cent in lemon-lime carbonated soft drinks in Portugal, but, as the market share of KAS was only one per cent, the Commission concluded that the conditions of competition in the market would not change. In *Procordia/Erbamont*, M323, 1993, the Commission emphasised that the overlap between the activities of the parties was minimal in clearing, for example, a market share of over 78 per cent for local anaesthetics in Italy. In *Degussa/Ciba-Geigy*, M317, 1993, Degussa held market shares of 40 per cent in glass colours and of 50 per cent in silver pastes, whereas Ciba-Geigy had market shares of less than 10 per cent and less than 5 per cent in the same products. The Commission concluded that Degussa's competitive position would only be reinforced to an insignificant extent by the concentration, emphasising, among other factors, the comparatively low volume of sales of the products concerned.

[499] *Mannesmann/VDO*, M164, 1991.

[500] *Lucas/Eaton*, M149, 1991.

decision was that Lucas and Eaton were neither actual nor potential competitors in the EC. Eaton had tried to enter the EC market in the 1970s but had been obliged to withdraw unsuccessful. The Commission concluded, therefore, that Eaton would not have been likely to try to re-enter the EC market alone.

In contrast, in *Aérospatiale-Alenia/de Havilland* the loss of potential competition between the parties was a factor taken into account by the Commission in declaring the concentration incompatible with the common market: de Havilland would be eliminated as a potential competitor in the market for turbo-props of 60 seats and over in which ATR had a 76 per cent market share.[501]

(6) Non-competition factors

(a) *Technical and economic progress: relevance of industrial policy*
The obligation on the Commission under art. 2(1) of the regulation to take account of the development of technical and economic progress in assessing the compatibility of a concentration with the common market sits somewhat uncomfortably with the other competition-orientated criteria which the Commission must apply. The question arises as to whether this obligation can allow compatibility to be determined partially on industrial policy grounds, such as, for example, preventing a key EC company falling under third country control, preventing a merger which would lead to considerable unemployment or creating a Euro-champion to revive a declining EC industry.

The concept of technical and economic progress is taken from art. 85(3) of the treaty and the Commission itself has stated that the concept must be understood in the light of the principles enshrined in art. 85(3) of the treaty, as interpreted by the case law of the Court of Justice.[502] This might suggest that a concentration which fails the compatibility test on pure competition grounds (i.e., the equivalent of infringing art. 85(1)) could none the less be granted an exemption on technical or other economic grounds (i.e., as under art. 85(3)). This interpretation would, however, appear incorrect.

A concentration will be deemed impermissible under the regulation if it is judged to create or strengthen a dominant position in a manner which

---

[501] *Aérospatiale-Alenia/de Havilland* OJ 1991 L334/42, at p. 50 (para. 31). In *Renault/Volvo*, M004, 1990, the parties were not actual competitors in the bus markets in the UK (in which Volvo had a 64 per cent market share) and France (in which Renault had a 69.9 per cent market share). However, the Commission accepted that, following public procurement liberalisation, the companies would have been potential competitors. Despite the very high market shares, it was concluded that the strength of other competitors prevented the loss of potential competition from creating or strengthening a dominant position in a way which significantly impeded competition.

[502] See accompanying statements entered in the minutes of the EC Council concerning Council Regulation 4064/89, interpretative statement by the Commission concerning the application of art. 2(1)(b), *Nineteenth Report on Competition Policy*, p. 266.

¶639

significantly impedes effective competition. From the wording of the regulation, there is no possibility of an exemption being granted to a concentration which is judged to have such an effect on competition.[503] The development of technical and economic progress is, therefore, apparently to be seen as one factor to be applied in determining the effect of the concentration on competition. However, the wording of art. 2(1)(b) expressly states that the development of technical and economic progress is only relevant if 'it is to consumers' advantage and does not form an obstacle to competition'. It is arguable that these qualifications, especially the second, make the reference to economic and technical development largely meaningless. If the purpose of applying the criteria in art. 2(1)(b) is to assess whether a concentration obstructs competition, how can it be a precondition of the application of certain of these criteria that they should not have the very effect which their application is supposed to evaluate?[504]

(b)   *Economic cohesion*

In addition to the apparent inconsistency of the text of the regulation in relation to the concept of technical and economic progress, further confusion as to whether non-competition factors have any role in the Commission's evaluation is provided by the thirteenth recital of the preamble to the regulation. This states that:

'the Commission must place its appraisal within the general framework of the achievement of the fundamental objectives referred to in Article 2 of the Treaty, including that of strengthening the Community's economic and social cohesion, referred to in Article 130A [of the Treaty].'

The references to art. 2 and 130A suggest that the special interests of the less-developed regions of the EC and the need to reduce economic imbalances within the EC should be taken into account in assessing the compatibility of concentrations. The Commission itself reinforced this view by declaring in a statement entered in the minutes of the EC Council concerning art. 2(1) and the thirteenth recital that:

'among the factors to be taken into consideration for the purposes of

---

[503] During the negotiation of the regulation certain draft proposals did provide for a two-stage substantive analysis comprising a review of the effects of the concentration on competition followed by a review of its eligibility for an exemption.

[504] It should be noted that, even under the two stage test of art. 85, the final requirement for the grant of an exemption under art. 85(3) – that the undertakings concerned should not be afforded the possibility of eliminating competition for a substantial part of the products in question – shows that the justification of technical and economic progress is strictly qualified. The benefits of an agreement cannot cure the restrictions which it contains unless a substantial degree of competition remains in the market, and this will never be the case if the parties have a dominant position (see Commission notice concerning the assessment of co-operative joint ventures pursuant to art. 85 of the treaty, OJ 1993 C43/2, at p. 11 (para. 58).

¶639

establishing the compatibility or incompatibility of a concentration – factors as referred to in Article 2(1) and explained in recital 13 – account should be taken in particular of the competitiveness of undertakings located in regions which are greatly in need of restructuring owing *inter alia* to slow development.'

Thus the restructuring of firms in the less developed regions of the EC is seen as desirable in the belief that it will make such firms more competitive vis-à-vis firms in the economically stronger member states. The difficulty in reconciling this with the provisions of art. 2 of the regulation is clear, and as recitals are to be taken into account in interpreting Community legislation,[505] it is further evidence of the internal inconsistency of the regulation on the question of the relevance of non-competition factors.

(c)   *Commission practice*
In the cases, the Commission has avoided taking a position on the meaning of the text of the regulation on technical and economic progress by dismissing the arguments of the parties as factually incorrect.

In *Aérospatiale-Alenia/de Havilland*[506] the Commission considered two arguments made by the applicants: first that the merger was necessary to prevent production being phased out at de Havilland in the medium to long term (the failing firm defence) and second that the merger would increase economic efficiency by reducing costs, including currency fluctuation risk. Without admitting the relevance of such considerations for a substantive analysis of compatibility, the Commission decided that there was no likelihood of production being phased out at de Havilland, that cost savings were minimal and that in any event ATR had an excellent position on the market.[507] The Commission further stressed that, even had the concentration contributed to the development of technical and economic progress, this would not have been to the advantage of consumers since the dominance resulting from the concentration would make it rational for ATR/de Havilland to enter into a price war which would drive all their competitors from the market.[508] Thus, as technical and economic benefits could not prevent power of price, they would be irrelevant.[509]

---

[505] *Hydrotherm Gerätebau GmbH v Compact del Dott Ing Mario Andreoli & C sas*, [1984] ECR 2999, at pp. 3018–3019 (para. 18–21).
[506] *Aérospatiale-Alenia/de Havilland*, OJ 1991 L334/42.
[507] Id., at p. 51 (para. 31) and p. 59ff. (para. 65–68).
[508] Id., at p. 60 (para. 69–70).
[509] This seems to reflect the views of Commissioner Brittan, the Commissioner responsible for merger control until the end of 1992. In a speech to the Centre for European Studies, Brussels, on 24 September 1990, he declared:

'Lest there be any doubt, let me stress that no words plucked from the regulation can give rise to a defence against the finding of a dominant position as a result of which effective competition is significantly impeded . . . I

¶639

In *Accor/Wagons-Lits* the Commission concluded that the parties had failed to show that the merger would result in any improvement in technical or economic progress to the benefit of the consumer, that in any event, this progress could be achieved by different means.[510] Accor's claims of cost savings in the motorway catering markets were rejected as unproven, and Accor was thought unlikely to pass on any cost savings to the consumer given the low level of demand elasticity in those markets.[511]

On a practical level, the Commission may of course take account of industrial policy considerations without this being apparent from its legal reasoning. As has been seen in this chapter, the Commission is required to apply a number of very imprecise concepts in its review, in particular the definition of product and geographic market and the degree of constraint placed on the merged firms by actual and potential competitors. Thus if the Commission wished to build a Euro-champion, it could deny the creation of a dominant position by emphasising the strength of the third country competitors. It might be said that in *Aérospatiale-Alenia /de Havilland* (which is still after more than three years of EC merger control the only case in which a finding of incompatibility was made) this was not possible because most of the main competitors were EC or EFTA firms (British Aerospace, Fokker, Saab, Dornier and Casa).[512]

¶640 Oligopolies and joint dominance

(1) Joint dominance under art. 86 and the regulation

One important element of uncertainty concerning the application of the merger regulation after its adoption was whether it could only be used to prevent the creation or strengthening of a dominant position by a single entity or whether it could also be used to prevent the creation or tightening of an oligopoly in which no one firm could be regarded as dominant. As it may be irrational for firms to compete in a narrow oligopoly owing to their mutual interdependence, it is strongly arguable that the prevention of the creation of such an oligopoly is a valid goal of a merger control system.[513] The wording of

---

do not see how a dominant position which impedes competition could give rise to technical or economic progress of the sort which competition policy could endorse. There may be some short-term technical progress available to a monopolist, but it would not last for long when one considers the well-known debilitating effect of monopoly. As for economic progress, apart from monopoly rents which would accrue, there would be no progress at all.'

[510] *Accor/Wagons-Lits*, OJ 1992 L204/1, at p. 9 (para. 25(4)). The reference to achieving the same economic and technical benefits by other means is reminiscent of the application of art. 85(3) to joint ventures. In a number of cases the Commission has stressed that an exemption can only be granted if the benefit of a joint venture cannot be obtained through less restrictive forms, such as a licence (see ¶509). Under this approach, a merger, which eliminates all competition between the parties, would be seen as the most restrictive form of achieving the benefit.

[511] *Id.*, at p. 10 (para. 26(2)(f)).

[512] *Aérospatiale-Alenia/de Havilland*, OJ 1991 L334/42.

[513] The merger control legislation in·the USA, Germany, France and the UK can be applied to control concentrations in oligopolistic markets.

¶640

the regulation, however, makes no express reference to the control of oligopolistic markets.

Under art. 86 of the treaty the Commission has developed the concept of joint or collective dominance, which has been accepted in principle by the Court of First Instance.[514] This implies that in circumstances in which no single firm has sufficient market power to be regarded as holding a dominant position, two or more firms between whom there is little or no competition can be judged together to have sufficient market power to be deemed jointly dominant.[515] By applying a concept of joint dominance under the regulation, it was apparent that the Commission might be able to restrict structural changes in oligopolistic markets.

There are textual arguments both for and against the application of a concept of collective dominance under the regulation. The text of art. 86 specifically refers to joint dominance in its opening words: '[a]ny abuse by one or more undertakings of a dominant position.'[516] Consequently, the absence of similar wording in the regulation could, *a contrario*, be said to deny the Commission the right to apply the concept under the regulation. However, it is equally arguable that the precise wording of the compatibility test in art. 2(2) and (3) of the regulation is neutral as to the issue of sole and joint dominance. The first requirement in art. 2(1)(a) 'to preserve and develop effective competition within the common market' might be interpreted to justify control extending beyond individual dominance.

(2)   Commission practice under the regulation

The Commission finally decided in *Nestlé/Perrier*[517] that it did have power under the regulation to prevent the creation or strengthening of joint dominance. Relying on art. 3(f) of the treaty and the absence of wording in the regulation expressly excluding oligopolistic dominance, the Commission adopted a teleological interpretation:

> 'The EC's Merger Regulation obliges the Commission to prevent the creation or reinforcement of a dominant position as a result of which

---

[514] See *Società Italiano Vetro (SIV) SpA & Ors v EC Commission ('Flat Glass')* [1992] 2 CEC 33, in which the Court of First Instance stated:

> 'There is nothing, in principle, to prevent two or more independent economic entities from being, on a specific market, united by such economic links that, by virtue of that fact, together they hold a dominant position vis-à-vis the other operators on the same market' (at para. 358).

The court found on the facts that the Commission had failed to prove the existence of a collective dominant position.

[515] The views of the Commission and of the court on what can be relied upon to prove collective dominance under art. 86 appear to a large extent irreconcilable (see ¶247).

[516] See *Società Italiano Vetro (SIV) SpA & Ors v EC Commission ('Flat Glass')* [1992] 2 CEC 33, at para. 357–358.

[517] *Nestlé/Perrier*, OJ 1992 L356/1, on appeal.

¶640

effective competition is significantly impeded. This applies to oligopolies as well as to single firm dominance, a concept accepted and upheld in practice by most competition authorities, including those of Germany, France, the United Kingdom and the United States. Restriction of the concept to single firm dominance would create a serious legal and institutional loophole by enabling oligopolistic market power to avoid control if it results from mergers with a Community dimension.'[518]

In the early cases the Commission addressed oligopoly concerns relatively rarely. *Alcatel/AEG Kabel*[519] and *Thorn EMI/Virgin Music*[520] were the only two cases in which joint dominance was addressed at length[521] prior to *Nestlé/ Perrier*.[522] Each of these decisions will be considered below.

In *Alcatel/AEG Kabel* the issue of joint dominance was raised by the German Bundeskartellamt, and the Commission expressly reserved judgment on whether art. 2 of the merger regulation applied to positions of joint dominance.[523] In the German power cables market the parties' combined market share was 25 per cent, the next two operators having 23 per cent (Siemens) and 10 per cent (Felten & Guilleaume) respectively. The Commission stated that under German law the fact that three companies have a combined market share of over 50 per cent leads to a presumption that they form a dominant oligopoly and thus reverses the burden of proof of dominance. It confirmed, however, that no such presumption applies under the regulation, and that the burden is on the Commission:

'... to demonstrate in all cases that effective competition could not be

---

[518] Commission press release of 22 July 1992 (IP(92)617).

[519] *Alcatel/AEG Kabel*, M165, 1991.

[520] *Thorn EMI/ Virgin Music*, M202, 1992.

[521] For completeness, reference should also be made to three other cases, *Varta/Bosch, Fiat Geotec/Ford New Holland* and *Henkel/Nobel*. In *Varta/Bosch*, OJ 1991 L320/26, an allegation of joint dominance in the replacement market for starter batteries in Spain appears to have been made in the statement of objections, but was later dropped after the oral hearing. In the decision, having noted that the market share of the new entity would be 44.5 per cent in that market, the Commission stated:

'The existence of an equally strong competitor, Tudor SA, could lead for several reasons to alignment of the behaviour of both competitors. In particular the absence of other large actual competitors able to counter any alignment of the behaviour of main competitors on the Spanish market is noted' (at p. 30, para. 32).

In *Fiat Geotec/Ford New Holland*, M009, 1991, the Commission showed itself aware of the development of an oligopoly in the combine harvester market, in which three producers would have around 80 per cent of the market in the EC, but reserved its position for future mergers. It stated that it was 'conscious of the increased level of concentration on the combine harvester market resulting from the operation, which would necessitate very close scrutiny of any further additional mergers on this market in the future.' (para. 23). In *Henkel/Nobel*, M186, 1992, it was noted that the market for toothpaste in France and Germany and soap in France was highly concentrated, with three or four companies accounting for 50–75 per cent of the market. However, the market was judged dynamic, as substitute products placed competitive pressure on the market leaders, as did strong competitors and strong buyers.

[522] *Nestlé/Perrier*, OJ 1992 L356/1, on appeal.

[523] Ibid.

expected on structural grounds between the leading companies in a highly concentrated market'.

On the facts, the Commission considered that there was effective competition on the market prior to the concentration and that there was no evidence to suggest that there would be a lack of effective competition in the future. It pointed to a 20 per cent price decrease in the previous ten years, the bargaining strength of the buyers and the increasing opening-up of the market through EC legislation on public procurement. This was despite the Bundeskartellamt's assertion that conscious parallel behaviour was likely, especially given that the market was both mature and transparent, and demand was declining.

In *Thorn EMI/Virgin Music* the Commission stated that the structural features of the highly concentrated markets for recorded music could have indicated collective dominance.[524] However, the Commission concluded that there was no evidence that the markets had been operating in an anti-competitive manner or that the increase in the degree of concentration resulting from the transaction would imply a perceptible reduction in competition.

In *Nestlé/Perrier* the Commission decided for the first time that two firms would hold a position of collective dominance on a market.[525] According to the Commission, Nestlé and BSN would be jointly dominant in the market for bottled source water in France, on which they would have a market share of 82 per cent by value. On the facts of the case, the Commission stressed that the bottled water market had been characterised by a low degree of competition in the years prior to the decision. This was highlighted by a steady pattern of parallel price rises by the major brands which had been facilitated by the ready availability of pricing and sales data among the three main suppliers. The Commission judged that this had already resulted in the charging of supra-competitive prices. This situation had been able to develop because competition from other French producers was weak and because the French market was virtually closed to outside competitors by high barriers to entry, as shown by the very low level of imports and the poor record of new market entrants. Following the concentration, the Commission judged that

---

[524] *Thorn EMI/Virgin Music*, M202, 1992. In the pop music market the five leading producers accounted for 77 per cent of sales in the EC prior to the concentration and 83 per cent thereafter. Features which might have suggested possible collective dominance included:

- the fact that Virgin was the last remaining substantial independent on the market;
- the failure of market entrants to weaken the very strong market position of the small number of market leaders;
- the limited scope for price competition;
- the existence of co-operative agreements between the market leaders;
- the competitive advantage of the market leaders derived from the very significant revenues earned from their back catalogues.

[525] *Nestlé/Perrier*, OJ 1992 L356/1, on appeal.

¶640

competition between Nestlé and BSN would be irrational: they were both very large firms, they had similar market shares, they had similar cost structures and there was little prospect of competition through product development. The way in which they had joined forces to prevent an outsider from buying Perrier (the third major producer on the market), and had then agreed to divide the corporate spoils between them (Nestlé had agreed to sell the Volvic brand to BSN), had shown their communality of interests.

Following the *Nestlé/Perrier* decision,[526] the Commission had cause to consider collective dominance in two cases involving Rhône-Poulenc and SNIA, although the Commission did not find there to be collective dominance in either case. In the first case,[527] in which the three market leaders would account for two-thirds of the market for carpet fibres and threads, the Commission emphasised that there was competition among manufacturers in product quality and in the development of new and differentiated products. Indeed, by creating a strong third force to compete with Du Pont and ICI (who would be stronger than the merged entity), the concentration was considered likely to improve competition in the market. In the second case,[528] in which only two companies would account for two-thirds of the market, the Commission found the constraints imposed on the competitive conduct of these manufacturers by the price sensitivity of powerful buyers to be an important factor inconsistent with a finding of collective dominance. Other factors relied on by the Commission included the degree of competition among manufacturers in the development of new and improved products and the fact that prices were not transparent and that products were not homogeneous.[529]

(3) Relevant factors in considering joint dominance

In the light of the limited number of cases considered to date, the most important factors in an assessment of collective dominance can be summarised as follows:

(a) *High and balanced level of concentration*

The first precondition of a finding of collective dominance is a high level of concentration in the market. In *Nestlé/Perrier* two companies had a combined market share of 82 per cent.[530] Under German law, which provides a useful point of reference, there is a rebuttable presumption of dominance if three or fewer firms have a market share of at least 50 per cent or if five or fewer firms

---

[526] Ibid.
[527] *Rhône-Poulenc/SNIA*, M206, 1992.
[528] *Rhône-Poulenc/SNIA (II)*, M355, 1993.
[529] The Commission also considered joint dominance in *Linde/Fiat*, M256, 1992.
[530] *Nestlé/Perrier*, OJ 1992, L356/1, on appeal.

¶640

have a market share of at least two-thirds.[531] In addition, the oligopolists should also be of similar strength on the market. In *Rhône-Poulenc/SNIA* the oligopoly was not symmetrical, as Du Pont and ICI had certain competitive advantages which gave them a stronger position on the market than the merged entity.[532]

(b)   *Ability to act independently of actual and potential competition*
As with sole dominance, the members of the oligopoly will only be regarded as dominant if they are judged able to act independently of actual and potential competition on the market. In this respect the analysis in ¶638 is applicable. In *Nestlé/Perrier* actual competitors were weak, the market was mature, barriers to entry were high and there appeared little prospect of new entrants to the French market.[533] In contrast, in *Alcatel/AEG Kabel*, even though the market was mature and demand declining, public procurement liberalisation was undermining national markets and strengthening the bargaining position of buyers.[534]

(c)   *Price transparency*
A high degree of price transparency on the market will facilitate the parallel conduct associated with collective dominance. In *Nestlé/Perrier*[535] the market was judged to be transparent because the product was sold at list prices and competitive sales and pricing data was readily available to manufacturers. In *Rhône-Poulenc/SNIA (II)*[536] on the other hand, prices were not transparent because they were individually negotiated with customers.

(d)   *Homogeneous product*
Parallelism will also be facilitated if products are homogeneous. In *Rhône-Poulenc/SNIA (II)*[537] it was held that competition would be maintained on the market partly through product differentiation and product innovation. On the other hand, a situation in which the products sold by competing manufacturers are homogeneous and unlikely to be subject to further development – as was the case in *Nestlé/Perrier*[538] – is compatible with collective dominance.

---

[531] GWB, s. 22(3)(2).
[532] *Rhône-Poulenc/SNIA*, M206, 1992. See also *Rhône-Poulenc/SNIA (II)*, M355, 1993.
[533] *Nestlé/Perrier*, OJ 1992, L356/1, on appeal.
[534] *Alcatel/AEG Kabel*, M165, 1991.
[535] *Nestlé/Perrier*, OJ 1992 L356/1, on appeal.
[536] *Rhône-Poulenc/SNIA (II)*, M355, 1993.
[537] Id. See also *Rhône-Poulenc/SNIA*, M206, 1992.
[538] *Nestlé/Perrier*, OJ 1992 L356/1, on appeal.

¶640

(e)   *Evidence of lack of competition on the market*

From the limited number of cases in which collective dominance has been considered, the manner in which the members of the oligopoly have acted on the market prior to the concentration appears to be regarded as a crucial part of the analysis. In *Nestlé/Perrier*[539] a pattern of parallel price increases leading to supra-competitive pricing was proven, whereas, on the other hand, in *Alcatel/AEG Kabel*[540] the Commission emphasised the fall in prices that had occurred. It is submitted that without evidence of past parallel conduct in the market it may be difficult for the Commission to provide sufficient evidence that the companies concerned will not compete in the future.

(f)   *Links between the members of the oligopoly*

Evidence of actual links between the companies concerned, for example common board members or commercial agreements, is likely to facilitate a finding of collective dominance under the regulation.[541]

¶641   Relationship between quality of control and compatibility

As explained in ¶621 above, the Commission regards the transformation of a joint venture into a company solely controlled by one of its parents as a concentration. The Commission considers that the position on the affected market of the acquiring parent company is strengthened as a consequence of the move from joint to sole control. Whereas competition between the parent company and the joint venture may have been unlikely under joint control, the parent company did not have the sole ability to determine the market behaviour of the joint venture company.

Thus, in transactions comprising a move from joint to sole control, the Commission has scrutinised the horizontal and vertical market relationship of acquiring parent and joint venture.[542] The Commission has, however, shown appreciation of the fact that the market strength of the acquiring parent may previously have been stronger than its own market share suggested. In *Eridania/ISI* the fact that Eridania already had joint control of ISI, and the extent of its prior involvement in the commercial operations of ISI were factors cited by the Commission in concluding that no dominance was created despite

---

[539]   *Nestlé/Perrier*, OJ 1992 L356/1, on appeal.

[540]   *Alcatel/AEG Kabel*, M165, 1991. See also *Rhône-Poulenc/SNIA (II)*, M355, 1993.

[541]   Under art. 86, the Court of First Instance seems to regard such links as the basis of joint dominance. See *Società Italiano Vetro (SIV) SpA & Ors v EC Commission ('Flat Glass')* [1992] 2 CEC 33, at para. 358. In *Nestlé/Perrier*, however, it was the pattern of parallel pricing which was the strongest evidence relied upon by the Commission.

[542]   See *ICI/Tioxide*, M023, 1990; *Eridania/ISI*, M062, 1991; *Solvay-Laporte/Interox*, M197, 1992; and *ABB/BREL*, M221, 1992.

¶641

the very high combined market shares of Eridania and ISI.[543] The obvious risk with such an approach is that the Commission comes close to denying its own justification for a review of the effect on competition of a change in the quality of control.

This risk is particularly acute as a consequence of the Commission's use of the concept of industrial leadership in relation to concentrative joint ventures.[544] The Commission has on occasions considered that, even if one parent remained in the same market as a joint venture which it jointly controlled, the joint venture was none the less concentrative because that parent would exercise industrial leadership in the joint venture. Indeed it appears that Eridania may have had 'industrial leadership' of ISI.[545] However, given the degree of control over the market conduct of the joint venture which the exercise of industrial leadership seems to imply, it is difficult to see how a later acquisition of sole control by the industrial leader will have any significant effect on the degree of competition in the relevant market. In such circumstances, a substantive review of the acquisition of sole control would serve no purpose.

¶642   Ancillary restrictions: general principles

The 25th recital of the preamble to the merger regulation states that the regulation will still apply in situations where the undertakings to the concentration accept restrictions which are 'directly related and necessary to the implementation of the concentration'. In art. 8(2) of the regulation it is provided that any decision which declares that a concentration is compatible with the common market will also apply to such restrictions.[546] Thus, if restrictions agreed upon by the parties to the concentration can be shown to be directly related and necessary to the implementation of the concentration or 'ancillary', the permissibility of such restrictions will be analysed together with the concentration under the regulation and clearance of the concentration will result in clearance of the ancillary restrictions.[547]

While the treatment of ancillary restrictions is therefore certain, the consequences of restrictions being deemed not ancillary must also be considered. Sections II.3 and III.B.3 of the notice on ancillary restrictions both

---

[543] *Eridania/ISI*, M062, 1991. Eridania had previously determined the day-to-day operation of ISI through the appointment of the managing director. In addition it alone of the two parent companies of ISI had been active on the sugar markets, and therefore it had played a major role in determining the market behaviour of ISI.

[544] See ¶626(4) for a discussion of industrial leadership.

[545] *Eridania/ISI*, M062, 1991.

[546] The Commission notice regarding restrictions ancillary to concentrations, OJ 1990 C203/5 (hereinafter the 'notice on ancillary restrictions') states, however, that '[t]he 'restrictions' [which could be so covered] are those agreed upon between the parties to the concentration which limit their own freedom of action in the market. They do not include restrictions to the detriment of third parties.'

[547] For a consideration of ancillary restrictions in the context of co-operative operations, see ¶506.

suggest that a conclusion that a restriction is not ancillary results in the concentration remaining subject to the regulation and the non-ancillary restriction being considered against the relevant requirements of member state and EC competition law, particularly art. 85 of the treaty. In practical terms, however, non-ancillary restrictions are likely to be challenged in the context of the regulation procedure and amended or deleted in order to obtain clearance.

Regarding whether particular restrictions are ancillary to the concentration of which they are a part, art. 8(2) of the merger regulation states that ancillary restrictions are those which are directly related and necessary to the implementation of the concentration.

With regard to the first requirement, that restrictions must be directly related to the implementation of the concentration, the Commission has indicated that ancillary restrictions must be 'subordinate in importance to the main object of the concentration'[548] but have a direct link with the concentration. The requirement of direct linkage will not be met if the only connection between the restriction and the concentration is that they occur in the same context. Similarly, regarding concentrations carried out in stages, restrictions which relate to the period prior to the creation of a concentration, with the possible exception of those discussed at ¶643(4) below, shall not be deemed ancillary.[549]

The second requirement, that the restrictions must be necessary to the implementation of the concentration in order to be deemed ancillary, is interpreted by the Commission to mean:

'... that in their absence the concentration could not be implemented or could only be implemented under more uncertain conditions, at substantially higher cost, over an appreciably longer period or with considerably less probability of success'.[550]

In addition, the restriction must not exceed, in its duration, field of application or subject matter, that which is reasonably required to implement the concentration.

¶643 Ancillary restrictions: application of the principles

The general principles discussed above may be applied to three common types of agreements which often accompany transfers and concentrative joint ventures: (1) non-competition clauses, (2) licences and (3) purchase, service and supply agreements. In addition, joint acquisitions which result in the

---

[548] Notice on ancillary restrictions, II.4. See *Courtaulds/SNIA*, M113, 1991, where the Commission indicated that '[t]he four lease agreements concerning the premises are among the elements constituting the concentration; therefore the question as to whether they have to be qualified as ancillary restrictions does not arise'; and *Rhône-Poulenc/SNIA*, M206, 1992.

[549] See *Solvay-Laporte/Interox*, M197, 1992 and notice on ancillary restrictions, II.4.

[550] Notice on ancillary restrictions, II.5.

¶643

division of the acquired business will also be considered in so far as they give rise to restrictions which may also be considered ancillary.[551]

(1)   Non-competition clauses

In the context of a transfer of an undertaking, a non-competition clause binding the seller is often necessary in order for the purchaser to acquire the full value of the intangible assets transferred[552] and thus to allow the transfer to take place. In these circumstances, certain types of non-competition clauses will be considered ancillary.[553] Ancillary non-competition clauses have been deemed to include undertakings not to compete with the transferred business, undertakings not to solicit employees or customers[554] and undertakings not to use certain trade marks in the marketing and sale of certain products.[555] The Commission makes it clear, however, that non-competition clauses accompanying transfers of purely physical assets are not typically necessary for the implementation of such transfers and will not generally be considered ancillary.[556] Because the purchasers of exclusive industrial and commercial property rights will have a right of action against the seller if such rights are infringed, it will also not be necessary for these purchasers to enter into non-competition agreements with the seller. As a result, such non-competition agreements will also not be considered ancillary.[557] In addition, an ancillary non-competition agreement may not be used to prevent the purchase of shares for investment purposes only.[558]

(a)   *Proportionality*

Even if the non-competition clause in question relates to a transfer which meets the above requirements, the substance of the clause must not be excessive in relation to the legitimate purpose which it is meant to serve. In this regard, a non-competition obligation of five years will probably be considered

---

[551] Although these are the types of provisions which have been identified in the notice on ancillary restrictions and the decisions, the doctrine as set out above should not be considered to be limited to these categories. For example, a loan agreement between a purchaser and one of its competitors was deemed ancillary in *CCIE/GTE*, M258, 1992. This determination allowed the loan to be approved along with the rest of the transaction in spite of the finding that it could weaken competition between these two parties.

[552] Similarly, in *BTR/Pirelli*, M253, 1992, the seller's agreement that the acquired business would not carry out business other than in the normal course between the date of the agreement and completion was deemed ancillary.

[553] With respect to non-competition clauses, the notice on ancillary restrictions is, in significant measure, based on the Commission's decision in *Nutricia/de Rooij*, OJ 1983 L376/22, upheld in *Remia BV & Ors v EC Commission* [1985] ECR 2545.

[554] See e.g. *Solvay-Laporte/Interox*, M197, 1992; and *Volkswagen/VAG (UK)*, M304, 1993.

[555] *Linde/Fiat*, M256, 1992 (in the joint venture context).

[556] Notice on ancillary restrictions, III.A.1.

[557] Notice on ancillary restrictions, III.A.1.

[558] *Tesco/Catteau*, M301, 1993.

¶643

reasonable if the transfer includes both goodwill and know-how.[559] If the transfer includes only goodwill, the likely maximum duration is shortened to two years.[560] Particular circumstances may, however, justify longer periods.[561]

It is also worth noting that in *Inchcape/IEP*[562] a prohibition on the disclosure and use of confidential information regarding a transferred company was limited to the same duration as the non-competition clause: three years. This outcome may suggest that provisions regarding confidential information may function as non-competition clauses and will be treated as such by the Commission if they do. This outcome was also reached, in part, in *Solvay-Laporte/Interox*[563] where the parties had agreed to indefinite confidentiality and non-use obligations regarding commercial information and technical know-how. Regarding the technical know-how, the indefinite nature of the obligation was deemed permissible. Regarding the commercial information, however, the indefinite duration of the obligation was deemed unacceptable in so far as it would have the result of effectively prolonging the protection of the acquirer from competitive acts of the vendor beyond the period of the non-competition clause.

With regard to geographic scope, the Commission regards 'the area where the vendor had established the products or services before the transfer' as being the maximum allowable scope of a non-competition clause.[564] Similarly, the purchaser may only be protected from competition from the seller regarding the economic activity transferred if the non-competition clause is to be regarded as ancillary.[565]

(b) *Joint ventures*
In the context of concentrative joint ventures, non-competition clauses which bind the parents will generally be considered ancillary if they express 'the reality of the lasting withdrawal of the parents from the businesses in question'.[566] Such non-competition clauses have been allowed to extend for the duration of the relevant agreements,[567] for some fixed period beyond the

---

[559] *Fiat Geotech/Ford New Holland*, M009, 1991 (five-year non-competition clause deemed ancillary); *VIAG/Continental Can*, M081, 1991 (three-year non-competition clause deemed ancillary); *Digital/Philips*, M129, 1991 (five-year non-competition clause deemed ancillary); *Thorn EMI/Virgin Music*, M202, 1992 (less than five-year non-competition clause deemed ancillary); *BTR/Pirelli*, M253, 1992 (five-year non-competition clause deemed ancillary); *GECC/AVIS*, M234, 1992 (five-year non-competition clause deemed ancillary); and *Tesco/Catteau*, M301, 1993 (three-year non-competition clause deemed ancillary in view of the limited know-how transferred).
[560] Notice on ancillary restrictions, III.A.2.
[561] Notice on ancillary restrictions, III.A.2. See ICL/Nokia Data, M105, 1991.
[562] *Inchcape/IEP*, M182, 1991.
[563] *Solvay-Laporte/Interox*, M197, 1992.
[564] Notice on ancillary restrictions, III.A.3. See *Tesco/Catteau*, M301, 1993.
[565] Notice on ancillary restrictions, III.A.
[566] See e.g. *Sanofi/Sterling Drug*, M072, 1991; and *Rhône-Poulenc/SNIA*, M206, 1992.
[567] *Sanofi/Sterling Drug*, M072, 1991; and *Lucas/Eaton*, M149, 1991.

¶643

duration of the relevant agreements[568] or for the duration of the relevant agreements but, in any case, some minimum period.[569] The ancillary non-competition agreement in *Dräger/IBM/HMP* in favour of the newly-created joint venture was, however, only valid for 18 months.[570]

In another concentrative joint venture,[571] one of the parents which remained in the field of activity of the joint venture agreed not to acquire any business competing with the joint venture without granting the joint venture a right of first refusal. This agreement was deemed ancillary in so far as it indicated such parent's 'intention to develop [the relevant business] through the joint venture'. Another unilateral non-competition clause in the joint venture context was deemed ancillary in *British Airways/TAT*.[572]

(c)   *Protection of the seller*
Lastly, while the Commission has indicated that non-competition agreements which protect the seller will, in the context of a transfer of an undertaking, not usually be considered ancillary,[573] in *TNT/Canada Post & Ors* restraints on the activities which the joint venture could engage in were regarded to be ancillary. This conclusion was reached in view of the fact that the restraints placed upon the joint venture went beyond the transferred businesses and the recognition that the parents would define the scope of the joint venture in any event.[574]

(2)   Licences of industrial and commercial property rights and of know-how
With regard to certain transfers or the creation of certain joint ventures, the purchaser or the joint venture will not acquire all of the industrial or commercial property rights or know-how of the seller or the parents because such party or parties will continue to use such rights or know-how in the conduct of a non-transferred business.[575] Under these circumstances, the implementation of the concentration will require that the purchaser or the joint venture receive a licence to make use of such rights or know-how.[576] Such licences and agreements to enter into such licences may therefore be considered ancillary. The ancillary licences may restrict the use of the rights or know-how to the activities transferred but may normally not include territorial

---

[568]   *Thomson/Pilkington*, M086, 1991 (life of venture plus two years); *Courtaulds/SNIA*, M113, 1991 (life of venture plus two years); *Ingersoll-Rand/Dresser*, M121, 1991 (life of venture plus one year); and *Steetley/Tarmac*, M180, 1992 (life of venture plus two years).

[569]   *Ericsson/Kolbe*, M133, 1991; and *Volvo/Atlas*, M152, 1991 (co-extensive with agreement but at least five years).

[570]   *Dräger/IBM/HMP*, M101, 1991. See also *Avesta/British Steel/NCC*, M239, 1992, where the non-competition agreement was valid for five years.

[571]   *Thomson/Pilkington*, M086, 1991.

[572]   *British Airways/TAT*, M259, 1992, on appeal.

[573]   Notice on ancillary restrictions, III.A.

[574]   *TNT/Canada Post, DBP Postdienst, La Poste, PTT Post and Sweden Post*, M102, 1991.

[575]   See e.g. *Thomson/Pilkington*, M086, 1991 and *Avesta/British Steel/NCC*, M239, 1992.

[576]   In *Mannesmann/Hoesch*, M259, 1992, however, the seller was the beneficiary of certain arrangements which were deemed ancillary. See also *Harrisons & Crosfield/AKZO*, M310, 1993.

limitations.[577] The Commission has suggested that such ancillary licences should be granted for a period co-extensive with the life of the intellectual property right being licensed,[578] although in *Fiat Geotech/Ford New Holland*, trade mark licences of four and ten years were none the less deemed ancillary.[579] Ongoing exchanges of information might also be deemed ancillary in this context.[580]

This principle was also applied in the context of a research and development agreement entered into between the purchaser in one transaction and the purchaser in a parallel transaction, where the two divisions purchased were previously controlled by a single company.[581] In so far as the agreement was entered into for a finite ten-year period, contained incentives for the beneficiary to develop its own R&D capacity and attempted generally to recreate the position of the two divisions prior to the operation, it was determined to be ancillary. This determination was reached even though the two parties are competitors and the agreement was deemed capable of further weakening competition between them.

(3)   Purchase and supply agreements

In some cases, an undertaking or part of an undertaking being transferred was previously incorporated into the seller so as to have provided such undertaking with internal sources of supply or services or internal outlets for its products or services. Under such circumstances, a transfer may be potentially disruptive to such a degree so as to make service, purchase or supply agreements between the seller and the purchaser necessary.[582] Depending on the circumstances, such ancillary agreements may benefit the seller or the purchaser.[583]

---

[577]   Notice on ancillary restrictions, III.B, V.B.

[578]   Notice on ancillary restrictions, III.B, V.B.

[579]   *Fiat Geotech/Ford New Holland*, M009, 1991. See also *Grand Metropolitan/Cinzano*, M184, 1992; *BTR/Pirelli*, M253, 1992; *Linde/Fiat*, M256, 1992; *British Airways/TAT*, M259, 1992, on appeal; and *AHOLD/ Jerónimo Martins*, M263, 1992.

[580]   *BTR/Pirelli*, M253, 1992.

[581]   *CCIE/GTE*, M258, 1992.

[582]   These considerations will also arise in the context of concentrative joint ventures and the existence of service, purchase or supply agreements between such ventures and their parents. In such cases, the Commission has indicated that the applicable principles will be the same as those relevant to the complete or partial sale of an undertaking: notice on ancillary restrictions, V.C. See e.g. *Avesta/British Steel/NCC*, M239, 1992, where far-reaching post-completion supply and services agreements between one of the parents and the joint venture were authorised for a maximum of two years. Such agreements also included a sales agency arrangement. These issues also arose in *British Airways/TAT*, M259, 1992, on appeal; and *Matra/Cap Gemini Sogeti*, M272, 1993. See also *Solvay-Laporte/Interox*, M197, 1992, for service and supply agreements which arose upon the dissolution of a joint venture. Another context in which these principles may be applied is the purchase by two separate undertakings of two divisions previously held by the same company. In *CCIE/GTE*, M258, 1992, non-exclusive, arm's length supply agreements entered into between two such purchasers were deemed ancillary.

[583]   In *Fiat Geotech/Ford New Holland*, M009, 1991, a transitional services agreement by which the seller agreed to provide to the purchaser 'upon its request and during a four-year period, all those services' that Ford New Holland previously obtained from the seller's group was deemed ancillary. In *Thomas Cook/LTU/West LB*, M229, 1992, agreements intended to ensure that the purchaser would continue to benefit from the use of the seller as a distribution channel were deemed ancillary, as well as agreements which functioned so as to put certain

¶643

In addition, it may in some cases be necessary to create purchase or sale obligations for fixed quantities and in such cases these agreements will be deemed ancillary.[584] In any case, purchase or supply agreements must be limited to an objectively justified transition period after which the purchase or supply relationship must be replaced with a relationship of greater commercial autonomy.[585]

The notice on ancillary restrictions strictly applies the general requirements of relatedness and necessity in the context of exclusive purchase and supply agreements. In this regard, it is suggested that only exceptional circumstances such as the 'absence of a market or the specificity of products'[586] are sufficient to render an exclusive purchase or supply contract necessary to the implementation of a transaction and thus ancillary. As in other contexts, the parties will be bound to consider whether less restrictive means exist to accomplish the same ends, such as fixed-quantity agreements. None the less, in *RVI/VBC/ HEULIEZ*[587] a 'clause of exclusivity of manufacture' entered into by one of the parents (VBC) in favour of the joint venture (Heuliez Bus) was considered to be ancillary. Also in the joint venture context, the agreement among the parents that the *TNT/Canada Post & Ors* joint venture would have exclusive access to the parents' postal outlets for two years was also deemed necessary in order for the parents to 'transfer the value' of the express delivery business to the joint venture[588] and therefore ancillary.

(4)   Ancillary restrictions in the context of joint acquisitions

In the context of joint acquisitions leading to the division of the acquired

---

arrangements which had previously existed between the seller and the sold enterprise on an 'arm's length basis' between the seller and the purchaser. These ancillary agreements were, however, limited to a maximum duration of five years.

The reverse situation may be found in *Otto/Grattan*, M070, 1991, where the ancillary agreement bound the purchaser to continue to supply certain services, through the purchased subsidiary, to the seller for periods ranging from six months to four years. In *ICL/Nokia Data*, M105, 1991, the seller and the purchaser agreed that both the seller and the transferred company would 'make available to each other any supplies required in the conduct of their respective businesses for an initial period of one year'. This agreement was also considered ancillary. See also *BTR/Pirelli*, M253, 1992, where reciprocal supply arrangements were deemed ancillary.

[584] Notice on ancillary restrictions, III.C.

[585] In *Digital/Philips*, M129, 1991, supply agreements which allowed the purchaser to obtain additions and spare parts needed to supply the acquired customer base were deemed ancillary. The duration of the agreements was linked to the period during which the seller would phase out manufacture of the products, after which time the purchaser could supply the acquired customer base with additions and spare parts manufactured within its own group. In *Courtaulds/SNIA*, M113, 1991, a non-exclusive supply agreement benefiting the joint venture was deemed ancillary although its duration was limited to an undisclosed period less than five years. See also *Solvay-Laporte/Interox*, M197, 1992 (five-year limitation imposed); and *GECC/AVIS*, M234, 1992. In *Steetley/ Tarmac*, M180, 1992, an agreement whereby the joint venture purchased certain materials and services from its parents for two years was deemed ancillary in so far as it was 'necessary to ensure the smooth transition of ownership and control'.

[586] Notice on ancillary restrictions, III.C. For a consideration of the scarcity of supply in the context of an ancillary supply contract, see *Rhône-Poulenc/SNIA*, M206, 1992.

[587] *RVI/VBC/HEULIEZ*, M092, 1991.

[588] *TNT/Canada Post, DBP Postdienst, La Poste, PTT Post and Sweden Post*, M102, 1991. See also *Harrisons & Crosfield/AKZO*, M310, 1993.

¶643

business, a different set of ancillary restrictions arise. In the first part of such joint acquisitions, it is necessary for the joint acquirers to obtain control. Secondly, the joint acquisition of control must be followed by a division of the assets or undertakings acquired.

(a) *Acquisition of the assets or undertakings*
With regard to the joint acquisition of control which forms the prelude to the division, the Commission has indicated that agreements between the acquirers to refrain from making individual competing offers for, or otherwise individually obtaining control of, the assets or undertakings being acquired jointly may be considered ancillary.[589] Careful attention should, however, be given as to whether this view is defensible. It might be concluded that agreements such as those described above which are effective before a concentration may be deemed to have arisen are rightly subject to art. 85 and 86 and national legislation. Moreover, in pre-regulation cases, the Commission held the view that such agreements facilitating joint acquisition were prima facie violations of art. 85(1).[590] Although in these earlier cases the joint operation of the acquired undertaking which was envisioned in the second stage would have been co-operative under the regulation, this need not alter the Commission's conclusion that certain agreements between undertakings to acquire joint control in the first stage fall within art. 85(1).

This conclusion is supported by the notice on ancillary restrictions itself which states that 'for concentrations which are carried out in stages ... the contractual arrangements relating to the stages before the establishment of control' remain subject to art. 85 and 86 for as long as control is not established.[591] As a result of these factors, some caution should be exercised in relying on the Commission's view that the agreements between joint acquirers described above may be ancillary and thus outside of art. 85(1). Except in cases where agreements regarding joint acquisition are closely coupled with agreements regarding the ultimate acquisition and division of the acquired undertaking or assets (which render the transaction clearly concentrative), a conclusion that an agreement between acquirers not to individually obtain control is outside art. 85(1) may be more difficult to defend than is suggested by the Commission.

(b) *Division of the assets or undertakings*
With regard to the second stage of what is referred to as a 'joint acquisition', the Commission has indicated that:

---

[589] Notice on ancillary restrictions, IV.2.
[590] See *Irish Distillers, Eighteenth Report on Competition Policy*, point 80.
[591]. Notice on ancillary restrictions, II.4.

¶643

'[r]estrictions limited to putting the division into effect are to be considered directly related and necessary to the implementation of the concentration'.[592]

In this regard, the division of the various tangible and intangible assets may not give rise to future co-ordination of behaviour between the acquiring undertakings. In addition, it is acknowledged by the Commission that a complete division may not always be immediately possible and that transitional arrangements may also be ancillary under these circumstances. Such arrangements will be judged according to the principles discussed for purchase and supply agreements above.[593]

¶644   Procedure: introduction

Merger cases are dealt with by the Merger Task Force, which is part of DG IV,[594] but has its own registry, internal organisation, management system and working methods.[595] It has a director,[596] who oversees three units, each managed by a head of unit. There are currently about 50 officials working in the Task Force.

The basic procedure falls into two main parts:

- phase 1 – the notification and preliminary examination (which takes one month); and

- phase 2 – the full proceeding (which takes up to a further four months).

The Commission will only initiate a phase 2 proceeding if, at the end of its phase 1 preliminary examination, it has serious doubts about the notified operation's compatibility with the common market. Thus, barring referral to a member state, phase 1 preliminary examinations result in one of three outcomes:

- a finding that the regulation is inapplicable;

- a clearance on the grounds that the Commission has no serious doubts about the compatibility of the operation with the common market; or

- the initiation of a phase 2 proceeding.

If a phase 2 proceeding is initiated, it will result in one of two outcomes:

---

[592] Notice on ancillary restrictions, IV.3.
[593] Notice on ancillary restrictions, IV.4.
[594] Directorate-General IV of the EC Commission, responsible for competition policy.
[595] The Task Force has prepared its own manual of procedure. Much internal work is done by meetings rather than written correspondence. There is an informal weekly meeting of all staff at which current cases as well as general issues and problems of interpretation are discussed. See Overbury, 'Politics or Policy? The Demystification of EC Merger Control', *Annual Proceedings of the Fordham Corporate Law Institute, International Antitrust Law & Policy*, 1992, at p. 557.
[596] At the time of writing, the director of the Merger Task Force was Philip Lowe.

- a clearance (with or without conditions) on the grounds that the operation is compatible with the common market; or

- a prohibition.[597]

The relevant procedural provisions are contained in the merger regulation itself, and in Regulation 2367/90,[598] (the 'implementing regulation'). They deal with, amongst other things, the form and content of notifications, suspension, referrals to or from member states, the form and content of decisions, time limits, requests for information by the Commission, investigations, hearings, confidentiality, fines and periodic payments. Whilst some of the procedures under the regulation are similar to those that apply generally in EC competition law, particularly Regulation 17/62,[599] others, such as those relating to suspension,[600] are quite different.

¶645 Whether or not to notify

Concentrations with a Community dimension must be notified to the EC Commission within one week of the conclusion of the agreement, announcement of a public bid or acquisition of a controlling interest. Failure to notify within the prescribed time limit may lead to fines of between ECU 1,000 and ECU 50,000.[601] The regulation is silent as to the effect of a failure to notify on the validity of an agreement entered into, but not yet put into effect or implemented. Although such an agreement may not be void, it may well be unenforceable.

Putting a concentration with a Community dimension into effect without notifying may lead to an additional fine of up to ten per cent of the turnover of the undertakings concerned.[602] The validity of transactions putting into effect a suspended[603] operation will depend on the eventual decision taken by the Commission.[604] It appears that the Commission may decide that a

---

[597] To 1 January 1994, 399 case numbers were issued and 190 notifications were made (including one request under Regulation 4064/89, art. 22(3)). In three of these cases, two different parts of the notified operation were considered separately. In one case three different parts of the operation were considered separately. Of the 195 separate operations notified, five were withdrawn, six found not to have a Community dimension, 16 found not to be concentrative (there being no acquisition of control, no autonomy, or risk of co-ordination), and two were referred to a member state. 153 operations were cleared after preliminary examination and 13 went to full assessment. Of those 13, 12 were eventually cleared and one was prohibited.

[598] Commission Regulation 2367/90 on the notifications, time limits and hearings provided for in Council Regulation 4064/89 on the control of concentrations between undertakings, OJ 1990 L219/5. Regulation 2367/90 was adopted on the basis of Regulation 4064/89, art. 23.

[599] Council Regulation 17/62 of 6 February 1962, implementing art. 85 and 86 of the treaty, JO 1962 13/204 (as amended JO 1962 58/1655, JO 1963 162/2696, JO 1971 L285/48); OJ 1959–1962 Eng. Spec. Ed., p. 86.

[600] See ¶652 below.

[601] Regulation 4064/89, art. 4(1) and 14(1)(a).

[602] Regulation 4064/89, art. 14(2)(b) and 7(1).

[603] See the section below concerning suspension.

[604] Regulation 4064/89, art. 7(5).

concentration is incompatible with the common market whether or not it has been notified,[605] and, if it has been implemented, require it to be reversed.[606]

The general principle is, therefore, that prior notification to the EC Commission of concentrations with a Community dimension is mandatory. This is in contrast to the position under the regulations implementing art. 85 of the treaty, particularly Regulation 17/62, where there is no obligation to notify, and no fine for failure to notify, although notification generally provides immunity from the risk of fines in respect of agreements which are eventually found by the Commission to infringe art. 85.

¶646   Notification under the merger regulation or under art. 85

The merger regulation and art. 85 are basically mutually exclusive jurisdictions. Sometimes an operation may be structured either as concentrative (falling under the regulation) or as co-operative (falling under art. 85). In such a case, consideration may be given to the advantages and disadvantages of falling within each of the two jurisdictions. It should be noted, however, that the Commission has indicated its intention to reduce some of these differences.[607]

Notifications under the regulation may be advantageous where time is a factor. A result may often be obtained within one month.[608] By contrast, decisions under art. 85 are not subject to such strict procedural time limits, and may take far longer. In addition, given the working methods of the Merger Task Force, the opportunities for other parts of the Commission or member states to comment on the proposed operation may be more limited than in the case of a notification made under art. 85.

The legal force of the Commission's findings should be considered. The outcome of a notification under the regulation would usually be a Commission decision clearing the operation, which may be relied upon before national courts. By contrast, under art. 85, formal Commission decisions are the exception. The more usual outcome would be a so-called 'comfort letter', which it may be more difficult to rely on before national courts.

A related issue is the treatment of clauses restrictive of competition. Under the regulation, these may be treated as ancillary restraints and effectively cleared by a Commission decision.[609] On the other hand, under art. 85, it may prove more difficult to persuade the Commission that clauses restrictive of

---

[605] Regulation 4064/89, art. 8(3).
[606] Regulation 4064/89, art. 8(4).
[607] See the widely circulated discussion paper attached to the draft Commission guidelines on co-operative joint ventures. The guidelines were published, without the discussion paper, as Commission notice concerning the assessment of co-operative joint ventures pursuant to art. 85 of the EEC Treaty, OJ 1993 C43/2. See also *The Future of EC Competition Policy*, speech given by Sir Leon Brittan, 7 December 1992, at p. 6 of the Commission press release of 8 December 1992.
[608] Of 190 notifications made to 1 January 1994, only 13 went to a phase 2 full proceeding.
[609] See the notice on ancillary restraints, discussed at ¶642.

¶646

competition should be treated as ancilliary and that they should not have the effect of placing the operation in breach of art. 85(1). The Commission may be more likely to consider the operation in breach of art. 85(1), but worthy of exemption under art. 85(3). A comfort letter issued in such a case would normally state that the Commission considers that the operation merits exemption under art. 85(3). Since this implies that the operation infringes art. 85(1), and national courts cannot grant an exemption under art. 85(3), this kind of comfort letter may actually be disadvantageous.[610]

Where a 'one stop shop' is a priority, or the parties have a preference for review by the Commission, it may be advantageous to structure the operation as a concentration. If above the thresholds, the Commission will have exclusive jurisdiction. If below the thresholds, the relevant national authorities would have jurisdiction. By contrast, under art. 85, there may be concurrent jurisdiction between the Commission and national authorities.

The burden of notification should also be considered. Form CO, on which notifications under the merger regulation must be made, requires considerably more detailed information than that which must be supplied on Form A/B, on which notifications under Regulation 17/62 must be made. Under the merger regulation the parties must provide 21 copies of the notification and 16 copies of supporting documents. Under Regulation 17/62, the parties need only provide 15 copies of the Form A/B and annex, three copies of the agreements, and one copy of other supporting documents.

In principle, confidentiality under the two jurisdictions is broadly the same. However, as a matter of practice, the Merger Task Force has put in place some stringent arrangements concerning confidentiality.[611] The Merger Task Force may therefore be preferred for confidential discussions involving price sensitive or other confidential information.

Regard should also be had to the provisions of the regulation relating to operations having both a concentrative element and a co-operative element. In this situation there are three broad possibilities for the Commission: in practice allow the co-operative element to be subsumed in the overall concentrative nature of the operation, possibly treating it as an ancillary restraint; treat the concentrative element under the merger regulation and the co-operative element under art. 85 (where the two are separable); or treat both elements under art. 85 (where the two are not separable).[612] In this respect, it may be helpful to bear in mind that in its decisions to date under the regulation, the

---

[610] The national court would normally suspend proceedings pending a Commission decision. See the notice on co-operation between national courts and the Commission in applying art. 85 and 86 of the EEC Treaty, OJ 1993 C39/6, at p. 9 (para. 24–30).

[611] A special unit of the Merger Task Force has responsibility for security, liaison with member states and the conduct of hearings. See Overbury, 'Politics or Policy? The Demystification of EC Merger Control', *Annual Proceedings of the Fordham Corporate Law Institute, International Antitrust Law & Policy*, 1993, at p. 557.

[612] See the concentrative/co-operative notice, para. 1.

¶646

Merger Task Force has shown a propensity to take jurisdiction in marginal cases, and a willingness to do some violence to the wording of the regulation in doing so. However, operations structured in a transparently artificial way may not necessarily be treated as falling within the jurisdiction intended by the notifying parties.

Finally, the implementing regulation provides that the Commission may, if requested by the parties, treat a notification made under the regulation in relation to an operation which is found not to constitute a concentration, as a notification made under one of the regulations implementing art. 85.[613]

¶647   Notifiable agreements

An agreement may be preceded by preliminary agreements or by a memorandum of understanding, and the question may arise as to the point in the negotiations at which a notification should be made. In practice, a notifiable agreement will need to bind the parties, i.e., be one which the parties cannot unilaterally rescind and one which it is intended should create a legal relationship between the parties on which they can rely. In this respect, the Merger Task Force has accepted notification of agreements that are conditional on some future event which the parties cannot control, such as regulatory authorisation.[614] The agreement will also need to be sufficiently precise for Form CO to be completed to the Commission's satisfaction, and for the Commission to assess whether or not the operation is concentrative, and if so, whether or not it is compatible with the common market. Doubtful cases should be discussed with the Commission during the pre-notification stage.

Agreements relating to future concentrations should be notified within one week from the conclusion of the agreement. However, where the period of time that will elapse before the concentration is to be put into effect is considerable (e.g., an agreement to acquire a minority shareholding of 20 per cent, increasing to 60 per cent after five years) the future structure of the market at the time of the concentration will be unknown to the Commission. The Commission may therefore consider that it is not yet possible to say whether the concentration will be compatible with the common market. Subject to discussions with the Merger Task Force, in these circumstances it would appear that the operation will need to be notified at or shortly before the time when the concentration will be put into effect.[615]

---

[613] Regulation 2367/90, art. 5. See ¶653(3) concerning conversion.

[614] *ICI/Tioxide*, M023, 1990. However, in *BNP/Dresdner Bank*, M021, 1990, time did not start to run until the necessary approval of the operation was received from the Hungarian authorities.

[615] Unfortunately, there is no clear legal basis for a Commission decision granting immunity from fines for failure to notify in the period between the conclusion of such an agreement and the eventual notification at the time of its implementation.

¶648   Pre-notification contact

Pre-notification contact allows discussion of issues such as whether or not the operation is concentrative or has a Community dimension. Given the complexity of the issues and the case-by-case approach of the Commission to date, pre-notification discussion will usually be desirable.[616] If necessary, there may be one or more pre-notification meetings between the parties and Commission officials, and a draft notification may be submitted by the parties for the Commission's initial comments before a formal notification is made. Discussions may be entered into on a no-names or confidential basis with the Merger Task Force.[617] However, the durability of any understandings reached during pre-notification discussions may depend upon whether or not the parties are prepared to extend the discussions, where necessary, to include other Commission services and/or the member states.

Once the case reaches a sufficiently advanced stage, and often well before formal notification, it will be allocated a case number and assigned to a case team, usually consisting of at least two case handlers and managed by a head of unit.

¶649   Completing Form CO

The notification must contain the information requested by Form CO, which is contained in annex 1 to the implementing regulation,[618] and must be correct and complete.[619] The information that must be provided to the Commission may be limited in two ways. First, if, in good faith, the notifying parties are able only to provide limited information, they may indicate this on the Form CO, giving reasons.[620] Second, if the notifying parties consider the provision of certain information unnecessary for the Commission's examination of the case, they may ask the Commission to dispense with the obligation to provide that information.[621] In practice, it is likely that the Commission may indicate whether or not it is prepared to consider such a dispensation during informal discussions prior to formal notification.[622]

Form CO is divided into eight sections. Sections 1, 3 and 4 require detailed information about the parties, including their ownership, control and personal and financial links. If the operation is a joint venture, section 2 requires the parties to explain the complex matter of why it is a concentrative as opposed to

---

[616]   399 case numbers were issued to 1 January 1994, whilst there were 190 notifications.

[617]   Regulation 2367/90, recital 8 of the preamble.

[618]   As amended by Regulation 3666/93, OJ 1993 L336/1, to take account of the entry into force of the EEA agreement.

[619]   Regulation 2367/90, art. 3(1).

[620]   Form CO, note A(a).

[621]   Form CO, note A(a) and Regulation 2367/90, art. 4(3).

[622]   Recital 8 to the preamble would appear to be the legal basis for a dispensation under Regulation 2367/90, art. 4(3) before notification.

a co-operative joint venture. However, the greatest time will be spent completing sections 5 and 6, on the basis of which the Commission will determine whether or not the concentration is compatible with the common market. Section 5 requires the parties to identify all the markets affected by the concentration (which may be a very large number as horizontal, vertical and conglomerate relationships must be considered) and to provide, for each market, detailed information on turnover, market share, prices, imports etc. Section 6 requires detailed information on the operation of the affected markets concerning market entry, R&D, distribution, the structure of supply and demand etc. Section 7 requires information about the effects of the operation on consumers and technical progress. It also requires the parties to state whether or not they wish the notification to be converted to a notification under one of the implementing regulations should the Merger Task Force consider that the operation is not concentrative. Section 8 is a declaration as to the accuracy of the information and estimates provided. Form CO requires that the completed notification be accompanied by:

- copies of the final or most recent versions of all documents bringing about the concentration;

- in a public bid, a copy of the offer document (if unavailable on notification, it should be submitted as soon as possible and not later than when it is posted to shareholders);

- copies of the most recent annual reports and accounts of all the parties to the concentration;

- copies of reports or analyses which have been prepared for the purposes of the concentration and from which information has been taken in order to provide the information requested in sections 5 and 6 regarding affected markets;

- a list containing the name and position of the author and a short description of the contents of all other analyses, reports, studies and surveys prepared by or for any of the notifying parties for the purpose of assessing or analysing the proposed concentration with respect to competitive conditions, competitors (actual and potential), and market conditions.

Twenty-one copies of each notification and 16 copies of supporting documents must be submitted to the Commission.[623] The supporting documents must be originals or copies of originals confirmed as true and complete by the notifying parties.[624] Notification must be made in one of the

---

[623] Regulation 2367/90, art. 2(2), as amended by Regulation 3666/93, OJ 1993 L336/1. Certain other documents, relating to the concentration but not directly relied on in the notification, must be listed and supplied to the Commission on request. See Form CO, note C(e).
[624] Regulation 2367/90, art. 2(3).

official languages of the Community, which will then be the language of the proceeding for the notifying parties. In cases involving joint notifications by undertakings from different member states, the parties will therefore have to select at the outset which one language will be the language of the proceeding. Supporting documents must be submitted in their original language, with a translation into the language of the proceeding if the original language is not one of the official languages of the Community.[625]

In most cases, the completion of Form CO is a very detailed and time-consuming exercise. Although some of the information requested will be readily available to notifying parties from pre-existing sources, a large portion of the necessary data will in many cases require additional research and computation.

Particular difficulties may arise in determining the companies in respect of which information must be provided in section 3. These include those directly or indirectly controlled by the parties, controlling the parties, and controlled by the undertakings or persons which control the parties. The reference to directly or indirectly means that companies more than one level away in the group hierachy are also included. Control is specified as control within the meaning of art. 3(3) of the regulation (discussed in detail at ¶620 above). In each case the nature and means of control must be specified. In certain cases it may be unclear whether or not an undertaking is controlled within the meaning of art. 3(3). Some guidance may be taken from whether or not the companies in question are consolidated in the accounts of an undertaking concerned, since the language of the regulation is similar to that used in Community legislation relating to consolidation of company accounts.[626] In practice, it is advisable to state in section 3 of Form CO the definition of control on the basis of which undertakings have been included or excluded.

In addition, the exact determination of affected markets in section 5 of the form, and the provision of general information about affected markets required by section 6, is often difficult, especially because much of this information depends on the market determination, which will not yet have been definitively made.

Although the form does not require the notifying parties to set out and defend their view of the notified transaction, the broad and in many cases open-ended nature of Form CO certainly provides them with the opportunity to do so.

---

[625] Regulation 2367/90, art. 2(4).
[626] See Directive 83/349 on consolidated accounts (the seventh company law directive), art. 1.

¶649

¶650   Notification

Concentrations with a Community dimension must be notified to the Commission not more than one week from the earliest of the conclusion of an agreement, the announcement of a public bid[627]or the acquisition of a controlling interest.[628] In the case of a merger or a joint acquisition of control, notification must be made jointly on a single Form CO[629] by the parties merging or acquiring joint control.[630] In all other cases the notification must be made by the person or undertaking acquiring control.[631]

Notifications will be effective on the date on which they are received by the Commission. If they are incomplete in a material respect, the Commission must inform the notifying parties without delay in writing, specifying an appropriate time for completion of the information. In this case, the notification will only become effective from the date on which the complete information is received. The Commission must acknowledge without delay receipt of the notification and of any reply to a request for further information.[632] Time will only start to run against the Commission once it has received a correct and complete notification.[633] In general, notifications must either be received by the Commission at the address shown on the Form CO, or have been despatched by registered post, before the expiry of the relevant period.[634] A notification will not be invalid simply because it is late, but the notifying parties may be subject to fines if they fail to notify on time, or supply incomplete or misleading information.[635] Any material changes in the facts specified in the notification which the notifying parties know or ought to have known must be communicated to the Commission without delay.[636]

---

[627] For cases involving contested take-over bids, see e.g. *AT&T/NCR*, M050, 1991; and *La Redoute/Empire*, M080, 1991. For examples of public offers generally, see *Tetra Pak/Alfa-Laval*, OJ 1991 L290/35; *Usinor/ASD*, M073, 1991; *EDS/SD-Scion*, M112, 1991; *GEHE AG/OCP SA*, M328, 1993; *IBM France/CGI*, M336, 1993; and *AKZO/Nobel Industrier*, M390, 1993.

[628] Regulation 4064/89, art. 4.

[629] Regulation 2367/90, art. 2(1). Where the parties do not wish to disclose confidential information to each other, it should be placed in separate annexes. The notification should be submitted by a joint representative, authorised to transmit and receive documents on behalf of all notifying parties. See Regulation 2367/90, art. 1(3).

[630] Since it appears that, in the Commission's view, the parents of a joint venture will usually be undertakings concerned, regardless of the precise legal mechanism by which the joint venture arises, they may jointly have an obligation to notify. Parties may therefore wish to consider incorporating in JV contracts clauses providing for where the costs of notification should fall.

[631] Regulation 4064/89, art. 4(2).

[632] Regulation 2367/90, art. 4. See e.g. *Rhône-Poulenc/SNIA (II)*, M355, 1993.

[633] Regulation 4064/89, art. 10; and Form CO, note A(b) and (c).

[634] Regulation 2367/90, art. 18, contains general provisions on the receipt of documents by the Commission. Art. 19 provides for the definition of Commission working days.

[635] Regulation 4064/89, art. 14.

[636] Regulation 2367/90, art. 3(2).

¶651 Professional secrecy

When completing Form CO, information covered by an obligation of professional secrecy should be submitted with each page marked 'Business secrets', and a statement of the reasons why it should not be divulged or published.[637] Information acquired by the Commission may only be used by the Commission for the purposes of the relevant request, investigation or hearing. Officials of the Commission and of the competent authorities of the member states may not disclose any information acquired as a result of the application of the regulation which is covered by the obligation of professional secrecy. This will not, however, prevent the publication of general information or surveys which do not contain information relating to particular undertakings or associations of undertakings.[638]

¶652 Suspension of the concentration

Concentrations with a Community dimension must not be put into effect before notification or within three weeks of notification.[639] This does not prevent the implementation of a notified public bid, provided that the acquiror does not exercise the voting rights attached to the securities in question other than on the basis of a derogation granted by the Commission and in order to maintain the full value of those investments.[640]

Following preliminary examination, the period of suspension may be extended by the Commission, within the first three weeks following notification, for all or part of the operation, if it is necessary to ensure the effectiveness of decisions to be taken later following a phase 2 full proceeding.[641] In practice, the suspension period may be extended either where a proceeding is initiated, or where a member state makes a request for referral. It may also be extended to cover the fourth week following notification, where the Commission has not yet determined what its phase 1 decision will be. Alternatively, the Commission may dispense with a formal extension decision and accept an undertaking from the parties not to implement the concentration.

The Commission may grant a derogation from suspension obligations on

---

[637] Form CO, note E. In the case of joint notifications information which should not be disclosed to the other notifying party or parties may be submitted separately and referred to in the notification as an annex, in which case the notification will be considered complete on receipt of all the annexes; Form CO, note E.

[638] Regulation 4064/89, art. 17. These provisions are without prejudice to art. 4(3) (publication of notification), art. 18 (access to file) and art. 20 (liaison with member states and consultation of the Advisory Committee on Concentrations).

[639] Regulation 4064/89, art. 7(1) and (2), and recital 7 of the preamble. The conclusion of the agreement itself or the acquisition of a controlling interest not preceded by an agreement would appear, by implication from art. 4, to be permissible.

[640] Regulation 4064/89, art. 7(3).

[641] Regulation 4064/89, art. 7(2).

request at any time before or after notification or completion of the transaction, in order to prevent serious damage to any undertaking or third party. Such a derogation may be subject to conditions and obligations.[642]

In principle, the parties have the right to be heard before the Commission decides to extend the suspension period, or before the Commission takes a decision relating to an application for a derogation which is unfavourable to the parties. The Commission must inform them in writing of its objections, and fix a time limit within which they may make their view known.[643] However, the Commission may also take a provisional decision without the parties having an opportunity to be heard, provided that they are given that opportunity as soon as possible after the provisional decision is taken.[644] In such circumstances the Commission must send a text of the provisional decision to the parties without delay, and in any event before the expiry of the initial suspension period, fixing a time limit within which they may make their views known. Once the parties have made their views known, the Commission will take a final decision annulling, amending or confirming the provisional decision. If the parties have not made their views known within the time limit fixed, the provisional decision will become final at the expiry of that period.[645] The parties may make their views known orally or in writing. They may confirm their oral statements in writing.

The validity of transactions carried out in contravention of a suspension depends on the Commission's eventual decision as to whether or not the concentration is compatible with the common market.[646] The Commission may impose fines not exceeding ten per cent of the aggregate turnover of the undertakings concerned where they intentionally or negligently put into effect a suspended concentration,[647] and periodic penalty payments of up to ECU 25,000 per day for failure to comply with a derogation obligation.[648]

---

[642] Regulation 4064/89, art. 7(4). See e.g. *Deutsche Bank/Banco de Madrid*, M341, 1993.

[643] Regulation 4064/89, art. 18(1) and Regulation 2367/90, art. 11(1).

[644] Regulation 4064/89, art. 18(2).

[645] Regulation 4064/89, art. 18 and Regulation 2367/90, art. 11(2).

[646] Regulation 4064/89, art. 7(5), para. 1. By virtue of art. 7(5), para. 2, art. 7 will have no effect on the validity of transactions in securities admitted to regularly operating and publicly accessible markets regulated and supervised by publicly recognised bodies where both buyer and seller are unaware that the transaction contravenes art. 7(1) or (2).

[647] Regulation 4064/89, art. 14(2)(b)

[648] Regulation 4064/89, art. 15(2)(a).

¶652

¶653   Preliminary examination of the notification

(1)   Publication of notice of prior notification

The Commission must examine the notification as soon as it is received.[649] If the Commission finds that a notification falls within the scope of the merger regulation it must publish the fact of the notification.[650] In practice, the Commission publishes in the 'C' series of the *Official Journal* a 'Prior notification of a concentration', usually including a preliminary finding that the operation could fall within the scope of the regulation (but reserving its position on this point). The notice is typically published four or five days after the date of notification, although this delay sometimes extends to seven or eight days.[651] It will state the date of the notification, the parties, their business activities, and the nature of the concentration and invite interested third parties to comment, generally within ten days of publication of the notice.

(2)   Liaison with the member states

The Commission must transmit to the competent authorities of the member states copies of notifications within three working days and, as soon as possible, copies of the most important documents lodged with or issued by the Commission.[652] The Commission is under an obligation to remain in close and constant liaison with the competent authorities of the member states, which may express their views on the procedure.[653] The Commission is not obliged, however, to consult the Advisory Committee on Concentrations before taking a decision at the end of the phase 1 preliminary assessment.[654]

(3)   Initial screening: conversion

In practice, the question of whether or not an operation is concentrative or co-operative may be one of the most difficult to resolve. The Commission has recognised this, and has established a special screening group to examine this issue. If the Commission finds that the operation is not a concentration, it must inform the parties in writing. The notification may, at the request of the parties, and subject to the provision of any necessary additional information, be

---

[649] Regulation 4064/89, art. 6(1).

[650] Regulation 4064/89, art. 4(3). The published notice must indicate the names of the parties, the nature of the concentration, and the economic sectors involved, taking account of the legitimate business secrets of the parties concerned.

[651] In one case, *Eurocard/Eurocheque – Europay*, M241, 1992, no notice of notification was published in the *Official Journal*.

[652] Regulation 4064/89, art. 19(1).

[653] Regulation 4064/89, art. 19(2). Half of the Merger Task Force officials were initially recruited from member state authorities, a fact which contributes to 'practical and rapid liaison'. See Overbury, 'Politics or Policy? The Demystification of EC Merger Control', *Annual Proceedings of the Fordham Corporate Law Institute, International Antitrust Law & Policy*, 1993, at p. 557.

[654] Regulation 4064/89, art. 19(3). See the discussion below concerning the Advisory Committee.

converted into a notification or application under one of the regulations implementing art. 85. Provided that any additional information requested by the Commission is supplied within the time fixed, the operation will be treated as having been notified on the original date of notification.[655] The fact of conversion is usually recorded in the art. 6(1)(c) decision taken by the Commission at the end of phase 1.[656]

(4) Verification, requests for information, and investigations
The essential facts contained in the notification will be verified by the Commission, if necessary by enquiries with competitors and customers. The Commission may request further information,[657] carry out investigations,[658] or request investigations to be carried out by the competent authorities of member states.[659] The procedures concerning requests for information and investigations are discussed in the section below concerning phase 2 proceedings (¶655).

(5) Hearings
The parties concerned and third parties showing a sufficient interest, may request to be heard orally.[660] In practice, throughout phase 1, the case handlers will be available for informal discussion. The procedure relating to hearings is discussed in the section below concerning phase 2 proceedings (¶655).

(6) Inter-service meeting
A preliminary examination report is prepared by the case handlers and submitted to an inter-service meeting, including members of the Commission legal service. If the information is complete and there is agreement, a draft decision is then prepared, which will be re-submitted to the inter-service meeting for approval.[661]

---

[655] Regulation 2367/90, art. 5.
[656] See e.g. *Philips/Thomson/Sagem*, M293, 1992.
[657] Regulation 4064/89, art. 11. If the information should have been provided in Form CO, the notification may be treated as incomplete, and time will not start to run against the Commission until the full notification has been received.
[658] Regulation 4064/89, art. 13.
[659] Regulation 4064/89, art. 12.
[660] Regulation 4064/89, art. 18, and Regulation 2367/90, art. 11–15.
[661] Colin Overbury, whilst head of the Merger Task Force, commented as follows on the streamlined nature of the operations of the unit:

'We operate a non-paper-based management system. Following every notification the Task Force makes an initial evaluation of the case. A report of this goes to an inter-service meeting where there is an agreed position or not as the case may be. The issues are at least identified and if necessary investigations and verifications are carried out. There is then a final report and a draft decision put to an inter-service meeting. It is on the basis of this meeting that a decision for submission to the Commission is drafted. Attendance at the meetings is the only way to have your view taken into consideration. This does not exclude horizontal contacts at a high level as between Director Generals or the College of Commissioners, but at the level of Directorates that has been agreed as the way we should operate; and it works.

¶653

(7)   Modification of the operation, conditions and obligations

Should it appear that the Commission may have doubts about the operation, the parties may wish to try and modify it, or give undertakings, with a view to obtaining a clearance under art. 6(1)(b) of the regulation. It is unclear, however, what the legal basis for such modifications might be, since art. 6 and 8 suggest that modifications may only be possible in the context of a phase 2 proceeding. Furthermore, the Commission's powers to enforce undertakings may appear to be limited in the case of phase 1 decisions. Despite this, the Commission's practice has been to accept modifications and undertakings or conditions in the context of a decision under art. 6(1)(b), subject to hearing interested third parties and consulting with the member states.[662]

However, in the interests of reducing the risk of having to re-notify a modified operation or face a phase 2 proceeding, parties should strive, particularly during the pre-notification stage but also following notification, to anticipate any problems that may arise, and discuss them with the case handlers at the earliest possible stage.

(8)   Decision

Barring a referral to a member state, the Commission must take one of the following decisions[663] within one month[664] from the day following receipt of the complete notification (the effective date of notification):

- the notified concentration does not fall within the scope of the regulation;
- the notified concentration falls within the scope of the regulation, but does not raise serious doubts as to its compatibility with the common market; or
- the notified concentration falls within the scope of the regulation and does raise serious doubts as to its compatibility with the common market, and a phase 2 proceeding should therefore be initiated.

The power of decision in phase 1 has been delegated to the Commissioner responsible, who must, however, consult with the President of the Commission before opening a phase 2 proceeding.[665] No decision will be taken to clear the

---

We are lucky not to have the massive translation problems of the rest of our colleagues in DG IV. All our decisions under art. 6 are in one language – the language of the case – and we only have one set of documents that have to be translated into all languages (namely the decisions taken under art. 8 of the regulation). At the moment, once there is a public version we send out art. 6 decisions to anyone who has a legitimate interest and asks for them.'

See P. Donoghy, 'The EC Merger Task Force: interview with Colin Overbury', *Lawyers in Europe* Sep./Oct. 1991, pp. 4 and 5.

[662]   See ¶656.

[663]   Regulation 4064/89, art. 6.

[664]   By virtue of Regulation 4064/89, art. 10(1), this period may be extended to six weeks if the Commission receives a request from a member state in accordance with art. 9(2) (referral to the competent national authorities of that member state).

[665]   See Overbury, 'Politics or Policy? The Demystification of EC Merger Control', *Annual Proceedings of the*

¶653

operation until at least three weeks has elapsed from the date on which the member states received copies of the notification.

If the Commission fails to take a decision clearing the operation or opening a phase 2 proceeding within one month (six weeks if there has been a request for referral by a member state), the concentration is deemed to have been declared compatible with the common market.[666]

(9)   Notification and publication of the decision

The Commission must notify its decision to the undertakings concerned and to the competent authorities of the member states without delay.[667] Although it is not obliged to do so, the Commission subsequently publishes, in the 'C' series of the *Official Journal*, a notice recording any decision taken at the end of the preliminary examination to close the case, entitled either 'Inapplicability of the regulation to a notified operation' or 'Non-opposition to a notified concentration'. The notice usually states the date and legal basis of the decision, and indicates that non-confidential copies of the full text of decisions may be obtained from the Merger Task Force by third parties showing a sufficient interest. Initially, the Commission did not publish decisions to open phase 2 proceedings, or a notice recording such a decision, and copies of these decisions were not available to third parties. However, it now publishes a notice entitled 'Initiation of proceedings' in the 'C' series of the *Official Journal*.[668]

¶654   Procedure for referral to member state authorities

The Commission must transmit to the competent authorities of the member states copies of notifications within three working days of receipt and, as soon as possible, copies of the most important documents lodged with or issued by the Commission.[669] A member state may inform the Commission within three weeks of receipt of the notification by that member state that a concentration threatens to create or to strengthen a dominant position as a result of which effective competition would be significantly impeded on a market within that member state which presents all the characteristics of a distinct market, whether or not it is a substantial part of the common market.[670] In the event that

---

Fordham Corporate Law Institute, International Antitrust Law & Policy, 1993, at p. 557. At the time of the refusal to clear the *Aérospatiale-Alenia/de Havilland* merger, this habilitation power had come under strong attack, notably from the Commissioner in charge of EC industry and the internal market. The opponents to the habilitation power of the Commissioner in charge of competition felt that they should be involved earlier in the decision-making process. Their involvment only at the end of the proceeding leaves little scope for having a meaningful impact on the result in view of the strict time limits under the regulation. Nevertheless, the attack failed, essentially because the Merger Task Force consults widely with other sections of the Commission throughout the proceeding.

[666]   Regulation 4064/89, art. 10(6).
[667]   Regulation 4064/89, art. 6(2).
[668]   See *Mannesmann/Vallourec/Ilva*, M315, 1993. The notice is published in OJ 1993 C265/5.
[669]   Regulation 4064/89, art. 19(1).
[670]   Regulation 4064/89, art. 9(2).

the Commission is so informed, the period of time in which the preliminary examination must be completed is extended from one month to six weeks, and the Commission may well take a decision extending the period of suspension.[671]

If it has received such a request from a member state, the Commission must then take one of the following decisions:

- there is a threat to a distinct market, but the Commission will deal with the case itself and not refer it to the member state;
- there is a threat to a distinct market, and the Commission will refer the case to the competent authorities of that member state; or
- there is not a threat or a distinct market, and adopt a decision to that effect addressed to the member state concerned.

For a full discussion of these issues, see ¶631.

¶655 Full assessment

(1) Initiation of proceedings

As discussed above, art. 6 and 8 of the merger regulation suggest that the possibilities for modification and the imposition of conditions, and their enforceability, may be limited in the context of phase 1 decisions. The Commission might therefore have interpreted these provisions as compelling it to open a phase 2 proceeding where it wished to impose conditions. It has not, however, done so, but has interpreted the relevant provisions as allowing modification and the imposition of conditions during phase 1. In fact, to 1 January 1993, of 135 notifications, a phase 2 proceeding had been initiated in only ten cases. The decision to initiate phase 2, which will be taken by the Commissioner, who must consult with the President of the Commission, will be notified to undertakings concerned. Initially, no notice recording the decision was published or available to third parties. However, such a notice entitled 'Initiation of proceedings' was published in the *Official Journal*[672] in *Mannesmann/Vallourec/Ilva*,[673] and this may mark a new development in the Commission's practice. The notice records the fact of the phase 2 proceeding and invites interested parties to comment within 15 days of its publication. Whilst the decision should show grounds on which serious doubts are based, it does not define the scope of the subsequent proceeding. That is done by the statement of objections. A decision to initiate proceedings will probably be accompanied by a decision to extend the period of suspension.[674]

Once a phase 2 proceeding is initiated, the Merger Task Force may request

---

[671] Regulation 4064/89, art. 10(1).
[672] OJ 1993 C265/5.
[673] *Mannesmann/Vallourec/Ilva*, M315, 1993.
[674] See ¶652.

additional information or carry out investigations. It will then draw up a statement of objections, there will be hearings, and a draft decision will be submitted to the Advisory Committee on Concentrations and subsequently the Commission.

(2) Requests for information[675]

The Commission may obtain all necessary information from governments, the competent authorities of member states and persons, undertakings or associations of undertakings concerned. Copies of requests for information sent to persons, undertakings or associations of undertakings concerned must be sent at the same time to the competent authorities of the member state where they are resident or have their seat. The request must state the legal basis on which it is made, its purpose, and the penalties set out in art. 14(1)(c) of the regulation for supplying incorrect information. The information must be provided by the owners or representatives of undertakings, or, in the case of legal persons, companies or firms or associations having no legal personality, by the persons authorised to represent them by law or by their statutes.[676]

If the complete information requested is not supplied within the period specified by the Commission, the Commission must issue a decision, specifying the information required, fixing an appropriate deadline and stating the penalties set out in art. 14(1)(c) and 15(1)(a) of the regulation, and the right to have the decision reviewed by the Court of First Instance. A copy of the decision must be sent at the same time to the competent authorities of the member state where the addressee is resident or has its seat.[677]

Failure to provide the information requested within the time limit, or supplying incorrect information, may lead to fines[678] and/or periodic payments,[679] and to the extension of the four-month period within which the Commission must reach a decision.[680]

(3) Investigations[681]

The Commission may make all necessary investigations, including the examination, taking or demanding copies of or extracts from the books and other business records, oral on-the-spot explanations, and entering any premises, land or means of transport. In exercising their powers, Commission officials must produce an authorisation in writing specifying the subject-matter

---

[675] See also the procedure under Regulation 17/62, discussed at ¶1107.
[676] Regulation 4064/89, art. 11(1)–(4).
[677] Regulation 4064/89, art. 11(5) and (6). There are special provisions relating to the transmission of documents and the receipt of documents by the Commission. See Regulation 2367/90, art. 16 and 18.
[678] Regulation 4064/89, art. 14(1)(c) (ECU 1,000–ECU 50,000).
[679] Regulation 4064/89, art. 15(1)(a) (ECU 25,000 for each day of delay).
[680] Regulation 4064/89, art. 10(4).
[681] See also the procedure relating to Regulation 17/62, discussed at ¶1107.

and purpose of the investigation and the penalties set out in art. 14(1)(d) of the regulation, if incomplete information is provided. The competent authorities of the member state where the investigation is to be carried out must be informed in good time before the investigation of the fact of the investigation and the identity of the officials taking part.[682]

Undertakings must submit to an investigation ordered by Commission decision, which must specify the subject-matter and purpose of the investigation, appoint the date on which it will begin, and state the penalties under art. 14(1)(d) and 15(1)(b) of the regulation, and the right to have the decision reviewed by the Court of First Instance. The competent authorities of the member state where the investigation will be carried out must be informed in writing in good time of the Commission's intention to take such a decision, and the Commission must hear the authority before taking its decision. Officials of the member state authority may assist in the investigation. Furthermore, if the undertaking opposes the investigation, the member state must assist the Commission to carry out the investigation.[683]

At the request of the Commission, investigations may be carried out by the competent authorities of a member state, with or without the assistance of the Commission.[684]

Failure to submit to an investigation or the provision of incomplete records may lead to fines[685] and/or periodic payments,[686] and to the extension of the four-month period within which the Commission must reach a decision.[687]

(4)   Liaison with member states
The Commission is required to stay in close and constant liaison with the member states, which may express their opinions, throughout the proceeding.[688]

(5)   Possible modifications to the concentration
At this stage of the proceeding, the parties may obtain some indication from the case handlers as to whether or not the Commission intends to issue a statement of objections. They may consider proposing modifications to the concentration with a view to obtaining a clearance under art. 8(2), para. 1.

---

[682] Regulation 4064/89, art. 13(1) and (2).
[683] Regulation 4064/89, art. 13(3)–(6) and recital 21 of the preamble.
[684] Regulation 4064/89, art. 12.
[685] Regulation 4064/89, art. 14(1)(d) (ECU 1,000–ECU 50,000).
[686] Regulation 4064/89, art. 15(1)(b) (ECU 25,000 for each day of delay).
[687] Regulation 4064/89, art. 10(4).
[688] Regulation 4064/89, art. 19.

¶655

(6)   Possible draft decision to clear under art. 8(2), para. 1.
Once the Commission has collected and verified all of the information it deems necessary, it may consider that the proposed concentration, which may or may not have been modified, would not create or strengthen a dominant position, in which case it will prepare a draft decision clearing the concentration under art. 8(2), para. 1 of the regulation. If, on the other hand, the Commission considers that conditions or obligations should be imposed under art. 8(2), para. 2, or that the concentration should be prohibited under art. 8(3), it will prepare a so-called statement of objections.

(7)   Statement of objections
Before taking a decision imposing conditions or prohibiting a concentration, the Commission must give the parties the opportunity to make their views known on the objections raised against them.[689] A statement of objections or a communication proposing amendments to the operation will be prepared, setting out the grounds on which an eventual decision may be taken,[690] and sent to the parties. It will specify a time within which the parties may make their views known. The Commission may base its eventual decision only on the objections in respect of which the parties have been able to submit their observations.[691]

(8)   Access to the file; written response to statement of objections
The parties will have an opportunity to have access to the file, subject to the legitimate interest of undertakings in the protection of their business secrets,[692] and to submit their written observations on the statement of objections.[693]

(9)   Hearings of the parties and of third parties[694]
Before taking any decision relating to clearance subject to conditions, prohibition, reversal, revocation, fines or periodic payments, the Commission must give the undertakings concerned the opportunity to make their views known, at every stage of the procedure up to the consultation of the Advisory Committee on Concentrations. Decisions relating to the extension of the period of suspension may be taken provisionally without the undertakings concerned having the opportunity of making their views known, provided that the Commission gives them such an opportunity as soon as possible after any such decision.[695]

---

[689] Regulation 4064/89, art. 18(1).
[690] Regulation 2367/90, art. 12.
[691] Regulation 4064/89, art. 18(3).
[692] Regulation 4064/89, art. 18(3) and Regulation 2367/90, art. 12(2).
[693] Regulation 2367/90, art. 12(4).
[694] See also Regulation 2367/90, art. 11–15, which deal with hearings of the parties and of third parties.
[695] Regulation 4064/89, art. 18(1) and (2).

¶655

In so far as the Commission or the competent authorities of the member states deem it necessary, other natural or legal persons may also be heard. Those showing sufficient interest, especially members of the administrative or management bodies of the undertakings concerned or the recognised representatives of their employees are entitled, on application, to be heard.[696]

(10)   The Advisory Committee on Concentrations

Given the general requirement for close liaison between the member states and the Commission, the Advisory Committee on Concentrations has somewhat broader powers than its equivalent under Regulation 17/62. It must be consulted before any decision is taken in phase 2, or before any fines or periodic payments are imposed.[697]

It consists of representatives of the member states, and is chaired by a member of the Commission. It is convened at the invitation of the Commission, with at least 14 days' notice (which period may exceptionally be shorter in order to avoid serious harm to an undertaking concerned). A summary of the case with an indication of the most important documents and a preliminary draft decision must be provided with the invitation.[698]

The committee must deliver an opinion, if necessary by vote. The Commission must take the utmost account of the opinion, and must inform the committee of the manner in which its opinion has been taken into account.[699] The Committee may recommend publication of its opinion.[700]

(11)   Decision

The Commission must close a full proceeding by means of a decision[701] clearing or prohibiting the concentration within not more than four months[702] of the date on which proceedings are initiated.[703] If it fails to take a decision

---

[696]   Regulation 4064/89, art. 18(3) and (4).

[697]   Regulation 4064/89, art. 19(2).

[698]   Regulation 4064/89, art. 19(5).

[699]   Regulation 4064/89, art. 19(6). See e.g. *Accor/Wagons-Lits*, OJ 1992 L204/1; and opinion of the Advisory Committee on Concentrations given at the 15th meeting on 7 April 1993 concerning a preliminary draft decision relating to Case IV/291 – *KNP/Bührmann/Tetterode/VRG*, OJ 1993 C231/5. It may, however, decline to follow the commitee's opinion. See *Varta/Bosch*, OJ 1991 L320/26, at p. 31 (para. 36); and Opinion of the Advisory Committee on Concentrations given at the seventh meeting on 17 July 1991 concerning a preliminary draft decision relating to Case IV/M012–*Varta/Bosch*, OJ 1991 C302/6.

[700]   Regulation 4064/89, art. 19(7).

[701]   Without prejudice to Regulation 4064/89, art. 9 (referral to the competent authorities of the member states).

[702]   By virtue of Regulation 4064/89, art. 10(4), this may exceptionally be extended where, owing to circumstances for which one of the undertakings concerned is responsible, the Commission has had to request information by decision pursuant to art. 11 or had to order an investigation by decision pursuant to art. 13.

[703]   Regulation 4064/89, art. 8(2), (3) and 10(2), (3). A third possible outcome is referral to a member state where such referral is requested after initiation of a full investigation but before preparatory steps for an art. 8

within the relevant time, the concentration will be deemed to have been cleared.[704]

The Commission may decide either to clear a concentration by declaring it compatible with the common market (with or without conditions attached), or to prohibit it by declaring it incompatible with the common market.[705] The Commission may attach to a clearance conditions and obligations intended to ensure that the undertakings concerned comply with any commitments they have given to the Commission regarding the modification of the original transaction, and covering any restrictions directly related to and necessary for the implementation of the concentration.[706] For a full discussion of these issues see ¶656.

If the Commission prohibits a concentration which has been implemented, it may require concentrated assets to be separated, or any other action appropriate to restore conditions of effective competition.[707] The Commission may revoke a clearance at any time if it has been obtained by deceit or is based on incorrect information for which one of the undertakings is responsible or if the undertakings concerned breach an obligation attached to the clearance.[708]

There is no delegation for phase 2 decisions, which must be considered by the full Commission. If there is consensus at the level of the *Chefs de Cabinet*, the case may be formally adopted by the Commission without detailed discussion. Otherwise it will be debated and voted on by majority, i.e. at least nine votes irrespective of how many Commissioners are present.[709]

(12) Publication of the decision

The Commission must publish decisions taken at the end of a phase 2 proceeding in the *Official Journal of the European Communities*.[710]

---

decision have been taken by the Commission. A decision as to whether or not to refer in such a case must be taken within three months of notification, and a referral shall be deemed to have been made if within that period, despite a reminder from the member state, no decision or preparatory steps have been taken (see art. 9(4) and (5) and ¶631). In practice this outcome is unlikely since the Commission does not generally initiate full investigations until four weeks after notification, by which time the deadline for referral requests (three weeks from receipt of the notification by the member state) should have passed.

[704] Regulation 4064/89, art. 10(6). Regulation 2367/90, art. 6–10, contain detailed provisions concerning the beginning, end and suspension of the time limits, and the treatment of holidays.

[705] Regulation 4064/89, art. 8(2) and (3).

[706] Regulation 4064/89, art. 8(2).

[707] Regulation 4064/89, art. 8(4).

[708] Regulation 4064/89, art. 8(5) and (6).

[709] Treaty establishing a single Council and a single Commission of the European Communities of 8 April 1965, art. 17

[710] Regulation 4064/89, art. 20.

¶655

¶656   Conditional clearances: introduction

In a number of cases the Commission has accepted the compatibility of a concentration with the common market only after the parties have agreed to make changes to the concentration. Article 8(2) of the regulation provides that the Commission may attach to a decision declaring a concentration compatible with the common market

> '... conditions and obligations intended to ensure that the undertakings concerned comply with the commitments which they have entered into vis-à-vis the Commission with a view to modifying the original concentration plan.'

Furthermore, if the parties commit a breach of such an obligation, the Commission has the power under art. 8(5)(b) to revoke the decision declaring the compatibility of the concentration. It should be noted that these provisions only apply to decisions taken at the end of proceedings initiated under art. 6(1)(c). Consequently, if the Commission clears a concentration after one month by taking a decision under art. 6(1)(b), it would not have the power to enforce any commitments which the parties may have made during the preliminary review.

Strictly speaking, the Commission has no right to impose changes on the parties; it only has the right to hold them to whatever commitments they themselves choose to make. Thus if it becomes clear during the course of the review that the Commission intends to take a decision declaring the concentration incompatible with the common market, the parties will need to be ready to propose changes to the concentration which address the major concerns identified in the proceeding unless, of course, any change would make the transaction no longer viable. If it is clear from the outset that a planned concentration raises serious competition issues, the acceptability of possible concessions should be considered by the parties at an early stage, as time is very short at the end of a proceeding. A senior official has suggested:

> 'The process may assume the quality of a poker game, but it is a poker game in which the parties themselves are always the dealer.'[711]

However, as long as the companies are interested in saving their deal, they will be under considerable pressure to co-operate fully and accept whatever amendments will satisfy the case handlers, because the prospect of losing a deal and facing a long court battle is unlikely to be attractive to most companies. This is all the more so in view of the typical antipathy of the European Court of Justice towards interfering with discretionary findings of the Commission.

---

[711] See Overbury, 'Politics or Policy? The Demystification of EC Merger Control', *Annual Proceedings of the Fordham Corporate Law Institute, International Antitrust Law & Policy*, 1993, at p. 557.

¶656

¶657 Commission practice on conditional clearances

The cases reveal that the changes made to concentrations in order to obtain clearance have become increasingly imaginative and complex as time has progressed. The basic purpose of the changes is to alter the structure of the market so as to reduce the strength of the merging parties and to increase competition from third parties. As the Commission may not declare a concentration compatible with the common market if it creates or strengthens a dominant position which significantly impedes effective competition, the effect of the undertakings given by the parties should be to prevent the merged entity from having market power. There is no possibility for concentrations which fail the compatibility test to be granted an exemption, and thus the giving of undertakings by the parties is the only way of saving a concentration which will prevent effective competition on the market.

In the undertakings given, notifying parties have agreed to sell-off businesses, to sever equity links, to terminate or modify exclusive distribution arrangements and to make available facilities to competitors. The following is a brief summary of the undertakings given as part of decisions taken under art. 8(2).

In *Alcatel/Telettra*[712] the Commission required that Telefonica, the monopsonistic buyer of certain telecommunications equipment from the parties, should divest itself of the equity stakes which it held in the parties. These equity holdings were seen as a significant disincentive to the implementation by Telefonica of a diversified purchasing policy and thus as an important barrier to entry to competitors of the parties. The elimination of such a barrier to entry was crucial given that the parties had combined market shares as high as 83 per cent.[713]

In *Magnetti Marelli/CEAc*[714] the proposed concentration would have led to a combined market share of 60 per cent in the French replacement starter-battery market. The Commission was able to clear the transaction when Fiat, the parent of Magnetti Marelli, agreed to reduce its holding in the number two player in the French battery market, CFEC, to ten per cent.[715]

In *Varta/Bosch*[716] the Commission cleared the concentration once one of the parties (Varta) had agreed to sever all links with Deta/Mareg, which, following the concentration, would be the strongest competitor of the merged entity on the replacement market for starter batteries in Germany (on which the merged entity would have a market share of 44.3 per cent). The links were based on overlapping board membership and a long-term licence granted by Varta to

---

[712] *Alcatel/Telettra*, OJ 1991 L122/48.
[713] Id., at p. 51 (para. 20–22) and pp. 54–55.
[714] *Magnetti Magnelli/CEAc*, OJ 1991 L222/38.
[715] Id. at pp. 40–41 (para. 19–20).
[716] *Varta/Bosch*, OJ 1991 L320/26.

Deta/Mareg, the terms of which the Commission regarded to be incompatible with full competition between licensor and licensee.[717]

In *Accor/Wagons-Lits*[718] the acquisition by Accor of Wagons-Lits would have led in the motorway catering sector to combined market shares in France of 89 per cent for catering in the strict sense and 69 per cent for light meals. Emphasising the combination of these very high market shares and high barriers to market entry, the Commission reached the view that Accor would have a dominant position. In order for the acquisition of Wagons-Lits to proceed, Accor agreed to sell off these motorway catering activities.[719]

In *Nestlé/Perrier*[720] the acquistion by Nestlé of Perrier would have led to Nestlé and BSN being jointly dominant on the market for bottled source water in France with a combined market share of over 82 per cent by value. The Commission cleared the concentration after Nestlé agreed to sell a number of brand names and water sources to a single, independent buyer, who would have to be approved by the Commission and further agreed not to re-acquire any of these for ten years. The buyer was to constitute a third force on the market to prevent the collective dominance of Nestlé and BSN, and thus the Commission would have to be satisfied that it would have sufficient financial resources and relevant commercial expertise to exercise this role. Before the sale, Nestlé agreed not to carry out any structural changes to Perrier and not to transfer confidential commercial and proprietary information to Nestlé. Nestlé also agreed, given the narrow oligopolistic structure of the market, not to provide any data on its sales volumes less than one year old liable to be supplied to competitors which would enable competitors to identify Nestlé's exact sales volumes.[721]

In *Du Pont/ICI*,[722] Du Pont would have had a dominant position in the market for nylon carpet fibres in the EC after acquiring ICI's nylon interests with a market share of 43 per cent. The concentration was cleared when Du Pont agreed to supply an independent third party with up to 12,000 tonnes of nylon staple fibre, to transfer to it a carpet research and development installation, to give incentives for sufficient sales staff to accompany the transfer of activities and to license or assign it an ICI trade mark.[723]

In *KNP/BT/VRT*[724] the Commission concluded that the merged entity would have a dominant position in the markets for the distribution and servicing of printing presses in the Netherlands and Belgium because it would be the

---

[717] Id., at pp. 30, 32–34.
[718] *Accor/Wagons-Lits*, OJ 1992 L204/1.
[719] Id., at pp. 11–12 (para. 29–31).
[720] *Nestlé/Perrier*, OJ 1992 L356/1, on appeal.
[721] Id., at pp. 29–31 (para. 136–138).
[722] *Du Pont/ICI*, OJ 1993 L7/13.
[723] Id., at pp. 22–23 (para. 48).
[724] *KNP/BT/VRG*, OJ 1993 L217/35.

¶657

exclusive distributor of the two leading manufacturers of printing presses in these countries. Clearance was granted subject to an undertaking from the parties to terminate the relationship with one of the two manufacturers and to divest of the assets related to these distribution and servicing activities.[725]

Observations

The statistics on the Commission's settlement practice are revealing: in all but three of the ten cases in which a full review had been completed and a decision published by 1 January 1994, the Commission has cleared the operation after undertakings have been given.[726] The Merger Task Force sees this as evidence of its wish to seek a remedial rather than a prohibitory solution wherever posssible.[727] In addition, in a number of decisions taken within one month of notification under art. 6(1)(b), the Commission has taken account of undertakings given by the parties in declaring the concentration compatible with the common market.[728] This is despite the fact that the wording of art. 8 of the regulation would provide no support for any attempt to enforce these undertakings.

However, the extent to which the changes agreed by the parties will in fact remedy the threats to competition identified by the Commission in its substantive review of each case cannot yet be known. Moreover, even assuming that the parties comply with all the increasingly detailed obligations placed upon them, the parties themselves will have no control over the effect which the changes may have on competition in the market. For example, in *Nestlé/ Perrier*[729] the aim was to create a new strong competitor on the market to offset the market power of Nestlé and BSN. However, even if Nestlé fulfils its own obligations as to the transfer of the brands and water sources, there can be no guarantee that the Commission's reconstruction of the market will succeed. If it does not succeed, and Nestlé and BSN are perceived to dominate the market in two years time, the Commission will be powerless as it may only revoke a decision under art. 8(5) of the regulation if the parties themselves fail to fulfil their obligations.

Furthermore, certain of the undertakings which have been given by the parties will require continuous monitoring by the Commission of the future

---

[725] Id., at pp. 44–45 (para. 66–71).

[726] As for the three other cases, *Aérospatiale-Alenia/de Havilland* OJ 1991 L334/42, was declared incompatible with the common market; and *Tetra Pak/Alfa-Laval* OJ 1991 L290/35 and *Mannesmann/Hoesch* OJ 1993 L114/34 were cleared without changes.

[727] See Overbury, 'Politics or Policy? The Demystification of EC Merger Control', (1992) *Fordham Corporate Law Institute* (conference version).

[728] See *Fiat Geotech/Ford New Holland*, M009, 1991; *TNT/Canada Post, DBP Postdienst, La Poste, PTT Post and Sweden Post*, M102, 1991; *Courtaulds/SNIA*, M113, 1991; *Air France/Sabena*, M157, 1992; *Grand Metropolitan/Cinzano*, M184, 1992; *Ifint/EXOR*, M187, 1992; *Elf Aquitaine/Thyssen/Minol*, M235, 1992; *British Airways/TAT*, M259, 1992, on appeal.

[729] *Nestlé/Perrier*, OJ 1992 L330/1, on appeal.

conduct of the parties on the market. Reference can be made to the prohibition on Nestlé from supplying certain sales data liable to be disclosed to competitors whilst the market remains a narrow oligopoly[730] and the obligation on the EC postal authorities in *TNT/Canada Post & Ors* to treat competitors of their joint venture in a non-discriminatory manner in respect of the supply of services.[731] In respect of the latter case, even if the postal administrations breached their undertaking, the Commission would not be able to revoke its decision because it was taken under art. 6(1)(b).

Thus, whilst industry may welcome the Commission's settlement practice as evidence of a flexible approach to mergers, whether it will be successful in preventing the development of market power remains to be seen.

¶658 Conclusion

Based on the first few years of operation of EC merger control, some general comments may be appropriate.

First, the Community's implementation of the regulation defies critics who expected that the Brussels' bureaucracy would never have been able to adhere to the strict time limits set in the regulation.

A second striking feature is the user-friendly and pragmatic approach of the Merger Task Force. This attitude is in line with the idea expressed in the preamble to the regulation that mergers

'... must be welcomed as being in line with dynamic competition and capable of increasing the competitiveness of European industry, improving the conditions of growth and raising the standard of living in the Community'.

Commission officials have stressed, indeed, that only in a last resort will they use their powers to block a concentration, and the prevalence of 'negotiated settlements', combined with the fact that only one concentration has been prohibited thus far, may support this contention.

Needless to say, the speed with which the Merger Task Force has been able to handle cases and its flexible approach are in contrast with the slowness and rigidity which tend to characterise ordinary competition proceedings under art. 85 and 86 of the EC Treaty. Hence, there is increased pressure on DG IV to streamline its normal procedures as well.

A third and perhaps more fundamental comment that can appropriately be made is the great discretion enjoyed in the day-to-day application of the merger regulation. In keeping with this administrative flexibility, the Task Force has adopted a rather teleological approach in interpreting the text of the merger

---

[730] Ibid.
[731] *TNT/Canada Post, DBP Postdienst, La Poste, PTT Post and Sweden Post*, M102, 1991.

regulation itself, which has not always found sympathy with lawyers thirsting for legal certainty. The view that the merger regulation applies to the creation or strengthening of both sole and joint dominance is an example of this dynamic approach. The danger with this approach is that the Commission holds itself out as both law maker and judge because the limited scope for judicial review by the EC courts offers little protection.

The apparent willingness of the Task Force to adopt something of an ad hoc approach to merger control, and to avoid the laying down of fixed rules, may have worked to the benefit of industry up until now. However, there is no guarantee that the current favourable approach of the Commission toward restructuring will continue. Indeed, the wide discretion enjoyed by the Commission when assessing mergers under the regulation is something of a double edged sword. An overnight change of policy by the Commission could easily lead to the regulation being used much more frequently to block mergers.[732]

---

[732] As stated by Professor F M Scherer in his article 'Lessons for the EC from the US experience' in *The Financial Times* of 24 January 1990:

'If Europe learns from [the] history [of US merger control], it can move to economically sound market definition criteria. If it fails to do so, considerable wheel-spinning is likely to ensue before the loser in some disputed merger case carries its appeal to the Court of Justice and wins a victory that forces the EC authorities to rationalise their efforts.

Clearly articulated market definition and efficiency standards could have an important fringe benefit. Vague criteria leave bureaucrats in Brussels considerable discretion to impose personal preferences; sharply articulated criteria limit that discretion.

In America, the Madisonian-Jeffersonian tradition places substantial weight on limiting the arbitrary exercise of governmental power. In Europe, such power has been tolerated more readily. However, the implementation of a new European Community merger policy permits a fresh choice on whether business affairs are to be governed by a rule of law or a rule of men.'

¶658

7 Trade Associations, Trade Fairs, Exhibitions and Exchanges

INTRODUCTION

¶701 Scope of the discussion

Trade associations generally involve competitors acting together. While their activities may bring about the same restrictive effects as a cartel among individual undertakings, they give rise to some common problems. Thus, this chapter discusses separately trade associations, and the most common types of trade association activities, including research and development, advertising, product standardisation and certification. In addition, attention will be devoted to the problem of trade association rules that may lead to a collective refusal to deal. Finally, this chapter discusses trade fairs, exhibitions and exchanges.

TRADE ASSOCIATIONS

¶702 Definition

A trade association is an organisation that reflects, encourages and promotes the interests of a given industry or economic sector. In its 'typical' form, a trade association is composed of undertakings that are competitors at the same level of manufacture and distribution. However, trade associations may also involve firms at more than one level, or firms providing different kinds of services, such as in the case of agreements between associations of manufacturers and wholesalers, or associations of wholesalers and retailers.[1]

Normally, undertakings come together to share experiences and ideas that may contribute to a general improvement of the industry. In fact, trade

---

[1] See *Pabst & Richarz/BNIA*, OJ 1976 L231/24 (association of producers, co-operatives, distillers and brokers of Armagnac).

associations' main goals are to represent the interests of an industry vis-à-vis the public, political and administrative bodies and other sectors of the economy, and to promote the development of the industry.[2] Therefore, trade associations are different from co-operatives and consortia, such as those organised in the form of a 'European Economic Interest Grouping'.

¶703   Overview of trade associations under EC competition law

Trade associations are expressly subject to EC competition rules: art. 85 of the Treaty of Rome prohibits 'decisions of associations of undertakings' and art. 86 prohibits any abuse by 'one or more undertakings' in a dominant position. In most of the cases concerning trade associations, the competition authorities relied on art. 85 and interpreted widely the concepts of 'decisions' and 'concerted practice'.[3]

As a general rule, art. 85 applies to any activity of trade associations in so far as it is calculated to produce anti-competitive results.[4] Undertakings may not escape the application of the competition rules by acting through the intermediary of a trade association. Article 85 applies to any kind of association, irrespective of its legal form,[5] and even if it does not have a separate legal personality. In addition, a trade association need not be engaged in economic activities on its own, and may be subject to the prohibition of art. 85 even if it is not a profit-making body,[6] or if its members are undertakings entrusted with the operation of public services.[7]

Trade association activities may violate the competition rules because of their effects on the behaviour of their members. By belonging to the association, members are deemed to have accepted its constitution and have empowered it to undertake obligations on their behalf. Consequently, even when a member did not actually sign an agreement concluded by a trade association, but did not oppose it, it may be held to have acquiesced in the agreement.[8]

---

[2] See *Milchförderungsfonds*, OJ 1985 L35/35 (creation of special fund to promote the dairy industry).

[3] This broad application of art. 85 to trade associations may help explain the fact that cases are rarely brought under art. 86.

[4] *NV IAZ International Belgium v EC Commission* [1983] ECR 3369, at p. 3410; *Van Landewyck Sàrl & Ors v EC Commission* [1980] ECR 3125, at p. 3250; *FRUBO v EC Commission* [1975] ECR 563, at p. 583; *Sorema v High Authority* [1964] ECR 151, at p. 162.

[5] See Chapter 2.

[6] *Van Landewyck Sàrl & Ors v EC Commission* [1980] ECR 3125, at p. 3250.

[7] See e.g. *NAVEWA/ANSEAU*, OJ 1982 L167/39, corrigendum: OJ 1982 L325/20, 48; on appeal: *NV IAZ International Belgium v EC Commission* [1983] ECR 3369, where the Commission applied art. 85 to the activities of a trade association that included water supply companies. The Commission held that although these companies were entrusted with the operation of services of general economic interest within the meaning of art. 90(2), this did not exempt them from the obligation to comply with art 85 to the extent that such compliance does not interfere with the performance of the tasks assigned to them.

[8] See *FEDETAB*, OJ 1978 L224/30, at p. 38, on appeal: *Van Landewyck Sàrl & Ors v EC Commission* [1980] ECR 3125.

¶703

It is not necessary for trade association decisions to be binding on members for art. 85 (1) to apply.[9] An informal decision and even a decision made by a body that does not normally have the power to adopt a decision may be sufficient for the purposes of art. 85,[10] provided that the compliance with this decision has an appreciable effect on the market.[11] In *Van Landewyck Sàrl & Ors v EC Commission*[12] the court considered certain undertakings as parties to a trade association recommendation because they informed the Commission that they wanted to be party to the notification of the recommendation and for several years they adhered to it. Thus, the court held that the recommendation was a 'faithful expression of the applicants' intention to conduct themselves'[13] in the cigarette market. It also produced appreciable effects on competition in this market because it was implemented by seven undertakings controlling a substantial part of the market.

As they are subject to the competition rules, trade associations may be fined, even in cases where fines are also imposed on their members on an individual basis.[14] In deciding whether to impose a fine on a trade association, the decisive factor is whether it has played a separate role in carrying out the infringement of competition law.[15] Associations that do not actively participate will generally not be fined, even in cases where the association may be used by its members to give a stronger and wider impact to a restrictive agreement.[16]

---

[9] Trade association decisions usually consist of resolutions by governing bodies, such as the board of directors, but may also take the form of bylaws, articles of incorporation, recommendations and circulars.
See *Lloyd's Underwriters' Association and The Institute of London Underwriters*, OJ 1993 L4/26 at p. 30. The absence of sanctions, in a head of a price-fixing agreement, other than 'strong criticism' from other members of the association did not, according to the Commission, mean that there was no violation of art. 85(1) since the signature of such an agreement restricted competition, which is explicitly prohibited by art. 85(1).

[10] See *Verband der Sachversicherer eV v EC Commission* [1987] ECR 405, at p. 454.

[11] On their face, trade association decisions are unilateral acts. However, they are drafted with the object of being applied by the trade association members. Thus, they give raise to agreements between undertakings when they are expressly accepted by the members, or to concerted practices, when the members merely comply with them. See *NV IAZ International Belgium v EC Commission* [1983] 3369, at. 3410, where the court described the effects of a recommendation issued by an association to implement an agreement concerning the use of conformity labels. The court held that the recommendation produced a situation in which the water supply companies, which were members of the association, carried out checks on consumers' premises to determine whether machines connected with the water-supply system were provided with the conformity label. In this way, the recommendation determined the conduct of the members and exerted an appreciable effect on competition.

[12] *Van Landewyck Sàrl & Ors v EC Commission* [1980] ECR 3125, at p. 3250.

[13] Id. See also *Distribution of railway tickets by travel agents*, OJ 1992 L366/47.

[14] See *Roofing felt*, OJ 1986 L232/15, on appeal: *Belasco & Ors v EC Commission* [1989] ECR 2117; *NAVEWA/ANSEAU*, OJ 1982 L167/39, corrigendum: OJ 1982 L325/20, on appeal: *NV IAZ International Belgium v EC Commission* [1983] ECR 3369.

[15] See *Åhlström & Ors v EC Commission* [1988] ECR 5193, at p. 5245; *Hudson Bay/Dansk Pelsdravlerforening*, OJ 1988 L316/43, at p. 48, on appeal: *Dansk Pelsdravlerforening v EC Commission*, Case T-61/89, judgment of 2 July 1992 (not yet reported); *NAVEWA/ANSEAU*, OJ 1982 L167/39, at p. 50, corrigendum: OJ 1982 L325/20, on appeal: *NV IAZ International Belgium v EC Commission* [1983] ECR 3369.

[16] *Welded Steel Mesh*, OJ 1989 L260/1, at p. 42.

¶703

¶704   Trade association activities generally

As a general rule, activities that are lawful when engaged in by competitors acting jointly are lawful for trade associations. Conversely, activities that are unlawful when engaged in by individuals acting together are quite simply unlawful when undertaken by trade associations. Since trade associations and their members are subject to the same rules as other groups of competitors acting together, this chapter will not discuss activities such as price fixing, information exchanges and market sharing discussed at length elsewhere.[17] Instead, it will discuss the most common activities of trade associations and the limits within which they must be carried out.

In particular, three types of activities will be analysed. First, those concerning the maintenance of professional standards by rules on training, registration of members and codes of conduct. In respect of these activities, attention will be focused on the risk that they may give rise to a collective refusal to deal.

Secondly, activities concerning common studies and research and development on matters of common interest relevant for all the members of the association will be analysed. These activities are lawful unless they are part of anti-competitive or discriminatory schemes. Therefore, their legality under EC competition law depends on their purpose and effects.

Thirdly, attention will be devoted to activities tending to improve the industry as a whole, such as the publication and dissemination of trade journals, programmes designed to promote plant safety, joint advertising and programmes related to industry-wide quality control.[18] The primary condition for the legality of any programme undertaken by a trade association is that its benefits must be available to all members and that such a programme is not associated with anti-competitive schemes. The following activities are discussed below: joint advertising and promotion, product standardisation, certification and quality labels and uniform sales conditions.

¶705   Membership

Trade association membership should be voluntary. In other words, undertakings that are not affiliated with the association should not be compelled to join in order to be able to enter a market and trade with the members of the association.[19] Since a trade association represents industry-

---

[17] See Chapter 8.

[18] See, e.g., *Industrieverband Solnhofener Naturstein-platten eV*, OJ 1980 L318/32, where activities such as quality control, sales promotion by means of advertising, training of skilled labour, and technical, economic and legal assistance to members were considered to be lawful by the Commission.

[19] See *PHC, Eighth Report on Competition Policy*, points 81–82, where the Commission considered that the rules of an association of pharmaceutical manufacturers, importers and dealers infringed art. 85, inter alia because, as a result of these rules, manufacturers, importers and dealers who were not affiliated with the association were compelled to become members and accept the obligations deriving from the membership if they wanted to trade with the association members.

wide interests, trade association membership should be open to any interested party in that industry. To maintain professional standards, however, trade associations may establish rules governing admission which deal with such matters as the requirements for admission, the body entitled to decide on admission,[20] and the right to resign from the association.[21] In addition, trade association articles may provide for proceedings to appeal the decisions on admission or exclusion of members.[22]

Membership rules should be based on reasonable, objective standards. In *Retel 1988*,[23] the Commission determined that a set of rules established by two Dutch trade associations for the purpose of enabling installers of telematics equipment to obtain the status of a 'recognised' installer did not infringe art. 85(1). The Commission emphasised that the criteria for receiving the 'recognised' status were objective, qualitative criteria relating mainly to the applicant's technical aptitude, and non-discriminatory treatment was ensured by an elaborate appeals procedure. The Commission also noted that an installer did not need to be 'recognised' to carry out his business or obtain supplies of equipment, that installers from other member states could obtain this status and that the fee for the associations did not constitute a barrier to market entry.[24]

See also *EATE levy*, OJ 1985 L219/35, on appeal: *Association nationale des travailleurs indépendants de la batellerie (Antib) v EC Commission* [1987] ECR 2201.

[20] See *Cauliflowers*, OJ 1978 L21/23, where the Commission held that the admission rules of a trade association of vegetable dealers infringed art. 85 because they required a favourable decision of a majority of the board of directors. Since the board was composed of competitors of the applicant, the Commission considered that it was unlikely that the board would have voted for the admission of a new competitor. See also *Department Stores, Ninth Report on Competition Policy*, points 89–90.

[21] While members may be required to pay a resignation fee, the financial cost of this obligation should not represent a substantial barrier to members wishing to leave the association. See, e.g. *Campina, XXIst Report on Competition Policy for 1991*, points 83–84, where the Commission objected to the obligation imposed on the members of a co-operative to pay ten per cent of the average annual milk price obtained as a resignation fee. In *Milk Marketing Board, XXIInd Report on Competition Policy for 1992*, points 161–166, the Commission decided that it would closely monitor the effects of the leaving terms of the new milk marketing co-operative for England and Wales, and in particular the two per cent penalty payable on a three months' notice. If real competition would be prevented over an initial period of two years, the Commission would have to decide whether or not the present leaving terms could be maintained. If, on the other hand, real competition would emerge, the Commission could decide to give more freedom to the new co-operative in the choice of the contract terms.

[22] In *Centraal Bureau voor der Rijwielhandel*, OJ 1978 L20/18, the Commission struck down the provisions of a regulation enacted by the Dutch trade association for bicycles and related goods concerning the appeal proceeding against the decision taken under this regulation. These provisions did not provide the right to take action before the ordinary courts. The Commission stated that: '[t]he ouster of jurisdiction of the ordinary courts relates to matters involving the application and scope of the competition rules of the Treaty and therefore falls within Article 85 (1) and prevents any competitive action which is permissible under these rules.' Id. at p. 25.

[23] *Retel 1988*, OJ 1991 C121/2.

[24] In *National British Cattle and Sheep Breeders' Associations, XXIInd Report on Competition Policy for 1992*, p. 416, the Commission objected to the rules and decisions of the Associations which effectively prevented a non-discriminatory access to the economic activities of its 200 affiliated breeders' societies. Application for membership by a French breeder was rejected without explanation. This barred the breeder from participating in the economic activities organised by the societies because they were open only to members. In addition, registered imported sheep could not be resold within a period of 18 months after registration. Following the Commission's intervention, the Associations undertook to establish objective criteria for membership, to reason its opinions on a rejection and to organise a non-discriminatory appellate procedure.

¶705

Membership rules of a trade association and, in particular, requirements for admission may be found unlawful when they are designed in such a way that the access to the association for certain undertakings is made more difficult. In *Centraal Bureau voor de Rijwielhandel*,[25] the Commission struck down a regulation enacted by a trade association which set up a system organising the market for the distribution and servicing of bicycles and related goods. The network established by the association was open to all undertakings which obtained the status of 'recognised dealer'. The Commission held that some requirements for recognition were unlawful. In particular, it objected to the requirement that dealers do business in premises in the Netherlands because this requirement put firms not established in the Netherlands at a competitive disadvantage.[26] The Commission also held that the requirements as to stocks, premises and presentation restricted competition because the ability to compete of firms which did not meet or did not wish to meet these requirements was substantially reduced.[27]

¶706   Codes of conduct

In the face of 'unfair' trade practices (e.g. a competitor undercutting prices), trade associations are sometimes tempted to draft codes of conduct outlining rules of 'acceptable' behaviour for association members. The line that separates normal competitive behaviour from unfair competition is not always clear, and there is a likelihood that the Commission will find that such a provision prevents, distorts or restricts competition. The Commission in a number of decisions has found such 'codes of conduct', 'rules of fair trade', etc., to be restrictive of competition.[28] Where the code provides for the imposition of fines or other sanctions to enforce the conduct, this will also constitute a violation of art. 85(1).[29] However, in the context of a computerised reservations

---

[25] *Centraal Bureau voor de Rijwielhandel*, OJ 1978 L20/18.

[26] See also *Papiers Peints de Belgique*, OJ 1974 L237/3, on appeal: *Papiers Peints v EC Commission* [1975] ECR 1419, where the membership of the association was restricted to wallpaper manufacturers established in Belgium. The Commission held that this provision had the object of restricting competition because '. . . undertakings from other States which have no establishment in Belgium find difficulty of access to the Belgian market'. Id. at p. 7.

[27] In *Cauliflowers*, OJ 1978 L21/23, the Commission found that the obligation to have a packaging centre imposed on vegetable dealers by virtue of an agreement between an agricultural co-operative and the dealers' association restricted competition because it made entry to the market more difficult for new dealers.

[28] *Vimpoltu*, OJ 1983 L200/44 (decision establishing 'fair trading rules'); *SSI*, OJ 1982 L232/1; *Stichting Sigarettenindustrie & Ors v EC Commission* [1985] ECR 3831 ('rules of conduct' for sales in cigarette trade); *IFTRA rules for producers of virgin aluminium*, OJ 1975 L228/3 (agreement to halt 'destructive sales below cost', 'dumping', and related practices); *Agreement between manufacturers of glass containers*, OJ 1974 L160/1 (agreement preventing participants from offering lower prices than those of competitor when delivering goods in territory of competitor). See also *Building and construction industry in the Netherlands*, OJ 1992 L92/1.

[29] In *Vimpoltu*, OJ 1983 L200/44, the Vimpoltu decision establishing 'fair trading rules' provided that in the event of suspected breaches of its provisions, importers were subject to investigation either by independent accountants or by submission of a report of their own accountants. If a breach was then established, substantial fines were imposed, depending upon the gravity of the offence. The Commission considered that 'the procedure for dealing with suspected infringements . . . and the provision for imposing fines . . . aggravate the restrictive

system (CRS) for the car rental industry, the Commission took a favourable position with regard to a code of conduct for car rental companies operating through CRS vendors.[30]

¶707   Collective boycott

To the extent that a trade association's rules, bylaws or regulations require members to deal only with recognised or approved third parties, this may constitute an unlawful collective boycott.[31] For example, in *Sarabex*,[32] the British Bankers'Association (BBA) and the Foreign Exchange and Currency Deposit Brokers'Association (FECDBA) had to amend an agreement under which approved banks using services of FECDBA's members in the London foreign exchange market agreed not to use the services of other brokers. To overcome the Commission's objections, a system was established pursuant to which brokers who met certain objective criteria could become 'recognised brokers' with whom banks could deal.[33]

Not only may trade associations not restrict the entry of competitors into the market, but they also may not enact rules obliging their members to deal exclusively with other members. In *Centraal Bureau voor de Rijwielhandel*,[34] the Commission struck down the clauses of a regulation enacted by an association of bicycle traders preventing its members from trading in bicycles and related goods with non-recognised undertakings. The Commission found that this restriction denied non-recognised firms access to the majority of the bicycle traders in the Netherlands market.[35]

A collective refusal to deal by a trade association may also exist in cases involving the termination or elimination of a customer or of a supplier for his trading practices. In *Papiers Peints de Belgique*,[36] an independent wholesaler refused to comply with the price levels imposed by the Belgian wallpaper manufacturers' association, and refused to ensure that these prices were applied by his customer, a chain of self-service discount stores. Therefore, the association and its members decided to no longer supply the wholesaler. The Commission found that this decision infringed art. 85(1) because it restricted competition between the wholesaler and the other dealers and was motivated

---

effect of the Vimpoltu decision by encouraging importers to comply with it strictly'. Id. at p. 48. See also *Building and construction industry in the Netherlands*, OJ 1992 L92/1.

[30] *Acriss*, OJ 1993 C149/9. For a more detailed discussion on CRS, see ¶1030(4) and ¶1035.

[31] For a more general discussion of boycotts, see Chapter 8.

[32] *Sarabex, Eighth Report on Competition Policy*, points 35–37.

[33] See also *Netherlands Insurers, Sixth Report on Competition Policy*, points 120–121, where the Commission asked an association of major transport insurers in the Netherlands to change a rule prohibiting its members from concluding reinsurance contracts with non-members; *Irish timber importers association, XXth Report on Competition Policy*, point 90.

[34] *Centraal Bureau voor de Rijwielhandel*, OJ 1978 L20/18. See also *Central Heating*, JO 1972 L264/22.

[35] Id., at p. 23.

[36] *Papiers Peints de Belgique*, OJ 1974 L237/3, on appeal: *Papiers Peints v EC Commission* [1975] ECR 1491.

by the association's desire to enforce its general sales conditions, particularly its pricing policy. It rejected this motivation as a justification for the boycott because the sales conditions and pricing policy were themselves infringements of art. 85 and the wholesaler could refuse to comply with them.[37]

¶708   Research and development

Trade associations often co-ordinate joint research and development programmes carried out by some or all of their members. On the one hand, these activities are considered essential to innovation[38] and, sometimes, are indispensable for traders who may not be able to undertake them individually. On the other hand, joint research and development programmes may be problematic to the extent that they involve co-operation among competitors. The Commission has with these issues in *Eurogypsum*,[39] which involved an association formed for the purpose of promoting the development of the plaster, gypsum and anhydrite industry in Europe. This purpose was achieved through joint studies and research on scientific and technical problems relating to gypsum and plaster, and by dissemination of the results of its research by means of plant tours, technical conferences, presentations of technical films and publication of studies in technical trade journals. All members of the association, regardless of size, were entitled to benefit equally from the results of the work organised by the association. Moreover, these results were frequently made public. The Commission, in granting a negative clearance, considered that the co-operation of the members of the association in the joint financing and organisation of technical and scientific research relating to the production and uses of plaster did not have the effect of preventing, restricting or distorting competition because the results obtained were widely disseminated.

¶709   Joint publicity and promotion

Trade associations may legally engage in joint advertising intended to draw the consumer's attention to the products of an industry or to a common brand, so long as participating undertakings are not prohibited from advertising their own brands.[40] The Commission has noted, however, that joint advertising by undertakings of a certain size might violate Community competition laws where, for example, a market may be characterised as an oligopoly.[41] Joint

---

[37] For another example of a joint refusal to supply, see *FEDETAB*, OJ 1978 L224/29, on appeal: *Van Landewyck Sàrl & Ors v EC Commission* [1980] ECR 3125.
[38] See Chapter 5.
[39] *Eurogypsum*, OJ 1968 L57/9.
[40] See *ASBL pour la promotion du tube d'acier soudé électriquement*, JO 1970 L153/14. The Commission has struck down joint advertising agreements that limited individual advertising. See *Papiers Peints de Belgique*, OJ 1974 L237/7, at p. 8, on appeal: *Papiers Peints v EC Commission* [1975] ECR 1491.
[41] *First Report on Competition Policy*, points 36–37.

advertising may be unlawful when it is part of an agreement which also provides for restrictions on prices and for production quotas.[42]

A joint advertising programme aimed at promoting a particular brand may also run foul of the competition rules. In *Milchförderungsfonds*,[43] a Milk Promotion Fund was established with the task of promoting the quality and sale of milk and dairy products by, inter alia, carrying out a programme of systematic advertising. The Commission found that as it concerned one particular product (i.e., semi-hard cheese exported to Italy), the sales promotion and advertising programme strengthened the competitive position of the German exporters because 'these measures related to particular brands'.[44] The Commission considered that the programme constituted a violation of art. 85(1), but noted that had the advertising and sales promotion been of a general nature (i.e., not brand oriented) its decision would have been different. 'In such a case the promotion would benefit all competitors and there would not be an appreciable distortion of competition.'[45]

¶710   Product standardisation

Several decisions have shown that the Commission is not opposed to the efforts of associations of producers to improve the quality of their products by means of certain measures of standardisation (which may include, for example, the use of a common trade mark, and industry publicity and promotion), on condition that competition between the parties to the agreement or access to the agreement by other producers is not excluded.[46] Not only may standardisation agreements serve to improve a sector by rationalising production, but they may also benefit consumers by improving the interchangeability of the products in question.[47] Nevertheless, the Commission has noted that certain problems may

---

[42] See *Roofing felt*, OJ 1986 L232/15, on appeal: *Belasco & Ors v EC Commission* [1989] ECR 2117. See also notice concerning agreements, decisions and concerted practices in the field of co-operation between enterprises, JO 1968 C75/3, corrigendum : JO 1968 C84/14.

[43] *Milchförderungsfonds*, OJ 1985 L35/35.

[44] Id., at p. 40.

[45] Id., at p. 41. See also *Roofing felt*, OJ 1986 L232/15 (joint promotion of collective trade mark found to limit scope of trade association members to compete with each other through product differentiation); *Industrieverband Solnhofener Natursteinplatten*, OJ 1980 L318/32 (association's advertising activities also benefit non-members); *Papiers Peints de Belgique*, OJ 1974 L237/3 (limitation on individual advertising by members restricts competition), on appeal: *Papiers Peints v EC Commission* [1975] ECR 1491; *Wild-Leitz*, JO 1972 L61/27 (parties not competing as regards products covered by joint advertising); *ASBL pour la promotion du tube d'acier soudé électriquement*, JO 1970 L153/14 (members free to advertise own products).

[46] *First Report on Competition Policy*, points 37–39. See *Roofing felt*, OJ 1986 L232/15; *Central Heating*, JO 1972 L264/22; *ASBL pour la promotion du tube d'acier soudé électriquement*, JO 1970 L153/14; *Transocean Marine Paint Association*, JO 1967 L163/10, extended: OJ 1974 L18/18, OJ 1980 L39/73 and [1989] 1 CEC 2,003; OJ 1989 L351/40.

[47] For example, in *Transocean Marine Paint Association*, JO 1967 L163/10, an exemption was granted to an association consisting of medium-sized producers established in different countries. The association was established to develop marine paints by utilising joint technical knowledge, and the members agreed to manufacture paint of the same quality and to sell it under the same trade mark in order to make themselves more

arise from agreements that concern solely the uniform application of standards and types: where the effectiveness of standardisation agreements is linked with the obligation to manufacture or sell only those products subject to fixed standards, they may come under the general ban on cartels.

Thus, in *Central Heating*,[48] where an association of heating equipment manufacturers and an association of heating installation engineers created a system of equipment approval in Belgium, the Commission found the arrangement to violate art. 85(1). The parties had established an Accreditation Committee to issue certificates of accreditation for heating equipment. Under the terms of the agreement the participating installers, who controlled approximately 70 per cent of the Belgian market, undertook to purchase only approved equipment. The Commission found that the technical standards used by the Accreditation Committee as the basis for its approval were identical to those set by the official Belgian Standardisation Institute. While the latter association regularly granted certificates of conformity to manufacturers from other member states, the Committee limited itself to approving primarily Belgian manufacturers. The Commission concluded that the system constituted a hindrance to the normal system of equipment classification with regard to the installers party to the agreement, that the effect of the arrangement was to exclude a considerable amount of equipment manufactured in other member states, and that competition was restricted in violation of art. 85(1).

¶711   Certification and quality labels

Programmes awarding certificates or seals of approval and quality labels are often launched within the framework of trade associations. By attesting the quality of the products holding it, the certificate or label is of considerable value to consumers. In order to comply with Community competition rules, however, the programme must meet certain requirements: first, all producers whose products objectively meet the stipulated standards must have access to the certificate or label on the same conditions as members of the association;[49]

---

competitive with the biggest international groups on the market. The Commission considered that buyers were thus able to obtain, whenever they required it, marine paints of identical quality in a large number of countries.

[48] *Central Heating*, JO 1972 L264/22.

[49] Notice on agreements, decisions and concerted practices in the field of co-operation between enterprises, JO 1968 C75/3, corrigendum: JO 1968 C84/14.

'Such associations for the joint use of a quality label do not restrict competition if other competitors, whose products objectively meet the stipulated quality requirements, can use the label on the same conditions as the members. Nor do the obligations to accept quality control of the products provided with the label, to issue uniform instructions for use, or to use the label for the products meeting the quality standards constitute restraints of competition. But there may be restraint of competition if the right to use the label is linked to obligations regarding production, marketing, price formation or obligations of any other type, as is for instance the case when the participating enterprises are obliged to manufacture or sell only products of guaranteed quality.'

secondly, the standards imposed must be reasonable and objective;[50] and finally, the programme must not restrict the producer's right to sell and advertise products other than those certified.[51]

NAVEWA/ANSEAU[52] involved an agreement concerning the use of a conformity label for washing machines and dishwashers. NAVEWA/ ANSEAU is a non-profit association founded to safeguard the common interests of water-supply companies in Belgium. The agreement in issue required that appliances intended for use in Belgium carry a conformity label certifying that they complied with the general safety requirements established by water companies. The agreement had the stated purpose of preventing, 'in the interests of public health, any deterioration in the quality of the water supplied due to contamination or pollution, particularly when washing machines or dishwashers are connected to the drinking-water supply.'[53] The agreement further provided that the conformity label would be distributed solely by the Communauté de l'Electricité (CEG), a non-profit association comprised of electric utilities, manufacturers and importers of electrical appliances, professional associations and technical bodies concerned with the application of electricity, and that the label could only be obtained through manufacturers or sole importers. NAVEWA/ANSEAU was charged with carrying out random checks to determine whether the machines placed in commercial distribution bore the conformity label and, if so, whether they in fact met the specified technical requirements. Any machine not qualifying for a label was required to undergo an individual inspection, the cost of which was prohibitive in relation to the selling price of the machine.

The Commission considered that both the text of the agreement and the manner in which it was implemented had the purpose of preventing competition within the Community. Moreover, the programme of conformity checks had the effect of discriminating against importers other than sole importers. The only way that an importer other than the sole importer could obtain the conformity label was to apply to the sole importer. In the event of

---

See *Poroton, Tenth Report on Competition Policy*, points 130–132, where the Commission considered that forced participation in an association in order to have access to a standards certificate violated art. 85(1); and *ASBL pour la promotion du tube d'acier soudé électriquement*, JO 1970 L153/14, where the Commission granted a negative clearance for a certification programme because it was open to all producers meeting objectively established quality standards.

[50] *ASBL pour la promotion du tube d'acier soudé électriquement*, JO 1970 L153/14.

[51] Notice on agreements, decisions and concerted practices in the field of co-operation between enterprises, JO 1968 C75/3, corrigendum: JO 1968 C84/14. See *ASBL pour la promotion du tube d'acier soudé électriquement*, JO 1970 L153/14; *Vereniging van Vernis-en Verffabrikanten in Nederland*, JO 1969 L168/22. *APB* [1990] 1 CEC 2,060; OJ 1990 L18/35, in which the Commission also found that the exclusion of some distributors from a control system did not infringe art. 85(1), since this restriction of competition could not be regarded as appreciable in the circumstances of the case.

[52] *NAVEWA/ANSEAU*, OJ 1982 L167/39, corrigendum: OJ 1982 L325/20, on appeal: *NV IAZ International Belgium v EC Commission* [1983] ECR 3369.

[53] *Id.*, at p. 40.

refusal, each machine had to be individually examined, a method that was prohibitively expensive. The Commission concluded that these provisions allowed sole importers to block parallel imports and take restrictive measures to prevent them. Finding the violation to be very serious and in some instances deliberate, the Commission imposed substantial fines.

In *APB*,[54] the Commission granted a negative clearance to a standard agreement between the Association Pharmaceutique Belge (APB) and individual manufacturers of pharmaceutical products concerning the distribution of parapharmaceutical products in Belgian pharmacies. Under this agreement, Belgian and foreign manufacturers had the right to place the APB stamp on such products, which was the guarantee that they had been checked and approved by APB. In order to obtain negative clearance, the APB had to amend the clause providing that the manufacturers were allowed to sell, directly or indirectly, the products concerned, whether bearing the stamp or not, only through pharmacies. In the final version of the contract, the manufacturers were free to sell the parapharmaceuticals both to pharmacies and to other retail outlets; however, they could place the APB stamp only on products intended for sale through pharmacies.[55]

¶712   Uniform sales conditions

The Commission has noted that the application of uniform conditions by a group of undertakings may constitute a concerted practice in violation of Community competition rules.[56] Nevertheless, the use of standardised printed forms will not be objectionable so long as it is not combined with an undertaking or tacit agreement on uniform prices, rebates or sales conditions.[57] Thus, a trade association may prepare and disseminate standard sales conditions, provided that members remain free to adopt different sales

---

[54] *APB*, OJ 1990 L18/35.

[55] Id., at p. 38. The Commission took the view that the amended agreement still restricted competition because distributors other than pharmacies were excluded from the APB quality stamp system. However, this restriction was not considered to be appreciable because the distributors were free to create their own quality stamp and, in any event, the quality of the products was only one means of competition among the distributors. *Lloyd's Underwriters' Association and the Institute of London Underwriters*, OJ 1993 L4/26.

[56] See *Publishers Association – Net Book Agreement*, OJ 1989 L22/12, on appeal: *Publishers Association v EC Commission* [1992] 2 CEC 219 (uniform sale conditions on sale of books).

[57] Notice on agreements, decisions and concerted practices in the field of co-operation between enterprises, JO 1968 C75/3, corrigendum: JO 1968 C84/4: 'Application of uniform conditions by all participating firms may constitute a case concerted practice, and the making of joint price comparisons may have the same result. In this connection, no objection can be raised against the use of standardised printed forms; their use must however not be combined with an understanding or tacit agreement on uniform prices, rebates or conditions of sale.'
See *Fire Insurance (D)*, OJ 1985 L35/20, on appeal: *Verband der Sachversicherer eV v EC Commission* [1987] ECR 405 (non-binding recommendations on premiums); *Nuovo CEGAM*, OJ 1984 L99/29 (exemption granted to agreement imposing standard basic tariff); *Vimpoltu*, OJ 1983 L200/44 (maximum discounts, standard delivery and payment terms, and rules on sales promotions); *Fedetab*, OJ 1978 L224/29 (collective and uniform fixing of payment terms); *Papiers Peints de Belgique*, OJ 1974 L237/3 (standardisation of credit terms, minimum purchases by customers, fixing of dates, prices and conditions for clearance sales, prohibition of cash discounts).

conditions. To the extent that a trade association attempts to force its members to use specific sales conditions, the programme will be found to violate Community competition rules.

TRADE FAIRS AND EXHIBITIONS

¶713   Introduction

By bringing together manufacturers, distributors and importers from a given industrial sector, trade fairs benefit both industry and its customers. For industry, they allow comparison of competing products and permit the promotion of a range of products with a minimum of effort. Moreover, they offer manufacturers an effective means of marketing their products in other member states, thus facilitating the achievement of a single European market. This advantage may be particularly important for small and medium-sized companies because it may be the only means they have of gaining a foothold in the markets of other member states. Customers are provided with more information and better guidance, and are given an overview of the entire market without having to make several trips.

Despite these advantages, trade fairs and exhibitions may present problems under the competition rules. In particular, problems are likely to arise when the organisers – typically trade associations – prohibit participants from exhibiting at other trade fairs and exhibitions for a given period of time or use a selective admissions policy.

¶714   Restraint periods

The Commission has intervened in many cases involving a 'restraint period', that is, a period, generally before and after a trade fair, during which participants are prohibited from exhibiting at other trade fairs.[58] Restraint periods may restrict competition between manufacturers, importers and distributors by preventing them from promoting their products in competition with each other at other trade fairs. Restraint periods may also restrict competition between organisers of exhibitions by preventing organisers of one trade show from securing the participation of exhibitors in another trade show during the restraint period.

---

[58] *British Dental Trade Association – BDTA*, OJ 1988 L233/15 (dental supplies); *Internationale Dentalschau*, OJ 1987 L293/58 (dental supplies); *VIFKA*, OJ 1986 L291/46 (office equipment); *SMM&T*, OJ 1983 L371/1 (motor vehicles); *BPICA*, OJ 1977 L299/18, extended OJ 1982 L156/16 (motor vehicles); *UNIDI*, OJ 1975 L228/17, extended OJ 1984 L322/10, on appeal *ANCIDES v EC Commission* [1987] ECR 3131 (dental supplies); *CEMATEX*, JO 1971 L227/26, extended OJ 1983 L140/27 (textile machinery); *European Machine Tool Exhibitions*, JO 1969 L69/13, extended OJ 1979 L11/16, OJ 1989 L37/11 (machine tools); *EUMAPRINT*, *Third Report on Competition Policy*, point 57 (printing and papermaking machinery).

¶714

Consistently, the Commission has been willing to exempt rules imposing restraint periods on participants under art. 85(3), though often after requiring the organisers to amend these rules. As a practical matter, such rules mean that most exhibitors will take part in the same major trade fairs. Getting the exhibitors together under one roof helps ensure that a full range of products will be displayed and is likely to generate livelier competition in the exhibition hall. It also may lead to lower distribution costs that can be passed on to customers because manufacturers can limit their marketing efforts to a few major fairs. Customers also benefit because they avoid having to travel from one trade fair to another to see all the available products.

The restraint period should not be so long that it prevents exhibitors from participating in rival trade fairs. As a general rule, this period should not be longer than the 'open' period during which exhibitors are free to participate in other fairs.[59] For example, in *UNIDI*,[60] the Commission exempted trade fair rules that provided that the fair would be held every 18 months and that imposed a restraint period of nine months immediately prior to the fair. Several years later, UNIDI amended these rules to provide that the trade fair would be held once a year and to shorten the restraint period to six months. Again, the Commission granted an exemption.[61]

---

[59] With one exception, the period of restraint has never been longer than the 'open' period. See *VIFKA*, OJ 1986 L291/46 (exhibition held every other year; restraint period limited to exhibition year); *SMM&T*, OJ 1983 L376/1 (same); *UNIDI*, OJ 1975 L228/17 (exhibition held every 18 months; restraint period limited to nine months following exhibition), extended OJ 1984 L322/10 (exhibition held every nine months; restraint period limited to six months following exhibition), upheld on appeal *ANCIDES v EC Commission* [1987] ECR 3131; *CEMATEX*, JO 1971 L227/26, extended OJ 1983 L140/27 (exhibition held every four years; restraint period limited to two years); *European Machine Tool Exhibition*, JO 1969 L69/13, extended OJ 1979 L11/16 (exhibition held every other year; restraint period limited to year of exhibition). In recent cases, the ratio has been less than 1:1. See *British Dental Trade Association – BDTA*, OJ 1988 L233/15 (exhibition held every year; restraint period limited to four months before exhibition, one month after); *Internationale Dentalschau*, OJ 1987 L293/58 (exhibition held every three years; restraint period limited to three months before exhibition, two months after)
In *BPICA*, OJ 1977 L299/18, extended OJ 1982 L156/16, however, the Commission exempted a restraint period that amounted to a permanent prohibition on participation in events not authorised by the trade association. The Commission's attitude in this case may have been influenced by the numerous exceptions to this prohibition; in particular, it only applied to international exhibitions, so exhibitors remained free to participate in national and regional exhibitions.

[60] *UNIDI*, OJ 1975 L228/17, extended OJ 1984 L322/10, upheld on appeal *ANCIDES v EC Commission* [1987] ECR 3131.

[61] The organiser of a competing trade fair, ANCIDES, contested this second exemption decision. According to ANCIDES, UNIDI usually held its trade fair at the end of June. This meant that ANCIDES could only hold its trade fair in the immediately following six months, of which three were lost to summer vacation, so that, as a practical matter, ANCIDES only had a window of three months in which to hold a competing trade fair. Advocate General Slynn seemed to acknowledge that, in the abstract, this argument could have merit. It emerged at the hearing, however, that the most recent UNIDI exhibition was, in fact, held at the end of September. The Advocate General tactfully noted that, after this revelation, 'ANCIDES seems to place less reliance on this part of its case.' ([1987] ECR 3131, at p. 3147). Not surprisingly, the court also rejected the argument.

¶715   Admission rules

Admission rules may restrict competition by limiting the number of exhibitors of a given product.[62] However, the Commission has been willing to exempt selective admissions procedures under art. 85(3).[63] The Commission recognises that organisers of trade fairs may be bound by certain space limitations which necessitate a restriction on the number of participants.[64] In fact, such limitations may be desirable in that they enable the organisers to rationalise costs, thus producing savings that may be passed on to consumers. A selective admissions policy may not only reduce costs, but it may also help ensure that the range of articles on display is as extensive as space limitations permit. Specifically, a selective policy ensures that multiple displays of the same article do not prevent a complete range of articles from being displayed.

The selection procedure itself must be based on objective criteria. In *Internationale Dentalschau*,[65] the Commission exempted an admissions procedure based on the following order of priority: manufacturers; importers or dealers appointed by manufacturers; other importers or dealers in the order in which their application was received. In the Commission's view, it is appropriate for the manufacturer to be given priority over the dealer because the manufacturer is in the best position to present his products. Likewise, if it is necessary to choose among several dealers, the dealer appointed by the manufacturer should be given priority because this dealer may be assumed to enjoy the confidence of the manufacturer. In *Sippa*,[66] the selection procedure was even more refined in that it gave priority to dealers intending to display products not already being displayed by a manufacturer or its primary authorised dealer over dealers who had a secondary delegation of authority from the manufacturer, but who intended to display products already being displayed by others. In exempting this procedure, the Commission again highlighted its concern over seeing an the widest range of products as possible would be on display.

While admissions procedures and restraint periods have received the most attention, other aspects of trade fair regulations have also raised competition law concerns. In *Sippa*[67] a rule that required participants in the trade fair to

---

[62] *Internationale Dentalschau*, OJ 1987 L293/58; *Sippa.* OJ 1991 L60/19.

[63] Id.

[64] In *Internationale Dentalschau*, OJ 1987 L293/58, at p. 61, a participant could only be excluded on the grounds of limited space:

'Admissions to the exhibition can be restricted only if the multiple display of the same products would prevent other products from being exhibited because of lack of space. The organizer cannot use this as a pretext for refusing admission, since, in the event of arbitration proceedings, it is up to him to prove that admission was refused solely because of lack of space.'

[65] *Internationale Dentalschau*, OJ 1987 L293/58.

[66] *Sippa*, OJ 1991 L60/19.

[67] Id.

display documents and prices and actively canvas visitors only with respect to products actually shown on the stand was found to infringe art. 85(1). The Commission granted an exemption under art. 85(3), however, on the grounds that this rule simply forced exhibitors to focus on the primary purpose of the trade fair – informing buyers about the products on display – rather than on other matters such as competing for orders, an activity which was more appropriate outside of the fair. Also, the rule did not prevent exhibitors from engaging in 'passive' canvassing, so that they could answer questions from customers concerning products not on display. The Commission's position on this point would seem at odds with its concern over making the most efficient use of the available space.

Participation in trade fairs must be open to companies from throughout the EC on a non-discriminatory basis. In *EUMAPRINT*,[68] the Commission condemned an attempt to reserve participation in so-called 'national' exhibitions to local companies and companies from other member states with a local presence through, for instance, a subsidiary, distributor or agent. Companies from other member states without a local presence could only participate in 'international' exhibitions. In the Commission's view, such a system penalised companies that were not large enough to have a presence abroad by preventing them from exhibiting their products abroad and meeting prospective agents or distributors. In *British Dental Trade Association*,[69] the trade association learned that the Commission had not changed its position on this issue. In that case, the association's use of a similar system that discriminated against companies from other member states drew a fine of ECU 100,000.[70]

EXCHANGES

¶716   Status under EC competition rules

The Commission has issued negative clearances for several sets of rules and regulations of certain institutions which organise commodity exchanges.[71]

---

[68] *EUMAPRINT, Third Report on Competition Policy,* point 57 (printing and paper making machinery).
[69] *British Dental Trade Association – BDTA,* OJ 1988 L233/15.
[70] As in *EUMAPRINT,* the association sponsored a dual system of international and national trade fairs, and restricted the ability of companies from other member states to participate in the latter. In addition, the association discriminated against companies from other member states even with respect to their participation in international exhibitions: participation was by invitation only, which were only issued if space remained after local companies had completed their bookings.
    The Commission did not object to charging non-members higher admission fees in view of the extra costs and financial risks involved in organising the exhibitions, which were borne by members of the association.
[71] *London Sugar Futures Market Ltd,* OJ 1985 L369/25; *London Cocoa Terminal Market Association Ltd,* OJ 1985 L369/28; *Coffee Terminal Market Association of London Ltd,* OJ 1985 L369/31; *London Rubber Terminal Market Association Ltd,* OJ 1985 L369/04; *Petroleum Exchange of London Ltd,* OJ 1987 L3/27; *The GAFTA Soya*

These decisions elaborate on a position which the Commission adopted previously in the *Sarabex* case.[72]

The establishment of such exchanges is regarded favourably by the Commission, because they provide a market floor for trading and price-making in the product concerned. Moreover, the commodity exchanges considered by the Commission provided, in most cases, the mechanism by which the principal global markets of the products in question operated and the Commission found that 'they contribute to the stability and smooth operation of world trade and to world pricing mechanisms'.[73]

However, the grant of a negative clearance occurred only after the existing rules had been modified in what the Commission considered to be two key areas:

(1) *Prices*: the original rules generally amounted to a form of price-fixing in that they established minimum net rates of commission which could be charged by floor members, and varied according to who was paying and who was receiving. The highest rate of commission applied where the payer was a non-member. The new rules mostly require that 'a' commission be charged but the rates are freely negotiable.[74]

(2) *Membership rules*: the existence of different classes of members is not inconsistent with art. 85(1) as long as the criteria for access to the different classes are fully objective.[75] The number of the class of full floor members may be limited. The modified rules now typically require that a refusal of an application for membership states reasons and can be

---

Bean Meal Futures Association, OJ 1987 L19/18; *The London Grain Futures Market*, OJ 1987 L19/22; *The London Potato Futures Association Ltd*, OJ 1987 L19/26; *The London Meat Futures Exchange Ltd*, OJ 1987 L19/30; *Baltic International Freight Futures Exchanges Ltd*, OJ 1987 L222/24; this decision does not involve a commodity market, but a market dealing in standardised freight futures contracts for shipowners, charterers and users of shipping transport in general. In *Hudson's Bay/Dansk Pelsdyravlerforening*, OJ 1988 L316/43 on appeal: *Dansk Pelsdyravlerforening v EC Commission*, Case T-61/89, judgment of 2 July 1992 (not yet reported) and *VBA/Bloemenveilingen Aalsmeer*, OJ 1988 L262/27, the Commission adopted a negative attitude and refused to grant a negative clearance or an exemption.

[72] See *Eighth Report on Competition Policy*, points 35–37.

[73] Observation made by the Commission in, inter alia, *London Sugar Futures Market Ltd*, OJ 1985 L369/25; *Petroleum Exchange of London Ltd*, OJ 1987 L3/27; *The GAFTA Soya Bean Meal Futures Association*, OJ 1987 L19/18.

[74] In *Sarabex*, which involved the British foreign exchange broking market, the Commission allowed the establishment of both maximum and minimum rates for dealings in each currency. No specific explanation was given. See *Eighth Report on Competition Policy*, points 35–37. Compare: *Belgische Vereniging der Banken/ Association Belge des Banques*, OJ 1987 L7/27 where a convention between banks on the collection of cheques and commercial bills originating abroad was held to be contrary to art. 85(1), because it established the mere principle of, and the procedures for, charging a commission, without, however, setting any minimum or maximum tariffs.

[75] The Commission decisions do not provide extensive details on the nature of such criteria. The decisions indicated, however, that the criteria in question may for instance involve the financial standing of prospective members and proof of a continuous interest in the trade of the commodity concerned (See, e.g., *London Cocoa Terminal Market Association Ltd*, OJ 1985 L369/28, at p. 30; *Petroleum Exchange of London Ltd*, OJ 1987 L3/27 at p. 29; *The London Grain Futures Market*, OJ 1987 L19/22 at p. 24).

¶716

challenged in an appeal procedure. Some exchanges provide for an ultimate recourse to an ordinary civil court.[76]

Apart from the sensitive areas just mentioned, the organisation running the market appears to have some leeway to determine what the Commission calls 'various technical questions', such as standard contract terms (not involving any price terms) and quality specifications as to the products traded. Moreover, it is allowed for such organisations to procure the provision of clearing and settlement facilities.

However, in two recent decisions, the Commission condemned anti-competitive conduct by auction associations. In *Bloemenveilingen Aalsmeer*[77] the Commission reviewed agreements between a flower auctioneer and the wholesalers established on its premises. Since the wholesalers could sell only those products acquired through the auctioneer or approved by it, the Commission found that competition between the suppliers offering their goods for sale through the auctioneer was restricted. In *Hudson's Bay/Dansk Pelsdyravlerforening* (DPF),[78] the Commission condemned the rules issued by a Danish auction association, compelling its members to sell their entire production to a subsidiary of the association. The Commission found that the members were prevented from exporting part of their production and that the agreement aimed at limiting market entry by competitors, by virtually monopolising the supply and sale of the products in Denmark.[79]

---

[76] See for instance *London Sugar Futures Market Ltd*, OJ 1985 L369/25 at p. 27.

[77] *Bloemenveilingen Aalsmeer*, OJ 1988 L262/27; see also *Bloemenveilingen Aalsmeer*, notice, OJ 1989 C83/3.

[78] *Hudson's Bay/Dansk Pelsdyravlerforening* OJ 1988 L316/43, on appeal: *Dansk Pelsdyravlerforening v EC Commission*, Case T-61/89, judgment of 2 July 1992 (not yet reported).

[79] On this point, the Court of First Instance upheld the Commission decision.

at first glance, do not appear to constitute price-fixing have been condemned under art. 85(1):

(1) an agreement to refrain from advertising rebates;[7]

(2) an agreement to refrain from making 'destructive sales below costs', to engage in dumping or to sell below published prices;[8]

(3) an agreement fixing discounts to be offered to customers;[9]

(4) agreements fixing target prices;[10]

(5) an agreement setting up a compensation system for equalising proceeds of domestic and foreign sales;[11]

---

[7] *Papiers Peints v EC Commission* [1975] ECR 1491, at p. 1511 (para. 10), 'If a system of fixed selling prices is clearly in conflict with [art. 85(1)], a price-list system under which the announcement of rebates on these prices is prohibited is equally so.'

[8] *IFTRA rules for producers of virgin aluminium*, OJ 1975 L228/3, at pp. 8–10. (1) Regarding sales below cost: 'The clause concerned with "destructive sales below cost" is alleged to have as its object "the protection and promotion of true competition". In the present case the principal object of [that clause] cannot reasonably be said to be the "protection and promotion of true competition" [because it creates] a framework which facilitates and encourages the suppression of commercial initiatives which, whilst being inconvenient to the other parties to the agreement, are not "destructive" in the reasonable sense of that term; i.e. such as to imperil the existence of a competitor.' (2) Regarding dumping: 'It is . . . difficult to predict whether a proposed sale will constitute unlawful dumping, and in consequence a reciprocal undertaking to refrain from dumping will necessarily discourage the parties from sales which may indeed inconvenience other parties in their national markets, but which would not ultimately be found contrary to the rules concerning dumping. Moreover, the threat of the institution of "procedures" by a competitor and the imposition of contractual penalties . . . are further inducements not to distort the markets of competitors by any measures of price competition.' (3) Regarding sales below published prices: '[The clause discouraging] the signatories from selling at prices below those they have published . . . under colour of protecting customers against discrimination, provide[s] the parties with means of shelter from competition to the extent that the parties are enabled to predict each other's price policy with a reasonable degree of certainty.'

[9] *German ceramic tiles manufacturers*, JO 1971 L10/15.

[10] *Cementhandelaren v EC Commission* [1972] ECR 977, at p. 989, where the court stated: 'If a system of imposed selling prices is clearly in conflict with [art. 85(1)], the system of target prices is equally so . . . It cannot . . . be supposed that the clauses of the agreement concerning the determination of "target prices" are meaningless . . . In fact, the fixing of a price, even one which merely constitutes a target, affects competition because it enables all the participants to predict with a reasonable degree of certainty what the pricing policy pursued by their competitors will be.'

In *Polypropylene*, OJ 1986 L230/1, at p. 29, the Commission stated that even though 'the achieved price level generally lagged behind the "targets" and that price initiatives tended to run out of momentum, sometimes eventually resulting in a sharp drop in prices . . ., [prices] show a regular pattern over the years of close parallel movement of target and actual levels'. On appeal, in *ICI v EC Commission*, [1992] ECR II-1021, at para. 310–311, the Court of First Instance qualified the target price agreement as a price-fixing agreement because it had the same anti-competitive object as the latter, i.e., it attempted to alter the normal evolution of market prices. The Commission's decision was also the subject of an appeal in *Rhône-Poulenc, Petrofina, Atochem v EC Commission* [1991] ECR II-867, II-1087 and II-1177 respectively; in *BASF, Enichem Anic, Hercules Chemicals, DSM v EC Commission* [1991] ECR II-1523, II-1623, II-1711 and II-1833 respectively (DSM appealed an order by the Court of First Instance of 4 November 1992 which dismissed as inadmissible an application for revision on purely procedural grounds of the judgment of 17 December 1991) and in *Hüls, Hoechst, Shell International Chemical Company, Solvay, Montedipe, Chemie Linz v EC Commission*, [1992] ECR II-499, 629, 757, 907, 1155 (hereinafter '*Polypropylene Cases*'). See also *PVC*, OJ 1989 L74/1, on appeal: *BASF & Ors v EC Commission*, [1992] II-ECR-315; [1992] 1 CEC 519 (Commission decision annulled on purely procedural grounds) (hereinafter '*PVC Cases*'); *LdPE*, OJ 1989 L74/91.

¶803

(6) an agreement setting up a delivered price system;[12]

(7) an agreement imposing fixed profit margins and standard terms of payment;[13]

(8) agreements restricting or limiting rebates;[14]

(9) an agreement applying index-linked general price increases;[15]

(10) agreements fixing purchase prices of raw materials;[16]

(11) an agreement refraining from giving free gifts to customers or selling at a loss;[17]

---

[11] *Cimbel*, JO 1972 L303/24. A group of Belgian cement manufacturers formed a common organisation, Cimbel, which, inter alia, supervised a programme whereby their receipts from certain sales were pooled. The parties claimed that the pooling established solidarity among the manufacturers and enabled them to follow a joint competition policy on foreign markets. The generally higher profits derived from sales on the Belgian domestic market were used to subsidise their exports. The Commission considered that, 'the agreement ... has the object and the effect of artificially strengthening the competitive position of the various Belgian manufacturers on the export market. Because of the existence of this pool fund, which essentially functions as a private subsidy, the manufacturers of other Member States are in fact not in competition with one another but with the Cimbel members as a whole, i.e., the collective Belgian Industry. ... In addition to the manufacturers of other Member States, Belgian cement consumers are placed at a disadvantage by the pooling of receipts – which is closely linked to the elimination of price competition on the Belgian market. Exports are financed by the excessive profits realised on the domestic market. Absent such a pooling of receipts and imposed prices, these profits would have to be lower.'

[12] *Agreement between manufacturers of glass containers*, OJ 1974 L160/1, at p. 14, where the Commission stated: 'The system of prices free at ultimate destination ... consists in applying ... uniform delivered prices which in providing for an averaged freight charge do not reflect the actual cost of transport of goods from place of origin to destination. This system ... has the object of nullifying any competitive advantage which a producer of glass containers might gain from the proximity to his customers. It favours distant customers at the expense of those who are near.'

[13] *Fedetab*, OJ 1978 L224/29, on appeal: *Van Landewyck v EC Commission* [1980] ECR 3125.

[14] *Lloyd's Underwriters Association and The Institute of London Underwriters*, OJ 1993 L4/26 (negative clearance of two agreements relating to marine hull and machinery insurance after clauses fixing rebates and minimum premium increases were deleted and a market-sharing agreement was abandoned by the parties); *Flat-glass sector in Benelux*, OJ 1984 L212/13 (maximum discount reduced from 25 per cent to 15 per cent); *Vimpoltu*, OJ 1983 L200/44 (discount limited to 25 per cent of recommended retail price); SSI, OJ 1982 L232/1, on appeal: *Stichting Sigarettenindustrie & Ors v EC Commission* [1985] ECR 3831. See also *Vereniging van Vlaamse Reisbureaus v Sociale Dienst van de Plaatselijke en Gewestelijke Overheidsdiensten* [1987] ECR 3801; *Distribution of railway tickets by travel agents*, OJ 1992 L366/47, on appeal: *Union Internationale des Chemins de Fer v EC Commission*, Case T-14/93, not yet decided.

[15] *Cast iron and steel rolls*, OJ 1983 L317/1.

[16] *Zinc producers group*, OJ 1984 L220/27. In that case, the Zinc Producers Group (ZPG), an organisation composed of nearly all the zinc mining and smelting companies in the Western world, decided to fix a common price, the so-called 'producer price' for zinc, and to substitute this price for that quoted on the London Metal Exchange (LME), the world-wide commodities exchange for metals (the LME price at the time was £140 per ton, but the producer price was set at £125, with the ultimate goal being £100). The Commission considered that by agreeing on the producer price, the parties had restricted their freedom to negotiate their purchase prices with mining companies. In the Commission's view, the agreement had the object and effect of restricting price competition, and it was irrelevant that the producer price was not always actually applied in contracts with mining companies or that discounts were sometimes granted. 'The decisive point is that the agreed producer price was always used as a basis for the actual prices stipulated in purchase and supply contracts for zinc ... The agreement of a producer price was thus a constant, at least indirect influence on the firms' pricing behaviour' (at p. 38). See also *Belgian agreement on industrial timber, Fifth Report on Competition Policy*, point 36.

[17] *Roofing felt*, OJ 1986 L232/15; on appeal: *Belasco & Ors v EC Commission* [1989] ECR 2117.

(12) an agreement guaranteeing a minimum market share thereby artificially stabilising market prices.[18]

(13) an agreement relating to charges connected with environmental protection.[19]

¶804   Price discrimination

Article 85(1)(d) expressly prohibits agreements between undertakings or concerted practices which 'apply dissimilar conditions to equivalent transactions with other trading parties, thereby placing them at a competitive disadvantage'. Thus, an agreement whereby competitors undertake to discriminate among their customers as regards pricing terms constitutes a form of prohibited agreements. Although neither the Commission nor the court have frequently relied on art. 85(1)(d) in justifying their decisions, discriminatory pricing has been 'consistently condemned', especially when it has the object or effect of partitioning markets within the Community.[20]

In *Fedetab*,[21] an agreement among tobacco manufacturers relating to maximum margins to be granted to certain defined categories of wholesalers and retailers was condemned. By a series of agreements and decisions the manufacturers divided wholesalers and retailers into several precisely defined categories (based, inter alia, on annual sales and number of brands sold) and specified profit margins for each of them. The Commission found that the system:

'constituted a restriction of competition for both manufacturers and wholesalers, since the manufacturers no longer had the opportunity of competing against each other on mark-ups, and the wholesalers in the services they render to the manufacturers. What the intermediary earns is his category's standard percentage of the price, irrespective of the competitive quality or extent of the services he himself may render.[22] ... [T]he link between these margins and the number of brands stocked by each intermediary means that competition is substantially restricted ... since they

---

[18] *Solvay, CFK*, OJ 1991 L152/16. In return for CFK moderating its pricing behaviour, Solvay guaranteed CFK an annual minimum sales tonnage on the German market by buying the shortfall from CFK if its sales fell below the guaranteed minimum.

[19] *VOTOB, XXIInd Report on Competition Policy for 1992*, points 177–186. The Commission pointed out that although it is in favour of an improvement of the environmental conditions of a given sector, it has to ensure that such an improvement does not take place at the expense of competition.

[20] *The Distillers Company*, notice pursuant to art. 19(3) of Council Regulation 17/62, OJ 1983 C245/3.

[21] *Fedetab*, OJ 1978 L224/29, on appeal: *Van Landewyck v EC Commission* [1980] ECR 3125.

[22] Id., at p. 38. The Commission considered that 'the various criteria considered in classifying [the wholesalers] and retailers took no account of the other services that intermediaries in each category might be good or bad at providing, such as delivery rate, product display, sales incentive, response to emergency requests for stocks, etc. The limitation of wholesalers' margins, notwithstanding any competitive endeavour on their part, to those prescribed for the category in which [the manufacturers] placed them, deprived them in turn of any possibility of competing with each other on resale prices to retailers.'

are obliged to keep stocks of slow-moving brands of cigarette, thus tying up part of their working capital.'[23]

A special kind of discrimination is involved in aggregated rebate systems where competing suppliers agree among each other to grant more favourable purchase terms, e.g. rebates or discounts, to customers who buy their requirements from the cartel instead of from some independent supplier. The Commission has found such systems to be in violation of art. 85(1). Thus, in *Papiers peints de Belgique*,[24] it condemned an aggregated rebate system set up by Belgian wallpaper manufacturers who were members of the Groupement des Fabricants de papiers peints de Belgique. The Groupement had adopted general sales conditions containing a scaled system of rebates, whereby an increasing percentage of rebate was granted depending on the total volume of purchases made from the Groupement. The Commission found this system to restrict competition from other wallpaper producers who were not members of the Groupement. It noted:

'The aggregated rebate system leads to a concentration of orders with members of the Groupement. The fact that the rate of rebate varies with quantities purchased encourages those who have already covered part of their requirements from members of the Groupement to buy their entire requirements from those members, in order to obtain the highest possible rebate ... The scale of aggregated rebates thus applies dissimilar conditions to similar transactions with other trading parties. A Belgian customer who buys a certain quantity of wallpaper from a member of the Groupement and then buys a further quantity of wallpaper from another member of the Groupement will get a higher rebate than the customer who buys the same amount and quality of wallpaper from the first manufacturer but who makes his further purchase from one not belonging to the Groupement. The purchase from the manufacturer not belonging to the Groupement is not taken into account when calculating the amount of the rebate due to the second customer.'[25]

In *Gas water-heaters and bath-heaters*,[26] the Commission also condemned an aggregated rebate system even though it included purchases from suppliers who were not party to the agreement. In the Commission's view, such a system

---

[23] Id., at p. 40. See also, *Vereeniging van Cementhandelaren v EC Commission* [1972] ECR 977 (agreement to supply customers belonging to a certain trade association on terms more advantageous than to those not belonging to the association).

[24] *Papiers Peints de Belgique*, OJ 1974 L237/3, on appeal: *Papiers Peints v EC Commission* [1975] ECR 1491.

[25] Id., at p. 8. See also *SSI*, OJ 1982 L232/1, on appeal: *Stichting Sigarettenindustrie & Ors v EC Commission* [1985] ECR 3831; *German ceramic tile manufacturers*, JO 1971 L10/15; *Dutch manufacturers of liquorice, Second Report on Competition Policy*, point 34.

[26] *Gas water-heaters and bath-heaters*, OJ 1973 L217/34.

¶804

can infringe art. 85(1) where it concerns a substantial proportion of the suppliers and purchasers on the market in question and where its effect is sufficient, because of product characteristics and market conditions, to distort competition appreciably and to affect trade between member states. Because the appliances were of a relatively homogeneous type with selling prices thus uniform, the market share of the parties to the agreement exceeded 70 per cent and the intermediaries obtained 94 per cent of their supplies from the parties to the agreement, the Commission considered that the system 'perceptibly distorts competition' in the market.[27] Even where an aggregated rebate system extends to purchases from third parties, they are liable, according to the Commission, 'to afford undue protection to domestic manufacturers by maintaining preferences in favour of traditional suppliers.'[28]

In *Nederlandse Sigarenwinkeliers Organisatie v EC Commission*,[29] the court confirmed the Commission's position that aggregated rebate systems are prohibited under art. 85(1). However, the court avoided the question whether such systems are discriminatory in the sense of art. 85(1)(d). While the Commission explicitly relied on this provision, the court stated that, given the anti-competitive effect of the bonus scheme concerned, there was no need to examine this question.[30]

¶805 Ancillary agreements

The parties to a price-fixing arrangement may be tempted to conclude additional agreements to ensure the maximum effectiveness of its provisions. The obvious purpose of such ancillary agreements is to supplement the main agreement. As shown in various decisions,[31] an ancillary agreement in support of a price-fixing agreement is no less illegal than the price-fixing agreement itself.

In *Zinc producer group*,[32] the price of zinc was, until 1964, determined on a daily basis according to supply and demand on the market. This price was quoted on the London Metals Exchange (LME) as the 'producer price'. Because the LME producer price was susceptible to daily fluctuations, price quotations under long-term contracts were rendered quite uncertain. To correct this uncertainty the major western zinc mining and smelting companies, members of the Zinc Producer Group (ZPG), agreed to introduce a common

---

[27] Id., at p. 37.
[28] *Third Report on Competition Policy*, point 54.
[29] *Nederlandse Sigarenwinkeliers Organisatie v EC Commission* [1985] ECR 3801.
[30] Id., at p. 3824.
[31] *Roofing felt*, OJ 1986 L232/15, on appeal: *Belasco & Ors v EC Commission* [1989] ECR 2117; *Polypropylene*, OJ 1986 L230/1, on appeal: *Polypropylene Cases* cited at footnote 10 (restriction of production and/or sales, control of stock and diversion of supplies to overseas markets found to be intended to secure favourable climate for price increases); *Zinc producer group*, OJ 1984 L220/27; *White lead*, OJ 1979 L21/16 (delivery quotas).
[32] *Zinc producer group*, OJ 1984 L220/27.

producer price to replace that quoted on the LME. The common producer price was substantially lower than that quoted on the LME. The parties supported their common producer price in a number of ways:

(1) They engaged in collective abstention from selling zinc on the LME. The result was that the LME's stocks of zinc were severely reduced to the extent that it often was handling only lower-quality zinc from eastern bloc countries.

(2) The parties engaged in intervention buying if the LME producer price fell below a predetermined level. Two methods were used. Initially, support buying was done through special companies incorporated by ZPG and capitalised with contributions from its members. Later, beginning in 1974, each member was assigned a quota of zinc that it was to purchase on the LME. Instead of buying zinc on the LME, each member had the option of reducing production in line with its quota or transferring an equivalent tonnage of its production to its stocks (or at least not placing it on the market).

(3) They agreed to curtail zinc production. The purpose of the production cuts was both 'to obtain a planned reduction in supply so as to remove the temptation for ZPG members with surplus zinc that could not be sold at the producer price to offer it for sale on the LME or directly to zinc consumers [thereby causing] the LME price to fall and [endangering] the producer price' and to prevent 'any surplus zinc being sold in the home market or "area of influence" of another ZPG member, perhaps at lower prices'.[33] Once again, each member had the option not to reduce production if it stockpiled an equivalent amount of its production.

The Commission condemned each of these practices:

'The obligation undertaken by the firms not to sell zinc on the LME and under certain circumstances to buy up zinc before it reached the LME and to engage, themselves or through third companies, in buying to support the quoted price also constituted a restriction of competition. Its object and effect was to influence the LME zinc price so that it did not diverge too far from the producer price and so to relieve market pressures on ZPG members to change the producer price. The producers thereby brought the LME price, which was determined by supply and demand, into line with the fixed producer price, thus reducing the competitive pressure exerted by the LME price.'[34]

---

[33] Id., at p. 33.
[34] Id., at p. 38.

¶805

Regarding production curtailments, the Commission declared: 'The agreement … to keep within collectively agreed and allocated production quotas … restricted competition. These agreements … imposed restrictions on the producers' own commercial independence.'[35] The Commission concluded that 'the mere fact of agreement on … production restrictions … is likely to have inhibited the firms' commercial and competitive independence, since they would have to answer for any breaches of the agreements to the ZPG.'[36]

The Commission's opposition to ancillary agreements was reiterated in its *Roofing felt* decision.[37] Seven Belgian manufacturers of roofing felt undertook, inter alia, not to sell, assign, lease or loan their production plants or equipment to third parties without the consent of the others. In the event, if one of the parties were declared bankrupt or his production plan seized on behalf of creditors, members undertook to contribute to the cost of buying up the plan on their joint account. In 1980, following the bankruptcy of one of the members, the remaining members took joint action to stop a takeover by interested foreign firms lest this 'upset the already very precarious balance on the market.'[38] The Commission found that the members' objective was not to acquire the plant themselves, but to ensure that it did not fall into the hands of competitors who were not members of the cartel. Instead of facing fragmented supply by competing national producers, actual or potential foreign suppliers:

'had to contend with a unified front of the large majority of producers, acting together to distort competition through a comprehensive cartel. The effect was to transform the basis for decision by foreign suppliers to enter the market, and the competitive conditions they would have to face, including the prospect of collective retaliation by the cartel against competitive pricing by importers.'[39]

¶806   Concerted pricing practices

When a company adjusts its prices, its competitors will usually follow suit. Price uniformity among competitors, short of a price-fixing agreement, does not normally give rise to problems under art. 85(1). Where, however, such objective parallel-pricing behaviour gives way to concerted practices between competitors, it violates art. 85(1).[40]

---

[35] Ibid.
[36] Ibid.
[37] *Roofing felt*, OJ 1986 L232/15, on appeal: *Belasco & Ors v EC Commission* [1989] ECR 2117.
[38] Id., at p. 22.
[39] Id., at p. 28.
[40] For a discussion of the notion of 'concerted practice', see Chapter 2.

¶807　Restriction of competition

The wording of art. 85 initially caused the court to rule that 'for the purpose of applying art. 85(1), there is no need to take account of the concrete effects of an agreement once it appears that it has as its object the prevention, restriction or distortion of competition.'[41] In the context of horizontal price-fixing agreements and concerted practices the Commission has repeatedly adhered to this principle, stating that the demonstration of the agreement's effect is not 'strictly necessary', given the 'manifestly anti-competitive object' of the agreement.[42] In order to determine whether an agreement has such a 'manifestly anti-competitive object', the Commission will look both to the reasonable construction of the terms of the agreement and to the question whether a restriction of competition would be the natural and probable consequence of its application. Labelling an agreement between competitors as a 'code of conduct', 'fair trading rules', 'rules against unfair competition' and the like, is not sufficient to remove it from the scope of art. 85(1) if the underlying object is to restrict competition between the parties to the detriment of their customers.[43] The Commission's approach has been approved by the court.[44]

This approach has three consequences. First, in order to have an anti-competitive object, it is sufficient for an agreement to be susceptible of creating anti-competitive effects.[45] Both the Commission and the court have held that art. 85(1) is violated even if the agreement in question actually has never been implemented and the prices agreed upon have not been respected. Thus, in *Flat-glass sector in Benelux*,[46] the Commission stated that the question 'whether or not the prices were always implemented by the parties does not alter the fact that agreements ... existed which are in themselves infringements of art. 85. Furthermore, even if the agreements were not always observed, this does not mean they did not nevertheless have a significant effect on the firms' behaviour.'[47] In *Belasco & Ors v EC Commission*,[48] the applicants claimed that the Commission had itself conceded that the agreed prices had not been

---

[41] *Consten and Grundig v EC Commission* [1966] ECR 299, at p. 342. In *Scottish Salmon Board*, OJ 1992 L246/37, at p. 43, the Commission went so far as to say that '[a]n agreement to fix prices *per se* limits competition within the meaning of Article 85(1)'.

[42] *Polypropylene*, OJ 1986 L230/1, at p. 29; on appeal: see *Polypropylene Cases* cited at footnote 10; *French-West African shipowner's committees*, OJ 1992 L134/1, at p. 74; *PVC* [1989] 1 CEC 2,167; OJ 1989 L74/1, at p. 13; on appeal: *PVC Cases* cited at footnote 10; LdPE [1989] 1 CEC 2,193; OJ 1989 L74/21, at p. 34; *Roofing felt*, OJ 1986 L232/15, at p. 26, on appeal: *Belasco & Ors v EC Commission* [1989] ECR 2117.

[43] *Vimpoltu*, OJ 1983 L200/44; SSI, OJ 1982 L232/1, on appeal: *Stichting Sigarettenindustrie & Ors v EC Commission* [1985] ECR 3831; *IFTRA rules for producers of virgin aluminium*, OJ 1975 L228/3; *Agreement between manufacturers of glass containers*, OJ 1974 L160/1.

[44] See e.g. *Verband der Sachversicherer eV v EC Commission* [1987] ECR 405, at p. 457.

[45] *ICI v EC Commission* [1992] ECR II-1021.

[46] *Flat-glass sector in Benelux*, OJ 1984 L212/13.

[47] Id., at p. 19.

[48] *Belasco & Ors v EC Commission* [1989] ECR 2117, at para. 11.

respected in practice. The court rejected this argument by stating[49] that, even if this were true, the decision in question nevertheless had the object of restricting competition.[50]

Secondly, the Commission's approach may be interpreted as preventing the application of the de minimis rule with respect to horizontal price-fixing agreements and concerted practices. So far, both the Commission and the court have only referred to the de minimis rule in the context of (mostly vertical) agreements which do not belong to the category of 'classical' cartels. It should be noted, however, that the court has at least implicitly accepted the applicability of the de minimis rule to vertical pricing arrangements.[51]

The Commission may still inquire into the effect of the arrangement for the purpose of assessing the gravity of the infringement and deciding on the fines to be imposed. In taking a cumulative approach of combining object and effect, the Commission stated in *Roofing felt*[52] that 'not only the restrictive intent, but also the effects of a cartel must be taken into consideration when it comes to assessing the gravity of the infringements'.

Thirdly, if the Commission has established that the agreement has an anti-competitive object, a further inquiry into the effects will only be relevant for the assessment of the gravity of the infringement and of the amount of the fines to be paid.[53]

It is also worth noting that for a violation of art. 85(1), it is sufficient for the Commission to establish that the agreement or concerted practice itself, in which the parties participated, has an anti-competitive object or effect. Thus, the Commission does not have to prove that each individual participation of each party in the agreement had such an object or effect.[54]

---

[49] Id., at para. 15.

[50] See *Fire Insurance*, OJ 1985 L35/20, on appeal: *Verband der Sachversicherer eV v EC Commission* [1987] ECR 405; *Zinc producer group*, OJ 1984 L220/27; *Vegetable parchment*, OJ 1978 L70/54; *Preserved mushrooms*, OJ 1975 L29/26; *Franco-Japanese ballbearings agreement*, OJ 1974 L343/19; *International Quinine Cartel*, JO 1969 L192/5.

[51] *Distillers v EC Commission* [1980] ECR 2229, at p. 2265 (para. 27–28):

'[T]he applicant maintains that the price terms do not fall within the prohibition of Article 85(1) ... because its sales in the member countries other than the United Kingdom are minimal in relation to the sales of other spirits ... Although an agreement may escape the prohibition in Article 85(1) when it affects the market only to an insignificant extent, having regard to the weak position which those concerned have in the market in the products in question, the same considerations do not apply in the case of a product of a large undertaking responsible for the entire production.'

[52] *Roofing felt*, OJ 1986 L232/15, at p. 26, on appeal: *Belasco & Ors v EC Commission* [1989] ECR 2117.

[53] *Montedipe SpA v EC Commission* [1992] ECR II-1155, at para. 264. In response to an argument of one of the parties, the court referred to the 'per se-like' character of the violation of art. 85(1) (a), (b) and (c). See also *Roofing felt*, OJ 1986 L232/15, at p. 26, on appeal: *Belasco & Ors v EC Commission* [1989] ECR 2117.

[54] *Enichem Anic v EC Commission* [1991] ECR II-1623 (at para. 213–216) and *Hercules Chemicals v EC Commission* [1991] ECR II-1711 (at para. 269–272), and *Hüls v EC Commission* (at para. 304–306), *Solvay v EC Commission* (at para. 270–273) and *Chemie Linz v EC Commission* [1992] ECR II-499, 907, 1275 (at para. 314–316).

¶808   Effect on trade between member states

The requirement of the existence of an effect on trade between member states is in the opinion of Commission and court easily met for the establishment of an infringement of art. 85 in the context of pricing cartels. First, it is irrelevant whether the parties involved are established in one member state,[55] in different member states[56] or even in third countries.[57] Furthermore, the Commission and the court have repeatedly found trade between member states to be affected in cases where the arrangement in question only applied within one member state.[58] In *Papiers Peints v EC Commission* the court, endorsing the decision of the Commission, declared that:

> 'the fact that a price-fixing agreement of the type in question only covers the marketing of products in a single Member State does not rule out the possibility that trade between Member States may be affected. In fact, a restrictive agreement extending over the whole of the territory of a Member State is by its very nature liable to have the effect of reinforcing the compartmentalization of markets on a national basis, thereby holding up the economic interpenetration which the Treaty is designed to bring about and protecting domestic production'.[59]

---

[55] *Flat glass* [1989] 1 CEC 2,077; OJ 1989 L33/44, on appeal: *Società Italiano Vetro (SIV) SpA & Ors v EC Commission* [1992] ECR II-1403; [1992] 2 CEC 33; *Roofing felt*, OJ 1986 L232/15, on appeal: *Belasco & Ors v EC Commission* [1982] ECR 2117; *Papiers Peints v EC Commission* [1975] ECR 1491; *Cimbel*, JO 1972 L303/24; *VVVF*, JO 1969 L168/22. The question whether a price-fixing agreement between undertakings in the same member state falls under the prohibition of art. 85(1) is a question of fact to be determined according to such circumstances as the relative position of the parties and the importance of the agreement in the market in question, and the general economic context of the agreement; *SSI*, OJ 1982 L232/1, on appeal: *Stichting Sigarettenindustrie & Ors v EC Commission* [1985] ECR 3831; *Fedetab*, OJ 1978 L224/29, on appeal: *Van Landewyck v EC Commission* [1980] ECR 3225.

[56] *LdPE* [1989] 1 CEC 2,193; OJ 1989 L74/21; *PVC* [1989] 1 CEC 2,167; OJ 1989 L74/1, on appeal: *PVC Cases* cited at footnote 10; *Polypropylene*, OJ 1986 L230/1, on appeal: *Polypropylene Cases* cited at footnote 10; *Zinc producer group*, OJ 1984 L212/13; *Flat-glass sector in Benelux*, OJ 1984 L212/13; *Peroxygen products*, OJ 1985 L35/1; *Cast iron and steel rolls*, OJ 1983 L317/1; *Vegetable parchment*, OJ 1978 L70/54; *IFTRA rules for producers of virgin aluminium*, OJ 1975 L228/3; *Agreements between manufacturers of glass containers*, OJ 1974 L160/1; *Dyestuffs*, JO 1969 L195/11, on appeal: *ICI v EC Commission* [1972] ECR 619; *International Quinine Cartel*, JO 1969 L192/5.

[57] *LdPE*, OJ 1989 L74/29, *PVC*, OJ 1989 L74/1, on appeal: *PVC Cases* cited at footnote 10. *Polypropylene*, OJ 1986 L230/1, at p. 30, where the Commission stated: 'Article 85 of the EEC Treaty applies to restrictive agreements which may affect trade between Member States even if the undertakings involved are established or have their headquarters outside the Community', on appeal: *Polypropylene Case* cited at footnote 10; *Aluminium Imports from Eastern Europe*, OJ 1985 L92/1; *Wood pulp*, OJ 1985 L85/1, on appeal: *Åhlström & Ors v EC Commission* [1988] ECR 5193 (ruling with regard to the jurisdictional aspects of the case) and *Åhlström & Ors v EC Commission* [1993] 1 CEC 466; *Preserved mushrooms*, OJ 1975 L29/26; *Franco-Japanese ballbearings agreement*, OJ 1974 L343/19; *Dyestuffs*, JO 1969 L195/11, on appeal: *ICI v EC Commission* [1972] ECR 619.

[58] *Solvay, CFK*, OJ 1990 L152/16; *Assurpol*, OJ 1992 L37/16, at p. 22; *Roofing felt*, OJ 1986 L232/15, on appeal: *Belasco & Ors v EC Commission* [1989] ECR 2117; *Vimpoltu*, OJ 1983 L200/44; *SSI*, OJ 1982 L232/1, on appeal: *Stichting Sigarettenindustrie v EC Commission*, [1985] ECR 3831; *Papiers Peints de Belgique*, OJ 1974 L237/3, on appeal: *Papiers Peints v EC Commission* [1975] ECR 1491; *Gas water-heaters and bath-heaters*, OJ 1973 L217/34; *Vereeniging van Cementhandelaren*, JO 1972 L13/34, on appeal: *Cementhandelaren v EC Commission* [1972] ECR 977; *German ceramic tiles manufacturers*, JO 1971 L10/15; *Woollen fabrics (UIB)*, Twelfth Report on Competition Policy, point 71.

[59] *Papiers Peints v EC Commission* [1975] ECR 1491, at p. 1513.

Secondly, for the assessment of such effect, account has to be taken of such circumstances as the relative position of the parties, the importance of the agreement in the market in question and the general economic context in which it exists.[60] It is noteworthy that, again, the goal of market integration plays an important role in the interpretation of what affects intra-Community trade, thus making it highly unlikely that horizontal arrangements, even if restricted to one member state, will escape the prohibition of art. 85(1).[61]

Thirdly, with regard to the restrictive effect or object of an agreement,[62] it is sufficient for a violation of art. 85(1) that the agreement or concerted practice itself, in which the undertakings participated, has an appreciable effect on trade between member states. Thus, it is not necessary for the Commission to prove that each individual participation by each undertaking has such an appreciable effect.[63]

Finally, in order to have an appreciable effect on trade between member states, it is sufficient for an agreement to be susceptible to create an effect. Thus, it is unnecessary for the Commission to prove actual effects on trade between member states.[64]

¶809   State intervention

State intervention will only exculpate undertakings if it takes compulsory forms, while lesser forms of government involvement will not remove the case from the ambit of art. 85. This strict approach remains particularly valid with respect to horizontal price-fixing agreements. Thus, in *AROW/BNIC*[65] the Commission condemned the fixing of minimum prices for the sale of cognac by way of industry-wide agreements despite the fact that these agreements were subsequently made compulsory for the whole Cognac region through an interministerial order. They were concluded under the auspices of the Bureau National Interprofessionnel du Cognac (BNIC), a trade association which was created by the French government in order to supervise the manufacture and distribution of cognac and to ensure quality control. In 1976, a decision by the Government Commissioner fixed minimum prices for the sale of cognac in

---

[60] Id., at p. 1514.

[61] See *Flat glass* [1989] 1 CEC 2,077; OJ 1989 L33/44, at p. 358; on appeal : *Società Italiano Vetro (SIV) SpA & Ors v EC Commission* [1992] ECR II-1403; [1992] 2 CEC 33.

[62] See ¶807.

[63] *Petrofina v EC Commission* [1991] ECR II-1087, (at para. 226–227); *Enichem Anic v EC Commission* [1991] ECR II-1623 (at para. 223–225), *Hercules Chemicals v EC Commission* [1991] ECR II-1711 (at para. 279–280), *Hüls v EC Commission* (at para. 313–315), *ICI v EC Commission* (at para. 304–306), *Montedipe v EC Commission* [1992] ECR II-499, 1021, 1155 (at para. 253–254). Consequently, it is irrelevant that the participating undertakings in the agreement or concerted practice hold only a small share of the relevant market. *Enichem Anic v EC Commission* [1991] ECR II-1623, at para. 224.

[64] *DSM v EC Commission* [1991] ECR II-1833, at para. 249–250. (DSM has appealed against an order of the Court of First Instance of 4 November 1992, OJ 1992 C334/10, which dismissed as inadmissible an application for revision on purely procedural grounds of the judgment of 17 December 1991).

[65] *AROW/BNIC*, OJ 1982 L379/1.

order 'to maintain the traditional quality of cognac, to guarantee ... a quality corresponding to the price ... and to avoid any manipulation with the aim of artificially reducing prices'.[66] In December 1978, the BNIC members concluded an industry agreement on cognac prices. This agreement, initially binding only upon BNIC members, was subsequently extended by interministerial order to all 'growers, cooperative cellars, distillers and wholesale shippers' in the Cognac region. The order was based on a French law which provided that such agreements may be extended by the competent authority where they would improve in particular the application, subject to state control, of rules of marketing, prices, terms of payment, product quality and other goals. In the following years, similar agreements were concluded within the framework of BNIC and extended by interministerial decree to all relevant traders. The Commission rejected the idea that this type of governmental intervention was sufficient to exculpate the members of BNIC, stating that the agreements constituted acts distinct from the subsequent extending orders made by the public authorities. It continued:

'Each year since 1978 the industry agreements have been concluded before the extending orders. Each year there has been a period of between three weeks and two-and-a-half months during which the agreements concluded within the BNIC were binding only on the firms which are members of the professional and trade organization of the BNIC ... Lastly, the notion of an extending order implies that there are rules to extend which are binding on their signatories. The effect of the extending order is only to make these rules binding on parties other than the signatories. Article 2 of the Law of 10 July 1975 ... explicitly states that an agreement must first of all be concluded, that there is no obligation to extend it, and that the extension may relate to part of its provisions only.'[67]

However, the Commission took the state intervention into account when it came to assessing the gravity of the infringement and the fines to be imposed.[68]

In two subsequent rulings under art. 177 of the treaty,[69] involving industry agreements concluded within the framework of the BNIC and later extended by the French authorities in the way described above, the court confirmed the Commission's position.

Similarly, in *SSI*[70] price agreements between manufacturers and/or importers were drawn up only after consultation with the Dutch government. The

---

[66] Id., at p. 4.
[67] Id., at p. 11.
[68] Id., at p. 14. See also *Building and construction industry in the Netherlands*, OJ 1992 L92/1, at pp. 27–28, on appeal: *Vereniging van Samenwerkende en Prijsregelende Organisaties in de Bouwnijverheid v EC Commission*, Case T-29/92, not yet decided.
[69] *BNIC v Clair* [1985] ECR 391; *BNIC v Aubert* [1987] ECR 4789; [1989] 1 CEC 363.
[70] *SSI*, OJ 1982 L232/1, on appeal: *Stichting Sigarettenindustrie & Ors v EC Commission* [1985] ECR 3831.

Commission condemned a bonus scheme even though it had been established with the backing of the Ministry of Economic Affairs in an effort to support the specialist retailers in their struggle with supermarkets. It held that this was no justification for engaging in a concerted practice contrary to the Community competition rules.[71] On appeal,[72] the applicants argued that the Dutch authorities put pressure on the undertakings in order to influence the setting of prices and margins. However, the court avoided answering the question of whether such pressure would remove the agreements from the ambit of art. 85(1) by stating that, beyond the mere fact that consultations took place, no proof was established in this respect.[73]

In conclusion, it might be said that the Community authorities will not accept state intervention as a valid defence unless it amounts to direct compulsion which deprives the undertakings concerned at least partly of their freedom to refrain from the anti-competitive arrangements. However, it remains unclear what degree of compulsion is necessary and to what extent precisely the freedom of the parties has to be restricted. If, on the other hand, the arrangement is merely prepared in consultation with the public authorities or subsequently reinforced in one way or the other, the prohibition of art. 85(1) continues to apply. This is particularly true for cases where the private action is a necessary precondition for the public measure to take effect.[74]

¶810   Exemptions under art. 85(3)

As stated before, the Commission regards price competition as one of the essential forms of competition, and any interference with it as a particularly severe infringement of art. 85(1). Consequently, the Commission has almost always refused to exempt horizontal price-fixing arrangements under art. 85(3). In most cases, the contested agreements and practices had not been notified to the Commission, so that the Commission could not grant an exemption anyway.[75] But even where such notification actually had taken place,[76] the Commission usually summarily stated that the conditions of art. 85(3) were not met. Alleged justifications have consistently been rejected. For example, in *AROW/BNIC*[77] the Commission rejected BNIC's contention that minimum

---

[71] Id., at p. 31.

[72] *Stichting Sigarettenindustrie & Ors v EC Commission* [1985] ECR 3831, at p. 3871.

[73] Id., at pp. 3871–3872.

[74] See more extensively Chapter 2, ¶213.

[75] See e.g. *Roofing felt*, OJ 1986 L232/15, at p. 29, on appeal: *Belasco & Ors v EC Commission* [1989] ECR 2117; *Meldoc*, OJ 1986 L348/50, at p. 63; *Flat glass* [1989] 1 CEC 2,077; OJ 1989 L33/44, at p. 64, on appeal: *Società Italiano Vetro (SIV) SpA & Ors v EC Commission* [1992] ECR II-1403; [1992] 2 CEC 33.

[76] See e.g. *Papiers Peints de Belgique*, OJ 1974 L237/3, at p. 9, on appeal: *Papiers Peints v EC Commission* [1975] ECR 1491; *SSI*, OJ 1982 L232/1, at pp. 32–34, on appeal: *Stichting Sigarettenindustrie & Ors v EC Commission* [1985] ECR 3831; *Fire insurance*, OJ 1985 L35/20, at p. 27, on appeal: *Verband der Sachversicherer eV v EC Commission* [1987] ECR 405; *Ansac*, OJ 1990 L152/54.

[77] *AROW/BNIC*, OJ 1982 L379/1, at pp. 12–13.

prices had to be fixed in order to guarantee the quality and characteristics of the product. Similarly, in *Building and Construction Industry in the Netherlands*, the Commission rejected the argument that an agreement organising price tendering and partially consisting of price-fixing was justified because it served 'to promote and administer orderly competition, to prevent improper conduct in tendering and to promote the formation of economically justified prices'.[78]

There are very few exceptions to this rule. In *Nuovo CEGAM*,[79] a large number of direct insurers formed an association for the dissemination of statistical information on the basis of which a common tariff of basic premiums for various types of risk would be applied. The members had surrendered the right to fix independently the basic premium rates used to calculate the actual commercial rates of premiums which they charged to those seeking insurance. In granting an individual exemption, the Commission considered that the:

'determination of standard tariffs of basic premiums by the Association's organs is acceptable given that it does not impede the members' freedom to determine the final premiums for a particular risk in the light of their own commercial policy or business considerations. Hence, the insured ... still has a choice between insurers offering different final premiums. Without a standard basic tariff the Association would have found it harder to achieve its aims of improving production and distribution. ...'[80]

In *TEKO*,[81] the Commission exempted an agreement on gross premium calculations in the sector of machinery loss of profits insurance and in the sector of space insurance. When considering an exemption, the Commission took into account the fact that the limited number of insurance contracts in these sectors and the diversity of risks generated insufficient statistical information to calculate net premium rates. In addition, competition was not eliminated because the insurers were still free to decide whether or not 'to pass the reinsurance commission in whole or in part to the policyholder or to refund part of the premium where loss experience [was] favourable'.[82]

Furthermore, the Commission has repeatedly exempted price-fixing

---

[78] *Building and construction industry in the Netherlands*, OJ 1992 L92/1, at p. 2, on appeal: *Vereniging van Samenwerkende en Prijsregelende Organisaties in de Bouwnijverheid*, Case T-29/92, not yet decided.

[79] *Nuovo CEGAM*, OJ 1984 L99/29.

[80] Id., at p. 34. See also *Concordato Incendio*, OJ 1989 L15/25; *Assurpol*, OJ 1992 L37/16. In *Tariff structures in the combined transport of goods*, OJ 1993 L73/38, as amended by OJ 1993 L145/38, the Commission used similar arguments to exempt an agreement on a common tariff structure and a flat rate of one per cent for incidental costs in the combined transport sector. In Commission Regulation 3932/92 on the application of art. 85(3) of the treaty to certain categories of agreements, decisions and concerted practices in the insurance sector, OJ L398/7, art. 1(a) and art. 2, the Commission has granted an exemption by way of a block exemption for collective basic premium calculations provided that they are only used for reference purposes and that they do not contain 'in any way loadings for contingencies, income deriving from reserves, administrative or commercial costs ... anticipated profits'.

[81] *TEKO*, OJ 1989 L13/43, at p. 38.

[82] Id., at p. 30.

agreements in the banking sector,[83] which are discussed in more detail in Chapter 10.

¶811 Article 86

In *Flat glass*,[84] the Commission found a horizontal cartel not only to be in violation of art. 85(1), but also to infringe art. 86 of the treaty. The case involved a horizontal price-fixing and market-sharing cartel between three producers of flat glass in Italy. The Commission found the existence of an abuse of a dominant position by reference to the same facts which it had already used in its assessment of the cartel under art. 85.

The Court of First Instance, however, annulled the Commission decision with regard to art. 86. The court did not exclude the possibility that conduct which constituted a violation of art. 85(1) might also 'have effects which are incompatible with art. 86 of the Treaty'.[85] Yet, the court continued,

'it should be pointed out that for the purposes of establishing infringement of art. 86 of the Treaty, it is not sufficient, as the Commission's agent claimed at the hearing, to 'recycle' the facts constituting an infringement of art. 85, deducing from them the finding that the parties to an agreement or to an unlawful practice jointly hold a substantial share of the market, that by virtue of that fact alone they hold a collective dominant position, and that their unlawful behaviour constitutes an abuse of that collective dominant position. Amongst other considerations, a finding of a dominant position, which is in any case not in itself a matter of reproach, presupposes that the market in question has been defined ...'[86]

The court thus annulled this aspect of the Commission decision on the ground that the Commission had not properly established the market share of the companies and had adduced insufficient proof.

---

[83] See e.g. *Uniform Eurocheques*, OJ 1985 L35/43; *Belgian Bank Association*, OJ 1987 L7/27; *ABI*, OJ 1987 L43/51.

[84] *Flat glass* [1989] 1 CEC 2,077; OJ 1989 L33/44, at pp. 64–66, on appeal: *Società Italiano Vetro (SIV) SpA & Ors v EC Commission* [1992] ECR II–1403; [1992] 2 CEC 33.

[85] Id., at para. 359. The court referred to the text of art. 8(2) of Council Regulation 4058/86 on maritime transport which implicitly recognised the possibility that the same conduct could constitute a double infringement.

[86] Id., at para. 360. In two subsequent decisions, *Cewal, Cowac and Ukwal*, OJ 1993 L34/20, on appeal: *Compagnie Maritime Belge Transport NV and Compagnie Maritime Belge NV, Dafra Lines A/S, Deutsche Afrika-Linien GmbH & Co and Nedlloyd Lijnen BV v Commission*, Cases T-24/93, T-25/93, T-26/93 and T-28/93, not yet reported and *Warner-Lambert/Gillette & Ors*, OJ 1993 L116/21, the Commission made separate analyses under art. 85(1) and 86, presumably in an effort to avoid the problems raised in *Flat glass*.

MARKET-SHARING ARRANGEMENTS

¶812   Introduction

Like price-fixing arrangements, market-sharing in its various forms is prohibited under the EC competition rules. Article 85(1)(c) expressly mentions the sharing of markets or sources of supply as an anti-competitive practice and art. 85(1)(b) condemns, inter alia, the limitation or control of production.

In their most typical form, market-sharing arrangements provide for mutual respect of different markets, usually determined along national borders, with the result that each market remains insulated from the others. Given that the main goal of the EC Treaty is market integration, it is not surprising that the Community authorities have taken a particularly strict view of such arrangements. As early as in its *First Report on Competition Policy*,[87] the Commission noted that 'restriction on competition and practices which jeopardize the unity of the Common Market are proceeded against with special vigour. Cases in point are agreements on market-sharing by dividing areas, agreements to allocate customers, and collective exclusive dealing agreements'.[88]

The incompatibility of market-sharing arrangements with the EC competition rules is further enhanced by the fact that they often form part of a larger unlawful cartel involving other elements such as price-fixing or information exchange.[89] For example, in *Flat glass*,[90] the Commission applied art. 85 to a horizontal cartel, which involved both price-fixing and various forms of market-sharing.

---

[87] *First Report on Competition Policy*, at p. 15.

[88] The Commission's emphasis on market integration is further witnessed by the following paragraph on market-sharing arrangements, taken from the same report, at p. 25:

'Market-sharing agreements are particularly restrictive of competition and contrary to the achievement of a single market. Agreements or concerted practices for the purpose of market-sharing are generally based on the principle of mutual respect of the national markets of each Member State for the benefit of producers resident there. The direct object and result of their implementation is to eliminate the exchange of goods between the Member States concerned. The protection of their home market allows producers to pursue a commercial policy – particularly a pricing policy – in that market which is insulated from the competition of other parties to the agreement in other Member States, and which can sometimes only be maintained because they have no fear of competition from that direction. The fixing of delivery quotas in relation to total sales, combined in some cases with a compensation scheme to ensure that the quotas are respected, means that the members of the group give up any possibility of obtaining an advantage over their competitors by applying an individual sales policy. Maintenance of the equilibrium as fixed by the quotas directly endangers intra-Community trade as soon as the sales quotas are applied to one or more markets within the Community'.

First Report on Competition Policy, point 2. The importance of the integration of the EC market and the harmful effects of market-sharing agreements was recently reiterated by the Commission in its *XXth Report on Competition Policy*, point 1.

[89] See e.g. *Polypropylene*, OJ 1986 L230/1, on appeal: *Polypropylene Cases* cited at footnote 10; *Roofing felt*, OJ 1986 L232/15, on appeal: *Belasco & Ors v EC Commission* [1989] ECR 2117; *PVC* [1989] 1 CEC 2,167; OJ 1989 L71/1, on appeal: *Polypropylene Cases* cited at footnote 10; LdPE [1989] 1 CEC 2,193; OJ 1989 L74/21; *Flat glass* [1989] 1 CEC 2,077; OJ 1989 L33/44; *Solvay, CFK*, OJ 1990 L152/16 (see also footnote 18).

[90] *Flat glass* [1989] 1 CEC 2,077; OJ 1989 L33/44

This section will discuss geographical division as the most common type of market-sharing (¶813), as well as arrangements restricting production or sources of supply (¶814) and arrangements allocating customers or products (¶815).

¶813 Geographical market-sharing

Territorial divisions

Early Commission interventions in the context of market-sharing dealt with territorial divisions. Characterising this type of agreement as 'so obviously contrary to Community rules of competition', the Commission noted that every investigation it undertook resulted in the offending agreements being terminated without the necessity of a formal decision being taken.[91] The common element in all of these cases was that each of the undertakings involved had agreed to stay out of the others' national markets.[92]

International Quinine Agreement[93] was the first case in which a formal decision was issued. The parties had concluded a 'gentlemen's agreement' by which their respective national markets remained the 'reserved' territory of each local producer. This agreement was combined with an additional agreement allocating export quotas and fixing prices so as to discourage sales between member states. The Commission found that the agreements on prices, protection of national markets and export quotas complemented each other and constituted such a serious violation that, for the first time, it decided to impose fines. On appeal, the court concluded that the agreements guaranteed protection of each domestic market for the producers in the various member states and confirmed to a large extent the Commission's decision.[94]

The next decision, *Tuberies Julien/Van Katwijk*,[95] involved a 'typical market-sharing agreement' whereby a Dutch undertaking was banned from selling in the Belgian market and a Belgian undertaking voluntarily limited its

---

[91] *First Report on Competition Policy*, points 3–4.

[92] *Cleaning Products*, *Eighth General Report on the Activities of the Communities*, point 64 (agreement safeguarding respective national markets of Belgian and Dutch producers supported by export prohibitions imposed on customers); *Construction equipment*, *First Report on Competition Policy*, point 4 (agreement surrendering right to export to a member state); *Semi-finished metallic products*, *First General Report on the Activities of the Communities*, points 52–53 (agreement between undertakings of one member state to prevent deliveries on their internal market from other member states); *International Cable Development Corporation*, EC Bull. No 5–69, Chapter 6, (reciprocal protection of national markets by means of prohibitions on investment or participation, refusals to make deliveries to buyers in other countries, and agreements to forgo advertising in other countries); *Sheet Glass*, EC Bull. No 8–70, Chapter 7, 8–9 (mutual respect of members' national markets and their existing level of export sales).

[93] *International Quinine Cartel*, JO 1969 L192/5.

[94] *ACF Chemiefarma v EC Commission* [1970] ECR 661; *Buchler v EC Commission* [1970] ECR 733; *Boehringer v EC Commission* [1970] ECR 769. The court affirmed the Commission's findings as concerns the undertakings' protection of domestic markets, but reversed the Commission's findings as regards the duration of the joint determination of prices and quotas, and consequently reduced the amount of the fines.

[95] *Julien/Van Katwijk*, JO 1970 L242/18.

exports to 20 per cent of Dutch domestic consumption. Interestingly, when the Dutch company notified its Belgian counterpart of its intention to comply with the treaty, it was prevented from doing so by a Dutch national court that held that the parties were obliged to comply with the terms of their contract. The Commission concluded that the partitioning of outlets erected 'an artificial barrier against trade between the two countries [which] could hinder the attainment of the objectives of a single market between the states'.[96] Even though the Commission had found that the agreement infringed art. 85, it imposed no fine because the agreement had been promptly notified.

In a recent case, the Commission again strongly opposed the partitioning of the market. In *Cewal, Cowac and Ukwal*,[97] agreements were made between different liner conferences whereby they '[would] not compete with each other as outsiders in their respective areas of operation'.[98] The Commission qualified these agreements as 'partition[ing] the European Atlantic coast into several separate areas, with each area taking in one or more Member States, in breach of art. 85(1)(c).'[99]

Sometimes horizontal agreements on export and import bans among producers are supplemented by vertical agreements between producers, distributors and final consumers. In *Ijsselcentrale*[100] four Dutch electricity generating companies set up a new company which served as a vehicle for co-operation. They reserved the Dutch market of electricity supply for themselves by agreeing not to export or import electricity unless through the new company. They also agreed to impose the same bans on the distributors in their supply agreements. Finally, the distributors included an exclusive purchasing provision in their agreements with the final consumers. The Commission found that this scheme infringed art. 85(1) and could not be exempted under art. 85(3) or under art. 90(2).

Less direct means of market-sharing

Besides direct export and import bans, geographical market-sharing can be achieved by more subtle means, such as the ones used in *European Sugar Industry*.[101] The European sugar industry had traditionally been characterised by close co-operation between quasi-governmental national market associations and domestic producers and by strict compartmentalisation.

---

[96] Id., at p. 19.
[97] *Cewal, Cowac and Ukwal*, OJ 1993 L34/20, on appeal: *Compagnie Maritime Belge Transport NV and Compagnie Maritime Belge NV, Dafra Lines A/S, Deutsche Afrika-Linien GmbH & Co and Nedlloyd Lijnen BV v EC Commission*, Cases T-24/93, T-25/93, T-26/93 and T-28/93, not yet decided.
[98] Id., at p. 28.
[99] Ibid.
[100] *Ijsselcentrale*, OJ 1991 L28/32; on appeal: *Rendo & Ors v EC Commission*, Case T-16/91, judgment of 18 November 1992, not yet reported.
[101] *European Sugar Industry*, OJ 1973 L140/17, on appeal: *Suiker Unie & Ors v EC Commission* [1975] ECR 1663.

¶813

Beginning on 1 July 1968, when the various national market organisations were replaced by a common market organisation, the parties were accused of having engaged in concerted practices designed to control the sugar trade within the member states so as to guarantee to each producer the protection of its respective national market. However, because certain areas of the Community were faced with sugar shortages, a number of intra-Community sales were necessary. To get around the possible competitive effects of trade between member states, the producers agreed to make deliveries in other member states only through local producers in the importing country.[102] The effect of this agreement was to allow the importing producer to sell the purchased sugar at the same price, on the same conditions and under the same trade mark as its own sugar. Because the parties knew or should have known that the measures taken were 'obviously contrary' to the aims of market integration, the Commission imposed substantial fines.

On appeal, the court upheld the Commission's finding that a large part of the arrangement is contrary to art. 85(1), but annulled part of the Commission's decision on other grounds. In particular, the court held that the national regulation which existed on the Italian market besides the Community regime eliminated any room for competition, thus excluding any possible infringement of art. 85 by private parties.

Similar forms of market-sharing arrangements have been condemned in a number of decisions. In *Vegetable parchment*,[103] the only British producer of vegetable parchment wanted to reserve the entire British and Irish markets for itself. To this end, it entered into a concerted practice with the continental manufacturers, whereby it purchased the quantity needed to fill the gap between its own production and the demand on the UK markets from those manufacturers. In turn, the latter refrained from directly supplying customers on this market. In line with its strict scrutiny of any arrangements designed to isolate national markets in the Community, the Commission condemned the practice without a more detailed analysis of its anti-competitive effects.[104]

---

[102] In its *Second Report on Competition Policy*, at point 28, the Commission revealed further details of the system:

'[D]eliveries to dealers and customers of the country of destination were refused, or bids were made only at higher prices, adapted to those being charged on the market of the destinee country; restrictive clauses were written into the contracts concluded with the national dealers and customers, so as to prevent the latter from disturbing the sales policy pursued by the producers concerned; and the bids made by the producers – especially the French and Belgian producers – submitted for the auctions organized by the Commission with a view to granting export refunds on exports to non-member countries were concerted so that the quantities of surplus sugar remaining within the Common Market could be controlled and would exert no competitive pressure'.

[103] *Vegetable parchment*, OJ 1978 L70/54.

[104] *Solvay, ICI* OJ 1990 L152/1, involved facts similar to *Vegetable parchment*. In that case ICI purchased a substantial amount of soda-ash from Solvay to meet the demands of its customers in return for Solvay's agreement to stay out of the UK market. The Commission noted that such an arrangement does not always constitute a per se violation, but considered it as evidence of a wider concertation to eliminate competition between the two companies. In another case decided on that same day, the Commission fined Solvay and CFK for

The Commission also held art. 85(1) to be violated by an agreement between a German and a Japanese manufacturer of numerical controls, granting each other exclusive selling rights in Europe and Asia respectively.[105] It based its reasoning on the fact that the agreement was concluded between manufacturers of competing products and isolated the Community market as a whole.[106] The application of the block exemption Regulation 67/67 was also precluded because the parties were actual competitors.[107] The Commission further refused an individual exemption, not only because the agreement had not been notified, but also because it gave rise to market-sharing and therefore could not benefit consumers.[108]

Other cases where the Commission found infringements of art. 85 because of market-sharing involved arrangements on mutual respect of established distribution channels[109] or on the alignment with competitors' prices for sales made in a reserved territory.[110]

In addition to the more typical 'you-take-France-and-I'll-take-Germany' type of agreement, geographical market-sharing may be accomplished by means of sales quotas or of export or delivery quotas.[111] In *Cementregeling voor Nederland*,[112] Dutch, Belgian and German cement manufacturers agreed to divide the supplying of the Dutch market among themselves. Delivery quotas were established based on annual cement consumption. If one of the parties exceeded its quotas, it was obliged to take whatever measures were necessary to correct the imbalance. The Commission found that the system of delivery quotas 'does not allow the parties to freely determine the quantity of cement

---

a market-sharing agreement whereby CFK was guaranteed a minimum share of the German market. In that case, the parties agreed that if CFK's sales in Germany fell below a guaranteed minimum, Solvay would buy the shortfall from CFK. In return, CFK would refrain from 'disruptive' pricing behaviour. *Solvay, CFK*, OJ 1990 L152/16.

[105] *Siemens/Fanuc*, OJ 1985 L376/29.

[106] See also *EMI v CBS* [1976] ECR 811, 871 and 913, where the court held, at p. 848, that '[a] restrictive agreement between traders within the Common Market and competitors in third countries that would bring about an isolation of the Common Market as a whole ... might be of such a nature as to affect adversely the conditions of competition within the Common Market'. In *Quantel International – Continuum/Quantel SA*, OJ 1992 L235/9, at p. 15, the Commission stated that such a sharing among competitors of the world market whereby the EC market is reserved for one of them 'represents a serious infringement of Article 85 because, on a specific market, it contributes to the technological and commercial isolation of the common market from a third country by preventing [the other competitors] from manufacturing and marketing those products.'

[107] Article 3(a) of Regulation 67/67.

[108] *Fifteenth Report on Competition Policy*, at p. 60. While the Commission recognised that, in general, a reciprocal exclusive distribution agreement between competitors may improve distribution in the sense of art. 85(3), it noted, at p. 36 of the decision, that in the present case the two parties were both strong parties and that any possible benefit could not outweigh the anti-competitive effects of the arrangement.

[109] *COBELPA/VNP*, OJ 1977 L242/10.

[110] *Agreements between manufacturers of glass containers*, OJ 1974 L160/1.

[111] See *Centraal Stikstof Verkoopkantoor*, OJ 1978 L242/15, involving a joint sales agency set up by two Dutch manufacturers, discussed at ¶525; *French-West African shipowners' committees*, OJ 1992 L134/1, at p. 14, involving a shipowners' agreement which had the effect of sharing among its members the market for cargoes carried by liner vessel between France and 11 African states.

[112] *Cementregeling voor Nederland*, JO 1972 L303/7.

they sell in the Netherlands'.[113] The system 'impairs the freedom to export Belgian and German cement to the Netherlands and the freedom of international trade in cement between Belgium and the Federal Republic of Germany on the one hand, and the Netherlands on the other, in such a way as to jeopardize the realization of the objective of a single market between states'.[114] The Commission rejected the parties' claims that the objective of the system was to guarantee 'adequate production capacities' for the Dutch cement market which would contribute to production improvements, and consequently refused to grant an exception under art. 85(3).[115]

¶814 Restrictions of production or sources of supply

Article 85(1)(b) expressly prohibits agreements and concerted practices that limit or control production. Thus, the allocation of production quotas among competitors has been condemned by the Community authorities without exception. In *International Quinine Cartel*[116] a series of gentlemen's agreements among Dutch, German, French and British producers prohibited the French and British parties from manufacturing quinine without the approval of the other parties, in exchange for territorial protection of their respective home markets. The Commission found art. 85(1) to be infringed, and rejected the parties' contention that the French and British companies were unable to manufacture quinidine in any event because of their lack of technical experience.[117] On appeal, the court confirmed the Commission's findings.[118]

In *Italian cast glass*,[119] the Commission condemned a system of production quotas established by Italian glass manufacturers, finding that the quotas were intended to preserve each company's respective market share. By having limited production, the parties 'no longer had any incentive to reduce their prices to win a larger market share as, if they had done so, they would have

---

[113] Id., at p. 14.

[114] Id., pp. 14–15.

[115] See also, *Roofing felt*, OJ 1986 L232/15 (sales quotas), on appeal: *Belasco & Ors v EC Commission* [1989] ECR 2117; *Polypropylene*, OJ 1986 L230/1, on appeal: *Polypropylene Cases* cited at footnote 10 (sales quotas); *Peroxygen products*, OJ 1985 L35/1; *Zinc producer group*, OJ 1984 L220/27 (export and delivery quotas); *Flat-glass sector in Benelux*, OJ 1984 L212/13; *Polistil/Arbois*, OJ 1984 L136/9; *Cast iron and steel rolls*, OJ 1983 L317/1 (export quotas); *Cimbel*, JO 1972 L303/24 (delivery quotas).

[116] *International Quinine Cartel*, JO 1969 L192/5; on appeal: *ACF Chemiefarma v EC Commission* [1970] ECR 661; *Buchler v EC Commission* [1970] ECR 733; *Boehringer Mannheim GmbH v EC Commission* [1970] ECR 769.

[117] Id., at p. 21.

[118] 'The fact relied upon that, when the gentlemen's agreement was concluded, the French undertakings were not in a position to manufacture synthetic quinidine does not render lawful such a restriction which entirely precluded them from taking up this activity. That the French undertakings should accede to this restriction of their freedom of action is explicable in terms of their interest – owing to the particularly high prices which they maintained for their products in France – in preserving the territorial protection which they enjoyed on their domestic market.' (*ACF Chemiefarma v EC Commission* [1970] ECR 661, at p. 629 (para. 156–157)). See also *Agreements restricting production and sale of fruit*, Fifth Report on Competition Policy, point 38.

[119] *Italian cast glass*, OJ 1980 L383/19.

forfeited the opportunity of drawing the maximum benefit from their production quotas'.[120]

In line with its general attitude towards market-sharing arrangements, the Commission has usually refused to grant exemptions under art. 85(3). In some cases, exemptions were granted after the parties had removed the provisions fixing production quotas. Thus, in *Synthetic fibres*,[121] the Commission only granted an individual exemption to a so-called 'crisis cartel',[122] intended to reduce overcapacities, after the allocation of production quotas had been dropped.[123] In *Fine paper*,[124] the Commission objected to production quotas in the context of a specialisation agreement among the principal French manufacturers of fine paper, granting an exemption only after the parties had terminated that part of the agreement establishing production quotas.

It is also possible that parties to a market-sharing agreement deprive customers of the benefits of a competitive market by cutting off sources of supply. In *Cewal, Cowac and Ukwal*,[125] agreements between liner conferences, which held dominant position on their respective markets, not to operate in each other's areas not only constituted classical territorial market-sharing agreements, but also had the effect of cutting off 'the supply of transport services available to shippers from each conference area'.[126] By controlling the supply of available transport services, the members of the liner conference were able to maintain their market-sharing agreement.

¶815   Allocation of customers and/or products

Market-sharing may result not only from geographical divisions and production restrictions, but by allocation of customers and products as well. In *BP Kemi-DDSF*,[127] BP Kemi supplied all of DDSF's ethanol needs. The parties agreed that DDSF would enjoy the exclusive right for sales of ethanol in Denmark, except for those customers whose annual consumption exceeded 100,000 litres. BP Kemi directly sold to such large customers, but its direct sales were limited to 25 per cent of the combined annual sales of the two parties. The scheme was found to be unacceptable by the Commission because it fixed the customers to be supplied by each party and removed BP Kemi's incentive to sell ethanol to new customers.

---

[120] Id., at p. 24.
[121] *Synthetic fibres*, OJ 1984 L207/17.
[122] For further details see ¶820.
[123] See also *Eleventh Report on Competition Policy*, at p. 41.
[124] *Fine paper*, OJ 1972 L182/24.
[125] *Cewal, Cowac and Ukwal*, OJ 1993 L34/20, on appeal: *Compagnie Maritime Belge Transport NV and Compagnie Maritime Belge NV, Dafra Lines A/S, Deutsche Afrika-Linien GmbH & Co and Nedlloyd Lijnen BV v EC Commission*, Cases T-24/93, T-25/93, T-26/93 and T-28/93, not yet decided.
[126] Id., at p. 28; See also *French-West African shipowners'committees*, OJ 1992 L134/1, at p. 14.
[127] *BP Kemi-DDSF*, OJ 1979 L286/32.

In *Building and construction in the Netherlands,*[128] a complete system was set up to regulate and monitor prices and tenders in the Dutch construction sector. According to the Commission, the predesignation, during the meeting of the bidders of an 'entitled bidder' or 'preferred bidder' having the exclusive right to negotiate the terms of the contract with the client, amounted to an impermissible sharing of customers. Indeed, this predesignation prevented the competing bidders from further competition. They were even prohibited from contacting the client once the entitled bidder was designated.

In *Roofing felt,*[129] the Commission found a violation of art. 85(1) where seven Belgian producers of roofing felt agreed, under the cloak of 'stability of clientele', to stick to their own customers. During the course of the investigation, the parties admitted that the object was to prevent one member's customers being approached by other members. Moreover, in the face of the price-cutting policy adopted by one competitor, the parties agreed to divide among themselves the competitor's customers, making them offers with maximum discounts so as to take business away from the competitor and induce it to abandon its price cutting. This practice, needless to say, was condemned in the strongest terms by the Commission.

Two other cases, in which the agreements were amended without the need for a formal decision, illustrate the Commission's opposition to this form of market-sharing. The first involved an agreement between two pharmaceutical companies restricting the resale of the drug ampicillin. The agreement provided that the drug could only be sold for consumer use (effectively prohibiting bulk sales) and that it could only be sold for human consumption. The obligation to sell solely for human consumption, to the exclusion of sales for veterinary purposes, amounted to an unjustifiable restriction. The Commission stated that 'restrictions on the form in which raw material may be resold or on the use to which it may be put are quite as prejudicial to the maintenance of free competition in the Community as geographical market-sharing'.[130] The second case involved an agreement among three manufacturers of fertilisers, one Belgian and two German. The agreement provided that every month the Belgian manufacturer sold each of the German companies an agreed quantity of fertiliser. The product was packaged in sacks bearing the German company's name, and was delivered, not in Germany, but to the German

---

[128] *Building and construction industry in the Netherlands,* OJ 1992 L92/1, on appeal: *Vereniging van Samenwerkende en Prijsregelende Organisaties in de Bouwnijverheid v EC Commission,* Case T-29/92, not yet decided. This agreement was also found to be a violation of art. 85(1) as it involved elements of price-fixing and an impermissible information-exchange arrangement. See ¶803 and ¶823.
[129] *Roofing felt,* OJ 1986 L232/15, on appeal: *Belasco & Ors v EC Commission* [1989] ECR 2117. See also *Lloyd's Underwriters' Association and the Institute of London Underwriters,* OJ 1992 L4/26, where the Commission gave a negative clearance after the parties abandoned a market-sharing agreement which effectively ensured that insurers who had first insured the risk could continue to underwrite the risk at renewal.
[130] *Beecham Pharma-Hoechst, Sixth Report on Competition Policy,* points 129–133.

companies' Belgian customers. Likewise, every month the German producers sold the same quantity of fertiliser to the Belgian company, but delivered the product to the Belgian company's customers in Germany. The Commission found that the system restricted trade between Belgium and Germany, and rejected the parties' argument that without the reciprocal arrangement, freight costs and small profit margins would have prevented them from supplying their export customers.[131]

In *Flat glass*,[132] two producers, SIV and FP, decided to share the supplies of flat glass to a large consumer, Piaggio, equally. In order to achieve their goal, they agreed to implement differentiated price increases, which resulted in a reduced supply quota for FP and an increased supply quota for SIV. The Commission found that 'through these agreements and practices, which institute[d] clear infringements, the two producers developed a long-term strategy designed to get the customer in question to aportion its order in accordance with what they had decided, thus depriving Piaggio, through the system of differentiated prices, of any economic scope for choosing its own sources of supply.'[133] The court qualified the agreements as both price-fixing and market-sharing, caught by art. 85(1)(a) and (e) with clear anti-competitive objects.[134]

¶816   Exemptions under art. 85(3) and non-applicability of art. 85(1)

It follows from the Commission's strong objections to all forms of market-sharing arrangements, that it generally does not grant exemptions under art. 85(3). The thread running through the Commission's case law is its conviction that fair and undistorted competition is the best guarantee of market supply, rather than allowing the producers to determine for themselves how a given market is to be supplied. Consequently, the Community authorities have rejected asserted justifications for market-sharing, such as alleviation of shortages of raw materials[135] or the maintenance or improvement of adequate production and supply.[136]

The only occasion where the Commission exempted a major geographical

---

[131] *Agreement between manufacturers of nitrogenous fertilisers*, Sixth Report on Competition Policy, points 126–128.

[132] *Flat glass*, OJ 1989 L33/44; on appeal: *Società Italiano Vetro (SIV) SpA & Ors v EC Commission* [1992] ECR II-1403; [1992] 2 CEC 33.

[133] Id., at p. 63.

[134] *Società Italiano Vetro SpA, Fabbrica Pisano SpA, PPG Vernante Pennitalia SpA v EC Commission*, Cases T-68/89, T-77/89, T-78/89, judgment of 10 March 1992, at para. 336. It should be noted that the Court of First Instance partially annulled the Commission's decision, but not with respect to the market-sharing agreements discussed here or price-fixing. See discussion at ¶811.

[135] *ACF Chemiefarma v EC Commission* [1970] ECR 661, at p. 695.

[136] *Cementregeling voor Nederland*, JO 1972 L303/7; *Roofing felt*, OJ 1986 L232/15, at p. 29, on appeal: *Belasco & Ors v EC Commission* [1989] ECR 2117.

market-sharing arrangement is *Transocean Marine Paint Association*.[137] It involved an agreement by an association of 18 medium-sized producers of marine paint, each of which was established in a different country, with five EC producers participating. The agreement provided that all parties would produce marine paint according to a uniform formula established by the association and would sell it under identical packaging and under the same trade mark. The purpose of the agreement was to allow these medium-sized producers to compete more effectively with large international groups of manufacturers of marine paints by permitting them to offer marine paints of identical composition and quality in all the larger ports of the world. Each producer sought to obtain orders in the territory of the country in which it was established, but was allowed to sell outside its own country. Local producers were afforded a degree of protection in that sales made by one producer in another territory were subject to the payment of a commission to the local producer and, depending upon the product involved, required the consent of the local producer.

The Commission considered that the agreement limited the opportunities for economic activities in the various countries, even though consent was, in principle, required to be given, because it complicated and delayed the execution of export orders within the Community. Nevertheless, finding that the agreement contributed to the improvement of the distribution of goods by rationalising and intensifying the sale of marine paints manufactured under the same trade mark, the Commission granted an exemption under art. 85(3). Under the circumstances a flexible system of geographical division ensured that marine paints would be offered and stocked regularly and in sufficient quantities in a large number of ports.[138]

The main reason for the Commission's leniency in this case should be attributed to its policy of encouraging co-operation between small and medium-sized firms so as to permit them to compete more effectively with larger companies. In its assessment under art. 85(3), the Commission explicitly noted that the agreement did not eliminate competition for a substantial part of

---

[137] *Transocean Marine Paint Association*, JO 1967 L163/10.
[138] The Commission further stated (Id., at p. 14.):

'The members of the association are, therefore, in a position to deal as well with buyers who want to be able to obtain marine paints of uniform quality used by them whenever and wherever they need them. Without the agreement, the members would have had to create their own distribution network in a large number of countries, which would have involved investments and risks excessive for medium-sized undertakings (the need to open branches or agencies, to maintain warehouses and after-sales service). The association and the coordination of the various sales networks of the members allow them, even though medium-sized undertakings, to compete more actively with the large marine paint manufacturers already represented in all the major countries; this results in an increase in the supply of the products and to an improvement in the sales structure in the marine paint industry. The agreement thus produces perceptible objective advantages for the distribution of the products, in comparison to the situation that would exist without it.'

¶816

the products because the members of the association were faced with 'lively competition', in particular from large manufacturers.

The exemption was renewed for the first time in 1973, although subject to new conditions.[139] On appeal, the court annulled one of these newly attached conditions on procedural grounds.[140] A revised exemption was granted in 1975[141] and twice renewed in 1980[142] and 1988.[143]

It is useful to note that a geographical market-sharing clause in a share transfer agreement does not come under the prohibition of art. 85(1) under certain conditions.[144] Such a clause is normally allowed for a limited period of time and intended to protect the vendor, with his particularly detailed knowledge of the transferred undertaking, from being able to regain his former clients immediately after the sale.[145]

¶817   Collective boycotts

A collective boycott is traditionally considered among the most pernicious violations of competition law. It consists of a concerted refusal by a group of competitors at one stage of the distribution chain to deal with either one or more customers or suppliers. The aim of such a boycott usually is to punish or eliminate the 'troublesome' customer/supplier for his trading practice. Therefore, it constitutes a deliberate violation of art. 85. A refusal among members of a trade association to deal with non-members may have the same effect. In view of the intent to restrain the freedom of competitors to deal with others as they see fit, a collective boycott is such an obvious infringement of art. 85 that there are few reported cases.[146]

In *Papiers Peints de Belgique*,[147] Belgian wallpaper manufacturers had established a trade association that regulated price ranges and quality levels in the industry. An independent wholesaler refused to comply with the price

---

[139] OJ 1974 L19/18.

[140] *Transocean Marine Paint v EC Commission* [1974] ECR 1063.

[141] OJ 1975 L286/24.

[142] OJ 1980 L39/73.

[143] OJ 1988 L351/40. The latest version of the articles of association and of three supplementary agreements now expressly provides for a prohibition on members to actively canvass sales outside allocated territories. Passive sales, on the contrary, are authorised.

[144] See *Remia BV & Ors. v EC Commission* [1985] ECR 2545 and Commission notice regarding restrictions ancillary to concentrations, OJ 1990 C203/5, both discussed in ¶616.

[145] In *Quantel International-Continuum/Quantel SA*, OJ 1992 L235/9, the parties had agreed to a protocol which provided for a division of the markets worldwide, whereby the European market was reserved for Quantel SA, the vendor. When Quantel SA took measures to prevent Quantel International, its former US subsidiary, from entering the European market, the Commission refused to accept the non-applicability of art. 85(1), as it did in the *Remia* case, because of the excessive duration (8 to 9 IS1/ID2 years) of the protocol. In addition, the agreement in question was designed to protect the vendor (Quantel SA) instead of the purchaser (Quantel International).

[146] On the other hand, purely unilateral refusals to deal which do not involve any horizontal concertation are of less concern for competition law purposes. They may nevertheless amount to a restrictive practice within the context of exclusive or selective distribution systems, or constitute an abuse of a dominant position.

[147] *Papiers Peints de Belgique*, OJ 1974 L237/3, on appeal: *Papiers Peints v EC Commission* [1975] ECR 1491.

levels imposed by the association, and refused to ensure that they were applied by his customer, a chain of self-service discount stores. The association and its members decided not to supply the wholesaler any longer. The Commission found that this decision constituted a restraint on the wholesaler's competition with other dealers and was motivated by the association's desire to enforce its general sales conditions, particularly its pricing policy. It rejected this motivation as a justification for the boycott because the sales conditions and pricing policy were themselves infringements of art. 85 which the wholesaler could refuse to comply with. Furthermore, the fact that the wholesaler had debts with one member of the association was no justification for the other members to refuse supplying him. In fixing the fines, the Commission classified the boycott as 'one of the most serious infringements of the rules of competition' and 'an intentional infringement of art. 85(1)'.[148]

Collective discrimination is often found as part of trade association rules. The Commission has dealt with a number of cases where the rules, regulations or by-laws of a trade association required their members to deal only with parties recognised by the association.[149] Only in unusual cases will there be a reasonable and objective justification for such rules, qualifying the agreement for exemption under art. 85(3). For example, in *Netherlands Insurers*,[150] an association of the major transport insurers in the Netherlands included a rule prohibiting the members from concluding reinsurance contracts with non-members. The Commission asked the association to change the rule because it found it to be a 'restriction of competition ... which serves to intensify the continuing isolation of national markets ...'

CRISIS CARTELS

¶818 Introduction

Difficult economic times and declining or stagnant industries present special problems for the Community competition policy. Despite the Community institutions' hostile position toward price-fixing, quotas and other traditional cartel restraints, the Commission has occasionally taken a more tolerant

---

[148] *Papiers Peints de Belgique*, OJ 1974 L237/3, at p. 10. See also *Fourth Report on Competition Policy*, point 66; *Fedetab*, OJ 1978 L224/29, where in response to a number of large distribution firms reducing the number of brands of cigarette they stocked, tobacco manufacturers agreed to withhold all supplies of cigarettes until the firms reverted to their previous number of brands, on appeal: *Van Landewyck & Ors v EC Commission* [1980] ECR 3125.

[149] *Sarabex*, *Eighth Report on Competition Policy*, points 35–37; *Netherlands insurers*, *Sixth Report on Competition Policy*, points 120–121; *Gas water-heaters and bath-heaters*, OJ 1973 L217/34; *Pottery convention* EC Bull. Nos 5–64, Annex II; *Seventh General Report on the Activities of the Community*, point 67; *Irish Timber Importers Association*, *XXth Report on Competition Policy*, point 98.

[150] *Netherlands Insurers*, *Sixth Report on Competition Policy*, points 120–121.

position towards so-called 'crisis cartels' in industries or sectors of industries faced with structural overcapacity and general recessionary pressures. The purpose of such 'crisis cartels' is to ensure not only the maintenance of the competitive position of the industry concerned, but sometimes its very existence in often highly competitive markets. Agreements that restrict competition by reducing surplus capacity or by co-ordinating plant closures may be pro-competitive in the long term and may have beneficial effects in a broader social context, for example by preserving jobs. The Commission none the less takes the view that such agreements are in fact anti-competitive and prohibited by art. 85(1) but may deserve exemption under art. 85(3) when they merely reduce overcapacity and do not, at the same time, fix prices, quotas, production or sales.[151] As is the case for all exemptions under art. 85(3), a notification of the agreement is required.[152]

¶819   Structural overcapacity

According to the Commission, structural overcapacity exists where, over a prolonged period, an entire economic sector has been experiencing a significant reduction in the rates of capacity utilisation, a drop in output accompanied by substantial operating losses, and where the information available does not indicate that any lasting improvement can be expected in this situation in the medium term.[153]

There are two approaches to 'restructuring' industries characterised by overcapacity and declining or stagnant demand. First, there can be a sectoral reduction in capacity involving all or almost all firms in the industry.[154] Secondly, firms can enter into bilateral agreements to specialise or rationalise production.[155] Whatever type of solution is chosen, the Commission will always verify whether, after the reorganisation programme is completed, there will still be a sufficient number of Community manufacturers left to maintain effective competition in the Community.[156]

¶820   Sectoral agreements

'Crisis cartels' which provide for participation of the majority of the undertakings of the sector concerned will only be eligible for an exemption

---

[151] *Eleventh Report on Competition Policy*, point 46.
[152] In *Montedipe v EC Commission*, Case T-14/89, judgment of 10 March 1992, not reported, at para. 271, the Court of First Instance rejected the argument that undertakings could take measures of self discipline in a situation of economic crisis since the EC Treaty did not provide a counterpart to art. 58 of the ECSC Treaty which provides for measures to be taken by the High Authority. The court stressed that only Community authorities, i.e. the Commission, could unite undertakings in exceptional circumstances of economic crisis.
[153] *Twelfth Report on Competition Policy*, point 38.
[154] See e.g. *Synthetic fibres*, OJ 1984 L207/17.
[155] See e.g. *BPCL/ICI*, OJ 1984 L212/1.
[156] *Twelfth Report on Competition Policy*, point 40.

under art. 85(3) if they are aimed solely at achieving a coordinated reduction of overcapacity, without otherwise restricting free decision-making by the parties.[157] The Commission has noted that it will not exempt arrangements which involve a strict code of internal discipline covering all the economic activities of the parties as well as protection against competition by outsiders.[158] In particular, the Commission will only find the requirements of art. 85(3) to be met if the agreement satisfies the following conditions:[159]

(1) the agreement must contain a detailed and binding programme of closures and must prevent the creation of any new capacity, except for replacement capacities provided for in the reorganisation programme;

(2) consumers must not be deprived of the freedom of choice between competitors or the benefits of continued competition between the participating companies;

(3) any information-exchange arrangement under the agreement must be solely with a view to supervising capacity reductions, and may not serve to co-ordinate policy on the use of remaining capacity or to align sales conditions; and

(4) the agreement must be for a specifically stated limited period.

In *Italian cast glass*[160] the Commission expressed a rather unfavourable opinion with regard to sectoral crisis cartels. First, it noted that the agreement in question did not merit exemption because it shielded more than half of the Italian production of cast glass from competition, thus eliminating competition in respect of a substantial part of the product.[161] With respect to the sectoral crisis situation which the parties put forward in justification of the agreement, the Commission stated:

'On the one hand, [art. 85(3)] makes no reference to such a situation and, on the other, no decision genuinely to reduce the productive capacities of the undertakings which took part in the practice in question (which might have been appropriate to the structural crisis situation) was taken; it was merely decided unilaterally to set quantitative shares for sales of cast glass on the Italian market, to the benefit exclusively of the manufacturers, without any advantage for consumers. It is therefore not possible to allow, in the guise of a crisis cartel, restrictions of competition which are not indispensable.'[162]

---

[157] *Twelfth Report on Competition Policy*, point 39.
[158] *Eleventh Report on Competition Policy*, point 46. See also Sharpe, 'The Commission's Proposals on Crisis Cartels', 17 CML Rev 75 (1980).
[159] *Twelfth Report on Competition Policy*, point 39.
[160] *Italian cast glass*, OJ 1980 L383/19.
[161] Id., at p. 25.
[162] Id., at p. 26.

¶820

In subsequent cases, the Commission dropped the need for a reference in art. 85(3) to a sectoral crisis situation as a basic condition for exemption without, however, taking an unambiguously favourable view towards this type of agreement. The *Synthetic fibres* case evidences some of the Commission's hesitancies with respect to sectoral agreements. In 1972, the European producers of cut polyester fibres notified an agreement 'designed to ensure co-ordination of investment and rationalisation of production with a view to eliminating or preventing excess capacity in the industry'.[163] The question of whether such an agreement could be acceptable under art. 85 remained unsettled because the particular agreement contained features which were found to be clearly incompatible with art. 85(3), and the notification was subsequently withdrawn.[164] The structural problems of the industry as a whole worsened. In 1977, capacity utilisation had dropped to an average of 70 per cent and the Commission asked the member states not to grant the industry assistance that might increase production capacity.[165]

In 1978, the industry notified a new agreement.[166] Along with a cutback in production capacity, the agreement provided for a system of production and sales quotas that the Commission found unacceptable. After numerous amendments to the proposal, a formal exemption was finally granted in 1984.[167] The exempted agreement, concluded in October 1982 and lasting until the end of 1985, provided that the ten largest European manufacturers would, inter alia, reduce their production capacity for six types of synthetic textiles by 18 per cent.[168]

Although clearly in violation of art. 85(1), the agreement was nevertheless deemed to have fulfilled the conditions of art. 85(3). In particular, the Commission noted that the agreement improved production, allowed greater specialisation by each party, provided for the restructuring operations to be carried out in 'socially acceptable' ways (e.g., by making suitable arrangements for the redeployment of workers laid off), granted consumers a fair share of the benefits resulting from the improvements (i.e., after the reorganisation, by a healthy industry offering better goods at competitive terms and, during the

---

[163] *Second Report on Competition Policy*, point 31.
[164] Ibid.
[165] *Seventh Report on Competition Policy*, point 204.
[166] *Eighth Report on Competition Policy*, point 42.
[167] *Synthetic fibres*, OJ 1984 L207/17.
[168] By the terms of the agreement, the parties also undertook: (1) to supply to a trustee all relevant information concerning the capacity to be dismantled and to accept the principle of inspection of their plants by independent experts; (2) to consult each other in the event of important changes on the market, with a view to identifying appropriate solutions; (3) not to sell all or any of their dismantled plants in Western Europe, and not during the lifetime of the agreement to increase the capacity which they had themselves determined; and (4) to pay compensation to the other participants should they fail to implement the projected reductions. See also *Stichting Baksteen*, OJ 1993 C34/11, where the Commission announced its intention to take a favourable stand on the implementation of an agreement between Dutch brick manufacturers intended to manage the overcapacity in this sector.

¶820

reorganisation, by continued competition between the participants), related only to reduction of overcapacity, and was of limited duration. The Commission considered that because the agreement did not affect the parties' marketing behaviour and because substitute and non-Community products were freely available on the market, competition in the goods in question would continue to be strong.

Similarly, in *Zinc shutdown agreement*,[169] the six largest Community zinc producers, faced with substantial world-wide overcapacity and heavy financial losses, notified the Commission of an agreement whereby each company would reduce such capacity as it considered advisable, and not create any new capacity. Each company that actually cut capacity was to be compensated by the others, particularly for social costs. The Commission proposed to exempt the agreement 'in view of the heavy financial losses in the European zinc industry and the fact that the agreement was to last for a fixed period', but the zinc market improved before a formal Decision could be issued, and the agreement was terminated by the parties.[170]

¶821   Bilateral agreements

In *Rovin*[171] the Commission took a similar position towards bilateral agreements as it had done for sectoral agreements. In the face of overcapacity in the petrochemical market, Shell and Akzo concluded a restructuring agreement whereby they created a joint venture company, Rovin, for the manufacture of polyvinylchloride (PVC), a product derived in part from vinylchloride monomers (VCM). Shell placed its PVC plant at the exclusive disposal of Rovin, and Akzo did likewise with its VCM plant.

Production capacity was placed under Rovin's exclusive control. The agreement became effective on 1 October 1982, and was to last for an indefinite period (but at least to 1 January 1987). Both parties agreed not to engage in the production of VCM or PVC except through the joint venture.

The Commission noted that the European VCM and PVC markets were served by companies having vertically integrated production and marketing operations, and that prior to the agreement, neither Shell nor Akzo possessed such integrated operations. Since neither party was able to produce VCM and PVC independently, their agreement allowed them to integrate the vertical production process and marketing of the products, thereby facilitating a better match between supply and demand of prime materials, a better utilisation rate for their facilities and the maintenance of constant quality-specifications. Finding that the agreement achieved a structural improvement of capacity-

---

[169] *Zinc shutdown agreement, Thirteenth Report on Competition Policy*, point 58.
[170] Ibid.
[171] *Rovin, Fourteenth Report on Competition Policy*, point 85.

utilisation and thus a healthier structural situation in the sector, the Commission issued a 'comfort letter' to the parties.

In *BPCL/ICI*,[172] two British companies, ICI and BPCL, concluded an agreement for the restructuring of the petrochemical sector in the UK. The restructuring involved specialisation of production by which ICI would assume sole production of low density polyethylene (LdPE). While the deal was essentially an asset transfer, it was one that necessitated plant closures. ICI sold its most modern UK LdPE production plant to BPCL, and BPCL sold its most modern UK PVC production plant to ICI. ICI then closed all remaining UK LdPE plants (but had two LdPE plants remaining on the Continent), thereby abandoning the production of LdPE in the UK, and BPCL likewise closed its PVC plants.

The closure of the plants served to eliminate an important and active producer in the UK for each of the two products in question, and was seen as a violation of art. 85(1). Nevertheless, the Commission felt that an exemption under art. 85(3) was warranted. The closure of the older plants served to reduce capacity in a sector that was suffering from overcapacity. As a result of the agreement, each of the parties was able to greatly improve production efficiency. In the Commission's view, the closures stemmed a loss-making activity for both producers, and thus released resources for investment that would help promote technical progress.

The planned transfer of the respective businesses and the nature of the plant closures were also seen to benefit the consumer. In view of the losses being suffered, the plants might have been threatened by unilateral closure by the producers, thereby causing individual customers to be faced with a disruption of supplies. By permitting each party to (partially) withdraw from a loss-making product line, the agreement would permit consumers to benefit in the long run since this would allow the specialising party to be able to liberate resources to finance long-term investment and research and development rather than to cover operating costs.

Following the swap deal with ICI in 1984 which was approved by the Commission,[173] BPCL entered into a second round of restructuring which was looked upon favourably by the Commission. The Commission noted that the agreements between Bayer, BPCL and EC[174] were intended to reorganise and rationalise their respective petrochemical businesses, particularly in the polyethylene sector, a sector suffering from structural overcapacity. It was also stated that, as a result of these agreements, each party would be able to increase capacity in more modern plants, thus reducing manufacturing costs per unit for

---

[172] *BPCL/ICI*, OJ 1984 L212/1.
[173] *BPCL/ICI*, OJ 1984 L212/1.
[174] *Bayer/BP Chemicals*, OJ 1988 L150/35.

¶821

the products in which it would be specialising. Furthermore, these agreements provided for an exchange of technical information, technical co-operation and a restructuring of the distribution system. The Commission decided that the latter measures would help bring about both a healthier industrial structure and a more efficient production.

An obligation was imposed on the parties to inform the Commission on a regular basis about any changes in their agreements, variations in their respective capacities and especially to send reports concerning the implementation of the operations allowed by the Commission.

There seems to exist a tendency in recent Commission decisions to control the closure of old plants and the opening of new plants more strictly than in the past. The validity of the exemption of the agreements between Bayer, PBCL and EC depended on the further development of the market in question. The closing down of plants had already been subject to prior agreements.[175] While the Zinc shutdown agreement never gave rise to a formal decision by the Commission because the situation on the zinc market improved, in *BPCL/ICI* the closing down of plants as a part of the restructuring programme was exempted by the Commission. A possible change of the market, however, was not taken into account.

In *Bayer/BP Chemicals*, the parties had the obligation to open a new plant before June 1991 and to close down two facilities by the end of 1991. Fulfilment of the latter condition could, however, be postponed upon a finding by the Commission that a postponement was objectively justified by the situation in the polyethylene sector at that time.

In *ENI/Montedison*[176] an exemption under art. 85(3) was granted in respect of agreements which aimed at restructuring the Italian petrochemical industry. These agreements provided for the reciprocal transfer of parts of the petrochemical businesses of ENI and Montedison, notably cracking-products, thermoplastics and certain rubbers. In addition, supply and plant management contracts were entered into in order to cope with the new situations created by the dual ownership of plants following the execution of the restructuring plan. Although competition between ENI and Montedison was reduced by these agreements, the Commission nevertheless granted an exemption under art. 85(3) since the agreements were deemed necessary to restructure the petrochemical sector which is suffering from serious structural overcapacity in the whole Community. The agreements enabled the parties to rationalise more quickly and radically than would have been possible individually. By granting such an exemption it was also ensured that competition remained at a workable level and that the benefits were passed on to the consumer.

---

[175] *BPCL/ICI*, OJ 1984 L212/1; *Zinc shutdown agreement, Thirteenth Report on Competition Policy*, point 58.
[176] *ENI/Montedison*, OJ 1987 L5/13.

In *Enichem/ICI*[177] two petrochemical companies, Enichem (Italy) and ICI (UK) set up a joint venture, European Vinyls Corporation ('EVC'), which would operate on the vinyl chloride monomer (VCM) and the polyvinylchloride (PVC) markets. Both parent companies agreed to shut down, reduce the capacity of or convert certain plants or facilities.

The Commission held that the agreements would restrict competition under art. 85(1) for a number of reasons, including the fact that EVC was dependent on continued co-operation of each parent company as well as on the latter's services, raw materials, technology, patents and personnel, the parent companies and the joint venture remained each other's potential[178] and, to a certain extent, actual competitors and the parties did not transfer their assets to the joint venture.

The agreements were exempted under art. 85(3) because they were deemed to allow in the short term major progress in the rationalisation of the parent companies' petrochemical businesses and because concentration on more modern plants would allow them to be utilised at a higher level of capacity. The Commission also enumerated specific benefits accruing to the parent companies as a result of the joint venture, e.g. the companies did not have to reduce their range of types, qualities and grades currently offered to customers and a reallocation of production units closer to their natural markets would be concomitant.

It is interesting to note that in this decision the Commission conditioned the exemption on an obligation for the parent companies and the joint venture to refrain from maintaining any interests in competing production or distribution undertakings within the Community, lest this participation be of a purely financial nature.

INFORMATION-EXCHANGE ARRANGEMENTS

¶822   General

The Commission has always been suspicious of exchanges of industrial data between competitors. As a general rule, an exchange of information which leads to market co-ordination or which could induce the participating firms to act in the same way is regarded by the Commission as a violation of art. 85(1).[179]

---

[177] *Enichem/ICI*, OJ 1988 L50/18.

[178] Potential competition was inferred from the active presence which both parent companies retained in the upstream business of the joint venture which would make it comparatively easy and cheap for them to re-enter the joint venture's. In addition, the parent companies were considered to be potential competitors because of their retention of certain activities on the joint venture's market. For an analysis of the concept of potential competition see ¶506.

[179] In *COBELPA/VNP*, OJ 1977 C242/10, at p. 27, the Commission stated with regard to an information exchange arrangement on prices:

Because of the variety of arrangements that are possible and the diversity of information that can be exchanged, it is very difficult to discern which arrangements are permissive and which are not. Consequently, each case is assessed individually by the Commission taking into account all the specific circumstances.[180]

Notwithstanding this case-by-case assessment of such arrangements, the large number of cases in this area makes it possible to draw some general conclusions. As a general rule, the Commission will be particularly sensitive to the structure of the market, to the benefits for the consumer and to the nature, and more specifically the detail, of the information exchanged.[181]

First, the Commission will pay very close attention to information exchange arrangements in highly concentrated markets. In such a market, the exchange of sensitive information can lead to restrictions of competition for several reasons. It will increase the already high barriers of entry for non-participants in the exchange, whether they choose to become members of the exchange or not.[182] Indeed, if they choose not to reveal their own information, they will not be able to compete on an equal footing with the members of the exchange who can act on the basis of more detailed and more accurate market information. On the other hand, if they choose to become members of the exchange, they will have to reveal their own confidential information, on the basis of which the established competitors can take immediate action.

In addition, this exchange of information could give rise to a degree of market transparency which would prevent any form of hidden competition on the oligopolistic market. In this connection, the Commission has stated that: '[i]ndeed active competition in these market conditions becomes possible only if each competitor can keep its actions secret or even succeeds in misleading its rivals'.[183] In the absence of external competitive pressure, because of the high barriers of entry, this market will stabilise completely and any form of competition will become impossible.

The Commission's treatment of information-exchange agreements in the insurance sector illustrates the importance that it attaches to the degree of competition on the market. For example, in *Nuovo CEGAM*,[184] the parties to

---

'These concerted practices thus resulted in the establishment of a system of solidarity and mutual influence designed to coordinate business activities. They replaced the normal risks of competition by practical cooperation, resulting in conditions of competition differing from those obtaining in a normal market situation.'

The Commission's view is based on the opinion of the Court of Justice in respect of concerted practices in *ICI v EC Commission* [1972] ECR 619, at para. 64, and in *Suiker Unie & Ors v EC Commission* [1975] ECR 1663 as discussed in ¶212 above.

[180] *Seventh Report on Competition Policy*, point 7.
[181] Ibid.
[182] *UK Agricultural Tractor Registration Exchange*, OJ 1992 L68/19, at p. 28.
[183] *UK Agricultural Tractor Registration Exchange*, OJ 1992 L68/19, at p. 26.
[184] *Nuovo CEGAM*, OJ 1984 L99/29, at p. 35.

¶822

the agreement were not considered to be in a position to eliminate competition because they held only 26 per cent of the Italian market for engineering insurance. In Regulation 3932/92, the Commission inserted maximum thresholds of ten per cent and 15 per cent for a combined market share so as to ensure that competition remained.[185] In *TEKO*, the Commission stated that competition between parties to the agreement was still possible because, although the insurance companies were bound to apply the premiums calculated by TEKO, they 'still were able to choose to pass part of the reinsurance commission to policy holders or refund them part of the premium'.[186] However, in *UK Tractor*,[187] which is discussed at length in ¶823, the Commission found that an information-exchange agreement between competitors which held 88 per cent of the UK tractor market violated art. 85(1).

Secondly, the Commission will pay close attention to whether the consumer will derive any benefit from the exchange or instead will suffer harm as a result of this exchange. Indeed, the Commission stated on several occasions that such an exchange of information between competitors in a highly concentrated market only benefited the producers and deprived consumers of any benefit of hidden competition.[188]

However, in *X Open Group*,[189] the Commission cleared an arrangement among a group of software producers and AT&T, the developer of a widely used operating system, to exchange both market and technical information in furtherance of an 'open system' as an industry standard. The development of such a system increased the possibilities for the consumer to mix hardware and software from different suppliers. The Commission decided to clear this arrangement because the information exchanged related exclusively to the requirements of the consumer in order for the producers to determine and better react to consumer needs. In this case, according to the Commission, competition was enhanced instead of restricted.

Thirdly, the Commission will see to it that industrial data of individual firms, which are usually regarded as business secrets, are not exchanged directly

---

[185] Article 11 of Commission Regulation 3932/92, on the application of art. 85(3) of the treaty to certain categories of agreements, decisions and concerted practices in the insurance sector, OJ 1992 L398/7.

[186] *TEKO*, OJ 1989 C13/34, at p. 38. See also *Assurpol*, OJ 1992 L37/16, at p. 24, and *Concordato Incendio*, OJ 1990 L15/25, at p. 29.

[187] *UK Agricultural Tractor Registration Exchange*, OJ 1992 L68/19.

[188] The Commission stated in its *Seventh Report on Competition Report*, at point 7(3): '[Such an information exchange arrangement] debars buyers from exploiting whatever "concealed competition" subsists between sellers in oligopolistic markets ...' See also *UK Agricultural Tractor Registration Exchange*, OJ 1992 L68/19, at p. 26; *X/Open group*, OJ 1987 L35/36; *COBELPA/VNP* OJ 1977 L242/10, at p. 15; *Agreements between manufacturers of glass containers* OJ 1974 L166/1, at para. 54.

[189] *X/Open group*, OJ 1987 L35/36. With regard to the benefits to the consumers, see the Commission's analyses under art. 85(3) of information exchange agreements in the insurance sector: *Assurpol* OJ 1992 L37/16 at p. 23; *TEKO* OJ 1989 L13/34, at p. 38; *Concordato Incendio*, OJ 1989 L 15/25, at p. 28; *Nuovo CEGAM* OJ 1984 L99/29, at p. 34, and Commission Regulation 3932/92.

¶822

between the different competitors[190] or by way of inference from aggregate statistical figures for the whole industry.[191] For example, in *Peroxygen products*, the three producers who supplied the French market with these products provided sales and production figures to a statistics collecting body. However, due to the limited number of producers, it was very easy for each of them to deduce the market share of the other two producers. Thus, each of them could check whether the others were upholding the arrangement they had made to share the French market for peroxygen products.[192]

Yet, the Commission does not object to the sharing among competitors of collated industry-wide statistical data which does not allow the identification of an individual business.[193] The Commission neither objects to the dissemination among competitors of 'market information [of individual firms] relating to past transactions [which became] truly historic' because it 'no longer has any real impact on future behaviour.'[194]

Other kinds of information-exchange arrangements which have been examined by the Commission include the following :

(1) compilation of statistics by trade associations;[195]

---

[190] Information may be exchanged between the undertakings themselves or through a body acting as an intermediary, such as a trade association.

[191] For cases dealing with the inference of figures of industrial firms from aggregate figures, see *Seventh Report on Competition Policy*, point 7(1); *UK Agricultural Tractor Registration Exchange*, OJ 1992 L 68/19 (as discussed at ¶823 below); *Peroxygen products*, OJ 1985 L 35/1, at p. 9.

[192] *Peroxygen products*, OJ 1985 L35/1, at pp. 9–10.

[193] See e.g. *European Wastepaper Information Service, Eighteenth Report on Competition Policy*, point 63.

[194] *UK Agricultural Tractor Registration Exchange*, OJ 1992 L68/19, at p. 29. (one-year-old sales are regarded as truly historic). See also *Fatty Acids*, OJ 1987 L3/17, at p. 22 and *Flat-glass sector in the Benelux*, OJ 1984 L212/13, at p. 20 (a quarterly exchange of sensitive information was regarded as a violation of art. 85(1)).

[195] Commission notice on agreements, decisions and concerted practices in the field of co-operation between the undertakings, JO 1968 C75/3, corrigendum JO 1968 C84/14, at para. II(1). The Commission stated that agreements limited to an exchange of opinion or experience (see *Department Stores, Ninth Report on Competition Policy*, point 89), joint market research, joint comparative studies of enterprises or industries, and joint preparations of statistics and calculation models generally fall outside the scope of art. 85(1). However, in case these agreements include recommendations or if the calculation models contain specified rates of calculation (see *IFTRA rules for manufacturers of virgin aluminum*, OJ 1975 L228/3), there may be a restraint of competition.

A distinction should also be made between agreements on statistical information which contain only aggregate industry-wide figures and those which reveal the identity of individual firms. See *UK Agricultural Tractor Registration Exchange*, OJ 1992 L68/19, at p. 32, as discussed above in ¶823; *European Wastepaper Information Service, Eighteenth Report on Competition Policy*, point 63 (negative clearance for an exchange among competitors of aggregate and average figures on stocks, consumption and prices); *X Open Group*, OJ 1987 L35/36; *Peroxygen products* OJ 1985 L35/1 (information exchange agreement in support of a market-sharing agreement); *Vegetable parchment*, OJ 1978 L70/54, at p. 62 (to provide the trade association with individualised invoices is an indication of a concerted practice, because totals of invoices suffice for the calculation of aggregate figures); *COBELPA/VNP*, OJ 1977 L242/10, at p. 15; *Seventh Report on Competition Policy*, point 7.

The Commission has, on several occasions, exempted agreements under art. 85(3) in the insurance sector which involve, among other things, the exchange of information on claims experience and the joint calculation of premiums. See Commission Regulation 3932/92 on the application of art. 85(3) of the treaty to certain categories of agreements, decisions and concerted practices in the insurance sector, OJ 1992 L398/7, art. 1(a) and art. 2. This block exemption covers exchange of statistical information, common calculation of tables, figures and basic premium rates. The information should serve a purely referential or illustrative purpose and the undertakings should not be bound by these premiums or tables. See *Assurpol*, OJ 1992 L37/16; *TEKO*, OJ 1989 L13/34; *Concordato Incendio*, OJ 1989 L15/25; *Nuovo CEGAM*, OJ 1984 L99/29. These cases concern, among other

¶822

(2) information-exchange on output and sales figures;[196]

(3) information-exchange on prices, costs and general business terms;[197]

(4) exchange of information related to distributors;[198]

---

things, calculation of net premium rates except for *TEKO*, where the Commission stated that, due to the limited number of contracts and the diversity of risks, there was insufficient statistical information for the calculation of net premiums and only the calculation of gross premiums was possible.

[196] *UK Agricultural Tractor Registration Exchange*, OJ 1992 L68/19, as discussed above at ¶823; *Welded Steel Mesh*, OJ 1989 L260/1; *LdPE*, OJ 1989 L74/21; *PVC* 1989 L74/1, on appeal: *PVC Case* cited at footnote 10; *Flat glass*, OJ 1989 L33/44, on appeal: *Società Italiana Vetro (SIV) SpA & Ors v EC Commission* [1992] ECR II-1403; [1992] 2 CEC 33 (in these three cases, *LdPE*, *PVC* and *Flat glass*, sales figures were exchanged in support of market-sharing and price-fixing arrangements); *Fatty Acids* OJ 1987 L3/17, at p. 22 (exchange of global sales volumes from which the parties' market shares could be deduced); *Polypropylene*, OJ (1986) L230/1, on appeal: *Polypropylene Cases* cited at footnote 10 (exchange of information on sales and prices which served as proof of a concerted practice); *Peroxygen products*, OJ 1985 L35/1 (exchange of information on production and sales figures); *Zinc producer group*, OJ 1984, L220/27, at p. 38 (exchange of information on investment and production cuts: objectionable if approval is needed or recommendations are made); *Flat-glass sector in the Benelux*, OJ 1984 L212/13, at p. 19 (quarterly exchange of sales figures in support of a market-sharing agreement); *SSI*, OJ 1982 L232/1, at p. 22, on appeal: *Stichting Sigarettenindustrie & Ors v EC Commission* [1985] ECR 3831 (inference of market share of other producers from sales data provided by the retailers to a producers' committee in order for these retailers to receive a bonus); *Italian cast glass* OJ 1980 L383/19, at para. 99(g) (information exchange on sales and prices of each type of products); *BP Kemi/DDSF*, OJ 1979 L286/32, at para. 78 (information exchange on sales made to each customer); *White Lead*, OJ 1979 L21/16, at para. 25–26 (information exchange on export figures); *Vegetable parchment*, OJ 1978 L70/54, at pp. 62–63 (information exchange on selling prices and export figures); *COBELPA/VNP*, OJ 1977 L242/10, at p. 15 (information exchange on sales and output figures and on prices); *S.C.P.A.-Kali und Salz*, OJ 1973 L217/3 (exchange of information on stocks, current production, production forecast, orders received and forecast trends in demand); *Cimbel*, OJ 1972 L303/24 (information exchange arrangement on sales figures in support of a market-sharing agreement based on sales quotas); *Ships' cables, Fifth Report on Competition Policy*, point 40 (compilation of delivery schedules by trade associations).

[197] *Irish Club Rules*, OJ 1991 C166/6 and OJ 1993 C263/6 (exchange of information on costs, rates and service agreements). The Commission has clarified its view on the common calculation of basic premium rates i.e. the average cost of risk cover in the insurance sector on several occasions: Commission Regulation 3932/92, OJ 1992 L398/7; *Assurpol*, OJ 1992 L37/16; *TEKO*, OJ 1989 L13/34, *Concordato Incendo*, OJ 1989 L15/25; *Nuovo CEGAM*, OJ 1984 L99/29; *Wood Pulp*, OJ 1985 L5/1, on appeal: *Åhlström & Ors v EC Commission* [1988] ECR 5193 (only on the jurisdictional aspects of the case), [1993] 1 CEC 466 (price announcements and exchange of price information); *Vimpoltu*, OJ 1983 L200/47, at p. 48 (exchange of price lists before new prices come into effect); *Italian Cast glass*, OJ 1980 L383/19; *Vegetable parchment*, OJ 1978 L70/54, at p. 62; *COBELPA/VNP*, OJ 1977 L242/10 (exchange of information on prices and business terms); *IFTRA rules for producers of virgin aluminum*, OJ 1975 L228/3 (information exchange on prices and cost calculation); *Agreement between manufacturers of glass containers* OJ 1974 L160/10, at para. 40–45 ; *VVVF*, JO 1969 L168/22 (negative clearance for an agreement which contains restrictions of competition, such as the communication of prices, which only have an effect on markets outside the EC); Commission notice on agreements, decisions and concerted practices in the field of co-operation between undertakings, JO 1968 C75/3, corrigendum JO 1968 C84/4 (joint calculation models; *European Paper Machine Wire manufacturers, Sixth Report on Competition Policy*, point 134 (exchange of prices, terms of delivery and payment and invoices); *Dutch Sporting Cartridges Agreement, Third Report on Competition Policy*, point 55 (an agreement among producers of sporting cartridges containing a reciprocal prior notification of price changes).

[198] *UK Agricultural Registration Exchange*, OJ 1992 L68/19, at pp. 30–31 (data on dealer sales of own company provided by a trade association of producers is not objectionable as long as it does not reveal the sales figures of competitors and does not interfere with parallel imports; see also discussion in ¶823); *Hasselblad*, OJ 1982 L161/18, at p. 27 (exchange of information between a producer and its sole distributors is objectionable under art. 85(1) if it is designed to prevent parallel imports); *SABA*, OJ 1976 L28/9, at p. 26 (obligation of sole distributor to provide the producer with information on its sales is not a restriction of competition as long as it is not used by the producers to interfere with the distributors' export and pricing policies).

¶822

(5) information-exchange on consumers enquiries;[199] and

(6) other sensitive information.[200]

It is also worth noting that the Commission, when exempting an exchange of sensitive information, will see to it that the information will not be used for other purposes than those for which the Commission has granted an exemption.[201]

¶823   An example: UK Tractor[202]

The Commission's decision in *UK Tractor* is worth examining in some detail because it provides a good example of the Commission's approach in this area.

The case concerned an information exchange organised under the umbrella of a trade association. The participants in the exchange were all of the major suppliers of tractors in the UK. Together they held some 87 per cent to 88 per cent of the UK tractor market. The remaining 12 per cent of the market was shared by several smaller manufacturers who were not members of the exchange.

The information exchanged between the participants was mainly taken from the official forms used for the registration of tractors with the UK Department of Transport. The Department of Transport had agreed to make the registration documents available to the trade association for industry analysis. With the assistance of a computer bureau, the trade association made the information on the registration forms available to its members by way of reports and analyses and also in the form of direct computer access. In its review of the exchange, the Commission made a distinction between three types of information that were thus made available: aggregate industry data, data identifying sales of individual competitors and data on sales made by a participant's own dealers.

The Commission did not object to aggregate industry data being made available to the members of the exchange. It did not matter that the data were

---

[199] *Building and construction industry in the Netherlands*, OJ 1992 L92/1 (information exchange between competitors in a bidding procedure); *Cast iron and steel rolls*, OJ 1983 L317/1, at pp. 11–13 (an exchange of customer enquiries in support of a price-fixing and market-sharing agreement).

[200] *International Energy Agency*, OJ 1983 L376/30 (exchange of information on origin of oil, quality, tanker and refinery capacity, storage capacity and other sensitive information as part of an emergency plan organised by the OECD in case of a shortage of oil supply in the European Countries; the Commission reaffirmed its position in this case in its decision *International Energy Agency*, OJ 1994 L68/35 and extended the exemption until 2003; *Non-ferrous semi-manufacturers*, *Fifth Report on Competition Policy*, point 39 (exchange of information on R & D, production, sales promotion, raw material supplies, commercial management, data processing and general business strategy); *Belgian agreement on industrial timber*, *Fifth Report on Competition Policy*, points 36–37 (exchange of information needed for the preparation of buying programmes).

[201] E.g. *Ford/Volkswagen*, OJ 1993 L20/14. The Commission granted an exemption under art. 85(3) for a joint venture between Ford and VW for the development and manufacturing of a new multi-purpose vehicle on the condition that 'all competitively sensitive non-public, information ... does not reach employees of the other company [and that] employees who have to know shall sign a confidentiality agreement.' Id. at art. 2(2).

[202] *UK Agricultural Tractor Registration Exchange*, OJ 1992 L68/19.

broken down by horsepower groupings, drive line or different geographic areas (e.g. the UK, counties, dealer territories, postcode sectors) and that they were made available for yearly, quarterly, monthly and weekly time periods. The sole concern raised by the Commission with regard to aggregate industry data was that they should not identify the retail sales of the individual members of the exchange. Therefore, the Commission objected to the exchange of aggregate industry data to the extent that the reports would contain less than ten tractor units for any specific breakdown by territory, product or time period. In the Commission's opinion, there would be a high risk that even aggregate data would allow, directly or indirectly, the identification of exact sales volumes of individual competitors in cases where less than ten units would have been recorded.

Through the exchange, the members also obtained data identifying sales of individual competitors. The data thus exchanged included the volume of retail sales and the market shares of each member of the exchange for a number of geographic areas (i.e. national, regional, county, dealer territory, postcode sector); the volume of retail sales and the market shares both of every specific model and for a number of horsepower groupings; and the daily and monthly retail sales and market shares in the UK. The Commission concluded that by means of this exchange of information the members were able to follow the sales performance and market penetration of each competitor on a yearly, quarterly, monthly and daily basis in respect of all relevant products, even within the smallest geographic areas.

In its assessment of the part of the exchange dealing with data identifying the sales of individual participants, the Commission attached particular importance to the following factors :

- the market structure (i.e. the level of concentration, the existence of high barriers to entry and the level of competition coming from outside the Community);
- the nature of the information (in this case: exact quantities of retail sales and exact market share figures);
- the detail of the information exchanged (i.e. specificity of product and geographic breakdowns and relevant time frames); and
- organisational aspects (in this case: the fact that members met regularly which gave them a forum for contacts).

On the basis of these factors, the Commission arrived at the conclusion that the exchange of information on individual competitors amounted to a restriction of competition. The main arguments in support of that conclusion were that this part of the exchange (1) created a degree of market transparency between the suppliers in a highly concentrated market which was likely to destroy any

¶823

remaining hidden competition and (2) increased barriers to entry for non-members.

The Commission's appraisal of this part of the exchange should not be taken to suggest that any exchange of detailed information between competitors necessarily constitutes a problem under art. 85 of the treaty. In the *UK Tractor* case the Commission suggests at least two instances where such an exchange could receive more favourable treatment, namely in cases where:

- the market concerned is competitive and presents a low degree of concentration and the transparency resulting from the exchange of information is directed towards or of benefit to consumers; or[203]

- truly historic data is exchanged which no longer has any real impact on future behaviour.[204]

In addition to aggregate industry data and data on competitors, the exchange also revealed to each individual manufacturer detailed information about the retail sales of its own dealers. The Commission analysed both the horizontal and the vertical implications of this part of the exchange.

With regard to the horizontal impact, the Commission's concerns were identical to those expressed in relation to the other types of information described above. Indeed, the Commission objects to such own-company information being made available if it would facilitate, in combination with industry-wide information, identification of the exact sales made by individual competitors or dealers of competitors. This risk was said to exist in the case of the tractor market where the number of total industry sales for any given breakdown was less than ten units.

The possible vertical impact of this part of the exchange is best understood in the context of the Commission's policy concerning parallel trade and market integration. The potential anti-competitive effects were described by the Commission as follows :

'The dealer import and dealer export analyses show for each dealer territory the exact number of sales made to customers within that territory both by the local dealer and by other dealers of the same network. These analyses further show in which dealer territories outside his own a dealer makes sales. The Exchange thus reveals the exact destination of each specific tractor and reveals the export activities of each dealer into the territories of other dealers in the United Kingdom. This monitoring of dealers' sales outside their allocated territory allows manufacturers to exercise pressure on dealers

---

[203] Id., at p. 26, para. 37.
[204] On that basis, the Commission accepted an annual exchange of one-year old sales figures of individual competitors at the UK, MAFF region and land use level and with a breakdown by model. *UK Agricultural Tractor Registration Exchange*, OJ 1992 L68/19 at p. 29, para. 50.

¶823

engaging in any perceived excessive export activity. It is the very nature of such reports to give rise to misuse which in most cases cannot be controlled a posteriori (a manufacturer could, for instance, reduce supplies to a dealer who sells too many tractors in other dealers' territories). The import/export analyses are thus highly likely to reduce intrabrand competition with the result that dealers can maintain higher profit margins for both themselves and the manufacturers.'[205]

If this strong statement is taken to reflect the Commission's current thinking on the issue, the significance of the *UK Tractor* decision may extend beyond information exchanges organised in a trade association context and may also affect various information systems that are typically set up in a distribution context to monitor the performance of the network.[206]

---

[205] *UK Agricultural Tractor Registration Exchange*, OJ 1992 L68/19 at p. 30, para. 55.
[206] See also *Ford Agricultural*, OJ 1993 L20/1, in which the Commission relied, inter alia, on the use made by Ford of (the own-company) information obtained through the Tractor exchange to condemn Ford for interference with parallel trade.

9 Abuse of dominant position

¶901 Introduction: the concept of 'abuse'

Article 86 of the treaty prohibits 'any abuse by one or more undertakings in a dominant position within the Common Market or in a substantial part of it ... in so far as it may affect trade between Member States'. The concept of dominant position, as well as the required effect on trade has been dealt with in Chapter 2 (¶234–¶252). The present chapter examines the concept of 'abuse'.

Exploitative abuses and anti-competitive abuses

Article 86 does not define what may constitute an 'abuse', but it lists examples of abusive conduct: unfair prices and unfair trading conditions generally; restriction of production, markets or technical developments; discrimination and tying.[1] These examples refer to cases where dominant market power is directly exploited to the detriment of suppliers or customers. The nature of the examples of abuse listed in art. 86 had led many early commentators on art. 86[2] to conclude that art. 86 was not concerned with monopolisation practices but rather with direct exploitation of market power (what has sometimes been referred to as 'exploitative abuses'). This interpretation, however, was challenged by the Commission. Eager to expand its jurisdiction, the Commission took the view that art. 86 could also reach practices of dominant undertakings that result in a lessening of competition such as mergers and acquisitions or predatory price-cutting (sometimes referred to as 'anti-

---

[1] The abuses listed in art. 86 are:

(1) directly or indirectly imposing unfair purchase or selling prices or other unfair trading conditions;
(2) limiting production, markets or technical development to the prejudice of consumers;
(3) applying dissimilar conditions to equivalent transactions with other trading parties, thereby placing them at a competitive disadvantage; and
(4) making the conclusion of contracts subject to acceptance by the other parties of supplementary obligations which, by their nature or according to commercial usage, have no connection with the subject of such contracts.

The court has declared that this list is not an exhaustive enumeration of possible infringements, but is only illustrative. See, e.g. *Europemballage Corp and Continental Can Co Inc v EC Commission* [1973] ECR 215, at p. 245 (para. 26).
[2] See e.g. Joliet, *Monopolization and Abuse of Dominant Position: A Comparative Study of American Approaches to the Control of Economic Power*, The Hague, Martinus Nijhoff, 1967.

competitive abuses').[3] On this issue, as on many other jurisdictional issues, the Commission's expansive interpretation was backed by the court. In the 1973 *Continental Can* judgment the court said that art. 86 'is not only aimed at practices which may cause damage to consumers directly, but also at those which are detrimental to them through their impact on an effective competitive structure, such as is mentioned in Article 3(f) of the Treaty'.[4] The court upheld the Commission's view that mergers and acquisitions may constitute an abuse if they substantially restrict competition.[5] Ironically, the definition of the concept of abuse which is currently most often cited – the *Hoffmann-La Roche* decision in which the court said that the concept of abuse in art. 86 relates to

'the behaviour of an undertaking in a dominant position which is such as to influence the structure of a market where, as a result of the very presence of the undertaking in question, the degree of competition is weakened and which, through recourse to methods different from those which condition normal competition in products or services on the basis of the transactions of commercial operators has the effect of hindering the maintenance of the degree of competition still existing in the market or the growth of that competition.'[6]

– almost completely overlooks the fact that exploitative abuses, which historically were the main subject of art. 86, are also covered by art. 86.

Abusive behaviour by dominant undertakings

Another aspect of the concept of abuse in art. 86 also deserves to be highlighted. Despite the inferences that could be drawn from the text of art. 86,

---

[3] For example, in 1966, the Commission issued a study entitled, *Le Problème de la Concentration dans le Marché Commun*, Etudes CEE, Série Concurrence, No. 3, in which it mentioned as abusive conduct prohibited under art. 86 a 'merger of an undertaking occupying a dominant position and another undertaking which has the effect of eliminating competition that would otherwise continue to exist on the market and of creating a monopolistic position' and 'price competition that is engaged in for the purpose of ousting from the market a competitor who does not have sufficient financial sources to withstand for a longer period sales below cost' (at p. 26).

[4] *Europemballage Corp and Continental Can Co Inc v EC Commission* [1973] ECR 215, at p. 245 (para. 26).

[5] The *Tetra Pak I (BTG licence)* decision (OJ 1988 L272/27, at p. 43 (para. 60)) constitutes a recent application of this principle:

'The Commission considers that, at the time of the acquisition of the Liquipak group and the assignment of the licence to it, Tetra occupied a dominant position in the EEC market for the production of machines incorporating technology for sterilizing cartons, used for filling under aseptic conditions board cartons with UHT-treated liquids, including in particular milk. Tetra abused its dominant position by the acquisition of this exclusive licence which had the effect of strengthening its already dominant position, further weakening existing competition and rendering even more difficult the entry of any new competition'.

[6] *Hoffmann-La Roche v EC Commission* ('*Vitamins*') [1979] ECR 461 at p. 541 (para. 91).

it is established case law that there need not be a causal relationship between the market power resulting from the existence of a dominant position and the abuse. In other words, the dominant position does not have to be the means by which the abuse is committed. In practice, this means that a finding of abuse cannot be negated by providing evidence that the course of conduct in question has also been adopted by non-dominant undertakings, or is a normal practice in the market concerned.[7] This indicates that art. 86 imposes a special responsibility on undertakings found to hold a dominant position. Their scope of action is limited by the existence of a special set of rules that do not apply to non-dominant undertakings.

Abusive practices

Since the abuse prohibited by art. 86 may take many forms, this chapter analyses the types of abuse which have been dealt with thus far in the case law except mergers and acquisitions which are discussed in Chapter 6. Depending upon the circumstances, practices other than those discussed here might also constitute an abuse. The practices reviewed in this chapter include:

(1) pricing practices (¶902–¶906);

(2) refusals to supply (¶907–¶911);

(3) discrimination (¶912 and ¶913);

(4) unfair terms and conditions (¶914);

(5) miscellaneous abuses:

- exclusive dealing obligations (¶915);

- abusive registration of trade marks (¶916);

- restrictions on resales (¶917);

- tying (¶918);

- abusive licensing practices (¶919);

- market-sharing agreements (¶920);

- abusive conduct by undertakings holding a collective dominant position (¶921);

- abusive conduct on the part of a dominant purchaser (¶922).

---

[7] *Europemballage Corp and Continental Can Co Inc v EC Commission* [1973] ECR 215, at p. 245 (para. 27).

¶901

PRICING PRACTICES

¶902   Abusive behaviour

A number of cases under art. 86 have dealt with pricing practices. It follows from these cases that a dominant undertaking may commit an abuse of dominant position by:

- charging excessive prices (see ¶903);
- engaging in geographical price discrimination (see ¶904);
- offering certain types of discounts or rebates to its customers (see ¶905);
- charging unduly low 'predatory' prices (see ¶906).

¶903   Excessive prices

Article 86 expressly provides that an abuse may consist in directly or indirectly imposing 'unfair selling prices'. The cases of alleged excessive prices dealt with thus far by the Commission fall into two distinct categories:

(1) excessive prices as a form of alleged exploitation of market power; and

(2) excessive prices as a means of discouraging parallel imports.

Excessive prices as a form of exploitation of market power

Article 86 is clearly based on the assumption that, unless some form of control is established, dominant undertakings will take advantage of their market power to charge excessive prices. The first example of abuse listed in art. 86 consists of 'directly or indirectly imposing unfair purchase or selling prices or other unfair trading conditions'. One of the remarkable features of the enforcement practice of the EC competition authorities is the small number of cases in which allegations of unfair pricing have been made. As a matter of fact, there has been only one case in which the Commission found that a dominant undertaking had exploited its customers through the charging of excessive prices (as distinguished from situations in which the excessive prices are only a means of discouraging parallel imports) – the 1975 *Chiquita* decision[8] – but this finding of abuse was overruled by the court on appeal.

Chiquita bananas: the Commission's decision

In *Chiquita*, the Commission held that, apart from engaging in geographic market discrimination, United Brands had also violated art. 86 by charging excessive prices for its branded Chiquita bananas in Belgium, the Netherlands,

---

[8] *Chiquita*, OJ 1976 L95/1; on appeal: *United Brands v EC Commission* [1978] ECR 207. See also, *British Airways, Tenth Report on Competition Policy*, points 136–138.

¶902

Luxembourg, Denmark and Germany. This finding essentially rested on three factors.

(1) First, the Commission relied on a comparison between the prices charged by United Brands in Ireland, on the one hand, and the generally higher prices (sometimes by as much as 100 per cent according to the Commission) charged in Belgium, the Netherlands, Luxembourg, Denmark and Germany. According to the Commission, this comparison showed that the prices charged by United Brands in the latter countries had produced a 'very substantial profit'.

(2) Secondly, the Commission relied on a comparison between the prices charged by United Brands for its branded Chiquita bananas and those charged for second grade unbranded bananas. The Commission alleged that the price differential between the two grades of bananas – on average 30 to 40 per cent – was not justified by corresponding cost and quality differences.

(3) Finally, the Commission also compared the prices charged by United Brands for Chiquita bananas and those charged by competing (non-dominant) suppliers for their own brands. The Commission noted that the prices of competing brands were generally lower than those of Chiquita bananas.

The Commission concluded:

'UBC's prices are excessive in relation to the economic value of the product supplied. This is confirmed by the substantial difference of 30 to 40 per cent between the prices of unbranded bananas sold by UBC and those sold under the Chiquita brand, although the quality of unbranded bananas is only slightly lower than that of Chiquita bananas. At the very most, half of this difference in price cannot be accounted for by differences in quality or the costs of advertising campaigns. Furthermore, UBC's prices for its customers in all the Member States involved, except those in Ireland, are currently higher than the prices of competing brands of bananas which are of a quality comparable with Chiquita bananas. UBC's principal competitors still operate at a profit notwithstanding their lower prices, and are indeed constantly seeking to enlarge their sales. In these circumstances, for the purposes of this Decision, it would be sufficient if UBC were to reduce its price levels to prices at least 15 per cent below those currently charged to its customers in Denmark and Germany (other than to the Scipio Group). In conclusion, the prices which are currently charged to customers in the BLEU, Denmark, Germany (other than to the Scipio Group) and the

¶903

Netherlands are unfair and therefore constitute an abuse by UBC of its dominant position.'[9]

As United Brands pointed out in its appeal to the court, the Commission's suggestion that United Brands should reduce its prices by 15 per cent made little sense. Prices for bananas, a highly perishable agricultural commodity, are subject to wide fluctuations over short periods of time; United Brands charged weekly prices which could vary substantially from one week to another. In such a volatile context, it was hard to visualise how United Brands could implement the Commission's injunction to reduce its prices – which prices? As a matter of fact, in its defence to United Brands' application for suspension of the decision, the Commission disclaimed any intention of requiring United Brands to reduce its prices or to charge any given level of prices.[10]

Chiquita bananas: the Court's ruling
The finding of abuse was finally annulled by the court. The court ruled that there was no support for the allegation that United Brands had made a 'very substantial profit' since the prices charged by United Brands in Ireland (from which the Commission had inferred that the higher prices charged in the other member states were unduly profitable) had produced losses. All the court said on the issue of excessive prices was that 'charging a price which is excessive because it has no reasonable relation to the economic value of the product supplied is ... an abuse'.[11] The court did not elaborate much further on this point, limiting itself to the statement that '[t]his excess could, inter alia, be determined objectively if it were possible for it to be calculated by making a comparison between the selling price of the product in question and its cost of production'.[12] No indication was given as to what might constitute an 'excessive' profit margin.

Restrictions on the application of art. 86 to excessive prices
United Brands was the Commission's first venture into the area of price control in the context of art. 86. It may also be the last in view of the inconclusive results

---

[9] *Chiquita*, OJ 1976 L95/1, at pp. 15–16.
[10] *United Brands v EC Commission* (Order of the President of the Second Chamber of the Court) [1976] ECR 425.
[11] *United Brands v EC Commission* [1978] ECR 207, at p. 301 (para. 250).
[12] Id., at p. 301 (para. 251). See also *Sterling Airways*, *Tenth Report on Competition Policy*, points 136–138, where a Danish private airline filed several complaints with the Commission against SAS and the Danish Government, alleging inter alia that the Danish Government, by approving SAS' tariffs for certain flight routes, had allowed SAS to charge excessively high prices. For example, Sterling Airways alleged that it could profitably fly the London–Copenhagen route for DKr 600, while SAS charged DKr 2,560. Yet, the Commission preferred to compare costs and revenues of SAS instead of making a comparison between the prices charged by the different airline companies because the services offered by the companies might not be equivalent and because the cost structure of the companies might be different,

of that case. In its *Fifth Report on Competition Policy*, the Commission recognised the difficulty of determining whether or not a given price is 'fair':

'[M]easures to halt the abuse of dominant positions cannot be converted into systematic monitoring of prices. In proceedings against abuse consisting of charging excessively high prices, it is difficult to tell whether in any given case an abusive price has been set for there is no objective way of establishing exactly what price covers costs plus a reasonable profit margin'.[13]

The *Chiquita* decision reflects a concern about excessive prices that would seem no longer to have the relevance that it did when the decision was issued in 1975. In trying to apply art. 86 to excessive prices in *Chiquita*, the Commission was following the lead of UK and German antitrust authorities which had similarly sought in the early 1970s to deal with instances of perceived excessive prices under their domestic legislation. This concern about excessive prices seems to have largely receded. In addition, the cases have shown the difficulty of defining what constitutes a 'fair' price.[14] Instances in which the prohibition of art. 86 will be applied to excessive prices will therefore probably remain exceptional.

Excessive prices as a means of discouraging parallel imports
Apart from the *Chiquita* case, the Commission has applied art. 86 in cases where the excessive prices charged by the dominant undertaking were not motivated by the intention of exploiting customers but rather were a means of discouraging parallel exports.

A typical example is *General Motors Continental*.[15] The Commission ruled in that case that General Motors had infringed art. 86 in charging excessive prices for the issue of certificates of conformity (over which it had a legal monopoly) for new imported cars in Belgium. The price for this formality had been raised from BFr 2,500 to BFr 5,000 while the price charged by other firms for the same service was generally BFr 2,500. A fine of ECU 100,000 was imposed by the Commission. On appeal, the court upheld the validity of the Commission's approach but nevertheless annulled the decision on the ground that General

---

[13] *Fifth Report on Competition Policy*, point 3. In *Bodson v SA Pompes Funèbres* [1988] ECR 2479; [1990] 1 CEC 3, the court held that in order to establish whether or not undertakings, holding concessions for funeral services granted by the local authorities, were charging unfair prices, a comparison could be made between the prices charged by the group of undertakings which held concessions and the prices charged by other undertakings, particularly the prices charged by suppliers in municipalities where the services had been liberalised. This comparison would not be decisive in itself, but would provide a basis for assessing if the prices were unfair.

[14] Substantial differences between the prices or tariffs practised in the various member states may constitute an indication of an abuse of a dominant position (*Ministère public v Tournier* [1989] ECR 2521, para. 34ff.; *Lucazeau v Sociétés des auteurs, compositeurs et éditeurs de musique (SACEM)* [1989] ECR 2811, para. 21ff.).

[15] *General Motors Continental*, OJ 1975 L29/14; on appeal: *General Motors v EC Commission* [1975] ECR 1367. See also, *BL*, OJ 1984 L207/11, on appeal: *BL plc v EC Commission* [1986] ECR 3263.

Motors had voluntarily reduced its price for the service concerned and reimbursed the excess amount as soon as it realised the excessive character of its price.

In this case, what General Motors was allegedly seeking to achieve was not to obtain abnormal profits for its legal monopoly over the issue of certificates of conformity for cars imported through parallel channels. The conduct challenged by the Commission was allegedly motivated by the desire to discourage parallel imports of Opel cars into Belgium, a market over which General Motors clearly holds no dominant position. This case shows that EC competition authorities do not shy away from using narrow market definitions (in this case the carrying out of a compulsory administrative formality ancillary to the sale of a product)[16] in order to find a dominant position and so apply art. 86 to an undertaking that clearly holds no dominant position on the market in which it sells its products.

¶904   Geographical price discrimination

The charging of discriminatory prices by a dominant undertaking may constitute an abuse of a dominant position within the sense of art. 86. Article 86(c) provides that an abuse may consist in 'applying dissimilar conditions to equivalent transactions with other trading parties, thereby placing them at a competitive disadvantage'.

As illustrated by the *Chiquita* decision,[17] geographical price discrimination along national lines may constitute an abuse of a dominant position under certain circumstances. The facts of the case are as follows. United Brands had traditionally sold its bananas to ripeners–distributors in Europe at different prices according to the member state where the ripener–distributor was established. The Commission found this practice to be an abuse of a dominant position falling under art. 86(c). In its decision the Commission stressed that the bananas in question were all freighted on the same ships, were unloaded at the same cost in Rotterdam and Bremerhaven and were sold under the same conditions of sale and terms of payment. United Brands argued in its defence that its prices were not discriminatory since they only reflected differences in the anticipated resale price of the bananas among the various member states due to factors beyond United Brands' control such as the weather, the different availability of competing seasonal fruit, holidays, strikes, etc. The Commission and the court, however, refused to take into account differences in market conditions at the ripener-distributor's level as an 'objective justification' for price differences at the supplier's level. The Commission and the court took the view that the price differences fell under art. 86(c) because they put at a

---

[16] See also *Volvo Italy, Seventeenth Report on Competition Policy*, point 82.
[17] *Chiquita*, OJ 1976 L95/1.

competitive disadvantage those of United Brands' customers who wished to resell the bananas in a member state other than that in which they were established.

The refusal of EC competition authorities to accept differences in market conditions at the ripener/distributor's level as an objective justification for price differences at the supplier's level is typical of the bias against any form of contractual integration between suppliers and distributors which characterises most of the EC law on distribution arrangements.[18] The case, however, should not be read as meaning that dominant undertakings are in all cases subject to an obligation to charge uniform prices for their products throughout the EC. One of the essential features of the *Chiquita* case was that, as the Commission stressed in its decision, the product was sold at the same place at different prices depending upon the location of the buyer.[19] In addition, it is important to bear in mind that the Commission and the court had also accused United Brands of seeking to prevent arbitrage among the ripeners/distributors by imposing upon them a prohibition on the resale of green bananas; what the court referred to as a 'rigid partitioning of national markets'. In the absence of those rather exceptional circumstances, different prices charged in different member states should not as such be treated as an abuse of a dominant position under art. 86.

¶905   Rebates

Another form of price discrimination that may constitute an abuse under art. 86 is the grant of certain types of rebates. The cases have thus far dealt with the following types of rebate:

- loyalty rebates,
- target rebates, and
- top-slice rebates.

Loyalty rebates

The first type of rebate that was found to be abusive is the so-called 'loyalty' or 'fidelity' rebate. In *Suiker Unie*,[20] the court affirmed the Commission's finding that the practice by SZV – a group of sugar producers located in the southern

---

[18] See Chapter 3.

[19] In *Chiquita*, OJ 1976 L95/1, at p. 15, the Commission noted:

'UBC's bananas are practically all sold at the same place, the ports of Bremerhaven and Rotterdam, and at the same time, the time of arrival in the EEC. Differences in transport costs, taxes and duties or marketing conditions might justify different levels in price on resale at the retail level. These differences can, however, never justify objectively UBC's different prices to its distributor/ripeners for equivalent transactions at Bremerhaven and Rotterdam, and still less so given that the quantities of bananas sold to each such distributor/ripener are approximately the same.'

[20] *Suiker Unie & Ors v EC Commission* [1975] ECR 1663.

part of Germany – to grant a rebate of DM 0.3 per 100 kg, provided the customer met his annual requirements exclusively from members of SZV, constituted an abuse within the meaning of art. 86. Fidelity rebates differ from purely quantitative rebates in that they are not exclusively linked to the volume of purchases from the producer concerned. They reward a purchaser for his loyalty or fidelity. Different purchasers who buy the same quantities are treated differently if one buys all his requirements from the supplier, while the other uses several suppliers to meet his requirements. If they are competitors, the difference in treatment may put the latter at a competitive disadvantage within the meaning of art. 86(c).[21]

At the same time, fidelity rebates are challenged by the Commission because they tend to restrict the access of competing producers to the market.[22] They are designed, through the grant of a financial advantage, to induce customers not to obtain their supplies from competing producers.[23] Where the dominant firm grants fidelity rebates, it may be difficult for smaller competitors to gain some business at the expense of the dominant firm. The rebates that smaller competitors would have to grant to the clients of the dominant undertaking to make it sufficiently attractive for them to forgo the fidelity rebate would be out of proportion to the rebate granted by the dominant undertaking. In *Suiker Unie*, the Commission found that lower prices of up to DM 20 per metric tonne offered by outside suppliers did not outweigh the disadvantage of losing the fidelity rebate of a mere DM 0.3 per 100 kg (i.e., DM 3 per metric tonne).[24]

The above analysis of fidelity rebates was confirmed and substantially elaborated upon in *Hoffmann-La Roche*.[25] In the view of the court:

---

[21] Id., at p. 2004 (para. 522–525). See also *Soda-ash–Solvay*, OJ 1991 L152/21 at p. 36, (on appeal: *SA Solvay et Cie v EC Commission*, Joined cases T-30 to T-32/91, not yet decided), where the rebates and other financial inducements did not reflect possible differences in costs based on the quantities supplied but were designed to secure the whole or the largest possible percentage of the customer's requirements (para. 62 et seq.).

[22] See *Coca Cola Export Corporation, Filiale Italiana*, Commission press release IP(88) 615 of 13 October 1988. In this case the Commission inter alia condemned a system of fidelity rebates applied by an Italian branch of Coca Cola. This system was found by the Commission to prevent or hinder competing producers from entering the Italian colas market. The resulting undertaking offered by Coca Cola Export which excluded, inter alia, the possibility of Coca Cola Export granting its customers fidelity rebates, would, in the words of the Commission, 'have the effect of ensuring that competition in the soft drinks markets of the European Community will be strengthened to the advantage of both competitors of Coca Cola Export and consumers in general. Indeed, competitors of Coca Cola Export will have fuller opportunities of access to commercial outlets selling beverages and may freely develop and launch new products. Consumers will therefore have a choice between a larger range of drinks' (Commission press release IP(90) 7 of 8 January 1990). See also *BPB Industries* [1989] 1 CEC 2,008; OJ 1989 L10/50. In this case the Commission found that BPB Industries, the only producer of plasterboard in Great Britain and Ireland, had abused its dominant position by penalising merchants who intended to import plasterboard into Ireland. Rebates were offered to all merchants willing to purchase exclusively from BPB. The Commission, at p. 68, held that these measures 'not only made it difficult for imported plasterboard to enter and compete in the market, but also put pressure on the merchants to cease importing altogether'.

[23] *Hoffmann-La Roche v EC Commission* (*'Vitamins'*) [1979] ECR 461, at p. 540 (para. 90). See also *BPB Industries plc & Anor v EC Commission* [1993] 1 CEC 713, at para. 119–120 (on appeal: *BPB Industries plc & Anor v EC Commission*, Case C-310/93P, not yet decided).

[24] *Suiker Unie & Ors v EC Commission* [1975] ECR 1663, at pp. 2000–2001 (para. 499–501).

[25] *Hoffmann-La Roche v EC Commission* (*'Vitamins'*) [1979] ECR 461.

'An undertaking which is in a dominant position on a market and ties purchasers – even if it does so at their own request – by an obligation or promise on their part to obtain all or most of their requirements exclusively from the said undertaking abuses its dominant position within the meaning of Article 86 of the Treaty whether the obligation in question is stipulated for without further qualifications or whether it is undertaken in consideration of the grant of a rebate. The same applies if the said undertaking, without tying the purchasers by a formal obligation, applies, either under the terms of agreements concluded with these purchasers or unilaterally, a system of fidelity rebates, that is to say discounts conditional on the customer's obtaining all or most of its requirements – whether the quantity of its purchases be large or small – from the undertaking in a dominant position.'[26]

In that case, it was made clear that discounts (even if granted at the request of the customer) that are conditional on the customer's obtaining most of his requirements, or a high percentage of his requirements, should also be considered as fidelity rebates. As the concept of abuse is an objective one,[27] the conduct of an undertaking in a dominant position may be regarded as abusive within the meaning of art. 86 even in the absence of any fault. An undertaking in a dominant position has a special responsibility not to allow its conduct to impair genuine undistorted competition in the common market.[28]

English clauses
It was further made clear in *Hoffmann-La Roche* that the inclusion in the agreement of a so-called 'English clause' or 'competition clause' did not adequately remedy the anti-competitive effects of a fidelity rebate. An English clause allows the purchaser to obtain his supplies from another producer, without losing the benefit of the fidelity rebate, when that producer offers more favourable terms which the main supplier does not want to meet. The court said that the English clause was a remedy for some, though not all, of the negative consequences of the practice of fidelity rebates. It further stressed that an English clause, owing to its very nature, provided Hoffmann-La Roche with

---

[26] Id., at p. 539 (para. 89). See also *BPB Industries plc & Anor v EC Commission* [1993] 1 CEC 713, at para. 68, (on appeal: *BPB Industries plc & Anor v EC Commission*, Case C-310/93P, not yet decided), where the court held that where an economic operator holds a strong position in the market, the conclusion of exclusive supply contracts in respect of a substantial proportion of purchases constitutes an unacceptable obstacle to entry to that market. The fact that the promotional payments made in that case represented a response to requests and to the growing buying power of the merchants did not justify the inclusion in the supply contracts of an exclusivity clause.

Some guidance as to the types of schemes that the Commission is likely to accept may be found in the three art. 19(3) notices published concerning British Gypsum's revised rebate schemes, see OJ 1992 C321/9–12.

[27] *Hoffmann-La Roche v EC Commission* ('*Vitamins*') [1979] ECR 461, at p. 541 (para. 91); *BPB Industries & Anor v EC Commission* [1993] 1 CEC 713, at para. 70, (on appeal: *BPB Industries plc & Anor v EC Commission*, Case C-310/93P, not yet decided).

[28] *Michelin v EC Commission* [1983] ECR 3461 at p. 3511 (para. 57).

competitive information which might be of great value to it. That was considered an aggravation of the abuse committed by Hoffmann-La Roche.[29]

In *Solvay*,[30] the Commission viewed the different types of competition clauses as strengthening the tie between Solvay and the customer and exclusionary in both object and effect. They allowed Solvay to be fully informed of the details of competitors' activity while effectively excluding the possibility of a competitor actually obtaining any business. In the words of the Commission:

> '[c]ompetition clauses which give the dominant supplier the option of terminating the whole agreement if the customer obtains even a small part of its supplies from a competitor are already a deterrent to competition: the customer is extremely unlikely to jeopardize its security of supply in such circumstances'.[31]

Group fidelity

In *Napier Brown/British Sugar*[32] the Commission found that a special system of fidelity rebates infringed art. 86. British Sugar offered to grant a rebate to the members of a group of purchasers if all the members of the group were willing to purchase exclusively from British Sugar in the future. In this way pressure was put on those members of the group who were not purchasing from British Sugar to resume doing so because they would then benefit from the bonus. Furthermore, if they purchased from another supplier, the remaining members of the group would not benefit from the bonus.

Target rebates

Michelin[33] discusses another kind of rebate – the so-called 'target rebates'. These are rebates which are conditional upon the attainment of sales targets. In *Michelin*, the targets were fixed in common agreement by the distributor and Michelin at the beginning of each year. They reflected the number of tyres which the distributor was likely to sell during the following year, based on the previous year's sales. If the distributor reached, or exceeded that target, he was entitled to a 0.2 per cent to 0.4 per cent discount.[34] Target rebates differ from fidelity rebates in that they are not based on an explicit or implicit undertaking by the purchaser to obtain all or most of his supplies from the supplier. On the

---

[29] *Hoffmann-La Roche v EC Commission* [1979] ECR 461, at pp. 545–546 (para. 107). See also *ECS/AKZO*, OJ 1985 L374/1, at p. 22.

[30] *Soda-ash–Solvay*, OJ 1991 L152/21, (on appeal: *SA Solvay et Cie v EC Commission*, Joined cases T-30 to T-32/91, not yet decided).

[31] Id., at p. 35.

[32] *Napier Brown/British Sugar*, OJ 1988 L284/41.

[33] *Michelin*, OJ 1981 L353/33; on appeal: *Michelin v EC Commission* [1983] ECR 3461.

[34] See *Michelin*, OJ 1981 L353/33, at pp. 37–39.

¶905

other hand, target rebates can be distinguished from quantity rebates because the targets are individually set for each producer, whereas in a purely quantitative system the rebates depend only on the quantity of the purchases made by the buyer.[35]

Rebate schemes with long reference periods
In a key paragraph of its judgment in *Michelin*, the court held that the system of target rebates, as applied by Michelin, amounted to an abuse. The rationale invoked by the court goes, however, far beyond the mere question of the legitimacy of target rebates. In deciding *Michelin*, the court ruled upon all rebate systems that are based on relatively long reference periods (e.g. one year) and which reward the buyer on the basis of the quantities he purchases from the supplier during that period.[36] Such rebate schemes have in common that at the end of the reference period they put the purchaser under considerable pressure to reach the target, or lose the rebate. Since the rebate is calculated over the total annual purchases made by the buyer, even a relatively small rebate, for example 0.2 per cent to 0.4 per cent, can have a considerable impact on the profit margin of the distributor.[37] The court said that this constitutes an abuse since the pressure at the end of the reference period discourages the buyers from choosing freely at all times between the offers made by different suppliers.[38] Neither the desire to increase sales, nor the ability to programme the production were considered to justify the use of target rebates by a dominant undertaking.

Additional factors
In *Michelin*, the court also took into account additional factors such as the opacity of the rebate system and the fact that Michelin did not confirm in writing the amount and the conditions of the rebate to the distributors, as elements which increase the pressure on the distributors.[39] In practice, this means that it is advisable for dominant undertakings to pursue clarity and simplicity in the discount schemes which they want to apply. On the other hand, it would appear that these elements are of secondary importance only, since even a crystal-clear and simple target rebate system with a long reference

---

[35] *Suiker Unie & Ors v EC Commission* [1975] ECR 1663, at p. 2003 (para. 518); *Hoffmann-La Roche v EC Commission* ('*Vitamins*') [1979] ECR 461, at p. 540 (para. 90); *Michelin v EC Commission* [1983] ECR 3461, at p. 3515 (para. 72).
[36] *Michelin v EC Commission* [1983] ECR 3461, at p. 3517 (para. 81).
[37] Ibid.
[38] Id., at p. 3518 (para. 85).
[39] Id., at p. 3518 (para. 83). See also *Soda-ash–Solvay*, OJ 1991 L152/21, at p. 34, (on appeal: *SA Solvay et Cie v EC Commission*, Joined cases T-30 to T-32/91, not yet decided), where the ability of a second supplier to displace Solvay for a part of the business of a major customer was rendered even more difficult by the obligation of secrecy with regard to the percentage rebate and the cheque payment.

period will most probably be considered abusive when practised by a dominant undertaking.

Other long-term rebate schemes

The ruling in *Michelin* not only affects target rebate schemes with a long reference period, but any rebate scheme that induces buyers to obtain higher quantities and which is calculated over a relatively long period of time. For example, certain kinds of quantity rebate schemes appear to be affected by the *Michelin* rule. The traditional rebate scheme, which rewards the buyer for obtaining increasing quantities from the supplier with increasing rebate rates will almost certainly be treated in the same way as a target rebate. At the end of the reference period, or even throughout the reference period, the buyer will be induced to obtain more from the supplier, because at certain thresholds the increase in the rate of the rebate will be so attractive to the buyer that offers by outside suppliers will not be considered by him.

Michelin should therefore be read as a warning against rebate schemes in which rebates are calculated over an excessively long reference period. Since the pressure on the buyer, and therefore the abuse, is directly linked to the length of the reference period, it should be sufficient to reduce the reference period to a reasonable length. Reference periods of three to four months would appear to meet the standard. The Commission recently accepted a unilateral undertaking offered by Coca-Cola Export whereby the latter undertook not to include target rebate provisions exceeding three consecutive months[40] in agreements with any of its large distributers in the EC.

In addition, if the customer contracts for a tonnage which is in fact equivalent or close to its requirements, such arrangements may be exclusionary under art. 86 particularly if they are of long duration. The Commission in *Solvay* considered the 24-month notice period in the case of 'evergreen' contracts (supply contracts of indefinite duration) to be excessive.[41]

---

[40] See *Coca-Cola Export* settlement, Commission press release IP(90)7 of 9 January 1990.

[41] 'It prevents the customer from reacting in an informed or competitive manner to changes in market conditions. Since it is impossible to predict with any certainty what conditions will prevail in two years' time, the long period of notice acts as a strong deterrent against terminating the link with Solvay', *Soda-ash–Solvay*, OJ 1991 L152/21 at p. 35, (on appeal: *SA Solvay et Cie v EC Commission*, Joined cases T-30 to T-32/91, not yet decided). In *BPB Industries & Anor v EC Commission* [1993] 1 CEC 713, at para. 73 (on appeal: *BPB Industries plc & Anor v EC Commission*, Case C-310/93P, not yet decided), the court disregarded the fact that the merchants were free to cancel their contractual arrangements with the supplier at any time or to refuse promotional payments and continue to sell imported plasterboard. In its view, the right to terminate a contract in no way prevents its actual application until such time as the right to terminate it has been exercised. An undertaking in a dominant position is powerful enough to require its customers not only to enter into such contracts but also to maintain them, with the result that the legal possibility of termination is in fact rendered illusory.

Top-slice rebates

Another example of a rebate scheme that may have exclusionary effects is the 'top-slice' rebate. Some customers prefer to have one main supplier for their 'core' requirements (75 per cent – 85 per cent) and another secondary supplier to supply the remainder of their requirements. In order to reduce the effectiveness of this secondary supplier, certain dominant undertakings develop a two-tier pricing system whereby they charge the usual price for the customer's 'core' tonnage which the customer would have bought from it anyway and, in addition, offer a further increased 'top-slice' (and usually secret) discount for the remaining quantity that the customer would normally have bought from the second supplier. In *Solvay*,[42] the dominant supplier gave not only a top-slice discount of 20 per cent, but also a variable cheque rebate. As a result, competitors attempting to enter as second supplier by obtaining from Solvay part of the customer's business (i.e. the marginal tonnage) would have to offer a price below their costs if they wished to get any business. While this competitor had to offer this unprofitably low price on all the tonnage offered, Solvay only had to do so on the marginal tonnage.

'The Commission's objections to the rebate system apply not only to cases where Solvay has complete exclusivity but also to those where it is the principal, but not the sole, supplier. In such cases, the progressive rebates contribute to the maintenance of Solvay's overall dominant position by securing its share of the customer's business. The rigidity of the market is preserved since it is extremely difficult for any second supplier to break into Solvay's "core" business.'[43]

According to the Commission, there is no need, in order for such practices to fall under art. 86, for a legal obligation or express stipulation requiring the customer to obtain its supplies exclusively from the dominant firm: '[i]t is sufficient if the object or result of the inducement offered is to tie customers to the dominant producers.'[44]

Discount and rebate schemes with tie-in aspects

In *Hoffmann-La Roche*, the court considered it a violation of art. 86(d) to apply a fidelity rebate calculated on the overall purchases made by the purchaser, when it was established that the various groups of products to which the rebate applies constituted separate product markets. The court held that this was a practice which made purchases of one category of products conditional upon

---

[42] *Soda-ash–Solvay*, OJ 1991 L152/21, (on appeal: *SA Solvay et Cie v EC Commission*, Joined cases T-30 to T-32/91, not yet decided).
[43] Id., at p. 34.
[44] *Soda-ash–ICI*, OJ 1991 L152/40, at p. 51, (on appeal: *Imperial Chemical Industries plc (ICI) v EC Commission*, Case 37/91, not yet decided).

the purchase of another category of products.[45] Presumably that holding applies only to fidelity rebates and not to other rebates such as, for example, quantitative rebates. The effect of a fidelity rebate applied to different categories of products is that a competing producer will be prevented from supplying customers of the dominant undertaking because the customers would lose the benefits of the rebate not only on the product category in question, but on all products covered by the rebate scheme. A purely quantitative rebate scheme does not have that effect. Customers can obtain supplies from competing producers without losing the benefits of the rebate earned on other products.

Michelin appears to confirm this interpretation. Neither the court, nor the Commission, objected to the application by Michelin of a variable annual discount on car tyres, although that discount was calculated on the total volume of purchases of all categories of tyres.[46] The Commission, however, objected to a 0.5 per cent increase of that discount on car tyres which was introduced by Michelin to compensate dealers for not being able to meet the agreed sales target for heavy-vehicle tyres. Due to a temporary shortage of supplies Michelin could not meet demand for heavy-vehicle tyres. The Commission interpreted the 0.5 per cent increase as a commercial practice covered by art. 86(d) because, in its interpretation, the 0.5 per cent extra bonus which was granted on purchases of heavy-vehicle tyres was made conditional upon the attainment of a sales target fixed in respect of car tyres.[47] The court annulled the Commission's decision on this point because Michelin could establish that the Commission's interpretation was erroneous in fact. The extra bonus had been limited to sales of car tyres according to a target set for those tyres, and was not dependent on the volume of heavy-vehicle tyres sold.[48]

Objective justification

In *Eurofix-Bauco v Hilti*,[49] a rebate system with a tie-in effect was found by the Commission to infringe art. 86. Hilti, a producer of nail-guns and consumables

---

[45] *Hoffmann-La Roche v EC Commission* ('*Vitamins*') [1979] ECR 461, at p. 547 (para. 111). See also *Coca-Cola Export Corporation, Filiale Italiana*, Commission press release IP(88) 615 of 13 October 1988. The Commission found therein that a rebate system violated art. 86 since the rebates were made conditional on the purchase of a series of products belonging to separate markets. The press release did not mention what type of rebate was concerned. In the *Coca-Cola Export* settlement, Commission press release IP(90) 7 of 9 January 1990, Coca-Cola Export undertook not to include in any of its agreements with large distributors provisions that conditioned rebates upon the customer's purchase of one or more additional beverages produced by Coca-Cola Export along with the purchase of 'Coca-Cola'. Coca-Cola Export similarly undertook not to include provisions under which a target rebate is paid on the basis of the customer reaching a total aggregate purchase of both 'Coca-Cola' and other beverages produced by Coca-Cola Export.

[46] See *Michelin v EC Commission* [1983] ECR 3461, at pp. 3520–3522 (para. 92–99) and the opinion of Advocate-General Verloren van Themaat, at p. 3544.

[47] Id., at p. 3520 (para. 93).

[48] Id., at p. 3521 (para. 97–98).

[49] *Eurofix-Bauco v Hilti*, OJ 1988 L65/19.

(i.e. the nails for its use), applied a different discount system to supported and unsupported plant-hire companies. This policy of classifying their dealers was applied unilaterally and without explanation by Hilti. The Commission held that this particular policy was part of Hilti's strategy to prevent competition from independent nail-makers. A dealer who purchased consumables from competitors would lose its status as supported dealer. The Commission concluded:

'Therefore, the policy of lower discounts to unsupported dealers when not based on considerations of quantity uniformly applied or not objectively justified constitutes an abuse of a dominant position. This is particularly so when the criteria for selection are kept secret and the policy applied unilaterally by Hilti without any explanation.'[50]

Apparently the idea of considerations being 'objectively justified' was determinative in *Coca-Cola Export Corporation, Filiale Italiana*[51] in which the following rebates were considered acceptable:

(1) rebates conditional on the purchase of a series of sizes of the same product;

(2) rebates conditional on the carrying out by the distributor of a particular activity (rearrangement and resupply of the shelves, use of advertising materials, etc.).

¶906   Predatory prices

In its 1966 memorandum on concentration, the Commission said that an abuse of a dominant position may consist of 'price competition that is engaged in for the purpose of ousting from the market a competitor who does not have sufficient financial resources to withstand for a longer period sales below cost price'. It was not until 1985, in the *AKZO* case, that the Commission had the occasion to apply this notion.

AKZO Chemie, a company belonging to the multinational AKZO group of companies, was found guilty by the Commission of an attempt to drive ECS, a small UK competitor, out of the flour-additives market in the UK and Ireland. The Commission said that AKZO tried to eliminate its competitor in that market because the latter intended to use the profits derived from its flour-additive operations in the UK to expand into another, far more important

---

[50] Id., at pp. 28 and 38. See also *BPB Industries*, OJ 1989 L10/50, at pp. 65–66, where the Commission found that tie-in aspects existed in a system whereby BPB rewarded the loyalty of customers who obtained all their requirements from BPB by offering them promotional payments. The scheme in question was not based on objective criteria and, according to the Commission, served to strengthen the ties between BPB and the individually selected customers and to exclude competitors from access to those customers. The Commission accordingly found that the tying of the merchants in question to BPB amounted to an abuse.

[51] *Coca-Cola Export Corporation, Filiale Italiana*, Commission press release IP(88) 615 of 13 October 1988.

market in which AKZO was also deemed to be dominant – the organic peroxides market of the EC. AKZO allegedly first threatened to cut its prices in the UK flour-additives market unless ECS would abstain from entering the organic peroxides market. When ECS did not give in, AKZO allegedly executed its threat by adopting a long-term policy of charging 'uneconomic' prices.[52]

The decision is remarkable for its rejection of any strict cost-based standard for the determination of what constitutes a predatory price. Instead, the Commission inferred the abusive nature of AKZO's prices from the exclusionary effects of AKZO's pricing behaviour upon the complainant and the anti-competitive intent allegedly displayed by AKZO. Advocate General Lenz[53] devised a different criterion of legitimacy, namely one based on cost structure. The Advocate General opined that in deciding whether prices in an oligopolistic market (such as the present one) were artificially or unreasonably low, it was necessary to analyse the cost structure of all the oligopolists so that a reliable picture could be obtained of the price level that was in fact economically justified. The fact that the Commission only investigated AKZO's capacity, and not that of its two main competitors, meant that the examination of the relevant economic sector was not as thorough as it ought to have been. Advocate General Lenz concluded that 'since there are no reliable findings regarding the costs and the production capacity of two of the three main market participants, the Court will be unable to arrive at any view with regard to the question of the prices that were economically justifiable or reasonable'.[54]

Advocate General Lenz attached particular importance to the fact that AKZO's behaviour could also be explained by an intention other than that imputed to it by the Commission. This concerned the notion of 'the meeting of competition'. ECS had made offers to AKZO's traditional customers (albeit at their request) at prices considerably below those of AKZO. In the Advocate General's view, this behaviour could have been interpreted by AKZO as giving it the right to initiate an active pricing policy.[55] This view would seem to suggest that a 'meeting of competition' defence may possibly be raised to refute an allegation of predatory pricing.

Unfortunately, the court[56] did not address this point. Instead, it developed a

---

[52] *ECS/AKZO*, OJ 1985 L374/1. See *Tetra PAK II*, OJ 1992 L72/1, at pp. 34, 36.

[53] [1991] ECR I-3396. The Advocate General recommended that the court declare the Commission decision void for not having proven that AKZO occupied a dominant position within the meaning of art. 86. If the court were not to follow the Advocate General's assessment concerning the issue of dominance, he recommended that the Commission decision would be declared void on a substantial number of the findings of abusive conduct and that the fine be decreased from ECU 10m to ECU 500,000.

[54] [1991] ECR I-3396, at para. 36.

[55] [1991] ECR I-3396, at para. 215. The Advocate General did not consider it necessary, in justifying such an alternative explanation of behaviour, to examine what ECS's intention was in making such offers.

[56] *AKZO Chemie BV v EC Commission* [1991] ECR I-3359.

¶906

criterion of legitimacy different to that used by Advocate General Lenz, namely one based on the costs and the strategy of the dominant undertaking. It rejected AKZO's argument that the Commission should have investigated the cost structure of all three market participants. It held that in view of the criterion to be used, i.e. the costs and the strategy of the dominant undertaking, AKZO's arguments with respect to the inadequacy of the Commission's investigation of the cost structure and pricing policy of its competitors were irrelevant. After having stated that not all competition by means of price can be regarded as legitimate, the court developed the following test:

'Price below average variable costs (that is to say, those which vary depending on the quantities produced) by means of which a dominant undertaking seeks to eliminate a competitor must be regarded as abusive. A dominant undertaking has no interest in applying such prices except that of eliminating competitors so as to enable it subsequently to raise its prices by taking advantage of its monopolistic position, since each sale generates a loss, namely the total amount of the fixed costs (that is to say, those which remain constant regardless of the quantities produced) and, at least part of the variable costs relating to the unit produced.

Moreover, prices below average total costs, that is to say, fixed costs plus variable costs, but above average variable costs, must be regarded as abusive if they are determined as part of a plan for eliminating a competitor. Such prices can drive from the market undertakings which are perhaps as efficient as the dominant undertaking but which, because of their smaller financial resources, are incapable of withstanding the competition waged against them.'[57]

In *Tetra Pak II*,[58] the Commission stated that:

'in certain circumstances the pursuit of activities having inadequate profitability to cover all the costs involved may indeed be economically justified in the short term, provided income remains above variable costs and the activities contribute in part to covering fixed costs ; but, on the contrary, an entrepreneur must normally give up any activities whose profits remain permanently inadequate to cover variable costs, let alone those which do not cover direct variable costs'.[59]

---

[57] *AKZO Chemie BV v EC Commission* [1991] ECR I-3359 at para. 71–72. Some economic experts have been fairly critical of the court's judgment in the *AKZO* case, for example, Philips and Moras, 'The AKZO Decision: A Case of Predatory Pricing?' Journal of Industrial Economics, Vol. 41, Sept. 1993, no. 3, pp. 315–321. The authors come to the conclusion that this is a case of active competition, not of predation.

[58] *Tetra Pak II*, OJ 1992 L72/1.

[59] Id., at p. 33. See also pp. 34–36.

In *Napier Brown/British Sugar*[60] the Commission made an analysis of costs in order to establish that British Sugar had abused its dominant position. British Sugar was dominant in the markets for both raw materials (i.e. industrial sugar) and the corresponding derived product (i.e. retail sugar). By maintaining a very low margin between the price it charged for raw materials to the companies competing in the production of the derived product and the price it charged for the derived product, competition in the retail sugar market was restricted. The margin was found by the Commission to be insufficient to reflect British Sugar's own cost of transformation (i.e. repackaging). The Commission stated:

> 'It is clear from the facts as set out above that should BS have maintained this margin in the long term, Napier Brown, or any company equally efficient in repackaging as BS without a self-produced source of industrial sugar, would have been obliged to leave the United Kingdom retail sugar market.'[61]

The Commission concluded that, taking some other abusive practices into account, the intention, or natural and foreseeable consequence of the maintenance of the pricing policy was the removal of Napier Brown from the British retail sugar market and consequently the pricing policy constituted an abuse of a dominant position.

'Fighting ships'

The use of so-called 'fighting ships', as described in the *Cewal* case,[62] is yet another form of predatory pricing. Fighting ships are ships designated by members of a liner conference to sail in competition with the ships of non-member carriers. The fighting ships are scheduled to sail on the same dates, or on neighbouring dates, as the ships of the independent competitor at freight rates which are lower than the tariffs agreed between the members of the conference. The resulting loss of revenue is shared by the members of the conference. The use of fighting ships differs from the predatory conduct stigmatised in the *AKZO* case because of its multilateral character. It is a strategy characterised by the use of a concerted, exceptional price with the aim of removing a competitor. The issue that arose in the *AKZO* case was different, namely how to distinguish between predatory prices and aggressive, but legitimate, price competition engaged in unilaterally by a dominant company.

---

[60] *Napier Brown/British Sugar*, OJ 1988 L284/41.
[61] Id., at pp. 54–55.
[62] *Cewal, Cowal and Ukwal*, OJ 1993 L34/20.

REFUSALS TO SUPPLY

¶907 Introduction

Even though the text of art. 86 does not impose a duty to supply on dominant undertakings, it follows from a series of cases that, unless objectively justified, refusals to supply by a dominant undertaking may constitute an abuse within the meaning of art. 86. Such an abuse may occur where an undertaking that is dominant in one market attempts to use its power in that market to eliminate or to hinder effective competition in a separate but related market (¶908), or where a dominant undertaking withdraws supplies from an established customer on a completely separate market (¶909). The dominant undertaking may have a defence where the refusal to supply is the result of shortages (¶910). The Commission has also had cause to address particular forms of refusal to deal in the air transport sector (¶911).

¶908 Refusal to supply competitor

Refusal to supply prohibited: the Commercial Solvents case

The first case to deal with a refusal to supply by a dominant undertaking was *Commercial Solvents*.[63] Commercial Solvents Corporation (CSC) was the only producer of raw materials for the industrial production of ethambutol, a product which is needed for the production of certain drugs used to treat tuberculosis. CSC challenged this finding, but the evidence it adduced was rejected by the court. Thus, it was held that CSC had a monopoly position for the production and sale of certain raw materials which are necessary for the manufacture of ethambutol. Until 1970, an Italian company – Istituto Chemioterapico Italiana (Istituto) – acted as reseller of these raw materials produced by CSC. In that capacity it had been supplying Zoja, an Italian producer of ethambutol, for a number of years. CSC and Istituto were related undertakings and were found to have acted as an economic unit for the purposes of the proceedings. In 1970, the CSC group changed its commercial policy and decided to stop supplying within the EC the raw materials necessary for the manufacture of ethambutol. Instead it started (through Istituto) itself to manufacture ethambutol and to develop specialities based on ethambutol. Its refusal to supply Zoja was considered an abuse of a dominant position by the Commission.[64]

The court confirmed the decision on appeal. It held that a manufacturer that has a dominant position in the production of a raw material and which is therefore about to control the supply to manufacturers of derivatives, may not

---

[63] *Commercial Solvents v EC Commission* [1974] ECR 223.
[64] *ZOJA/CSC–ICI*, JO 1972 L299/51.

¶908

refuse to supply these raw materials when such refusal risks eliminating all competition on the part of an important manufacturer of derivative products.[65] A decision by the dominant producer to enter the market for derivatives is not a justification for the refusal to supply.

A similar set of facts can be found in two other cases: *Hugin* and *CLT* (see below).

Spare parts, accessories etc: the Hugin case

In *Hugin*, the Commission considered it abusive for Hugin Kassaregister AB, a Swedish manufacturer of cash registers, to stop supplying spare parts to Liptons, a small UK company which was active in the market for the repair and maintenance of cash registers. Hugin was held to be dominant in the market for its own spare parts and therefore was not entitled to refuse to supply a competitor with spare parts, lest all competition from that competitor be eliminated.[66]

The court did not have to rule on the question of whether Hugin's refusal to supply Liptons with spare parts was abusive, because it found that the conduct in issue was not capable of affecting trade between member states.[67]

Supply of services: the CLT case

Subsequent case law shows that an undertaking that is dominant with regard to the production and supply of certain products which are necessary to compete in another market may not refuse to supply these products and thereby reserve that market for itself. *CLT* confirmed that this principle also applies to the supply of services by a dominant undertaking.[68]

In that case, the service related to an advertisement technique called 'tele-marketing', i.e. the indication in the advertisement of a telephone number which the public can call to obtain further information on the product which is being advertised. The service consists of making available to advertisers telephone lines and a team of telephone operators to provide information to persons who respond to the advertisements. Compagnie Luxembourgeoise de Télédiffusion (CLT), which runs the RTL television station, and its subsidiary, Information Publicité Benelux (IPB), which is CLT's exclusive agent for television advertising aimed at the Benelux countries, were held by the Vice-President of the Brussels Commercial Court to be in a dominant position on the market in television advertising aimed at viewers in French-speaking Belgium.[69] One of the questions which he referred to the Court of Justice for a

---

[65] *Commercial Solvents v EC Commission* [1974] ECR 223, at pp. 250–251 (para. 25).
[66] *Hugin/Liptons*, OJ 1978 L22/23.
[67] *Hugin v EC Commission* [1979] ECR 1869.
[68] *Telemarketing v CLT* [1985] ECR 3261.
[69] Id., at p. 3272 (para. 6).

¶908

preliminary ruling was whether an undertaking like CLT had the right to reserve for itself, or for a subsidiary under its control, to the exclusion of any other undertaking, an auxiliary activity – i.e. the provision of tele-marketing services – which could be carried out by a third undertaking. The third undertaking in this case was Centre Belge d'Etudes de Marché – Télé-marketing SA, a Belgian trading company which had studied the tele-marketing concept and which had already conducted tele-marketing operations on the RTL channel. The court answered as follows on the question submitted for a preliminary ruling:

> 'An abuse within the meaning of Article 86 is committed where, without any objective necessity, an undertaking holding a dominant position on a particular market reserves to itself or to an undertaking belonging to the same group an auxiliary activity which might be carried out by another undertaking as part of its activities on a neighbouring but separate market, with the possibility of eliminating all competition from such undertaking.'

In its judgment, the court explicitly referred to its prior holding in *Zoja*.[70]

Application of the rationale to subsequent cases

Commercial Solvents, *Hugin* and *CLT* have in common that an undertaking which is dominant in one market may not use its power in that market to eliminate or to hinder effective competition in a separate but related market. In all three cases the dominant firm had taken a general decision no longer to supply to any firm operating in the related market.

The rationale underlying these three cases appears to have been used in subsequent proceedings. For example, one of the important issues in *IBM* was whether IBM was under an obligation to supply other manufacturers in sufficient time with the technical information needed to permit competitive peripheral products to be used with IBM's System/370 computer. The Commission claimed that IBM's refusal to provide timely information concerning the interfaces hindered effective competition in the market for peripheral equipment, which can be considered auxiliary to the market for mainframe computers in which IBM was allegedly dominant.[71]

Exercise of industrial property rights
Likewise, in proceedings against *Ford Motor Company Ltd*, the Commission claimed that Ford was attempting to exclude manufacturers of body panels

---

[70] Id., at pp. 3277–3278 (para. 25–27).
[71] The IBM proceedings were settled on 1 August 1984 pursuant to a unilateral undertaking by IBM to modify its business practices against which the Commission had taken issue. See, *IBM* settlement, *Fourteenth Report on Competition Policy*, points 94–95. See also, for further developments, *Sixteenth Report on Competition Policy*, point 75; *Seventeenth Report on Competition Policy*, point 85; *Eighteenth Report on Competition Policy*, point 78.

from the market for Ford compatible body panels by invoking its copyrights under UK law and by refusing to grant licences.[72] With respect to computer programs the Commission recently indicated that under certain circumstances 'the exercise of copyright as to the aspects of a computer program, which other companies need to use in order to write compatible programs', could amount to an abuse of a dominant position within the meaning of art. 86.[73]

On the other hand, in *AB Volvo v Erik Veng (UK)*,[74] the court held that a refusal by the proprietor to grant a licence of a registered design, even in return for reasonable royalties, did not in itself amount to an abuse. But the court also mentioned:

> 'It must however also be noted that the exercise of an exclusive right by the proprietor of a registered design ... may be prohibited by Article 86 if it involves ... certain abusive conduct such as the arbitrary refusal to supply spare parts to independent repairers, the fixing of prices for spare parts at an unfair level or a decision no longer to produce spare parts for a particular model even though many cars of that model are still in circulation ...'.[75]

Refusal to supply coupled with refusal to honour guarantee

In *Eurofix-Bauco v Hilti*,[76] one of the practices by Hilti which constituted an abuse consisted in the refusal to supply cartridges for nail-guns to long-standing customers because it objected to their possible resale to independent nail-makers. In doing so, Hilti allegedly tried to prevent the free availability of Hilti-compatible cartridge strips with the aim of blocking the entry of competitors into another market, namely of nails compatible with Hilti nail-guns.[77]

In addition, Hilti refused to honour guarantees on nail-guns if nails of another mark had been used. This refusal was likewise part of Hilti's policy to attempt to block the sale of nails by independent nail-manufacturers. The Commission considered that it could be legitimate not to honour a guarantee if nails of lower quality caused malfunctioning, premature wear or breakdown. But in this case the refusal amounted to an abuse since it hindered customers from being supplied by other manufacturers and Hilti had not shown that the use of non-Hilti nails was more likely to cause any of the problems mentioned with Hilti guns than the use of Hilti nails.[78]

---

[72] *Ford Motor Company Ltd, Fifteenth Report on Competition Policy*, point 49. See also *Ford body panel settlement*, Commission press release IP(90) 4 of 10 January 1990.

[73] Commission conclusions decided on the occasion of the adoption of the Commission's proposal for a Council directive on the legal protection of computer programs, OJ 1989 C91/16.

[74] *AB Volvo v Erik Veng (UK)* [1988] ECR 6211. See also *CICRA & SpA Maxicar v Régie Nationale des Usines Renault* [1988] ECR 6039.

[75] *AB Volvo v Erik Veng (UK)* [1988] ECR 6211, at p. 6235 (para. 9).

[76] *Eurofix-Bauco v Hilti*, OJ 1988 L65/19.

[77] Id., at p. 36.

[78] Id., at p. 37.

Refusal to supply established customer with no objective justification
Similarly, in *Napier Brown/British Sugar*,[79] the only processor of sugar beet in the UK refused to supply industrial sugar to Napier Brown, an established customer. British Sugar claimed that it could not supply the quantities demanded since the EC sugar regime only gave it limited supplies of sugar for sale and that a system of quotas was needed in order to ensure continuity. The Commission, on the basis of documents found on the premises of British Sugar, showed that the system of quotas was only a pretext to justify British Sugar's refusal to supply Napier Brown and it concluded 'that BS ha[d] abused its dominant position by refusing to supply industrial sugar to NB without objective necessity, the intention or foreseeable result of which would have been to precipitate the removal of NB from the United Kingdom retail sugar market, thereby reducing competition in that market'.[80]

¶909 Refusal to supply non-competing customer

Refusal to supply prohibited: United Brands case
United Brands discussed another kind of refusal to supply. United Brands was not active in the market in which its customers were operating. It refused to supply bananas to Olesen, a Danish distributor/ripener, because the latter had taken part in an advertising campaign by one of the UBC's competitors: Standard Fruit. Olesen was the exclusive distributor of Standard Fruit in Denmark. United Brands further argued that Olesen started selling less of its bananas and did not take sufficient care in the ripening process.[81]

To challenge the Commission's finding of an abuse in this respect, United Brands argued that its reasons to stop supplying Olesen constituted an objective justification. Furthermore, United Brands' decision not to supply Olesen any longer did not adversely affect competition on the Danish market. United Brands argued that the Commission had turned art. 86 upside down by requiring proof from the dominant firm that its refusal to supply was objectively justified, whereas it is up to the Commission to establish that, in the particular circumstances of a specific case, the refusal to supply amounts to an abuse.[82]

In a far-reaching statement, the court said that:

'... an undertaking in a dominant position ... cannot stop supplying a long-standing customer who abides by regular commercial practice, if the orders placed by that customer are in no way out of the ordinary'.[83]

---

[79] *Napier Brown/British Sugar*, OJ 1988 L284/41, at pp. 44 and 54.
[80] Ibid.
[81] *United Brands v EC Commission* [1978] ECR 207, at pp. 290–291 (para. 163–175).
[82] Id., at pp. 257–258.
[83] Id., at p. 292 (para. 182).

It further held that the arguments advanced by United Brands to justify its refusal to supply were irrelevant. It merely conceded, as a matter of principle, that even dominant firms are entitled to protect their own commercial interests, provided the measures taken are proportionate to the threat, and provided their actual purpose is not to strengthen the dominant position and abuse it.[84] A refusal to supply did not meet these criteria: it was an excessive sanction for Olesen's behaviour and might have a deterrent effect on other distributor/ripeners because it might discourage them from participating in advertising campaigns for other brand names.

Justifications rejected
United Brands puts dominant firms under a positive duty to supply, unless objective reasons justify the decision not to supply. Given the court's cursory treatment of the arguments advanced by United Brands to justify its position, it would appear that only exceptional circumstances can justify a refusal to supply by a dominant firm. Obviously, a refusal to supply because the distributor does not follow the supplier's restrictive export policy is not a valid justification.[85]

The Commission, in a decision providing for interim measures, considered that the refusal by a manufacturer of musical instruments, dominant in the market of brass band instruments, to supply two established customers constituted a sufficient prima facie case of abuse.[86] The two customers had formed a company for the purpose of manufacturing instruments themselves. In that context, the Commission observed:

'A dominant undertaking may always take reasonable steps to protect its commercial interests, but such measures must be fair and proportional to the threat. The fact that a customer of a dominant producer becomes associated with a competitor or a potential competitor of that manufacturer does not normally entitle the dominant producer to withdraw all supplies immediately or to take reprisals against that customer.

There is no obligation placed on a dominant producer to subsidize competition to itself. In the case where a customer transfers its central activity to the promotion of a competing brand it may be that even a dominant producer is entitled to review its commercial relations with that customer and on giving adequate notice terminate any special relationship. However, the refusal of all supplies to GHH and RCN and the other actions

---

[84] Id., at p. 293 (para. 189). Korah rightly remarks that '[t]o allow a dominant firm to protect its commercial interests when they are attacked but not if this strengthens its position, poses difficulty. To repel the threat is in itself to strengthen its position'. See Korah, *An Introductory Guide to EEC Competition Law and Practice,* London ESC Publishing, (1985), at p. 144.

[85] *Suiker Unie & Ors v EC Commission* [1975] ECR 1663, at p. 1983 (para. 396–400).

[86] *BBI/Boosey & Hawkes: Interim measures,* OJ 1987 L286/36. The complaint was withdrawn following a settlement on terms agreed by the two parties involved (see, *Eighteenth Report on Competition Policy,* point 71)

B&H has taken against them as part of its reaction to the perceived threat of BBI, would appear in the circumstances of the present case to go beyond the legitimate defence of B&H's commercial interests.'[87]

Likewise, refusing to supply because the order is too big for the local market, or even for the European market has been held by the Commission to be abusive. In *Polaroid/SSI Europe* the Commission added that supplying on the condition that the customer reveals the geographical destination of the goods, or the identity of its proper customers, is a practice which will be considered in the same way as a refusal to supply.[88]

¶910 Shortages

A refusal to supply an occasional customer in times of shortage may, under certain circumstances, be justified. In *ABG*, the court annulled the Commission's decision that a number of oil companies had abused their dominant position by refusing to supply oil to ABG. ABG acted as a purchasing co-operative on behalf of the Dutch company AVIA Nederland BV during the 1973–74 oil crisis.[89] Although the Commission recognised that occasional customers should not be placed on equal footing with traditional customers who are bound by the terms of an agreement, it argued that the difference in treatment may not put at stake the very existence of these customers.[90] The court disagreed for a number of reasons. It mainly held that, given the situation of shortage, supplying to ABG would have implied a considerable diminution of deliveries which the contractual customers legitimately expected. Under art. 86, there is no obligation for dominant undertakings to apply similar rates of reduction to all their customers in times of shortage. Such measures can only be imposed either by the national authorities, or by the Community authorities pursuant to art. 103.[91]

However, the Commission has indicated in its *BPB* decision[92] that a dominant firm has to supply its goods at the time of shortage according to criteria which are objectively justified. In this decision, the Commission condemned a delivery scheme, pursuant to which customers who were not trading in imported plasterboard were to be treated more favourably as regards supplies of plaster at a time of temporary plaster shortage. The Commission stated that:

---

[87] Id., at p. 41.
[88] *Polaroid/SSI Europe, Thirteenth Report on Competition Policy*, points 155–157.
[89] *ABG-oil companies operating in the Netherlands*, OJ 1977 L117/1; on appeal: *BP v EC Commission* [1978] ECR 1513.
[90] *BP v EC Commission* [1978] ECR 1513, at p. 1522.
[91] Id., at p. 1528 (para. 34).
[92] *BPB Industries* [1989] 1 CEC 2,008; OJ 1989 L10/50.

'... the adoption and implementation of a policy of reserving priority orders for plaster for customers who were not stockists of imported plasterboard was an abuse of BG's dominant position in the supply of plasterboard, for the criterion for the selection of those merchants who were eligible for priority supplies of plaster was not objectively justified, but designed only to reward merchants dealing exclusively in BG plasterboard while treating less favourably those dealing in imports.'[93]

¶911   Refusals to deal in the air transport sector

Refusal of access to computerised reservation system

A special type of a refusal to deal was considered by the Commission in *London European/Sabena*.[94] Sabena refused to grant London European access to its Saphir computerised reservation system. London European operated between Luton and Brussels and wanted access to the Saphir system in order to be listed on the terminals of Belgian travel agencies, which made most of their reservations using this system. One of the reasons for Sabena's refusal was aimed at placing pressure on London European to fix a higher level of fares and to conclude a ground-handling contract with Sabena.[95]

Refusal to interline

A similar type of abuse was challenged by the Commission in *British Midland v Aer Lingus*.[96] Aer Lingus had cancelled interlining facilities previously granted to British Midland when that airline announced its intentions to start operating a London (Heathrow) – Dublin service. Interlining essentially consists of an agreement pursuant to which airlines are authorised to sell each other's services. As a result, a single ticket can be issued which comprises segments to be performed by different airlines. Travel agents prefer to avoid the loss of time and the extra work involved in issuing separate tickets. Furthermore, a significant number of passengers consider the possibility to change tickets and to organise complex journeys on a single ticket as necessary. For the airline involved, interlining is attractive because it allows an airline with a low frequency service to reap the benefits of a high frequency service which its rival may have developed, usually at a very significant cost. This was the main reason

---

[93] Id., at p. 68. This view was upheld by the Court of First Instance on appeal: *BPB Industries plc & Anor v EC Commission*, [1993] 1 CEC 713, at p. 734 (para. 94); on appeal: *BPB Industries plc & Anor v EC Commission*, Case C-310/93P, not yet decided.
[94] *London European/Sabena* [1989] 1 CEC 2,278; OJ 1988 L317/47.
[95] Id., at p. 52. The Council adopted Regulation 2299/89 on a code of conduct for computerised reservation systems, OJ 1989 L220/1 (amended at OJ 1993 L278/1). Article 9 of the regulation provides inter alia that a 'system vendor shall make any of the distribution facilities of a [computerised reservation system] available to any subscriber on a non-discriminatory basis'.
[96] *British Midland v Aer Lingus*, OJ 1992 L 96/34.

why Aer Lingus decided not to maintain the interlining arrangement with British Midland.

However, the Commission did not accept this line of defence. It held that entry into the airline sector is always very difficult. When an airline commences a new service, it will normally expect to incur some losses during an initial period. Denying interline facilities is likely to increase the entry barrier. A new entrant without interlining facilities is likely to be considered in this respect as a second-rate airline. The Commission considered that refusing to interline is not normal competition on the merits, because interlining has for many years been accepted industry practice with widely acknowledged benefits for both airlines and passengers.

DISCRIMINATION

¶912   Nationals or residents of different member states

As already discussed, a dominant undertaking may violate art. 86 by engaging in price discrimination. Article 86 also applies to another type of discriminatory treatment by a dominant firm: discrimination between nationals or residents of different member states.

Discrimination by a dominant firm between nationals or residents of different member states has been held to be abusive from the outset. In 1971, the Commission condemned the German collecting society GEMA for refusing admission to nationals of other member states.[97] In *Sacchi*, the court confirmed that discrimination between undertakings or products of a given member state and those of other member states as regards access to television advertising would no doubt be abusive if practised by a dominant firm.[98]

Subsequent case law has confirmed the strict application of the duty of dominant firms not to treat nationals of different member states in a discriminatory manner. In *GVL*, the Commission reiterated its holding that discriminatory treatment by a dominant undertaking on grounds of nationality must be regarded automatically as an infringement of art. 86.[99] GVL, a German collecting society engaged in the exploitation of performers' rights, had refused to conclude management agreements with foreign artists who had no residence in Germany. One of the reasons it invoked for doing so was that the extent of copyright protection differed from member state to member state. As a result of that disparity, the rights of foreign artists, which are established outside Germany, are governed by laws that do not recognise royalties in respect of the

---

[97] *GEMA*, JO 1971 L134/15.
[98] *Sacchi* [1974] ECR 409, at p. 430 (para. 17).
[99] *GVL*, OJ 1981 L370/49; on appeal: *GVL v EC Commission* [1983] ECR 483.

¶912

secondary exploitation of copyright. Although German law recognised these royalties, GVL argued that only nationality or residence were sufficiently strong connecting factors for that law to be applicable. Essentially, its position was that the differential treatment was not based on nationality or residence, but on the nature of the rights vested in the artists. The differential treatment was a result of the disparity in the national laws of the member states. This defence was rejected by the court.

In *Basset v SACEM*,[100] the court did not find the charging of a royalty called 'supplementary mechanical reproduction fee', in addition to a performance royalty on the public performance of sound recordings, to be discriminatory, even though such a supplementary fee was not provided for in the member state where those recordings were lawfully placed on the market. The supplementary fee was charged irrespective of the origin of the recordings and the company levying the fee was only using the possibilities offered by the national legislation concerning copyright. Furthermore, the level of the charge was not considered unfair.

¶913   Discriminatory conditions imposed on customers

According to art. 86(c), an abuse may consist in 'applying dissimilar conditions to equivalent transactions with other trading parties, thereby placing them at a competitive disadvantage'. In *Napier Brown/British Sugar*, the Commission held that British Sugar had abused its dominant position in refusing to supply sugar, originating from sugar beet, to Napier Brown, when Napier Brown specifically requested it and by delivering cane-origin sugar instead. Napier Brown claimed that other clients received sugar of exclusively beet origin on request. Napier Brown attached importance to receiving sugar of beet origin because it would receive an EC storage rebate for storing EC-produced beet-origin sugar, which it would not receive if British Sugar delivered cane-origin sugar. The Commission thus concluded that British Sugar had imposed discriminatory conditions of the kind referred to in art. 86(c).[101]

The cases of *Eurofix-Bauco v Hilti*[102] and *Napier Brown/British Sugar*[103] show that a policy implemented by a dominant undertaking to try and attract customers from its competitors by offering certain customers particularly favourable prices and terms may constitute an abuse according to art. 86. In the first case, Hilti made a selection of the most important customers of its competitors and offered them especially favourable conditions. Since the other customers of Hilti buying similar quantities did not receive these special

---

[100] *Basset v SACEM* [1987] ECR 1747.
[101] *Napier Brown/British Sugar*, OJ 1988 L284/41, at pp. 49 and 55.
[102] *Eurofix-Bauco v Hilti*, OJ 1988 L65/19.
[103] *Napier Brown/British Sugar*, OJ 1988 L284/41

conditions, such conditions were found by the Commission to be selective and discriminatory.[104] In the second case, British Sugar intended to offer major outlets for retail sugar excellent prices if they 'de-listed' or refused to stock Napier Brown products.[105] The Commission clearly objected to such behaviour:

'An aggressive price rivalry is an essential competitive instrument. However, a selective discriminatory pricing policy by a dominant firm designed purely to damage the business of, or deter market entry by, its competitors, whilst maintaining higher prices for the bulk of its other customers, is both exploitive of these other customers and destructive of competition. As such, it constitutes abusive conduct by which a dominant firm can reinforce its already preponderant market position.'[106]

In *BPB Industries*,[107] the Commission held that favouring certain customers by giving priority to their orders in times of temporary shortages can amount to an abuse of a dominant position. BPB gave priority to orders from customers who were not also trading in imported plasterboard. Since BPB was the only producer of plasterboard in Great Britain and Ireland, the only competition came from imported plasterboard. The Commission objected to the fact that the only criterion for giving priority was whether the customer appeared on a list of merchants who were trading in imported plasterboard and that no regard was paid to whether the merchant was a good customer in any other sense, such as being effective or successful in selling or promoting BPB's products. The Commission concluded:

'[T]he adoption and implementation of a policy of reserving priority orders of plaster for customers who were not stockists of imported plasterboard was an abuse of [BPB's] dominant position in the supply of plasterboard, for the criterion for the selection of those merchants who were eligible for priority supplies of plaster was not objectively justified, but designed only to reward merchants dealing exclusively in [BPB] plasterboard while treating less favourably those dealing in imports. Consequently, the arrangements were liable to affect the future behaviour of [BPB] customers by encouraging them to sell only [BPB] plasterboard'.[108]

---

[104] *Eurofix-Bauco v Hilti*, OJ 1988 L65/19, at p. 37.
[105] *Napier Brown/British Sugar*, OJ 1988 284/41, at pp. 43 and 44. However, the Commission did not take any decision related to this issue, since it did not establish any case in which 'de-listing' proved successful.
[106] *Eurofix-Bauco v Hilti*, OJ 1988 L65/19, at p. 37.
[107] *BPB Industries* [1989] 1 CEC 2,008; OJ 1989 L10/50.
[108] Id., at p. 68. See *BPB Industries plc & Anor v EC Commission* [1993] 1 CEC 713, at p. 734 (para. 94); on appeal: *BPB Industries plc & Anor v EC Commission*, Case C-310/93P, not yet decided. See also *Tetra Pak II*, OJ 1992 L71/1, at pp. 25, 30 and 36.

UNFAIR TERMS AND CONDITIONS

¶914   The prohibition

Article 86 prohibits not only the imposition of unfair prices, but also the direct or indirect imposition of unfair trading conditions.

Copyright management societies requiring assignment of copyright

In *BRT v SABAM*,[109] the court addressed the issue of unfair trading conditions in the context of copyrights. SABAM, the Belgian copyright-collection society required its members to assign all their present and future copyrights and to allow it to exercise these rights for five years after their withdrawal from the association. One of the questions referred to the court for an art. 177 preliminary ruling asked whether an undertaking such as SABAM, enjoying a de facto monopoly for the management of copyrights, was imposing unfair trading conditions within the meaning of art. 86.

The court, noting that the association operated 'to protect the rights and interests of individual members against, in particular, major exploiters and distributors', stated that any appraisal must balance between the requirement of maximum freedom for authors to dispose of their works and that of the effective management of their rights.[110] The association's practices should not exceed 'the limit absolutely necessary for the attainment of [its] object'.[111] The court considered that the compulsory assignment of all copyrights, both present and future, may constitute an unfair condition, 'especially if such assignment is required for an extended period after the members' withdrawal'.[112] The court thus concluded that:

> 'the fact that an undertaking entrusted with the exploitation of copyrights and occupying a dominant position ... imposes on its members obligations which are not absolutely necessary for the attainment of its object and which thus encroach unfairly upon a member's freedom to exercise his copyright can constitute an abuse'.[113]

---

[109] *BRT v SABAM* [1974] ECR 313.
[110] Id., at pp. 316–317 (para. 8–9).
[111] Id., at p. 317 (para. 11).
[112] Id., at p. 317 (para. 12).
[113] Id., at p. 317 (para. 15). See also *GEMA*, JO 1971 L134/15, where the Gesellschaft für musikalische Aufführungs – und mechanische Vervielfältigungsrechte (GEMA) ('Company for Musical Performance and Mechanical Reproduction Rights'), which granted and managed musical copyrights, was found to have abused its dominant position by binding its members with unnecessary obligations. GEMA required the assignment of authors' rights for all categories and for the entire world. The Commission considered that it was necessary for GEMA's members to be given the freedom to decide: whether to assign to GEMA or to another copyright society all or part of their rights for the countries in which GEMA does not operate directly; or whether to assign to GEMA all their rights for countries in which GEMA does operate directly or to divide them by categories among several copyright societies; and whether to withdraw from GEMA the administration of certain categories after due notice at the end of the year; and *GEMA Statutes*, OJ 1982 L94/12, granting a negative clearance to GEMA

Unilateral price-fixing and extension of lease

In *Alsatel v Novasam*,[114] the court recognised that certain clauses in a rental and maintenance contract for telephone installations constituted an abuse. Alsatel imposed an obligation on its customers to have any modifications to the telephone connection or installation carried out exclusively by Alsatel and the charge for such modifications was determined by Alsatel on a case-by-case basis. The contracts had a duration of 15 years and could be extended for another 15 years if the initial rental increased by 25 per cent or more as a result of modifications to the installations. The court held that the obligation not to call on third parties to carry out modifications of the installations could be justified as necessary to protect Alsatel's property, but that the fact that no fixed price was laid down for such modifications and that Alsatel determined the charges unilaterally could be regarded as unfair trading conditions. Also, the automatic prolongation of the contract if the rental increased by 25 per cent or more was considered by the court as contrary to art. 86(a).

Excessive prices

The court has also held that a national copyright society in a dominant position imposes unfair terms of contract when the fees it applies to discotheques in one member state are significantly higher than those charged in other member states in so far as the comparison has been made on a similar basis. It would, however, not be seen as unfair terms if the copyright society could justify this price difference as a result of objective and pertinent divergences in the copyright management provided in the member state concerned, compared with that provided in other member states.[115]

Binding customers through restrictions on sale or long leases

Probably the most extensive analysis by the Commission of the imposition by an undertaking of unfair terms and conditions arose in *Tetra Pak II*.[116] The Commission held that Tetra Pak had abused its dominant position by 'the imposition on users of Tetra Pak products in all Member States of numerous contractual clauses ... having the essential object of unduly binding them to Tetra Pak and of artificially eliminating potential competition'.[117] In particular, Tetra Pak was found to have imposed abusive contractual conditions governing

---

for a provision in its statutes intended merely 'to prevent those contacts whereby the users seek, by exploiting certain works frequently and taking no account of public taste and qualitative criteria, to share in the royalties collected by GEMA, helping themselves, as it were, without any restrictions. In this way GEMA protects its membership as a whole'.
[114] *Alsatel v Novasam* [1988] ECR 5987; [1990] 1 CEC 248.
[115] *Ministère Public v Tournier* [1989] ECR 2521. See also *Lucazeau v SACEM, SACEM v Debelle* and *SACEM v Soumagnac* [1989] ECR 2811.
[116] *Tetra Pak II*, OJ 1992 L72/1; on appeal.
[117] Ibid., at art. 1(2).

¶914

the sale and leasing of Tetra Pak equipment and cartons, which have no link with the purpose of the contracts and some of which distort the very nature thereof.

Thus, concerning the sale of Tetra Pak equipment, for example, purchasers were prohibited from adding accessory equipment to the machine, from modifying the machine and adding or removing parts, and from moving the machine. The Commission found, inter alia, that such provisions deprived the purchasers of certain of their property rights. The requirement that Tetra Pak's agreement be obtained for the resale or transfer of use of equipment was similarly condemned by the Commission. Furthermore, the Commission condemned the imposition of clauses whereby Tetra Pak had an exclusive right to maintain and repair equipment, beyond the guarantee period for the entire life of the equipment. In addition to binding the purchaser to Tetra Pak, the Commission found that such a clause gave Tetra Pak an indirect means of control over the purchaser to ensure that he complied with other contractual provisions. The fact that the guarantee itself was linked to the fulfilment of all the customer's contractual obligations, including the exclusive use of Tetra Pak cartons, was further condemned by the Commission.

Concerning the leasing of Tetra Pak equipment, the Commission found, inter alia, that the three to nine year minimum duration of Tetra Pak's leases was 'in any case excessive', and therefore constituted an abuse of art. 86. In particular, the nine-year term for a lease was found to be equal to or to exceed the technological (up to obsolescence) if not physical life of the machines. As for the three-year term, the Commission considered that it also constituted an abuse 'in so far as, in a sector in which there is rapid technological development, it unduly binds the leaseholder to Tetra Pak ...'.

MISCELLANEOUS ABUSES

¶915   Exclusive dealing obligations

As illustrated by *Hachette*,[118] a case that was settled after the issuance of a statement of objections, the imposition of exclusive supply obligations by an undertaking in a dominant position may constitute an abuse of a dominant position. The case involved exclusive distribution arrangements imposed by the defendants on the majority of French publishers for exports of French newspapers and periodicals to the other EC countries, and on the major publishing houses in the other EC countries for imports of foreign newspapers and periodicals into France. The Commission took the view that these

---

[118] *Hachette, Eighth Report on Competition Policy*, points 114–115,

extensive exclusive distribution arrangements made it 'very difficult if not impossible' for other newspaper distributors to penetrate the market. The undertakings concerned voluntarily agreed to terminate these arrangements and, as a result, the case was settled.

In *Hoffmann-La Roche*, the court similarly held that:

'[a]n undertaking which is in a dominant position on a market and ties purchasers – even if it does so at their request – by an obligation or promise on their part to obtain all or most of their requirements exclusively from the said undertaking abuses its dominant position within the meaning of Article 86'.[119]

This language was endorsed by the court in *AKZO*[120] and by the Court of First Instance in *BPB*.[121]

In *Istituto/IMC and Angus*,[122] the Commission investigated the practices of two American firms, IMC and Angus, which together held a dominant position in the market for aminobutanol. Following the intervention of the Commission, IMC and Angus modified their contracts for delivery. They terminated exclusive purchasing agreements and a resale ban for aminobutanol, the latter being considered by the Commission as closing-off the market to new entrants.

Similarly, in its *BPB* decision,[123] the Commission condemned BG's policy of offering special promotional payments to individually selected merchants who undertook to purchase plasterboard exclusively from BG. This part of the Commission's decision was upheld by the Court of First Instance in *BPB*.[124]

Exclusivity arrangements were also condemned by the Commission in *Soda-ash–Solvay*,[125] even though the supply agreement was sometimes expressed in the form of a 'tonnage' contract (i.e. the tonnage contracted for was equivalent or close to the customer's total requirements). Although in *Soda-ash–Solvay* the exclusivity sometimes constituted consideration for certain financial inducements offered to the customer, in *Soda-ash–ICI*[126] the Commission stated that, for the purposes of establishing an abuse of a dominant position in such circumstances, 'it is irrelevant whether the (exclusivity) obligation in question is stipulated for without further qualification or whether it is undertaken in consideration of the grant of a rebate'. Exclusive supply arrangements were also condemned in *Tetra Pak II*.

---

[119] *Hoffmann-La Roche v EC Commission* ('*Vitamins*') [1979] ECR 461, at pp. 539–540 (para. 89).
[120] *AKZO v Commission* [1991] ECR I-3359 (at para. 149)
[121] *BPB Industries plc & Anor v EC Commission* [1993] 1 CEC 713, at p. 730 (para. 68).
[122] *Istituto/IMC and Angus*, Sixteenth Report on Competition Policy, point 76.
[123] *BPB Industries* [1989] 1 CEC 2,008; OJ 1989 L10/50, at p. 65.
[124] *BPB Industries plc & Anor v EC Commission* [1993] 1 CEC 713.
[125] *Soda-ash–Solvay*, OJ 1991 L152/21.
[126] *Soda-ash–ICI*, OJ 1991 L152/40.

¶915

A more detailed analysis of exclusive purchasing agreements from the point of view of both art. 85 and 86 is contained in Chapters 2 and 3.

¶916   Abusive registration of trade marks

In *Osram/Airam*, the Commission stated that an undertaking 'in a dominant position in a substantial part of the Common Market which registers a trade mark when it knows or ought to have known that that mark is already used by a competitor in other Member States may infringe Article 86 [because] this registration restricts the competitor's opportunities for penetrating the market dominated by the firm concerned'.[127]

This statement related to a Commission investigation of Osram GmbH, one of the main lamp producers in the EC, following a complaint lodged by OY Airam AB, a small Finnish manufacturer. When the Finnish firm tried to register its 'Airam' trade mark, Osram objected on the ground of possible confusion with its 'Osram' mark. Subsequently, Osram defensively registered the 'Airam' trade mark in Germany. After Commission intervention, the parties came to a settlement whereby OY Airam AB could use 'Airam' as part of its trade name and trade mark everywhere in the Community, provided that its corporate descriptions (i.e. 'OY' and 'AB') and the word 'Finland' (or other country of manufacture) figure as prominently on the label as does the 'Airam' trade mark.

¶917   Restrictions on resales

As illustrated by the *Chiquita*[128] decision, the imposition on purchasers by a dominant undertaking of restrictions on resales constitutes an abuse under art. 86. In *Chiquita* the Commission objected to a clause in United Brands' sales conditions prohibiting the resale of bananas in green condition by its ripener–distributors. The Commission and the court analysed this restriction as being equivalent to a ban on exports. The clause was found to be illegal even though there was no evidence that it had actually been enforced as a market-partitioning device and the perishable nature of the product in practice prevented resales across borders.

¶918   Tying

The last example of abuse listed in art. 86 is tying which consists of 'making the conclusion of contracts subject to acceptance by the other parties of supplementary obligations which, by their nature or according to commercial

---

[127] *Osram/Airam, Eleventh Report on Competition Policy*, point 97.
[128] *Chiquita*, OJ 1976 L95/1. See also *European Gas Producers* settlement, Commission press release IP(89) 426 of 7 June 1989.

¶916

usage, have no connection with the subject of such contracts'. In other words, an undertaking that enjoys a dominant position on the market for a product or a service may not make the sale of this product or the provision of this service conditional upon the sale of another product or the provision of another service.

Thus, the Commission considered that IBM was abusing its dominant position by not offering its most powerful range of computers (the System 370) without a capacity of main memory ('memory bundling') and the basic software ('software bundling') included in the price. A proceeding under art. 86 was initiated by the Commission but was terminated without a formal decision after IBM had undertaken to offer its System 370 in the EC either without main memory or with only such capacity as is strictly required for testing and to take further measures to enable competing companies in the EC to attach both hardware and software products of their design to System 370.[129]

Fiat Auto had imposed an obligation on their dealers and authorised repairers to sell and use only lubricants sold and manufactured by Fiat under the brand name of Oliofiat. Since the Commission considered that this practice could have closed the market for competing lubricant suppliers in a significant part of the Italian market, it intervened. As a result of the Commission intervention, Fiat sent a circular letter to its dealers and workshops modifying the obligation, indicating that from then on the Fiat network members should use Fiat lubricants or the lubricants of other manufacturers if they meet quality standards and specifications necessary to preserve the correct performance of the vehicles.[130]

Tying not justified by safety concerns

In *Eurofix-Bauco v Hilti*,[131] the Commission found that Hilti, a producer of fastening systems used in the building industry, was abusing its dominant position by supplying cartridge strips to certain end-users or distributors only when purchased with the necessary complement of nails. The company also reduced discounts for orders of cartridges without nails, because the customer was buying the nails from a competitor.

The Court of First Instance upheld the position of the Commission and rejected the justification advanced by Hilti.[132] In its defence, Hilti alleged that the nails manufactured by Eurofix and Bauco revealed significant deficiencies which rendered them incompatible for use in the Hilti system and, hence, potentially unsafe. When asked why it took no other actions, legal or otherwise,

---

[129] *IBM* settlement, *Fourteenth Report on Competition Policy*, points 94–95.
[130] *Oliofiat, Seventeenth Report on Competition Policy*, point 84.
[131] *Eurofix-Bauco v Hilti*, OJ 1988 L65/19, at pp. 25, 26 and 36. See also, *Fifteenth Report on Competition Policy*, point 49.
[132] *Hilti AG v EC Commission* [1991] ECR II-1439, on appeal: [1994] 1 CEC 590.

¶918

than to tie the sale of its cartridge strips to the purchase of its nails, Hilti answered on the one hand that it had considered the problem as a local one and did not want to provoke legal action by issuing public warnings, and on the other hand that recourse to the competent authorities would have caused greater harm to the interests of Bauco and Eurofix than the conduct which it in fact pursued. The court rejected this defence and stressed that member states' law provided for penalties when dangerous products are sold and when misleading claims are made regarding the characteristic of products.

'In those circumstances it is clearly not the task of an undertaking in a dominant position to take steps on its own initiative to eliminate products which, rightly or wrongly, it regards as dangerous or at least as inferior in quality to its own products.'[133]

The lesson to be drawn from the *Hilti* case is that if a dominant undertaking has reasons to believe that a competitor's products are unsafe, it should address itself to the public authorities and let them handle the problem, rather than taking steps on its own initiative.[134]

Rebates equivalent to tying

In *Hoffmann-La Roche*,[135] both the Commission and the court considered that the system of rebates offered by Hoffmann-La Roche to its customers amounted to a tying practice since the rebates were calculated on overall purchases of goods belonging to separate markets.

Absence of connection between tied products

When condemning tying practices, the Commission usually emphasises the absence of connection between the tied products or services. Thus, in *British Telecommunications*,[136] the Commission challenged the practice whereby BT, a public corporation with a statutory monopoly for the running of tele-communication systems throughout the UK, prevented message-forwarding agencies in the UK from relaying telex messages both originating in and for delivery outside the UK. This practice, which was aimed at protecting the revenues of other national telecommunication authorities, was condemned on the ground that it '[made] the use of telephone and telex installations subject to obligations which have no connection with the assignment of telephone or telex services'.[137] The Commission further noted that 'the scope of BT's

---

[133] Ibid., at para. 118.
[134] However, for a case where an approach made to the public authorities was considered abusive, see *French-West African shipowners' committees* OJ 1992 L134/1.
[135] *Hoffmann-La Roche v EC Commission* ('*Vitamins*') [1979] ECR 461, at p. 547 (para. 110–111).
[136] *British Telecommunications*, OJ 1982 L360/36.
[137] Id., at p. 40. See also, *London European/Sabena* [1989] 1 CEC 2,278; OJ 1988 L317/47, at p. 52. In this case Sabena refused to grant London European access to its computer reservation system unless London European

monopoly in the relevant legislation is the exclusive privilege of running telecommunications systems, not the offering of services making use of such systems'.[138]

Subsequently, in a preliminary ruling under art. 177, the court objected to the practice whereby a television station subjected the sale of broadcasting time for telemarketing operations to the use of the telephone number of an exclusive advertising agent belonging to the same group. The court stressed inter alia that telemarketing (an activity whereby an advertiser places in one media, here television, an advertisement carrying a telephone number which those at whom the advertisement is aimed may call either to obtain information on the product offered or to respond to the advertising campaign in some other way) constitutes a 'neighbouring but separate' market from that of the chosen advertising medium.[139]

In *Napier Brown/British Sugar*,[140] British Sugar refused to supply sugar to customers who did not accept delivery of the sugar by British Sugar. The Commission considered that delivery was a separate but ancillary activity which could be undertaken by an individual contractor acting alone. The Commission concluded that British Sugar had abused its dominant position by refusing to grant its customers an option between purchasing sugar on an ex-factory or delivered price basis.[141]

Tying not justified by integrated nature of business

In *Tetra Pak II*, the Commission considered standard contractual terms obliging purchasers of Tetra Pak packaging machines to use only Tetra Pak cartons supplied exclusively by Tetra Pak to be abusive. The Commission found this to be a serious restriction on intra-brand as well as inter-brand competition. This system of tied sales limited outlets and made contracts subject to acceptance of conditions which had no connection with their purpose. The restrictions on competition were strengthened given Tetra Pak's integrated distribution system and its patent policy (the patenting of minor technical characteristics and of the slightest modification to them). They made the carton market totally dependent on the machine market, and were an incentive to discriminatory and loss making pricing on the latter. The Commission rejected Tetra Pak's arguments that the conditions could be justified on the grounds of the integrated nature of its business, for technical

---

agreed to give the ground-handling contract to Sabena. The Commission found that the two contracts were not connected and held the behaviour of Sabena contrary to art. 86(d).

[138] *British Telecommunications*, OJ 1982 L360/36, at p. 41.
[139] *Telemarketing v CLT* [1985] ECR 3261, at pp. 3276–3278 (para. 19–27).
[140] *Napier Brown/British Sugar*, OJ 1988 L284/41.
[141] Id., at p. 55.

reasons, for considerations of product liability and health and by the need to protect its reputation. Tetra Pak was fined ECU 75m.[142]

Computer program copyright

With respect to the exercise of copyright over aspects of a computer program, the Commission recently stated that under certain circumstances an abuse of a dominant position may be found 'if a dominant company tries to use its exclusive rights in one product to gain an unfair advantage in relation to one or more products not covered by these rights'.[143]

¶919   Abusive licensing practices

Abusive acquisition of licence

Tetra Pak I[144] illustrates the Commission's thinking that a dominant company has 'a special responsibility not to allow its conduct to impair genuine undistorted competition on the Common Market'.[145] The Tetra Pak Group was dominant in the markets of machines incorporating technology for sterilising cartons for UHT treated liquids (mainly milk) and the supply of those cartons. In 1986, Tetra Pak took over Liquipak, which had an exclusive licence from the British Technology Group (BTG) on new technology which facilitated the adaptation of gable top cartons, which previously could only be fresh filled, to aseptic filling for UHT treated liquids. Due to this takeover, Tetra Pak acquired the licence and obtained an advantage which its competitors did not possess. The Commission referred to *Continental Can*,[146] where the court stated that there may be an abuse if a dominant firm strengthens its position so that the degree of dominance reached substantially fetters competition. The Commission found these conditions were fulfilled since Tetra Pak's acquisition of the licence prevented or at least delayed the entry of a new competitor, Elopak, into the market. A new entrant into the market was almost the only way to challenge Tetra's dominance because only minimal competition existed. Elopak had in fact co-operated with Liquipak in developing an aseptic packaging machine incorporating the new technology, but as Tetra Pak took over Liquipak, Tetra Pak got exclusive access to the BTG technology. Since technology was the key element to entering the market, the Commission found that Tetra Pak had considerably raised the barriers to entry, perhaps even to an insurmountable level. The Commission concluded:

---

[142] *Tetra Pak II*, OJ 1992 L72/1, at para. 116–120.
[143] Commission conclusions decided on the occasion of the adoption of the Commission's proposal for a Council directive on the legal protection of computer programs, OJ 1989 C91/16.
[144] *Tetra Pak I (BTG licence)*, OJ 1988 L272/27.
[145] *Michelin v EC Commission* [1983] ECR 3461, at p. 3511.
[146] *Europemballage Corp and Continental Can Co Inc. EC Commission* [1973] ECR 215.

'Consequently, the acquisition of the exclusive licence not only strengthened Tetra's already considerable dominant position, but also had the effect of reducing even further the possibility of any effective competition. This behaviour therefore constitutes an abuse of its dominant position. This abuse continued as long as Tetra had the exclusivity to the licence in question.'[147]

Abusive refusals to license

In *Tetra Pak*, the dominant company was the licensee, but there are also cases in which the dominant company was the licensor.

In *AB Volvo v Erik Veng (UK)*[148] and *Maxicar v Renault*[149] the court held that a refusal by the proprietor to grant a licence of a registered design, even in return for reasonable royalties, did not in itself amount to an abuse, but that certain exercises by the proprietor of an exclusive right can be abusive.[150]

In *Magill TV Guide/ITP, BBC & RTE*,[151] three television broadcasting companies refused to license the Magill TV Guide to reprint their respective advance weekly programme listing. By their licensing policy, the three companies restrained undertakings seeking to publish a weekly TV Guide with the result that no comprehensive weekly TV Guide existed in Ireland or the UK. Viewers who wished to obtain advance weekly programme information were forced to buy three separate guides published by the three companies respectively. The Commission held that the companies had abused their dominant position in preventing the introduction of a new product to the market and that they had used copyright in a manner which falls outside the specific subject matter of that right. Another element of the abuse was the fact that the companies kept the market for weekly television guides to themselves.

The Court of First Instance confirmed the Commission's decision and developed the following analytical framework to reconcile the exercise of exclusive rights derived from national intellectual property law with the principles of freedom of competition as expressed in art. 86. The starting point for the analysis was the by then well-established principle that the holder of an intellectual property right – copyright in the case at hand – may exercise the specific subject-matter of his right (including the right to refuse to grant licences to third parties) without this being in itself contrary to art. 86. However, if such right is exercised in a manner or in circumstances so as to pursue an aim which is manifestly contrary to art. 86, that principle would no longer apply.[152] The

---

[147] *Tetra Pak I (BTG licence)*, OJ 1988 L272/27, at p. 40.
[148] *AB Volvo v Erik Veng (UK)* [1988] ECR 6211.
[149] *CICRA and SpA Maxicar v Régie Nationale des Usines Renault* [1988] ECR 6039; [1990] 1 CEC 267.
[150] See ¶908.
[151] *Magill TV Guide/ITP, BBC & RTE* [1989] 1 CEC 2,223; OJ 1989 L78/43; on appeal: *Radio Telefis Eireann v EC Commission* [1991] ECR II-485; *Independent Television Publications Ltd v EC Commission* [1991] ECR II-535 and *BBC v EC Commission* [1991] ECR II-575.
[152] See *BBC v EC Commission* [1991] ECR II-575, at para. 58.

¶919

Court of First instance stressed that this would have to be judged in the light of the details of each individual case.

The court then listed the individual circumstances which, in its view, showed that the applicants had gone beyond what was necessary to protect the specific subject-matter of their copyright.

These individual circumstances were essentially the following. The applicants were found to have prevented the emergence on the market of a new product, a comprehensive weekly TV guide (as opposed to weekly TV guides containing only the individual applicants' programme listings), for which there was a potential consumer demand and which was likely to compete with their own product. In so doing, the applicants had used their copyright monopoly in the derivative market of weekly television guides. According to the court, the arbitrary nature of the refusal to grant licences to third parties was shown by the absence of any justification flowing from the specific needs peculiar to the publishing of television guides. The publication of the broadcasters' own weekly TV Guides would still have been economically viable even if third parties were authorised to publish weekly listings.

The Court of First Instance also stressed that this analysis was in line with the opinion of the Court of Justice in the *Volvo v Veng*[153] and *Maxicar v Renault*[154] cases. As mentioned above,[155] the court stated:

> 'It must however also be noted that the exercise of an exclusive right by the proprietor of a registered design ... may be prohibited by Article 86 if it involves ... certain abusive conduct such as the arbitrary refusal to supply spare parts to independent repairers, the fixing of prices for spare parts at an unfair level or a decision no longer to produce spare parts for a particular model even though cars of that model are still in circulation ...'.[156]

In addition, the Court of First Instance stated that the failure of the broadcasters to take into account the needs and demands of the consumers was comparable to the decision by a car manufacturer not to produce spare parts any longer although there were still many cars in circulation.[157]

Although the *Magill TV Guide* cases pay extensive lip service to *Volvo v Veng* and *CICRA v Renault*, one cannot avoid having the impression that the ruling in these landmark cases may have been turned on its head. The primary ruling in these cases stated that a refusal by a proprietor to license, even in return for reasonable royalties, is part of the subject-matter of the exclusive right and is therefore not, in itself, abusive.[158] This fundamental principle, which

---

[153] *AB Volvo v Erik Veng (UK)* [1988] ECR 6211.
[154] *CICRA and SpA Maxicar v Régie Nationale des Usines Renault* [1988] ECR 6039.
[155] See ¶908.
[156] *AB Volvo v Erik Veng (UK)* [1988] ECR 6211, at para. 9.
[157] See *BBC v EC Commission* [1991] ECR II-575, at para. 61.
[158] *AB Volvo v Erik Veng (UK)* [1988] ECR 6211, at p. 6235, at para. 8.

is essential to maintain a proper balance between intellectual property rights and competition law, risks being undermined if the right-holder must show a justification for his refusal to grant licences to third parties. The president of the Court of First Instance had already indicated in an order for interim measures during the first appeal that the owner of an exclusive copyright is not obliged to license.[159] In the meantime, RTE and ITP have appealed the judgment of the Court of First Instance.[160] It is now up to the Court of Justice to clarify this point of law.

¶920   Market-sharing agreements

A dominant firm which requires competitors to enter into market-sharing agreements is likely to abuse its dominant position. In *Decca Navigator System*,[161] Racal Decca enjoyed a dominant position in the market for commercial receivers of DNS signals. Through agreements with some other undertakings, it reserved the market for commercial receivers for itself and left the market for pleasure-boat receivers to the other companies. Decca reinforced the effect of this arrangement by making changes in the DNS signals (Decca was also dominant in the market for the transmission of DNS signals), causing malfunctioning of the devices sold by competitors unwilling to enter into the market sharing agreements. The Commission found that Decca had abused its dominant position by the said actions, but did not impose a fine since it was not established that Decca's infringement of art. 86 was intentional or even due to negligence because of the complexity of the legal assessment of the case and the lack of precedents.

¶921   Abusive conduct by undertakings holding a collective dominant position

In *Flat glass*, the Commission found that the companies concerned, three Italian manufacturers of flat glass, were in a collective dominant position. Thereby, the Commission was able to construct infringements of art. 85 as also constituting an abuse within the meaning of art. 86. The actions taken by the three firms were considered abusive since they restricted the consumers' ability to choose sources of supply and limited the market outlets of the Community's other producers of flat glass. Their business conduct consisted of:

---

[159] *Radio Telefis Eireann & Ors v EC Commission*, order of the President of the Court of 11 May 1989, [1989] ECR 1141, at para. 13.
[160] *Radio Telefis Eireann and Independent Television Publications v EC Commission*, Cases C-241/91 and C-242/91, not yet decided.
[161] *Decca Navigator System* [1989] 1 CEC 2,137; OJ 1989 L43/27.

(1) communication of identical prices to their customers on dates close to each other;

(2) identical discounts;

(3) identical classification of the main customers by category or level; and

(4) elements of concerted practices between the producers which consisted of meetings or other contacts between the producers in which the uniformity of the prices, discounts and classification was agreed upon.[162]

On appeal, the Court of First Instance held that the Commission had not sufficiently substantiated the finding of a collective dominant position and annulled the Commission decision in so far as it referred to an infringement of art. 86.[163] The court did not consider it necessary to discuss whether the business conduct of the firms concerned was indeed abusive or not. The court established, however, that 'recycling' facts constituting an infringement of art. 85 is insufficient to establish a dominant position or an abuse thereof. This statement does not affect the general principle that the same agreement or practice may infringe both art. 85 and 86.

In two other cases involving maritime transport, the Commission found that the members of shipowners' committees or shipping conferences held a collective dominant position.[164] In the first case, *French-West African Shipowners' Committee*,[165] the Commission considered that those practices by which the members of the committee endeavoured to eliminate effective competition from non-committee shipping lines constituted an abuse of a dominant position. Such practices consisted of involvement in the imposition of fines by the authorities on non-committee shipowners and in the imposition of conditions of admission to newcomers so as to make their access to the trade virtually impossible. The conduct found abusive by the Commission was broadly the same as that which had been held to infringe art. 85 of the treaty. This leaves certain doubts as to whether this conduct constitutes a simple 'recycling' of the facts, and is therefore insufficient to establish an abuse of a dominant position, or not. The analysis made by the Commission, however, seems to go further than a simple 'recycling' of the facts.

In the second case, *Cewal*,[166] the Commission considered that Cewal, one of

---

[162] *Flat glass* [1989] 1 CEC 2,077; OJ 1989 L33/44. This decision has been referred to as the first time the Commission used the concept of a collective dominant position. However, in *European Sugar Industry*, OJ 1973 L140/17, the Commission considered two undertakings having a dominant position together on the Dutch sugar market. See Chapter 2 above.

[163] *Società Italiano Vetro SpA & Ors v EC Commission* [1992] 2 CEC 33. On the notion of collective dominance, see Chapter 2, ¶247.

[164] On the notion of collective dominance, see Chapter 2, ¶247.

[165] *French-West African Shipowners' Committees* OJ 1992 L134/1, at p. 17. For a detailed analysis of the case, see Chapter 10.

[166] *Cewal* OJ 1993 L 34/20, at p. 31. For a detailed analysis of the case, see Chapter 10.

the shipping conferences operating between Europe and west and central Africa, had abused its collective dominant position in three different ways:

(1) concluding an agreement with governmental authorities with the effect of restricting competition by the exclusion of non-member lines from participation in the trade;

(2) using the 'fighting ships' method, a practice which was treated by the Commission as predatory pricing and as an imposition of dissimilar conditions to equivalent transactions; and

(3) imposing excessive conditions in its loyalty contracts.

¶922   Abusive conduct on the part of a dominant purchaser

When Tabacalera SA, the Spanish tobacco monopoly holder, increased its own production of ordinary cigarette filters from 44 per cent to 100 per cent of its requirements, its supplier of cigarette filters, Filtrona, lodged a complaint with the Commission. Following the Commission's rejection of the complaint, Filtrona brought an action before the court to obtain a judgment as to whether Tabacalera abused its dominant position as a purchaser by virtue of its vertical expansion.[167] The Court of First Instance did not have to decide the matter as the appeal was ruled inadmissible.[168]

---

[167] OJ 1989 C211/9.
[168] *Filtrona Española v EC Commission* [1990] ECR II-393 (summary publication only).

10 Special Sectors

¶1001 Outline

When defining the scope of application of art. 85 and 86 of the treaty, attention must be given to the fact that a number of special sectors of the economy are either in whole or in part exempt from the application of the EC competition rules. Other sectors present such particular features that a sector-specific application of the EC competition rules has been developed.

The special sectors that will be discussed in this chapter are the following: coal and steel (¶1002); nuclear energy (¶1003); agriculture (¶1004); the military sector (¶1005); transport by rail, road and inland waterway (¶1006); maritime transport (¶1007–¶1020); air transport (¶1021–¶1042); banking (¶1043–¶1050); insurance (¶1051–¶1054); and telecommunications (¶1055–¶1066).

¶1002 Coal and steel

Pursuant to art. 232(1) of the EC Treaty, coal and steel are outside the scope of the treaty.[1] They are instead covered by the Treaty establishing the European Coal and Steel Community ('ECSC') which contains its own provisions on competition.[2] However, due to the limited scope of the ECSC Treaty, the EC Treaty and the ECSC Treaty may apply to different parts of the same agreement in the coal and steel industry.[3] Indeed, the EC Treaty, because of its general application, covers every aspect of the coal and steel industry which is not covered by the ECSC Treaty.

It is also worth mentioning that the ECSC Treaty will expire in 2002. It will

---

[1] What exactly is meant by 'coal' and 'steel' is defined in Annex 1 to the ECSC Treaty.

[2] Article 65 of the ECSC Treaty deals with agreements and art. 66 with the abuse of a dominant position and with merger control. Article 60 prohibits unfair and discriminatory pricing.

[3] In *Jahrhundertvertrag*, OJ 1993 L50/14, an agreement was reached between the General Association of the German Coalmining industry (GVSt) on the one hand and the Association of the German Public Electricity Supply Industry (VDEW) and the Association of Industrial Producers of Electricity (VIK) on the other hand, for the sale and purchase of specific amounts of coal for the purpose of generating electricity. Because art. 80 and art. 65 limit the application of the ECSC Treaty to undertakings which are engaged in the production or distribution of coal and steel, the Commission could only exempt the agreements among the mining companies and the decisions of GVSt to make such an overall agreement with the electricity industry under art. 66 of the ECSC Treaty. However, because of the broad scope of art. 85(1) of the EC Treaty, the agreements with the electricity industry (VDEW and VIK) could be exempted under art. 85(3).

It is also worth noting that the EC Treaty also applies to the coal and steel industry in respect of those coal and steel products which are not mentioned in Annex 1 to the ECSC Treaty.

not be renewed because, according to the Commission, special treatment for coal and steel is no longer justified.[4] In order to enable a smooth transition the Commission has decided to align as far as possible its practices under the two treaties.

¶1003   Nuclear energy

Pursuant to art. 232(2) of the EC Treaty, the treaty provisions may not derogate from those of the Treaty establishing the European Atomic Energy Community.

The Euratom Treaty does not have any competition rules of its own. Hence, art. 85 and 86 of the EC Treaty apply to nuclear energy.[5] However, the Euratom Treaty contains specific provisions on the establishment of joint ventures,[6] and prices of nuclear materials which need to be taken into account.[7]

¶1004   Agriculture

Application of competition rules to agriculture

The Treaty of Rome (as amended by the Union Treaty) provides for the establishment of a common agricultural policy (art. 3(d)) and for the principle of undistorted competition (art. 3(g)). Since these two essential objectives of the Community may be conflicting, special provisions are set out in art. 39–46 of the treaty in order to determine under which conditions the rules on competition laid down in the treaty apply to the production of and trade in agricultural products.

According to art. 38(3) of the treaty, the products subject to the provisions of art. 39–46 are listed in Annex II to the treaty. The list in Annex II does not wholly coincide with the definition of agricultural products given in art. 38(1). The definition in art. 38(1) is only indicative. The binding definition is that contained in art. 38(3) which refers to Annex II.[8]

Article 42 of the treaty declares with respect to agricultural products:

'The provisions of the chapter relating to rules on competition shall apply to

---

[4] *XXIst Report on Competition Policy*, point 207.

[5] See e.g. *United Reprocessors*, OJ 1976 L51/7; *KEWA*, OJ 1976 L51/15; *Amersham Buchler*, OJ 1982 L314/34; *Scottish Nuclear, Nuclear Energy Agreement*, OJ 1991 L178/31 (exemption under art. 85(3) of agreement between the Scottish nuclear power generating company and the Scottish distributor of electricity for the reorganisation and privatisation of the production, supply and distribution of electricity in Scotland); *Twinning Programme Engineering Group*, OJ 1992 C148/8 (notification for negative clearance of an agreement among seven electricity generating enterprises and associations for the carrying out and co-ordination of studies and technical solutions for the improvement of safety in VVER nuclear power plants operating in eastern Europe).

[6] Article 45–51 of the EAEC Treaty.

[7] Id., art. 67–69.

[8] de Cockborne, J.E., 'Les règles communautaires de concurrence applicables aux entreprises dans le domaine agricole', Rev. Trim. Dr. Eur., No. 24(2), avril–juin 1988, p. 293. See also, *Coöperatieve Stremsel en Kleurselfabriek v EC Commission* [1981] ECR 851

production of and trade in agricultural products only to the extent determined by the Council within the framework of Article 43(2) and (3) and in accordance with the procedure laid down therein, account being taken of the objectives set out in Article 39.'

Regulation 26/62[9] was adopted by the Council on 4 April 1962. Article 1 of the regulation states that the competition rules (art. 85–90 of the treaty and provisions made to implement the treaty rules) shall apply to all agreements, decisions and practices relating to the production of or trade in the products listed in Annex II to the treaty.

Exceptions

Article 2(1) of Regulation 26/62 provides for two substantial exceptions to the rule of art. 1. Pursuant to art. 2(1), art. 85(1) of the treaty shall not apply to such of the agreements, decisions and practices:

(1) as form an integral part of a national market organisation; or

(2) as are necessary for the attainment of the objectives set out in art. 39 of the treaty.[10]

These two exceptions are further defined as including:

'agreements, decisions and practices of farmers, farmers' associations or associations of such associations belonging to a single Member State which concern the production or sale of agricultural products or the use of joint facilities for the storage, treatment or processing of agricultural products, and under which there is no obligation to charge identical prices, unless the Commission finds that competition is thereby excluded or that the objectives of Article 39 of the Treaty are jeopardized'.

Article 2(2) of the same regulation gives the Commission the sole power, subject to review by the Court of Justice, to determine, by a decision that is to be published, which agreements, decisions and practices fulfil the conditions specified in art. 2(1).

---

[9] Council Regulation 26/62 applying certain rules of competition to production of and trade in agricultural products, JO 1962 993. In addition, it should be noted that concentrations on the market for agricultural products are subjected to Council Regulation 4064/89 of 21 December 1989 on the control of concentrations between undertakings, OJ 1990 L257/13.

[10] The objectives of art. 39 are to:

- increase agricultural productivity;
- ensure a fair standard of living for the agricultural community;
- stabilise markets;
- assure the availability of supplies;
- ensure that supplies reach consumers at reasonable prices.

¶1004

On several occasions, the Commission and the court have refused to grant the benefit of an exception.[11]

National market organisations

With respect to the first art. 2(1) exception concerning national market organisations, the Commission determined in the *New Potatoes* case[12] that the conditions specified in art. 2(1) were fulfilled. This was the first decision clarifying the meaning of 'national organisations'. A 'national organisation' was defined as a totality of legal devices placing the regulation of the market in the products in question under the control of the public authority, with a view to ensuring the realisation of the objectives of art. 39.

In that particular case the regulation of the French new potato market was entrusted to producer groups recognised by the Ministry for Agriculture and to authorised economic committees. These private-law bodies implemented the regulation of the market in question by means of decisions and agreements. Although the regulation of the French new potato market was thus entrusted to professional organisations, the Commission found that the whole organisation took the form of a 'national organisation' within the meaning of art. 2(1) of Regulation 26/62 because both the constitution of the professional organisations in question and their relevant decisions and agreements were placed under the control of the French public authority.

The Commission also considered that the agreements in question, even though they placed restrictions on the freedom to produce and market products, did not jeopardise the implementation of the fundamental principles of the treaty and did not exclude competition and in particular price competition. Consequently, the provisions of art. 85(1) of the EC Treaty were declared inapplicable to the agreements in question.

Objectives of art. 39

With respect to the second art. 2(1) exception, concerning the objectives set out in art. 39, the Commission held in its *Cane Sugar* decision,[13] without further justification, that a long-term purchase contract for the supply of African and Caribbean cane sugar to the Community was 'within the objectives contemplated by Article 39'.

In its *Bloemenveilingen Aalsmeer* decision of 26 July 1988,[14] the Commission

---

[11] See e.g. *Cauliflowers*, OJ 1978 L21/23; *Frubo v EC Commission* [1975] ECR 563 at pp. 582 and 583 (para. 22–27); *Suiker Unie & Ors v EC Commission* [1975] ECR 1663, at pp. 1948–1950 (para. 211–255) and at p. 2020 (para. 603–605); *Preserved Mushrooms*, OJ 1975 L29/26; *Nungesser v EC Commission (Maize seed)* [1982] ECR 2015; *Milchförderungsfonds*, OJ 1985 L35/35; *Sugar beet*, OJ 1989 L31/32.

[12] *New Potatoes*, OJ 1987 L159/2.

[13] *Cane sugar*, OJ 1980 L39/64.

[14] *Bloemenveilingen Aalsmeer*, OJ 1988 L262/27. On 26 July 1988, the 'Verenigde Bloemenveilingen Aalsmeer' (VBA) notified new rules which had entered into force on 1 May 1988 and which it amended at the

refused to grant the benefit of an exception. This case involved exclusive dealing arrangements in favour of producer groups cultivating flowers and other ornamental plants. The decision is interesting because the Commission explained at great length why the provisions of the exclusive dealing arrangements were not necessary for the attainment of the objectives set out in art. 39 of the EC Treaty.

In that case, the object of the exclusive dealings to further the interests of the members of the group was achieved mainly through the holding of auction sales, at which not only members' products, but also products of other Dutch and foreign growers were put up for auction by the growers themselves or by dealers. One of the dealers, who wished to sell larger quantities than he had agreed to sell, applied to the Commission to challenge the whole system.

The Commission considered first that the provisions did not form an integral part of a market organisation. The Commission then ruled that, to that date, in no sector of the common agricultural policy had an exclusive dealing arrangement in favour of producers been regarded as a means of attaining the objectives of art. 39 of the EC Treaty. According to the Commission, such a binding arrangement could lead to a situation in which the individual member had no choice but to sell his products through the group because the direct sales channels were blocked. The group contended in response to the objections raised by the Commission that, according to the recitals of Regulation 234/68, promoting the rational marketing of production and ensuring stable market conditions were important objectives of the common agricultural policy in the field of live plants and floricultural products. The Commission held that such an argument was untenable, at least in so far as it related to the contractual relations between the group and the purchasers admitted to it. Lastly, the group argued that the restrictions of competition placed on its tenants were indispensable to the running of its auctions. The Commission also rejected this argument on the grounds that the vertical integration of dealers into the system went beyond what was legally acceptable.

Other exceptions

Apart from the two exceptions mentioned in Regulation 26/62, agreements and decisions with respect to agricultural products can also benefit from an exemption under art. 85(3) of the treaty[15] or they can be part of specific community measures on the basis of art. 42 and 43 of the treaty, enhancing the conclusion of agreements in the agricultural domain.

Commission's instigation. In its notice (see *Bloemenveilingen Aalsmeer*, OJ 1989 C83/3) the Commission proposed to take a favourable decision on the decisions and agreements summarised there.

[15] See de Cockborne, J.E., 'Les règles communautaires de concurrence applicables aux entreprises dans le domaine agricole', Rev. Trim. Dr. Eur., No. 24(21), avril–juin 1988, pp. 308–314.

¶1005   Military sector

Article 223(1)(b) of the EC Treaty provides that:

> 'Any Member State may take such measures as it considers necessary for the protection of the essential interests of its security which are connected with the production of or trade in arms, munitions and war material; such measures shall not adversely affect the conditions of competition in the common market regarding products which are not intended for specifically military purposes.'[16]

Furthermore, art. 225 empowers the European Commission to examine, together with the member state concerned, how measures taken pursuant to art. 223 can be adjusted to the rules laid down in the treaty.

Thus, it is clear that military products are not as such exempted from the operation of art. 85 and 86. Article 223 only authorises the member states to take measures derogating from the rules of the treaty which they consider necessary for the protection of the essential interests of their security. This authority is itself subject, however, to the express condition found in art. 223 that such measures shall not adversely affect the conditions of competition regarding products which are not intended specifically for military purposes.

Among the scarce case law on the subject, it is noteworthy to mention that in 1979 the Commission in the *French State/Suralmo* case,[17] caused the French Government, represented by the Direction Nationale d'Interventions Domaniales, to amend a clause that restricted the rights of the licensee, Suralmo, to grant sub-licences for applying a patented invention to military equipment.[18] As reported in the *Ninth Report*:

> 'The Commission informed the parties to the agreement that, in its opinion, the different terms for the exercise of Suralmo's right to grant sub-licences, depending on whether these related to applications for military or civilian use, constituted a field-of-use restriction and could therefore fall within the prohibition in Article 85(1) of the EEC Treaty.

> Further, Article 223 of the Treaty could not in the Commission's view be invoked in this case, since the engines to which the patents related, far from being intended for specifically military purposes, were on the contrary intended primarily for nonmilitary use. The right that Article 223 gives any

---

[16] As long ago as 15 April 1958, the EEC Council of Ministers formulated a list of products covered by art. 223(1)(b). This list is not publicly available. Nevertheless, pursuant to a decision of the representatives of the member states at their 265th meeting on 17–19 July 1963, nationals of the member states who can show a sufficient interest may obtain a copy of the list from their national governments.

[17] *Suralmo, Ninth Report on Competition Policy*, points 114 and 115.

[18] Under the clause, Suralmo was required to obtain prior written consent from the Directeur Technique des Armements Terrestres before granting any sub-licences for military applications.

Member State to take such measures as it considers necessary for the protection of the essential interests of its security and which are connected with the production of or trade in war material, even if these measures adversely affect the conditions of competition in the Common Market, is subject to the provision that the measures must concern only products intended for specifically military purposes.'

This case shows that the Commission construes art. 223 narrowly rather than viewing it as a blanket exemption for any government action in the military field.

In 1982, the Commission intervened against a production sharing agreement between two private French companies active in the field of ballistic missiles – Forgeal and Cruisot-Loire. As a result of the Commission's intervention, the charter and by-laws of their joint venture company – Air Forge – had to be amended. In particular, the rules providing for order allocation under a system of fixed quotas had to be deleted.[19] While it is possible that the question of the applicability of art. 223 was never raised in this case as the Commission's report of the case makes no mention of art. 223, this case suggests that the competition rules apply to agreements between private parties even if military equipment is involved.[20]

The writing on the wall seems to be that defence contracts are increasingly open to antitrust scrutiny in the EC. Hence, those drafting such contracts will have to assess carefully the respective roles of government and private industry in order to define the private company's exposure.

¶1006   Transport by rail, road and inland waterway

Scope
Council Regulation 1017/68 regulates the application of the EC competition rules in the sector of transport by rail, road and inland waterway.[21] The scope of this regulation is defined in art. 1 as including agreements, decisions and concerted practices on transport rates and conditions, the supply of transport, the sharing of transport markets, the application of technical improvements, technical co-operation or the joint financing or acquisition of transport equipment or supplies. The regulation also contains provisions on the abuse of

---

[19] *Twelfth Report on Competition Policy*, point 85.
[20] In a more recent case, *GEC-Siemens/Plessey*, OJ 1990 C239/2, which involved an agreement between private companies that included defence electronics, the Commission expressly declined to rule on the application of the competition rules to products used exclusively for defence purposes.
[21] JO 1968 L175/1.

a dominant position on the transport market. All these provisions also apply to operations of providers of services ancillary to transport.[22]

Restrictive practices

The substantive provisions of this regulation are similar to the general provisions on competition in the EC Treaty. Article 2 of the regulation corresponds to the prohibition, contained in art. 85(1) of the EC Treaty, of agreements between undertakings which have as their object or effect the prevention, restriction or distortion of competition on the EC market. Article 7 of the regulation takes over the rule of art. 85(2) in that it declares the prohibited agreements automatically void. The prohibition of abuse of dominant positions of art. 8 coincides with the rule spelled out in art. 86 of the EC Treaty. Finally, art. 9 provides for specific rules for public enterprises similar to those contained in art. 90 of the EC Treaty.

In *French inland waterway charter traffic: EATE levy*,[23] the French boatmen's co-operative EATE and the French National Federation of Inland Waterway Forwarding Agents agreed on the establishment of a ten per cent levy (the EATE levy) on all charters with an international destination arranged in France through the official inland waterway freight exchange system. The levy was to be collected by the forwarding agents and was to be used for the benefit of the entire trade. The members of EATE could apply for a refund.

The Commission found the agreement to violate art. 2 of the regulation on several accounts. First, the levy placed the international carriers at a competitive disadvantage. Indeed, the levy was only charged on international traffic while the funds collected through this system were in fact used exclusively for the promotion and expansion of traffic to French destinations in which foreign carriers could only play an insignificant role because of French Government regulation in this sector. Secondly, the fact that foreign carriers were barred from membership in EATE prevented them from applying for a refund of the levy and thus again placed them at a competitive disadvantage. Finally, according to the Commission, 'the promise of a refund of the levy was too strong an inducement for the [French] carriers to resist. [T]his measure [was] contrary to competition rules since it restric[ted] the commercial independence of the carriers.'[24]

---

[22] For example, the activities of freight forwarding agents. See *French inland waterway charter traffic: EATE levy*, OJ 1985 L219/35, on appeal: *Association nationale des travailleurs indépendants de la batellerie (Antib) v EC Commission* [1987] ECR 2201.

[23] Ibid.

[24] Id., at p. 42.

¶1006

Exemptions

The principle of art. 85(3) of the EC Treaty is adopted in art. 5 of the regulation, but is adapted to the specific situation of the transport sector. In addition, art. 3 of the regulation provides for a negative clearance of agreements of which the sole object and effect is the achievement of technical improvement or technical co-operation by use of a range of means enumerated in art. 3(1)(a)–(g). Further, art. 4 contains a block exemption for certain agreements between small or medium-sized inland waterway or road traffic companies. Finally, art. 6 provides for an individual exemption, subject to certain specific conditions, of agreements helping to reduce disturbances on the market in case of a state of crisis in the industry.

In *Tariff structures in the combined transport of goods*,[25] the railway companies that were members of the International Railways Union notified the Commission of an agreement on a common tariff structure for the sale of rail haulage. The agreement included a flat rate charge of one per cent of the total rail haulage price for incidental costs. The Commission concluded that the agreement could not be cleared under art. 3 of the regulation although the establishment of a tariff structure is mentioned in art. 3(1)(g), because the agreement did not have the object and effect of applying technical improvements or achieving technical co-operation. Indeed, the agreement was aimed at the prevention of a further reduction in the revenue of the railways and had an effect on prices. In addition, in breach of art. 3(1)(g), part of the tariff (the one per cent charge for incidental costs) had been fixed.

However, the Commission exempted the agreement under art. 5 of the regulation because of the many benefits it entailed. A common tariff structure and the fixing of a common rate for incidental costs made it easier for operators to compare prices which increased efficiency and enhanced competition. Although the agreement on a flat rate of one per cent for incidental costs constituted a fixing of price, the Commission regarded this as a negligible restriction necessary in view of the specific market situation at that time.

Procedure

The procedural provisions of art. 10–28 of the regulation are similar to those contained in Regulation 17/62 on the implementation of art. 85 and 86 of the EC Treaty.[26] However, in contrast to the procedure for an exemption under art.

---

[25] *Tariff structures in the combined transport of goods*, OJ 1993 L73/38. See also *Eurotunnel*, OJ 1988 C292/2 and *Nineteenth Report on Competition Policy*, point 57, where the Commission exempted a market-sharing agreement between the French and British railway companies on the usage of the Channel Tunnel. The agreement also established the utilisation rules for the tunnel.
[26] Regulation 17/62 implementing art. 85 and 86 of the treaty, JO 1962 L13/204.

¶1006

85(3), in order to be eligible for an exemption under art. 5 of the regulation, the agreement does not have to be notified.[27]

In addition, the Commission further implemented Regulation 1017/68 by Regulation 1629/69 and Regulation 1630/69.[28]

MARITIME TRANSPORT

¶1007   Introduction

Liner conferences

Since the last century, international maritime transport services have been characterised by the operation of 'liner conferences'. A liner conference is :

> 'a group of two or more vessel-operating carriers which provides international liner services for the carriage of cargo on a particular route or routes within specified geographical limits and has an agreement or arrangement, whatever its nature, within the framework of which they operate under uniform or common freight rates and any other agreed conditions with respect to the provision of liner services'.[29]

The liner conference was developed in response to problems of overcapacity and rate undercutting, caused by the effects of the technological implications of the nineteenth century industrial revolution on an industry with an inelasticity of supply. The liner conference enabled the industry to impose remunerative rates, fixed in advance by the conference members, and prohibited the members from undercutting these rates. Subsequently, additional provisions were also introduced into liner conference arrangements, such as cargo sharing between the members and strict membership criteria.

Despite the cartellisation of international maritime trade by liner conferences, governments traditionally acknowledged the particular economic circumstances prevalent in this sector,[30] and welcomed the stability and reliability of service to which they gave rise. Consequently, governments

---

[27] *French inland waterway charter traffic: EATE levy*, OJ 1985 L219/35 at p. 43, on appeal: *Association nationales des travailleurs indépendantes de la batellerie (Antib) v EC Commission* [1987] ECR 2201. In this case the parties had not notified the Commission for an exemption. See also recitals 14 and 15 of Regulation 1017/68.

[28] Regulation 1629/69 on the form, content and other details of the complaint pursuant to art. 12 and to notifications pursuant to art. 14(1) of Regulation 1017/68, JO 1969 L209/1; Regulation 1630/69 on the hearings provided for in art. 26(1) and (2) of Regulation 1017/68, JO 1969 L209/11.

[29] Regulation 4056/86, art. 1(3)(b), as taken from the United National Convention on a Code of Conduct for Liner Conferences.

[30] See, for example, recital 6 of Regulation 4056/86, which refers to 'the distinctive characteristics of maritime transport'.

initially abstained from imposing excessive regulatory requirements, and largely permitted liner conferences to function through self-regulation.[31]

However, governmental intervention did emerge in response to the wishes of certain developing countries intent upon securing for their nascent shipping lines a percentage of their foreign trade with the developed world. The liner conference system underwent formal international codification in 1974 by virtue of the United Nations Convention on a code of conduct for liner conferences.[32] The UN liner code covers both relations between the conferences and their users, and relations between the conference members inter se. Thus, for example, art. 7 of the UN liner code governs the use of loyalty arrangements, whereas art. 1 thereof contains provisions concerning the membership of national and non-national shipping lines to the conference. However, the UN liner code does little to open competition in the world's cartelised liner trades.

Intervention of EC law

Although certain EC member states had for many years condoned the participation of their national shipping lines in liner conferences, and were prepared to ratify the UN liner code, conceptual difficulties arose concerning the compatibility of the UN liner code with the application of the general principles of Community law. In particular, despite the conflicting views of the Council based on a liberal interpretation of art. 84(2) of the EC Treaty, the European Court of Justice ruled in the *French Seamen* case[33] that the general principles contained in the EC Treaty, including the competition rules provided for in art. 85 and 86, were of universal application. The immediate effect of the court's *French Seamen* judgment was the need to assess the compatibility of the UN liner code, which was concluded two days after the court's judgment, with the general principles of Community law. Concern was expressed as to the code's compatibility with art. 6 (formerly art. 7), 52, 85, 86 and 113 of the EC Treaty.

The short-term remedy to inconsistencies between the general principles of Community law and the UN liner code was the adoption by the EC Council of the so-called 'Brussels package',[34] which was designed to ensure that the ratification by the EC member states of the code did not conflict with their obligations under the EC Treaty. However, in the long-term the jurisprudence of the EC Court of Justice led to the development of the Community's common

---

[31] One should note that, despite (what are now) art. 3(f) and (g) of the EC Treaty, no Community measures concerning the operation of liner conferences emerged until over 25 years after the Treaty of Rome.
[32] UN Doc TD/CODE/11/Rev.1 (1974).
[33] *EC Commission v France* [1974] ECR 359.
[34] Council Regulation 954/79 of 15 May 1979, OJ 1979 L121/1.

maritime transport policy. It was in this manner that the Council adopted, on 16 December 1986, the so-called '1986 package', comprising:

(1) Council Regulation 4055/86 applying the principle of freedom to provide services to maritime transport between member states and between member states and third countries;[35]

(2) Council Regulation 4056/86 laying down detailed rules for the application of art. 85 and 86 of the treaty to maritime transport;[36]

(3) Council Regulation 4057/86 on unfair pricing practices in maritime transport;[37]

(4) Regulation 4058/86 concerning co-ordinated action to safeguard free access to cargoes in ocean trades.[38]

¶1008   Application of competition rules to international maritime transport services: Regulation 4056/86

Policy

Regulation 4056/86 (hereinafter 'the regulation') sets out detailed rules concerning the application of art. 85 and 86 to certain international maritime transport services operating into or out of the territory of the Community. Although the stated aim of the regulation is to implement the competition rules of the EC Treaty in the maritime transport sector, it is important to note that the regulation forms part of the 1986 package, and therefore part of the Community's maritime transport policy. Thus, unlike the Community legislation applying art. 85 and 86 in the air transport sector, the regulation has a dual legal basis, comprising both art. 84(2) and 87 of the EC Treaty.[39]

The dual policy objectives of the regulation have given rise to certain anomalies relative to the application of the Community's competition rules in other areas of economic activity. In particular, the regulation, drafted by the Council, contains a block exemption for liner conferences, despite their central function of fixing the freight rates to be levied by conference members. This block exemption is unlimited in duration. Recital 8 of the regulation justifies this block exemption on the basis of the historically acknowledged 'stabilising effect' of liner conferences, and their provision of 'reliable services' for shippers. Whether such reasoning meets the four substantive conditions for exemption enumerated in art. 85(3) of the EC Treaty remains uncertain. On

---

[35] OJ 1986 L378/1.
[36] OJ 1986 L378/4.
[37] OJ 1986 L378/14.
[38] OJ 1986 L378/21.
[39] The Community legislation implementing art. 85 and 86 in the inland transport and air transport sectors (Council Regulation 1017/68 and Council Regulation 3975/87 respectively) has art. 87 as its exclusive legal basis.

the assumption that the criteria of art. 85(3) are met, the regulation attaches a condition and certain obligations to the block exemption in order to ensure that the fulfilment of these criteria is maintained. However, one such obligation provides for the negotiation of loyalty agreements with transport users, despite the Community's condemnation of the use of loyalty rebates in other areas. Indeed, a block exemption is provided for any such agreements concluded with transport users. In addition, it is only in the case of a breach of the single condition[40] that the liner conference agreements become automatically void. The breach of the four obligations may result in the removal of the block exemption only in the last resort. Clearly, a more rigorous policy could have been pursued by including the four obligations as conditions.

In short, the regulation provides for the continuation of the liberal policy traditionally adopted towards liner conferences within the international maritime transport sector. However, the liner conference system has for some years been in crisis, which has undermined its effectiveness as a means of organising international maritime transport services. Shipowners have had to adjust their activities accordingly. EC competition law, as applied by the Commission, has had to take account of these developments. It would appear that, in doing so, the Commission is now introducing a more restrictive policy towards the application of art. 85 and 86 in the maritime transport sector, in a manner more consistent with the application of EC competition rules in other areas.

¶1009   Regulation 4056/86: subject-matter and scope

Article 1(1) of the regulation defines its subject-matter broadly as 'maritime transport services'. However, art. 1(2) narrows the scope of the regulation to 'international maritime transport services from or to one or more Community ports, other than tramp vessel services'.[41]

Services from or to one or more Community ports

Sea transport services between two non-Community ports remain unaffected by the provisions of Regulation 4056/86,[42] as do transport services operated within the boundaries of one member state, i.e. cabotage. Furthermore, in the event that an agreement provides for the carriage of goods over both sea and land-legs, the regulation is applicable to the sea-leg of the journey only.[43]

---

[40] Regulation 4056/86, art. 4.

[41] The jurisdictional scope of the regulation is in contrast to that of Regulation 3975/87, which does not cover international flights between the Community and third countries (see ¶1026).

[42] However, EC competition rules may be applied to such services by virtue of the judgment of the EC Court of Justice in the *Wood Pulp* case, *Åhlström & Ors v EC Commission* [1988] ECR 5193.

[43] The application of the regulation in general, and the liner conference block exemption contained therein in particular, to multi-modal transport operations is discussed below at ¶1020.

Tramp vessel services

All maritime transport services[44] fall within the scope of the regulation, with the exception of tramp vessel services. The regulation is therefore principally concerned with the provision of scheduled liner services. Tramp vessel services are defined as those services providing for:

> '… the transport of goods in bulk or break-bulk in a vessel chartered wholly or partly to one or more shippers on the basis of a voyage or time charter or any other form of contract for non-regularly scheduled or non-advertised sailings where the freight rates are freely negotiated case by case in accordance with the conditions of supply and demand'.[45]

The exclusion of tramp vessel services from the scope of the regulation is justified by the fact that tramp vessel rates are generally set on the basis of market forces.[46] In the event that tramp rates fail to be set in this manner, for example as a result of a pricing agreement between tramp vessel operators or the unilateral conduct of a single dominant tramp vessel operator, the service supplied on the basis of such rates would no longer fall within the definition of tramp vessel services contained in art. 1(3)(a). The quasi-tramp vessel service would therefore fall into the residual category of maritime transport services covered by the regulation.

Two problems may result from this treatment of tramp vessel services in the regulation. First, regulatory difficulties may result in circumstances where it is uncertain whether the rates have been freely set, i.e., in circumstances where the application of the regulation is unclear. Either the national authorities could act using provisions of national law, or the Commission could intervene in respect of such quasi-tramp vessel services on the basis of the full regulatory powers contained in the regulation. Secondly, such regulatory uncertainty is compounded by the legal uncertainty surrounding the substantive treatment of such quasi-tramp vessel services in the event that the regulation is applied. Is the Commission's traditional policy towards restrictions on price competition to be continued, or is the Community's more lenient policy on the application of art. 85(3) of the EC Treaty in the maritime transport sector to be followed,[47] thereby providing relief for quasi-tramp vessel service operators by virtue of the opposition procedure contained in art. 12 of the regulation?[48]

---

[44] Thus, the carriage of both cargo and passengers is regulated by the provisions of the regulation.
[45] Regulation 4056/86, art. 1(3)(a).
[46] Regulation 4056/86, recital 4.
[47] In particular, see the block exemption for liner conferences contained in art. 3 of the regulation.
[48] It is often claimed that such uncertainty serves to undo much of the benefit originally intended for tramp vessel operators by the express exclusion of such services from the scope of the regulation.

¶1010   Regulation 4056/86: technical agreements

Like the legislation implementing art. 85 and 86 of the EC Treaty in the inland[49] and air[50] transport sectors, the regulation provides that the prohibition laid down in art. 85(1) of the treaty shall not apply to certain 'white listed' practices.[51] According to the regulation, such practices 'do not, as a general rule, restrict competition'.[52]

Technical agreements include common standards, pooling of vessels or staff, setting up of successive operations,[53] co-ordination of timetables, consolidation of individual consignments (i.e. less than container loads ('LCLs')) and common rules for the application of tariffs. The regulation provides that this list may be modified by the Council following a proposal from the Commission.[54]

However, such agreements are only white listed to the extent that their 'sole object or effect is to achieve technical improvements or co-operation'.[55] This would appear to preclude the use of arrangements which, in addition to purely technical benefits, might also give rise to certain commercial advantages.[56] However, it is unclear whether it is both the 'improvements' and 'co-operation' which must be exclusively technical in nature, or only the 'improvements', thereby white listing the use of commercially advantageous co-operation.[57] The Commission apparently favours the former, more restrictive, interpretation.[58]

---

[49] Council Regulation 1017/68 of 19 July 1968 applying the rules of competition to transport by rail, road and inland waterway; see art. 3.

[50] Council Regulation 3975/87 of 14 December 1987 laying down the procedure for the application of the rules on competition to undertakings in the air transport sector; see art. 2.

[51] Regulation 4056/86, art. 2.

[52] Regulation 4056/86, recital 7.

[53] Despite an earlier Commission statement implying the contrary, it would appear that the Commission does not regard art. 2(1)(c) of the regulation as including multi-modal (land and sea-leg) operations (see Kreis, 'European Community Competition Policy and International Shipping', *Fordham International Law Journal*, Vol. 13, 411, at pp. 431–433). Thus, according to the Commission, consecutive sea-legs only may fall within this provision. This interpretation is substantiated by the reference in the equivalent art. 3 of Regulation 1017/68 on inland transport to 'successive ... *combined* transport operations' (emphasis supplied). The disapplication of art. 85(1) to the land and sea-legs of multi-modal operations would, therefore, need to be addressed under art. 2 of the regulation and art. 3 of Regulation 1017/68 separately.

[54] Regulation 4056/86, art. 2(2).

[55] Regulation 4056/86, art. 2.

[56] The increasingly common consortium agreement could constitute such commercially advantageous co-operation. Similarly, it is likely that agreements concluded by conferences with outsiders concerning the calculation of freight surcharges would be viewed as constituting commercially beneficial agreements for the purposes of art. 2 of the regulation.

[57] This uncertainty is fuelled by the inclusion in art. 3 of Regulation 1017/68 of the term 'technical' before both the words 'improvements' and 'co-operation', whereas art. 2 of Regulation 3975/87 adopts the same terminology as that contained in art. 2 of Regulation 4056/86.

[58] The strict approach adopted by the Commission in its *Secrétama* and *Cewal* decisions (see below at ¶1018) confirms this, as does the Commission's refusal to treat consortia agreements as technical agreements (see below at ¶1019).

¶1011   Regulation 4056/86: block exemption for liner conferences

(1)   Introduction

The main practical effect[59] of the regulation derives from the block exemption for liner conferences contained in art. 3 thereof. This block exemption applies to agreements, decisions and concerted practices of all or part of the members of one or more liner conferences[60] in the event that they have as their objective the fixing of rates and conditions of carriage and, 'as the case may be', the co-ordination of shipping timetables, the determination of the frequency of sailings, the co-ordination or allocation of sailings among members of the conference, and the regulation of the carrying capacity of each member or the allocation of cargo or revenue among members.

(2)   Duration

Unusually for a block exemption, no term is expressly provided for art. 3 of the regulation. Thus, the block exemption for liner conferences will apply indefinitely to the relevant liner conference agreements until such time as the Commission withdraws the benefit thereof in accordance with either art. 7(2) or 8(2) of the regulation.

(3)   Substance

Both the definition of liner conferences contained in art. 1(3)(b) of the regulation, and the wording of art. 3 of the regulation itself clearly provide for the block exemption to apply despite, and indeed because of, members of a liner conference or several liner conferences agreeing to fix cargo rates and conditions of carriage. It is exceptional that horizontal price fixing[61] between competitors is expressly tolerated by the Community institutions.

(a)   *Agreements without the fixing of rates or conditions of carriage*
Since the adoption of the regulation, doubt had existed as to whether the block exemption would apply to liner conference agreements that do not provide for the fixing of rates or the conditions of carriage.[62] This matter was clarified by the *Secrétama* and *Cewal* decisions, wherein the Commission stated that the block exemption contained in art. 3 of the regulation is not

---

[59] As discussed below, the crisis in the liner conference system has to a certain extent reduced the practical value of the liner conference block exemption for the international shipping industry.

[60] As defined by art. 1(3)(b) of the regulation.

[61] Commission Regulation 1617/93 in the air transport sector provides for consultation on tariffs only. Such consultations must be non-binding in nature (art. 4).

[62] This issue arose principally as a result of the inclusion in the block exemption regulations for patent licensing and specialisation agreements of a provision whereby the block exemptions would apply to agreements providing for obligations on the parties of a lesser scope than those expressly permitted by the regulations (see art. 1(3) of Regulation 2349/84 and art. 2(2) of Regulation 417/85 respectively).

applicable to liner conference agreements whose objectives do not include the fixing of rates.[63] This interpretation is consistent with the historical origins of the liner conference system, of which rate-fixing was the essential element.

(b) *Independent rate action*

Less certain is the application of the liner conference block exemption to conferences operating under US law, whose members are guaranteed the right to take independent rate action ('IRA') by virtue of the US 1984 Shipping Act.[64] Attention has focused on the apparent inconsistency between IRA and the art. 3 requirement that rates be fixed by the conference. However, although liner conferences as defined by the regulation do function on the basis of fixed, common rates, this does not mean that identical rates are always applied by the individual conference members. Variations in the rate actually charged may result from seasonal adjustments in the price of the cargo or from the variety of methods of rate calculation. In addition, art. 5 of the regulation provides for the use of certain loyalty rebates, thereby resulting in the application of different rates for different shippers, depending on the amount of the latter's cargo carried by that particular conference member. Thus, to the extent that it may result in different rates being applied by different conference members, it would be misleading to state that the notion of IRA as provided for in US legislation is wholly inconsistent with the practice of conferences specifically targeted by art. 3 of the regulation.

Furthermore, art. 3 of the regulation provides a block exemption for those liner conference agreements which have as their *objective* the fixing of rates and conditions of carriage. No equivalent requirement is made in respect of the *effect* of the agreement. It is arguable that, while the effect of a conference providing for IRA may be the application of different rates in practice, it nevertheless remains true that the principal objective of such a conference is the fixing of rates and conditions of carriage. The possibility for IRA by individual members of the conference would not appear to be inconsistent with such an objective.

It could be said, therefore, that liner conference agreements providing for IRA should fall within the scope of the art. 3 block exemption. However, it

---

[63] It would appear that this interpretation is in conformity with the wishes of the authors of the regulation, for the text finally adopted differed from that originally proposed by the Commission (OJ 1981 C282/4), which stated that liner conference agreements were to be exempted 'when they have one or more of the following objectives: (a) the fixing of ... rates and conditions of carriage and, as the case may be; (b) the co-ordination of ...'. Thus, in its originally proposed form, the regulation did not envisage that the fixing of rates should be a prerequisite for the application of the block exemption.

[64] S. 5(b)(8). Under the US IRA procedure, a conference member may offer shippers a lower rate than the general conference rate, although at least ten days' notice must be given of this under-cutting to the remaining conference members. These other members may then decide whether to follow the IRA of the single operator.

¶1011

should be recalled that the historical justification for the liner conference block exemption provided in recital 8 of the regulation refers expressly to the 'stabilising effect' thereof. A conference system providing for IRA may not result in the requisite degree of stability necessary to justify (i.e. meet the conditions imposed by art. 85(3) of the EC Treaty) the application of the block exemption. In these circumstances, the Commission may be compelled to remove the benefit of the block exemption by virtue of art. 7 of the regulation. Consequently, the application of the art. 3 block exemption to conferences providing for IRA by its members should be assessed by the Commission on a case-by-case basis, with particular emphasis on the degree of stability provided by the conference agreement in question.

(c)   *Passenger services*

The scope of the art. 3 block exemption is restricted by the definition of a liner conference contained in art. 1(3)(b) of the regulation. This provision expressly states that the liner conferences envisaged by the regulation are those concerned with the carriage of cargo only.[65] Agreements between liner conferences concerning the carriage of passengers are not, therefore, covered by the art. 3 block exemption.[66]

(d)   *Open/closed conferences*

Although liner conferences throughout the world generally developed strict membership criteria in the absence of governmental regulation, this is not true of conferences operating in US waters. In particular, the 1916 US Shipping Act confers antitrust immunity on so-called 'open' conferences only, i.e. conferences which any vessel owner operating on the trade covered by the conference may join or leave as of right. The question arises in practice whether the block exemption contained in art. 3 of the regulation applies to both closed and open conferences.

The liner conference definition contained in art. 1(3)(b) of the regulation does not expressly refer to either closed or open liner conferences. However, according to recital 3 of the regulation, 'as far as conferences subject to the Code of Conduct are concerned, the regulation should supplement the Code or make it more precise'. Since the UN liner code applies to closed conferences only, this recital would appear to suggest that the regulation and, therefore, art. 3 thereof, is directed principally at closed liner conferences. However, the absence of any reference to membership criteria in the definition of liner conferences apparently prevents any conclusion that the block exemption is applicable to closed liner conferences exclusively.

---

[65] The definition of liner conferences originally proposed by the Commission included services for the carriage of both cargo and passengers (OJ 1981 C282/4).

[66] However, passenger service agreements do remain within the scope of the regulation itself.

¶1011

¶1012   Regulation 4056/86: condition and obligations attached to liner conference block exemption

Despite the broad scope of the liner conference block exemption contained in the regulation, any exemption granted by virtue of art. 85(3) of the EC Treaty must maintain a certain degree of effective, 'workable' competition within the sector concerned,[67] in order to ensure compliance with the four substantive criteria set out in art. 85(3) of the EC Treaty. A single condition and several obligations have been attached to the liner conference block exemption in order to ensure that these criteria are[68] met by liner conference agreements in practice.[69]

(1)   Condition of non-discrimination

Article 4 of the regulation provides that the block exemption for liner conferences[70] is granted subject to the condition[71] that the agreement shall not, within the Community, cause any 'detriment' to 'certain' ports, transport users or carriers as a result of the application of different rates or conditions of carriage for the 'same' goods according to the country of origin or destination of the goods, or the port of loading or discharge, unless such different rates or conditions of carriage may be 'economically justified'.[72]

The text of art. 4 of the regulation expressly provides that this condition should be respected as regards 'certain' ports, transport users or carriers only. It remains unclear which ports, transport users or carriers are referred to in this regard. In order to ensure consistency with the absolute prohibition of discrimination on grounds of nationality contained in art. 6 of the EC Treaty, it is suggested that liner conferences should respect this provision in their dealings with all ports, users or carriers within the EC or of Community nationality.

Further uncertainty surrounds the precise meaning of 'detriment', and the notion of 'same' goods. Unlike, for example, the Community's legislation on anti-dumping,[73] no additional indication of the meaning of these words is

---

[67] *Metro v EC Commission* [1977] ECR 1875, at para. 20.

[68] As noted above, there remains some doubt as to whether the liner conference block exemption meets the criteria for exemption imposed by art. 85(3) of the EC Treaty.

[69] Regulation 4056/86, recital 9.

[70] This condition is also applicable to the block exemption for agreements between transport users and conferences concerning the use of scheduled maritime transport services provided for in art. 6 of the regulation.

[71] Recitals 9 and 10 of the regulation refer to 'conditions' in the plural, reflecting an earlier draft of the regulation which provided for the loyalty arrangement obligation to be classified as a condition. Given the significant effect of the breach of a condition relative to the breach of an obligation (discussed below at ¶1012), the fact that this earlier draft was amended presumably reflects the desire of certain parties that a less stringent approach be adopted towards the operation of the liner conference block exemption.

[72] This provision expressly incorporates into the regulation the general principle of non-discrimination on the grounds of nationality contained in (what is now) art. 6 of the EC Treaty.

[73] Council Regulation 2423/88 of 11 July 1988 on protection against dumped or subsidised imports from countries not members of the European Community, OJ 1988 L209/1. See, in particular, art. 4 thereof, which

contained in the regulation. Further clarification might also have been provided concerning the type of economic justification sufficient to authorise a prima facie breach of this condition.

Breach of condition
The effect of a breach of this condition is to remove the protection afforded to the agreement by the block exemption.[74] The agreement would therefore be automatically void[75] in accordance with art. 85(2) of the EC Treaty.

(2) Obligations
Four obligations are imposed[76] on the beneficiaries of the block exemption for liner conferences. These obligations relate to consultations, loyalty arrangements, services not covered by freight charges and the availability of tariffs and the notification of any arbitration awards to the Commission. Only the first two obligations merit any additional comment.

(a) *Consultations*
Article 5 of the regulation imposes an obligation on conferences to consult with transport users in relation to the rates, conditions and quality of scheduled maritime transport services.[77] Any agreements resulting from such consultations are exempted from the application of art. 85(1) of the EC Treaty by virtue of the block exemption contained in art. 6 of the regulation.

Recital 12 of the regulation justifies the obligation to consult on the basis that it may give rise to a 'more efficient operation of maritime transport services which takes better account of users' requirements'. Furthermore, such treatment of consultations is consistent with the traditional international policy towards maritime transport, which has been characterised by self-regulation. Indeed, such operator/shipper consultation was provided for in the UN liner code,[78] which sought to provide a detailed 'mandatory' framework within which consultation[79] should take place. However, such consultation has never been

---

provides an indication of the injury to be sustained by the Community industry before anti-dumping measures may be adopted, and the definition of 'like' goods contained in art. 2(12) thereof.
[74] Regulation 4056/86, art. 4.
[75] As with infringements of art. 85(1) and 86 generally, the automatic nullity sanction only applies to those provisions or features in the agreement or practice that violate art. 85(1) or 86. Provided they are severable, any remaining provisions are unaffected by the nullity sanction.
[76] Regulation 4056/86, art. 5. Interestingly, art. 3 itself does not refer to any such obligations, but only to the condition contained in art. 4 of the regulation.
[77] In the light of the traditional EC competition law policy towards contact or information exchange between actual or potential competitors (see, for example, *Suiker Unie & Ors v EC Commission* [1975] ECR 1663), the obligation on conferences to collectively consult with transport users may be viewed with some surprise.
[78] Article 11.
[79] Such consultation had taken place, for example, within the Consultative Shipping Group ('CSG'), established in 1963 and made up of the transport ministers of western European countries and Japan. The CSG led to the creation of the Committee of European National Shipowners' Associations ('CENSA') and the European Shippers' Councils ('ESC').

seen to be particularly effective, and is often perceived as having a bias in favour of the liner conferences. Article 5 of the regulation has done little to remedy this, particularly given the unsatisfactory drafting of this provision.[80] Added to such considerations is the limited effect of a breach of this obligation, discussed below. Indeed, given the unsatisfactory consideration of 'users' requirements' under the regulation, in 1991 CENSA and the ESC developed their own consultation procedure, to be followed by dispute-settlement provisions at a later date.

(b)   *Loyalty arrangements*

One of the objects of consultations envisaged by the regulation is the form and terms of loyalty arrangements negotiated between liner conferences and transport users. Such arrangements fall expressly within the scope of the block exemption contained in art. 6 of the regulation. It should be noted that the authorisation for conferences to enter into loyalty arrangements with transport users is generally inconsistent with the Community institutions' policy towards such rebate arrangements in other areas of economic activity.[81] Despite this special treatment for loyalty rebates entered into by liner conferences, the regulation does not contain any justification in its recitals for this approach.

Nevertheless, the regulation does seek to provide shippers with some protection by requiring that loyalty arrangements must comply with certain conditions. Thus, the loyalty arrangements 'shall be based on the contract system or any other system which is also lawful', and shall be the result of negotiations between the conference and the users.[82] In addition, transport users must be given the opportunity to choose between the use of immediate or deferred rebate systems, and must be able to negotiate the derogation of certain products from these loyalty arrangements. 100 per cent loyalty arrangements may be entered into, but may not be 'unilaterally imposed'.[83] The conference is further obliged to list the cargo that is to be subject to the loyalty

---

[80] For example, art. 5 fails to provide for any framework within which the consultations should take place, and does not contain any procedural rules for the conclusion of agreements resulting from such consultations. The paucity of detail in art. 5 should be compared with the relatively extensive nature of the consultation provisions contained in art. 11 of the UN Liner Code. In addition, the inconsistent language in recital 12 ('associations of users') on the one hand and art. 5 and 6 ('transport users') on the other has caused uncertainty as to whether the consultations provided for by art. 5 envisage participation by shippers' organisations, or whether individual shippers should engage in dialogue with liner conferences on their own account.

[81] In relation to art. 85 of the EC Treaty, the Court of Justice has upheld Commission decisions condemning and refusing to grant an individual exemption for collective aggregated rebate schemes amongst competitors (see, for example, *Van Landewyck Sàrl & Ors v EC Commission* [1980] ECR 3125 ; *Nederlandse Sigarenwinklers Organisatie v EC Commission* [1985] ECR 3801). Similarly, the Commission has consistently applied art. 86 to the use of loyalty rebates by dominant undertakings (see, for example, *Suiker Unie & Ors v EC Commission* [1975] ECR 1663; *Hoffmann-La Roche v EC Commission* [1979] ECR 461).

[82] Regulation 4056/86, art. 5(2).

[83] The Commission has indicated that a dominant conference offering shippers 100 per cent loyalty arrangements does not satisfy this non-imposition criterion (see the Commission's *Cewal* decision, discussed at ¶1018 below).

¶1012

arrangement, and cite those circumstances (which are sometimes obligatory) in which the transport user shall be released from its obligation of loyalty. However, it is widely perceived that such conditions do little to protect the interests of shippers and other transport users in practice. Furthermore, loyalty arrangements have increasingly been replaced by time/volume service contracts. The regulation has failed to address this development.

(c)   *Breach of an obligation*

The breach of an obligation attached to the art. 3 liner conference agreement block exemption by virtue of art. 5 may result in the EC Commission addressing a recommendation to the party concerned.[84] Thereafter, and only in the event that these recommendations are not observed, may the Commission adopt a decision preventing or requiring certain acts to be carried out, or withdrawing the benefit of the block exemption, with or without granting an individual exemption.[85]

¶1013   Regulation 4056/86: monitoring of exempted agreements

Despite the imposition of the aforementioned condition and obligations, art. 7(2) of the regulation recognises that the block exemptions provided for in art. 3 and 6 may nevertheless result in effects that are incompatible with art. 85(3) of the EC Treaty, particularly concerning the existence of outsider competition. Indeed, art. 7(2) provides the following, non-exhaustive examples of the 'special circumstances' in which such effects may arise: acts of conferences or a change in market conditions that result in[86] the elimination of competition, acts of conferences that hinder technical or economic progress or user participation in the benefits and acts of third countries[87] that restrict outside competition, impose unfair tariffs on conference members or impose arrangements which otherwise impede technical or economic progress. The type of Commission intervention – which must follow the procedural rules set

---

[84] Regulation 4056/86, art. 7(1).

[85] Regulation 4056/86, art. 7(1). The Commission has in practice overcome the procedural shortcomings of art. 7(1) concerning the breach of an obligation. Thus, in its *Cewal* decision the Commission treated the imposition of 100 per cent loyalty rebates as an abuse of a dominant position, thereby enabling more effective Commission intervention by virtue of art. 8 of the regulation.

[86] Certain shipowners have maintained that the reference to acts of conferences or market conditions 'resulting in' the absence or elimination of actual or potential competition would exclude Commission intervention in those circumstances where actual or potential competition is merely restricted, rather than totally eliminated. However, given the non-exhaustive nature of this list of special circumstances, the Commission has been reluctant to accept this rather literal interpretation of the regulation.

[87] The possibility of Commission intervention following acts by third countries which result in effects incompatible with art. 85(3) of the EC Treaty is in addition to the more general provisions concerning relations with third countries contained in art. 9 of the regulation.

out in Section II of the regulation – will depend on the special circumstance in question, although it may ultimately result in the withdrawal of the block exemptions.

¶1014   Regulation 4056/86: abuse of dominant position

Article 8 of the regulation prohibits the abuse of a dominant position within the meaning of art. 86 of the EC Treaty in the international maritime services sector. Where the Commission finds that in a particular case the conduct of a conference, although exempted under the regulation, nevertheless has effects which are incompatible with art. 86 of the EC Treaty,[88] it is empowered to withdraw the block exemption.

Article 86 and block exemptions

For some time there had been uncertainty as to whether an agreement benefiting from a block exemption could legitimately be deemed by the Commission to infringe art. 86 of the EC Treaty, therefore questioning the validity of the approach adopted by the Council in the regulation. However, this issue was resolved in the affirmative by the Court of First Instance in its 1990 *Tetra Pak* ruling[89] concerning the Commission's *Tetra Pak* decision,[90] wherein special reference to art. 8 of the regulation was made.

Collective dominance

Some doubt had also arisen as to whether undertakings could be considered to enjoy a collective dominant position for the purposes of the application of art. 86 of the EC Treaty. Thus, it was uncertain whether members of a conference, while not in a dominant position individually, could nevertheless be considered as dominant when their market status was assessed jointly. This issue was also resolved in the affirmative by the Court of First Instance, which made a specific reference to art. 8 of the regulation while confirming the Commission's approach in this regard.[91] More specifically, the collective dominance of liner conferences has been upheld by the Commission in its *Secrétama*[92] and *Cewal*[93] decisions.

---

[88] For arguments to the effect that the conference system per se is based on abusive conduct, see Rakovsky, 'Sea Transport Under EC Competition Law', *Nineteenth Annual Fordham Corporate Law Institute Antitrust Law & Policy*, 22–23 October 1992.

[89] *Tetra Pak Rausing SA v EC Commission* [1990] ECR II-309.

[90] Decision of 26 July 1988, OJ 1988 L272/27.

[91] *Società Italiano Vetro SpA & Ors v EC Commission*, [1992] ECR II-1403; [1992] 2 CEC 33.

[92] *French–West African shipowners' committees*, OJ 1992 L134/1, discussed below at ¶1018.

[93] *Cewal, Cowac and Ukwal*, OJ 1993 L34/20, discussed below at ¶1018.

¶1015   Regulation 4056/86: conflicts of international law

The regulation imposes a duty on the Commission to consult with the authorities of third countries in the event that the application of the regulation may enter into conflict with the provisions laid down by the law, regulation or administrative action of third countries and compromise important Community trading and shipping interests. The Commission must undertake consultations aimed at reconciling the aforementioned interests with respect for Community law.[94] However, the majority of problems incurred by the Community's carriers engaged in international maritime transport have concerned access to trades, which the Commission has sought to resolve through consultation provided for by Regulation 4058/86.[95]

¶1016   Regulation 4056/86: procedural rules

With regard to procedural rules, it is necessary to bear in mind that some articles (namely art. 16, 18, 20 and 23) are very similar to those provided for in Regulation 17/62 or in Regulation 1017/68.

Proceedings to terminate infringements

Procedures to terminate infringements of art. 85 and/or 86 may be triggered by a complaint submitted by a member state, or by any person claiming a legitimate interest, or will be initiated by the Commission itself. The Commission may then find either that there has been an infringement, or that there are no grounds for intervention under art. 85(1) or 86, or that the conditions of both art. 85(1) and 85(3) are met and that it will therefore issue a decision applying art. 85(3).

Individual exemptions

Article 12 lays down the conditions for the application of individual exemptions under art. 85(3) by a simplified opposition procedure,[96] while art. 13 deals with the duration and revocation of decisions applying art. 85(3) taken pursuant to art. 11(4) or art. 12(4) of the regulation.

The Commission is granted the sole power to impose obligations under art. 7 and to issue decisions pursuant to art. 85(3) (art. 14), and it must carry out the

---

[94] Regulation 4056/86, art. 9.
[95] See for example, *Eighteenth Report on Competition Policy*, point 32.
[96] To date, eight notices have been published by the Commission by virtue of art. 12(2) of the regulation: Case IV/32.385: *Sealink–SNCF*, OJ 1989 C17/8; Case IV/32.383: *Sealink–SMZ*, OJ 1989 C17/12; Case IV/33.168: *Agreement 1237*, OJ 1990 C59/2; Case IV/33.304: *Gulfway Agreement*, OJ 1990 C130/3; Case IV/33.677: *Irish Club Rules*, OJ 1991 C166/6; Case IV/33.592: *Baltic Shipping Co/Witass*, OJ 1991 C179/6; Case IV/33.626: *Agreements establishing joint transhipment services between Helsingborg and Helsingor*, OJ 1992 C36/5; Case IV/34.250: *Europe Asia trades agreement*.

procedures provided for in the regulation in liaison with the member states (art. 15).

Commission powers

The Commission has wide powers of inquiry (art. 16 and 18). It is permitted to ask for the assistance of the competent authorities of the member states (art. 17) and it may impose both fines[97] and periodic penalty payments (art. 19 and 20), subject only to review by the Court of First Instance (art. 21). Before taking any of the decisions listed in art. 11, 12(3), 12(4), 13(3), 19 and 20, the Commission is obliged to grant the undertakings concerned the opportunity of being heard (art. 23).[98]

Implementing powers

The Commission's power, provided for by art. 26, to adopt implementing provisions concerning the scope of the obligation of communication pursuant to art. 5(5), concerning the form, content and other details of complaints pursuant to art. 10, applications pursuant to art. 12 and also the hearings provided for in art. 23(1) and (2) resulted in the adoption of Regulation 4260/88[99] on the communications, complaints and applications and the hearings provided for in Council Regulation 4056/86.

Regulation 4260/88 includes two sections, the first dealing with notifications, complaints and applications, the second dealing with hearings. Article 1 of Regulation 4260/88 deals with notifications provided for by art. 5(5) of the regulation. Article 2 of Regulation 4260/88 deals with complaints described in art. 10 of the regulation, and art. 3 and 4 of Regulation 4260/88 indicate the persons entitled to submit applications under art. 12 of the regulation and the form of those applications.[100] Finally, the other provisions of Regulation 4260/88 deal with the hearings provided for by art. 23(1) and (2) of the regulation.

---

[97] Fines have been imposed by the Commission on four occasions. Two fines were imposed on Ukwal (OJ 1992 L121/45) and Mewac (OJ 1993 L20/6) for their refusal to submit to a Commission investigation. Two fines were imposed on the members of French–West African shipowners' committees (OJ 1992 L134/1) and on certain members of the Cewal conference (OJ 1993 L34/20) as a result of substantive Commission decisions applying art. 85 and 86 of the EC Treaty (see below at ¶1018). The decision concerning the members of Cewal is currently subject to judicial review before the EC Court of First Instance (see Cases T-24/93, T-25/93, T-26/93 and T-28/93).

[98] The Commission is obliged by art. 23(3) to publish a notice when it intends to apply art. 85(3) of the EC Treaty following such a hearing. Two such notices have been published: notice pursuant to art. 23(3) of Regulation 4056/86 and art. 26(3) of Regulation 1017/68 concerning Cases IV/32.380 and IV/32.772: *Eurocorde Agreements*; and notice pursuant to art. 23(3) of Regulation 4056/86 concerning Case IV/33.677: *Irish Club Rules*.

[99] OJ 1988 L376/1.

[100] Applications pursuant to art. 12 of Regulation 4056/86 have to be submitted on form MAR set out in Annex 1 to Regulation 4260/88.

¶1016

¶1017   The demise of the liner conference system

Just as the conference system first emerged in response to certain technological developments, more recent events are now undermining the leading role of the conference system in the organisation of international maritime transport services. In particular, as in other areas of transport, the international maritime transport sector has been revolutionised by freight containerisation. Containerisation has led to larger vessels and reduced cargo handling times in port, thereby increasing the volume of cargo which may be carried by a single vessel over a period of time. Significant overcapacity has resulted. In addition, in order to benefit from the full economies of scale afforded by containerisation, and to increase vessel productivity, vessels of greater tonnage have been requisitioned since the 1970s. The technological innovation and re-equipment costs necessary to meet this challenge have resulted in a significant increase in the level of capital investment required to acquire and operate a vessel. The traditional liner conference system has proved unable to meet these new challenges. Consequently, those vessel owners operating within conferences have sought alternative methods of operation. Thus, agreements have been concluded between conference members for the exclusion of outsider competition, the widespread use of consortia agreements has emerged and multi-modal transport operations have been developed. EC competition law has been applied accordingly.[101]

¶1018   The restriction of outsider competition

Although vessel owners operating within the rigid framework imposed by the liner conference system have experienced difficulty in adjusting to the advent of containerisation, the cost efficiencies resulting from containerisation have been exploited to the full by the more flexible independent lines. Consequently, shippers have been able to use cheaper services offered by such independent liner services operating alongside the traditional liner conference operator. Almost inevitably, liner conferences have sought to restrict such outsider competition. To date, the Commission has condemned such conduct on two occasions, although at least one additional investigation has been settled amicably.[102]

---

[101] Sir Leon Brittan QC, then EC Commissioner responsible for competition policy, stated in 1991 that as a result of 'the visible cartellisation' of entire trades, '[t]he time has therefore come for the Commission to seek the most appropriate instruments for safeguarding competition in a changing technical and commercial environment' ('Developments and prospects for the Community', address to the Institut Français de la Mer, Paris, 8 March 1991).

[102] It is likely that further intervention on the part of the Commission will arise on other routes where the great majority of cargo is carried by conference members, such as on the Mediterranean trades.

Shipowners' committees

The first substantive decision adopted by the Commission on the basis of the regulation followed complaints lodged by the Danish Shipowners' Association and the Danish Government against the activities of shipping companies operating between French ports and the ports serving certain west and central African states. These shipping companies had set up shipowners' committees, regulated by the Committee's Secretariat (Secrétama), in order to administer the application of certain shipping rules adopted by the relevant west and central African states within the context of resolutions adopted by the Ministerial Conference of the States of West and Central Africa for Maritime Transport (CMEAOC). The CMEAOC resolutions were based on the cargo-sharing principles of the 1974 UN liner code, and invited its member states to adopt shipping rules aimed at giving their national lines priority in the allocation of freight and at implementing freight monitoring systems on the basis of the 40:40:20 cargo allocation rule.[103]

The shipowners' committees were established by the shipping companies in order to administer the application of such national rules. Although principally comprised of conference members, the shipowners' committees also had non-conference members. Thus, in addition to administering the allocation of the conference cargo along the lines of the 40:40:20 cargo allocation rule, the committees extended this rule to cover all liner cargo (i.e. conference and non-conference) carried on the relevant trades. The activities of independent liner carriers were, therefore, significantly reduced.

The Commission condemned the operation of such shipowners' committees on the basis of both art. 85 and 86 of the EC Treaty, rejecting the defence that the committees had been established as a result of obligations imposed by the relevant national authorities. With regard to art. 85(1)(b) and (c) of the EC Treaty,[104] the Commission found that all the shipping services on the relevant trades had been regulated, and not just those offered by the conference members. The Commission found that outside, non-conference competition

---

[103] Article 2 of the UN Liner Code advocates the principle that equal shares of the conference cargo should be allocated to the home traders at both ends of a given bilateral trade, while the balance should be allocated to the shipping companies of third countries that are members of the same conference. This principle, although not mandatory in nature, has become known as the 40:40:20 cargo allocation rule.

[104] The requisite effect on intra-Community trade was deemed to result from the partitioning of trade between the Community and the 11 African states concerned, whereby the French national carriers benefit to the detriment of the national shipping lines of other member states. In addition, the Commission also referred to the distortion of competition between shippers operating in the Community, to the detriment of French shippers relative to shippers operating from other ports in the Community. Similarly, the Commission referred to the so-called deflections of trade resulting from such discrimination against French shippers, with trade for export to the relevant west and central African states encouraged to move through other Community ports adjacent to France instead. The Commission's findings as to the requisite effect on intra-Community trade are, therefore, generally in conformity with recital 6 to the regulation. However, for a criticism of the finding of any effect on intra-Community trade in such circumstances, see Forwood, 'Jurisdictional Limits to the Application of EC Competition Rules to International Maritime Transport', *Nineteenth Annual Fordham Corporate Law Institute International Antitrust Law & Policy*, 22–23 October 1992.

¶1018

had effectively been eliminated. In condemning the creation of the shipowners' committees, the Commission refused to accept that the agreements providing for their creation constituted technical agreements within the meaning of art. 2 of the regulation. The Commission further rejected the application of the liner conference block exemption contained in art. 3 of the regulation, since non-conference members were parties to the agreements and such agreements did not have as their objective the fixing of rates. Article 85(3) was deemed inapplicable.

Concerning the application of art. 86 of the EC Treaty, the Commission found that the shipowners' committees had abused their collective[105] dominant position on all the liner services involved in the carriage of general cargo between France and the 11 west and central African states concerned.[106] The Commission's finding of an abuse of such collective dominant position was broadly based on the same conduct as that which had been held to have infringed art. 85 of the EC Treaty.[107] As a result of the infringements of both art. 85 and 86 of the EC Treaty, fines of between ECU 2,400 and 11,628,000 were imposed on those shipping companies operating within the shipowners' committees.

Euro-African shipping conferences
The second, and latest, decision under the regulation was adopted by the Commission on the basis of a similar desire by conference members to restrict the activities of independent operators offering liner services between northern Europe and, principally, Zaire. In particular, the Commission found that three conferences (Cewal, Cowac and Ukwal) had entered into an agreement whereby the members of each conference would not compete as outsiders in the trades covered by the other two conferences. The Commission further found that Cewal had (1) entered into a co-operation agreement with Ogefrem, the Zairian Maritime Freight Administration, as a result of which foreign currency was only issued by the Zairian banks to shippers using Cewal's services and by which Cewal was in principle given monopoly rights on its

---

[105] See ¶1014 above.

[106] Shipowners have argued that the relevant geographic market for the application of art. 86 in this sector should be the world market, given the reference in recital 8 of the regulation to the mobility of fleets. However, the approach adopted by the Commission in the *Secrétama* decision is in conformity with the definition of relevant geographic markets used in the air transport sector (see the judgment of the Court of Justice in *Ahmed Saeed* and the Commission's *Air France/Sabena* merger control decision).

[107] The Commission's *Secrétama* decision was published shortly after the judgment of the Court of First Instance in the *Italian Flat Glass* case, wherein the court condemned the Commission's 'recycling' of the same facts for the application of both art. 85 and 86 of the treaty. Although it is possible that the Commission did not have sufficient time to consider this judgment before adopting the *Secrétama* decision, it is interesting that the Commission's *Cewal* decision, while finding infringements of both art. 85 and 86 of the treaty, imposes fines for the infringement of art. 86 only.

¶1018

trades, (2) imposed 100 per cent loyalty rebates on shippers and (3) employed fighting ships in order to exclude non-conference companies.

Agreement between conferences

The Commission decided that the Cewal/Cowac/Ukwal agreement infringed art. 85(1)(b) and (c) of the EC Treaty. In particular, the Commission found that the agreement was not a liner conference agreement within the meaning of art. 3 of the regulation, for it did not provide for the fixing of common or uniform rates. No fine was imposed by the Commission for such infringement of art. 85.[108]

Abusive conduct by Cewal

The Commission treated the remaining conduct by Cewal as an abuse of the collective dominant position held by the members of that conference on its routes between northern Europe and Zaire, contrary to art. 86 of the EC Treaty. With regard to the Cewal-Ogefrem co-operation agreement, the Commission referred to a 1987 resolution of the OECD Council concerning common principles of shipping policy and liberalisation of operations relating to maritime transport,[109] which cites as an example of 'possible practices in which conferences might indulge with regard to non-conference lines, which could be regarded as abuse of their dominant position' the 'deliberate conclusion of agreements with governmental or quasi-governmental authorities which have the effect of restricting competition by the exclusion of non-member lines from participation in the trade or of placing them at a substantial disadvantage vis-à-vis conference lines'. The Commission rejected the defence that such conduct resulted solely from obligations imposed by public authorities.

Concerning the use of fighting ships, the Commission found that this practice constituted an abuse of Cewal's dominant position on two counts. First, the Commission treated the use of fighting ships as predatory pricing adopted with the aim of removing the sole independent competitor. Secondly, the Commission further considered that such conduct could be treated as an abuse of art. 86(c) of the EC Treaty, since shippers using non-fighting ships must pay higher rates for the carriage of their goods in comparison with the rates applicable when those same goods are carried by fighting ships.

As for the use of 100 per cent loyalty agreements, the Commission found that such loyalty agreements had been abusively imposed on shippers. In particular, the Commission considered that offering shippers 100 per cent loyalty rebates when shippers may only occasionally use the services of a single non-

---

[108] See footnote 107 above.
[109] OECD Document C(87) 11 (final).

¶1018

conference shipping company, and depend for the rest on the services provided by Cewal, was tantamount to imposing such 100 per cent loyalty rebates. The Commission considered such imposition of 100 per cent loyalty rebates to constitute an abuse of Cewal's dominant position since it is contrary to the express conditions set out for loyalty agreements in art. 5(2)(b) of the regulation, and restricted the freedom of users. The Commission also found that the imposition of 100 per cent loyalty rebates reduced the ability of the sole non-conference shipping company to maintain its activity on a durable basis, and that such conduct amounted to Cewal applying dissimilar conditions to equivalent transactions with its trading partners, thereby placing some of them at a competitive disadvantage. Fines of between ECU 100,000 and ECU 9.6m were imposed accordingly.[110]

East African Maritime Conference

In October 1991, the Commission initiated a proceeding against the East African Maritime Conference (EAMC) on the basis of art. 85 and 86 of the treaty. The EAMC agreement provided that shipping lines wishing to leave the conference were required to give a minimum of 12 months notice. Such notice could only expire at the end of a calendar year. According to the Commission,[111] this notice provision constituted an infringement of art. 85(1) which fell outside the scope of the block exemption contained in art. 3 of the regulation. In particular, the Commission considered that such notice provision restricted the ability of a conference member to leave the conference and operate as an outsider for as much as two years. The Commission informed the EAMC that, in its opinion, the maximum period of notice should not exceed six months. The EAMC revised the terms of the agreement accordingly, whereupon the Commission terminated its investigation without adopting any formal measures.

¶1019   Consortia arrangements

Shipping consortia emerged in response to the increased capital requirements of shipowners seeking to obtain large and cost effective vessels of the type necessitated by the advent of containerisation in the international maritime transport sector.[112] Although prevalent at the time of the adoption of the 1986 package, no measures concerning shipping consortia were included within the

---

[110] These fines are currently subject to judicial review by the EC Court of First Instance (see Cases T-24/93, T-25/93, T-26/93 and T-28/93).

[111] Press release IP(93)739.

[112] According to the opinion of the Economic and Social Committee on the proposal for a Council regulation on the application of article 85(3) of the treaty to certain categories of agreements, decisions and concerted practices between shipping companies (OJ 1991 C69/16), '(c)onsortia are fairly recent phenomena born out of the container revolution in the 1960s/70s which called for the building of much larger ships to effect economies of scale and increase ship productivity. The degree of investment needed to re-equip to meet such technology

terms of this legislation. However, the Commission undertook at that time to provide the Council with a report on the need for legislation concerning, inter alia, consortia. This report was published by the Commission on 18 June 1990,[113] accompanied by a proposal for a block exemption.[114] This proposal, with amendments, was adopted by the Council on 25 February 1992.[115]

The need for such a proposal resulted from the legal uncertainty which has surrounded consortia arrangements. First, the industry attempted to classify such arrangements as concentrations falling within the scope of the merger regulation. However, this approach was rejected by the Commission as a result of the co-operative nature of existing consortia agreements, as confirmed in its 1990 report. The Commission has similarly rejected the definition of consortia agreements as purely technical agreements, within the meaning of art. 2 of Regulation 4056/86. In addition, the Commission has also declined to consider shipping consortia as liner conferences within the meaning of art. 3 of Regulation 4056/86, since consortia agreements generally contain restrictive arrangements that go beyond those exempted by the aforementioned art. 3. The resultant legal uncertainty required the notification of consortia agreements to the Commission for individual exemption, in accordance with art. 12 of Regulation 4056/86.

The Council's 1992 block exemption regulation was adopted in order to facilitate the use of consortia agreements through overcoming the uncertainty surrounding their operation. However, unlike its block exemption in relation to liner conferences, the Council's block exemption on shipping consortia does not contain detailed provisions. Rather, as in the case of other areas of essentially anti-competitive activity exempted by it en masse, the Council has merely provided the legislative framework within which the Commission may introduce more detailed provisions. One should note that the Council's enabling legislation is based 'in particular' on art. 87 of the EC Treaty. Unlike the regulation, therefore, the Commission's block exemption regulation will not be based on art. 84(2) of the EC Treaty. Thus, the conflict between transport policy and competition policy, which had led to such a liberal regime for liner conferences, should not dictate the substance of the shipping consortia

---

innovation was beyond the capability of most single shipowners. It became clear then that the vast majority of existing liner companies were no longer the optimum commercial unit for raising the huge capital sums involved.

Many of the shipping lines which once provided conventional liner-cargo services grouped together to form consortia, first at national level and then also internationally.'

[113] Communication by the Commission: 'Report on the possibility of a group exemption for consortia agreements in liner shipping', COM(90) 260 final. Originally, the Commission had undertaken to supply the report within one year. However, the drafting of the report was significantly delayed as a result of the industry's failure to co-operate.

[114] Proposal for a Council regulation on the application of art. 85(3) of the treaty to certain categories of agreements, decisions and concerted practices between shipping companies, COM(90) 260 final.

[115] Regulation 479/92 on the application of art. 85(3) of the treaty to certain categories of agreements, decisions and concerted practices between liner shipping companies (consortia), OJ 1992 L55/3.

¶1019

block exemption. In addition, the Commission's regulation will only apply for a period of five years, in contrast with the principally unlimited duration of the liner conference block exemption contained in art. 3 of the regulation.

The Commission has published its draft block exemption regulation.[116] The draft block exemption does not apply to rate fixing[117] by consortia operating outside of conferences, and would not appear to apply in respect of multi-modal operations. The draft block exemption will similarly not apply when consortia arrangements impose capacity restrictions on members. In addition, the draft block exemption is rendered subject to certain conditions and obligations, which provide inter alia for effective competition inside or outside the consortium, and place limits on the shares held by the consortium of the direct trade into and out of the ports covered by the agreement. Furthermore, the draft block exemption regulation provides a detailed framework for consultation between consortia and transport users. Although the Commission's regulation remains in draft form, there is some indication that this text may mark the application of a more stringent competition policy in the EC maritime transport sector.

¶1020   Multi-modal transport operations

Similarly, containerisation has opened the way for extensive multi-modal transport operations. For practical and administrative convenience, liner conferences engaging in such operations introduced so-called 'through rates', which cover both the land and sea-legs of containerised transportation. The application of art. 85(1) of the EC Treaty has become relevant as a result of the restriction of price competition between the providers of the land and sea-legs.

Multi-modal operations do not fall outside the scope of art. 85(1) by virtue of being technical agreements within the meaning of art. 2 of the regulation.[118] However, arguments to the effect that such agreements may benefit from the liner conference block exemption contained in art. 3 of the regulation have been advanced as a result of the wording of art. 5 of the regulation, which refers to the user's choice as to 'inland transport operations'[119] and the obligation on the conference members to provide tariff information setting out 'the exact

---

[116] Draft of a Commission Regulation (EC) on the application of article 85(3) of the EC Treaty to certain categories of agreements, decisions and concerted practices between liner shipping companies (consortia), OJ 1994 C63/8.

[117] However, recital 14 of the draft block exemption regulation indicates that individual exemptions 'may often be granted' for rate fixing by consortia operating outside of a conference 'in view of the increased competition they provide in relation to rates or quality of service with regard to liner conferences operating on the routes in question'.

Similarly, the draft block exemption regulation does not provide for tariff consultations within consortia operating outside of a conference. In the air transport sector, such tariff consultations are covered by the block exemption contained in art. 1 of regulation 1617/93.

[118] See ¶1010 above.

[119] Regulation 4056/86, art. 5(3).

extent of the services covered by the freight charge in proportion to the sea transport and the land transport'.[120] The Commission has rejected these arguments,[121] and in January 1993 initiated a proceeding against the Far Eastern Freight Conference in respect of agreements to fix inland transport rates. Despite expectations to the contrary, the Commission's draft block exemption regulation for shipping consortia would not appear to apply to consortia arrangements providing for multi-modal operations (see ¶1019 above).

AIR TRANSPORT

¶1021   Introduction

The enforcement of EC competition law within the air transport sector warrants special consideration for three reasons. First, the procedural framework in which the competition rules are enforced in the air transport sector is usually different from the general framework in which the competition rules are applied in other sectors. Secondly, a body of substantive competition law unique to the air transport sector has developed which is essential to any consideration of air transport competition questions. Finally, the ongoing liberalisation of air transport within the EC is also an important factor contributing to the distinctive quality of competition law issues within the air transport sector.

This chapter will consider each of these elements. The first section (¶1022) briefly considers the liberalisation of the Community air transport sector. Although this book does not provide the proper forum for a full discussion of EC air transport liberalisation, the brief summary provided below is an important accompaniment to the sections that follow it. The second section (¶1023–¶1031) will describe the three different procedural frameworks in which competition law is applied in the air transport sector and the circumstances under which each applies. This description will include a consideration of the applicable block exemptions (¶1030) and the effect of the merger regulation (¶1031). The third section (¶1032–¶1042) will review the substantive application of the merger regulation and art. 85 and 86 in the air transport sector.

---

[120] Regulation 4056/86, art. 5(4).

[121] The Commission's stance would appear to be based principally on the scope of the regulation, which refers to international *maritime* transport services only. This restricted scope of the regulation was maintained by the Transport Council despite requests by the European Parliament and the Economic and Social Committee that the regulation should expressly be applied to 'intermodal transport' also. The Commission argues that the scope of the block exemption cannot exceed that of the regulation within which it is contained.

¶1021

¶1022   Market liberalisation

The liberalisation of the air transport sector is of such ongoing importance that it warrants brief inclusion in this chapter.[122] As a result of three successive liberalisation 'packages', Community carriers benefit from increased access to routes within the Community and increased freedom in setting tariffs.[123] The third package of air transport liberalisation measures, enacted by the Council in 1992, established a Community-wide licensing framework for EC carriers,[124] opened certain previously protected routes to all Community carriers as of 1 January 1993 with the expectation of opening all other routes as of 1 April 1997[125] and further liberalised the member state-based fare approval system in the EC.[126] These liberalisation measures are an important part of the backdrop against which the competition rules are applied in the air transport sector, especially given Commission statements that the competition rules must be used to secure and protect the increased opportunities made possible by liberalisation.[127] It should also be noted that, as of early 1994, the Commission was considering the liberalisation of ground handling services and published a consultation paper on this subject.[128]

In addition, the third liberalisation package fares regulation[129] itself contains the basis for the prohibition of air fares which are 'excessively high' or which are so low so as to result in 'widespread losses among all air carriers concerned'.[130] Although these provisions regulate pricing conduct in a manner similar to competition law, they must be seen as a supplement to, rather than a substitute for, the application of competition law to air transport pricing. The general requirements of EC competition law, and particularly art. 86, will apply to air transport pricing conduct whether or not such conduct complies with the above described requirements of the fares regulation.[131]

---

[122] One of the important underlying ideas which appears to be guiding Community liberalisation policy in the air transport sector is the desire to avoid what are often seen to be the ill effects of liberalisation in the US.

[123] For a description of the first package of liberalisation measures, see the *Seventeenth Report on Competition Policy*, points 43–46. For a description of the second package of liberalisation measures, see the *XXth Report on Competition Policy*, points 70 and 71.

[124] Council Regulation 2407/92 of 23 July 1992 on licensing of air carriers, OJ 1992 L240/1.

[125] Council Regulation 2408/92 of 23 July 1992 on access for Community air carriers to intra-Community air routes, OJ 1992 L240/8. See Commission decision on a procedure relating to the application of Regulation 2408/92 (Case VII/AMA/I/93 – *Viva Air*), OJ 1993 L140/51. Regarding the application of the second package route access regulation, see Commission decision examining, by virtue of art. 10(4) of Council Regulation 2343/90, the application of art. 10(3) of the same regulation to the increase of frequencies on existing services on the route London (Heathrow)–Brussels, OJ 1992 L353/32, Commission information note P-58(92).

[126] Council Regulation 2409/92 of 23 July 1992 on fares and rates for air services, OJ 1992 L240/15.

[127] See *XXth Report on Competition Policy*, point 69.

[128] Consultation paper regarding ground handling services (94/C41/02), OJ 1994 C41/2.

[129] Council Regulation 2409/92 of 23 July 1992 on fares and rates for air services, OJ 1992 L240/15.

[130] Id., art. 6.

[131] See Commission decision on the compliance of certain air fares with the requirements of art. 3(1) of Council Regulation 2342/90, Annex III, 3.3, para. 7, OJ 1992 L220/35. This regulation has been superseded by Regulation 2409/92, above.

¶1023 Procedural framework for enforcement of competition law in the air transport sector: overview

The procedural framework within which competition law is enforced in the air transport sector varies depending both on the exact nature of the services in question and where such services are provided. As will be discussed in greater detail below, art. 85 and 86 apply to services ancillary to air transport, such as ground handling services and computerised reservation systems, in the same way the competition rules are applied in other sectors, by way of Regulation 17/62.[132] With regard to the actual provision of air transport services, the applicable procedural framework depends on whether or not the flight in question is a flight between Community airports. If it is, the air transport enabling regulations, Regulation 3975/87[133] and Regulation 3976/87,[134] will apply. If, on the other hand, the flight in question is between the Community and a third country, for the time being only the limited transitional regime of art. 88 and 89 of the treaty will apply.

Thus, there are three different procedural frameworks in which competition law is applied in the air transport sector:

(1) through the general implementing regulation, Regulation 17/62, as far as services ancillary to air transport are concerned;

(2) through the limited regime of art. 88 and 89 of the treaty, as far as flights between the Community and third countries are concerned; and

(3) through the air transport implementing regulations, Regulation 3975/87 and Regulation 3976/87, as far as flights between Community airports are concerned.

Each of these categories will be considered below.

¶1024 Services ancillary to air transport[135]

Regulation 17/62, the general implementing regulation regarding art. 85 and 86 of the treaty, was made inapplicable to certain aspects of the transport sector by

---

[132] Council Regulation 17/62 of 6 February 1962 implementing art. 85 and 86 of the treaty, JO 1962 13/204; amended JO 1962 58/1655, JO 1963 162/2696, JO 1971 L285/48.

[133] Council Regulation 3975/87 of 14 December 1987 laying down the procedure for the application of the rules on competition to undertakings in the air transport sector, OJ 1987 L374/1.

[134] Council Regulation 3976/87 of 14 December 1987 on the application of art. 85(3) of the treaty to certain categories of agreements and concerted practices in the air transport sector, OJ 1987 L374/9.

[135] The block exemptions relating to services ancillary to air transport are discussed in the general section on block exemptions in ¶1030 below.

virtue of Regulation 141/62.[136] In the *Olympic Airways*[137] decision of 1985 and the *London European–Sabena*[138] decision of 1988, the Commission specified the scope of Regulation 141/62 more precisely and therefore clarified those segments of the air transport sector that are still covered by Regulation 17/62. The Commission stated that, notwithstanding Regulation 141/62, Regulation 17/62 still applies to activities that are ancillary to air transport. Such ancillary activities include ground handling services,[139] computer reservation systems[140] and computerised air cargo information systems.[141]

As a result, alleged violations of art. 85 and 86 of the EC Treaty that relate to services ancillary to air transport will be subject to the same Regulation 17/62 procedural framework as alleged violations in other sectors. It is only alleged violations that relate to the actual provision of air transport services which are subject to a different regulatory regime.

¶1025   Air transport services

As noted above at ¶1024, Regulation 17/62 does not apply to air transport services. Thus, until the enactment of Regulation 3975/87 and Regulation 3976/87,[142] which implemented the competition rules in the air transport sector, the Commission had no power of direct enforcement with regard to air transport, and was dependent upon member state co-operation to restrain anti-competitive conduct in this sector. Since Regulation 3975/87 and Regulation 3976/87, as amended, only apply to flights within the Community,[143] however, the limited regime that applied prior to the enactment of those regulations is still relevant to flights between the EC and third countries. Therefore, with regard to air transport services as such, the applicable procedural framework depends on the exact nature of the route in question.

---

[136] Council Regulation 141/62 exempting transport from the application of Council Regulation 17/62, JO 1962 L124/2751.

[137] OJ 1985 L46/51, see also *Fifteenth Report on Competition Policy*, points 33 and 74.

[138] OJ 1988 L317/47.

[139] *Olympic Airways*, OJ 1985 L46/51.

[140] *London European–Sabena*, OJ 1988 L317/47.

[141] Notice pursuant to art. 19(3) of Council Regulation 17/62 concerning Case IV/34.177 – *Global Logistics System*.

[142] Council Regulation 3975/87 of 14 December 1987 laying down the procedure for the application of the rules on competition to undertakings in the air transport sector, OJ 1987 L374/1; Council Regulation 3976/87 of 14 December 1987 on the application of art. 85(3) of the treaty to certain categories of agreements and concerted practices in the air transport sector, OJ 1987 L374/9.

[143] As originally enacted, Regulations 3975/87 and 3976/87 applied only to international flights between Community airports, thus excluding domestic Community flights from their scope. As a result of Council Regulation 2410/92 of 23 July 1992 amending Regulation 3975/87 laying down the procedure for the application of the rules on competition to undertakings in the air transport sector, OJ 1992 L240/18 and Council Regulation 2411/92 of 23 July 1992 amending Regulation 3976/87 on the application of art. 85(3) of the treaty to certain categories of agreements and concerted practices in the air transport sector, OJ 1992 L240/19, the scope of Regulations 3975/87 and 3976/87 was extended to cover flights within a single member state.

¶1026   Air transport services: flights between the Community and third countries

(1)   Present system

With regard to flights between the Community and third countries, Regulation 17/62 does not apply.[144] Moreover, the specific enabling regulations for the air transport sector, Regulations 3975/87 and 3976/87, only govern flights within the Community and are therefore also inapplicable. Thus, although the court has made it clear that the competition rules apply to air transport even in the absence of enabling legislation,[145] the relevant procedural framework is limited.

In the absence of enabling legislation applicable to flights between the Community and third countries, art. 88 and 89 of the EC Treaty apply.[146] Article 88 establishes the power of authorities in member states to apply art. 85 and 86 to areas concerning which implementing legislation has not yet been passed by the Council pursuant to art. 87. Article 89 grants limited authority to the Commission to investigate suspected infringements of art. 85 and 86. Article 89 does not, however, give the Commission itself the power to bring such infringements to an end. On the contrary, the Commission may only publish a decision and authorise member states to take the necessary measures.[147]

In the absence of EC enabling legislation, it is also important to consider the jurisdiction of national courts. With regard to flights between the Community and third countries, national courts do not have the authority to apply art. 85.[148] This reflects the fact that it would be contrary to the general principle of legal certainty for art. 85(1) and (2) to be applied by member state courts unless it was possible to determine whether the exemption of art. 85(3) was

---

[144] See ¶1025 above.

[145] *Ministère Public v Asjes & Ors* [1986] ECR 1425; see also Bellis, '"Nouvelles Frontières" and EEC Competition Law in the Air Transport Sector: A Restatement of Classical Jurisdictional Rules', 27 Swiss Review of International Competition Law 51 (1986), and *EC Commission v France* [1974] ECR 359.

[146] *Ministère Public v Asjes & Ors* [1986] ECR 1425; *Ahmed Saeed Flugreisen & Anor v Zentrale zur Bekämpfung unlauteren Wettbewerbs* [1989] ECR 803.

[147] In 1986, before the enactment of Regulation 3975/87, the Commission made use of art. 89(1) to charge Aer Lingus, Air France, Alitalia, British Airways, British Caledonian, KLM, Lufthansa, Olympic Airways, Sabena and SAS with entering into capacity and revenue sharing arrangements, joint ventures, tariff concertations and other agreements in violation of art. 85. The proceedings were expanded in 1987 to cover Iberia, Luxair and TAP. With respect to Alitalia, Lufthansa and Olympic Airways, the Commission proceeded to adopt reasoned decisions under art. 89(2). These decisions were allowed to lapse, however, when the carriers agreed to co-operate with the Commission along with the other carriers. The art. 89 proceedings regarding all carriers lapsed upon the entry into force of Regulation 3975/87 and the changes required by the Commission were made by the carriers in order to qualify for the applicable block exemption, see *Sixteenth Report on Competition Policy*, point 36; *Seventeenth Report on Competition Policy*, point 46. The Commission also acted under art. 89 in response to complaints made by Sterling Airways against SAS and the Danish Government, see *Tenth Report on Competition Policy*, points 136–138.

[148] *Ministère Public v Asjes & Ors* [1986] ECR 1425; *Ahmed Saeed Flugreisen & Anor v Zentrale zur Bekämpfung unlauteren Wettbewerbs* [1989] ECR 803.

¶1026

applicable.[149] Since national courts cannot directly apply art. 85(3) and the Commission cannot grant exemptions under art. 85(3) with regard to flights between the Community and third countries, national courts cannot apply art. 85(1) and (2) regarding such flights.[150]

The same reasoning has, however, been held not to apply to art. 86 because it contains no exemption provision comparable to art. 85(3).[151] As a result, art. 86 may be applied by national courts to flights between the Community and third countries as well as to flights within the Community and services ancillary to air transport services.[152]

(2) Possibility of future extensions

Proposals exist to extend the scope of Regulation 3975/87 to cover international flights between the Community and third countries,[153] and apply art. 85(3) of the treaty to international air transport between the Community and third countries.[154] The Commission has maintained an active interest in receiving the additional authority which these proposals would confer. In a 1992 communication to the Council, the Commission indicated that:

> 'proper enforcement of the competition rules in respect of air transport to third countries is therefore urgently required. The Commission has made proposals to give it the normal powers of fact-finding, exemption of useful cooperation and termination of infringements which it has in other fields. The Council is requested to give these proposals urgent consideration. In order to remove legal uncertainty and to ensure the benefit of the application of the competition rules, the Commission would have no alternative, in the absence of proper enforcement powers, but to make use of its residual powers under Article 89 of the EEC Treaty.'[155]

---

[149] Id.

[150] By the same logic, member state courts may apply art. 85(1) and (2) regarding international or domestic flights between Community airports and services ancillary to air transport services.

[151] *Ahmed Saeed Flugreisen & Anor v Zentrale zur Bekämpfung unlauteren Wettbewerbs* [1989] ECR 803.

[152] The application of art. 86 by national courts to the air transport sector may, however, prove difficult in practice, as demonstrated in the case of *Malibu Travel Inc v Koninklijke Luchtvaart Maatschappij NV* [1991] ECC 281. This case concerned summary proceedings before the District Court of Amsterdam, in which the plaintiffs sought an injunction and damages against KLM on the basis of art. 86, since the latter's pricing policy and conditions of use attached to the London–Amsterdam–Accra tickets allegedly constituted an abuse of its dominant position on the relevant market. The proceedings were dismissed by the court since, in the absence of case law indicating how the relevant market should be defined, the court could not make this determination with sufficient certainty for the purposes of issuing a ruling.

[153] Proposal for a Council regulation amending Regulation 3975/87 of 14 December 1987 laying down the procedure for the application of the rules on competition to undertakings in the air transport sector, OJ 1989 C248/7.

[154] Proposal for a Council regulation on the application of art. 85(3) of the treaty to certain categories of agreements and concerted practices in the air transport sector, OJ 1989 C248/10, modified at OJ 1991 C153/21.

[155] *Air Transport Relations with Third Countries*, para. 37, COM(92) 434 final of 21 October 1992.

(3) Relations between EC member states and third countries

In addition to the application of the EC competition rules to flights between the Community and third countries, two additional issues are briefly considered in this section: (i) the negotiation of bilateral air transport agreements with third countries; and (ii) agreements between the EC and third countries that extend the application of EC air transport legislation.

The Commission has proposed legislation under which it would obtain the authority to negotiate bilateral air transport agreements with third countries on behalf of member states.[156] The Commission has argued at length that a combined EC negotiating block is necessary, particularly in view of the alleged disadvantage suffered by individual member states negotiating against powerful third countries such as the US.[157] Despite the Commission's eagerness, the member states have so far been reluctant to grant it such authority, especially in view of the perceived failure of the Commission to set out explicitly the exact basis on which it would engage in such negotiations and to address fully certain difficulties regarding the allocation of rights to which its external relations proposal seems to give rise. In March 1993, the Council concluded that the member states should remain fully responsible in the field of aviation external relations unless action is taken by the Council authorising negotiations at a Community level.[158]

Regarding the extension of EC air transport legislation, including the competition rules, to third countries, the Community has already entered into an agreement to this effect with Norway and Sweden.[159] Although the agreement was originally intended to lapse upon the entry into force of the European Economic Area agreement, additional legislation has been integrated into the agreement with Norway and Sweden and the duration of the agreement has been extended as far as certain legislation is concerned.[160] In addition, the Commission has suggested that '[a]n extension of the Community regulatory framework [in air transport] which has been established with the EFTA countries should also be considered as a follow up to the association agreements with the countries in Eastern Europe.'[161] Of more immediate

---

[156] Proposal for a Council decision on a consultation and authorisation procedure for agreements concerning commercial aviation relations between member states and third countries (COM(90) 17 final of 23 February 1990, amended by COM(92) 434 final of 21 October 1992).

[157] *Air Transport Relations with Third Countries*, COM(92) 434 final of 21 October 1992.

[158] Council press release 5333/93 (Presse 36-G), 15 March 1993.

[159] Council Decision 92/384 concerning the conclusion of an agreement between the EEC, the Kingdom of Norway and the Kingdom of Sweden on civil aviation, OJ 1992 L200/20. See also Council Notice dated 30 April 1993, OJ 1993 L105/36, regarding the entry into force of the agreement on 6 July 1992.

[160] Council Decision 93/453 concerning the amendment of the agreement between the EEC, the Kingdom of Norway and the Kingdom of Sweden on civil aviation, OJ 1993 L212/17. See also notice dated 22 September 1993, OJ 1993 L237/35. With respect to the EEA agreement generally, see ¶272.

[161] *Air Transport Relations with Third Countries*, para. 57 (see also, para. 17), COM(92) 434 final of 21 October 1992. See also opinion on the agreement between the EEC and the Republic of Slovenia in the field of transport, OJ 1993 C201/21, at para. 2. For a discussion of the association agreements, see ¶273.

¶1026

effect, discussions have taken place regarding the extension of EC air transport legislation to Switzerland.

¶1027   Air transport services: flights between Community airports

Within the framework of the 1987 'civil aviation package',[162] the Council adopted Regulation 3975/87 and Regulation 3976/87 implementing art. 85 and 86 with regard to international air transport between Community airports. As a result of two subsequent amendments, the scope of Regulation 3975/87 and Regulation 3976/87 was extended to cover all flights between Community airports, both international and domestic.[163]

¶1028   Flights between Community airports: the enforcement procedure under Regulation 3975/87

Regulation 3975/87 largely parallels Regulation 17/62 and Regulations 1017/68[164] and 4056/86[165] for inland and maritime transport.[166] The enforcement procedure to be followed under Regulation 3975/87 is, however, distinctive in the following two areas:

(1) the Commission's powers relating to the granting of exemptions; and

(2) the opposition procedure.

Individual exemptions

The Commission's powers to grant individual exemptions under Regulation 3975/87 differ from the Commission's powers under Regulation 17/62 in several respects. Under the former, the Commission may grant an exemption without prior notification of the agreement in question.[167] According to art. 4(3) of Regulation 3975/87, the Commission is obliged to grant an exemption whenever it finds that an agreement satisfies the requirements of art. 85(3), even if no notification has been submitted. Regulation 17/62, on the other hand, explicitly provides that no art. 85(3) decision may be taken until there has been a notification.[168]

---

[162] Council Regulation 3975/87 of 14 December 1987 laying down the procedure for the application of the rules on competition to undertakings in the air transport sector, OJ 1987 L374/1; Council Regulation 3976/87 of 14 December 1987 on the application of art. 85(3) of the treaty to certain categories of agreements and concerted practices in the air transport sector, OJ 1987 L374/9; Council Directive 87/601 of 14 December 1987 on fares for scheduled air services between member states, OJ 1987 L374/12 (repealed by Regulation 2342/90, OJ 1990 L217/1); Council Decision 87/602 of 14 December 1987 on the sharing of passenger capacity between air carriers on scheduled air services between member states and on access for air carriers to scheduled air-service routes between member states, OJ 1987 L374/19.
[163] See footnote 21 above.
[164] JO 1968 L175/1.
[165] OJ 1986 L378/4.
[166] See Argyris, 'The EEC Rules of Competition and the Air Transport Sector', (1989) 26 CML Rev 5, at p. 11.
[167] See recital 9 of Regulation 3975/87.
[168] Regulation 17/62, art. 4(1).

¶1027

Moreover, an exemption granted by the Commission under Regulation 3975/87 may take effect prior to the date of any notification,[169] or, in the absence of a notification, prior to the date of decision.[170] In contrast, an exemption granted by the Commission under Regulation 17/62 may not take effect earlier than the date of notification.[171] As a result of these factors, a company may feel less compelled to notify an arrangement which may fall within art. 85(1) and which is governed by Regulation 3975/87. Nonetheless, notification does under normal circumstances provide immunity from fines as of the date of the notification.[172]

Opposition procedure
The second distinctive feature is the opposition procedure, as set out in art. 5 of Regulation 3975/87. If an agreement, decision or concerted practice has been notified and has been judged generally admissible, the Commission will publish a notice in the *Official Journal* inviting all interested third parties and the member states to submit their comments. Unless the Commission notifies the applicant to the contrary within a period of 90 days from the date of publication, the agreement, decision or concerted practice shall be deemed exempt for a period not to exceed six years. The opposition procedure has been used widely, e.g. in a number of joint operation agreements between airlines relating to certain routes,[173] for a co-operation agreement between two carriers on cross-chartered flights[174] and for the IATA cargo tariff co-ordination system.[175]

Unlike the situation under Regulation 17/62, the Commission is obliged under Regulation 3975/87 to arrive at a decision regarding notifications it has received within a certain time-frame. As a result, the Commission may respond more rapidly to a notification received under Regulation 3975/87 than to a notification received under Regulation 17/62. This shorter response period may, in some cases, make notification under Regulation 3975/87 a more attractive alternative.

Implementing provisions
Regulation 3975/87 provides in art. 19 that the Commission has the power to adopt implementing provisions regarding complaints submitted to the

---

[169] Regulation 3975/87, art. 5(4).
[170] Regulation 3975/87, art. 4(3).
[171] Regulation 17/62, art. 6(1).
[172] Regulation 3975/87, art. 12(5).
[173] See e.g. OJ 1989 C204/3, OJ 1990 C29/3 and OJ 1991 C124/5. The opposition procedure was also used in a joint venture between British Airways, KLM and Sabena, OJ 1990 C82/7.
[174] *Air France/Air Inter cross-chartered flights*, OJ 1989 C190/4.
[175] *IATA cargo tariff co-ordination*, OJ 1989 C228/2.

¶1028

Commission and applications and hearings. Pursuant to this the Commission has adopted a regulation.[176]

Power to adopt interim measures

In 1991, the Council enacted Regulation 1284/91,[177] which amends art. 4 of Regulation 3975/87. Regulation 1284/91 is intended to allow the Commission to act quickly in order to protect a carrier against the anti-competitive practices of a competitor (e.g. the introduction of predatory pricing or excessive capacity by a carrier with a dominant position).

Under the amended regulation, the Commission has the power to take an interim decision ordering an airline to cease practices if it has clear prima facie evidence that the practices in question infringe the competition rules. Furthermore, those practices must have the 'object or effect of directly jeopardising the existence of an air service', and circumstances must be such that 'recourse to normal procedures may not be sufficient to protect the air service or the airline company concerned'.[178] Such interim decision will only apply for a period of six months, although it can be renewed for a further three months. During that time, the Commission will, before taking a definitive decision, carry out its normal full investigation. If a carrier fails to comply with an interim decision, the Commission has the power to fine the carrier from ECU 50 to 1000 per day.

Before taking an interim decision under the regulation as amended, the Commission must inform the carrier concerned of the allegations made against it, and will have to allow it the right to be heard.[179] The Commission will still be obliged to consult the Advisory Committee on Agreements and Dominant Positions in Air Transport (which comprises representatives of the national authorities of the member states) before taking a decision under the expedited procedure, but the Commission may do so orally on very short notice, rather than being obliged to submit a preliminary draft decision.[180] Although the Commission is not obliged to follow the view of the Committee, the Committee none the less provides a means for the member states to seek to influence the action of the Commission.

The authority of the Commission to take interim decisions in competition cases has already been confirmed by the EC Court of Justice.[181] Thus, while the

---

[176] Commission Regulation 4261/88 of 16 December 1988 on the complaints, applications and hearings provided for in Regulation 3975/87, OJ 1988 L376/10.

[177] Council Regulation 1284/91, amending Regulation 3975/87 laying down the procedure for the application of the rules on competition to undertakings in the air transport sector, OJ 1991 L122/2.

[178] Regulation 1284/91, art. 1(1).

[179] Regulation 1284/91, art. 1(3).

[180] See *XXIst Report on Competition Policy for 1991*, point 39. However, as a consequence of art. 1(2) of the regulation, if the Commission wishes to use its power to extend the validity of an interim decision beyond the six-month limit by a further three months, it must consult the Committee by convening a meeting on at least 14 days notice.

[181] See e.g. *Camera Care v EC Commission* [1980] ECR 119. Interim measures are discussed in greater detail in ¶1116.

¶1028

amendment may clarify the Commission's powers by replacing judge-made law with specific legislation, it would not appear to add significantly to them.

¶1029   The Commission's power to grant block exemptions under Regulation 3976/87

Within the framework of the 1987 'civil aviation package', the Council also adopted Regulation 3976/87[182] empowering the Commission to grant block exemptions to certain categories of agreements in the air transport sector. These categories include agreements concerning air transport services as such as well as agreements concerning services ancillary to air transport.[183]

The Commission may adopt block exemption regulations with respect to

'agreements, decisions or concerted practices which have as their object any of the following:

- joint planning and co-ordination of airline schedules;
- consultations on tariffs for the carriage of passengers and baggage and of freight on scheduled air services;
- joint operations on new or less busy scheduled air services;
- slot allocation at airports and airport scheduling in accordance with the Code of Conduct adopted by the Council;
- common purchase, development and operation of computer reservation systems relating to timetabling, reservations and ticketing by air transport undertakings in accordance with the Code of Conduct adopted by the Council.'[184]

Regulation 3976/87 also provides for the procedure to be followed, and the measures to be taken in cases where an agreement does not meet the conditions attached to a block exemption or where an agreement meets such conditions, but none the less is inconsistent with art. 85(3) or is prohibited by art. 86.[185]

---

[182] Council Regulation 3976/87 on the application of art. 85(3) of the treaty to certain categories of agreements and concerted practices in the air transport sector, OJ 1987 L374/9; amended by Council Regulation 2344/90, OJ 1990 L217/15 which extended the validity of any block exemption regulation adopted under Regulation 3976/87 to 31 December 1992 and allowed an exemption to be adopted concerning consultations on cargo rates; further extended by Council Regulation 2411/92, OJ 1992 L240/19, which also modifies those areas concerning which block exemption regulations may be adopted.

[183] See recital 1 of Regulation 3976/87. See also Argyris, 'The EEC Rules of Competition and the Air Transport Sector', (1989) 26 CML Rev 5, at pp. 19–20.

[184] Regulation 3976/87, as amended, art. 2. This list differs to some degree from the list originally included in Regulation 3976/87. Originally, a block exemption for certain revenue-sharing plans was authorised as well as block exemptions for certain ground handling services and in-flight catering services. On the other hand, the regulation as amended authorises the Commission to adopt block exemption regulations with regard to freight tariff consultations and joint operations, neither of which were provided for in the original regulation.

[185] Regulation 3976/87, art. 7.

¶1030   Block exemption regulations

The Commission has made use of its powers to grant block exemptions by adopting:

- Regulation 1617/93 on the application of art. 85(3) of the treaty to certain categories of agreements and concerted practices concerning joint planning and co-ordination of schedules, joint operations, consultations on passenger and cargo tariffs on scheduled air services and slot allocation at airports;[186]

- Regulation 3652/93 on the application of art. 85(3) of the treaty to certain categories of agreements between undertakings relating to computerised reservation systems for air transport services.[187]

(1)   Tariff consultation

Price-fixing is expressly prohibited under art. 85(1)(a) of the treaty. Consequently, the court stated in *Nouvelles Frontières*[188] that the fixing of air tariffs within the framework of IATA might trigger the application of art. 85. However, the Community enforcement authorities have not attacked mere tariff consultations as price fixing. By virtue of Regulation 1617/93 and its predecessors,[189] the Commission has granted a block exemption to certain consultations regarding both passenger and cargo tariff rates on scheduled air services between Community airports.[190]

The exemption is subject to strict conditions to ensure that the consultations do not amount to tariff fixing in practice.[191] It only applies if participation in such consultations is voluntary and open to any carrier who operates or intends to operate direct or indirect services on the route concerned, and any proposal may not be binding on the participants. The participants in consultations may only discuss air fares and cargo rates for a scheduled service, as well as the

---

[186] Commission Regulation 1617/93 on the application of article 85(3) of the treaty to certain categories of agreements and concerted practices concerning joint planning and co-ordination of schedules, joint operations, consultations on passenger and cargo tariffs on scheduled air services and slot allocation at airports, OJ 1993 L155/18.

[187] Commission Regulation 3652/93 on the application of art. 85(3) of the treaty to certain categories of agreements between undertakings relating to computerised reservation systems for air transport services, OJ 1993 L333/37.

[188] *Ministère Public v Asjes & Ors* [1986] ECR 1425.

[189] Commission Regulation 2671/88 on the application of art. 85(3) to certain categories of agreements between undertakings, decisions of associations of undertakings and concerted practices concerning joint planning and co-ordination of capacity, sharing of revenue and consultations on tariffs on scheduled air services and slot allocation at airports, OJ 1988 L239/9 and Commission Regulation 84/91 on the application of art. 85(3) of the treaty to certain categories of agreements, decisions and concerted practices concerning joint planning and co-ordination of capacity, consultations on passenger and cargo tariff rates on scheduled air services and slot allocation at airports, OJ 1991 L10/14.

[190] Regarding the application of Regulation 84/91 to tariff consultations, see *British Midland v Aer Lingus*, OJ 1992 L96/34.

[191] See recital 5 of Regulation 1617/93.

related conditions. The consultations may not extend to the capacity which will be made available and may not include an agreement on agents' remuneration 'or other elements of the tariffs discussed'.[192] Furthermore, the Commission and the member states must be entitled to send observers to such consultation meetings in order to verify that the conditions are respected.

In addition, tariff consultations 'must not exceed the aim of facilitating interlining' and must be 'limited to fares and rates which give rise to actual interlining'.[193] Accordingly, with regard to the types of tariffs and seasons which were the subject of the consultations, air transport users must be able to purchase a single ticket combining services of more than one carrier and, provided it is permitted by the conditions of the initial reservation, to change a reservation to another service on the same route operated by another carrier.[194]

Finally, the tariffs that are discussed in the consultations must be applied without discrimination based on the nationality or place of residence of passengers within the EC or the origin of freight within the EC.

(2) Joint planning and co-ordination of schedules

Under Regulation 1617/93, the Commission also exempted arrangements on the joint planning and co-ordination of the schedules of air services between Community airports. Such joint planning and co-ordination of capacities may include connecting flights between different airlines.[195] The basic objective of all such arrangements is to foster the maintenance of services at less busy times of the day, during less busy periods or on less busy routes and the development of onward connections,[196] thus benefiting the air traveller. Unlike its predecessor, Regulation 1617/93 allows planning and co-ordination regarding the minimum capacity to be provided on services, the connection of which has been co-ordinated between carriers.[197] However, in order to benefit from the block exemption, planning and co-ordination may not limit the capacity to be provided by participating carriers or serve to share capacity.

Regulation 1617/93 also provides that the establishment of schedules which facilitate interline connections between co-ordinating parties, as well as the minimum capacity to be utilised on such schedules, may be achieved by means

---

[192] Regulation 1617/93, art. 4(1)(f).
[193] Recital 5 of Regulation 1617/93.
[194] A carrier participating in tariff consultations may, however, refuse to allow the combination of its services with those of another participating carrier or refuse to allow voluntary changes of reservations 'for objective and non-discriminatory reasons of a technical or commercial nature, in particular where the air carrier effecting carriage is concerned with the credit worthiness of the air carrier who would be collecting payment', Regulation 1617/93, art. 4(1)(b).
[195] *XXth Report on Competition Policy*, point 71.
[196] Recital 3 of Regulation 1617/93.
[197] Regulation 1617/93, art. 2(a)(ii).

¶1030

of a binding arrangement.[198] All other planning and co-ordination must be achieved by way of non-binding arrangements.

The participating carriers must be free to introduce additional services or to withdraw from the co-operation altogether for future seasons without incurring penalties or being required to give more than three months notice. Finally, the conditions require that the planning and co-ordination does not attempt to influence the schedules of non-participating carriers.

(3) Slot allocation and airport scheduling

Another type of agreement exempted under Regulation 1617/93 concerns slot allocation and airport scheduling concerning air services between Community airports because it 'can improve the utilization of airport capacity and airspace, facilitate air traffic control and help spread out the supply of air transport services from the airport'.[199] The exemption requires the open and non-discriminatory application of the agreed-upon measures. Thus, in order to be exempted from art. 85(1), consultations on slot allocation and airport scheduling must be open to all interested airlines and any rules of priority may not be related to carrier identity or nationality or category of service, either directly or indirectly. As in the case of tariff consultations, the Commission and the member states must be allowed to send observers to the consultations.

For the exemption to apply, new entrants[200] must have priority regarding 50 per cent of newly-created, unused or given-up slots. In addition, carriers participating in the consultations must be granted access to certain information relating to slot allocation. If a carrier's request for slots is not accepted, the carrier is entitled to a statement of reasons.

(4) Computerised reservation systems

Under Commission Regulation 3652/93,[201] agreements between two or more undertakings that have as their purpose:

- the purchase or development of a computerised reservation system ('CRS'),
- the creation of a system vendor which operates the system, or
- the regulation of the distribution of the services,

may be exempted from the application of art. 85(1) of the treaty.

However, the exemption may only apply to obligations:

---

[198] Id.

[199] Recital 6 of Regulation 1617/93.

[200] For the purposes of Regulation 1617/93, new entrants are defined with reference to art. 2(b) of Council Regulation 95/93 on common rules for the allocation of slots at Community airports, OJ 1993 L14/1. Regulation 95/93 sets out the framework for the allocation of slots at congested Community airports.

[201] Commission Regulation 3652/93, OJ 1993 L333/37, superseding Commission Regulation 83/91, OJ 1991 L10/9, which expired on 31 December 1993.

¶1030

- not to directly or indirectly engage in the development, marketing or operation of another CRS,

- on system vendors to appoint parent carriers or participating carriers as distributors regarding all or certain subscribers in defined areas,

- on system vendors to grant exclusive distribution rights to all or certain subscribers in defined areas, and

- on system vendors not to permit distributors to sell other system vendors' distribution facilities.

The reason for granting the block exemption was that, while CRS's have become increasingly important to the successful marketing of air transport services, the creation and operation of such systems involves large investments which only a few European undertakings could make on their own.[202] The block exemption was originally enacted in order to improve the Community's competitive position, particularly with regard to two European joint ventures, Amadeus and Galileo.[203]

The exemption is subject to several conditions, the most important of which is that the system must be operated in a neutral and non-discriminatory way, i.e. the display of information may not be biased in favour of one or more particular airlines.[204] The exemption is also subject to the following additional obligations:

- subject to certain conditions, a parent carrier must provide information to, accept reservations from and distribute its services through another CRS to the same extent as its own CRS;

- the system vendor must offer participation in the system to any carrier on an equal and non-discriminatory basis, as long as capacity is available;

- the fees charged by the system vendor must be non-discriminatory and reasonably related to the cost of providing the service;

- undertakings providing the CRS with information must ensure that the data they submit is accurate and complete;

- the system vendor must ensure that the CRS is separated from any carrier's individual computer system;

---

[202] See recital 5 of Regulation 3652/93.

[203] See Argyris, 'The EEC Rules of Competition and the Air Transport Sector', (1989) 26 CML Rev 5, at p. 30.

[204] To the same end, the Council adopted Regulation 2299/89 on a code of conduct for computerised reservation systems, OJ 1989 L220/1, amended by Regulation 3089/93, OJ 1993 L278/1, which parallels to a large extent the provisions of the block exemption. See also, explanatory note on the EEC code of conduct for computerised reservation systems, OJ 1990 C184/2. In this regard, consideration might be given to the circumstances in which the computerised reservation system code of conduct would become relevant in an actual case, given the general application of art. 85 and 86 in this context. It would appear that the code of conduct is relevant with respect to unilateral conduct (not governed by art. 85) by a non-dominant carrier (not governed by art. 86) in the field of computerised reservation systems. Under these circumstances, the code of conduct may represent the only means of prohibiting impermissible CRS conduct under the EC competition rules.

¶1030

- limitations must be respected regarding the availability of information generated by the CRS; and

- any participating carrier or subscriber to the system must be entitled to terminate its contract on short notice and without paying more than the costs directly related to the termination of the contract.

The CRS block exemption contains a number of additional requirements governing, inter alia, the obligations of system vendors regarding information provided by participating carriers and contractual terms, loading and processing facilities, display requirements, relations with subscribers, billing, competition between system vendors and reciprocity.

(5) Joint operations

Regulation 1617/93, unlike its predecessor,[205] provides for a block exemption regarding 'the joint operation of a scheduled air service on a new or on a low-density route between Community airports'.[206] The joint operation must take the form of one carrier sharing the revenues and costs of a scheduled air service operated by another carrier.[207] There must have been either no direct service on the route in question for the four traffic seasons preceding the commencement of the joint operation or the capacity on the route covered by the joint operation must not exceed 30,000 seats annually in each direction. This limitation may be doubled on routes longer than 750 km for which there is no more than a twice-daily direct service.

In addition, in order to benefit from the block exemption, the carrier operating the service must not offer a capacity (not including the joint operation) of more than 90,000 seats annually at both of the airports in question. The annual revenues from air transport within the EC of the operating carrier, together with the annual revenues from air transport within the EC of any other carriers which, directly or indirectly, control the operating carrier, may not exceed ECU 400m. Finally, neither participating carrier may be prevented from operating additional services on its own account on the route in question and independently establishing the fares, capacity and schedules regarding such services, the joint operation may not extend beyond three years and both parties must be able to terminate the arrangement as of the end of a traffic season by giving notice of not more than three months.[208]

---

[205] Commission Regulation 84/91, OJ 1991 L10/14.
[206] Regulation 1617/93, art. 1.
[207] Regulation 1617/93, art. 3(a).
[208] These conditions suggest that the terms according to which a block exemption is available are, in general, similar to the established case law regarding joint operations: see ¶1033 below.

¶1030

¶1031 Procedural framework: the merger regulation

On 21 December 1989, the Council adopted Regulation 4064/89 on the control of concentrations between undertakings.[209] Since the entry into force of the regulation on 21 September 1990, concentrations with a Community dimension have been subject to notification to the EC Commission.[210] The complex system described above, whereby the procedural framework within which competition law is enforced in the air transport sector depends both on the exact nature of the services and where such services are provided, is greatly simplified with respect to concentrations as defined under the merger regulation. In accordance with art. 22(2) of the merger regulation, Regulation 17/62 and Regulation 3975/87 do not apply to concentrations as defined under the merger regulation.

As a result, any concentration with a Community dimension, including such concentrations in the air transport sector, will be subject solely to the requirements of the merger regulation.[211] With respect to concentrations without a Community dimension, including such concentrations in the air transport sector, these transactions will, in general, be subject neither to the merger regulation nor to the enabling regulations discussed above.[212]

¶1032 Substantive application of the merger regulation in the air transport sector

(1) Delta/PanAm

Delta/PanAm[213] marked the first concentration in the air transport sector evaluated under the merger regulation. The decision is interesting in its consideration of Community-wide turnover as well as its examination of the relevant market. With regard to the former, the *Delta/PanAm* decision suggests three possible methods of calculating the Community-wide turnover attributable to air transport services. The alternative methods of allocating revenues suggested were:

- by country of destination;
- by country of origin and country of final destination on a 50/50 basis; or
- based on where the ticket sale occurred.

---

[209] Council Regulation 4064/89 of 21 December 1989 on the control of concentrations between undertakings, OJ 1990 L257/14.

[210] See ¶610.

[211] There are exceptions to this generalisation, including the member states' right to take measures to protect other legitimate interests and the possibility of the referral of a notified transaction to member state authorities (see ¶629).

[212] For a more detailed description of the treatment of concentrations without a Community dimension, see ¶633.

[213] Case IV/M.130 – *Delta Air Lines/PanAm*.

These alternatives were discussed without arriving at any conclusion as to which of the three methods should be used, since each of them resulted in the conclusion that the concentration had a Community dimension.

With regard to the determination of the relevant market, the decision suggested that the market could be defined with each individual route itself being a distinct market or, alternatively, on the basis of a bundle of routes. In the latter case, the exact routes included in each bundle would depend on the degree of demand-side substitutability. As with the turnover calculation, however, the final determination of the relevant market was deemed unnecessary since both alternatives resulted in the concentration being deemed permissible.

(2) Air France/Sabena

The *Air France/Sabena* decision,[214] relating to Air France's acquisition of a minority holding in Sabena, also addressed the allocation of turnover and the determination of relevant markets in the air transport sector. Regarding the allocation of turnover, the decision cited the *Delta/PanAm* decision and repeated the three options set out therein. The *Air France/Sabena* decision also avoided definitively endorsing one of the three options since application of all three led to the conclusion that the concentration had a Community dimension. Nonetheless, the decision suggests that the second method of calculating air transport turnover (by country of origin and country of final destination on a 50/50 basis) is closer to the spirit of the merger regulation. On that basis, it might be speculated that this method is the most likely to be employed in cases where a choice among the three possibilities is necessary.

Regarding the determination of relevant markets in air transport, the *Air France/Sabena* decision generally fits within the framework established by the *Delta/PanAm* decision. The *Air France/Sabena* decision was, however, much more specific in its description of the factors underlying demand-side substitutability.[215] With regard to the routes between Belgium and France, the relevant markets were determined to be each individual route. In a second category, flights between Paris and certain destinations were deemed substitutable with flights between Brussels and such destinations.[216] In a third

---

[214] Case IV/M.157 – *Air France/Sabena*, OJ 1992 C272/5.

[215] The decision states as general principles that (i) the longer the distance of the routes in question, the greater the substitutability between routes; (ii) the closer together the points served by different routes, the greater the substitutability between such routes; and (iii) as the frequency on individual routes increases, the substitutability between routes decreases.

[216] Paris–Ankara and Brussels–Ankara were deemed substitutable routes and Paris–Budapest and Brussels–Budapest were deemed substitutable.

¶1032

category, the relevant markets were deemed to include the flights between certain destinations and all EC or EFTA airports serving such destinations.[217]

In addition to air transport routes themselves, however, the *Air France/ Sabena* decision also addressed the competitive implications of take-off and landing slots and airport facilities. In general, the decision stated that airport facilities (runways, terminals, take-off and landing slots and air traffic control facilities) must be considered as factors of production which are indispensable and for which substitutes are not easily obtained. As a result, the decision acknowledged that in some cases control of such facilities can erect barriers to entry or create vertical links which create or strengthen dominant positions in the relevant air transport market.

With regard to slots, the decision concluded that the notified concentration could result in the creation of a dominant position regarding air routes departing from Brussels in virtue of the accumulation of slots at Zaventem airport.

With regard to airport facilities, it should be noted that one of the consequences of the Air France acquisition of a minority holding in Sabena is the anticipated creation of a 'hub and spoke' network based in Brussels. The decision found that the creation of such a network could strengthen the dominant position of Air France and Sabena regarding routes between Belgium and France and erect barriers to entry for competitors who do not benefit from their own European hub and spoke network.

In total, therefore, Air France's acquisition of a minority holding in Sabena was deemed to create a number of potential problems under the merger regulation: (1) a combined monopoly position on the Brussels–Lyon, Brussels–Nice and Brussels–Paris routes, (2) very high combined market positions on the Brussels or Paris–Ankara market and the Brussels or Paris–Budapest market, (3) very strong combined market positions regarding certain African destinations,[218] (4) control of a large number of slots at Zaventem airport, and (5) anticipated control of a European hub and spoke network centred in Zaventem.

The concentration was nonetheless deemed compatible with the common market, but only after a number of undertakings were granted by Air France, Sabena and the French and Belgian Governments. These parties agreed to enable other carriers to compete on the routes between France and Belgium and, regarding two of the three routes,[219] agreed that either Air France or

---

[217] This was determined to be the case concerning routes between Europe and francophone sub-Saharan Africa. For example, the routes Paris–Douala, Brussels–Douala, Geneva–Douala and Frankfurt–Douala were all determined to be part of the same market.

[218] Ouagadougou (Burkina Faso), Bujumbura (Burundi), Bamako (Mali), Niamey (Niger) and Kigali (Rwanda).

[219] Brussels–Lyon and Brussels–Nice.

¶1032

Sabena would discontinue its services for the benefit of a competitor. Similar undertakings were entered into regarding the African routes. Regarding the Ankara and Budapest markets, the parties agreed to multi-designation on the routes in question after a certain level of annual traffic was reached. Regarding take-off and landing slots, Air France and Sabena agreed to limit the number of slots held by both of them at Zaventem to no more than 65 per cent of all available slots during any two hour period and no more than 75 per cent of all available slots during any one hour period. Finally, in response to concerns related to the development of a hub and spoke network centred in Zaventem, the French Government agreed to permit the creation or the development of a hub airport comparable to the anticipated Zaventem facility if such a facility is requested by competitors of Air France or Sabena.[220]

(3) British Airways/TAT

The *British Airways/TAT* decision[221] considered the acquisition by British Airways of a 49.9 per cent interest in TAT European Airlines. In considering the combined position of British Airways and TAT EA, it was concluded that there was an overlap regarding only two routes: Paris–London and Lyon–London. In the consideration of these two routes, the question of substitutability between different airports in the same city took on considerable importance.[222]

Regarding the Paris–London route, British Airways operated from both Heathrow and Gatwick and TAT EA operated only from Gatwick. Regarding London–Lyon, BA only operated from Heathrow and TAT EA only operated from Gatwick. In order to assess the affect on competition as a result of BA's acquisition, therefore, the substitutability between Heathrow and Gatwick had to be evaluated.

Concerning such substitutability, the Commission arrived at the conclusion that an overall analysis of the London market would appear to be appropriate. However, the congestion of both Heathrow and Gatwick airports was seen to limit the relevance of their partial substitutability. In this regard, it was noted that BA held a substantial portion of the total slots at both Gatwick and Heathrow. It was also noted that BA was the only airline capable of operating on both the Paris–London and London–Lyon routes from both Heathrow and Gatwick airports.

In view of these structural factors, the Commission concluded that the transaction could significantly impede competition on the two routes in question. These concerns were overcome, however, in view of slot

---

[220] The practical relevance of the French Government's undertakings regarding such a hub airport may be called into question, especially given their seemingly limited nature.
[221] *British Airways/TAT* Case IV/M.259, OJ 1992 C326/16.
[222] See also *British Midland v Aer Lingus*, OJ 1992 L 96/34 at pp 37 and 20.

undertakings given by British Airways. Regarding the London–Paris route, BA agreed to make up to 12 daily slots available at Gatwick when a carrier or carriers wishing to commence services or increase pre-existing services is unable to obtain the necessary slots from the airport co-ordinator. Regarding London–Lyon, BA entered into a similar undertaking to make up to four slots available at Gatwick, but only if traffic on the route exceeds a certain threshold.

(4) British Airways/Dan Air

The Commission's decision in *British Airways/Dan Air*[223] was issued in response to a request from the Belgian Government pursuant to art. 22 of the merger regulation.[224]

From an air transport perspective, the decision is interesting in its analysis as to whether British Airways' acquisition of the non-chartered activities of Davies and Newman Holdings plc creates or strengthens a dominant position held by BA on the Brussels–London route.[225] In reaching its conclusion that British Airways did not hold a dominant position on the Brussels–London route after the acquisition, the Commission took BA's overall market share of less than 50 per cent into account.

In addition, the Commission attached great importance to the success of British Midland at capturing 18 per cent of the market in less than one year. Although British Midland's performance on the route was only possible because it possessed slots at Heathrow that could be transferred from other routes, British Midland's dramatic showing was nonetheless seen to demonstrate the vulnerability of BA's market share to competition. Finally, the Commission also considered the fact that British Airways' market share was falling, that there were three strong carriers as well as a number of smaller competitors on the route and that traffic on the route was increasing steadily. Based on these factors, the Commission determined that British Airways was not capable of acting independently of competitors and customers on the Brussels–London route and could therefore not be considered dominant.

The Commission also briefly considered the possibility of the acquisition enhancing BA's entire network. In view of Dan Air's previous market position, however, it was concluded that the effect on BA's general position in the Community would not be significant.

---

[223] *British Airways/Dan Air*, Case IV/M.278, OJ 1993 C68/5, press release IP(93) 106.

[224] See ¶633. For a discussion of the circumstances leading to the request, see press releases IP(92) 1048 and IP(93) 63.

[225] Although the Commission considers BA's possible dominance on the Brussels–London route as a whole, the possibility of Heathrow and Gatwick airports constituting separate markets is left open since, in either case, the transaction would be deemed permissible.

¶1032

¶1033   Substantive application of art. 85[226] in the air transport sector: joint operation agreements

In the summer of 1988, 12 joint operation agreements between airlines were notified to the Commission.[227] Although the Commission's response to the 12 agreements varied significantly, each agreement provided for the joint operation of particular intra-Community routes. The arrangements provided that the flights themselves would be operated by one of the two parties to the agreement, the programmes and schedules would be decided jointly, the carriers would co-operate commercially and costs and revenues would be shared.

Three of the joint operation agreements were terminated following discussion with the Commission.[228] Of the remaining nine agreements, the Commission took a favourable view of three, all of which combined the marketing network of a large airline with a small carrier operating a new route.[229] Even as regards these three agreements, however, the Commission made it clear that it intended to reconsider whether they are still indispensable and whether sufficient competition still exists after two or three years of operation.[230] The Commission refused to grant exemptions to the six other agreements[231] because they did not appear indispensable to the maintenance of services on the routes and because of the likelihood that they would eliminate competition in the provision of air transport services between the cities in question.

In 1991, an agreement relating to joint operation of the Copenhagen–Cologne/Bonn route between Maersk Air and Deutsche Lufthansa was notified. The parties contended that the agreement ensured continued operation on an otherwise loss-generating route, would create cost savings and was important to a 'route-concept' plan to increase passenger choice in the relevant region of Germany.[232] The agreement may be deemed exempt from

---

[226] In addition to the cases examined hereunder, consideration should also be given to the charges made by the Commission under art. 89 which are discussed in footnote 147 above.

[227] *XIXth Report on Competition Policy*, point 25.

[228] Agreements between British Airways and Air France concerning the Paris–Manchester and Nice–Manchester routes and between British Airways and Alitalia concerning the London–Genoa route.

[229] The agreements between Air France and NFD Luftverkehrs AG concerning the Nürnberg–Paris, Munich–Lyon and Munich–Marseille routes, a summary of which was published in OJ 1989 C204/3; between Air France and Brymon concerning the Paris–London City Airport route, a summary of which was published in OJ 1989 C204/6; and between London City Airways and Sabena concerning the London City Airport–Brussels route, a summary of which was published in OJ 1989 C204/12.

[230] *XIXth Report on Competition Policy*, point 25.

[231] The agreements between Air France and Iberia relating to the Paris–Bilbao–Santiago de Compostela route, a summary of which was published in OJ 1989 C204/4; Air France and Alitalia relating to the Paris–Milan and Paris–Turin routes, a summary of which was published in OJ 1989 C204/5; Air France and Sabena relating to the Paris–Brussels route, the Bordeaux–Brussels and Toulouse–Brussels routes and the Brussels–Lyon–Marseille route, summaries of which were published in OJ 1989 C204/7–10; and Aer Lingus and Sabena relating to the Brussels–Dublin route, a summary of which was published in OJ 1989 C204/11.

[232] OJ 1991 C124/5.

the application of art. 85(1) in view of the fact that the Commission raised no objections during the 90-day period provided for in art. 5 of Regulation 3975/87.[233]

In 1989, a joint operation agreement between Air France and Air Inter was notified.[234] The agreement consisted of an exchange, the result of which would have been that Air Inter would have operated certain flights between France and the rest of the EC under the Air France 'flag' and Air France would have operated certain domestic flights under the Air Inter 'flag'. The agreement provided for profit and loss sharing between the parties, joint promotion and the continued association of the route with the carrier which originally served it. The parties argued that an exemption pursuant to art. 85(3) of the treaty was justified in view of the development of improved domestic services and Paris connections, the introduction of new fares at reduced levels and the absence of impermissible restrictions on competition given the essential independence of the parties. Nonetheless, the Commission informed the parties that it had serious doubts as to the applicability of art. 85(3) and art. 85(1) therefore prohibited the joint operation arrangement.

¶1034   Substantive application of art. 85 in the air transport sector: framework co-operation agreements

Air France and Lufthansa entered into a framework co-operation agreement which created a permanent structure through which information regarding the position of the carriers could be regularly exchanged and which enhanced co-operation between the carriers with regard to certain commercial and technical activities.[235] The agreement involved a co-ordination committee composed of senior executives and an organised exchange of executives between the two airlines.

The Commission concluded that in view of the highly regulated character of the air transport market and the position of large airlines, the agreement would quite likely be inconsistent with the development of 'healthy competition'. In addition to not instituting the co-operative measures described above, the parties agreed to inform the Commission of any new co-operative measures agreed to between them.

---

[233] An additional joint operation between Maersk Air and Sabena on the Brussels–Billund route, notified at OJ 1991 C235/3, was allowed by the Commission based on its assessment in press release IP(92) 5.

[234] OJ 1989 C190/4.

[235] *XXth Report on Competition Policy*, point 106.

¶1035   Substantive application of art. 85 in the air transport sector: CRS co-operation agreements

Although the parties ultimately broke off negotiations because of irreconcilable differences, the Commission approved a partnership agreement entered into between the owners of Amadeus and Sabre, the largest computerised travel reservation systems in Europe and the US.[236] The approved agreement provided for co-operation in marketing and distribution as well as technology development. The undertakings obtained by the Commission as a condition for approval obliged the carriers holding an interest in Amadeus or Sabre not to discriminate against other computerised reservation systems, not to prevent non-associated carriers from using other computerised reservation systems and to treat all carriers using their systems in a non-discriminatory fashion. The Commission also indicated its intention to obtain similar assurances from the owners of Galileo and Worldspan, two other CRSs operating in the EC.

On 17 April 1993, the Commission published a notice stating its favourable view regarding the combination of the computerised reservation systems operated by Galileo and Covia and the operation of a new system called Galileo International.[237] According to the Commission, the new system held a 34.6 per cent share of the Community market for CRS services.

¶1036   Substantive application of art. 85 in the air transport sector: computerised cargo information systems

In a notice dated 18 March 1993, the Commission announced its intention to take a favourable view of a set of agreements entered into by Lufthansa, Air France, Cathay Pacific and JAL which create a global air cargo logistics system.[238]

Such logistics system facilitates the tracking and tracing of air cargo shipments, the placement of booking requests and access to information and allows the preparation of detailed shipping plans. The system will not itself offer cargo booking and marketing services. The Commission's approval was conditional on the parties' agreement to respect the requirements of the CRS block exemption,[239] which may be taken to confirm the Commission's view that the potential competition concerns created by a computerised cargo

---

[236] *XXIst Report on Competition Policy for 1991*, points 93–95 and press release IP(91) 784. Amadeus is owned by Air France, Iberia Airlines and Lufthansa and Sabre is owned by AMR Corp, American Airlines' parent company.

[237] Notice pursuant to art. 19(3) of Regulation 17/62 concerning Case IV/34.632 – *Agreements relating to the combination of the Galileo and Covia CRSs*, OJ 1993 C107/4.

[238] Notice pursuant to art. 19(3) of Regulation 17/62 concerning Case IV/34.177 – *Global Logistics System*, OJ 1993 C76/5.

[239] Commission Regulation 83/91 on the application of art. 85(3) of the treaty to certain categories of agreements between undertakings relating to computer reservation systems for air transport services, OJ 1991 L10/9 (superseded since 1 January 1994, see ¶1030(4))

distribution system are very similar to those which arise in the CRS context. This conclusion is also supported by the Commission's assessment of the Encompass cargo logistics information system.[240]

¶1037   Substantive application of art. 85 in the air transport sector: IATA programmes

In 1991 the Commission granted exemptions to the IATA Passenger Agency Programme[241] and the IATA Cargo Agency Programme,[242] subject to a number of amendments adopted by IATA.[243] The exempted programmes provide for collective networks of agencies that sell passenger and freight services and establish the requirements for becoming an agent and the relationship between IATA airlines and agents. Although the Commission found that the amended resolutions still restricted competition, it concluded that there was enough potential benefit to justify the exemptions. The Commission had issued a statement of objections in 1989 regarding an earlier version of the IATA passenger agency programme.[244]

IATA also notified its cargo tariff co-ordination arrangements in 1989.[245] In addition to certain technical issues, the most important elements of the arrangements related to the establishment of fees and charges for the transportation and handling of cargo and related services. After receiving submissions from third parties and identifying certain goods for which air transport was the only satisfactory means of transport, the Commission informed IATA that there were serious doubts as to whether the resolutions met the requirements of art. 85(3).[246]

¶1038   Substantive application of art. 85 in the air transport sector: hub and spoke operation

In 1989, British Airways, KLM and Sabena entered into an agreement whereby BA and KLM would each acquire a 20 per cent holding in Sabena World Airlines, a subsidiary of Sabena. The agreement, which would have created a hub and spoke system at Brussels' Zaventem airport, encountered strong opposition from several small airlines. It was also referred to the EC Commission and the UK Monopolies and Mergers Commission and an action

---

[240] Notice pursuant to art. 19(3) of Regulation 17/62 concerning Case IV/34.276 – *Encompass Europe (GLV/ELTS BV)*, OJ 1992 C233/2.

[241] OJ 1991 L258/18.

[242] OJ 1991 L258/29.

[243] *XXIst Report on Competition Policy for 1991*, points 101–103.

[244] *Nineteenth Report on Competition Policy*, point 58.

[245] OJ 1989 C228/2.

[246] Press release IP(89) 928. In this context it should be noted that a block exemption is now available for freight tariff consultations, see ¶1030(1).

¶1038

was filed against the agreement under Belgian law in the Brussels Commercial Court.

After having previously applied for clearance,[247] in June 1990 the participants received a statement of objections stating that the arrangement infringed art. 85(1) and formal replies were made. The statement of objections outlined a number of risks to competition posed by the agreement, particularly reduced competition at Zaventem, collaboration between Sabena and KLM which serve overlapping routes and co-operation regarding long-haul routes.[248] Although further discussions took place between the parties and the Commission, Sabena, KLM and BA announced the abandonment of the plan on 31 December 1990.

¶1039   Substantive application of art. 86 in the air transport sector: take-overs and acquisitions

(1)   Acquisition of British Caledonian by British Airways

Only two weeks after the Commission had acquired its new powers under Regulation 3975/87, it opened an inquiry into the abuse of a dominant position by BA following its acquisition of British Caledonian. The Commission was concerned that the merger would strengthen the position of BA in the scheduled air transport services market in Europe, a market on which it already held a strong position. The companies were previously direct competitors on 11 intra-Community routes and BA had retained the licences of British Caledonian on these routes following the acquisition, thereby restricting competition. In addition, BA kept all the slots allocated to British Caledonian at London Gatwick Airport.

The inquiry was closed by the Commission upon undertakings given by BA. The company agreed to apply for the British Caledonian licences on certain routes and to withdraw applications for other routes. It also agreed to limit its slots at Gatwick to a maximum of 25 per cent. Given the guarantees which had already been obtained from BA by the UK Monopolies and Mergers Commission, the Commission felt that sufficient competition was assured.

(2)   Air France acquisition of UTA

In February 1990 the EC Commission announced that the acquisition by state-owned Air France of French independent UTA constituted a prima facie abuse of a dominant position in violation of art. 86 of the EC Treaty. As a result of this acquisition, Air France also gained a 56 per cent stake in, and thus indirect control of, the domestic carrier Air Inter. With its new group structure,

---

[247] OJ 1990 C82/7.
[248] *XXth Report on Competition Policy*, point 108.

Air France controlled 97 per cent of routes within France and 44 per cent of all flights from Paris.

An agreement was reached under which the merger was cleared.[249] In exchange for this clearance, however, the French Government and Air France were required to make concessions. In general, Air France was required to dispose of its holding in the fourth largest French carrier, TAT; a number of domestic routes were opened up to competition from a carrier outside the Air France group; the French Government agreed to designate a second carrier on international routes if certain capacity or frequency thresholds were exceeded;[250] and the French Government agreed to give priority to carriers outside the Air France group in respect of international routes which were not currently operated.[251]

(3) KLM take-over of Transavia

Although the Commission ultimately approved the increase by KLM from 40 per cent to 80 per cent of its stake in Dutch independent, Transavia,[252] it was originally concerned about the effect of both the 40 per cent and 80 per cent holding on (a) the market for charter services out of Amsterdam; (b) the market for scheduled services out of Amsterdam and (c) the possible consolidation of KLM's dominant position 'on the Dutch market for the sale of air transport to and from the Netherlands.'[253]

Approval regarding both the original agreement and the increased shareholding was therefore only given following the agreement by the Dutch Government to grant a total of 35 route licences on scheduled international routes (for which slots would be made available at Amsterdam) to Dutch and other EC carriers outside the KLM group according to a fixed timetable which extends to 1994. In addition, it was agreed that licences would be granted to Dutch carriers on ten domestic routes, restrictions on charter services would be reduced and that KLM would not pursue any further Dutch acquisitions or seek to influence Dutch airlines outside of its group. The Commission concluded that the opening up of so many routes to inter-carrier competition would off-set the potential harm to competition which the take-over by KLM of one of the largest Dutch charter carriers and the main Dutch carrier outside the KLM group would have otherwise caused. This settlement is, therefore, very similar in purpose to the settlement which was made in relation to the take-over

---

[249] See, press release IP(90)870 of 30 October 1990.
[250] This could be a non-French EC carrier if the home country of that carrier was prepared to grant reciprocal treatment to French carriers.
[251] See *XXth Report on Competition Policy*, point 116.
[252] Press release IP(91)658 of 5 July 1991.
[253] *XXIst Report on Competition Policy for 1991*, point 91.

¶1039

by Air France of UTA and Air Inter and the take-over by British Airways of British Caledonian.

¶1040   Substantive application of art. 86 in the air transport sector: interlining

The Commission has held that a dominant carrier's refusal to enter into or maintain an interlining relationship with another carrier may constitute an abuse of art. 86.[254] An interlining agreement allows a carrier to issue tickets involving travel on more than one carrier. Thus, for example, if two airlines have entered into an interlining agreement, a ticket may be issued for travel to an intermediate destination on the first carrier and from the intermediate to some final destination on the second carrier. Interlining arrangements are also closely related to the voluntary change of tickets which allows travellers to use tickets issued by one airline for travel on another if, for example, the flight for which the original reservation was made is missed or becomes inconvenient.

Most recently, the Commission determined that Aer Lingus abused its dominant position on the London–Dublin route by terminating its interlining agreement with British Midland.[255] Although such termination did not endanger British Midland's continued presence on the route, the Commission's decision was based on the notion that Aer Lingus made it more difficult for British Midland to compete.[256] The duty to interline imposed by the Commission was limited to two years following the decision, subject to review at the end of such period.

In 1990, Lufthansa agreed to re-establish interlining with Air Europe following intervention by the Commission. Lufthansa had previously withdrawn from its interlining relationship with Air Europe in view of increased price competition between the two carriers on the London–Munich route. As a result, Air Europe filed a formal complaint with the Commission alleging violation of art. 86, the resolution of which was a two-year settlement agreement re-establishing interlining. The press release describing the settlement[257] makes it clear that under some circumstances the relevant market in air transport may be as narrow as travel between two airports. The press release states that '[w]here an airline has a large share of a particular market between two airports, a refusal to interline may hinder the maintenance or development of competition on that route or on connecting routes, and thus constitute an abuse of that dominant position'.

---

[254] See *XXth Report on Competition Policy*, points 73–76.
[255] *British Midland v Aer Lingus*, OJ 1992 L96/34.
[256] Ibid, at pp. 39–41. See also press release IP(92) 132.
[257] Press release IP(90) 384 of 14 May 1990.

¶1041   Substantive application of art. 86 in the air transport sector: computerised reservation systems

As regards the application of art. 86 to vendors of computerised reservation systems, the Commission found in *London European/Sabena*[258] that Sabena had infringed art. 86 by refusing to grant London European access to its computerised reservation system on the grounds that London European's tariffs were significantly lower than the IATA rate and that it had not entrusted the ground handling of its aircraft to Sabena.

The Commission initiated proceedings in the case in May 1987, eight months before the entry into force of Regulation 3975/87. However, this did not impede the Commission from exercising its full power of implementing the EC competition rules, since the activities in question were ancillary to air transport and therefore fell within Regulation 17/62.[259]

With regard to art. 86, the Commission had some difficulty establishing that Sabena occupied a dominant position in the relevant market. In accordance with the case law of the court, the Commission defined the geographical market as being restricted to Belgium and the product market to be CRSs. It argued that although other non-computerised reservation methods still exist, computerised reservation is important for the successful marketing of air transport and will in the near future replace all other forms of reservation. The Commission stated that the relevant market thus defined had two facets: the provision of computerised reservation services to travel agencies and the provision of such services to other air transport companies. Once it had found that Sabena occupied a dominant position in respect of both facets of the market, the Commission had no difficulty in finding that the tying between access to the Saphir system on the one hand, and London European's fares and the ground handling contract on the other constituted an abusive practice expressly covered by art. 86(d).

¶1042   Substantive application of art. 86 in the air transport sector: frequent flyer programmes

In so far as certain frequent flyer programmes may bind customers to a particular carrier or constitute an impermissible barrier to entry, the Commission may also be expected to take an interest in frequent flyer programmes offered by dominant carriers. Such programmes may violate art. 86 if, for example, they include deadlines on which all previously acquired unused points are lost or award points in a non-linear fashion in an attempt to bind certain customers. Awarding different points on otherwise comparable

---

[258] *London European–Sabena*, OJ 1988 L317/47.
[259] See ¶1024.

routes in an attempt to disadvantage a competitor may, under certain circumstances, also constitute an abuse.[260]

BANKING

¶1043   The applicability of the competition rules to the banking sector

At present it is clearly established that the competition rules apply to the banking sector. Over the past few years, the Commission has considerably broadened its application of the competition rules to the banking sector. As early as its *Second Report on Competition Policy*, the Commission stated that the treaty rules on competition are of general application and thus applicable to the banking sector as long as no special regulation under art. 87(2)(c) has been adopted.[261] Up to this date, no such regulations have been adopted.

In *Züchner*,[262] it was argued that banks are not subject to the competition rules since they are undertakings 'entrusted with the operation of services of general interest' within the meaning of art. 90(2) of the treaty, by reason of the special nature of the services provided by banks and the vital role which they play in transfers of capital. According to art. 90(2), the competition rules should therefore not apply if their application would obstruct the performance, in law or in fact, of the particular task assigned to them. The court, however, did not agree with this line of reasoning:

> 'Although the transfer of customers' funds from one Member State to another normally performed by banks is an operation which falls within the special task of banks, particularly in connexion with international movements of capital, that is not sufficient to make them undertakings within the meaning of Article 90(2) of the Treaty unless it can be established that in performing such transfers the banks are operating a service of general economic interest with which they have been entrusted by a measure adopted by the public authorities.'[263]

This is in line with the court's position in *BRT v SABAM*[264] where the court held that the exception contained in art. 90(2) needs to be narrowly interpreted.

In *Uniform Eurocheques*,[265] the Commission held that art. 90(2) did not

---

[260] The Commission was, at the time of this writing, in the process of preparing a notice on frequent flyer programmes. The Commission was also examining the possibility of publishing guidelines for the consideration of complaints in this area and a Council regulation providing a frequent flyer programme code of conduct has been discussed.

[261] *Second Report on Competition Policy*, point 50.

[262] *Züchner v Bayerische Vereinsbank AG* [1981] ECR 2021.

[263] *Züchner v Bayerische Vereinsbank AG* [1981] ECR 2021, at p. 2030 (para. 7).

[264] *BRT v SABAM* ('*BRT II*') [1974] ECR 313, at p. 318 (para. 19).

[265] *Uniform Eurocheques*, OJ 1985 L35/43, at p. 48.

apply due to the fact that the Eurocheque system was set up on the initiative of private financial institutions, which therefore did not perform a task entrusted to them by public authorities. The express approval of the competent authorities in the countries concerned and, in some countries, explicit legal acts facilitating the operation of the system did not have any influence on the Commission's assessment.

In *Züchner*, the court also rejected an argument that art. 104ff. concerning the 'economic policy' of the member states should support the non-applicability of the competition rules to the banking sector. According to the court, these provisions fail to exempt banks from the competition rules since they are merely concerned with the co-ordination between member states of economic policy where it concerns balance of payments matters and with the provision of collaboration between certain national administrative departments and central banks.[266]

According to the Commission, the *Züchner* judgment 'makes it clear that the banking sector is only exempted from the competition rules to the extent that any anti-competitive conduct by banks is imposed on them by the monetary authorities'.[267] In addition, it should be noted that under certain conditions, banks are excluded from Council Regulation 4064/89 on the control of concentrations between undertakings.[268]

¶1044   Charges and commissions

The case law distinguishes between interbank agreements on commissions to be charged to the customers and interbank agreements regarding the commissions to be paid between the banks themselves. Whereas the former category would not appear to be eligible for an exemption, the latter category may benefit from an exemption provided that certain conditions are met.

¶1045   Commissions charged to customers

In *Züchner*, the court ruled that the uniform application of a general service charge imposed on customers for transfers of capital and other payments between banks within the common market could amount to a concerted

---

[266] *Züchner v Bayerische Vereinsbank AG* [1981] ECR 2021, at p. 2030 (para. 8).

[267] *Eleventh Report on Competition Policy*, point 61.

[268] Pursuant to art. 3(5) of the regulation, a concentration shall not be deemed to arise provided that banks acquire securities in an undertaking with a view to reselling them, that they do not exercise voting rights in respect of those securities with a view to determining the competitive behaviour of that undertaking, or that they only exercise such voting rights with a view to preparing the sale of all or part of that undertaking or of its assets or the sale of those securities and that any such sale takes place within one year of the date of organisation. This one-year period may be extended by the Commission on request when the banks justify the fact that the sale was not reasonably possible within the set period. Furthermore, art. 5(3) sets out a special rule to determine whether a merger involving banks has a Community dimension. Instead of the turnover of the companies involved, which is the normal rule, one tenth of the total assets multiplied by the ratio between loans and advances to credit institutions and customers in transactions with Community residents and the total sum of those loan and advances, is the relevant figure. See Regulation 4064/89, OJ 1989 L395/1.

practice. The plaintiff in the main proceedings argued that the charge was imposed at the same rate in other member states and by all the banks in Germany and that this was an indication of a concerted practice among the banks. The defendant argued that the similarity was due to the costs involved in the transfers and that the levy only represented a partial contribution towards the total costs of the transfers. The court held:

> 'The fact that the charge in question is justified by the costs involved in all transfers abroad normally effected by banks on behalf of their customers, and that it therefore represents partial reimbursement of such costs, debited uniformly to all those who make use of such service, does not exclude the possibility that parallel conduct in that sphere may, regardless of the motive, result in coordination between banks which amounts to a concerted practice within the meaning of Article 85 of the Treaty.'[269]

The court held that such a concerted practice would fall within the prohibition of art. 85(1) if it enabled the banks to 'congeal conditions in their present state thus depriving their customers of any genuine opportunity to take advantage of services on more favourable terms which would be offered to them under normal conditions of competition'.[270]

In order to decide whether there existed a concerted practice, the court stated that it should be considered whether there were contacts or exchanges of information between the banks on the subject of, inter alia, the rate of the charges actually imposed for comparable transfers and whether, with regard to market conditions, the rate of commission uniformly imposed is no different from that which would have resulted from free competition. The court also mentioned that consideration should be given to the number and importance of the participating banks and the volume of transfers affected by the practice as compared with the total volume of transfers.

Pre-Züchner cases

Prior to the *Züchner* judgment, the Commission had already investigated the issue of commissions charged to customers for particular banking services, but had not established a clear principle governing the application of art. 85 in this matter. In respect of commissions charged for cashing travellers cheques denominated in foreign currencies in Belgium, the Commission even went so far as to accept that, in view of the high costs for the banks, a minimum commission rate was justified.[271] In *Sarabex*,[272] the rules of the Foreign

---

[269] *Züchner v Bayerische Vereinsbank AG* [1981] ECR 2021, at p. 2032 (para. 17).
[270] *Züchner v Bayerische Vereinsbank AG* [1981] ECR 2021, at p. 2033 (para. 20).
[271] *Eighth Report on Competition Policy*, point 34. The Commission also made similar observations concerning commissions for cashing Eurocheques in France.
[272] *Eighth Report on Competition Policy*, points 35, 37.

Exchange and Current Deposit Brokers' Association prohibited its members from charging commissions differing from the agreed rates. The Commission intervened with the result that the system was modified in such a way that a maximum and a minimum rate was set for dealings in each currency, thus leaving a margin for competition between brokers operating in the sector.

Post-Züchner: no exemption for agreements on commission

The Commission's case law in the post-Züchner period indicates that interbank agreements that affect trade between member states and that determine the commissions to be charged to customers do run counter to art. 85(1) and are not eligible for an exemption pursuant to art. 85(3). When granting an exemption in *Uniform Eurocheques*,[273] the Commission expressly stated that the decision did not cover national agreements between banks or decisions by national banking associations to fix the level of commission that individual issuing institutions should charge to their customers. The Commission added that 'national agreements or decisions of that type, which would eliminate residual competition between institutions issuing uniform Eurocheques . . ., could not in any circumstances be regarded as indispensable within the meaning of Article 85(3)(a) of the Treaty'.[274] Similarly, in *Belgische Vereniging der Banken/ Association Belge des Banques*[275] and *ABI*,[276] the Commission attached importance to the fact that the agreements benefiting from an exemption did not govern relations between banks and their customers.

In *Dutch Banks*,[277] the Commission objected to several provisions in regulations, decisions and circulars issued by the Dutch Bankers' Association and notified to the Commission. These provisions were withdrawn or amended following the Commission's statement of objections. The Commission disapproved of the agreements on minimum commissions to be charged to customers, since they unjustifiably restricted the banks concerned in their freedom to determine rates and charges to be applied to their customers. A proposal to replace certain minimum commissions to be charged to customers by minimum commissions which banks would charge each other was not accepted by the Commission.[278]

More recently in *Eurocheque: Helsinki Agreement*,[279] the Commission

---

[273] *Uniform Eurocheques*, OJ 1985 L35/43, at pp. 50 and 51.
[274] *Uniform Eurocheques*, OJ 1985 L35/43, at p. 50.
[275] *Belgische Vereniging der Banken/Association Belge des Banques*, OJ 1987 L7/27, at pp. 34 and 35. The Commission noted, at p. 29, that following the Commission's statement of objections, the association had abandoned certain restrictive practices. In particular, all the provisions related to charges and fees payable by customers were deleted.
[276] *ABI*, OJ 1987 L43/51, at pp. 60 and 61.
[277] *Dutch Banks* [1989] 2 CEC 2,032; OJ 1989 L253/1.
[278] Id., at p. 5.
[279] *Eurocheque: Helsinki Agreement*, OJ 1992 L95/50. The Commission's decision has been appealed to the Court of First Instance: *Eurocheque International SC v EC Commission*, Case T-40/92, not yet decided.

imposed fines on Eurocheque International SC and the Groupement des Cartes Bancaires CB, an organisation representing all French banks that are members of the Eurocheque system, for the operation of an anti-competitive agreement regarding the conditions governing the acceptance of foreign Eurocheques in the trading sector in France. Under the agreement, generally referred to as the 'Helsinki Agreement', French banks agreed to charge French traders a commission on purchases paid for by Eurocheques drawn on a foreign bank. In addition, the agreement provided that the rate of commission should not be higher than that applicable to payments made by other means, such as credit cards. The Commission indicated that these conditions constituted a clear restriction of competition and that the agreement was inconsistent with the general agreement governing the operation of the Eurocheque system previously exempted by the Commission. A basic principle of that agreement is that the payee, i.e. the trader receiving a Eurocheque, would receive the full amount of the cheque. According to the Commission, it was precisely this aspect of the Eurocheque system – which differs from typical credit card operations – that led to its success. The Commission held that the Helsinki Agreement rendered the use of Eurocheques less attractive for traders in France and impeded the development of the Eurocheque system in that country.

In refusing to grant an exemption to the Helsinki Agreement, the Commission stressed that it did not improve distribution or services as required by art. 85(3). In addition, only the French banks benefited as they were paid twice for the same service, first by the traders under the Helsinki Agreement, and, secondly, by the foreign banks, the drawers of the Eurocheques, pursuant to the general agreement establishing the Eurocheque system. The Commission also noted that the Helsinki Agreement was aimed at preventing the development of competition between bank cards and Eurocheques.

¶1046   Commissions charged between banks

Although the Commission has adopted a very negative attitude towards interbank agreements on commissions to be charged to customers, a slightly more favourable treatment is awarded to interbank agreements relating to commissions to be charged between the banks themselves.

In *Uniform Eurocheques*,[280] the Commission held it to be a restriction of competition that the Eurocheque organisation decided the fixed and uniform commissions to be paid to the payee banks for uniform Eurocheques drawn in local currency on a bank in a foreign country. The commission, which was set at 1.25 per cent of the amount of the cheque, with no minimum rate, was not

---

[280]   *Uniform Eurocheques*, OJ 1985 L35/43, at pp. 47, 49 and 50.

charged when the cheque was cashed but when the cheque was reimbursed by the clearing centre. The national clearing centre in the country of the drawee bank was free to charge an extra commission on top of the 1.25 per cent to cover its own processing and clearing costs. The drawee bank, which issued the cheques, was also free to charge an extra commission to its customers. The Eurocheque agreement was granted an exemption since the restrictions of competition were considered necessary as the Eurocheque system could not function effectively otherwise. The banks provide a service of accepting cheques issued by banks situated abroad, which is neither balanced nor compensated by an equivalent reciprocal service. Hence, it is necessary, according to the Commission, to determine in common the terms and conditions for accepting and clearing the cheques. The absence of a common and uniform determination of the remuneration would imply bilateral negotiations between the 15,000 participating banks, which would mean that centralised clearing would be made impossible and that the processing cost for Eurocheques would increase considerably.

In *Belgische Vereniging der Banken/Association Belge des Banques*,[281] the Commission found that three conventions, concluded by the members of the Belgian Banking Association (BVB/ABB), had the effect of restricting competition. Two of the conventions were found to be restrictive of competition because they prevented banks from determining bilaterally charges for services they provide to each other, thereby preventing them from negotiating on an individual basis better terms than those laid down in the convention. The first convention concerned transactions in securities and fixed the amount of the rebates, calculated as a percentage, on commissions received for services of intermediation by registrar banks to other banks. The second convention fixed the maximum amount of payment commission that may be charged between banks on international payment transactions originating abroad. The restriction of competition was found to be particularly pronounced in the convention on payments originating abroad since that convention set uniform rates expressed in absolute amounts. The third convention, dealing with the collection of cheques and commercial bills originating abroad did not fix any rates, but was considered to have anti-competitive effects because the banks agreed upon the principle of charging commissions and upon who would be permitted to collect them. According to the Commission, the conventions appreciably restricted the freedom of action of the banks.[282] The conventions were, however, granted an exemption since the Commission considered the conditions of art. 85(3) to be met.

---

[281] *Belgische Vereniging der Banken/Association Belge des Banques*, OJ 1987 L7/27, at pp. 32 and 33.
[282] Id., at p. 33.

The Commission's reasoning was similar in *ABI*[283]and *Dutch Banks*,[284] where it found that agreements were restrictive of competition due to the fact that they limited the possibility for banks to agree bilaterally on more favourable terms and conditions provided for by the agreements. *ABI* concerned commissions provided for in agreements on, inter alia, the collection of bills and documents and the service of collecting bank cheques and similar instruments. The Commission applied a similar reasoning as in *Uniform Eurocheques* and *Belgische Vereniging der Banken/Association Belge des Banques* in order to grant those agreements an exemption.

In *Dutch Banks*, the Commission was not willing to grant an exemption for certain interbank agreements on commissions to be charged between banks. It found that the parties had not met their burden of proof since they had 'not shown that such agreements on interbank commissions would actually be necessary for the successful implementation of certain forms of cooperation positive in themselves, between a number of banks'. The Commission continued:

> 'only in the exceptional cases, where such a necessity is established, may agreements on interbank commissions be capable of obtaining an exemption under Article 85(3)'.[285]

These particular agreements were subsequently withdrawn. However, the Commission found that agreements between Dutch banks concerning transfers relating to fund-raising acceptances and the commission to be charged thereon restricted competition, but nevertheless decided not to take action under art. 85 as the arrangements did not affect trade between member states.

¶1047   Value dates

In *Dutch Banks*, the Commission opposed uniform value dates provided for in circulars concerning simplified clearing procedures for cheques denominated in guilders and foreign currencies. The uniform value dates were to be applied not only in dealings between banks but also by banks vis-à-vis their customers. The Commission considered that 'banks should be free in their value dating policy they apply vis-à-vis customers and foreign banks and that restrictions on such freedom are not necessary to ensure proper interbank cooperation in clearing cheques, as aimed by the circular.' The circulars were adjusted

---

[283] *ABI*, OJ 1987 L43/51.

[284] *Dutch Banks* [1989] 2 CEC 2,032; OJ 1989 L253/1; on appeal: *Nederlandse Bankiersvereniging and Nederlandse Vereniging van Banken v EC Commission* Case T-138/89, judgment of 17 September 1992, not yet reported.

[285] Id., at pp. 5 and 6.

accordingly.[286] The rules on uniform value dates in the dealings between the relevant Dutch banks were considered to indirectly restrict competition for customers, but an exemption was granted under art. 85(3).[287]

¶1048   Interest rates

The court held in *Van Eycke*[288] that it is not permissible for a member state, by way of legislation, to require or incite deposit-holders to follow the terms of a previous agreement between credit institutions laying down maximum rates of interest in order to benefit from tax exemptions. The credit institutions in Belgium had agreed to limit the rate of interest for deposit accounts to seven per cent. Since all the credit institutions did not respect this agreement, the Belgian government, seeking lower rates of interest, enacted legislation which determined the maximum interest rate allowed in order for the client of the bank to benefit from the tax exemption. Even though the court objected to the practice of a member state using national legislation to force banks to respect existing agreements between themselves, it did find it permissible for the Belgian Government to decide independently through national legislation the maximum rate of interest to be paid on deposit accounts in order to benefit from the tax exemptions.[289] The court's assessment of the conduct of the Belgian state from the viewpoint of art. 3(f) (previous version of the treaty), 5 and 85 of the treaty entails a finding, at least implicitly, that interbank agreements on interest rates which affect trade between member states run counter to art. 85(1).

Following the *Van Eycke* judgment, it is now clear that the Commission fully intends to apply art. 85(1) to interbank agreements on interest rates.[290] Thus far, only a few interbank agreements on interest rates have been notified to the Commission and no formal decisions have yet been adopted.[291] In response to the position taken by the Commission, some banking associations have argued that a degree of co-ordination of interest rate levels is a necessary and legitimate objective of monetary policy.[292] It has been pointed out that, in general, strong competition exists in the banking sector and that any occasional coincidental changes in interest rates by banks in different parts of the EC are

---

[286] Notice in OJ 1988 C282/4, at p. 7; see also *Dutch Banks* [1989] 2 CEC 2,032; OJ 1989 L253/1, at p. 7.

[287] *Dutch Banks* [1989] 2 CEC 2,032; OJ 1989 L253/1, at pp. 9–11; see also *ABI*, OJ 1987 L43/51, at pp. 57 and 60, where the Commission similarly held agreements on value dates to restrict competition, but granted an exemption under art. 85(3).

[288] *Van Eycke v ASPA SA* [1988] ECR 4769.

[289] Id., para. 18–20.

[290] See Commission press release IP(91)520 of 5 June 1991; Commission press release IP(89) 869 of 16 November 1989.

[291] Commission press release IP(92)625 of 24 July 1992.

[292] See *XXIst Report on Competition Policy for 1991*, point 33.

often the result of pressure from monetary authorities and should not be confused with restrictive practices.[293]

¶1049   Agreements not restricting competition

In several cases, the Commission has found that interbank agreements do not restrict competition within the meaning of art. 85(1). In *Irish Banks*, the Commission held that agreements concerning bank opening hours, clearing rules and a direct debiting scheme did not restrict competition.[294] Furthermore, in *Dutch Banks*, the Commission held that several provisions did not restrict competition since they did not concern charges and fees or other terms and conditions affecting competition.[295] In the same decision the Commission granted a negative clearance for a regulation issued by the Dutch Bankers' Association regarding foreign exchange transactions, which fixed a middle rate, used as a reference basis for foreign currencies. The rules were established by procedures which took account of market developments and the middle rates were not mandatory.[296] Also in *Dutch Banks*, the Commission cleared decisions concerning charges for the use of postage-paid envelopes and the value of gift vouchers, a circular concerning additional security to be provided by the customer in connection with transactions in foreign securities (not mandatory) and an agreement concerning gifts and bonuses offered as an incentive to savers. According to the Commission, these practices did not appreciably restrict competition.[297] In *ABI*, the Commission held that an agreement which imposed a penalty on banks which did not effectuate certain transfers within a set time limit was merely a technical instrument and that it did not restrict the banks' competitive activity.[298]

In recent years, the Commission has received notifications of several dozen bilateral co-operation agreements signed by banks or their national associations.[299] Most of these agreements passed the Commission's scrutiny unamended. In fact, the Commission sent 'comfort letters' in response to most of the notifications indicating that after preliminary investigation, the Commission would not take action against the agreements involved. In some

---

[293] Id.

[294] *Irish Banks*, OJ 1986 L295/28.

[295] *Dutch Banks* [1989] 2 CEC 2,032; OJ 1989 L253/1, at p. 8. The provisions in question concerned:

- certain articles on dealing with documentary credits and orders for acceptance and collection,
- a regulation concerning the 'Valutanoteringscommissie',
- a decision concerning charges for the use of postage-paid envelopes,
- a decision concerning the sale of gift vouchers,
- a circular concerning forward transactions in foreign currencies,
- an agreement concerning gifts and bonuses offered as an incentive to savers.

[296] *Dutch Banks* [1989] 2 CEC 2,032; OJ 1989 L253/1, at pp. 6, 8 and 9.

[297] *Dutch Banks* [1989] 2 CEC 2,032; OJ 1989 L253/1, at p. 9.

[298] *ABI*, OJ 1987 L43/51.

[299] See *XXIst Report on Competition Policy* for 1991, point 31.

cases, the Commission requested amendments to the agreements before granting its approval.

The Commission has confirmed that it is not opposed to interbank agreements that promote greater efficiency and facilitate movement by savings banks' customers from one member state to another.[300] However, the Commission did object to the following clauses in the agreements which it found were restrictive of competition:

- commitments not to enter into each others' territory;
- commitments not to conclude similar agreements with other credit institutions in the territory;
- exclusivity granted to each partner in its respective home country for distributing and dealing in common products;
- a priori control of national associations over bilateral agreements signed by their members.[301]

Another form of co-operation among savings banks that has attracted the attention of the Commission is co-operation aimed at making the automated teller machines of savings banks interoperable. In this connection, the Commission advised the promoters of a co-operation arrangement among national associations of European savings banks that the interbank commission provided for in the arrangement should be a maximum and that banks should remain free to negotiate bilateral agreements setting lower commissions.[302] In connection with its monitoring of co-operation between savings banks, the Commission has also investigated agreements in the form of EEIGs.[303]

¶1050   Effect on trade between member states

It is clear that following the court's judgment in *Züchner*, the concept of 'trade' also includes monetary transactions.[304] The Commission has found interbank agreements capable of affecting trade between member states, even though the banks involved were all situated in the same member state. In these instances the Commission has focused on the internationalisation of banking activities, the possible isolation of national markets and the nature of the service.

In several cases, the Commission has found that interbank agreements did not affect trade between member states. In *Dutch Banks*,[305] the Commission found that the decision by the Dutch Bankers' Association on uniform

---

[300] Id.
[301] Id.
[302] Id., point 35.
[303] Id., point 36; *Tepar*, OJ 1991 C209/9.
[304] *Züchner v Bayerische Vereinsbank AG* [1981] ECR 2021, at p. 2032 (para. 18).
[305] *Dutch Banks*, OJ 1989 L253/1.

conditions for renting safes did not appreciably affect trade because of the nature of the service and since branches of banks from other member states did not normally offer this type of service. Similarly, in *ABI*,[306] it was held that agreements on minimum charges for safe deposit and safe custody services cannot appreciably affect competition by virtue of the very object of the service.

In other cases, the Commission has found an effect on inter-state trade, but has generally granted an exemption under art. 85(3). In *Belgische Vereniging der Banken/Association Belge des Banques*,[307] the Commission noted that branches of foreign banks form an integral part of those banks and are therefore involved in trade between member states. In *ABI*,[308] the Commission found that trade between member states was affected since all export and import operations of goods were settled through the agency of banks.

THE INSURANCE SECTOR

¶1051   The applicability of the competition rules to the insurance industry

The question whether or to what extent the competition rules are applicable to the insurance sector has given rise to a protracted debate and the principles governing this question have been agreed upon only recently.

The Commission's point of view was, never the less, clear from the outset. As early as its *Second Report on Competition Policy* the Commission considered that in principle the insurance industry should be subject to the treaty's rules on competition and the implementing regulations thereof. This, the Commission added, would be different only if special regulations comparable to those for agriculture and road, rail and inland waterway transport were to be adopted for the insurance industry.[309]

The Commission stated that the information available to it did not warrant the conclusion that art. 87(2)(c) should be relied upon in the insurance sector. It should, however, be noted that the Commission indicated in the same report that it was 'aware that application of the competition rules must take account of the peculiar characteristics of certain industries or must constitute one of the components of a common policy defined for a specific industry'.[310]

---

[306] *ABI*, OJ 1987 L43/51.
[307] *Belgische Vereniging der Banken/Association Belge des Banques*, OJ 1987 L7/27.
[308] *ABI*, OJ 1987 L43/51. See also *Dutch Banks*, OJ 1989 L253/1.
[309] *Second Report on Competition Policy*, point 50.
[310] *Second Report on Competition Policy*, point 56.

The instances in which the Commission actually applied the competition rules to the insurance industry remained rare until 1984.[311] In that year the first two formal decisions, i.e. *Nuovo CEGAM*[312] and *Fire Insurance (D)*,[313] were issued.

In *Verband der Sachversicherer*,[314] on appeal against the *Fire Insurance (D)* decision of the Commission, the Court of Justice was directly asked whether the competition rules are applicable to the insurance industry. The court considered the arguments advanced against submitting insurance companies to the competition rules. The main focus of the insurers' objection was that the calculation of premiums based on statistics which are subject to a large degree of uncertainty is an operation unique to the insurance industry. As single undertakings are not in a position to calculate accurately premiums based on their own experience, it is necessary that they co-operate among each other in order to calculate the reserves to hold in case an insured risk materialises, otherwise they risk insolvency. However, it was held that a given industry is only exempt from the applicability of those rules if the EC Treaty has made an express derogation to that effect. The court therefore agreed with the Commission that art. 85 and 86 of the treaty as well as the provisions of Regulation 17/62 apply without restriction to the insurance industry. The court also added that the Commission, within the framework of its power under art. 85(3) to grant individual or block exemptions, could take the specific features of the insurance sector into account.

¶1052   Block exemption regulation

Since the judgment in *Verband der Sachversicherer*, the Commission has published Regulation 3932/92 on the application of art. 85(3) of the treaty to certain categories of agreements, decisions and concerted practices in the insurance sector.[315] The regulation came into effect on 1 April 1993 and is applicable until 31 March 2003. The main objective of the Commission in adopting this regulation is to create legal certainty within the insurance sector and to offer clear guidelines to insurers on where to draw the line between

---

[311] Aside from the three cases commented upon in the *Second Report on Competition Policy*, the Commission merely reiterated in the *Thirteenth Report on Competition Policy*, point 67, that insurance companies are in principle to be put on the same footing as any other undertaking for competition law purposes.

[312] *Nuovo CEGAM*, OJ 1984 L99/29.

[313] *Fire Insurance (D)*, OJ 1985 L35/20.

[314] *Verband der Sachversicherer v EC Commission* [1987] ECR 405, at p. 447. It should be noted that in *Van Ameyde v UCI* [1977] ECR 1091, the court considered whether or not the business of a national motor vehicle insurance bureau was compatible with art. 85 and 86. The court did not, however, deal with the specific issue of whether the competition rules apply to the insurance sector.

[315] Commission Regulation 3932/92 of 21 December 1992, OJ 1992 L398/7.

acceptable and unacceptable agreements,[316] and to benefit the consumer with the resulting improvement in services and greater efficiency in the industry.[317]

The categories of agreements covered by Regulation 3932/92 are the following:

(1) the establishment of common risk-premium tariffs;

(2) the establishment of standard policy conditions;

(3) the common coverage of certain types of risk; and

(4) the establishment of common rules on the testing and acceptance of security devices.[318]

(1)   Establishment of common risk-premium tariffs

As mentioned earlier,[319] a unique factor of the insurance industry is that insurance companies co-operate in the compilation of statistics because, alone, they do not have the capacity to gather sufficient information to rate risks accurately. Prior to the adoption of the block exemption regulation, a number of agreements had been notified to the Commission which contained clauses concerning co-operation relating to loss statistics and premiums. The Commission held that agreements of this nature constituted a restriction of competition under art. 85(1). However, the Commission then decided that the conditions for an exemption under art. 85(3) were fulfilled as these arrangements provided an improvement in the service for consumers and generally increased efficiency, as a result of pooling information.[320]

Co-operation agreements of this nature are governed by the provisions of art. 2, 3 and 4 of the regulation. Article 2(a) sets out the subject-matter to which the agreements must relate in order to benefit from the exemption, which include 'the calculation of the average cost of risk cover (pure premiums) or the establishment and distribution of mortality tables ...'. Such agreements must specify that any tables or calculations distributed are of an illustrative nature only, as any mandatory imposition of premium levels would restrict competition.[321] In addition, when the tables are being compiled they must exclude any loadings for contingencies, administrative or commercial costs,

---

[316] See *XXIst Report on Competition Policy for 1991*, point 37.

[317] See Brittan, 'Financial Services – The Role of Competition Policy' Eur. Bus. Rev., April 1992.

[318] These categories of agreements are among those categories with respect to which the Commission is empowered to adopt a block exemption regulation under Regulation 1534/91, OJ 1991 L143/1. Other categories listed in that regulation with respect to which the Commission has not yet adopted a block exemption are agreements concerning (1) the settlement of claims; and (2) registers of, and information on, aggravated risks.

[319] See ¶1051.

[320] See *Assurpol*, OJ 1992 L37/16; *TEKO*, OJ 1990 L13/34; *Concordato Incendio*, OJ 1990 L15/25.

[321] Regulation 3932/92, art. 3(a). See also *Nuovo CEGAM*, OJ 1984 L99/29, where the Commission decided that the determination of standard tariffs or basic premiums was acceptable provided that it did not prevent participating insurers from calculating the final premium for a particular risk in the light of their own commercial policy.

¶1052

commissions payable to intermediaries or anticipated profits, nor may they make any reference to undertakings party to the agreement.[322] Undertakings or associations who agree among themselves or who oblige others not to use calculations or tables which differ from those formulated under the provisions of art. 2(a) may not benefit from the block exemption.[323] These conditions imposed by the Commission serve to ensure that any restrictions exempted by the regulation are purely necessary to attain the objectives of the agreement.

(2)   Establishment of standard policy conditions

Standard policy conditions for direct insurance, and common models illustrating profits to be realised from an insurance policy involving an element of capitalisation established by co-operation agreements are exempted under the regulation.[324] The Commission considers that such agreements are necessary to create greater efficiency in the insurance sector and to facilitate consumers in their dealings with insurance companies.[325] Also, this type of co-operation confers benefits on the consumer by improving the comparability of insurance cover and allowing risks to be more uniformly classified.[326]

However, these agreements must not lead to the standardisation of products or the creation of too captive a customer base.[327] Moreover, the regulation provides that standard policy conditions must be accessible to policyholders and any interested parties in order to ensure a genuine benefit for consumers.[328] Thus, standard conditions and illustrative models may serve only as a reference guide, otherwise they will be excluded from the benefit of the exemption.[329]

In cases where standard policy conditions exclude any specific type of risk without the possibility of inclusion by agreement, the exemption does not apply.[330] The regulation also offers the consumer significant protection with regard to, inter alia, contractual relationships with insurers, the duration of certain types of policies and the imposition by the insurer of conditions that go beyond the initial object of the policy.[331]

In the realm of risk category insurance agreements that exclude coverage of certain risks because of characteristics associated with the policyholder, the regulation will not apply.[332] However, the Commission stresses that this

---

[322] Regulation 3932/92, art. 3(b) and (c).
[323] Id., art. 4
[324] Id., art. 5.
[325] See *Assurpol*, OJ 1992 L37/16, at p. 23; *Concordato Incendio*, OJ 1990 L15/25, at p. 28.
[326] Regulation 3932/92, recital 7 to the preamble.
[327] Id.
[328] Id., art. 6(1)(c).
[329] Id., art. 6(1)(a) and (2).
[330] Id., art. 7(1)(a).
[331] Id., art. 7.
[332] Id., art. 8.

¶1052

exclusion is without prejudice to any particular insurance conditions established for 'social or occupational categories of the population'.[333]

(3) Common coverage of certain types of risks

The Commission takes a favourable approach to the establishment of co-insurance or co-reinsurance groups because arrangements of this type encourage companies to enter the market and, consequently, increases the capacity to cover large or undeterminable risks, which are traditionally difficult to insure due to their scale, rarity or novelty.[334]

For example, in a decision concerning a co-reinsurance agreement for the covering of environmental risks, the Commission found the agreement and certain decisions regarding the activities of the co-reinsurance pool to be restrictive of competition.[335] The Commission, never the less, granted an individual exemption under art. 85(3) on the grounds that the agreement would enable insurers to obtain financial and technical expertise in this difficult area of insurance. The Commission also decided that the agreement benefited consumers as the increased capacity of the pool would enable risks of both small and medium-sized enterprises to be covered.

Under Regulation 3932/92, the exemption applies to 'agreements or concerted practices which have as their object the setting up and operation of groups of insurance undertakings or of insurance undertakings and reinsurance undertakings for the common coverage of a specific category of risks in the form of co-insurance or co-reinsurance.'[336] Both co-insurance and co-reinsurance groups are defined in the regulation, and these include, for example, co-reinsurance groups established by insurance companies, possibly aided by reinsurance companies, with the aim of mutually reinsuring all their liabilities, or part of them, in respect of a specific risk category.[337]

By their very nature, co-insurance and co-reinsurance arrangements are susceptible of restricting competition, particularly to the extent that they necessitate the adoption of common features such as policy conditions and commercial premiums. The regulation specifically allows the parties to agree on certain matters concerning the common arrangement.[338] To ensure that such arrangements do not have an unduly restrictive effect on competition, however, the Commission has stipulated that the exemption is only available to those groups whose participants do not hold a share of the relevant market in excess of 15 per cent in the case of co-reinsurance groups and ten per cent in the

---

[333] Id.
[334] Regulation 3932/92, recital 10 to the preamble.
[335] *Assurpol*, OJ 1992 L37/16.
[336] Regulation 3932/92, art. 10(1).
[337] Id., art. 10(2).
[338] Id., art. 10(3), 12 and 13.

¶1052

case of co-insurance groups.[339] Catastrophe risks and aggravated risks benefit from a derogation from this provision as their representative percentage is calculated with reference only to the market share of the group itself.[340]

Regulation 3932/92 sets out the obligations that may legitimately be imposed on undertakings that participate in a co-insurance or co-reinsurance group, without being restrictive of competition.[341] Accordingly, it is permissible to subject any cover the group may give to a risk to certain stipulations, including the acceptance of insurance conditions used by the group, the approval of claims by the group before settlement and the acceptance of the group's entitlement to negotiate on behalf of all participants.

(4) Establishment of common rules on the testing and acceptance of security devices

In connection with the EC's new approach in the field of technical harmonisation and standardisation and certification and testing developed in conjunction with the internal market programme,[342] the Commission has decided to allow insurance companies to co-operate in the field of standardisation of security devices. In accordance with Regulation 3932/92, agreements relating to technical standards, certification measures and evaluation provisions, in particular those which as far as possible conform to a European level, are exempt from the provisions of art. 85(1).[343] The regulation defines the conditions under which the establishment of technical specifications and procedures for certifying such security devices and the companies installing or maintaining them are authorised.[344] The Commission requires that any formulation and distribution of technical standards and other specifications must be accompanied by a statement allowing insurance companies to accept other security devices or maintenance or installation companies, if they choose to do so.[345]

---

[339] Id., art. 11(1).

[340] Id., art. 11(2).

[341] Id., art. 12 and 13.

[342] See Council resolution of 7 May 1985 on a new approach to technical harmonisation and standardisation, OJ 1985 C136/1; Council resolution of 21 December 1989 on a global approach to conformity assessment, OJ 1990 C10/1.

[343] Regulation 3932/92, art. 14. According to the Commission, '[c]ooperation in the evaluation of security devices and of the undertakings installing and maintaining them is useful insofar as it removes the need for individual evaluation.' Id., recital 17 preamble.

[344] Id., art. 15. The purpose of these conditions is to ensure that all manufacturers and installation and maintenance companies may apply for evaluation, and that the evaluation and certification are guided by objective and well-defined criteria. Id., recital 17 preamble.

[345] Id., art. 15(c).

¶1053   Insurance intermediaries

The Commission indicated that it intended to grant an exemption to agreements between insurance companies pertaining to the fixing of maximum rates of commissions for their intermediaries (agents and brokers).[346] Similarly in *Nuovo CEGAM*[347] the Commission did not object to a clause whereby maximum commissions were laid down.[348] Also, the Commission granted an exemption under art. 85(3) from an agreement whereby a sales intermediary for life insurance and other investment business was 'appointed' by the life insurance company as its representative. The Commission did not oppose the fact that the agent could not represent other life insurers but objected, however, to the clauses relating to the prohibition of the appointment by the insurer of other representatives and to the prohibition of commission rebating. Both clauses were deleted at the request of the Commission.[349]

¶1054   Marine mutual insurance

In *P & I Clubs*[350] the Commission ruled on a number of issues in the field of marine mutual insurance.

On 18 June 1981, 17 Protection and Indemnity Clubs ('P & I Clubs'), representing 90 per cent of world shipping tonnage in 1979 and 1980, entered into an agreement, known as the International Group Agreement ('IGA'). Protection and Indemnity Clubs are associations of shipowners, charterers, operators and managers of ships who agree to share each other's third-party liabilities on a non-profit-making basis. The IGA was set up as a framework agreement which intended to provide rules delineating the rights and duties of the clubs inter se. The IGA contained rules which had as their effect a reduction of competition between the clubs by imposing limitations on the rights of each club to give a quote both for vessels already insured with another club and for new or newly acquired vessels. The Commission considered that the said provisions, as modified pursuant to three years of discussion with the Commission, could be exempted under art. 85(3).

The Commission objected to a system of rules of transition whereby premiums charged by the new club (i.e. the club intending to insure the vessel in the future) could not be lower than the 'holding' club's rates (i.e. the rate

---

[346] *Insurance Intermediaries*, Commission notice, OJ 1987 C120/5.
[347] *Nuovo CEGAM*, OJ 1984 L99/29.
[348] In *Re Meng*, Case C-2/91, judgment of 17 November 1993, not yet reported, the Court of Justice ruled that a German law prohibiting insurance agents from transferring to their clients all or part of the commissions paid by insurance companies is not precluded by art. 85(1) of the treaty. Similarly in *Re Ohra Schadeverzekeringen*, Case C-245/91, judgment of 17 November 1993, not yet reported, a Dutch law preventing insurance companies operating in the Netherlands from granting rebates and other financial advantages directly to policy-holders was also found by the court not to infringe art. 85(1).
[349] *Halifax Building Society and Standard Life Assurance Co*, Commission notice, OJ 1992 C131/2.
[350] *P & I Clubs*, OJ 1985 L376/2.

charged by the club currently insuring the ship). In addition, it was held that the clauses relating to release calls, i.e. the amount members who withdraw a vessel or a fleet from a club are charged to cover their share of the liabilities incurred during their membership but which are not settled at the time of withdrawal, could be used to reinforce restrictions on transfers between clubs. The rules relating to a minimum 'estimated total cost' for tankers, i.e. minimum basic rates to be observed by the clubs in their under-writing of tanker business, were also found to be objectionable.

The IGA rules, as amended following the Commission's intervention, provide for a system whereby shipowners can transfer vessels already insured or new vessels to a new club provided, first, that they obtain a contractually binding commitment at the quoted rate, to be adjusted on the basis of certain criteria, by 30 September of the year preceding that for which the new insurance policy is to be effective and, secondly, that they notify the holding club within three days from the date the commitment was entered into. The ship operator therefore remains free to transfer one or more vessels of his fleet to a new club provided that the rate quoted by the new club is not 'unreasonably low'. An expert committee decides, upon a timely application by the holding club, whether the quoted rate is reasonable.

In the final version of the IGA rules the minimum rate for tankers, as originally notified, was deleted and substituted by a flexible formula according to which all quotations for tankers must make fair and adequate provision for a limited number of cost factors.

It is submitted that the decision of the Commission in *P & I Clubs* is a 'cas d'espèce' and should therefore not be extrapolated to other sectors of mutual insurance. It can be noted that in an obiter dictum the Commission indicated that mutual insurance systems in themselves do not constitute a restriction of competition.[351]

The problems in the sector of marine mutual insurance are indeed very fact-specific. The Commission's decision to grant an individual exemption under art. 85(3) was largely based on the four objectives crucial to the mutual P & I Clubs system, i.e. continuity of membership, preservation of the principle of mutuality, stability of premiums and continuity of pool arrangements.[352]

In *Lloyd's Underwriters' Association and the Institute of London*

---

[351] *P & I Clubs*, OJ 1985 L376/2.

[352] *P & I Clubs*, OJ 1985 L376/2. Pools are associations of clubs which collectively reinsure liabilities in excess of certain thresholds. It can also be noted that the Commission has objected to a so-called Flag Ownership Management Warranty ('FOM Warranty') in the marine insurance sector whereby business granted under a treaty, dealing with the insurance of hulls of vessels as well as with reinsurance, would be restricted to the national flag vessels of the one who had granted the business. The Commission considered that this warranty infringed art. 85 because it would effectively restrict foreign insurers' access to the London reinsurance market. See Commission press release IP(89) 260 of 19 April 1989.

Underwriters,[353] the Commission granted negative clearance to two agreements notified to it concerning marine hull and machinery insurance. The Joint Hull Understandings (JHU) and the Respect of Lead Agreement (RLA) were notified to the Commission in 1989. Following the Commission's examination of the agreements, three clauses in the JHU were deleted and the entire text of the RLA was modified to avoid restricting competition. The offending clauses in the JHU, limited the freedom of the members of Lloyd's Underwriters' Association (LUA) and the Institute of London Underwriters (ILU) to determine their own prices, particularly on renewal of insurance policies. The terms of the RLA prevented underwriters competing for renewals as it ensured that the same insurers who first insured the risk would continue to do so as the policy would automatically be renewed with them. The RLA also restricted competition between the ILU and LUA by providing that there should be two underwriters from each association on every slip (order). Both the clauses in the JHU and the provisions of the RLA ceased to be effective from 25 April 1991. According to the terms of the new RLA any competing group or groups of underwriters are permitted to challenge the existing group of policy insurers. The existing underwriters are also obliged to make their records available if so requested by their competitors.

TELECOMMUNICATIONS

¶1055   Introduction

In 1987, the Commission embarked on an ambitious programme to both liberalise and harmonise the EC's telecommunications sector with the publication of a 'green paper'.[354] The impetus for this programme can be attributed to at least three factors.[355] First, technological developments are rapidly making traditional monopolies in this sector obsolete. For example, a shortage of frequencies was often cited as a reason for creating public monopolies for radio and television broadcasting. With the development of cable and satellite broadcasting, this justification is no longer valid. Moreover, the plethora of new products and services available on the market has put pressure on member states to liberalise telecommunications markets to enable consumers to have access to these products and services which the national

---

[353] *Lloyd's Underwriters' Association and the Institute of London Underwriters*, OJ 1993 L4/26.

[354] Communication by the Commission: *Towards a Dynamic European Economy, Green Paper on the Development of the Common Market for Telecommunications Services and Equipment*, COM(87) 290, 30 June 1987. The Council broadly endorsed the programme outlined in the green paper in a resolution adopted in June 1988. Council resolution of 30 June 1988 on the development of the common market for telecommunications services and equipment up to 1992, OJ 1988 C257/1.

[355] See generally Ehlermann, 'Managing Monopolies: The Role of the State in Controlling Market Dominance in the European Community' [1993] 5 ECLR 61.

PTTs have been unable to provide. The importance of technology as a driving factor in the liberalisation of the telecommunications market is readily apparent when one compares the progress towards liberalisation in other sectors, such as the energy sector, where technology advances at a slower pace.

Secondly, the existence of national monopolies is at odds with the goal of creating a single internal market. In particular, the cross-border supply of telecommunications services is essential to the eventual creation of trans-European telecommunications networks. Until national barriers are broken down, telecommunications costs in the EC will remain higher than those in the US and Japan, thus putting EC industry at a disadvantage as they attempt to compete on global markets. Thirdly, some member states have come under pressure to privatise their PTTs in order to finance the huge capital outlays required in the telecommunications sector, thus forcing PTTs to become more market-oriented. Relatedly, some member states have chosen to auction off licences for telecommunications services such as mobile telephones to the highest bidder as a means of raising cash for the public purse, which also leads to greater competition.

To achieve the liberalisation and harmonisation of the EC telecommunications sector, the Commission has adopted a three-pronged strategy:

(1) the creation of EC-wide standards in the telecommunications sector by means of directives adopted under art. 100A of the EC Treaty;

(2) the liberalisation of the telecommunications sector by means of directives adopted under art. 90(3) of the EC Treaty; and

(3) the ongoing liberalisation of the telecommunications sector through the application of the competition rules set out in art. 85 and 86 of the EC Treaty.

This section will focus on the latter two aspects of this basic strategy because it is these that directly involve principles of competition law. In so far as the harmonisation of standards is concerned, it is worth noting that substantial progress has been made. In the area of telecommunications equipment, a directive has been adopted that calls for the mutual recognition of terminal equipment.[356] In the area of services, a series of directives and recommendations establishes the principle of open network provision, which is concerned with harmonising conditions necessary to ensure open access to public telecommunications networks.[357]

---

[356] Directive 91/263 on the approximation of the laws of the member states concerning telecommunications terminal equipment, OJ 1991 L128/1.

[357] Council Directive 90/387 on the establishment of the internal market for telecommunications services through the implementation of open network provision, OJ 1990 L192/1; Council Directive 92/44 on the

¶1056   Liberalisation of the telecommunications market through art. 90(3) directives

Central to the Commission's effort to open up the telecommunications market to competition are two directives adopted by virtue of the powers conferred on the Commission by art. 90(3): the 'terminal equipment directive' of May 1988,[358] and the 'services directive' of June 1990.[359] In essence, art. 90(3) gives the Commission the power to adopt directives or decisions addressed to the member states to ensure the application of art. 90 which, broadly, requires the member states to abide by the treaty rules, particularly the competition rules. The art. 90(3) procedure offered the Commission a means of implementing the liberalisation strategy announced in its green paper without giving protectionist member states the opportunity to interfere. As discussed below (¶1057 and ¶1058), this approach was highly controversial and was challenged before the Court of Justice.

¶1057   Terminal equipment

The basic purpose of the terminal equipment directive (Directive 88/301) is to open up the EC market for telecommunications terminal equipment, particularly telephones, modems and telex terminals, by abolishing the monopolies of national telecommunications authorities. Member states must withdraw special or exclusive rights that have been granted to national authorities for the importation, marketing, connection, bringing into service and maintenance of terminal equipment, and must ensure that these rights are available to private companies.[360] Member states must also ensure that users have access to new public termination points so that they can connect the equipment of their choice.[361] In addition, because the technical characteristics of the networks in the member states are different, the member states are required to publish all technical specifications and type-approvals so that manufacturers can adapt their equipment to the characteristics of each national network.[362] To avoid having national telecommunications authorities that compete in the equipment market also establish the rules governing that market, the directive requires member states to vest the powers to adopt

---

application of open network provision to leased lines, OJ 1992 L165/27; Council Recommendation 92/382 on the application of open network provision to public switched data services, OJ 1992 L200/1; Council Recommendation 92/383 on the application of open network provision to ISDN, OJ 1992 L200/10; Common Position adopted by the Council on 30 June 1993 with a view to adopting a directive on the application of open network provision to voice telephony, 6957/2/93/Rev 2.

[358] Commission Directive 88/301 of 16 May 1988 on competition in the markets in telecommunications terminal equipment, OJ 1988 L131/73.

[359] Commission Directive 90/388 of 28 June 1990 on competition in the markets for telecommunications services, OJ 1990 L192/10.

[360] Terminal equipment directive, art. 2 and 3.

[361] Id., art. 4.

[362] Id., art. 4–6 and 8.

technical specifications and type-approval procedures in an independent entity.[363] Finally, the directive requires member states to ensure that their national telecommunications authorities give their customers the opportunity to terminate long-term leases – concluded when the authority had exclusive rights – to enable customers to obtain equipment elsewhere if they wish.[364]

Challenge to the directive

The adoption of the terminal equipment directive stirred controversy because, for the first time, the Commission had used art. 90(3) as a basis for a directive of general application to all member states rather than a decision aimed at a particular member state.[365] By adopting this approach, the Commission bypassed the Council, where there was a lack of political consensus for such far-reaching action, and used art. 90 to break up a legal monopoly rather than simply regulate the way in which it operated. France, later joined by Belgium, Germany, Greece and Italy, challenged the Commission's actions before the Court of Justice, arguing that the Commission had exceeded its powers. More specifically, it was argued that an art. 90(3) directive was not the appropriate means of achieving liberalisation; rather, this goal could have been achieved through more traditional means such as legislative proposals from the Council based on art. 100A designed to harmonise disparate national rules or by means of actions brought by the Commission against individual member states under art. 169 for violations of EC rules.

Ruling of the Court of Justice

In *France v EC Commission*,[366] the Court of Justice upheld the validity of the terminal equipment directive, though it annulled those provisions referring to 'special rights' and requiring the termination of long-term lease contracts. The court squarely rejected the argument that monopoly rights are per se compatible with the treaty; rather, they must be evaluated in light of the different treaty rules mentioned in art. 90(1).[367] In examining the validity of specific provisions of the directive in light of these rules, the court was careful to distinguish between exclusive and special rights, both of which are explicitly mentioned in art. 90(1), but nowhere defined. With respect to exclusive rights, the court upheld the Commission's authority under art. 90(3) to require member states to abolish exclusive rights regarding terminal equipment as

---

[363] Id., art. 6.

[364] Id., art. 7.

[365] The Commission has issued decisions addressed to individual member states under art. 90(3) on several occasions. See e.g. *International Express Courier Services – Spain*, OJ 1990 L233/19; *Express Delivery Services – Netherlands*, OJ 1990 L10/47. The Commission's power to issue such decisions was confirmed in *Netherlands and PTT Nederland v EC Commission* [1991] ECR I-565.

[366] *France v EC Commission* [1991] ECR I-1223.

[367] Id., at p. I-1265 (para. 22).

incompatible with the principle of the free movement of goods laid down in art. 30. The court expressed particular concern over both the ability of national PTTs to supply the range and quality of products demanded by consumers and the requisite installation and maintenance services.[368] The court annulled the provisions of the directive dealing with special rights, noting that the Commission had neither defined these rights nor justified their abolition.[369]

The court agreed with the Commission on the separation of the regulatory and commercial functions of the PTTs.[370] To allow a PTT to retain regulatory functions, such as type-approval of its competitor's equipment, would result in a clear conflict of interest. Finally, the court annulled the provision of the directive allowing customers to terminate long-term equipment leasing or maintenance agreements. In the court's view, art. 90 is concerned only with state action, and not with commercial contracts entered into by PTTs on their own initiative without any encouragement from the state.[371] The court noted that, to the extent that such contracts are anti-competitive, they may be dealt with on a case-by-case basis under art. 85 or 86.

¶1058   Telecommunications services

In June 1990, two years after the adoption of the terminal equipment directive, the Commission adopted a similar directive aimed at opening most telecommunications services to competition. The services directive seeks to abolish restrictions on the freedom to provide services imposed by PTTs to which member states have granted special or exclusive rights and the elimination of abuses by the PTTs of the dominant position they hold for the creation and exploitation of the network. The directive applies to all telecommunications services except for the following services that were specifically excluded from its scope: radio and television broadcasting,[372] telex, mobile radio telephony, paging and satellite services.[373]

Reserved and non-reserved services

The directive requires member states to withdraw all special or exclusive rights for the supply of telecommunications services other than so-called 'reserved services', i.e. voice telephony and, until the end of 1992, packet and

---

[368] Id.; at pp. I-1268 and I-1269 (para. 35 and 42).
[369] Id.; at p. I-1270 (para. 45).
[370] Id.; at p. I-1271 (para. 31 and 32).
[371] Id.; at p. I-1272 (para. 55 and 56).
[372] Services directive, art. 1(1).
[373] Id., art. 1(2).

circuit-switched data services.[374] At the time, it was considered that the liberalisation of voice telephony could threaten the financial stability of the PTTs because this was their primary source of revenue.[375] Member states may make the supply of non-reserved services subject to licensing or declaration procedures aimed at compliance with certain essential requirements,[376] provided that such procedures are public, objective and non-discriminatory.[377]

The directive also requires member states to take the necessary measures to make conditions governing access to their networks objective and non-discriminatory, and publish them, which will in particular enable companies to obtain leased lines within a reasonable period.[378] Like the terminal equipment directive, the services directive requires member states to separate regulatory and operational functions[379] and allows customers to terminate long-term contracts existing at the time of the directive's adoption.[380]

Challenge to the directive

The validity of the services directive was challenged by Spain, France, Italy and Belgium. In *Spain v EC Commission*,[381] a judgment similar in many respects to its judgment on the terminal equipment directive, the Court of Justice upheld the validity of the services directive. Following its earlier ruling, the court held that the Commission has the power, on the basis of art. 90(3), to adopt a directive laying down general rules that specify the member states' obligations under the treaty. Again, the court struck down the provisions of the directive dealing with special rights on the grounds that it did not make it clear precisely what special rights were envisaged and how any such rights might be contrary to the treaty. Likewise, as in its judgment on the terminal equipment directive, the court annulled the provision of the directive allowing customers to terminate long-term contracts for the supply of telecommunications services.

The court's judgment left open the issue of special rights first raised in its judgment on the terminal equipment directive. While these rights are not defined in the treaty, they would appear aimed at a situation where one or more

---

[374] Id., art. 2 and 3.

[375] Since then, the position has changed. In June 1993, the Council established a timetable for the liberalisation of voice telephony services under which these services would be liberalised by 1 January 1998 with the following exceptions: Spain, Ireland, Greece and Portugal were granted a five-year transitional period, and member states with 'very small networks' – thought to be Luxembourg and possibly Belgium – were given a two-year transitional period. See Council Resolution of 22 July 1993, OJ 1993 C213/1.

[376] Essential requirements are defined as 'the non-economic reasons in the general interest which may cause a member state to restrict access to the public telecommunications network or public telecommunications services. These reasons are security of network operations, maintenance of network integrity, and, in justified cases, interoperability of services and data protection.' Id., art. 1(1).

[377] Id., art. 2.

[378] Id., art. 4.

[379] Id., art. 7.

[380] Id., art. 8.

[381] *Spain & Ors v EC Commission*, Joined cases C-271/90, C-281/90 and C-289/90, judgment of 17 November 1992 (not yet reported).

entities other than the PTT has the right to provide a telecommunications service, but the number of these entities is limited.[382] In light of the confusion surrounding the notion of special rights, it is conceivable that member states may attempt to escape their obligations under the services directive by simply establishing duopolies for various telecommunications service sectors rather than opening-up these sectors to full-fledged competition. The issue of special rights could also become significant in sectors such as mobile phones and satellites not covered by the services directive as member states gradually introduce competition into these sectors. To avoid the uncertainty attached to the concept of special rights, one approach would be to move toward the broader notion of market dominance to evaluate whether member states have met their obligations. Thus, special rights could be objectionable in cases where a company holding such rights has a dominant position on the market.[383]

¶1059   Future liberalisation

The terminal equipment and services directives launched an ambitious programme of liberalisation and established important legal precedent regarding the Commission's power under art. 90(3). Ironically, the use of this new-found legislative power may be rare in the future. The emphasis given to the concept of subsidiarity in the context of the debate surrounding the Maastricht Treaty will make it increasingly difficult for the Commission to make use of a legislative route that involves neither the Council nor the Parliament. In these circumstances, it is likely that the Commission will resort with increasing frequency to the more traditional approach of harmonisation directives coupled with a case-by-case application of art. 85 and 86 to complete the task that it began with the art. 90(3) directives.[384] However, even the threat of the use of art. 90(3) may prove to be a potent inducement to member states to proceed with the process of liberalisation and harmonisation.

¶1060   Application of the competition rules: overview

As noted, the application of art. 85 and 86 to the telecommunications sector is likely to acquire increasing significance as a means of completing the liberalisation process begun by the terminal equipment and services directives. Resort to the competition rules will not only help fill in gaps left by these directives, but also will extend the liberalisation process to services excluded

---

[382] See opinion of Advocate General Jacobs in *Spain & Ors v EC Commission*, Joined cases C-271/90, C-281/90 and C-289/90, judgment of 17 November 1992 (not yet reported).

[383] See Id., at para. 51.

[384] This appears to be the strategy that the Commission has adopted with respect to the liberalisation of the gas and electricity markets. In these sectors, the Commission has issued proposals to the Council for harmonisation directives and has pursued individual infringement proceedings against certain member states. See *XXIInd Report on Competition Policy*, points 49–53 and 513.

¶1059

from the scope of these directives such as satellites, paging and mobile phones. Indeed, many of the Commission's more recent decisions in the telecommunications field have involved these reserved services.[385]

The application of art. 85 and 86 to the telecommunications sector is tempered by industrial policy concerns. In this connection, the Commission appears particularly willing to adopt a lenient attitude towards co-operation arrangements among European firms, including structural arrangements such as joint ventures and mergers, that will help develop trans-European networks and enable these firms to become more competitive on world markets.[386]

¶1061   State action

In considering the application of the competition rules in the telecommunications sector, a threshold issue is whether the restrictive conduct is the result of state action or that of an undertaking. If the conduct is the result of state action, art. 85 and 86 apply by virtue of art. 90(1).[387] If the conduct is that of an undertaking, art. 85 and 86 apply directly. As discussed below, the concept of undertaking in this context includes PTTs acting in their commercial capacity.

¶1062   Commission guidelines

Before examining the application of the competition rules in the telecommunications sector, it is important to note that, in September 1991, the Commission issued guidelines on the subject.[388] The guidelines are intended to clarify the Commission's approach in this sector without committing the Commission to a specific course of action in the future, thus allowing it to follow a case-by-case approach.[389] The guidelines essentially concern the direct application of art. 85 and 86 to undertakings, leaving aside issues concerning the application of art. 90 to member states.[390] They confirm that art. 85 and 86

---

[385] See e.g. *Astra*, OJ 1993 L20/23 (satellites); *Eirpage*, OJ 1991 L306/22 (paging); *Konsortium ECR 900*, OJ 1990 L228/31 (mobile phones).

[386] In the preface to its guidelines on the application of EC competition rules in the telecommunications sector, OJ 1991 C233/2, the Commission noted that the guidelines 'should ... be seen as one aspect of an overall Community policy towards telecommunications, and notably of policies and actions to encourage and stimulate those forms of cooperation which promote the development and availability of advanced communications for Europe.' In its resolution of 16 June 1993 on the situation in the telecommunications sector, the Council endorsed this approach, recognising 'the importance of competition rules in the new regulatory environment, taking into account the need for co-operation inter alia for trans-European services, and the situation of operators in European and non-European telecommunications markets.' See Council Resolution of 22 July 1993, OJ 1993 C213/1.

[387] For a more detailed discussion of art. 90, see Chapter 13.

[388] Guidelines on the application of EC competition rules in the telecommunications sector, OJ 1991 C233/2 (the 'guidelines').

[389] The Commission notes that it 'will apply these principles also to future individual cases in a flexible way, and taking the particular context of each case into account.' Id., at para. 9. The guidelines are not binding. Id., at para. 10.

[390] Id., at para. 12.

apply both to private companies and public telecommunications operators including telecommunications administrations and recognised private operating agencies, which are referred to collectively as Telecommunications Organisations or 'TOs'.[391]

¶1063   Relevant markets

In the guidelines, the Commission addresses the problem of defining the relevant product and geographic markets for the purposes of applying art. 85 and 86. For services, the Commission suggests that distinct markets would seem to exist for terrestrial network provision, voice communication, data communication and satellites.[392] Distinct service markets may also be identified for mobile communications including cellular telephone, paging, telepoint, cordless voice and cordless data communication.[393] For equipment, the following areas are mentioned as relevant for the purposes of market definition: public switches, private switches, transmission systems including telephone sets, modems, telex terminals, data transmission terminals and mobile telephones.[394]

The definition of the relevant product market can be particularly difficult in the telecommunications sector because fast-moving technology means that market definitions change frequently.[395] For example, as technical developments allow additional features to be added to paging systems, the boundary between the market for paging systems and that for other mobile communication systems may become blurred.[396]

To the extent that value-added services are aimed at a distinct group of users, they may be considered to constitute a distinct market. For example, the Commission has held that the market for express courier services is distinct from that for the basic postal service.[397] Express services meet the needs of business customers who must have a guarantee that their packages will arrive within a given time, while the basic service meets the needs of the general public where price is at least as important as speed.

With regard to the relevant geographic market, the Commission generally considers that each member state forms a separate market because the lack of a pan-European regulatory structure and common standards for equipment

---

[391] Id., at para. 20.

[392] Id., at para. 27. The Commission recognises that these markets may be broken down further into separate markets. For example, it is possible to identify several markets for satellite services. Id., at para. 29.

[393] Id., at para. 30.

[394] Id., at para. 28.

[395] See Id., at para. 30.

[396] In *Eirpage*, OJ 1991 L306/22, at p. 28, the Commission determined that the market for paging services is distinct from the market for mobile telephones generally because pagers are not as unwieldy as mobile telephones and the service is cheaper. The Commission noted that, while this distinction will become blurred in the future, paging will continue to be cheaper because it is one-way.

[397] *International Express Courier Services, Spain*, OJ 1990 L 233/19, at p. 20.

tends to isolate national markets.[398] However, as the single market gradually becomes a reality, the relevant geographic market will be extended accordingly.[399]

¶1064 Application of art. 85 to agreements typical to the sector

In the guidelines, the Commission discusses categories of agreements that are typical in the telecommunications industry. The principal categories are examined below together with the relevant case law.

(1) Agreements between TOs on reserved services

As noted, 'reserved services' are those that are not yet liberalised – notably network infrastructure and voice telephony – so that they continue to be provided by the TOs. Agreements between TOs relating to these services may restrict competition to the extent that they dampen 'hub competition', that is, the competition among the TOs for the business of major users who want to centralise their telecommunications activities in a given member state.[400] For instance, agreements between TOs on prices, discounting or collection charges for international services is likely to restrict hub competition because price competition is a crucial element of customer choice.[401] However, agreements concerning only the setting up of common tariff structures may be eligible for exemption under art. 85(3) to the extent that they improve transparency, thus making it easier for users to compare prices.[402]

Apart from agreements concerning prices, other agreements between TOs susceptible of restricting competition include the following:

(a) agreements on other conditions for the provision of facilities such as restricting the uses to which leased circuits may be put;[403]

(b) agreements on the choice of telecommunications routes;[404]

---

[398] Id., at para. 32. In *Alsatel v Novasam* [1988] ECR 5987, the court held that the relevant geographic market was France as a whole rather than a region of France, presumably because the authorisation for the installation of the telephone equipment at issue in that case was granted on a national rather than a regional basis. However, the court seemed to suggest that the regional market could become relevant in a case if there was sufficient evidence to show that the regional installers of equipment held a collective dominant position.

[399] Guidelines at para. 32.

[400] Id., at para. 42.

[401] Id., at para. 44 and 45. In *CEPT* and *CCITT*, *XXth Report on Competition Policy*, points 56 and 57, the Commission raised objections to recommendations issued by international organisations to which TOs belong concerning the pricing of certain services.

[402] Id., at para. 46.

[403] Id., at para. 47.

[404] Id., at para. 48.

(c) agreements on the imposition of technical and quality standards on the services provided on the public network;[405]

(d) agreements reserving special treatment for TOs' terminal equipment or other companies' equipment for the interconnection or interoperation of terminal equipment with reserved services and facilities;[406]

(e) agreements on the exchange of information.[407]

(2) Agreements on the supply of non-reserved services and terminal equipment

Agreements between TOs for the supply of non-reserved services and terminal equipment are susceptible of restricting competition within the meaning of art. 85(1) to the extent that they limit the services offered or make it more difficult for third parties to offer similar services.[408] However, such agreements may be eligible for exemption under art. 85(3) where they bring about benefits such as a European-wide service based on the principle of a one-stop shop, European-wide standardisation, cost reductions and a general improvement of public infrastructure.[409] In one case, the Commission indicated that it was willing to exempt a co-operation agreement among TOs for the supply of managed data network services on the condition that the TOs would neither discriminate against private service suppliers nor cross-subsidise their own activities.[410]

Co-operation between TOs and private telecommunications operators is becoming more frequent as the markets for various telecommunications services are gradually deregulated. This co-operation often takes the form of a joint venture agreement. Such agreements may infringe art. 85(1) to the extent that they restrict actual or potential competition between the partners.[411] Generally, the TO is at least a potential competitor on the market because it has the financial capacity and technical and commercial skills necessary to enter the market. Likewise, the private operator is generally a potential entrant because, typically, it already operates a system on other geographic markets.[412] The arrangement may also restrict competition from third parties because they will be discouraged from entering a market where a joint venture involving the local TO is already present.[413] However, such arrangements may be eligible for exemption under art. 85(3). For example, in *Eirpage*,[414] the Commission

---

[405] Id., at para. 49. The Commission notes that standardisation agreements will generally be eligible for exemption under art. 85(3) to the extent that they bring more openness and facilitate pan-European networks.

[406] Id., at para. 52.

[407] Id., at para. 53.

[408] Id., at para. 56–62.

[409] Id., at para. 63.

[410] *MDNS, XXth Report on Competition Policy*, point 58.

[411] Guidelines at para. 66.

[412] Id.

[413] Id., at para. 67.

[414] *Eirpage*, OJ 1991 L306/22. For an example of a joint venture arrangement in the satellite sector that was denied an exemption, see *Astra*, OJ 1993 L20/23.

¶1064

exempted a joint venture arrangement between the Irish PTT and Motorola for the construction and operation of a paging system in Ireland, citing the following reasons:

- the joint venture would provide nationwide service to less profitable rural areas that had not been served in the past;
- the joint venture would provide enhanced services such as direct contact with the paging service subscriber via interconnection to the public network; and
- neither party alone could have offered services of the same quality as rapidly.

Before granting the exemption, the Commission sought assurances from the TO that companies interested in competing with the joint venture would be treated on exactly the same footing as the joint venture with respect to matters such as the availability of facilities, frequency allocation and licensing requirements.[415]

The Commission has stressed that, in assessing joint ventures in the telecommunications sector, it attaches particular importance to whether the joint venture promotes technical progress and whether it makes European companies more competitive on world markets.[416] For example, in *Optical Fibres*,[417] the Commission granted an exemption to a series of joint venture agreements between Corning, a US company, and various European companies. The Commission noted that the joint venture would enable the European partners to produce a high-technology product and facilitate a more rapid transfer of Corning's optical fibre technology than would otherwise be possible, thus enabling them to withstand competition from US and Japanese producers.

(3) Research and development agreements

As a general rule, the Commission takes a favourable view of research and development agreements in the telecommunications sector. In the guidelines, the Commission notes that it is prepared to consider full-range co-operation between even large firms if such co-operation would improve the structure of European industry and enable it to meet competition on the world market.[418]

---

[415] In other cases involving joint ventures in which TOs participated, the Commission has shown a similar concern with ensuring that the participation of the TO did not give the joint venture an unjustified advantage over its competitors. See *Infrax*, OJ 1993 C117/3; *Infonet*, OJ 1992 C7/3; *Mercury/DGCT: International Telex Link*; *XXIst Report on Competition Policy for 1991*, p. 335.

[416] Guidelines at para. 137 and 138.

[417] *Optical Fibres*, OJ 1986 L236/30. See also *Aérospatiale/Alcatel Espace*, OJ 1994 C47/6; *Canon/Olivetti*, OJ 1988 L52/51.

[418] Guidelines at para. 77. For examples of the Commission's approach with respect to R&D agreements in the telecommunications sector, see *Alcatel Espace/ANT Nachrichtentechnik*, OJ 1990 L32/19; *Konsortium ECR 900*, OJ 1990 L228/31.

¶1064

¶1065   Abuse of dominant position

Application of art. 86 to TOs

Fcr many years it was unclear to what extent the activities of TOs were subject to art. 86. In its landmark judgment in *British Telecom*,[419] however, the Court of Justice held that TOs operating as commercial providers of telecommunications services are as much subject to art. 86 as those in the private sector. That case arose when British Telecom, having at the time a statutory monopoly for the provision of telecommunications services in the UK, prohibited private message-forwarding agencies from providing their services in the UK in competition with its own services. The court confirmed the Commission's view that British Telecom was subject to art. 86 because the provision of telecommunication services to a user for a fee was essentially a business activity. The court rejected the argument that the measures adopted by British Telecom were covered by art. 90(2) because, unless British Telecom were able to protect itself against the activities of the message-forwarding agencies, its ability to carry out its public task would be jeopardised. The court found no evidence that these activities harmed British Telecom or that the Commission's censure of British Telecom's actions jeopardised British Telecom's ability to perform its public tasks.

Formal Commission decisions involving the application of art. 86 to the telecommunications sector have been rare, presumably because private operators are reluctant to complain about a TO's practices to the Commission or national authorities out of fear of retaliation or, in some cases, of antagonising a potential business partner. It appears likely that this situation will only change to the extent that the Commission is able to satisfy industry concerns over the need to keep the identity of complainants confidential.

Dominant position

Apart from areas where they have a dominant position because of special or exclusive rights granted by a member state, TOs may hold dominant positions because they continue to have high market shares even after liberalisation of the market.[420] Even if the market share alone is not enough for a finding of dominance, the market share combined with other factors such as the monopoly over the network or other related services and a powerful distribution network could result in dominance.[421] Similarly, private operators may be dominant based on their market share, or their market share taken into consideration with other factors such as technological advance and the

---

[419] *Italy v EC Commission* ('*British Telecom*') [1985] ECR 873. See also Written Question No. 792/88, OJ 1989 C103/24.
[420] Guidelines at para. 80.
[421] Id.

possession of information concerning access protocols or interfaces necessary to ensure interoperability of software or hardware.[422]

Abuse

In the guidelines, the Commission catalogues the types of abuse that are most prone to arise in the telecommunications sector. Particular attention is paid to the danger of a TO attempting to extend its dominant position in one market, such as network provision, to a neighbouring market such as message-forwarding services. This type of abuse was dealt with in *CBEM-Télémarketing*,[423] where the Court of Justice condemned the refusal of a Luxembourg television station to sell television time to a telephone marketing company that competed with the station's own telephone marketing activities. The court held that art. 86 is infringed where, without any objective necessity, an undertaking holding a dominant position on a particular market reserves for itself an ancillary activity which might be carried out by another undertaking on a neighbouring but separate market, with the possibility of eliminating all competition of that undertaking.

The extension of a dominant position in one market to a neighbouring market may constitute an abuse not only when this is a result of an undertaking's own action, as was the case in *CBEM-Télémarketing*, but also when it is the result of state action. In *RTT v GB-Inno-BM*,[424] the court held that Belgium's grant to the Belgian PTT – which held a monopoly for the operation of the basic telephone network – of the right to grant authorisations for the connection of telephones to the public network constituted a violation of art. 86 read in conjunction with art. 90(1). The court emphasised that the mere possession of this right sufficed to establish an infringement and that it was not necessary to prove that the PTT had exercised this right in a discriminatory manner.[425] The court noted that the need to ensure that telephones met essential requirements such as the security of users and the protection of the public network against harm could be met by publishing the specifications for the telephones and establishing a procedure to ensure that these specifications were met. This case is also significant because it confirms

---

[422] Id., at para. 81.
[423] *CBEM-Télémarketing v Compagnie Luxembourgeoise de Télédiffusion (CLT) and Information Publicités Benelux (IPB)* [1985] ECR 3261. See also *International Express Courier Services – Spain*, OJ 1990 L233/19, where the Commission found that a TO with a dominant position on the market for basic postal service abused this position when, without any objective necessity, it reserved to itself an ancillary activity – express courier services.
[424] *RTT v GB-Inno-BM* [1991] ECR I-5941. See also *RTT, XXth Report on Competition Policy*, point 55, where the Commission objected to the Belgian PTT's attempt to impose certain conditions on companies wishing to lease lines on its network. Following the Commission's intervention, the PTT agreed not to impose any conditions other than that they should not carry out a simple transfer of data.
[425] See also *Spain & Ors v EC Commission*, Joined cases C-271/90, C-281/90 and C-289/90, judgment of 17 November 1992, not yet reported, para. 35 and 36, where the court reached the same conclusion with respect to the extension of a TO's network monopoly to the market for telecommunications services.

¶1065

the view taken by the Commission in the services directive that it constitutes an abuse of art. 86 for a TO to perform both regulatory and commercial functions.[426]

The court's ruling in *RTT v GB-Inno-BM* highlights the fact that a member state may breach the competition rules if it grants exclusive rights to an undertaking that put the undertaking in a situation where the mere exercise of those rights will inevitably give rise to an abuse. The court dealt with this same notion in *ERT*.[427] In that case, Greece granted exclusive rights over the transmission of its own television broadcasts as well as the retransmission of broadcasts from other member states. The court held that art. 90(1) of the treaty is violated where the grant of such rights is 'liable to create a situation in which [the] undertaking is led to infringe Article 86 by virtue of a discriminatory broadcasting policy which favours its own programmes, unless the application of Article 86 obstructs the performance of the particular tasks entrusted to it.'[428]

Another area of particular concern to the Commission is the cross-subsidisation of activities open to competition by those reserved to TOs.[429] Cross-subsidisation allows a TO to use revenues from one part of its business to beat competitors in others. Cross-subsidisation may take many forms, including the funding of activities with capital provided at interest rates that are below market rates, or providing land, equipment, personnel or services at prices that are not negotiated at arms' length.[430] Cross-subsidisation may also take the form of predatory pricing, in which case it would be prohibited by *AKZO* and its progeny.[431] Cross-subsidisation principles may also be applied to private companies such as US-based telecommunications companies that attempt to subsidise their EC operations out of revenues earned in the US.[432] In cases of agreements involving TOs, the Commission may require the parties to submit accounts on a periodic basis that shows how costs are allocated between various activities.[433]

---

[426] Similar issues were raised in *Procureur du Roi v Lagauche & Ors*, Joined Cases C-46/90 and C-93/91, judgment of 27 October 1993, not yet reported, which involved challenges to the Belgian PTT's right to draw up specifications and grant type-approval to cordless phones while competing on the same market for the supply of goods and services in the telecommunications sector. The court noted that art. 6 of the terminal equipment directive requires a clear separation of these functions. See also the ruling of the court in *Ministère Public v Taillandier*, Case C-92/91, judgment of 27 October 1993, not yet reported.

[427] *ERT v DEP & Ors* [1991] ECR I-2925. See also *Corbeau*, Case C-320/91, judgment of 19 May 1993, not yet reported, para. 11; *Höfner and Elsner v Macrotron* [1991] ECR I-1979, at p. I-2018 (para. 28–31); opinion of Advocate General Van Gerven, para. 35–40, *Netherlands & PTT Nederland v EC Commission* [1992] ECR I-565.

[428] Id., at para. 38.

[429] Cross-subsidisation between reserved services does not raise competition problems because there is no competition to be restricted. See guidelines at para. 103.

[430] Id., at para. 104.

[431] See Chapter 9.

[432] Guidelines at para. 110.

[433] For instance, in *Eirpage*, OJ 1991 L306/22, the Commission sought written assurances from a chartered accountant that a joint venture in which a TO was involved and to which the TO provided certain services paid full costs and expenses to the TO. See generally, guidelines at para. 102–110.

¶1065

¶1066   Services of general economic interest

Article 90(2) is frequently raised as a defence by member states and TOs in art. 86 cases. Article 90(2) provides as follows:

'Undertakings entrusted with the operation of services of general economic interest or having the character of a revenue-producing monopoly shall be subject to the rules contained in this Treaty, in particular to the rules on competition, in so far as the application of such rules does not obstruct the performance, in law or in fact, of the particular tasks assigned to them. The development of trade must not be affected to such an extent as would be contrary to the interests of the Community.'

Thus, art. 85 and 86 apply to TOs unless their application would obstruct their performance of the particular tasks assigned to them. Typically, it is argued that a TO's monopoly over a given service or restrictions imposed on private operators are necessary to allow the TO to perform the particular tasks assigned to it.

A review of the cases reveals that both the Commission and the court have placed a restrictive gloss on the art. 90(2) exception. For example, in *Express Delivery Services – Netherlands*,[434] the Commission found that the Dutch PTT's obligation to provide a basic postal service was not threatened by competition in the market for express deliveries. In reaching this conclusion, the Commission pointed out that the PTT's profits had risen despite this competition, that the PTT enjoyed certain advantages in carrying out its tasks, and that the PTT had been successful in withstanding competition from private couriers, primarily because of its ability to adjust its tariff structure to take into account cost differences.

Restrictions to ensure compliance with 'essential requirements'

In *RTT v GB-Inno-BM*,[435] the court found that, by virtue of its operation of the public telephone network, the Belgian PTT provided a service of general economic interest within the meaning of art. 90(2). However, the court held that restrictions placed on the ability of private operators to provide telephones to be connected to this network could not be justified as necessary to allow the PTT to carry out this service of general economic interest. According to the court, the production and sale of telephones is an activity that must be open to

---

[434] *Express Delivery Services – Netherlands*, OJ 1990 L10/47, on appeal: *Netherlands & PTT Nederland v EC Commission* [1992] ECR I-565 (reversing Commission decision on procedural grounds). See also *International Express Courier Services*, OJ 1990 L233/19. For cases involving the application of art. 90(2) in the electricity sector, see *Jahrhundertvertrag/VIK-GVSt*, OJ 1993 L50/14; *IJsselcentrale*, OJ 1991 L28/32.
[435] *RTT v GB-Inno-BM* [1991] ECR I-5941.

any undertaking. Moreover, to ensure that these telephones met certain 'essential requirements' such as ensuring the security of users, the security of those operating on the network and the protection of the network against harm, it sufficed for the PTT to publish equipment specifications and establish a procedure for verifying compliance with these specifications.

The concept of 'essential requirements' referred to by the court in that case was that developed by the Commission in the services directive. According to that directive, member states may make the grant of licences to provide telecommunications services conditional upon compliance with certain 'essential requirements', which are defined as follows:

> 'the non-economic reasons in the general interest which may cause a member state to restrict access to the public telecommunications network or public telecommunications services. These reasons are security of network operations, maintenance of network integrity, and, in justified cases, interoperability of services and data protection.'[436]

While essential requirements may be invoked by a member state to justify certain restrictions on the provision of telecommunications services that would otherwise be impermissible, it would appear difficult for TOs to invoke such requirements in the context of art. 90(2). In particular, it would seem difficult for a TO to explain why it must impose certain restrictions on network access when the member state that granted the TO its rights in the first place did not consider such restrictions necessary to safeguard essential requirements.[437]

Provision of universal service

An argument that may prove more successful in the context of art. 90(2) is based on the TO's obligation to provide universal service. In the services directive, the Commission noted that the particular task assigned to TOs within the meaning of art. 90(2) was 'the provision and exploitation of a universal network, i.e. one having general geographical coverage, and being provided to any service provider or user upon request within a reasonable period of time.'[438] The Commission decided to exclude voice telephony from the scope of the

---

[436] Services directive, art. 1(1) and 2. Recital 9 of the preamble elaborates on this definition as follows:

'the security of network operations means ensuring the availability of the public network in case of emergency. The technical integrity of the public network means ensuring its normal operation and the interconnection of public networks in the Community on the basis of common technical specifications. The concept of interoperability of services means complying with such technical specifications introduced to increase the provision of services and the choice available to users. Data protection means measures taken to warrant the confidentiality of communications and the protection of personal data.'

[437] See guidelines at para. 22.

[438] Recital 18 of the preamble to the services directive. See generally Council Resolution 94/C48/01 of 7 February 1994 on universal service principles in the telecommunications sector, OJ 1994 C48/1, which sets out the elements constituting universal service.

directive because, if TOs were subjected to competition in this sector, it could jeopardise their ability to accomplish this task. More specifically, their financial stability could be threatened as the financial resources for the development of the network come primarily from voice telephony.

In *Corbeau*,[439] the Court of Justice expanded on this line of reasoning. That case arose when criminal proceedings were brought against Corbeau for operating a courier service in the city of Liège, Belgium, in contravention of the law conferring the monopoly for postal services on the Belgian PTT. The court had little trouble establishing that the PTT performed a service of general economic interest within the meaning of art. 90(2) in so far as it was responsible for providing postal service of similar quality and at uniform rates throughout Belgium regardless of the profitability of each individual delivery.

The court then turned to the question of whether a monopoly over postal services was necessary to enable the PTT to perform its task. At the outset, the court established the basic premise that the PTT's obligation to provide this universal service rested on the assumption that the PTT could subsidise its unprofitable activities from its profitable ones and could restrict competition with respect to the more profitable activities. Otherwise, private operators who chose to concentrate their efforts on the profitable activities would be in a position to offer lower prices than the PTT because, unlike the PTT, they were not burdened with the extra costs of providing a universal service. The court emphasised, however, that this rationale did not justify a monopoly with respect to specific services that could be distinguished from services of general economic interest in that they were designed to meet the individual needs of companies that demanded certain additional services that the traditional postal service did not supply such as home collection of mail, more rapid delivery and the possibility of changing destination in transit. The court added that such additional services, either by their nature or the conditions under which they were offered such as their geographical coverage, should not jeopardise the financial stability of the basic service.

---

[439] *Corbeau*, Case C-320/91, judgment of 19 May 1993, not yet reported.

PART III

PROCEDURE

11 Procedure

INTRODUCTION

¶1101 Rules of procedure generally

Article 87 of the EC Treaty entrusted the Council of Ministers with the task of devising the rules of procedure to enforce art. 85 and 86. Pending the adoption of such rules, the enforcement of the EC antitrust provisions remained the joint responsibility of the authorities in member states[1] and the Commission.

The Council enacted Regulation 17/62, the first regulation implementing art. 85 and 86 of the treaty, on 6 February 1962.[2] This first regulation lays down in considerable detail the various rules of procedure that need to be followed in order to apply art. 85 and 86. Thus, it provides for the registration of agreements, for means of investigation, for the right to be heard, for the adoption of cease-and-desist orders, for the granting of negative clearances and exemptions, and for the imposition of fines and periodic penalty payments. In addition, Regulation 17/62 does away with the concurrent jurisdiction of the national authorities who only remain competent 'as long as the Commission has not initiated any procedure'.[3]

Shortly thereafter, pursuant to a delegation of authority contained in Regulation 17/62, the Commission itself issued two regulations, one dealing with the notification procedure,[4] and the other with the organisation of hearings.[5]

More than 12 years after Regulation 17/62 had come into effect, the Council enacted a regulation providing for limitation periods in EC competition law.[6]

---

[1] i.e., the national authorities, whether administrative or judicial, in charge of the application of local competition laws. See *BRT v SABAM* (*'BRT I'*) [1974] ECR 51.

[2] Council Regulation 17/62 of 6 February 1962 implementing art. 85 and 86 of the treaty, JO 1962 13/204; amended JO 1962 58/1655, JO 1963 162/2696, JO 1971 L285/49.

[3] The term 'initiation of any procedure' has been interpreted to mean an act of the Commission reflecting authority instead of mere administration. See *Brasserie de Haecht v Wilkin* (*'Haecht II'*) [1973] ECR 77, at pp. 87–88 (para. 14–18).

[4] Commission Regulation 27/62 of the Commission implementing Council Regulation 17/62, JO 1962 35/1118.

[5] Commission Regulation 99/63 on the hearings provided for in art. 19(1) and (2) of Council Regulation 17/62, JO 1963 127/2268.

[6] Council Regulation 2988/74 concerning limitation periods in proceedings and the enforcement of sanctions under the rules of the European Economic Community relating to transport and competition. OJ 1974 L319/1.

The absence of such a provision in Regulation 17/62 had been an issue in two proceedings before the Court of Justice.[7] The court, however, failed to read the existence of such a fundamental principle into Community law.

The Commission has, on its own initiative, albeit in response to criticism voiced by the Bar and business circles, introduced a number of practical improvements to its rules of procedure aimed at making the proceedings more transparent and fair, and at accelerating them.[8]

Last but not least, the Commission's procedure has been influenced by the judicial review exercised by the Court of Justice in competition cases and, to a lesser extent, by the interest expressed by the European Parliament and the Economic and Social Committee in some of the activities of the Commission in the competition field.

These various ongoing influences from other institutions, together with the wealth of experience gained by the Commission in its day-to-day practice, explain why the application of the basic rules of procedure laid down in Regulation 17/62 is not a rigid process but one that keeps changing over the years.

¶1102   Nature of Commission proceedings

The proceedings before the Commission are of an administrative nature. Article 15(4) of Regulation 17/62 expressly provides that decisions of the Commission by which fines are imposed 'shall not be of a criminal law nature'.[9]

The procedure before the Commission is largely written and inquisitorial. The powers of fact-finding, prosecution and decision-making are all vested in the same institution, the Commission, without any clear separation.[10] Hence, the Commission cannot be regarded as a 'tribunal' within the meaning of art. 6(1) of the European Convention for the Protection of Human Rights.[11] The Commission, instead, acts as an executive body of the Community.

---

[7] *ACF Chemiefarma v EC Commission* [1970] ECR 661; *ICI v EC Commission* [1972] ECR 619.

[8] See e.g. ¶1111 on access to the file. See also the *XXIInd Report on Competition Policy for 1992*, point 115 et seq; point 122 et seq.

[9] The procedure is expressly said to be of a non-criminal law nature because a number of member states would have objected to any criminal jurisdiction being delegated to the Commission. See the opinion of Advocate General Mayras in *Boehringer v EC Commission* [1972] ECR 1281, at p. 1291. In contrast, Advocate-General Darmon stated in *Åhlström & Ors v EC Commission* ('*Wood Pulp*'), [1993] 1 CEC 446, his opinion at para. 451:

'A regulation of general application cannot be required to state in minute detail the reasons which led to its adoption. A Commission decision in the field of competition is another matter entirely, particularly where it orders a trader to pay a fine and is therefore manifestly of a penal nature.'

[10] The scope of the Commission's powers was criticised by the European Parliament, which suggested that 'the Commission should, within its internal procedures, make a distinction between its investigatory, examinatory and decision-making functions regarding restrictive agreements and abuses of dominant positions'. See *XXth Report on Competition Policy*, point 89.

[11] In *Musique Diffusion Française v EC Commission* [1983] ECR 1825, at p. 1880 (para. 6–7), the Court of Justice made the following statement:

'MDF maintains that the contested decision is unlawful by the mere fact that it was adopted under a system in

Even though, in theory at least, the decisions in competition cases are adopted by the Commission as a collegiate body, the parties to the proceedings never face their judges, the 17 members of the Commission; they have access only to members of the Commission's staff.

In view of the fact that the Commission combines the role of prosecutor and judge, EC competition proceedings tend to move with greater dispatch than in a system offering more checks and balances.[12] The rules of procedure are fairly simple in the EC and are applied with little formalism. The obvious advantage is that protracted litigation can be avoided and remedies obtained earlier. The drawback is that the rules of due process are not as well developed as they could be.[13]

The Commission's enforcement of art. 85 and 86 of the treaty is twofold. On the one hand the Commission adopts individual measures – notably decisions ordering the termination of infringements, decisions granting negative clearance and exemption decisions pursuant to art. 85(3) – and on the other hand the Commission adopts measures of general application, such as block exemptions and notices. Individual measures are considered at ¶1103–¶1131 and general measures are described at ¶1132–¶1134.

INDIVIDUAL MEASURES ADOPTED BY THE COMMISSION

¶1103   Decision-making power of the Commission

When the Commission takes a decision it acts in a quasi-judicial capacity. The Commission's decision-making power includes the power to adopt three broad categories of decisions:

(1) decisions finding an infringement;

(2) decisions granting a negative clearance;

(3) decisions providing for an exemption under art. 85(3).

The last two categories of decisions (see ¶1121–¶1127) are the culmination of the notification procedure set in motion by at least one of the parties to the agreements concerned, whereas the first category of decisions (see ¶1104–

---

which the Commission combines the functions of prosecutor and judge, which is contrary to Article 6(1) of the European Convention for the Protection of Human Rights. That argument is without relevance. As the Court [of Justice] held in its judgment ... in ...*Van Landewyck v EC Commission* [1980] ECR 3125, the Commission cannot be described as "a tribunal" within the meaning of Article 6 of the European Convention for the Protection of Human Rights.'

[12] It remains to be seen how the Court of First Instance will in the long term influence the development of EC competition law. See ¶1135 et seq.

[13] See e.g. House of Lords, Session 1981–1982, *8th Report*, para. 6 and 9.

¶1120) are the result of an investigation which may have been triggered in a number of different ways (see ¶1105).

¶1104   Infringement proceedings: overview

Article 3 of Regulation 17/62 provides that whenever the Commission establishes the existence of an infringement of art. 85 and 86, it may by decision require the offender to bring such infringement to an end.

The administrative process leading to such a decision implies an investigation of the facts by the Commission, which employs considerable powers of discovery to that effect.

Provided that the results of the investigation warrant the initiation of a proceeding, the parties concerned will be notified by the Commission of such initiation and will receive a so-called 'statement of objections' in which the principal objections of the Commission against the agreement or practice involved are set out in some detail. The recipients of the statement of objections are allowed to comment on the charges put forward by the Commission, both in writing within a given time-limit and orally at a hearing.

If the Commission proceeds with the case, notwithstanding the comments and arguments made by the parties concerned, it must consult with the Advisory Committee, composed of representatives of the antitrust authorities of the member states and chaired by a Commission official, before the draft decision can be finally adopted by the members of the Commission.

Of course, not every case started by the Commission gives rise to a formal decision. According to the available statistical information, settlements outnumber decisions by far. However, in view of the scarce information that is published on settlements, the criteria which underlie the Commission's settlement practice are not entirely clear.

Before reaching a final decision, or a settlement, in a given case, the Commission may adopt interim relief if the urgency of the situation so warrants.

Instead of taking a decision requiring the termination of an infringement, the Commission is also empowered to issue a non-binding recommendation to that effect. Until now, however, the Commission has only rarely made use of this possible approach.

The procedure involved in reaching a decision which establishes the existence of an infringement, and the consequences of such a decision, are explained in ¶1105 to ¶1120.

¶1105   Opening of investigation

The Commission may become aware of a possibly restrictive agreement or practice as a result of its own investigation, or because of an application for negative clearance or a notification for exemption, or because of the receipt of a complaint.

Complaint

From the Commission's *Annual Reports on Competition Policy* it is clear that complaints are being made more frequently. 110 complaints were filed with the Commission in 1992, 83 in 1991 and 97 in 1990. This is to be compared with 66 in 1985 and 45 in 1981. On 31 December 1992, 1,562 cases were pending before the Commission, 287 of which were complaints from companies.

It is also interesting to note that the filing of complaints is no longer a typical means of defence reserved for the weak market operator against the strong, but that it is nowadays also being used by large corporations as a strategic weapon against their major competitors. This phenomenon can best be illustrated by the complaint filed by the Reynolds Tobacco company against the acquisition of an interest by Philip Morris in Rothmans.[14]

Member states and any natural or legal person claiming a legitimate interest may file a complaint with the Commission.[15] The Commission has drawn up a special form (amended following the entry into force of the EEA Agreement) for the filing of complaints, but its use is not compulsory.[16] A simple letter will suffice. However, as a minimum the complaint should provide the following information:

(1) identification of the complainant and of the subject of the complaint;

(2) an indication of the complainant's legitimate interest in the matter;

(3) a precise description of the restrictive agreement or practice complained about; and

(4) evidence of authority, if the complaint is signed by a representative of the complainant.

Private complainants do not automatically have the right to obtain from the Commission a decision on whether or not an infringement of EC competition rules exists. It is up to the Commission to decide whether or not to initiate an investigation.[17] In this regard, priority will be granted to cases presenting a 'Community interest'. As a consequence, the Commission may refer a

---

[14] *Fourteenth Report on Competition Policy*, points 98–100. See also *BAT & Reynolds v EC Commission* [1987] ECR 4487.

[15] Trade unions may have a legitimate interest within the meaning of art. 3(2) of Regulation 17/62 to lodge a complaint (*Sixteenth Report on Competition Policy, BP/TGWU-Llandarcy Refinery*, point 43).

[16] Form C. In maritime and air transport matters, the Commission leaves it to the discretion of the complainants to decide on the form, content and details of the complaints (see Regulation 4260/88, recital 3; Regulation 4261/88, recital 2).

[17] The situation is different where the complaint is made by a member state: in this case, the Commission is obliged to initiate an investigation; see art. 89(1) of the treaty and *Automec Srl v EC Commission* ('*Automec II*') [1992] ECR II-2223, at p. 2275 (para. 76).

complaint to the appropriate national authority for cases where no important Community interest is at stake, provided that redress is available at the national level.[18] Depending on the circumstances of the case, complainants should therefore consider whether their request would be dealt with more efficiently by national authorities.[19]

In assessing the 'Community interest', the Commission has a wide discretionary power but is nevertheless under a duty to examine carefully each complaint it receives.[20] In *Automec I*,[21] the Court of First Instance clarified the administrative procedure to be followed in examining a complaint, distinguishing three stages in the procedure leading to the rejection of a complaint.

First, the Commission collects information concerning the complaint, which may include an informal exchange of views and information between the Commission and the complainant with a view to clarifying the factual and legal

---

[18] See *Automec Srl v EC Commission* ('*Automec II*'), footnote 17 above. In this case, the Court of First Instance stated that the Commission had not violated the rights of the complainant by refusing to initiate proceedings since the competent national court was entitled to apply art. 85(1) of the EC Treaty and declare the anti-competitive agreement void pursuant to art. 85(2).

In its Notice on co-operation between national courts and the Commission in applying art. 85 and 86 of the EEC Treaty (OJ 1993 C39/6, at p. 7), the Commission confirmed the general rule set out in *Automec II*:

'14. The Commission intends, in implementing its decision-making powers, to concentrate on notifications, complaints and own-initiative proceedings having particular political, economic or legal significance for the Community. Where these features are absent in a particular case, notifications will normally be dealt with by means of comfort letter and complaints should, as a rule, be handled by national courts or authorities.

15. The Commission considers that there is not normally a sufficient Community interest in examining a case when the plaintiff is able to secure adequate protection of his rights before the national courts. (*Automec Srl v EC Commission* ... para. 91–94.) In these circumstances the complaint will normally be filed.'

In *Automec II*, at p. 2280 (para. 95), the Court of First Instance also pointed out that the applicability of a block exemption regulation to the agreement(s) concerned was a factor the Commission could take into account in assessing the Community interest. The principal objective of block exemptions is to limit the need for notifications and their existence should facilitate the application of competition law by national courts.

[19] Complaints which concern exclusively, or almost exclusively, a single member state should be dealt with directly by the national authorities. A few months after the judgment in *Automec II*, the Commission referred back to the French competition authorities a complaint filed several years previously against the French copyright management society SACEM. The complainants argued that SACEM infringed art. 86 by charging excessive royalties for music reproduction. On the basis of a comparative study of royalties charged by different copyright management societies in other member states, the Commission concluded that the effect of a possible abuse by SACEM would mainly arise in France. In its letter referring the complaint to the French authorities, the Commission recalled its wide margin of discretion, as described in the *Automec II* case, when assessing the 'Community interest' of a complaint; see press release IP(92) 977 of 27 November 1992. Two actions for annulment have been lodged with the Court of First Instance against the Commission's decision: *Benim v EC Commission*, Case T-114/92, not yet decided, OJ 1993 C43/25 and *Roger Tremblay & Ors v EC Commission*, Case T-5/93, not yet decided, OJ 1993 C43/26.

[20] Examination of the facts of the case and assessment of Community interest are subject to judicial review. In the same *Automec II* case (see footnote 17 above), at p. 2277 (para. 85), the Court of First Instance held that the Commission has to clearly state the reasons of fact and law which led it to conclude that there was no Community interest. In this regard, the Court of First Instance recently annulled a decision by which the Commission rejected a complaint. The court found that the Commission had failed to take account of documents 'whose conclusiveness could not, at first sight, be ruled out without a thorough examination'. (See *SA Asia Motor France & Ors v EC Commission* [1993] ECR II-669).

[21] *Automec Srl v EC Commission* ('*Automec I*') [1990] ECR II-367, at pp. 382–383 (para. 45–47).

issues and allowing the complainant to expand on his allegations in the light of any initial reaction from the Commission.

Secondly, if the Commission finds that, based on the information in its possession, there are insufficient grounds for pursuing the matter or that the complaint presents no Community interest, the Commission gives the complainant notice under art. 6 of Regulation 99/63. This notice may be described as a statement of objections in reverse in that the Commission gives a full explanation of the reasons why it does not act on the complaint and affords the complainant the opportunity to submit further written comments by a given date. This notice is designed to protect the procedural rights of the complainant by letting him know why the Commission intends not to start an investigation.[22]

In the third stage, the Commission considers any further comments submitted by the complainant. It may decide either to open an investigation if new facts have been disclosed, or reject the complaint for lack of merit.[23] Even though the applicable regulation only provides that the Commission must inform the complainant of its intention not to act on the complaint and, anomalously, does not require the Commission to inform the complainant of the final rejection of his complaint, the Commission has nevertheless adopted the practice of supplying the complainant who so requests with a definitive ruling rejecting his complaint in order to allow him to appeal the matter before the Court of First Instance.[24]

If, instead of rejecting the complaint, the Commission takes up the case but later in its final decision rejects, whether expressly or implicitly, some of the

---

[22] Like a statement of objections, the notice does not constitute a final decision that may be challenged under art. 173 of the treaty before the Court of First Instance. Id. at pp. 382–383 (para. 46); see also *XXth Report on Competition Policy*, point 165.

[23] In its *Seventeenth Report on Competition Policy*, point 111, the Commission noted that complainants, once they have made submissions in reaction to the Commission's letter according to art. 6 of Regulation 99/63, have no further right of reply until the final decision rejecting the complaint has been taken. This is so even though the Commission may use in its final decision new arguments to refute the complainant's submissions. See also *BAT & Reynolds v EC Commission* [1987] ECR 4487, at p. 4574 (para. 26–27).

[24] *Eleventh Report on Competition Policy*, point 118, *Fifteenth Report on Competition Policy*, point 1. In *Demo-Studio Schmidt v EC Commission* [1983] ECR 3045, at p. 3063 (para. 12), the Court of Justice noted that the Commission did 'not dispute the fact that its decision on the applicant's complaint does constitute a measure which the Court may be called upon to declare void, since a 'notice' or 'communication' of that kind is definitive'. In *CICCE v EC Commission* [1985] ECR 1105, the Commission had argued that the submission relating to matters set out in the complaint but not repeated in the comments filed pursuant to art. 6 of Regulation 99/63 should be declared inadmissible. The Court of Justice, however, refused to draw such a distinction between arguments based on information contained in the complaint and arguments based on information contained in the comments submitted pursuant to said art. 6. Hence, the court rejected the Commission objection of inadmissibility (para. 20). It is interesting to note, however, that the Commission did not raise the admissibility issue in connection with the fact that the 'decision' by which the complaint was rejected was not a decision signed by a member of the Commission but was a mere administrative letter signed by the Director-General. See *Fifteenth Report on Competition Policy*, point 127.

In *BAT & Reynolds v EC Commission* [1987] ECR 4487, at pp. 4570–4571 (para. 11–12), the Court of Justice stated that the letters of the Commission rejecting the complaints of BAT and Reynolds were drawn up in the form of a decision. The court held that the 'letters have the content and effect of a decision, in as much as they close the investigation, contain an assessment of the agreements in question and prevent the applicants from requiring the re-opening of the investigation unless they put forward new evidence'.

arguments raised by the complainant, the latter will likewise be entitled to file an appeal against the Commission's decision.[25]

As to a complainant's right to participate in the proceedings before the Commission once his complaint has been accepted, mention ought to be made of the fact that the Commission grants him access to the file and allows him to take part in the hearing.[26]

Other events triggering an investigation

In addition to complaints filed with the Commission, there are a number of other factors which may cause the Commission to start an investigation on its own initiative, for example:

- informal or anonymous complaints;
- reports in the press;
- questions raised in the European Parliament;
- information received from national antitrust authorities;
- information gathered during a sector inquiry.

During the last few years, the number of proceedings opened by the Commission on its own initiative was as follows:

1987 – 30	1990 – 77
1988 – 44	1991 – 23
1989 – 67	1992 – 43

Last but not least, every year a number of investigations are started as a result of information received by the Commission via the notification process.

---

[25] *Metro v EC Commission* [1977] ECR 1875, at p. 1901 (para. 13).

[26] See *Thirteenth Report on Competition Policy*, point 74b, where it is stated that:

'Although complainants do not automatically have a right to see the file during the course of the examination of the complaint by the Commission, the Commission in practice ensures that a complainant receives the replies and observations regarding the complaint, sometimes in summary form, submitted by the undertaking(s) against which the complaint was lodged.'

In *Ancides* [1987] ECR 3131, at pp. 3153–3154 (para. 7–10), the Court of Justice held that a third party, despite the fact that it had made written submissions in reaction to a published notice, did not have the right to be admitted to the subsequent proceedings, unless the conditions of art. 19(2) of Regulation 17/62 were met. See also *Seventeenth Report on Competition Policy*, point 111, where the Commission stated that if:

'the third party wishes to make further submissions it must ask the Commission's leave to do so under the second sentence of Article 19(2) of Regulation 17 and demonstrate a sufficient interest'.

In *BAT & Reynolds v EC Commission* [1987] ECR 4487, at p. 4574 (para. 24), the Court of Justice stated that the complainants had no right to be kept informed of the progress made in the discussions between the Commission and Philip Morris in order to bring the agreements in conformity with the treaty. The court held that:

'the legitimate interests of the complainants are fully protected when they are informed of the outcome of the negotiations in the light of which the Commission proposes to close the proceedings'

For the rights of third parties to have access to the file and to be heard, see ¶1111 and ¶1114.

¶1106   Discovery procedure

Since it is the Commission's duty to detect and prosecute infringements of the competition rules, it is only natural that it has at its disposal powers of discovery to that effect.

The Commission's powers of discovery consist essentially of the right to send a request for information and to carry out on-the-spot investigations. They are described in detail at ¶1107–¶1111.

For many years the exercise by the Commission of its power of discovery has been at the centre of a critical debate in favour of more 'due process'.[27] As a result of this drive, the Commission has introduced some procedural safeguards among which the defendant's right of access to the file is clearly the most significant (see ¶1111).

¶1107   Discovery: requests for information

In instances of suspected infringement of art. 85 or 86, the Commission, pursuant to art. 11 of Regulation 17/62, may seek to obtain all necessary information from the companies involved, from third parties and from the national authorities of the member states.[28] 'Necessary' information is information that might enable the Commission to verify the existence of the presumed infringement referred to in the request which justified the initiation of the inquiry.[29]

It is a two-step procedure in that a formal Commission decision compelling the addressee to supply certain information must be preceded by a simple request for information which he may, but need not, answer. However, if the company decides to reply to a simple request and provides incomplete information, the Commission may impose a fine. Both in the case of a simple request and a request by way of a formal decision, the Commission must state the legal basis and purpose of the request.[30]

The Commission's power to send out requests for information has, of course, never been disputed. As a result, case law on the subject tends to deal only with fine points rather than with the broad principle. Some of these issues are nevertheless worth mentioning. For example, the Commission has ruled that questions raised in a request for information must be answered in good faith and in their proper context. In other words, a legalistic approach will not do and

---

[27] See e.g. House of Lords, Session 1983–84, *18th Report*.

[28] For an example of a request for information addressed to national authorities, see *Cast iron and steel rolls*, OJ 1983 L317/1.

[29] *NV SEP v EC Commission* [1991] ECR II-1497, at pp. 1509–1510 (para. 25).

[30] Article 11(3) and (5) of Council Regulation 17/62 of 6 February 1962 implementing art. 85 and 86 of the treaty, JO 1962 13/204. See also *Solvay v EC Commission* [1989] ECR 3355, *Orkem v EC Commission* [1989] ECR 3283, at p. 3346 (para. 9).

fines will apply if significant facts are being concealed.[31] Furthermore, in the *Telos* case, the Commission defined incorrect information as being

'any statement ... which gives a distorted picture of the true facts asked for, and which departs significantly from reality on major points. Where a statement is thus false or so incomplete that the reply taken in its entirety is likely to mislead the Commission about the true facts, it constitutes incorrect information within the meaning of Article 15(1)(b)'.[32]

Therefore, if the question is ambiguous, as sometimes happens, the answer should be drafted in clear terms to avoid any misunderstanding later.

As an important caveat, the Court of First Instance has held that the request for information should be proportionate to the purpose of the investigation.[33]

In connection with the Commission's active encouragement of private enforcement, it is to be noted that a complainant in a Commission proceeding or an intervener in a court proceeding will eventually have access to the non-confidential part of the Commission's file. Hence, the reply given to a questionnaire may be subject to discovery. Thus, a complainant or intervener can obtain documents which could later be used as evidence in a damage suit before a national court. When preparing the answer to a questionnaire it is therefore essential to mark clearly as confidential any information supplied which constitutes a business secret.

However, the Court of First Instance made it clear in the *SEP* case that an undertaking cannot refuse to transmit a confidential document on the grounds that the Commission might forward it to the authorities of the member states.[34] The national authorities are bound by the obligation to preserve professional secrecy imposed by art. 20 of Regulation 17/62 and must take all appropriate measures to ensure that confidentiality is not breached. While the authorities of the member states must have access to information provided to the Commission under art. 11, they must not use this information as evidence in the exercise of their jurisdiction to apply national and Community rules on competition.[35]

The question of whether the Commission's power to request information extends to companies located outside the EC has not yet been ruled upon. However, in the *Zoja* case, the Commission apparently sent an informal request for information to the Commercial Solvents Corporation in New York

---

[31] See e.g. *National Panasonic (Belgium)*, OJ 1982 L113/18; *National Panasonic (France)*, OJ 1982 L211/32; *Comptoir Commercial d'Importation*, OJ 1982 L27/31; *Peugeot*, OJ 1986 L295/19. For a critical assessment of the Commission's approach, see Korah, 'Misleading Replies to Requests for Information', (1982) 3 BLR 69.

[32] *Telos*, OJ 1982 L58/19.

[33] *NV SEP v EC Commission*, [1991] ECR II-1497, at p. 1518 (para. 51).

[34] *NV SEP v EC Commission*, footnote 33 above, at para. 53 et seq.

[35] *Dirección General de Defensa de la Competencia v Asociación Española de Banca Privada & Ors* [1992] ECR I-4785. See ¶1110.

¶1107

which remained unanswered.[36] Needless to say, if the information requested from a company inside the EC is embodied in documents located outside the EC – even though such documents ought normally to be kept at the company's offices in the EC – the Commission is likely to order the production of such documents by imposing a daily penalty for non-compliance on the company located in the EC. In this connection the following paragraphs from the Commission's *CSV* decision are of interest:

'The reason given by CSV for refusing to comply with the request is unacceptable. The information requested concerns the business activity of the Dutch firms belonging to CSV and of CSV itself. The information is available within the Community and the Commission is entitled to call for it. The Commission's staff may not disclose any information acquired if it is covered by the obligation of professional secrecy.

Part of the information has also been supplied to an international combine established in Switzerland. However, the fact that information has been supplied to a body governed by Swiss law does not mean that it can no longer be supplied to the Commission. Nor are the Commission and its staff released from their obligation of professional secrecy simply because the information has been supplied to the combine based in Switzerland.

Even if Swiss law could be interpreted to mean that the supply of information to the Commission amounted to unlawful disclosure, this would still not warrant delaying the performance of obligations imposed by the Commission in order to enforce the rules of competition.'[37]

If questions are raised in the form of a decision rather than by way of a simple letter, the Commission tends to indicate with greater precision why the gathering of the information is 'necessary'.[38] However, case law on this matter seems to be limited to a marginal review of whether the Commission's request for information is truly necessary.

In *Solvay*,[39] the applicant argued that the information requested by the Commission was not necessary because the Commission already had in its possession the evidence of the participation of the applicant in the infringement. The Court of Justice simply recalled that the Commission is vested by Regulation 17/62 with wide powers of verification and information. Even though the Commission already has some elements evidencing an infringement of the competition rules of the treaty, further information may be

---

[36] *Zoja/CSC–ICI*, JO 1972 L299/51.

[37] *CSV*, OJ 1976 L192/27.

[38] See e.g. *RAI/UNITEL*, OJ 1978 L157/39; *Fire Insurance*, OJ 1982 L80/36; *Deutsche Castrol Vertriebsgesellschaft*, OJ 1983 L114/26.

[39] *Solvay v EC Commission* [1989] ECR 3355; see also *Orkem v EC Commission* [1989] ECR 3283, at pp. 3347–3348 (para. 13–15).

required in order to define better the scope of the infringement, by the determination of its duration or of the circle of the undertakings concerned. The court has also specified that the Commission is empowered under art. 11 of Regulation 17/62 to request the communication of documents, even though it has already carried out on-the-spot investigations.[40]

The Court of Justice in the *Solvay* and *Orkem* cases attempted to define the limits of the Commission's powers under art. 11 of Regulation 17/62. In both cases the Commission required the companies to describe all procedures or concerted measures envisaged or decided in order to support price-initiatives, or the methods of quota-fixing between the participants in the agreement. The parties argued that this was against the principle of non self-incrimination. The court pointed out that legal persons cannot invoke a right of non self-incrimination as this principle is not common to the legal orders of all member states. However, the court ruled that certain limits should be imposed on the Commission's powers in order to preserve the undertakings' rights of defence. Since the burden of proof rests on the Commission to demonstrate the infringement, the Commission should not be permitted to ask questions, the answers to which would oblige the company to admit the existence of the infringement. In this regard, the Court of Justice decided in the *Orkem* case, that the Commission could not require details on concerted measures envisaged or adopted to support price initiatives and to allocate sales target or quotas to the participants.[41]

This principle, however, does not extend to proceedings under national civil law between private parties as long as these proceedings cannot directly or indirectly result in a sanction imposed by a public authority.[42] It does not mean either that a company is released from the obligation to communicate documents, even though these documents could serve to establish the existence of an infringement.

Admittedly, the court's position on this matter is not totally clear as the right of an undertaking not to answer certain kinds of questions would seem to amount to a recognition of the principle of non self-incrimination. Further case law specifying the exact scope of the Commission's power under art. 11 will clearly be welcomed by defence counsel.

¶1108   Discovery: sectoral inquiries

In addition to its right to obtain all the necessary information in instances of suspected infringement of the competition rules from the companies involved,

---

[40] *Solvay v EC Commission*, footnote 39 above; see also *Orkem v EC Commission*, note 39 supra, at p. 3347 (para. 14).
[41] Id., at p. 3352 (para. 38–39).
[42] *Otto BV v Postbank NV*, Case C-60/92, judgment of 10 November 1993, not yet reported.

the Commission is also authorised to conduct a general enquiry into an entire sector of the economy if circumstances suggest that competition in that sector is restricted.[43]

When undertaking a sector inquiry, the Commission may in particular request every company or association of companies active in that sector to submit all agreements and concerted practices which are not subject to the notification requirement. The Commission may also ask companies whose size suggests that they have a dominant position to supply all particulars on their structure and market conduct which are necessary for an assessment under art. 86 of the treaty.

Before starting a sectoral enquiry, the Commission must consult the Advisory Committee on Restrictive Practices and Monopolies.

The Commission has hitherto only rarely used its authority to investigate an entire sector of the economy.[44]

¶1109   Discovery: on-the-spot investigations

In a case of suspected infringement of art. 85 or 86, the Commission, pursuant to art. 14 of Regulation 17/62, may undertake all necessary investigations into companies and trade associations (including third parties). This right of inspection by Commission officials includes the right to enter any premises, land and means of transport of undertakings; examine the books and other business records and to take copies of same; and ask for oral explanations on the spot.

As in the case of requests for information, there is no sanction for refusing to submit to an investigation unless and until the Commission adopts a formal decision to that effect, which is subject to review by the Court of First Instance. However, in the case of on-the-spot investigations, the Commission is not required to seek voluntary compliance first; it may immediately adopt a decision compelling a company to submit to an investigation.[45]

Initially, companies in need of time to prepare for an investigation had a clear interest in refusing voluntary compliance because it would take the Commission many months to adopt a formal decision. Since 1980, this time factor is no longer present because the Commissioner in charge of competition matters has been delegated the power to take the decision on behalf of all his

---

[43] See art. 12 of Council Regulation 17/62 of 6 February 1962 implementing art. 85 and 86 of the treaty, JO 1962 13/204.

[44] The Commission has investigated the margarine and brewery sectors (*First Report on Competition Policy*, point 124), the oil sector (*Third Report on Competition Policy*, point 14) and the motor-vehicle sector (*XXIst Report on Competition Policy for 1991*, point 121). This last investigation was triggered by the existence of car-price differences between the different member states.

[45] *National Panasonic (UK) v EC Commission* [1980] ECR 2033.

colleagues.[46] Hence, the delay involved has become a matter of days or even hours rather than months.

Companies will not be deemed to have fully co-operated merely by granting access to their premises. Co-operation is interpreted by the Commission as an ongoing obligation which runs from the beginning to the end of the investigation. In this context, any obstacle to the officials' exercise of power, even temporary, may be considered as a refusal to submit.[47] In addition, it should also be noted that, as in the case with requests for information, voluntary compliance by a company does not entitle it to submit to the investigation less fully than if it were acting under a formal order.[48]

Since an on-the-spot investigation, especially when carried out by surprise (often referred to as a 'dawn raid'), constitutes a dramatic intrusion into privacy, it is only natural that the increasing use by the Commission of this power has given rise to difficult situations and stirred up considerable debate.[49]

Commission's memorandum
In an attempt to clarify the issues, the Commission has issued an 'explanatory memorandum', for attachment to inspectors' warrants, defining the powers of the officials and the rights of the companies concerned.[50] The memorandum consists of two explanatory notes. The first note relates to investigations carried out upon production of the authorisation in writing specified in art. 14(2) of Regulation 17/62, which does not compel the company to submit to the investigation. The second note relates to investigations carried out under a formal decision adopted in accordance with art. 14(3) of the regulation. Unfortunately, these documents are rather short and they do not go as far as the European Parliament wished, since they do not contain the internal rules of procedure and instructions to which the inspectors are subject.[51]

Nevertheless, the Commission's memorandum constitutes a step in the right direction. It confirms the company's right to have its counsel present, provided

---

[46] By an unpublished 'authorisation' of 5 November 1980. The question of the validity of this delegation of authority was raised in *AKZO v EC Commission* [1986] ECR 2585, at p. 2615 (para. 34–40). With regard to the compatibility of that system with the principle of collegiate responsibility, the Court of Justice ruled that the Commission could, within certain limits and subject to certain conditions, authorise its members to adopt certain decisions in its name without the principle of collegiate responsibility being impaired by this authorisation. Decisions adopted under a delegation of authority are adopted in the name of the Commission and may be subject to an action for annulment. However, this system of delegation of authority is limited to specific categories of measures of management or administration. Such is the case for a decision ordering an undertaking to submit to an investigation; see also *Hoechst v EC Commission* [1989] ECR 2859, at pp. 2930–2931 (para. 44–46).

[47] See *CSM-Sugar*, OJ 1992 L305/16, at p. 17.

[48] *Fédération Nationale de l'Industrie de la Chaussure de France*, OJ 1982 L319/12.

[49] See e.g. House of Lords, Session 1983–84, *18th Report*. See also Answer to Written Question No. 677/79, OJ 1979 C310/30.

[50] Explanatory note to authorisation to investigate under art. 14(2) of Regulation 17/62, *Thirteenth Report on Competition Policy*, annex.

[51] See the Resolution of the European Parliament on the *Twelfth Report on Competition Policy*, at para. 53 annexed to the *Thirteenth Report on Competition Policy* at p. 246.

¶1109

the inspection is not unduly delayed as a result.[52] The explanatory memorandum also establishes the company's right to obtain from the inspectors a signed inventory of the copies taken and a copy of the minutes, if any, drawn up regarding oral explanations given on the spot.

Subject-matter of the inquiry

Article 14(2) and (3) of Regulation 17/62 expressly provide that the officials of the Commission, when exercising their powers on the basis of an authorisation in writing or a decision, shall specify the subject-matter and purpose of the investigation. This requirement is also contained in the explanatory memorandum.

A detailed description of the subject-matter of the investigation may allow the company to identify more readily the materials and documents that are relevant to the investigation. The Commission's memorandum stresses the importance to the company of drawing the inspectors' attention to any favourable factors. Admittedly, fairness requires that the inspectors should listen to whatever exculpating factors the company subject to the investigation is able to show. Obviously, in order to produce such factors, it is necessary that the company be provided with as much information as possible. This may not always be the case. A copy of the complaint, if any, is usually given much later in

---

[52] In *Mewac*, OJ 1993 L20/6, the Commission imposed a fine on a group of shipping companies pursuant to art. 19 of Council Regulation 4056/86 laying down detailed rules for the application of art. 85 and 86 of the treaty to maritime transport. The Commission officials presented themselves at the premises of the Conference in Marseille on 28 June 1989 at 10.00 a.m. to carry out an on-the-spot investigation under art. 18(3) of Regulation 4056/86. The Secretary-General of the Conference who was in Paris at that time, considered that, in his absence and in the absence of any lawyer representing the company, the officials were not allowed to proceed with the investigation until his return on the following day at 8.30 a.m. The Commission imposed a fine for non-compliance, stating in its decision:

'Naturally the Commission's representatives are prepared to wait for a lawyer to be present before commencing an inspection, provided that the delay is reasonable and that no documents are removed from the premises or destroyed in the meantime. In the present case, there was no material reason why the Commission decision could not be implemented: had the Conference so wished, the Commission officials could have been joined either promptly by any legal representative or adviser designated by the Conference or, later in the day, by the Secretary-General himself or his Paris-based lawyer; in the latter case, the Conference could have allowed the Commission officials, with the help of the Conference staff present at the time, to begin an initial examination of documents relating to the subject-matter of the investigation, on the understanding that the Secretary-General or his representative could, as soon as they arrived, add any appropriate comments.

In the circumstances, there are no grounds for claiming that the absence of the Secretary-General from the headquarters of the Conference (four hours and 40 minutes away by train and less by plane) constituted exceptional circumstances preventing the investigation from taking place. Furthermore, in view of the difficulties experienced by the Secretary-General, the Commission officials sought to assist him by offering to allow him a reasonable period of time to return to Marseille and to delay the start of the investigation. Even if the Secretary-General had believed the circumstances to be exceptional, he could have invited the Commission officials, also by way of exception, to remain on the Conference's premises after normal business hours.'

the proceedings. Human nature being what it is, inspectors may be tempted to obtain a maximum of information from the company with a minimum of disclosure from their side. As stated by an experienced Commission inspector:

> '... it is not appropriate to expect the authorizations to provide a great deal of detail, since the Commission officials, before beginning the investigation, give the business the opportunity to request explanations on the object of the investigation.
>
> Such explanations should neither get bogged down in general discussion of the applicability of Articles 85 and 86 of the EEC Treaty to the particular case, nor should they result in the Commission officials as it were laying their cards on the table, in a way that could jeopardize the purpose of the investigation, before business decides whether or not it is prepared for the investigation.'[53]

In *Hoechst*, the Court of Justice ruled that the Commission was not obliged to disclose to the company all the information that was in its possession at the date of the investigation.[54] More specifically, the exact definition of the product and geographical market or the exact nature and duration of the infringement are not necessary conditions for the validity of the investigation.[55] However, the court recalled that the Commission is under an obligation to state clearly the alleged facts that it intends to verify.[56] The fact that the Commission must consult the national authorities prior to the investigation may help to ensure that the Commission provides a sufficiently detailed description of the subject-matter and purpose of the investigation.[57]

Such a description may also allow the company to check whether the officials exceed the scope of their investigating powers. Indeed, the officials' power is limited to the examination of the documents or business records which are related to the subject-matter of the investigation. In practice, however, this

---

[53] Kreis, 'EEC Commission Investigation Procedures in Competition Cases', (1983) 17 Int. Law 36.

[54] *Hoechst v EC Commission* [1989] ECR 2859, at pp. 2929–2930 (para. 41).

[55] See e.g. *Dow Benelux v EC Commission* [1989] ECR 3137, at p. 3153 (para. 10).

[56] *Hoechst v EC Commission* [1989] ECR 2859, at pp. 2929–2930 (para. 41); *Dow Benelux v EC Commission* [1989] ECR 3137, at p. 3152 (para. 9).

[57] In an answer to a Parliamentary Question (Answer to Question No. 677/79, OJ 1979 C310/30), the Commission had explained that the standard administrative practice followed in the consultation process 'is for the Commission officials responsible for the investigation to visit the national authority concerned, when they produce the full text of the draft decision ordering an investigation and supply any further explanation requested. The facts and findings of consultations are recorded in writing.'

However, in certain cases, the consultation process has proved to be less formal. In the *AKZO* case, the Commission only contacted the British authorities by telephone and no minute of the consultation was drawn up. The Court of Justice considered that the informality of this consultation was 'of little importance' as the Commission must be able to adopt a decision under art. 14(3) of Regulation 17/62 'without being made subject to conditions of a formal nature which would have the effect of delaying such adoption'; see *AKZO v EC Commission* [1986] ECR 2585, at p. 2612 (para. 24). It is interesting to note that, in the *Hercules* case, the Court of First Instance stated with regard to access to the file that '(t)he Commission may not depart from rules which it has ... imposed on itself'; see *Hercules v EC Commission* [1991] ECR II 1711, at p. 1799 (para. 53).

limit may be difficult to apply since it is for the Commission to determine which relevant documents must be presented for examination. The Commission's conduct during an investigation is nevertheless subject to judicial review. The company can lodge an action for annulment with the Court of First Instance against the investigation decision if it considers that the officials have exceeded their powers. The annulment of the decision would prevent the Commission from using the documents unlawfully acquired as evidence supporting an infringement.[58]

Right of entry and possible right of search

It is unfortunate that the memorandum of the Commission does not offer any practical guidance on how the investigation should actually be organised. Indeed, whereas in law the officials have a right of entry, but not a right to search, this distinction may be hard to apply in practice:

> 'Nevertheless, the fact that the Commission does not have a right to search cannot mean that the Commission officials must sit waiting in some conference room in the business to see whether any of the documents requested are going to be produced to them and, if so, which ones.
> Rather, in order to attain the purpose of the investigation, it may be necessary for the Commission officials, in accordance with their right of entry, to see for themselves whether certain records are available.'[59]

The Court of Justice has stated in a series of judgments[60] that the right of entry would be useless if Commission officials were only able to retrieve documents which they had previously identified. According to the court, the right of entry also allows officials to obtain documents whose existence was unknown to the officials prior to entry. Therefore, depending on the circumstances, it may prove to be difficult to prevent an inspector from rummaging through the files, though in principle this ought to be resisted in order to avoid the inspection exceeding its precise scope and degenerating into a fishing expedition. The executive in charge of 'welcoming' the Commission's inspection team will in most instances be hard-pressed to find a compromise solution between the inspectors' interest in keeping 'eye-contact' with the relevant filing cabinets (to avoid possible removal or destruction of pertinent documents) and the company's interest in limiting the intrusion to a minimum so that the exercise does not become too 'open-ended' and disruptive of the company's operations.

---

[58] See *CSM-Sugar*, OJ 1992 L305/16, at p. 18.
[59] Kreis, 'EEC Commission Investigation Procedures in Competition Cases', (1983) 17 Int. Law 36 at p. 44; Joshua, 'The Element of Surprise', (1983) 8 E.L. Rev. 3, at p. 11.
[60] See e.g. *Hoechst v EC Commission* [1989] ECR 2859, at p. 2926 (para. 27); *Dow Benelux v EC Commission* [1989] ECR 3137, at p. 3159 (para. 38); *Dow Ibérica v EC Commission* [1989] ECR 3165, at p. 3188 (para. 24).

However, in *Hoechst*, the Commission stated that it did have a right to search in case of a refusal to co-operate. In that case, Hoechst had refused to submit to the investigations arguing that the Commission's purpose was in fact to carry out a search in the premises. The Commission argued before the Court of Justice that a right to search was within the scope of its powers in the case of non-co-operation on the part of the undertaking. After recalling the principle whereby the right to search was not allowed in the case of co-operation, the Court of Justice stated that a different situation pertained where there was obstruction on the part of the company. The Commission is, in such a case, entitled to carry out investigations without the co-operation of the company, but it must be assisted by the national authorities who must ensure that national procedural rules of safeguard are complied with in order to respect the company's rights of defence, and that the means of investigation are not arbitrary or excessive with regard to the object of the investigation.[61] The court's judgment does not provide very much guidance as to the precise limits under which the Commission must conduct its investigations. For the sake of legal certainty, it is hoped that more specific guidelines will be laid down in future cases.

Duty to assist
Furthermore, it is to be noted that the company must do more than passively undergo the inspection. In the *Italian glass* case, the Commission made it clear that the company is under a positive duty to assist the inspectors in their quest for certain documents:

> 'The argument that Fabbrica Pisana has satisfactorily fulfilled its obligations by generally putting all its files at the investigator's disposal must be rejected, since the obligation on undertakings to supply all documents required by Commission inspectors must be understood to mean not merely giving access to all files but actually producing the specific documents required.
>
> Nor can the argument that the Commission's inspectors did not examine the business records of the administration department be accepted, as none of the undertaking's representatives has told them that the documents requested were, or might be, kept in that department and where there was

---

[61] *Hoechst v EC Commission* [1989] ECR 2859, at p. 2928 (para. 34–35). Participation of the authorities of member states is also envisaged under the provisions of art. 13 of Regulation 17/62 which empowers the Commission to request on-the-spot investigations to be carried out on its behalf by the national authorities of the member states. Article 13 raises a particular point of interest at a time when the Commission seems prepared to use this provision more often than in the past. Recourse to art. 13 leaves open the question as to whether national officials must carry out the investigation in conformity with their respective national laws. In this last hypothesis, the powers of the national officials would vary depending on the legislation of the member state in which the investigation is being carried out. This may even give rise to the national officials having wider powers than those of Commission officials, e.g., if under their national laws, they are allowed to carry out a search in the company's premises.

otherwise no reason to suppose that documents of that nature might be found there.'[62]

The absence of a 'right to search' on the part of inspectors, therefore, is in any event compensated by a 'duty to find' imposed on the company concerned.

Oral explanations

Another problem area on which the memorandum is regretfully silent concerns the inspector's right to ask for 'oral explanations on the spot'. It is generally accepted that the inspectors have no right to 'interrogate' company officers or employees and that the questions they are entitled to ask must, one way or another, be related to the books and records that are being examined. Again, however, it may be difficult in practice to draw the line between a question properly arising from an examination of the books and records and a question that lends itself better to a written request for information.[63]

Although the Court of Justice ruled on self-incrimination only in relation to art. 11 of Regulation 17/62, the same principle would seem a fortiori applicable to on-the-spot oral explanations which could lead to self-incrimination on the part of the undertaking.

The question of 'who' within the company should provide the oral explanation is likewise not dealt with in the Commission's memorandum. While legal arguments can be found in favour of restricting the supply of oral explanations to persons who are duly authorised to represent the company, there may be situations where the inspector will want to hear the information 'from the horse's mouth':

'It would thus appear eminently reasonable for the Commission officials to ask the author of the document or anyone else who can provide an explanation. Indeed, refusal to let the inspectors see the persons who can most easily provide explanations could in an extreme case so obstruct the investigation as to amount to a refusal to submit.'[64]

So again, this is an area where in the heat of the debate conflicting views may well emerge.

---

[62] *Fabbrica Pisana*, OJ 1980 L73/30.

[63] In *National Panasonic (UK) v EC Commission* [1980] ECR 2033, at p. 2056 (para. 15), the Court of Justice, obiter, stated that the inspectors may ask questions 'arising from the books and business records which they examine'. According to an authoritative scholar this would mean that the Commission is entitled 'to ask questions about the conduct under investigation as opposed to simply the books or their contents, provided such questions arise from the examination of such books' (Kerse, *EEC Antitrust Procedure*, (1988), at p. 105). Admittedly, this is still a grey area.

[64] Joshua, 'The element of surprise', (1983) 8 E.L. Rev. 3, at p. 12.

Legal privilege

A further point to note in connection with the Commission's powers of discovery in on-the-spot investigations is the Commission's stand on the thorny issue of legal privilege. The Commission, when interpreting the *AM & S* case[65] in its *Twelfth Report on Competition Policy*, made the following comments:

'The inspectors may no longer have access to written communications between an independent lawyer entitled to practise his profession in one of the Member States and an undertaking for the purposes and in the interests of the latter's right of defence, i.e., all written communications exchanged after the initiation of administrative enquiries and all earlier written communications which have a relationship to the subject matter of those enquiries. The Commission is, however, entitled to inspect all other pages.'[66]

In *Hilti*,[67] the Court of First Instance specified the scope of the protection granted by legal privilege. The company concerned had claimed privilege in respect of legal advice given by an outside lawyer and reported in internal memoranda distributed among managerial staff. The court made it clear that 'the principle of the protection of written communications between lawyer and client may not be frustrated on the sole ground that the content of those communications and of that legal advice was reported in documents internal to the undertaking.'[68] Therefore, it seems that any internal documents reporting the content of advice from outside counsel and protected by legal privilege can also benefit from the same protection. However, it is clear that legal advice given by in-house counsel cannot qualify for any legal privilege.[69]

The position, as stated by the Court of Justice in the *AM & S* case, later evolved in that the Commission is prepared to extend legal privilege to independent lawyers from outside the Community by way of bilateral agreements on the basis of reciprocity:

'In the interest of international equity and to avoid any deterioration of relations between the Community and countries in which the same professional ethics are respected, the Commission believes that it may be useful for the Community to conclude bilateral international agreements with interested third countries, on the basis of reciprocity, with the aim of extending legal privilege to the lawyers of these countries. These agreements would be an addition to the existing Community rules in this domain and would therefore not require an amendment of Regulation 17.'[70]

---

[65] *AM & S v EC Commission* [1982] ECR 1575.
[66] *Twelfth Report on Competition Policy*, point 33.
[67] *Hilti v EC Commission*, Order of the Court of First Instance [1990] ECR II-163.
[68] Id. at II-170 (para. 18).
[69] In *John Deere*, OJ 1985 L35/58, at p. 61, and in *Bayo-n-ox*, OJ 1990 L21/71 at p. 78, the Commission relied on memoranda of in-house counsel to establish the intentional nature of the infringement.
[70] *Thirteenth Report on Competition Policy*, point 78. For a comprehensive article on the various considerations that influenced the Commission in reaching the position it did, see Kroin, 'The AM & S Judgment

Preparation

Since an on-the-spot investigation may be carried out by surprise, it is important to be prepared at all times for such an event. More and more companies have prepared internal guidelines to that effect.

Company guidelines for an investigation should at least achieve the following.

(1) Explain in layman's terms the basic rules governing investigations. For clarity's sake, it might, for instance, prove useful to reproduce a sample of a Commission authorisation and decision in order to make it easier for the person concerned to ascertain which type of investigation is being carried out.

(2) Lay down responsibilities for the supervision of the investigation. The following questions should be addressed:

(a) Who, in each location of the company, will be responsible for supervising investigations? If inspectors show up, do the reception personnel know to whom the matter should be referred?

(b) Have adequate arrangements been worked out with in-house or outside lawyers to ensure their prompt arrival in the event of an investigation?

(c) Will the company voluntarily submit to the investigation or will it require the issuance of a formal decision? What criteria are most relevant in connection with this question?

(d) Are the competent employees and executives familiar with the company's rights and obligations in case of investigation?

(3) Give common-sense advice as to how to handle most effectively the investigation, such as:

(a) a record should be taken of all the documents seen by inspectors;

(b) two copies (one for the inspectors, one for the company) should be made of each document requested by the inspectors;

(c) notes should be taken of the discussions held in the course of the investigation;

(d) a post mortem of the investigation should be held to determine

---

of the European Court of Justice and its Consequences within and outside the Community', (1984) 20 Swiss Rev., Int. Comp. L. 3. As to the impact on in-house counsel, see Burkard, 'Attorney-Client Privilege in the EEC: The Perspective of Multinational Corporate Counsel', (1986) 20 Int. Law 677.

On 9 October 1984, the Commission submitted a recommendation for a Council decision, authorising the Commission to open negotiations with a view to the conclusion of agreements between the European Economic Community and certain third countries concerning the protection of legal papers in connection with the application of the rules of competition, COM(84) 548 final. However, it should be noted that so far the Council has not acted upon the negotiating mandate proposed by the Commission.

¶1109

whether additional information or documents should be supplied to the inspectors, etc.

The preparation of guidelines on how to handle an investigation should not only cover the immediate aspects inherent in any investigation but should also address the more fundamental question of the company's normal 'document retention' policy. It is, indeed, of no use and physically impossible to keep documents forever. Furthermore, the actual organisation of the filing system deserves attention: what is kept, where and by whom? Ideally, for instance, files should be kept by subject-matter rather than simply on a chronological basis since otherwise it may prove to be difficult to stay within the precise scope of the investigation. By the same token, legal opinions, confidential and other sensitive information are better being kept at one location rather than being spread over numerous establishments of the company.

¶1110   Discovery: professional secrecy

Information received by the Commission pursuant to a request for information, a sector enquiry or an on-the-spot investigation may only be used 'for the purpose of the relevant request or investigation'.[71] The Court of Justice explained this point further in the *Dow Benelux* case.[72] Dow Benelux argued that the on-the-spot investigation carried out by the Commission at its premises was ill-founded because it was based on information acquired during a previous investigation, which had been carried out at the premises of another company for a different purpose. The court stated that it would have been illegal for the Commission officials to use such information as evidence against Dow Benelux, as it was clearly the use of information for purposes other than those for which it had been gathered. However, the court added that the Commission is not prevented from relying on information obtained during earlier investigations to initiate a new inquiry.

The obligation to use information only for the purpose for which it has been gathered must also be respected by the authorities of the member states. The Court of Justice confirmed this principle in *Tribunal de Defensa de la Competencia* where it stated that, in applying national and Community rules on competition, authorities of the member states may not use as evidence unpublished information obtained by the Commission in replies to requests made under art. 11 of Regulation 17/62, or pursuant to applications and notifications made under art. 2, 4 and 5 of the regulation.[73]

---

[71] Regulation 17/62, art. 20(1).
[72] *Dow Benelux v EC Commission* [1989] ECR 3137.
[73] *Dirección General de Defensa de la Competencia v Asociación Española de Banca Privada & Ors* [1992] ECR I-4785, at p. 4837 (para. 55). Although the Court of Justice did not have to rule on this particular point, the same principle should apply to information gathered in the framework of an on the spot investigation.

In this case, the Spanish competition authorities initiated proceedings against several Spanish banks for an alleged infringement of Spanish competition law. The initiation was based on information received by the Commission in the framework of a notification and forwarded to the Spanish authorities in application of art. 10 of Regulation 17/62. The court held that the Spanish authorities could not use this information as proof in the framework of any national legal proceedings initiated for infringement of national or Community competition law, as the information had not been collected for this purpose. Such information could only constitute a basis for the national authorities to open an investigation in the framework of which they could gather their own evidence.[74]

Furthermore, the officials of the Commission as well as those of the relevant authorities of the member states, may not disclose information received in application of Regulation 17/62 when such information is 'of the kind covered by the obligation of professional secrecy'.[75]

¶1111   Discovery: access to the file

Except for certain documents regarded by the Commission as 'confidential' and hence not accessible (documents containing other companies' business secrets; internal Commission documents such as notes, drafts or other working papers; any information disclosed to the Commission subject to an obligation of confidentiality), companies 'involved in a procedure' are now entitled to inspect the file on their case.[76]

A defendant's right of access to the file is the single most important procedural innovation introduced by the Commission.[77] In introducing this

---

[74] Id., at pp. 4833–4834 (para. 42–43).

[75] Regulation 17, art. 20(2). In *Van Landewyck v EC Commission* [1980] ECR 3125, at p. 3239 (para. 46), the Court of Justice, after balancing a complainant's right to be heard with the duty of the Commission to respect the confidentiality requirement, stated as follows: '... Article 19(2) gives [the complainant] a right to be heard and not a right to receive confidential information'. In the event a dispute arises on the question of whether a document is confidential or not, the Court of First Instance, which is now competent to rule on litigation between undertakings and the Commission, should have the last word. This principle of judicial review on confidentiality was established in *AKZO v EC Commission* [1986] ECR 2585.

In *Adams v EC Commission* [1985] ECR 3539, the Court of Justice ordered the Commission to pay damages in accordance with art. 215 of the treaty because of a negligent breach of the obligation of professional secrecy which enabled Hoffmann-La Roche to identify Mr Adams as the supplier of incriminating evidence. In the wake of this judgment the Commission has revised its internal security procedures; see *Fifteenth Report on Competition Policy*, point 51.

[76] *Twelfth Report on Competition Policy*, point 34. See also *XXth Report on Competition Policy*, point 89. As to the right of access to the file by complainants, see *Thirteenth Report on Competition Policy*, point 74b, where it is stated that:

'Although complainants do not automatically have a right to see the file during the course of the examination of the complaint by the Commission, the Commission in practice ensures that a complainant receives the replies and observations regarding the complaint, sometimes in summary form, submitted by the undertaking(s) against which the complaint was lodged.'

[77] See e.g. *Zinc Producer Group*, OJ 1984 L220/27, at p. 37, one of the first cases where the Commission granted access to the entire file with the exception of internal and confidential documents.

practice, the Commission went beyond the requirements imposed by existing case law, which obliged the Commission to disclose only the documents on which it chose to rely.[78] As a result of this case law, a number of documents in the Commission's file which might have been favourable to the defendant's position remained inaccessible.

Although the right of access to the files is a major breakthrough in the field of due process, it is capable of further improvement, especially with regard to the timing. The Commission is only prepared to grant access as of the moment that the statement of objections against the defendant is issued.[79] In a number of instances this may be too late. Since years often elapse between the Commission's fact finding and the release of the statement of objections in a particular case, it may become increasingly difficult to verify or refute certain assertions of facts. In addition, the danger exists that in the meantime more Commission officials will have built their conviction on elements which the inspector perhaps has misunderstood but which the defendant has been unable to 'nip in the bud'.

Confidentiality

As stated above, the documents that the Commission considers confidential are not accessible. In this connection, for example, it is interesting to note that the

---

[78] In *SA Hercules Chemicals v EC Commission* [1991] ECR II-1711, at pp. 1739–1740 (para. 53–54), the Court of First Instance stated that

'... in establishing a procedure for providing access to the file in competition cases, the Commission imposed on itself rules exceeding the requirements laid down by the Court of Justice.... The Commission may not depart from rules which it has thus imposed on itself.... It follows that the Commission has an obligation to make available to the undertakings involved in Article 85(1) proceedings all documents, whether in their favour or otherwise, which it has obtained during the course of the investigation...'.

See also on this point *SA Cimenteries CBR & Ors v EC Commission* [1992] ECR II-2667, at p. 2683 (para. 40–41).

On the requirements imposed by case law see, e.g. *Consten and Grundig v EC Commission* [1966] ECR 299, at p. 338; *ACF Chemiefarma v EC Commission* [1970] ECR 661, at p. 686; *Chiquita*, OJ 1976 L95/1; on appeal: *United Brands v EC Commission* [1978] ECR 207. See also *VBVB and VBBB v EC Commission* [1984] ECR 19, at p. 59 (para. 23–25). See also *Hoffmann-La Roche v EC Commission* ('*Vitamins*') [1979] ECR 462, at p. 512 (para. 14), where the Court of Justice ruled on the one hand that the non-disclosure by the Commission to the defendant of certain documents relied upon in the administrative proceeding constitutes a violation of the rights of the defence if these non-disclosures affect the defendant's right to be heard on the facts stated therein, or on the conclusions drawn by the Commission therefrom, but, on the other hand, accepted the principle that the Commission had cured the defect by submitting the documents before the court on appeal. The latter part of the court's ruling is surprising. It could be interpreted to mean that even if the Commission's decision does violate 'an essential procedural requirement' under art. 173 of the treaty, the Commission may be given a 'second chance', so to speak, to remedy the defect in its administrative proceeding in the course of the subsequent judicial proceeding.

Likewise, in the aforementioned *Hercules* case, at p. 1740 (para. 56), the applicant, in the course of the judicial procedure, had access to certain documents, i.e. the other producers' replies to the statements of objections, which the Commission had previously refused to disclose in the framework of the administrative procedure. The Court of First Instance did not deem it necessary to examine whether this refusal constituted a violation of the rights of the defence as the the documents examined before the court did not contain any evidence in favour of the applicant's position. Consequently, the court stated that, even in the absence of a refusal from the Commission, the outcome of the procedure would not have been any different.

[79] *Thirteenth Report on Competition Policy*, point 74b; *Fourteenth Report on Competition Policy*, point 1(vii).

Commission in its *Thirteenth Report on Competition Policy* agreed to release the purely factual reports drawn up by the inspectors after an on-the-spot investigation but not their 'final assessment report'.[80]

The Court of Justice judgments in *AKZO v EC Commission* and *BAT & Reynolds v EC Commission* have incited the Commission 'to take particular care in handling confidential information'.[81] According to the *Eighteenth Report on Competition Policy*, confidentiality will be afforded to any document, the disclosure of which might have a 'significant adverse effect' upon the supplier of the information.[82] In particular, confidential (sensitive) information given by third parties will in principle not be made accessible to parties involved in the proceedings.[83]

When several competing firms are involved in proceedings, access to the file may not lead to an exchange of confidential information between them. It is the task of the Commission to ensure that this rule is complied with, even if the undertakings agree to waive reciprocally the confidentiality of this information.[84]

The confidential nature of the documents should not preclude their disclosure where the Commission relies upon the information in question as necessary evidence of an alleged infringement of the EC competition rules.[85]

In the event of a dispute arising on the question of whether or not a document is confidential, it is for the Commission to decide the issue but it must allow the party concerned the possibility to file an appeal to the Court of First Instance against its decision which may only be implemented after, and in accordance with, the court's verdict.[86]

---

[80] *Thirteenth Report on Competition Policy*, point 74b. It is also interesting to note that, in *SA Cimenteries CBR v EC Commission*, see footnote 78 above, at p. 2680 (para. 30), the Commission interpreted confidentiality as covering documents obtained by the Commission in the framework of its investigatory powers and not used against the companies. The Court of First Instance did not have the opportunity to rule on this issue as the companies' applications were declared inadmissible; see footnote 95 below.

[81] *AKZO v EC Commission* [1986] ECR 2585; *BAT & Reynolds v EC Commission* [1987] ECR 4487; *Eighteenth Report on Competition Policy*, point 43.

[82] *Eighteenth Report on Competition Policy*, point 43.

[83] Ibid.

[84] Ibid. In the *Hercules* case, the Commission denied the applicant access to the replies to the statement of objections supplied by the other companies involved in the same proceedings. On the position of the Court of First Instance, see footnote 78 above.

[85] *Eighteenth Report on Competition Policy*, point 43.

[86] *AKZO v EC Commission* [1986] ECR 2585. It is interesting to note that the European Parliament had suggested that the hearing officer be entrusted with a role of mediation in the case of a dispute related to the confidentiality requirement but that the Commission had rejected such suggestion:

'It is thus too early to respond to some of the suggestions made by the Parliament in this regard, but the following clarifications can already be made now: in connection with access to files, it would seem inappropriate for the Hearing Officer to act as an arbiter in disputes regarding the confidentiality of documents when access to the file is given before the oral hearing takes place. If parties feel they have not been able to adequately prepare their response to the statement of objections because certain documents in the file were erroneously held to be of a confidential nature and thus not accessible, they can bring this matter up before the Hearing Officer during the oral phase of the procedure, who at that point can deal with the problem in the light of his mandate. Finally, it should be remembered that where an undertaking makes a request to consult a document which is not

¶1112   Initiation of procedure

When the facts resulting from the investigation so warrant, the Commission will formally open proceedings. The decision to commence proceedings rests with the Commissioner in charge of competition matters.[87]

The main significance of the initiation of procedure formality is that, as of that moment, the national antitrust authorities lose their concurrent jurisdiction in favour of the Commission.[88] In addition, the initiation of a procedure is an act which causes the time to stop running under the 'statute of limitation'.[89]

A decision to open a proceeding is not a decision against which an appeal can be filed with the Court of First Instance under art. 173 of the treaty because it is only the start and not the culmination of a procedure.[90]

¶1113   Statement of objections

After the opening of a proceeding, the Commission must notify the defendant of its objections against the agreement or practice in question.[91] This document in which the Commission's charges are set out, is called the statement of objections. It discusses the facts and legal reasoning on the basis of which the Commission reaches the provisional conclusion that there is an infringement of art. 85 and/or art. 86 of the treaty and will make it clear whether the Commission considers imposing a fine.

The statement of objections sets the parameters of the case. Any decision adopted by the Commission at the end of the proceeding may only deal with the charges raised in the statement of objections on which the parties have had the opportunity of being heard.[92] Thus, any subsequent changes to the charges

accessible, the Commission may make a non-confidential summary available.' (*Fourteenth Report on Competition Policy*, point 1(vii)).

[87] A collegiate decision was previously required to commence proceedings in the absence of a complaint. The power of opening a proceeding has in the meantime been delegated to the Commissioner in charge of competition matters, irrespective of there being a complaint or not. See Kerse, *EEC Antitrust Procedure*, (1988) at p. 188.

[88] Regulation 17/62, art. 9(3).

[89] See ¶1120.

[90] *IBM v EC Commission* [1981] ECR 2639.

[91] The authority to determine the contents of the statement of objections belongs to the Commissioner in charge of competition matters. In practice, however, the statement of objections is usually signed by the Director-General. The validity of such delegation of signature, as opposed to a delegation of authority, has been accepted by the Court of Justice in *ICI v EC Commission* [1972] ECR 619; see also *Cementhandelaren v EC Commission* [1972] ECR 977; and *VBVB and VBBB v EC Commission* [1984] ECR 19, at pp. 56–57 (para. 13–14).

[92] Regulation 99/63, art. 4. See *Åhlström & Ors v EC Commission* ('*Wood Pulp*') [1993] 1 CEC 466, where an article of the Commission's decision was annulled for failure to comply with this rule. As a consequence, only the documents mentioned in the statement of objections may be treated as admissible evidence against a company. In *ICI v EC Commission* [1992] ECR II-1021, at p. 1044 (para. 34–35), the Court of First Instance stated that 'if ... documents [are] not mentioned in the statement of objections, the undertaking concerned [is] entitled to take the view that they [are] of no importance for the purposes of the case .... As far as the documents which are appended to the statement of objections but which are not mentioned in the Decision are concerned, they may be used in the Decision as against the applicant only if the applicant could reasonably deduce from the statements of objections the conclusions which the Commission intended to draw from them.'

brought in the initial statement of objections would require the Commission to issue a supplementary statement of objections.[93] The defendant should then again have the opportunity to reply in writing and orally to the objections as amended.

On the question of how much detail should be provided in the statement of objections, the Court of Justice has ruled that the defendant need only be informed of 'the essential elements of fact on which the objections are based'.[94]

In proceedings involving more than one defendant, the Commission may send the same statement of objections to all of them as long as the individual charges and the evidence on which they are based are set out clearly.[95]

As a practical matter, defendants usually receive the statement of objections, duly signed by the Director-General of DG IV, together with a cover letter from the latter, in which mention is made of the fact that a proceeding has been initiated and of the time-limit within which the reply, if any, must be filed and a hearing applied for.

If a defendant is located outside the Community, service may validly take place either by sending the statement of objections to an establishment in the Community,[96] or by sending it by mail directly to the foreign defendant outside the EC.[97]

¶1114   Hearing

The right to be heard may be exercised both in writing and orally.

A defendant who has been served with a statement of objections must be given the opportunity to reply in writing on 'the matters to which the

---

[93] In *Åhlström & Ors v EC Commission* ('*Wood Pulp*'), footnote 92 above, at para. 40–54, the Court of Justice annulled an article of the Commission's decision because the Commission relied on documents collected after the statement of objections concerning which the parties had no right to defend themselves.

[94] See e.g. *ICI v EC Commission* [1972] ECR 619, at pp. 650–651, where the Court of Justice confirmed the views on this issue as laid down in *Consten and Grundig v EC Commission* [1966] ECR 299, at p. 338, and in *ACF Chemiefarma v EC Commission* [1970] ECR 661; *Europemballage and Continental Can v EC Commission* [1973] ECR 215, at p. 240 (para. 4–6); *Musique Diffusion Française v EC Commission* [1983] ECR 1825, at pp. 1881–1882 (para. 14). In other words, it is not necessary for the Commission to include in the statement of objections facts that exonerate the alleged offender. However, in such a case the Commission would run the risk that its decision might be quashed for incorrect assessment of the evidence. See *AEG-Telefunken v EC Commission* [1983] ECR 3151.

[95] *Suiker Unie & Ors v EC Commission* [1975] ECR 1663, at pp. 1989–1990 (para. 423–428). Several companies involved in a procedure opened by the Commission to investigate an alleged cartel in the cement market filed an action for the annulment of a decision taken by the Commission whereby it refused to communicate to them the entire contents of the statement of objections. The Commission informed each company of the allegations concerning their respective national markets, but refused to communicate the chapters relating to the infringements that allegedly occurred in other member states and the corresponding documents of the file on the grounds that those chapters did not 'in any way' concern them. The Court of First Instance dismissed the application as it was filed at a preparatory stage and not against the final decision of the Commission. See *SA Cimenteries and others v EC Commission* [1992] ECR II-2667.

[96] *Europemballage and Continental Can Corp v EC Commission* [1973] ECR 215, at p. 241 (para. 9–10).

[97] *Geigy v EC Commission* [1972] ECR 787, at pp. 823–824 (para. 10–11).

Commission has taken objection',[98] and thus set out 'all matters relevant to their defence'.[99]

The Commission, when it fixes the time-limit within which the defendant must file his comments, must have regard to the time required for the preparation of such comments and the urgency of the matter.[100]

The addressees of a statement of objections may, in their written reply, apply to be heard orally.

Parties invited

Hearings are not public.[101] Only the following persons may attend the oral hearing.

(1) Addressees of a statement of objections. Their request to be heard orally may not be refused if they show a 'sufficient interest' or if the Commission intends to impose fines;[102]

(2) Third parties, i.e. persons other than the addressees of the statement of objections. Their application to be heard must be granted, provided they show a 'sufficient interest'.[103] The Court of Justice has attributed a wide discretion to the Commission in the interpretation of the 'sufficient interest' criterion;[104]

(3) Third parties whose presence at the hearing is considered necessary by the Commission or by the competent authorities of the member states;[105]

(4) The representatives of the Commission and of the competent authorities of the member states;[106]

(5) The representative of an interested non-EC government as an observer, provided the companies concerned do not object to the invitation.[107]

---

[98] Regulation 17/62, art. 19(1).

[99] Regulation 99/63, art. 3(2).

[100] Id., art. 11(1). In *Suiker Unie & Ors v EC Commission* [1975] ECR 1663 at pp. 1927–1928 (para. 94–99), the Court of Justice held that a two-month time limit was reasonable. In *Commercial Solvents v EC Commission* [1974] ECR 223, at p. 274, the advocate general found 15 days to be 'patently unreasonable' and 'oppressive'.

[101] Regulation 99/63, art. 9(3). This article further provides for the possibility of hearing persons 'separately' if business secrets are involved.

[102] Id., art. 7(1) which implements art. 19(1) of Regulation 17/62.

[103] Regulation 17/62, art. 19(2). In *ANCIDES v EC Commission* [1987] ECR 3131, at pp. 3153–3154 (para. 5–10), the Court of Justice rejected the argument that ANCIDES had been deprived of the right to a fair hearing. Third parties which have a sufficient legal interest to be heard, can only require a hearing if they apply to be heard. Since ANCIDES had not requested a hearing, the court held that the Commission had not infringed the provisions in question. The court also held that ANCIDES had already had the opportunity to put forward its views when it replied to the notice published in the *Official Journal* pursuant to art. 19(3) of Regulation 17/62. See also *BAT & Reynolds v EC Commission* [1987] ECR 4487, at pp. 4572–4573 (para. 19–20). The Commission in its *Seventeenth Report on Competition Policy*, point 111, concluded that this judgment 'makes it clear that complainants cannot claim the same right to a hearing as the defendants to the allegations'.

[104] See, e.g., *VBVB and VBBB v EC Commission* [1984] ECR 19, at pp. 57–58 (para. 17–18).

[105] Regulation 17/62, art. 19(2).

[106] Regulation 99/63, art. 8(2).

[107] This happened in the 1982 hearing of the case against IBM

Legal representation

The legal representation of parties summoned to attend is regulated as follows:

'Persons summoned to attend shall appear either in person or be represented by legal representatives or by representatives authorized by their constitution. Undertakings and associations of undertakings may moreover be represented by a duly authorized agent appointed from among their permanent staff.

Persons heard by the Commission may be assisted by lawyers or university teachers who are entitled to plead before the Court of Justice of the European Communities in accordance with Article 17 of the Protocol on the Statute of the Court, or by other qualified persons.'[108]

Two points emerge from this provision. First, it is clear that the role of lawyers is limited to assistance, not representation.[109] Secondly, it is clear that lawyers do not enjoy a monopoly to assist the persons heard by the Commission: university teachers allowed to plead[110] and 'other qualified persons' may likewise assist the person who is being heard.

Even though art. 9(2), cited above, leaves no doubt that if the person heard is assisted by a lawyer, it must be a lawyer 'entitled to plead before the Court of Justice', i.e. a lawyer who is qualified in one of the member states,[111] the Commission has nevertheless as a practical matter allowed lawyers from third countries to attend the hearing in order to assist their client. The Commission then views such third country lawyers as 'other qualified persons'.

Hearing Officer

In view of the monolithic structure of the Commission, within which the role of prosecutor tends to prevail over the adjudicatory function, it was generally felt

---

[108] Regulation 99/63, art. 8(2).

[109] In *BASF v EC Commission* [1972] ECR 713, at p. 730 (para. 10–12), the Court of Justice stated as follows:

'10. The applicant complains that the Commission refused to allow it to be represented at the hearing of the parties concerned by its lawyer.

It is argued that if that refusal is in conformity with Article 9(2) of Regulation 99/63, then that provision is contrary to the treaty because the administration may not exercise control over the undertakings' method of choosing their representatives in a procedure which may lead to the imposition of a fine.

11. Article 9(2) of Regulation 99/63, which provides that undertakings may be represented only by a duly authorised agent appointed from among their permanent staff or by legal representatives or representatives authorised by their constitution, is justified by the fact that as a general rule those persons are the best informed as to the facts and technical or economic aspects of their undertakings' actions which may be of decisive importance in applying the rules on competition. The hearing of the parties concerned cannot serve any useful purpose if those persons do not take part.

12. The complaint as to illegality put forward by the applicant is therefore unfounded.'

[110] This is the case with law professors in Germany.

[111] See Rules of Procedure of the Court of Justice of the European Communities of 19 June 1991, OJ 1991 L176/7, art. 38(3). See Rules of Procedure of the Court of First Instance of the European Communities of 2 May 1991, OJ 1991 L136/1, art. 44(3).

¶1114

by defence counsel that hearings were not a very meaningful exercise because they had to plead their client's case in front of a chairman who had been responsible for bringing the action in the first place.[112] In order to remedy this situation the Commission in 1982 created, within its antitrust administration, a new post of 'Hearing Officer'.

The task entrusted to the Hearing Officer is to ensure that the hearing is properly conducted, that the rights of defence are respected and that in the preparation of the subsequent decision due account is taken of all the relevant facts, 'whether favourable or unfavourable to the parties concerned'.[113] Specifically, the Hearing Officer has responsibility for: (1) organising preparations for the hearing (fixing the date, duration and place as well as the issues on which the presentations ought to focus); (2) conducting the hearing (e.g. determining which new documents may be submitted, whether witnesses may be heard, etc.); and (3) submitting, after the hearing, comments to the Director-General for Competition on the continuation of the procedure (e.g. need for additional information, withdrawal of certain objections or filing of an additional statement of objections). The Hearing Officer's report is considered to be an internal document and is not required to be disclosed to the defendant for comment.[114]

In theory, the presence of the Hearing Officer should create a better atmosphere because it is not only important that justice be done but also that justice be seen to be done. Furthermore, the involvement of the Hearing Officer should in principle reduce the 'shadow boxing' aspect of Commission hearings in that the Hearing Officer will have a direct line of access to the Commission member in charge of competition matters. In practice, however, it is the authors' experience that the Commission's staff have tended to resist his playing too independent a role. This unfortunate development is confirmed by the Commission's refusal to allow the Hearing Officer to intervene in the event of a dispute arising regarding the parties' right of access to the file or in connection with 'surprise' inspection visits undertaken by Commission officials.[115] Furthermore, the fact that the Hearing Officer has no staff of his own, except for a secretary, would seem to make it physically impossible for him to study all the facts he needs to know to perform his function meaningfully at the hearing.

---

[112] See e.g. Van Bael, 'EEC Antitrust Enforcement and Adjudication as seen by Defense Counsel', (1979) 7 Swiss Rev. Int. Comp. L.1, at p. 16.

[113] Article 2 of Commission decision of 23 November 1990 on the implementation of hearings in connection with procedures for the application of art. 85 and 86 of the EEC Treaty and art. 65 and 66 of the ECSC Treaty, Annex to the *XXth Report on Competition Policy*, p. 312.

[114] *Petrofina SA v EC Commission* [1991] ECR II-1087, at p. 1113 (para. 53).

[115] The Commission rejected suggestions of the European Parliament to that effect. See *Fourteenth Report on Competition Policy*, point 1(vii). See also the resolution of the European Parliament on the *Fourteenth Report on Competition Policy*, at para. 47, Annex to the *Fifteenth Report on Competition Policy*, at p. 239, and the Commission's outright refusal in the *Fifteenth Report on Competition Policy*, point 1(iii).

The Commission made a positive evaluation of the role of the Hearing Officer in its *Eighteenth Report on Competition Policy*. It noted significant improvements in the preparation of the hearings in the more than 50 hearings that the Hearing Officer had presided over since the post was created. The fact that the Hearing Officer had pointed out gaps or errors in the presentation of facts had, according to the Commission, led to the withdrawal of certain objections in several cases. The Commission also noted, however, that the Hearing Officer had only in very few cases made use of his right to refer his observations directly to the member of the Commission responsible for competition matters.[116]

Typical hearing

The hearing usually starts by a short presentation of the case by the case-handler or 'rapporteur' of the Commission's staff. It is followed by oral argument by the defendant and possibly by comments of the complainant, if any.

Thereafter, in addition to raising questions of his own, the Hearing Officer will invite the representatives of the Commission and of the national authorities to put their questions regarding the presentations made at the hearing.

If a party at the hearing offers 'witnesses' or experts to be heard, their testimony and reports may likewise give rise to questions, though the Commission has no right to cross-examine witnesses or otherwise hear any person present at the hearing under oath.

Except for an unusually complex case, the hearing in which only one defendant is involved will not take more than one day. Hearings involving several defendants can take more than one week and will require some effort of streamlining and co-ordination to avoid repetition in the briefs of the various defendants.

Hearings currently take place in the Borschette Centre in Brussels in rooms where simultaneous translation facilities are available.

On balance, it pays to make use of the right to be heard because it is the only time that the defendant can put his case directly to the representatives of the national authorities and to the representative of the Commission's Legal Service.

Record

According to art. 9(4) of Regulation 99/63, the 'essential content' of the statements made by each person who has been heard will be recorded in minutes, subject to the person's approval.

---

[116] *Eighteenth Report on Competition Policy*, point 44.

¶1114

For many years the Commission followed the practice of making available a full transcript of the hearing based on magnetic tapes. Currently, however, the Commission is only providing a summary of what transpired at the hearing.

¶1115   Advisory Committee

The Advisory Committee on Restrictive Practices and Monopolies ('Advisory Committee') is the vehicle for the necessary liaison between the Commission and the authorities of the member states provided for in Regulation 17/62.

The Advisory Committee is composed of 'officials competent in the matter of restrictive practices and monopolies'.[117] They receive a copy of all applications for negative clearance and notifications for exemption as well as copies of complaints and of the most important documents filed with the Commission.[118] Where the case falls under the rules of the EEA Agreement, the Advisory Committee is attended by representatives of the EFTA Surveillance Authority and EFTA states who will have received a copy of the application or notification.

The Advisory Committee must be consulted prior to the adoption of any of the following decisions:[119]

(1) a decision establishing the existence of an infringement of art. 85 and/or 86;

(2) a decision granting negative clearance;

(3) a decision granting an exemption under art. 85(3), or concerning the renewal, amendment or revocation of same;

(4) a decision imposing a fine or periodic penalty payment.[120]

The consultation of the Advisory Committee takes place in Brussels at a meeting which must not be held earlier than 14 days after dispatch of the convocation notice. Such notice must be accompanied by 'a summary of the case together with an indication of the most important documents, and a preliminary draft decision'.[121] The meeting is typically chaired by a Director of DG IV.

As suggested by the title of the Committee, its opinion on the case is only of an advisory nature instead of being binding on the Commission.

---

[117] Regulation 17/62, art. 10(4).

[118] Id., art. 10(1).

[119] Id., art. 10(3).

[120] The Committee needs to be heard only before the final imposition of the periodic penalty payment; see *Hoechst v EC Commission* [1989] ECR 2859, at pp. 2932–2933 (para. 55–56).

[121] Regulation 17/62, art. 10(5). In this regard, the lack of a communication to the representatives of a transcript of the hearing may constitute a breach of the rights of the defence of the undertakings if the hearing raised new important points not mentioned in the statement of objections; see *Radio Telefis Eireann v EC Commission* [1991] ECR II-485, at pp. 500–502 (para. 22–25).

The Advisory Committee's opinion will be attached to the draft decision which will be put before the Commission but is not otherwise made public.[122] The fact that this essential element of the file remains secret has frequently been criticised but the Court of Justice has refused to rule that the non-disclosure of the opinion would violate the defendant's right to a fair trial.[123]

¶1116   Interim measures

Neither the EC Treaty nor the implementing Regulation 17/62 provide for any express authority for the Commission to adopt interim relief, pending the final outcome of a proceeding. The Court of Justice, however, in its *Camera Care* judgment of 1980[124] has read such authority into Regulation 17/62 by interpreting art. 3 of the regulation, i.e. the Commission's power to adopt decisions to bring infringements to an end, in the sense that it grants the Commission the implied power 'to take interim measures which are indispensable for the effective exercise of its functions ...' since otherwise the Commission's power to make final decisions might become 'ineffectual or even illusory because of the actions of certain undertakings'.[125]

The Court of Justice, when granting the Commission authority to adopt interim relief by way of a formal decision, set certain criteria for the exercise of such authority. According to the court, interim measures should only be taken 'in cases proved to be urgent in order to avoid a situation likely to cause serious and irreparable damage to the party seeking their adoption, or which is intolerable for the public interest'. In addition, the Court of Justice made it clear that the interim relief must by definition be of a temporary and conservatory nature and that the Commission must pay due regard 'to the legitimate interests of the undertaking concerned'. Furthermore, the court insisted that 'the essential safeguards guaranteed to the parties concerned' by Regulation 17/62, in particular by art. 19, be maintained.[126] Hence, the parties concerned should have the opportunity of making written and oral observations on the Commission's statement of objections. Thus, the procedure to be followed by the Commission is the same as that followed in the preparation of a final decision, except that, in view of the urgency of the matter, the Commission need only be concerned that there is a prima facie

---

[122] Id., art. 10(6). The situation is slightly different if the merger regulation applies. Article 19(7) of the merger regulation provides that 'the Advisory Committee may recommend publication of the opinion' and that 'the Commission may carry out such publication'.

[123] *Musique Diffusion Française v EC Commission* [1983] ECR 1825, at pp. 1886–1887 (para. 34–36).

[124] *Camera Care v EC Commission* [1980] ECR 119 (para. 12–21).

[125] Id., at p. 131 (para. 18).

[126] Id., at p. 131 (para. 19).

infringement and that the conditions of granting interim measures are met, without, however, prejudging the final outcome of the case.[127]

Thus far, the Commission has only adopted a decision ordering interim relief on six occasions.[128] In the *Ford* case, an appeal was filed with the Court of Justice and the interim decision was quashed on the ground that the Commission had exceeded its power by adopting relief which was outside the framework of the final decision which the Commission could take under art. 3 of Regulation 17/62.[129] In a more recent case,[130] the Commission erred too far in the opposite direction. In that case, the Court of First Instance annulled a decision whereby the Commission had refused to grant interim measures to allow the French private broadcaster 'la Cinq' to gain access to international sports events broadcast through Eurovision. The court recalled that, for the adoption of interim measures, only prima facie evidence of an infringement is required and not the establishment of a clear and obvious infringement. It also recalled that 'irreparable damage' is defined as damage which cannot be remedied by the decision taken by the Commission at the end of the administrative procedure.[131]

¶1117   Recommendations

Before adopting a decision by which an infringement is established and the companies concerned are required to bring such infringement to an end, the Commission may issue a recommendation for termination of the infringement.[132]

Unlike interim measures, a recommendation is not binding on its addressees. The Court of Justice has described the Commission's power to issue

---

[127] The criteria for the adoption of interim measures are strictly applied by the Commission. In 1992, two requests for interim measures were rejected on grounds of insufficient evidence of serious and irreparable harm suffered by the complainant (*EBU-Eurovision System*; *TESN/Football authorities*) and one such request was rejected for lack of prima facie evidence (*Phoenix/IBM*); see *XXIInd Report on Competition Policy for 1992*, points 592–594.

[128] *Ford Werke AG – interim measures*, OJ 1982 L256/20; *ECS/AKZO – interim measures*, OJ 1983 L252/13; *BBI/Boosey & Hawkes – interim measures*, OJ 1987 L286/36; *Peugeot*, press release IP(90) 233 of 27 March 1990, upheld by the Court of First Instance on appeal: *Peugeot v EC Commission* [1990] ECR II-195 and [1991] II-653; *Mars*, press release IP(92) 222 of 25 March 1992, partly suspended on appeal: *Langnese-Iglo GmbH and Schöller Lebensmittel GmbH & Co KG v EC Commission* [1992] ECR II-1839; *Sealink*, press release IP(92) 478 of 11 June 1992, on appeal: *Sealink Stena Line (Holdings) Limited v EC Commission*, OJ 1992 C290/13, not yet decided. On a number of occasions the mere initiation of interim proceedings by the Commission has induced defendants to cease or modify their practices. See e.g. *Amicon Corp/Fortia AB and Wright Scientific Ltd, Eleventh Report on Competition Policy*, point 112; *Hilti, Fifteenth Report on Competition Policy*, point 49; *Ford Motor Company Ltd*, ibid.

[129] *Ford of Europe Inc. and Ford Werke AG v EC Commission* [1984] ECR 1129.

[130] *La Cinq SA v EC Commission* [1992] ECR II-1.

[131] The Commission had interpreted this notion too strictly in so far as it argued before the court that only damage that could not be remedied by any subsequent decision, such as cessation of activities, could be considered as 'irreparable'.

[132] Regulation 17/62, art. 3(3).

recommendations as a means of informing the companies concerned '... of its assessment of the situation with regard to the Community law in order to persuade them to comply with its point of view without immediately resorting to legal enforcement'.[133]

The Commission has hardly ever made use of its power to issue recommendations.[134]

¶1118   Final decision

A final decision adopted by the Commission will order certain relief, and needs to comply with a number of formal requirements.[135]

Possible relief

When the Commission establishes the existence of an infringement of art. 85 or 86 of the treaty, 'it may by decision require the undertakings or associations of undertakings concerned to bring such infringement to an end'. If, however, the infringement has already been terminated prior to the adoption of a decision, the Commission's decision need not contain a cease-and-desist order but may be purely declaratory in nature.[136]

The Commission's power is not limited simply to requiring the parties concerned to terminate their infringement but includes the authority to order certain positive remedial action.[137] However, in *Automec II*, the Commission declared before the Court of First Instance that, in the circumstances of that case, it lacked the power to impose positive action on the parties as a means of

---

[133] *Camera Care* [1980] ECR 119, at p. 130 (para. 16).

[134] See e.g. *Convention Faience* Bull EC 5–1984.

[135] Regulation 17/62, art. 3(1).

[136] See e.g. *Pabst & Richarz/BNIA*, OJ 1976 L231/24; *ABG oil companies operating in the Netherlands*, OJ 1977 L117/1; *Video cassette recorders*, OJ 1978 L47/42; *Michelin*, OJ 1981 L353/33; *GVL*, OJ 1981 L370/49; *Windsurfing International*, OJ 1983 L229/1; *Aluminium Imports from Eastern Europe*, OJ 1985 L92/1; *Breeders' rights – roses*, OJ 1985 L369/9; *Sperry New Holland*, OJ 1985 L376/21; *Eurocheque: Helsinki Agreement*, OJ 1992 L95/50.

[137] In *Consten and Grundig v EC Commission* [1966] ECR 299, at pp. 345–346, the Court of Justice confirmed the principle that the Commission has the power to order positive relief and upheld the Commission's order requiring the defendants to abstain from measures preventing parallel imports. In *Continental Can*, JO 1972 L7/25 the Commission had ordered the defendant to submit a proposal for divestment within six months. The Commission's decision was quashed by the Court of Justice on other grounds, i.e. the inadequate definition of the product market (*Europemballage and Continental Can v EC Commission* [1973] ECR 215).

In *Commercial Solvents v EC Commission* [1974] ECR 223, at pp. 255–256 (para. 42–47), the Court of Justice held that the Commission was entitled to order the defendant to supply certain quantities of raw materials to remedy the refusal of supplies and to require it to submit proposals to prevent a repetition of the conduct complained of.

In *Soda-ash–Solvay*, OJ 1991 L152/21, at p. 37, the Commission called on Solvay 'to abandon its system of fidelity rebates and ... to notify ... the details of any new system of discounts or rebates in order to ensure its conformity with Community competition rules'. Solvay was also required to renegotiate all its supply agreements for soda-ash in the Community so as to comply with the requirements of the decision; see also *Tetra Pak II*, OJ 1992 L72/1, at p. 42.

In a number of decisions the Commission imposed an obligation on the defendant to inform interested parties about certain aspects of the defendant's compliance with the decision: *Chiquita*, OJ 1976 L95/1; *Gerofabriek*, OJ 1977 L16/8; *Fedetab*, OJ 1978 L224/29; *Johnson & Johnson*, OJ 1981 L377/16; *Hasselblad*, OJ 1982 L161/18; *VBBB/VBVB*, OJ 1982 L54/36; *ECS/AKZO*, OJ 1985 L374/1.

remedying an infringement of art. 85. In particular, it had no authority to require the parties to enter into an agreement. Such arrangement can only be imposed on the basis of the provisions of national law.[138]

Likewise, neither art. 85 nor Regulation 17/62 empowers the Commission to adopt a decision binding on member states.[139]

In addition, the Commission's decision may provide for a sanction: the imposition of fines and/or periodic penalty payments (see ¶1119).

Last but not least, mention must be made of the 'automatic nullity' provided for in art. 85(2) of the treaty, as the civil law consequence of an infringement of art. 85(1).[140]

Formal requirements

Certain procedural decisions (decisions initiating proceedings pursuant to art. 9(3) of Regulation 17/62, decisions rejecting complaints, decisions ordering the supply of certain information or the submission to an on-the-spot investigation) can be taken by the Commissioner in charge of competition matters.[141] All other decisions in application of the EC competition rules remain the responsibility of the full Commission, acting as a collegiate body.[142]

A Commission decision was struck down by the Court of First Instance for failure to comply with this rule in the *PVC* price-fixing cartel case.[143] The companies brought an action for the annulment of the decision taken by the Commission imposing fines on them, arguing that the decision had been adopted by a person who lacked the authority to do so. On the basis of the minutes of the relevant meeting of the Commissioners, the court found that the adoption of the decision in two of the languages used in the proceedings had not been made at this meeting, but had been delegated to the Commissioner who was, at that time, responsible for competition. The court specified that the delegation of authority to adopt a decision was only valid for those languages which were not used in the proceedings.[144]

---

[138] See *Automec Srl v EC Commission* (*'Automec II'*) [1992] ECR II-2223, where the Commission stated that it lacked the competence to adopt a decision ordering BMW to resume deliveries to its distributor, Automec, and to allow it to use certain of its trade marks.

[139] See *Nefarma v EC Commission* [1990] ECR II-797, at p. 817 (para. 70), where the Court of First Instance confirmed that art. 3(1) of Regulation 17/62 empowers the Commission to require undertakings to bring infringements of EC competition law to an end, but does not authorise the Commission to require a member state to adopt particular measures in its domestic law.

[140] The nullity sanction is discussed in Chapter 2.

[141] See ¶1109. The Commission may be prepared to delegate decisions under art. 15(6).

[142] In view of the heavy workload of the Commission, most of the competition decisions have in practice been adopted by the Commission without any debate but by the so-called 'written procedure', a procedure whereby the draft decision is circulated to the cabinet of each Commission member and is considered to be adopted if no objections are raised within a period of a few days. In *Buchler v EC Commission* [1970] ECR 733, at p. 754 (para. 21–23), the Court of Justice rejected the applicant's contention that the decision should be declared invalid because the members of the Commission had not received the complete file. For the court it was sufficient that they had been briefed 'regarding the essential points of the case and had access to the entire file'.

[143] *BASF AG & Ors v EC Commission* (*'PVC'*) [1992] ECR II-315.

[144] Under art. 16 of the Rules of Procedure of the Commission adopted on 17 February 1993, decisions adopted under the 'delegation procedure' are to be authenticated in the authentic language(s) by the signatures of the

Once a decision has been adopted, it must be notified to the parties concerned and it takes effect upon notification.[145]

The Commission may not make further amendments once the decision has been formally adopted and notified. In the *PVC* case, the Court of First Instance strictly applied this principle and concluded that the Commission had so seriously and manifestly violated its own rules of procedure as to render the decision non-existent.[146]

Except for procedural decisions dealing with requests for information, on-the-spot investigations, or sector inquiries, Commission decisions need to be published in the *Official Journal*. Such publication must state the names of the parties and the main content of the decision but shall duly consider the legitimate interest of the parties concerned in the protection of their business interests.[147]

The decisions of the Commission must be fully reasoned. For this basic requirement of art. 190 of the treaty to be satisfied it suffices that the decision mentions 'the principal issues of law and fact upon which it is based and which are necessary in order that the reasoning which had led the Commission to its decision may be understood'.[148] In other words, 'in non-judicial proceedings of this kind the administration is not required to give reasons for its rejection of

---

appropriate Commissioner and a designated official from the Secretariat-General.

[145] Article 191 of the treaty. In *ICI v EC Commission* [1972] ECR 619, at p. 652 (para. 39), the Court of Justice held that the notification required is 'external to the legal act'. Hence, if a notification were invalid, it would not affect the validity of the decision as such. Furthermore, the court ruled in the same case, at p. 652 (para. 42), that notification to a subsidiary within the EC, instead of to the parent company outside the EC was not improper as long as the parent had full knowledge of the text of the decision. On this question see also *Europemballage and Continental Can Corp v EC Commission* [1973] ECR 215. In *Bayer v EC Commission* [1991] ECR II-219, the Court of First Instance held that the dispatch of a letter with a postal notice of delivery constitutes valid notification. Consequently, the time-limit for bringing an action for annulment starts running from the date of the notice of delivery. In this context, an acknowledgment of receipt attached to the decision only constitutes an alternative means for the Commission to ascertain the company has received the decision.

[146] *BASF AG & Ors v EC Commission* ('*PVC*') [1992] ECR II-315. In this case, the Court of First Instance found certain inconsistencies between the texts of the decisions submitted at the meeting of the Commissioners and the text of the decisions notified to the parties. In addition, an extra paragraph had been added in several versions and the identity of one of the defendants was stated differently in the text notified to the parties. This judgment is particularly striking in so far as the ruling provoked intense speculation that older cases in which the Commission had adopted the same decision-making process could be reopened on the ground that the decision never existed. However, the Court of First Instance, less than one month later, dismissed certain companies' attempt to challenge on these grounds a decision whereby the Commission had fined them for a price-fixing cartel in the polypropylene sector. The court's reasoning was that the applicants had failed to invoke the non-existence of the decision when they lodged their first request for the annulment of the fines. See *ICI v EC Commission* [1992] ECR II-1021, at p. 1153 (para. 399–401). On appeal from the *PVC* ruling (*EC Commission v BASF AG & Ors* [1994] 2 CEC 152) the Court of Justice held that the procedural irregularities found by the Court of First Instance were not so grave that the Commission's decision had to be treated as legally non-existent. The failure of the Commission to observe its own rules of procedure did, however, amount to an infringement of an essential procedural requirement that was sufficiently serious to warrant annulling the decision. The Court of Justice did acknowledge that, in extreme and exceptional circumstances, acts could be tainted by an irregularity so grave that they had to be treated as non-existent.

[147] Regulation 17/62, art. 21. Premature publicity regarding a case, i.e. information released prior to the adoption of the decision, though held to be regrettable, does not affect the validity of the eventual decision. See *United Brands v EC Commission* [1978] ECR 207, at pp. 305–306 (para. 280–288).

[148] *ACF Chemiefarma v EC Commission* [1970] ECR 661, at p. 690 (para. 78). See also *Michelin v EC Commission* [1983] ECR 3461, at pp. 3499–3500 (para. 11–16).

the parties' submissions'.[149] According to case law, art. 190 of the treaty does not oblige the Commission to discuss all the matters of fact and of law which may have been dealt with in the administrative proceedings.[150]

¶1119   Fines and periodic penalty payments

In addition to the Commission's power to issue cease-and-desist orders and its authority to provide for other suitable relief, the breach of EC competition rules may also be penalised by the imposition of fines and periodic penalty payments.

Fines

Regulation 17/62 distinguishes between two kinds of fines: those imposed in connection with the notification procedure and with the Commission's powers of discovery, and those imposed either as a sanction for the violation of art. 85(1) and 86 or for non-compliance with an obligation provided for as a condition for an exemption granted pursuant to art. 85(3).

(1)   *Fines for procedural infringements*

The supply of incorrect or misleading information in an application for negative clearance or in a notification filed to obtain an exemption may be penalised by a decision imposing a fine ranging between a minimum of ECU 100 and a maximum of ECU 5,000.[151]

The supply of incorrect information in response to a request for information or a sector enquiry is similarly liable to a fine ranging between ECU 100 and ECU 5,000.[152] The same is true if the information is supplied after expiry of the time-limit set in the decisions requesting the information.

The refusal to submit to an on-the-spot investigation ordered by the decision or the incomplete submission of books or business records in the course of an

---

[149] *Consten and Grundig v EC Commission* [1966] ECR 299, at p. 338. See also *IAZ v EC Commission* [1983] ECR 3369, at pp. 3407–3408 (para. 9–11); *GVL v EC Commission* [1983] ECR 483, at p. 500 (para. 12); *Michelin v EC Commission* [1983] ECR 3461, at pp. 3499–3500 (para. 11–16); *Hasselblad v EC Commission* [1984] ECR 883, at p. 901 (para. 17–18); *VBVB and VBBB v EC Commission* [1984] ECR 19, at pp. 58–59 (para. 21–22).

[150] See e.g. *VBVB and VBBB v EC Commission* [1984] ECR 19, at pp. 58–59 (para. 21–22); *BAT & Reynolds v EC Commission* [1987] ECR 4487, at pp. 4585–4586 (para. 72–73); *Belasco v EC Commission* [1989] ECR 2117, at p. 2194 (para. 54–56). In *Petrofina SA v EC Commission* [1991] ECR II-1087, at pp. 1108–1109 (para. 39), the Court of First Instance specified that the Commission must set out the evidence upon which its decision is based, but need not provide an exhaustive list of all the evidence available, a blanket reference thereto being sufficient.

[151] Regulation 17/62, art. 15(1)(a). See, e.g. *Theal/Watts*, OJ 1977 L39/19. Article 19 of Regulation 4056/86 (maritime transport) and art. 12 of Regulation 3975/87 (air transport) enable the Commission to impose the same fines. The merger regulation, on the other hand, enables the Commission to impose substantially higher fines (art. 14 of Regulation 4064/89). See ¶646.

[152] Regulation 17/62, art. 15(1)(b). See e.g. *Telos*, OJ 1982 L581/19, and the decisions cited under *National Panasonic (Belgium)*, OJ 1982 L113/18; *National Panasonic (France)*, OJ 1982 L211/32; *Comptoir Commercial d'Importation*, OJ 1982 L27/31. See also *Peugeot*, OJ 1986 L295/19. For a critical assessment of the Commission's approach, see Korah, 'Misleading Replies to Requests for Information', (1982) 3 BLR 69

on-the-spot investigation may also call for the imposition of a fine of minimum ECU 100 and maximum ECU 5,000.[153]

The maximum fine of ECU 5,000 being a rather low ceiling, it is understandable that the Commission has almost invariably applied the maximum sanction.

(2)   *Fines penalising substantive breaches of competition rules*

Whereas the fines that the Commission may impose to penalise procedural infringements are rather modest, the situation is considerably different with respect to fines imposed to punish a breach of art. 85(1) or 86 or a violation of a condition imposed under art. 85(3). For such substantive infringements, Regulation 17/62 provides that the Commission may, on each of the companies involved, impose fines 'from [ECU] 1,000 to 1,000,000 ..., or a sum in excess thereof but not exceeding 10 per cent of the turnover in the preceding business year ...'.[154]

In its *XXIst Report on Competition Policy*, the Commission announced its intention to make fuller use of the possibility offered by Regulation 17/62 to impose fines of up to ten per cent of the annual turnover of the companies involved in order to reinforce the deterrent effect of penalties under Community competition law.[155]

In fixing the amount of the fine, the Commission must have regard both to the duration and the gravity of the infringement.[156]

When the Commission establishes the existence of an infringement, it will, in its decision, indicate the time period during which the infringement occurred. The longer an infringement has lasted, the greater must have been its effect on the competitive situation and, hence, the higher the fine should be.[157]

In order to assess the gravity of an infringement, a number of considerations may be pertinent:

(a) knowledge of parties;[158]

---

[153] Regulation 17/62, art. 15(1)(c). See e.g. *Fédération Nationale des Industries de la Chaussure de France*, OJ 1982 L319/12; *CSM-Sugar*, OJ 1992 L305/16.

[154] Regulation 17/62, art. 15(2). See also, art. 19 of Regulation 4056/86 (maritime transport) and art. 12 of Regulation 3975/87 (air transport). The merger regulation enables the Commission to impose substantially higher fines (art. 14 of Regulation 4064/89). See ¶646.

[155] See *XXIst Report on Competition Policy for 1991*, point 139.

[156] Regulation 17/62, art. 15(2)(b).

[157] In *Musique Diffusion Française v EC Commission* [1983] ECR 1825, at pp. 1909–1910 (para. 123–124), the Court of Justice partially annulled the Commission's decision because the duration of the infringement as specified in the decision was longer than the duration which had been mentioned in the statement of objections. The court reduced the fine accordingly. In *Tetra Pak II*, OJ 1992 L72/1, at p. 40, the Commission imposed a record fine of ECU 75m, inter alia, because of the lengthy duration of the infringements which were determined to have lasted at least 15 years.

[158] The Commission will impose a higher fine if an infringement is committed intentionally rather than negligently. For a definition of the terms 'intentionally or negligently' see the opinion of Advocate General Mayras in *General Motors v EC Commission* [1975] ECR 1367, at pp. 1388–1389. See also *John Deere*, OJ 1985

(b) nature of the restrictions on competition;[159]

(c) number and size of the companies concerned, their respective market shares and market situation at the time the infringement was committed;[160]

(d) importance of the product concerned;[161]

(e) responsibility of each of the companies concerned;[162]

L35/58, at pp. 61 and 63 where the Commission referred to opinions of in-house counsel to establish the illegal intent. Especially for large companies it may be difficult, if not impossible, to avoid a finding by the Commission that an infringement was committed at least negligently. The standards of care set in the context of judicial review are, indeed, very high. For example, the Commission had condemned United Brands (*Chiquita*, OJ 1976 L95/1), and Hoffmann-La Roche (*Vitamins*, OJ 1976 L223/27) for having abused a dominant position of which they may not have been aware because they were still subject to substantial competitive restraints. The fact that the Commission had in effect re-written the concept of a dominant position to include a mere status of pre-eminence was not considered by the Court of Justice to be a sufficient ground for reducing, let alone cancelling the fine (*United Brands v EC Commission* [1978] ECR 207; *Hoffmann-La Roche v EC Commission* ('*Vitamins*') [1979] ECR 461). In *Michelin*, OJ 1981 L353/33, the Commission condemned a yearly bonus system as an abuse committed 'intentionally or at any rate negligently', even though its features did not squarely fall within the concept of a 'loyalty bonus' as defined in *Hoffmann-La Roche*. In *Tipp-Ex v EC Commission* [1990] ECR I-261, the Court of Justice fully upheld the Commission decision imposing a fine of ECU 400,000, stating that Tipp-Ex could not have failed to be aware that a system of absolute territorial protection was a restriction of competition.

[159] For example, in *Pioneer*, OJ 1980 L60/21, at p. 36 (para. 90), the Commission stated as follows:

'All the undertakings knew or ought to have known that the prevention of parallel imports is a serious breach of Article 85(1), as has been established by a series of judgments of the Court of Justice of the EEC and decisions of the Commission. By participating in these concerted practices, the undertakings involved in this case sought to obstruct in respect of the distribution of Pioneer equipment one of principal aims of the EEC Treaty, namely the creation of a single market between Member States, or their conduct had at least the effect of such obstruction.'

In the *Thirteenth Report on Competition Policy*, point 63, the Commission, when commenting on the *Pioneer* case, described as 'serious infringements', those for which fines had been imposed in the past and had been confirmed in judgments of the Court of Justice, such as 'export bans, market-partitioning and horizontal and vertical price-fixing, in the realm of restrictive agreements, and in the sphere of abuses of dominant positions, refusals to supply, price discrimination, exclusive or preferential long-term supply agreements and loyalty rebates.'

In the *ECS/AKZO decision*, OJ 1985 L374/1, at p. 25, the Commission justified the ECU 10m fine as follows:

'The infringement in the present case involved the making of direct threats to a small competitor in order to deter it from expanding into a new market and providing an important element of competition to AKZO's position of market dominance. When AKZO's threats were ignored, AKZO sought in a systematic and determined manner to implement a plan to damage the business of ECS. AKZO employed its substantial resources to subsidise over a long period of time a course of conduct designed not only to harm ECS specifically but also to serve its policy of retaining by any means its dominant market position in an important industrial sector. By taking this action to prevent or punish the expansion of a small competitor to another Member State, AKZO was flouting one of the fundamental objectives of the Treaty, namely the creation of a single market between Member States. The seriousness of the infringement is heightened by the fact that AKZO continued its abusive behaviour long after proceedings had been taken in the High Court and indeed even after the Commission had issued a Decision ordering interim measures. The Commission also considers it a further aggravating factor that AKZO had given a totally misleading version of the events to the High Court and that given the difficulties of proof it would probably have succeeded in achieving its purpose of eliminating ECS had the Commission not discovered the evidence on which this Decision is based. It is further apparent that the aggressive behaviour against ECS was not an isolated event but occurred in the context of a settled corporate policy by AKZO to use its market power to discipline or destroy unwanted competitors.'

[160] See e.g. *Boehringer v EC Commission* [1972] ECR 1281, at pp. 805–806 (para. 52–57); *Soda-ash–Solvay, CFK*, OJ 1991 L152/16, at p. 20.

[161] See e.g. *Wood Pulp*, OJ 1985 L85/1, at p. 25.

[162] For examples of the Commission's assessment of the role played by each of the defendants, see *BMW Belgium*, OJ 1978 L46/33; *Pioneer*, OJ 1980 L60/21; *NAVEWA/ANSEAU*, OJ 1982 L167/39; *Flat glass in the*

(f) repeat offence;[163]

(g) deterrent effect;[164]

(h) actual effect of the infringement;[165]

(i) institutionalised nature of the infringement;[166]

(j) direct or indirect financial benefit derived from the infringement.[167]

(3) *Mitigating circumstances*

When assessing the amount of the fine the Commission may also take into account the existence of certain mitigating factors. The following examples of such factors are based on the Commission's practice as well as on the rulings of the Court of Justice and the Court of First Instance:

(a) early termination of the infringement;[168]

(b) co-operative attitude during the investigation;[169]

(c) introduction of a compliance policy;[170]

Benelux, OJ 1984 L212/13, at pp. 21–22; *Zinc producer group*, OJ 1984 L220/27; *Peroxygen products* OJ 1985 L35/1; *Wood Pulp* OJ 1985 L85/1; *Sperry New Holland*, OJ 1985 L376/21, at pp. 26–27; *Polypropylene* OJ 1986 L230/1; *Soda-ash-Solvay, CFK*, OJ 1991 L152/16, at p. 20; *Gosme/Martell-DMP*, OJ 1991 L185/23, at p. 30; *Eurocheque: Helsinki Agreement*, OJ 1992 L95/50, at p. 65; *Viho/Parker Pen*, OJ 1992 L233/27, at p. 32.

[163] *Flat glass in the Benelux*, OJ 1984 L212/13; *Soda-ash-Solvay, ICI*, OJ 1991 L152/1, at p. 14; *Soda-ash-Solvay, CFK*, OJ 1991 L152/16, at p. 20; *Soda-ash-Solvay*, OJ 1991 L152/21, at p. 38; *Soda-ash-ICI*, OJ 1991 L152/40, at p. 53.

[164] See *Musique Diffusion Française v EC Commission* [1983] ECR 1825, at pp. 1905–1906 (para. 105–106).

[165] See e.g. *Meldoc*, OJ 1986 L348/50.

[166] See e.g. *PVC* [1989] 1 CEC 2,167; OJ 1989 L74/1; *LdPE* [1989] 1 CEC 2,193; OJ 1989 L74/21; *Building and construction industry in the Netherlands*, OJ 1992 L92/1, at pp. 27–28 (para. 141).

[167] *Soda-ash-Solvay, ICI*, OJ 1991 L152/1, at p. 14; *Eurocheque: Helsinki Agreement*, OJ 1992 L95/50, at p. 65 (para. 80–81). In its *XXIst Report on Competition Policy for 1991*, point 139, the Commission noted:

'The financial benefit which companies infringing the competition rules have derived from their infringements will become an increasingly important consideration. Wherever the Commission can ascertain the level of this ill-gotten gain, even if it cannot do so precisely, the calculation of the fine may have this as its starting-point. When appropriate, that amount could then be increased or decreased in the light of the other circumstances of the case, including the need to introduce an element of deterrence or penalty in the sanction imposed on the participating companies.'

[168] See e.g., *Polistil/Arbois*, OJ 1984 L136/9; *Sperry New Holland*, OJ 1985 L376/21, at p. 28; *John Deere*, OJ 1985 L35/58, at pp. 63–64; *Konica* OJ 1988 L78/34, at p. 42; *London European-Sabena* [1989] 1 CEC 2,278, OJ 1988 L317/47, at p. 53; *Gosme/Martell-DMP*, OJ 1991 L185/23, at p. 30. In *Welded steel mesh* [1989] 2 CEC 2,051; OJ 1989 L260/1, at p. 41, the Commission took into account that some undertakings, which were originally involved in the forbidden agreements, later withdrew from the arrangements, thus reducing their effectiveness. In *Sandoz*, the Court of Justice took into account the fact that Sandoz removed the words 'export prohibited' from its invoices at the beginning of the procedure; see *Sandoz v EC Commission* [1990] ECR I-45 (para. 22). See also *Åhlström & Ors v EC Commission ('Wood Pulp')* [1993] 1 CEC 466, at para. 194.

[169] For example, *BL*, OJ 1984 L207/11; Answer to Written Question No. 2006/82, OJ 1983 C118/21; *Wood Pulp*, OJ 1985 L85/1, at p. 26; *Sperry New Holland*, OJ 1985 L376/21, at p. 26; *British Dental Trade Association*, OJ 1988 L233/15, at p. 24; *Hudson's Bay-Dansk Pelsdyravlerforening* [1989] 1 CEC 2,270; OJ 1988 L316/43, at p. 48; *Welded steel mesh* [1989] 2 CEC 2,051; OJ 1989 L260/1, at p. 41 (para. 141); *Viho/Toshiba*, OJ 1991 L287/39, at p. 43; *Building and construction industry in the Netherlands*, OJ 1992 L92/1, at p. 27; *Viho/Parker Pen*, OJ 1992 L233/27, at pp. 31–32 (para. 24). See also *ICI v EC Commission* [1992] ECR II-1021, at pp. 1150–1151 (para. 391–394).

[170] *National Panasonic (UK) Ltd.*, OJ 1982 L354/29, at p. 34; *John Deere*, OJ 1985 L35/58, at pp. 63–64; *Viho/Toshiba*, OJ 1991 L287/39, at p. 43; *Viho/Parker Pen*, OJ 1992 L233/27, at p. 32.

¶1119

(d) acceptance of an undertaking to remedy the situation;[171]

(e) illegal nature of the infringement not clear;[172]

(f) reliance on a Commission notice;[173]

(g) slow reaction by the Commission;[174]

(h) confusion resulting from national legislation or government action;[175]

(i) difficult economic situation;[176]

(j) pressure exercised on the infringing company by another company;[177]

(k) peripheral involvement in the infringement;[178]

(l) large proportion of European sales outside the Community.[179]

It is interesting to note that reliance on advice of counsel[180] and the different tax treatment of fines[181] have not been accepted as factors which need to be taken into account when setting the amount of the fine.

---

[171] See e.g. *Wood Pulp*, OJ 1985 L85/1, at p. 26. The Court of Justice ruled on the appeal against the Commission's decision in *Åhlström & Ors v EC Commission* [1993] 1 CEC 466, where the companies brought an action against their undertakings. The court declared the admissibility of this action, stating, at para. 181 of the judgment, that '(t)he obligations imposed on the applicants by the undertaking must be regarded in the same way as orders requiring an infringement to be brought to an end, as provided for in Article 3 of Regulation 17.... In giving that undertaking, the applicants thus merely assented, for their own reasons, to a decision which the Commission was empowered to adopt unilaterally.' Indeed, the undertakings were annulled insofar as they imposed obligations which did not relate to infringements upheld by the court. See also *Eurofix-Bauco v Hilti*, OJ 1988 L65/19, at p. 42; *Distribution of railway tickets by travel agents*, OJ 1992 L366/47; *Ford Agricultural*, OJ 1993 L20/1, at p. 4.

[172] See e.g. *Agreements between manufacturers of glass containers*, OJ 1974 L160/1; *Franco-Japanese ballbearings agreement*, OJ 1974 L343/19; *Vegetable parchment*, OJ 1978 L70/54, at p. 62; *Windsurfing International*, OJ 1983 L229/1; *Fatty Acids*, OJ 1987 L3/17, at p. 24; *British Dental Trade Association*, OJ 1988 L233/15, at p. 24; *Napier Brown/British Sugar*, OJ 1988 L284/41, at p. 58; *Decca Navigator System* [1989] 1 CEC 2,137; OJ 1989 L43/27, at p. 46; *Eco System/Peugeot*, OJ 1992 L66/1, at p. 12 (para. 34); *Ford Agricultural*, OJ 1993 L20/1, at p. 4 (para. 21).

[173] *Suiker Unie & Ors v EC Commission* [1975] ECR 1663, at p. 2010 (para. 556).

[174] *Commercial Solvents v EC Commission* [1974] ECR 223, at p. 257 (para. 51); *Eurocheque: Helsinki Agreement*, OJ 1992 L95/50, at p. 66 (para. 89).

[175] *ABG oil companies operating in the Netherlands*, OJ 1977 L117/1, at p. 12; *Welded steel mesh*, OJ 1989 L260/1, at p. 42; *Building and construction industry in the Netherlands*, OJ 1992 L92/1, at pp. 27–28 (para. 141).

[176] *Zinc producer group*, OJ 1984 L220/27; *Flat glass in the Benelux*, OJ 1984 L212/13; *Flat glass*, OJ 1989 L33/44, at p. 67; *PVC* [1989] 1 CEC 2,167; OJ 1989 L74/1, at p. 17; *LdPE*, OJ 1989 L74/21, at p. 39. In *Newitt/Dunlop Slazenger International & Ors*, OJ 1992 L131/32, at p. 45, the Commission took into account the financial problems faced by one of the participating undertakings.

[177] *Tipp-Ex*, OJ 1987 L222/1, at pp. 10–11; *Fisher-Price/Quaker Oats Ltd-Toyco*, OJ 1988 L49/19, at p. 22.

[178] See e.g. *LdPE*, OJ 1989 L74/21, at p. 39; [1989] 1 CEC 2,193; *Building and construction industry in the Netherlands*, OJ 1992 L92/1, at p. 28; see also *PVC* (OJ 1989 L74/1, at pp. 17–18) where the Commission found it reasonable to impose a significantly lower fine for one undertaking which operated on the periphery.

[179] See e.g. *LdPE*, OJ 1989 L74/21, at p. 39; [1989] 1 CEC 2,193

[180] See e.g. *Miller v EC Commission* [1978] ECR 131, at p. 152 (para. 17–18); *Tipp-Ex v EC Commission* [1990] ECR I-261.

[181] *Buchler v EC Commission* [1970] ECR 733, at p. 761 (para. 51).

(4)   *Double jeopardy*

According to the fundamental principle of law non bis in idem, the Commission must, when it imposes a fine, take account of fines already inflicted in a different jurisdiction for the same infringement.[182]

The Commission has also stated that, in principle, fines should not be applied cumulatively when two provisions of the treaty are infringed simultaneously by the same set of facts. The Commission considered that, in such a case, only fines for the more serious infringement should be imposed.[183] The fact that fines have already been imposed on undertakings for another infringement has also been taken into account by the Commission.[184]

(5)   *Maximum fines*

According to art. 15(2) of Regulation 17/62, the Commission may impose fines ranging from ECU 1,000 to ECU 1m, irrespective of the turnover of the company concerned. However, for fines in excess of ECU 1m it is provided in the same article that they may not exceed '10 per cent of the turnover in the preceding business year of each of the undertakings participating in the infringement'.

In its *Pioneer* judgment the Court of Justice made it clear that the ten per cent of turnover limit relates to the total turnover, i.e. sales of all products, worldwide, rather than being limited to the company's turnover in the relevant products and geographic markets involved in the infringement.[185]

However, in the same judgment the court also noted that the Commission could:

'have regard both to the total turnover of the undertaking, which gives an indication ... of the size of the undertaking and of its economic power, and to the proportion of that turnover accounted for by the goods in respect of which the infringement was committed, which gives an indication of the scale

---

[182] See *Walt Wilhelm v Bundeskartellamt* [1969] ECR 1. This is so, even if the different jurisdiction happens to be outside the EC, see *Boehringer Mannheim v EC Commission* [1972] ECR 1281, at pp. 1289–1290 (para. 4–6), where, however, the Court of Justice accepted cumulation because the facts calling for the sanctions were not the same.

[183] *Flat glass* [1989] 1 CEC 2,077; OJ 1989 L33/44, at p. 67. In this case, the Commission held that both art. 85 and 86 of the treaty had been infringed. Since it was the first time that the concept of 'collective dominant position' was used, the Commission considered that no fines should be imposed under art. 86.

[184] *PVC*, OJ 1989 L74/1, at p. 17; *LdPE*, 1989 L74/21, at p. 39.

[185] *Musique Diffusion Française v EC Commission* [1983] ECR 1825, at p. 1909 (para. 121).

of the infringement. On the other hand . . . it is important not to confer on one or other of these figures a disproportionate importance in relation to the other factors.'[186]

This last sentence can be interpreted as a word of caution against the mathematical application of the ten per cent rule which might very well be in conflict with a fundamental principle of Community law, i.e. the so-called 'proportionality rule'. In accordance with this principle, the fine must relate to the nature of the infringement, the size of the company concerned and its responsibility for the infringement.[187]

In the Commission's practice, the term 'preceding business year' refers to the year prior to the one in which the decision imposing the fine is adopted.

When several companies participated in the infringement, the ten per cent upper limit must be taken into account for each of them.

In a situation where the defendant companies include a parent and its subsidiary, however, the Commission is entitled, on the basis of the economic unit doctrine, to deviate from the requirement of fixing the fine on an individual basis. In such instance, it could fix one fine for the corporate group and provide for joint and several liability.[188] The ten per cent upper limit would then have to

---

[186] Ibid.

[187] The Commission feels bound to observe the principle of proportionality in its fining policy. See the *Thirteenth Report on Competition Policy*, point 64. See also the Answer to Written Question No. 2296/85, OJ 1986 C123/27, where Mr Sutherland stated as follows:

'The Commission bases its assessment on two principles.

   (i) proportionality, i.e. there must be a relationship between the amount of the fine on the one hand, and the gravity of the infringement, the size of the undertaking and its responsibility for the infringement, on the other;

   (ii) equity, i.e. non-discrimination between undertakings in comparable situations, whether in the same decision or in different decisions. The Commission has, however, gradually increased the general level of fines since 1979 so as to reinforce their deterrent effect. The upper limit fixed by Regulation No. 17 for fines in competition matters is one million ECU or 10 per cent of the undertaking's turnover in the previous financial year.'

By its *NAVEWA/ANSEAU* decision (OJ 1982 L167/39) the Commission amended an earlier decision and corrected its appreciation of the degree of involvement of one of the defendants.

In *Stichting Sigarettenindustrie & Ors v EC Commission* [1985] ECR 3831, the Court of Justice reduced the fine imposed on Reynolds, one of the applicants, because it appeared from the explanations furnished by the Commission that the fine was fixed on the basis of the same percentage of turnover for all the applicants, that means, without having taken into account the less active role played by Reynolds.

In *Musique Diffusion Française v EC Commission* [1983] ECR 1825, at pp. 1903–1904 (para. 98), the Court of Justice implicitly recognised the principle that an undertaking might not be held responsible for an infringement in a situation where its managers would have exceeded their powers.

Also in *Stichting Sigarettenindustrie & Ors v EC Commission*, the Court of Justice held that the Commission can take into account only those parts of an agreement from which the restriction of competition directly results, when it imposes a fine for an infringement of art. 85.

[188] See e.g., *Zoja/CSC-ICI*, JO 1972 L299/51. Similarly, a successor company is liable for payment of fines

be determined in reference to the turnover of the parent company and subsidiary combined.

(6) *Payment*

It is the Commission's practice to specify in its decision the amount of the fine both in ECUs and in the currency of a member state (usually the currency of the member state where the company concerned has its main establishment or is otherwise closely connected with). The decision will also specify the bank account(s) where payment should be made as well as the deadline for making the payment, usually three months from the date on which the decision was notified to the company concerned.

If payment is made in a currency different from the one specified in the decision, the conversion must be done at the free market rate on the payment date.[189]

The Commission makes the suspension of the collection subject to the supply of an appropriate bank guarantee covering the amount of the fine plus interest.[190] The interest rate is usually set one per cent above the going rate of the national bank of the member state in whose currency the fine is expressed.

In appropriate cases and having regard to the financial situation of the companies concerned, the Commission may allow payment to be deferred or effected in instalments. In such instances also, the Commission will request that a bank guarantee be provided.[191]

(7) *Levels of fine*

An examination of the table of fines[192] shows that the Commission has not endeavoured to establish a uniform tariff of fines but has, instead, made full use of the wide margin of discretion it enjoys when setting a fine. For example, in two cases brought around the same time and involving the same products (hi-fi equipment) and the same kind of infringement (export ban), the amount of the fines imposed by the Commission was ECU 6,950,000 in the one case[193] as against only ECU 450,000 in the other.[194]

Similarly, there have been cases where the Commission has refrained from imposing a fine on account of the novelty of the infringement,[195] whereas in

---

because it is held to be responsible for the actions of the firms taken over. See for example, *Zinc producer group*, OJ 1984 L220/27, at p. 41; *Peroxygen products*, OJ 1985 L35/1.

[189] *Société Anonyme Générale Sucrière v EC Commission* [1977] ECR 445.

[190] *Twelfth Report on Competition Policy*, points 60–61. See also *AEG-Telefunken v EC Commission* [1983] ECR 3151, at p. 3221 (para. 139–143).

[191] *Thirteenth Report on Competition Policy*, point 55.

[192] Annex 1 below.

[193] *Pioneer*, OJ 1980 L60/21.

[194] *National Panasonic (UK)*, OJ 1982 L354/29.

[195] See cases cited under note 170 above. See also *Eco System/Peugeot*, OJ 1992 L66/1. In other cases, the novelty of the infringement was only taken into account by the Commission among other mitigating factors in the

other instances it imposed fines notwithstanding the novel features of the infringement.[196]

According to art. 17 of Regulation 17/62, the courts have unlimited jurisdictions to review decisions in which the Commission has imposed a fine. The Court of Justice has, nevertheless, endorsed the wide discretion of the Commission and has even accepted that the Commission could from one day to another impose much higher fines than in the past. According to the court, 'the fact that the Commission, in the past, imposed fines of a certain level for certain types of infringement does not mean that it is estopped from raising the level within the limits indicated in Regulation 1762 if that is necessary to ensure the implementation of Community competition policy'.[197]

Periodic penalty payments

Pursuant to art. 16 of Regulation 17/62 the Commission may by decision impose periodic penalty payments of a minimum of ECU 50 and a maximum of ECU 1,000 per day in order to compel companies to terminate an infringement of art. 85(1) or 86, to comply with an obligation imposed under art. 85(3) or to supply information requested by decision or to submit to an on-the-spot investigation ordered by decision.[198]

If a company is compelled to satisfy more than one obligation, the Commission has interpreted art. 16(1) of Regulation 17/62 to mean that the maximum penalty of ECU 1,000 may be applied to each such obligation.[199]

When a company has satisfied the obligation sanctioned by a periodic penalty payment, the Commission may reduce the total amount of the periodic penalty payment, compared to the amount provided for in the original decision.[200]

---

reduction of the fine. See *Building and construction industry in the Netherlands*, OJ 1992 L92/1, at p. 28 (para. 141); *Eurocheque: Helsinki Agreement*, OJ 1992 L95/50, at p. 66 (para. 90). A striking example of the Commission's virtually unlimited discretion in setting fines may be found in the art. 86 cases dealing with predatory conduct. In *ECS/AKZO*, OJ 1985 L374/1, the Commission applied art. 86 for the first time to alleged predatory pricing and imposed a fine of ECU 10m. On appeal, the novelty of the infringement as well as its limited effects were, however, taken into account by the Court of Justice which reduced the amount of the fine to ECU 7.5m: *AKZO Chemie BV v EC Commission* [1991] ECR I-3359, at p. 3476 (para. 163). In *Napier Brown/British Sugar*, OJ 1988 L284/41, the Commission referred to the absence of case law dealing with predatory pricing as a factor to be taken into account in setting the amount of the fine. In that case, the Commission imposed a fine of ECU 3m. In *Decca Navigator System* [1989] 1 CEC 2,137; OJ 1989 L43/77, the Commission condemned predatory conduct of a non-pricing nature. No fine was imposed.

[196] See e.g. *Zoja/CSC-ICI*, JO 1972 L299/51, when the Commission dealt for the first time with a refusal to supply, and *Chiquita*, OJ 1976 L95/1 which dealt for the first time with price abuses.

[197] *Musique Diffusion Française v EC Commission* [1983] ECR 1825, at p. 1906 (para. 109).

[198] See also, art. 20 of Regulation 4056/86 (maritime transport); art.12 of Regulation 3975/87 (air transport); art. 14 of Regulation 4064/89 (the merger regulation).

[199] See e.g. *Zoja/CSC-ICI*, JO 1972 L299/51.

[200] Regulation 17/62, art. 16(2). For example, in *Baccarat*, OJ 1991 L97/16, the Commission imposed the maximum amount of ECU 1,000 per day, but reduced the amount of the periodic penalty payment to a total of ECU 10,000 after communication of the information requested by the Commission.

¶1119

¶1120 Limitation periods

Regulation 17/62 did not provide for any limitation periods. On two occasions the Court of Justice was faced with a claim that the Commission should have abstained from imposing fines since the infringements had taken place many years before the Commission had initiated its proceedings.[201] The court, however, rather than reading a 'statute of limitations' into Community law by reference to the existence of such a fundamental principle in the legal system of all member states, was of the opinion that the matter should be regulated by the Council. This the Council did in 1974 by adopting Regulation 2988/74.[202]

Under this regulation, the Commission's power to impose fines is subject to a limitation period of five years for substantive infringements of the EC competition rules. The limitation period is three years for procedural infringements, i.e. infringements relating to requests for information, investigations, applications for negative clearance and notifications.

The limitation period begins to run as of the day that the infringement is committed. However, if the infringement is continuing or repeated, time only starts running on the day on which the infringement ceases.[203]

The limitation period is interrupted by any action taken by the Commission for the purpose of 'the preliminary investigation of proceedings'. Such actions are said to include in particular the following:

(1) requests for information, including both simple requests and those ordered by a formal decision;

(2) on-the-spot investigations, including both those carried out on the basis of a simple mandate and those ordered by a formal decision;

(3) the initiation of proceedings;

(4) the notification of the Commission's statement of objections.[204]

The limitation period is interrupted as of the date on which the action of the Commission is notified to at least one of the participants in the infringement and will apply to all of them.

Each interruption causes time to start running afresh. However, the limitation period expires in any event after a period equal to twice the limitation period has elapsed without the imposition of a fine or a penalty.

It should be noted that the limitation period is suspended for as long as the Commission decision is the subject of proceedings pending before the Court of Justice or the Court of First Instance.

---

[201] *ACF Chemiefarma v EC Commission* [1970] ECR 661; *ICI v EC Commission* [1972] ECR 619.
[202] Council Regulation 2988/74, concerning limitation periods in proceedings and the enforcement of sanctions under the rules of the European Economic Community relating to transport and competition, OJ 1984 L319/1.
[203] *Zinc producer group*, OJ 1984 L220/27, at p. 42.
[204] Regulation 2988/74, art. 2(1).

Finally, the regulation provides for a five-year limitation period for the enforcement of sanctions.

¶1121   Decisions granting negative clearance or exemption

In addition to decisions establishing the existence of an infringement (see ¶1104–¶1120), the Commission also issues decisions granting a negative clearance to a particular agreement or practice.

A negative clearance is a decision in which the Commission, based on the facts available to it, comes to the conclusion that there are no grounds under art. 85(1) or art. 86 of the treaty for action on its part against the agreement or practice concerned.[205]

An agreement or practice which clearly restricts competition and thus would violate art. 85(1), may nevertheless escape prohibition provided it receives the benefit of an exemption pursuant to art. 85(3).[206] This exemption will be granted if the Commission, on balance, finds that the restrictive effects of the agreement are offset by the advantages derived from it.

Decisions granting negative clearance or exemption, and the procedure followed in such cases, are described at ¶1122–¶1128.

¶1122   The notification process

Unless a particular agreement belongs to a category of agreements that is expressly dispensed from the notification requirement or is covered by a so-called 'block exemption', a notification must be filed with the Commission in order possibly to qualify for an individual exemption under art. 85(3) from the prohibition contained in art. 85(1).[207]

Applications for negative clearance are usually combined with a notification of the agreement or practice concerned in order to seek an exemption under art. 85(3), because only by filing a notification does one secure immunity from fines for activities subsequent to the date of notification, in the event that the application for a negative clearance fails.[208]

(1)   Form A/B

At first, separate forms were used for applications for a negative clearance (Form A) and for notifications for an exemption (Form B). However, as a result of most parties' practice of combining the two requests, the Commission quickly developed a joint form: Form A/B. Separate forms have been

---

[205] Regulation 17/62, art. 2.
[206] Id., art. 4, 6 and 8; for new member states, art. 5, 7 and 25.
[207] Id., art. 4(1). The situation is different in the maritime and the air transport sectors. See ¶1007 and ¶1021.
[208] Id., art. 15(5). See, e.g. *John Deere*, OJ 1985 I 35/58

developed for applications for a negative clearance and for notifications for an exemption in the maritime and air transport sectors.[209]

As of 1 January 1986 the old Form A/B, in use since 1962, was replaced by a successor, and this form, as adjusted for the operation of the EEA Agreement from 1 January 1994, is the form currently used. This form goes into considerably more detail.[210]

The present form was apparently issued 'in order to make it easier for firms to use, and also allowing the Commission to give a quicker response'.[211] While it is true that Form A/B requires the notifying parties to give complete information which should allow the Commission to evaluate the agreement or practice speedily without having to send out further questionnaires, it is questionable whether the form is 'easier to use' than its predecessor. On the contrary, some of the information may be cumbersome to compile,[212] require difficult assessments of what the relevant market is,[213] or involve the supply of soul-searching comments, bordering on self-incrimination.[214]

Form A/B takes account of the procedural developments that occurred in the last decade. The parties may choose between requesting a negative clearance or an exemption, the benefit of the 'opposition procedure'[215] or a 'comfort letter'.[216]

Companies may also use Form A/B to file an application for a negative clearance to determine whether or not a given practice falls under art. 86 of the treaty.

---

[209] Forms MAR and AER respectively (Regulations 4260/88 and 4261/88 as adjusted by Regulation 3666/93 for the entry into force of the EEA Agreement).

[210] Form A/B as described by the Commission in the *Fifteenth Report on Competition Policy*, point 48:

'The new form consists of only one sheet of paper for the names of the undertakings concerned and the purpose of the notification. The legal and economic aspects of the arrangements are to be described in a compulsory annex to be drawn up on normal paper using specific headings and reference numbers. These headings and reference numbers are set out in a Complementary Note to the form which also explains the purpose of the Community rules on competition, the different types of decisions likely to be taken by the Commission and various procedural matters.'

The form was originally published as an annex to Regulation 27/62 and was superseded by Appendix 1 to Regulation 3666/93 (OJ 1993 L336/1) with effect from 1 January 1994 to be used in applying the competition rules in an EEA context.

[211] *Fourteenth Report on Competition Policy*, point 47, last paragraph.

[212] For example, under subheading 3.3 of the annex to Form A/B, the notifying parties are required to provide 'the sales or turnover of each party in the goods or services affected by the arrangements in the Community, in the territory of the EFTA states, in the EEA territory and world-wide'. Moreover, if the turnover in the Community or in the territory of the EFTA states or in the EEA territory is material, i.e. more than a five per cent market share, they must give such figures for each member state and each EFTA state and for previous years, as well as supply each party's sales targets for the future.

[213] For example, under heading 2 of the annex to Form A/B, the notifying parties are requested to describe the nature of the goods or services 'affected by the arrangements or behaviour' and to give a brief description of the structure of the market, including stating 'whether there are substitute products'.

[214] For example, under subheading 5.1 of the annex to Form A/B, the notifying parties are requested to 'state which provision or effects of the arrangements or behaviour might . . . raise questions of compatibility with the Community's and/or the EEA rules of competition'.

[215] The opposition procedure is explained at the end of ¶1122.

[216] Comfort letters are discussed at ¶1126.

¶1122

It is worth mentioning that the applicants are requested to state, with reasons, the urgency of their application or notification and to mention earlier proceedings or informal contacts with the Commission, national authorities or courts regarding the arrangements notified. The Commission has particularly stressed the importance of these informal contacts, which should take place prior to the notification process in order to ensure the companies will provide all necessary information.

Likewise noteworthy is the suggestion in the form that a separate annex be used, marked 'Business Secrets', to group all the information the disclosure of which by publication or otherwise would cause harm.

Incidentally, upon the entry into force of the European Economic Area ('EEA'), the information requested in Form A/B also has to be provided for the countries adhering to the EEA.

Use of Form A/B is mandatory. In the absence of a properly filed notification form, an agreement is not capable of benefiting from an individual exemption even if, as a practical matter, the Commission had received knowledge of the contents of the agreement, whether through discussions with the parties concerned or otherwise.[217]

An application or notification need not be filed by all the parties to the agreement or practice concerned. However, the party filing the papers must inform all the others.[218]

If the agreement in question is a standard contract, it need only be notified once.[219]

If the information supplied in Form A/B is incomplete or inaccurate, the notification may be considered defective and invalid.[220] However, the

---

[217] See e.g. *Van Landewyck v EC Commission* [1980] ECR 3125, at p. 3243 (para. 62); *Distillers v EC Commission* [1980] ECR 2229, at pp. 2263–2264 (para. 23–24). In *Metro-SB-Großmärkte GmbH & KG v EC Commission* [1986] ECR 3021, at para. 25–32 the Court of Justice specified that the use of Form A/B is only mandatory for the initial notification of an agreement. Subsequent requests for renewal or extension pursuant to art. 8(2) of Regulation 17/62 may be made by way of a simple letter. In *Peugeot/Eco System*, OJ 1992 L66/3, at p. 7, the Commission made it clear that the mere communication of the agreement to DG IV does not constitute valid notification.

[218] In heading 2 of Form A/B the notifying parties are requested to 'state what steps have been taken to inform these other parties of this application or notification'.

[219] See *Parfums Rochas v Bitsch* [1970] ECR 515, at p. 523 (para. 5). It is interesting to note that in *Chiquita*, OJ 1976 L95/2, at p. 271, the Commission accepted that a notification of sales conditions for the Netherlands also covered those applicable in other member states because they were 'substantially the same'. However, in *Sperry-New Holland*, OJ 1985 L376/21, at p. 27, the Commission came to the conclusion that the contracts used outside the UK were 'not substantially the same'.

[220] For example, in *Aluminium Imports from Eastern Europe*, OJ 1985 L92/1, the Commission considered the notification to be invalid because the text of the agreements concerned had not been attached to Form A/B:

'A notification must notify the terms of the agreements and must not leave the Commission to guess whether they exist or what they say. An undertaking cannot take advantage of a notification which is ambiguous (as this notification, even on the interpretation most favourable to it, is ambiguous) so as to obtain both protection from fines and, because the Commission has been misled, the opportunity to continue to practise unlawful behaviour.'

The fact that the agreements had been discussed with a Commission official prior to filing Form A/B could not cure the defect:

¶1122

Commission may be less formalistic as to the way in which the notification form is actually filled out as long as a copy of the agreement in question is attached to the form.[221]

If, after the application for negative clearance or notification for exemption has been filed, the arrangements in question undergo a 'material change', the applicants or notifiers need to inform the Commission of the change.[222]

The supply of 'incorrect or misleading' information may be penalised by a fine. In the complementary note to Form A/B it is stated that the Commission will use its power to impose a fine 'only where applicants or notifiers have, intentionally or negligently, provided false information or grossly inaccurate estimates or suppressed readily available information or estimates, or have deliberately expressed false opinions in order to obtain negative clearance or exemption'.[223]

(2) Agreements not requiring notification
In order to reduce the number of notifications, art. 4(2) of Regulation 17/62 lists certain categories of agreements which are deemed to be less harmful and therefore need not be notified in order to be eligible for an exemption under art. 85(3):

(1) agreements between parties located within one member state,[224] which 'do not relate either to imports or exports between Member States';[225]

(2) agreements involving only two parties and which:

'Preliminary meetings with Commission officials cannot absolve the parties from the duty to make a fair and accurate disclosure in the notification of the arrangements they have made. This duty the parties failed to perform.'
[221] *VBBB v Eldi Records* [1980] ECR 1137, at p. 1170 (para. 11).

'An agreement may be regarded as properly notified in its entirety and may therefore benefit from the effects of an agreement which has been notified, where its entire text has been attached to the notification form, even though only some of the clauses of the agreement are quoted on the form, provided that the description given there constitutes a fair and accurate record of the provisions which at the time were considered most important.'

[222] Point VI of the complementary note to Form A/B.
[223] Ibid.
[224] In *BP Kemi-DDSF* (OJ 1979 L286/32, at p. 48) the Commission looked at the economic reality and refused to accept that the agreement had been entered into by two parties located within one member state 'because one of the parties is selling only goods which are imported from a company in another Member State and this other company and the party in question are both controlled by the same third company'.
[225] In *Bilger v Jehle* [1970] ECR 127, at p. 135 (para. 5–6), the Court of Justice ruled that a requirements contract between a brewery and a bar did not relate to imports or exports between member states since its performance did not call for the crossing of national borders. Thus, the court's interpretation of the words 'relate to imports or exports' differs from its interpretation of the 'effect on trade' requirement in art. 85(1). The court more readily accepts that trade is affected than that there is a relation to imports or exports (see e.g. *Brasserie de Haecht v Wilkin* ('*Haecht I*') [1967] ECR 407). Similarly, in *Fonderies Roubaix v Fonderies Roux* [1976] ECR 111, at p. 120 the Court of Justice ruled that there was no relation to imports or exports even though the product concerned had first been imported before it was sold between companies operating in the same member state. The Commission, however, has a tendency to find that the agreement concerned does relate to imports or exports in an effort to restrict the benefit of art. 4(2). See, for example, *SSI*, OJ 1982 L232/1, at p. 34.

¶1122

(a) relate to resale prices or other conditions of sale; or which

(b) impose 'restrictions on the exercise of industrial property rights' or know-how by the licensee or user;[226]

(3) agreements having as their sole object:

(a) the development or uniform application of standards or types; or

(b) joint research and development; or

(c) specialisation in the manufacture of products, provided

(i) the products subject to specialisation do not represent more than 15 per cent of the volume of business done in identical or similar products, and

(ii) the parties' combined annual turnover does not exceed ECU 200m.[227]

It should be noted that agreements not requiring notification may nevertheless be notified to the Commission. Parties in doubt about whether their agreement fits one of the categories exempted from notification may find it to be in their interest to notify it. Notification also provides the only secure way to obtain immunity from fines.[228]

(3) Opposition procedure

In five block exemption regulations, i.e. those covering patent licensing,[229] research and development,[230] specialisation agreements,[231] franchising[232] and

---

[226] The key question is to know whether a given restriction falls within or outside the scope of the industrial property right granted. In this connection one should consult the block exemption applicable to certain categories of patent licensing and know-how licensing agreements as well as the Commission's case law on other industrial property rights. See Chapter 4. For example, in *Windsurfing International v EC Commission* [1986] ECR 611 the Court of Justice, at para. 100, concurred with the Commission 'that the restrictions laid down in the clauses at issue exceed the scope of the rights conferred by the patent because they also encompass the board, which is not covered by the patent, and because they include an obligation not to challenge Windsurfing International's trade marks and patent'. The court concluded that as a result the clauses at issue failed to benefit from the dispensation of the notification requirement and, not having been notified, they were not eligible for an exemption under art. 85(3).

[227] Parties to such agreements would be well advised to consult the block exemption covering certain categories of specialisation agreements, and certain categories of research and development co-operation agreements, rather than relying exclusively on the wording of art. 4(2) of Regulation 17/62 for not notifying a particular agreement.

[228] In *Stichting Sigarettenindustrie & Ors v EC Commission* [1985] ECR 3831 (para. 70–78), the Court of Justice ruled that a fine may be imposed on an agreement which is exempted from the notification requirement.

[229] Commission Regulation 2349/84 on the application of art. 85(3) of the treaty to certain categories of patent licensing agreements, OJ 1984 L219/15, corrigendum, OJ 1985 L113/34, as amended. Article 4 of this block exemption regulation provides for an opposition procedure.

[230] Commission Regulation 418/85 on the application of art. 85(3) of the treaty to categories of research and development agreements, OJ 1985 L53/5, as amended. Article 7 of this block exemption regulation provides for an opposition procedure.

[231] Commission Regulation 417/85 on the application of art. 85(3) of the treaty to categories of specialisation agreements, OJ 1985 L53/1, as amended. Article 4 of this block exemption regulation provides for an opposition procedure.

[232] Commission Regulation 4087/88 on the application of art. 85(3) of the treaty to categories of franchise

know-how licensing agreements,[233] the Commission has introduced the so-called 'opposition procedure'.

Pursuant to this procedure it is possible to notify to the Commission agreements which contain restrictions which are not expressly exempted or prohibited by the regulation concerned. Such restrictions will be deemed to be covered by the block exemption unless the Commission opposes exemption within six months.

The advantage of this procedure over the traditional notification procedure is that after a relatively short period the parties who made use of the opposition procedure know whether the terms of their agreement are benefiting from the block exemption or not.[234]

A notification claiming the benefit of an opposition procedure may be opposed by the Commission, on its own initiative or at the request of a member state, either because it is felt that the arrangements should not benefit from a block exemption or to allow for more information to be collected. The notification will then be treated as an application for an individual exemption decision, unless the Commission later withdraws its opposition.

¶1123 Subsequent procedure

The application or notification is registered in the Registry of the Directorate-General for Competition. The applicant or notifier will receive an acknowledgement of receipt, listing the number under which the file has been registered.[235] The Registry is not open to the public.

The national competition authorities of the member states automatically receive a copy of the applications or notifications filed with the Commission.[236]

---

agreements, OJ 1988 L359/46. Article 6 of this block exemption regulation provides for an opposition procedure.

[233] Commission Regulation 556/89 on the application of art. 85(3) of the treaty to certain categories of know-how licensing agreements, OJ 1989 L61/1, as amended. Article 4 of this block exemption regulation provides for an opposition procedure.

[234] Thus far, only a limited number of applicants have made use of the opposition procedure. The Commission only received two notifications pursuant to art. 6 of Regulation 4087/88 (franchising), one notification pursuant to art. 4 of Regulation 2349/84 (patent licensing) and one notification pursuant to art. 4 of Regulation 556/89 (know-how licensing agreements) in 1992 (see *XXIInd Report on Competition Policy for 1992*, points 272–273). In the context of the other block exemption regulations, the opposition procedure has been used to an even lesser extent.

[235] The registration carries no implications regarding the validity of the notification. As pointed out by the Commission in *Aluminium Imports from Eastern Europe*, OJ 1985 L95/1, at p. 52:

'The mere registration of a notification, or its physical receipt by a Commission official, cannot amount to the acceptance of its validity still less of its completeness or accuracy. All notifications are registered, but Article 15(1)(a) of Regulation 17 provides for fines should a notification be discovered to be inaccurate, while Article 15(5) extends protection only to those matters falling within the limits of the notification. In both cases the necessary examination can only take place after the fact of registration.'

[236] The EFTA Surveillance Authority also receives a copy of the form and annex: Form A/B together with the annex must be supplied in 15 copies (two for the Commission, one for each member state and one for the EFTA Surveillance Authority). However, only three copies of the relevant agreement itself, and only one copy of other supporting documents, need to be filed.

¶1123

Once an agreement or practice is notified to the Commission an investigation process is set in motion to determine whether the agreement or practice concerned should benefit from a decision granting a negative clearance or an exemption. Consequently, further information may be sought from the applicants or from third parties and changes may be suggested to make the notified arrangements acceptable.

Depending on the results of the Commission's enquiry, there are a number of possible outcomes:

(1) a provisional decision may be issued whereby the Commission informs the parties concerned that after preliminary examination it is of opinion that art. 85(1) applies and the application of art. 85(3) is not justified (see ¶1124);

(2) the Commission may initiate an infringement proceeding against the parties who filed the notification (see ¶1104, ¶1105);

(3) a formal decision granting a negative clearance or exemption may be adopted (see ¶1125);

(4) the file may be closed by the release of a so-called 'comfort letter' without any formal decision being adopted (see ¶1126).

¶1124   Provisional decision

The notification of an agreement or practice protects the parties against fines. However, to avoid possible abuse of the notification process, art. 15(6) of Regulation 17/62 authorises the Commission to terminate immediately the immunity from fines whenever 'after preliminary examination it is of opinion that Article 85(1) of the Treaty applies and that application of Article 85(3) is not justified'.

The Commission has hitherto made little use of its power to adopt a provisional decision in circumstances where an agreement or practice that has been notified is prima facie illegal and incapable of being granted an exemption.[237]

Regulation 17/62 is silent as to the procedure which the Commission needs to follow before taking a provisional decision. However, in accordance with fundamental principles of Community law, it is clear that the Commission must notify the parties concerned of its objections and afford them the opportunity

---

[237] In *Vichy*, OJ 1991 L75/57, the Commission applied art. 15(6) of Regulation 17/62 to a notified exclusive distribution system. This system provided that only qualified dispensing chemists could be appointed as authorised distributors whereas holders of a pharmacy diploma were excluded from the distribution network. In its decision, the Commission referred to a previous decision where a similar agreement was found to infringe art. 85(1) and to a judgment of the Court of Appeal of Paris holding that the Vichy distribution system was caught by art. 85(1).

of being heard.[238] In addition a provisional decision needs to be properly reasoned.

¶1125   Formal decision

A formal decision granting a negative clearance or an exemption may only be taken after providing the parties concerned with the opportunity to be heard[239] and after inviting third parties to comment on the summary of the application or notification as published in the *Official Journal*.[240] The Advisory Committee must likewise be consulted.[241]

(1)   Negative clearance

A formal decision granting a negative clearance is a decision by the Commission that, based on the facts in its possession, there is no ground for action under art. 85(1) or art. 86 against a particular agreement or practice.[242]

A decision of negative clearance is of a lesser legal value than a formal exemption in that a negative clearance would not preclude national courts and/or competition authorities from reviewing the facts of the matter nor from applying national law to the agreement or practice in question.[243]

(2)   Exemption

A formal decision granting an exemption is a decision by the Commission that the agreement or practice notified to it violates art. 85(1) but satisfies the criteria for exemption laid down in art. 85(3).[244]

A decision granting an exemption needs to be issued for a specific period of time but it may be renewed upon application. The exemption may be retroactive to the notification date. The exemption is usually made conditional upon compliance with certain obligations. The Commission may revoke or amend its decision.

An exemption decision offers greater legal certainty than a negative clearance because national courts and competition authorities would be

---

[238] However, it is clear that the Commission does not have to consult the Advisory Committee before the adoption of a provisional decision under art. 15(6) of Regulation 17/62: see *Vichy v EC Commission* [1992] ECR II-415, at p. 431 (para. 40).

[239] Regulation 17/62, art. 19(1).

[240] Id., art. 19(3). For an example of comments filed by third parties, see *SABA's EEC distribution system*, OJ 1983 L376/41, at p. 45.

[241] Regulation 17/62, art. 10.

[242] Id., art. 2.

[243] The Court of Justice has made this point clear with respect to so-called comfort letters, i.e. administrative letters whereby the Commission decides to close a file; *Procureur de la République v Giry and Guerlain (Perfumes)* [1980] ECR 2327 (para. 12–19). There being no major difference between a comfort letter and a decision of negative clearance, the court's reasoning is likely to apply to decisions of negative clearance as well.

[244] Regulation 17/62, art. 4, 6 and 8; for new member states, art. 5, 7 and 25.

precluded from reviewing the agreement or practice concerned under Community law and, arguably, from applying stricter national laws.

Exemption period

In each case the Commission must specify the period for which it grants an exemption.[245] Typically, the period ranges between five and ten years. If the exemption requirements continue to be satisfied, the Commission, upon application, may decide to renew the exemption.

Usually, the exemption is applied retroactively to the date of notification unless the agreement in question initially did not satisfy the criteria specified in art. 85(3).[246] In such an instance, the Commission applies the exemption as of the date the agreement was amended to meet the requirements of art. 85(3).

In four situations, however, the Commission may fix the beginning of the exemption period at a date earlier than the notification date:

(a) with respect to agreements dispensed from notification, the exemption may go back to the effective date of the agreement;[247]

(b) with respect to so-called 'old'[248] and 'accession'[249] agreements, notified within the time-limits set out in Regulation 17/62, the Commission may go back to the date Regulation 17/62 came into effect for 'old' agreements[250] and to the date of accession for 'accession' agreements;[251]

(c) with respect to agreements relating to rail, road and inland waterway transport,[252] maritime transport,[253] and air transport;[254]

(d) with respect to agreements in the insurance sector.[255]

Another advantage reserved for old and accession agreements is that the Commission may specify the period during which such an agreement is found to violate art. 85(1). This enables the parties to terminate or modify the agreement

---

[245] Id., art. 8(1).

[246] Id., art. 6(1). For an interesting application of the possibility of the Commission giving retroactive effect to its exemption see *Grundig's EEC distribution system*, OJ 1985 L233/1, at p. 8.

[247] Regulation 17/62, art. 6(1) and (2).

[248] So-called 'old' agreements are agreements which were in existence on the date of entry in force of Regulation 17/62, i.e. 13 March 1962.

[249] So-called 'accession' agreements are agreements which were in existence on the date of accession of new member states, i.e. 1 January 1973 for the UK, Ireland and Denmark, 1 January 1981 for Greece, and 1 January 1986 for Portugal and Spain.

[250] Regulation 17/62, art. 5(1).

[251] Id., art. 25.

[252] Council Regulation 1017/68 applying rules of competition to transport by rail, road and inland waterway, OJ 1968 L175/1, art. 12(4).

[253] Council Regulation 4056/86 laying down detailed rules for the application of art. 85 and 86 of the treaty to maritime transport, OJ 1986 L378/4, art. 12(4).

[254] Council Regulation 3975/87 laying down the procedure for the application of the rules on competition to undertakings in the air transport sector, OJ 1987 L374/1, as amended, art. 5(4).

[255] Council Regulation 1534/91 on the application of art. 85(3) of the treaty to certain categories of agreements, decisions and concerted practices in the insurance sector, OJ 1991 L 143/1, art. 3

to make it qualify for a negative clearance or an exemption while at the same time protecting them against private actions by declaring art. 85(1) inapplicable during the interim period.[256]

Special conditions

The Commission may make the granting of an exemption subject to certain conditions and obligations.[257] Typically, the Commission has imposed regular reporting requirements on the addressees of an exemption decision. In one case, however, the Commission required one of the joint venture partners to reduce its voting rights in the two joint venture companies that were the subject of the decision.[258]

Revocation

The Commission is entitled to revoke an exemption in any of the following circumstances:

(a) when a change occurs in any of the basic facts which underlie the decision;

(b) in the event of non-compliance by the parties with the condition(s) attached to the exemption;

(c) when the decision is based on incorrect information or was induced by deceit;

(d) where the parties abuse the exemption.[259]

Except for the first ground, i.e. changed circumstances, the revocation of an exemption may have retroactive effect. Thus far, the Commission has not made use of its power to revoke an individual exemption.[260]

¶1126 Comfort letter

The adoption of a formal decision granting a negative clearance or an exemption tends to be a lengthy affair, usually lasting a few years. The Commission is aware of that situation and intends to accelerate its decision-making process so as to respond more swiftly to the needs of the notifying

---

[256] Regulation 17/62, art. 7(1). For an example where the Commission found that the conditions of art. 7 were not satisfied, see *Velcro/Aplix*, OJ 1985 L233/22, at p. 31.

[257] Regulation 17/62, art. 8(1).

[258] *Optical fibres*, OJ 1986 L236/30.

[259] Regulation 17/62, art. 8(3).

[260] In *Schöller Lebensmittel GmbH*, OJ 1993 L183/1, the Commission decided to withdraw the benefit of block exemption Regulation 1984/83 relating to exclusive purchasing obligations to the extent that that regulation would have applied to the agreements concerned. In *Tetra Pak I ('BTG licence')*, OJ 1988 L272/27, at pp. 41–42, the Commission would have withdrawn the benefit of Regulation 2349/84 on patent licensing agreements if Tetra Pak had not renounced the exclusivity of the licence acquired from BTG. In *Eco System/Peugeot*, OJ 1992 L66/1, at pp. 11–12, the Commission likewise informed Peugeot that it would withdraw the benefit of the block exemption contained in Regulation 123/85 from its authorised dealers in Belgium and Luxembourg if Peugeot did not instruct those dealers to supply cars to Eco System.

parties. In this regard, it has already embarked on a practice of issuing so-called 'comfort letters' which take considerably less time to prepare.

A comfort letter is an administrative letter signed by an official of the Commission's Directorate-General for Competition stating that no action will be taken with respect to a particular agreement or practice.

The Commission follows this approach of closing the file and informing the companies concerned by means of comfort letters in cases 'which at first sight raise no problems with respect to the rules of competition and do not require a formal decision'.[261]

It is worth mentioning that the Commission is ready to introduce a similar instrument for cases which, at first sight, are liable to infringe the rules of competition, by issuing a so-called 'warning letter'.[262]

The comfort letter will usually indicate the reason why the Commission is of the opinion that no action need to be taken. Thus, for example, the letter may state 'that an agreement is *de minimis*, falls under a block exemption regulation, falls under one of the Commission's notices, for example on commercial agents or cooperation'.[263]

Effect of a comfort letter

Only limited comfort can be drawn from the receipt of a comfort letter. From the 1980 *Perfume* judgments,[264] it is clear that, as with a negative clearance, neither national courts, nor local competition authorities, nor third parties are bound by such a letter. They may, but need not, take the letter into account when assessing the compatibility of the agreement or practice concerned with the EC competition rules.

Concerning the question of whether the Commission is bound by the terms of its letter, the opinion has been put forward that the Commission should be estopped from re-opening the file 'in the absence of any new facts which came to its attention after the "comfort letter" or unless a judgment indicated that the Commission had been acting under a misapprehension as to the law'.[265] The addressees of the comfort letter are not barred from claiming that the agreement is void under Community law.[266]

---

[261] *Eleventh Report on Competition Policy*, point 15. See also Answer to Written Question 173/85, OJ 1985 C255/27. This would also be the case in situations where there is a lack of Community interest. See notice on co-operation between national courts and the Commission in applying art. 85 and 86 of the EEC Treaty, OJ 1993 C39/6, at p. 7.

[262] Another innovation may be the imposition of an internal deadline for the issuance of comfort or warning letters. This deadline would be two months for cases involving structural changes such as structural joint ventures. See *XXIInd Report on Competition Policy for 1992*, point 122 et seq. For other cases, the Commission intends to respect a short deadline of 'a few months'. See also ¶1127.

[263] *Fifteenth Report on Competition Policy*, point 1(iii).

[264] *Procureur de la République v Giry and Guerlain (Perfumes)* [1980] ECR 2327 and *L'Oréal v De Nieuwe AMCK* [1980] ECR 3775.

[265] Mackenzie Stuart, 'Legitimate Expectations and Estoppel in Community Law and English Administrative Law', (1983) 1 L.I.E.I. 53 citing in support the opinion of Advocate General Reischl in *L'Oréal v De Nieuwe AMCK* [1980] ECR 3775, at p. 3803.

[266] See e.g. the Commission's submissions in *De Bloos v Bouyer* [1977] ECR 2359

The Commission has also made the point that comfort letters do not have the status of decisions and are therefore not capable of appeal to the Court of First Instance.[267]

Procedural safeguards
In an effort to increase the rather limited legal authority of a comfort letter, the Commission has introduced a number of procedural safeguards. First, the Commission has decided to publish the essential contents of the notified agreements in the *Official Journal*, in order to invite comments from third parties.[268]

'In light of the reactions received after publication, it could then be decided either to close the procedure by way of a provisional letter, so as to simplify and shorten the procedure, or to carry on with proceedings culminating in a formal decision. A provisional letter will only be sent if the undertakings involved agree to the procedure being closed in this manner. It will state that under these circumstances the Directorate-General for competition does not consider it necessary to follow the formal procedure through to the proposal of a decision under Article 85(3) in accordance with Article 6 of Regulation No. 17.'[269]

Admittedly, this increased transparency is bound to foster the persuasive authority of the comfort letter.[270]

A second procedural safeguard introduced by the Commission is that arrangements have been made 'for the appropriate liaison with the Advisory Committee on Restrictive Practices and Dominant Positions'.[271] In other words, in addition to third parties being informed through a notice in the *Official Journal*, the member states will be kept in the picture via the Commission's regular liaison with the Advisory Committee.

A third safeguard consists of the fact that cases dealt with by way of a comfort letter, after publication of the essential contents in the *Official Journal*, are listed in the *Annual Report on Competition Policy*.[272]

---

[267] See Commission notice on procedures concerning notifications pursuant to art. 4 of Council Regulation 17/62, OJ 1983 C295/6.

[268] See Commission notice on procedures concerning applications for negative clearance pursuant to art. 2 of Council Regulation 17/62, OJ 1982 C343/4; see e.g. notice pursuant to art. 19(3) of Council Regulation 17/62 concerning Case IV/33.964 – *UTC (Pratt & Whitney)/MTU*, OJ 1992 C279/2; notice pursuant to art. 19(3) of Council Regulation 17/62 concerning an application for negative clearance pursuant to art. 85(1) or exemption pursuant to art. 85(3) of the EEC Treaty – Case IV/33.863 – *Saint Gobain/Asahi*, OJ 1993 C111/6; notice pursuant to art. 19(3) of Council Regulation 17/62 concerning Case IV/34.342 – *Acriss*, OJ 1993 C149/9.

[269] *Thirteenth Report on Competition Policy*, point 72.

[270] However, it must be mentioned that only eight comfort letters out of 176 sent were published in 1992; see *XXIInd Report on Competition Policy for 1992*, point 126.

[271] *Twelfth Report on Competition Policy*, point 30.

[272] For example, see the Annex to the *Sixteenth Report on Competition Policy*, at p. 259, where only one case was listed. Admittedly, this is a low number. In its subsequent annual reports, the Commission only listed the notices published pursuant to art. 19(3) of Regulation 17/62, without specifying if the case was settled by a 'comfort letter'. Perhaps, this is due to the fact that most of the notifying parties prefer to receive a 'comfort letter' in the old style, i.e. without any publicity, notwithstanding its arguably lesser authority.

¶1126

¶1127   Benefits and disadvantages of the notification procedure

Under EC law, there is no obligation to notify an agreement. The filing of Form A/B is only a prerequisite for the issuance of a negative clearance or an exemption.

When considering the question whether to notify or not to notify a particular agreement, it may be appropriate to review some of the advantages and disadvantages that may flow from the notification process.

Benefits

The most tangible benefit of notification is the immunity from fines. Other advantages that deserve to be mentioned are the increased enforceability of an agreement that has been notified and the more favourable attitude of the Commission towards agreements that have been notified.

(1)   *Immunity from fines*

Regulation 17/62 stipulates that the fines which the Commission may impose to penalise infringement of art. 85(1) or art. 86 shall not be imposed in respect of acts taking place after notification to the Commission and before its decision in application of art. 85(3) of the treaty.

Given the vagaries that have at times plagued the interpretation of Community competition law and the high fines that have nevertheless been imposed, the immunity from fines, obtained through notification, may, in a number of situations, be considered as a substantial benefit.

However, this immunity may be of marginal importance in the case of normal commercial arrangements, which, although representing technical violations of art. 85(1), would be unlikely to result in fines since they would be eligible for an exemption under art. 85(3) if notified. In particular, it would appear unlikely that the Commission would devote its limited resources to the prosecution of parties to such an agreement. The risk of fines may also be lower in the case of agreements containing clauses which have not been dealt with in past Commission decisions. It is unlikely that the Commission would impose high fines in such cases even though it might issue a decision in order to establish a legal precedent.

When filing a notification in order to eliminate the risk of ever becoming subject to fines in relation to a particular agreement or practice, it is essential to bear in mind that the immunity from fines for acts subsequent to the notification is subject to the important proviso that they must 'fall within the limits of the activity described in the notification'.[273] Thus, for example, in

---

[273] Regulation 17/62, art. 15(5)(a)

AEG/Telefunken, the Commission refused the benefit of immunity from fines for a selective distribution system that had been notified, because its anti-competitive application had not been mentioned on Form A/B.[274]

It is also important to note that if parts of a notification are considered to be defective, the notification as a whole may be deemed invalid if the notified practices are related to the activities that have not been described.[275]

It is therefore of the utmost interest to the notifying parties that the notification papers be filled out with the greatest care. Indeed, depending on the circumstances, the Commission might well be tempted to interpret the protection resulting from the notification rather narrowly. For example, in *Papiers Peints de Belgique*,[276] a fine was imposed even though the infringement at issue, a collective boycott, was nothing but the sanction for non-compliance with a resale price maintenance scheme which had been notified to the Commission. As a matter of fact, in the notification form filed by the defendants in October 1962 they had to indicate under No. 3(f) the 'sanctions which may be taken against participating undertakings (penalty clause, expulsion, withholding of supplies, etc.)'. In a decision adopted 12 years after the notification the Commission refused to grant immunity from fines because on the form the defendants had listed 'expulsion' as a sanction rather than mentioning the 'withholding of supplies'. In its *Chiquita* decision,[277] the Commission did not hesitate to impose severe fines even though the one abuse (i.e. the so-called 'green banana clause'), said to provide the basis for the three other abuses of which the company was convicted, had been notified in 1968, that is seven years prior to the Commission's decision. This development was all the more surprising in that the notified sales conditions had been the subject of correspondence with a number of Commission officials up to 1971 causing the company to delete certain clauses deemed to be in violation of art. 85, but not the one clause which four years later was branded as abusive.

(2) *Increased enforceability*
Notification may also make it more difficult for a party to an agreement to invoke an infringement of art. 85(1) as a defence to an action for the enforcement of certain provisions. A national judge would be less likely to hold an agreement to be unenforceable if he knows that the agreement has been notified to the Commission and that an exemption may be forthcoming.[278]

---

[274] *AEG Telefunken*, OJ 1982 L117/15. In its decision the Commission found that AEG had been implementing a selective distribution system 'under which certain dealers applying for admission are discriminated against and under which influence is brought to bear on prices' (p. 27). See also *Hasselblad*, OJ 1982 L161/18.

[275] See e.g. *SSI*, OJ 1982 L232/1.

[276] *Papiers Peints de Belgique*, OJ 1974 L237/3.

[277] *Chiquita*, OJ 1976 L95/1.

[278] See the Commission's submissions on question No. 5 referred to the Court of Justice in *De Norre v Brouwerij Concordia* [1977] ECR 65, at pp. 82–85.

In assessing the importance of this advantage, the likelihood that the other party would invoke such a defence should be considered. This likelihood might be lower in the case of partners in a joint venture as opposed to a manufacturer–dealer relationship. Also, the consequences in the event that the agreement is held to be unenforceable must be considered. In the case of agreements involving substantial investment or the licensing of industrial property rights, the consequences of having the agreement declared unenforceable may be unacceptable.

(3)   *Provisional validity*

So-called 'old' and 'accession' agreements that have been notified in time,[279] or which are excluded from the notification formality, enjoy more than a mere increase in enforceability. They benefit from the provisional validity doctrine established by the Court of Justice in its *Haecht II* judgment. In this case the court ruled that with respect to 'old' agreements, the general principle of contractual certainty requires, particularly when the agreement has been notified in accordance with the provisions of Regulation 17/62, that the (national) court may only declare it to be automatically void after the Commission has taken a decision by virtue of that regulation.[280] In a subsequent case the court confirmed its theory not only for old agreements which had been notified but also for those which are exempted from the notification requirement.[281]

Since in both cases the court based its ruling on the need to protect legal certainty, it can be assumed that, by analogy, national courts must also respect the provisional validity of accession agreements.[282]

(4)   *More lenient attitude of officials*

Another possible advantage of notification is that it may create a certain amount of goodwill with the Commission. The Commission may adopt a more favourable attitude towards an agreement which is notified as opposed to an agreement which comes to its attention by other means such as press reports.

---

[279] See footnotes 248 and 249 above.
[280] *Brasserie de Haecht v Wilkin* ('*Haecht II*') [1973] ECR 77, at p. 86 (para. 9). It should be noted that provisional validity is not only brought to an end by the adoption of a decision by the Commission whereby an exemption is granted or refused, but also by the issuance of a comfort letter (*Procureur de la République v Giry and Guerlain (Perfumes)* [1980] ECR 2327), or by the adoption of a decision pursuant to art. 15(6) of Regulation 17/62 (*Portelange SA v Smith Corona* [1969] ECR 309).
[281] *De Bloos v Bouyer* [1977] ECR 2359, at p. 2370 (para. 10–15).
[282] *Third Report on Competition Policy*, point 5(a).

¶1127

Disadvantages

When considering the possibility of notifying an agreement or practice to the Commission, the advantages of the notification procedure need to be balanced against its possible disadvantages.

First, notification may not necessarily provide any immediate legal certainty regarding the validity of the agreement. The Commission continues to be faced with a significant backlog of notified agreements.[283] In certain cases, companies had to wait years before the agreement was evaluated by the Commission.

The Commission nevertheless seems ready to modify its decision-making process so as to accelerate the procedure and to meet the need for legal certainty sought by companies which decide to notify their agreements.[284] For this purpose, the Commission intends to fix deadlines for the treatment of cases involving structural changes, such as joint ventures, mergers or acquisitions coming under art. 85(1).[285] In such cases, the Commission would take an initial position, either by sending a comfort letter or a warning letter, within two months from the complete notification of the case.[286] If the Commission intends to adopt a decision, it would provide the company with the specific timetable it intends to follow and the deadline by which the final decision is expected.

The Commission also intends to introduce a similar system for the treatment of those cases not involving a structural change. In these cases, the Commission would not take its initial position after two months, but after a short time-limit not exceeding a few months.

Secondly, notification also involves a substantial disclosure of information to the Commission. Since the introduction of Form A/B, the filing of a notification has become a complex exercise.

Thirdly, notification may bring unwelcome publicity to an agreement. If the Commission decides to exempt an arrangement, it publishes a notice in the *Official Journal* which summarises the provisions of the agreement and invites comments from third parties. Thus, by notifying an agreement to the Commission, a company may attract criticism from its competitors.

Finally, the notification may cause the Commission to intervene and require the parties to amend certain critical provisions of the agreement.

---

[283] On 31 December 1991, there were 1,732 applications or notifications pending, 328 complaints and 227 own-initiative proceedings. *XXIst Report on Competition Policy*, point 73. On 31 December 1992, there were 1,064 applications or notifications pending, 287 complaints and 211 own-initiative proceedings. *XXIInd Report on Competition Policy for 1992*, point 126.

[284] In its *XXIInd Report on Competition Policy for 1992*, at point 123, the Commission acknowledged that '(a)lthough a substantial reduction in workload has been achieved in recent years through a rationalization of DG IV's activities, [the] procedures are still considered to be too time-consuming. This is a general problem and the Commission is looking into ways of resolving it by improving working methods.'

[285] The Commission has already expressed its will to act more quickly in cases concerning co-operative joint ventures. In the *Appolinaris/Schweppes* case, the Commission concluded its inquiry on the notified agreement in a time-limit similar to that provided under the merger regulation in order to avoid procedural discrimination.

[286] For a definition of a 'warning letter' see ¶1126.

Thus, whether or not to notify is a simple question for which there may not be a simple answer. Before notifying an agreement one may wish to consider possible alternative solutions such as amending the agreement to eliminate the potential antitrust exposure.

¶1128   Settlements

The term 'settlement' is here used to describe those competition cases where the Commission, upon receipt of a complaint or after an investigation on its own initiative, has either already issued a statement of objections and opened a formal proceeding, or is considering doing so, but decides, nevertheless, to close the file and to terminate or suspend the proceeding because the agreement or conduct concerned is terminated by the parties or amended to conform with the competition rules.[287]

Commission practice

More than 90 per cent of all competition cases are settled by the Commission short of a formal decision. Notwithstanding the importance of the Commission's settlement practice in sheer numbers, very little information about what actually occurs becomes public.

An examination of the *Annual Reports on Competition Policy* and of the *Bulletins of the European Communities* reveals that less than five per cent of the settlements are mentioned, however briefly. The Commission itself has made it clear that it only feels bound to issue 'press releases' in 'cases of particular importance, either because points of law were raised or because of the economic power of the firms involved'.[288] Even taking into account the routine statement in the annual competition reports that '[m]any of the cases concerned distribution and licensing agreements, as in past years, which could be settled after having been brought into line with existing block exemptions or notices', there would seem to be a grey zone, consisting of those settlements which do not fall into the above categories and are not mentioned in Community publications either.

The apparent lack of consistency in the Commission's settlement practice illustrates the wide discretion it enjoys in settling or prosecuting a case.[289]

---

[287] See generally, Van Bael, 'The Antitrust Settlement Practice of the EEC Commission', (1986) Fordham Corporate Law Institute 759.

[288] *Sixth Report on Competition Policy*, p. 11. See also: Answer to Written Question No. 306/84, OJ 1984 C225/20. The transparency of the procedure has nevertheless slightly improved since then. See *XXIst Report on Competition Policy for 1991*, point 67.

[289] For example, Fiat and Alfa Romeo obtained settlements by agreeing to instruct their dealers to stop discouraging purchases of righthand-drive cars on the Continent which were sold at lower prices than those prevailing in the UK: EC Bull 11-1984. British Leyland plc received a fine even though it had made the same commitment as its Italian competitors (*BL*, OJ 1984 L207/11). However, it is clear that the Commission's discretion is, in any event, restricted by such fundamental principles as the proportionality rules, the principle of

Even though most settlements occur before a statement of objections is issued, it is still quite common for a settlement to be reached shortly after receipt of a statement of objections when the defendant, perhaps for the first time, realises the strength of the case brought against him.

It is less common for settlements to be reached towards the end of the formal proceeding when the parties involved and the Commission tend to remain frozen in their respective adversarial positions. Nevertheless, two important cases were settled 'at the last minute': the *Cigarette* case, involving the acquisition of a substantial interest by Philip Morris Inc. in Rothmans, and the suspension of proceedings against IBM.[290]

Legal value

The legal authority of most settlements is doubtful. Unlike the suspension of the proceeding against IBM which was decided by the full Commission, most settlements are reached at staff level. This implies that the settlement obtained may be declared invalid for lack of authority or a proceeding may be re-opened or continued notwithstanding compliance by the parties with the terms of the settlement. Indeed, in the past, written assurances given by high-ranking officials have not prevented the Commission from deciding differently.[291]

Even in a situation where a particular settlement is decided upon by the Commission as a collegiate body, its legal value is rather limited because the Commission remains at all times free to re-open the case when new facts come to light or circumstances change. Thus, in the end, the legal value of a settlement is very much akin to that of a negative clearance. This means that parties who are interested in legal certainty more than in speed may prefer to wait for a formal exemption decision, that is valid *erga omnes* and arguably offers protection against the application of stricter national laws. This may seem rather paradoxical, since an agreement receiving a negative clearance may not, or no longer, violate art. 85(1), whereas an agreement benefiting from an exemption under art. 85(3) by definition amounts to an infringement of art. 85(1). It is anomalous, indeed, that the less restrictive agreement or practice enjoys less legal certainty, compared with a more restrictive agreement that has received the benefit of an exemption.

¶1129 Compliance policy

Having discussed the procedure leading to decisions by the Commission establishing infringements and having assessed the merits of the

---

non-discrimination and the rule of law (see e.g. the opinion of Advocate-General Rozès in *Demo-Studio Schmidt v EC Commission* [1983] ECR 3045).

[290] *Fourteenth Report on Competition Policy*, respectively points 98–99 and 94–95. See also *BAT & Reynolds v EC Commission* [1987] ECR 4487.

[291] See e.g. *Frubo v EC Commission* [1975] ECR 563, at pp. 581–582 (para. 18–21); *Aluminium Imports from Eastern Europe*, OJ 1985 L92/1.

notification process, it may be appropriate to underline the importance for companies to follow a prophylactic approach.

In view of the vigorous enforcement policy of the EC Commission, the antitrust exposure for companies doing business in the EC is rather serious. Even if fines are not imposed, the costs of a Commission investigation may be very great. Such costs include the loss of management and staff time, lawyers' fees, damage to the reputation of the company concerned and, possibly, actions for damages instituted before the national courts of the member states.

The best way for a company to reduce its exposure under EC competition law is to introduce and implement an active compliance policy.[292]

Purpose

A compliance programme is designed to educate management and key personnel on the significance of EC antitrust law for their day-to-day operations.

Since the EC Commission and the courts readily assume that companies know the law or at least ought to know it, companies have no choice but to ensure that their policies are formulated clearly in all areas which carry the risk of infringements and that their personnel fully understand and implement the stated policies, having immediate access to expert legal advice when necessary.

Benefits

If management is made aware of the sensitivities of EC antitrust enforcement, it is in a better position to avoid such pitfalls.

If notwithstanding the implementation of an antitrust compliance programme, a company is found to infringe the law, the existence of the compliance programme will be viewed by the Commission as a mitigating factor, calling for a reduction of the fine.

This principle has been most clearly expressed in the *National Panasonic* case, where the Commission described the corrective action taken by Matsushita Electric Trading Company Ltd., 'MET', as follows:

'The Commission considers that such deliberate conduct designed to frustrate the aim of establishing a common market for the products in question justifies the imposition of a substantial fine.

Regard must, however, also be taken of the fact that MET has taken urgent steps to regulate the overall marketing policies of its subsidiaries in the EEC. In consultation with the Commission, MET has adjusted its guarantees so that consumers may have their purchases serviced throughout the

---

[292] On the subject of compliance policies in general, see e.g. Martin, 'Compliance Programmes for European Competition Law', [1981] ECLR 305,

¶1129

Community irrespective of where in the common market such purchases were made. MET has also conducted an audit of its legal practices in the Community and has issued codes of conduct to all its subsidiaries in the EEC which have the authority of the parent company.

This constructive attitude adopted by the management of MET since at least September 1981, has been taken into account in assessing the amount of the fine. The undertakings concerned have adopted a comprehensive practical detailed and carefully considered antitrust compliance programme, with appropriate legal advice.

Such action must be considered a positive step which contributes to an awareness at all levels of the group of the daily impact of competition policy. It tends to ensure that senior management is in a position to control the behaviour of the whole group in the market place and thereby to establish effective internal rules for the compliance with EEC competition law.

In taking this action of MET into account, therefore, the further examination of the grounds for imposing a fine in the amount which would otherwise have been justified has not been made.'[293]

The same principle was applied in *John Deere*,[294] *Sperry New Holland*,[295] *Hilti*,[296] *Napier Brown/British Sugar*[297] and in the *Toshiba* case.[298]

¶1130   Compliance policy: the compliance audit

Any compliance programme to be effective must be tailored to the specific needs of the company concerned. It must take the company's products and position on the market into account, as well as the reporting lines and decision making process.

In order to gather the company-specific information necessary to identify areas representing a potential antitrust risk, one should conduct an audit.

The procedures comprising such an audit typically require a detailed examination of selected company files and interviews with key personnel.

The document review is likely to focus on matters which in other EC antitrust cases have given rise to classic offences, e.g.:

- territorial restrictions and market sharing arrangements;
- pricing and discount policies;
- customer selection and refusals to deal;

---

[293] *National Panasonic*, OJ 1982 L354/28, at p. 34.
[294] *John Deere*, OJ 1985 L35/58, at pp. 63–64.
[295] *Sperry New Holland*, OJ 1985 L376/21, at p. 28.
[296] *Eurofix-Bauco/Hilti*, OJ 1988 L65/19, at p. 42.
[297] *Napier Brown/British Sugar*, OJ 1988 L284/41, at p. 58.
[298] *Toshiba*, OJ 1991 L287/39, at p. 43.

- sales literature and advertising;
- membership of trade associations;
- correspondence with competitors and suppliers;
- reports on mergers, acquisitions and joint ventures;
- R & D projects, licensing, standards;
- new products and business development;
- annual reports, releases to security analysts, etc.

The personnel selected for interviews should not only include the decision-makers but also those entrusted with the actual day-to-day implementation of the company policy in the field.

The organisation of the antitrust audit is better to be left in the hands of outside expert counsel. This is in order to secure the benefit of the attorney-client privilege, in addition to benefiting from their wide experience and independent judgement. Furthermore, outside counsel may more easily obtain the co-operation of management personnel, compared to inside counsel who may be either too close or perhaps, too subordinate, to management. Last but not least, outside counsel are more experienced in dealing with the delicate ethical considerations that may arise upon discovering a violation.

Once the audit is completed, senior management will have to be briefed on the company's performance and risk rating in the various areas that have been scrutinised. This report may include proposals for alternative business practices, offering no or less risk than the ones hitherto followed, together with recommendations for tightening up procedures and introducing a compliance package.

¶1131   Compliance policy: the compliance programme

It is not within the scope of this book to cover in detail what might be profitably included in a compliance programme. This may well differ from company to company. Nevertheless, some general observations may be in order.

Generally speaking, companies need to have a general policy statement, in addition to specific guidelines covering a wide variety of situations in which problems may arise.

(1)   General statement

This statement conveys the message that management is committed to the idea that the company should behave as a good corporate citizen and that compliance with the antitrust laws is the best guarantee for continued successful operations.

Thereafter, the document will restate the law in broad terms, focusing on possible problems arising in the company's relationship with competitors, customers and suppliers, and in connection with the company's market power.

In this connection, the following areas deserve particular attention:

(a) *Relations with competitors*

- prices and conditions of sale;
- market allocation;
- boycotts;
- participation in trade associations;
- specialisation agreements;
- joint purchasing agreements;
- joint R & D agreements;
- joint ventures.

(b) *Relations with customers and suppliers*

- resale prices;
- interference with imports and exports;
- tying arrangements;
- exclusive distribution arrangements;
- selective distribution systems;
- exclusive purchasing arrangements;
- refusals to deal;
- rebates;
- subcontracting agreements;
- reciprocal buying arrangements.

(c) *Abuse of market power*

Conduct on the part of a dominant company, i.e. a company holding a substantial share of the relevant market, is prohibited under art. 86 of the treaty if it amounts to an abuse of that dominance.

Practices most commonly found to be abusive include:

- the charging of 'unfair' prices, i.e. excessively high or unduly low 'predatory' prices;
- price discrimination, especially when practised on a geographical basis, i.e. when different prices are charged for the same product in different member states without any 'objective justification';

¶1131

- the granting of fidelity rebates;
- the granting of discounts that are not cost justified;
- refusals to deal when no 'objective justification' is present;
- tying practices.

(2) Specific guidelines
Companies may find merit in adopting a number of special guidelines covering specific high risk situations or dealing with specific problems.

(a) *Participation in trade associations*
There are no competition law problems with trade associations as such. The concern, however, is that a trade association meeting is typically a gathering of competitors, and such a meeting could lead to anti-competitive behaviour. Consequently, it may be wise for a company to devise specific rules for joining and participating in trade association activities. For example, in its *Pioneer* decision, the Commission drew adverse inferences from the fact that Pioneer had organised a meeting for its distributors in Antwerp for which there was no official agenda.

Thus, the items on the agenda of a trade association meeting deserve the utmost scrutiny. More importantly, the minutes of the meeting need to be carefully reviewed. For example, from the Commission's decisions in two price fixing cases, *Polypropylene*[299] and *Low Density Polyethylene*,[300] it follows that even companies that were absent from a particular meeting may find it difficult to exculpate themselves unless they unequivocally and promptly indicated their objections against what transpired at the meeting, as reflected in the minutes.

(b) *Proper business communications*
Careless language in business communications could have an extremely adverse effect on a company's position in an investigation or lawsuit involving the competition laws. While careful language will not avoid problems when the conduct being described is illegal, a poor choice of words may make lawful activity appear to be suspect. Furthermore, building a defence against language that is unclear, misleading, incorrect or provocative consumes time and money and may be unsuccessful.

---

[299] *Polypropylene*, OJ 1986 L230/1.
[300] *LdPE*, OJ 1989 L74/21.

¶1131

GENERAL MEASURES ADOPTED BY THE COMMISSION

¶1132   Examples of general measures

The Commission's enforcement policy is not exclusively implemented through individual measures applied to certain undertakings. It is also carried out by measures of general application, notably by the issuing of 'block exemptions' and 'notices'.

When the Commission takes a decision it acts in a quasi-judicial capacity, though these general measures are of a legislative nature. The latter are often the fruit of the experience gained by the Commission in its individual casework.

¶1133   Block exemptions

Article 85(3) of the treaty expressly provides for the possibility of a 'category' of agreements receiving an exemption from the prohibition of art. 85(1).

Pursuant to enabling regulations of the Council of Ministers,[301] the Commission has enacted a number of regulations under which the following categories of agreements are exempted as a group:

(1) exclusive distribution agreements;[302]

(2) exclusive purchasing agreements;[303]

(3) patent licensing agreements;[304]

(4) specialisation agreements;[305]

(5) selective distribution agreements for motor vehicles;[306]

---

[301] Council Regulation 19/65 of the Council enabling the Commission to adopt block exemptions for certain categories of agreements relating to exclusive dealing and industrial property rights, JO 1965 36/533. Council Regulation 2821/71 enabling the Commission to adopt block exemptions for certain categories of agreements dealing with the application of standards or types, research and development and specialisation, JO 1971 L285/46, as amended. Council Regulation 3976/87 on the application of art. 85(3) of the treaty to certain categories of agreements and concerted practices in the air transport sector, OJ 1987 L374/9, as amended. Council Regulation 4056/86 laying down detailed rules for the application of art. 85 and 86 of the treaty to maritime transport, OJ 1986 L378/4, itself contains a block exemption. See art. 3 and following. Council Regulation 1534/91 on the application of art. 85(3) of the treaty to certain categories of agreements, decisions and concerted practices in the insurance sector, OJ 1991 L143/1.

[302] Commission Regulation 1983/83 on the application of art. 85(3) of the treaty to categories of exclusive distribution agreements, OJ 1983 L173/1.

[303] Commission Regulation 1984/83 on the application of art. 85(3) to categories of exclusive purchasing agreements, OJ 1983 L173/30, corrigendum, OJ 1983 L281/24.

[304] Note 229 above.

[305] Note 231 above.

[306] Commission Regulation 123/85 on the application of art. 85(3) of the treaty to certain categories of motor vehicle distribution and servicing agreements, OJ 1985 L15/16.

(6) research and development agreements;[307]

(7) certain agreements in the air transport sector;[308]

(8) computer reservation systems for air transport services;[309]

(9) ground handling services;[310]

(10) franchise agreements;[311]

(11) know-how licensing agreements;[312]

(12) agreements in the insurance sector.[313]

In principle, these block exemptions do away with the need for filing individual notifications for agreements the terms of which are not more restrictive than the clauses specifically allowed in the block exemption. They are generally aimed at promoting legal certainty and alleviating the burden on the Commission staff. Especially, the so-called 'opposition procedure' may prove to be a useful instrument to that effect.

¶1134   Notices

From time to time the Commission has set out its views on certain categories of agreements in the form of a notice. Unlike block exemptions, notices have no binding force. They are for general guidance only. The Commission has, in particular, published the following notices:

(1) notice on exclusive dealing contracts with commercial agents;[314]

(2) notice on patent licence agreements;[315]

(3) notice on co-operation agreements;[316]

---

[307] Note 230 above.

[308] Commission Regulation 1617/93 on the application of art. 85(3) of the treaty to certain categories of agreements and concerted practices concerning joint planning and co-ordination of schedules, joint operations, consultations on passenger and cargo tariffs on scheduled air services and slot allocation at airports, OJ 1993 L155/18.

[309] Commission Regulation 3652/93 on the application of art. 85(3) of the treaty to certain categories of agreements between undertakings relating to computerised reservation systems for air transport services, OJ 1993 L333/37.

[310] Commission Regulation 82/91 on the application of art. 85(3) of the treaty to certain categories of agreements, decisions and concerted practices concerning ground handling services, OJ 1991 L10/7, expired on 31 December 1992.

[311] Commission Regulation 4087/88 on the application of art. 85(3) of the treaty to categories of franchise agreements, OJ 1988 L359/46.

[312] Note 233 above.

[313] Commission Regulation 3932/92 on the application of art. 85(3) of the treaty to certain categories of agreements, decisions and concerted practices in the insurance sector, OJ 1992 L398/7.

[314] Commission Notice on exclusive dealing contracts with commercial agents, JO 1962 139/2921. The Commission is currently drafting a new notice on contracts with commercial agents, see *XXIst Report on Competition Policy for 1991*, point 133.

[315] Notice on patent licence agreements ('Christmas message'), JO 1962 138/2922.

[316] Commission Notice concerning agreements, decisions and concerted practices in the field of co-operation between enterprises, JO 1968 C75/3, corrigendum, JO 1968 C93/3.

(4) notice on imports of Japanese goods;[317]

(5) notice on agreements of minor importance;[318]

(6) notice on subcontracting agreements;[319]

(7) notice on procedures concerning comfort letters;[320]

(8) notice on procedures concerning applications for exemption under art. 85(3);[321]

(9) notice on exclusive distribution and purchasing agreements;[322]

(10) notice on motor vehicle distribution and servicing agreements.[323]

(11) notice on restrictions ancillary to concentrations;[324]

(12) notice regarding the concentrative and co-operative operations under the merger regulation;[325]

(13) notice on activities of motor vehicle intermediaries (this notice being adopted to supplement the notice on motor vehicle distribution and servicing agreements);[326]

(14) notice on co-operation between national courts and the Commission in applying art. 85 and 86;[327]

(15) notice on the assessment of co-operative joint ventures under art. 85(1) and (3).[328]

The notices specified at (9) and (10) above are designed to assist in the interpretation of the block exemptions on the same subject.

---

[317] Commission Notice concerning imports into the Community of Japanese goods falling within the scope of the Rome Treaty, JO 1972 C111/13.

[318] Commission Notice on agreements, decisions and concerted practices of minor importance which do not fall under art. 85(1) of the treaty, OJ 1986 C231/2.

[319] Commission Notice concerning its assessment of certain subcontracting agreements in relation to art. 85(1) of the treaty, OJ 1979 C1/2.

[320] Commission Notice on procedures concerning application for negative clearance pursuant to art. 2 of Council Regulation 17/62, OJ 1982 C343/4.

[321] Commission Notice on procedures concerning notifications pursuant to art. 4 of Council Regulation 17/62, OJ 1983 C295/6.

[322] Commission Notice concerning Commission Regulations 1983/83 and 1984/83 on the application of art. 85(3) of the treaty to categories of exclusive distribution and exclusive purchasing agreements, OJ 1984 C101/2, amended OJ 1992 C121/2.

[323] Commission Notice concerning Regulation 123/85 on the application of art. 85(3) of the treaty to certain categories of motor vehicle distribution and servicing agreements, OJ 1985 C17/4.

[324] Commission Notice regarding restrictions ancillary to concentrations, OJ 1990 C203/5.

[325] Commission Notice regarding the concentrative and co-operative operations under Council Regulation 4064/89 on the control of concentrations between undertakings, OJ 1990 C203/10.

[326] Commission Notice concerning the clarification of the activities of motor vehicle intermediaries, OJ 1991 C329/20.

[327] Commission Notice on co-operation between national courts and the Commission in applying art. 85 and 86 of the EEC Treaty, OJ 1993 C39/6.

[328] Commission Notice concerning the assessment of co-operative joint ventures pursuant to art. 85 of the EEC Treaty, OJ 1993 C43/2.

¶1134

JUDICIAL REVIEW

¶1135   Jurisdiction and procedure generally

Decisions adopted by the Commission in the competition field are subject to review by the Court of Justice and the Court of First Instance. The Court of First Instance was, in fact, set up for the purpose of reducing the workload of the Court of Justice and of improving the judicial protection available to litigants, particularly in cases involving complex factual issues such as competition cases.

The Court of Justice is composed of 13 judges and assisted by six advocates general and by one registrar. It has jurisdiction to hear appeals against decisions of the Court of First Instance on points of law. Decisions adopted by the Commission under art. 85 and 86 may also be reviewed directly by the Court of Justice, where such decisions do not fall under the jurisdiction of the Court of First Instance. In addition, the Court of Justice may issue preliminary rulings on matters requiring the interpretation of Community law referred to it by national courts.

The Court of First Instance is composed of 12 judges and assisted by a registrar. It has jurisdiction to hear and determine, at first instance, competition law cases brought against an institution of the Communities by natural or legal persons. In addition, it has unlimited jurisdiction in regard to penalties, jurisdiction to entertain a plea of illegality and to suspend measures and grant other interim relief.

The procedure before the Court of Justice and the Court of First Instance is divided into two phases, a written and an oral phase. However, the procedure followed by the Court of Justice varies according to whether it is a direct action before the court or a request for a preliminary ruling. Also, in the case of a direct action, the procedure before the Court of Justice differs slightly depending on whether the action is brought on appeal following a decision by the Court of First Instance, or whether there was no such initial action before the Court of First Instance.

¶1136   Composition and organisation of the Court of Justice

The Court of Justice is composed of 13 judges and six advocates general who are appointed by common accord of the member states for a term of six years. They must be chosen 'from persons whose independence is beyond doubt and who possess the qualifications required for the appointment to the highest judicial offices in their respective countries or who are jurisconsults of recognised competence'.[329]

---

[329] Article 167 of the treaty.

The judges and advocates general are appointed by decision of a conference of representatives of the governments of the member states. In practice, each of the 12 member states nominates a judge for the court. The thirteenth judge comes from one of the five largest member states, on a rotation basis. By the same token, four of the six advocates general are appointed upon nomination by each of the four largest member states (Spain is not included), whereas the fourth and fifth are nominated by one of the remaining member states on a rotation basis.

The six-year term of office of the judges and advocates general is renewable.[330] In order to ensure the continuity of the court's membership, only one half of the members is up for re-election at triennial intervals. No compulsory retirement age is provided for.

The president of the court is elected by the judges for a renewable term of three years.[331] He directs the judicial business and administration of the court and presides at hearings and deliberations.[332] He also rules on requests for suspension of operation or enforcement and other interim measures.[333]

The court, in addition to sitting as a full court, is also divided into chambers.[334] Each of these chambers of the court likewise has a president, appointed by the court.

Role of the judge-rapporteur

When a case is registered, the president of the court assigns it to one of the chambers. One of the judges of that chamber will be nominated by the president of the court to act as judge-rapporteur on the case.[335]

Cases are assigned to a chamber or to the full court following the consideration of a preliminary report by the judge-rapporteur, and after hearing the advocate general.[336] This preliminary report is prepared by the judge-rapporteur at the end of the written procedure. In this report he puts the legal problems in their context, provides a summary of the submissions of the parties and suggests whether the court should order any measures of enquiry.

The judge-rapporteur is also the draftsman of the report for the hearing. This report is made available to the parties prior to the hearing to allow them to

---

[330] The point has been made that the six-year term, despite its possible renewal, is too short fully to secure judicial independence. See Brown and Jacobs, *The Court of Justice of the European Communities* (1977), at p. 28.

[331] Rules of Procedure of the Court of Justice of the European Communities of 19 June 1991, OJ 1991 L176/7, art. 7(1).

[332] Id., art. 8.

[333] Id., art. 85.

[334] Id., art. 9(1).

[335] Id., art. 9(2).

[336] Id., art. 95(2).

¶1136

comment. It contains a summary of the facts, a description of the procedure and the submissions of the parties.

Last but not least, the judge-rapporteur prepares the draft judgment in accordance with the majority opinion of the court.

Role of the advocates general

The role of the advocate general assigned to the case is 'to make, in open Court, reasoned submissions ... in order to assist the Court in the performance of the task assigned to it'.[337] To that effect, the advocate general, at the end of the oral procedure, delivers a non-binding opinion to the court covering both the facts and the legal issues of the case, and containing a proposal for deciding the matter. The advocate general does not participate in the court's deliberations. The office of advocate general is a form of institutionalised amicus curiae.

The activities of the advocates general are co-ordinated by one of them, the 'First Advocate General'. The title changes hands every year, on a rotation basis.

Administration of the court

The administration of the Court of Justice is the task of the registrar. He is appointed by the court for a renewable term of six years. He is responsible for the court's registry in which all pleadings and supporting documents are lodged. He also takes care of the acceptance, transmission, custody and service of documents and he draws up the minutes of hearings, judgments, orders and other decisions. The Court of Justice has issued detailed rules for the running of the registry in 'instructions to the registrar'.[338]

Each judge and advocate general is assisted by two law-clerks, usually referred to as 'legal secretaries'. They assist the judges and advocates general in their work.

¶1137 Composition and organisation of the Court of First Instance

The Court of First Instance consists of 12 members, one from each member state, appointed by common accord of the member states for a term of six years.

The qualifications required in order to become a judge at the Court of First Instance are slightly different from those required at the Court of Justice. The judges of the Court of First Instance are chosen 'from persons whose independence is beyond doubt and who possess the ability required for appointment to judicial office'.[339]

---

[337] Article 166 of the treaty.
[338] See Instructions to the Registrar, OJ 1982 C39/35.
[339] Article 168A(3) of the treaty.

The six-year term of office of the judges is renewable, and every three years one half of the members is up for re-election. Similarly to the rules pertaining to the Court of Justice, the members elect the president for a renewable term of three years.[340]

The role of the advocate general

The Court of First Instance has no permanent advocate general attached to it, but one of the judges may be called upon to perform the task of an advocate general on a case-by-case basis.[341] The criteria for the appointment of advocates general set out in the Rules of Procedure of the Court of First Instance are reasonably flexible. When the Court of First Instance sits in plenary session, an advocate general must be designated by the president of the court.[342] In cases dealt with by a chamber, however, an advocate general may be designated to assist the chamber only if the legal difficulty or the factual complexity of the case so requires.[343] The decision to designate an advocate general is taken by the court sitting in plenary session at the request of the chamber before which the case comes.[344] The parties to a case have no influence on the question of when and in what circumstances an advocate general should be appointed. The role of the advocate general at the Court of First Instance is identical to that which he plays before the Court of Justice. The judge acting as advocate general may not take part in the judgment of the case.

The organisation of sittings

The Court of First Instance sits in chambers of three or five judges[345] or, in certain cases, in plenary session. A case may be referred to the Court of First Instance sitting in plenary session whenever the legal difficulty or the importance of the case or special circumstances so justify.[346]

The role of the judge-rapporteur

When the case is registered, the president of the Court of First Instance assigns it to a chamber and designates one of its judges to act as judge-rapporteur.[347] The judge-rapporteur presents his preliminary report to the Court of First

---

[340] Rules of Procedure of the Court of First Instance of the European Communities of 2 May 1991, OJ 1991 L136/1, art. 7(1).

[341] Id., art. 2(2).

[342] Id., art. 17.

[343] Id., art. 18.

[344] Id., art. 19.

[345] Id., art. 12(1). Staff cases are assigned to chambers of three and all other cases are in principle assigned to chambers of five judges.

[346] Id., art. 14. This article has so far been applied by the Court of First Instance in *Tetra Pak v EC Commission* [1990] ECR II-309; *Automec Srl v EC Commission* ('*Automec II*'), [1992] ECR II-2223, and *Asia Motor France v EC Commission* [1992] ECR II-2285.

[347] Id., art. 13.

Instance at the end of the written procedure. In this report he suggests whether measures of organisation of procedure and measures of inquiry should be undertaken and whether the case should be referred to the Court of First Instance in plenary session or to a chamber composed of a different number of judges.[348]

The judge-rapporteur, as before the Court of Justice, also draws up the report for the hearing. This report contains a summary of the factual and legal material for the proceeding and is made available to the parties who may comment on it either orally or in writing.

Administration of the court

The Court of First Instance has its own registrar. The rules governing his service are contained in the Rules of Procedure of the Court of First Instance and are exactly the same as those governing the Registrar of the Court of Justice.[349] Apart from those matters, the Court of First Instance is structurally and administratively linked with the Court of Justice.[350]

¶1138   Jurisdiction of the Court of Justice and the Court of First Instance

The Court of Justice is the Community's supreme judicial authority. A matter may reach the court for review as a result of a direct action brought by one of the parties involved in a dispute; in competition law cases normally on appeal from the Court of First Instance, or as a result of a request for a preliminary ruling, filed by a national court.

Pursuant to art. 168A of the EC Treaty, which was added by the Single European Act, the Council established the Court of First Instance on 24 October 1988.[351] At that time, the Council did not confer jurisdiction on the Court of First Instance to the maximum extent permitted by the treaty, namely all actions brought by natural or legal persons, but only over four specific categories of cases brought by natural and legal persons:

(1) staff cases;

(2) certain categories of actions brought under the European Coal and Steel Treaty;

---

[348] Id., art. 52(1).

[349] The Protocol on the Statute of the Court of Justice, attached to the EC Treaty, art. 45 (amended by Council Decision 88/591 of 24 October 1989, establishing a Court of First Instance of the European Communities, OJ 1988 L319/1, corrected version, OJ 1989 C215/1, art. 7).

[350] Article 168A of the treaty provides that the Council 'may attach to the Court of Justice' a court of first instance. Most services, such as translation, interpretation for oral hearings, finance, recruitment and other personnel matters are common for the two courts. In most respects, the two courts thus form one institution.

[351] Council Decision 88/591 of 24 October 1988, establishing a Court of First Instance of the European Communities, OJ 1988 L319/1, corrected version at OJ 1989 C215/1.

(3) actions for annulment and failure to act concerning the EC competition rules applicable to undertakings; and

(4) actions for damages arising out of an act or failure to act subject to challenge by an applicant under one of the first three headings.

In June 1993, following a request by the court to the Council for an extension of the Court of First Instance's jurisdiction, the Council extended the Court of First Instance's jurisdiction to embrace all actions for annulment, failure to act and damages brought by natural and legal persons.[352] As a result of this extension, in addition to the four categories of cases listed above, the following actions brought by natural and legal persons are now included in the jurisdiction of the Court of First Instance:

(1) actions brought by natural and legal persons against the Commission in the field of state aid;

(2) actions for annulment and failure to act concerning trade protection measures in the field of dumping and subsidies;[353]

(3) all actions for damages caused by the Community's institutions or by its servants in the performance of their duties.

The nature of the cases that the Court of First Instance is competent to hear reflects a fundamental distinction between the role of the Court of Justice and the role of the Court of First Instance. The Court of Justice is generally considered as the proper forum for direct actions raising issues of constitutional significance and thus retains, in addition to references for preliminary rulings, jurisdiction in disputes between the institutions and between institutions and the member states which typically raise important issues concerning the institutional balance within the Community. The Court of First Instance, on the other hand, has responsibility at first instance for cases which are factually complex such as competition cases, state aids, anti-dumping and subsidy cases.

The Court of First Instance has limited jurisdiction, but plays an important role in the implementation of the EC competition rules since it determines at first instance cases in this area which are brought by natural or legal persons against an institution of the Communities, i.e. against Commission decisions.[354] The Court of First Instance is in principle not bound by judgments of the Court of Justice and may develop its own jurisprudence. In practice, however, the fact that decisions of the Court of First Instance can be set aside by the Court of Justice means that the Court of First Instance considers itself bound by the case law of the Court of Justice and frequently refers to the judgments of the Court

---

[352] Council Decision 93/350 of 8 June 1993 amending Council Decision 88/591, OJ 1993 L144/21.
[353] See Council Decision 94/149 OJ 1994 L66/29.
[354] Council Decision 88/591, art. 3(1)(c).

¶1138

of Justice in its reasoning. Appeals from the Court of First Instance to the Court of Justice may only be on points of law, which indicates that it is the Court of First Instance which, from the commencement of its operation in October 1989, has been responsible for the review at first and last instance of the factual circumstances underlying the decisions of the Commission in competition cases. So far the Court of First Instance has adopted a more activist and inquisitorial approach than the Court of Justice when reviewing the factual findings of the Commission.[355]

¶1139   Direct actions

The direct actions that are of special relevance in the context of the enforcement of EC competition law are the action for annulment (see ¶1140) and the action for failure to act (see ¶1141).

¶1140   Action for annulment

Judicial review of EC competition law is typically sought through an action for annulment under art. 173 of the treaty. With the establishment of the Court of First Instance, it is for that court to decide on most direct actions as such actions are normally instituted by undertakings against decisions of the Commission and thus fall under its jurisdiction.[356] The Court of First Instance has accordingly taken over the jurisdiction of the Court of Justice in this field.

In connection with such a review, questions may arise regarding the nature of the act which is the subject of the appeal, the person filing the appeal, the grounds for annulment, the persons entitled to intervene in the proceeding, and the outcome of the appeal.

Reviewable acts

According to art. 173 of the treaty the legality of regulations, directives and decisions of the Council and the Commission are capable of judicial review.

Among the decisions adopted by the Commission in the competition field, the following may clearly be the subject of an appeal:

(1) decisions finding an infringement;

(2) decisions granting negative clearance or exemption;

(3) provisional decisions;

---

[355] See e.g. *Filtrona Española SA v EC Commission* [1990] ECR II-393 and *Bayer v EC Commission* [1991] ECR II-219. See also *Societá Italiano Vetro SpA & Ors v EC Commission* [1992] 2 CEC 33, where the Court of First Instance required the Commission to present convincing evidence for the factual allegations in its decision and, after failure of the latter to produce such evidence, concluded that on several issues the evidence of the Commission was lacking or only gave a partial account of the facts.

[356] Council Decision 88/591, art. 3(1)(c).

(4) decisions ordering the supply of certain information or compelling a party to submit to an on-the-spot investigation;

(5) a final decision rejecting a complaint and closing the case;

(6) decisions declaring the non-applicability of the merger regulation to a notified concentration;

(7) decisions declaring a concentration compatible or incompatible with the common market.

However, in addition to these acts that constitute formal decisions of the Commission, there may be other acts which, though not labelled as a decision, may nevertheless have the essential features of a decision and as such be capable of judicial review.

In the *Cement* case, the court has interpreted the term 'decision' as:

'[any] measure which produces legal effects touching the interests of the undertakings by bringing about a distinct change in their legal position'.[357]

In addition to producing legal effects, the act must definitively lay down the position of the Commission, in other words, it must be final. In the *IBM* case the Court of Justice held that preparatory acts preceding the adoption of a final decision cannot form the object of an appeal.[358]

Locus standi

In accordance with art. 173 of the treaty, any natural or legal person is entitled to file an appeal against a decision of which he is an addressee.[359] Even if he is not an addressee, he may still file an appeal provided that the decision, though

---

[357] *Cimenteries v EC Commission* [1967] ECR 75, at p. 91. Subsequent case law has further clarified the nature and intensity of such legal effects. For instance, the Court of Justice has rejected as inadmissible appeals against acts that merely reproduced the provisions of a previous act that had not been challenged within the required time-limits or which merely clarified the logical consequences arising from another provision but without introducing any change. See, e.g. *SNUPAT v High Authority of the European Coal and Steel Community* [1961] ECR 53, at pp. 75–76 and *Hamboner v High Authority of the European Coal and Steel Community* [1960] ECR 493, at p. 503. In *Nefarma v EC Commission* [1990] ECR II-797, *Vereniging Nederlandse Ziekenfondsen & Ors v EC Commission* [1990] ECR II-827, and *Prodifarma & Ors v EC Commission* [1990] ECR II-843 (Omni-Partijen Akkoord judgments), the Court of First Instance held that a letter to the Dutch Government from the member of the Commission with special responsibility for competition policy, which was purely factual in nature, produced no legal effects and consequently was not an act capable of an appeal. See also *SA Cimenteries CBR & Ors v EC Commission* [1992] ECR II-2667, where the Court of First Instance stated that the measures by which the Commission refused, first, to disclose all the chapters of the statement of objections to the applicants and, secondly, to grant them access to all the documents in its file are not capable of producing legal effects of such a nature as to affect their interests immediately and held the appeal inadmissible.

[358] *IBM v EC Commission* [1981] ECR 2639, at p. 2654 (para. 21). See also *Automec Srl v EC Commission* ('*Automec I*') [1990] ECR II-367, where the Court of First Instance ruled that, in the procedure for investigating complaints, neither the preliminary observations made by the Commission at the beginning of such a procedure nor the communication to the complainant provided for in art. 6 of Regulation 99/63 may be regarded as decisions within the meaning of art. 173 of the EC Treaty, but as preparatory measures which cannot produce any legal effects and against which an action for annulment cannot be brought.

[359] This is so even in the absence of a fine being imposed, see, e.g. *BP v EC Commission* [1978] ECR 1513.

addressed to another person, is nevertheless of 'direct and individual concern' to him. Thus, for example, the appeal filed by a complainant in a competition case has been held admissible.[360]

Grounds for appeal

Article 173 enumerates four grounds on which an appeal may be based:

(1) lack of competence;

(2) infringement of an essential procedural requirement;

(3) infringement of the treaty or any rule of law relating to its application; and

(4) misuse of powers.

These four grounds have one point in common: they all seem to relate more to questions of law than of fact. However, in actual practice, especially in competition cases, the Court of Justice has often been called upon to review facts and it has proved to be quite willing to do so irrespective of the legal qualification of the infringement involved.

It is now the Court of First Instance that decides appeals against Commission decisions on the basis of the grounds enumerated in art. 173 of the EC Treaty. As pointed out above, the Court of First Instance has so far undertaken a more detailed analysis of the facts, and this is particularly relevant considering that appeals to the Court of Justice against decisions of the Court of First Instance can only relate to points of law.

Outcome of appeal

If the appeal is well founded, the relevant Community Court will declare all or part of the decision void.[361]

If the decision, subject to appeal, provided for a fine or periodic penalty payment, the court's jurisdiction is referred to as being 'unlimited', which means that the court may cancel, reduce or increase the fine or periodic penalty payment imposed.[362] Such unlimited jurisdiction is particularly relevant when the court partially annuls a Commission decision because it allows the

---

[360] *Metro v EC Commission* [1977] ECR 1875; *BAT & Reynolds v EC Commission* [1987] ECR 4487. Also, the court has treated as an addressee a member of the same group as the addressee. See e.g. *Ford v EC Commission* ('*Ford I*') [1984] ECR 1129, at p. 1159.

[361] Article 174 of the EC Treaty. Occasionally, the Community court not only partially quashed the decision of the Commission but also remanded the decision back to the Commission for corrective action, see *Transocean Marine Paint v EC Commission* [1974] ECR 1063, at p. 1081 (para. 22).
In *Societá Italiano Vetro SpA & Ors v EC Commission* [1992] 2 CEC 33, para. 319, the Court of First Instance held that the fact that a Community court may, as part of the judicial review of the acts of the Community administration, partially annul a Commission decision, does not mean that it has jurisdiction to remake the contested decision.

[362] See art. 172 of the EC Treaty. Regulation 17/62, art. 17. Thus far, the court has not made use of its power to increase the fines imposed in a competition case.

re-assessment of the level of the fine in the light of those parts of the Commission decision which have been annulled.[363]

¶1141 Action for failure to act

Pursuant to art. 175 of the EC Treaty a direct action may also be brought before the court in the event that the Council or the Commission fail to act in violation of the EC Treaty. Proceedings for failure to act have been brought and have been declared admissible only very rarely.

This type of action comes under the jurisdiction of the Court of First Instance when it is brought by a natural or legal person.[364]

A private party may bring such an action if he would be the potential addressee of an act which the Community institution would be obliged to take with regard to him.[365] An action brought under art. 175 is admissible only if the institution fails to define its position within two months of being called upon to act by either accepting or rejecting the request. The action may be then brought before the court within a further two months.

Thus, for example, in competition cases, a complainant could avail himself of the possibility of filing an action under art. 175 should the Commission fail to consider his complaint. However, once the Commission has defined its position, an action for failure to act would no longer be admissible.[366] The Court of Justice and the Court of First Instance have considered that the purpose of proceedings for failure to act is solely to obtain the adoption of the unadopted act. Thus, if the measure sought has been adopted after the proceeding was brought but before judgment was pronounced, the purpose of the proceeding

[363] See e.g. *Societá Italiano Vetro SpA & Ors v EC Commission*, [1992] 2 CEC 33, at para. 370–374 and *Petrofina SA v EC Commission*, [1991] ECR II-1087.

[364] Council Decision 88/591, art. 3(1)(c).

[365] See e.g. *Lord Bethell v EC Commission* [1982] ECR 2277, at p. 2291; *Emrich v EC Commission*, Order of the Court of 30 March 1990, [1990] ECR I-1555, (para. 5–6); *Asia Motor France v EC Commission*, Order of the President of the Court of 23 May 1990, [1990] ECR I-2181, at pp. 2184–2185, (para. 10–12); *Prodifarma v EC Commission*, Order of the Court of First Instance of 23 January 1991, [1991] ECR II-1, at p. 13, (para. 35).

The question whether the addressees of an act for the purposes of art. 175 should be extended to include persons who, even if not addressees, are directly and individually concerned by such an act has not yet explicitly been resolved. The court has made reference to this issue in several cases. See e.g. *Star Fruit Company v EC Commission* [1989] ECR 291, at p. 301 and *Prodifarma v EC Commission*, Order of the Court of First Instance of 23 January 1991, [1991] ECR II-1, at pp. 14–16, (para. 38–45). In favour of this approach, see e.g. opinion of Advocate General Dutheillet de Lamothe in *Mackprang v EC Commission* [1971] ECR 797 and opinion of Advocate General Lenz in *Star Fruit Company v EC Commission* [1989] ECR 291, at p. 296.

[366] *GEMA v EC Commission* [1979] ECR 3173, at pp. 3188–3190 (para. 14–23) where the Court of Justice considered that a notice given to the complainant under art. 6 of Regulation 99/63 is an act which constitutes a definition of the Commission's position within the meaning of art. 175 and dismissed the action for failure to act. It should be noted that such a notice has been regarded by the Court of First Instance as a preliminary measure against which an action for annulment is not available. See *Automec I*, note 358 supra. Thus, if the Commission only adopts a notice under art. 6 of Regulation 99/63, which is all it is bound to do under the regulation, the procedural rights of the complainant will be extinguished, as neither art. 175 nor art. 173 will be applicable. In practice, however, the Commission supplies a complainant who so requests with a final rejection of the complaint against which an action for annulment can be brought; *Lord Bethell v EC Commission* [1982] ECR 2277, at pp. 2290–2291 (para. 12–17).

ceases to exist.[367] Procedures for failure to act have also been brought in conjunction with an action for annulment under art. 173 where the legal nature of the communication from the Commission was unclear.[368]

¶1142   Appeal from decisions of the Court of First Instance

The scope of an appeal from decisions of the Court of First Instance is limited to points of law.[369] This limitation has the purpose of relieving the Court of Justice from the time-consuming process of an in-depth review of the facts of the case and makes it the supplementary judicial body competent to review questions of law rather than of fact, thus strengthening the role of the Court of Justice as the principal judicial authority of the Communities.

The appeal must be based on one or more of the following grounds:[370]

(1) lack of competence of the Court of First Instance;

(2) a breach of a procedural right which adversely affects the interest of the applicant;

(3) an infringement of Community law by the Court of First Instance.

Point (3) has the purpose of only permitting appeals concerning points of law and grants the Court of Justice a wide freedom of interpretation as to the line to be drawn between questions of law and questions of fact.

The persons entitled to bring an appeal are:[371]

- any party that has been unsuccessful, in whole or in part, in its submissions;
- interveners, when the decision of the Court of First Instance directly affects them;
- member states and Community institutions, even though they did not intervene in the case before the Court of First Instance;
- any person whose application to intervene has been dismissed, but only where the appeal concerns the right to intervene.

An appeal may be brought against final decisions of the Court of First Instance and decisions of that court disposing of substantive issues in part only or disposing of a procedural issue concerning a plea of lack of competence or of inadmissibility.[372] Furthermore, an appeal may be brought against a decision by which the Court of First Instance has dismissed an application to intervene and

---

[367] *Asia Motor France v EC Commission* [1992] ECR II–2285.
[368] *Camera Care v EC Commission* [1980] ECR 119, at p. 129.
[369] Article 168A(1) of the treaty.
[370] Protocol on the Statute of the Court of Justice, attached to the EC Treaty, art. 51.
[371] Id., art. 49 and 50.
[372] Id., art. 49.

against any decision by which it has suspended the application of an act (art. 185 of the treaty), prescribed interim measures (art. 186 of the treaty), or suspended the enforcement of a decision of the Commission imposing a pecuniary obligation (art. 192(4) of the treaty).[373]

Outcome of appeal

When the Court of Justice finds the appeal, in whole or in part, clearly inadmissible, or clearly unfounded, it can dismiss the appeal, in whole or in part, at any time.[374]

If the Court of Justice finds the appeal well-founded, it will quash the decision of the Court of First Instance, either by giving final judgment itself, where the state of the proceeding so permits, or by referring the case back to the Court of First Instance. In the latter case, the Court of First Instance is bound by the decision of the Court of Justice on points of law. The Court of Justice may also decide which of the effects of the decision of the Court of First Instance shall be considered definitive in cases where a well-founded appeal is brought by a member state or a Community institution, which did not intervene in the proceedings before the Court of First Instance.[375]

¶1143   Preliminary rulings

Under art. 177 of the treaty, the Court of Justice has jurisdiction to give 'preliminary rulings' at the request of national courts on questions concerning the interpretation or validity of provisions of Community law. Any national court or tribunal may request a preliminary ruling if it considers that a decision on a question of Community law is necessary to enable it to render a judgment. A court or tribunal from which there is no appeal must make such a request. When such a request is made, the proceedings in the national court are generally suspended until the court gives a ruling. In the context of a preliminary reference, the court has the power to interpret Community law, but not to apply it to the facts of the case. After the court has issued a ruling, the case is sent back to the national court which applies the ruling to the facts of the case.

---

[373] Id., art. 50.
[374] Rules of Procedure of the Court of Justice of the European Communities of 19 June 1991, OJ 1991 L176/7, art. 119.
[375] Protocol on the Statute of the Court of Justice, attached to the EC Treaty, art. 54.

¶1144   Procedure before the Court of First Instance

In May 1991 the Court of First Instance adopted its own Rules of Procedure which are to a large extent identical to the Rules of Procedure of the Court of Justice.[376]

The most significant innovation in the Rules of Procedure of the Court of First Instance is the possibility of adopting measures for the organisation of the procedure whose purpose is to ensure that cases are prepared for hearing, procedures carried out and disputes resolved under the best possible conditions.[377]

Measures of organisation are decided by the Court of First Instance after hearing the advocate general when appointed and typically upon recommendations made by the judge-rapporteur in his preliminary report as to whether these measures should be undertaken. Parties may express their views before the measures are prescribed if the circumstances so warrant.

The Court of First Instance may also prescribe any such measure at any stage of the proceedings and may do so on its own initiative or following a proposal from one or both parties in the case.[378]

The rules of procedure of the Court of First Instance also provide for measures of enquiry which correspond to those foreseen by the rules of procedure of the Court of Justice. However, in the Court of First Instance's practice measures of organisation have proved to be more important than orders relating to measures of inquiry and have particularly been introduced for the preparation of big cartel cases.[379]

---

[376] Until this was done, the Rules of Procedure of the Court of Justice were applied *mutatis mutandis*. The procedure before the Court of First Instance is furthermore governed by Title III of the Protocol on the Statute of the Court of Justice with the exception of art. 20, concerning preliminary rulings. The Court of First Instance will not give such rulings.

The following articles of the EC Treaty are declared applicable to the Court of First Instance except when otherwise provided for in the Council Decision establishing the Court of First Instance:

- art. 172 concerning unlimited jurisdiction as regards penalties;
- art. 174 concerning the possibility of limiting the effects of an annulment;
- art. 176 and 187 concerning the effects of judgments;
- art. 184 concerning pleas of illegality;
- art. 185 and 186 concerning suspensory effect;
- art. 192 concerning enforceability of pecuniary obligations on persons other than states.

[377] Rules of Procedure of the Court of First Instance of the European Communities of 2 May 1991, OJ 1991 L136/1, art. 64. Such measures may consist in particular of:

- putting questions to the parties;
- inviting the parties to make written or oral submissions on certain aspects of the proceedings;
- asking the parties or third parties for information on particulars;
- summoning the parties'agents or the parties in person to meetings.

[378] Id. art. 49. See e.g. *La Cinq v EC Commission* [1992] ECR II-1, where the Court of First Instance ordered measures of organisation during the written procedure.

[379] See e.g. *Societá Italiano Vetro SpA & Ors v EC Commission*, [1992] 2 CEC 33, where the judge-rapporteur held informal meetings with the legal representatives of the applicants before the oral hearing with a view to obtaining a complete summary of each of the parties' position and a common file of documents which the parties considered important. This facilitated the conduct of the oral hearing.

Measures of organisation are more informally taken than measures of inquiry given that a formal order does not have to be adopted as long as the parties co-operate.

The other rules of procedure are similar to those of the Court of Justice, which are described below.

¶1145   Procedure before the Court of Justice

The following pages contain a description of the procedure before the Court of Justice. As has been noted above, the form of procedure before the two courts is essentially identical. The Rules of Procedure of the Court of First Instance only depart from the Rules of Procedure of the Court of Justice with respect to a relatively small number of points. For the sake of convenience reference will be made to the relevant provisions of both courts' Rules of Procedure.

The filing of an appeal against decisions of the Commission is subject to certain formalities, the most important of which is the observance of the strict time-limits prescribed by the EC Treaty (see ¶1146).

The procedure in direct actions (see ¶1149–¶1151) is somewhat different from the procedure in preliminary rulings (see ¶1155). The procedure before the Court of Justice in appeals from the decisions of the Court of First Instance also presents certain specific characteristics (see ¶1152).

¶1146   Time-limits

The time-limits within which the appeal needs to be filed vary according to the type of action involved:

(1)   Actions for annulment

An action for annulment under art. 173 must be filed within two months of the publication of the measure, or of its notification to the plaintiff or, in the absence thereof, of the day on which it came to the knowledge of the plaintiff. The time-limit starts running from the day following the receipt of the notification of the measures[380] or, where the measure is published, from the fifteenth day after publication of the measure in the *Official Journal*.[381]

---

[380] A decision is duly notified once it has been communicated to the person to whom it is addressed and the latter is in a position to be aware of it. See *Ferriera Valsabbia v EC Commission* [1984] ECR 3089 and *Cockerill-Sambre SA v EC Commission* [1985] ECR 3749. More specifically, in *Bayer v EC Commission* [1991] ECR II-219 the Court of First Instance held that the dispatch of a registered letter with an advice of delivery was an appropriate means of notifying Commission decisions.

[381] Rules of Procedure of the Court of Justice of the European Communities of 19 June 1991, OJ 1991 L176/7, art. 81 and Rules of Procedure of the Court of First Instance of the European Communities of 2 May 1991, OJ 1991 L136/1, art. 102.

It should be noted that in accordance with art. 80 of the Rules of Procedure of the Court of Justice and art. 101 of the Rules of Procedure of the Court of First Instance, 'when a period expressed in days, weeks, months or years is to be calculated from the moment at which an event occurs or an action takes place, the day during which that occurs or that action takes place shall not be counted as falling within the period in question'. The Court of First

Furthermore, as the period is expressed in months, it will end with the expiry of whichever day in the second month falls on the same date as the day during which the notification or the publication took place. Also, the period of two months is extended by a given number of days, depending upon the applicant's country of residence.[382] These time-limits can be prolonged if the expiry is caused by the existence of unforeseeable circumstances or force majeure[383] or in the case of excusable error.[384]

(2) Actions for failure to act

The EC Treaty does not establish any time-limits within which the institution must be called upon to act in an action under art. 175. However, the court has ruled that the applicant must act within a reasonable time.[385] Once the institution has been called upon to act, it must do so within two months. If this two-month period elapses without any action, the applicant must bring the action before the competent court within a further period of two months.

Instance held in *Filtrona Española SA v EC Commission* [1990] ECR II-393 that both art. 81 and art. 80 of the Rules of Procedure of the Court of Justice (corresponding to art. 102 and 101 of the Rules of Procedure of the Court of First Instance) are complementary and aim to ensure for all parties the right to benefit from the full time-limit without granting a supplementary day. Thus, in the event of notification, the day following the receipt of the notification is included within the period of two months. The period then ends with the expiry of the day in the second month which falls on the same date as the day during which the notification took place.

[382] Article 1(3) of Annex II to the Rules of Procedure of the Court of Justice, which also applies to the Court of First Instance, provides for the following extension of time-limits on account of distance:

- Belgium: two days;
- Germany, the European territory of France and the European territory of the Netherlands: six days;
- the European territory of Denmark, Greece, Ireland, Italy, Spain, Portugal (with the exception of the Azores and Madeira), UK: ten days;
- other European Countries and territories: two weeks;
- the Azores and Madeira: three weeks;
- other countries, departments and territories: one month.

Periods shall include official holidays, Sundays and Saturdays and shall not be suspended during the judicial vacations. Furthermore, if the period would otherwise end on a Saturday, Sunday or official holiday, it shall be extended until the end of the first following working day. See art. 80(1)(d)(e) and art. 80(2) of the Rules of Procedure of the Court of Justice, and art. 101(1)(d)(e) and 101(2) of the Rules of Procedure of the Court of First Instance.

[383] Article 42 of the Protocol on the Statute of the Court of Justice. The court has stated that unforeseeable circumstances or force majeure require abnormal difficulties, independent of the will of the person concerned and apparently inevitable even if all due care is taken. This exception has been interpreted strictly by both the Court of Justice and the Court of First Instance. See e.g. *Busseni v EC Commission* [1984] ECR 557, *Ferriera Vittoria v EC Commission* [1984] ECR 2349, and *Filtrona Española SA v EC Commission* [1990] ECR II-393.

[384] *Schertzer v Parliament* [1977] ECR 1729, and *Orlandi v EC Commission* [1979] ECR 1613. The notion of excusable error has been narrowly interpreted by the Court of First Instance in *Bayer v EC Commission* [1991] ECR II-219. The court held that it could only relate to exceptional circumstances in which the institution concerned had adopted a course of conduct capable on its own or to a decisive degree of causing understandable confusion in the mind of an individual acting in good faith and exercising all the care that could be expected of a reasonably diligent operator.

[385] *Netherlands v EC Commission* [1971] ECR 639. See also opinion of Advocate General Darmon in *Irish Cement v EC Commission* [1988] ECR 6400.

(3)   Preliminary rulings

References by national courts to the Court of Justice for a preliminary ruling are not subject to any time-limit.

¶1147   Language

In references for preliminary ruling, the language of the referring court is to be used.

In direct actions the language is in principle chosen by the applicant from one of the official Community languages, unless the application is made against a member state or a natural or legal person having the nationality of a member state. The Court of Justice and the Court of First Instance may, however, authorise the use of another language at the joint request of the parties or at the request of one of the parties, after hearing the opposite party and the advocate general.[386]

The internal working language of both courts is French. Simultaneous translation is available during the oral argument.

¶1148   Legal representation

Whereas member states and Community institutions are represented before the court by an agent appointed for each case, private parties must be represented by a lawyer 'entitled to practice before the Court'.[387]

¶1149   Procedure in direct actions

The procedure before the competent court is essentially a written procedure (see ¶1150). The mere filing of an appeal does not stay the execution of the contested measures. However, a party may ask the competent court for interim relief, such as the suspension of the measure, in order to prevent 'irreversible' damage pending judgment. In addition, any person establishing an interest in a case submitted to either court for review may intervene in favour of one of the parties to the proceedings other than a member state or an EC institution. The plaintiff's application for appeal is filed with the competent court. The registrar will serve the application on the defendant, who normally has one month (this

---

[386]   Rules of Procedure of the Court of Justice of the European Communities of 19 June 1991, OJ 1991 L176/1, art. 29(2) and Rules of Procedure of the Court of First Instance of the European Communities of 2 May 1991, OJ 1991 L136/1, art. 35(2).

[387]   Protocol on the Statute of the Court of Justice, attached to the EC Treaty, art. 17. In accordance with art. 38(3) of the Rules of Procedure of the Court of Justice of 19 June 1991 L176/7 and art. 44(3) of the Rules of Procedure of the Court of First Instance of the European Communities of 2 May 1991, OJ 1991 L136/1: '[t]he lawyer acting for a party must lodge at the Registry a certificate that he is entitled to practise before a Court of a Member State'.

period is generally extended at the request of the interested party) to lodge a statement of defence. This initial exchange of briefs may be followed by a second round consisting of a reply by the applicant and a rejoinder from the defendant. After the close of the pleadings, the competent court may make further enquiries concerning specific issues of fact. In particular, the Court of First Instance may undertake measures of organisation as explained above.

At the hearing, each party is given an opportunity to elaborate upon its position and to reply to each other's arguments. The judges and the advocate general, if appointed before the Court of First Instance, may address questions to the parties during the course of the hearing. The advocate general delivers his opinion in open court, or sometimes in writing in the procedure before the Court of First Instance, after the hearing, in a separate hearing which concludes the oral procedure. This opinion is not binding upon the court, but is accorded substantial weight by the judges in arriving at their decision. The court's decision is reached by a simple majority vote. There is only one judgment of the court, without any separate concurring or dissenting opinions.

There is no appeal from the judgment of the Court of Justice. The judgment of the Court of First Instance may be appealed before the Court of Justice but, as noted above, only on points of law.

¶1150   Written procedure

The written procedure starts by lodging the application at the competent court.

In addition to identifying the applicant and the defendant(s), the application needs also to set out the subject-matter of the dispute, the grounds for the application, the evidence relied upon and the form of order sought by the applicant.[388] Thus, the application filed with the competent court constitutes the first written pleading of the applicant and sets the parameters of his case.

Each application lodged at the Court of Justice or at the Court of First Instance gives rise to the publication in the *Official Journal* of a short notice, mentioning the date of registration of the application, the identity of the parties, the subject-matter of the proceedings, the form of order sought by the applicant and a summary of the pleas in law and of the main supporting arguments.[389]

---

[388] Rules of the Court of Justice of the European Communities of 19 June 1991, OJ 1991 L176/7, art. 38(1) and Rules of Procedure of the Court of First Instance of the European Communities of 2 May 1991, OJ 1991 L136/1, art. 44.

[389] Id., art. 16(6) and 24(6).

(1)   Preliminary issues

A party applying to the competent court for a decision on a preliminary issue not going to the substance of the case must make the application by a separate document. The president must prescribe a period within which the other party may lodge a document containing a statement of the order sought by that party. The Court of Justice or the Court of First Instance must decide on the application after hearing the advocate general or reserve its decision for the final judgment.[390]

In cases where it is clear that the court to which an application is addressed has no jurisdiction to take cognisance of an action or where the action is manifestly inadmissible, that court may, by reasoned order, after hearing the advocate general and without taking further steps in the proceedings, give a decision on the action.[391]

(2)   Interim measures

The filing of an appeal does not in any way stay the execution of the measure which is the subject of the appeal.[392] To that effect, the applicant needs to file a separate application with the competent court, requesting the grant of total or partial suspension of the measure and/or any other interim measure which would be necessary.[393] Such application needs to specify the circumstances requiring urgent action and the factual and legal grounds setting out a prima facie case for the interim measures sought.[394]

The 'urgency' test has been defined to mean that interim relief must be necessary 'in order to avoid serious and irreparable harm before the decision of the Court in the main case'.[395] As to the 'prima facie' requirement, it has been

---

[390] Id., art. 91 and 114.

[391] Id., art. 92(1) and 111.

[392] Article 185 of the treaty.

[393] Rules of Procedure of the Court of Justice of the European Communities of 19 June 1991, OJ 1991 L176/7, art. 83(1) and Rules of Procedure of the Court of First Instance of the European Communities of 2 May 1991, OJ 1991 L136/1, art. 104(1).

[394] Id., art. 83 and 104(2).

[395] *Arbed v EC Commission* [1981] ECR 721; *Miles Druce v EC Commission* [1973] ECR 1049; *Montedipe SpA v EC Commission* [1986] ECR 2623; *Radio Telefis Eireann & Ors v EC Commission* [1991] 2 CEC 114. In *Ford v EC Commission* [1982] ECR 3091, the court held that it was necessary to consider whether there was a serious risk that the detrimental effects of a provisional measure adopted by the Commission will in the meantime cause damage exceeding the inevitable but short-lived disadvantages arising from such a measure. See also *Automobiles Peugot SA v EC Commission*, Order of the President of the Court of First Instance of 21 May 1990, [1990] ECR II-195. In *Dow Chemical Nederland BV v EC Commission* [1987] ECR 4367, the urgency requirement was not considered to be fulfilled in respect of a request for an interim order requiring the Commission to abstain from using various documents and information it had obtained during an investigation. The applicant argued that the investigation was not conducted in a proper manner and that the use of the evidence acquired therein would cause it serious and irreparable harm. The court held that the Commission would be prevented from using evidence it might have obtained in an investigation if the investigation decision was

said that the applicant must have 'at least an arguable case, in the main proceedings'.[396]

When applying these two criteria both the Court of Justice and the Court of First Instance may have to balance the interests of the applicant against the interest of the defendant and/or third parties.[397] Furthermore, interim measures are only designed to preserve the 'status quo ante' and may in no event prejudge the decision of the competent court on the substance of the main action.[398]

When an application for interim relief is filed with either court, the president will give the other side a short period of time to comment in writing or orally. The president will either decide on the application himself or refer the matter to the court.[399] In practice, most applications are decided by the president.

In view of the Commission's practice not to proceed with the collection of fines imposed pending the outcome of the appeal, provided a proper bank guarantee is set up, applications for stay of execution have been concerned with other aspects of the Commission's decision. In competition cases, a majority of the applications for interim relief have been granted.

---

subsequently annulled by the court and that the Commission decision 'might be annulled in so far as it is based on such evidence'. Accordingly the court did not find that the applicant would suffer serious and irreparable damage if it did not grant the interim order. In *Italy v EC Commission*, Order of the President of the Court of 17 March 1989, [1989] ECR 801, the President of the Court of Justice dismissed an application by the Italian Government on the grounds that the government had not given the necessary information to make possible an assessment of any damage caused to the Italian Republic. The President further added that had the firms concerned claimed themselves that recovery measures would cause them serious and irreparable damage, they would have had to show that the danger derived from recovery measures actually taken by the Italian authorities and could not be prevented by domestic remedies.

[396] *Camera Care v EC Commission* [1980] ECR 119. In *Publishers Association v EC Commission* [1989] ECR 1693, at para. 31, the court held that 'the application does not appear to be devoid of all foundation and that accordingly the requirement that a prima facie case must be established is satisfied'. See also *Hoechst AG v EC Commission* [1987] ECR 1549. In *La Cinq v EC Commission* [1992] ECR II-1, the Court of First Instance stated that the 'prima facie' case requirement does not require a clear and flagrant breach of competition rules.

[397] *Istituto Chemioterapico Italiano and Commercial Solvents v EC Commission* [1973] ECR 357; *Johnson and Firth Brown Ltd v EC Commission* [1975] ECR 1; *Metro v EC Commission* [1976] ECR 1353. See also *Publishers Association v EC Commission* [1989] ECR 1693, at para. 35–36. In *Langnese and Schöller v EC Commission*, Cases T-24/92 and T-28/92, order of the President of the Court of First Instance of 16 June 1992, not yet reported, the court arrived at a compromise solution and the suspension of the Commission's interim measure sought by the applicants was only partially granted.

[398] Rules of Procedure of the Court of Justice of the European Communities of 19 June 1991, OJ 1991 L176/7, art. 86(4) and Rules of Procedure of the Court of First Instance of the European Communities of 2 May 1991, OJ 1991 L136/1, art. 107(4).

[399] Id., art. 85 and 106.

¶1150

(3)   Third party intervention

Third parties having an interest in the result of a case brought before the Court of Justice or before the Court of First Instance may, within three months from the publication of the notice regarding the application originating the proceeding, lodge an application to intervene.[400]

The application needs to set out the reasons for the intervener's interest in the case, his submissions supporting or opposing the position of one of the parties to the original case, as well as the necessary evidence and documentation.[401]

The court will give the parties to the original case an opportunity to submit their written or oral comments on the application to intervene.[402]

If the court accepts the intervention, the intervener will receive a copy of the record of the proceedings and will have the opportunity to state in writing the grounds for his submissions.[403] Following the submission of the statement in intervention, the president of the court must, if necessary, prescribe a time-limit within which the parties may reply to that statement.[404]

In competition cases, competitors of the addressees, complainants, trade associations, consumer organisations and member states are the most likely third parties to intervene.

(4)   Exchange of briefs

Within one month after service on him, or her, of the application the defendant must lodge a defence, setting out the points of fact and law relied on, the supporting evidence and the form of order sought.[405]

The application originating the proceedings and the defence may be, and they usually are, supplemented by a reply from the applicant and by a rejoinder from the defendant.[406]

In a reply or rejoinder, a party may introduce further evidence, though it must give reasons for the delay in supplying it.[407] However, no fresh issue may

---

[400] Id., art. 93(1) and 115(1).
[401] Id., art. 93(1)2 and 115(2).
[402] Id., art. 93(2) and 116(1).
[403] Id., art. 93(3) and (5) and art. 116(2) and (4). By way of derogation from this principle, the president may, on the application by one of the parties, omit confidential information. In *Hilti v EC Commission* [1990] ECR II-163, where the applicant claimed confidential treatment for certain parts of its pleadings vis-à-vis two interveners, the court accepted the request of confidentiality of those documents covered by legal professional privilege, those constituting communications internal to the undertaking but reporting the content of legal advice and others that revealed business secrets. The court, however, rejected the applicant's request that the interveners could only use the pleadings and other procedural documents received for the purpose of the litigation.
[404] Id., art. 93(6) and 116(5).
[405] Id., art. 40 and 46.
[406] Id., art. 41 and 47(1).
[407] Id., art. 42(1) and 48(1).

¶1150

be raised unless it is based on matters of law or fact that came to light in the course of the procedure, i.e. until the judgment is issued.[408] This provision does not in any way provide for the possibility of an applicant transforming an application on grounds of failure to act into an application for annulment.[409] An act which, during the proceedings, replaces or extends the validity of the contested act must be regarded as a new factor enabling the applicant to amend its pleadings.[410] In case one of the parties raises a new issue, the president may, even after the expiry of the normal procedural time-limits, allow the other party to respond to that issue.

(5) Measures of enquiry

After the rejoinder has been lodged, the judge-rapporteur will present his preliminary report to the court. This report may recommend that certain measures of enquiry, and of organisation if the case is before the Court of First Instance, be undertaken.[411] If the court, after hearing the advocate general, follows the recommendation of the judge-rapporteur, it will prescribe the measures of enquiry that it considers appropriate by means of an order, or measures of organisation if the case is before the Court of First Instance, setting out the issues of fact to be determined.[412]

The court's measures of enquiry include:[413]

- the personal appearance of the parties;
- a request for information and production of documents;
- oral testimony;
- experts' reports;
- an inspection of the place or thing in question.

---

[408] Id., art. 42(2) and 48(2). See e.g. *Societá Italiano Vetro SpA v EC Commission* [1992] 2 CEC 33, para. 82, where the applicant introduced for the first time a plea in law based on the infringement of the European Convention for the Protection of Human Rights only at the reply stage, which was not accepted by the Court of First Instance.

[409] In *GEMA v EC Commission* [1979] ECR 3173, at p. 3191, para. 26, the Court of Justice seems to suggest that even when an applicant can raise a new plea in law based on matters of law or fact which came into light during the proceeding, he cannot introduce new conclusions other than those set out in his application and thus modify the object of the proceeding; see also *Asia Motor France v EC Commission* [1992] ECR II-2285 (para. 43–44).

[410] See *Alpha Steel Ltd v EC Commission* [1982] ECR 749, *Fabrique de fer de Charleroi SA & Anor v EC Commission* [1987] ECR 3639 and *Stahlwerke Peine-Salzgitter AG v EC Commission* [1988] ECR 4131. Nevertheless, the court has considered in *Automec Srl v EC Commission* ('*Automec I*') [1990] ECR II-367 that if the contested act is not a definitive measure but only a provisional one, a subsequent measure adopted while the action is in progress cannot be regarded as a new factor enabling the applicant to amend its conclusions. The reason for this is that a provisional measure cannot produce any legal effects which could be replaced or the validity of which could be extended by a subsequent measure.

[411] Id., art. 44(1) and 52(1).

[412] Id., art. 44(1) and 52(2).

[413] Id., art. 45 and 65.

¶1150

The Court of Justice has made little use of its formal powers of investigation in competition cases. In only very few cases did it hear witnesses.[414] Similarly, the appointment of experts occurred only rarely.[415]

(6)   Standard of proof

The Court of Justice has ruled that in order to successfully challenge the findings of the Commission:

> '... it is sufficient for the applicants to provide circumstances which cast the facts established by the Commission in a different light and which thus allow another explanation of the facts to be substituted for the one adopted by the contested decision.'[416]

In other words, if the applicant is able to create some doubt by offering a reasonable alternative explanation of the facts, he should prevail: in dubio pro reo.

Nevertheless, from the jurisprudence over the years, it is clear that the Court of Justice has often been reluctant to scrutinise the use the Commission has made of its discretionary powers in competition cases. As early as its judgment in *Grundig*, the court emphasised that :

> '... the exercise of the Commission's powers necessarily implies complex evaluations on economic matters. A judicial review of these evaluations must take account of their nature by confining itself to an examination of the relevance of the facts and of the legal consequences which the Commission deduces therefrom. This review must in the first place be carried out in respect of the reasons given for the decision which must set out the facts and considerations on which the said evaluations are based.'[417]

Although this extract from the ruling of the Court of Justice referred to the Commission's power to grant exemptions under art. 85(3), it accurately reflects the court's overall attitude concerning whatever economic evaluations the Commission makes in its decisions. As a matter of fact, 19 years later, in its *Remia* judgment,[418] in a case which the Commission had decided under art. 85(1), the court came to the same conclusion. It noted that the Commission's decision was based on an appraisal of complex economic situations. Hence, the

---

[414] *Suiker Unie & Ors v EC Commission* [1975] ECR 1663; *Musique Diffusion Française v EC Commission* [1983] ECR 1825; *AKZO Chemie BV and AKZO Chemie UK Ltd v EC Commission* [1986] ECR 2585.

[415] See e.g. *ICI v EC Commission* [1972] ECR 619, at pp. 647–648; *Åhlström & Ors v EC Commission* [1988] ECR 5193. The experts' report, though generally favourable to the defendant's thesis, was not discussed in the court's reasoning which went in favour of the Commission's point of view.

[416] *Compagnie Royale Asturienne des Mines SA and Rheinzink GmbH v EC Commission* [1984] ECR 1679, at p. 1702 (para. 16).

[417] *Grundig-Verkaufs GmbH v EC Commission* [1966] ECR 299 at p. 347.

[418] *Remia BV v EC Commission* [1985] ECR 2545.

court was of the opinion that it must limit its review of such an appraisal to verifying whether the relevant procedural rules have been complied with, whether the facts on which the choice is based have been accurately stated and whether there has been a manifest error of appraisal or a misuse of powers.

Thus, from the pronouncement of the Court of Justice in *Grundig* and *Remia*, it is clear that it is only inclined to intervene whenever the Commission's findings would appear to be wrong on the surface or totally lacking in support. In other words, the court, rather than double-checking the findings made by the Commission, will tend to give them full credit, unless, prima facie, there would appear to be something grossly wrong.

It is submitted that this attitude of the Court of Justice may occasionally create a situation where it remains for the defendant to prove his innocence. Indeed, it is not because the authorities have not committed any 'manifest error' when assessing the facts that they have properly discharged their burden of adducing sufficient evidence of a breach of the competition rules. Discretion cannot mask the standards of evidence on which such a breach can properly be based.

The reluctance of the Court of Justice to scrutinise the discretionary findings of the Commission in any depth is not cured by the court's willingness to review the question whether in a given case the relevant procedural rules have been complied with. Indeed, even in situations where the violation of a rule of due process is clearly established, the Court of Justice tends to refuse to quash the Commission's decision on the ground that even in the absence of any infringement of a principle of due process by the Commission, the outcome of the case would not have been different. The court appears to be of the opinion that the administrative nature of the proceedings before the Commission implies that lesser standards of care and fairness apply than in a judicial proceeding.[419]

The foregoing discussion makes it clear that from the very beginning the Court of Justice has perceived its role more as that of a Supreme Court than as a true Court of Appeal with wide fact-finding powers. In this context, the creation of the Court of First Instance for the purpose of trying the facts more fully,[420] has been generally welcomed.

---

[419] In *Pioneer Hi-Fi Ltd v EC Commission* [1983] ECR 1825 at p. 1880 (para. 6 and 7), the court made the following statement :

'MDF maintains that the contested decision is unlawful by the mere fact that it was adopted under a system in which the Commission combines the functions of prosecutor and judge, which is contrary to Article 6(1) of the European Convention for the Protection of Human Rights.
That argument is without relevance. As the Court held in its judgments of 29 October 1980 in Cases 209 to 215 and 218/78 (*Van Landewyck v Commission* [1980] ECR 3125), the Commission cannot be described as a "tribunal" within the meaning of Article 6 of the European Convention for the Protection of Human Rights.'

The Court of First Instance likewise held that the EC Commission is not an art. 6 tribunal; see *Shell International Chemical Co. Ltd v EC Commission* [1992] ECR II-757.

[420] As stated by Judge Vesterdorf, acting as advocate general in *Polypropylene* '   the very creation of the

Although it is probably too early to make any conclusive comments on the direction in which the Court of First Instance is steering its review of the factual findings of the Commission, it is nevertheless interesting to note that in its *Flat Glass* judgment the Court of First Instance left no doubt about the principle that the burden of proof should rest entirely on the Commission and that this burden had not been properly discharged.[421]

¶1151   Oral procedure

The oral procedure consists of the oral arguments of the parties and of the opinion of the advocate general.[422]

(1)   Hearing

After the parties have exchanged briefs and the court has completed its preparatory enquiry, if any, a hearing will be organised at which the parties have the opportunity to present their case orally.[423] In some cases, however, the Court of Justice, acting on a report from the judge-rapporteur, after hearing the advocate general and with the express consent of the parties, may decide that the procedure before the court will not include an oral hearing. This possibility was provided for in the last modification of the Rules of Procedure of the Court of Justice and tends to accelerate the proceedings in those cases where the oral procedure appears to be of no use or merely redundant.[424] This possibility, however, is not provided for in the Rules of Procedure of the Court of First Instance.

A few days prior to the hearing, the court and the parties receive a copy of the report for the hearing prepared by the judge-rapporteur. His report sets out the facts of the case and summarises the arguments of the parties. This document is very helpful because it will show which facts or arguments are already well understood and which points need to be explained more fully at the hearing.

At the hearing, counsel have the opportunity to present their clients' case to the court. The order of speeches is applicant, defendant, intervener. The president will give the parties a chance to reply briefly to each other's arguments. At times, the judges and the advocate general put many probing questions which liven up the debate considerably.

Court of First Instance as a court of both first and last instance for the examination of facts in cases brought before it is an invitation to undertake an intensive review in order to ascertain whether the evidence on which the Commission relies in adopting a contested decision is sound' (opinion of the Advocate General Vesterdorf in Joined Cases T-1 to 4/89 and T-6 to 15/89 delivered on 10 July 1991).

[421] *Societá Italiano Vetro SpA & Ors v Commission* [1992] 2 CEC 33. In para. 205 the court actually criticised the Commission for having engaged in 'cutting and pasting' evidence, gathered from uncertain sources.

[422] Protocol on the Statute of the Court of Justice of the European Community. art. 18.

[423] Rules of Procedure of the Court of Justice of the European Communities of 19 June 1991. OJ 1991 L176/7. art. 55.

[424] Id., art. 44(a).

(2) Advocate general's opinion

Usually, some time after the hearing, the advocate general will deliver his opinion in open court. However, in the procedure before the Court of First Instance, the judge acting as advocate general may make his reasoned submissions in writing.[425] As has been noted above, the inclusion of this kind of opinion does not always occur in the procedure before the Court of First Instance.

In his opinion, the advocate general deals with all the facts and issues of the case and recommends a particular solution. Though not binding on the court, his opinion, nevertheless, may be of considerable assistance to the Court of Justice.

Generally speaking, the opinion of an advocate general reflects greater freedom when dealing with the issues than a court judgment. Indeed, the court needs to take its previous case law into account and its judgments are often the result of a compromise reached in the deliberation room.

After the advocate general has rendered his opinion, the President will declare the oral procedure closed.[426] Thus the parties are not entitled to comment on the advocate general's opinion, unless the court orders the re-opening of the oral procedure in case new circumstances have arisen.[427] In cases where no advocate general has been appointed, the President shall declare the oral procedure closed at the end of the hearing and deliberation of the case begins.[428]

¶1152   Procedure on appeal from the Court of First Instance

The procedure before the Court of Justice in the case of an appeal from the Court of First Instance is rather similar to that in the case of an appeal from Commission decisions. Several procedural rules of the Court of Justice remain applicable to this particular procedure.[429] Among those not applicable are

---

[425] Council Decision 88/591, art. 46(3).

[426] Rules of Procedure of the Court of Justice of the European Communities of 19 June 1991, OJ 1991 L176/7, art. 59(2) and Rules of Procedure of the Court of First Instance of the European Communities of 2 May 1991, OJ 1991 L136/1, art. 61(2).

[427] Id., art. 61 and art. 62. In *United Brands v EC Commission* [1978] ECR 207, at pp. 305–306 (para. 280–288), the court dismissed United Brands' motion to re-open the oral procedure in view of alleged important factual errors in the advocate general's opinion (Financial Times, 1 December 1977, p. 2). Contrast the approach of the court in *Procureur de la République v Giry and Guerlain (Perfumes)* [1980] ECR 2327, and *AM & S v EC Commission* [1982] ECR 1575, where the court decided to re-open the oral procedure on its own initiative. In *Hüls AG v EC Commission* [1992] ECR II-499 the applicant applied for the re-opening of the proceeding to raise the same claim as in the PVC cartel cases. The Court of First Instance rejected the application on the grounds that it should have been raised beforehand and should have been supported by some evidence. The court concluded that since the applicant's arguments could not justify an application for revision, there was no question of accepting the applicant's request to re-open the oral proceeding.

[428] Rules of Procedure of the Court of First Instance of the European Communities of 2 May 1991, OJ 1991 L136/1, art. 60.

[429] Rules of Procedure of the Court of Justice of the European Communities of 19 June 1991, OJ 1991 L176/7, art. 118. Included are art. 42(2), 43, 44, 55 to 90, 93, 95 to 100 and 102.

notably the rules concerning preparatory enquiries since the Court of Justice does not, in this case, examine the facts.

The appeal can be lodged at the registry of the Court of Justice or at the registry of the Court of First Instance, and the applicant must attach to the appeal the decision appealed against.[430] As in the normal procedure, third party intervention is possible, but the Court of Justice decides upon the admissibility of the intervention without hearing the other parties.[431]

The subject-matter of the proceeding before the Court of First Instance may not be changed on appeal. This restriction does not, however, prohibit the introduction of new legal arguments in the appeal, provided that the subject matter is not thus modified.

The procedure consists of a written and an oral part. The Court of Justice may, however, after hearing the Advocate General and the parties, decide 'to dispense with the oral procedure unless one of the parties objects on the ground that the written procedure did not enable him fully to defend his point of view'.[432] It is possible that the Court of Justice will interpret this provision as giving it the power to dispense with the oral procedure, even if a party objects, when the court considers that the written procedure has permitted the party in question to defend his point of view fully.[433]

The written part consists of the appeal and a defence, and can further be supplemented by a reply and a rejoinder. However, there is no absolute right to submit a reply or a rejoinder since it will only be allowed if the President of the Court considers such further submissions necessary in order to enable a party to put forward his point of view or provide a basis for the decision on the appeal.[434]

¶1153   Judgment

The court's judgment is adopted by a simple majority vote and there are no dissenting opinions.

The court's judgment contains a summary of the facts,[435] the submissions of the parties, the grounds for the decision and the operative part of the judgment,

---

[430] Id., art. 111 and 112(2).

[431] Id., art. 123.

[432] Id., art. 120.

[433] See E. Van Ginderachter, 'Le Tribunal de Première Instance des Communautés Européennes', Cahiers du droit européen, 1989, p. 63, at p. 98.

[434] Rules of Procedure of the Court of Justice of the European Communities of 19 June 1991, OJ 1991 L176/7, art. 117(1).

[435] The court has discontinued its practice of distributing and publishing the 'Facts and Issues' part of its judgments. The essential content of that part is currently incorporated in the 'Decision' part of the judgment. The 'Decision' part, however, deals only summarily with the factual background. The judgment instead makes a reference to the Report for the Hearing, drawn up by the judge-rapporteur, which is published together with the judgment and the opinion of the advocate general.

including the decision as to costs.[436] It may be interesting to note that the judgments of the Court of First Instance tend to be consistently longer than those of the Court of Justice and contain a detailed summary of the facts, the procedure and the arguments of the parties.[437]

Costs

The unsuccessful party is ordered to pay the costs.[438] Where each party succeeds on some and fails on other counts, or where the circumstances are exceptional, the court may order that the parties bear their own costs in whole or in part.[439] The court may order a party, even if successful, to pay the costs that it has caused the opposite party to incur unreasonably or vexatiously.[440] Member states and the institutions that intervene in the proceedings must bear their own costs. The court may also order other interveners to bear their own costs.[441]

The recoverable costs include 'expenses necessarily incurred by the parties for the purpose of the proceedings, in particular the travel and subsistence expenses and the remuneration of agents, advisers or lawyers'.[442] In the event that a dispute arises regarding the costs to be recovered, the matter is decided by a chamber of the Court of Justice, or by the Court of First Instance itself.[443]

The same rules regarding costs are applicable in the case of an appeal from a decision of the Court of First Instance. However, when the appeal is unfounded or where the appeal is well-founded and the Court of Justice itself gives

---

[436] Rules of Procedure of the Court of Justice of the European Communities of 19 June 1991, OJ 1991 L176/7, art. 63 and Rules of Procedure of the Court of First Instance of the European Communities of 2 May 1991, OJ 1991 L136/1, art. 81.

[437] In some cases, the Court of First Instance has in its judgment completely restructured and reformulated the arguments of the parties. See, e.g. *Polypropylene* cases, see notes 299 and 420 above.

[438] Rules of Procedure of the Court of Justice of the European Communities of 19 June 1991, OJ 1991 L176/7, art. 69(2) and Rules of Procedure of the Court of First Instance of the European Communities of 2 May 1991, OJ 1991 L136/1, art. 87(2).

[439] Id., art. 69(3) and 87(3). See e.g. *General Motors v EC Commission* [1975] ECR 1367, at pp. 1388–1389. See also, *BASF & Ors v EC Commission* [1992] ECR II-315, where the court ordered the Commission to pay the costs even though it held that the applications were inadmissible and *Asia Motor France v EC Commission* [1992] ECR II-2285 where costs were shared given the exceptional circumstances of the case.

[440] Id.

[441] Rules of Procedure of the Court of Justice of the European Communities of 19 June 1991, OJ 1991 L176/7, art. 69(4) and Rules of Procedure of the Court of First Instance of the European Communities of 2 May 1991, OJ 1991 L136/1, art. 87(4).

[442] Id., art. 73 and 91.

[443] Id., art. 74(1) and 92(1). See e.g. *Europemballage Corp and Continental Can v EC Commission* [1975] ECR 495. In this case, the court stated as follows:

'As Community law contains no provisions as to scale fees, the Court must be free to consider the facts of the case, taking into account the object and nature of the action, its importance from the point of view of Community law and the difficulty of the case.'

The court then fixed the recoverable amount of legal fees in the currency of one of the member states and rejected a request for default interest. See also *Firma Gebrüder Dietz v EC Commission* [1977] ECR 2431, noted (1978) 3 E.L.Rev. 212. In this case, the Commission tried to recover legal fees for its agents. The court rejected the claim and allowed the Commission only to recover the travel and subsistence expenses of its agents because these expenses were not covered by their normal salary.

¶1153

judgment, the Court of Justice makes the decision as to costs.[444] In the case of a well-founded appeal brought by a member state or an institution which did not intervene in the proceedings before the Court of First Instance, the Court of Justice may order the parties to bear their own costs or that the member state or institution shall pay the costs which the appeal has caused the initial applicant to incur.[445]

Effective date
Only the operative part of the judgment is read in open court. The judgment is binding from the date of its delivery in court.[446]

Revision/rectification of judgments
The court's judgment is final unless an application for revision or a third party proceeding is successful. An application for revision may be filed only upon discovery of a fact 'which is of such a nature as to be a decisive factor, and which, when the judgment was given, was unknown to the Court and to the party claiming the revision'.[447] The application for revision needs to be made within three months of the date on which the applicant receives knowledge of the fact supporting his application.[448] However, no such application may be filed after ten years have elapsed from the date of the judgment.[449]

The court's judgment may also be modified as a result of third-party proceedings. An application originating third-party proceedings must be lodged within two months of the publication of the contested judgment.[450] Such application needs to state how the judgment is prejudicial to the rights of the third party and why it was unable to take part in the original case.[451] The contested judgment will be changed on the points on which the submissions of the third party are upheld.[452]

---

[444] Rules of Procedure of the Court of Justice of the European Communities of 19 June 1991, OJ 1991 L176/7, art. 122. As a consequence of this provision, it is probably the Court of First Instance which decides on the costs if the appeal is well-founded and referred back to the Court of First Instance.

[445] Ibid.

[446] Rules of Procedure of the Court of Justice of the European Communities of 19 June 1991, OJ 1991 L176/7, art. 65 and Rules of Procedure of the Court of First Instance of the European Communities of 2 May 1991, OJ 1991 L136/1, art. 83.

[447] Protocol on the Statute of the Court of Justice, attached to the EC Treaty, art. 41.

[448] Rules of Procedure of the Court of Justice of the European Communities of 19 June 1991, OJ 1991 L176/7, art. 98 and Rules of Procedure of the Court of First Instance of the European Communities of 2 May 1991, OJ 1991 L136/1, art. 123(1).

[449] Protocol on the Statute of the Court of Justice, attached to the EC Treaty, art. 41.

[450] Rules of Procedure of the Court of Justice of the European Communities of 19 June 1991, OJ 1991 L176/7, art. 97 and Rules of Procedure of the Court of First Instance of the European Communities of 2 May 1991, OJ 1991 L176/7, art. 123(1).

[451] Ibid.

[452] Id., art. 97(3) and 123(3).

If the court's judgment is not clear, a party to the proceedings may file an application for interpretation.[453] By the same token, if the Court of Justice should omit to give a decision on a particular point at issue or on costs, any party may within a month after service of the judgment apply to the court to supplement its judgment.[454]

The court may also, on its own motion, or on application by a party made within two weeks after the delivery of a judgment, rectify clerical mistakes, calculation errors and obvious slips.[455]

¶1154   Relationship between the courts

If a case is addressed to the wrong court, as a result of either a formal error or a mistake in appreciation of the competence of the court, the court lacking the necessary competence must refer the action to the competent court.[456] In order to avoid a negative conflict of jurisdiction, once a case has been transferred from the Court of Justice to the Court of First Instance, the latter cannot decline jurisdiction.[457] In cases where the Court of First Instance considers that it has jurisdiction and that it will decide the case, an appeal to the Court of Justice would be necessary in order to contest its competence.[458] Where an appeal is brought before the Court of Justice against a decision of the Court of First Instance disposing of a procedural issue concerning a plea of lack of competence, the Court of First Instance may stay the proceeding.

Should the two courts be seised at the same time of cases in which the same relief is sought, the same issue of interpretation is raised or the validity of the same act is called into question, the Court of First Instance may stay the proceeding before it until the Court of Justice has delivered its judgment. Before doing so, the Court of First Instance must hear the parties and the advocate general.[459] Where applications are made for the same act to be

---

[453] Id., art. 102 and 129. See e.g. *SA Générale Sucrière & Ors v EC Commission* [1977] ECR 445.

[454] Rules of Procedure of the Court of Justice of the European Communities of 19 June 1991, OJ 1991 L176/7, art. 67. The Rules of Procedure of the Court of First Instance only provide for the possibility of applying to supplement the judgment if a decision on costs has been omitted. See Rules of Procedure of the Court of First Instance of the European Communities of 2 May 1991, OJ 1991 L136/1, art. 85.

[455] Id., art. 66 and 84. See, e.g. the two orders of the court, dated 11 May and 26 June 1978, *United Brands v EC Commission* [1978] ECR 207, at pp. 305–306 (para. 280–288).

[456] Article 47, first and second para., of the Protocol on the Statute of the Court of Justice. See e.g. *Asia Motor France v EC Commission*, Order of the President of the Court of 23 May 1990, [1990] ECR I-2181 where the Court of Justice transferred the case to the Court of First Instance as the application concerned the implementation of competition rules applicable to undertakings.

[457] Protocol on the Statute of the Court of Justice, attached to the EC Treaty, art. 47(2). Rules of Procedure of the Court of First Instance of the European Communities of 2 May 1991, OJ 1991 L136/1, art. 80.

[458] Rules of Procedure of the Court of First Instance of the European Communities of 2 May 1991, OJ 1991 L136/1, art. 77(b).

[459] Protocol on the Statute of the Court of Justice, art. 47(3).

declared void, the Court of First Instance may also decline jurisdiction in order that the Court of Justice may rule on such applications. Following the same procedure, the Court of First Instance may order that the proceedings be resumed.[460]

¶1155   Procedure in preliminary rulings

The procedure in preliminary rulings differs from that involved in direct actions. The procedure is not of a adversarial nature. The parties do not initiate it. The procedure is initiated by the national court, which requests a preliminary ruling from the Court of Justice. When the Court of Justice receives the order for reference from the national court, the Registrar sends a copy to the parties to the proceedings before the national court, to the member states, the Commission and, where an act of the Council is involved, to the Council. They all may submit written observations within a period of two months.[461] At the hearing of the case, they may also make oral remarks, which is the only time that a party may respond to the arguments of other parties since, in contrast to direct actions, there is no defence, reply or rejoinder. The court may decide, however, not to organise an oral procedure provided that none of the persons entitled to submit written observations has asked to present oral arguments.[462] After the hearing, the procedure is the same as in direct actions.

If a question referred to the Court of Justice for a preliminary ruling is manifestly identical to a question on which the court has already ruled, the court may, after informing the national court which initiated the procedure and the involved parties, hearing the advocate general, give its decision by reasoned order in which reference is made to its previous judgment.[463]

Furthermore, the Court of Justice does not resolve the case that is referred to it. Once it has answered the questions of law which are the subject of the reference, the case is sent back to the national court which requested the preliminary ruling. The proceedings will then continue in the national court from the point at which they were suspended. The national court must apply Community law to the facts of the case in accordance with the Court of Justice's judgment.

All questions of interpretation of Community law arising before any national court may, at that court's discretion, be referred to the Court of Justice. If the

---

[460] Rules of Procedure of the Court of First Instance of the European Communities of 2 May 1991, OJ 1991 L136/1, art. 78.

[461] Rules of Procedure of the Court of Justice of the European Communities of 19 June 1991, OJ 1991 L176/1, art. 103(3).

[462] Id., art. 104(4).

[463] Id., art. 104(3).

national court is one of last resort, however, it is under a duty to make a reference for a preliminary ruling.[464]

Several important issues of EC competition law have been resolved by the Court of Justice by way of a preliminary ruling.[465]

---

[464] Article 177 of the treaty.

[465] See e.g. *Bosch v Van Rijn* [1962] ECR 45; *Société Technique Minière v Maschinenbau Ulm* [1966] ECR 235; *Brasserie de Haecht v Wilkin* [1967] ECR 407; *Parke, Davis v Centrafarm* [1968] ECR 55; *Wilhelm v Bundeskartellamt* [1969] ECR 1; *Völk v Vervaecke* [1969] ECR 295; *Sirena v Eda* [1971] ECR 69; *Deutsche Grammophon v Metro* [1971] ECR 487; *BRT v SABAM ('BRT I')* [1974] ECR 51; *Centrafarm v Sterling Drug* [1974] ECR 1147; *EMI Records v CBS UK* [1976] ECR 811; *Terrapin v Terranova* [1976] ECR 1039; *Coditel v Ciné Vog Films* [1980] ECR 881; *Procureur de la République v Giry and Guerlain (Perfumes)* [1980] ECR 2327; *Pronuptia de Paris v Schillgalis* [1986] ECR 353; *Ministère Public v Asjes & Ors* [1986] ECR 1425; *Vereniging van Vlaamse Reisbureaus v Sociale Dienst van de Plaatselijke en Gewestelijke Overheidsdiensten* [1987] ECR 3801; *Van Eycke v SA Apsa* [1988] ECR 4769; *AB Volvo v Erik Veng (UK) Ltd* [1988] ECR 6211

¶1155

PART IV

STATE AIDS

12 State Aids

INTRODUCTION

¶1201 Overview

Articles 92 to 94 of the EC Treaty aim at preventing member states from granting to undertakings aid that distorts or threatens to distort competition and affects trade between member states. Articles 92 to 94 are thus directed at the same objectives as art. 85 and 86, and are also included in the Chapter of the EC Treaty on competition policy. Unlike art. 85 and 86, however, the state aid rules are not couched in terms of an outright prohibition. Rather, art. 92(1) provides that state aid is 'incompatible' with the common market. This shift in tone reflects the more politically-sensitive nature of state aids: while art. 85 and 86 are aimed at the activities of private enterprise, the state aid rules are aimed at those of member states.

Since the mid-1980s, the Commission has progressively tightened its control over state aid. In large part, this increased vigilance is the direct result of the push towards a single internal market. In the Commission's view, companies will be reluctant to undertake the kind of pan-European activity necessary to achieve a single market if, in addition to their true competitors, they must also contend with the finance ministries of the member states into which they seek to expand.[1] Moreover, state aids may exacerbate the gap between the rich and

---

[1] In the *XXth Report on Competition Policy*, point 169, the Commission explained the importance of a strong state aid policy to the achievement of a single internal market as follows:

'[As the internal market nears completion and barriers to trade between member states are reduced,] hitherto partially protected national markets will become increasingly accessible to more competitors in other Member States. If Member States use aid to defend companies or industries coming under pressure from this increased competition, or grant aid to counteract the effect of assistance given in other Member States, competition will be distorted and there is a danger that industrial structures will become ossified. Furthermore, unless undistorted competition is allowed to restructure Community industry, very little of the macroeconomic gains which according to forecasts should result from the completion of the internal market ... will in fact be realized. Competition is the main vehicle for securing these advantages, and competition-distorting aid measures threaten the very rationale of the internal market. Consequently, a reinforced State aid policy is not only vital to the successful completion of the internal market but a necessary prerequisite if the projected gains from such integration are to be realized.'

See also *XXIst Report on Competition Policy for 1991*, point 10; *XXIInd Report on Competition Policy for 1992*, point 1.

poor regions in the Community, which runs counter to the goal of a single, integrated market.[2]

To tighten its control over state aids, the Commission has adopted a multi-faceted approach. First, it has introduced a series of procedural innovations designed to enhance its powers. For instance, it has established a framework for the notification and review of existing aid schemes as well as new aid schemes.[3] It has also put teeth in its enforcement policy, notably through the increased use of the power to order recovery of illegal aid from recipients.[4] Secondly, it has targeted new forms of aid for review. Aid to state-owned companies, which often went by unnoticed in the past, is now subject to strict scrutiny pursuant to an annual reporting system.[5] Also, the Commission is conducting a systematic review of existing aid schemes to determine which of these still qualify for clearance.[6]

Finally the Commission has sought to heighten awareness of the Community's state aid regime and increase the transparency of its work in this field. In an effort to make its policies clearer and more predictable, it has issued a series of guidelines and communications to the member states which discuss how it intends to treat various forms of aid.[7] For example, the Commission has fleshed out the meaning of the principles used to judge aid to state-owned companies – notably, the market economy investor principle – in a set of guidelines.[8] To improve communication with the member states, the Commission has begun holding regular (at least twice yearly) multilateral meetings with aid experts from the member states.[9] To obtain more

---

[2] In the *XXIst Report on Competition Policy for 1991*, point 13, the Commission stated:

'Examination of State aid, with regard both to new projects notified in 1991 and to existing schemes, has been geared to the overriding objective of ensuring strict control of aid granted in the most prosperous regions, so that the aid granted to help develop the least prosperous regions can achieve its objective, notably by facilitating the investment required to narrow the development gap separating them from the rest of the Community or to help them adjust structurally.'

See also id., point 158; *XXth Report on Competition Policy*, point 169.

[3] See ¶1227.

[4] See ¶1232.

[5] See ¶1229.

[6] See ¶1222.

[7] By issuing guidelines, the Commission largely avoids the political bargaining that would occur if it used more formal instruments such as regulations or directives that required the involvement of the Council. In a field such as state aids, which involves restrictions placed on member states, it would seem necessary to avoid such bargaining if the state aids policy is to be effective. The disadvantage of this approach is that the enforceability of guidelines may be challenged. See, for example, *France v EC Commission*, Case C-325/91, judgment of 16 June 1993 (not yet reported), in which the Court of Justice annulled the Commission communication on the application of art. 92 and 93 of the treaty and of art. 5 of Directive 80/723 to public undertakings in the manufacturing sector. Following the annulment, the Commission decided to adopt as a directive the contested obligation on member states to provide annual financial data (Directive 93/84, amending Directive 80/723, OJ 1993 L254/16) and to re-adopt the communication omitting the reporting requirement (OJ 1993 C307/3).

[8] See ¶1204.

[9] See *XXth Report on Competition Policy*, point 170.

¶1201

comprehensive information on state aid programmes, the Commission periodically conducts surveys on state aids in the Community.[10]

While the emerging principle of subsidiarity may affect the Commission's application of the competition rules, it may play a lesser role in the enforcement of the state aid rules.[11] First, it would seem unrealistic to expect member states to police their own activities in this field. Secondly, to the extent that the application of the state aid rules involves a balancing of local interests and Community interests, particularly with respect to regional aid, the Commission would seem in a better position to act as a neutral arbiter. Nevertheless, the subsidiarity principle may come into play in so far as many of the policies in the state aids field simply establish an overall framework within which member states are free to follow their own policies.[12]

The court has generally supported the Commission's policy in the state aids field, but it has also instituted some basic procedural safeguards for the parties involved. For example, the court has imposed deadlines on the Commission to ensure that the grant of legitimate aid is not unduly delayed by the need for Commission review.

The first part of this chapter considers which types of state aid fall within the scope of art. 92(1). The second part examines the categories of state aid that are or may be compatible with the common market pursuant to art. 92(2) and 92(3). The third part reviews the major procedural elements found in art. 93.

STATE AIDS WITHIN THE SCOPE OF ART. 92(1) OF THE EC TREATY

¶1202   Introduction

Article 92(1) states the basic rule on state aids as follows:

> 'Save as otherwise provided in this Treaty, any aid granted by a Member State or through state resources in any form whatsoever which distorts or threatens to distort competition by favouring certain undertakings or the production of certain goods shall, in so far as it affects trade between member states, be incompatible with the common market.'

---

[10] See e.g. Third Survey on State Aids in the European Community in the manufacturing and certain other sectors, IV/E-6(92)D (1992).

[11] See *XXIInd Report on Competition Policy for 1992*, point 121.

[12] For example, in the area of regional aid, the Commission has laid down general principles concerning which regions may benefit from aid and the maximum level that may be paid, but leaves it to the member states to decide matters such as what projects should receive aid.

Thus, a measure is only 'incompatible' with the common market within the meaning of art. 92(1) if the following conditions are met:

(1) an 'aid' exists;

(2) the aid is granted by a member state or through state resources;

(3) the aid distorts or threatens to distort competition;

(4) the aid favours certain undertakings or the production of certain goods;

(5) the aid affects trade between member states; and

(6) the aid is not specifically permitted by another treaty provision.

¶1203   Concept of 'aid': basic principles

The treaty does not contain a precise definition of 'aid'. The court and the Commission have interpreted this term broadly to include not only positive benefits such as subsidies, but also measures that, in various forms, reduce costs that would otherwise have to be borne by the company receiving the beneficial treatment.[13] While aid often involves a situation where the recipient receives something for nothing, this gratuitous element is not necessary for a finding of aid. If the state grants a loan to a company that could not have obtained a loan from a commercial bank, aid exists even though the company pays a normal commercial rate of interest to the state.[14] The critical feature is whether the recipient receives a benefit that he could not obtain under normal market conditions. This concept of the 'market economy investor' is explored in more detail below.

Article 92(1) provides that state aid can be granted 'in any form whatsoever'. The case law of the Commission and the court confirms that aid may take many forms, ranging from government assistance in paying for the disposal of surplus manure[15] to government financing of film production.[16] Some of the more

---

[13] In *Steenkolenmijnen v High Authority* [1961] ECR 1, at p. 19, the court explained that the concept of aid is wider than that of a subsidy:

'A subsidy is normally defined as a payment in cash or in kind made in support of an undertaking other than the payment by the purchaser or consumer for the goods or services which it produces. An aid is a very similar concept, which, however, places emphasis on its purpose and seems especially devised for a particular objective which cannot normally be achieved without outside help. The concept of aid is nevertheless wider than that of a subsidy because it embraces not only positive benefits, such as subsidies themselves, but also interventions which, in various forms, mitigate the charges which are normally included in the budget of an undertaking and which, without, therefore, being subsidies in the strict meaning of the word, are similar in character and have the same effect.'

See also *Amministrazione delle Finanze dello Stato v Denkavit Italiana* [1980] ECR 1205.
[14] For an example of such a loan, see *France v EC Commission* ('*Boussac*') [1990] ECR I-307.
[15] See *Dutch Manure Bank*, OJ 1992 L170/34.
[16] See *Greek Films*, OJ 1989 L208/38.

common forms of aid include the following: tax exemptions[17] and refunds,[18] reductions in social security[19] and medical insurance[20] contributions, employment premiums,[21] capital injections,[22] loans at reduced rates of interest,[23] state guarantees,[24] export[25] or investment subsidies,[26] and reductions in the price of real estate or assets owned by the state.[27]

¶1204   Concept of 'aid': market economy investor principle

The so-called 'market economy investor principle' has been used with increasing frequency to determine whether a given measure constitutes aid.[28]

---

[17] See e.g. *Mactac*, OJ 1991 L156/39; *Volkswagen Bruxelles*, OJ 1991 L123/46; *SA Sucrerie Couplet, Brunehaut-Wez*, OJ 1990 L186/21; *Belgian Shell*, OJ 1989 L106/34. The deferment of tax payments may also constitute aid. See e.g. *PMU*, OJ 1992 L14/35.

[18] See e.g. *Aid granted by the Italian Government to the forestry, pulp, paper and board industry and financed by means of levies on paper, board and cellulose*, OJ 1992 L47/19; *Aid granted in France to cereal farmers and producers, financed by the reimbursement of specific fiscal and parafiscal charges*, OJ 1990 L105/15; *Aid to declining industrial regions in France*, Seventeenth Report on Competition Policy, point 245; *Aid to Belgian textile and clothing industries*, Sixteenth Report on Competition Policy, point 216; *Irish export sales relief*, Tenth Report on Competition Policy, point 173.

[19] See e.g. *Italy v EC Commission* [1974] ECR 709; *EC Commission v France* [1983] ECR 3707; *Aid scheme in favour of the textile and clothing industry in France*, OJ 1983 L137/24; *Eighth Report on Competition Policy*, point 238.

[20] See e.g. *EC Commission v Italy* [1983] ECR 2525.

[21] See e.g. *Belgian aid to SMEs*, Eighth Report on Competition Policy, point 243.

[22] See cases cited at footnote 37 below.

[23] See e.g. *Intermills v EC Commission* [1984] ECR 3809; *Nuova Cartiera di Arbatax*, OJ 1992 L159/46; *Mactac*, OJ 1991 L156/39; *Reinhold KG*, OJ 1991 L156/33; *Bolzano Steelworks*, OJ 1991 L86/28; *Magefesa*, OJ 1991 L5/18; *MFL Group*, OJ 1990 L182/94; *Aluminia and Comsal*, OJ 1990 L118/42; *Peugeot*, OJ 1989 L123/52; *Valeo*, OJ 1989 L143/44; *International Harvester/Tenneco*, OJ 1988 L229/37.

[24] See e.g. *Schiffswerft Germersheim*, OJ 1991 L158/71; *Magefesa*, OJ 1991 L5/18; *Eighth Report on Competition Policy*, point 223.

[25] See e.g. *Hellenic Republic v EC Commission* [1988] ECR 2875; *EC Commission v France* [1969] ECR 523; *Greek Special Tax*, OJ 1989 L394/1; *Italian Forestry, Pulp, Paper and Board Industry*, OJ 1992 L47/19.

[26] See e.g. *Philip Morris Holland v EC Commission* [1980] ECR 2671; *Volkswagen Bruxelles*, OJ 1991 L123/46; *Sucrerie Couplet, Brunehaut-Wez*, OJ 1990 L186/21; *Belgian Shell*, OJ 1989 L106/34.

[27] See e.g. *Sony Berlin*, OJ 1993 C216/5; *Daimler-Benz*, OJ 1992 L263/15; *Toyota*, OJ 1992 L6/36.

[28] The Commission has applied this principle in numerous individual cases. See *IOR/Finalp*, OJ 1992 L183/30; *Hytasa*, OJ 1992 L171/54; *Nuova Cartiera de Arbatax*, OJ 1992 L159/46; *MFL Group*, OJ 1992 L182/94; *Imepiel*, OJ 1992 L172/76; *Sabena*, OJ 1991 L300/48; *Halkis Cement*, OJ 1991 L73/27; *Enasa*, OJ 1989 L367/62; *Veneziana Vetro*, OJ 1989 L166/60; *ENI–Lanerossi*, OJ 1989 L16/52; *Alfa Romeo*, OJ 1989 L394/9; *Renault*, OJ 1988 L220/30; *Pechiney*, OJ 1988 L121/57; *Boch*, OJ 1987 L228/39, OJ 1986 L223/30, OJ 1985 L59/21, OJ 1983 L91/32; *Boussac*, OJ 1987 L352/42; *Ideal Spun*, OJ 1984 L283/42; *Meura*, OJ 1984 L276/34; *Fabelta*, OJ 1984 L62/18; *Intermills*, OJ 1982 L280/30; *Leeuwarden*, OJ 1982 L277/15.

The Commission has explained this principle in detail in two Communications to member states: Commission communication concerning the application of art. 92 and 93 of the EEC Treaty and of art. 5 of Commission Directive 80/723 to public undertakings in the manufacturing sector (as re-adopted, OJ 1993 C307/3) ('Commission communication on state aids to public undertakings'); Commission communication on the application of art. 92 and 93 of the EEC Treaty to public authorities' holdings in company capital, Bulletin EC 9–1984.

The court has repeatedly upheld the use of this principle. See *Italy v EC Commission* ('*Aluminia and Comsal*') [1991] ECR I-4437; *Italy v EC Commission* ('*Alfa Romeo*') [1991] ECR I-1603; *Italy v EC Commission* ('*ENI-Lanerossi*') [1991] ECR I-1433; *Belgium v EC Commission* ('*Tubemeuse*') [1990] ECR I-959; *Belgium v EC Commission* ('*Boch*') [1986] ECR 2321; *Belgium v EC Commission* ('*Meura*') [1986] ECR 2263.

According to this principle, the provision of funds to a company constitutes aid if the company would not have been able to obtain the funds on the same terms from private capital markets.[29] To make this determination, it is necessary to ask whether, in similar circumstances, a private investor would have made the funds available and, if so, whether he would have done so on the same terms. This comparison of the behaviour of the state with that of a hypothetical investor is to be made as of the time when the funds were provided.[30]

The private investor whose behaviour is used as a benchmark is interested in obtaining a return on his investment; social, regional policy and sectoral considerations that might enter into a state's decision on how to use its funds are not relevant for the private investor and, thus, are not taken into account.[31] The hypothetical investor is of a size comparable to that of the body administering the aid[32] and, as a result, its perspective is not necessarily that of an investor looking for a speculative or short-term profit. In several cases, the court has held that this investor may be influenced by other, more long-term factors. For instance, in *Alfa Romeo*,[33] the relevant behaviour was deemed to be that of a private holding company pursuing a structural policy – whether general or sectoral – to obtain a profit over the long-term. Similarly, in *ENI-Lanerossi*,[34] the court recognised that a private investor may well inject new capital to enable a company to survive temporary difficulties to become profitable again. By the same token, a parent company may carry the losses of a subsidiary for a limited time to allow the latter to withdraw from an unprofitable business under favourable conditions to avoid tarnishing the

---

[29] In *Belgium v EC Commission* ('*Boch*') [1986] ECR 2321, at p. 2345 (para. 13), the court stated the test as follows:

'An appropriate way of establishing whether such a measure is a State aid is to apply the criterion ... of determining to what extent the undertaking would be able to obtain the sums in question on the private capital markets. In the case of an undertaking whose capital is almost entirely held by the public authorities, this test is, in particular, whether in similar circumstances a private shareholder, having regard to the foreseeability of obtaining a return and leaving aside all social, regional-policy and sectoral considerations, would have subscribed the capital in question.'

[30] Commission communication on state aids to public undertakings, at p. 10 (para. 28). See also *Italy v EC Commission* ('*Aluminia and Comsal*') [1991] ECR I-4437.

[31] With respect to such costs, the Commission has stated:

'If these costs were considered by the Commission, it would amount to granting Member States the power to rescue companies in difficulties on the basis of pure national interest. This situation, which could create serious distortions of competition contrary to the common interest, would be in contradiction with the principles of the EEC Treaty empowering the Commission to determine the compatibility of State assistance in the context of the Community as a whole and not in that of a single Member State. Putting the abovementioned costs together with those corresponding to the behaviour of the State as owner/shareholder of a company would amount to emptying the market-economic private-investor principle of its meaning.' (*Hytasa*, OJ 1992 L171/54, at pp. 59 and 60.

[32] *Italy v EC Commission* ('*Alfa Romeo*') [1991] ECR I-1603 (at para. 19).

[33] Id. (para. 20).

[34] *Italy v EC Commission* ('*ENI-Lanerossi*') [1991] ECR I-1433 (at para. 21). See also *Belgium v EC Commission* ('*Meura*') [1986] ECR 2263 (at para. 15).

¶1204

group's image or to redirect the group's activities.[35] In both of these cases, the state was a majority shareholder in the company receiving the aid, which would presumably give it a more long-term perspective than if it were only a minority shareholder.[36]

While the market economy investor principle was developed mainly in cases involving capital injections,[37] it is increasingly being applied to other forms of state intervention such as loans[38] and guarantees,[39] as well as to determine whether the state is receiving a normal return on its capital investments.[40] In its communication concerning aid to public enterprises,[41] the Commission offers a

---

[35] Id. See also *Conversion Activities of French Public Industrial Groups Outside the Steel and Coal Industries,* OJ 1992 L138/24, at p. 29 (conversion activities of certain public groups do not constitute aid because they offer indirect benefits such as 'indirect material profit', 'maintaining the group's image' and 'redirecting its activities').

[36] The Commission has suggested that the standard articulated in *ENI-Lanerossi* and *Alfa Romeo* only applies in cases where the state is a majority shareholder. See *Imepiel,* OJ 1992 L172/76 at p. 81. See also Commission communication on state aids to public undertakings at p. 10 (para. 30).

The Commission's decision in *Nuova Cartiera di Arbatax,* OJ 1992 L159/46, illustrates the confusion that may result if different standards are applied depending upon the circumstances. In that case, both public and private companies took shareholdings in a struggling newsprint producer. The Commission found that the provision of capital by the public companies constituted state aid because a private investor would not have made the investment. That a private company also provided capital did not change the Commission's appraisal because the private company was a large paper manufacturing group pursuing 'group strategic purposes' in which the newsprint producer could play a role. In this connection, the Commission also emphasised that the private company was in charge of the management of the newsprint producer. It is unclear why the public companies could not also have been said to be pursuing 'group strategic purposes', particularly as one of them was engaged in promoting the production and use of cellulose and paper. If the answer is that the public companies lacked managing control of the company, this would seem anomolous because the Commission went on to cite the fact that the shareholding of the private company had been significantly reduced in favour of the public shareholders as further evidence of state aid.

[37] See *Italy v EC Commission ('Aluminia and Comsal')* [1991] ECR I-4437; *Italy v EC Commission ('Alfa Romeo')* [1991] ECR I-1603; *Italy v EC Commission ('ENI-Lanerossi')* [1991] ECR I-1433; *France v EC Commission ('Boussac')* [1990] ECR I-307; *Belgium v EC Commission ('Tubemeuse')* [1990] ECR I-959; *Belgium v EC Commission ('Boch')* [1986] ECR 2321; *Belgium v EC Commission ('Meura')* [1986] ECR 2263; *Imepiel,* OJ 1992 L172/76; *Hytasa,* OJ 1992 L171/54; *Nuova Cartiera di Arbatax,* OJ 1992 L159/46; *Sabena,* OJ 1991 L300/48; *Enasa,* OJ 1989 L367/62; *Veneziana Vetro,* OJ 1989 L166/60; *Alfa Romeo,* OJ 1989 L394/9; *Renault,* OJ 1988 L220/30; *Pechiney,* OJ 1988 L121/57; *ENI-Lanerossi,* OJ 1989 L16/52; *Boch,* OJ 1987 L228/39, OJ 1986 L223/30, OJ 1985 L59/21, OJ 1983 L91/32; *Meura,* OJ 1984 L276/34; *Leeuwarden,* OJ 1982 L277/15; *Intermills,* OJ 1982 L280/30.

[38] *France v EC Commission ('Boussac')* [1990] ECR I-307; *Belgium v EC Commission ('Boch'),* [1986] ECR 2321 at p. 2345 (para. 12) ('no distinction can be drawn between aid granted in the form of loans and aid granted in the form of a subscription of capital'); *MFL Group,* OJ 1992 L182/94; *Nuova Cartiera di Arbatax,* OJ 1992 L159/46; *Halkis Cement Co.,* OJ 1991 L73/27; *Renault,* OJ 1988 L220/30; *Pechiney,* OJ 1988 L121/57.

[39] See *IOR/Finlap,* OJ 1992 L183/30 (state holding company became the sole owner of a company, which, under Italian law, made it responsible for all of the company's debts).

[40] See *Finsider/ILVA,* OJ 1989 L86/76 (Commission imposed conditions on grant of aid to ensure a minimum return on capital). See generally Commission communication on state aids to public undertakings, at p. 9 (para. 26).

[41] Commission communication to the member states on the application of art. 92 and 93 of the EEC Treaty and of art. 5 of Commission Directive 80/723 to public undertakings in the manufacturing sector, as re-adopted, OJ 1993 C307/3 (the 'Commission communication on state aids to public undertakings'). In *France v EC Commission,* Case C-325/91, judgment of 16 June 1993 (not yet reported), France successfully challenged the validity of this communication. It was re-adopted excluding the requirement to provide the Commission with annual financial data, with the latter obligation being included in Commission Directive 93/84, OJ 1993 L254/16, amending Directive 80/723.

While this communication is limited to the manufacturing sector, the Commission has noted that it may use the principles described in the communication in evaluating aid in other sectors (id., para. 3). The Commission appears particularly likely to apply these principles in service sectors such as banking and insurance, the

detailed analysis of the market economy investor principle, and outlines how it intends to apply this principle to diverse forms of aid granted to state-owned companies. Briefly, these principles are as follows:

(1) Capital injections

A capital injection is considered to be an aid when it is unlikely it will produce a normal return within a reasonable period.[42] A market economy investor would normally provide equity finance if the present value of expected future cash flows from the intended project exceeds the new outlay.[43] In evaluating the financial position of the company, the Commission will look at its profit and loss situation, financial indicators, financial projections and market trends.[44]

(2) Guarantees

The aid element in a guarantee is the difference between the rate which the borrower would pay in a free market and that actually obtained with the benefit of the guarantee, net of any premium paid for the guarantee.[45] In assessing this aid element, the Commission will analyse the borrower's financial situation on the basis of the factors listed above in connection with capital injections.[46]

(3) Loans

The aid element in a loan is the difference between the rate which the company should pay (which is dependent on its financial position and the security given for the loan) and that actually paid.[47] The Commission has indicated that it will scrutinise closely the value of the assets pledged by the borrower to secure the loan.[48]

(4) Return on investments

The state should expect a rate of return on its capital investments by way of dividends or capital gains equivalent to that obtained by comparable private companies.[49] The Commission measures the rate of return by profit (after depreciation but before taxation and disposals) expressed as a percentage of assets employed.[50]

---

audiovisual sector and the entertainment and leisure industries where there is competition between state-owned companies and private companies. See *XXIst Report on Competition Policy for 1991*, point 158.

[42] Commission communication on state aid to public undertakings, at p. 12 (para. 35).
[43] Id.
[44] Id., at p. 12 (para. 37).
[45] Id., at p. 13 (para. 38).
[46] Id.
[47] Id., at p. 14 (para. 41).
[48] Id. (para. 40).
[49] Id. (para. 43).
[50] Id.

¶1204

While the Commission denies that it substitutes its judgment for that of the investor when applying the market economy investor principle,[51] a review of the cases suggests that the Commission sometimes finds it hard to resist the temptation to second-guess investment decisions made by public authorities. For example, in *Boussac*,[52] the Commission found that capital investment by the French Government in a company constituted aid even though this investment was made on the basis of a favourable report by an independent financial consultant and in association with banks and private investors. Likewise, in *Tubemeuse*,[53] the Commission found that financial assistance given by the Belgian Government to a company constituted aid even though the investments were partly financed by an international banking consortium and on the basis of a report by an independent firm of business consultants.

¶1205   Entity granting state aid

Article 92(1) only covers aid 'granted by a Member State or through state resources'. The court has interpreted broadly the notion of 'state' to include regional and local governmental entities[54] as well as public and private bodies authorised by the state to administer aid.[55] In borderline cases, whether an entity constitutes the 'state' for art. 92 purposes turns on the degree of control that the state has over the entity. For example, in *ENI-Lanerossi*,[56] the court held that ENI, a public entity established by legislation, constituted the 'state' for the purposes of art. 92 even though, according to the terms of its enabling legislation, it was required to operate as an independent economic entity dependent on private capital markets for funds. In reaching this conclusion, the court pointed out that the members of ENI's governing board were appointed

---

[51]   In its communication on state aids to public undertakings, at p. 9 (para. 27–29), the Commission acknowledged that entrepreneurial investment decisions involve a wide margin of judgement, and stated that it would only find state aid in situations where 'it is beyond a reasonable doubt that there is no other plausible explanation for the provision of public funds'.

[52]   *France v EC Commission* ('*Boussac*') [1990] ECR I-307.

[53]   *Belgium v EC Commission* ('*Tubemeuse*') [1990] ECR I-959.

[54]   In *Germany v EC Commission* [1987] ECR 4013, at p. 4041 (para. 17), the court stated:

'the fact that the aid programme was adopted by a State in a federation or by a regional authority and not by the federal or central power does not prevent the application of Article 92(1) of the Treaty if the relevant conditions are satisfied. In referring to "any aid granted by a Member State or through State resources in any form whatsoever" Article 92(1) is directed at all aid financed from public resources. It follows tha aid granted by regional and local bodies of the Member States, whatever their status and description, must be scrutinized to determine whether it complies with Article 92 of the Treaty.'

[55]   See *Steinike und Weinlig v Germany* [1977] ECR 595 at p. 611 (para. 21) ('[t]he prohibition contained in Article 92(1) covers all aid granted by a Member State or through State resources without it being necessary to make a distinction whether the aid is granted directly by the State or by public or private bodies established or appointed by it to administer the aid.')

[56]   *Italy v EC Commission* ('*ENI-Lanerossi*') [1991] ECR I-1433.

by the Italian Government, that ENI did not enjoy complete autonomy as it was required to operate within the bounds of directives issued by a ministerial committee, and that the repayment of borrowed funds was guaranteed by the Italian Government.[57]

For an entity to be considered as controlled by the government, it is not necessary that the government hold a majority of shares or control the governing board; other indicia of control may suffice. In *Van der Kooy v EC Commission*,[58] the court held that a company constituted the 'state' for art. 92 purposes even though the Dutch Government only held 50 per cent of its shares (the other 50 per cent were held by private industry) and appointed only half of the members of the supervisory board. A key consideration for the court appeared to be that the Dutch Government had the ability to veto the price structure adopted by the company; for the court, it did not matter that, in practice, this veto power was wielded as a rubber stamp.

In *EC Commission v France*,[59] the court suggested that it does not take much to establish the necessary degree of state involvement. In that case, the Commission contested the legality of aid granted to French farmers out of surplus funds from the French National Agricultural Credit Fund. As the fund's surplus was generated by the management of private funds and not of government resources, and government representatives were in a minority on the fund's governing board, even the Commission had doubts concerning whether the fund could be considered as constituting the 'state' for art. 92 purposes. Thus, the Commission brought a claim on the basis of art. 169 rather than art. 92, arguing that the French Government's encouragement of a 'measure having an effect equivalent to state aid' constituted a breach of its general obligations under the treaty. The court rejected the Commission's claim on procedural grounds. However, it did not share the Commission's doubts concerning whether the grant to the farmers constituted aid. According to the court, this grant was 'state aid' within the scope of art. 92 because it 'was decided and financed by a public body and the implementation of which is subject to the approval of the public authorities, the detailed rules for the grant of which correspond to those for ordinary State aid and which, moreover, was put forward by the Government as forming part of a body of measures in favour of farmers which were all notified to the Commission in pursuance of Article 92(3).'[60]

This case demonstrates that it is not necessary for the aid to be financed by state funds as long as it is brought about by state action. Thus, a state aid has

---

[57] Id., para. 12 and 13. In *Italy v EC Commission* ('*Alfa Romeo*') [1991] ECR I-1603, the court engaged in a similar analysis to find that a public entity was effectively controlled by the Italian Government.

[58] *Van der Kooy v EC Commission* [1988] ECR 219.

[59] *EC Commission v France* [1985] ECR 439.

[60] Id., at p. 449 (para. 15).

been found in cases where the advantage was wholly or partially financed by contributions levied on the companies concerned.[61]

¶1206   Distortion of competition

Article 92(1) only applies to aid that 'distorts or threatens to distort competition.' This requirement is linked closely with the selectivity and inter-state trade requirements discussed below and, as a practical matter, it is often difficult to examine these factors in isolation.[62] If aid strengthens the position of a specific company, this company is then better off than its competitors engaged in inter-state trade, and, arguably by definition, competition is distorted. However, the court has made it clear that some minimal analysis is necessary to establish a distortion of trade. Specifically, the relevant market and the position of the aid recipient on that market must be examined along with the volume of inter-state trade in the product concerned.[63]

¶1207   Selectivity

Article 92(1) also contains a selectivity requirement because state aid may only be found incompatible with the common market if it favours 'certain undertakings or the production of certain goods'. Consequently, general measures that affect the economy as a whole are not caught by art. 92(1). The distinction between aids and general measures is often elusive.[64] A measure that may appear neutral on its face may, upon closer scrutiny, be held to constitute aid. For example, Italy introduced a plan to reduce employers' medical insurance contributions by having the Italian Government assume certain of the employers' obligations. The plan called for a greater reduction in employers' contributions to insurance plans for female employees than for male employees. While apparently neutral on its face, the court found that this

---

[61] *France v EC Commission* [1987] ECR 4393, at p. 4418 (para. 23); *Steinike und Weinlig v Germany* [1977] ECR 595, at p. 611 (para. 22); *Dutch Manure Bank*, OJ 1992 L170/34.

[62] For example, in *Philip Morris v EC Commission* [1980] ECR 2671, at pp. 2688–89 (para. 11), the court seemed to blend these requirements together: '[w]hen State financial aid strengthens the position of an undertaking compared with other undertakings competing in intra-Community trade the latter must be regarded as affected by that aid.'

[63] See *Netherlands and Leeuwarder Papierwarenfabriek v EC Commission* [1985] ECR 809, at p. 824 (para. 24).

[64] For an explanation of the economic rationale for the distinction between aids and general measures, see *Second survey on state aids in the European Community in the manufacturing and certain other sectors*, EC Commission, July 1990, para. 9–10 (the 'Second survey on state aids').

For the purposes of its periodic surveys on state aids, the Commission lists the following as 'general measures or other measures' that do not constitute state aid:

'– Differences between the various tax systems and general social security systems in Member States (depreciation, social security deficit, etc.)
– Customs duties, quotas, public procurement, market restrictions, technical standards
– Specific tax schemes (cooperatives, owner enterprises, self-employed, etc.)
– General reduction in VAT (for example, foodstuffs in the United Kingdom, certain products in the French overseas Departments).'

Id., at Annex I (footnotes omitted).

¶1207

measure constituted state aid rather than a general measure because it favoured industries employing a large number of women such as the textile, clothing, footwear and leather-goods sectors.[65] Similarly, the court has held that a preferential rediscount rate for exports constituted aid.[66] Apparently, the fact that this rate did not apply to companies that manufactured only for the domestic market was enough to satisfy the selectivity requirement.[67]

If state assistance does not reduce the costs that a particular company would otherwise be forced to bear, but rather constitutes part of a social policy measure intended to have more widespread benefits, it may not be considered to favour 'certain undertakings' within the meaning of art. 92(1). For example, if the state makes employee severance payments for which a company would otherwise be responsible, these payments normally constitute aid because they clearly represent benefit to that company. On the other hand, if the state pays employee benefits that go beyond those that the employer is obliged to make, these payments do not constitute aid because they do not benefit the company by reducing costs which, for instance, its competitors might be forced to bear.[68] In a similar vein, state assistance for vocational training will not generally constitute aid because it is simply one of the traditional responsibilities assumed by the state; however, if the training programme caters to the needs of a specific company, it may constitute aid.[69]

¶1208   Effect on trade between member states

State aid falls within the scope of art. 92(1) only 'in so far as it affects trade between member states'. As under art. 85 and 86, the requirement of an effect on inter-state trade has been interpreted liberally. Consequently, aid schemes generally will be deemed to affect inter-state trade except for those small enough to qualify for exemption under the de minimis rule discussed below.

In *Philip Morris v EC Commission*,[70] the court stated the basic criterion for

---

[65] *EC Commission v Italy* [1983] ECR 2525, at p. 2530 (para. 4).

[66] *EC Commission v France* [1969] ECR 523.

[67] On this point, the court seemed to follow the reasoning of Advocate General Roemer, who opined (id., at p. 552) as follows:

'First of all Article 92 requires that "certain undertakings or the production of certain goods" be favoured. Like the Commission I take it however that this does not mean only aid to individual sectors or geographical areas but also a measure which does not apply to all the undertakings in a Member State which is doubtless the case with aids to exports in relation to many undertakings which produce exclusively for domestic market.'

See also *EC Commission v Ireland* [1982] ECR 4005, in which the Commission argued that a state action favouring all domestic products as against imports is too general to fall within the scope of art. 92. In that case, the court did not reach this issue, but Advocate General Capotorti opined that the Irish Government's 'Buy Irish' campaign constituted a state aid because it reduced the advertising costs of Irish companies, which gave them an advantage over their competitors from other member states.

[68] See *MFL Group*, OJ 1992 L182/94; *Magefesa*, OJ 1991 L5/18.

[69] See *Ford/Volkswagen*, OJ 1991 C257/5; *Saint-Gobain*, OJ 1991 L215/11.

[70] *Philip Morris v EC Commission* [1980] ECR 2671, at p. 2688 (para. 11).

determining whether a given aid scheme affects inter-state trade as follows: 'when State financial aid strengthens the position of an undertaking compared with other undertakings competing in intra-Community trade the latter must be regarded as affected by that aid.' The court has placed a broad gloss on this principle. For inter-state trade to be affected, it is not necessary for the company receiving the aid to be engaged in inter-state trade. Rather, it suffices if the company manufactures a product subject to such trade. In such circumstances, aid given to a company engaged in domestic production affects inter-state trade because the aid allows the company to maintain or increase its domestic market share, thus preventing producers located in other member states from increasing their market share in the member state where the company receiving the aid is located.[71]

In *Tubemeuse*,[72] the court demonstrated how far it is willing to go to find the requisite effect on inter-state trade. In that case, it was argued that inter-state trade was not affected because Tubemeuse, the company receiving the aid in question, exported 90 per cent of its production outside of the Community. The court rejected this argument. The court stressed that Tubemeuse had announced its intention to withdraw from certain foreign markets, making it 'reasonably foreseeable that Tubemeuse would redirect its activities toward the internal Community market.'[73] Thus, it appears that the requisite effect on

---

[71] See e.g. *Italy v EC Commission* ('*ENI-Lanerossi*') [1991] ECR I-1433 at para. 26–29; *Italy v EC Commission* ('*Alfa Romeo*') [1991] ECR I-1603 at para. 25–27; *France v EC Commission* [1988] ECR 4067, at p. 4087 (para. 17–19). In *France v EC Commission*, id. (para. 19), the court stated:

'aid to an undertaking may be such as to affect trade between Member States and distort competition where that undertaking competes with products coming from other Member States, even if it does not itself export its products. Such a situation may exist even if there is no over-capacity in the sector at issue. Where a Member State grants aid to an undertaking, domestic production may for that reason be maintained or increased with the result that, in circumstances such as those found to exist ... undertakings established in other Member States have less chance of exporting their products to the market in that Member State. Such aid is therefore likely to affect trade between Member States and distort competition.'

[72] *Belgium v EC Commission* ('*Tubemeuse*') [1990] ECR I-959.

[73] Id., at p. I-1014 (para. 38). The court also noted that evidence had been presented to show that Tubemeuse's exports outside of the Community had begun to fall while sales within the Community had begun to rise. Id. (para. 39). It is unclear whether the requisite effect on inter-state trade would have been found in the absence of such a statement of intention. The court stated (id., at pp. I-1013 and I-1014 (para. 35)) that:

'having regard to the interdependence between the markets on which Community undertakings operate, it is possible that aid might distort competition within the Community, even if the undertaking receiving it exports almost all its production outside of the Community. The exportation of part of the undertaking's production to non-member countries is only one of a number of circumstances which must be considered.'

The court pointed out that most Community producers exported a large portion of their production outside the Community and that the world market for the product in question was highly competitive, leading to the conclusion that 'any advantage accorded to an undertaking in this sector is therefore likely to improve its competitive position in regard to other undertakings.' (Id., at p. I-1014 (para. 37)).

These statements suggest that aid to a Community producer active on a global market may be deemed to affect trade between member states to the extent that the aid gives the company an advantage over other Community producers active on the world market. Arguably, however, an effect on inter-state trade for the purposes of art. 92(1) requires evidence of an effect on the Community market. In *Tubemeuse*, the court was careful to point out that there were some outlets within the Community for the product in question. Id. (para. 36).

¶1208

inter-state trade is present if it is reasonably foreseeable that the aid in question will affect that trade.

The court requires the Commission to undertake at least a minimal level of analysis on the issue of inter-state trade, examining the relevant market, the position of the aid recipient on that market and the volume of inter-state trade in the product concerned.[74]

In 1992, the Commission introduced a de minimis rule in the field of state aids.[75] Under this rule, aid schemes offering not more than ECU 50,000 to a company over a three-year period are considered to have no appreciable effect on inter-state trade or competition.[76] The de minimis rule does not apply in sectors subject to special rules on state aid.[77]

¶1209   Exceptions

State aids that meet the conditions discussed above are incompatible with the common market 'save as otherwise provided in the Treaty'. As discussed in detail below, art. 92 and 93 contain specific exceptions to the general prohibition on state aids. Other areas in which exceptions have been carved out include agriculture (art. 42), transport (art. 77 and 80), public undertakings (art. 90(2)) and national defence (art. 223(1)(b)).

STATE AIDS COMPATIBLE WITH THE COMMON MARKET

¶1210   Introduction

A common thread that runs through the EC Treaty's chapter on competition policy is that the application of the competition rules may be tempered by the need to attain other Community objectives. Thus, agreements that restrict competition within the meaning of art. 85(1) may be exempted under art. 85(3). Likewise, under art. 90(2), the competition rules apply to companies providing

---

[74] See *Netherlands and Leeuwarder Papierwarenfabriek BV v EC Commission* [1985] ECR 809. In that case, the court found that the Commission had failed to give an adequate explanation because 'the contested decision did not contain the slightest information concerning the situation of the relevant market, the place of Leeuwarder in that market, the pattern of trade between Member States in the products in question or the undertaking's exports.' (Id., at p. 824 (para. 24)). See also *Germany v EC Commission* [1987] ECR 4013.

[75] This rule was introduced in the context of the Community guidelines on state aid for small and medium-sized enterprises, OJ 1992 C213/2, because such enterprises are considered the most likely to use this rule. However, there is no limit to the size of the company that can benefit from this rule. Prior to the adoption of these guidelines, the court had refused to apply by analogy the de minimis rule used in competition matters to state aid cases. See *Belgium v EC Commission* ('*Tubemeuse*'), [1990] ECR I-959, p. I-1015 (para. 42 and 43).

[76] Community guidelines on state aid for small and medium-sized enterprises (SMEs), OJ 1992 C213/2, at p. 5 (para. 3.2). In addition to meeting these tests, it must be an express condition of the award or scheme that any further aid the same firm may receive in respect of the same type of expenditure from other sources or under other schemes does not take the total aid the firm receives above the ECU 50,000 limit. Id.

[77] Id. For a listing of the sectors in which special rules apply, see ¶1218 below.

public services only to the extent that these rules do not interfere with the performance of the assigned tasks.

The state aid rules pick up this same thread. Aid that would otherwise fall within the scope of art. 92(1) may be allowed under art. 92(2) or (3). In short, not all aid is bad. It may help achieve Community-wide goals such as the restructuring of sectors struggling under the burden of overcapacity, reducing disparities among regions, making EC industry more competitive and fighting unemployment. Article 92(2) lists the types of state aid that are automatically deemed to be compatible with the common market. Article 92(3) lists the types of state aid that may be deemed to be compatible in the discretion of the Commission or the Council. As a practical matter, most aid is more likely to qualify for exemption under this second category.

¶1211   Aid that is automatically compatible with the common market

Article 92(2) lists three categories of aid that are automatically considered to be compatible with the common market. The first category is aid having a social character that is granted to individual consumers and is of a non-discriminatory nature in so far as the origin of the products is concerned.[78] The second category is emergency aid to alleviate the damage caused by natural disasters or other exceptional occurrences.[79] The third category is aid granted to certain areas of the Federal Republic of Germany to compensate for the adverse economic consequences caused by the post-war division.[80] In the past, aid to areas of the Federal Republic of Germany bordering on the former German Democratic Republic and to West Berlin were justified on this basis. As a result of the reunification of Germany, this aid is being phased out.[81] Conceptually, aid granted in the context of the reunification of Germany could conceivably fall within the scope of this third category. However, the Commission has chosen to treat this aid as regional aid falling under art. 92(3) instead,[82] so that this third category of aid is destined to become an historical anomaly.[83] The Commission takes a generally favourable attitude towards investment in the former GDR,

---

[78] Article 92(2)(a). An example of this kind of aid is the purchase of wheat by the state and its subsequent resale at a discount, which reduces bread prices. See *Benedetti v Munari* [1977] ECR 163 at p. 190 (opinion of Advocate General Reischl).

[79] Article 92(2)(b). Aid intended to promote the industrial development of an area hit by a natural disaster rather than to relieve the immediate effects of the disaster does not fall within this category; however, it may be eligible for exemption as regional aid under art. 92(3)(a) and (c). See *Aid to Areas of Mezzogiorno Affected by Natural Disasters*, OJ 1991 L86/23.

[80] Article 92(2)(c).

[81] See *XXIst Report on Competition Policy*, point 289; *XXth Report on Competition Policy*, point 178; *ERP Aufbauprogramm*, OJ 1992 C164/3.

[82] See e.g. *ERP-Aufbauprogramm*, OJ 1992 C164/3; *Mercedes-Benz*, OJ 1992 C68/8. For a review of regional aid programmes, see ¶1217 below.

[83] In the meantime, projects involving the former GDR may occasionally contain aid elements falling within the scope of art. 92(2)(c). For instance, in *Daimler-Benz*, OJ 1992 L263/15, the Commission found that the

but has established guidelines for the monitoring of aid granted by the German Government in the context of the privatisation of companies in the former GDR by the Treuhandanstalt to ensure that such aid does not unduly distort competition.[84]

If an aid measure falls within one of these three categories, this does not obviate the need to notify the aid to the Commission. As discussed below, the Commission is empowered to review all systems of aid.

¶1212   Aid that may be compatible with the common market

There exist six categories of aid that may be determined to be compatible with the common market. Four of these categories are subject to control by the Commission, and two by the Council. Article 92(3) lists the four types of aid that require Commission approval as follows:

(a) aid to promote the economic development of areas where the standard of living is abnormally low or where there is serious underemployment;

(b) aid to promote the execution of an important project of common European interest or to remedy a serious disturbance in the economy of a member state;

(c) aid to facilitate the development of certain economic activities or of certain economic areas, where such aid does not adversely affect trading conditions to an extent contrary to the common interest; and

(d) aid to promote culture and heritage conservation where that aid does not affect trading conditions and competition in the Community to an extent that is contrary to the common interest. (This category was added by virtue of the Union Treaty.)

With respect to the Council, art. 93(3) allows the Council to decide that additional categories of aid are compatible with the common market.[85] Also, pursuant to art. 93(2), the Council may authorise a given aid measure 'in derogation from the provisions of Article 92 or from the regulations provided for in Article 94, if such a decision is justified by exceptional circumstances'. In practice, the Council rarely uses its powers in this area[86] and, consequently, this section will focus on the categories of aid controlled by the Commission.

---

amount by which the purchase price for real estate in Berlin was reduced to compensate Daimler-Benz for agreeing to include a building considered to be an eyesore in its real estate project with a view to demolishing this building constituted aid compatible with the common market under art. 92(2)(c).

[84] See press release IP(92) 952 of 25 November 1992; *XXIInd Report on Competition Policy for 1992*, points 19 and 349. See also *Mercedes-Benz*, OJ 1992 C68/8.

[85] Article 92(3)(e). The Council must decide by qualified majority on a Commission proposal.

[86] The Council has used its powers under (what is now) art. 92(3)(e) with respect to shipbuilding, see Council Directive 90/684 of 21 December 1990 on aid to shipbuilding, OJ 1990 L380/27, and with respect to some agricultural products. The Council almost never uses its powers under art. 93(2), presumably because of the difficulty of reaching a decision to authorise aid that the Commission will have, in all probability, already condemned.

¶1213   General principles

The Commission enjoys a wide margin of discretion in deciding whether aid falls within one of the categories listed in art. 92(3).[87] In the exercise of this discretion, the Commission must make economic and social assessments in a Community context.[88] Thus, it is not enough that aid promotes purely local or national goals; rather, aid must be consistent with Community-wide goals.[89] The Commission has stated that it uses the following guidelines in determining whether to approve aid:

(a) the aid must promote a development that is in the interest of the Community as a whole; the promotion of national interests is not enough to justify the Commission exercising its discretionary powers under art. 92(3);

(b) the aid must be necessary to bring about that development, in that without the aid the measure in question would not be realised; and

(c) the modalities of the aid (e.g. intensity, duration, the problems which may be caused by transferring difficulties from one member state to another, and the degree of distortion of competition) must be commensurate with the importance of the objective of the aid.[90]

The Commission has consistently made it clear that it construes narrowly the exceptions provided for in art. 92(3).[91] These exceptions may be invoked only when the Commission is satisfied that 'without the aid, market forces alone would be insufficient to guide recipients towards patterns of behaviour that would serve one of the objectives of the said exceptions.'[92]

The court has consistently upheld the Commission's discretion with respect to whether an aid qualifies for one of the exceptions listed in art. 92(3).[93] While

---

[87] *Belgium v EC Commission* (*'Tubemeuse'*) [1987] ECR I-959, at p. I-1018 (para. 56).

[88] Id.

[89] For instance, in *Deufil v EC Commission* [1987] ECR 901, the court upheld the Commission's finding that even though regional aid designed to increase productive capacity might benefit the local economy, this aid was not compatible with the common market because the Community as a whole suffered from overcapacity for the product concerned. Thus, the creation of jobs in one region would lead to a loss of jobs in others.

[90] *Twelfth Report on Competition Policy*, point 160.

[91] For instance, in *Hytasa*, OJ 1992 L171/54, at p. 61, the Commission stated that '[i]n order to ensure the proper functioning of the common market, and having regard to the principle embodied in Article 3[(g)], the exceptions provided for in Article 92(3) must be construed narrowly when any aid scheme or individual aid award is scrutinized'.

[92] Id. The Commission endorsed this rationale in *Philip Morris v EC Commission* [1980] ECR 2671, at p. 2690 (para. 16 and 17).

[93] See e.g. *Italy v EC Commission* (*'ENI-Lanerossi'*) [1991] ECR I-1433 at para. 34; *Belgium v EC Commission* (*'Tubemeuse'*) [1990] ECR I-959, at p. I-1018 (para. 56); *Philip Morris v EC Commission* [1980] ECR 2671, at p. 2691 (para. 24).

the court may review the basis of the Commission's findings of fact,[94] it does not appear inclined to conduct a detailed review of the facts.[95]

¶1214 Aid to economically-depressed areas

Article 92(3)(a) provides that aid to promote the economic development of areas where the standard of living is abnormally low or where there is serious unemployment may be considered compatible with the common market. This type of aid has increased in importance with the advent of the single market programme because it was recognised that the least-favoured regions of the Community (basically, Greece, Portugal, Ireland and parts of Spain) needed assistance if the economic and social cohesion called for by this programme was to be achieved.[96] In this connection, in 1987, the Commission published a communication on the application of art. 92(3)(a) and (c) to regional aid schemes, which outlines a more systematic approach in this area and encourages the use of art. 92(3)(a) with respect to regional aid.[97] Pursuant to this communication, regions eligible for aid under art. 92(3)(a) are those where the per capita gross domestic product does not exceed 75 per cent of the Community average in purchasing power parities. This communication also provides for the grant of operating aid in exceptional circumstances and subject to certain conditions.

¶1215 Aid for projects of common European interest

Article 92(3)(b) provides that aid to promote important projects of common European interest or to remedy a serious disturbance in the economy of a member state are compatible with the common market. Important projects of common European interest generally form part of a transnational European programme supported jointly by a number of member states, or arise from concerted action by a number of member states to combat a common threat such as environmental pollution.[98] Examples of such projects include R&D related to new technologies such as high-definition television[99] or the development of new environmental protection standards.[100] At least as far as

---

[94] See *Germany v EC Commission* [1984] ECR 1451, at pp. 1499–1500 (opinion of Advocate General Slynn).
[95] See *Deufil v EC Commission* [1987] ECR 901. For a rare example of a case in which the court reviewed the substance of a Commission decision, see *Société Cdf Chimie & Anor v EC Commission* [1990] ECR I-3083. In that case, the court found that the Commission had committed manifest errors in its assessment of the facts.
[96] See *XXIst Report on Competition Policy for 1991*, point 55.
[97] Commission communication on the method for the application of art. 92(3)(a) and (c) to regional aid, OJ 1988 C212/2; updated at OJ 1989 C78/5, OJ 1990 C163/6, OJ 1992 C114/4.
[98] See *Exécutif Régional Wallon and Glaverbel v EC Commission* [1988] ECR 1573, at p. 1595 (para. 22).
[99] See *XXIst Report on Competition Policy for 1991*, point 180. Other important projects of common European interest for which aid has been authorised include the Eprom (semi-conductors) project; the DAB project involving the creation of an earth radio digital system; and a software factory project. *Nineteenth Report on Competition Policy*, point 144.
[100] The Commission's policy with respect to state aid related to environmental matters is set out in a set of guidelines released in 1994. See *Community guidelines on State aid for environmental protection*, OJ 1994 C72/2

R&D projects are concerned, the Commission has explained that the art. 92(3)(b) derogation 'can be applied to projects which are both qualitatively and quantitatively important, are transnational in character and are related to the definition of industrial standards that can allow Community industry to benefit from all the advantages of the single market.'[101] By the same token, aid to a single firm is unlikely to qualify for the art. 92(3)(b) derogation.[102]

Article 92(3)(b) also allows aid to remedy a serious disturbance in the economy of a member state. The Commission's approval of aid designed to assist companies experiencing difficulties in Greece due to a nation-wide economic crisis provides a rare example of a such a case.[103]

¶1216   Regional and sectoral aid: introduction

Article 92(3)(c) provides that aid 'to facilitate the development of certain economic activities or of certain economic areas' may be compatible with the common market. Thus, this provision concerns both regional and sectoral aid.

Initially, the Commission sought to restrict regional and sectoral aid. As discussed below, this policy is still evident in the Commission's treatment of aid towards various sectors, where it generally prohibits operating aid and insists that aid be associated with restructuring measures. In recent years, however, the Commission has recognised that aid can play a positive role in achieving Community-wide goals. For example, the Commission acknowledges that regional aid may help achieve the goal of a single market by reducing disparities among the Community's regions. Likewise, so-called 'horizontal aid' may contribute to Community-wide goals such as increased R&D, environmental protection and the promotion of SMEs.

¶1217   Regional aid

While regions eligible for aid under art. 92(3)(a) are those that are suffering severe economic problems when compared to the rest of the Community,[104] regions falling under art. 92(3)(c) are those with more general development problems in relation to the national as well as the Community situation.[105]

According to these guidelines, the Commission may authorise aid for important projects of European interest in the environmental field at higher rates than the limits laid down for aid authorised pursuant to art. 92(3)(c). To qualify, the aid 'must be necessary for the project to proceed and the project must be specific and well-defined, qualitatively important, and must make an exemplary and clearly identifiable contribution to the common European interest'. Id., at para. 3.7.

[101] *XXIst Report on Competition Policy for 1991*, point 180.

[102] See *Caulliez Frères*, OJ 1989 L223/22, at p. 26.

[103] See *Seventeenth Report on Competition Policy*, points 186 and 187. The Commission explained that 'the application of Article 92(3)(b), which would underline that it was dealing with an unprecedented situation, provided a more logical solution to the case in question than the application of Article 92(3)(c) which it had traditionally applied to schemes or individual rescue operations of companies in difficulty.'

[104] See ¶1214.

[105] *Eighteenth Report on Competition Policy*, point 167. See also *Germany v EC Commission* [1987] ECR 4013, at p. 4042 (para. 19).

Typically, art. 92(3)(a) regions are on the fringes of the Community and are predominantly rural areas with an underdeveloped industrial base or poor infrastructure; in contrast, art. 92(3)(c) regions are frequently located in the more central, prosperous parts of the Community and often are suffering because of a decline of traditional industries.[106] Until the disparity between these generally prosperous areas and the peripheral, poorer parts of the Community is greatly reduced, regional aid in the more prosperous member states is likely to meet with more resistance from the Commission than aid to regions in economically-depressed areas because the Commission considers it vital to smooth out broad disparities in the Community.[107]

In its 1987 communication on regional aid,[108] the Commission explained the criteria it uses when deciding whether a region is eligible for aid under art. 92(3)(c). The Commission uses two basic criteria: income per capita and structural unemployment, which are assessed in a national context. The better the position of a member state relative to the Community as a whole, the greater must be the disparity between the region and the member state to justify the award of aid. In short, the wealthier the member state in which the region is located, the poorer the region must be to qualify for aid. Unlike art. 92(3)(a) regions, the Commission does not in principle allow the award of operating aid in art. 92(3)(c) regions, which means that the aid must generally be linked to initial investment or job creation.

The importance that the Commission attaches to the elimination of disparities among regions is reflected by the introduction of a regional component into many of the aid codes. For example, the guidelines on aid for environmental protection authorises higher rates of assistance in areas qualifying for regional aid.[109]

¶1218   Sectoral aid

The Commission describes its attitude towards sectoral aid as 'basically negative.'[110] According to the Commission, interventionist sectoral policies are generally ineffective in promoting structural adjustment compared to horizontal measures.[111] In 1978, the Commission laid down its general policy

---

[106] *Eighteenth Report on Competition Policy*, point 167.

[107] See *XXIst Report on Competition Policy for 1991*, point 158 ('[t]he priority objective of economic aid and social cohesion requires a strict control of aid in the most prosperous areas to make sure that the impact of aid approved for the development of the less favoured regions of the Community is not offset by large amounts of aid distributed in richer areas'); *XXth Report on Competition Policy*, point 169 (announcing Commission's intention to tighten discipline on regional aid in rich regions).

[108] Commission communication on the method for the application of art. 92(3)(a) and (c) to regional aid, OJ 1988 C212/2; updated at OJ 1989 C78/5, OJ 1990 C163/6, OJ 1992 C114/4.

[109] Community guidelines on state aid for environmental protection, OJ 1994 C72/3. Higher rates of aid are also authorised in the Community guidelines on state aid for small and medium-sized enterprises, OJ 1992 C213/2, and in the Community framework for state aids for research and development, OJ 1986 C8/2.

[110] *XXIst Report on Competition Policy for 1991*, point 253.

[111] Id. On horizontal measures, see ¶1219.

guidelines on sectoral aid.[112] These guidelines have been reaffirmed since, and still provide a reliable guide to the Commission's approach in this area.[113] In these guidelines, the Commission emphasises that state aid is the exception, not the rule, and should be used to solve long-term problems, not preserve the status quo. To the extent possible, aid should be degressive, limited in time and clearly linked to objectives for restructuring of the sector concerned. Moreover, the granting of aid by one member state must not lead to the transfer of industrial problems and unemployment to other member states nor should it keep inefficient companies in existence to the detriment of their more efficient competitors.[114]

Guidelines have been adopted for assessing state aid granted to industrial sectors that are experiencing difficulties (such as overcapacity in a shrinking worldwide market) and, thus, are particularly likely targets for aid. These sectors are: synthetic fibres,[115] textiles and clothing,[116] motor vehicles,[117] shipbuilding,[118] coal[119] and steel.[120]

State aid is also controlled on a sectoral basis with respect to sectors for which common policies have been established under the EC Treaty. These sectors are: agriculture,[121] fisheries[122] and transportation.[123] In these sectors, state aid

---

[112] Communication to the Council on Commission policy on state aid schemes, COM(78)221 final (May 1978).

[113] See *Seventeenth Report on Competition Policy*, point 206.

[114] Id.

[115] Code on aid to the synthetic fibres industry, OJ 1992 C346/2. See also Commission communication, OJ 1989 C173/5; Commission communication, OJ 1991 C186/1; Commission letter to member states, SG(77) D/1190, dated 4 February 1977 and Annex (Doc. SEC(77) 317, 25 January 1977).

[116] Commission letter to member states, SG(77) D/1190 dated 4 February 1977 and Annex (Doc. SEC(77) 317, 25 January 1977).

[117] Community framework on state aid to the motor vehicle industry, OJ 1989 C123/3, renewed OJ 1991 C81/4, OJ 1993 C36/17.

[118] Council Directive 90/684 of 21 December 1990 on aid to shipbuilding, OJ 1990 L380/27 as amended by Council Directive 93/115 of 16 December 1993, OJ 1993 L326/62.

[119] Commission Decision 3632/93/ECSC of 28 December 1993 establishing Community rules for state aid to the coal industry, OJ 1993 L329/12. See also Commission Decision 341/94/ECSC of 8 February 1994 implementing Decision 3632/93/ECSC.

[120] Commission Decision 3855/91/ECSC of 27 November 1991 establishing Community rules for aid to the steel industry, OJ 1991 L362/57.

[121] The Commission has stated its intention to lay down the principal elements of state aid policy as it relates to the agricultural sector. See *XXIst Report on Competition Policy for 1991*, point 313.

[122] Guidelines for the examination of state aids in the fisheries and aquaculture sector, OJ 1992 C152/2. See also Council Regulation 4028/86 of 18 December 1986 on Community measures to improve and adapt structures in the fisheries and aquaculture sector, OJ 1986 L376/7, as amended by Council Regulation 3944/90 of 20 December 1990, OJ 1990 L380/1; Council Regulation 4042/89 of 19 December 1989 on the improvement of the conditions under which fishery and aquaculture products are processed and marketed, OJ 1989 L388/1.

[123] The bulk of aid granted in the land transport sector is that paid to national railways, either in compensation for public service obligations under Regulation 1191/69 on action by member states concerning the obligations inherent in the concept of a public service in transport by rail, road and inland waterway, JO 1969 L156/1, as amended by Council Regulation 1983/93, OJ 1991 L169/1, and Regulation 1192/69 of 26 June 1969 on common rules for the normalisation of the accounts of railway undertakings, JO 1969 L156/8, or as aid within the limits laid down by Regulation 1107/70 on the granting of aids for transport by rail, road and inland waterway, JO 1970 L130/1, as amended by Regulation 1100/89, OJ 1989 L116/24, and Regulation 3578/92, OJ 1992 L364/11.

With respect to sea transport, see Guidelines for the examination of state aids to Community shipping companies, Doc. SEC (89) 921, 3 August 1989. These guidelines are being adjusted by the Commission. See *XXIInd Report on Competition Policy for 1992*, point 501.

policy must be applied in a way that is consistent with the broader, common policies.[124]

The Commission takes a favourable view of aid in some sectors. For example, in the energy sector, the Commission considers that aid promoting certain Community objectives such as environmental protection and energy-saving may be acceptable.[125] Other sectors receiving favourable treatment include tourism[126] and the non-profit sector.[127]

While a detailed review of the Commission's policy in various sectors is beyond the scope of this chapter, it is worth noting some common threads running through the cases and policy guidelines. While these common principles are useful as general points of reference in attempting to understand how the Commission tends to approach state aids problems, they should not be viewed as hard-and-fast rules.

Operating aid

The Commission is generally opposed to operating aid, which is aid that covers operating costs otherwise borne by companies in the normal course of their affairs.[128] Operating aid is considered objectionable because it simply preserves the status quo and does not go to the root of the problem. Operating aid is deemed to distort competition at a sectoral level to such a degree that it generally will not be approved even if it may help attain other Community objectives.[129] Thus, the guidelines on aid to the motor vehicle industry state that operating aid should not be allowed in this sector even if the beneficiaries are located in disadvantaged regions.[130]

Operating aid may be approved in rare cases. For instance, it may be

---

The Commission has set forth the criteria that it uses to assess state aid in the air transport sector in Annex IV of Memorandum No. 2 on the development of the Community air transport policy, Doc. COM(84) 72 final. For a summary of these criteria and an evaluation of aid schemes in this sector, see Doc. SEC(92) 431, 11 March 1993.

[124] For example, art. 42 of the EC Treaty makes the application of the state aid rules in the agriculture sector subject to the basic legislation establishing the common agricultural policy. See *Sixteenth Report on Competition Policy*, points 283–289.

[125] See *XXIInd Report on Competition Policy for 1992*, points 448–453.

[126] *XXIst Report on Competition Policy*, point 271 ('[t]he Commission takes a favourable view of aid to promote tourism and craft activities inasmuch as they contribute to diversification, help maintain the economic base and create jobs in less favoured areas'). See also *XXth Report on Competition Policy*, points 302 and 303.

[127] *XXIst Report on Competition Policy for 1991*, point 272.

[128] In its Guidelines for the examination of state aids in the fisheries and aquaculture sector, OJ 1992, C152/2, the Commission gives the following definition of operating aid:

'[s]tate aids which are granted without imposing any obligation on the part of recipients and which are intended to improve the liquidity situation of their undertakings, the amount of which depends on the quantity produced or marketed, the prices of products, the unit of production or the factors of production and the result of which would be a reduction in the recipient's production costs or an improvement in the recipients's income are, as operating aids, incompatible with the common market.'

For examples of operating aid, see *Siemens*, OJ 1992 L288/31; *Nuova Cartiera di Arbatax*, OJ 1992 L159/53; *Spanish Fishing Fleet*, OJ 1990 L314/13.

[129] *Siemens*, OJ 1992 L288/31.

[130] Community framework on state aid to the motor vehicle industry, OJ 1989 C123/3, renewed OJ 1991 C81/4, OJ 1993 C36/17.

¶1218

acceptable for a limited period of time in order to allow a restructuring plan to take effect.[131] The Commission has also been willing to accept operating aid in the context of regional aid programmes directed towards the most depressed areas of the Community.[132] In the environmental field, the Commission has stated that it may authorise operating aid in certain well-defined circumstances, notably where the aid is only designed to compensate for extra production costs by comparison with traditional costs, and it is temporary and degressive so as to provide an incentive for reducing pollution or introducing more efficient uses of resources more quickly.[133]

Restructuring/elimination of excess capacity
In cases involving aid to sectors plagued by excess capacity, the Commission takes a critical view of aid,[134] and often conditions approval of the aid on the implementation of a restructuring plan designed to reduce the excess capacity.[135] The link between aid and restructuring has also been emphasised by the Court of Justice.[136] If an aid scheme in an industry suffering from overcapacity does not reduce this overcapacity, but simply maintains the status quo, it should normally bring about benefits in other areas such as improved product quality.[137] For firms in a precarious financial position, the Commission insists that the restructuring programme must lead to the long-term health of

---

[131] See e.g. Communication to the Council on Commission policy on state aid schemes, COM(78)221 final (May 1978).

[132] See Commission communication on the method for the application of art. 92(3)(a) and (c) to regional aid, OJ 1988 C212/2, updated at OJ 1989 C78/5, OJ 1990 C163/6, OJ 1992 C114/4.

[133] Community guidelines on state aid for environmental protection, OJ 1994 C72/3 at para. 3.4.

[134] See e.g. *Saint-Gobain* (*Eurofloat*), OJ 1991 L215/11.

[135] See e.g. *Enasa*, OJ 1989 L367/68; *Caulliez Frères*, OJ 1989 L223/22. See also *Boch*, OJ 1987 L228/39 (approval of aid conditioned on recipient's agreement not to grant operating aid or increase capacity for a period of at least three years). The Commission also follows this approach in the various guidelines that it has issued concerning aid to specific industrial sectors, most of which are burdened by overcapacity. For example, in the code on aid to the synthetic fibres industry, OJ 1992 C342/2, the Commission states:

'the Commission would inform the Member States and interested parties of its resolve to oppose any public financial support which would result in the installation of new capacity or even in the maintenance of existing capacity in the synthetic fibres industry. It intends to do this by making its authorization of the grant of aid conditional on a significant reduction in the production capacity of the assisted company.'

[136] In *Netherlands and Leeuwarder Papierwarenfabriek BV v EC Commission* [1985] ECR 809, at p. 825 (para. 26), the court stated:

'The contested decision merely states in the first place that the Netherlands aid "would not 'facilitate the development of … certain economic areas' within the meaning of that provision" … and in the second place that "developments in the paperboard-processing industry show that to maintain production capacity through the grant of State aid would not be in the common interest" and that "furthermore, the paperboard-processing industry's future prospects rule out the conclusion that the aid envisaged would not adversely affect trading conditions to an extent contrary to the common interest".… However, there is no indication whatsoever in the decision that the Commission took into consideration the essential fact, which might have caused it to make a different assessment, that the aid in question was accompanied by a restructuring of the recipient undertaking which, by diverting its production to high-quality products, led to a reduction in its production capacity and in its market share.'

[137] See e.g. *Technofibres*, OJ 1992 C301/2.

the company and must have other benefits as well such as contributing to the health of the sector involved by reducing capacity.[138]

Regional policy

An aid scheme that would normally be considered incompatible with the common market may be acceptable if it would benefit one of the poorer regions in the Community, thus helping to decrease the disparities among the Community's regions. In examining a given aid plan, the Commission must weigh the benefits to the region against possible disadvantages to the sector as a whole.[139] Thus, aid to build a plant in one of the poorest regions in the Community may not be acceptable if it concerns an industrial sector suffering from substantial overcapacity.

Horizontal policies

As discussed in greater detail below, the Community has developed a number of so-called 'horizontal policies'. These policies do not deal with aid aimed at any specific sector or region, but rather with aid in the context of broader, Community-wide policies concerning matters such as the environment, R&D, employment and the promotion of small and medium-sized enterprises ('SMEs'). An aid scheme that may otherwise be considered to be incompatible with the common market may be acceptable if it promotes one of these policies.[140]

¶1219   Horizontal aid

In addition to regional and sectoral aid, the Commission has developed policies with respect to so-called 'horizontal aid'. Such aid falls within the scope of the art. 92(3)(c) exemption to the extent that it 'facilitates the development of certain economic activities or of certain economic areas.'[141]

Research and development aid

R&D has become one of the largest, and in some member states the single largest, form of government support for industry.[142] This support may take

---

[138] See e.g., *Imepiel*, OJ 1992 L172/76.

[139] *SNIA-BPD Group*, OJ 1992 C166/2; *Ford/Volkswagen*, OJ 1991 C257/6.

[140] Horizontal policies are often referred to in the Commission's various guidelines on aids to specific sectors. For example, the code on aid to the synthetic fibres industry, OJ 1992 C346/2, states that '[i]n the case of aid coming under the frameworks on State aid for research and development and in environmental matters, the substantive examination of the aid schemes notified will be carried out applying the provisions of those frameworks.'

[141] In connection with small and medium-sized enterprises, the Commission has stated that '[i]n view of the positive externalities associated with SMEs, their importance for particular sectors of industry and for regional development, and the specific problems they face, there can be no doubt that State aid for SMEs "facilitates the development of certain economic activities or of certain economic areas".' (Community guidelines on State aid for small and medium-sized enterprises (SMEs), OJ 1992 C213/2.)

[142] *Sixteenth Report on Competition Policy*, point 247.

many forms, ranging from grants for basic industrial research to loans that must only be repaid if a project is successful.[143] Consistent with its approach under art. 85,[144] the Commission takes a generally favourable view of state aid for R&D projects.[145] The Commission recognises, however, that R&D aid is susceptible of distorting competition, particularly in so far as it may be concentrated in certain highly research-intensive sectors, on large firms and on the most developed regions.[146]

In 1986, the Commission outlined the basic principles for the assessment of aid to R&D.[147] Broadly, the Commission considers that aid levels should get progressively lower as the project gets nearer to the market.[148] The Commission seeks to ensure that aid received by firms does not take the place of their usual R&D expenditures, but rather enables them to carry out particularly risky projects or to explore areas which would not have been open to them with more limited resources.[149] In the Commission's view, as a result of aid received, firms should carry out more research than they would have done if they had not received the aid.[150] To verify whether this criterion is met, the Commission examines the structure and evolution of the R&D costs of the company over past years, notably R&D expenditure, R&D as a percentage of turnover and the number of employees working in R&D.[151]

Employment aid

The Commission is generally favourably disposed towards aid programmes intended to promote the employment of categories of workers experiencing particular difficulty in finding a job as long as these programmes are not confined to particular industries or firms.[152] These programmes may take the

---

[143] *XXIst Report on Competition Policy for 1991*, point 174.
[144] See Chapter 4.
[145] The Commission has explained its basic approach as follows (*Sixteenth Report on Competition Policy*, point 247):

'In examining the R&D schemes and projects notified to it, the Commission will exercise a general presumption in favour of such aid because of the contribution that R&D aid can make towards achieving Community goals ... because of the risks attached to R&D and the long pay-back periods which may be involved so that the activity would often not take place without aid, and finally because of the fact that aid for R&D by its nature may be less prone to distort trade between Member States than aid for investment which has a direct impact on production capacity and output. Furthermore, the Commission is aware that R&D is necessary to provide a constant stream of new products so as to sustain the growth, prosperity and worldwide competitiveness of Community industry and that State aids may have a role to play in this process.'

R&D aid may be exempted in cases of important projects of common European interest. See ¶1215.
[146] *XXIst Report on Competition Policy for 1991*, point 52.
[147] See Community framework for state aids for research and development, OJ 1986 C83/2.
[148] In its Community framework for state aids for research and development, OJ 1986 C83/2, the Commission stipulated that the level of aid for basic industrial research should not be more than 50 per cent of the gross costs of the project. The Commission generally allows up to 25 per cent for the subsequent stages of applied research and development. *XXIst Report on Competition Policy for 1991*, point 176.
[149] *XXIst Report on Competition Policy for 1991*, point 177.
[150] *XXIInd Report on Competition Policy for 1992*, point 355.
[151] Id.
[152] *XXIst Report on Competition Policy for 1991*, point 270; *XXth Report on Competition Policy*, point 280.

form of recruitment aid, the creation of new jobs and the promotion of self-employment.[153]

Environment

In addition to qualifying for exemption as supporting an important project of common European interest under art. 92(3)(b),[154] aid such as that to assist firms in developing new environmental protection measures that go beyond those required by law may be eligible for exemption under art. 92(3)(c) as aid to facilitate the development of certain economic activities.[155]

The Commission's approach to aid in this area is explained in a set of guidelines published in 1994.[156] The main concern is that some member states will grant aid to firms to help them make the investments necessary to comply with environmental standards, which will give these firms an advantage over those in member states that must meet the same requirements, but which do not receive aid.[157] Thus, the Commission is only willing to authorise the following types of environmental aid:

(1) aid for investment to comply with new mandatory standards;[158]

(2) aid for investment that allows firms to achieve higher levels of environmental protection than those mandated by law;[159]

(3) where there are no mandatory environmental standards, aid for investment that will significantly improve a firm's environmental performance or match that of firms in other member states where mandatory standards apply;[160]

(4) aid for information activities, training and advisory services;[161]

(5) operating aid in limited circumstances;[162] and

(6) aid for the purchase of environmentally friendly products.[163]

---

[153] *XXIst Report on Competition Policy for 1991*, point 270.

[154] See ¶1215.

[155] Aid for environmental purposes in regions eligible for aid pursuant to art. 92(3)(a) may be authorised under that article. Community guidelines on state aid for environmental protection, OJ 1994 C72/3 at p. 8 (para. 36).

[156] Id.

[157] Id., at p. 3 (para. 1.4).

[158] Id., at p. 6 (para. 3.2.3). Such aid may be authorised up to the level of 15 per cent gross of the eligible costs. Aid may only be granted for a limited period and only in respect of plant which has been in operation for at least two years when the new standards or obligations enter into force.

[159] Id. Such aid may be authorised up to a maximum of 30 per cent gross of the eligible costs. The level of aid actually granted for exceeding standards must be in proportion to the improvement of the environment that is achieved and to the investment necessary for achieving the improvement.

[160] Id.

[161] Id., at p. 7 (para. 3.3).

[162] Id., at p. 7 (para. 3.4).

[163] Id., at p. 8 (para. 3.5).

¶1219

General investment aid

The Commission takes a negative view towards general investment aid schemes, which are schemes that are not directed at a specific industry or region and do not pursue a specific Community objective.[164] Recently, the Commission conducted a broad-ranging review of such schemes, which led to the abolition of many and the amendment of others.[165] According to the Commission, investment is a normal business expense that is in a firm's own interest, and should not generally require government assistance.[166] Moreover, general investment aid is inconsistent with the goal of an integrated single market characterised by social and economic cohesion.[167] When investment aid is available in the more prosperous parts of the Community that do not need assistance, this reduces the attractiveness of the incentives offered in assisted areas, particularly those in the less-developed regions.[168]

Small and medium-sized enterprises ('SMEs')

The Commission recognises that SMEs play an important role in the economy[169] and that they may need assistance to overcome obstacles which larger, more established firms may not face such as raising capital or meeting the costs of complying with government regulations.[170] This aid may include education and training and the simplification of regulatory requirements as well as financial incentives for start-ups and investments.[171] The Commission takes a basically favourable view towards such aid and, in 1992, adopted guidelines on aid to SMEs designed to clarify its policy in this area.[172] These guidelines apply to SMEs in all sectors, but give way to any applicable sectoral rules on aid.[173] These guidelines clarify the definition of 'SME' to ensure that aid schemes benefit only SMEs and not larger firms, and describe the various

---

[164] *XXth Report on Competition Policy*, point 171. For examples of such schemes, see *XXIst Report on Competition Policy for 1991*, points 242–247.

[165] See *XXIst Report on Competition Policy for 1991*, points 240–247.

[166] Community guidelines on state aid for small and medium-sized enterprises (SMEs) (the 'SME guidelines'), OJ 1992 C213/2 at p. 6 (para. 4.1).

[167] Id.

[168] Id. See also *XXth Report on Competition Policy*, point 171.

[169] In its *XXIst Report on Competition Policy for 1991*, point 165, the Commission noted:

'SMEs play a disproportionate role in employment creation and a large number of them are in the forefront of innovation, making them a major source of competition and a motor of structural change and economic regeneration. The SME sector is also of fundamental importance for regional development and in parts of manufacturing industry which depend on subcontracting, the health of large enterprises being therefore also dependent on a strong SME sector.'

See also SME guidelines, OJ 1992 C213/2, para. 1.1–1.2.

[170] In the SME guidelines, at p. 2 (para. 1.3), the Commission noted that '[t]he compliance costs of small businesses with respect to government regulations on health and safety, financial accounting, etc., may be higher and the tax burden on them may be heavier, both in terms of the rates of tax they pay and the compliance costs of the tax system (e.g. collection of social security contributions and VAT).'

[171] *XXIst Report on Competition Policy for 1991*, point 165.

[172] In the Commission's view, the playing field should be tilted slightly in favour of SMEs. SME guidelines, at p. 2 (para. 1.4).

[173] Id., at p. 3 (para. 1.6).

types and intensities of aid which the Commission will normally be prepared to authorise. The Commission also takes a favourable view of aid programmes designed to improve the general business environment, particularly for SMEs, through the use of specialised consultants, training, the dissemination of advanced technology and the improvement of production and management methods.[174]

Rescue/restructuring aid

Rescue aid is granted to a company to keep it afloat for a limited time while it discovers the causes of its difficulties and works out a solution.[175] Restructuring aid is granted to a company to allow it to stay in business pending the implementation of a restructuring programme.[176] The Commission considers that such aid is particularly susceptible of distorting competition because it prevents market forces from working to weed out unproductive firms.[177] Consequently, it is only willing to approve rescue and restructuring aid in exceptional circumstances.[178] Both types of aid must be limited to the amount necessary to keep the company in business and must be limited in time.[179] It must be linked to a satisfactory restructuring plan, and may be granted only where it can be demonstrated that the Community interest is best served by keeping a manufacturer in business and by re-establishing its viability.[180]

Export aid

Member states devote a substantial amount of money to promote exports of national products to third countries.[181] The main types of export aid are export credit insurance programmes for short-term as well as medium and long-term risks, interest-rate subsidies and tied development aid assistance. The Commission has shown increasing concern over the distorting effect that

---

[174] *XXth Report on Competition Policy*, point 294.
[175] *Eighth Report on Competition Policy*, point 228.
[176] Id.
[177] See *Magefesa*, OJ 1991 L5/18, at p. 23.
[178] See *Alfa Romeo*, OJ 1989 L394/9. The Commission has signalled its intention to monitor such aids closely. See *Nineteenth Report on Competition Policy*, point 124.
[179] For specific criteria that rescue and restructuring aids must meet, see *Eighth Report on Competition Policy*, point 228. For examples of cases in which the Commission has applied these criteria, see *La Papelera Española*, OJ 1992 C234/8; *Magefesa*, OJ 1991 L5/18; *Alfa Romeo*, OJ 1989 L394/9; *Enasa*, OJ 1989 L367/62.
[180] See *Alfa Romeo*, OJ 1989 L394/9, at p. 17. In this connection, the Commission stated (id.) that:

'It is necessary for the Commission to ensure that the aid will not enable a beneficiary to increase its market share at the expense of its unaided competitors. In cases where certain companies still have excess capacity, the Commission may require reductions in capacity in order to ensure that the aid contributes to the overall recovery of the sector.'

[181] *XXIst Report on Competition Policy for 1991*, point 166.

¶1219

export aid can have on trade between member states,[182] and is currently preparing guidelines on the application of the state aid rules to short-term export credit insurance.[183]

Privatisations

In recent years, an increasing number of cases have involved aid granted in the context of privatisations.[184] Often, the aid takes the form of a capital injection or debt write-off intended to make the company's shares more attractive to potential buyers.[185] In the Commission's view, the sale of a public enterprise may involve aid unless the shares are sold to the highest bidder in an open and unconditional bidding procedure.[186]

¶1220   Cumulation of aids

To ensure that its policies on different kinds of state aid operate as a coherent whole, the Commission has adopted special rules on the cumulation of aids.[187] The Commission is particularly concerned with avoiding having the discipline imposed by its regional aid policy undermined by the award of aids with other policy objectives.[188]

Member states must notify to the Commission cases involving the cumulation of aids where the total investment in a project exceeds ECU 12m or where the cumulative intensity of the aids exceeds 25 per cent in net grant equivalent (basically, the cost of the project).[189] Notification is not necessary in the following cases:

(1) where the investment does not exceed ECU 3m;

(2) where the cumulative intensity does not exceed ten per cent; or

(3) where the intensity of all the aids to be granted for the investment project remains below the ceiling for any one of the aid schemes under which aid is being awarded to the project.[190]

The Commission will examine notified projects on a case-by-case basis within 30 working days, taking into account the overall situation in the region and

---

[182] Id.

[183] See *XXIInd Report on Competition Policy for 1992*, point 339.

[184] See *XXIInd Report on Competition Policy for 1992*, points 388, 417 et seq, 424 and 464–466; *XXXIst Report on Competition Policy*, points 248–252.

[185] See e.g. *XXIInd Report on Competition Policy*, points 417–421.

[186] *XXIst Report on Competition Policy for 1991*, point 248.

[187] Commission communication on rules applicable to cases of cumulation of aids for different purposes, OJ 1985 C3/2.

[188] *Fourteenth Report on Competition Policy*, point 199.

[189] Commission communication on rules applicable to cases of cumulation of aids for different purposes, OJ 1985 C3/2.

[190] Id.

sector concerned, the intensity of the cumulative aid as well as the effects on competition and the increase in aid levels.[191]

PROCEDURE

¶1221   Introduction

Clear, precise procedural rules are lacking in the field of state aid.[192] The treaty provisions themselves only provide a faint outline of a coherent procedure, and no implementing regulation analogous to Regulation 17/62 adopted in connection with art. 85 and 86 has ever been adopted in an effort to provide a comprehensive set of procedural rules.[193] In fact, the Commission may be reluctant to remedy this situation, fearful that the adoption of such a regulation could lead to a weakening of its powers in the field.[194] In the absence of a coherent procedural framework, the court has been left with the task of filling in procedural gaps on an ad hoc basis. While the court has increased the protection available to defendants and increased legal certainty in state aid proceedings, it may only deal with problems as they arise; such a piecemeal approach is clearly no substitute for a comprehensive legislative framework adopted after thorough study. Until such legislation is adopted, however, the case law of the court and the practice of the Commission remain the litigant's only guideposts in a state aid proceeding.

¶1222   Notification and review procedures: overview

In conjunction with its effort to tighten the Community's state aid regime, the Commission has actively encouraged member states to notify new aid schemes by making them more aware of their obligation to do so and by making more frequent use of its enforcement weapons, particularly the ability to force the

---

[191] *Fourteenth Report on Competition Policy*, point 199.

[192] In *Irish Cement v EC Commission* [1988] ECR 6473, at p. 6490 (para. 19), Advocate General Darmon observed that 'the field of State aids is a complex one where the most diligent undertaking may experience some difficulty in rapidly finding the "silver thread" of the applicable rules and systems.'

[193] Article 94 of the treaty (as amended by the Union Treaty) gives the Council the power to adopt such a regulation:

'The Council, acting by qualified majority on a proposal from the Commission and after consulting the European Parliament, may make any appropriate regulations for the application of articles 92 and 93 and may in particular determine the conditions in which article 93(3) shall apply and the categories of aid exempted from this procedure.'

Regulation 1107/70 on the granting of aids for transport by rail, road and inland waterway, JO 1970 L130/1, was partially based on art. 94 of the treaty.

[194] In 1990, the Commission resisted the suggestion made by several member states that it should propose a regulation to the Council under art. 94 aimed at making state aids policy more transparent. See *XXth Report on Competition Policy*, point 170. According to the Director-General of DG IV, '[p]roposals to the Council would no doubt have led to responsibility for the control of state aid being transferred to the Council, which would have been unacceptable to the Commission.' Ehlermann, 'The Contribution of EC Competition Policy to the Single Market,' 29 CML Rev 257, (1992), at p. 275.

repayment of aid granted illegally. The Commission has also begun systematically to review existing aid schemes. As a result of these efforts, the number of notifications has risen in recent years.[195] At the same time, the number of formal proceedings initiated by the Commission has dropped, suggesting that the dialogue between the Commission and the member states brought about by the notification process often results in settlements being reached during the preliminary stages of the notification procedure.[196]

This section examines the procedure for the notification and review of state aids. The applicable procedure depends on whether the aid is 'new' or 'existing', and, if 'new', whether it is 'notified' or 'unnotified'. This jargon can be confusing because it does not follow the ordinary meaning of the words. The difference between 'new' and 'existing' aid has nothing to do with whether the aid is already in existence. Rather, the difference depends on whether the aid has been notified to the Commission: 'new' aid has never been notified, while 'existing' aid has been notified. Thus, an aid scheme that has been in existence for years, but has never been notified to the Commission, is considered to be 'new' aid. Similarly, 'existing' aid that has been notified to the Commission, but is subsequently modified, is considered to be 'new' aid. For lack of a better term, this kind of aid is commonly called 'unnotified new aid' to distinguish it from new aid schemes that are notified to the Commission prior to implementation (called 'notified new aid').

¶1223 Notified new aids: basic rules

Article 93(3) establishes a system for examining plans to grant new aid or alter existing aid. It provides as follows:

> 'The Commission shall be informed, in sufficient time to enable it to submit its comments, of any plans to grant or alter aid. If it considers that any such plan is not compatible with the common market having regard to Article 92, it shall without delay initiate the procedure provided for in paragraph 2. The Member State concerned shall not put its proposed measures into effect until this procedure has resulted in a final decision.'

Thus, the treaty establishes a two-stage process for the review of proposals to grant new aid or to alter existing aid. First, the Commission conducts a preliminary examination under art. 93(3). If the Commission finds that the aid is compatible with the common market, the procedure is terminated. If the Commission finds that the aid is incompatible with the common market or at

---

[195] In 1986, there were 124 notifications; in 1992, 459. *XXIInd Report on Competition Policy for 1992*, point 129.

[196] In 1986, 47 proceedings were initiated; in 1992, only 26 proceedings were initiated despite nearly a four-fold increase in the number of notifications. The Commission has reported that 'the discussions which take place as part of the increased collaboration between Member States and the Commission result more often than in the past either in the amendment or in the withdrawal of the proposed aid measures initially notified'. *XXIst Report on Competition Policy for 1991*, point 76.

least has doubts on this point, it must open the second stage of the procedure, which is a more formal proceeding under art. 93(2). Each of these phases in the procedure are discussed below.

¶1224   Notified new aids: preliminary examination

The purpose of the preliminary examination under art. 93(3) is to allow the Commission to form a prima facie opinion on the compatibility of the aid with the common market to determine whether it is necessary to open formal proceeding under art. 93(2).[197] This preliminary examination is an informal proceeding and the Commission is not required to give other member states or other interested third parties an opportunity to submit their comments.[198] The court has ruled that the Commission should not use this preliminary proceeding as a substitute for the more formal art. 93(2) proceeding in which third parties have a right to be heard, and that it should open art. 93(2) proceedings in cases where it is not wholly convinced that an aid programme is compatible with the common market.[199] Despite this ruling, there would seem to be a risk that the interests of third parties will not be protected adequately because the Commission has a large measure of discretion in deciding whether to open an art. 93(2) proceeding.[200]

While the Commission is conducting its preliminary examination, the member state may not put the proposed aid plan into effect.[201] As art. 93(3) does not specify any time limit for the preliminary examination, this standstill obligation could seriously impede a member state's efforts to aid its industry if the Commission's examination were allowed to continue for months or years.

---

[197] *Germany v EC Commission* [1984] ECR 1451, at p. 1488 (para. 11). In this case, the court restated the procedural rules concerning the examination of state aids developed in earlier cases. See *Lorenz v Germany* [1973] ECR 1471; *Markmann v Germany* [1973] ECR 1495; *Nordsee v Germany* [1973] ECR 1511; *Lohrey v Germany* [1973] ECR 1527.

[198] Id.

[199] Id.

[200] For example, in *Matra v EC Commission* [1991] ECR I-5823 (order of the President of the Court) and judgment of 15 June 1993 (not yet reported), the Commission, after a preliminary examination conducted under art. 93(3), decided that an aid programme was compatible with the common market and that it was not necessary to commence formal proceedings under art. 93(2). During the course of these proceedings, a competitor of the recipient of the aid complained to the Commission that the aid would be incompatible with the common market and, after the Commission decided to close the procedure, took the matter to court. Although the competitor's willingness to pursue its argument to the court suggests the existence of at least a prima facie case that the aid was not compatible with the common market so that the Commission should have opened an art. 93(2) proceeding, the court upheld the Commission's decision not to open such a proceeding. The court noted that the Commission had examined in some detail the argument that the aid would lead to overcapacity in the sector.

In another case involving a challenge to a Commission decision not to open an art. 93(2) proceeding, *William Cook plc v EC Commission*, Case C-198/91, judgment of 19 May 1993 (not yet reported), the court made it clear that the Commission's discretion in deciding whether or not to open such a proceeding is not unfettered. In that case, the court annulled the Commission's decision not to open an art. 93(2) proceeding on the grounds that the factual assessments necessary to determine the effect of the aid were complex enough to warrant a more formal, in-depth investigation.

[201] Article 93(3).

¶1224

Recognising this problem, the court has held that, while it is necessary for the Commission to be allowed sufficient time to form a preliminary view on the compatibility with the common market of plans submitted to it, it must define its position within a reasonable period because the member state concerned might wish to act quickly.[202] By analogy to art. 173 and 175 of the treaty, the court fixed that period at two months.[203] In exceptional cases, the period has been extended beyond two months.[204] While some doubts exist as to precisely when this period starts running, the cases suggest that it begins when the Commission considers that it has received all of the relevant information,[205] and this is clearly the position followed by the Commission in practice. In an effort to ensure timely scrutiny of aid plans, the Commission has requested that member states notify aid plans at the draft stage using a form developed by the Commission.[206] Unless the Commission decides that aid is incompatible with the common market, the member state may implement the aid measures at the end of the two-month examination period after giving the Commission prior notice.[207]

If the Commission decides that an aid plan is compatible with the common market after its preliminary examination, it is not bound to adopt a formal decision, but it must at least inform the member state concerned.[208] Once the aid is implemented by the member state, it becomes an 'existing' aid within the meaning of art. 93(1) and, as discussed below, is subject to ongoing monitoring by the Commission.[209] As mentioned, if an 'existing' aid is modified, the modifications must be notified to the Commission in the same manner as other 'new' aid.

---

[202] *Lorenz v Germany* [1973] ECR 1471, at p. 1481 (para. 4).

[203] Id.

[204] See *France v EC Commission* ('*Boussac*') [1990] ECR I-307, at p. I-358 (para. 26 and 27) (three-month period considered reasonable due to difficulty in obtaining necessary information).

[205] Id. at pp. I-357 and 358 (para. 25–28) (nine-month period between member state's initial submission to the Commission under art. 93(3) and the Commission's decision to commence proceedings under art. 93(2) did not infringe principle of legal certainty because member state did not supply the facts necessary for the Commission to make an assessment in its initial submission to the Commission).

Thus far, the Commission does not appear to be overly concerned with strict adherence to the two-month limit, and it remains to be seen whether the court will require such strict adherence. In a case pending before the court, *Spain v EC Commission*, Case C-312/90, (judgment of 30 June 1992 on issue of admissibility only) (not yet reported), Spain had proceeded to implement its aid programme after the Commission had failed to open a formal proceeding under art. 93(2) within the two-month period. Subsequently, the Commission opened a formal proceeding and suspended the grant of the aid. Spain contests this action on the grounds that the aid in question was existing aid rather than new aid because it was granted after the expiry of the two-month preliminary examination period. Consequently, the aid could not be suspended pending the outcome of the proceeding.

[206] Communication to the member states concerning the procedures for the notification of aid plans and procedures applicable when aid is provided in breach of the rules of art. 93(3) of the EC Treaty, letter from the Commission to the member states SG (91) D/4577, reprinted in *XXIst Report on Competition Policy for 1991*, p. 302. The notification form is set out in an annex to this letter.

[207] *Germany v EC Commission* [1984] ECR 1451, at p. 1488 (para. 11).

[208] Id. (para. 12).

[209] Id.

¶1225   Notified new aids: formal proceeding

If the Commission is unable to decide whether an aid plan is compatible with the common market or decides that, on a prima facie basis, the plan is incompatible with the common market, it must initiate without delay. the second stage of the review process, which is a more formal examination procedure governed by art. 93(2).[210] The first two paragraphs of art. 93(2) describe this procedure as follows:

> 'If, after giving notice to the parties concerned to submit their comments, the Commission finds that aid granted by a State or through State resources is not compatible with the common market having regard to Article 92, or that such aid is being misused, it shall decide that the State concerned shall abolish or alter such aid within a period of time to be determined by the Commission.
>
> If the State concerned does not comply with the decision within the prescribed time, the Commission or any other interested State may, in derogation from the provisions of Articles 169 and 170, refer the matter to the Court of Justice direct.'

Thus, the art. 93(2) procedure begins with the Commission giving notice to the parties concerned to submit their comments. Typically, the Commission writes to the member state concerned asking it to submit its comments within one month and publishes a notice in the *Official Journal of the European Communities* requesting the other member states and interested parties to submit their comments within one month of the date of the notice. In contrast to proceedings under art. 85 and 86, there is no procedure in state aid cases involving the hearing of all the parties and the disclosure of information between them.[211] Nevertheless, the Commission must at least give the member state concerned the opportunity to make its views known on the comments submitted by interested third parties on which the Commission proposes to base its decision.[212] If the member state is denied its right to be heard, this may lead to the annulment of the Commission's decision if it is established that,

---

[210] Id. (para. 12 and 13).

[211] See *Belgium v EC Commission* ('*Meura*') [1986] ECR 2263, at p. 2288 (para. 26).

[212] *France v EC Commission* [1987] ECR 4393 at p. 4415 (para. 12). To the extent that the member state has not been afforded the opportunity to comment on the observations of third parties, the Commission may not take them into account in its decision. Id. See also *Belgium v EC Commission* ('*Meura*') [1986] ECR 2263.

but for this irregularity, the outcome of the proceeding would have been different.[213]

After the Commission has heard the comments of all the parties, it must adopt a formal decision on the compatibility of the aid with the common market.[214] While art. 93(2) does not set any time limit within which the Commission must make its decision, the Commission must act within a reasonable time or risk having its decision annulled for violating the principle of legitimate expectations.[215] If the Commission decides that aid is not compatible with the common market or is being misused, it may issue a decision ordering the member state to abolish or alter the aid within a specified period.[216]

Article 93(2) also gives member states the opportunity of taking their case directly to the Council, an option that serves to highlight again the sensitivity of the drafters of the treaty to the fact that state aid cases may touch on important national political interests. A member state may apply to the Council for a decision that, despite its incompatibility with art. 92 or regulations adopted under art. 94, the aid is justified by 'exceptional circumstances.'[217] If the Commission has already begun the review proceedings under art. 93(2), this application serves to suspend the Commission proceedings until the Council has 'made its attitude known.'[218] If the Council fails to act within three months, the Commission may issue a decision.[219]

---

[213] *France v EC Commission* [1987] ECR 4393, at p. 4415 (para. 13).

[214] The court has held that an examination instituted under art. 93(2) may only be terminated by the adoption of a decision within the meaning of art. 189 of the treaty. In practice, the Commission only adopts formal decisions in cases where it considers that the aid is incompatible with the common market, or is only compatible if certain conditions are met. See *Fédération Nationale du Commerce Extérieur des Produits Alimentaires v France* [1991] ECR I-5505 (para. 13) (Opinion of Advocate General Jacobs). Positive decisions are simply published as notices in the *Official Journal*.

[215] In *Fédération Nationale des Producteurs de Vins de Table et Vins de Pays v EC Commission* [1979] ECR 2425, the court held that the Commission has a reasonable period within which to complete the art. 93(2) procedure and may not be attacked under art. 175 for its failure to act within the two-month time limit laid down in that article once it has opened an art. 93(2) procedure.

In *RSV v EC Commission* [1987] ECR 4617, the court struck down a Commission decision finding the aid in question to be incompatible with the common market and ordering its refund. In that case, the Commission waited 26 months before adopting its decision. In the court's view, this delay could establish a legitimate expectation on the part of the member state that the aid was lawful. However, a long investigation period may be justified in cases where the member state is slow in providing the Commission with all of the relevant information. In *France v EC Commission* ('*Boussac*') [1990] ECR I-307, the court held that the Commission did not infringe the principle of legal certainty in waiting 32 months between the initiation of art. 93(2) proceedings and the adoption of the final decision because it did not receive all of the facts necessary for it to examine the compatibility of the aid with the common market until just two months before the adoption of its decision.

[216] Article 93(2). This decision must indicate to the member state the aspects of the aid which are incompatible with the treaty and subject to abolition or alteration. *Belgium v EC Commission* [1986] ECR 89, at p. 103 (para. 9); *EC Commission v Germany* [1973] ECR 813, at p. 831 (para. 20).

[217] Article 93(2), third subparagraph.

[218] Id.

[219] Id., at fourth subparagraph.

¶1226   Unnotified new aids

Despite the Commission's efforts to heighten enforcement of the obligation imposed on member states to notify aid schemes, member states continue to grant aid without notifying the aid scheme to the Commission.[220] In such cases, the Commission may challenge the scheme after learning of it from a press report, a Parliamentary question, a complaint from another member state or local and regional authorities or a complaint from one of the recipient's competitors.[221] The question has arisen of whether the Commission may declare such an aid scheme to be unlawful solely because it was not notified and require recovery of the aid without examining the details of the scheme to judge its compatibility with the common market. To allow the Commission to take such action would clearly punish member states that failed to notify aid schemes and would seem consistent with the last sentence of art. 93(3), which prohibits a member state from implementing a new aid scheme without first obtaining the authorisation of the Commission. On the other hand, allowing such action would mean that aid that is compatible with the common market may be declared unlawful simply because of procedural irregularities.

In *Boussac*,[222] the court struck a compromise. It held that the Commission must examine the case on its merits, but, in the meantime, may issue an interim decision requiring the member state to suspend immediately the payment of the aid pending the outcome of the examination of the aid and to provide the Commission with information concerning the aid.[223] If the member state fails to provide the information requested, the Commission may adopt a decision on the basis of the information available and order the recovery of aid already paid.[224] If the member state fails to suspend payment of the aid, the Commission may bring the matter directly before the court.[225]

Drawing on the court's judgment in *Boussac*, the Commission has developed a procedure to be followed in cases of unnotified aid.[226] First, the Commission will request the member state to supply full details of the aid in question within 30 days.[227] If the member state fails to reply or provides an unsatisfactory reply, the Commission may then:

(1) adopt a provisional decision requiring the member state to suspend immediately the application of the aid scheme or payment of aid

---

[220] In 1992, there were 102 cases of unnotified aid. *XXIInd Report on Competition Policy for 1992*, point 129.
[221] See *XXIInd Report on Competition Policy for 1992*, point 17.
[222] *France v EC Commission ('Boussac')* [1990] ECR I-307.
[223] Id., at p. I-356 (para. 19).
[224] Id. (para. 22).
[225] Id. (para. 23).
[226] Communication to the member states concerning the procedures for the notification of aid plans and procedures applicable when aid is provided in breach of the rules of art. 93(3) of the EC Treaty, letter from the Commission to the member states SG (91) D/4577 of 4 March 1991, reprinted in *XXIst Report on Competition Policy for 1991*, p. 302; see also *XXth Report on Competition Policy*, point 172.
[227] In urgent cases, this time limit may be shorter. Id.

unlawfully authorised and to inform the Commission within 15 days that this decision has been complied with;[228] and

(2) initiate the formal examination procedure under art. 93(2), giving the member state concerned notice to communicate within one month its comments and all information necessary to assess the compatibility of the aid with the common market.

If the member state fails to provide the information requested within the time limit, the Commission may adopt a final decision under art. 93(2) on the basis of the information available to it finding that the aid is incompatible with the common market. This decision will require recovery of the amount of aid already paid unlawfully in accordance with the relevant provisions of national law.[229] If the member state does not comply with the Commission's decisions (either the provisional decision or the final negative decision) the Commission may take the matter to the Court of Justice and, if necessary, apply for an interim order suspending payment of the aid.

¶1227 Existing aids

Article 93(1) establishes a procedure for the review of existing aids which has been used with increasing frequency in recent years in connection with the Commission's efforts to tighten control over aids.[230] Existing aids are:

(1) aids in operation when the treaty came into force or when new member states acceded to the treaty; and

(2) aids lawfully implemented after notification to the Commission, e.g.

- aids that were introduced after their notification and authorisation by the Commission, or

- aids that were notified to the Commission but, following the Commission's failure to either authorise them or begin a formal proceeding under art. 93(2) within the two-month period prescribed for preliminary examinations under art. 93(3), were put into effect by the member state concerned.[231]

As mentioned,[232] the term 'existing aid' is somewhat of a misnomer because it

---

[228] The Commission first adopted such a provisional decision in *PMU*, OJ 1992 L14/35.

[229] These provisions shall include those concerning interest due for late payment of amounts owing to the government, interest which should normally run from the date of the award of the unlawful aid in question.

[230] See *XXIst Report on Competition Policy for 1991*, points 240 and 241; *XXth Report on Competition Policy*, p. 15 and point 171. According to the Commission, the review of existing aid schemes is necessary 'because many of them were approved years ago at a time when the economic circumstances were different, for example during the recession of the second half of the 1970s and early 1980s, and when the Community market was more fragmented than is the case today'. Id.

[231] See *Spain v EC Commission*, Case C-312/90, judgment of 30 June 1992 (not yet reported); *Italy v EC Commission*, Case C-47/91, judgment of 30 June 1992 (not yet reported); *Italy v EC Commission* [1974] ECR 709, at p. 723 (opinion of Advocate General Warner); *Lorenz v Germany* [1973] ECR 1471, at p. 1481 (para. 4).

[232] See ¶1222.

does not refer to all existing aid schemes, but rather only those lawfully implemented after notification to the Commission. Apart from difficulties of terminology, the classification of aid as 'new' or 'existing' can be problematic. For example, Commission approval of a general aid programme often obviates the need to make a notification to the Commission each time an individual aid package is granted under this programme. However, it is not always clear whether a given aid package is covered by the general aid programme or whether it is a new aid that must be notified to the Commission.[233] Another situation in which the distinction between 'new' and 'existing' aid is prone to become blurred is when a member state proceeds to grant aid on the grounds that the two-month period under art. 93(3) has expired without any action by the Commission.[234] As discussed above, this period only begins to run once the Commission has received all pertinent information, a standard that may give rise to controversy concerning the calculation of this period.

The distinction between existing and new aid is a distinction with a difference. While the Commission may suspend the grant of new aid pending the completion of its examination under art. 93(2) and (3), it may not do so while examining existing aid.[235]

Article 93(1) provides that the Commission shall keep all systems of existing aids under review and that it shall propose 'any appropriate measures required by the progressive development or by the functioning of the common market'. Thus, if the Commission considers that an existing aid programme has become incompatible with the common market due to changed economic circumstances, it must present the member state with a specific proposal to remedy the problem. This proposal is not binding on the member state, but it is important as a mandatory step to the eventual opening of the art. 93(2) procedure discussed in the preceding section.[236]

If the member state decides to ignore the Commission's proposal, the Commission may commence the art. 93(2) procedure.

---

[233] See *Italy v EC Commission*, Case C-47/91, judgment of 30 June 1992 (not yet reported).
[234] See *Spain v EC Commission*, Case C-312/90, judgment of 30 June 1992 (not yet reported).
[235] Id.
[236] For an example of a case involving a review of an existing aid sceme, see *Regeling Bijzondere Financiering*, OJ 1992 C22/6. See also *XXIInd Report on Competition Policy for 1992* points 455, 462.

¶1227

¶1228   Aids of minor importance

The Commission has established an expedited notification procedure for aids of minor importance.[237] New aid schemes[238] do not need to be notified where:

(1) the aid scheme is limited to small and medium-sized enterprises;[239] and

(2) where the scheme has specific investment objectives, the aid intensity does not exceed 7.5 per cent of the investment cost;

(3) where the aid is designed to lead to job creation, it amounts to not more than ECU 3,000 per job created; or

(4) when, in the absence of specific investment or job creation objectives, the total volume of aid a beneficiary may receive is not more than ECU 200,000.[240]

The first criterion must be satisfied in all cases and at least one of the following three criteria must be satisfied as well. A similar system applies to existing aid schemes. Aid schemes qualifying for expedited treatment are notified on a short form provided by the Commission and the Commission will decide on the proposal in 20 working days.[241]

¶1229   Aid to state-owned companies

Member states must file an annual report with the Commission providing details on state intervention in state-owned companies.[242] This reporting requirement is not intended to replace the usual notification procedures

---

[237] Notification of an aid scheme of minor importance, OJ 1990 C40/2, as amended by OJ 1992 C213/10. See generally *Fourteenth Report on Competition Policy*, point 203.

[238] New aid schemes exclude those covered by specific sectoral rules. Notification of an aid scheme of minor importance, OJ 1991 C40/2, as amended by OJ 1992 C213/10.

[239] An SME is defined as any firm which

– has no more than 250 employees, and
– either
  – an annual turnover not exceeding ECU 20m, or
  – a balance sheet total not exceeding ECU 10m, and
– is not more than 25 per cent owned by one or more companies not falling within this definition, except public investment corporations, venture capital companies or, provided no control is exercised, institutional investors. Id.

[240] Id. All of these threshold figures are pre-tax.

[241] The notification form is set out in an annex to the Commission communication, OJ 1992 C213/10.

[242] Directive 80/723 of 25 June 1980 on the transparency of financial relation between member states and public undertakings, OJ 1980 L195/35, as amended by OJ 1985 L229/20 and OJ 1993 L254/16, art. 5A. Details of this reporting system were included in the original version of the Commission communication to the member states on the application of art. 92 and 93 of the EC Treaty and of art. 5 of Commission Directive 80/723 to public undertakings in the manufacturing sector, OJ 1991 C273/2. This communication was annulled by the Court of Justice as being beyond the Commission's powers as set out in Directive 80/723. Following the ruling by the court, the Commission incorporated the reporting requirement in the directive (Directive 80/723 as amended by Directive 93/84 (OJ 1993 L254/16)) and readopted the communication without references to the reporting requirement (OJ 1993 C307/3)).

Prior to the introduction of this annual reporting system, member states were only required to provide such information to the Commission upon a specific request pursuant to Directive 80/723. This directive was upheld by the Court in *France, Italy and UK v EC Commission* [1982] ECR 2545.

discussed above, but rather is intended to supplement them as a means of increasing transparency in an area that has proved troublesome in the past. These reports must be filed by member states with respect to public undertakings whose principal activity is manufacturing and which have an annual turnover of more than ECU 250m.

¶1230   Enforcement judicial review before the Court of Justice[243]

If the Commission decides that aid is compatible with the common market and closes the art. 93(2) procedure, this decision may be challenged within two months under art. 173 by a member state or a private party who is directly and individually concerned by the decision, such as a complainant that has taken an active part in the proceedings.[244] Pending the court's decision, the applicant may ask the court to enjoin the grant of the aid.[245] If the Commission decides that aid is not compatible with the common market, this decision may be challenged within two months by a member state or the aid recipient under art. 173. If the member state fails to do so, it may not later challenge the validity of the decision in the context of enforcement proceedings brought by the Commission.[246]

If the member state does not comply with the Commission's order to alter or abolish an aid scheme and/or to repay aid pursuant to a decision finding aid to be incompatible with the common market or does not observe the conditions on which the Commission approved the aid, art. 93(2) allows the Commission or any interested member state to refer the matter directly to the court and thus avoid the more cumbersome procedures set out in art. 169 and 170.[247] The Commission may not seek to enforce its decision by adopting a second decision designed to implement its initial decision unless this second decision is based on a new examination under art. 93(2).[248]

Instead of bringing proceedings under art. 93(2), the Commission may bring

---

[243] The Court of First Instance does not have jurisdiction to review state aid cases.

[244] See *COFAZ v EC Commission* [1986] ECR 391, in which the Court of Justice held that, as a complainant taking an active part in an art. 93(2) procedure, a trade association had standing under art. 173 to challenge a Commission decision to close the procedure. See also *Comité international de la rayonne et des fibres synthétiques v EC Commission*, Case C-313/90, judgment of 24 March 1993 (not yet reported).

[245] See *Matra v EC Commission* [1991] ECR I-5823, Case C-225/91R, Order of the President of the Court of 4 December 1991 (not yet reported).

[246] *EC Commission v Belgium* [1986] ECR 89, at p. 104 (para. 13).

[247] Art. 93(2), second sub-para. While the Commission or a member state may decide to bring proceedings under art. 169 or 170 instead of art. 93(2), they must use the procedure laid down in art. 93(2) if they wish to establish that an aid scheme is incompatible with the common market. See *EC Commission v France* [1985] ECR 439.

[248] See *British Aerospace and Rover Group Holdings v EC Commission* [1992] ECR I-493. If the Commission decides to open a new art. 93(2) procedure, it may take into account the circumstances already considered in any previous decision. *Italy v EC Commission* [1991] ECR I-4437.

proceedings under art. 169. According to the Court, however, it may only bring proceedings under art. 169 to have a measure declared incompatible with the common market under the state aid rules where a member state has failed to comply with a decision adopted by the Commission after having followed the procedure laid down in art. 93(2).[249] The Commission may not stop proceedings under art. 93(2) and use this alternate route as a means of circumventing the safeguards laid down in art. 93(2) for the benefit of member states.[250] Pending the court's judgment on its art. 93(2) petition, the Commission may ask for interim measures under art. 186 to enjoin the grant of aid.[251]

¶1231   Role of national courts

Article 92(1) does not have direct effect.[252] Thus, in contrast to the situation under art. 85, where national courts have the power to apply the substantive norm contained in art. 85(1) and declare a restrictive agreement to be void under art. 85(2), national courts do not have the power to apply the substantive norm embodied in art. 92(1) by ruling on the compatibility of an aid scheme with the common market. In the state aid field, only the Commission and the Council, have the power to make this determination.

While national courts may not rule on the compatibility of aid, they nevertheless have an important role to play in enforcing the state aid rules. The power of national courts in the state aid field is based on the standstill obligation set forth in art. 93(3). The Court of Justice has ruled that this provision has direct effect, which means that national courts have the power to prohibit member states from implementing an aid scheme that has not yet been authorised by the Commission.[253] Thus, a competitor of a recipient of aid may seek an injunction in a national court against a member state that seeks to implement an aid scheme without notifying the scheme to the Commission or,

---

[249] The Commission may bring proceedings under art. 169 at any time if it considers that a measure is contrary to treaty provisions other than those dealing with state aids. See *EC Commission v Hellenic Republic* [1990] ECR I-3125, at p. I-3154 (para. 11).

[250] *EC Commission v France* [1985] ECR 439, pp. 449 and 450 (para. 17).

[251] See e.g. *EC Commission v France* [1983] ECR 2621.

[252] See *Steinike und Weinlig v Germany* [1977] ECR 595, at pp. 608–610 (para. 5–15). The court explained that 'the prohibition in Article 92(1) is neither absolute nor unconditional since Article 92(3) and Article 93(2) give the Commission and the Council extensive power to admit aids in derogation from the general prohibition in Article 92(1).' Id., at p. 609 (para. 8). See also *Lorenz v Germany* [1973] ECR 1471; *Capolongo v Maya* [1973] ECR 611; *Costa v ENEL* [1964] ECR 585.

[253] In *Lorenz v Germany* [1973] ECR 1471, at p. 1483 (para. 8), the court stated that:

'[T]he prohibition on implementation referred to in the last sentence of Article 93(3) has a direct effect and gives rise to rights in favour of individuals, which national courts are bound to safeguard.

The immediately applicable nature of this prohibition extends to the whole of the period to which it applies.

Thus the direct effect of the prohibition extends to all aid which has been implemented without being notified and, in the event of notification, operates during the preliminary period, and where the Commission sets in motion the contentious procedure, up to the final decision.'

in the case of notified aid, before the scheme has been cleared by the Commission; in addition, an action may be brought to require the member state to recover aid already paid out. In cases where the Commission eventually declares the aid to be compatible with the common market, this does not affect a national court's ability to order recovery of aid already paid out.[254] In the court's view, the national court must be able to take such action to safeguard the rights of the parties to the proceeding pending the Commission's decision and to give effect to art. 93(3)'s standstill obligation.[255] The Commission encourages national courts to play an active role in this area as part of its effort to foster the decentralised application of the competition rules[256] and, as more persons become aware of the possibilities of seeking redress in national courts, an increasing number of cases involving state aid are likely to be litigated in the national arena.

¶1232   Repayment of unauthorised aid

While it has long been established that the Commission may require the repayment of aid illegally granted,[257] it was not until 1983 that the Commission announced its intention to make use of this possibility.[258] Since then, the Commission has made increasing use of this power as a means of putting teeth into its state aids policy.[259] Prominent examples of cases in which the Commission has exercised this power are *Renault*,[260] in which the Commission ordered repayment of FF 6 billion, and *Rover/British Aerospace*,[261] in which the Commission ordered repayment of £44.4 m.

The Commission generally allows the member state to decide the most

---

[254] *Fédération nationale du commerce extérieur des produits alimentaires v France* [1991] ECR I-5505, at para. 15 and 16. Advocate General Jacobs has suggested that a member state may be able to set off aid paid prematurely against aid payable under a plan found to be compatible with the common market, but an adjustment should be made to offset any competitive advantage that would otherwise accrue to the recipient by reason of the early payment. Id., opinion of Advocate General Jacobs, para. 28.

[255] *Fédération nationale du commerce extérieur des produits alimentaires v France* [1991] ECR I-5505, at para. 14.

[256] See *XXIst Report on Competition Policy for 1991*, point 71. The application of state aids rules by national courts is not mentioned in the Commission's Notice on co-operation between national courts and the Commission in applying art. 85 and 86 of the EC Treaty, OJ 1993 C39/6.

[257] This principle was first established by the court in *EC Commission v Germany* [1973] ECR 813, at p. 829 (para. 13).

[258] See Commission communication, OJ 1983 C318/3.

[259] In his answer to Written Question No. 181/88, OJ 1989 C151/9, Sir Leon Brittan, the Commissioner then in charge of competition policy, noted the exponential growth in the amount of aid subject to recovery:

'The total amount of aids illegally granted by Member States, which the Commission required them to withdraw, and to recover the actual economic benefit conferred, was of the order of ECU 5 million in 1985, ECU 11 million in 1986 and ECU 747 million in 1987.'

See also *Seventeenth Report on Competition Policy*, point 173.

[260] *Renault*, OJ 1991 C11/3. The Commission required the immediate payment of FF 3.5 billion, and the treatment of the remaining FF 2.5 billion as long-term debt.

[261] *Rover*, OJ 1991 C21/2, on appeal: *British Aerospace and Rover Group Holdings v EC Commission* [1992] ECR I-493.

suitable means of recovering aid. In pursuing the recovery of illegal aid, the member state must take care that the recovery takes place in accordance with national law subject to the proviso that the provisions of national law are applied in such a way that 'the recovery required by Community law is not rendered practically impossible and the interests of the Community are taken fully into consideration.'[262] In this connection, a member state may not plead provisions, practices or circumstances existing in its internal legal system to justify a failure to comply with obligations resulting from Community law.[263] Thus, it is no defence to a Commission decision ordering repayment of aid that the member state no longer has the responsibility for ordering recovery as a result of a government reorganisation that shifted such responsibility to the regional level.[264]

It appears that the only defence that a member state may raise to explain its failure to comply with a Commission decision ordering recovery of illegal aid is absolute impossibility.[265] In such cases, the member state must submit proposals to the Commission for amendments to the Commission's decision that would enable the member state to overcome the obstacles to the implementation of that decision, and the member state must work with the Commission in an attempt to overcome such obstacles.[266] Thus, absolute impossibility will be a successful defence only in rare cases, such as where the recipient has been dissolved.[267]

---

[262] *EC Commission v Germany* [1989] ECR 175, at p. 192 (para. 12).

[263] *EC Commission v Belgium* [1990] ECR I-491 (summary report only), para. 8.

[264] Id. See also *EC Commission v Hellenic Republic*, Case C-183/91, judgment of 10 June 1993 (not yet reported), where the court rejected the argument that the recovery of aid granted in the form of a tax exemption would be impossible because it would require the retroactive imposition of a tax in violation of the national constitution. In the court's view, there existed a simple practical solution to this problem: require the aid recipients to pay an amount equal to the tax exemption to the member state without calling it a tax.

[265] *EC Commission v Belgium ('Boch')* [1986] ECR 89, at p. 104 (para. 14).

[266] Id., at p. 105 (para. 16). The court has explained as follows (id.):

'[T]he fact that the only defence which a Member State to which a decision has been addressed can raise in legal proceedings such as these is that implementation of the decision is absolutely impossible does not prevent that State – if, in giving effect to the decision, it encounters unforeseen or unforeseeable difficulties or perceives consequences overlooked by the Commission – from submitting those problems for consideration by the Commission, together with proposals for suitable amendments. In such a case the Commission and the Member State concerned must respect the principle underlying Article 5 of the Treaty, which imposes a duty of genuine cooperation on the Member States and Community institutions; accordingly, they must work together in good faith with a view to overcoming difficulties whilst fully observing the Treaty provisions, and in particular the provisions on aid.'

See also *EC Commission v Hellenic Republic*, Case C-183/91, judgment of 10 June 1993 (not yet reported); *EC Commission v Germany ('Alcan')* [1989] ECR 175.

[267] For example, in *Belgium v EC Commission ('Tubemeuse')* [1990] ECR I-959, the aid recipient was insolvent, and the court held that the member state had complied with its obligations with regard to the recovery of aid by seeking to have its debt registered as an unsecured debt of the insolvent company and by lodging an appeal against the judgment of the national court rejecting that application. In contrast, in *EC Commission v Belgium ('Boch')* [1986] ECR 89, the inability of the recipient to repay the aid out of its profits did not constitute proof of impossibility because the aid could be recovered by instituting proceedings for winding up the recipient.

¶1232

In several cases, the defence of legitimate expectations has been raised against the repayment of aid.[268] The court has ruled that this defence will only be allowed in exceptional circumstances,[269] and has held that the interests of the Community must be taken into account in considering this defence.[270] The court has made it clear that a recipient of aid may not claim to have a legitimate expectation that aid is lawful where the recipient never bothered to check whether the aid was notified to the Commission and cleared under art. 93.[271] Nowadays, the Commission makes it more difficult for recipients to raise the defence of legitimate expectations by publishing a summary of aid proceedings in the *Official Journal* which expressly puts all concerned on notice of the possibility of repayment.[272] The court has also held that a member state whose authorities granted aid contrary to the procedural rules laid down in art. 93 may not rely on legitimate expectations of recipients to justify a failure to comply with a Commission decision instructing it to recover the aid.[273]

---

[268] See *Germany v EC Commission* [1990] ECR I-3437; *EC Commission v Germany* ('*Alcan*') [1989] ECR 175; *RSV v EC Commission* [1987] ECR 4617; *Deufil v EC Commission* [1987] ECR 901; *Deutsche Milchkontor v Germany* [1983] ECR 2633.

[269] *EC Commission v Germany* [1990] ECR I-3437, at p. I-3457 (para. 16). For a rare case in which this defence was invoked successfully, see *RSV v EC Commission* [1987] ECR 4617 (Commission's 26-month delay in adopting a decision on the aid in question established a legitimate expectation on the part of the recipient that such aid was lawful). See also *IOR/Finalp*, OJ 1992 L183/30.

[270] *EC Commission v Germany* ('*Alcan*') [1989] ECR 175; *Deutsche Milchkontor v EC Commission* [1983] ECR 2633.

[271] *EC Commission v Germany* [1990] ECR I-3437. In that case, the court noted that 'a diligent businessman should normally be able to determine whether [the art. 93] procedure has been followed.' Id., at p. I-3457 (para. 14).

[272] For a typical example of such a notice, see *Merco*, OJ 1992 C291/7.

[273] Id. (para. 17).

PART V

EC COMPETITION LAW AND THE MEMBER STATES

13 EC Competition Law and the Member States

¶1301 Overview

This chapter examines the relationship between the EC competition rules and the laws and activities of the member states. First, the problem of concurrent jurisdiction between Community law and the national laws of the member states is examined (¶1302–¶1304). Secondly, the powers of the national authorities and courts to apply EC competition rules are discussed, and some problems that may arise in connection with the enforcement of the EC competition rules by national courts are highlighted (¶1305–¶1311). Thirdly, member-state legislation that is inconsistent with the competition rules such as legislation favouring anti-competitive agreements by undertakings is discussed (¶1312–¶1316). Finally, the application of the competition rules to the public sector through art. 90 is examined (¶1317–¶1322).

CO-EXISTENCE OF EC COMPETITION RULES WITH THE LAWS OF THE MEMBER STATES

¶1302 Introduction

In addition to the EC rules on competition that are directly applicable throughout the EC, most of the member states have competition laws of their own.[1] Even though the precedence of EC law over national law has been clearly established in cases of conflict, cases involving concurrent jurisdiction can give rise to difficulties.

---

[1] The relevant laws of the member states are: Belgium – *Law on the protection of Economic Competition* 1991; Denmark – the *Competition Act* 1989; France – the *Ordinance 1986-1243 on the freedom of prices and on competition*; Germany – the *Act against Restraints of Competition* 1957; Greece – *Antitrust law 703/1977*; Ireland – The *Competition Act* 1989; Italy – *Law 287/90 on the Protection of Competition and the Market*; The Netherlands – *Economic Competition Act* 1956; Spain – *Law 16/89 on the Defence of Competition*; UK – *Fair Trading Act* 1973, *Restrictive Trade Practices Act* 1976, the *Competition Act* 1980.

¶1303   Supremacy of Community law: basic principles

In the event of a conflict between Community law and the national law of a member state, Community law prevails. This principle was established by the Court in its 1964 *Costa/ENEL* judgment.[2]

Guidance on the application of this principle to the field of competition law was offered by the court a few years later in *Wilhelm v Bundeskartellamt*.[3] In this case, the court discussed the scope for parallel proceedings under both EC law and national law with respect to the same offence. The court came to the following conclusion:

> 'Consequently, and so long as a regulation adopted pursuant to Article 87(2)(e) of the Treaty has not provided otherwise, national authorities may take action against an agreement in accordance with their national law, even when an examination of the agreement from the point of view of its compatibility with Community law is pending before the Commission, subject however to the condition that the application of national law may not prejudice the full and uniform application of Community law or the effects of measures taken or to be taken to implement it.'[4]

¶1304   Application of the supremacy rule in practice

The principle of concurrent jurisdiction as explained by the Court in *Wilhelm* is fairly straightforward: parallel application of national and Community law is possible as long as the application of national law does not imperil 'the full and uniform application of Community law'.[5] In practice the following situations may arise.

---

[2] *Costa v ENEL* [1964] ECR 585.

[3] *Wilhelm v Bundeskartellamt* [1969] ECR 1. By art. 87(2)(e), the Council was empowered to determine the relationship between the EC rules on competition and national laws. The Council, however, has never adopted any such regulation of a general nature in this respect. See, however, Council Regulation 4064/89 on the control of concentrations between undertakings, OJ 1990 L257/13.

[4] *Wilhelm v Bundeskartellamt* [1969] ECR 1, at p. 15 (para. 9). See also *Procureur de la République v Giry and Guerlain ('Perfumes')* [1980] ECR 2327, at p. 2374 (para. 15), where the court, after citing the *Wilhelm v Bundeskartellamt* case stated:

> 'Community law and national law on competition consider restrictive practices from different points of view. Whereas Articles 85 and 86 regard them in the light of the obstacles which may result from trade between Member States, national law proceeds on the basis of the considerations peculiar to it and considers restrictive practices only in that context. It follows that national authorities may also take action in regard to situations which are capable of forming the subject-matter of a decision by the Commission.'

See also *Dirección General de la Competencia v Asociación Española de Banca Privada & Ors*, Case C-67/91, judgment of 16 July 1992, not yet reported, at para. 11 and 12.

[5] The specific problems of allocation of jurisdiction between the Commission and national authorities under Regulation 4064/89 on the control of concentrations between undertakings, OJ 1990 L257/13, are discussed in Chapter 6.

(1)   An agreement or practice is prohibited by art. 85 or 86

Due to the supremacy of Community law over national law, the Community prohibition applies irrespective of a national provision or authorisation to the contrary.[6] The Community prohibition does not prevent the concurrent application of a national prohibition, or even a sanction.[7]

(2)   An agreement or practice does not infringe art. 85 or 86

In such a situation there is no joint application and thus no conflict. Hence, national law may be applied in full.[8]

(3)   An agreement or practice violates art. 85(1) but enjoys the benefit of an exemption under art. 85(3)

This situation is more complicated and controversial. The Commission has interpreted the *Wilhelm* judgment to mean that national authorities may not prohibit an agreement which received an exemption under art. 85(3).[9] Others

---

[6] See e.g. *VBVB and VBBB v EC Commission* [1984] ECR 19, at p. 64 (para. 40), where the court rejected the argument that the Commission should have been guided in its competition policy by the fact that resale price maintenance for books is an acceptable practice in all the member states.

[7] *Wilhelm v Bundeskartellamt* [1969] ECR 1, at p. 15 (para. 11), where the court stated that:

'[t]he possibility of concurrent sanctions need not mean that the possibility of two parallel proceedings pursuing different ends is unacceptable ... If, however, the possibility of two procedures being conducted separately were to lead to the imposition of consecutive sanctions, a general requirement of natural justice, such as that expressed at the end of the second paragraph of Article 90 of the ECSC Treaty, demands that any previous punitive decision must be taken into account in determining any sanction which is to be imposed.'

[8] See e.g. the proposed *GKN/Sachs* merger, *Sixth Report on Competition Policy*, points 110–113. The Commission had authorised the merger under art. 66 of the ECSC Treaty, after having verified under art. 86 of the EEC Treaty whether the merger did not constitute an abuse of a dominant position on the market for clutches. The German Federal Cartel Office, however, enjoined the merger under s. 24 of the *Act against Restraints of Competition* because it found that the proposed merger would have strengthened the dominant position of Sachs on the German market for clutches. The Commission's comments, at point 113, were as follows:

'In its decision authorizing the merger under Article 66 of the ECSC Treaty, all the Commission considered was the potential restriction on competition in the steel market. The Federal Cartel Office, on the other hand, considered the situation as regards competition on markets not covered by the ECSC Treaty. This, therefore, gave it the power to prohibit the merger without infringing the rule that Community law prevails. The Commission did not act under the rules of competition in the EEC Treaty, which would have restricted the freedom of the national authority to apply its own law. Its decision to refrain from action under Article 86 of the EEC Treaty in no way restricts the application of national law.

Nor does the authorization given under Article 66 of the ECSC Treaty prevent the Federal Cartel Office from prohibiting the merger. Admittedly, the Commission's decision must be regarded as a positive, though indirect, measure to attain the general objectives of the Treaty, and thus prevails over conflicting measures taken by the national authorities. However, in this case the authorization was given after analysis of only a minor aspect of the merger, so that the Cartel Office's decision to prohibit the merger could not create a situation of conflict requiring application of the principle that Community law prevails.'

See also, *Procureur de la République v Giry and Guerlain ('Perfumes')* [1980] ECR 2327, at p. 2375 (para. 18), where the court ruled that a comfort letter issued by the Commission does not prevent the application of stricter national law.

[9] See *Fourth Report on Competition Policy*, point 45, where the Commission rejected the so-called 'double barrier' theory as follows:

'The primacy of the Community law is equally valid as a principle in relation to exemptions from the ban on restrictive practices granted pursuant to Article 85(3). In the judgment of 13 February 1969 [i.e. the judgment in

¶1304

have argued that a distinction should be drawn between an exemption granted as a measure of Community policy as opposed to an exemption whereby an agreement or practice is merely declared to be consistent with the common market.[10]

(4) An agreement or practice violates art. 85(1) but might ultimately qualify for an exemption under art. 85(3)

In its *Wilhelm* judgment the court stated that:

'[w]here, during national proceedings, it appears possible that the decision to be taken by the Commission at the culmination of a procedure still in progress concerning the same arrangement may conflict with the effects of the decision of the national authorities, it is for the latter to take the appropriate measures'.[11]

The Commission has suggested that the following two solutions are the most likely 'appropriate measures' to be taken:

- Suspension of national proceedings until the Commission has given its decision. This would enable the national authorities to wait until they have received the Commission's decision and then align the decision which they are to take under national law with the decision taken under Community law.

- Consultation with the Commission before adopting the national decision. This would establish obligations for the authorities of the member states similar to those incumbent upon the Commission under Article 10 of Regulation No. 17. An essential function of the consultation would be the

---

Wilhelm], the Court rejected the argument that exemption by the Commission withdraws only the Community barrier to a restrictive practice under Article 85(1), leaving unimpaired the national authority's power to prohibit such a practice under its own law (double barrier theory).

This in accordance with the principle that the provisions of Article 85 must be seen as a whole and therefore applied as uniformly as possible.'

[10] See e.g. Markert, 'Some Legal Administrative Problems of the Coexistence of Community and National Competition Law in the EEC', (1974) 11 CML Rev 92, at p. 97, where the author stated that:

'It is highly doubtful to interpret the Court's formula of "positive, albeit indirect, action in order to promote a harmonious development of economic activities throughout the Community in accordance with Article 2 of the Treaty" as meaning all exemptions granted under Article 85(3). Rather, this formula seems to allude to other measures under the Treaty such as directives under Article 102 to member states to harmonize national laws. One has to rely therefore on the other formula of the Court that the application of national competition law must not "jeopardize the uniform application throughout the Common Market of the Community cartel rules or the full effect of measures taken under such rules". As regards the uniform application of Article 85, no jeopardy by national measures against an exempted agreement would arise, since such measures would not affect the legal status of the agreement as being exempted under Community Law. Similarly, if the exemption was merely a declaration of consistency with the Common Market, its full effect in the case of national measures against the agreement would remain untouched. Only where the exemption was given as a measure of Community policy, it would be arguable that its full effect would be jeopardized if a Member State takes action under its national law to prevent the agreement from being carried out.'

[11] *Wilhelm v Bundeskartellamt* [1969] ECR 1, at pp. 14 and 15 (para 8)

¶1304

mutual provision of detailed information on content and scope of the decisions which are expected to be taken. The authorities of the member states would thus be in a position to take account of the Commission's views without having to wait until the Commission had actually adopted a decision.'[12]

EC COMPETITION LAW APPLIED BY NATIONAL AUTHORITIES AND NATIONAL COURTS

¶1305   Introduction

National authorities and courts possess concurrent powers with the Commission for the application of art. 85(1), 85(2) and 86 of the treaty.[13] The distribution of powers between Community and national authorities raises a number of issues. For instance, the parallel application of Community competition rules may result in a conflict between decisions of the Commission on the one hand, and of the national authority on the other. This section describes the power of the national authorities and courts to apply EC competition rules, and discusses practical aspects of the decentralisation of the enforcement of the EC competition rules.

¶1306   Decentralisation

In view of its limited resources and the increasing number of cases, the Commission has, for many years, pushed for the decentralisation of the enforcement of the EC competition rules by encouraging civil actions before national courts. Such increased private enforcement would enable the Commission to devote its resources to the really important cases that involve cross-border transactions.

This desire to decentralise enforcement can be traced back to the *Thirteenth Report on Competition Policy* (for 1983), where the Commission stated:

'Improved and more intense contact between national courts and the Commission would help tighten up enforcement... [a]nother step in the enforcement of Community competition law by national courts would be to develop the existing practice whereby the court asks the Commission to give

---

[12] *Fourth Report on Competition Policy*, point 46. These issues are discussed in more detail in the section on national courts, at ¶1305ff.

[13] Compare the merger regulation, where the Commission has the exclusive power to assess the compatibility with the common market of operations having a Community dimension.

an opinion on issues arising from cases before it, since such clarifications can only be conducive to a good administration of justice.'[14]

Two court judgments – *Delimitis*[15] and *Automec*[16] – provide support to the Commission's campaign for greater private enforcement at the national level. In *Delimitis*, the Court of Justice discussed the basic principles governing the relationship between national courts and the Commission in applying competition law. The court noted that only the Commission could take exemption decisions under art. 85(3), but that both the Commission and national courts could apply art. 85(1) and art. 86 as those provisions have direct effect. The court then elaborated on the practical application of these principles and made some suggestions concerning co-operation between national courts and the Commission.

In *Automec*, the Court of First Instance upheld the Commission's rejection of a complaint because of a lack of sufficient Community interest and advised the complainant to seek relief before a national court. From a practical standpoint, this case is significant because it established that the Commission is not required to investigate every complaint it receives. Rather, it is only obliged to take a decision on matters that fall within its exclusive competence, such as the withdrawal of an exemption granted under art. 85(3).[17] Consequently, the Commission may give priority to those cases which represent a particular political, economic or legal interest to the Community.[18]

Finally, decentralisation of the enforcement of the competition rules is a logical consequence of the growing importance of the concept of subsidiarity. In the context of EC competition law, subsidiarity means that cases where the Community has an important economic, political or legal interest at stake should be handled by the Commission, and national authorities should deal with agreements or practices that only affect national markets.

It is in this context that the Commission's notice on co-operation between national courts and the Commission was issued.[19] The purpose of the notice is to facilitate the application of EC competition rules by national courts. In the notice, the Commission sets out the principles of how it intends to assist the national courts by closer co-operation in the application of art. 85 and 86 in individual cases.[20]

---

[14] *Thirteenth Report on Competition Policy*, points 217 and 218. See also *Fifteenth Report on Competition Policy*, points 38 and 39; *Sixteenth Report on Competition Policy*, point 41; *Seventeenth Report on Competition Policy*, point 55; and *XXIst Report on Competition Policy for 1991*, point 69.

[15] *Delimitis v Henninger Bräu AG* [1991] ECR I-935.

[16] *Automec v EC Commission*, Case T-24/90, judgment of 18 September 1992, not yet reported.

[17] *Automec v EC Commission*, Case T-24/90, judgment of 18 September 1992, not yet reported, at para. 74 and 75.

[18] *Automec v EC Commission*, Case T-24/90, judgment of 18 September 1992, not yet reported, at para. 85.

[19] Notice on co-operation between national courts and the Commission in applying art. 85 and 86 of the EEC Treaty, OJ 1993 C39/6 [hereinafter referred to as the 'notice'].

[20] Notice, para. 3. See also *XXIInd Report on Competition Policy for 1992*, point 299.

¶1306

¶1307 Advantages and disadvantages of procedure before national courts

For private parties, the application of the competition rules by national courts has some advantages compared to the procedure before the Commission. In its notice, the Commission mentions, for example, that only national courts can award damages for losses suffered as a result of an infringement of the EC competition rules; that a national court can grant interim measures more quickly than the Commission; that it is possible to combine a claim under EC law with a claim under national law; and that in some member states legal costs can be reimbursed, which is never possible before the Commission.[21]

It should be noted, however, that there may be certain disadvantages in seeking relief before a national court rather than the Commission which the Commission fails to mention in its notice. A disadvantage frequently cited is that the procedure before the Commission is free of charge whereas a plaintiff in a national court proceeding is likely to incur substantial legal fees. However, it should be mentioned that this assumption is not necessarily true. The expense of a complaint before the Commission in a complex case can be high, especially if the Commission opens a proceeding and is prepared to allow the complainant to play an ongoing role in the case. Furthermore, as more and more member states establish competition authorities, procedures before national authorities may also be conducted free of charge.

A second disadvantage in filing a complaint with a national court is that the Commission may depart from its previous decisions if it no longer considers them appropriate, thus enabling competition policy to evolve over time. In contrast, national courts may feel constrained by existing case law developed by the Commission and the Community courts in addressing an issue of EC competition law. Thirdly, the Commission is normally in a better position to make complex economic assessments, which a national judge not specialised in competition law might find difficult to make. Fourthly, given its substantial powers, the Commission can carry out Community-wide investigations whereas it can be difficult for a plaintiff under national procedural rules to provide evidence, particularly where the plaintiff has to obtain evidence outside the territory of the national court. Fifthly, the identity of the complainant may remain confidential in Commission proceedings, at least at the initial stages. This may make a small company more willing to file an art. 86 complaint against a dominant undertaking on which it depends. Finally, it is only the Commission that may grant an exemption under art. 85(3). While national courts may apply the block exemption regulations, they do not have the power to issue individual exemptions.

---

[21] Notice, para. 16.

It should be noted that the inability of the national courts to grant an exemption under art. 85(3) may be a factor relevant to the decision of a potential litigant whether to seek relief before a national court or the Commission. This limitation of the power of the national court may, in some circumstances, work to the advantage of the plaintiff. For instance, if the plaintiff files a complaint against an agreement between two of its competitors before a national court, it is obviously an advantage for the complainant that the national court cannot grant an exemption under art. 85(3).

¶1308   The powers of the national authorities

National authorities entitled to apply EC competition law are divided into two categories: 'national authorities' that apply art. 85 and 86 by virtue of art. 88,[22] and 'national courts' that apply art. 85 and 86 by virtue of their direct effect.[23]

National authorities

National authorities include both administrative authorities in charge of applying domestic competition law and, in certain member states, national courts especially entrusted with the task of applying domestic competition legislation and of ensuring the legality of that application by the administrative authorities.[24] These national authorities apply art. 85(1) and 86 on a direct basis, i.e. they take action against undertakings in order to establish whether an infringement has occurred. However, national authorities have to renounce their power when the Commission initiates a procedure of its own.[25] In this context, the initiation of a procedure must be an authoritative act on the part of the Commission which states its intention to take a decision under art. 2, 3 and 6 of Regulation 17/62.[26] It should be noted that a proceeding is not initiated when the Commission issues an acknowledgement of receipt of a request for a negative clearance or of a notification to obtain an exemption under art. 85(3).[27]

---

[22] Article 88 provides as follows:

'Until the entry into force of the provisions adopted in pursuance of Article 87, the authorities in member states shall rule on the admissibility of agreements, decisions and concerted practices and on abuse of a dominant position in the common market in accordance with the law of their country and with the provisions of Article 85, in particular paragraph 3, and of Article 86.'

In addition, art. 9(3) of Regulation 17/62 provides that:

'As long as the Commission has not initiated any procedure under Articles 2, 3 or 6, the authorities of the member states shall remain competent to apply Article 85(1) and Article 86 in accordance with Article 88 of the Treaty; they shall remain competent in this respect notwithstanding that the time limits specified in Article 5(1) and in Article 7(2) relating to notification have not expired'.

[23] *BRT v SABAM ('BRT I')* [1974] ECR 51, at p. 62 (para. 15). On the problem of defining the term 'national authorities', see *Bilger v Jehle* [1970] ECR 127, at p. 136 (para. 9).

[24] *BRT v SABAM ('BRT I')* [1974] ECR 51, at p. 63 (para. 19). See also *Ministère Public v Asjes & Ors* [1986] ECR 1425, at p. 1468 (para. 55).

[25] Regulation 17/62, art. 9(3).

[26] *Brasserie de Haecht v Wilkin-Janssen* [1973] ECR 77, at p. 88 (para. 16).

[27] Id.

In its notice, the Commission is only concerned with co-operation with the national courts rather than with the national authorities even though the national authorities have substantial experience in applying competition law at the national level and, arguably, offer plaintiffs certain advantages in competition cases such as low costs and wide investigative powers. Presumably, the Commission feels a need to focus on improving co-operation with national courts because it already has significant contacts with national authorities, particularly within the framework of the Advisory Committee.

National courts
Unlike the national authorities, national courts are not responsible for matters relating to policy orientation and enforcement of art. 85 and 86. Rather, national courts are responsible for applying these provisions in the context of civil litigation between private parties. National courts have the power to deal with these cases by virtue of the doctrine of direct effect according to which art. 85(1) and 86 may be invoked by private individuals and firms in national courts without further action on the part of public authorities or the enactment of implementing legislation.[28] Unlike the national authorities, national courts do not lose jurisdiction when the Commission initiates a proceeding of its own concerning the same matter because, otherwise, individuals might be deprived of the rights which they hold under the treaty.[29]

National courts are typically called upon to apply art. 85 and 86 in two types of situations: (1) actions relating to contracts, where the defendant argues that the contract is null and void by virtue of art. 85(2); and (2) actions for damages where the prohibitions contained in art. 85 and 86 are generally relevant in determining whether the conduct which has given rise to the alleged injury is illegal. As a general rule, the remedies available to private parties are a matter of national law, but they must not be less favourable than those granted for claims under national – as opposed to EC – law.[30] They usually consist of declarations of nullity or illegality of prohibited agreements, injunctions to prohibit restrictive behaviour, restitution of moneys paid, or damages for harm caused by the violation of the competition rules.

National courts have the power to decide whether an agreement or practice infringes art. 85(1) making it void under art. 85(2), or to decide whether a company is abusing its dominant position on a given market under art. 86. However, the national courts do not have the power to decide that the agreement or practice is eligible for an exemption under art. 85(3) because only

---

[28] *BRT v SABAM ('BRT I')* [1974] ECR 51, at p. 62 (para. 16). See also *Delimitis v Henninger Bräu AG* [1991] ECR I-935, at p. 992 (para. 45); *Marty v Estée Lauder* [1980] ECR 2481, at p. 2500 (para. 13).
[29] *BRT v SABAM ('BRT I')* [1974] ECR 51, at p. 63 (para. 17).
[30] *Rewe-Handelsgellschaft Nord mbH & Anor v Hauptzollamt Kiel* [1981] ECR 1805, at p. 1838 (para. 44). See also *Amministrazione delle Finanze dello Stato v San Giorgio* [1983] ECR 3595, at pp. 3613 and 3614 (para. 16).

the Commission has the power to grant exemptions under art. 85(3).[31] Likewise, national courts do not have the power to rule on the validity of so-called 'old agreements', i.e. agreements concluded before the entry into force of Regulation 17/62 in the original six member states, and which were notified within the time limits of Regulation 17/62 or dispensed from notification. Such agreements are considered to be provisionally valid and national courts may not rule on their validity until the Commission has dealt with the matter by issuing a decision refusing exemption or issuing a comfort letter closing the file.[32]

¶1309 Application of art. 85 and 86 by national courts

In applying art. 85 and 86, national courts risk issuing decisions that conflict with those of the Commission unless they take into account the Commission's powers in applying these same provisions. In its *Delimitis* judgment, the court offered some guidelines as to how national courts could avoid such conflicts which were elaborated upon in the notice. This section focuses on the application of art. 85 and 86 by the national courts in practice.

Application of art. 85(1) and (2) and art. 86

The first question faced by national courts is whether the agreement or practice at issue infringes art. 85(1) or art. 86. In addressing this issue, the national courts may examine whether the agreement or practice has been dealt with by the Commission. While decisions, comfort letters or other statements of the Commission concerning the applicability of art. 85(1) and art. 86 are not binding on national courts, they may provide a useful source of information.[33] If the Commission has not dealt with the particular agreement or practice at issue, the national courts may look to the case law of the Community courts as well as previous decisions of the Commission. Also, the Commission has specified in a

---

[31] Regulation 17/62, art. 9(1), provides that:

'Subject to review of its decision by the Court of Justice, the Commission shall have sole power to declare Article 85 (1) inapplicable pursuant to Article 85 (3) of the Treaty.'

See also *Delimitis v Henninger Bräu AG* [1991] ECR I-935, at p. I-991 (para. 44). In the past, the Commission has suggested that national courts may apply art. 85 (3) in cases in which Community practice and case law leave no reasonable doubt that a particular agreement is entitled to benefit from such an exemption. See *De Norre v NV Brouwerij Concordia* [1977] ECR 65, at pp. 82, 83 and 89; *Procureur de la République & Ors v Giry and Guerlain SA & Ors* [1980] ECR 2327, at p. 2369. However, the Commission has not yet indicated that it is willing to give up its monopoly in applying art. 85(3) in favour of national courts.

[32] See *Delimitis v Henninger Bräu AG* [1991] ECR I-936, at p. I-992 (para. 48); *Lancôme v Etos* [1980] ECR 2511, at p. 2534 (para. 16); *De Bloos v Bouyer* [1977] ECR 2359, at pp. 2369 and 2370; and *Brasserie de Haecht v Wilkin-Jansen* [1973] ECR 77, at pp. 86 and 87. If the Commission has taken a prohibition decision or issued a comfort letter closing the file, the national courts may then invalidate an agreement. See *Lancôme v Etos* [1980] ECR 2511, at p. 2535 (para. 17); notice, para. 31.

The provisional validity doctrine can also be applied by analogy to agreements which become subject to art. 85 following the accession of new member states. For further discussion of this issue, see Chapter 11.

[33] *Procureur de la République v Giry and Guerlain* ('*Perfumes*') [1980] ECR 2327, at p. 2375 (para. 18)

number of notices the categories of agreements that are not caught by the prohibition of art. 85(1) that may be used for guidance by national courts.[34]

If the Commission has initiated a case concerning the agreement or practice in question, the national court may, but need not, stay its proceedings to await the outcome of the Commission's action or to seek the Commission's views in accordance with the co-operation procedure discussed below. Otherwise, there would seem to be a risk of conflicting decisions; for example, it is conceivable that the Commission could rule that an agreement is caught by art. 85(1) even though a national court had previously ruled to the contrary.

Application of art. 85(3) by national courts

If a national court determines that an agreement or practice is caught by art. 85(1), it must examine whether it has been granted an exemption under art. 85(3) by the Commission. If the Commission has issued a decision granting an exemption, the national court is bound by this decision and must regard the agreement as enforceable.[35] It should be noted, however, that an exemption decision under art. 85(3) does not prevent the national court from applying art. 86 to the agreement by virtue of the Court of First Instance's ruling in *Tetra Pak*.[36]

If the Commission issues a comfort letter instead of a formal exemption decision stating that it does not intend to take any action against the agreement or conduct in question, a national court is not prevented from applying art. 85 and 86 to the agreements in question.[37] In other words, a national court may, but need not, take into account the comfort letter in its evaluation of the

---

[34] See the notices on: exclusive dealing contracts with commercial agents (JO 1962, p. 2921/62); agreements decisions and concerted practices in the field of co-operation between enterprises (JO 1968 C77/3, as corrected in OJ 1968 C84/14); assessment of certain subcontracting agreements (OJ 1979 C1/2); and agreements of minor importance (OJ 1986 C231/2).

[35] In *NV L'Oréal & Anor v PVBA De Nieuwe AMCK* [1980] ECR 3775, at pp. 3792 and 3793 (para. 22 and 23), where the court held that decisions to grant an exemption under art. 85(3) confer rights on the parties to an agreement subject to such a decision. These parties may rely on the decision against third parties who claim that the agreement is void under art. 85(2). See also notice, para. 25(a).

It should be noted that mere notification of an agreement to obtain an exemption does not oust the jurisdiction of the national courts. See *Brasserie de Haecht v Wilkin-Janssen* [1973] ECR 77, at p. 87 (para. 10).

[36] *Tetra Pak Rausing SA v EC Commission* [1990] ECR II-309. At para. 42 of that case, the Court of First Instance held that:

'there is nothing to justify limiting the power of national courts to apply Article 86 on the ground that the practice in question has been granted exemption under Article 85(3). [. . .] On the contrary, when applying Article 86, in particular to conduct which is exempted under Article 85(3), the national courts are acting as Community courts of general jurisdiction. They will merely be applying – as they are bound to do by virtue of the primacy and direct effect of the Community rules on competition – the principles of Community law governing the relationship between Article 85(3) and Article 86.'

[37] See *L'Oréal v De Nieuwe AMCK* [1980] ECR 3775; *Lancôme v Etos* [1980] ECR 2551; *Marty v Estée Lauder* [1980] ECR 2481; *Procureur de la Républic v Giry and Guerlain ('Perfumes')* [1980] ECR 2327. For a discussion of comfort letters, see ¶1126.

agreement under art. 85(3).[38] National courts may be reluctant to give too much weight to a non-binding comfort letter, particularly as this could be deemed inconsistent with the basic rights of the parties in the national proceedings. Also, to the extent that a comfort letter states that the agreement in question infringes art. 85(1), but would appear to qualify for an exemption under art. 85(3), this would be of little help to the national court because, technically speaking, the Commission has not issued an exemption under art. 85(3) and the national court has no power to do so.

If a block exemption has been issued for the type of agreement in dispute, the national court must determine whether the agreement is covered by the block exemption, and, if so, declare the agreement valid under EC competition law.[39] However, the national court may not modify the scope of the block exemption.[40] If it is unclear whether a specific agreement is covered by a block exemption, the national court may make a reference to the Court of Justice by virtue of art. 177. Even if an agreement is covered by a block exemption, this would not seem to prevent a national court from applying art. 86 to the agreement in light of the *Tetra Pak* judgment.

If an agreement has not been the object of a decision by the Commission granting an exemption or is not covered by a block exemption, the national court may be placed in a difficult position. Strictly speaking, until an exemption under art. 85(3) is granted, a national court must view an agreement as void under art. 85(2). However, there is a danger that the Commission might later issue a decision reaching a different result, particularly in cases where the agreement has been notified to the Commission and would appear to satisfy the conditions for exemption.

In *Delimitis*,[41] the court offered some suggestions as to how a national court might avoid such conflict in cases where an agreement has been duly notified to the Commission; these suggestions were elaborated upon by the Commission in the notice.[42] Where the agreement falls within art. 85(1) and, in light of prior case law and the block exemption regulations, clearly does not qualify for exemption under art. 85(3), the national court should proceed to deliver its judgment. Where the national court considers that the agreement may be

---

[38] In its notice, para. 25(a), the Commission notes that national courts may take account of comfort letters as factual elements.

[39] Notice, para. 26(b).

[40] See *Delimitis v Henninger Bräu AG* [1991] ECR I-935, at p. I-992 (para. 46).

Some of the block exemptions provide for a so-called 'opposition procedure' pursuant to which it is possible to notify to the Commission agreements that contain restrictions that are neither expressly exempted or prohibited by the block exemption in question. Such restrictions will be deemed to be covered by the block exemption if the Commission does not oppose exemption within six months. The effect of the non-opposition by the Commission is uncertain because non-opposition is not a formal exemption decision. Therefore, it could be argued that, upon expiry of the six-month period, national courts retain the power to deal with clauses not expressly exempted.

[41] *Delimitis v Henninger Bräu AG* [1991] ECR I-935, at pp. I-993 and I-994 (para. 50–54).

[42] Notice, para. 28–32.

eligible for exemption, it should suspend the proceedings pending a decision on the case by the Commission. At the same time, the national court may adopt appropriate interim measures. The national courts may also seek assistance from the Commission in the manner described below.

¶1310 Co-operation between national courts and the Commission

In the notice, the Commission stresses that it intends to work towards closer co-operation with national courts and offers to provide information to national courts on various aspects of competition law.[43] First, a national court may ask the Commission for information of a procedural nature, such as whether a case is pending before the Commission, whether a certain agreement has been notified and, if so, whether the Commission has formally opened proceedings or taken a position by means of a decision or comfort letter. If necessary, national courts may also ask the Commission to give an opinion as to how much time is likely to be required before it decides whether to grant an exemption. Secondly, the Commission has offered to assist the national courts on points of law.[44] Finally, national courts may obtain factual information from the Commission, such as statistics, market studies and economic analyses as long as such information is not confidential.[45]

If a national court refers a case to the Commission on points of law, the Commission may grant an interim opinion. Although such an interim opinion is not binding on the court requesting it and is given only to provide guidance for resolving the dispute,[46] this referral procedure may give rise to problems. First, the Commission's interim opinion will probably be based on facts submitted to it by the national court. It does not appear that the parties will have the opportunity to express their views to the Commission.[47] The lack of any procedure to allow input from the parties raises the issue of whether the rights of the defendant would be unduly restricted. Secondly, it is likely that the interim opinion will affect the position of the parties in the national

---

[43] Notice, para. 33–44.

[44] The Commission suggests that the national courts consult the Commission when the application of art. 85(1) or 86 is particularly difficult or where it is doubtful whether an agreement is eligible for an exemption under art. 85(3). The national courts may also consult the Commission on its customary practice in relation to the Community law at issue without considering the merits of the case, para. 38 of the notice.

[45] Notice, para. 40. The legal and factual information may be provided only under certain conditions: the requested data must be at the Commission's disposal and they may be communicated only in so far as permitted by the principle of sound administration, para. 41.

[46] Notice, para. 39.

[47] At para. 42 of the notice, the Commission notes:

'As *amicus curiae*, the Commission is obliged to respect legal neutrality and objectivity. Consequently, it will not accede to requests for information unless they come from a national court, either directly or indirectly through parties which have been ordered by the court concerned to provide certain information. In the latter case, the Commission will ensure that its answer reaches all the parties to the proceedings.'

proceedings, thus becoming a sort of informal judgment outside the scope of the normal procedural safeguards. Since the interim opinion in most cases will presumably be supplied by an official of DG IV of the Commission, there might also be a question as to the legal validity of such an interim opinion. Furthermore, if the Commission gives opinions on the interpretation of Community law, there may also be some question of whether the Commission is not in fact usurping the court's power under art. 177.

Thirdly, if the national court seeks an interim opinion from the Commission concerning the eligibility of an agreement for exemption, it would seem that this opinion would only be useful to the national court if it is negative, as the national court could proceed to rule that the agreement is ineligible for exemption. If the Commission issued a positive opinion on this matter, this opinion would seem to be of limited use to the national court because it would not seem to constitute a formal exemption decision on the basis of which the national court could act, but rather an informal opinion similar to a comfort letter. In fact, unless the Commission gives the national court reason to believe that a formal decision will be forthcoming, the national court might feel compelled to invalidate the agreement under art. 85(2) on the grounds that it has not been exempted under art. 85(3).

A final issue that arises is whether a national court is allowed under national procedural rules to refer a legal question to the Commission. In some member states, it is not clear that the national court would even be permitted to seek the advice of an authority such as the Commission. Moreover, it may be questionable whether reports of the Commission could be entered into evidence before the national court as in some jurisdictions they might constitute hearsay that could not be checked through cross-examination.

¶1311   Conclusion

The Commission Directorate General for Competition has rather limited human resources compared to other jurisdictions such as the US or Germany. The problems resulting from this shortage of staff have been exacerbated by the increase in the workload arising from the introduction of merger control, the application of the competition rules to new sectors of the economy such as telecommunications, air and sea transport etc., and the enforcement of EC competition law in the EEA.

It remains to be seen, however, whether the promotion of decentralised enforcement will actually ease the burden on the Commission's staff. The vagaries inherent in the co-operation procedure provided for in the notice may indeed create more legal problems than the notice purports to solve. Differing interpretations of Community law by national judges will surely take years to correct via the Community's judicial order. Hence the Commission might be tempted to remedy the emerging distortions by enacting more detailed legislation, thereby burdening its human resources even further.

Perhaps a more effective way for the Commission to reduce its workload would be to adopt a 'rule of reason' approach under art. 85(1), as is the case in the US, instead of conducting this balancing exercise only under art. 85(3) upon the filing of a notification.

Similarly, a significant reduction of the Commission's case load could be achieved by a less liberal interpretation of the required effect on trade between member states. Clearly, if the subsidiarity concept is to have any real meaning it is essential for the Commission to change its practice of finding the necessary effect on inter-state commerce all too easily.

NATIONAL LEGISLATION INCONSISTENT WITH EC COMPETITION RULES

¶1312   Introduction

Apart from the issue of co-existence of EC competition rules with competition laws of the member states and the enforcement of the competition law to the national level, other facets of the relationship between EC competition law and the conduct of member states exist which require further analysis. In particular, case law of the court points out that member states that support anti-competitive agreements in their legislation may infringe art. 3(g), 5, 85 and 86 of the EC Treaty.

¶1313   National legislation and art. 3(g), 5, 85 and 86 of the EC Treaty

The court scrutinised in *NV GB-Inno-BM v ATAB*,[48] for the first time, national legislation on the basis of (what is now) art. 3(f), 5, 85 and 86 of the treaty. The court, in summarising its approach, stated:

'First, the single market system which the Treaty seeks to create excludes any national system of regulation hindering directly or indirectly, actually or potentially, trade within the Community. Secondly, the general objective set out in Article 3[g] is made specific in several Treaty provisions concerning the rules on competition, including Article 86, which states that any abuse by one or more undertakings of a dominant position shall be prohibited as incompatible with the Common Market in so far as it may affect trade between the Member States. Accordingly, while it is true that Article 86 is

---

[48] *NV GB-Inno-BM v ATAB* [1977] ECR 2115.

directed at undertakings, nonetheless it is also true that the Treaty imposes a duty on member states not to adopt or maintain in force any measure which could deprive that provision of its effectiveness. [...] Likewise, member states may not enact measures enabling private undertakings to escape from the constraints imposed by Articles 85 to 94 of the Treaty.'[49]

Although the court formulated the principle that national legislation can infringe (what is now) art. 3(g), 5, 85 and 86 of the treaty, it failed to provide much guidance as to the precise circumstances under which such a violation would be found. The subsequent case law of the court discusses three possible ways in which conduct of the member states may be incompatible with the treaty:

(1) member states impose or favour the adoption of anti-competitive agreements, decisions or concerted practices;

(2) member states reinforce the effects of existing anti-competitive agreements, decisions or concerted practices;

(3) member states entrust undertakings with the power of a public authority thereby depriving legislation of its state character.

¶1314 Legislation imposing or favouring the adoption of anti-competitive conduct

The court has repeatedly stated that national legislation which requires the adoption of anti-competitive agreements, or which favours the adoption of such agreements, runs counter to (what is now) art. 3(g), 5 and 85 of the treaty.[50] The court, however, has thus far never applied this principle against a member state in an actual case.

¶1315 Legislation reinforcing the effects of anti-competitive conduct

In several cases the court has held that national legislation which reinforces the effects of existing anti-competitive agreements violates (what is now) art. 3(g), 5 and 85 of the treaty. *Bureau national interprofessionnel du cognac v Aubert*[51]

---

[49] Id., at pp. 2144 and 2145 (para. 28–31, 33). See also *Elliniki Radiophonia Tiléorassi AE v Dimotiki Etaireia Pliroforissis & Ors* [1991] ECR I-2925, at p. I-2962 (para. 35).

[50] *Association des Centres Distributeurs Edouard Leclerc v Sarl 'Au Blé Vert'* [1985] ECR 1, at p. 32 (para. 15); *Cullet and Chambre syndicale des réparateurs automobiles et détaillants de produits pétroliers v Centre Leclerc Toulouse and Centre Leclerc Saint-Orens-de-Gameville* [1985] ECR 305, at p. 320 (para. 17); *Ministère Public v Asjes & Ors* [1986] ECR 1425, at p. 1471 (para. 72); *Vereniging van Vlaamse Reisbureaus v Sociale Dienst van de Plaatselijke Gewestelijke Overheidsdiensten* [1987] ECR 3801, at p. 3826 (para. 10); *Syndicat des libraires de Normandie v L'Aigle distribution SA* [1988] ECR 4457; *Van Eycke v SA ASPA* [1988] ECR 4769, at p. 4791 (para. 17).

[51] *Bureau national interprofessionnel du cognac v Aubert* [1987] ECR 4789

concerned an inter-trade agreement on maximum production quotas which was made binding on all the members of the profession by a ministerial order. The court referred to *Inno v ATAB*,[52] and stated that a member state which extends an inter-trade agreement, such as the one concerned, by ministerial order infringes (what is now) art. 3(g), 5 and 85 of the treaty.[53]

Both in *Asjes* and in *Ahmed Saeed*[54] the court considered whether homologation of aviation tariff-agreements by member states violated the treaty. The court reiterated the principle that member states, by approving agreements which infringe art. 85 and thereby reinforcing their effects, violate their treaty obligations. When *Asjes* was decided, implementing measures as prescribed by art. 87 of the treaty had yet to be taken. Therefore, a violation of the treaty could only exist, the court decided, if national authorities had taken a measure under art. 88 or if the Commission had issued a decision under art. 89, para. 2. In *Ahmed Saeed*,[55] the implementing measures of art. 87 had been taken[56] and the court decided, without further qualification, that the homologation was contrary to the treaty.

In *Vereniging van Vlaamse Reisbureaus v Sociale Dienst van de Plaatselijke en Gewestelijke Overheidsdiensten*,[57] the same issue was addressed. The social services provided public service employees with a reduction on the tariffs of tours as fixed by the tour operators thereby passing on the commission normally paid to the travel agents. This policy was considered contrary to a Belgian Royal decree which bound travel agents to the agreed or legally imposed tariffs and prohibited them from sharing commissions with clients.[58] The court first considered whether an anti-competitive agreement existed. After reviewing the rules drafted by the Belgian Association of Travel Agencies, the standard agreements governing contractual relations between tour operators and travel agents, and the Royal decree, the court decided that this was the case. The court concluded that these agreements aimed to prevent travel agents from engaging in price competition by passing on part of their commission to their clients.[59] The court then analysed if the Belgian Royal decree reinforced the effects of these anti-competitive agreements. The affirmative conclusion of the court was based on three reasons:

---

[52] *NV GB-Inno-BM v ATAB* [1977] ECR 2115.
[53] *Bureau national interprofessionnel du cognac v Aubert* [1987] ECR 4789, at p. 4815 (para. 23 and 24). See also *Nederlandse Associatie van de Farmaceutische Industrie 'Nefarma' and Bond van Groothandelaren in het Farmaceutische Bedrijf v EC Commission* [1990] ECR II-797.
[54] *Ministère Public v Asjes & Ors* [1986] ECR 1425, at p. 1471 (para. 72); *Ahmed Saeed Flugreisen & Anor v Zentrale zur Bekämpfung unlauteren Wettbewerbs eV* [1989] ECR 803.
[55] *Ahmed Saeed Flugreisen & Anor v Zentrale zur Bekämpfung unlauteren Wettbewerbs eV* [1989] ECR 803.
[56] Regulation 3975/87.
[57] *Vereniging van Vlaamse Reisbureaus v Sociale Dienst van de Plaatselijke en Gewestelijke Overheidsdiensten* [1987] ECR 3801.
[58] Belgian Royal decree of 30 June 1966, art. 22.
[59] *Vereniging van Vlaamse Reisbureaus v Sociale Dienst van de Plaatselijke en Gewestelijke Overheidsdiensten* [1987] ECR 3801, at p. 3826 (para. 13–17).

¶1315

(1) When a contractual prohibition was transformed into a legislative provision, the prohibition acquired a permanent character and could no longer be rescinded by the parties.

(2) The Royal decree allowed a travel agent who complied with the rules to bring proceedings for a restraining order against travel agents who, not being a party to the agreement, did not comply with these rules.

(3) The possible revocation of an operating licence for failure to observe the rules constituted a highly effective sanction, with regard both to the parties to the agreements and to third parties.[60]

Finally, the Court in *Van Eycke v SA ASPA*[61] addressed the question whether a Belgian Royal decree, under which holders of savings deposits were entitled to tax advantages if the interest they received did not exceed a maximum amount,[62] infringed (what is now) art. 3(g), 5 and 85 of the treaty. The alleged anti-competitive agreement preceding the Royal decree was a self-disciplinary agreement between banks and financial institutions. In line with its previous case law, the court examined whether this Royal decree was intended to reinforce the effects of a pre-existing restrictive practice. The court considered this to be the case where state legislation merely incorporates wholly or in part the terms of an agreement concluded between firms and makes compliance with those terms compulsory or encourages such compliance by means of incentives. The court found no evidence in the case at hand that the Royal decree concerned constituted a mere confirmation of the pre-existing agreements. However, the court left a final decision in this matter to the national judge.[63]

The case law discussed above indicates that, in assessing whether particular legislation violates the treaty, the court typically considers whether an anti-competitive agreement existing prior to the enactment of the legislation is reinforced as a result of such legislation. This does not mean, however, that legislation enacted under pressure by interested parties necessarily runs counter to art. 3(g), 5 and 85 of the treaty.[64]

---

[60] Id., at p. 3829 (para. 23).

[61] *Van Eycke v SA ASPA* [1988] ECR 4769.

[62] Belgian Royal decree of 13 March 1986.

[63] *Van Eycke v SA ASPA* [1988] ECR 4769, at p. 4792 (para. 18). See also *Re Marchandise & Ors* [1991] ECR I-1027, at p. I-1043 (para. 23), where national legislation prohibiting the employment of workers in retail shops on Sundays was held not to infringe (what is now) art. 3(g), 5 and 85 of the treaty since it did not reinforce the effects of pre-existing agreements, decisions or concerted practices.

[64] See Joliet, 'National Anti-Competitive Legislation and Community Law', *Fordham International Law Journal*, 1989, Vol. 12, 163 at p. 188.

¶1316   Legislation deprived of its state character

Member states that deprive their legislation of its state character by entrusting to undertakings the powers to make decisions and to assume, in other words, the powers of a public authority, can thereby violate the treaty.[65]

In *Leclerc v Sarl 'Au Blé Vert'*,[66] the court considered a French law requiring editors and importers of books to fix retail prices for the books which they handled. Under the law, a retail trader who sold books at a price lower than 95 per cent of the fixed retail price would be subject to sanctions. The issue, according to the court, was whether a national law transferring the responsibility for fixing binding retail prices to private enterprises violates (what is now) art. 3(g), 5 and 85 of the treaty. At the time of the judgment, the Commission had yet to devise specific measures relating to this subject. Consequently, the court refused to find a violation because the obligations imposed on the member states under art. 3(f) (now art. 3(g)), 5 and 85 of the treaty had yet to be determined with sufficient specificity. This refusal was based on the court's desire to promote legal certainty and should not be understood as a fundamental interpretation of the obligations of member states under the treaty.[67]

In *Cullet v Leclerc*, the court held that a French law that imposed a minimum retail price for fuel did not violate art. 3(f) (now art. 3(g)), 5 and 85 of the treaty. The court reasoned that:

> '[...], rules such as those concerned in this case are not intended to compel suppliers and retailers to conclude agreements or to take any other action of the kind referred to in Article 85(1) of the Treaty. On the contrary, they entrust responsibility for fixing prices to the public authorities, which for that purpose consider various factors of a different kind. The mere fact that the ex-refinery price fixed by the supplier – which, moreover, may not exceed the ceiling price fixed by the competent authorities – is one of the factors taken into account in fixing the retail selling price does not prevent rules such as those concerned here from being State rules and is not capable of depriving the rules on competition applicable to undertakings of their effectiveness.'[68]

In *Van Eycke v SA ASPA*,[69] the court likewise emphasised that the authorities had not delegated to the undertakings the power to determine the

---

[65] *Van Eycke v SA ASPA* [1988] ECR 4769.

[66] *Association des Centres Distributeurs Edouard Leclerc v Sarl 'Au Blé Vert'* [1985] ECR 1.

[67] See Joliet, 'National Anti-Competitive Legislation and Community Law', *Fordham International Law Journal*, 1989, Vol. 12, 163, at p. 173.

[68] *Cullet and Chambre syndicale des réparateurs automobiles et détaillants de produits pétroliers v Centre Leclerc Toulouse and Centre Leclerc Saint-Orens-de-Gameville* [1985] ECR 305, at p. 320 (para. 17).

[69] *Van Eycke v SA ASPA* [1988] ECR 4769, at p. 4792 (para. 19).

maximum interests allowed. This, according to the court, confirmed the state character of the measure concerned.

In the view of the court, the mere fact that legislation may restrict competition is not the deciding factor as to whether such legislation infringes art. 3(f) (now art. 3(g)), 5 and 85 of the treaty. The basic criterion for the evaluation of legislation in the light of these treaty provisions is the extent to which the powers of public authorities are transferred to the undertakings. Undertakings may operate under the supervision of the public authorities, but they must not be entrusted with powers of a public authority. This would explain the emphasis which the court put in *Cullet v Leclerc*[70] and in *Van Eycke v SA ASPA*[71] on the fact that, respectively, the minimum retail price and the maximum interests were fixed by the public authorities and not by the undertakings.

THE PUBLIC SECTOR

¶1317 Introduction

For many years, public sector activities – notably, the production and distribution of gas and electricity, telecommunications,[72] postal services, transportation and certain financial services – did not receive much attention from the Community, despite their considerable size .and economic importance. This situation began to change gradually in the late 1970's, but it was not until the Community introduced the single market programme in 1985 that significant changes began to take place. As a result of this programme, the Commission began to develop a more systematic approach to the application of the competition rules to the public sector and to the use of its powers under art. 90(3). The Commission's activism in this area gave rise to a number of cases so that, in recent years, the court has began to develop a substantial body of case law in this area.

The reasons for the increased emphasis that is put by the Community on the application of the competition rules to the public sector can be summarised by the following statement by the Commission in its *XXIInd Report on Competition Policy for 1992*:

'The existing form of organization is based on a market divided along national lines and is therefore intrinsically incompatible with the Community competition rules, something which has become steadily clearer in the

---

[70] *Cullet and Chambre syndicale des réparateurs automobiles et détaillants de produits pétroliers v Centre Leclerc Toulouse and Centre Leclerc Saint-Orens-de-Gameville* [1985] ECR 305.
[71] *Van Eycke v SA ASPA* [1988] ECR 4769, at p. 4792 (para. 19).
[72] For a discussion on the application of art. 90 in the telecommunications sector, see Chapter 10.

judgments of the Court of Justice. It is a structure which will often facilitate the abuse of a dominant position. It restricts freedom to supply services and the free movement of goods. It is often accompanied by discrimination on grounds of nationality.'[73]

This section will focus on art. 90, which, subject to certain limitations, submits public undertakings to the same rules as private ones. If this were not the case, member states could use their influence or nationalise industries and thereby avoid the application of the competition rules. However, a level playing field is not necessarily achieved by merely applying the EC competition rules to public and private undertakings alike. It is often the member states themselves that, through their influence on the public undertakings, in some way induce these undertakings to infringe the competition rules without there being any action on the part of the undertaking itself. In such cases, the member states are held responsible under art. 90.

The purpose of art. 90 of the treaty is to specify the conditions under which art. 85 and 86 will apply to public undertakings, to undertakings granted special or exclusive rights by the member states and to undertakings entrusted with the operation of services in the general economic interest.[74] Pursuant to art. 90(3), the Commission is responsible for ensuring compliance with art. 90, for issuing appropriate directives to the member states and for issuing decisions. The Commission is able to take action against member states either under art. 90(3) or by initiating proceedings under art. 169 of the treaty.

¶1318 Application of the treaty rules to the public sector: art. 90(1)

Article 90(1) provides that 'in the case of public undertakings and undertakings to which member states grant special or exclusive rights, member states shall neither enact nor maintain in force any measure contrary to the rules contained in this Treaty'. First of all, it should be noted that art. 90(1) imposes an obligation on member states, rather than on undertakings, and is not limited to preventing breaches of art. 85 and 86. However, the discussion in this section will be limited to the application of the competition rules.

Public undertakings
As is the case under art. 85 and 86, the concept of undertaking is broad, referring to all entities performing economic activities regardless of their legal form. Even where the primary purpose of the entity is non-economic, it may

---

[73] *XXIInd Report on Competition Policy for 1992*, point 24. See also *XXIst Report on Competition Policy for 1991*, points 3 and 168.
[74] *Bodson v Pompes Funèbres des Régions Libérées SA* [1988] ECR 2479, at p. 2512 (para. 16).

have the status of an undertaking to the extent that it engages in economic activity. For instance, a broadcasting organisation may be entrusted with a task of a cultural or informative nature but it behaves as an undertaking, for example, when it sells advertising time or purchases programmes. In addition, an entity may be regarded as a 'public undertaking' within the meaning of art. 90, even when it is integrated into the state administration and does not have a separate legal personality provided it is carrying out economic activities of an industrial or commercial nature.[75]

In view of the fact that there exist several definitions as to 'private' and 'public' undertakings within the legal systems of the member states, the Community has yet to provide a definition of the concept of 'public undertaking' under Community law. However, in the first transparency directive, the Commission defined public undertaking as any undertaking over which the public authorities may directly or indirectly exercise a dominant influence.[76] Such influence is presumed when the public authorities directly or indirectly:

(1) hold a major part of the undertaking's subscribed capital;

(2) control a majority of votes; or

(3) can appoint more than half of the administrative, managerial or supervisory positions within the undertaking.[77]

Thus, it is the state's influence over an undertaking that is of importance in determining whether an undertaking will be considered to be 'public' or not. The Commission has, for example, held the Netherlands post office, a company governed by private law but wholly-owned by the state, to be a public undertaking within the meaning of art. 90(1).[78]

Special or exclusive rights
The reason for the inclusion of undertakings enjoying special or exclusive rights in art. 90 would appear to stem from the possibility that the state may influence their behaviour, under threat of withdrawing the rights. A special or exclusive right can be given to either a private or a public undertaking. A special right puts an undertaking in a stronger market position than it would have without the right, whereas an exclusive right extends this right to a monopoly. The

---

[75] See *EC Commission v Italy* [1987] ECR 2599, at p. 2623 (para. 13), concerning the Italian tobacco monopoly, a state administrative entity.

[76] Article 2 of Commission Directive 80/723 on the transparency of financial relations between member states and public undertakings, OJ 1980 L195/35. Admittedly this definition was given only 'for the purpose of this directive', *France, Italy and UK v EC Commission* [1982] ECR 2545, at p. 2578 (para. 24), but it nevertheless provides a useful indication of the Commission's view.

[77] Commission Directive 80/273, art. 2(2), OJ 1980 L195/35.

[78] *Express Delivery Services in the Netherlands*, OJ 1990 L10/47, at p. 49. See also *Re International Express Courier Services in Spain*, OJ 1990 L233/19.

treaty does not contain a definition of special and exclusive rights. However, in a directive dealing with the telecommunications sector, the Commission defines them as 'the rights granted by a Member State or a public authority to one or more public or private bodies through any legal, regulatory or administrative instrument reserving them the right to provide a service or undertake an activity'.[79] It is therefore reasonably clear that when a member state grants to a single undertaking the sole right to, for example, provide a service or operate a network, that undertaking enjoys an exclusive right within the meaning of art. 90. While the definition of an exclusive right is fairly straightforward, the definition of a special right poses more problems and remains somewhat unsettled. It has been suggested that special rights are rights granted to more than one undertaking, but where the number of such undertakings is limited, and chosen in a discriminatory and subjective manner by the state concerned.[80]

To be considered a special right within the meaning of art. 90, the right must be granted by the state to a limited number of undertakings and not to an indefinite group of undertakings. Thus, for instance, in *NV GB-Inno-BM v ATAB*, a member state had given certain undertakings the possibility of fixing compulsory selling prices among themselves to customers. The court found it questionable whether this amounted to a special right since the right was open to all those which fulfilled certain criteria.[81] The court has, for example, regarded the following to be special or exclusive rights granted by member states: the right granted to an airline to operate an air route alone or with one or two other undertakings;[82] the exclusive right granted to a port undertaking to carry out port operations;[83] an exclusive concession granted to funeral enterprises on the condition that they charged particularly high prices;[84] and the exclusive right given to a national PTT for the collection, transport and distribution of mail.[85]

Measures contrary to the treaty

Under art. 90(1), member states are prohibited from taking or maintaining any measure involving a public undertaking or an undertaking to which it has granted special or exclusive rights which is contrary to the competition rules.

---

[79] Commission Directive 90/388 on competition in the markets for telecommunications services, OJ 1990 L192/10, art. 1.

[80] See opinion of Advocate General Jacobs in *Spain & Ors v EC Commission*, Cases C-271/90, C-281/90 and C-289/90, judgment of 17 November 1992, not yet reported, at para. 50. In this connection, it may be questionable whether a special right can be granted to an undertaking which holds a dominant position on the market in question. Id., at para. 51.

[81] *NV GB-Inno-BM v ATAB* [1977] ECR 2115, at p. 2146 (para. 41).

[82] *Ahmed Saeed Flugreisen & Anor v Zentrale zur Bekämpfung unlauteren Wettbewerbs eV* [1989] ECR 803.

[83] *Merci Convenzionali Porto di Genova SpA v Siderurgica Gabriella SpA* [1991] ECR I-5889.

[84] *Bodson v Pompes Funèbres des Régions Libérées SA* [1988] ECR 2479.

[85] *Procureur du Roi v Corbeau*, Case C-320/91, judgment of 19 May 1993, not yet reported.

For many years, the court seemed to make a distinction between the existence and the exercise of a right granted to an undertaking. The court suggested that member states are free to grant special or exclusive rights as they choose, but the exercise of these rights by the beneficiaries must comply with the treaty. However, more recent cases seem to blur the distinction between the existence and exercise of a right by indicating that not merely the exercise, but even the structure of a monopoly, may be contrary to art. 90. It would appear from recent court cases and Commission decisions that the mere grant of a special or exclusive right might infringe art. 90(1) in conjunction with, for example art. 86, when this necessarily leads to or induces an infringement of the treaty and no objective justification exists. The circumstances under which the grant of special or exclusive rights may be contrary to the competition rules are examined below. It should be emphasised that, while it is possible to identify some common themes in the cases, this is a rapidly evolving area of the law and many issues are not entirely settled.

Grant of right distinguished from exercise

The wording of art. 90 presupposes the existence of public undertakings and undertakings given special or exclusive rights by the state. Therefore, it has for a long period of time been argued that the mere granting by the state of special or exclusive rights to undertakings in itself did not constitute an infringement of any treaty rule. This view received support from the court's ruling in *Sacchi*, a case concerning provisions which reserved to the Italian State the right to broadcast television transmissions, and, in particular, cable television transmissions. In that case, the court held that:

> 'Article 90(1) permits member states *inter alia* to grant special or exclusive rights to undertakings. Nothing in the Treaty prevents Member States, for considerations of public interest, of a non-economic nature, from removing radio and TV transmissions, including cable transmissions, from the field of competition by conferring on one or more establishments an exclusive right to conduct them.'[86]

The court also stated that, for the performance of their task, the undertakings were subject to the prohibition against discrimination and, as far as their activities were of an economic nature, to the competition rules as well.[87]

---

[86] *Sacchi* [1974] ECR 409, at pp. 429 and 430 (para. 14). See also *Elliniki Radiophonia Tiléorassi AE v Dimotiki Etairia Pliroforissis & Ors* [1991] ECR I-2925, at p. I-2957 (para. 10).
[87] *Sacchi* [1974] ECR 409, at pp. 429 and 430 (para. 14).

¶1318

Grant of right itself objectionable

However, it appears that the court in recent cases has gone further than in the *Sacchi* judgment and limited the freedom of the state to grant special or exclusive rights. The recent cases seem to imply that member states are in breach of art. 90(1) when they place undertakings in a situation where they cannot help but commit an abuse under art. 86, such as where a state measure influences the structure of the market in such a way that it makes anti-competitive behaviour by the undertaking inevitable.

For instance, in *France v EC Commission*,[88] the Commission directive on competition in the market for telecommunications terminal equipment[89] was challenged by France, supported by other member states. The principal issue was whether the effects inherent in the grant of exclusive and special rights over terminal equipment were sufficient for the Commission to invoke art. 90(1), together with art. 30, 59, 85 and 86. France argued that, as art. 90(1) presupposed the existence of such rights, the Commission could only intervene against the manner in which those rights were used by those to whom they had been granted. The court declared that even if art. 90 presupposed the existence of undertakings having special or exclusive rights, it did not follow that all such rights were necessarily to be considered compatible with the treaty. The question of their compatibility with the treaty depended on the rules to which art. 90(1) referred.[90]

The court picked up on this theme in *Höfner and Elser v Macrotron*.[91] In this case, the court held that the simple fact of creating a dominant position by granting an exclusive right within the meaning of art. 90(1) is not as such incompatible with art. 86 of the treaty. It concluded that even the granting of a right in itself must conform with the treaty in cases where the undertaking in question, merely by exercising the exclusive right granted to it, cannot avoid abusing its dominant position.[92]

Undertaking with exclusive right incapable of satisfying demand

Recent cases suggest that a member state is more likely to be found in breach of art. 90(1) if it creates a situation whereby the undertaking to which it has given an exclusive right is not capable of satisfying consumer demand. For example, in the case concerning the validity of the directive on telecommunications terminal equipment,[93] the court upheld the Commission's demand for the withdrawal of exclusive rights for the importation, marketing, connection

---

[88] *France v EC Commission* [1991] ECR I-1223.
[89] Commission Directive 88/301 on competition in the markets in telecommunications terminal equipment, OJ 1988 L131/73.
[90] *France v EC Commission* [1991] ECR I-1223, at p. I-1265 (para. 22).
[91] *Höfner and Elser v Macrotron GmbH* [1991] ECR I-1979.
[92] Id., at p. I-2018 (para. 29).
[93] *France v EC Commission* [1991] ECR I-1223.

¶1318

and/or maintenance of terminal equipment. In reaching this conclusion, the court pointed out that the market for terminal equipment was characterised by a diversity of technical products, and that there was no certainty that a monopolist could satisfy consumer demand. The grant of such a right can only be allowed in so far as there is a public service justification, such as the safety of users or employees.[94]

The court used the same reasoning in *Höfner and Elser*, where the German labour exchange monopoly, which had been given the exclusive right to executive recruitment activities, was held to be 'manifestly incapable of satisfying the demand prevailing on the market'.[95]

Other recent cases emphasise that a member state may infringe the competition rules when it grants exclusive rights to an undertaking that puts the undertaking in a situation in which the undertaking by the mere exercise of those rights, abuses its dominant position. In *ERT*,[96] the Greek State had granted an exclusive right to ERT to transmit and to retransmit television broadcasting. ERT claimed that a competing television station infringed its exclusive right. The court referred to the *Sacchi* judgment, where it had held that the treaty did not oppose the grant, for reasons of public interest, of a TV-monopoly of a non-economic nature, but added that the arrangements for organising and operating such a monopoly must infringe neither the provisions of the treaty on free movement of goods and services nor the competition rules. Article 90(1) was found to prohibit the granting of an exclusive right to transmit and to retransmit television broadcasting in one undertaking where this would create a situation in which the undertaking was induced to infringe art. 86 due to a discriminatory broadcasting policy which favours its own programmes.[97]

Similarly, in *Port of Genoa*,[98] the court found that an undertaking to which the state had granted exclusive rights had abused its dominant position simply by exercising those rights. Here, an Italian law granted an exclusive right to carry out the loading and unloading of goods in Italian ports only to undertakings that employed only Italian nationals. The court found that this provision infringed art. 90(1) and 86 because the undertakings concerned were induced to abuse their dominant position by, for example, charging disproportionately high prices.[99]

---

[94] Id., at p. I-1268 (para. 35–37).
[95] *Höfner and Elser v Macrotron GmbH* [1991] ECR I-1979, at p. I-2018 (para. 31). The word 'manifestly' seems to indicate that it must be established that the undertaking falls far short of satisfying demand.
[96] *Elliniki Radiophonia Tiléorassi AE v Dimotiki Etairia Pliroforissis & Ors* [1991] ECR I-2925.
[97] Id., at pp. I-2962 and I-2963 (para. 37 and 38).
[98] *Merci Convenzionali Porto di Genova SpA v Siderurgica Gabriella SpA* [1991] ECR I-5889.
[99] Id., at para. 19.

Extension of monopoly to neighbouring market

Another example of a state measure that is likely to be found in breach of art. 90(1) and 86, and which also illustrates that the mere exercise of exclusive rights by an undertaking may induce the undertaking to abuse its dominant position, is where a monopoly is extended by state action to a neighbouring market without any objective justification. In *RTT*,[100] a case concerning the Belgian telecommunications monopoly, the court was faced with the issue of the compatibility with the competition rules of national rules granting to the RTT the responsibility for establishing and operating a public telephone network, the right to supply telephones and the power to license for connection to the network telephones which it had not supplied itself. Belgium argued that designating as the licensing authority a body which was in competition with applicants for licences did not in itself constitute an abuse under art. 86 in the absence of a specific abuse, such as the discriminatory application of the rules relating to the grant of the licences. The court rejected that argument, ruling that the extension, without objective justification, of the monopoly for the setting up and running of the telephone network to the market for telephones was in itself contrary to art. 86 in conjunction with art. 90(1). The court stressed that the mere possession of this right to authorise the connection of telephones was sufficient to establish a breach, without it being necessary to verify that the monopoly had been exercised in a discriminatory manner.[101]

A further example of a state measure extending an exclusive right to an adjacent market that may be judged contrary to art. 90(1) is provided in the Commission's decision on *Express Delivery Services in the Netherlands*.[102] In this case, the Commission found that a Dutch law preventing private couriers from delivering letters weighing up to 500 grammes in competition with the express delivery service operated by the Dutch PTT was contrary to art. 90(1). By extending the exclusive right given to the PTT for basic postal service to the express delivery market, the Dutch Government had enabled PTT to extend its dominant position to an ancillary activity which might be offered by private express couriers.[103]

---

[100] *Régie des Télégraphes et des Téléphones (RTT) v SA GB-Inno-BM* [1991] ECR I-5941. Similar issues were raised in *Procureur du Roi v Lagauche & Ors*, Joined Cases C-46/90 and C-93/91, judgment of 23 October 1993, not yet reported, concerning challenges to the right of RTT to grant authorisations for cordless phones.

[101] Id., at para. 24. The court reached the same conclusion in a case where the monopoly was extended to the market for telecommunications services. *Spain & Ors v EC Commission*, Joined Cases C-271/90, C-281/90 and C-289/90, judgment of 17 November 1992, not yet reported, at para. 35 and 36. These judgments diverge considerably from the court's holding in *Sacchi*, where the court held that '[...] the fact that an undertaking to which a Member State grants exclusive rights has a monopoly is not as such incompatible with Article 86' and that it is '[...] the same as regards an extension of exclusive rights following a new intervention by this State'. *Sacchi* [1974] ECR 409, at p. 430 (para. 14).

[102] *Express Delivery Services in the Netherlands*, OJ 1990 L10/47. See also *Re International Courier Services in Spain*, OJ 1990 L233/19.

[103] The Commission appeared to take a different approach in a case concerning the French Telecommunications Act reported at *XXIst Report on Competition Policy for 1991*, point 324.

Conclusion

To conclude, it would appear that it is no longer only the performance of the undertakings that have been granted special or exclusive rights which must not be discriminatory or inconsistent with the competition rules. The cases referred to above indicate that the mere granting of special or exclusive rights might infringe art. 90(1) in conjunction with, for example art. 86, when this necessarily leads to or induces an abuse by the privileged undertaking through, for example, a discriminatory policy or an incapability of satisfying consumer demands and no objective justification exists.

¶1319   Exceptions to the general rule: art. 90(2)

Article 90(2) provides as follows:

> 'Undertakings entrusted with the operation of services of general economic interest or having the character of a revenue-producing monopoly shall be subject to the rules in this Treaty, in particular to the rules on competition, in so far as the application of such rules does not obstruct the performance, in law or in fact, of the particular tasks assigned to them. The development of trade must not be affected to such extent as would be contrary to the interests of the Community.'

Article 90(2) concerns two types of undertakings: undertakings that have been entrusted with the operation of services of general economic interest, and undertakings having the character of a revenue-producing monopoly. While art. 90(2) reaffirms the principle that the treaty rules apply to those undertakings, it contains, however, an exception to the principles discussed above, which is frequently used as a defence in proceedings involving member states and different monopolies.

There are two requirements that have to be fulfilled in order to apply the exception.[104] First, the performance of the task assigned to the undertakings must be obstructed by the application of the competition rules. Secondly, trade within the Community must not be affected to a degree contrary to the interest of the Community. It should be noted that, while the terminology used for the undertakings referred to in art. 90(2) is not the same as for those in art. 90(1), from both the broad interpretation by the court of the term 'public undertakings' and from economic realities, it seems clear that most

---

[104] In *France v EC Commission* [1991] ECR I-1223, at p. I-1263 (para. 12), the court declared that this 'provision seeks to reconcile the Member States' interest in using certain undertakings, in particular in the public sector, as an instrument of economic or fiscal policy with the Community's interest in ensuring compliance with the rules on competition and the preservation of the unity of the Common Market.'

undertakings referred to in art. 90(2) would also qualify as 'public undertakings' under art. 90(1).[105]

Entrusted undertakings

The word 'entrusted' indicates that art. 90(2) only applies if the undertaking has been actually entrusted by an act of the public authority with a task of general economic interest.[106] This means that the state must have taken legal steps to secure the provision of the service by the undertaking in question. Consequently, an undertaking created by a private initiative, although performing a service of general economic interest, may not be considered to be an 'entrusted' undertaking. An example of entrusted undertakings is provided in a case concerning Dutch generators and distributors of electricity, in which case the Commission found the undertakings in question to be entrusted undertakings within art. 90(2), since they were assigned their tasks on the basis of concessions granted by the Minister for Economic Affairs.[107] However, in *Uniform Eurocheques*,[108] the Commission stated that art. 90(2) did not apply because the founders of the Eurocheque system, private financial institutions, had not at any time been entrusted with the operation of a service of general economic interest by the public authorities. The Commission reached this conclusion notwithstanding the fact that the competent authorities had approved and, in some countries, legally upheld the Eurocheque system.

Services of general economic interest

The notion 'operation of services' suggests that the services must be performed on an ongoing, regular basis such as the operation of a public utility. It would seem that a service will be of general economic interest when it involves an economic activity (although the aim may be non-economic) and is operated in the interest of the general public. It has been suggested that the concept of 'general economic interest' is very wide.[109] The following undertakings have been found by the court to operate services of a 'general economic interest' within the meaning of art. 90(2):

---

[105] However, this does not imply that the undertakings in art. 90(1) always come under art. 90(2) as well. It is quite possible for an undertaking granted a special or exclusive right not to perform a service of general economic interest.

[106] *BRT v SABAM* ('*BRT II*') [1974] ECR 313, at p. 318 (para. 22); *Ahmed Saeed Flugreisen & Anor v Zentrale zur Bekämpfung unlauteren Wettbewerbs eV* [1989] ECR 803, at p. 853 (para. 55–57).

[107] *IJsselcentrale & Ors*, OJ 1991 L28/32, at p. 43.

[108] *Uniform Eurocheques*, OJ 1985 L35/43 at p. 48; see also *Züchner v Bayerische Vereinsbank AG* [1981] ECR 2021.

[109] See the opinion of the Advocate General in *Ministère Public Luxembourg v Muller* [1971] ECR 723, at p. 739, who suggested that the concept of 'general economic interest' is extremely broad and therefore 'the authors of the Treaty chose it in preference to the concept which is more traditional in certain national laws but is probably narrower, that of economic public service or of public service of an industrial and commercial nature'.

- an entity entrusted with ensuring the navigability of the state's most important waterway;[110]
- a monopoly over the broadcasting of television advertising;[111]
- the operation of air routes that are not commercially viable;[112]
- postal services;[113]
- the operation of a public telephone network, but not the providing of telephone equipment;[114] and
- the operation of the national public electricity supply and the generators that supply the distributors.[115]

However, in *Port of Genoa*,[116] the court, without giving any reasons, did not consider undertakings carrying out dock work, i.e. loading, unloading, transhipment and storage of goods in a port, to be entrusted with a service of a general economic interest.[117]

Revenue-producing monopolies

A revenue-producing monopoly is an undertaking that has been given an exclusive right solely for the purpose of creating revenue for the member state, e.g. the tobacco and alcohol monopolies in some countries. This type of monopoly appears to be of decreasing importance in the Community. Furthermore, they have to operate within the constraints of art. 37 regarding state monopolies.[118] There have so far not been any judgments by the court or Commission decisions defining this kind of monopoly. However, since the court's ruling in *Sacchi*,[119] it would appear that only public interests of a non-economic nature will justify the creation of monopolies. Therefore, it is difficult to see how a revenue-producing monopoly can be justified, since it scarcely can be of a non-economic nature.

---

[110] *Ministère Public Luxembourg v Muller* [1971] ECR 723.
[111] *Sacchi* [1974] ECR 409.
[112] *Ahmed Saeed Flugreisen & Anor v Zentrale zur Bekämpfung unlauteren Wettbewerbs eV* [1989] ECR 803.
[113] *Procureur du Roi v Corbeau*, Case C-320/91, judgment of 19 May 1993, not yet reported.
[114] *Régie des Télégraphes et des Téléphones (RTT) v SA GB-Inno-BM* [1991] ECR I-5941 (para. 16 and 22). Notably, the court held that the public telephone network was a service of general economic interest at the present state of Community development.
[115] *IJsselcentrale & Ors*, OJ 1991 L28/32, at p. 43.
[116] *Merci Convenzionali Porto di Genova SpA v Siderurgica Gabriella SpA* [1991] ECR I-5889 at p. I-5931 (para. 28).
[117] However, Advocate General Van Gerven held that the management of a port is an activity of general economic interest, whereas carrying out or organising the dock-work is not. If these latter activities would be considered to be of general economic interest then almost all economic activities would fall within this concept. According to the Advocate General, it is decisive for whether an activity would come within the concept in question that the services are of direct benefit to the society as a whole ([1991] ECR I-5889, at p. I-5919 (para. 27).
[118] For a discussion of state monopolies, see ¶1322.
[119] *Sacchi* [1974] ECR 409.

¶1319

Obstruction of assigned task

An exemption under art. 90(2) can only be given to an undertaking in so far as the application of treaty rules would obstruct the performance of its tasks. In this regard, it is not sufficient that compliance with the treaty rules would make the performance of the task more difficult. For example, the Commission has stated that an exemption is only possible if the undertaking concerned has no other technically and economically viable means of performing its task.[120] Thus, it is very difficult to satisfy the conditions for a derogation under art. 90(2).

In *RTT*,[121] for example, the court found that the extension of RTT's monopoly over the public telephone network to include the market for telephone equipment and the approval of such equipment would lead to the restriction or exclusion of competition on the market for telephone equipment, and was not justified as necessary for RTT to carry out its service of general economic interest. According to the court, it was not necessary to have a monopoly on the market for telephone equipment to meet such essential requirements as the safety of the users because a less restrictive alternative was available, namely, the publication of specifications and a procedure that made it possible to verify that these specifications were fulfilled.[122]

While it is generally difficult to successfully invoke the exception set forth in art. 90(2), the Commission appears more willing to admit this exception in cases where the monopoly is under an obligation to provide a universal service, and its ability to do so may be jeopardised if competition is allowed. In the field of telecommunications, the Commission has defined the concept of universal service as a service 'having general geographical coverage, and being provided to any service provider or user upon request within a reasonable period of time.'[123] The court recently had the opportunity to develop this line of reasoning concerning postal services in the *Corbeau*[124] case.

In *Corbeau*, a case which concerned a private courier service competing with the Belgian PTT that had been granted a monopoly over such services, the court was faced with the question of whether a monopoly over postal services was necessary to enable the Belgian PTT to perform its task. According to the court, it must be assumed that the PTT's obligation to provide this universal service is based on the assumption that the PTT could subsidise its unprofitable activities from the more profitable ones and could restrict competition with respect to the more profitable activities. Otherwise, other operators who chose to concentrate their efforts on the profitable activities would be in a position to

---

[120] *NAVEWA-ANSEAU*, OJ 1982 L167/39, at p. 48.
[121] *Régie des Télégraphes et des Téléphones (RTT) v SA GB-Inno-BM* [1991] ECR I-5941.
[122] Id., at para. 22.
[123] Commission Directive 90/388 on competition in the markets for telecommunications services, OJ 1990 L192/10, preamble, recital 18.
[124] *Procureur du Roi v Corbeau*, Case C-320/91, judgment of 19 May 1993, not yet reported.

offer lower prices than the PTT because, unlike the PTT, they were not burdened with the extra costs of providing a universal service. The court emphasised, however, that this reason did not justify a monopoly with respect to specific services of general economic interest in that they were designed to meet the individual needs of companies that demanded certain additional services that the traditional postal service did not supply such as home collection of mail, more rapid delivery and the possibility of changing destination in transit. The court added that such additional services, either by their nature or the conditions under which they were offered such as their geographical coverage, should not jeopardise the financial stability of the basic service.[125]

Similar reasoning may be found in *Ahmed Saeed*,[126] where the court held that art. 90(2) may be applied to all carriers that may be obliged by the public authorities to operate on routes which are not commercially viable, but which are necessary for reasons of general interest. Also, in a recent case concerning a set of agreements between the German coal mining industry, the German public electricity supply industry and the industrial producers of electricity, by which the two latter parties had undertaken to purchase a certain amount of German coal for the purpose of generating electricity, the Commission considered that the application of art. 85 to the agreements would not prevent the provision of basic supply of electricity since the basic security of public electricity supplies was not ensured only by these agreements.[127]

¶1320   Procedural aspects of art. 90(1) and (2)

After having outlined the possibilities of qualifying for the exception under art. 90(2), the question remains as to who can apply the exception, i.e. whether only the Commission has the authority to do so or whether national authorities and courts may also apply the exception.

Since art. 90(1) prohibits member states from enacting or maintaining in force any measure contrary to a rule that has direct effect, it has been suggested that art. 90(1) itself has direct effect, i.e. it confers rights or obligations on individuals which national courts are bound to recognise and enforce.[128] However, the question of direct effect and the application of competition rules in national courts is more complicated as regards art. 90(2). Given the wording of art. 90(2), in particular the condition that the development of trade must not be affected contrary to the interest of the Community, it would appear that the

---

[125] Id., at para. 17–19. See also the Commission's decisions in *Re International Express Courier Services in Spain*, OJ 1990 L233/19 at p. 22, and *Express Delivery Services in the Netherlands*, OJ 1990 L10/47.

[126] *Ahmed Saeed Flugreisen & Anor v Zentrale zur Bekämpfung unlauteren Wettbewerbs eV* [1989] ECR 803, at p. 853 (para. 55).

[127] 'Jahrhundertvertrag', OJ 1993 L50/14, at p. 22.

[128] See e.g. Advocate General Jacobs in *Höfner and Elser v Macrotron GmbH* [1991] ECR I-1979, at p. I-2008.

Commission is the competent body to apply the derogation. This view is supported by, for example, the court's holding in *Muller*, where it held that art. 90(2) does not 'create individual rights which national courts must protect'.[129] This position was strongly reinforced by the court's statement in the *British Telecom* case:

'the application of Article 90(2) is not left to the discretion of the Member State, which has entrusted an undertaking with the operation of a service of general economic interest. Article 90(3) assigns to the Commission the task of monitoring such matters, under the supervision of the court'.[130]

However, other case law indicates that art. 90(2) cannot preclude national courts from giving effect to rules such as art. 85 and 86.[131] Thus, the court established in the *BRT v SABAM* case that it is 'the duty of the national court to investigate whether an undertaking which invokes the provisions of Article 90(2) [...] has in fact been entrusted by a Member State with the operation of a service of general economic interest.'[132] The judgments in *Ahmed Saeed*[133] and *ERT*[134] suggest that the national court is competent to decide whether the application of the treaty rules would obstruct the performance of the particular tasks assigned to the undertaking. In *ERT*, the court found that:

'it is for the national court to determine whether the practices of such an undertaking are compatible with Article 86 and to verify whether those practices, if they are contrary to that provision, may be justified by the needs of the particular task with which the undertaking have been entrusted.'[135]

These cases hold that if the national court establishes that the rights entrusted to the undertaking are disproportionate to the task to be accomplished, it may refuse to apply the exception and apply the competition rules. If the national court, however, is of the opinion that the undertaking could not perform the task assigned to it if it were subject to the competition rules, the national court seems to have three options:

---

[129] *Ministère Public Luxembourg v Muller* [1971] ECR 723, at p. 730 (para. 16). See also Advocate General Lenz in *Ministère Public v Asjes & Ors* [1986] ECR 1425, at p. 1445.

[130] *Italy v EC Commission* [1985] ECR 873, at p. I-888 (para. 30).

[131] Advocate General Jacobs stated in *Höfner and Elser v Macrotron GmbH* [1991] ECR I-1979, at p. I-2008, that 'what is really meant when Article 90(2) is denied direct effect is simply that the partial derogation that it makes from the ordinary rules of the Treaty in favour of certain undertakings does not have direct effect.'

[132] *BRT v SABAM ('BRT II')* [1974] ECR 313, at p. 318 (para. 22). See also *Sacchi* [1974] ECR 409, at p. 430 (para. 18), where the court held that 'even within the framework of Article 90, therefore, the prohibitions of Article 86 have a direct effect and confer on interested parties rights which the national courts must safeguard.'

[133] *Ahmed Saeed Flugreisen & Anor v Zentrale zur Bekämpfung unlauteren Wettbewerbs eV* [1989] ECR 803, at p. 853 (para. 55–57).

[134] *Elliniki Radiophonia Tiléorassi AE v Dimotiki Etairia Pliroforissis & Ors* [1991] ECR I-2925.

[135] Id., at p. I-2962 (para. 34). This holding was repeated by the Court of First Instance in *Rendo NV & Ors v EC Commission*, Case T-16/91, judgment of 18 November 1992, not yet reported, at para. 99.

¶1320

(1) the national court can request a preliminary ruling from the court under art. 177 of the treaty;

(2) the national court may stay the proceedings and ask the Commission for its opinion; or

(3) the national court may grant the derogation.

The ruling in *ERT* seems to suggest that the national court is competent to decide whether the exception under art. 90(2) applies. This would not, however, appear to be the position of the Commission.[136]

¶1321   Application by the Commission: art. 90(3)

Article 90(3) provides that:

'The Commission shall ensure the application of the provisions of this Article and shall, where necessary, address appropriate directives or decisions to the Member States.'

Article 90(3) requires the Commission to ensure that the member states observe the obligations imposed on them in relation to the undertakings referred to in art. 90(1) and (2) by addressing directives or decisions to the member states. In some recent cases, the court has clarified the scope of the Commission's powers under art. 90(3).

In *France v EC Commission*,[137] the court dealt with the Commission's power to adopt directives under art. 90(3). In that case, France contested the legality of the directive on telecommunications terminal equipment, which was adopted by the Commission pursuant to art. 90(3).[138] The court held that the Commission has the power to adopt general directives setting out member states' obligations in concrete terms resulting from art. 90(1) and (2). However, a directive cannot be used to make a finding that a member state has failed to fulfil a particular obligation under the treaty, since this power of the

---

[136] The Commission claims in its guidelines on the application of EEC competition rules in the telecommunications sector, OJ 1991 C233/2, para. 23, that it has exclusive competence to decide that art. 90(2) derogation applies. Paragraph 23 reads in full:

'The Commission infers from the case law of the Court of Justice that it has exclusive competence, under the control of the Court, to decide that the exception of Article 90(2) applies. The national authorities, including judicial authorities, can assess that this exception does not apply, when they find that the competition rules clearly do not obstruct the performance of the task of general economic interest assigned to the undertakings. When those authorities cannot make a clear assessment in this sense they should suspend their decision in order to enable the Commission to find that the conditions for the application of that provision are fulfilled.'

[137] *France v EC Commission* [1991] ECR I-1223.

[138] Commission Directive 88/301 on competition in the markets in telecommunications terminal equipment, OJ 1988 L131/73.

Commission does not allow it to consider the actual situation in a particular member state.[139]

The Commission's power to adopt decisions under art. 90(3) is somewhat different from that concerning directives. This distinction was outlined by the court in the *Dutch PTT*[140] case, in which the Commission's decision,[141] based on art. 90(3), concerning the Dutch express delivery services was contested. The Dutch Government argued that the Commission was not entitled to adopt a decision under art. 90(3) ruling that a member state had infringed art. 90(1). At most, art. 90(3) allowed the Commission to specify in general terms the obligations arising from art. 90(1). If a specific breach was established, the Commission must bring an action against the member state under art. 169. The court rejected this argument and stated that the nature and role of directives and decisions was distinct. Decisions are adopted in relation to a specific situation in one or more member states. In taking such a decision, the Commission would necessarily have to assess that situation under Community law, and determine the consequences which would follow for the member state concerned.[142] The court concluded that, should the Commission not have the power to find a specific measure taken by a member state to be incompatible with the treaty and to indicate what measures member states have to adopt in order not to infringe the treaty, art. 90(3) would be deprived of all effectiveness.[143]

Decisions adopted

The Commission has used this power to issue decisions pursuant to art. 90(3) against, for example, Greek legislation requiring all public property in Greece be insured by Greek public sector insurance companies; Greek legislation requiring the staff of Greek state-owned banks to recommend to their customers insurance with companies owned or controlled by the public

---

[139] *France v EC Commission* [1991] ECR I-1223, at p. I-1263 (para. 14 and 17), reiterated in *Spain & Ors v EC Commission*, Joined Cases C-271/90, C-281/90 and C-289/90, judgment of 17 November 1992, not yet reported, at para. 12.

[140] *Netherlands & Ors v EC Commission* [1992] ECR I-627.

[141] *Express Delivery Services in the Netherlands*, OJ 1991 L10/47.

[142] *Netherlands & Ors v EC Commission* [1992] ECR I-627, at para. 27.

[143] Id., at para. 28.

banking sector;[144] Spanish and Dutch laws reserving express courier services below certain weights and tariffs to the national PTT;[145] and preferential air fares available under Spanish legislation for travel on the national carrier to Spanish nationals resident on the Canary and Balearic islands.[146]

Directives adopted

Thus far, the Commission has adopted four directives based on art. 90(3). The first two directives concerned the transparency of financial relations between member states and public undertakings.[147] The other two directives adopted under art. 90(3) both concerned the telecommunications sector, namely the directives abolishing exclusive rights to terminal equipment[148] and services other than voice telephony.[149] The legality of these directives have been confirmed by the court.[150] Considering the increasing importance of the concept of subsidiarity it may prove politically difficult for the Commission to make use of this legislative power which neither involves the Council nor the Parliament. Therefore, it is likely that the Commission will resort to the adoption of harmonisation directives based on art. 100A together with a case-by-case application of art. 85 and 86.[151]

¶1322   State monopolies under art. 37

In addition to the Commission's recent activities in respect of the public sector carried out on the basis of art. 90, brief mention should be made of the position of certain state monopolies under art. 37 of the treaty. Article 37 is one of the treaty provisions governing the free movement of goods. It requires member states progressively to adjust state monopolies that affect imports and exports

---

[144] *Insurance in Greece of Public Property and Loans Granted by the Greek State-owned Banks*, OJ 1985 L152/25. Since Greece did not comply with the decision, the Commission later initiated court proceedings. See *EC Commission v Hellenic Republic* [1988] ECR 3611.

[145] *Express Delivery Services in the Netherlands*, OJ 1990 L10/47 and *Re International Express Courier Services in Spain*, OJ 1990 L233/19.

[146] *Air and Sea Transport Fares for Spanish Nationals Resident in the Canary and Balearic Islands*, OJ 1987 L194/28. There have been renewed complaints about this alleged discrimination on grounds of nationality since the public sector sea company has introduced new reductions, which the Spanish Government claims are set on a strictly commercial basis. Since it is the Commission's opinion that Spain has failed to put an end to an infringement of art. 90(1), it has decided to initiate proceedings against Spain under art. 90(3), *XXIInd Report on Competition Policy for 1992*, point 523.

[147] Commission Directive 80/723 on the transparency of financial relations between member states and public undertakings, OJ 1980 L195/35, as amended by Commission Directive 85/413, OJ 1985 L229/20.

[148] Commission Directive 88/301 on competition in the markets in telecommunications terminal equipment, OJ 1988 L131/73.

[149] Commission Directive 90/388 on competition in the markets for telecommunications services, OJ 1990 L192/10.

[150] *France v EC Commission* [1991] ECR I-1223 (terminal equipment) and *Spain & Ors v EC Commission*, Joined Cases C-271/90, C-281/90 and C-289/90, judgment of 17 November 1992, not yet reported (telecommunications services). For a detailed discussion of these cases, see Chapter 10.

[151] It would appear that this is the strategy the Commission has adopted concerning the energy sector. In this sector, it has recently adopted two directives intended to complete the internal market in electricity and natural gas, the legal basis of which is art. 100A rather than art. 90(3).

to ensure that, by the end of the transitional period for the abolition of customs duties and quantitative restrictions, no discrimination exists between nationals of member states with regard to the conditions under which goods are procured or marketed.[152] In recent years, the bulk of the cases under art. 37 have arisen with respect to the traditional state monopolies of new member states and it is likely that art. 37 will come into play in the context of the potential accession of Austria, Finland, Norway and Sweden and other states to the Community.

Article 37 only applies to state monopolies for goods although it may apply to monopolies for services to the extent that they may have an influence on intra-state trade in goods, such as where the services monopoly leads to discrimination against imported goods as opposed goods of domestic origin.[153] For the purposes of art. 37, a state monopoly is defined broadly as 'any body through which a Member State, in law or in fact, either directly or indirectly supervises, determines or appreciably influences imports or exports between Member States' as well as 'monopolies delegated by the State to others.'[154] Examples of state monopolies include monopolies for alcohol,[155] tobacco,[156] oil,[157] gas and electricity,[158] fertilisers[159] and telephones.[160]

Article 37 does not prohibit state monopolies. Rather it requires that they be operated in a way that ensures that there is no discrimination between foreign and domestic goods with respect to how they are procured or marketed.[161] Thus national monopolies may not maintain exclusive import rights, and producers from other member states must be able to sell their products directly in the member state where the state monopoly exists. An example of the Commission's approach in this area is provided by the *Spanish Oil Monopoly* case.[162] Initially, the Commission required Spain to allow independent producers to set up distribution networks parallel to that of the state oil monopoly. In this connection, the Commission required the Spanish authorities to change rules concerning the minimum distance between service

---

[152] Article 37, para. 1, provides as follows:

'Member States shall progressively adjust any State monopolies of a commercial character so as to ensure that when the transitional period has ended no discrimination regarding the conditions under which goods are procured and marketed exists between nationals of Member States.'

[153] See e.g. *Bodson v Pompes Funèbres des Régions Libérées SA* [1988] ECR 2479.

[154] Article 37, para. 2.

[155] See e.g. *Seventeenth Report on Competition Policy*, point 295.

[156] See e.g. id., point 292.

[157] See e.g. *XXIst Report on Competition Policy for 1991*, points 330 and 332; *XXth Report on Competition Policy*, points 361 and 362.

[158] See e.g. *XXIst Report on Competition Policy for 1991*, point 328.

[159] See e.g. *XXIst Report on Competition Policy for 1991*, points 338 and 339; *XXth Report on Competition Policy*, point 363.

[160] See e.g. *Sixteenth Report on Competition Policy*, point 294.

[161] *EC Commission v Italy* [1983] ECR 1955, at pp. 1967 and 1968 (para. 11).

[162] See *XXIst Report on Competition Policy for 1991*, point 332; *XXth Report on Competition Policy*, point 362; *Eighteenth Report on Competition Policy*, point 312.

stations so that new service stations could be set up in profitable areas. When it became clear that the parallel service station network was having trouble getting established, the Spanish authorities were then required to change the regulations that required service stations operated by the state monopoly to obtain their supplies domestically, thus allowing foreign suppliers to use the service station network of the state monopoly.

Annexes

Annex 1

FINES FOR SUBSTANTIVE INFRINGEMENTS

Case	COMMISSION					COURT OF JUSTICE	
	Ref.	Art.	Infringement	Company	Fine (ECU)	Ref.	Decision
1. *International Quinine Agreement*	Decision 69/240 JO 1969 L192/5	85	Market-sharing price-fixing and production	ACF Chemiefarma	210,000	Case 41/69 *ACF Chemiefarma v EC Commission* [1970] ECR 661	Fines of ACF Chemiefarma, Boehringer and Buchler were each reduced by 10,000
				Boehringer	190,000	Case 44/69 *Buchler v EC Commission* [1970] ECR 733	
				Buchler	65,000	Case 45/69 *Boehringer Mannheim v EC Commission* [1970] ECR 769	
				Nogentaise	12,000		
				Pharmacie Centrale	10,000		
				Pointet-Girard	12,000		
2. *Dyestuffs*	Decision 69/243 JO 1969 L195/11	85	Price-fixing	ACNA	40,000	Case 57/69 *ACNA v EC Commission* [1972] ECR 933	ACNA's fine reduced to 30,000
				BASF	50,000	Case 49/69 *BASF v EC Commission* [1972] ECR 713	Decision upheld
				Bayer	50,000	Case 51/69 *Bayer v EC Commission* [1972] ECR 745	Decision upheld
				Ciba	50,000		
				Geigy	50,000	Case 52/69 *Geigy v EC Commission* [1972] ECR 787	Decision upheld

Case	COMMISSION Ref.	Art.	Infringement	Company	Fine (ECU)	COURT OF JUSTICE Ref.	Decision
				Hoechst	50,000	Case 56/69 *Hoechst v EC Commission* [1972] ECR 927	Decision upheld
				ICI	50,000	Case 48/69 *ICI v EC Commission* [1972] ECR 619	Decision upheld
				Mainkur	50,000	Case 55/69 *Casella v EC Commission* [1972] ECR 887	Decision upheld
				Sandoz	50,000	Case 53/69 *Sandoz v EC Commission* [1972] ECR 845	Decision upheld
				Société Française MC	50,000	Case 54/69 *Francolor v EC Commission* [1972] ECR 851	Decision upheld
3. *Pittsburgh Corning Europe*	Decision 72/403 JO 1972 L272/35	85	Price discrimination in lieu of export ban	Pittsburgh Corning Europe	100,000	—	—
4. *Zoja CSC ICI*	Decision 72/457 OJ 1972 L299/51	86	Refusal to deal	Istituto Chemioterapico Italiano (reseller) Commercial Solvents Corp (US) (fine imposed jointly and severally)	200,000	Joined Cases 6 & 7/73 *ICI v EC Commission* [1974] ECR 223	Fine reduced to 10,000

		COMMISSION					COURT OF JUSTICE	
Case	Ref.	Art.	Infringement	Company	Fine (ECU)	Ref.	Ref.	Decision
5. *WEA-Filipacchi*	Decision 72/480 OJ 1972 L303/52	85	Export ban	WEA-Filipacchi	60,000	—	—	Fines quashed or reduced
6. *European Sugar Industry*	Decision 73/109 OJ 1973 L140/17	85 86	Market-sharing Ancillary practices	AIE	100,000	Joined Cases 40–48, 50, 54–56, 111, 113, 114/73 *Suiker Unie & Ors v EC Commission* [1975] ECR 1663		quashed
				Béghin	700,000			100,000
				Cavarzare	200,000			quashed
				Centrale Suiker	600,000			150,000
				Eridania	1,000,000			quashed
				Générale Sucrière	400,000			80,000
				Pfeifer & Langen	800,000			240,000
				SADAM	100,000			quashed
				Société des Raffin	500,000			80,000
				Sucres & Denrées	1,000,000			100,000
				Süddeutsche Zucker	700,000			quashed
				Südzucker	200,000			40,000
				Suiker Unie	800,000			200,000
				Tirlemontoise	1,500,000			600,000
				Volano	100,000			quashed
				Zuccheri	300,000			quashed
7. *Deutsche Philips*	Decision 73/322 OJ 1973 L293/40	85	Export ban	Deutsche Philips	60,000	—	—	—
8. *Papiers Peints de Belgique*	Decision 74/431 OJ 1974 L237/3	85	Price-fixing boycott	SC Usines Peters Lacroix	135,000	Case 73/74 *Papiers Peints v EC Commission* [1975] ECR 1491		Decision annulled

Case	COMMISSION				Fine (ECU)	COURT OF JUSTICE	
	Ref.	Art.	Infringement	Company		Ref.	Decision
				Les Papetries de Genval	120,000		
				Vanderborght Frères	36,000		
				Papiers Peints Brepols	67,500		
9. *General Motors Continental*	Decision 75/75 OJ 1975 L29/14	86	Unfair pricing, in lieu of export ban	General Motors Continental	100,000	Case 26/75 *General Motors v EC Commission* [1975] ECR 1367	Decision annulled
0. *Preserved Mushrooms*	Decision 75/77 OJ 1975 L29/26	85	Market-sharing, price-fixing	Blanchard Euroconserves Champifrance Faval Champex-Centre	32,000 32,000 26,000 2,000 8,000	—	—
1. *Miller International*	Decision 76/915 OJ 1976 L357/40	85	Export ban	Miller International Schallplatten (wholly owned subsidiary of MCA Records, US)	70,000	Case 19/77 *Miller International Schallplatten v EC Commission* [1978] ECR 131	Decision upheld
12. *Vitamins*	Decision 76/642 OJ 1976 L223/27	86	Requirement contracts, fidelity rebates	Hoffmann-La Roche	300,000	Case 85/76 *Hoffmann-La Roche v EC Commission* [1979] ECR 461	Fine reduced to 200,000
1=. *Chiquita*	Decision 76/353 OJ 1976 L95/1	86	Export ban, refusal to deal, unfair and discriminatory prices	United Brands	1,000,000	Case 27/76 *United Brands v EC Commission* [1978] ECR 207	Fine reduced to 850,000

Case	Ref.	Art.	COMMISSION Infringement	Company	Fine (ECU)	COURT OF JUSTICE Ref.	Decision
14. *Theal-Watts*	Decision 77/129 OJ 1976 L39/19	85	Export ban	Tepea BV Cecil E Watts Ltd	10,000 10,000	Case 28/77 *Tepea v EC Commission* [1978] ECR 1391	Decision upheld
15. *BMW Belgium*	Decision 78/155 OJ 1978 L46/33	85	Export ban	BMW Belgium 5 local dealers 3 local dealers 39 local dealers	150,000 2,000 1,500 1,000	Joined Cases 32, 36–82/78 *BMW Belgium & Ors v EC Commission* [1979] ECR 2435	Decision upheld
16. *Hugin/Liptons*	Decision 78/68 OJ 1978 L22/23	86	Refusal to deal	Hugin Kassaregister AB Hugin Cash Registers Ltd (UK subsidiary) (fine imposed jointly and severally)	50,000	Case 22/78 *Hugin v EC Commission* [1979] ECR 1869	Decision annulled
17. *Vegetable Parchment Producers*	Decision 78/252 OJ 1978 L70/54	85	Price-fixing, boycott	Dalle and Lecompte Feldmühle Nicolaus Rube Scheipen Serlachius	25,000 15,000 25,000 10,000 25,000 15,000	—	—
18. *Kawasaki*	Decision 79/68 OJ 1979 L16/9	85	Export ban	Kawasaki Motors (UK) Ltd	100,000	—	—
19. *Floral*	Decision 80/182 OJ 1980 L39/51	85	Export cartel	CFA GE SCC	85,000 85,000 85,000	—	—

Case	COMMISSION Ref.	Art.	Infringement	Company	Fine (ECU)	COURT OF JUSTICE Ref.	Decision
20. *Pioneer*	Decision 80/256 OJ 1980 L60/21	85	Export ban	Pioneer Electronic Europe (subsidiary of Pioneer, Japan) Exclusive distributors: Musique Diffusion Français C Melchers Pioneer High Fidelity	4,350,000 850,000 1,450,000 300,000	Joined Cases 100–103/80 *Musique Diffusion Français & Ors v EC Commission* [1983] ECR 1825	Fine reduced 2,000,000 600,000 400,000 200,000
21. *Johnson & Johnson*	Decision 80/1283 OJ 1980 L377/16	85	Export ban	Johnson & Johnson Wholly owned subsidiaries: Cilag Chemie GmbH Cilag Chemie AG Ortho Pharmaceutical (fines imposed jointly and severally)		—	—
22. *Michelin*	Decision 81/969 OJ 1981 L353/33	86	Discriminatory pricing	NV Nederlandsche Banden-Industrie Michelin	680,000	Case 322/81 *NV Nederlandsche Banden-Industrie Michelin v EC Commission* [1983] ECR 3461	Fine reduced to 300,000
23. *Moët et Chandon*	Decision 82/203 OJ 1982 L94/7	85	Export ban	Moët-Hennessey	1,100,000	—	—

	COMMISSION					COURT OF JUSTICE	
Case	Ref.	Art.	Infringement	Company	Fine (ECU)	Ref.	Decision
24. *Hasselblad*	Decision 82/367 OJ 1982 L161/18	85	Export ban, selective distribution, price resale maintenance	Hasselblad (GB) Ilford Telos Prolux Victor Hasselblad	165,000 10,000 10,000 10,000 560,000	Case 86/82 *Hasselblad (GB) Ltd v EC Commission* [1984] ECR 883	Fine on Hasselblad (GB) reduced to 80,000
25. *Navewa/ Anseau*	Decision 82/371 OJ 1982 L167/39	85	Prevention of parallel imports through conformity labelling	Bauknecht ACEC AEG Philips Miele, Industriepark Associated Consumer Brands Bosch Association Nationale des Services d'Eau (Anseau) Van Assche Hoover Zanker Disem-Andries Artsel IAZ Electrolux-Martin Siemens Van Maercke	76,500 38,500	Joined Cases 96– 102, 104, 105, 108 & 110/82 *NV IAZ Int'l Belgium & Ors v EC Commission* [1983] ECR 3369	Decision upheld

| Case | COMMISSION | | | | Fine (ECU) | COURT OF JUSTICE | |
	Ref.	Art.	Infringement	Company		Ref.	Decision
				Despagne Asogem Hobart Indesit Bell-Telephone BBC Hausgeräte GmbH (succ. belge)	9,500		
26. *AEG Telefunken*	Decision 82/267 OJ 1982 L117/115	85	Selective distribution; price resale maintenance	AEG-Telefunken	1,000,000	Case 107/82 *AEG-Telefunken AG v EC Commission* [1983] ECR 3151	Decision upheld AEG must pay default interest on fines
27. *Cigarettes*	Decision 82/506 OJ 1982 L232/1	85	Price-fixing	British-American Tobacco Co	350,000	Joined Cases 240–242, 261, 262, 268 & 269/82 *Stichting Sigarettenindustrie & Ors v EC Commission* [1985] ECR 3831	Decision upheld
				Sigarettenfabriek Ed Laurens BV	425,000		Decision upheld
				De Koninklijke Bedrijven Theodorus Niemeyer BV	100,000		Decision upheld
				Philip Morris Holland BV	125,000		
				RJ Reynolds Tobacco BV	150,000		Reynolds' fine reduced to 100,000
				Turmac Tobacco Co BV	325,000		Decision upheld
				Fines based on market share			Decision upheld

Case	COMMISSION Ref.	Art.	Infringement	Company	Fine (ECU)	COURT OF JUSTICE Ref.	Decision
28. *National Panasonic*	Decision 82/853 OJ 1982 L354/28	85	Export ban	National Panasonic (wholly owned subsidiary of Matsushita – Japan)	450,000	—	—
29. *Rolled Zinc Products*	Decision 82/866 OJ 1982 L362/40	85	Market-sharing, production control	CRAM Rheinische Zinkwalzwerk	400,000 500,000	Joined Cases 29 & 30/83 *Compagnie Royale Asturienne des Mines SA and Rheinzink GmbH v EC Commission* [1984] ECR 1679	Fine cancelled
30. *AROW/BNIC*	Decision 82/896 OJ 1982 L379/1	85	Price-fixing	BNIC	160,000	—	—
31. *Toltecs/Dorcet*	Decision 82/897 OJ 1982 L379/19	85	Extension of no-challenge clause	BAT Cigaretten-Fabrieken	50,000	Case 35/83 *BAT Cigaretten-Fabrieken GmbH v EC Commission* [1985] ECR 363	Fine cancelled
32. *Windsurfing International*	Decision 83/400 OJ 1983 L229/1	85	Exclusive patent licensing, export ban	WSI Licensees: Ostermann Akutec Klepper Shark WSC	50,000 15,000 10,000 10,000 5,000 5,000	Case 193/83 *Windsurfing International Inc v EC Commission* [1986] ECR 611	Fine on WSI reduced to 25,000
33. *Cast Iron and Steel Rolls*	Decision 83/546 OJ 1983 L317/1	85	Market-sharing, price-fixing	Fines imposed on 26 companies	8,000– 100,000	—	—

Case	COMMISSION Ref.	Art.	Infringement	Company	Fine (ECU)	COURT OF JUSTICE Ref.	Decision
34. *IPTC Belgium*	Decision 83/667 OJ 1983 L376/7	85	Conformity labelling, prevention of parallel imports	IPTC Belgium	5,000	—	—
35. *Polistil Arbois*	Decision 84/282 OJ 1984 L136/9	85	Prevention of parallel imports	Polistil Arbois	30,000 30,000	—	—
36. *BL*	Decision 84/379 OJ 1984 L207/11	86	Refusal to deal	BL	350,000	Case 226/84 *British Leyland (BL) plc v EC Commission* [1986] ECR 3263	Decision upheld
37. *Flat-glass Sector in the Benelux Countries*	Decision 84/388 OJ 1984 L212/13	85	Price-fixing, market-sharing	BSN Glaverbel Compagnie de Saint-Gobain Glaceries de Saint-Roch	935,000 850,000 1,450,000 765,000	—	—
38. *Zinc Producers*	Decision 84/405 OJ 1984 L220/27	85	Market-sharing, price-fixing, resale ban, production control	Billiton Nederland Metallgesellschaft Société Minière et Métallurgie de Penarroya Preussag Rio Tinto Zinc Corporation Union Minière	350,000 500,000 500,000 500,000 500,000 950,000	—	—
39. *Peroxygen Products*	Decision 85/74 OJ 1985 L35/1	85	Marekt-sharing, price-fixing	Solvay et Cie Laporte Industries Degussa AG L'Air Liquide SA Atochem	3,000,000 2,000,000 3,000,000 500,000 500,000	—	—

Case	COMMISSION Ref.	Art.	Infringement	Company	Fine (ECU)	COURT OF JUSTICE Ref.	Decision
40. *John Deere*	Decision 85/79 OJ 1985 L35/58	85	Export ban	Deere & Co	2,000,000	—	—
41. *Wood Pulp*	Decision 85/202 OJ 1985 L85/1	85	Price-fixing, export ban, resale bans	British Columbia Forest Products Ltd	100,000	Joined Cases 89, 104, 114, 116, 117 & 125–129/85 *Åhlström Oy & Ors v EC Commission* [1993] 1 CEC 466	Fine cancelled
				Canadian Forest Products Ltd	125,000		Canfor's fine reduced to 20,000
				McMillan Bloedel Ltd	150,000		McMillan's fine reduced to 20,000
				St Anne-Nackawick Pulp & Paper Co Ltd	200,000		St Anne's fine reduced to 20,000
				Weldwood of Canada Ltd	50,000		Fine cancelled
				Westar Timber Ltd	150,000		Westar's fine reduced to 20,000
				Bowater Incorporated	500,000		Fine cancelled
				Chesapeake Corp	50,000		Fine cancelled
				Crown Zellerbach	50,000		Fine cancelled
				Federal Paper Board Company, Inc	100,000		Fine cancelled
				Georgia-Pacific Corporation	150,000		Fine cancelled
				International Pulp Sales Company	250,000		Fine cancelled
				The Mead Corporation	50,000		Application dismissed
				Scott Paper Company	50,000		Fine cancelled

Case	COMMISSION			Company	Fine (ECU)	COURT OF JUSTICE	
	Ref.	Art.	Infringement			Ref.	Decision
				Weyerhaeuser Company	50,000		Fine cancelled
				Pulp, Paper and Paperboard Export Association of the United States (KEA)	50,000		Fine cancelled
				Åhlström Oy	50,000		Fine cancelled
				Ensos-Gutzeit Oy	200,000		Fine cancelled
				Joutenso-Pulp Co	50,000		Fine cancelled
				Kaukas AB Oy	100,000		Fine cancelled
				Kemi Oy	50,000		Fine cancelled
				Metsä-Botnia AB Oy	100,000		Fine cancelled
				Oulu Oy	100,000		Fine cancelled
				Wilh Schaumann AB Oy	100,000		Fine cancelled
				Veitsiluoto Oy	150,000		Fine cancelled
				Finncell	100,000		Decision upheld
				Billerud-Uddeholm			
				Iggesunds Bruk AB	50,000	—	—
				Kopparfors AB	50,000	—	—
				Korsnäs-Marma AB	50,000	—	—
				MoDoCell AB	50,000		
				Norrlands Skogägares Cellulosa AB	150,000	—	—
				Södra Skogsägarna AB	150,000	—	—

Case	COMMISSION				Fine (ECU)	COURT OF JUSTICE	
	Ref.	Art.	Infringement	Company		Ref.	Decision
				Stora Kopparbergs-Bergslags AB	200,000	—	—
				Svenska Cellulosa AB (SCA)	150,000	—	—
				Svenska Cellulosa- Och Papperbruks Föreningen	50,000	—	—
42. *Siemens/Fanuc*	Decision 85/618 OJ 1985 L376/29	85	Exclusive selling rights	Fanuc Ltd Siemens AG	1,000,000 1,000,000	—	—
43. *ECS/AKZO*	Decision 85/609 OJ 1985 L374/1	86	Unfair commercial practices, price cutting, discriminatory prices	AKZO Chemie BV	10,000,000	Case 62/86 *AKZO Chemie BV v EC Commission* [1993] 2 CEC 115	AKZO's fine reduced to 7,500,000
44. *Sperry New Holland*	Decision 85/617 OJ 1985 L376/32	85	Export ban, refusal to supply	Sperry New Holland Sperry NV	750,000	—	—

Case	COMMISSION				Fine (ECU)	COURT OF FIRST INSTANCE		COURT OF JUSTICE	
	Ref.	Art.	Infringement	Company		Ref.	Decision	Ref.	Decision
45. *Polypropylene*	Decision 86/398 OJ 1986 L230/1	85	Price-fixing, market-sharing, exchange of information	ANIC SpA	750,000	Case T-6/89 *Enichem Anic SpA v EC Commission* [1991] ECR II-1623	ANIC's fine reduced to 450,000	Case C-49/92 P *EC Commission v Enichem Anic SpA*, not yet decided	

Case	Ref.	COMMISSION Art.	Infringement	Company	Fine (ECU)	COURT OF FIRST INSTANCE Ref.	Decision	COURT OF JUSTICE Ref.	Decision
				Atochem	1,750,000	Case T-3/89 Atochem SA v EC Commission [1991] ECR II-1177	Decision upheld	—	—
				BASF AG	2,500,000	Case T-4/89 BASF Aktiengesellschaft v EC Commission [1991] ECR II-1523	Fine reduced to 2,125,000	Case C-255/92 P BASF Aktiengesellschaft v EC Commission, not yet decided	
				DSM NV	2,750,000	Case T-8/89 DSM NV v EC Commission [1991] ECR II-1833	Decision upheld	Case C-5/93 P DSM NV v EC Commission, not yet decided	
				Hercules Chemicals NV	2,750,000	Case T-7/89 SA Hercules Chemicals NV v EC Commission [1992] 1 CEC 207	Decision upheld	Case C-51/92 P SA Hercules NV v EC Commission, not yet decided	
				Hoechst AG	9,000,000	Case T-10/89 Hoechst Aktiengesellschaft v EC Commission [1992] ECR II-629	Decision upheld	Case C-227/92 P Hoechst Aktiengesellschaft v EC Commission, not yet decided	

Case	COMMISSION		Company	Fine (ECU)	COURT OF FIRST INSTANCE		COURT OF JUSTICE	
	Ref.	Art. Infringement			Ref.	Decision	Ref.	Decision
			Hüls AG	2,750,000	Case T-9/89 Hüls Aktiengesellschaft v EC Commission [1992] ECR II-499	Hüls' fine reduced to 2,337,500	Case C-199/92 P Hüls Aktiengesellschaft v EC Commission, not yet decided	
			ICI plc	10,000,000	Case T-13/89 Imperial Chemical Industries plc v EC Commission [1992] ECR II-1021	ICI's fine reduced to 9,000,000	Case C-200/92 P Imperial Chemical Industries plc v EC Commission, not yet decided	—
			Chemische Werke LINZ	1,000,000	Case T-15/89 Chemi Linz AG v EC Commission [1992] ECR II-1275	Decision upheld	—	
			Montedipe	11,000,000	Case T-14/89 Montedipe SpA v EC Commission [1992] ECR II-155	Decision upheld	Case C-235/92 P Montecatini SpA (formerly Montedipe SpA) v EC Commission, not yet decided	

| Case | COMMISSION | | Company | Fine (ECU) | COURT OF FIRST INSTANCE | | COURT OF JUSTICE | |
	Ref.	Art. Infringement			Ref.	Decision	Ref.	Decision
			Petrofina SA	600,000	Case T-2/89 *Petrofina SA v EC Commission* [1991] ECR II-1087	Petrofina's fine reduced to 300,000	—	—
			Rhône-Poulenc SA	500,000	Case T-1/89 *Rhône-Poulenc SA v EC Commission* [1991] ECR II-867	Decision upheld	—	—
			Shell International Chemical Co Ltd	9,000,000	Case T-11/89 *Shell International Chemical Co Ltd v EC Commission* [1992] ECR II-757	Shell's fine reduced to 8,100,000	Case C-234/92 P *Shell International Chemical Co Ltd v EC Commission*, not yet decided	—
			Solvay & Cie	2,500,000	Case T-12/89 *SA Solvay et Compagnie v EC Commission* [1992] ECR II-907	Decision upheld	—	—

| Case | COMMISSION | | | | Fine (ECU) | COURT OF FIRST INSTANCE | | COURT OF JUSTICE | |
	Ref.	Art.	Infringement	Company		Ref.	Decision	Ref.	Decision
				Statoil Den Norske Stats Oljeselskap AS (now incorporating SAGA Petrokjemi)	1,000,000	—	—	—	—
46. *Roofing Felt*	Decision 86/399 OJ 1986 L232/15	85	Price-fixing, setting of quotas for sales, co-ordinating product ranges	Antwerps Teeren Asfaltbedrijf NV	420,000	—	—	Case 246/86 *Belasco & Ors v EC Commission* [1989] 2 CEC 912	Decision upheld
				Compagnie Générale des Asphaltes SA	150,000	—	—		Decision upheld
				Lummerzheim & Co NV	20,000	—	—		Decision upheld
				Limburgse Asfalt-fabrikien PvbA	30,000	—	—		Decision upheld
				Kempische Asfaltbedrijf NV	75,000	—	—		Decision upheld
				De Boer & Co NV	75,000	—	—		Decision upheld

Case	COMMISSION Ref.	Art.	Infringement	Company	Fine (ECU)	COURT OF FIRST INSTANCE Ref.	Decision	COURT OF JUSTICE Ref.	Decision
48. *Fatty Acids*	Decision 87/1 OJ 1987 L3/17	85	Prevention of parallel imports	Unichema Henkel Oleofina	50,000 50,000 50,000	—	—	— —	— —
49. *Tipp-Ex*	Decision 87/406 OJ 1987 L222/1	85	Prevention of parallel imports	Tipp-Ex Vertrieb GmbH & Co KG Beiersdorf AG	400,000 10,000	—	—	Case 279/87 *Tipp-Ex GmbH & Co KG v EC Commission* [1990] ECR I-261	Decision upheld
50. *Sandoz*	Decision 87/409 OJ 1987 L222/28	85	Export ban	Sandoz PF	800,000	—	—	Case 277/87 *Sandoz Prodotti Farmaceutici SpA v EC Commission* [1990] ECR I-45	Sandoz's fine reduced to 500,000
51. *Fisher Price/ Quaker Oats Ltd – Toyco*	Decision 88/86 OJ 1988 L49/19	85	Export ban	Quaker Oats	300,000	—	—	—	—
52. *Konica*	Decision 88/172 OJ 1988 L78/34	85	Export ban, prevention of resale parallel imported products	Konica UK Ltd Konica Europe GmbH	75,000 75,000	—	—	— —	— —

Case	Ref.	Art.	COMMISSION Infringement	Company	Fine (ECU)	COURT OF FIRST INSTANCE Ref.	COURT OF FIRST INSTANCE Decision	COURT OF JUSTICE Ref.	COURT OF JUSTICE Decision
53. *Eurofix-Bauco/Hilti*	Decision 88/138 OJ 1988 L65/19	86	Refusal to supply	Hilti AG	6,000,000	Case T-30/89 *Hilti AG v EC Commission* [1992] 1 CEC 155	Decision upheld	Case C-53/92 P *Hilti AG v EC Commission*, not yet reported	Upheld
54. *BDTA*	Decision 88/477 OJ 1988 L233/15	86	Discriminatory refusal to promote products	BDTA	100,000	—	—	—	—
55. *Napier Brown/British Sugar*	Decision 88/518 OJ 1988 L284/41	86	Refusal to sell, discrimination, fidelity discounts	British Sugar plc	3,000,000	—	—	—	—
56. *Hudson's Bay – Dansk Pelsdyravlerforening*	Decision 88/587 [1989] 1 CEC 2,270	85	Forcing members to deal exclusively with OPF	Danish Fur Breeders Association	500,000	Case T-61/89 *Dansk Pelsdyravlerforening v EC Commission* [1992] ECR II-1931	Dansk's fine reduced to 300,000	—	—
57. *London European – Sabena*	Decision 88/589 [1989] 1 CEC 2,278	86	Act to drive competitor from market	Sabena	100,000	—	—	—	—
58. *BPB Industries plc*	Decision 89/22 [1989] 1 CEC 2,008	86	Fidelity rebates	British Gypsum Ltd BPB Industries plc	3,000,000 150,000	Case T-65/89 *BPB Industries plc & Anor v EC Commission* [1993] 1 CEC 713	Decision upheld	Case C-310/93 P *BPB Industries plc & Anor v EC Commission*, not yet decided	—

Case	Ref.	COMMISSION Art.	Infringement	Company	Fine (ECU)	COURT OF FIRST INSTANCE Ref.	COURT OF FIRST INSTANCE Decision	COURT OF JUSTICE Ref.	COURT OF JUSTICE Decision
59. *Flat Glass*	Decision 89/93 [1989] 1 CEC 2,077	85 & 86	Market-sharing, price-fixing	Fabbrica Pisana SpA	7,000,000	Joined Cases T-68/89, T-77/89 & T-78/89 *Società Italiano Vetro SpA (SIV) & Ors v EC Commission* [1992] 2 CEC 33	Fabbrica Pisana's fine reduced to 1,000,000	—	—
				Società Italiana Vetro-SIV SpA	4,700,000		Italiana Vetro's fine reduced to 671,428	—	—
				Vernante Pennitalia SpA	1,700,000	—	Fine cancelled	—	—
60. *PVC*	Decision 89/190 [1989] 1 CEC 2,167	85	Market-sharing, price-fixing	Atochem SA	3,200,000	Joined Cases T-79/89, T-84/89–T-86/89, T-89/89–T-91/89, T-92/89, T-94/89, T-96/89, T-98/89, T-102/89 & T-104/89 *BASF AG & Ors v EC Commission* [1992] 1 CEC 519	Decision non-existent	Case C-137/92 P *EC Commission v BASF Aktiengesellschaft & Ors* [1994] 2 CEC 152	
				BASF AG	1,500,00				
				DSM NV	600,000				
				Enichem SpA	2,500,000				
				Hoechst AG	1,500,000				
				Huels AG	2,200,000				
				Imperial Chemical Industries plc	2,500,000				
				Limburgse Vinyl Maatschappij	750,000				
				Montedison SpA	1,750,000				

| Case | COMMISSION | | | | | COURT OF FIRST INSTANCE | | COURT OF JUSTICE | |
	Ref.	Art.	Infringement	Company	Fine (ECU)	Ref.	Decision	Ref.	Decision
				Société Artésienne de vinyl	400,000				
				Shell International Chemical Co Ltd	850,000				
				Wacker Chemie GmbH	1,500,000				
				Solvay et Cie	3,500,000				
				Norsk Hydro AS	750,000				
61. *LdPE*	Decision 89/91 [1989] 1 CEC 2,193	85	Price-fixing, sale quotas	Atochem SA	3,600,000	Case T-90/89 *Atochem SA v EC Commission*, not yet decided			
				BASF AG	5,500,000	Case T-80/89 *BASF Aktiengesellschaft v EC Commission*, not yet decided			
				BP Chemicals Ltd	750,000	—			
				Bayer AG	2,500,000	Case T-88/89 *Bayer AG v EC Commission*, not yet decided	—		

| Case | Ref. | COMMISSION | | Company | Fine (ECU) | COURT OF FIRST INSTANCE | | COURT OF JUSTICE | |
		Art.	Infringement			Ref.	Decision	Ref.	Decision
				Chemie Holding AG	500,000	Case T-107/89 *Chemie Holding AG v EC Commission,* not yet decided			
				Dow Chemical Co	2,250,000	Case T-112/89 *Dow Chemical Co v EC Commission,* not yet decided			
				DSM NV	3,300,000	Case T-83/89 *DSM NV and DSM Kunststoffen BV v EC Commission,* not yet decided			
				Enichem SpA	4,000,000	Case T-95/89 *Enichem SpA v EC Commission,* not yet decided			
				Hoechst AG	1,000,000	Case T-97/89 *Hoechst Aktiengesellschaft v EC Commission,* not yet decided			

Case	COMMISSION			Company	Fine (ECU)	COURT OF FIRST INSTANCE		COURT OF JUSTICE	
	Ref.	Art.	Infringement			Ref.	Decision	Ref.	Decision
				Imperial Chemical Industries plc	3,500,000	Case T-99/89 *Imperial Chemical Industries plc v EC Commission,* not yet decided			
				Montedison SpA	2,500,000	Case T-105/89 *Montedison SpA v EC Commission,* not yet decided			
				Monsanto Co	150,000	Case T-81/89 *Monsanto Co v EC Commission,* not yet decided			
				Neste Oy	1,000,000	Case T-100/89 *Neste Oy v EC Commission,* not yet decided			
				Orkem SA	5,000,000	Case T-87/89 *Orkem SA v EC Commission,* not yet decided			
				Repsol Quimica SA	100,000	Case T-101/89 *Repsol Quimica SA v EC Commission,* not yet decided			

Case	COMMISSION				Fine (ECU)	COURT OF FIRST INSTANCE		COURT OF JUSTICE	
	Ref.	Art.	Infringement	Company		Ref.	Decision	Ref.	Decision
62. *Welded Steel Mesh*	Decision 89/515 [1989] 2 CEC 2,051	85	Price-fixing, delivery quotas, market-sharing	Shell International Chemical Co Ltd	850,000	Case T-103/89 *Shell International Chemical Co Ltd v EC Commission*, not yet decided			
				Statoil-Den Norske Stats Oljeselskap AS	500,000	Case T-93/89 *Den Norske Stats Oljeselskap AS (Statoil) v EC Commission*, not yet decided			
				Tréfilunion SA (TU)	1,375,000	Case T-148/89 *Société Tréfilunion v EC Commission*, not yet decided			
				Société Métallurgique de Normandie (SMN)	50,000	Case T-147/89 *Société Métallurgique de Normandie v EC Commission*, not yet decided			
				Société des Treillis et Panneaux Soudés (STPS)	150,000	Case T-151/89 *Société des Treillis et Panneaux Soudés (STPS) v EC Commission*, not yet decided			

Case	Ref.	COMMISSION		Company	Fine (ECU)	COURT OF FIRST INSTANCE		COURT OF JUSTICE	
		Art.	Infringement			Ref.	Decision	Ref.	Decision
				Sotralentz SA	228,000	Case T-149/89 *Sotralentz SA v EC Commission*, not yet decided			
				Tréfilarbed Luxembourg Saarbrüken Sarl	1,143,000	Case T-141/89 *Société Tréfilarbed Luxembourg-Saarbrüken Sarl v EC Commission*, not yet decided			
				Steelinter SA	315,000	Case T-144/89 *Steelinter SA v EC Commission*, not yet decided			
				NV Usines Gustave Boël, Afdeling Trébos	550,000	Case T-142/89 *Usines Gustave Boël SA v EC Commission*. not yet decided			
				Thibo Bouwstaal BV	420,000	—	—		
				Van Merksteijn Staalbouw BV	375,000	—	—		
				ZND Bouwstaal BV	42,000	—	—		

Case	COMMISSION Ref.	Art.	Infringement	Company	Fine (ECU)	COURT OF FIRST INSTANCE Ref.	Decision	COURT OF JUSTICE Ref.	Decision
				Baustahl-gewebe GmbH (BStG)	4,500,000	Case T-145/89 *Baustahlgewebe GmbH v EC Commission*, not yet decided			
				ILRO Spa	13,000	Case T-152/89 *ILRO SpA v EC Commission*, not yet decided			
				Ferriere Nord SpA (Pittini)	320,000	—			
				GB Martinelli fu GB Metallurgica SpA	20,000	Case T-150/89 *GB Martinelli fu GB Metallurgica SpA v EC Commission*, not yet decided			
63. *Bayo-n-ox*	Decision 90/38 [1990] 1 CEC 2,066	85	Export ban, market-sharing	Bayer AG	500,000	Case T-12/90 *Bayer AG v EC Commission* [1991] ECR II-219	Application dismissed	Case C-195/91 P *Bayer AG v EC Commission*, not yet decided	
64. *Soda-ash – Solvay, ICI*	Decision 91/297 [1991] 2 CEC 2,003	85	Market-sharing	Solvay et Cie SA	7,000,000	Case T-30/91 *SA Solvay et Cie v EC Commission*, not yet decided			

| Case | COMMISSION | | | | Fine (ECU) | COURT OF FIRST INSTANCE | | COURT OF JUSTICE | |
	Ref.	Art.	Infringement	Company		Ref.	Decision	Ref.	Decision
				Imperial Chemical Industries plc	7,000,000	Case T-36/91 *Imperial Chemical Industries plc (ICI) v EC Commission*, not yet decided			
65. *Soda-ash – Solvay, CFK*	Decision 91/298 [1991] 2 CEC 2,022	85	Market-sharing	Solvay et Cie SA	3,000,000	Case T-31/91 SA *Solvay et Cie v EC Commission*, not yet decided			
				Chemische Fabrik Kalk GmbH	1,000,000				
66. *Soda-ash – Solvay*	Decision 91/299 [1991] 2 CEC 2,029	86	'Unofficial' exclusivity agreements, fidelity rebates	Solvay et Cie SA	20,000,000	Case T-32/91 SA *Solvay et Cie v EC Commission*, not yet decided			
67. *Soda-ash – ICI*	Decision 91/300 [1991] 2 CEC 2,053	86	Rebates 'unofficial' exclusivity agreements	Imperial Chemical Industries plc	10,000,000	Case T-37/91 *Imperial Chemical Industries plc (ICI) v EC Commission*, not yet decided			

Case	COMMISSION Ref.	Art.	Infringement	Company	Fine (ECU)	COURT OF FIRST INSTANCE Ref.	Decision	COURT OF JUSTICE Ref.	Decision
68. *Gosmel Martell – DMP*	Decision 91/335 [1991] 2 CEC 2.110	85	Export ban, discouragement of parallel trade	Martell et Cie SA	300,000	—	—		
				Distribution Martell Piper SA	50,000	—	—		
69. *Viho/Toshiba*	Decision 91/532 [1991] 2 CEC 2,196	85	Export ban	Toshiba Europa (IE) GmbH	2,000,000	—	—		
70. *Tetra Pak II*	Decision 92/163 [1992] 1 CEC 2,145	86	Restriction of supplies, market division, tying arrangement, discrimination between users, practices intended to eliminate competitors	Tetra Pak International SA	75,000,000	Case T-83/91 *Tetra Pak International SA v EC Commission*, not yet decided			
71. *Building and Construction Industry in the Netherlands*	Decision 92/204 [1992] 1 CEC 2,220	85	Exchange of information, concerted action on prices, market-sharing	Amsterdamse Aannemers Vereniging	1,451.250	Case T-29/92 *Vereniging van Samenwerkende Prijsregelende Organisaties in de Bouwnijverheid v EC Commission*, not yet decided			

Case	COMMISSION					COURT OF FIRST INSTANCE		COURT OF JUSTICE	
	Ref.	Art.	Infringement	Company	Fine (ECU)	Ref.	Decision	Ref.	Decision
				Algemene Aannemers- vereniging voor Water- bouwk- undige Werken	436,500				
				Aannemers- vereniging van Boor- ondernemers en Buizen- leggers	436,500				
				Aannemers- vereniging Velsen Beverwijk en Omstreken	202,500				
				Aannemers Vereniging Haarlem- Bollenstreek	337,500				
				Aanemers- vereniging Veluwe en Zuidelijke IJsselmeer- polders	445,000				

| Case | COMMISSION | | | | | COURT OF FIRST INSTANCE | | COURT OF JUSTICE | |
	Ref.	Art. Infringement	Company	Fine (ECU)		Ref.	Decision	Ref.	Decision
			Combinatie van Aannemers in het Noorden	198,000					
			Vereniging Centrale Prijsregeling Kabelwerken	180,000					
			Delftse Aannemers Vereniging	162,000					
			Economisch Nationaal Verbond van Aannemers van Sloopwerken	184,500					
			Aannemersvereniging 'Gouda en Omstreken'	249,750					
			Gelderse Aannemers Vereniging inzake Aanbestedingen	996,750					
			Gooise Aannemers Vereniging	270,000					

Case	COMMISSION Ref.	Art. Infringement	Company	Fine (ECU)	COURT OF FIRST INSTANCE Ref.	Decision	COURT OF JUSTICE Ref.	Decision
			's-Gravenhaagse Aannemersvereniging	1.188.000				
			Leidse Aannemersvereniging	317,250				
			Vereniging Markeer Aannemers Combinatie	38,250				
			Nederlandse Aannemers- en Patroonsbond voor de Bouwbedrijven (NAPB Dordrecht)	324,000				
			Noord-hollandse Aannemers Vereniging voor Waterbouwkundige Werken	238,500				
			Oostnederlandse Vereniging Aanbestedings Regeling	1,116,000				

| Case | Ref. | COMMISSION | | Company | Fine (ECU) | COURT OF FIRST INSTANCE | | COURT OF JUSTICE | |
		Art.	Infringement			Ref.	Decision	Ref.	Decision
				Provinciale Vereniging van Bouwbe-drijven in Groningen en Drenthe	474,750				
				Rotterdamse Aanemers-vereniging	2,103,750				
				Aannemers-vereniging 'de Rijn-streek'	96,750				
				Stichting Aan-bestedings-regeling van de Samen-werkende Bouwbed-rijven in Friesland	384,750				
				Samenwerk-ende Prijs-regelende Vereniging Nijmegen en Omstreken	200,250				

| Case | COMMISSION | | | | | COURT OF FIRST INSTANCE | | COURT OF JUSTICE | |
	Ref.	Art.	Infringement	Company	Fine (ECU)	Ref.	Decision	Ref.	Decision
				Samenwerkende Patroons Verenigingen in de Bouwbedrijven Noord-Holland-Noord	670,500				
				Utrechtse Aannemers Vereniging	1,055,250				
				Vereniging Wegenbouw Aannemers Combinatie Nederland	4,792,500				
				Zuid Nederlandse Aannemers Vereniging	3,948,750				
72. *Eurocheque: Helsinki Agreement*	Decision 92/212 [1992] 1 CEC 2.275	85	Price-fixing agreement	Groupement des cartes bancaires 'CB'	5,000,000	Case T-39/92 *Groupement des cartes bancaires 'CB' v EC Commission* [1994] 1 CEC 494	CB's fine reduced to 2,000,000		

Case	COMMISSION Ref.	Art.	Infringement	Company	Fine (ECU)	COURT OF FIRST INSTANCE Ref.	Decision	COURT OF JUSTICE Ref.	Decision
73. *British Midland v Aer Lingus* (Fine imposed pursuant to art. 12(2) of Regulation 397/87)	Decision 92/213 [1992] 1 CEC 2,261	85 & 86	Unlawful participation in a tarrif consultation, refusal to grant interline	Eurocheque International SC	1,000,000	Case T-40/92 *Eurocheque International SC v EC Commission*	Decision annulled		
				Aer Lingus plc	750,000	—	—		
74. *Newitt/ Dunlop Slazenger International & Ors*	Decision 92/261 [1992] 2 CEC 2,003	85	Export ban, dissuasive measures aimed at strengthening the export ban	Dunlop Slazenger International Ltd	5,000,000	Case T-43/92 *Dunlop Slazenger International Ltd v EC Commission*, not yet decided			
				All Weather Sports Benelux BV	150,000	Case T-38/92 *All Weather Sports Benelux BV v EC Commission* [1994] 2 CEC 3	Fine cancelled		

Case	Ref.	COMMISSION				COURT OF FIRST INSTANCE		COURT OF JUSTICE	
		Art.	Infringement	Company	Fine (ECU)	Ref.	Decision	Ref.	Decision
75. *French-West African Shipowners' Committees* (Fine imposed pursuant to art. 19(2) of Regulation 4056/86)	Decision 92/262 [1992] 2 CEC 2,028	85 & 86	Allocation of cargo quotas, application of a system of penalties for breach of the quota rules, application of a co-option mechanism excluding shipowners from the trade	Delmas (L Martin and Maurel and Prom included)	11,628,000	—	—		
				Hoegh SWAL	651,000	—	—		
				RMS Afrika	2,400	—	—		
				UWAS	56,400	—	—		
				Splosna Plovba	2,800	—	—		
				Deep Sea Shipping	3,400	—	—		
				East Asiatic Co WAS	55,800	—	—		
				I Messina	4,600	—	—		
				Lloyd Triestino	32,800	—	—		
				Transmare	12,800	—	—		
				Van Uden	10,100	—	—		
				Nedlloyd	25,800	—	—		
				Compagnie Maritime Belge	46,000	—	—		
				Mac Lines	10,100	—	—		
				Société Navale de l'Ouest	1,751,000	—	—		
				Société Navale Caennaise	970,000	—	—		
				Deutsche Afrika Linien-Woermann	43,200	—	—		

Case	COMMISSION Ref.	Art.	Infringement	Company	Fine (ECU)	COURT OF FIRST INSTANCE Ref.	Decision	COURT OF JUSTICE Ref.	Decision
76. *Vitho/Parker Pen*	Decision 92/246	85	Export ban	Parker Pen Ltd	700,000	Case T-77/92 *Parker Pen Ltd v EC Commission*, not yet decided			
				Herlitz AG	40,000	Case T-66/92 *Herlitz AG v EC Commission*, not yet decided			
77. *Distribution of Railway Tickets by Travel Agents*	Decision 92/568 [1993] 1 CEC 2,078	85	Imposition of conditions for the approval of travel agencies, single rate of commission, prohibition on agencies from passing on part of their commission to customers	International Union of Railways	1,000,000	Case T-14/93 *International Union of Railways v EC Commission*, not yet decided			
78. *Cewal & Ors* (Fine imposed pursuant to art. 19(2) of Regulation 4056/86)	Decision 93/82 [1993] 1 CEC 2,144	85	Market-sharing	Compagnie Maritime Belge	9,600,000	Case T-24/93 *Compagnie Maritime Belge v EC Commission*, not yet decided			

| Case | COMMISSION | | | | Fine (ECU) | COURT OF FIRST INSTANCE | | COURT OF JUSTICE | |
	Ref.	Art.	Infringement	Company		Ref.	Decision	Ref.	Decision
				Dafra Line	200,000	Case T-25/93 *Dafra-Lines A/S v EC Commission*, not yet decided			
				Nedlloyd Lijnen BV	100,000	Case T-28/93 *Nedlloyd Lijnen BV v EC Commission*, not yet decided			
				Deutsche Afrika Linien-Woermann Linie	200,000	Case T-26/93 *Deutsche Afrika-Linien GmbH v EC Commission*, not yet decided			
79. *HOV SVZ/ MCN*	Decision 94/210 [1994] 1 CEC 2.163	86	Discriminatory pricing	Deutsche Bahn	11,000,000				

Annex 2

MERGER CONTROL CASES
NOTIFICATIONS PUBLISHED IN OJ 1990

Case	Parties	Notification	Decision	Outcome	Sector/Product
M004	Renault/Volvo	04.10.90 C-254/3 of 09.10.90	06.11.90 C-281/2 of 09.11.90	NC	Motor vehicles
M018	Groupe AG/Amev	19.10.90 C-268/8 of 24.10.90	21.11.90 C-304/27 of 04.12.90	NSD	Insurance
M023	ICI/Tioxide	30.10.90 C-278/15 of 06.11.90	28.11.90 C-304/27 of 04.12.90	NSD	Chemicals
M025	Arjomari-Prioux/Wiggins Teape Appleton	08.11.90 C-285/18 of 13.11.90	10.12.90 C-321/16 of 21.12.90	NCOD	Pulp & Paper
M027	Promodes/Dirsa	15.11.90 C-290/16 of 20.11.90	17.12.90 C-321/16 of 21.12.90	NSD	Retail distribution
M026	Cargill/Unilever	20.11.90 C-293/8 of 23.11.90	20.12.90 C-327/14 of 29.12.90	NSD	Agricultural merchanting
M024	Mitsubishi/UCAR	26.11.90 C-300/8 of 29.11.90	04.01.91 C-5/7 of 09.01.91	NSD	Carbon & Graphite
M037	Matsushita/MCA	03.12.90 C-307/2 of 07.12.90	10.01.91 C-12/15 of 18.01.91	NSD	Consumer electronics & Entertainment
M050	AT & T/NCR	07.12.90 C-310/23 of 11.12.90	18.01.91 C-16/20 of 24.01.91	NSD	Information technology
M042	Alcatel/Telettra	10.12.90 C-315/13 of 14.12.90	12.04.91 L-122/48 of 17.05.91	C	Telecommunications
M043	Magneti Marelli/CEAc	10.12.90 C-315/14 of 14.12.90	29.05.91 L-222/38 of 10.08.91	C	Automotive/Batteries

Outcome: NC = not concentration, NCOD = no community dimension, MS = referred to Member State, NSD = no serious doubts, C = compatible, I = Incompatible

NOTIFICATIONS PUBLISHED IN OJ 1991

Case	Parties	Notification	Decision	Outcome	Sector/Product
M021	BNP/Dresdner Bank	21.12.90 C-5/7 of 09.01.91	04.02.91 C-34/20 of 09.02.91	NSD	Banking
M058	Baxter/Nestlé/Salvia	04.01.91 C-7/3 of 11.01.91	06.02.91 C-37/11 of 13.02.91	NC	Clinical nutrition
M009	Fiat Geotech/Ford New Holland	07.01.91 C-8/7 of 12.01.91	08.02.91 C-118/14 of 03.05.91	NSD	Agricultural machinery
M065	ASKO/Omni	21.01.91 C-18/13 of 26.01.91	21.02.91 C-51/12 of 27.02.91	NSD	Diverse
M057	Digital/Kienzle	22.01.91 C-18/15 of 26.01.91	22.02.91 C-56/16 of 05.03.91	NSD	Computers
M017	Aerospatiale/MBB	23.01.91 C-18/14 of 26.01.91	25.02.91 C-59/13 of 08.03.91	NSD	Helicopters
M069	Kyowa/Saitama Banks	06.02.91 C-36/15 of 12.02.91	07.03.91 C-66/13 of 14.03.91	NSD	Banking
M068	Tetra Pak/Alfa-Laval	06.02.91 C-36/15 of 12.02.91	19.07.91 L-290/35 of 22.10.91	C	Packaging
M070	Otto/Grattan	22.02.91 C-51/5 of 27.02.91	21.03.91 C-93/6 of 11.04.91	NSD	Mail order
M012	Varta/Bosch	25.02.91 C-55/4 of 02.03.91	31.07.91 L-320/26 of 21.11.91	C	Batteries
M073	Usinor/ASD	22.03.91 C-84/7 of 28.03.91	29.04.91 C-193/34 of 24.07.91	NSD	Steel
M063	Elf/Ertoil	22.03.91 C-84/8 of 28.03.91	29.04.91 C-124/13 of 14.05.91	NSD	Petrochemicals

Outcome: NC = not concentration, NCOD = no community dimension, MS = referred to Member State, NSD = no serious doubts, C = compatible, I = Incompatible

NOTIFICATIONS PUBLISHED IN OJ 1991

Case	Parties	Notification	Decision	Outcome	Sector/Product
M080	La Redoute/Empire	25.03.91 C-87/10 of 04.04.91	25.04.91 C-156/10 of 14.06.91	NSD	Mail order
M082	ASKO/Jacobs/ADIA	09.04.91 C-100/18 of 17.04.91	16.05.91 C-132/13 of 23.05.91	NSD	Diverse
M010	Conagra/Idea	25.04.91 C-118/14 of 03.05.91	30.05.91 C-175/18 of 06.07.91	NSD	Meat
M092	RVI/VBC/Heuliez	29.04.91 C-119/12 of 04.05.91	03.06.91 C-149/15 of 08.06.91	NSD	Motor vehicles
M081	VIAG/Continental Can	30.04.91 C-119/13 of 04.05.91	06.06.91 C-156/10 of 14.06.91	NSD	Packaging
M072	Sanofi/Sterling Drug	03.05.91 C-123/28 of 09.05.91	10.06.91 C-156/10 of 14.06.91	NSD	Pharmaceuticals
M085	Elf/Occidental	13.05.91 C-126/7 of 16.05.91	13.06.91 C-160/20 of 20.06.91	NSD	Petrochemicals
M053	Aérospatiale-Alenia/de Havilland	13.05.91 C-128/13 of 18.05.91	02.10.91 L-334/42 of 05.12.91	I	Aviation
M098	Elf/BC/Cepsa	16.05.91 C-132/12 of 23.05.91	18.06.91 C-172/8 of 03.07.91	NSD	Petrochemicals
M097	Péchiney/Usinor-Sacilor	21.05.91 C-135/15 of 25.05.91	24.06.91 C-175/18 of 06.07.91	NSD	Steel
M093	Apollinaris/Schweppes	22.05.91 C-137/18 of 28.05.91	24.06.91 C-203/14 of 02.08.91	NC	Beverages
M099	Nissan/R. Nissan	27.05.91 C-142/10 of 31.05.91	28.06.91 C-181/21 of 12.07.91	NSD	Motor vehicles/Distribution

Outcome: NC = not concentration, NCOD = no community dimension, MS = referred to Member State, NSD = no serious doubts, C = compatible, I = Incompatible

NOTIFICATIONS PUBLISHED IN OJ 1991

Case	Parties	Notification	Decision	Outcome	Sector/Product
M101	Dräger/IBM/HMP	27.05.91 C-142/11 of 31.05.91	28.06.91 C-236/6 of 11.09.91	NSD	Information technology
M076	Lyonnaise des eaux Dumez/Hans Brochier	10.06.91 C-156/9 of 14.06.91	11.07.91 C-188/20 of 19.07.91	NSD	Utilities
M105	ICL/Nokia Data	14.06.91 C-162/10 of 21.06.91	17.07.91 C-236/6 of 11.09.91	NSD	Computers
M112	EDS/SD-Scicon	18.06.91 C-162/11 of 21.06.91	17.07.91 C-237/44 of 12.09.91	NSD	Information technology
M088	Elf/Enterprise	21.06.91 C-166/16 of 26.06.91	24.07.91 C-203/14 of 02.08.91	NC	Oil & Gas
M111	BP/Petromed	28.06.91 C-172/9 of 03.07.91	29.07.91 C-208/24 of 09.08.91	NSD	Petrochemicals
M062	Eridania/ISI	04.07.91 C-175/19 of 06.07.91	30.07.91 C-204/12 of 03.08.91	NSD	Sugar
M116	Kelt/American Express	18.07.91 C-189/25 of 20.07.91	20.08.91 C-223/38 of 28.08.91	NSD	Oil & Gas
M124	BNP/Dresdner Bank – Czechoslovakia	24.07.91 C-198/27 of 27.07.91	26.08.91 C-226/28 of 31.08.91	NSD	Banking
M129	Digital/Philips	30.07.91 C-206/9 of 07.08.91	02.09.91 C-235/13 of 10.09.91	NSD	Computers
M110	ABC/Générale des Eaux/ Canal-+/W H Smith TV	07.08.91 C-209/17 of 10.08.91	10.09.91 C-224/5 of 19.09.91	NSD	Broadcasting
M130	Delta/Pan Am	09.08.91 C-213/20 of 15.08.91	13.09.91 C-289/14 of 07.11.91	NSD	Air transport

Outcome: NC = not concentration, NCOD = no community dimension, MS = referred to Member State, NSD = no serious doubts, C = compatible, I = Incompatible

NOTIFICATIONS PUBLISHED IN OJ 1991

Case	Parties	Notification	Decision	Outcome	Sector/Product
M134	Mannesmann/Boge	22.08.91 C-223/39 of 28.08.91	23.09.91 C-265/8 of 11.10.91	NSD	Automotives/Shock absorbers
M119	Metallgesellschaft/ Feldmühle	11.09.91 C-242/7 of 17.09.91	14.10.91 C-276/4 of 23.10.91	NSD	Metals
M122	Paribas/MBH	16.09.91 C-245/16 of 20.09.91	17.10.91 C-277/18 of 24.10.91	NSD	Wholesale distribution
M137	Bank America/Security Pacific	23.09.91 C-251/10 of 26.09.91	24.10.91 C-289/14 of 07.11.91	NSD	Banking
M146	Metallgesellschaft/Safic Alcan	04.10.91 C-265/7 of 11.10.91	08.11.91 C-300/22 of 21.11.91	NSD	Rubber
M141	UAP/Transatlantic/ Sun Life	07.10.91 C-264/12 of 10.10.91	11.11.91 C-296/12 of 15.11.91	NSD	Insurance
M086	Thomson/Pilkington	20.09.91 C-250/31 of 25.09.91	23.10.91 C-279/19 of 26.10.91	NSD	Optronics
M102	TNT/Canada Post, DBP Postdienst, La Poste, PTT Post and Sweden Post	28.10.91 C-284/23 of 31.10.91	02.12.91 C-322/19 of 13.12.91	NSD	Mail
M156	Cereol/Continentale	30.10.91 C-288/13 of 06.11.91	27.11.91 C-7/7 of 11.01.92	NCOD	Oil seed
M165	Alcatel/AEG Kabel	05.11.91 C-292/16 of 09.11.91	18.12.91 C-6/23 of 10.01.92	NSD	Cables
M149	Lucas/Eaton	06.11.91 C-293/11 of 12.11.91	09.12.91 C-328/15 of 17.12.91	NSD	Automotive/Brakes

Outcome: NC = not concentration, NCOD = no community dimension, MS = referred to Member State, NSD = no serious doubts, C = compatible, I = Incompatible

NOTIFICATIONS PUBLISHED IN OJ 1991

Case	Parties	Notification	Decision	Outcome	Sector/Product
M164	Mannesmann/VDO	12.11.91 C-297/10 of 16.11.91	13.12.91 C-88/13 of 09.04.92	NSD	Automotive
M126	Accor/Wagons-Lits	14.11.91 C-298/23 of 19.11.91	28.04.92 L-204/1 of 21.07.92	C	Travel & tourism
M147	Eurocom/RSCG	15.11.91 C-300/21 of 21.11.91	18.12.91 C-332/16 of 21.12.91	NSD	Advertising
M138	Campsa	19.11.91 C-302/19 of 22.11.91	19.12.91 C-344/23 of 28.12.91	NSD	Petrochemicals/Distribution
M113	Courtaulds/SNIA	19.11.91 C-304/18 of 23.11.91	19.12.91 C-333/16 of 24.12.91	NSD	Textiles
M121	Ingersoll Rand/Dresser	19.11.91 C-304/19 of 23.11.91	18.12.91 C-86/15 of 07.04.92	NSD	Industrial pumps
M167	Gambogi/Cogei	19.11.91 C-304/20 of 23.11.91	19.12.91 C-334/23 of 28.12.91	NSD	Construction
M139	VIAG/EB-Brühl	19.11.91 C-306/17 of 26.11.91	19.12.91 C-333/16 of 24.12.91	NSD	Automotive/Engine blocks
M159	Mediobanca/Generali	27.11.91 C-310/35 of 30.11.91	19.12.91 C-334/23 of 28.12.91	NC	Insurance
M176	Sunrise	27.11.91 C-312/23 of 03.12.91	13.01.92 C-18/15 of 24.01.92	NC	Broadcasting
M178	Saab Ericsson Space	29.11.91 C-314/24 of 05.12.91	13.01.92 C-17/10 of 23.01.92	NSD	Aerospace
M152	Volvo/Atlas	05.12.91 C-302/12 of 11.12.91	14.01.92 C-17/10 of 23.01.92	NSD	Automotive/Hydraulics

Outcome: NC = not concentration, NCOD = no community dimension, MS = referred to Member State, NSD = no serious doubts, C = compatible, I = Incompatible

NOTIFICATIONS PUBLISHED IN OJ 1991

Case	Parties	Notification	Decision	Outcome	Sector/Product
M182	Inchcape/IEP	10.12.91 C-325/26 of 14.12.91	21.01.92 C-21/27 of 28.01.92	NSD	Motor vehicles/Distribution
M133	Ericsson/Kolbe	11.12.91 C-329/23 of 18.12.91	22.01.92 C-27/14 of 04.02.92	NSD	Telecommunications
M183	Schweizer Rück/Elvia	16.12.91 C-331/19 of 20.12.91	14.01.92 C-27/14 of 04.02.92	NSD	Insurance

Outcome: NC = not concentration, NCOD = no community dimension, MS = referred to Member State, NSD = no serious doubts, C = compatible, I = Incompatible

NOTIFICATIONS PUBLISHED IN OJ 1992

Case	Parties	Notification	Decision	Outcome	Sector/Product
M180	Steetley/Tarmac	20.12.91 C-1/13 of 04.01.92	12.02.92 C-50/25 of 25.02.92	NSD MS	Construction
M179	SPAR/Dansk Supermarked	20.12.91 C-6/21 of 10.01.92	03.02.91 C-29/18 of 06.02.92	NSD	Food retailing
M184	Grand Metropolitan/Cinzano	06.01.92 C-6/22 of 10.01.92	07.02.92 C-47/23 of 21.02.92	NSD	Beverages
M162	James River/Rayne	10.01.92 C-11/10 of 17.01.92	13.02.92 C-43/19 of 18.02.92	NSD	Paper
M090	BSN-Nestlé/Cokoladovny	16.01.92 C-16/15 of 22.01.92	17.02.92 C-47/23 of 21.02.92	NC	Foodstuffs
M166	Torras/Sarrio	22.01.92 C-21/26 of 28.01.92	24.02.92 C-58/20 of 05.03.92	NSD	Pulp & Paper
M187	Ifint/EXOR	30.01.92 C-27/15 of 04.02.92	02.03.92 C-88/13 of 09.04.92	NSD	Mineral water
M186	Henkel/Nobel	20.02.92 C-52/16 of 27.02.92	23.03.92 C-96/23 of 15.04.92	NSD	Cosmetics
M190	Nestlé/Perrier	25.02.92 C-53/19 of 28.02.92	22.07.92 L-356/1 of 05.12.92	C	Mineral water
M189	Generali/BCHA	05.03.92 C-62/3 of 11.03.92	06.04.92 C-107/24 of 28.04.92	NSD	Insurance
M168	Flachglas/Vegla	11.03.92 C-68/21 of 17.03.92	13.04.92 C-120/30 of 12.05.92	NC	Glass
M192	Banesto/Totta	13.03.92 C-70/19 of 19.03.92 corr. C-73/18 of 24.03.92	14.04.92 C-107/24 of 28.04.92	NSD	Financial services

Outcome: NC = not concentration, NCOD = no community dimension, MS = referred to Member State, NSD = no serious doubts, C = compatible, I = Incompatible

NOTIFICATIONS PUBLISHED IN OJ 1992

Case	Parties	Notification	Decision	Outcome	Sector/Product
M211	BSN/EXOR	17.03.92 C-72/24 of 21.03.92	01.04.92 C-115/43 of 06.05.92	withdrawn	Foodstuffs
M202	Thorn EMI/Virgin Music	20.03.92 C-75/12 of 26.03.92	27.04.92 C-120/30 of 12.05.92	NSD	Music
M207	Eureko	20.03.92 C-75/13 of 26.03.92	27.04.92 C-113/12 of 01.05.92	NC	Insurance
M188	Herba/IRR	24.03.92 C-77/15 of 28.03.92	28.04.92 C-120/30 of 12.05.92	NC	Cereals
M197	Solvay/Laporte-Interox	26.03.92 C-82/11 of 02.04.92	30.04.92 C-165/26 of 02.07.92	NCOD NSD	Chemicals
M210	Mondi/Frantschach	07.04.92 C-92/12 of 11.04.92	12.05.92 C-124/19 of 16.05.92	NSD	Pulp & Paper
M218	Eucom/Digital	14.04.92 C-103/22 of 23.04.92	18.05.92 C-140/20 of 03.06.92	NSD	Telecommunications
M208	Scott/Mölnlycke	21.04.92 C-107/22 of 28.04.92	18.05.92 C-135/20 of 26.05.92	withdrawn	Paper
M224	Volvo/Lex	21.04.92 C-107/23 of 28.04.92	21.05.92 C-142/18 of 04.06.92	NSD	Motor vehicles/Distribution
M221	ABB/BREL	22.04.92 C-109/10 of 29.04.92	26.05.92 C-142/18 of 04.06.92	NSD	Rail
M213	Hong Kong and Shanghai Bank/Midland	23.04.92 C-113/11 of 01.05.92	21.05.92 C-157/18 of 24.06.92	NSD	Banking
M214	DuPont/ICI	30.04.92 C-116/13 of 07.05.92	30.09.92 L-7/13 of 13.01.93	C	Chemicals

Outcome: NC = not concentration, NCOD = no community dimension, MS = referred to Member State, NSD = no serious doubts, C = compatible, I = Incompatible

NOTIFICATIONS PUBLISHED IN OJ 1992

Case	Parties	Notification	Decision	Outcome	Sector/Product
M220	Bibby/Finanzauto	25.05.92 C-139/17 of 02.06.92	29.06.92 C-275/8 of 23.10.92	NSD	Earth moving equipment
M222	Mannesmann/Hoesch	27.05.92 C-142/17 of 04.06.92	12.11.92 L-114/34 of 08.05.93	C	Steel
M236	Ericsson/Ascom	05.06.92 C-151/14 of 16.06.92	08.07.92 C-201/26 of 08.08.92	NSD	Telecommunications
M241	Eurocard/Eurocheque-Europay	10.06.92 Not published	13.07.92 C-182/19 of 18.07.92 corr. C-193/12 of 31.07.92	NCOD	Financial services
M242	Promodes/BRMC	12.06.92 C-152/23 of 17.06.92	13.07.92 C-232/14 of 10.09.92	NSD	Foodstuffs/Distribution
M234	GECC/AVIS	12.06.92 C-153/18 of 18.06.92	15.07.92 C-201/26 of 08.08.92	NSD	Car Leasing
M229	Thomas Cook/LTU/West LB	16.06.92 C-154/29 of 19.06.92	14.07.92 C-199/12 of 06.08.92	NSD	Travel
M160	Elf Atochem/Rohm & Haas	24.06.92 C-161/31 of 27.06.92	28.07.92 C-201/27 of 08.08.92	NSD	Chemicals
M206	Rhône-Poulenc/SNIA	08.07.92 C-177/20 of 14.07.92	10.08.92 C-212/23 of 18.08.92	NSD	Chemicals
M198	Péchiney/VIAG	10.07.92 C-181/21 of 17.07.92	10.08.92 C-307/7 of 25.11.92	NSD	Metals
M249	Northern Telecom/Matra Télécommunication	10.07.92 C-181/22 of 17.07.92	10.08.92 C-240/15 of 19.09.92	NSD	Telecommunications
M232	PepsiCo/General Mills	13.07.92 C-187/18 of 24.07.92	05.08.92 C-228/6 of 04.09.92	NSD	Beverages

Outcome: NC = not concentration, NCOD = no community dimension, MS = referred to Member State, NSD = no serious doubts, C = compatible, I = Incompatible

NOTIFICATIONS PUBLISHED IN OJ 1992

Case	Parties	Notification	Decision	Outcome	Sector/Product
M253	BTR/Pirelli	15.07.92 C-186/31 of 23.07.92	17.08.92 C-265/5 of 14.10.92	NSD	Automotive
M117	Koipe-Tabacalera/Elosua	17.07.92 C-185/17 of 22.07.92	28.07.92 C-227/10 of 03.09.92	NC	Edible oil
M239	Avesta/ British Steel/NCC	03.08.92 C-204/14 of 12.08.92	04.09.92 C-258/9 of 07.10.92	NSD	Stainless steel
M235	Elf Aquitaine-Thyssen/ Minol	03.08.92 C-200/18 of 07.08.92	04.09.92 C-232/14 of 10.09.92	NSD	Petrochemicals
M251	Allianz/DKV	07.08.92 C-207/19 of 14.08.92	10.09.92 C-258/9 of 07.10.92	NSD	Insurance
M261	Volvo/Lex (2)	12.08.92 C-208/15 of 15.08.92	04.09.92 C-239/11 of 18.09.92	NSD	Motor vehicles/Distribution
M258	CCIE/GTE	24.08.92 C-225/14 of 01.09.92	25.09.92 C-258/10 of 07.10.92	NSD	Lighting
M238	Siemens/Philips Kabel	26.08.92 C-227/9 of 03.09.92	11.11.92 C-300/14 of 17.11.92*	withdrawn	Cables
M263	Ahold/Jerónimo Martins	28.08.92 C-226/8 of 02.09.92	29.09.92 C-261/10 of 10.10.92	NSD	Food retail
M256	Linde/Fiat	27.08.92 C-227/10 of 03.09.92	28.09.92 C-258/10 of 07.10.92	NSD	Handling equipment
M157	Air France/Sabena	07.09.92 C-232/15 of 10.09.92	05.10.92 C-272/5 of 21.10.92	NSD	Air transport

Outcome: NC = not concentration, NCOD = no community dimension, MS = referred to Member State, NSD = no serious doubts, C = compatible, I = Incompatible
* Withdrawn and renotified at the same time. The Commission decided on 23.12.92 to proceed with 2nd phase investigation. The notification was withdrawn a second time of 08.01.93 (C-11/5 of 16.01.93).

NOTIFICATIONS PUBLISHED IN OJ 1992

Case	Parties	Notification	Decision	Outcome	Sector/Product
M265	VTG/BPTL	09.09.92 C-240/14 of 19.09.92	12.10.92 C-279/8 of 28.10.92	NC	Petrochemicals
M254	Fortis/La Caixa	05.10.92 C-261/19 of 10.10.92	05.11.92 C-297/4 of 13.11.92	NSD	Insurance
M259	British Airways/TAT	23.10.92 C-283/10 of 31.10.92	27.11.92 C-326/16 of 11.12.92	NSD	Air transport
M266	Rhône-Poulenc Chimie/ SITA	23.10.92 C-288/6 of 05.11.92	26.11.92 C-319/6 of 05.12.92	NSD	Waste
M277	Del Monte/Royal Foods/ Anglo American	09.11.92 C-298/10 of 14.11.92	09.12.92 C-331/13 of 16.12.92	NSD	Foodstuffs
M283	Waste Management International plc/SAE	18.11.92 C-307/7 of 25.11.92	21.12.92 C-10/5 of 15.01.93	NSD	Waste management
M290	Sextant/BTG-VDO	23.11.92 C-312/8 of 28.11.92	21.12.92 C-9/3 of 14.01.93	NSD	Aircraft equipment
M289	PepsiCo/KAS	25.11.92 C-315/2 of 02.12.92	21.12.92 C-8/2 of 13.01.93	NSD	Beverages
M296	Crédit Lyonnais/BFG Bank	01.12.92 C-322/16 of 09.12.92	11.01.93 C-45/18 of 17.02.93	NSD	Banking
M278	British Airways/Dan Air	30.11.92 C-328/4 of 12.12.92*	22.02.93 C-68/5 of 11.03.93	NSD	Air transport
M291	KNP/Bührmann- Tetterode/VRG	08.12.92 C-329/2 of 15.12.92	04.05.93 L-217/35 of 27.08.93	C	Paper & Board
M293	Philips/Thomson/Sagem	08.12.92 C-331/14 of 16.12.92	18.01.93 C-22/2 of 26.01.93	NC	Electronics

Outcome: NC = not concentration, NCOD = no community dimension, MS = referred to Member State, NSD = no serious doubts, C = compatible, I = Incompatible
* Request pursuant Article 22(3). Full request received by the Commission on 19.01.93.

NOTIFICATIONS PUBLISHED IN OJ 1993

Case	Parties	Notification	Decision	Outcome	Sector/Product
M301	Tesco/Catteau	23.12.92 C-4/2 of 08.01.93	04.02.93 C-45/18 of 17.02.93	NSD	Foodstuffs/Distribution
M304	VWAG/VAG (UK)	23.12.92 C-5/3 of 09.01.93	04.02.93 C-38/12 of 12.02.93	NSD	Motor vehicles/Distribution
M299	Sara Lee/BP Food Division	06.01.93 C-9/3 of 14.01.93	08.02.93 C-39/12 of 13.02.93	NSD	Processed meat
M216	CEA Industrie/France Télécom/Finmeccanica/ SGS-Thomson	21.01.93 C-27/3 of 30.01.93	22.02.93 C-68/5 of 11.03.93	NSD	Semi-conductors
M292	Ericsson/Hewlett-Packard	11.02.93 C-48/9 of 19.02.93	12.03.93 C-83/5 of 24.03.93	NSD	Telecommunications
M312	Sanofi/Yves St Laurent	12.02.93 C-46/10 of 18.02.93	15.03.93 C-89/3 of 31.03.93	NSD	Cosmetics
M272	Matra/Cap Gemini Sogeti	16.02.93 C-52/5 of 23.02.93	17.03.93 C-88/8 of 30.03.93	NSD	Aerospace
M295	SITA-RPC/Scori	18.02.93 C-53/10 of 24.02.93	19.03.93 C-88/9 of 30.03.93	NSD	Waste
M300	Kingfisher/Darty	19.02.93 C-55/11 of 26.02.93	22.03.93 C-87/8 of 27.03.93	NSD	Consumer electronics/ Distribution
M286	Zürich/MMI	01.03.93 C-64/3 of 06.03.93	02.04.93 C-112/4 of 22.04.93	NSD	Insurance
M317	Degussa/Ciba-Geigy	04.03.93 C-66/14 of 09.03.93	05.04.93 C-104/10 of 15.04.93	NSD	Ceramics
M328	Gehe/OCP	04.03.93 C-67/12 of 10.03.93	05.04.93 C-114/5 of 24.04.93	NSD	Pharmaceuticals

Outcome: NC = not concentration, NCOD = no community dimension, MS = referred to Member State, NSD = no serious doubts, C = compatible, I = Incompatible

NOTIFICATIONS PUBLISHED IN OJ 1993

Case	Parties	Notification	Decision	Outcome	Sector/Product
M318	Thomson/Shorts	08.03.93 C-71/7 of 13.03.93	14.04.93 C-136/4 of 15.05.93	NSD	Missile systems
M322	Alcan/Inespal/Palco	11.03.93 C-75/11 of 17.03.93	14.04.93 C-114/5 of 24.04.93	NSD	Packaging
M320	Ahold/Jerónimo Martins/ Inovaçao	12.03.93 C-79/5 of 20.03.93	19.04.93 C-117/2 of 28.04.93	NSD	Food retail
M335	Schweizerische Kreditanstalt/ Schweizerische Volksbank	24.03.93 C-91/5 of 01.04.93	29.04.93 C-147/6 of 27.05.93	NSD	Banking
M310	Harrisons & Crosfield/ AKZO	24.03.93 C-91/6 of 01.04.93	29.04.93 C-128/5 of 08.05.93	NSD	Chemicals
M323	Procordia/Erbamont	25.03.93 C-88/9 of 30.03.93	29.04.93 C-128/5 of 08.05.93	NSD	Pharmaceuticals
M237	DASA/Fokker	02.04.93 C-104/10 of 15.04.93	10.05.93 C-136/4 of 15.05.93	NSD	Aviation
M284	Wacker/Hoechst	02.04.93 C-105/4 of 16.04.93	10.05.93 C-171/4 of 22.06.93	NSD	PVC
M336	IBM France/CGI	16.04.93 C-113/2 of 23.04.93	19.05.93 C-151/5 of 02.06.93	NSD	Information technology
M344	Codan/Hafnia	23.04.93 C-120/2 of 30.04.93	28.05.93 C-171/4 of 22.06.93	NSD	Insurance
M341	Deutsche Bank/Banco de Madrid	26.04.93 C-121/5 of 01.05.93	28.05.93 C-175/11 of 26.06.93	NSD	Banking
M349	Aegon/Scottish Equitable	27.05.93 C-147/7 of 27.05.93	25.06.93 C-181/4 of 03.07.93	NSD	Insurance

Outcome: NC = not concentration, NCOD = no community dimension, MS = referred to Member State, NSD = no serious doubts, C = compatible, I = Incompatible

NOTIFICATIONS PUBLISHED IN OJ 1993

Case	Parties	Notification	Decision	Outcome	Sector/Product
M326	Toyota Motor Corporation/Walter Frey Holding/Toyota France	28.05.93 C-154/8 of 05.06.93	01.07.93 C-187/4 of 09.07.93	NSD	Motor vehicles/Distribution
M350	West LB/Thomas Cook	28.05.93 C-157/3 of 09.06.93	30.06.93 C-216/4 of 11.08.93	NSD	Travel
M346	JCSAT/SAJAC	01.06.93 C-158/6 of 10.06.93	30.06.93 C-219/14 of 13.08.93	NSD	Satellite communications
M285	Pasteur Mérieux/Merck	04.06.93 C-159/2 of 11.06.93	05.07.93 C-188/10 of 10.07.93	NC	Vaccines
M334	Costa Crociere/Chargeurs/Accor	17.06.93 C-173/15 of 24.06.93	19.07.93 C-204/5 of 28.07.93	NSD	Travel
M343	Société Générale de Belgique/Générale de Banque	30.06.93 C-188/9 of 10.07.93	03.08.93 C-225/2 of 20.08.93	NSD	Banking & Financial services
M357	Commerzbank/CCR (Paribas)	06.07.93 C-191/6 of 15.07.93	09.08.93 C-221/4 of 17.08.93	NSD	Banking & Financial services
M308	Kali+Salz/MdK/Treuhand	14.07.93 C-196/9 of 20.07.93		C	Potash
M355	Rhône-Poulenc/SNIA (II)	22.07.93 C-205/4 of 29.07.93	08.09.93 C-272/6 of 08.10.93	NSD	Chemicals
M319	BHF/CCF/Charterhouse	27.07.93 C-209/16 of 03.08.93	30.08.93 C-247/4 of 10.09.93	NSD	Banking & Financial services
M366	Alcatel/STC	28.07.93 C-225/2 of 20.08.93	13.09.93 C-259/3 of 23.09.93	NCOD	Submarine telecommunications

Outcome: NC = not concentration, NCOD = no community dimension, MS = referred to Member State, NSD = no serious doubts, C = compatible, I = Incompatible

NOTIFICATIONS PUBLISHED IN OJ 1993

Case	Parties	Notification	Decision	Outcome	Sector/Product
M358	Pilkington-Techint/SIV	30.07.93 C-213/13 of 06.08.93		C	Glass
M353	British Telecom/MCI	11.08.93 C-226/3 of 21.08.93	13.09.93 C-259/3 of 23.09.93	NC NC NCOD	Telecommunications
M362	Nestlé/Italgel	13.08.93 C-226/4 of 21.08.93	15.09.93 C-270/3 of 06.10.93	NSD	Frozen foods
M315	Mannesmann/Vallourec/ Ilva	18.08.93 C-228/17 of 24.08.93	26.01.94	C	Steel
M360	Arvin/Sogefi	23.08.93 C-235/10 of 31.08.93	23.09.93 C-305/11 of 11.11.93	NSD	Automotive/Exhausts
M354	Cyanamid/Shell	01.09.93 C-243/2 of 07.09.93	01.10.93 C-273/6 of 09.10.93	NSD	Agrochemicals
M365	Thyssen/Balzer	01.09.93 C-244/5 of 08.09.93	30.09.93 C-276/18 of 14.10.93	NSD	Steel
M196	Volvo/Procordia	09.09.93 C-252/3 of 16.09.93	11.10.93 C-281/4 of 19.10.93	NSD	Foodstuffs
M330	McCormick/CPC/ Rabobank/Ostmann	14.09.93 C-256/3 of 21.09.93		MS	Herbs & Spices
M337	Allied Signal/Knorr- Bremse	14.09.93 C-257/2 of 22.09.93	15.10.93 C-298/6 of 04.11.93	NSD	Automotive/Air brakes
M376	Synthomer/Yule Catto	21.09.93 C-262/3 of 28.09.93	22.10.93 C-303/5 of 10.11.93	NSD	Chemicals/Synthetic rubber
M342	Fortis/CGER	11.10.93 C-278/3 of 16.10.93	15.11.93 C-23/13 of 27.01.94	NSD	Banking & Insurance

Outcome: NC = not concentration, NCOD = no community dimension, MS = referred to Member State, NSD = no serious doubts, C = compatible, I = Incompatible

NOTIFICATIONS PUBLISHED IN OJ 1993

Case	Parties	Notification	Decision	Outcome	Sector/Product
M363	Continental/Kaliko/ DG-Bank/Benecke	25.10.93 C-298/6 of 04.11.93	29.11.93 C-336/11 of 11.12.93	NSD	Plastics
M384	UAP/VINCI	27.10.93 C-300/11 of 06.11.93	01.12.93 C-3/5 of 05.01.94	NSD	Insurance
M382	Philips/Grundig	29.10.93 C-302/3 of 09.11.93	03.12.93 C-336/11 of 11.12.93	NSD	Consumer electronics
M392	Hoechst/Schering	19.11.93 C-321/12 of 27.11.93	22.12.93 C-9/3 of 13.01.94	NSD	Agrochemicals
M394	Mannesmann/RWE/ Deutsche Bank	19.11.93 C-321/13 of 27.11.93	22.12.93 C-9/3 of 13.01.94	NSD	Telecommunications
M391	BAI/Banca Popolare di Lecco	25.11.93 C-324/2 of 01.12.93	20.12.93 C-4/3 of 06.01.94	NSD	Banking
M390	AKZO/Nobel Industrier	29.11.93 C-332/6 of 08.12.93	10.01.94 C-19/13 of 22.01.94	NSD	Chemicals
M368	SNECMA/TI	09.12.93 C-339/13 of 16.12.93	17.01.94 C-42/12 of 12.02.94	NSD	Aviation

Outcome: NC = not concentration, NCOD = no community dimension, MS = referred to Member State, NSD = no serious doubts, C = compatible, I = Incompatible

NOTIFICATIONS PUBLISHED IN OJ 1994

Case	Parties	Notification	Decision	Outcome	Sector/Product
M388	Unilever France/Ortiz Miko	21.12.93 C-5/3 of 07.01.94	C-39/5 of 09.02.94	Withdrawn	Frozen foods
M399	Rhône-Poulenc-SNIA/ Nordfaser	22.12.93 C-6/3 of 08.01.94	03.02.94 C-42/13 of 12.02.94	NSD	Chemicals

Outcome: NC = not concentration, NCOD = no community dimension, MS = referred to Member State, NSD = no serious doubts, C = compatible, I = Incompatible

Annex 3

COMMISSION DECISIONS – CHRONOLOGICAL ORDER

1964

March 11   *Grosfillex-Fillistorf*, JO 1964 915
June 1   *Bendix-Mertens & Straet*, JO 1964 1426
July 30   *Nicholas Frères-Vitapro*, JO 1964 2287
Sept. 23   *Grundig-Consten*, JO 1964 2545
Oct. 22   *Dutch Engineers & Contractors Association (DECA)*, JO 1964 2761

1965

July 8   *DRU-Blondel*, JO 1965 2194
Sept 17   *Hummel-Isbecque*, JO 1965 2581
Dec. 17   *Jalatte-Voss and Jalatte-Vandeputte*, JO 1966 37

1967

June 27   *Transocean Marine Paint Association*, JO 1967 10

1968

Feb. 26   *Eurogypsum*, JO 1968 L57/9
July 17   *Alliance de Constructeurs français de machines-outils*, JO 1968 L201/1
            SOCEMAS, JO 1968 L201/7
            ACEC-Berliet, JO 1968 L201/7
Nov. 6   *Cobelaz-Usines de Synthèse*, JO 1968 L276/13
            Cobelaz-Cokeries, JO 1968 L276/19
            CFA, JO 1968 L276/29
            Reickermann/AEG-Elotherm, JO 1968 L276/25

1969

March 13   *European Machine Tool Exhibitions*, JO 1969 L69/13
May 5   *Convention Chaufourniers*, JO 1969 L122/8
June 18   *Christiani & Nielsen*, JO 1969 L165/12
June 25   *VVVF*, JO L168/22
June 30   *SEIFA*, JO L173/8
July 16   *International Quinine Agreement*, JO 1969 L192/5
July 22   *Clima-Chappée/Buderus*, JO 1969 L195/1
            Jaz-Peter, JO 1969 L195/5

July 24   *Dyestuffs*, JO 1969 L195/11
Dec. 5   *Pirelli SpA-Société Dunlop*, JO 1969 L242/41

1970

June 29   *Electrically-welded steel tubes*, JO 1970 L153/14
June 30   *Kodak*, JO 1970 L147/24
            ASPA, JO 1970 L148/9
Oct. 28   *Julien-Van Katwijk*, JO 1970 L242/18
            OMEGA, JO 1970 L242/22
Dec. 23   *Supexie*, JO 1971 L10/12
Dec. 29   *Ceramic tiles*, JO 1971 L10/15

1971

Feb. 1   *CICG-ZWEI/ZPÜ*, JO 1971 L34/13
May 28   *FN/CF*, JO 1971 L134/6
June 2   *GEMA*, JO 1971 L134/15
June 18   *Inquiry into market for beer*, JO 1971 L161/2
July 2   *Asphaltoid-Keller, SA*, JO 1971 L161/32
Sept. 24   *CEMATEX*, JO 1971 L227/26
Nov. 9   *SIAE*, JO 1971 L254/15
Nov. 25   *Boehringer*, JO 1972 L282/46
Dec. 9   *Continental Can*, JO 1972 L7/25
Dec. 16   *VCH*, JO 1972 L13/34
            SAFCO, JO 1972 L13/44
Dec. 20   *SOPELEM/LANGEN*, JO 1972 L13/47
Dec. 22   *Burroughs-Delplanque*, JO 1972 L13/50
            Burroughs-Geha, JO 1972 L13/53
Dec. 23   *Henkel-Colgate*, JO 1972 L14/14
            NCH, JO 1972 L22/16

1972

Jan. 17   *MAN-SAVIEM*, JO 1972 L31/29
Feb. 23   *Wild-Leitz*, JO 1972 L61/27
June 9   *Davidson Rubber Co*, JO 1972 L143/31
            Raymond-Nagoya, JO 1972 L143/39
July 6   *GEMA*, JO 1972 L166/22
July 26   *Fine Paper*, JO 1972 L182/24
Sept. 28   *Rodenstock*, JO 1972 L267/17
            Misal, JO 1972 L267/20
Oct. 20   *Central Heating*, JO 1972 L264/22
Nov. 23   *Pittsburgh Corning Europe – Formica Belgium – Hertel*, JO 1972 L272/35
Dec. 14   *ZOJA/CSC – ICI*, JO 1972 L299/51
Dec. 18   *Cementregeling voor Nederland – 1971*, JO 1972 L303/7
Dec. 22   *CIMBEL*, JO 1972 L303/24
            Wea-Filipacchi Music S.A., JO 1972 L303/52
            Decisions by GISA – association, JO 1972 L303/45

1973

Jan. 2	*European Sugar Industry*, OJ 1973 L140/17
May 11	*SCPA-Kali und Salz*, OJ 1973 L217/3
June 14	*Du Pont de Nemours Deutschland*, OJ 1973 L194/27
July 3	*Gas water-heaters and bath-heaters*, OJ 1973 L217/34
Oct. 5	*Deutsche Philips GmbH*, OJ 1973 L293/40
Oct. 8	*PRYM-BEKA*, OJ 1973 L296/24
Dec. 21	*Transocean Marine Paint Association*, OJ 1974 L19/18
	Kali und Salz/Kali-Chemie, OJ 1974 L19/22

1974

May 15	*Agreements between manufacturers of glass containers*, OJ 1974 L160/1
July 23	*Papiers Peints de Belgique*, OJ 1974 L237/3
July 24	*Advocaat Zwarte Kip*, OJ 1974 L237/12
July 25	*FRUBO*, OJ 1974 L237/16
Nov. 29	*Franco-Japanese ballbearings agreement*, OJ 1974 L343/19
Dec. 13	*Bayerische Motorenwerke*, OJ 1975 L29/1
Dec. 19	*Goodyear Italiana-Euram*, OJ 1975 L38/10
	Duro-Dyne – Europair, OJ 1975 L29/11
	General Motor Continental, OJ 1975 L29/14
Dec. 20	*Rank/Sopelem*, OJ 1975 L29/20
	SHV-Chevron Oil Europe, OJ 1975 L38/14

1975

Jan. 8	*Preserved mushrooms*, OJ 1975 L29/26
March 5	*Sirdar/Phildar*, OJ 1975 L125/27
June 3	*Stoves and Heaters*, OJ 1975 L159/22
July 14	*Intergroup*, OJ 1975 L212/23
July 15	*IFTRA rules for producers of virgin aluminium*, OJ 1975 L228/3
July 17	*UNIDI*, OJ 1975 L228/17
July 18	*Kabelmetal-Luchaire*, OJ 1975 L222/34
July 25	*Bronbemaling v Heidemaatschappij*, OJ 1975 L249/27
Oct. 23	*Transocean Marine Paint Association*, OJ 1975 L286/24
Nov. 21	*Bomée-Stichting*, OJ 1975 L329/30
Dec. 2	*AOIP/Beyrard*, OJ 1976 L6/8
Dec. 15	*Bayer/Gist-Brocades*, OJ 1976 L30/13
	SABA, OJ 1976 L28/19
Dec. 17	*Chiquita*, OJ 1976 L95/1
Dec. 23	*KEWA*, OJ 1976 L51/15
	United Reprocessors GmbH, OJ 1976 L51/7

1976

June 9	*Vitamins*, OJ 1976 L223/27
June 25	*CSV*, OJ 1976 L192/27
July 26	*Pabst & Richarz/BNIA*, OJ 1976 L231/24
	Reuter/BASF, OJ 1976 L254/40
Dec. 1	*Miller International Schallplatten GmbH*, OJ 1976 L357/40
Dec. 21	*Theal/Watts*, OJ 1977 L39/19
	Junghans, OJ 1977 L30/10
Dec. 22	*GERO-fabriek*, OJ 1977 L16/8

1977

Jan. 20	*Vacuum Interrupters Ltd*, OJ 1977 L48/32
Apr. 19	*ABG oil companies operating in the Netherlands*, OJ 1977 L117/1
July 25	*De Laval-Stork*, OJ 1977 L215/11
Sept. 8	*COBELPA/VNP*, OJ 1977 L242/10
Nov. 7	*BPICA*, OJ 1977 L299/18
Nov. 23	*GEC-Weir Sodium Circulators*, OJ 1977 L327/26
Dec. 2	*Centraal Bureau voor de Rijwielhandel*, OJ 1978 L20/18
	Cauliflowers, OJ 1978 L21/23
Dec. 8	*Hugin/Liptons*, OJ 1978 L22/23
	Freiformschmieden, OJ 1978 L10/32
Dec. 20	*The Distillers Company Ltd, Conditions of Sale and Price Terms*, OJ 1978 L50/16
	Video cassette recorders, OJ 1978 L47/42
Dec. 21	*Sopelem/Vickers*, OJ 1978 L70/47
	Spices, OJ 1978 L53/20
Dec. 23	*Vegetable parchment*, OJ 1978 L70/54
	Jaz-Peter, OJ 1978 L61/17
	BMW Belgium NV and Belgian BMW dealers, OJ 1978 L46/33
	Campari, OJ 1978 L70/69
	Penneys, OJ 1978 L60/19

1978

May 26	*RAI/UNITEL*, OJ 1978 L157/39
June 12	*SNPE-LEL*, OJ 1978 L191/41
July 20	*GB-INNO-BM – Fedetab*, OJ 1978 L224/29
	Central Stikstof Verkoopkantoor, OJ 1978 L242/15
July 28	*Wm. Teacher and Sons Ltd – conditions of sale*, OJ 1978 L235/20
	Arthur Bell and Sons Ltd – conditions of sale, OJ 1978 L235/15
Sept. 21	*Breeders' rights – maize seed*, OJ 1978 L286/23
Oct. 20	*WANO Schwarzpulver*, OJ 1978 L322/26
	Zanussi, OJ 1978 L322/36
Dec. 7	*EMO*, OJ 1979 L11/16
Dec. 12	*Kawasaki*, OJ 1979 L16/9
	White Lead, OJ 1979 L21/16

1979

Jan. 10   *Vaessen/Moris*, OJ 1979 L19/32
Jan. 17   *Beecham/Parke Davis*, OJ 1979 L70/11
Jan. 30   *Fides, Milan*, OJ 1979 L57/33
July 6   *AM & S Europe Ltd, Bristol*, OJ 1979 L199/31
Sept. 5   *BP Kemi-DDSF*, OJ 1979 L286/32
Nov. 28   *Floral*, OJ 1980 L39/51
Dec. 5   *Rennet*, OJ 1980 L51/19
Dec. 7   *Cane Sugar Supply Agreements*, OJ 1980 L39/64
Dec. 12   *Transocean Marine Paint Association*, OJ 1980 L39/73
Dec. 14   *Pioneer Hi-Fi Equipment*, OJ 1980 L60/21
Dec. 20   *Fabbrica Pisana, Pisa*, OJ 1980 L75/30
            Fabbrica Lastre di Vetro Pietro Sciarra, Rome, OJ 1980 L75/35

1980

April 17   *Krups*, OJ 1980 L120/26
July 9   *National Sulphuric Acid Association*, OJ 1980 L260/24
July 22   *The Distillers Co Ltd – Victuallers*, OJ 1980 L233/43
Sept. 18   *IMA Rules*, OJ 1980 L318/1
Oct. 16   *Industrieverband Solnhofener Natursteinplatten*, OJ 1980 L318/32
Nov. 25   *Johnson & Johnson*, OJ 1980 L377/16
Dec. 11   *Vacuum Interrupters Ltd*, OJ 1980 L383/1
            Hennessy-Henkell, OJ 1980 L383/11
Dec. 17   *Italian cast glass*, OJ 1980 L383/19

1981

Sept. 28   *Italian flat glass*, OJ 1981 L326/32
Oct. 7   *Bandengroothandel Frieschebrug BV/NV Nederlandse Banden-Industrie
            Michelin*, OJ 1981 L353/33
Oct. 29   *GVL*, OJ 1981 L370/49
Nov. 17   *Comptoir commercial d'importation*, OJ 1982 L27/31
Nov. 17   *Langenscheidt/Hachette*, OJ 1982 L39/25
Nov. 25   *VBBB/VBVB*, OJ 1982 L54/36
            Telos, OJ 1982 L58/19
Nov. 26   *Sopelem-Vickers*, OJ 1982 L391/1
Nov. 27   *Moët et Chandon (London) Ltd*, OJ 1982 L94/7
Dec. 2   *Hasselblad*, OJ 1982 L161/18
Dec. 4   *GEMA statutes*, OJ 1982 L94/12
Dec. 9   *Fire Insurance*, OJ 1982 L80/36
Dec. 11   *SA National Panasonic (Belgium) NV*, OJ 1982 L113/18
Dec. 17   *NAVEWA-ANSEAU*, OJ 1982 L167/39

1982

Jan. 6   *AEG-Telefunken*, OJ 1982 L117/15

April 15	*BPICA*, OJ 1982 L156/16
June 21	*National Panasonic (France) SA*, OJ 1982 L211/32
July 15	*SSI*, OJ 1982 L232/1
Aug. 18	*Distribution system of Ford Werke AG – interim measure*, OJ 1982 L256/20
Oct. 27	*Fédération nationale de l'industrie de la chaussure de France*, OJ 1982 L319/12
Oct. 29	*Amersham Buchler*, OJ 1982 L314/34
Nov. 4	*NAVEWA-ANSEAU*, OJ 1982 L325/20
Dec. 7	*National Panasonic*, OJ 1982 L354/28
Dec. 10	*British Telecommunications*, OJ 1982 L360/36
	Cafeteros de Colombia, OJ 1982 L360/31
Dec. 14	*Rolled zinc products and zinc alloys*, OJ 1982 L362/40
Dec. 15	*AROW/BNIC*, OJ 1982 L379/1
	Toltecs/Dorcet, OJ 1982 L379/19

1983

Jan. 10	*Deutsche Castrol Vetriebsgesellschaft GmbH*, OJ 1983 L114/26
May 24	*Cematex*, OJ 1983 L140/27
July 11	*Windsurfing International*, OJ 1983 L229/1
July 13	*Vimpoltu*, OJ 1983 L200/44
	Rockwell/Iveco, OJ 1983 L224/19
July 29	*ECS/AKZO – interim measures*, OJ 1983 L252/13
Oct. 17	*Cast iron and steel rolls*, OJ 1983 L317/1
Nov. 16	*Distribution system of Ford Werke AG*, OJ 1983 L327/31
Dec. 5	*Murat*, OJ 1983 L348/20
	SMM & T Exhibition Agreement, OJ 1983 L376/1
	IPTC Belgium, OJ 1983 L376/7
	VW-MAN, OJ 1983 L376/11
Dec. 6	*Schlegel/CPIO*, OJ 1983 L351/20
Dec. 8	*Carbon Gas Technologie*, OJ 1983 L376/17
Dec. 12	*Nutricia/de Rooij and Nutricia/Zuid-Hollandse Conservenfabriek*, OJ 1983 L376/22
	International Energy Agency, OJ 1983 L376/30
Dec. 21	*SABA's EEC distribution system*, OJ 1983 L376/41

1984

March 30	*Nuovo CEGAM*, OJ 1984 L99/29
April 18	*IBM personal computer*, OJ 1984 L118/24
May 16	*Polistil/Arbois*, OJ 1984 L136/9
July 2	*BL*, OJ 1984 L207/11
July 4	*Synthetic fibres*, OJ 1984 L207/17
July 12	*Carlsberg*, OJ 1984 L207/26
July 19	*BPCL/ICI*, OJ 1984 L212/1
July 23	*Agreements and concerted practices in the flat-glass sector in the Benelux countries*, OJ 1984 L212/13

Aug. 6   *Zinc producer group*, OJ 1984 L220/27
Nov. 23   *UNIDI*, OJ 1984 L322/10
            Peroxygen products, OJ 1985 L35/1
Dec. 5   *Fire insurance (D)*, OJ 1985 L35/20
Dec. 7   *Milchförderungsfonds*, OJ 1985 L35/35
Dec. 10   *Grohe's distribution system*, OJ 1985 L19/17
            Ideal-Standard's distribution system, OJ 1985 L20/38
            Uniform Eurocheques, OJ 1985 L35/43
Dec. 12   *Mecaniver-PPG*, OJ 1985 L35/54
Dec. 14   *John Deere*, OJ 1985 L35/58
Dec. 19   *Wood pulp*, OJ 1985 L85/1
            Aluminium imports from eastern Europe, OJ 1985 L92/1

1985

Jan. 23   *Olympic Airways*, OJ 1985 L46/51
July 10   *Grundig's EEC distribution system*, OJ 1985 L233/1
            French inland waterway charter traffic: EATE levy, OJ 1985 L219/35
July 12   *Velcro/Aplix*, OJ 1985 L233/22
Nov. 27   *Ivoclar*, OJ 1985 L369/1
Dec. 2   *BP/Kellogg*, OJ 1985 L369/6
Dec. 13   *Breeders' rights: roses*, OJ 1985 L369/9
            Sole distribution agreements for whisky and gin, OJ 1985 L369/19
            London Sugar Futures Market Limited, OJ 1985 L369/25
            London Cocoa Terminal Market Association Ltd, OJ 1985 L369/28
            Coffee Terminal Market Association of London Ltd, OJ 1985 L369/31
            London Rubber Terminal Market Association Ltd, OJ 1985 L369/34
Dec. 14   *ECS/AKZO Chemie*, OJ 1985 L374/1
Dec. 16   *Sperry New Holland*, OJ 1985 L376/21
            P & I Clubs, OJ 1985 L376/2
            Villeroy & Boch, OJ 1985 L376/15
Dec. 18   *Siemens/Fanuc*, OJ 1985 L376/29

1986

April 23   *Polypropylene*, OJ 1986 L230/1
July 10   *Roofing felt*, OJ 1986 L232/15
July 14   *Optical fibres*, OJ 1986 L236/30
Sept. 25   *Peugeot*, OJ 1986 L295/19
Sept. 30   *VIFKA*, OJ 1986 L291/46
            Irish Banks' Standing Committee, OJ 1986 L295/28
Nov. 26   *MELDOC*, OJ 1986 L348/50
Dec. 2   *Fatty Acids*, OJ 1987 L3/17
Dec. 4   *Petroleum Exchange of London Ltd*, OJ 1987 L3/27
            ENI/Montedison, OJ 1987 L5/13
Dec. 10   *The GAFTA Soya Bean Meal Futures Association*, OJ 1987 L19/18
            The London Grain Futures Market, OJ 1987 L19/22

The London Potato Futures Association Ltd, OJ 1987 L19/26
The London Meat Futures Exchange Ltd, OJ 1987 L19/30
Dec. 11 *Belgische Vereniging der Banken/Association Belge des Banques*, OJ 1987 L7/27
Dec. 12 *ABI*, OJ 1987 L43/51
Dec. 15 *X/Open Group*, OJ 1987 L35/36
Boussois/Interpane, OJ 1987 L50/30
Dec. 17 *Mitchell Cotts/Sofiltra*, OJ 1987 L41/31
Pronuptia, OJ 1987 L19/39
Yves Rocher, OJ 1987 L8/49

1987

July 10 *Tipp-Ex*, OJ 1987 L222/1
July 13 *Computerland*, OJ 1987 L222/12
Baltic International Freight Futures Exchange Ltd, OJ 1987 L222/24
Sandoz, OJ 1987 L222/28
July 29 *BBI/Boosey & Hawkes: Interim measures*, OJ 1987 L286/36
Sept. 18 *Internationale Dentalschau*, OJ 1987 L293/58
Dec. 18 *Fisher-Price/Quaker Oats Ltd – Toyco*, OJ 1988 L49/19
Konica, OJ 1988 L78/34
New potatoes, OJ 1988 L59/25
Dec. 22 *De Laval-Stork*, OJ 1988 L59/32
Eurofix-Bauco v *Hilti*, OJ 1988 L65/19
Rich Products/Jus-rol, OJ 1988 L69/21
ARG/Unipart, OJ 1988 L45/34
Enichem/ICI, OJ 1988 L50/18
Olivetti/Canon, OJ 1988 L52/51

1988

May 5 *Bayer/BP Chemicals*, OJ 1988 L150/35
July 11 *British Dental Trade Association – BDTA*, OJ 1988 L233/15
July 18 *Napier Brown – British Sugar*, OJ 1988 L284/41
July 20 *IVECO/FORD*, OJ 1988 L230/39
July 26 *Bloemenveilingen Aalsmeer*, OJ 1988 L262/27
Tetra Pak I (BTG licence), OJ 1988 L272/27
Oct. 11 *BBC Brown Boveri* [1989] 1 CEC 2,234; OJ 1988 L301/68
Continental/Michelin [1989] 1 CEC 2,241; OJ 1988 L305/33
Oct. 13 *Delta Chemie/DDD* [1989] 1 CEC 2,254; OJ 1988 L309/34
Oct. 24 *Eurotunnel* [1989] 1 CEC 2,266; OJ 1988 L311/36
Oct. 28 *Hudson's Bay-Dansk Pelsdyravlerforening* [1989] 1 CEC 2,270; OJ 1988 L316/43
Nov. 4 *London European – Sabena* [1989] 1 CEC 2,278; OJ 1988 L317/47
Nov. 14 *ServiceMaster* [1989] 1 CEC 2,287; OJ 1988 L332/38
Dec. 2 *Transocean Marine Paint Association* [1989] 1 CEC 2,003; OJ 1989 L351/40
Charles Jourdan [1989] 1 CEC 2,119; OJ 1989 L35/31

Dec. 5   *BPB Industries plc* [1989] 1 CEC 2,008; OJ 1989 L10/50
Dec. 7   *Flat glass* [1989] 1 CEC 2,077; OJ 1989 L33/44
Dec. 12   *Publishers Association – Net Book Agreements*, OJ 1989 L22/12
Dec. 19   *Uniform Eurocheques* [1989] 1 CEC 2,111; OJ 1989 L36/16
Dec. 20   *EMO* [1989] 1 CEC 2,130; OJ 1989 L37/11
Dec. 21   *Decca Navigator System* [1989] 1 CEC 2,137; OJ 1989 L43/27
            PVC [1989] 1 CEC 2,167; OJ 1989 L74/1
            LdPE [1989] 1 CEC 2,193; OJ 1989 L74/21
            Magill TV Guide/ITP, BBC and RTE [1989] 1 CEC 2,223; OJ 1989 L78/43

1989

April 20   *German restriction of competition in the shipbuilding industry*, OJ 1990
            L118/39
May 3   *Italian aid to the newsprint industry*, [1990] 1 CEC 2, 144; OJ 1990 L114/25
May 24   *Aluminina and Comsal*, [1990] 1 CEC 2155; OJ 1990 L118/42
June 9   *National Sulphuric Acid Association* [1989] 2 CEC 2,006; OJ 1989 L190/22
July 12   *UIP* [1989] 2 CEC 2,019; OJ 1989 L226/25
July 19   *Dutch banks* [1989] 2 CEC 2,032; OJ 1989 L253/1
Aug. 2   *Welded steel mesh* [1989] 2 CEC 2,051; OJ 1989 L260/1
Sept. 15   *Film purchases by German television stations* [1989] 2 CEC 2,109; OJ 1989
            L284/36
Dec. 13   *Bayo-n-ox* [1990] 1 CEC 2,066; OJ 1990 L21/71
Dec. 14   *APB*, OJ 1990 L18/35
Dec. 19   *Sugar beet*, OJ 1990 L31/32
Dec. 20   *Belgian aid to the pharmaceutical industry*, OJ 1992 L182/89
Dec. 20   *MFL Group*, [1992] 2 CEC 2,084; OJ 1992 L182/94
Dec. 20   *TEKO* [1989] 1 CEC 2,045; OJ 1990 L13/34
            Concordato Incendio [1990] 1 CEC 2,053; OJ 1990 L15/25

1990

Jan. 12   *Alcatel Espace/ANT Nachrichtentechnik*, [1990] 1 CEC 2,096; OJ 1990
            L32/19
Jan 31   *Re SA Sucrerie Couplet*, [1990] 2 CEC 2,027; OJ 1990 L186/21
Feb. 14   *Spanish fishing fleet*, OJ 1990 L314/13
Feb. 21   *Re Aid to German motor vehicle industry*, [1990] 2 CEC 2,043; OJ 1990
            L188/55
March 23   *Moosehead/Whitbread*, [1990] 1 CEC 2,127; OJ 1990 L100/32
May 2   *Halkis Cement Co*, [1991] 1 CEC 2,080; OJ 1991 L73/27
May 8   *C. Walker & Sons (Holding) Ltd/British Steel plc*, OJ 1990 L131/27
June 26   *Metaleurop SA*, [1990] 2 CEC 2,033; OJ 1990 L179/41
July 2   *Netherlands Programme of Agricultural Income Aid*, OJ 1990 L174/63
July 4   *Belgian grant of long-term credit to shipowners*, OJ 1990 L338/21
July 13   *Elopak/Metal Box – Odin*, [1990] 2 CEC 2,066; OJ 1990 L209/15
July 18   *Cold-rolled stainless steel flat products*, OJ 1990 L220/28
July 18   *Re Aid to Hamburg*, OJ 1991 L215/1

July 25	*Bolzano Steelworks*, OJ 1991 L86/28
July 25	*Industrie Ottiche Riunite SpA (IOR)*, [1992] 2 CEC 2,091; OJ 1992 L183/30
July 25	*Re Aid to the Mezzogiorno*, [1991] 1 CEC 2,086; OJ 1991 L86/23
Oct. 15	*Cekacan*, [1990] 2 CEC 2,099; OJ 1990 L299/64
Nov. 28	*Bayer/Dental*, [1991] 1 CEC 2,003; OJ 1990 L351/46
Nov. 28	*Volkswagen Bruxelles SA*, [1991] 1 CEC 2,121; OJ 1991 L123/46
Dec. 1	*Re CNIH*, OJ 1991 L123/51
Dec. 19	*D'Ieteren Motor Oils*, [1991] 1 CEC 2,025; OJ 1991 L20/42
Dec. 20	*Magefesa*, [1991] 1 CEC 2,071; OJ 1991 L5/18

1991

Jan. 24	*Re Mactac SA*, [1991] 2 CEC 2,093; OJ 1991 L156/39
March 13	*Re Belgian aid to shipowners*, OJ 1991 L203/105
March 20	*Re nut and/or locust bean producers*, OJ 1991 L100/35
March 26	*Saint-Gobain (Eurofloat)*, [1991] 2 CEC 2,134; OJ 1991 L215/11
March 26	*Textilwerke Deggendorf GmbH*, OJ 1991 L215/16
May 28	*Re Aid to the Friuli Venezia Giulia region*, OJ 1991 L262/29
May 29	*Magneti Marelli/CEAc*, [1991] 2 CEC 2,146; OJ 1991 L222/38
June 11	*Pari Mutuel Urbain (PMU)*, [1992] 1 CEC 2,003; OJ 1992 L14/35
July 5	*Sardinian aid to Ferriere Acciaierie Sarde*, OJ 1991 L298/1
July 19	*Tetra Pak/Alfa-Laval*, [1991] 2 CEC 2,203; OJ 1991 L290/35
July 24	*Re Aid to Sabena*, [1991] 2 CEC 2,124; OJ 1991 L300/48
July 31	*Toyota Motor Corp*, [1992] 1 CEC 2,011; OJ 1992 L6/36
July 31	*Varta/Bosch*, OJ 1991 L320/26
Aug. 16	*Italian aid to the Mezzogiorno*, OJ 1991 L254/14
Aug. 24	*Re Ente Nazionale per la Cellulosa e per la Carta (ENCC)*, [1992] 1 CEC 2,087; OJ 1992 L47/19
Nov. 27	*Italian aid to the public steel sector*, OJ 1992 L9/16
Nov. 27	*Nuova Cartiera di Arbatax (NCA)*, [1992] 2 CEC 2,098; OJ 1992 L159/46
Nov. 27	*Re French public industrial conversion activities*, OJ 1992 L138/24
Dec. 12	*Re Aid to a German shipyard*, [1991] 2 CEC 2,080; OJ 1991 L158/71
Dec. 17	*Re Reinhold KG*, [1991] 2 CEC 2,086; OJ 1991 L156/33
Dec. 18	*Re aid to Deggendorf textile works*, OJ 1992 L183/36
Dec. 19	*Re Spanish durum wheat*, OJ 1992 21/32

1992

March 11	*Re Dutch Aid for Enviromentally Sound Manure Disposal*, [1992] 2 CEC 2,135; OJ 1992 L170/34
March 25	*Eurocheque: Helsinki Agreement*, [1992] 1 CEC 2,275; OJ 1992 L95/50
March 25	*Hilaturas y Tejidos Andaluces SA (Hytasa)*, [1992] 2 CEC 2,143; OJ 1992 L171/54
March 25	*Industrias Mediterraneos de la Piel SA*, [1992] 2 CEC 2,157; OJ 1992 L172/76
March 25	*Intelhorce SA/GTE General Textil España SA*, OJ 1992 L176/57
April 6	*Ukwal*, [1992] 1 CEC 2,297; OJ 1992 L121/45
April 15	*Daimler-Benz AG*, [1992] 2 CEC 2,230; OJ 1992 L263/15
April 28	*Accor/Wagon-Lits*, [1992] 2 CEC 2,170; OJ 1992 L204/1

June 22   *Swedish and Norwegian civil aviation agreement*, OJ 1992 L200/20
June 24   *Siemens SA*, OJ 1992 L288/25
June 30   *Re temporary compensation for German farmers*, OJ 1992 L215/100
July 22   *Nestlé/Perrier*, [1993] 1 CEC 2,018; OJ 1992 L356/1
July 22   *Re German/Spanish coach service*, OJ 1992 L222/69
July 25   *Re State Aid in Decree-Laws*, OJ 1992 L207/47
July 31   *Danish and Dutch Aid to the steel sector*, OJ 1992 L223/28
July 31   *Re transitional compensation for German farmers*, OJ 1992 L257/43
Sept. 30   *Du Pont/ICI*, [1993] 1 CEC 2,055; OJ 1993 L7/13
Nov. 4   *Spanish aid to the agricultural processing industry*, OJ 1993 L55/54
Nov. 11   *Re aid to promote economic growth and scientific methods*, OJ 1993 L55/61
Nov. 12   *Mannesmann/Hoesch*, [1993] 2 CEC 2,003; OJ 1993 L114/34
Dec. 9   *Aid to the Mezzogiorno*, OJ 1993 L117/22
Dec. 22   *Jahrhundertvertrag*, [1993] 1 CEC 2,186; OJ 1993 L50/14
Dec. 23   *AIMA aid to exporters of citrus fruit to Eastern Europe*, OJ 1993 L74/84
Dec. 23   *French aid for the creation of industrial enterprises*, OJ 1993 L85/22
Dec. 23   *French exploration for, or extraction of, oil or gas*, OJ 1993 L12/19

1993

Jan. 12   *AIMA Italian aid for carrot storage*, OJ 1993 L61/52
Jan. 20   *Rhineland-Palatinate*, OJ 1993 L61/55
Feb. 10   *AIMA Italian aid for hazelnut storage*, [1993] 2 CEC 2,029; OJ 1993 L117/28
Feb. 24   *Tariff structures in the combined transport of goods*, [1993] 1 CEC 2,218; OJ 1993 L73/38
March 9   *Re aid to Madrid*, OJ 1993 L145/25
March 9   *Rover Group (No. 2)*, [1993] 2 CEC 2,053; OJ 1993 L143/7
April 6   *German aid for the electronics sector*, OJ 1993 L185/43
May 4   *KNP/BR/VRG*, [1993] 2 CEC 2,156; OJ 1993 L217/35
May 10   *Re Basque tax concessions*, OJ 1993 L134/25
May 26   *Tariff structures in the combined transport of goods*, OJ 1993 L145/31
June 9   *Re tax credit for professional road hauliers*, OJ 1993 L233/10
June 22   *Zera/Montedison and Hinkens/Stähler*, [1994] 1 CEC 2,003; OJ 1993 L272/28
June 30   *CNSD*, [1993] 2 CEC 2,173; OJ 1993 L203/27
July 7   *Italian aid to the ceramics industry*, OJ 1993 L238/38
July 14   *UK exploration for, or extraction of, oil or gas*, OJ 1993 L196/55
July 22   *Cartiere del Garda*, [1994] 1 CEC 2,026; OJ 1993 L273/51
July 22   *Cenemesa Group (CCC)/Asea-Brown Boveri*, [1994] 1 CEC 2,044; OJ 1993 L309/21
July 22   *Swedish and Norwegian civil aviation agreement*, OJ 1993 L212/17
July 28   *Re temporary compensation for German farmers*, OJ 1993 L222/51
Sept. 22   *Pari Mutuel Urbain (PMU) II*, [1994] 1 CEC 2,035; OJ 1993 L300/15
Sept. 22   *Re aid for the Valtellina*, [1994] 1 CEC 2,130; OJ 1994 L79/24
Nov. 24   *Auditel*, [1994] 1 CEC 2,070; OJ 1993 L306/50
Dec. 7   *Merco*, [1994] 2 CEC 2,080; OJ 1994 L154/37

Dec. 21   *Aer Lingus*, [1994] 1 CEC 2,101; OJ 1994 L54/30
Dec. 21   *Grundig's EC distribution system II*, [1994] 1 CEC 2,091; OJ 1994 L20/15
Dec. 21   *Pilkington-Techint/SIV*, [1994] 2 CEC 2,031; OJ 1994 L158/24
Dec. 21   *Re Access to facilities of Port of Rødby*, [1994] 1 CEC 2,116; OJ 1994 L55/52
Dec. 21   *Sea Containers v Stena Sealink*, [1994] 1 CEC 2,077; OJ 1994 L15/8
Dec. 21   *SST-Garngesellschaft mbH*, [1994] 1 CEC 2,198; OJ 1994 L114/21

1994

Jan 26   *Groupe Bull*, [1994] 1 CEC 2,195; OJ 1994 L107/61
Jan 31   *Mannesmann/Vallourec/Ilva*, [1994] 1 CEC 2,136; OJ 1994 L102/15
Feb. 16   *Re fines for restrictive practices by steel beam producers*, Commission press
           release IP(94) 134
Feb. 21   *International Energy Agency (IEA)*, [1994] 1 CEC 2,123; OJ 1994 L68/35
March 29   *HOV SVZ/MCN*, [1994] 1 CEC 2,163; OJ 1994 L104/34
April 13   *Stichting Certificatie Kraanverhuurbedrijf and the Federatie van Nederlandse
           Kraaverhuurbedrijven*, OJ 1994 L117/30
April 29   *Stichting Baksteen*, [1994] 2 CEC 2,051; OJ 1994 L131/15
May 18   *Exxon/Shell*, [1994] 2 CEC 2,060; OJ 1994 L144/20

Annex 4

COURT ORDERS – CHRONOLOGICAL ORDER

1971

Aug. 18   *GEMA v EC Commission*, Case 45/71R, [1971] ECR 791

1972

March 21   *Europemballage and Continental Can v EC Commission*, Case 6/72R, [1972] ECR 157

1973

March 14   *Istituto Chemioterapico Italiano and Commercial Solvents v EC Commission*, Joined Cases 6 and 7/73R, [1973] ECR 357

Oct. 11   *Miles Druce v EC Commission*, Joined Cases 160 and 161/73R, [1973] ECR 1049

1974

April 3   *Kali-Chemie v EC Commission*, Case 20/74R, [1974] 337
July 8   *Kali-Chemie v EC Commission*, Case 20/74RII, [1974] ECR 787
Oct. 25   *FRUBO v EC Commission*, Case 71/74R and RR, [1974] ECR 1031

1975

Oct. 22   *National Carbonising Company v EC Commission*, Case 109/75R, [1975] ECR 1193

1976

April 5   *United Brands v EC Commission*, Case 27/76R, [1976] ECR 425
July 23   *Metro v EC Commission*, Case 26/76R, [1976] ECR 1353

1978

Oct. 30   *Heintz van Landewyck SARL & Ors v EC Commission*, Joined Cases 209 to 215 and 218/78R, [1978] ECR 2111

1980

Jan. 17   *Camera Care Ltd v EC Commission*, Case 792/79R, [1980] ECR 119

1981

July 7   *IBM v EC Commission*, Joined Cases 60/81R and 190/81R, [1981] ECR 1857

1982

March 29   *AEG-Telefunken AG v EC Commission*, Case 107/82R, [1982] ECR 1179
March 31   *VBVB/VBBB v EC Commission*, Joined Cases 43 and 63/82R, [1982] ECR 1241
May 6   *AEG-Telefunken AG v EC Commission*, Case 107/82R, [1982] ECR 1549
May 18   *AM & S v EC Commission*, Case 155/79, [1982] ECR 1616
Sept. 6   *Ford of Europe Incorporated and Ford-Werke AG v EC Commission*, Case 229/82R, [1982] ECR 2849
Sept. 29   *Ford of Europe Incorporated and Ford-Werke AG v EC Commission*, Joined Cases 228 and 229/82R, [1982] ECR 3091

1983

July 12   *Société d'Initiatives et de Co-opération Agricole and Société Interprofessionnelle des Producteurs et Expéditeurs-Fruits, Légumes v EC Commission*, Case 114/83R, [1983] ECR 2315

1986

April 30   *AKZO Chemie BV v EC Commission*, Case 62/86R, [1986] ECR 1503
Sept. 24   *Montedipe SpA v EC Commission*, Case 213/86R, [1986] ECR 2623

1987

March 26   *Hoechst AG v EC Commission*, Case 46/87R, [1987] ECR 1549
Oct. 28   *Dow Chemical Nederland BV v EC Commission*, Case 85/87R, [1987] ECR 4367

1989

March 17   *Italy v EC Commission*, Case 303/88R, [1989] ECR 801
May 11   *Radio Telefis Eireann & Ors v EC Commission*, Joined Cases 76, 77 and 91R, [1989] ECR 1141
June 13   *Publishers Association v EC Commission*, Case 56/89R, [1989] ECR 1693

1990

May 21   *Automobiles Peugeot SA and Peugeot SA v EC Commission*, Case T-23/90R, [1990] ECR II-195
Nov. 21   *Samenwerkende Elektriciteits-produktiebedrijven NV v EC Commission*, Case T-39/90R, [1990] ECR II-649
Dec. 6   *Cosimex GmbH v EC Commission*, Case T-131/89R, [1990] ECR II-1

1991

May 17   *Comité International de la Rayone et des Fibres Synthétiques & Ors v EC Commission*, Case C-313/90R, [1991] ECR I-2557

Dec. 4   *Matra SA v EC Commission*, Case C-225/91R, Order, [1991] ECR I-5823

1992

Mar. 23   *Cimenteries CBR SA & Ors v EC Commission*, Joined Cases T-10 to T-12, T-14 and T-15/92R, [1992] ECR II-1572

Mar. 26   *BASF AG v EC Commission*, Case T-4/89 Rev, [1992] ECR II-1592

Mar. 29   *Rendo NV & Ors* v *EC Commission*, Case T-2/92, not yet reported

1994

March 2   *Hilti AG v EC Commission*, Case C-53/92P, [1994] 1 CEC 590

Annex 5

COURT JUDGMENTS – CHRONOLOGICAL ORDER

1962

April 6   *Kledingverkoopbedrijf de Geus v Bosch and van Rijn*, Case 13/61, [1962] ECR 45

1964

July 15   *Flaminio Costa v ENEL*, Case 6/64, [1964] ECR 585

1966

June 30   *Société Technique Minière v Maschinenbau Ulm GmbH MBU*, Case 56/65, [1966] ECR 235

July 13   *Etablissement Consten SARL & Grundig-Verkaufs-GmbH v EC Commission*, Joined Cases 56 & 58/64, [1966] ECR 299
Government of the Italian Republic v EC Council and EC Commission, Case 32/65, [1966] ECR 389

1967

March 15   *Cimenteries v EC Commission*, Joined Cases 8–11/66, [1967] ECR 75
Dec. 12   *SA Brasserie de Haecht v Wilkin and Wilkin*, Case 23/67, [1967] ECR 407

1968

Feb. 29   *Parke, Davis & Co v Probel, Reese, Beintema-Interpharm and Centrafarm*, Case 24/67, [1968] ECR 55

1969

Feb. 13   *Wilhelm & Ors v Bundeskartellamt*, Case 14/68, [1969] ECR 1
July 9   *Völk v Etablissements J Vervaecke*, Case 5/69, [1969] ECR 295
SA Portelange v SA Smith Corona Marchant International & Ors, Case 10/69, [1969] ECR 309

1970

March 18   *Brauerei A Bilger Söhne GmbH v Jehle and Jehle*, Case 43/69, [1970] ECR 127

June 30   *Parfums Marcel Rochas Vertriebs-GmbH v Helmut Bitsch*, Case 1/70, [1970]
            ECR 515
July 15   *ACF Chemiefarma NV v EC Commission*, Case 41/69, [1970] ECR 661
            Buchler & Co v EC Commission, Case 44/69, [1970] ECR 733
            Boehringer Mannheim GmbH v EC Commission, Case 45/69, [1970] ECR
            769

1971

Feb. 18   *Sirena Srl. v Eda Srl. & Ors*, Case 40/70, [1971] ECR 69
May 6   *Société Anonyme Cadillon v Firam Höss, Maschinenbau KG*, Case 1/71,
            [1971] ECR 351
June 8   *Deutsche Grammophon GmbH v Metro-SB-Großmärkte GmbH & Co KG*,
            Case 78/70 [1971] ECR 487
Nov. 25   *Béguelin Import Co & Ors v SAGL Import Export & Ors*, Case 22/71, [1971]
            ECR 949

1972

July 14   *Imperial Chemical Industries Ltd v EC Commission*, Case 48/69, [1972]
            ECR 619
            Badische Anilin- und Soda-Fabrik AG v EC Commission, Case 49/69, [1972]
            ECR 713
            Farbenfabriken Bayer AG v EC Commission, Case 51/69, [1972] ECR 745
            JR Geigy AG v EC Commission, Case 52/69, [1972] ECR 787
            Sandoz AG v EC Commission, Case 53/69, [1972] ECR 845
            SA Française des Matières Colorantes (Francolor) v EC Commission, Case
            54/69, [1972] ECR 851
            Cassella Farbwerke Mainkur AG v EC Commission, Case 55/69, [1972]
            ECR 887
            Farbwerke Hoechst AG v EC Commission, Case 56/69, [1972] ECR 927
            Azienda Colori Nazionali – ACNA SpA v EC Commission, Case 57/69,
            [1972] ECR 933
            Vereniging van Cemethandelaren v EC Commission, Case 8/72, [1972] ECR
            977
Dec. 14   *Boehringer Mannheim GmbH v EC Commission*, Case 7/72, [1972] ECR
            1281

1973

Feb. 6   *SA Brasserie de Haecht v Wilkin-Janssen*, Case 48/72, [1973] ECR 77
Feb. 21   *Europemballage Corp and Continental Can Company Inc v EC
            Commission*, Case 6/72, [1973] ECR 215

1974

Jan. 30   *Belgische Radio en Televisie & Anor v SV SABAM and NV Fonior*, Case
            127/73, [1974] ECR 51

March 9   *Société Anonyme Générale Sucrière & Ors v EC Commission*, Joined Cases 41, 43 and 44/73, [1977] ECR 445

May 24   *Hoffmann-La Roche v Centrafarm Vertriebsgesellschaft Pharmazeutischer Erzeugnisse mbH*, Case 107/76, [1977] ECR 957

June 9   *Srl. Ufficio Henry van Ameyde v Srl. Ufficio Centrale Italiano de Assistenza Assicurativa Automobilisti in Circolazione Internazionale (UCI)*, Case 90/76, [1977] ECR 1091

Oct. 25   *Metro SB-Großmärkte GmbH & Co KG v EC Commission*, Case 26/76, [1977] ECR 1875

Nov. 16   *NV GB-INNO-BM v Vereniging van de Kleinhandelaars in Tabak (ATAB)*, Case 13/77, [1977] ECR 2115

1978

Feb. 1   *Miller International Schallplatten GmbH v EC Commission*, Case 19/77, [1978] ECR 131

Feb. 14   *United Brands Co and United Brands Continentaal BV v EC Commission*, Case 27,76, [1978] ECR 207

May 23   *Hoffmann-La Roche & Co AG v Centrafarm Vertiebsgesellschaft Pharmazeutischer Erzeugnisse mbH*, Case 102/77, [1978] ECR 1139

June 20   *Tepea BV v EC Commission*, Case 28/77, [1978] ECR 1391

June 29   *Benzine en Petroleum Handelsmaatschappij BV & Ors v EC Commission*, Case 77/77, [1978] ECR 1513

Oct. 10   *Centrafarm BV v American Home Products Corporation*, Case 3/78, [1978] ECR 1823

1979

Feb. 13   *Hoffmann-La Roche & Co AG v EC Commission*, Case 85/76, [1979] ECR 461

May 31   *Hugin Kassaregister AB and Hugin Cash Registers Ltd v EC Commission*, Case 22/78, [1979] ECR 1869

June 12   *BMW Belgium SA & Ors v EC Commission*, Joined Cases 32/78 and 36 to 82/78, [1979] ECR 2435

Oct. 18   *Sirena Srl. v Eda Srl. & Ors*, Case 40/70, [1979] ECR 3169
GEMA, Gesellschaft für musikalische Aufführungs- und mechanische Vervielfältigungsrechte v EC Commission, Case 125/78, [1979] ECR 3173

Oct. 25   *Greenwich Film Production v Société des Auteurs, Compositeurs et Editeurs de Musique (SACEM) & Anor*, Case 22/79 [1979] ECR 3275

1980

March 18   *SA Compagnie Générale pour la Diffusion de la Télévision, Coditel, & Ors v SA Ciné Vog Films & Ors*, Case 62/79, [1980] ECR 881

March 20   *Vereniging ter Bevordering van de Belangen des Boekhandels & Ors v Eldi Records BV*, Case 106/79 [1980] ECR 1137

June 26   *National Panasonic (UK) Ltd v EC Commission*, Case 136/79, [1980] ECR 2033

July 10   *Distillers Co Ltd v EC Commission*, Case 30/78, [1980] ECR 2229
           Procureur de la République & Ors v Bruno Giry and Guerlain SA & Ors, Joined Cases 253/78 and 1 to 3/79, [1980] ECR 2327
           Anne Marty SA v Estée Lauder SA, Case 37/79, [1980] ECR 2481
           SA Lancôme and Cosparfrance Nederland BV v Etos BV and Albert Heyn Supermarkt BV, Case 99/79, [1980] ECR 2511

Oct. 29   *Van Landewyck Sàrl & Ors v EC Commission*, Joined Cases 209 to 215 and 218/78 [1980] ECR 3125

Dec. 11   *NV L'Oréal and SA L'Oréal v PBVA De Nieuwe AMCK*, Case 31/80, [1980] ECR 3775

1981

Jan. 22   *Dansk Supermarket A/S v A/S Imerco*, Case 58/80, [1981] ECR 181

March 25   *Coöperatieve Stremsel- en Kleurselfabriek v EC Commission*, Case 61/80, [1981] ECR 851

June 16   *Salonia v Poidomani & Anor*, Case 126/80, [1981] ECR 1563

July 14   *Züchner v Bayerische Vereinsbank AG*, Case 172/80, [1981] ECR 2021

Nov. 11   *International Business Machines Corporation (IBM) v EC Commission*, Case 60/81, [1981] ECR 2639

1982

May 18   *AM & S Europe Ltd v EC Commission*, Case 155/79, [1982] ECR 1575

June 8   *LC Nungesser KG & Anor v EC Commission*, Case 258/78, [1982] ECR 2015

July 10   *William v EC Commission*, Case 246/81, [1982] ECR 2277

Sept. 9   *Keurkoop BV v Nancy Kean Gifts BV*, Case 144/81, [1982] ECR 2853

Oct. 6   *Coditel, SA Compagnie Générale pour la Diffusion de la Télévision, & Ors v Ciné-Vog Films SA & Ors*, Case 262/81, [1982] 3381

1983

March 2   *Gesellschaft zur Verwertung von Leistungs-schutzrechten mbH*, Case 7/82, [1983] ECR 483

June 7   *SA Musique Diffusion Française & Ors v EC Commission*, Joined Cases 100–103/80, [1983] ECR 1825

Oct. 11   *Oswald Schmidt, trading as Demo-Studio Schmidt v EC Commission*, Case 210/81, [1983] ECR 3045

Oct. 25   *Allgemeine Elektricitäts-Gesellschaft AEG-Telefunken AG v EC Commission*, Case 107/82, [1983] ECR 3151

Nov. 8   *NV IAZ International Belgium & Ors v EC Commission*, Joined Cases 96 to 102, 104, 105, 108 and 110/82, [1983] ECR 3369

Nov. 9   *NV Nederlandsche Banden-Industrie Michelin v EC Commission*, Case 322/81, [1983] ECR 3461

Nov. 29   *Roussel Laboratoria BV & Ors v Netherlands*, Case 181/82, [1983] ECR 3849
Dec. 14   *Société de Vente de Ciments et Bétons de l'Est SA v Kerpen & Kerpent GmbH & Co. KG*, Case 319/82, [1983] ECR 4173

1984

Jan. 17   *Vereniging ter Bevordering van het Vlaamse Boekwezen, VBVB, and Vereniging ter Bevordering van de Belangen des Boekshandels, VBBB v EC Commission*, Joined Cases 43 and 63/82, [1984] ECR 19
Feb. 7   *Duphar BV & Ors v Netherlands State*, Case 258/82, [1984] ECR 523
Feb. 21   *Hasselblad (GB) Ltd v EC Commission*, Case 86/82, [1984] ECR 883
Feb. 28   *Ford of Europe Incorporated & Anor v EC Commission*, Joined Cases 228 and 229/82, [1984] ECR 1129
March 28   *Compagnie Royale Asturienne des Mines SA and Rheinzink GmbH v EC Commission*, Joined Cases 29 and 30/83, [1984] ECR 1679
April 5   *Criminal proceedings against Jan van de Haar and Kaveka de Meern BV*, Joined Cases 177 and 178/82, [1984] ECR 1797
July 5   *Société d'Initiatives et de Coopération Agricoles and Société Interprofessionnelle des Producteurs et Expéditeurs de Fruits, Légumes, Bulbes et Fleurs d'Ile-et-Vilaine v EC Commission*, Case 114/83, [1984] ECR 2589
July 12   *Hydrotherm Gerätebau GmbH v Compact det Dott Ing Mario Andreoli & C sas*, Case 170/83, [1984] ECR 2999
Dec. 13   *GAARM – Groupement des Associations Agricoles pour l'Organisation de la Production et de la Commercialisation des Pommes de Terre et Légumes de la Région Malouine & Ors*, Case 289/83, [1984] ECR 4295

1985

Jan. 10   *Association des Centres distributeurs Edouard Leclerc & Ors v Sàrl 'Au blé vert' & Ors*, Case 229/83, [1985] ECR 1
Jan. 29   *Cullet and Chambre syndicale des réparateurs automobiles et détaillants de produits pétroliers v Centre Leclerc Toulouse and Centre Leclerc Saint-Orens-de-Gameville*, Case 231/83, [1985] ECR 305
Jan. 30   *BAT Cigaretten-Fabriken GmbH v EC Commission*, Case 35/83, [1985] ECR 363
            Bureau national interprofessionnel du cognac v Clair, Case 123/83, [1985] ECR 391
March 20   *Italy v EC Commission*, Case 41/83, [1985] ECR 873
March 28   *Comité des industries cinématographiques des Communautés européennes (CICCE) v EC Commission*, Case 298/83, [1985] ECR 1105
July 3   *SA Binon and Cie v SA Agence et messageries de la presse*, Case 243/83, [1985] 2015
July 11   *SA Saint-Herblain distribution, Centres distributeurs Leclerc & Ors v Syndicate des Libraires de Loire-Océan*, Case 299/83, [1985] ECR 2515
            Remia BV & Ors v EC Commission, Case 42/84, [1985] ECR 2545

Sept. 17   *Ford-Werke AG and Ford of Europe Inc v EC Commission*, Joined Cases 25 and 26/84, [1985] ECR 2725

Oct. 3   *Centre belge d'études de marché – Télémarketing (CEBM) SA v Compagnie luxembourgeoise de télédiffusion SA and Information publicité Benelux SA*, Case 311/84, [1985] ECR 3261

Dec. 10   *Nederlandse Sigarenwinkeliers Organisatie v EC Commission*, Case 260/82, [1985] ECR 3801
Stichting Sigarettenindustrie & Ors v EC Commission, Joined Cases 240 to 242, 261, 262, 268 and 269/82, [1985] ECR 3831
ETA Fabriques d'Ebauches SA v DK Investment SA & Ors, Case 31/85, [1985] ECR 3933

1986

Jan. 28   *Pronuptia de Paris GmbH v Pronuptia de Paris Irmgard Schillgalis*, Case 161/84, [1986] ECR 353

Feb. 25   *Windsurfing International Inc v EC Commission*, Case 193/83, [1986] ECR 611

April 30   *Ministère Public v Lucas Asjes & Ors*, Joined Cases 209, 210, 211 and 213/84, [1986] ECR 1425

June 24   *AKZO Chemie BV and AKZO Chemie UK Ltd v EC Commission*, Case 53/85, [1986] ECR 1965

Sept. 23   *AKZO Chemie BV and AKZO Chemie UK Ltd v EC Commission*, Case 5/85, [1986] ECR 2585

Oct. 22   *Metro-SB-Großmärkte GmbH & Co KG v EC Commission*, Case 75/84, [1986] ECR 3021

Nov. 11   *British Leyland Public Co v EC Commission*, Case 226/84, [1986] ECR 3263

Dec. 18   *VAG France SA v Etablissements Magne SA*, Case 10/86, [1986] ECR 4071

1987

Jan. 27   *Verband der Sachversicherer eV v EC Commission*, Case 45/85, [1987] ECR 405

April 9   *Basset v Société des Auteurs, Compositeurs et Editeurs de Musique (SACEM)*, Case 402/85, [1987] ECR 1747
Ministère Public v Verbrugge, Case 160/86, [1987] ECR 1783

May 20   *Association nationale des travailleurs indépendants de la batellerie (Antib) v EC Commission*, Case 272/85, [1987] ECR 2201

May 21   *ALBAKO Margarinefabrik Maria von der Linde GmbH & Co KG v Bundesanstalt für Landwirtschaftliche Marktordnung*, Case 249/85, [1987] ECR 2345

July 9   *Associazione Nazionale Commercianti Internazionali Dentali e Sanitari (Ancides) v EC Commission*, Case 43/85, [1987] ECR 3131

Oct. 1   *VZW Vereniging van Vlaamse Reisbureaus v VZW Sociale Dienst van de Plaatselijke en Gewestelijke Overheidsdiensten*, Case 311/85, [1987] ECR 3801

Nov. 17   *British American Tobacco Ltd and RJ Reynolds Industries, Inc v EC Commission*, Joined Cases 142 and 156/84, [1987] ECR 4487.
Dec. 3   *Bureau National Interprofessionnel du Cognac v Aubert*, Case 136/86, [1987] ECR 4789; [1989] 1 CEC 363

1988

March 3   *Allen and Hanburys Ltd v Generics (UK) Ltd*, Case 434/85, [1988] ECR 1245
April 10 *Louis Erauw-Jacquery SPRL v La Hesbignonne*, Case 27/87, [1988] ECR 1919; [1989] 2 CEC 637
May 4   *Corinne Bodson v Pompes Funèbres des Régions Libérées SA*, Case 30/87, [1988] ECR 2479; [1990] 1 CEC 3
May 17   *Warner Brothers Inc., Metronome Video ApS v Christiansen*, Case 158/86, [1988] ECR 2605; [1990] 1 CEC 33
July 14   *Syndicat des Librairies de Normandie v L'Aigle Distribution SA & Ors*, Case 254/87, [1988] ECR 4457; [1990] 1 CEC 94
Sept. 21 *Van Eycke v ASPA NV*, Case 267/86, [1988] ECR 4769
Sept. 27 *Ahlström Osakeyhtiö & Ors v EC Commission*, Joined Cases 89, 104, 114, 116, 117 and 125 to 129/85, [1988] ECR 5193; [1993] 1 CEC 466
          Société Bayer AG v Société de constructions mécaniques Hennecke GmbH, Case 65/86, [1988] ECR 5249
Oct. 5   *Consorzio Italiano della Componentistica di Ricambio per Autoveicoli and Maxicar v Régie Nationale des Usines Renault*, Case 53/87, [1988] ECR 6039; [1990] 1 CEC 267
          AB Volvo v Erik Veng (UK) Ltd, Case 238/87, [1988] ECR 6211
          ALSATEL – Société Alsacienne et Lorraine de Télécommunications et d'Electronique v SA NOVASAM, Case 247/86, [1988] ECR 5987; [1990] 1 CEC 248

1989

Jan. 24   *EMI Electrola GmbH v Firma Patricia Im-und Export Verwaltungsgesellschaft mbH & Ors*, Case 341/87, [1989] ECR 79; [1990] 1 CEC 322
April 11 *Ahmed Saeed Flugreisen and Silver Line Reisebüro GmbH v Zentrale zur Bekämpfung unlauteren Wettbewerbs eV*, Case 66/86, [1989] ECR 803; [1989] 2 CEC 654
May 12   *Ottung v Klee & Weilbach A/S and Thomas Schmidt A/S*, Case 320/87, [1989] ECR 1177; [1990] 2 CEC 674
May 18   *R v The Royal Pharmaceutical Society of Great Britain, ex parte the Association of Pharmaceutical Importers & Ors*, Case 266/87, [1989] ECR 1295; [1989] 2 CEC 415
July 11   *SC Belasco & Ors v EC Commission*, Case 246/86, [1989] ECR 2117; [1990] 2 CEC 912
July 13   *Ministère public v Tournier*, Case 395/87, [1989] ECR 2521; [1990] 2 CEC 815

March 21   *Italy & Ors v EC Commission*, Case C-303/88, [1991] ECR I-1433; [1993] 1 CEC 210

Italy v EC Commission, Case C-305/89, [1991] ECR I-1603

April 23   *Höfner & Anor v Macroton*, Case C-41/90, [1991] ECR II-1979

May 29   *Bayer v EC Commission*, Case T-12/90, [1991] ECR II-219; [1993] 2 CEC 305

June 18   *Elliniki Radiophonia Tileorassi – AE v Dimotiki Etairia Pliroforissis (DEP) & Ors*, Case C-260/89, [1991] ECR I-2925; [1993] 2 CEC 167

July 3   *AKZO Chemie BV v EC Commission*, Case C-62/86, [1991] ECR I-3359; [1993] 2 CEC 115

July 10   *Radio Telefis Eireann, British Broadcasting Corporation and Independent Television Publications Ltd v EC Commission*, Joined Cases T-69 – 70/89 and T-76/89, [1991] ECR II-485; [1991] 2 CEC 114

July 12   *Automobiles Peugeot SA and Peugeot SA v EC Commission*, Case T-23/90, [1991] ECR II-653

Oct. 3   *Italy v EC Commission*, Case C-261/89, [1991] ECR I-4437; [1993] 2 CEC 584

Oct. 24   *Rhône-Poulenc SA v EC Commission*, Case T-1/89, [1991] ECR II-867

Petrofina SA v EC Commission, Case T-2/89, [1991] ECR II-1087

Atochem SA v EC Commission, Case T-3/89, [1991] ECR II-1177

Fédération Nationale du Commerce Extérieur des Produits Alimentaires & Ors v France, Case C-354/90, [1991] ECR I-5505

Dec. 10   *Merci Convenzionali Porto di Genova Spa v Siderurgica Gabrielli Spa*, Case C-179/90, [1991] ECR I-5889; [1994] 1 CEC 196

Dec. 12   *Hilti AG v EC Commission*, Case T-30/90, [1991] ECR II-1439; [1992] 1 CEC 155

NV Samenwerkende Elektriciteits-produktiebedrijven v EC Commission, Case T-39/90, [1991] ECR II-1497

Dec. 13   *Régie des Télégraphes et des Téléphones (RTT) v GB-Inno-BM SA*, Case C-18/88, [1991] ECR I-5941; [1994] 1 CEC 117

Dec. 17   *BASF Aktiengesellschaft v EC Commission*, Case T-4/89, [1991] ECR II-1523

Enichem Anic Spa v EC Commission, Case T-6/89, [1991] ECR II-1623

SA Hercules Chemicals NV v EC Commission, Case T-7/89, [1991] ECR II-1711; [1992] 1 CEC 207

DMS NV v EC Commission, Case T-8/89, [1991] ECR II-1833

1992

Jan. 24   *La Cinq SA v EC Commission*, Case T-44/90, [1992] ECR II-1; [1993] 2 CEC 629

Feb. 4   *British Aerospace (BA) plc and Rover Group Holdings plc v EC Commission*, Case C-294/90, [1992] ECR I-493 [1992] 2 CEC 136

Feb. 12   *Netherlands & Ors v EC Commission*, Joined Cases C-48 and C-66/90, not yet reported

Feb. 27   *BASF & Ors v EC Commission*, Joined Cases T-79, T-84–86, T-89, T-91–92, T-94, T-96, T-98, T-102 and T-104/89, [1992] ECR II-315; [1992] 1 CEC 519
Société d'Hygiène Dermatologique de Vichy v EC Commission, Case T-19/91, [1992] ECR II-415; [1993] 1 CEC 318

March 10   *Hüls v EC Commission*, Case T-9/89, [1992] ECR II-499
Hoechst Aktiengesellschaft v EC Commission, Case T-10/89, [1992] ECR II-629
Shell International Chemical Company Ltd v EC Commission, Case T-11/89, [1992] ECR II-757
Solvay et Compagnie SA v EC Commission, Case T-12/89, [1992] ECR II-907
Imperial Chemical Industries plc v EC Commission, Case T-13/89, [1992] ECR II-1021
Montedipe SpA v EC Commission, Case T-14/89, [1992] ECR II-1155
Chemie Linz AG v EC Commission, Case T-15/89, [1992] ECR II-1275
Società Italiana Vetro SpA, Fabbrica Pisana Spa, Vernante Pennitalia v EC Commission, Joined Cases T-68, T-77 and T-78/89, [1992] ECR II-1403; [1992] 2 CEC 33

March 11   *Compagnie Commerciale de l'Ouest & Ors v Receveur Principal des Douanes de la Pallice Port*, Joined Cases C-78 – 83/90, [1992] ECR I-1847; [1994] 1 CEC 351

March 19   *Re Batista Morais*, Case C-60/91, [1992] ECR I-2085

June 30   *Spain v EC Commission*, Case C-312/90, not yet reported
Italy v EC Commission, Case C-47/91, not yet reported

July 2   *Dansk Pelsdyravlerforening v EC Commission*, Case T-61/89, not yet reported

July 9   *Publishers Association v EC Commission*, Case T-66/89, [1992] 2 CEC 219

July 16   *Dirección General de Defensa de la Competencia v Asociación Española de Banca Privada & Ors*, Case T-67/91, not yet reported

Sept. 17   *NBV & NVB v EC Commission*, Case T-138/89, not yet reported

Sept. 18   *Automec v EC Commission*, Case T-24/90, not yet reported
Asia Motor France v EC Commission, Case T-28/90, not yet reported

Nov. 17   *Spain & Ors v EC Commission*, Joined Cases C-271, C-281 and C-289/90, [1993] 2 CEC 378

Nov. 18   *Rendo NV & Ors v EC Commission*, Case T-16/91, not yet reported
SA Cimenteries CBR & Ors v EC Commission, Joined Cases T-10 – T-12 and T-15/92, not yet reported

1993

March 24   *CIRFS & Ors v EC Commission*, Case C-313/90, not yet reported

March 31   *Åhlström & Ors v EC Commission*, Joined Cases C-89, C-104, C-114, C-116 – C-117 and C-125 – C-129/85, [1993] 1 CEC 466

April 28   *Italy v EC Commission*, Case C-364/90, not yet reported

May 18   *Belgium v EC Commission*, Joined Cases C-356/90 and C-180/91, not yet reported

May 19   *Procureur du Roi v Corbeau*, Case C-320/91, not yet reported
           William Cook plc v EC Commission, Case C-198/91, not yet reported
June 10   *EC Commission v Hellenic Republic*, Case C-183/91, not yet reported
June 15   *Matra SA v EC Commission*, Case C-225/91, not yet reported
June 16   *France v EC Commission*, Case C-325/91, not yet reported
Oct. 27   *Ministère Public v Decoster & Ors*, Case 69/91, not yet reported
           Ministère Public v Taillandier, Case C-92/91, not yet reported
Oct. 28   *Zunis Holdings SA & Ors v EC Commission*, Case T-83/93, [1994] 1 CEC
           531
Nov. 10   *Petróleos de Portugal – Petrogal SA v Correia, Simões & Companhia,*
           Limitada & Ors, Case C-39/92, not yet reported
           Otto BV v Postbank NV, Case C-60/92, not yet reported
Nov. 17   *Re Meng*, Case C-2/91, not yet reported
           Bundesanstalt für den Güterfernverkehr v Gebrüder Reiff Gmbh & Co KG,
           Case C-185/91, not yet reported
           Re Ohra Schadeverzekeringen NV, Case C-245/91, not yet reported

1994

Jan. 13   *Metro SB-Großmärkte GmbH & Co. KG v Cartier SA*, Case C-376/92,
           [1994] ECR I-15; [1994] 1 CEC 399
Jan. 19   *SAT Fluggesellschaft mbH v Eurocontrol*, Case C-364/92, [1994] ECR I-43;
           [1994] 1 CEC 541
Feb. 23   *Groupement des Cartes Bancaires 'CB' & Anor v EC Commission*, Joined
           Cases T-39 and 40/92, [1994] ECR II-49; [1994] 1 CEC 494
March 2   *Hilti AG v EC Commission*, Case C-53/92P, [1994] ECR I-667; [1994] 1 CEC
           590
March 9   *TWD Textilwerke Deggendorf GmbH v Bundesrepublik Deutchland*, Case
           C-188/92, [1994] ECR I-833
March 15   *Banco de Crédito Industria SA, devenue Banco Exterior de España SAv*
           Ayuntamiento, Case C-387/92, [1994] ECR I-877
March 24   *Société anonyme à participation ouvrière nationale Air Francev EC*
           Commission, Case T-3/93, [1994] ECR I-121; [1994] 1 CEC 613
April 13   *Federal Republic of Germany & Anor v EC Commission*, Joined Cases
           C-324/90 & C-342/90, not yet reported
           HJ Banks & Co Ltd v British Coal Corp, Case C-128/92, not yet reported
April 27   *Gemeente Almelo & Ors v Energiebedrijf IJsselmij NV*, Case C-393/92,
           [1994] 2 CEC 281
May 17   *Corsica Ferries Srl v Corpo dei Piloti del Porto di Genova*, Case C-18/93, not
           yet reported
May 18   *Bureau Européen des Unions de Consommateurs (BEUC) & Anor v EC*
           Commission, Case T-37/92, not yet reported
May 19   *Samenwerkende Elektriciteits-productiebedrijven (SEP) v EC Commission*,
           Case C-36/92P, not yet reported
           Compagnie Nationale Air France v EC Commission, Case T-2/93, not yet
           reported

June 9   *Federal Republic of Germany v Delta Schiffahrts- und Speditionsgesellschaft mbH*, Case C-153/92, not yet reported

June 15   *EC Commission v BASF AG & Ors*, Case C-137/92P, [1994] 1 CEC 641

June 16   *Syndicat Français de l'Express International & Ors v EC Commission*, Case C-39/93P, not yet reported

Automobiles Peugeot & Anor v EC Commission, Case C-322/93P, not yet reported

Bibliography

General

Bellamy and Child, *Common Market Law of Competition*, fourth edn. (London, 1993) Sweet & Maxwell.

Bellis, 'International Trade and the Competition Law of the European Economic Community' (1979) 16 CML Rev. 647.

Bentil, 'Common Market Antitrust Law and Restrictive Business Agreements or Practices prompted by National Regulatory Measures' [1988] ECLR 354.

Cownie, 'State Aids in the Eighties' (1986) 11 ELRev. 247.

Ehlermann, 'The contribution of EC Competition Policy to the Single Market' (1992) 29 CMLRev. 257.

Gleiss/Hirsch, Burkert, *Kommentar zum EG Kartellrecht – Band 1* (Heidelberg, 1993) Verlag Recht und Wirtschaft.

Goyder, *EEC Competition Law*, second edn. (Oxford, 1993) Clarendon Press.

Green, *Commercial Agreements and Competition Law Practice and Procedure in the UK and EEC*, (London, 1986) Graham & Trotman.

Green, 'Article 85 in Perspective: Stretching Jurisdiction, Narrowing the Concept of a Restriction and Plugging a Few Gaps' [1988] ECLR 190.

Gyselen, 'State Action and the Effectiveness of the EEC Treaty's Competition Provisions' (1989) 26 CML Rev. 33.

Hawk, *United States, Common Market and International Antitrust: a Comparative Guide*, second edn. (New York, 1985) Law and Business Inc., looseleaf.

Hawk, 'North American and Common Market Antitrust and Trade laws' (1988) Fordham Corporate Law Institute, Matthew Bender.

Jacobs and Stewart-Clark, *Competition Law in the European Community*, second edn. (Kogan Page, 1991).

Joliet, *The Rule of Reason in Antitrust Law*, (The Hague, 1967) Martinus Nijhoff.

Joliet, 'National Anti-Competitive Legislation and Community Law' (1989) Fordham Int. L.J., vol. 12, 163.

Jones, Lewis and Van der Woude, *EEC Competition Law Handbook*, fourth edn. (London, 1993) Sweet & Maxwell.

Korah, 'The Rise and Fall of Provisional Validity – The Need for a Rule of Reason in EEC Antitrust' (1981) 3 Northwestern J. of Int. L. & Bus. 320.

Korah, *An Introductory Guide to EEC Competition Law and Practice*, fourth edn. (Oxford/London, 1990) ESC/Sweet & Maxwell.

Marenco, 'Competition between National Economies and Competition Between Businesses, a Response to Judge Pescatore' (1987) Fordham Int. L.J. 420.

Mattera, *Le Marché Unique Européen: Ses Règles, Son Fonctionnement*, (Paris, 1988) Jupiter.

Mendes, *Antitrust in a World of Inter-related Economics: The Interplay between Antitrust and Trade Policies in the US and the EEC*, (1991) Brussels University Editions.

Merkin and Williams, *Competition Law: Antitrust Policy in the UK and the EEC*, (London, 1984) Sweet & Maxwell.

Montagnon, *European Competition Policy* (1990) RIIA/Printer Publishers.

Mortelmans, 'The Compensatory Justification Criterion in the Practice of the Commission on State Aids', (1984) 21 CML Rev. 405.

Papaconstantinou, *Free Trade and Competition in the EEC Law, Policy and Practice*, (London, New York, 1988) Routledge.

Pathak, 'Articles 85 and 86 and Anti-competitive Exclusion in EEC Competition Law' [1989] ECLR 74 and 256.

Quigley, 'The Notion of a State Aid in the EEC' (1988) 13 ELRev. 242

Raybould, Firth, *Law of Monopolies, Competition Law and Practice in the USA, EEC, Germany and UK* (London/Boston, 1991) Graham & Trotman.

Riley, 'Nailing the Jellyfish: The Illegality of the EC/US Government Competition Agreement' [1992] 3 ECLR 101.

Ritter, Rawlinson, Braun, *EEC Competition Law: A Practitioner's Guide* (1991) Kluwer, Law and Taxation Publishers.

Ross, 'Challenging State Aids: the Effect of Recent Developments' (1986) 23 CML Rev. 867.

Schina, *State Aids under the EEC Treaty Articles 92 to 94*, (Oxford, 1987) ESC.

Slot and van der Woude, *Exploiting the Internal Market: Co-operation and Competition Towards 1992*, (Deventer, 1988) Kluwer.

Steindorff, 'Article 85 and the Rule of Reason' (1984) 21 CML Rev. 639.

Toepke, *EEC Competition Law*, (New York) John Whiley & Sons, looseleaf.

Van Bael and Bellis, *World Law of Competition*, vol. 1 and 2 (New York) Matthew Bender, looseleaf.

Van Bael et Bellis, *Droit de la Concurrence de la Communauté Economique Européenne* (Bruxelles, 1991) Bruylant.

Van Der Esch, 'Some Aspects of "Extra-Territorial" Infringement of EEC Competition Rules' (1985) Fordham Corporate Law Institute 285.

M. Waelbroeck, 'Competition, Integration and Economic Efficiency in the EEC from the Point of View of the Private Firm' (1984) vol. 82, 5–6 Mich. LRev. 1439.

Wiedeman, *Kommentar zu den Gruppenfreistellungsverordnungen des EWG-Kartellrechts Band I – Algemeiner Teil* (Köln, 1989) *und Band II – Besonderer Teil* (Köln, 1990) Verlag Dr. Otto Schmidt KG.

Distribution

Baden Fuller, 'Price Variations – the Distillers Case and Article 85 EEC' (1979) 28 ICLQ 128.

Chard, 'The Economics of the Application of Article 85 to Selective Distribution Systems' (1982) 7 ELRev. 83.

Daoût, 'Distribution under EEC Law – an Official View' (1983) Fordham Corporate Law Institute 44.

De Cockborne, 'The New Block Exemption on Franchising' (1989) Fordham Int. L.J., No. 2, 275.

Fine, 'EEC Consumer Warranties: A new Antitrust Hurdle Facing Exporters' [1989] ECLR 233.

Gast, *Les Procédures Européennes du Droit de la Concurrence et de la Franchise*, (Paris, 1989) Jupiter.

Groves, 'Motor Vehicle Distribution: the Block Exemption' [1987] ECLR 77.

Goyder, *EEC Competition Law*, (Oxford, 1988) Clarendon Press.

Goyder, *EC Distribution Law*, (London, 1992) Chancery Law Publishing.

Gyselen, 'Vertical Restraints in the Distribution Process: Strength and Weakness of the Free Rider Rationale under EEC Competition Law' (1984) 21 CML Rev. 648.

Horner, *Parallel Imports*, (London, 1987) Collins.

Kenyon-Slade, Thornton, *Schmithoff's Agency and Distribution Agreements* (London, 1992) Sweet & Maxwell & The Institute of Export.

Korah, 'Goodbye, Red Label: Condemnation of Dual Pricing by Distillers' (1979) 4 ELRev. 1.

Korah, *Exclusive Dealing Agreements in the EEC – Regulation 67/67 replaced*, (London, 1984) ELC.

Korah and Marenco, 'L'Article 85 du Traité CEE et les Contrats d'Agence' (1987) Cah. Dr. Eur. 603.

Korah, 'Franchising and the Draft Group Exemption' [1987] ECLR 124.

Korah, *Franchising Agreements and the EEC Rules: Regulation 4087/88* (London, 1989) ESC/Sweet & Maxwell.

Korah, Rothnie, *Exclusive Distribution and the EEC Competition Rules – Regulations 1983/83 & 1984/83* (London, 1992) Sweet & Maxwell.

Lasok, 'Assessing the Economic Consequences of Restrictive Practices: A Comment on the Delimitis Case' [1991] 5 ECLR 194.

Mendelsohn, Harris, *Franchising and the block exemption Regulation* (London, 1991) Longman.

Pathak, 'Vertical Restraints in EEC Competition Law' (1988) LIEI 15.

Pathak, 'Articles 85 and 86 and Anti-Competitive Exclusion in EEC Competition Law' [1988] ECLR 58 and 256.

Schödermeier, 'La Distribution selective et les Parfums – Une nouvelle Logique dans le Raisonnement de la Commission ?' 5-6 Cah. Dr. Eur. 649.

Toepke, 'EEC Law of Competition: Distribution Agreements and their Notification' (1985) vol. 19, 1 Int. Law. 117.

Van Bael, 'Heretical Reflections on the Basic Dogma of EEC Antitrust: Single Market Integration' (1980) 10 Swiss Rev. of Int. Comp. L. 39.

Van Bael, 'The Draft EEC Regulation on Selective Distribution of Motor Vehicles: a Daydream for Free Riders – a Nightmare for Industry' (1983) 19 Swiss Rev. of Int. Comp. L. 3.

Van Houtte, 'Les Contrats d'Agence au Regard de l'Article 85 CEE: Agir Pour le Compte d'Autrui et Intégration dans Son Entreprise' (1989) Cah. Dr. Eur. 345.

Willemart, 'Distribution automobile' (1983) 11 RDCB 677.

Warwick, *Parallel Imports* (London, 1993) Sweet & Maxwell.

Industrial and Commercial Property Rights

Bellis, 'After Polydor – The Territoriality of the Community Doctrine of Exhaustion of Industrial Property Rights' (1982) 16 Swiss Rev. Int. Comp. L. 17.

Bellis, 'Collecting Societies and EEC law' in *Collecting Societies in the Music Business* (Peeperkorn & Van Rij eds.) (1989) MAKLU.

Bellis, L'Ecluse, 'The Meaning of Competition for Information Technology in Europe' in *The Law of Information Technology in Europe 1992 – A Comparison with the USA* (Meijboom & Prins eds.) (1991) Kluwer.

Cabanellas, Massagner, *Know-How Agreements and EEC Competition* (Munich, 1992) IIC Studies, VCH.

Cawthra, *Patent Licensing in Europe*, second edn. (London, 1986) Butterworths.

Demaret, 'Patents, Territorial Restrictions and EEC Law' (1978) IIC. Studies, vol. 2.

Forrester, 'Software Licensing in the Light of Current EC Competition Law Considerations' [1992] 1 ECLR 5.

Friden, 'Recent Developments in EEC Intellectual Property Law; The Distinction between Existence and Exercise Revisited' (1989) 26 CML Rev. 193.

Guttuso, S., 'Know-How Agreements' (1986) Fordham Corporate Law Institute, 477.

Jeanrenaud, 'Exclusive Licences of Patent Rights and Territorial Restraints in the EEC – Certainty vs Flexibility' (1986) 26 Swiss Rev. Int. Comp. L. 21.

Johannes, *Industrial Property and Copyright in European Community Law*, (Leyden, 1976) Sijthoff.

Joliet, 'Territorial and Exclusive Trademark Licensing under the EEC Law of Competition' (1984) IIC 21.

Joliet, Marenco, Banks, 'Intellectual Property and the Community Rules on Free Movement: Discrimination Unearthed' (1990) 15 ELRev. 224.

Joliet, 'Trade Mark Law and the Free Movement of Goods: the Overruling of the Judgment in Hag I' (1991) IIC 303 and *Droit des Marques et Libre Circulation des Marchandises: l'Abandon de l'Arrêt Hag I* (1991) 2 Rev. trim. Dr. Eur. 187.

Korah, *Patent Licensing and EEC Competition Rules: Regulation 2349/84*, (London 1985) ESC/ Sweet & Maxwell.

Korah, *Know-How Licensing Agreements and EEC Competition Rules: Regulation 556/89* (London, 1989) ESC/ Sweet & Maxwell.

Kunze, 'Waiting for Sirena III – Trademark Assignment in the Case Law of the European Court of Justice, (1991) 22 IIC 319.

Odle, Zeyen, 'The EC Block Exemption Regulation 556/89 on Know-How: Practical Difficulties and Legal Uncertainties' [1991] 6 ECLR 231.

OECD, *Competition Policy and Intellectual Property Rights*, (Paris, 1989), OECD.

Orr and Farr, 'Know-How and Competition Rules of the EEC Treaty' (1988) World Comp. L. and EC Rev. 5.

Plottier, 'EEC Regulations on Patent Licensing and R&D: Analysis, Developments and Interface' (1986) 27 Swiss Rev. of Int. Comp. L. 25.

Price, 'The Secret of Know-how Block Exemption' [1989] ECLR 273.

Rose, 'Passing Off. Unfair Competition and Community Law' (1990) EIPR 123.

Shaw, 'Music to their Ears' (1990) 15 ELRev. 68.

Van Bael, 'Reflexions sur l'Arrêt "Semences de Maïs": des Semences d'Espoir?' (1983) Cah. Dr. Eur. 176.

Venit, 'EEC Patent Licensing Revisited: The Commission's Patent Licensing Regulation' (1985) 30 Antitrust Bull. 457.

Vinje, 'Compliance with Article 85 in Software Licensing' [1992] 4 ECLR 165.

M. Waelbroeck, 'The Effect of the Rome Treaty on the Exercise of National Industrial Property Rights' (1976) 21 Antitrust Bull. 99.

D. Waelbroeck, 'Know-How Licensing and EEC Competition Rules: a Commentary on Regulation No. 556/89' (1992) Antitrust Bull. 1047

Winn, 'Commission Know-How Regulation 556/89: Innovation and Territorial Exclusivity, Improvements and the Quid Pro Quo' [1990] 4 ECLR 135.

Co-operation Agreements

Caspari, 'Joint Ventures – the Intersection of Antitrust and Industrial Policy in the EEC' (1985) Fordham Corporate Law Institute 449.

Faull, 'Joint Ventures Under the EEC Competition Rules', [1984] ECLR 358.

Hawk, 'Joint Ventures under EEC Law' (1991) Fordham Int. L.J. 303.

Korah, *Research and Development – Joint Ventures and EEC Competition Rules – Regulation 418/85*, (London, 1986) ESC/ Sweet & Maxwell

Korah, 'Collaborative Joint Ventures for Research and Development where Markets are Concentrated: The Competition Rules of The Common Market and The Invalidity of Contracts' (1991) Fordham Int. L.J. 248.

OECD, *Competition Policy and Joint Ventures*, (Paris, 1989), OECD.

Ritter and Overbury, 'An Attempt at a Practical Approach to Joint Ventures under the EEC Rules of Competition' (1977) 14 CML Rev. 601.

Scherf, 'Kooperative Gemeinschaftsunternehmen im europäischen Wettbewerbsrecht' (1993) RIW 297.

Venit, 'Oedipus Rex: Recent Developments in the Structural Approach to Joint Ventures under EEC Competition Law' (1991) World Competition and Economics Review 5.

Whish, 'The Commission's Block Exemptions on Research and Development Agreements' [1985] ECLR 84.

White, 'Research and Development Joint Ventures Under EEC Competition Law' (1985) IIC 663.

Mergers and Acquisitions

Bach, *Der Marktbeherrschungsbegriff in der EG – Fusionskontrolle, auch im Vergleich zum deutschen Kartellrecht* (1993) Wirtschaft und Wettbewerb 805.

Cook, Kerse, *EEC Merger Control-Regulation 4064/89* (London, 1991) Sweet & Maxwell.

Davies, Lavoile, 'EEC Merger Control, A Half-Term Report Before the 1993 Review?' (1993) 3 World Competition Law and Economics Review 27.

Einsele, 'Auswirkungen der europäischen Fusionskontrollverordnung auf Gemeinschaftsunternehmen' (1992) RIW Beilage 2 zu Heft 8.

Fine, *Mergers and Joint Ventures in Europe: The Law and Policy of the EEC*, second edn. (London, 1994) Graham & Trotman/Martinus Nijhoff.

Hawk, 'The EEC Merger Regulation: The First Step toward one-stop Merger Control' (1990) Antitrust L.J. 195.

Hornsby, 'National and Community Control of Concentrations in a Single Market: Should Member States be Allowed to Impose Stricter Standards?' (1988) 13 ELRev. 295.

Jenny, *EEC Merger Control: Economies as an Antitrust Defence or an Antitrust attack?* (1992) Fordham Corporate Law Institute 591.

Jones, González, Díaz, *The EEC Merger Regulation* (London, 1992) Sweet & Maxwell.

Kleemann, 'First Year of Enforcement under the EEC Merger Regulation: a Commission View' (1991) Fordham Corporate Law Institute 623.

Kleinmann, Bechtold *Kommentar zur Fusionskontrolle* (1989) R&W.

Kleinmann, 'Die Anwendbarkeit der EG-Fusionskontrollverordnung auf Gemeinschaftsunternehmen', (1990) RIW 605.

Overbury, 'Politics or Policy? The Demystification of EC Merger Control' (1992) Fordham Corporate Law Institute.

Pathak, 'The EC Commission's Approach to Joint Ventures: A Policy of Contradictions' [1991] 5 ECLR 171.

Pheasant, 'Joint Ventures in Light of the Merger Regulation' (1990) European Corporate Legal Advisers Review 23.

Sibree, 'EEC Merger Control and Joint Ventures' (1992) 12 ELRev. 91.

Siragusa, Subiotto, 'The EEC Merger Control Regulation: The Commission's Evolving Case Law' (1991) 28 CML Rev. 877.

Soames, 'The "Community dimension" in the EEC Merger Regulation: The Calculation of the Turnover Criteria' [1990] 5 ECLR 213.

Van Der Esch, 'Merger Controls, Joint Ventures and Concentration Studies', (1974) Fordham Corporate Law Institute 153.

Venit, 'The "Merger" Control Regulation: Europe comes of age ... or Caliban's Dinner' (1990) 27 CML Rev 7.

Venit, 'The Evaluation of Concentrations under the Merger Control Regulation: The Nature of the Beast' (1990) Fordham Int. L.J. 412.

Venit, 'Oedipus Rex: Recent Developments in the Structural Approach To Joint Ventures Under EEC Competition Law' (1991) World Competition Law and Economics Review 5.

Weitbrecht, 'Drei Jahre europäische Fusionskontrolle-eine Zwischenbilanz' (1993) 22 EuZW 687.

Merger Control in the EEC, (London, 1988) Kluwer Law and Taxation Publishers.

Trade Associations

Brown, 'Trade Fairs and Fair Trade: the Commission's Exemption Policy' [1992] 2 ECLR 66.

Corones, 'The Application of Article 85 of the Treaty of Rome to the Exchange of Market Information between Members of a Trade Association' [1982] ECLR 67.

Reynolds, 'Trade Associations and the EEC Competition Rules' (1985) 23 Swiss Rev. of Int. Comp. L. 49.

Temple Lang, 'Trade Associations and Self-Regulation under EEC Antitrust Law' (1984) Fordham Corporate Law Institute 605.

Price-Fixing; Market-Sharing; Boycotts and Crisis Cartels

Gylstra and Murphy, 'Some Observations on the Sugar Case' (1977) 14 CML Rev. 45.

Mann, 'The Dyestuffs Case in the Court of Justice of the European Communities' (1973) 22 ICLQ 35.

Toepke, 'Pricing of Products in the EEC', (1982) Int. Law. 233.

Abuses of Dominant Position

Baden Fuller, 'Article 86 EEC: Economic Analysis of the Existence of a Dominant Position', (1979) 4 ELRev. 423.

Bruges Week, ed. Van Damme, *Regulating the Behaviour of Monopolies and Dominant Undertakings in Community Law*, (Bruges, 1977) De Tempel.

Fejoe, *Monopoly Law and Markets Studies of EC Competition Law with US Antitrust Law as a Frame of Reference and supported by Basic Market Economics* (Deventer, 1990) Kluwer.

Fox, 'Abuse of a Dominant Position under the Treaty of Rome – a Comparison with US Law' (1983) Fordham Corporate Law Institute 367.

Gyselen and Kyriazis, 'Article 86 EEC: The Monopoly Power Measurement Revisited' (1986) 11 ELRev. 34.

Gyselen, 'Abuse of Monopoly Power within the Meaning of Article 86 of the EEC Treaty: Recent Developments 1992 and EEC/US Competition Trade Law' (1989) Fordham Corporate Law Institute 360.

Joliet, *Monopolization and Abuse of Dominant Position: A Comparative Study of American and European Approaches to the Control of Economic Power*, (The Hague, 1967) Martinus Nijhoff.

L'Ecluse, 'Software Copyright after Magill' (1991) 15 Managing IP 991.

Price, 'Abuse of a Dominant Position, The Tale of Nails, Milk Cartons and TV Guides' [1990] 2 ECLR 80.

Temple Lang, 'Some Aspects of Abuse of Dominant Positions in European Community Antitrust Law' (1979) 3 Fordham Int. L. Forum 1.

Zanon, 'Price Discrimination Under Article 86 of the EEC Treaty: a Comment on the UBC Case' (1982) 31 ICLQ 36.

Special Sectors

Argyris, 'The EEC Rules of Competition and the Air Transport Sector' (1989) 26 CML Rev. 5.

Bredima-Savopoulou and Tzoannos, *The Common Shipping Policy of the EC* (1990) T.M.C. Asser Institut.

Clough and Randolph, *Shipping and EC Competition Law* (1991) Current EC Legal Developments Series, Butterworths.

Coleman, 'European Competition Law in the Telecommunications and Broadcasting Sectors' [1990] 5 ECLR 204.

Darnton, Wuersh, 'The European Commission's Progress Towards a New Approach for Competition in Telecommunications' (1992) IBL 111.

Dassesse and Isaacs, *EEC Banking Law*, (London, 1985) Lloyd's of London Press.

De Cockborne, 'Les Règles Communautaires de Concurrence Applicables aux Entreprises dans le Domaine Agricole' (1988) Rev. trim. Dr. Eur. 293.

Ehlermann, 'L'huile et le Sel: le Secteur bancaire et le Droit européen de la Concurrence' (1993) 3 Rev. trim. Dr. Eur. 457.

Eisen, Müller, Zweifel, 'Dangers of Delegated Regulation: The Case of the EEC and Insurance' (1990) World Competition and Economics Review 7.

Falkner, 'European Community Competition Policy and Financial Services: An Overview' [1991] 3 ECLR 113.

Forwood, 'Jurisdictional Limits to the Application of EC Competition Rules to International Maritime Transport' (1992) Fordham Corporate Law Institute 907.

Greaves, *EC Competition Law: Banking and Insurance* (London, 1992) Chancery Law Publishing.

Green, 'Competition and Maritime Trade: a Critical View' (1988) Journal of Law and Economics 612.

Green, *Consortia and Multi-modal Transport* (Antwerp, February 1991) The Second EEC Shipping Law Conference.

Gruson, Feuring, 'The New Banking Law of the European Economic Community' 1991 IBL 1.

Kreis, 'Maritime Transport and EEC Competition Rules' (1988) ETL 562.

Kreis, 'European Community Competition Policy and International Shipping' (1989) Fordham Int. L.J. 433.

Kreis, *Conferences and Outsiders* (Antwerp, February 1991) The Second EEC Shipping Law Conference.

Long, 'The European Commission's Guidelines on the Application of EEC Competition Rules in the Telecommunications Sector' (1991) Ent. L.R. 193.

Long, 'Air Transport in the EEC – Community Antitrust Law Aspects' (1991) Fordham Corporate Law Institute 287.

Ottervanger, 'Antitrust and Agriculture in the Common Market' (1989) Fordham Corporate Law Institute 203.

Overbury and Ravaioli, 'The Application of EEC Law to Telecommunications' (1989) Fordham Corporate Law Institute 271.

Rakovsky, 'Sea Transport Under EC Competition Law' (1992) Fordham Corporate Law Institute.

Ratliff, Tupper, Curschmann, 'Competition Law and Insurance: Recent Developments in the European Community' (1990) World Competition and Economics Review 67 and (1990) IBL 352.

Rycken, 'European Antitrust Aspects of Maritime and Air Transport' (1987) ETL 487.

Schmid, 'Air Transport within the European Single Market – how will it look after 1992?' (1992) Air & Space Law 199.

Schrier, Nadel and Rifas, *Outlook for the Liberalisation of Maritime Transport* (1985) Trade Policy Research Centre.

Simmonds, 'The Community's Declaration upon Signature of the UN Convention on the Law of the Sea' (1986) 23 CML Rev. 521.

Slot and Dagtoglou, *Toward a Community Air Transport Policy, The Legal Dimension* (1989) Kluwer Law and Taxation Publishers.

Van Houtte, 'Community Competition in the Air Transport Sector' (1993) Air & Space Law 61 and 275.

Welsh, *The Shipper's Viewpoint* (Antwerp, February 1991) The Second EEC Shipping Law Conference.

Yannopoulos, *Shipping Policies for an Open World Economy*, (Routledge, 1989).

Procedure

Brown, 'Notification of Agreements to the EC Commission: Whether to Submit to a Flawed System' (1992) 17 ELRev. 323.

Caspari, 'EEC Enforcement Policy and Practice: an Offical View' (1985) Antitrust L.J. 599.

de Bronett, 'Eröfnung und Abschluss von Wettbewerbsverfahren im Anwendungsbereich der VO Nr. 17 des Rates' (1989) Wirtschaft und Wettbewerb 459.

Edwards, 'Constitutional Rules of Community Law in EEC Competition Cases' (1989) Fordham Int. L.J. 111.

Gyselen, *Die Bemessung von Geldbussen im EG-Kartellrecht* (1993) Wirtschaft und Wettbewerb 561.

Joshua, 'The Element of Surprise' (1983) 8 ELRev. 3.

Joshua, 'The Right to be heard in EEC Competition Procedures' (1991) Fordham Int. L.J. 16.

Kamburoglou, Pirriwitz, 'Reichweite und Vollstreckung von Nachprüfungsentscheidungen' (1990) RIW 263.

Kennedy, 'The Essential Minimum: The Establishment of the Court of First Instance' (1989) 14 ELRev. 7.

Kerse, *EEC Antitrust Procedure*, third edn. (London, 1993) ELC.

Kreis, 'EEC Commission Investigation Procedures in Competition Cases' (1984) Int. Law. 19.

Lavoie, 'The Investigative Powers of the Commission with respect to Business Secrets under Community Competition Rules' (1992) 17 ELRev. 20.

Lenz, Mölls, '"Due Process" im Wettbewerbsrecht der EWG' (1991) Wirtschaft und Wettbewerb 771.

Pitt, 'Legal Privilege in EC Commission Antitrust Investigation' (1982) BLR 197.

Reynolds, 'Practical Aspects of Notifying Agreements' (1985) Fordham Corporate Law Institute 705.

Reynolds, 'EC Commission Policy on Fines' (1992) EBL 263.

Siragusa, 'Notifications of Agreements in the EEC – To notify or not to notify?' (1986) Fordham Corporate Law Institute 243.

Slot, Mcdonnel (eds.), *Procedure and Enforcement in EC and US Competition Law – Proceedings of the Leiden Europa Instituut Seminar on User-friendly Competition Law* (London, 1993) Sweet & Maxwell.

Stanbrook and Ratliff, 'EEC Antitrust audit' [1988] ECLR 334.

Van Bael, 'EEC Antitrust Enforcement and Adjudication as seen by Defense Counsel' (1979) 7 Swiss Rev. of Int. Comp. L. 1.

Van Bael, 'A Practitioner's Guide to Due Process in Antitrust and Anti-Dumping Proceedings' (1984) 18 Int. Law. 841.

Van Bael, 'The Antitrust Settlement Practice of the EEC Commission' (1986) Fordham Corporate Law Institute 759 and (1986) 23 CML Rev. 61.

Van Bael, 'Insufficient Judicial Control of the EC Competition Law Enforcement' (1992) Fordham Corporate Law Institute 733.

Vesterdorf, 'The Court of First Instance of the European Communities after two full years in operation' (1992) 29 CML Rev. 897.

Waelbroeck, 'Judicial Review of Commission Action in Competition Matters' (1983) Fordham Corporate Law Institute 179.

D. Waelbroeck, 'New Forms of Settlement of Antitrust Cases and Procedure Safeguards: is Regulation 17 Falling into Abeyance?' (1986) 11 ELRev. 268.

State aids

Doney-Bartholme, 'La Notion d'Aide d'Etat' (1993) 3–4 Cah. Dr. Eur. 399.

Ehlermann, 'Les Entreprises publiques et le Contrôle des Aides d'Etat' (1992) 360 Rev. MC 613.

Gyselen, 'La Transparence en Matière d'Aides d'Etat: Les Droits des Tiers' (1993) 3–4 Cah. Dr. Eur. 417.

Hancher, Ottervanger, Slot *EC State Aids* (UK, 1993) European Practice Library, Chancery Law Publishing.

Lasok, 'State Aids and Remedies under the EEC Treaty' [1986] ECLR 53.

Leibrock, 'Der Rechtsschutz im Beihilfeausichtsverfahren des EWG Vertrages' (1990) 25 Europarecht 20.

Schina, *State Aids under the EEC Treaty Articles 92 to 94* (Oxford, 1987) ESC/Sweet & Maxwell.

Slot, 'Procedural Aspects of State Aids: The Guardian of Competition versus the Subsidiary Villains ?' (1990) 27 CML Rev. 741.

Steindorff, Ernst 'Rückabwicklung unzulässiger Beihilfen nach Gemeinschaftsrecht' (1988) 152 Zeitschrift für Gesamte Handelsrecht und Wirtschaftsrecht 474.

Struys, 'Questions choisies de Procédure en Matière d'Aides d'Etat' (1993) 1 Rev. trim. Dr. Eur. 17.

Rengeling, 'Grundlagen des Subventionsrecht und Kompetenzen aus der Sicht von Bund und Ländern' (1988) 152 Zeitschrift für das Gesamte Handelsrecht und Wirtschaftsrecht 455.

National Courts

Cienfuegos Mateo, 'L'Application de la Nullité de l'Article 85 §2.2., du Traité CEE par les Jurisdictions nationales (avec un Examen particulier du Domaine des Transports aériens). Conséquences dans l'Ordre juridique interne' (1991) 3–4 Cah. Dr. Eur. 317.

Jacobs, 'Civil Enforcement and EEC Antitrust Law' (1984) Michigan LRev. 1364.

Korah, 'The Judgement in Delimitis: A Milestone towards a Realistic Assessment of the Effects of an Agreement or a Damp Squib ?' (1992) EIPR 167.

Lasok, 'Assessing the Economic Consequences of Restrictive Agreements: A Comment on the Delimitis Case' [1991] 5 ECLR 194.

Markert, 'Some Legal and Administrative Problems of the Co-existence of Community and National Competition Law in the EEC' (1974) 11 CML Rev. 92.

Picanol, 'Remedies in National Law for Breach of Articles 85 and 86 of the EEC Treaty – A review' (1983) 2 LIEI 1.

Steiner, 'How to make the Action Suit the Case – Domestic Remedies for Breach of EEC Law' [1987] ECLR 102.

Temple Lang, 'EEC Competition Actions in Member States' Courts – Claims for Damages, Declaration and Injunctions for Breach of Community Antitrust Law' (1984) Fordham Int. L.J. 389.

Verstrynge, 'The Relationship between National and Community Antitrust Law' (1981) 3 Northwestern J. of Int. L. & Bus. 358.

Vesterdorf, 'Complaints concerning infringements of Competition Law within the context of European Community Law' (1994) 31 CML Rev. 77.

Whish, 'The Enforcement of EC Competition Law in the Domestic Courts of Member States' [1994] 2 ECLR 60.

Public Enterprises

Ehlermann, 'Managing Monopolies: The Role of the State in Controlling Market Dominance in the European Community' [1993] 2 ECLR 61.

Esteva Mosso, 'La Compatibilité des Monopolies de Droit du Secteur des Télécommunications avec les Normes de Concurrence du Traité CEE' (1993) 3–4 Cah. Dr. Eur. 455.

Pais Antunes, 'L'Article 90 du Traité CEE, Obligations des Etats Membres et Pouvoirs de la Commission' (1991) 2 Rev. trim. Dr. Eur. 187.

Pappalardo, 'State Measures and Public Undertakings: Article 90 of the EEC Treaty Revisited' [1991] 1 ECLR 29.

Slot, 'Public Enterprises under EEC Law: The Lame Ducks of the Nineties' (1991) Fordham Corporate Law Institute 255.

Wainwright, 'Public Undertakings under Article 90' (1989) Fordham Corporate Law Institute 239.

Case Table

The following table lists alphabetically all cases and Commission decisions cited in the book. References are to paragraph numbers.

References to 'CEC' are to CCH's full text reporting service, European Community Cases.

Paragraph

A

ABG – Oil Companies Operating in the Netherlands (Decision 77/327) OJ 1977 L117/1 .... 113; 242; 247; 250; 910; 1118; 1119

ABI (Decision 87/103) OJ 1987 L43/51 .... 803; 810; 1045; 1046; 1047; 1049; 1050

Accor/Wagons-Lits (Decision 92/385) OJ 1992 L204/1; [1992] 2 CEC 2,170 .... 615; 636; 637; 638; 639; 655; 657

Acriss (Notice) OJ 1993 C149/9 706

ACF Chemiefarma NV v EC Commission (Case 41/69) [1970] ECR 661 .... 210; 216; 813; 814; 816; 1101; 1111; 1113; 1118; 1120

Adams v EC Commission (Case 145/83) [1985] ECR 3539 1110

Advocaat Zwarte Kip (Decision 74/432) OJ 1974 L237/12 403

AEG-Telefunken (Decision 82/267) OJ 1982 L117/15 1127

Aer Lingus/Sabena (Brussels/Sabena) (Notice) OJ 1989 C204/11 1033

Aérospatiale/Alcatel Espace (Notice) OJ 1994 C47/6 1064

Aérospatiale-Alenia/de Havilland (Decision 91/619) OJ 1991 L334/42; [1992] 1 CEC 2,034 .... 614; 618; 624; 635; 636; 638; 639; 657

Agreements and Concerted Practices in the Flat-glass Sector in the Benelux Countries (Decision 84/388) OJ 1984 L212/13 .... 217; 803; 807; 808; 813; 822; 1119

Agreements between Manufacturers of Glass Containers (Decision 74/292) OJ 1974 L160/1 .... 706; 803; 807; 808; 813; 822; 1119

Paragraph

Agreements relating to the combination of the Galileo and Covia CRSs (Notice) OJ 1993 C107/4 1035

Åhlström (A) Osakeyhtiö & Ors v EC Commission (Joined Cases 89, 104, 114, 116, 117 & 125–129/85) [1988] ECR 5193 .... 210; 211; 213; 256; 703; 802; 822; 1009; 1150

Åhlström (A) Osakeyhtiö & Ors v EC Commission ('Woodpulp') (Joined Cases 89, 104, 114, 116, 117 & 125–129/85) 31 Mar. 1993, [1993] 1 CEC 466 .... 212; 802; 808; 822; 1102; 1113; 1119

Ahmed Saeed Flugreisen & Anor v Zentrale zur Bekämpfung unlauteren Wettbewerbs eV (Case 66/86) [1989] ECR 803; [1989] 2 CEC 654 .... 201; 251; 1018; 1026; 1315; 1318; 1319; 1320

Air and Sea Transport Fares for Spanish Nationals Resident in the Canary and Balearic Islands (Decision 87/359) OJ 1987 L194/28 1321

Air France/Air Inter (Notice) OJ 1989 C190/4 .... 1028; 1033

Air France/Air Inter/UTA XXth Comp. Rep. EC. 1990 point 116 603

Air France/Alitalia (Paris/Milan, Paris/Turin routes) (Notice) OJ 1989 C204/5 1033

Air France/Iberica (Paris/Bilbao/Santiago de Compostela route) (Notice) OJ 1989 C204/4 1033

Legislation Finding List

This Legislation Finding List is divided into two sections:
- *Treaties, Conventions and International Agreements lists alphabetically EC and related Treaties, Conventions and International Agreements.*
- *Secondary Legislation lists Regulations, Directives and Decisions of the EC in that order.*

References are to paragraph numbers.

Note: References to art. 85 and 86 of the EC Treaty are not included in this list.

Index

References are to paragraph (¶) numbers.